Spectrum Health

Our gift to you.

LONGMAN

Handy Learner's DICTIONARY OF AMERICAN ENGLISH

NEW EDITION

PEARSON
Longman

Pearson Education Limited,
*Edinburgh Gate, Harlow, Essex CM20 2JE, England
and Associated Companies throughout the World*

Visit our website: http://www.longman.com/dictionaries

© Pearson Education Limited, 2000
*All rights reserved; no part of this publication may be reproduced,
stored in a retrieval system, or transmitted in any form or by any
means, electronic, mechanical, photocopying, recording, or
otherwise, without the prior written permission of the Publishers.*

First published 1993
This edition published 2000
Eighth impression 2006

ISBN-13: 978-0-582-36472-1
ISBN-10: 0-582-36472-8

Library of Congress Cataloging-in-Publication Data

British Library Cataloguing-in-Publication Data
A catalogue record for this book is available from the British Library.

Set in 5.5/7 pt Nimrod
Printed in China
NPCC/08

Acknowledgments

Director
Della Summers

Editorial Director
Adam Gadsby

Publisher
Laurence Delacroix

Production Editor
Michael Brooks

Pronunciation Editor
Beverley Britton Steiner

Cover
Sarah Hounsell

Production
Clive McKeough

Contents

Page

Pronunciation table — inside front cover

Guide to the dictionary — iv

Grammar Codes — vi

Symbols used with words in the same family — vi

The dictionary — 1

Word beginnings — 513

Word endings — 515

Irregular verbs — 518

Short forms and labels — inside back cover

Guide to the dictionary

Spelling

different spelling

> **age·is·m, agism** /ˈeɪdʒɪzəm/ n [U] the making of unfair differences between people because of their age, esp. treating young people more favorably than old people **agist** adj, n

irregular plurals

> **ox** /ɑks/ n **oxen** /ˈɑksən/ large animal of the cattle type, esp. male

irregular verbs

> **a·rise** /əˈraɪz/ vi **arose** /əˈroʊz/, **arisen** /əˈrɪzən/ happen; appear

Pronunciation/stress

pronunciations are shown using symbols from the International Phonetic Alphabet – see inside front cover

> **ba·by** /ˈbeɪbi/ n **1** very young child: (fig.) the baby of the class (= the youngest) **2** very young animal or bird: a baby monkey **3** infml person, esp. a girl or woman **4** infml one's special responsibility ~**ish** adj like a baby

stress syllables are clearly marked

> **bal·loon** /bəˈlun/ n **1** bag filled with gas or air so that it can float **2** small rubber bag that can be blown up and used as a toy

Meaning

clear and simple explanations using a limited defining vocabulary

> **beam**[1] /bim/ n long heavy piece of wood, esp. used to support a building

words with the same spelling but different use or meaning

> **an·tique** /ænˈtik/ adj old and therefore valuable ◆ n valuable old object

more than one meaning

> **be·come** /bɪˈkʌm/ v **became**, **become 1** begin to be: become kind | become warmer **2** vt be suitable for: Such behavior hardly becomes someone in your position.

Words that you may not know are written like THIS. You can find all these words in the dictionary.

> **be·drag·gled** /bɪˈdrægəld/ adj wet, LIMP, and muddy

common idioms and phrases are shown in dark type

bee /biː/ *n* **1** stinging insect that makes honey **2 a bee in one's bonnet** fixed idea; OBSESSION **3 the bee's knees** *infml* the best person or thing

phrasal verbs (= verbs which have a special meaning when they are used with a particular adverb or preposition)

boil¹ /bɔɪl/ *vi/t* **1** bring or come to the temperature at which a liquid changes to gas: *212°F is the boiling point of water.* **2** cook at this temperature: *to boil eggs* **3 boil down** boil till almost no water remains ♦ *n* [S]: *Bring the soup to a boil.*

boil away *phr vi* disappear by boiling
boil down to *phr vt* be no more than: *It all boils down to a question of money.*

examples showing how to use the word or phrase

boil over *phr vi* **1** (of a boiling liquid) flow over the sides of the container **2** get out of control (and develop into): *The conflict boiled over into war.*

labels showing style, region, etc.

close call /ˌkləʊs ˈkɔːl/ *n infml* situation in which something dangerous or very unpleasant is only just avoided

---

Grammar

parts of speech

bone-dry /ˌ·ˈ·◂/ *adj* perfectly dry
bon·fire /ˈbɒnfaɪə/ *n* large outdoor fire

words which are part of the same word family and which have different parts of speech are shown like this

boy /bɔɪ/ *n* young male person **~hood** *n* time of being a boy **~ish** *adj* like a boy

countable and uncountable nouns

choco·late /ˈtʃɒklɪt/ *n* **1** [U] solid brown substance eaten as candy **2** [C] small candy covered with this **3** [U] hot drink made from this ♦ *adj* dark brown

intransitive and transitive verbs

co·in·cide /ˌkəʊɪnˈsaɪd/ *vi* **1** happen at the same time **2** (of opinions, etc.) agree
com·pli·ment² /ˈkɒmpləˌment/ *vt* express admiration of

Grammar codes

[C] countable: a noun that can be counted and has a plural form: *This is a* **dictionary**. | *There are many* **dictionaries** *in the library.*

[U] uncountable: a noun that cannot be counted, and that has no plural form: *We drink* **milk** *with our dinner.* | *There isn't much* **milk** *left.* | *The book contained some interesting* **information** *about the town.*

[P] plural: a noun that is used only with a plural verb or pronoun, and that has no singular form: *These* **pants** *are too tight.*

[S] singular: a noun that is used only in the singular, and that has no plural form: *There was a* **babble** *of voices.* | *Let me take a* **look** *at it.*

[*the*] a noun that is the name of an actual place, organization, etc., and that is always used with the definite article: *The* **White House** | *This land belongs to the* **State**

vt a transitive verb: a verb that is followed by a direct object, which can be either a noun phrase or a clause: *She* **rides** *a bicycle to school.* | *He* **made up** *a good excuse.* | *We* **decided** *to leave.* | *I've* **given up** *eating meat.*

vi an intransitive verb: a **verb** that has no direct object: *They all* **came** *yesterday.* | *The plane took* **off** *at 7 o'clock.*

Symbols used with words in the same family

Words which are related to the headword are often given at the end of an entry. Sometimes they have a definition. Sometimes, if their meaning is clear, there is no definition. Sometimes a word is exactly the same as the headword, and so it is not written again. Sometimes a word has a different ending from the headword, and so the new ending is shown.

The following symbols are used to show exactly how these related words are formed:

♦ shows that a related word is exactly the same as the headword

~ shows that a related word is formed by adding an ending directly to the headword

— shows that the form of the headword changes slightly before the new ending can be added

an·ger /ˈæŋgə/ *n* [U] fierce displeasure and annoyance ♦ *vt* make angry

an·nounce /əˈnaʊns/ *vt* state loudly or publicly: *He announced the winner of the competition.* ~**ment** *n* public statement

a·nom·a·ly /əˈnɒməli/ *n fml* something different from the usual type: *A cat with no tail is an anomaly.* –**lous** *adj*

ap·pro·pri·ate² /əˈprəʊprieɪt/ *vt* **1** set aside (money) for a purpose **2** take for oneself –**ation** /əˌprəʊpriˈeɪʃən/ *n* [C;U]

A

A, a /eɪ/ the 1st letter of the English alphabet

a /ə; *strong* eɪ/ also (*before a vowel sound*) **an** — *indefinite article, determiner* **1** one: *a pencil | a doctor | a thousand dollars* **2** (*before some words of quantity*): *a few weeks | a little water* **3** for each: *6 times a day | $2 a dozen*

a·back /ə'bæk/ *adv* **be taken aback** be suddenly shocked

ab·a·cus /'æbəkəs/ *n* frame with sliding balls on wires, used for counting

a·ban·don /ə'bændən/ *vt* **1** leave completely **2** give up: *to abandon our search* **3** give (oneself) up completely to a feeling: *He abandoned himself to grief.* ~**ment** *n* [U]

a·bashed /ə'bæʃt/ *adj* uncomfortable and ashamed

a·bate /ə'beɪt/ *vi fml* (of wind, pain, etc.) become less fierce ~**ment** *n* [U]

ab·bey /'æbi/ *n* house of religious men or women; MONASTERY or CONVENT

ab·bre·vi·ate /ə'briviˌeɪt/ *vt* make shorter –**ation** /əˌbriviˈeɪʃən/ *n* short form of a word

ab·di·cate /'æbdɪˌkeɪt/ *vi/t* give up (a position or right) officially –**cation** /ˌæbdɪˈkeɪʃən/ *n* [U]

ab·do·men /'æbdəmən, æb'doʊ-/ *n* part of the body containing the stomach **abdominal** /æb'dɑmənl, əb-/ *adj*

ab·duct /æb'dʌkt, əb-/ *vt* take (a person) away illegally; KIDNAP ~**ion** /-'dʌkʃən/ *n* [U]

ab·er·ra·tion /ˌæbəˈreɪʃən/ *n* [C;U] difference from usual behavior

a·bet /ə'bɛt/ *vt* -**tt**- aid and abet *law* give help to (a crime or criminal) ~**tor** *n*

ab·hor /əb'hɔr, æb-/ *vt fml* hate very much ~**rent** /əb'hɔrənt, -'hɑr-, æb-/ *adj* deeply disliked ~**rence** *n* [U]

a·bide /ə'baɪd/ *vt* **abided** or **abode** /ə'boʊd/, **abode** bear; TOLERATE: *I can't abide rudeness.*

 abide by *phr vt* obey (laws, etc.)

a·bid·ing /ə'baɪdɪŋ/ *adj* without end: *an abiding love*

a·bil·i·ty /ə'bɪləti/ *n* [C;U] mental or physical skill

ab·ject /'æbdʒɛkt, æb'dʒɛkt/ *adj fml* **1** deserving great pity: *abject poverty* **2** without respect for oneself; HUMBLE: *an abject apology* ~**ly** *adv*

a·blaze /ə'bleɪz/ *adj* **1** on fire; burning **2** shining brightly

a·ble /'eɪbəl/ *adj* **1** having the power, time, etc., to do something: *Will you be able to come?* **2** intelligent; skilled

ab·nor·mal /æb'nɔrməl, əb-/ *adj* not ordinary; unusual ~**ly** *adv* ~**ity** /ˌæbnɔr'mæləti, -nə-/ *n* [C;U]

a·board /ə'bɔrd, ə'boʊrd/ *adv, prep* on or onto (a ship, airplane, etc.)

a·bol·ish /ə'bɑlɪʃ/ *vt* legally end something –**ition** /ˌæbə'lɪʃən/ *n* [U]

a·bom·i·na·ble /ə'bɑmənəbəl/ *adj* terrible; very bad –**bly** *adv*

ab·o·rig·i·nal /ˌæbə'rɪdʒənl◂/ *adj* (of people and living things) having lived in a place from the earliest times **aboriginal** *n*

ab·o·rig·i·ne /ˌæbə'rɪdʒəni/ *n* an aboriginal, esp. in Australia

a·bort /ə'bɔrt/ *v* **1** *vt* deliberately cause (a child) to be born too soon for it to live **2** *vi/t* end before the expected time: *abort the space flight* ~**ive** *adj* unsuccessful; coming to nothing ~**ion** /ə'bɔrʃən/ *n* [C;U] medical operation to abort a child

a·bound /ə'baʊnd/ *vi* [(in, with)] exist or have in large numbers or great quantity

a·bout¹ /ə'baʊt/ *prep* **1** on the subject of: *a book about cats* **2** near; close to: *He's about my height.* **3** concerning: *She told us all about the stars.* **4** **what/ how about: a** (making a suggestion): *How about a drink?* **b** what news or plans do you have concerning: *What about Jack?*

about² *adv* **1** a little more or less than: *about 5 miles* **2** nearly; almost: *He's about ready.* **3** **be about to** be going to: *We're about to leave.*

about-face /-ˌ-ˈ-, ˌ-ˈ-ˌ-/ *n* change to the opposite position or opinion

a·bove¹ /ə'bʌv/ *prep* **1** higher than; over: *fly above the clouds* **2** more than **3** above all most important of all **4** too good, honest, etc. for: *He's not above stealing.*

above² *adv* **1** higher: *the clouds above* **2** more: *aged 20 and above* **3** earlier in a book: *the facts mentioned above | the above-mentioned facts*

a·bove·board /əˈbʌvˌbɔrd, -ˌboʊrd/ adj without any trick or attempt to deceive

a·bra·sive /əˈbreɪsɪv, -zɪv/ adj 1 causing the rubbing away of a surface 2 rough and annoying: an abrasive personality

a·breast /əˈbrɛst/ adv 1 side by side 2 **keep/be abreast of** know the most recent facts about

a·bridge /əˈbrɪdʒ/ vt make (a book, etc.) shorter **–ment** n

a·broad /əˈbrɔd/ adv to or in another country

a·brupt /əˈbrʌpt/ adj 1 sudden and unexpected: an abrupt stop 2 (of behavior, etc.) rough and impolite **~ly** adv **~ness** n [U]

ab·scess /ˈæbsɛs/ n swelling on or in the body, containing PUS

ab·scond /əbˈskɑnd, əb-/ vi fml go away suddenly because one has done something wrong

ab·sence /ˈæbsəns/ n 1 [C;U] (period of) being away: absence from work 2 [U] lack: the absence of information about the crime

ab·sent[1] /ˈæbsənt/ adj 1 not present 2 showing lack of attention: an absent look on his face

ab·sent[2] /əbˈsɛnt, æb-/ vt fml keep (oneself) away

ab·sen·tee /ˌæbsənˈtiː/ n person who is absent from a place

absent-mind·ed /ˌ··ˈ···◂/ adj so concerned with one's thoughts as not to notice what is happening, what one is doing, etc.

ab·so·lute /ˈæbsəˌlut, ˌæbsəˈlut/ adj 1 complete; undoubted: an absolute ruler 3 not measured by comparison with other things; not RELATIVE **~ly** /ˌæbsəˈlutli◂/ adv 1 completely: I'm absolutely sure 2 certainly: "Do you think so?" "Absolutely."

ab·solve /əbˈzɑlv, -ˈsɑlv/ vt free (someone) from fulfilling a promise, or from punishment

ab·sorb /əbˈsɔrb, -ˈzɔrb/ vt 1 take in (liquids, heat, etc.) 2 fill the attention of: I was absorbed in a book. | an absorbing task **~ent** adj able to ABSORB (1) **absorption** /-ˈsɔrpʃən/ n

ab·stain /əbˈsteɪn/ vi 1 keep oneself from doing something unhealthy, bad, etc. 2 not vote **~er** n

ab·ste·mi·ous /əbˈstimiəs/ adj not allowing oneself much food, etc.

ab·sten·tion /əbˈstɛnʃən/ n [C;U] act of abstaining, esp. from voting

ab·sti·nence /ˈæbstənəns/ n [U] abstaining, esp. from alcoholic drink

ab·stract /ˈæbstrækt, æbˈstrækt, əbˈstrækt/ adj 1 existing as a quality or CONCEPT rather than as something real or solid: Beauty is abstract but a house is not. | The word 'hunger' is an **abstract noun.** 2 general rather than particular: an abstract discussion of crime, without reference to actual cases 3 (in art) not showing things as a camera would see them ♦ /ˈæbstrækt/ n 1 abstract work of art 2 short form of a statement, speech, etc.

ab·surd /əbˈsɜd, -ˈzɜd/ adj unreasonable; (funny because) false or foolish **~ly** adv **~ity** /əbˈsɜdəti, -ˈzɜ-/ n [C;U]

a·bun·dant /əˈbʌndənt/ adj more than enough **~ly** adv **–dance** n [S;U] an abundance of food

a·buse[1] /əˈbyuz/ vt 1 do cruel or violent things to 2 say bad things to or about 3 use badly: abuse one's power

a·buse[2] /əˈbyus/ n 1 [U] cruel or violent behavior towards 2 [U] cruel or rude words 3 [C;U] wrong use: the abuse of drugs **abusive** adj using cruel or rude words

a·bys·mal /əˈbɪzməl/ adj very bad

a·byss /əˈbɪs/ n large hole that seems to have no bottom

AC n [U] AIR-CONDITIONING

ac·a·dem·ic /ˌækəˈdɛmɪk◂/ adj 1 about schools and education 2 not related to practical situations; theoretical (THEORY): a purely academic question. ♦ n 1 university teacher 2 someone who values skills of the mind more than practical skills **~ally** adv

a·cad·e·my /əˈkædəmi/ n 1 private high school 2 school for training in a special skill: a military academy 3 society of people interested in the advancement of art, science, or literature

ac·cede /ækˈsid, ək-/ vi fml 1 agree to a demand, etc. 2 come to a high position

ac·cel·e·rate /əkˈsɛləˌreɪt/ vi/t 1 (cause to) move faster 2 (cause to) develop or happen faster **–ration** /əkˌsɛləˈreɪʃən/ n [U]

ac·cel·e·ra·tor /əkˈsɛləˌreɪtə/ n instrument in a car, etc., that is used to increase its speed

ac·cent[1] /ˈæksɛnt/ n 1 particular way of speaking, usu. connected with a place or a nationality **2** mark written over or under a letter, such as that on the 'e' of 'café' **3** importance given to a word or part of a word by saying it with more force

ac·cent² /ˈæksɛnt, ækˈsɛnt/ vt say with added force

ac·cen·tu·ate /əkˈsɛntʃueɪt, æk-/ vt give extra importance to

ac·cept /əkˈsɛpt/ v **1** vi/t receive (something offered), esp. willingly **2** vt believe or agree to: *Did she accept your reasons for being late?* ~**able** adj good enough; worth accepting: *an acceptable gift* ~**ance** n [C;U]

ac·cess¹ /ˈæksɛs/ n [U] **1** way in; entrance **2** means of using or getting something: *Students need access to books.* ~**ible** /əkˈsɛsəbəl/ adj easy to get or get to ~**ibility** /əkˌsɛsəˈbɪləti/ n [U]

access² vt obtain (stored information) from a computer's memory

ac·ces·so·ry /əkˈsɛsəri/ n **1** thing that is added but is not a necessary part: *car accessories such as a radio* | *a black dress with matching accessories* (= hat, bag, shoes, etc.) **2** *law* person who is not present at a crime but who helps in doing it

ac·ci·dent /ˈæksədənt, -ˌdɛnt/ n something, usu. unpleasant, that happens unexpectedly: *serious accidents on the freeway* | *I met her* **by accident**. ~**al** /ˌæksəˈdɛntəl/ adj ~**ally** adv

ac·claim /əˈkleɪm/ vt give public approval **acclaim** n [U]

ac·cli·mate /ˈækləˌmeɪt, əˈklaɪmɪt/ vi/t make or get used to the weather in a new place **acclimation** /ˌækləˈmeɪʃən/ n [U]

ac·co·lade /ˈækəˌleɪd/ n strong praise

ac·com·mo·date /əˈkɑːməˌdeɪt/ vt fml **1** provide with a place to live in **2** help by making changes: *to accommodate your wishes* –**dating** adj helpful –**dation(s)** /əˌkɑːməˈdeɪʃənz/ n [P] room and food

ac·com·pa·ni·ment /əˈkʌmpənimənt/ n **1** something which is used or provided with something else **2** music played at the same time as singing or another instrument

ac·com·pa·nist /əˈkʌmpənɪst/ n player of a musical accompaniment

ac·com·pa·ny /əˈkʌmpəni/ vt **1** go with, as on a journey **2** happen at the same time as: *Lightning usually accompanies*

thunder. **3** play a musical accompaniment to

ac·com·plice /əˈkʌmplɪs/ n person who helps someone to do wrong

ac·com·plish /əˈkʌmplɪʃ/ vt succeed in doing ~**ed** adj skilled ~**ment** n **1** [C] something one is skilled at **2** [U] act of accomplishing something

ac·cord /əˈkɔrd/ n [U] **1 in accord (with)** in agreement (with) **2 of one's own accord** without being asked; willingly

ac·cord·ance /əˈkɔrdns/ n **in accordance with** in a way that agrees with

ac·cord·ing·ly /əˈkɔrdɪŋli/ adv because of what has happened; therefore

according to /ˈ...ˈ/ prep **1** from what is said or written: *According to my watch, it's 4 o'clock.* **2** in a way that agrees with: *paid according to the amount of work done*

ac·cor·di·on /əˈkɔrdiən/ n musical instrument played by pressing the middle part together to force air through holes controlled by KEYS¹ (3) worked by the fingers

ac·cost /əˈkɔst, əˈkɑst/ vt go up and speak to (esp. a stranger), often threateningly

ac·count¹ /əˈkaʊnt/ n **1** report; description: *give an account of what happened* | **By all accounts**, (= according to what everyone says) *she's a good player.* **2** **accounts** record of money received and paid out **3** money kept in a bank or other institution where one saves money **4** arrangement that lets one buy goods and pay for them later **5** customer: *one of our biggest accounts* **6 bring/call someone to account** cause (someone) to give an explanation **7 on account of** because of **8 on no account/not on any account** not for any reason **9 take into account/take account of** give thought to; consider

account² v **account for** phr vt **1** give or be an explanation for **2** give a statement showing how money has been spent

ac·count·a·ble /əˈkaʊntəbəl/ adj responsible –**bility** /əˌkaʊntəˈbɪləti/ n [U]

ac·count·ant /əˈkaʊntənt, -ˈtnt/ n person who controls and examines money accounts

ac·cred·it·ed /əˈkrɛdɪtɪd/ adj **1** officially recognized as reaching a certain standard or quality: *an accredited college* **2** officially representing one's government in a foreign country **3** having the power to act for an organization

ac·crue /əˈkruː/ vi fml come as an increase or advantage

ac·cu·mu·late /əˈkjuːmjəˌleɪt/ vi/t make or become greater; collect into a mass **–lation** /əˌkjuːmjəˈleɪʃən/ n [C;U]

ac·cu·ra·cy /ˈækjərəsi/ n [U] being accurate; exactness

ac·cu·rate /ˈækjərɪt/ adj exactly correct **~ly** adv

ac·cu·sa·tion /ˌækjəˈzeɪʃən/ n [C;U] (statement) accusing someone of something

ac·cuse /əˈkjuːz/ vt charge (someone) with doing wrong: *He was accused of murder.* | *The accused (men) were found guilty.* **accuser** n **accusingly** adv

ac·cus·tom /əˈkʌstəm/ vt **be accustomed to** be in the habit of; be used to

ace /eɪs/ n **1** playing card with one mark or spot on it **2** person of the highest skill. **3** (in tennis) very fast and strong SERVE that the opponent cannot hit back ♦ adj infml very good or very skilled ♦ v infml receive the highest possible grade on a test

a·cer·bic /əˈsəbɪk/ adj (of a person or manner) clever in a rather cruel way

ache /eɪk/ vi have a continuous dull pain: *My head aches.* **ache** n: *a headache*

a·chieve /əˈtʃiːv/ vt **1** finish successfully **2** get by effort: *achieve results* **~ment** n **1** [U] successful finishing of something **2** [C] something achieved

a·chiever /əˈtʃiːvə/ n person who achieves a lot: *high achiever*

A·chil·les' heel /əˌkɪliz ˈhiːl/ n small but important weakness

ac·id /ˈæsɪd/ adj sour; bitter **acid** n **1** [C;U] chemical substance containing HYDROGEN **2** [U] sl the drug LSD

acid rain /ˌ· ˈ·/ n [U] rain containing harmful quantities of acid as a result of industrial pollution (POLLUTE)

acid test /ˌ· ˈ·/ n test of the value of something

ac·knowl·edge /əkˈnɒlɪdʒ/ vt **1** admit; recognize as a fact: *to acknowledge defeat* | *an acknowledged expert* **2** show one is grateful for **3** state that one has received: *acknowledge a letter* **4** show that one recognizes (someone) as by smiling, etc. **–edgment**, **–edgement** n [C;U]

ac·ne /ˈækni/ n [U] skin disorder common among young people, in which pimples appear on the face and neck

a·corn /ˈeɪkɔːn, ˈeɪkən/ n nut of the OAK tree

a·cous·tics /əˈkuːstɪks/ n **1** [U] scientific study of sound **2** [P] qualities that make a place good or bad for hearing in **acoustic** adj

ac·quaint /əˈkweɪnt/ vt fml **1 acquaint someone with** tell; make known to **2 be acquainted (with)** have met socially; know **~ance** n **1** [C] person whom one knows slightly **2** [S;U (with)] knowledge gained through experience

ac·qui·esce /ˌækwiˈes/ vi agree, often unwillingly **–escent** adj

ac·quire /əˈkwaɪə/ vt gain; come to possess

ac·qui·si·tion /ˌækwəˈzɪʃən/ n **1** [U] act of acquiring **2** [C] something acquired **–tive** /əˈkwɪzətɪv/ adj in the habit of acquiring things

ac·quit /əˈkwɪt/ vt -tt- decide that (someone) is not guilty: *The jury acquitted him (of murder).* **~tal** n [C;U]

a·cre /ˈeɪkə/ n a measure of land equal to 4,840 square yards

a·cre·age /ˈeɪkərɪdʒ/ n [S;U] area measured in acres

ac·rid /ˈækrɪd/ adj (of taste or smell) bitter; stinging

ac·ri·mo·ny /ˈækrəˌməʊni/ n [U] bitterness of manner or language **–nious** /ˌækrəˈməʊniəs◄/ adj

ac·ro·bat /ˈækrəˌbæt/ n person skilled in walking on ropes, etc., esp. at a CIRCUS **~ic** /ˌækrəˈbætɪk◄/ adj **~ics** n [P;U]

ac·ro·nym /ˈækrənɪm/ n word made from the first letters of a name, such as NATO

a·cross /əˈkrɒs/ adv, prep from one side to the other; on or to the other side (of): *a bridge across the river* | *Can you swim across?*

a·cross-the-board /ˌ·ˌ· ˈ·/ adj influencing or having effects on people or things of all types or at every level **across-the-board** adv

acryl·ic /əˈkrɪlɪk/ adj made from chemicals, rather than natural materials: *acrylic paint*

act¹ /ækt/ v **1** vi do something: *She acted on my suggestion.* | *The doctor acted correctly.* **2** vi/t perform in a play or film **3** vi produce an effect: *Does the drug take long to act?*

act up phr vi behave badly

act² n **1** something that one has done; an action of a particular kind: *an act of ter-*

rorism \ *a kind act* **2** law made by congress, etc. **3** main division of a stage play **4** short event in a stage or CIRCUS performance **5** example of insincere behavior used for effect: *She was just putting on an act.* **6** get one's act together *infml* do things in a more effective way — see also ACT OF GOD

act·ing¹ /'æktɪŋ/ *adj* appointed to do the duties of a position for a short time

acting² *n* [U] job or skill of representing a character in a play, movie, etc.

ac·tion /'ækʃən/ *n* **1** [U] process of doing something: *We must* **take action** *quickly.* **2** [C] something done; ACT: *Her prompt action saved his life.* **3** [C] way something works **4** [U] effect: *the action of light on photographic film* **5** [C;U] military fighting or a fight **6** [U] main events in a book, play, etc.: *The action takes place in Italy.* **7** [C;U] *law* legal charge of guilt: *bring an action against him* **8 in/into action** in/into operation **9 out of action** not working **10 take action** begin to act — see also JOB ACTION

ac·tiv·ate /'æktɪˌveɪt/ *vt* make active **–ation** /ˌæktəˈveɪʃən/ *n*

ac·tive /'æktɪv/ *adj* doing things; able to take action **~ly** *adv*

ac·tiv·ist /'æktɪvɪst/ *n* person taking an active part in politics

ac·tiv·i·ty /æk'tɪvəti/ *n* **1** [U] movement or action: *political activity* **2** [C] something done, esp. for interest or pleasure: *leisure activities*

act of God /ˌ · · ˈ·/ *n* major event that can't be controlled, like a flood or EARTHQUAKE

ac·tor /'æktər/ *actress* /'æktrɪs/ *fem.* — *n* person who acts in a play, film, etc.

ac·tu·al /'æktʃuəl, 'ækʃuəl/ *adj* existing as a fact; real **~ly** /'æktʃuəli, -tʃəli, 'ækʃuəli/ *adv* **1** in fact; really **2** (showing surprise): *He actually offered me a drink!*

ac·u·men /əˈkyumən, 'ækyəmən/ *n* [U] *fml* ability to judge quickly

ac·u·punc·ture /'ækyəˌpʌŋktʃər/ *n* [U] method of curing diseases by putting special needles into certain parts of the body

a·cute /əˈkyut/ *adj* **1** severe; very great: *acute shortage of water* **2** (of the mind or of senses) working very well **3** (of an angle) less than 90° **4** (of a mark) put above a letter, e.g. é, to show pronunciation **~ly** *adv* **~ness** *n* [U]

ad /æd/ *n infml* advertisement

A.D. (in the year) since the birth of Christ: *in 1492 A.D.*

ad·age /'ædɪdʒ/ *n* old wise phrase; PROVERB

ad·a·mant /'ædəmənt/ *adj fml* refusing to change one's mind

Ad·am's ap·ple /ˌædəmz ˈæpəl/ *n* lump at the front of the throat that moves when one talks or swallows

a·dapt /əˈdæpt/ *vt* make suitable for new conditions **~able** *adj* able to change **~ability** /əˌdæptəˈbɪləti/ *n* [U] **~ation** /ˌædəpˈteɪʃən, ˌædæp-/ *n* [C;U] act of adapting: *an adaptation of the play for television*

a·dapt·er, -or /əˈdæptər/ *n* electrical PLUG allowing more than one piece of equipment to run from the same SOCKET

add /æd/ *v* **1** *vt* put with something else: *add a name to the list* **2** *vi/t* join (numbers) together **3** *vt* say also

add to *phr vt* increase: *His absence added to our difficulties.*

add up *phr vi* make sense; seem likely: *The facts just don't add up.*

ad·dict /'ædɪkt/ *n* person who cannot stop a harmful habit **~ion** /əˈdɪkʃən/ *n* [C;U] **~ive** /əˈdɪktɪv/ *adj* habit forming

ad·dic·ted /əˈdɪktɪd/ *adj* dependent on something, esp. a drug

ad·di·tion /əˈdɪʃən/ *n* **1** [U] act of adding **2** [C] something added **3 in addition (to)** as well (as) **~al** *adj* as well; added **~ally** *adv* also

ad·di·tive /'ædətɪv/ *n* substance, esp. a chemical one, added to something else

add-on /ˈ· ·/ *n* piece of equipment that can be connected to a computer that increases its usefulness

ad·dress /əˈdrɛs, 'ædrɛs/ *n* **1** number, town, etc., where someone lives **2** speech made to a group of people ♦ *vt* **1** write a name and ADDRESS (1) on **2** direct a speech to: *She addressed the crowd.*

ad·ept /əˈdɛpt/ *adj* highly skilled

adept /'ædɛpt/ *n* person who is adept at something

ad·e·quate /'ædəkwɪt/ *adj* enough; good enough **~ly** *adv* **–quacy** /-kwəsi/ *n* [U]

ad·here /ədˈhɪr/ *vi* stick firmly, as with glue **adherence** *n* [U] **adherent** *n* loyal supporter of something

adhere to *phr vt* remain loyal to (an idea, plan, etc.)

adhesive

ad·he·sive /ədˈhiːsɪv, -zɪv/ n, adj (a substance such as glue) that can stick –**sion** /ədˈhiːʒən/ n [U]

ad hoc /ˌæd ˈhɒk, -ˈhəʊk/ adj made for a particular purpose

ad·ja·cent /əˈdʒeɪsənt/ adj fml very close; (almost) touching

ad·jec·tive /ˈædʒɪktɪv/ n word which describes a noun, such as black in a black hat –**tival** /ˌædʒɪkˈtaɪvəl◁/ adj

ad·join /əˈdʒɔɪn/ vi/t fml be next to (one another)

ad·journ /əˈdʒɜːn/ vi/t stop (a meeting, etc.) for a while –**ment** n [C;U]

ad·ju·di·cate /əˈdʒuːdɪkeɪt/ vi/t fml act as a judge; decide about –**cator** n –**cation** /əˌdʒuːdɪˈkeɪʃən/ n [U]

ad·junct /ˈædʒʌŋkt/ n something added without being a necessary part

ad·just /əˈdʒʌst/ vi/t change slightly so as to make right ~**able** adj ~**ment** n [C;U]

ad lib /ˌæd ˈlɪb/ adv spoken, played, performed, etc., without preparation **ad-lib** vi -**bb**- invent and say without preparation **ad-lib** adj

ad·min·is·ter /ədˈmɪnɪstə/ vt fml 1 manage (business affairs, etc.) 2 (to) give: administer medicine/punishment

ad·min·is·tra·tion /ədˌmɪnɪˈstreɪʃən/ n 1 [U] management or direction of the affairs of a business, government, etc. 2 [C] national government: the Bush Administration 3 [U] act of administering –**trative** /ədˈmɪnəˌstreɪtɪv, -strə-/ adj –**trator** /-ˌstreɪtə/ n

ad·mi·ra·ble /ˈædmərəbəl/ adj very good –**bly** adv

ad·mi·ral /ˈædmərəl/ n naval officer of high rank

ad·mire /ədˈmaɪə/ vt regard with pleasure; have a good opinion of **admiring** adj **admirer** n **admiration** /ˌædməˈreɪʃən/ n [U] feeling of pleasure and respect

ad·mis·si·ble /ədˈmɪsəbəl/ adj that can be accepted or considered

ad·mis·sion /ədˈmɪʃən/ n 1 [U] being allowed to enter a building, join a club, etc. 2 [U] cost of entrance: Admission $1 3 [C] statement admitting something; confession (CONFESS)

ad·mit /ədˈmɪt/ vt -**tt**- 1 allow to enter; let in 2 agree to the truth of (something bad) ~**tance** n [U] right to enter ~**tedly** adv it must be agreed that

ad·mon·ish /ədˈmɒnɪʃ/ vt fml scold gently; warn –**ition** /ˌædməˈnɪʃən/ n [C;U]

ad nau·se·am /ˌæd ˈnɔːziəm/ adv repeatedly and to an annoying degree

a·do /əˈduː/ n without further more ado with no further delay

ado·be /əˈdəʊbi/ n [U] mixture of clay and straw used for building houses

ad·o·les·cent /ˌædlˈesənt◁/ adj, n (of) a boy or girl who is growing up –**cence** n [S;U]

a·dopt /əˈdɒpt/ vt 1 take (someone else's child) into one's family forever 2 take and use (a method, suggestion, etc.) ~**ive** adj having adopted a child ~**ion** /əˈdɒpʃən/ n [U]

a·dore /əˈdɔː, əˈdʊə/ vt 1 love and respect deeply; worship 2 like very much **adorable** adj very lovable **adoring** adj loving **adoration** /ˌædəˈreɪʃən/ n [U]

a·dorn /əˈdɔːn/ vt add beauty to; decorate ~**ment** n [U]

a·dren·a·lin /əˈdrenlɪn/ n [U] chemical made by the body during anger, etc., causing quick or violent action

a·drift /əˈdrɪft/ adv, adj (of boats) floating loose; not fastened

a·droit /əˈdrɔɪt/ adj quick and skillful ~**ly** adv

ad·u·la·tion /ˌædʒəˈleɪʃən/ n [U] fml praise or admiration that is more than is necessary or deserved

ad·ult /ˈædʌlt, əˈdʌlt/ n a fully grown person or animal

adult adj 1 completely grown 2 typical of or appropriate for an adult

a·dul·ter·ate /əˈdʌltəreɪt/ vt make impure by adding something of lower quality

a·dul·ter·y /əˈdʌltəri/ n [U] sexual relations between a married person and someone outside the marriage **adulterer** /əˈdʌltərə/, **adulteress** /-trɪs/ fem. — n –**terous** adj

ad·vance /ədˈvɑːns/ vi/t go or bring forward in position, development, etc. **advanced** adj 1 far on in development 2 modern

advance n 1 forward movement or development 2 money provided before the proper time 3 **in advance** before in time ♦ adj coming before the usual time

advanced de·gree /ˌ·ˈ·, ·ˌ·/ n degree higher than a BACHELOR'S

ad·vanc·es /ədˈvɑːnsɪz/ n [P] efforts to become friends or lovers with someone

ad·van·tage /ədˈvɑːntɪdʒ/ n 1 [C] something that may help one to be successful

2 [U] profit; gain **3 take advantage of: a** make use of somebody, as by deceiving them **b** make use of; profit from ~**ous** /ˌædvænˈteɪdʒəs, -vən-/ adj

ad·vent /ˈædvent/ n **the advent of** the coming of (an important event, etc.)

ad·ven·ture /ədˈventʃə/ n **1** [C] exciting and perhaps dangerous experience **2** [U] excitement; risk –**turer** n **1** person who has or looks for adventures **2** person who hopes to make a profit by taking risks with his/her money –**turous** adj **1** also **adventuresome** /ədˈventʃəsəm/ fond of adventure **2** exciting

ad·verb /ˈædvɜːb/ n word which adds to the meaning of a verb, an adjective, another adverb, or a sentence, for example, *slowly*, *tomorrow*, and *here* –**ial** /ˈædˈvɜːbiəl/ n, adj

ad·ver·sa·ry /ˈædvəˌseri/ n fml opponent; enemy –**sarial** /ˌædvəˈseriəl/ adj

ad·verse /ˈædvɜːs, æd-, ˈædvɜːs/ adj fml unfavorable: *adverse comments* ~**ly** adv –**sity** /ədˈvɜːsəti, æd-/ n [C;U] bad luck; trouble

ad·ver·tise /ˈædvəˌtaɪz/ vi/t make (something for sale) known to people, e.g. in a newspaper –**tiser** n –**tising** n [U] business of doing this ~**ment** /ˌædvəˈtaɪzmənt, ədˈvɜːtɪz-, ədˈvɜːtɪs-/ also **ad** infml — n notice of something for sale or wanted

ad·vice /ədˈvaɪs/ n [U] opinion given to someone about what to do

advice col·um·nist /ˈ· ˌ···/ n person who gives advice in the part of a newspaper or magazine that contains letters from readers about their personal problems

ad·vise /ədˈvaɪz/ vt **1** give advice to **2** [(of)] fml inform: *Please advise me of the cost.* **3 well-advised/ill-advised** wise/unwise **advisory** giving advice **adviser** also **advisor** n **advisable** adj sensible; wise

ad·vo·cate /ˈædvəkət, -ˌkeɪt/ n person who speaks in defense of another person or of an idea; supporter **advocate** /-ˌkeɪt/ vt strongly support a particular way of doing things ~**cacy** /-kəsi/ n [U]

ae·gis /ˈiːdʒɪs/ n **under the aegis of** with the protection or support of

aeon, eon /ˈiːən, -ɑn/ n indefinitely long period of time

aer·i·al[1] /ˈeriəl/ n wire, rod, etc., that receives radio or television signals

aerial[2] /ˈeriəl/ adj in or from the air: *aerial photography*

aer·o·bat·ics /ˌerəˈbætɪks/ n [U] ACRO-BATIC tricks done in an aircraft **aerobatic** adj

aer·o·bic /eˈroʊbɪk/ adj relating to exercise to strengthen heart and lungs

aer·o·bics /eˈroʊbɪks/ n [U] active physical exercise done to music

aer·o·dy·nam·ics /ˌeroʊdaɪˈnæmɪks/ n [U] science of movement through the air **aerodynamic** adj **1** concerning aerodynamics **2** using the principles of aerodynamics

aer·o·nau·tics /ˌerəˈnɔtɪks/ n [U] science of the flight of aircraft

aer·o·sol /ˈerəˌsɔl, -ˌsɑl/ n container from which liquid is forced out in a fine mist

aer·o·space /ˈeroʊˌspeɪs/ n [U] the air around the Earth and space beyond it

af·fa·ble /ˈæfəbəl/ adj friendly and pleasant –**bly** adv

af·fair /əˈfer/ n **1** event; set of events **2** something to be done; business **3** sexual relationship outside marriage – see also FOREIGN AFFAIRS

af·fect /əˈfekt/ vt cause a change in; influence: *Smoking affects your health.* ~**ed** adj not natural; pretended ~**ation** /ˌæfekˈteɪʃən/ n [U] unnatural behavior

af·fec·tion /əˈfekʃən/ n [U] gentle, lasting fondness ~**ate** adj ~**ately** adv

af·fi·da·vit /ˌæfəˈdeɪvɪt/ n law written statement for use as proof

af·fil·i·ate /əˈfiliˌeɪt/ vi/t (esp. of a group) join to a larger group –**ation** /əˌfiliˈeɪʃən/ n [C;U] **affiliate** /əˈfiliət/ n [C] small company or organization controlled by a larger one

af·fin·i·ty /əˈfinəti/ n [C;U] close connection or liking

af·firm /əˈfɜm/ vt fml declare; state ~**ative** n, adj (statement) meaning 'yes' ~**ation** /ˌæfərˈmeɪʃən/ n [C;U]

af·firm·a·tive ac·tion /əˌfɜmətɪv ˈækʃən/ n [U] action to provide equal job possibilities for everyone regardless of race, sex, age, etc.

af·fix[1] /əˈfiks/ vt fml fix; fasten

af·fix[2] /ˈæfiks/ n group of letters added to the beginning or end of a word to change its meaning or use (as in "*un*tie", "kind*ness*")

af·flict /əˈflɪkt/ vt cause to suffer; trouble ~**ion** /əˈflɪkʃən/ n [C;U] fml

af·flu·ent /ˈæfluənt/ adj wealthy; rich —**ence** n [U]

af·ford /əˈfɔːrd, əˈfoʊrd/ vt 1 be able to pay for 2 be able to risk: *I can't afford to neglect my health.*~**able** adj not expensive

af·front /əˈfrʌnt/ vt be rude to; offend **affront** n

a·fi·cio·na·do /əˌfiʃəˈnɑːdoʊ/ n -**dos** someone who is keenly interested in a particular activity or subject

a·field /əˈfiːld/ adv **far afield** far away

AFL-CIO n [the] American Federation of Labor and Congress of Industrial Organizations; an association of American labor unions

a·float /əˈfloʊt/ adv, adj 1 floating 2 on a ship 3 out of debt

a·fore·said /əˈfɔːrsed/ adj said or named before

a·fraid /əˈfreɪd/ adj 1 frightened: *afraid of the dark* 2 sorry for something that has happened or is likely to happen: *"Are we late?" "I'm afraid so."*

a·fresh /əˈfreʃ/ adv fml again

Af·ri·can-Ameri·can /ˌ··· ·ˈ···◂/ n an American whose family originally comes from the part of Africa south of the Sahara Desert

af·ter /ˈæftər/ prep, conj 1 later than: *after breakfast* | *after you leave* 2 following: *Your name comes after mine in the list.* | *It rained day after day.* 3 because of: *After what he did I don't want to see him.* 4 in spite of: *After I packed it so carefully, the clock arrived broken.* 5 looking for: *The police are after him.* 6 fml in the style of: *a painting after Rembrandt* 7 **after all** in spite of everything ♦ adv later; afterwards

af·ter·ef·fect /ˈæftərəˌfekt/ n effect (usu. unpleasant) that follows some time after the cause

af·ter·life /ˈæftərˌlaɪf/ n [sing] life that is believed to exist after death

af·ter·math /ˈæftərˌmæθ/ n period following a bad event: *the aftermath of the war*

af·ter·noon /ˌæftərˈnuːn◂/ n [C;U] time between noon and sunset

af·ter·shave /ˈæftərˌʃeɪv/ n [C;U] pleasant-smelling liquid that a man puts on his face after he SHAVEs

af·ter·taste /ˈæftərˌteɪst/ n [usu. sing] taste left in the mouth after eating or drinking

af·ter·thought /ˈæftərˌθɔt/ n idea that comes later; something added later

af·ter·wards /ˈæftərwərdz/ adv later; after that

a·gain /əˈgen/ adv 1 once more; another time: *Say it again.* 2 back to the original place or condition: *He's home again now.* 3 besides; further: *I could eat as much (= the same amount) again.* 4 **again and again** very often

a·gainst /əˈgenst/ prep 1 in the direction of and meeting or touching: *The rain beat against the windows.* 2 in opposition to: *Stealing is against the law.* 3 as a protection from: *They were vaccinated against cholera.* 4 having as a background: *The picture looks good against that red wall.*

age /eɪdʒ/ n 1 [C;U] length of time someone has lived or something has existed: *What are the children's ages?* 2 [U] one of the periods of human life: *to look after her in her old age* 3 [C] period of history: *This is the nuclear age.* 4 [C] long time: *We haven't met for ages.* 5 **of age** old enough (usu. at 18 or 21) to be responsible in law for one's own actions 6 **under/over age** too young/too old to be legally allowed to do something ♦ vi/t make or become old **aged** adj 1 /eɪdʒd/ of the stated number of years: *a boy aged 10* 2 /ˈeɪdʒɪd/ very old: *an aged man*

age·is·m, agism /ˈeɪdʒɪzəm/ n [U] the making of unfair differences between people because of their age, esp. treating young people more favorably than old people **ageist, agist** adj, n

a·gen·cy /ˈeɪdʒənsi/ n work or business of an agent: *an employment agency*

a·gen·da /əˈdʒendə/ n -**das** list of things to be talked about at a meeting

a·gent /ˈeɪdʒənt/ n 1 person who does business for other people: *A travel agent arranges travel.* 2 person or thing that produces a result: *Soap is a cleansing agent.*

ag·gra·vate /ˈægrəˌveɪt/ vt 1 make worse 2 annoy: *an aggravating delay* –**vation** /ˌægrəˈveɪʃən/ n [C;U]

ag·gre·gate /ˈægrəgɪt/ n [C;U] total

ag·gres·sion /əˈgreʃən/ n 1 starting a quarrel or war without just cause –**sor** /əˈgresər/ n person or country that does this

ag·gres·sive /əˈgresɪv/ adj 1 always ready to attack 2 brave and determined

ag·grieved /əˈgriːvd/ adj fml showing hurt feelings

a·ghast /ə'gæst/ *adj* surprised and shocked

ag·ile /'ædʒəl, 'ædʒaɪl/ *adj* able to move quickly **agility** /ə'dʒɪləti/ *n* [U]

ag·i·tate /'ædʒəteɪt/ *v* **1** *vt* shake (a liquid) **2** *vt* make anxious; worry **3** *vi* [(for)] argue strongly in public **–tated** *adj* very nervous, anxious, or upset **–tator** *n* person who agitates for political or social change **–tation** /ˌædʒə-'teɪʃən/ *n* [U]

ag·nos·tic /æg'nɑstɪk, əg-/ *n, adj* (person) believing that nothing can be known about God **~ism** /-tɪˌsɪzəm/ *n* [U]

a·go /ə'goʊ/ *adj, adv* back in time from now: *a week ago*

ag·o·nize /'ægənaɪz/ *vi infml* make a long and anxious effort when trying to make a decision, etc. **–nized** *adj* expressing great pain **–nizing** *adj* causing great pain or difficulty

ag·o·ny /'ægəni/ *n* [C;U] great suffering

ag·o·ra·pho·bi·a /ˌægrə'foʊbiə/ *n* [U] fear of open spaces

a·grar·i·an /ə'grɛriən/ *adj fml* of land, esp. farmland

a·gree /ə'gri/ *v* **1** *vi/t* share the same opinion; say 'yes': *I agree with you.* | *We agreed to go home.* | *They met at the agreed place.* **2** *vi* (of statements, etc.) be the same; match **~able** *adj* pleasant **~ably** *adv* **~ment** *n* **1** [U] state of agreeing: *The 2 sides cannot reach agreement.* **2** [C] arrangement between people or groups; CONTRACT: *to break an agreement*

  agree with *phr vt* **1** suit the health of **2** be in accordance with

ag·ri·cul·ture /'ægrɪˌkʌltʃər/ *n* [U] growing crops; farming **–tural** /ˌægrɪ-'kʌltʃərəl◂/ *adj*

ag·ron·o·my /ə'grɑnəmi/ *n* [U] science of managing soil and growing crops

a·ground /ə'graʊnd/ *adv, adj* (of a ship) on or onto the shore or bottom of a sea, lake, etc.

a·head /ə'hɛd/ *adv, adj* **1** in front **2** into the future: *to plan ahead* **3** [(of)] in advance; succeeding better: *to get ahead of our rivals*

A.I. *n* [U] ARTIFICIAL INTELLIGENCE

aid /eɪd/ *n* **1** [U] help: *She came to my aid at once.* | *to collect $1,000* **in aid of** *medical research* **2** [C] person or thing that helps: *an aid in learning a language* – see also FIRST AID ♦ *vt fml* help

aide /eɪd/ *n* person who helps

AIDS, Aids /eɪdz/ *n* [U] Acquired Immune Deficiency Syndrome; very serious disease caused by a VIRUS which breaks down the body's natural defenses against infection

ail·ing /eɪlɪŋ/ *adj* sick: *an ailing child*

ail·ment /'eɪlmənt/ *n* illness

aim /eɪm/ *v* **1** *vi/t* point (a weapon, etc.) towards **2** *vi* direct one's efforts; intend: *I aim to be a writer.* ♦ *n* **1** act of directing a shot **2** desired result; purpose: *What is your aim in life?* **~less** *adj* without purpose

ain't /eɪnt/ *nonstandard*: am not, is not, are not, has not, *or* have not

air¹ /ɛr/ *n* **1** [U] mixture of gases that we breathe **2** [U] space above the ground: *travel by air* **3** [C] general character of a person or place: *an air of excitement at the meeting* **4** clear the air get rid of misunderstanding, etc., by stating the facts clearly **5 in the air: a** (of stories, talk, etc.) being passed on from one person to another **b** uncertain **6 on/off the air** broadcasting/not broadcasting – see also HOT AIR, THIN AIR **airs** *n* [P] unnatural behavior to make one seem important

air² *v* **1** *vi/t* make or become fresh by letting in air: *to air the room* **2** *vt* let people know: *He's always airing his opinions.* **3** *vt* broadcast **airing** *n* [C;U]

  air out *phr v* air² (1)

air·bag /'ɛrbæg/ *n* bag in a car that fills with air for protection in accidents

air·borne /'ɛrbɔrn, -boʊrn/ *adj* **1** carried by the air **2** (of aircraft) flying

air con·di·tion·ing /'· ·ˌ···/ also AC *n* [U] system using machines (**air conditioners**) to control the indoor air temperature **–tioned** *adj*

air·craft /'ɛrkræft/ *n* **-craft** flying machine

aircraft car·ri·er /'·· ˌ···/ *n* military ship that carries aircraft

air·fare /'ɛrfɛr/ *n* [U] price of a plane trip

air·field /'ɛrfild/ *n* place where aircraft can land

air·force /'ɛrfɔrs/ *n* branch of a country's military forces that fights in the air

air·head /'ɛrˌhɛd/ *n sl* stupid person

air·i·ly /'ɛrəli/ *adv* in a light AIRY (2,3) manner

air·lift /ˈɛɹˌlɪft/ n carrying of large numbers of people or amounts of supplies by aircraft, esp. to or from a place that is difficult to get to **airlift** vt

air·line /ˈɛɹlaɪn/ n business that carries passengers and goods by air

air·lin·er /ˈɛɹˌlaɪnə/ n large passenger aircraft

air·mail /ˈɛɹmeɪl/ n [U] system of sending letters, etc., by air

air·plane /ˈɛɹpleɪn/ n flying vehicle with wings and one or more engines

air·port /ˈɛɹpɔrt, -poʊrt/ n place where aircraft regularly land, with buildings for waiting passengers, etc.

air·space /ˈɛɹspeɪs/ n [U] sky above a country, regarded as that country's property

air strike /ˈ· ˌ·/ n an attack in which military aircraft drop bombs on a place

air·strip /ˈɛɹstrɪp/ n piece of ground where aircraft can land if necessary

air·tight /ˈɛɹtaɪt/ adj not letting air in or out

air time /ˈ· ˌ·/ n [U] time taken to broadcast a radio or television show

air-to-air /ˌ· · ˈ· ◂/ adj to be fired from one aircraft to another

air·wor·thy /ˈɛɹˌwəði/ adj (of an aircraft) in safe working condition **–thiness** n [U]

air·y /ˈɛri/ adj 1 open to the fresh air 2 not practical; **airy** notions 3 cheerful and careless

aisle /aɪl/ n passage between seats in a church, theater, etc.

a·jar /əˈdʒɑr/ adv, adj (of a door) slightly open

a.k.a. abbrev. for: also known as

a·kin /əˈkɪn/ adj [(to)] like; similar

à la carte /ˌɑlɑˈkɑrt, ˌælɑ-, ˌɑlɑ-/ adj (of food on a MENU) having a separate price for each

a·lac·ri·ty /əˈlækrəti/ n [U] fml quick and willing readiness

à la mode /ˌɑlɑˈmoʊd, ˌælɑ-, ˌɑlɑ-/ adj served with ice cream

a·larm /əˈlɑrm/ n 1 [C] warning of danger 2 [U] sudden fear 3 [C] apparatus that gives a warning: a burglar **alarm** 4 [C] clock that can be set to make a noise at any time to wake people: set the **alarm** (clock) for 6:30 ♦ vt frighten: **alarming** news **~ist** n person who always expects danger, often without good reason, and says so to others **~ist** adj

a·las /əˈlæs/ interj lit (cry expressing sorrow)

al·be·it /ɔlˈbi-ɪt, æl-/ conj fml even though: an important, albeit small, mistake

al·bi·no /ælˈbaɪnoʊ/ n person or animal with white skin, very light hair, and pink eyes

al·bum /ˈælbəm/ n 1 book for sticking photographs, etc., into 2 long-playing record

al·co·hol /ˈælkəˌhɔl, -ˌhɑl/ n [U] (drinks containing) the liquid that makes one drunk **~ism** n [U] diseased condition caused by the continued drinking of too much alcohol **~ic** /ˌælkəˈhɔlɪk ◂, -ˈhɑ-/ adj, n person unable to stop drinking alcohol

al·cove /ˈælkoʊv/ n small partly enclosed space in a room for a bed, etc.

ale /eɪl/ n [U] kind of beer

al·der·man /ˈɔldəmən/ n -woman /-ˌwʊmən/ low-level elected city government official

a·lert /əˈlət/ adj quick to see and ask; watchful ♦ n 1 warning of danger 2 **on the alert** ready to deal with danger ♦ vt warn

al·fal·fa /ælˈfælfə/ n small green SALAD plant

al·gae /ˈældʒi/ n [P] very small plants that live in or near water

al·ge·bra /ˈældʒəbrə/ n [U] branch of MATHEMATICS using letters to represent values

a·li·as /ˈeɪliəs/ n -ases false name used esp. by a criminal ♦ adv also called: Edward Ball, alias John Smith

al·i·bi /ˈæləˌbaɪ/ n proof that a person charged with a crime was somewhere else when it happened

a·li·en /ˈeɪliən/ n 1 foreigner who has not become a citizen of the country where he or she lives 2 (in films and stories) a creature from another world ♦ adj 1 foreign 2 different and strange

a·li·en·ate /ˈeɪliəˌneɪt/ vt make unfriendly **–ation** /ˌeɪliəˈneɪʃən/ n [U]

a·light /əˈlaɪt/ adj burning: Several cars were set alight ♦ vi **alighted** or alit /əˈlɪt/ fml get down; come down: to alight from a train

a·lign /əˈlaɪn/ vi/t 1 come or put into a line 2 **align** oneself with come into agreement with: They aligned themselves with the army. **~ment** n [C;U]

a·like /əˈlaɪk/ adj, adv like one another; the same

al·i·mo·ny /ˈælɪˌmoʊni/ n [U] money that one must pay regularly to a former wife or husband

a·live /əˈlaɪv/ adj **1** living; in existence: (fig.) *The argument was kept alive by the politicians.* **2** full of life; active **3 alive to** AWARE of **4 alive with** covered with (insects, etc.)

all[1] /ɔl/ determiner the whole of; every one of: *all the bread* | *all these questions* | *He ate it all.*

all[2] adv **1** completely: *It's all dirty.* | *He's all alone.* **2** for each side: *The score was 3 all.* **3 all along** from the beginning **4 all at once** also **all of a sudden** suddenly **5 all out** using all possible strength and effort **6 all over a** everywhere **b** finished **7 all right: a** safe or satisfactory **b** I agree; yes **8 all the by** so much: *If you help, we'll finish all the sooner.* **9 all there** having a good quick mind **10 all the same** even so; in any case **11 all the same** to making no difference to: *It's all the same to me what you do.* **12 all told** all together **13 all up** at an end; ruined **14 not all that** infml not very

all[3] pron **1** everyone or everything: *This is all I have.* | *I brought all of them.* **2 all in all** considering everything **3 (not) at all** (not) in any way: *I don't agree at all.* **4 in all** counting everyone or everything **5 once and for all** for the last time

Al·lah /ˈælə, ˈɑlə, əˈlɑ/ n (the Muslim name for) God

all-Ameri·can /ˌ.ˈ...ᵈ/ adj typical of America or Americans

all-around /ˌ.ˈ.ᵈ/ adj good at many different things: *the best all-around player*

al·lay /əˈleɪ/ vt fml make (fear, etc.) less

all clear /ˌ.ˈᵈ/ n [the+S] **1** signal that danger is past **2** GO AHEAD

al·lege /əˈlɛdʒ/ vt fml declare without proof: *an alleged thief* **allegedly** /əˈlɛdʒɪdli/ adv **allegation** /ˌælɪˈgeɪʃən/ n fml unproved statement

al·le·giance /əˈlidʒəns/ n [U] loyalty to a leader, country, etc.

al·le·go·ry /ˈæləˌgɔri, -ˌgoʊri/ n [C;U] (style of) story, poem, etc., in which the characters represent ideas and qualities

al·ler·gy /ˈælədʒi/ n condition of being made ill by a particular food, drug, etc. **-gic** /əˈlədʒɪk/ adj

al·le·vi·ate /əˈliviˌeɪt/ vt make (pain, etc.) less **-ation** /əˌliviˈeɪʃən/ n [U]

al·ley /ˈæli/ n **1** narrow street or path between larger streets **2** track along which balls are rolled in BOWLING **up/down one's alley** suitable

al·li·ance /əˈlaɪəns/ n **1** [C] close agreement or connection made between countries, etc., for a shared purpose **2** [U] act of forming an alliance or state of being in an alliance

al·li·ga·tor /ˈæləˌgeɪtə/ n animal like a CROCODILE

all-in·clu·sive /ˌ. .ˈ.. ◂/ adj including everything: *an all-inclusive price*

all-night /ˌ. ˈ./ adj open or happening all night: *an all-night pharmacy*

al·lo·cate /ˈæləˌkeɪt/ vt give as a share **-cation** /ˌæləˈkeɪʃən/ n [C;U]

al·lot /əˈlɑt/ vt **-tt-** allocate

al·lot·ment /əˈlɑtˈmənt/ n [C;U] allocation

al·low /əˈlaʊ/ vt **1** let (someone) do something without opposing them; let (something) be done; permit: *They allowed him to come.* **2** provide (esp. money or time) **~able** adj **~ance** n **1** money provided regularly **2 make allowances** take something into consideration

allow for phr vt take into consideration: *We must allow for the train being late.*

al·loy /ˈælɔɪ/ n mixture of metals

all right /ˌ. ˈ./ adj, adv **1** safe, unharmed, or healthy **2** acceptable **3** I/we agree **4** infml beyond doubt **5 That's/It's all right** (used as a reply when someone thanks you or says they are sorry for something they have done)

al·lude /əˈlud/ v **allude to** phr vt fml speak about indirectly **allusion** /əˈluʒən/ n [C;U]

al·lure /əˈlʊr/ vt attract or charm by the offer of something pleasant: *an alluring smile*

al·ly /ˈælaɪ, əˈlaɪ/ n person, country, etc., that helps one or agrees to help ♦ /əˈlaɪ, ˈælaɪ/ vt **1** unite by agreement, marriage, etc. **2 allied (to)** related or connected (to)

al·ma ma·ter /ˌælmə ˈmɑtə, ˌɑl-/ n school, college, etc., which one attended

al·ma·nac /ˈɔːlmənæk/ n book giving general information

al·might·y /ɔːlˈmaɪti/ adj very great

al·mond /ˈɑːmənd, ˈæm-/ n kind of nut

al·most /ˈɔːlməʊst, ɔːlˈməʊst/ adv very nearly; almost everyone | almost finished

alms /ɑːmz/ n [P] money, food, clothes, etc., given to poor people

a·loft /əˈlɒft/ adv fml high up

a·lone /əˈləʊn/ adv, adj 1 without others: He lives alone. 2 only: You alone can do it. 3 **leave/let alone**: a leave untouched or unchanged b allow to be by oneself

a·long /əˈlɒŋ/ adv 1 forward; on: Come along! 2 with others: Bring your sister along (with you). ♦ prep 1 from end to end of: walk along the road 2 somewhere on the length of

a·long·side /əˌlɒŋˈsaɪd/ adv, prep close to the side (of)

a·loof /əˈluːf/ adj, adv distant in feeling; not friendly ~**ness** n [U]

a·loud /əˈlaʊd/ adv in a voice that can be heard: to read aloud

al·pha·bet /ˈælfəbet/ n letters used in writing ~**ical** /ˌælfəˈbetɪkəl◂/ adj in the order of the alphabet

al·read·y /ɔːlˈredi/ adv 1 by or before an expected time; Are you leaving already? 2 before now: I've seen the film twice already.

al·right /ɔːlˈraɪt/ adj, adv ALL RIGHT

al·so /ˈɔːlsəʊ/ adv 1 as well; besides 2 **not only . . . but also . . .** both . . . and . . .

also-ran /ˈ·· ˌ·/ n person who has failed to win at a sport or in an election

al·tar /ˈɔːltə/ n table used in a religious ceremony

al·ter /ˈɔːltə/ vi/t make or become different ~**ation** /ˌɔːltəˈreɪʃən/ n [C;U]

al·ter·ca·tion /ˌɔːltəˈkeɪʃən/ n [C;U] noisy argument or quarrel

al·ter e·go /ˌɔːltə ˈiːgəʊ/ n **alter egos** 1 very close and trusted friend 2 part of one's personality which people do not usually see

al·ter·nate¹ /ˈɔːltənɪt/ adj (of two things) happening in turns; first one and then the other He works on alternate days. ~**ly** adv

al·ter·nate² /ˈɔːltəneɪt/ vi/t happen or follow by turns **–nation** /ˌɔːltəˈneɪʃən/ n [C;U]

al·ter·na·tive /ɔːlˈtɜːnətɪv/ adj 1 to be done or used instead; other 2 different from what is usual or traditional (TRADITION): alternative medicine 3 not based on or not accepting the established standards of ordinary society: alternative theater ♦ n [(to)] something that can be done or used instead ~**ly** adv

al·though /ɔːlˈðəʊ/ conj though

al·ti·tude /ˈæltɪtjuːd/ n height above sea level

al·to /ˈæltəʊ/ n **-tos** (person with) a singing voice between SOPRANO and TENOR

al·to·geth·er¹ /ˌɔːltəˈgeðə◂/ adv 1 completely: altogether different 2 considering everything together: Altogether, it was a good trip.

altogether² n **in the altogether** NUDE

al·tru·is·m /ˈæltruˌɪzəm/ n [U] unselfishness **–ist** n **–istic** /ˌæltruˈɪstɪk◂/ adj

al·u·min·um /əˈluːmənəm/ n [U] light silver-white metal

aluminum foil /·ˌ··· ˈ·/ n [U] very thin bendable sheet of shiny metal

al·ways /ˈɔːlweɪz, -wɪz, -wɪz/ adv 1 at all times: The sun always rises in the east. 2 for ever: I'll always love you. 3 very often and annoyingly: He's always complaining.

am /m, əm; strong æm/ v 1st person sing. present tense of BE

a.m., AM abbrev. for: 1 ante meridiem = (Latin) before noon (used after numbers expressing time) 2 amplitude modulation, the part of the radio band used by most stations: We broadcast on 670 AM and 98.2 FM.

a·mal·gam /əˈmælgəm/ n mixture or combination

a·mal·gam·ate /əˈmælgəmeɪt/ vi/t (of businesses, etc.) unite; combine **–ation** /əˌmælgəˈmeɪʃən/ n [C;U]

a·mass /əˈmæs/ vt gather or collect in great amounts

am·a·teur /ˈæmətʃə, -ˌtʃʊr, -tə/ n person who does something for enjoyment and without being paid: amateur actors | amateur sport ~**ish** /ˌæməˈtɜːrɪʃ, -ˈtɜːrɪʃ/ adj lacking skill

a·maze /əˈmeɪz/ vt fill with great surprise: I was amazed to hear the news. | an amazing film ~**ment** n [U] **amaz·ingly** adv

am·a·zon /ˈæməzən, -zən/ n tall, strong woman

am·bas·sa·dor /æmˈbæsədə/ n official of high rank representing his/her own country in another country

am·ber /ˈæmbə/ n [U] (yellow color of) a hard substance used for jewels

am·bi·dex·trous /ˌæmbɪˈdekstrəs/ adj able to use both hands equally well

am·bi·ence /ˈæmbɪəns, ˌɑmbiˈɑns/ n feeling of a place; ATMOSPHERE (3)

am·big·u·ous /æmˈbɪgyuəs/ adj having more than one meaning; not clear –uity /ˌæmbəˈgyuəti/ n [C;U]

am·bi·tion /æmˈbɪʃən/ n 1 [U] strong desire for success 2 [C] whatever is desired in this way: to achieve one's ambitions –tious adj –tiously adv

am·biv·a·lent /æmˈbɪvələnt/ adj having opposing feelings about something –lence n [U]

am·ble /ˈæmbəl/ vi walk at an easy gentle rate

am·bu·lance /ˈæmbyələns/ n motor vehicle for carrying sick people

am·bush /ˈæmbʊʃ/ n [C;U] surprise attack from a place of hiding **ambush** vt

a·me·li·o·rate /əˈmilyəˌreɪt/ vt fml improve –ration /əˌmilyəˈreɪʃən/ n [U]

a·men /ˌeɪˈmen, ˌɑ-/ interj (at the end of a prayer) may this be true

a·me·na·ble /əˈminəbəl, əˈmɛ-/ adj willing to be influenced

a·mend /əˈmend/ vt change and improve

a·mend·ment /əˈmendmənt/ n agreed change to an existing law, esp. the US Constitution

a·mends /əˈmendz/ n [P] **make amends** pay for harm or damage done

a·me·ni·ty /əˈmenəti, əˈmi-/ n something (e.g. a park or swimming pool) that makes life pleasant

Ameri·cana /əˌmerəˈkɑnə/ n [U] objects, stories, etc. typical of America

Ameri·can Dream /ˌ····ˈ·/ n [sing] belief that everyone in U.S. can be successful with hard work

Ameri·can·ism /əˈmerəkəˌnɪzəm/ n English word or phrase used in the US

am·e·thyst /ˈæməθɪst/ n [C;U] (purple color of) a stone used in jewelry

a·mi·a·ble /ˈeɪmiəbəl/ adj good tempered; friendly –bly adv

am·i·ca·ble /ˈæmɪkəbəl/ adj done in a friendly way: reach an amicable agreement –bly adv

a·mid /əˈmɪd/ also **amidst** /əˈmɪdst/ — prep fml among

a·miss /əˈmɪs/ adj, adv fml 1 wrong(ly) or imperfect(ly) 2 **take something amiss** be offended

ammo /ˈæmoʊ/ n [U] infml ammunition

am·mo·ni·a /əˈmoʊnyə/ n [U] 1 gas with a strong smell, used in explosives and chemicals 2 liquid used in house cleaning

am·mu·ni·tion /ˌæmyəˈnɪʃən/ n [U] bullets, bombs, etc.

am·ne·si·a /æmˈniːʒə/ n [U] loss of memory

am·nes·ty /ˈæmnəsti/ n general act of forgiveness, esp. by a state to people guilty of political offences

a·moe·ba, ameba /əˈmibə/ n -bas or -bae /-bi, -baɪ/ living creature that consists of only one cell –bic /-bɪk/ adj

a·mok /əˈmʌk, əˈmɑk/ also **amuck** — adv **run amok** run wildly about trying to kill people

a·mong /əˈmʌŋ/ also **amongst** /əˈmʌŋst/ — prep 1 in the middle of: a house among the trees 2 in the group of; one of: He's among the best of our students. | They talked about it among themselves. (= together) 3 to each of (more than 2): Divide it among the 5 of you.

a·mor·al /ˌeɪˈmɔrəl, eɪˈmɑrəl, æ-/ adj having to no understanding of right or wrong

am·o·rous /ˈæmərəs/ adj feeling or expressing love, esp. sexual love ~ly adv

a·mor·phous /əˈmɔrfəs/ adj having no fixed form or shape

a·mount¹ /əˈmaʊnt/ n quantity; total; large amounts of money

amount² v **amount to** phr vt be equal to

amp /æmp/ also **ampere** /ˈæmpɪər/ — n standard measure of the quantity of electricity

am·phet·a·mine /æmˈfɛtəˌmin, -mɪn/ n [C;U] drug used esp. illegally, by people wanting excitement

am·phib·i·an /æmˈfɪbiən/ n animal, such as a FROG, that can live both on land and in water –ious adj

am·phi·the·a·ter /ˈæmfəˌθiətə/ n open building with rows of seats round a central space

am·ple /ˈæmpəl/ adj enough; plenty **amply** adv

am·pli·fy /ˈæmpləˌfaɪ/ vi/t fml 1 explain in more detail 2 make (esp. sound) stronger –fier n instrument for making sound louder –fication /ˌæmpləfəˈkeɪʃən/ n [U]

am·pu·tate /ˈæmpyəˌteɪt/ *vi/t* cut off (part of the body) for medical reasons **–tation** /ˌæmpyəˈteɪʃən/ *n* [C;U]

a·muck /əˈmʌk/ *adv* AMOK

a·muse /əˈmyuz/ *vt* **1** cause to laugh: *an amusing story* **2** cause to spend time pleasantly **~ment** *n* **1** [U] state of being amused **2** [C] something that passes the time pleasantly

amusement park /·ˈ·· ˌ·/ *n* park with amusements and machines to ride on

an /ən; *strong* æn/ *indefinite article, determiner (used before a vowel sound)* a: *an elephant*

a·nach·ro·nis·m /əˈnækrəˌnɪzəm/ *n* person, thing, or idea placed in the wrong period of time: *To say 'Julius Caesar looked at his watch' is an anachronism.* **–nistic** /əˌnækrəˈnɪstɪk◄/ *adj*

an·a·gram /ˈænəˌgræm/ *n* word made by changing the order of the letters in another word: *'Silent' is an anagram of 'listen'.*

a·nal /ˈeɪnl/ *adj* of, concerning the ANUS

an·al·ge·sic /ˌænlˈdʒizɪk, -sɪk/ *n, adj* (substance) which makes one unable to feel pain

a·nal·o·gy /əˈnælədʒi/ *n* **1** [C] degree of likeness **2** [U] explaining one thing by comparing it to something else **–gous** /-gəs/ *adj* like or alike in some ways

a·nal·y·sis /əˈnæləsɪs/ *n* **1** [C;U] examination of something; analyzing **2** [U] PSYCHOANALYSIS **analyst** /ˈænl-ɪst/ *n* **analytic** /ˌænlˈɪtɪk◄/ *adj*

an·a·lyze /ˈænlˌaɪz/ *vt* examine carefully, often by dividing something into parts

an·ar·chy /ˈænərki/ *n* [U] **1** absence of government **2** social disorder **–chism** *n* [U] **–chist** *n* person who wishes for this **–chic** /æˈnɑrkɪk/ *adj*

a·nath·e·ma /əˈnæθəmə/ *n* something hated

a·nat·o·my /əˈnætəmi/ *n* **1** [U] scientific study of living bodies **2** [C] way a living thing works: (fig.) *the anatomy of modern society* **–mical** /ˌænəˈtɑmɪkəl◄/ *adj*

an·ces·tor /ˈænˌsɛstər/ *n* person from whom one is descended **–tral** /ænˈsɛstrəl/ *adj*

an·ces·try /ˈænˌsɛstri, -səstri/ *n* [C;U] all one's ancestors

an·chor /ˈæŋkər/ *n* **1** piece of heavy metal for lowering into the water to stop a ship from moving **2** something that makes one feel safe ♦ *v* **1** *vi* lower the anchor **2** *vt* fix firmly in position **~age** *n* place where ships may anchor **3** anchorperson

an·chor·per·son /ˈæŋkərˌpɜsən/ also **–man** /-ˌmæn/ *masc.*,**–woman** /-ˌwʊmən/ *fem.* — *n* broadcaster usu. on television, in charge of a news broadcast, to connect one part of the broadcast with the next

an·cho·vy /ˈænˌtʃoʊvi, -tʃə-, ænˈtʃoʊvi/ *n* **-vies** or **-vy** small fish with a strong taste

an·cient /ˈeɪnʃənt/ *adj* **1** of times long ago: *ancient Rome* **2** very old

an·cil·la·ry /ˈænsəˌlɛri/ *adj* providing additional help

and /ənd, ən; *strong* ænd/ *conj* **1** (joining 2 things) as well as: *John and Sally* | *We're cold and hungry* **2** then; therefore: *Water the seeds and they will grow.* **3** (showing that something continues without stopping): *we ran and ran.* **4** (used instead of **to** after **come, go, try**): *Try and open it.*

an·drog·y·nous /ænˈdrɑdʒənəs/ *adj* **1** (of person) looking like male and female at the same time **2** (of plant or animal) having both male and female parts

an·droid /ˈændrɔɪd/ *n* (in stories) ROBOT in human form

an·ec·dote /ˈænɪkˌdoʊt/ *n* short interesting story that is true **–dotal** /ˌænɪkˈdoʊtl/ *adj* containing or telling anecdotes

a·ne·mi·a /əˈnimiə/ *n* [U] also **anaemia** lack of enough red blood cells **–mic** *adj*

an·es·the·sia /ˌænəsˈθiʒə/ *n* [U] state of being unable to feel pain, etc.

an·es·thet·ic /ˌænəsˈθɛtɪk/ *n* [C;U] substance that stops one from feeling pain, either in a part of the body (**a local anesthetic**) or in the whole body, making one unconscious (**a general anesthetic**) **–thesia** *n* [U] use of these in medicine **–thetist** /əˈnɛsθətɪst/ *n* **–thetize** *vt*

a·new /əˈnu/ *adv* again

an·gel /ˈeɪndʒəl/ *n* **1** messenger of God **2** very kind and beautiful person **~ic** /ænˈdʒɛlɪk/ *adj*

an·ger /ˈæŋgər/ *n* [U] fierce displeasure and annoyance ♦ *vt* make angry

an·gle¹ /ˈæŋgəl/ *n* **1** space between 2 lines that meet, measured in degrees **2** corner

3 point of view **4 at an angle** not upright or straight ♦ *vt* **1** turn or move at an angle **2** represent (something) from a particular point of view

angle[2] *vi* catch fish with a hook and line

angler *n* someone who fishes for enjoyment

angle for *phr vt* try to get, by tricks or indirect questions: *to angle for an invitation*

an·go·ra /æŋˈɡɔrə/ *n* [U] soft wool made from fur of some goats or rabbits

an·gry /ˈæŋɡri/ *adj* **1** full of anger **2** (of the sky or clouds) stormy **angrily** *adv*

angst /æŋst/ *n* [U] anxiety and anguish caused esp. by considering the sad state of the world

an·guish /ˈæŋɡwɪʃ/ *n* [U] great suffering, esp. of the mind **~ed** *adj*

an·gu·lar /ˈæŋɡjələr/ *adj* **1** having sharp corners **2** (of a person) thin

an·i·mal /ˈænəməl/ *n* **1** living creature that is not a plant **2** all these except human beings **3** MAMMAL **4** person considered as lacking a mind and behaving like a wild nonhuman creature ♦ *adj* **1** of animals **2** of the body

an·i·mate[1] /ˈænəmɪt/ *adj* alive

an·i·mate[2] /ˈænəˌmeɪt/ *vt* give life or excitement to **~mated** *adj* cheerful and excited: *an animated discussion* **~mation** /ˌænəˈmeɪʃən/ *n* [U] **1** cheerful excitement **2** process of making CARTOONS

an·i·mos·i·ty /ˌænəˈmɒsəti/ *n* [C;U] powerful hatred

an·kle /ˈæŋkəl/ *n* thin part of the leg, above the foot

an·nals /ˈænlz/ *n* [P] history or record of events, etc., produced every year: *It will go down in the annals* (= history) *of modern science.*

an·nex /æˈnɛks, ˈænɪks/ *n* building added to a larger one **annex** /əˈnɛks, ˈænɛks/ *vt* take control of (land, etc.) **~ation** /ˌænɛkˈseɪʃən/ *n* [C;U]

an·ni·hi·late /əˈnaɪəˌleɪt/ *vt* destroy completely **–lation** /əˌnaɪəˈleɪʃən/ *n* [U]

an·ni·ver·sa·ry /ˌænəˈvɜrsəri/ *n* day that is an exact number of years after something happened

an·no·tate /ˈænəˌteɪt, ˈænoʊ-/ *vt fml* add notes to (a book) **–tation** /ˌænəˈteɪʃən/ *n*

an·nounce /əˈnaʊns/ *vt* state loudly or publicly: *He announced the winner*

of the competition. **~ment** *n* public statement

an·nounc·er /əˈnaʊnsər/ *n* person who reads the news, etc., on radio or television

an·noy /əˈnɔɪ/ *vt* make a little angry; cause trouble to: *an annoying delay* **~ance** *n* [C;U]

an·nu·al[1] /ˈænyuəl/ *adj* **1** happening once every year **2** for one year: *my annual salary* **~ly** *adv*

annual[2] *n* **1** plant that lives for one year **2** book produced each year with the same name but new contents

an·nu·i·ty /əˈnuəti/ *n* fixed sum of money paid each year to someone

an·nul /əˈnʌl/ *vt* **-ll-** cause (a marriage, etc.) to stop existing **~ment** *n* [C;U]

an·o·dyne /ˈænəˌdaɪn/ *adj* unlikely to offend or annoy anyone

a·nom·a·ly /əˈnɒməli/ *n fml* something different from the usual type: *A cat with no tail is an anomaly.* **–lous** *adj*

a·non[1] /əˈnɒn/ *adv lit* soon

anon[2] *abbrev. for* ANONYMOUS

a·non·y·mous /əˈnɒnəməs/ *adj* without a name; not giving the name: *an anonymous letter* **–mity** /ˌænəˈnɪmət̬i/ *n* [U]

an·o·rex·i·a /ˌænəˈrɛksiə/ *n* [U] dangerous condition in which there is a loss of desire to eat **–ic** *adj*

an·oth·er /əˈnʌðər/ *determiner, pron* **1** one more: *Have another drink.* **2** a different one: *I'll do it another time.* **3** more; in addition: *It'll cost you another $20.* **4 one another** each other

an·swer[1] /ˈænsər/ *n* **1** what is said or written when someone asks a question or sends a letter; reply **2** something discovered by thinking: *I'm getting fat — the answer is to eat less.*

answer[2] *v* **1** *vi/t* give an answer (to): *She answered with a smile.* **2** *vi/t* attend or act in reply to (the telephone ringing, a knock at the door, etc.): *Answer the phone, will you!* | *The dog answers to the name of Fred.* **3** *vi/t* be as described in: *He answers to the description you gave.* **4** *vt* be satisfactory for **~able** *adj* **1** able to be answered **2** responsible: *The school is answerable to your parents for your safety.*

answer back *phr vi/t* reply rudely (to)

answer for *phr vt* **1** be responsible for **2** pay or suffer for

an·swer·ing ma·chine /ˈ··· ·ˌ·/ *n* machine that records telephone calls when someone cannot answer them

ant /ænt/ *n* insect living on the ground and famous for hard work

ant·acid /æntˈæsɪd/ *n* medicine to help with stomach problems after having eaten or drunk too much

an·tag·o·nize /ænˈtægəˌnaɪz/ *vt* make into an enemy **–nism** *n* [U] hatred; opposition **–nist** *n* opponent **–nistic** /ænˌtægəˈnɪstɪk/ *adj*

Ant·arc·tic /æntˈɑrktɪk, -ˈɑrtɪk/ *adj, n* (of or concerning) the very cold most southern part of the world

an·te·bel·lum /ˌæntɪˈbɛləm/ *adj* before the American CIVIL WAR

an·te·ced·ents /ˌæntəˈsɪdnts/ *n* [P] *fml* past family or past history

an·te·cham·ber /ˈæntɪtˌʃeɪmbə/ also **anteroom** — *n* small room leading to a larger one

an·te·di·lu·vian /ˌæntɪdəˈluviən◂/ *adj* very old-fashioned

an·te·lope /ˈæntɪˌloʊp/ *n* **-lopes** *or* **-lope** graceful animal like a deer

an·ten·na /ænˈtɛnə/ *n* **1** *pl.* **-nae** /-ni/ insect's FEELER **2** AERIAL¹

an·them /ˈænθəm/ *n* religious or national song of praise

an·thol·o·gy /ænˈθɑlədʒi/ *n* collection of poems or other writings

an·thro·poid /ˈænθrəˌpɔɪd/ *adj* like a person

an·thro·pol·o·gy /ˌænθrəˈpɑlədʒi/ *n* scientific study of the human race **–gist** *n*

an·thro·po·mor·phic /ˌænθrəpəˈmɔrfɪk/ *adj* regarding a god, animal, etc., as having human qualities

an·ti·bi·ot·ic /ˌæntɪbaɪˈɑtɪk, ˌæntaɪ-/ *n* medical substance, such as PENICILLIN, that can kill harmful bacteria in the body

an·ti·bod·y /ˈæntɪˌbɑdi/ *n* substance produced in the body which fights disease

an·tic·i·pate /ænˈtɪsəˌpeɪt/ *vt* **1** expect: *We anticipate trouble.* **2** do something before (someone else) **3** guess (what will happen) and act as necessary **–pation** /ænˌtɪsəˈpeɪʃən/ *n* [U]

an·ti·cli·max /ˌæntɪˈklaɪmæks, ˌæntaɪ-/ *n* unexciting end to something exciting

an·tics /ˈæntɪks/ *n* [P] strange, amusing movements or behavior

anti·de·pres·sant /ˌæntɪdɪˈprɛsənt, ˌæntaɪ-/ *n* drug used for treating DEPRESSION

an·ti·dote /ˈæntɪˌdoʊt/ *n* something that prevents the effects of a poison or disease

an·ti·freeze /ˈæntɪˌfriz/ *n* [U] chemical put in water to stop it freezing, esp. in car engines

anti·his·ta·mine /ˌæntɪˈhɪstəmin, -mɪn/ *n* drug used for treating an ALLERGY or COLD

an·ti·nu·cle·ar /ˌæntɪˈnukliə, ˌæntaɪ-/ *adj* opposing the use of NUCLEAR power or weapons: *an antinuclear demonstration*

an·tip·a·thy /ænˈtɪpəθi/ *n* [C;U] fixed strong dislike; hatred

anti·per·spi·rant /ˌæntɪˈpəspərənt/ *n* substance used under the arms to prevent SWEATing

an·ti·quat·ed /ˈæntɪˌkweɪtɪd/ *adj* old-fashioned

an·tique /ænˈtik/ *adj* old and therefore valuable ♦ *n* valuable old object

an·tiq·ui·ty /ænˈtikwəti/ *n* **1** [U] great age **2** [U] ancient times **3** [C] something remaining from ancient times

an·ti·Sem·i·tis·m /ˌæntɪ ˈsɛməˌtɪzəm, ˌæntaɪ-/ *n* hatred of Jews **–Semitic** /-səˈmɪtɪk◂, ˌæntaɪ-/ *adj*

an·ti·sep·tic /ˌæntɪˈsɛptɪk◂/ *n, adj* (chemical substance) preventing disease by killing bacteria

an·ti·sla·ve·ry /ˌæntɪˈsleɪvəri, ˌæntaɪ-/ *n* opposition to slavery

an·ti·so·cial /ˌæntɪˈsoʊʃəl◂, ˌæntaɪ-/ *adj* **1** harmful to society **2** not liking to mix with people

an·tith·e·sis /ænˈtɪθəsɪs/ *n* **-ses** /-siz/ *fml* direct opposite

an·ti·trust /ˌæntɪˈtrʌst, ˌæntaɪ-/ *adj* (of laws) opposing practices that limit competition

ant·ler /ˈæntˑlə/ *n* horn of a deer

an·to·nym /ˈæntəˌnɪm/ *n* word opposite in meaning to another word

ant·sy /ˈæntsi/ *adj infml* nervous

a·nus /ˈeɪnəs/ *n* hole through which solid waste leaves the bowels

an·vil /ˈænvɪl/ *n* iron block on which metals are hammered to the shape wanted

anx·i·e·ty /æŋˈzaɪəti/ *n* **1** [C;U] fear and worry **2** [U] strong wish: *anxiety to please him*

anx·ious /'æŋkʃəs, 'æŋʃəs/ *adj* **1** worried and frightened **2** causing worry **3** wishing strongly: *anxious to please them* **~ly** *adv*

an·y /'ɛni/ *determiner, pron* **1** no matter which: *Take any you like.* **2** some; even the smallest number or amount: *Are there any letters for me?* **3 in any case** also **at any rate** — a whatever may happen **b** besides ♦ *adv* at all: *I can't stay any longer.*

an·y·bod·y /'ɛnɪˌbɑdi, -ˌbʌdi, -bədi/ *pron* anyone

an·y·how /'ɛnɪˌhaʊ/ *adv* **1** carelessly **2** in spite of everything

an·y·more /ˌɛnɪ'mɔr/ *adv* **not anymore** used to say that something that did happen or exist does not now: *She doesn't live here anymore.*

an·y·one /'ɛniˌwʌn, -wən/ *pron* **1** all people; no matter who: *Anyone can cook.* **2** even one person: *Is anyone listening?*

an·y·place /'ɛniˌpleɪs/ *adv infml for* ANYWHERE

an·y·thing /'ɛnɪˌθɪŋ/ *pron* **1** any object, act, event, etc.; no matter what: *He'll do anything for a quiet life.* **2** even one thing: *Can you see anything?* **3 anything but** not at all **4 anything like** at all like **5 as easy as anything** very easily

an·y·way /'ɛniˌweɪ/ *adv* in spite of everything; anyhow

an·y·where /'ɛniˌwɛr, -ˌhwɛr/ *adv* **1** at or to any place **2 anywhere near** at all near or nearly

a·or·ta /eɪ'ɔrtə/ *n* largest ARTERY in the body

a·part /ə'pɑrt/ *adv* **1** distant; separated: *towns 3 miles apart* **2** into parts: *to take a clock apart* **3 apart from:** **a** except for **b** as well as **4 tell/know apart** be able to see the difference between

a·part·heid /ə'pɑrtaɪt, -teɪt, -taɪd/ *n* [U] (in South Africa) the system established by government of keeping different races separate

a·part·ment /ə'pɑrt⌐mənt/ *n* room or set of rooms on one floor of a building

apartment build·ing /·'·· ˌ·'·/ *n* building containing a number of apartments

apartment com·plex /·'·· ˌ·'·/ *n* group of similar apartment buildings

ap·a·thy /'æpəθi/ *n* [U] lack of interest in things **–thetic** /ˌæpə'θɛtɪk◀/ *adj*

ape /eɪp/ *n* **1** large monkey with no tail **2 go ape/apeshit** *sl* become extremely angry ♦ *vt* copy (behavior) stupidly

a·per·i·tif /əˌperə'tif, ɑ-/ *n* alcoholic drink before a meal

ap·er·ture /'æpətʃə, -ˌtʃʊə/ *n* hole; opening

a·pex /'eɪpɛks/ *n* **-es** /'eɪpəsiz/ highest point: *the apex of a triangle*

aph·o·rism /'æfəˌrɪzəm/ *n* short wise saying

aph·ro·dis·i·ac /ˌæfrə'dɪziˌæk/ *n, adj* (drug, etc.) causing sexual excitement

a·piece /ə'pis/ *adv* each: *They cost 10c apiece.*

a·plomb /ə'plɑm/ *n* [U] calm selfcontrol

a·poc·a·lypse /ə'pɑkəlɪps/ *n* [U] (writing about) the end of the world **–lyptic** /əˌpɑkə'lɪptɪk◀/ *adj* telling of great future misfortunes

a·poc·ry·phal /ə'pɑkrəfəl/ *adj* (of a story) probably untrue

a·pol·o·get·ic /əˌpɑlə'dʒɛtɪk◀/ *adj* making an apology **~ally** *adv*

a·pol·o·gize /ə'pɑləˌdʒaɪz/ *vi* say one is sorry for a fault **–gy** *n* statement of sorrow for a fault, for causing trouble, etc.

ap·o·plex·y /'æpəˌplɛksi/ *n* [U] sudden loss of ability to move, feel, think etc.; STROKE[1] (5) **–plectic** /ˌæpə'plɛktɪk◀/ *adj* **1** of or concerning apoplexy **2** violently excited and angry

a·pos·tle /ə'pɑsəl/ *n* **1** one of the 12 first followers of Christ **2** leader of a new faith

a·pos·tro·phe /ə'pɑstrəfi/ *n* the sign ('), as in *I'm*

a·poth·e·o·sis /əˌpɑθi'oʊsɪs, ˌæpə'θiəsɪs/ *n* **-ses** /-siz/ **1** highest possible honor and glory **2** perfect example

ap·pall /ə'pɔl/ *vt* shock deeply: *We were appalled to hear the news.* **–ing** *adj* **1** shocking **2** of very bad quality **~ingly** *adv*: *an appallingly bad driver*

ap·pa·ra·tus /ˌæpə'rætəs, -'reɪtəs/ *n* [C;U] set of instruments, tools, etc. needed for a purpose

ap·par·el /ə'pærəl/ *n* [U] *fml* clothes

ap·par·ent /ə'pærənt, ə'per-/ *adj* **1** easily seen: *The reason became apparent.* **2** not necessarily real; seeming: *her apparent lack of concern* **~ly** *adv* it seems that: *Apparently, he's gone to China.*

ap·pa·ri·tion /ˌæpə'rɪʃən/ *n* GHOST

ap·peal /əˈpiːl/ n 1 [C;U] strong request for something: *an appeal for forgiveness* 2 [U] attraction; interest: *He doesn't have much sex appeal.* 3 [C;U] formal request (in law, sports) for a new decision ♦ vi 1 make a strong request: *to appeal for money* 2 please; attract: *Does the job appeal to you?* 3 ask for a new decision ~**ing** adj attractive

ap·pear /əˈpɪər/ vi 1 come into sight: *Spots appeared on my skin.* | *They finally appeared* (= arrived) *at 9:00.* 2 come in view of the public: *Her new book appears next month.* | *He's appearing* (= performing) *at Caesar's Palace.* 3 seem: *He appears to be angry.* 4 be present officially, as in a court of law ~**ance** n [C;U] 1 (an example of) the act of appearing 2 way a person or thing looks: *He changed his appearance by growing a beard.* 3 **put in/make an appearance (at)** attend (a meeting, party, etc.), esp. for a short time only

ap·pease /əˈpiːz/ vt satisfy, esp. by agreeing to demands ~**ment** n [C;U]

ap·pel·la·tion /ˌæpəˈleɪʃən/ n fml name; title

ap·pend /əˈpend/ vt fml add (esp. something written onto the end of a letter) ~**age** n something added to, or hanging from, something else

ap·pen·di·ci·tis /əˌpendəˈsaɪtɪs/ n [U] disease of the appendix (1)

ap·pen·dix /əˈpendɪks/ n -**dixes** or -**dices** /-dəsiz/ 1 small organ leading off the bowel 2 something added at the end of a book

ap·per·tain /ˌæpəˈteɪn/ v **appertain to** phr vt fml belong to

ap·pe·tite /ˈæpətaɪt/ n [C;U] desire, esp. for food

ap·pe·tiz·er /ˈæpətaɪzər/ n something eaten to increase the appetite -**tizing** adj causing appetite: *appetizing smells*

ap·plaud /əˈplɔːd/ vi/t 1 praise by striking one's hands together; CLAP 2 approve strongly **applause** /əˈplɔːz/ n [U] loud praise

ap·ple /ˈæpəl/ n kind of hard round juicy fruit — see also ADAM'S APPLE

ap·pli·ance /əˈplaɪəns/ n apparatus; machine

ap·plic·a·ble /ˈæplɪkəbəl, əˈplɪkəbəl/ adj having an effect; related: *The rule is applicable only to US citizens.*

ap·pli·cant /ˈæplɪkənt/ n person who applies for a job, etc.

ap·pli·ca·tion /ˌæplɪˈkeɪʃən/ n 1 [C;U] request: *to write applications for jobs* 2 [U] act of putting something to use 3 [C] particular practical use: *the industrial applications of this discovery* 4 [C;U] putting something on a surface 5 [U] careful effort

ap·pli·ca·tor /ˈæplɪˌkeɪtər/ n special brush, tool etc. for putting a substance, medicine, etc. on or in something

ap·ply /əˈplaɪ/ v 1 vt request officially: *apply for a job* 2 vt use for a purpose: *apply the brakes* 3 vt put onto a surface: *apply ointment to your skin* 4 vi/t give or have an effect: *Does the rule apply to me?* 5 vt cause to work hard: *apply oneself to the task* **applied** adj practical: *applied physics*

ap·point /əˈpɔɪnt/ vt 1 choose for a job 2 fml fix; decide: *the appointed time* ~**ment** n [C;U] (arrangement for) a meeting

ap·por·tion /əˈpɔːrʃən, əˈpoʊr-/ vt divide and share out

ap·po·site /ˈæpəzɪt/ adj fml completely appropriate

ap·praise /əˈpreɪz/ vt fml judge the value of **appraisal** n

ap·pre·cia·ble /əˈpriːʃəbəl, -ʃiə-/ adj noticeable: *an appreciable difference* -**bly** adv

ap·pre·ci·ate /əˈpriːʃieɪt/ v 1 vt be thankful for 2 vt understand and enjoy the good qualities of: *She appreciates good wine.* 3 vt understand fully: *I appreciate your difficulties.* 4 vi (of property) increase in value -**ciative** /-ʃətɪv, -ʃiə-/ adj: *an appreciative audience* -**ciation** /əˌpriːʃiˈeɪʃən/ n [C;U]

ap·pre·hend /ˌæprɪˈhend/ vt fml ARREST

ap·pre·hen·sion /ˌæprɪˈhenʃən/ n [U] anxiety; fear -**sive** /-sɪv, -zɪv/ adj worried

ap·pren·tice /əˈprentɪs/ n person learning a skilled trade ♦ vt [(to)] send as an apprentice: *apprenticed to an electrician* ~**ship** n [C;U]

ap·prise /əˈpraɪz/ vt fml tell or inform

ap·proach¹ /əˈproʊtʃ/ v 1 vt/t come near 2 vt make an offer or request to: *approach him about borrowing the money* 3 vt begin to consider or deal with

approach² n 1 act of approaching: *the approach of winter* 2 way of getting in 3 method of doing something 4 speaking to someone for the first time ~**able** *adj* easy to speak to or deal with

ap·pro·pri·ate¹ /ə'proupri-ıt/ *adj* correct; suitable ~**ly** *adv*

ap·pro·pri·ate² /ə'proupri,eɪt/ *vt* **1** set aside (money) for a purpose **2** take for oneself –**ation** /ə,proupri'eɪʃən/ *n* [C;U]

ap·prov·al /ə'pruvəl/ *n* [U] **1** favorable opinion **2** official permission **3 on approval** (of goods from a store) to be returned without payment if unsatisfactory

ap·prove /ə'pruv/ *v* **1** *vi* [(**of**)] have a favorable opinion: *I don't approve of smoking.* **2** *vt* agree officially to by **approvingly** *adv*

ap·prox·i·mate /ə'praksəmıt/ *adj* nearly correct but not exact ~**ly** *adv*: *approximately 300* ♦ /-,meɪt/ *vi* come near –**mation** /ə,praksə'meɪʃən/ *n* [C;U]

a·pri·cot /'æprı,kat, 'eɪ-/ *n* **1** [C] round orange or yellow fruit with a pit **2** [U] color of this fruit

A·pril /'eɪprəl/ *n* **1** the 4th month of the year **2 April fool** /ꞏꞏ ꞏ/ *n* (person who has been deceived or made fun of by) a trick played on April 1st

a·pron /'eɪprən/ *n* garment worn to protect the front of one's clothes

apt /æpt/ *adj* **1** likely: *apt to slip* **2** exactly suitable: *an apt remark* **3** quick to learn ~**ly** *adv* ~**ness** *n* [U]

apt. abbreviation of APARTMENT

ap·ti·tude /'æptə,tud/ *n* [C;U] natural ability

aptitude test /'··· ,/ *n* test used for finding out what someone's best skills are

aq·ua·ma·rine /,ækwəmə'rin◄/ *n* **1** [C] glass-like stone used for jewelry **2** [U] its blue-green color

a·quar·i·um /ə'kwɛriəm/ *n* –**iums** or –**ia** /-iə/ glass container for live fish

a·quat·ic /ə'kwætɪk, ə'kwɑtɪk/ *adj* living or happening in water

aq·ue·duct /'ækwə,dʌkt/ *n* bridge that carries water across a valley

Ar·a·bic /'ærəbık/ *n* main language of North Africa and the Middle East ♦ *adj: The signs 1, 2, 3, etc., are* **Arabic numerals.**

ar·a·ble /'ærəbəl/ *adj* (of land) used for growing crops

ar·bi·ter /'arbətə/ *n* someone who is in a position to make influen·tial judgments or to settle an argument

ar·bi·trage /'arbə,traʒ/ *n* [U] process of buying something (esp. a CURRENCY or COMMODITY) in one place and selling it at another place at the same time in order to profit from differences in price between the two places

ar·bi·tra·ry /'arbə,trɛri/ *adj* **1** based on chance rather than reason **2** typical of uncontrolled power –**rily** /,arbə'trɛrəli/ *adv* –**riness** /'arbə,trɛrınıs/ *n* [U]

ar·bi·trate /'arbə,treıt/ *vi/t* act as judge in an argument –**trator** *n* –**tration** /,arbə'treıʃən/ *n* [U] settlement of an argument by the decision of a person or group chosen by both sides: *go to arbitration*

arc /ark/ *n* part of the curve of a circle

ar·cade /ar'keıd/ *n* passage or building covered by an arch or arches, esp. one containing amusements

ar·cane /ar'keın/ *adj* mysterious and secret

arch /artʃ/ *n* curved part over a doorway or under a bridge ♦ *vi/t* make an arch: *The cat arched her back.*

ar·chae·ol·o·gy /,arki'alədʒi/ *n* [U] study of ancient remains –**gist** *n* –**gical** /,arkiə'ladʒıkəl/ *adj*

ar·cha·ic /ar'keı-ık/ *adj* no longer used; old

arch·bish·op /,artʃ'bıʃəp◄/ *n* chief BISHOP

ar·cher /'artʃə/ *n* person who shoots with a BOW² (1) ~**y** *n* [U]

ar·che·type /'arkı,taıp/ *n* **1** original of which others are copies **2** perfect example –**typal**, –**typical** /,arkı'tıpıkəl◄/ *adj*

ar·chi·pel·a·go /,arkə'pɛlə,gou/ *n* area with many small islands

ar·chi·tect /'arkə,tɛkt/ *n* person who plans buildings ~**ure** /-,tɛktʃə/ *n* [U] art of designing buildings; way of building

ar·chives /'arkaıvz/ *n* [P] **1** historical records **2** place where these are kept

arch·way /'artʃweı/ *n* an ARCH or a passage or entrance under an arch

Arc·tic /'arktık, 'artık/ *n, adj* **1** (*cap.*) (of or concerning) the very cold most northern part of the world **2** very cold

ar·dent /'ardənt/ *adj* very eager ~**ly** *adv*

ar·dor /'ardə/ *n* [C;U] *fml* strong excitement

ar·du·ous /'ardʒuəs/ *adj fml* needing effort; difficult ~**ly** *adv*

are /ə, *strong* ar/ *v* present tense pl. of BE

ar·e·a /ˈɛriə/ *n* **1** [C;U] size of a surface **2** [C] part of the world's surface: *a parking area behind the restaurant* **3** [C] subject of activity: *the area of language teaching*

area code /ˈ··· ˌ·/ *n* three numbers before a U.S. telephone number used when calling someone outside the local area

a·re·na /əˈrinə/ *n* **1** enclosed space used for sports **2** place of competition: *the political arena*

aren't /ˈɑrənt/ *v short for:* **1** are not **2** (in questions) am not

ar·gue /ˈɑrgyu/ *v* **1** *vi* express disagreement; quarrel **2** *vi/t* give reasons for or against something **arguable** *adj* perhaps true, but not certain **arguably** *adv:* *Arguably, the criminal is a necessary member of society.*

ar·gu·ment /ˈɑrgyəmənt/ *n* **1** [C] quarrel **2** [C;U] reason given for or against; use of reason ~**ative** /ˌɑrgyəˈmɛntət̮ɪv/ *adj* liking to argue too much

ar·id /ˈærɪd/ *adj* **1** (of land) very dry **2** uninteresting; dull

Aries /ˈɛriz/ *n* **1** first sign of the ZODIAC, represented by a RAM **2** person born between March 21 and April 19

a·rise /əˈraɪz/ *vi* **arose** /əˈrouz/, **arisen** /əˈrɪzən/ happen; appear

ar·is·toc·ra·cy /ˌærəˈstɑkrəsi/ *n* government by people of the highest social class –**rat** /əˈrɪstəkræt/ *n* person of high birth –**ratic** /ˌærɪstəˈkræt̮ɪk◂/ *adj*

a·rith·me·tic /əˈrɪθmət̮ɪk/ *n* calculation by numbers –**al** /ˌærɪθˈmɛt̮ɪkəl/ *adj*

ark /ɑrk/ *n* large ship, esp. the one described in the Bible

arm¹ /ɑrm/ *n* **1** upper limb **2** something shaped like this: *the arm of a chair* **3** part of a garment that covers the arm **4** part or division of the armed forces **5** **arm and a leg** high price **6** **arm in arm** (of 2 people) with arms joined **7** **keep someone at arm's length** avoid being friendly with someone **8** **with open arms** gladly and eagerly — see also ARMS

arm² *vi/t* supply with weapons ~**ed** *adj* carrying or supplied with weapons: *armed robbers*

ar·ma·da /ɑrˈmɑdə, -ˈmeɪ-/ *n* collection of armed ships

Ar·ma·ged·don /ˌɑrməˈgɛdn/ *n* (esp. in the Bible) great battle or war causing terrible destruction and bringing the end of the world

ar·ma·ment /ˈɑrməmənt/ *n* **1** [C] weapons or other fighting equipment of an army, etc. **2** [U] act of preparing for war

arm·chair /ˈɑrmtʃɛr/ *n* chair with supports for the arms ♦ *adj* ready to give advice or pass judgment, but not taking an active part

armed forc·es /ˌ· ˈ··/ *n* [P] see FORCES

ar·mi·stice /ˈɑrməstɪs/ *n* agreement to stop fighting for a time

ar·mor /ˈɑrmər/ *n* [U] **1** protective covering for the body in battle **2** protective metal covering on military vehicles: *an armored car* ~**y** *n* place where weapons are stored

arm·pit /ˈɑrmˌpɪt/ *n* hollow place under one's arm

arms /ɑrmz/ *n* [P] **1** weapons **2** **lay down one's arms** stop fighting and yield **3** **take up arms** get ready to fight with weapons **4** **up in arms** very angry and ready to argue: *They're up in arms over/about the low pay.* — see also SMALL ARMS

arms con·trol /ˈ· ·ˌ·/ *n* [U] attempt by countries to limit the number of war weapons that exist

ar·my /ˈɑrmi/ *n* **1** military forces that fight on land **2** large group: *an army of ants*

a·ro·ma /əˈroumə/ *n* pleasant smell ~**tic** /ˌærəˈmæt̮ɪk◂/ *adj*

aroma·thera·py /əˌroumə'θɛrəpi/ *n* [U] use of pleasant-smelling oils to improve one's health –**therapist** *n*

a·rose /əˈrouz/ *past t. of* ARISE

a·round /əˈraʊnd/ *adv, prep* **1 a** in various places: *I'll show you around (the house).* **b** somewhere near: *Is there anyone around?* **2 a** a little more or less than; about: *around 10 o'clock* **3 a** moving in a circle; measured in a circle: *turn around and around* | *3 yards around* **b** on all sides: *The children gathered around.*

a·rouse /əˈraʊz/ *vt* **1** *fml* cause to wake **2** make active; excite: *arouse suspicion*

ar·range /əˈreɪndʒ/ *v* **1** *vt* put in order: *arrange flowers* **2** *vi/t* plan: *arrange to meet her* **3** *vt* set out (music) for different instruments, etc. ~**ment** *n* **1** [C;U] (act of making) an agreement or plan: *make* *arrangements for the wedding* | *I have an arrangement with the bank.* **2** [C] something that has been put in order: *a beautiful flower arrangement* **3** [C] (example of) the setting out of a piece of music in a certain way

ar·ray /əˈreɪ/ *n* fine show, collection, or ordered group

ar·rears /əˈrɪrz/ *n* [P] money owed from the past: *He was two weeks in arrears with the rent.* (= he owed rent for two weeks)

ar·rest /əˈrɛst/ *vt* **1** seize by the power of the law 2 (a process) **3** attract (attention) ♦ *n* [C;U] act of arresting

ar·riv·al /əˈraɪvəl/ *n* **1** [U] act of arriving **2** [C] person or thing that has arrived: *to welcome the new arrivals*

ar·rive /əˈraɪv/ *vi* **1** reach a place: *arrive home* **2** happen; come: *The day arrived.* **3** win success

arrive at *phr vt* reach; come to: *arrive at a decision*

ar·ro·gant /ˈærəgənt/ *adj* proud in a rude way ~**ly** *adv* –**gance** /-gəns/ *n* [U]

ar·row /ˈæroʊ/ *n* **1** pointed stick to be shot from a BOW² (1) **2** sign (→) used to show direction

ar·se·nal /ˈɑrsənl/ *n* place where weapons are stored

ar·se·nic /ˈɑrsənɪk, ˈɑrsnɪk/ *n* [U] very poisonous substance

ar·son /ˈɑrsən/ *n* [U] crime of setting fire to property ~**ist** *n*

art /ɑrt/ *n* **1** [U] the making or expression of what is beautiful, e.g. in music, literature, or esp. painting **2** [U] things produced by art, esp. paintings: *an art gallery* **3** [C;U] skill in doing anything: *the art of conversation* **arts** *n* [P] subjects of study that are not part of science – see also FINE ARTS

ar·te·ry /ˈɑrtəri/ *n* **1** tube that carries blood from the heart **2** main road, passage, etc.

art·ful /ˈɑrtfəl/ *adj* **1** cleverly deceitful **2** skilfully put together ~**ly** *adv*

ar·thri·tis /ɑrˈθraɪtɪs/ *n* [U] painful disease of the joints –**tic** /ɑrˈθrɪtɪk/ *adj*

ar·ti·choke /ˈɑrtɪˌtʃoʊk/ *n* [C;U] **1** also **globe artichoke** — plant whose leafy flower is eaten **2** also **Jerusalem artichoke** — plant whose potato-like root is eaten

ar·ti·cle /ˈɑrtɪkəl/ *n* **1** thing; object: *an article of clothing* **2** piece of writing in a

newspaper **3** complete or separate part in a written law agreement **4** word used with nouns, such as *a, an,* and *the* in English

ar·tic·u·late¹ /ɑrˈtɪkyəlɪt/ *adj* **1** (of people) able to express thoughts and feelings clearly in words **2** (of speech) having clear separate sounds and words ~**ly** *adv*

ar·tic·u·late² /ɑrˈtɪkyəˌleɪt/ *v vi/t* speak or say clearly –**lation** /ɑrˌtɪkyəˈleɪʃən/ *n* [U]

ar·ti·fact /ˈɑrtəˌfækt/ *n* something made by people

ar·ti·fice /ˈɑrtəfɪs/ *n* **1** [C] clever trick **2** [U] CUNNING

ar·ti·fi·cial /ˌɑrtəˈfɪʃəl◂/ *adj* **1** made by people; not natural **2** not sincere ~**ly** *adv* ~**ity** /ˌɑrtəfɪʃiˈælɪti/ *n* [C;U]

artificial in·tel·li·gence /ˌ···· ·/··/ *n* [U] branch of computer science which aims to produce machines that can understand, make judgments, etc., in the way humans do

artificial res·pi·ra·tion /ˌ·····'·, ·ˌ··· ··/ *n* [U] making someone breathe again by pressing the chest, blowing into the mouth, etc.

ar·til·le·ry /ɑrˈtɪləri/ *n* [U] (part of the army that uses) large guns

ar·ti·san /ˈɑrtəzən, -sən/ *n* CRAFTSMAN

art·ist /ˈɑrtɪst/ *n* **1** person who works in one of the arts, esp. painting **2** inventive and skilled worker **3** professional singer, dancer, etc., who performs in a show ~**ry** *n* [U] inventive imagination and ability ~**ic** /ɑrˈtɪstɪk/ *adj* **1** of art or artists **2** showing skill in art ~**ically** *adv*

art·less /ˈɑrtlɪs/ *adj* simple and natural; almost foolish ~**ly** *adv*

artsy /ˈɑrtsi/ *adj infml* interested in art or knowing a lot about art

as¹ /əz; *strong* æz/ *adv, prep* **1** (used in comparisons and examples) equally; like: *He's as old as me.* | *small animals such as cats and dogs* | *She escaped dressed as a man.* **2** when considered as being: *As a writer, she's wonderful.* **3** **as far as** to the degree that

as² *conj* **1** (used in comparisons): *He's as old as I am.* **2** in the way that: *Do as I say!* | *Leave it as it is.* **3** because: *As I have no car, I can't go.* **4** when; while: *He saw her as she was getting off the bus.* **5** though: *Tired as I was, I tried to help.* **6** **as for** /ˌæz-/ when we speak of; concerning **7** **as if/though** in a way that seems **8** **as it is** /ˌæz-/ in reality **9** **as it were** as one might say **10 as of** /ˌæz-/ starting from (a time) **11 as yet** *fml* up until now

a.s.a.p. /ˌeɪ es eɪ ˈpi, ˈeɪsæp/ *abbrev. for*: as soon as possible

as·bes·tos /æsˈbestəs, æz-, əs-, əz-/ *n* [U] soft gray material that protects against fire or heat

as·cend /əˈsend/ *vi/t fml* **1** go up **2 ascend the throne** become king or queen ~**ancy**, ~**ency** *n* [U] controlling influence; power ~**ant**, ~**ent** *n* **in the ascendant** having or nearly having a controlling power or influence

as·cent /əˈsent/ *n* **1** [C;U] act or process of **2** [C] ascending; way up

as·cer·tain /ˌæsərˈteɪn/ *vt fml* discover; make certain ~**able** *adj*

as·cet·ic /əˈsetɪk/ *n*, *adj* (a person) avoiding physical pleasures and comforts, esp. for religious reasons ~**ism** /əˈsetəˌsɪzəm/ *n* [U]

as·cribe /əˈskraɪb/ *v* ascribe to *phr vt* believe to be the work of: *He ascribes his success to luck.*

a·sex·u·al /ˌeɪˈsekʃuəl/ *adj* **1** without sex **2** not interested in sex

ash /æʃ/ *n* [U] also **ashes** *pl.* — powder left when something has been burned ~**en** *adj* pale gray **ashes** [P] remains of a dead body after burning

a·shamed /əˈʃeɪmd/ *adj* feeling shame

a·shore /əˈʃɔr, əˈʃoʊr/ *adv* on or to the shore

ash·tray /ˈæʃtreɪ/ *n* dish for tobacco ash

a·side /əˈsaɪd/ *adv* to the side: *She stepped aside to let them pass.* ♦ *n* remark not intended to be heard by everyone present

ask /æsk/ *v* **1** *vi/t* say a question: *"Where is it?" she asked.* | *Ask him where to go.* **2** *vi/t* make a request for: *She asked him to wake her at 6:00.* **3** *vt* invite: *Ask them for dinner.* **4 ask for trouble/it** behave so as to cause (something bad): *If you park there, you're really asking for trouble!*

ask after *phr vt* ask for news of

a·skance /əˈskæns/ *adv* **look askance** without liking or pleasure

a·skew /əˈskyu/ *adv* not properly straight

a·sleep /əˈslip/ *adj* **1** sleeping **2** (of an arm or leg) unable to feel

as·par·a·gus /əˈspærəgəs/ *n* [U] plant whose stems are eaten as a vegetable

as·pect /ˈæspekt/ *n* **1** particular side of a plan, problem, etc. **2** direction in which a room, building, etc., faces

as·per·sion /əˈspɜrʒən, -ʃən/ *n fml* unkind or harmful remark: *They cast aspersions on my new book.*

as·phalt /ˈæsfɔlt/ *n* [U] black material used for road surfaces

as·phyx·i·ate /æsˈfɪksiˌeɪt, əs-/ *vt* kill by lack of air –**ation** /æsˌfɪksiˈeɪʃən, əs-/ *n* [U]

as·pire /əˈspaɪr/ *vi* direct one's hopes and efforts **aspiration** /ˌæspəˈreɪʃən/ *n* [C;U] strong desire

as·pirin /ˈæspərɪn/ *n* -**rin** *or* -**rins** (TABLET of) medicine that lessens pain and fever

ass /æs/ *n* **1** *taboo sl* BOTTOM (2) **2** DONKEY **3** foolish person

as·sail /əˈseɪl/ *vt fml* attack ~**ant** *n fml* attacker

as·sas·sin /əˈsæsən/ *n* person who assassinates

as·sas·sin·ate /əˈsæsəˌneɪt/ *vt* murder a ruler, politician, etc. –**ation** /əˌsæsəˈneɪʃən/ *n* [C;U]

as·sault /əˈsɔlt/ *n* [C;U] sudden violent attack assault *vt*

as·sem·ble /əˈsembəl/ *vi/t* gather or put together: *to assemble radios* | *A crowd assembled.*

as·sem·bly /əˈsembli/ *n* **1** [C] group of people gathered together for a purpose **2** group of people elected to make laws in some states **3** [U] assembling of machine parts

assembly line /ˈ··· ·/ *n* arrangement of workers and machines in which each person has a particular job, the work being passed from one worker to the next until the product is complete

as·sem·bly·man /əˈsemblimən/ **-wom·an** /-ˌwʊmən/ *n* member of a state assembly

as·sent /əˈsent/ *vi fml* agree ♦ *n* agreement

as·sert /əˈsɜrt/ *vt* **1** declare forcefully **2** make a strong claim to: *He asserted his authority.* **3 assert oneself** act in a way that shows one's power ~**ive** *adj* forceful; showing CONFIDENCE ~**ion** /əˈsɜrʃən/ *n* forceful statement or claim

as·sess /əˈses/ *vt* judge the value or amount of ~**ment** *n* [C;U]

as·set /ˈæset/ *n* **1** property that has value and may be sold **2** valuable quality or skill

asset-strip-ping /ˈ.. ˌ.-/ n practice of buying a company cheaply, selling all its assets to make a profit, and closing it down

ass-hole /ˈæs-houl/ n taboo **a** the ANUS **b** stupid annoying person

as-sid-u-ous /əˈsɪdjuəs/ adj with careful attention ~**ly** adv

as-sign /əˈsaɪn/ vt **1** give as a share or duty **2** decide on; name: assign a day for the meeting ~**ment** n **1** [C] duty or piece of work **2** [U] act of assigning

as-sig-na-tion /ˌæsɪgˈneɪʃən/ n (secret) meeting, usu. for sex

as-sim-i-late /əˈsɪməˌleɪt/ vi/t take in and accept (food, ideas, foreign people) –**lation** /əˌsɪməˈleɪʃən/ n [U]

as-sist /əˈsɪst/ vi/t fml help ~**ance** n fml ~**ant** n person who helps

as-so-ci-ate /əˈsoʊʃiˌeɪt, -siˌeɪt/ v **1** vi/t join as friends or partners **2** vt connect in the mind ♦ /əˈsoʊʃi-ɪt, -si-ɪt/ n: He's a business associate.

as-so-ci-a-tion /əˌsoʊʃiˈeɪʃən, -siˈeɪ-/ n **1** [C] society of people joined together **2** [U] act of joining together **3** [C;U] connecting things in the mind

as-sort-ed /əˈsɔrtɪd/ adj of various types; mixed

as-sort-ment /əˈsɔrtˈmənt/ n mixture

as-suage /əˈsweɪdʒ/ vt fml reduce (suffering)

as-sume /əˈsum/ vt **1** believe without proof: Let's assume he isn't coming. **2** begin to use or perform: to assume control **3** pretend to have: to adopt an assumed name

as-sump-tion /əˈsʌmpʃən/ n **1** [C] something believed without proof **2** [U] act of assuming

as-sure /əˈʃʊr/ vt **1** tell firmly; promise **2** make (oneself) sure or certain **assur-ance** n **1** [U] belief in one's own powers **2** [C] firm promise **assured** adj certain, esp. of one's own powers

as-te-risk /ˈæstərɪsk/ n star-like mark*

as-te-roid /ˈæstəˌrɔɪd/ n very small PLANET

asth-ma /ˈæzmə/ n [U] disease that causes difficulty in breathing ~**tic** /æzˈmætɪk/ adj

as-ton-ish /əˈstɒnɪʃ/ vt surprise greatly: His rudeness astonished me. ~**ment** n [U] surprise

a-stray /əˈstreɪ/ adj, adv off the right path

a-stride /əˈstraɪd/ adv, prep with a leg on each side (of)

as-trin-gent /əˈstrɪndʒənt/ adj **1** able to tighten the skin and stop bleeding **2** bitter; severe

as-trol-o-gy /əˈstralədʒi/ n [U] study of the supposed influence of the stars on events and character –**ger** n –**gical** /ˌæstrəˈlɑdʒɪkəl-/ adj

as-tro-naut /ˈæstrəˌnɔt/ n traveler in a spacecraft

as-tron-o-my /əˈstranəmi/ n [U] scientific study of the sun, stars, etc. –**mer** n –**mical** /ˌæstrəˈnɑmɪkəl-/ adj **1** of astronomy **2** very large; astronomical sums of money

as-tro-phys-ics /ˌæstroʊˈfɪzɪks, ˌæstrə-/ n [U] science of the nature of the stars and the forces that influence them –**ical** adj

AstroTurf /ˈæstroʊ ˌtɜrf/ n [U] tdmk artificial grass for playing sports on

as-tute /əˈstut/ adj able to see quickly something that is to one's advantage ~**ly** adv ~**ness** n [U]

a-sy-lum /əˈsaɪləm/ n **1** [U] protection and shelter **2** [C] MENTAL hospital

a-sym-met-ric /ˌeɪsəˈmetrɪk, ˌæ-/ also –**rical** /-kəl/ — adj having sides that are not alike

at /ət; strong æt/ prep **1** (showing where): at the airport **2** (showing when): at Christmas **3** towards: Look at me. **4** by: surprised at the news **5** (showing how someone does something): good at games **6** (showing a state or continued activity): at school | at war **7** (showing price, level, age, etc.): sold at 10 cents each | to stop work at 60 **8** at **a/an** in only one: He went up the stairs 2 at a time.

ate /eɪt/ past t. of EAT

a-the-is-m /ˈeɪθiˌɪzəm/ n [U] belief that there is no God –**ist** n

ath-lete /ˈæθlit/ n person who practices athletics

ath-let-ics /æθˈletɪks/ n [U] physical exercises such as running and jumping **athletic** adj **1** of athletics **2** physically strong and active

at-las /ˈætləs/ n book of maps

ATM n Automated Teller Machine; machine in a public place at which money can be taken out of one's bank account

at·mo·sphere /ˈætˀməsˌfɪr/ n 1 gases surrounding a heavenly body, esp. the Earth 2 air 3 general feeling of a place −**spheric** /ˌætˀməsˈfɛrɪk◂/ adj 1 of or concerning the Earth's atmosphere 2 mysteriously beautiful and strange: atmospheric music

at·oll /ˈætɒl, ˈætɑl, ˈætoʊl/ n ringshaped CORAL island

at·om /ˈætəm/ n smallest unit of an ELEMENT ~**ic** /əˈtɑmɪk/ adj 1 of atoms 2 using the power that comes from splitting atoms

atom bomb /ˌ·· ˈ·/ also **atomic bomb** /ˌ··· ˈ·/ — n bomb that uses the explosive NUCLEAR power produced by splitting atoms

a·tone /əˈtoʊn/ vi make repayment (for a crime, etc.) ~**ment** n [U]

a·tro·cious /əˈtroʊʃəs/ adj very cruel or bad ~**ly** adv

a·troc·i·ty /əˈtrɑsəti/ n 1 very cruel act 2 something very ugly

at·ro·phy /ˈætrəfi/ vi/t (cause to) lose flesh and muscle; weaken **atrophy** n [U]

at·tach /əˈtætʃ/ vt 1 fasten 2 cause to join: He attached himself to another group of tourists. 3 regard as having (special meaning or importance) 4 **be attached to** be fond of ~**ment** n [C;U]

at·tach·é /ˌætəˈʃeɪ, ˌætæ-/ n person who helps an AMBASSADOR

at·tack /əˈtæk/ n 1 [C;U] (act of) violence 2 [C] words intended to hurt 3 [C] sudden illness ♦ vt 1 make an attack 2 begin (something) with eagerness and interest ~**er** n

at·tain /əˈteɪn/ vt fml succeed in; reach ~**able** adj ~**ment** n 1 [U] act of attaining 2 [C] a skill

at·tempt /əˈtɛmpt/ vt try: I attempted to leave. ♦ n 1 effort made to do something 2 **attempt on someone's life** effort to murder someone

at·tend /əˈtɛnd/ v 1 vt be present at: attend the meeting 2 vi give attention 3 vi look after ~**ance** n 1 [C;U] act of being present 2 [C] number of people present: a large attendance ~**ant** n person who looks after a place or people

at·ten·tion /əˈtɛnʃən/ n [U] 1 careful thought: pay attention to the teacher 2 particular care or consideration: Old cars need lots of attention. 3 **at attention** (of a soldier) standing straight and still

at·ten·tive /əˈtɛntɪv/ adj 1 listening carefully 2 politely helpful ~**ly** adv ~**ness** n [U]

at·ten·u·ate /əˈtɛnyuˌeɪt/ vi/t (cause to) become thin, weak, less valuable, etc.

at·test /əˈtɛst/ vt fml 1 declare to be true 2 be proof of: His success attests (to) his ability.

at·tic /ˈætɪk/ n room below the roof of a house

at·tire /əˈtaɪr/ n fml clothes ♦ vt put on clothes

at·ti·tude /ˈætəˌtud/ n 1 way of feeling and behaving 2 fml position of the body

at·tor·ney /əˈtɜrni/ n person whose profession is the LAW (2)

attorney gen·er·al /ˌ··· ˈ···/ n chief attorney of a state or country who represents the government

at·tract /əˈtrækt/ vt 1 excite the admiration or interest of: He was attracted by her smile. 2 draw towards: Flowers attract bees. ~**ive** adj interesting, pleasing −**ively** adv ~**iveness** n [U] state of being attractive ~**ion** /əˈtrækʃən/ n 1 [U] power of attracting 2 [C] something attractive

at·tri·bute[1] /ˈætrəˌbyut/ n 1 quality that belongs to a person or thing 2 something regarded as a sign of a person or position

at·tri·bute[2] /əˈtrɪbyət/ v **attribute** to phr vt 1 believe to be the result of: He attributes his success to hard work. 2 ASCRIBE to

at·tri·tion /əˈtrɪʃən/ n [U] process of tiring, weakening, or destroying by continual worry, hardship, or repeated attacks: a war of attrition

at·tune /əˈtun/ v **attune** to phr vt make used to or ready for

a·typ·i·cal /eɪˈtɪpɪkəl/ adj not typical ~**ly** adv

au·burn /ˈɔbən/ adj, n [U] (esp. of hair) reddish brown

auc·tion /ˈɔkʃən/ n public meeting to sell goods to whoever offers the most money ♦ vt sell by auction

auc·tio·neer /ˌɔkʃəˈnɪr/ n person in charge of an auction, who calls out the prices

au·da·cious /ɔˈdeɪʃəs/ adj 1 (foolishly) daring 2 disrespectful ~**ly** adv −**city** /ɔˈdæsəti/ n [U]

au·di·ble /ˈɔdəbəl/ adj able to be heard −**bly** adv

au·di·ence /'ɔdiəns/ n **1** people listening to or watching a performance **2** formal meeting with someone important: *have an audience with the Pope*

au·di·o /'ɔdiou/ adj of sound radio signals

audio-vis·u·al /ˌ··· '···◄/ adj of both sight and hearing

au·dit /'ɔdɪt/ vt examine (business accounts) officially **audit** n ~**or** n

au·di·tion /ɔ'dɪʃən/ n test performance given by a singer, actor, etc. **audition** vi

au·di·to·ri·um /ˌɔdə'tɔriom, -'tour-/ n space where an AUDIENCE (1) sits

aug·ment /ɔg'mɛnt/ vi/t fml increase

au·gur /'ɔgə/ vi fml augur well/ill (for) be a sign of good/bad things in the future (for): *This rain augurs well for farmers.*

au·gust /ɔ'gʌst/ adj noble and grand

Au·gust /'ɔgəst/ the 8th month of the year

aunt /ænt, ɑnt/ n sister of one's father or mother, or wife of one's uncle

au pair /ˌou 'pɛr/ n young foreigner who lives with a family and helps with work in their house

au·ra /'ɔrə/ n effect or feeling produced by a person or place

au·ral /'ɔrəl/ adj of or related to the sense of hearing

aus·pic·es /'ɔspəsɪz, -ˌsɪz/ n [P] fml under the auspices of helped by

aus·pi·cious /ɔ'spɪʃəs/ adj fml showing signs of future success ~**ly** adv

aus·tere /ɔ'stɪr/ adj **1** without comfort; hard: *an austere life* **2** without decoration; plain ~**ly** adv –**terity** /ɔ'stɛrəti/ n [C;U]

au·then·tic /ɔ'θɛntɪk/ adj known to be real; GENUINE ~**ally** adv ~**ate** vt prove to be authentic ~**ation** /ɔˌθɛntɪ'keɪʃən/ n [U] ~**ity** /ˌɔθɛn'tɪsəti, ˌɔθən-/ n [U] quality of being authentic

au·thor /'ɔθə/ authoress /'ɔθərɪs/ fem. — n **1** writer **2** person who thinks of an idea or plan ~**ship** n [U]

au·thor·i·tar·i·an /əˌθɔrə'tɛriən, əˌθɑr-/ n, adj (person) demanding total obedience to rules ~**ism** n [U]

au·thor·i·ta·tive /ə'θɔrəˌteɪtɪv, ə'θɑr-/ adj deserving respect; to be trusted ~**ly** adv

au·thor·i·ty /ə'θɔrəti, ə'θɑr-/ n **1** [U] power to command: *Who is in authority here?* **2** [C] person or group with this power **3** [C] authoritative person, book, etc.: *He's an authority on plants.*

au·thor·ize /'ɔθəˌraɪz/ vt give formal permission for –**ization** /ˌɔθərə'zeɪʃən/ n [C;U]

au·to·bi·og·ra·phy /ˌɔtəbaɪ'ɑgrəfi/ n written account of one's own life –**phical** /ˌɔtəˌbaɪə'græfɪkəl/ adj

au·to·crat /'ɔtəˌkræt/ n **1** ruler with unlimited power **2** person who behaves like that ~**ic** /ˌɔtə'krætɪk◄/ adj

au·to·graph /'ɔtəˌgræf/ n SIGNATURE of someone famous ♦ vt sign one's name on

au·to·mate /'ɔtəˌmeɪt/ vt change (a process, etc.) to automation

auto·mat·ic /ˌɔtə'mætɪk◄/ adj **1** (esp. of a machine) able to work by itself **2** done without thought **3** certain to happen ♦ n (automatic) gun ~**ally** adv

au·to·ma·tion /ˌɔtə'meɪʃən/ n [U] use of machines that need no human control

au·tom·a·ton /ɔ'tɑmət°n/ n -**ta** /-tə/ or -**tons** **1** thing or machine that works by itself **2** person who acts without thought or feeling

au·to·mo·bile /ˌɔtəmə'bil, 'ɔtəməˌbil/ n fml for car

au·to·mo·tive /ˌɔtə'moutɪv/ adj relating to cars: *the automotive industry*

au·ton·o·mous /ɔ'tɑnəməs/ adj governing itself

au·ton·o·my /ɔ'tɑnəmi/ n [U] government or control (esp. of a country) by the people who live there

au·top·sy /'ɔˌtɑpsi/ n POSTMORTEM

au·tumn /'ɔtəm/ n [C;U] season between summer and winter ~**al** /ɔ'tʌmnəl/ adj — see FALL²

aux·il·i·a·ry /ɔg'zɪlyəri, -'zɪləri/ adj helping; adding support **auxiliary** n **1** helper **2** foreign soldier in the service of a country at war **3** an auxiliary verb

a·vail /ə'veɪl/ vi avail oneself of fml make use of ♦ n [U] help of/to no avail of no use; without success

a·vai·la·ble /ə'veɪləbəl/ adj able to be gotten, used, etc.: *Those shoes are not available in your size.* –**bility** /əˌveɪlə'bɪləti/ n [U]

av·a·lanche /'ævəˌlæntʃ, -ˌlɑntʃ/ n mass of snow crashing down a mountain: (fig.) *an avalanche of letters*

av·ant-garde /ˌavɑnt¹ ¹gard, ˌæ-◄/ adj, n [U] (of) people who produce the newest ideas, esp. in the arts

av·a·rice /¹ævərɪs/ n GREED for wealth **avaricious** /ˌævə¹rɪʃəs◄/ adj

a·venge /ə¹vendʒ/ vt punish for harm done; REVENGE: to avenge his death

av·e·nue /¹ævənu/ also Ave. written abbrev. — n 1 wide road, esp. between 2 rows of trees 2 way to a result

av·e·rage /¹ævrɪdʒ/ n 1 [C] amount found by adding quantities together and then dividing by the number of quantities 2 [C;U] level regarded as usual ♦ adj: the average rainfall | girls of average intelligence ♦ vt 1 calculate the average of 2 be or do as an average: I average 8 hours' work a day.

a·verse /ə¹vɜrs/ adj not liking

a·ver·sion /ə¹vɜrʒən, -ʃən/ n 1 [S;U] strong dislike 2 [C] hated person or thing

a·vert /ə¹vɜrt/ vt 1 prevent from happening: avert accidents 2 fml turn away (one's eyes)

a·vi·a·ry /¹eɪviˌɛri/ n cage for keeping birds in

a·vi·a·tion /ˌeɪvi¹eɪʃən/ n [U] flying in aircraft **-tor** /¹eɪviˌeɪtər/ n

av·id /¹ævɪd/ adj extremely enthusiastic **~ly** adv

av·o·ca·do /ˌævə¹kadoʊ, ˌɑ-/ n **-dos** or **-does** green tropical fruit

a·void /ə¹vɔɪd/ vt keep away from, esp. on purpose **~able** adj **~ance** n [U]

a·vowed /ə¹vaʊd/ adj openly admitted: his avowed supporters

a·vun·cu·lar /ə¹vʌŋkyələr/ adj of or like an uncle

a·wait /ə¹weɪt/ vt fml wait for

a·wake¹ /ə¹weɪk/ adj not asleep

a·wake² also **awaken** /ə¹weɪkən/ — vi/t awake awoke /ə¹woʊk/ or awakened, awoken /ə¹woʊkən/ or awaked wake: (fig.) People must be awakened to the dangers of nuclear weapons.

a·wak·en·ing /ə¹weɪkənɪŋ/ n 1 act of waking from sleep: (fig.) her awakening to social injustice 2 rude awakening sudden consciousness of an unpleasant state of affairs

a·ward /ə¹wɔrd/ vt give officially: award prizes ♦ n something awarded

a·ware /ə¹wɛr/ adj having knowledge or understanding: politically aware **~ness** n [U]

a·way¹ /ə¹weɪ/ adv 1 to or at another place: Go away! | She lives 3 miles away. 2 so as to be gone: The sounds died away. 3 continuously: He's hammering away.

away² adj (of a sports match) played at the place, sports field, etc., of one's opponent

awe /ɔ/ n [U] respect mixed with fear

awe-in·spir·ing /¹· ·ˌ··/ adj causing feelings of awe

awe·some /¹ɔsəm/ adj 1 causing feelings of awe 2 sl surprisingly good

aw·ful /¹ɔfəl/ adj 1 very bad: awful weather 2 very great: an awful lot of work **~ly** adv very

a·while /ə¹waɪl, ə¹hwaɪl/ adv short period of time: wait awhile

awk·ward /¹ɔkwərd/ adj 1 not moving skillfully: CLUMSY 2 difficult to handle 3 inconvenient: They came at an awkward time. 4 EMBARRASS·ing: an awkward silence **~ly** adv **~ness** n [U]

awn·ing /¹ɔnɪŋ/ n movable cloth roof put up as a protection against sun or rain

a·woke /ə¹woʊk/ past t. of AWAKE

a·wok·en /ə¹woʊkən/ past p. of AWAKE

AWOL /¹eɪˌwɔl, ¹eɪˌwɑl, ˌeɪˌdʌbəlyu ˌoʊ ¹ɛl/ adj, adv absent without leave: AWOL soldiers/He went AWOL.

a·wry /ə¹raɪ/ adj, adv 1 not in the planned way 2 twisted or bent

ax /æks/ n 1 tool for cutting down trees 2 **have an ax to grind** have a selfish reason for one's actions ♦ vt put a sudden end to (jobs, plans, etc.)

ax·i·om /¹æksiəm/ n principle accepted as true **~atic** /ˌæksiə¹mætɪk◄/ adj not needing proof

ax·is /¹æksɪs/ n axes /¹æksiz/ 1 line around which something spins: the Earth's axis 2 fixed line against which positions are measured on a GRAPH

ax·le /¹æksəl/ n bar on which a wheel turns

a·ya·tol·lah /ˌaɪə¹tɑlə/ n Shiite Muslim religious leader

aye /aɪ/ n, adv (person who votes) yes

az·ure /¹æʒər/ adj, n [U] bright blue

B

B, b /biː/ the 2nd letter of the English alphabet

b *abbrev. for*: born

baa /bɑ, bæ/ *vi, n* (make) the sound a sheep makes

bab·ble /ˈbæbəl/ *vi/t* talk quickly and foolishly **babble** *n* [S]

babe /beɪb/ *n* **1** *lit* baby **2** *sl* woman

ba·boon /bæˈbuːn/ *n* kind of large monkey

ba·by /ˈbeɪbi/ *n* **1** very young child: (fig.) *the baby of the class* (= the youngest) **2** very young animal or bird: *a baby monkey* **3** *infml* person, esp. a girl or woman **4** *infml* one's special responsibility ~**ish** *adj* like a baby

baby boom·er /ˈ·· ˌ·/ *n infml* someone born between 1946 and 1965 when many babies were born

babysit·ter /ˈbeɪbiˌsɪtə/ *n* person who looks after children while their parents are out **baby-sit** *vi* –*sat*; *pres. p.* –**sitting**

bach·e·lor /ˈbætʃələ/ *n* unmarried man

bachelor's de·gree /ˈ··· ˌ·/ *n* degree given after four years' college or university study

back¹ /bæk/ *n* **1** the part of one's body opposite the chest, from the neck to the bottom of the SPINE (1) **2** the part furthest from the direction that something moves in or faces: *the back of the aircraft/of the house | the back wheel of a bicycle* **3** the less important side of something **4** the part of a chair that one leans against **5** the end of a book or newspaper **6 back to back** with the backs facing each other **7 behind someone's back** without their knowledge **8 be flat on one's back** be helpless because of illness etc. **9 get off someone's back** stop annoying someone **10 have/with one's back to the wall** (be) in the greatest difficulties **11 turn one's back on someone** leave someone (esp. when one should stay) ~**less** *adj*: *a backless dress*

back² *adv* **1** in or into an earlier place: *Put the book back on the shelf.* **2** towards the back: *Lean back.* **3** away from the

speaker: *Stand back!* **4** in reply: *Call me back.* **5** in an earlier time: *back in 1983* **6 back and forth** in one direction, then in the opposite direction

back³ *v* **1** *vi/t* move backwards: *back the car down the road* **2** *vt* support and encourage **3** *vt* risk money on (the result of a horse race, etc.) **4** *vt* be or make the back of: *curtains backed with satin* ~**er** *n* **1** someone who supports a plan with money **2** someone who risks money on a horse, etc.

back down also **back off** *phr vi* give up an argument

back onto *phr vt* (of a place) have at the back: *a house backing onto the river*

back out *phr vi* not fulfill a promise

back up *phr vt* **1** support in an argument, etc. **2** move a vehicle backwards **3** copy a computer FILE

back·ache /ˈbækˌeɪk/ *n* [C;U] pain in the back

back·bit·ing /ˈbækˌbaɪtɪŋ/ *n* [U] unkind talk about someone who is absent

back·bone /ˈbækboʊn/ *n* **1** [C] SPINE (1): (fig.) *She's the backbone* (= main support) *of the parents' committee.* **2** [U] strength of character

back·break·ing /ˈbækˌbreɪkɪŋ/ *adj* (of work) very hard

back·date /ˌbækˈdeɪt, ˈ··/ *vt* make effective from an earlier date

back·drop /ˈbækdrɒp/ *n* background

back·fire /ˈbækfaɪə/ *vi* **1** (of a car, etc.) make a noise because the gas explodes too soon **2** have the opposite effect to that intended

back·ground /ˈbækgraʊnd/ *n* **1** scenery behind the main object **2** (information about) conditions existing when something happens or happened **3** person's family, experience, education, etc.

back·hand /ˈbækhænd/ *n* stroke (in tennis, etc.) with the back of the hand turned in the direction of movement [U] writing that leans to the left ~**ed** *adj* **1** using or made with a backhand **2** (of a remark) indirect, esp. sarcastic (SARCASM) ~**er** *n* backhand

back·ing /ˈbækɪŋ/ *n* **1** help; support **2** something that makes the back of an object

back is·sue /ˌ· ˈ··/ *n* newspaper, etc., earlier than the most recent one

back·lash /ˈbæklæʃ/ n sudden violent movement, esp. against a political or social movement

back·log /ˈbækˌlɒg, -ˌlɑg/ n things (esp. work) remaining to be done

back·pack /ˈbækpæk/ n a large bag carried on the back; esp. by walkers, etc. ~**er** n ~**ing** n [U]: to go backpacking in the mountains ♦ vi walk distances with a backpack

back·ped·al /ˈbækˌpedl/ vi 1 PEDAL backwards 2 take back a statement; change an earlier opinion

back·road /ˈbækˌroud/ n road away from the main roads in the country

back seat /ˌ ˈ·ˈ/ n 1 [C] seat at the back of a car 2 [S] less important position

back·side /ˈbæksaid/ n one's BOTTOM¹ (2)

back·slap·ping /ˈbækˌslæpɪŋ/ adj (of behavior) too friendly and noisy

back·slide /ˈbækˌslaid/ vi go back to a worse condition ~**slider** n

back·stage /ˌbækˈsteidʒ◄/ adv, adj 1 behind a theater stage 2 in private

back·stroke /ˈbækˌstrouk/ n way of swimming on one's back

back-to-back /ˌ ˈ · ˈ·◄/ adj 1 happening one after the other: back-to-back events 2 with backs against each other

back·track /ˈbæktræk/ vi 1 go back over the same path 2 BACKPEDAL (2)

back·up /ˈbækʌp/ n [C;U] 1 thing or person ready to be used in place of or to help another 2 line of traffic stretching back from where its flow has been halted (HALT)

back·ward /ˈbækwəd/ adj 1 towards the back 2 late in development: a backward child ~**ness** n [U]

back·wards /ˈbækwədz/ adv 1 towards the back, the beginning, or the past: say the alphabet backwards 2 with the back part in front: put one's hat on backwards 3 **know something backwards and forwards** know something perfectly

back·wa·ter /ˈbækˌwɒtə, -ˌwɑtə/ n 1 part of a river outside the current 2 place not influenced by outside events

back·woods /ˈbækwʊdz/ adj thought to lack good manners because of not living in the city

back·yard /ˌbækˈyɑrd◄/ n 1 yard behind a house 2 area under one's personal control

ba·con /ˈbeikən/ n [U] pig meat, smoked or preserved in salt

bac·te·ri·a /bækˈtɪriə/ n sing. -**rium** /-ˌriəm/ [P] very small living creatures that may cause disease

bad /bæd/ adj **worse** /wəs/, **worst** /wəst/ 1 unpleasant: bad news 2 morally wrong 3 unhealthy: Smoking is bad for you. 4 not of acceptable quality 5 severe: a bad cold 6 ROTTEN: The apples went bad. 7 disobedient: a bad boy 8 **feel bad about** be sorry or ashamed about 9 **have/get a bad name** lose or have lost people's respect 10 **in a bad way** very ill or in trouble 11 **not bad/not so bad** good ~**ly** adv 1 in a bad way: We played badly. 2 seriously: We were badly beaten. 3 a great deal: He needs help badly.

bad blood /ˌ ˈ/ n [U] angry or bitter feeling

bad debt /ˌ ˈ/ n debt that is unlikely to be paid

bade /bæd, beid/ past t. and p. of BID²

badge /bædʒ/ n something worn to show one's rank, membership, etc.

bad·ger¹ /ˈbædʒə/ n black and white night animal that lives in holes in the ground

badger² vt ask again and again

bad·lands /ˈbædˌlændz/ n rocky uneven land

badly-off /ˌ· ˈ·◄/ adj 1 poor 2 lacking

bad·min·ton /ˈbædˌmɪntˈn/ n [U] game similar to tennis, played with a SHUTTLECOCK over a high net

bad-mouth /ˈ· ·/ vt sl speak badly of

baf·fle /ˈbæfəl/ vt be too difficult for (someone): a baffling question

bag¹ /bæg/ n 1 soft container that opens at the top: a shopping bag 2 **in the bag** certain to be won, gained, etc.

bag² v -**gg**- 1 vt put into a bag 2 vt kill (animals or birds) 3 vt take possession of 4 vi be baggy

ba·gel /ˈbeigəl/ n hard round bread with a hole in the centre

bag·gage /ˈbægidʒ/ n [U] LUGGAGE

bag·gy /ˈbægi/ adj hanging in loose folds: baggy jeans

bag lady /ˈ· ˌ·/ n derog woman who lives in the streets, carrying all her possessions in bags

bag·pipes /ˈbægpaips/ n [P] musical instrument with pipes and a bag of air

bail¹ /beil/ n [U] 1 money paid so that a prisoner may be set free until tried (TRY¹ (3)) 2 **go/stand bail** pay this money

bail² *v* **bail out** *phr v* **1** *vt* pay bail for someone **2** *vt* help someone with money **3** *vi/t* remove water from a boat **4** *vi* escape from an aircraft

bai·liff /ˈbeɪlɪf/ *n* **1** law officer in a court **2** farm manager

bait /beɪt/ *n* [S;U] food used to attract fish, etc., to be caught ♦ *vt* **1** put bait on (a hook, etc.) **2** make (an animal or a person) angry intentionally

bake /beɪk/ *v* **1** *vi/t* (cause to) cook in an OVEN **2** *vi/t* (cause to) become hard by heating **3** *vi* become hot: *I'm baking!*

baker *n* person who bakes bread for sale

bakery place where bread is baked (and sold)

bak·ing pow·der /ˈ·· ˌ·-/ *n* [U] powder used to make bread and cakes light

baking so·da /ˈ·· ˌ·-/ *n* powder used to make cakes, etc. rise

bal·ance¹ /ˈbæləns/ *n* **1** [S;U] state in which weight is evenly spread: *It was difficult to keep my balance on the icy path.* **2** [C] instrument for weighing **3** [C] amount remaining somewhere: *my bank balance* **4** **in the balance** uncertain(ly) **5** **on balance** considering everything

balance² *v* **1** *vi/t* keep steady **2** *vi* (of 2 things, esp. debts) be equal **3** *vt* compare (2 things): *balance the advantages against the disadvantages*

balance of pay·ments /ˌ··· ·ˈ· ·/ *n* [(the) S] the difference between the amount of money coming into a country and the amount going out, including trade in insurance, between banks, etc.

balance of trade /ˌ··· ·ˈ·/ *n* [(the) S] the difference in value between a country's IMPORTS and EXPORTS

bal·co·ny /ˈbælkəni/ *n* **1** piece of floor that sticks out from an upstairs wall **2** upstairs seats in a theater

bald /bɔːld/ *adj* **1** with no hair on the head **2** plain: *a bald statement* ~**ing** *adj* becoming bald ~**ness** *n* [U]

bale¹ /beɪl/ *n* large tightly tied mass of esp. soft material: *a bale of cotton*

bale² *v* **bale out** *phr vi/t* remove water from a boat

balk /bɔːk/ *vi* be unwilling to agree: *I balked at the price.*

ball¹ /bɔːl/ *n* **1** round object used in games **2** round mass: *a ball of string/clay* **3** round part of the body: *eyeballs* **4** **on the**

ball showing up-to-date knowledge and readiness to act **5 play ball** COOPERATE **6 start/keep the ball rolling** begin/ continue something **balls** [P] *taboo sl* TESTICLES

ball² *n* **1** formal occasion for dancing **2** **have a ball** have a very good time

bal·lad /ˈbæləd/ *n* **1** poem that tells a story **2** popular love song

bal·last /ˈbæləst/ *n* [U] heavy material carried to keep a ship steady, or to be thrown from a BALLOON (1) to make it rise higher ♦ *vt* fill or supply with ballast

ball·cock /ˈbɔːlkɑk/ *n* hollow floating ball that opens and closes a hole through which water flows

bal·le·ri·na /ˌbæləˈriːnə/ *n* female ballet dancer

bal·let /bæˈleɪ, ˈbæleɪ/ *n* **1** [C] dance with music in which a story is told **2** [C] music for such a dance **3** [S;U] art of doing such a dance **4** [C] group of ballet dancers

ball game /ˈ· ·/ *n infml* state of affairs

bal·lis·tic /bəˈlɪstɪk/ *adj* **go ballistic** suddenly become very angry

bal·lis·tic mis·sile /ˌ·· ˈ·-/ *n* MISSILE that is guided as it rises into the air but then falls freely

bal·lis·tics /bəˈlɪstɪks/ *n* [U] science of the movement of objects, such as bullets fired from a gun **ballistic** *adj*

ball of wax /ˌ· · ˈ·/ *n infml* matter, affair, thing

bal·loon /bəˈluːn/ *n* **1** bag filled with gas or air so that it can float **2** small rubber bag that can be blown up and used as a toy **3** line around words thought or spoken by a CARTOON character ♦ *vi* swell up like a balloon

bal·lot /ˈbælət/ *n* **1** [S;U] (paper used in a) secret vote **2** [C] number of votes recorded ♦ **1** *vi* vote or decide by secret ballot **2** *vt* find out the views (of a group) by holding a vote

ballot box /ˈ·· ·/ *n* box in which voters put their BALLOTS

ball park /ˈ· ·/ *n* **1** park where BASEBALL is played **2** [S] *infml* range of numbers, prices, etc., within which the correct figure is likely to be

ball·point /ˈbɔːlpɔɪnt/ *n* pen with a ball at the end that rolls thick ink onto the paper

ball·room /ˈbɔːlrum, -rʊm/ *n* large room suitable for a BALL² (1)

balm /bɑm/ n [C;U] oily liquid used to lessen pain

balm·y /ˈbɑmi/ adj 1 (of air) soft and warm 2 sl foolish: crazy

ba·lo·ney /bəˈlouni/ n, interj [U] nonsense

bal·sa /ˈbɔlsə/ n [C;U] (light wood of) a tropical tree

bal·us·trade /ˈbæləˌstreɪd/ n upright posts with a bar along the top, guarding an edge where people might fall

bam·boo /ˌbæmˈbuː/ n -boos [C;U] (hollow jointed stems of) a tropical plant of the grass family

ban /bæn/ vt -nn- forbid ♦ n order forbidding something

ba·nal /bəˈnæl, bəˈnɑl, ˈbeɪnl/ adj uninteresting because ordinary ~ity /bəˈnælət̬i/ n [C;U]

ba·na·na /bəˈnænə/ n long yellow tropical fruit

banana split /ˌ·· ˈ·/ n ICE CREAM served between banana halves topped with whipped cream

band¹ /bænd/ n 1 narrow piece of material for fastening, or putting round something: a rubber band 2 STRIPE (1) 3 broadcasting range over which radio stations can be received: fm band

band² n group of people, esp. musicians playing popular music — see also ONE-MAN BAND; STEEL BAND

band³ v band together phr vi unite for a purpose

ban·dage /ˈbændɪdʒ/ n narrow piece of cloth for tying around a wound ♦ vt tie up with a bandage

Band-Aid /ˈ· ·/ n tdmk (a thin band of) material that can be stuck to the skin to protect small wounds

B&B /ˌbi ən ˈbi/ abbrev. for: (small hotel providing) bed and breakfast

ban·dit /ˈbændɪt/ n armed robber

band·stand /ˈbændstænd/ n raised place open to the air, used for a band to play on

band·wa·gon /ˈbændˌwægən/ n jump on a bandwagon join something that is popular, for personal gain

ban·dy /ˈbændi/ vt bandy words quarrel

bane /beɪn/ n cause of trouble ~ful adj harmful

bang¹ /bæŋ/ vi/t hit violently and noisily: I banged my head against the ceiling. **bang** n

bang² adv exactly: bang in the middle

ban·gle /ˈbæŋgəl/ n band worn as decoration on the wrist

bangs /bæŋz/ n [P] hair hanging over the forehead

ban·ish /ˈbænɪʃ/ vt 1 send away as a punishment 2 stop thinking about ~ment n [U]

ban·is·ter /ˈbænəstə/ n also **banisters** — upright posts with a bar along the top, beside a flight of stairs

ban·jo /ˈbændʒoʊ/ n -jos or -joes stringed instrument used esp. to play popular music

bank¹ /bæŋk/ n 1 land beside a river or lake 2 raised heap of earth, etc. 3 mass of snow, clouds, etc.

bank² n 1 place where money is kept and paid out on demand 2 place where something is kept for use: a blood bank ~er n person who owns, works in, or controls a BANK² (1)

bank³ vi/t keep (money) in a bank
  bank on phr vt depend on

bank⁴ vi (of an aircraft, etc.) raise one side while turning

bank·ing /ˈbæŋkɪŋ/ n [U] business of a BANK² (1)

bank note /ˈ· ·/ n piece of paper money

bank·roll /ˈbæŋkroʊl/ n supply of money ♦ vt infml supply money for or pay the cost of (a business, plan, etc.)

bank·rupt /ˈbæŋkrʌpt/ adj unable to pay one's debts: (fig.) morally bankrupt (= completely without morals) ♦ n person who is bankrupt ♦ vt make bankrupt or very poor ~cy n [C;U] state of being bankrupt

ban·ner /ˈbænə/ n 1 lit flag 2 piece of cloth with a political message on it, carried by marchers

ban·quet /ˈbæŋkwɪt/ n formal dinner banquet vi

ban·ter /ˈbæntə/ n [U] light joking talk banter vi

bap·tis·m /ˈbæptɪzəm/ n 1 [C;U] Christian religious ceremony of touching or covering a person with water 2 baptism by fire: a soldier's first experience of war b any unpleasant first experience –tize /ˈbæptaɪz, bæpˈtaɪz/ vt perform baptism on

bar /bɑr/ n 1 long narrow piece of solid material: a bar of soap | (fig.) bars of sunlight 2 length of wood or metal across a window, etc. 3 group of musical notes **4** place where drinks, etc., are served **5** bank of sand or stones under water **6** BARRIER (7) (*cap.*) the legal profession: *She was called to the Bar.* (= became a lawyer) **8 behind bars** in prison ♦ *vt* **-rr- 1** close with a bar: *They barred themselves in.* | (fig.) *to bar the way to success* **2** forbid; prevent: *He was barred from playing football.* ♦ *prep* **1** except **2 bar none** with no exception

barb /bɑrb/ *n* sharp point of a fish hook, etc., with a curved shape **~ed** *adj* **1** with short sharp points: *barbed wire* **2** (of speech) sharply unkind

bar·bar·i·an /bɑrˈbɛriən/ *n* wild uncivilized person

bar·bar·ic /bɑrˈbærɪk/ *adj* **1** very cruel 2 like a barbarian **–barism** /ˈbɑrbərɪzəm/ *n* [U] condition of being a barbarian **–barous** /ˈbɑrbərəs/ *adj* **-ity** /bɑrˈbærəti/ *n* [C:U] great cruelty

bar·be·cue /ˈbɑrbɪkyu/ *n* **1** [C] party where meat etc. is cooked outdoors **2** [C] metal frame on which this is done **3** [U] meat cooked in this way ♦ *vt* cook on a barbecue

bar·ber /ˈbɑrbə/ *n* person who cuts men's hair

bar·bi·tu·rate /bɑrˈbɪtʃərɪt, -ˌreɪt/ [C;U] drug that makes people sleep

bard /bɑrd/ *n* **1** poet **2 the Bard** Shakespeare

bar code /ˈ· ˌ·/ *n* set of lines on a product read by a computer to determine the price, etc.

bare /bɛr/ *adj* **1** without clothes or covering **2** with nothing added: *the bare facts* **3** empty: *a room bare of furniture* ♦ *vt* bring to view; EXPOSE **~ly** *adv* hardly

bare·back /ˈbɛrbæk/ *adj, adv* riding, esp. a horse, without a SADDLE (1)

bare bones /ˌ· ˈ·/ *n* [P] simplest but most important parts or facts

bare·faced /ˈbɛrfeɪst/ *adj* shameless

bare·foot /ˈbɛrfʊt/ *adv* without shoes

bar·gain¹ /ˈbɑrgɪn/ *n* **1** agreement to do something in return for something else **2** something sold cheap **3 into the bargain** besides everything else

bargain² *vi* talk about the conditions of a sale, etc.

bargain for/on *phr vt* take into account; expect

bar·gain·ing chip /ˈ··· ˌ·/ *n* something that gives an advantage in a deal

barge¹ /bɑrdʒ/ *n* boat with a flat bottom

barge² *vi* move heavily and rudely

barge in *phr vi* rush in rudely; interrupt

bar hop /ˈ· ˌ·/ *n sl* visit to several bars

bar·i·tone /ˈbærəˌtoʊn/ *n* (man with) a singing voice between TENOR and BASS[1]

bark¹ /bɑrk/ *v* **1** *vi* make the noise dogs make **2** *vt* say in a fierce voice **3** **bark up the wrong tree** *infml* have a mistaken idea ♦ **bark** *n* **1** sharp loud noise made by a dog **2 his bark is worse than his bite** *infml* he is not as bad-tempered, unfriendly, etc., as he appears

bark² *n* [U] outer covering of a tree

bar·ley /ˈbɑrli/ *n* [U] grasslike grain plant grown as a food crop

barn /bɑrn/ *n* farm building for storing things in

bar·na·cle /ˈbɑrnəkəl/ *n* small SHELLFISH that collects on rocks, ships, etc.

ba·rom·e·ter /bəˈrɑmətə/ *n* instrument for measuring air pressure so as to judge what weather is coming: (fig.) *a barometer of public opinion*

bar·on /ˈbærən/ *n* powerful man in business

ba·roque /bəˈroʊk, bəˈrɑk/ *adj* **1** in a decorated style fashionable in 17th-century Europe **2** (too) greatly ornamented

bar·racks /ˈbærɪks/ *n* building where soldiers live

bar·rage¹ /bəˈrɑʒ/ *n* heavy gunfire: (fig.) *a barrage of questions*

bar·rage² /ˈbɑrɪdʒ/ *n* bank of earth, etc., built across a river

bar·rel /ˈbærəl/ *n* **1** round wooden container: *a beer barrel* **2** long part of a gun, etc. that is shaped like a tube **3 over a barrel** in a difficult position

bar·ren /ˈbærən/ *adj* **1** unable to produce children, fruit, crops, etc. **2** useless; empty: *a barren discussion* **~ness** *n* [U]

bar·ri·cade /ˈbærəˌkeɪd, ˌbærəˈkeɪd/ *n* something quickly built to block a street, etc. ♦ *vt* close or defend with a barricade

bar·ri·er /ˈbæriə/ *n* something placed in the way to prevent movement: (fig.) *a barrier to success* | *the sound barrier*

bar·ring /ˈbɑrɪŋ/ *prep* except for

bar·row /ˈbæroʊ/ *n* **1** small cart to be pushed **2** WHEELBARROW

bar·tend·er /ˈbɑːrˌtɛndə/ n person who serves drinks in a BAR (4)

bar·ter /ˈbɑːrtə/ vi/t exchange goods for other goods **barter** n [U]

base¹ /beɪs/ n 1 part of a thing on which a thing stands 2 origin from which something develops or is made 3 center from which something is controlled, plans made, etc. 4 center for military operations, stores, etc. 5 main part or substance of a mixture: a vegetable base 6 point which a player must touch in BASE-BALL while running 7 not get to first base (with) not even begin to succeed (with) 8 off base wrong or unacceptable ♦ vt provide with a center: a company based in Paris ~less adj without good reason

base on/upon phr vt form by using something else as a starting point: a firm based on a novel

base² adj 1 esp. lit (of people or behavior) dishonorable 2 (of metal) not regarded as precious ~ly adv ~ness n [U]

base·ball /ˈbeɪsbɔːl/ n 1 [U] outdoor ball game played by 2 teams of 9 players each 2 [C] ball used in this game

base·board /ˈbeɪsbɔːrd, -bɔːrd/ n board fixed along the base of an inside wall

base·ment /ˈbeɪsmənt/ n room in a house below ground level

bas·es /ˈbeɪsiːz/ n pl. of BASIS

bash /bæʃ/ vt hit hard ♦ n 1 hard blow 2 party

bash·ful /ˈbæʃfəl/ adj SHY ~ly adv

ba·sic /ˈbeɪsɪk/ adj most necessary; FUNDAMENTAL: basic principles ~ally adv in spite of surface behavior or details; in reality

basics /ˈbeɪsɪks/ n [P] basic parts or principles

ba·sin /ˈbeɪsən/ n 1 round container for liquids; bowl 2 SINK² 3 hollow place where water collects 4 large valley

ba·sis /ˈbeɪsɪs/ n bases /ˈbeɪsiːz/ 1 the facts, principles, etc., from which something is formed, started, or developed: the basis of an opinion 2 the stated way of carrying out an action, process, etc.: working on a part-time basis

bask /bæsk/ vi lie in enjoyable warmth: (fig.) She basked in (= enjoyed) her employer's approval.

bas·ket /ˈbæskɪt/ n light woven container: a shopping basket

bas·ket·ball /ˈbæskɪtˌbɔːl/ n 1 [U] game in which players try to throw a ball into a basket 2 [C] large ball used in this game

basket case /ˈ·· ˌ·/ n person who can't deal with a situation

bass¹ /beɪs/ n 1 (man with) the lowest human singing voice 2 instrument with the same range of notes as this: a bass guitar 3 DOUBLE BASS

bass² /bæs/ n kind of fish that can be eaten

bass fid·dle /ˌbeɪs ˈfɪdl/ n DOUBLE BASS

bas·soon /bəˈsuːn, bæ-/ n large WOODWIND musical instrument

bas·tard /ˈbæstəd/ n 1 child of unmarried parents 2 sl unpleasant person 3 sl man of the stated kind: You lucky bastard!

baste /beɪst/ vt 1 pour fat over (meat) during cooking 2 sew loosely

bas·ti·on /ˈbæstʃən/ n 1 part of a castle wall that sticks out 2 place where a principle is defended: a bastion of freedom

bat¹ /bæt/ n stick for hitting the ball in BASEBALL, etc.

bat² /bæt/ vi/t 1 strike or hit (as if) with a bat 2 vt not bat an eyelid show no sign of shock

bat³ /bæt/ n 1 mouselike animal that flies at night 2 as blind as a bat not able to see well

batch /bætʃ/ n group; set

bat·ed /ˈbeɪtɪd/ adj with bated breath too frightened or excited to breathe

bath /bæθ/ n baths /bæðz, bæθs/ 1 act of washing one's whole body at one time 2 liquid in a container used for some special purpose: an eyebath 3 BATHTUB 4 place with baths for public use

bathe /beɪð/ v 1 vi take a BATH (2) 2 vt put in liquid: bathe your eyes

bath·ing suit /ˈ·· ˌ·/ n piece of clothing to swim in

ba·thos /ˈbeɪθɒs/ n [U] sudden change from beautiful ideas to ordinary foolish ones

bath·robe /ˈbæθroʊb/ n DRESSING GOWN worn before or after bathing

bath·room /ˈbæθrum, -rʊm/ n room with a bath and a TOILET (1)

bath·tub /ˈbæθtʌb/ n container in which one sits to wash the whole body

bat·on /bəˈtɒn, bæ-/ n short stick used by the leader of an ORCHESTRA, or as a weapon by a policeman, etc.

bat·tal·ion /bəˈtælyən/ n army unit of 500–1,000 soldiers

bat·ten /ˈbætˈn/ v **batten down** phr vt fasten with boards

bat·ter[1] /ˈbætə/ vi/t **1** beat hard and repeatedly **2** cause to lose shape by continual use

batter[2] n [U] mixture of flour, eggs, and milk for making PANCAKES, etc.

batter[3] n player in BASEBALL who tries to hit the ball with a BAT[1] (1)

bat·ter·ing ram n (in former times) heavy log used for breaking down castle doors

bat·ter·y /ˈbætəri/ n **1** apparatus for producing electricity **2** army unit of big guns **3** set of things together: a battery of tests

bat·tle /ˈbætl/ n short fight between enemies or opposing groups ♦ vi fight; struggle

bat·tle·ax /ˈbætlˌæks/ n axes **1** heavy ax for fighting **2** fierce woman

bat·tle·field /ˈbætlˌfild/ n place where a battle is fought

bat·tle·ments /ˈbætlmənts/ n [P] wall around a castle roof, with spaces to shoot through

bat·tle·ship /ˈbætlˌʃɪp/ n large ship with big guns, used in war

bat·ty /ˈbæti/ adj sl slightly crazy

bau·ble /ˈbɔbəl/ n cheap jewel

bawd·y /ˈbɔdi/ adj about sex in a rude, funny way **–ily** adv **–iness** n [U]

bawl /bɔl/ vi/t **1** shout loudly **2** CRY[1](1)

bay[1] /beɪ/ n **1** wide opening along a coast **2** division of a large room or building, separated by shelves, etc.

bay[2] vi make the deep cry of a large hunting dog

bay[3] n **hold/keep at bay** keep (an enemy, etc.) away

bay·o·net /ˈbeɪənɪt, -ˌnɛt, ˌbeɪəˈnɛt/ n knife on the end of a RIFLE ♦ vt drive a bayonet into

bay win·dow /ˌ ˈ·/ n window with three sides sticking out from a wall

ba·zaar /bəˈzɑr/ n **1** sale to get money for some good purpose **2** market in an Eastern town

ba·zoo·ka /bəˈzukə/ n long gun that rests on the shoulder and fires ROCKETS

BBQ written abbrev. for: BARBECUE

B.C. abbrev. for: before (the birth of) Christ

be[1] /bi; strong bi/ v aux pres. t. sing. **I am**, you **are**, he/she/it **is**; pres. t. pl. we/you/they **are**; past t. sing. **I was**, you **were**, he/she/it **was**; past t. pl. we/you/they **were**; past p. **been**; pres. p. **being 1** (forms continuous tenses with –ing): I am/was reading. **2** (forms passives with –ed): We are/were invited. **3** (used with **to**) **a** must: You are not to smoke. **b** (shows future plans): They are to be married soon.

be[2] v **1** (shows that something is the same as the subject): Today is Tuesday. **2** (shows where or when): He's upstairs. **3** (shows a group or quality): She's a doctor. | I'm cold. | Be careful! **4** (shows that something exists): There's a hole in your sock.

beach /bitʃ/ n sandy or stony shore ♦ vt move (a boat) onto a beach

beach ball /ˈ· ·/ n large light ball to play with on the beach

beach·comb·er /ˈbitʃˌkoumə/ n **1** person who lives on a beach **2** person who searches a beach for useful things to sell

beach·head /ˈbitʃhɛd/ n area on an enemy's shore that has been won by an opposing force

beach·wear /ˈbitʃwɛr/ n [U] clothing for the BEACH

bea·con /ˈbikən/ n fire or flashing light that gives warning

bead /bid/ n **1** small ball with a hole through it, for putting on string **2** drop of liquid: beads of sweat ~ed adj

bead·y /ˈbidi/ adj (of eyes) small and bright

bea·gle /ˈbigəl/ n hunting dog with short legs

beak /bik/ n bird's hard horny mouth

bea·ker /ˈbikə/ n glass cup used in chemistry

beam[1] /bim/ n long heavy piece of wood, esp. used to support a building

beam[2] n **1** line of light from some bright object **2** radio waves sent out to guide aircraft, etc. **3** bright look or smile ♦ v **1** vi (of the sun, etc.) send out light (and heat) **2** vt send out (esp. radio or television signals) in a certain direction **3** vi smile brightly

bean /bin/ n **1** seed or POD of any of various plants, esp. used as food: baked beans | coffee beans **2 full of beans a** full of life and eagerness **b** consisting of nonsense **3 spill the beans** tell a secret

bear[1] /bɛr/ n large, heavy furry animal that eats meat, fruit, and insects

bear[2] v bore /bɔr, boor/ borne /bɔrn, boorn/ **1** vt carry **2** vt support (a weight) **3** vt have; show: *The letter bore no signature. | to bear a famous name* **4** vt suffer or accept (something unpleasant) without complaining **5** vt fml give birth to **6** vi/t produce (a crop or fruit) **7** vi move in the stated direction: *Cross the field, bear left, and you'll see the house.* **8** vt be suitable for: *His words don't bear repeating.* **9** vt fml keep (a feeling toward someone) in one's mind: *I don't bear him a grudge.* **10 bear in mind** remember to consider **11 bring something to bear (on)** direct something, e.g. force or persuasion (on); EXERT ~able adj tolerable (TOLERATE) ~ably adv

bear down phr v **1** vt fml defeat **2** vi use all one's strength and effort

bear down on/upon phr vt come towards forcefully and threateningly, esp. at high speed

bear on/upon phr vt relate to

bear out phr vt support the truth of

bear up phr vi show courage or strength in spite of difficulties

bear with phr v show patience towards

beard /bɪrd/ n hair on the face below the mouth ~ed adj

bear·er /'bɛrə/ n **1** person who brings or carries something, e.g. the body at a funeral **2** person to whom a check is to be paid

bear·ing /'bɛrɪŋ/ n **1** [S;U] way of behaving **2** [S;U] connection; relevance (RELEVANT): *This has no bearing on the subject.* **3** [C] direction shown by a compass **4** understanding of one's position: *get/lose one's bearings*

bear mar·ket /ˌ· '··/ n situation in which the value of STOCK MARKET decreases

beast /bist/ n **1** animal with four feet **2** person or thing one does not like ~ly adj bad; nasty

beat[1] /bit/ v beat, beaten /'bit̩n/ or beat **1** vt hit again and again, esp. with a stick: *beat a drum | the rain beating against the windows* **2** vt mix with a fork, etc.: *beat the eggs* **3** vi move regularly: *I could hear his heart beating.* **4** vt defeat: *I beat him at tennis.* **5 beat about the**

bush talk indirectly about something **6 Beat it!** infml Go away! **7 beat one's brains out** try very hard to think or remember **8 beat the rap** avoid punishment **9 beat time** make regular movements to measure the speed or music ~er n tool for beating things ~ing ♦ n **1** act of giving repeated blows, usu. as punishment **2** defeat

beat[2] n **1** single stroke or blow: *the beat of the drum* **2** regular STRESS (4) in music or poetry **3** usual path followed by someone on duty

be·a·tif·ic /ˌbiə'tɪfɪk◄/ adj showing joy and peace: *a beatific smile*

beau·ti·cian /byu'tɪʃən/ n person who cuts women's hair and gives beauty treatments

beau·ti·ful /'byutəfəl/ adj giving pleasure to the mind or senses ~ly adv ~tify /-faɪ/ vt make beautiful

beat-up /ˌ· '·◄/ adj infml old and slightly damaged

beau·ty /'byuti/ n **1** [U] quality of being beautiful **2** [C] someone or something beautiful

beauty par·lor /'·· ˌ·/ n place where women get beauty treatments for face, hair, etc.

bea·ver /'bivə/ n animal like a big rat that builds walls of sticks etc. across streams

be·came /bɪ'keɪm/ past t. of BECOME

be·cause /bɪ'kɔz, -'kʌz/ conj **1** for the reason that: *I do it because I like it.* **2 because of** as a result of: *I came back because of the rain.*

beck /bɛk/ n **at one's beck and call** always ready to do what one asks

beck·on /'bɛkən/ vi/t call with a movement of the finger

be·come /bɪ'kʌm/ v became, become **1** begin to be: *become king | become warmer* **2** vt be suitable for: *Such behavior hardly becomes someone in your position.* **becoming** adj **1** attractive **2** suitable

bed[1] /bɛd/ n **1** [C] piece of furniture to sleep on **2** bottom or base: *bed of a river* **3** [C] piece of ground for plants **4** [U] making love; sex

bed[2] v -dd- **1** put in or on a bed: *a machine bedded in cement* **2** plant **3** have sex with

bed down phr v **1** vt make (a person or animal) comfortable for the night **2**

vi make oneself comfortable for the night

bed·clothes /'bɛdkloʊz, -kloʊðz/ *n* [P] sheets, etc., on a bed

bed·ding /'bɛdɪŋ/ *n* [U] materials for a person or animal to sleep on

bed·fel·low /'bɛdˌfɛloʊ/ *n* 1 person who shares a bed 2 close companion; partner

bed·lam /'bɛdləm/ *n* [S;U] place of wild noisy activity

bed of ros·es /ˌ· '· ·/ *n* [S] happy comfortable state

bed·pan /'bɛdpæn/ *n* container for a sick person's body waste

be·drag·gled /bɪˈdrægəld/ *adj* wet, LIMP, and muddy

bed·rid·den /'bɛdˌrɪdn/ *adj* too ill or old to get out of bed

bed·room /'bɛdrum, -rʊm/ *n* room for sleeping in

bed·side /'bɛdsaɪd/ *n* 1 side of a bed: *bedside lamp* 2 **bedside manner** way in which a doctor behaves when visiting a sick person

bed·sore /'bɛdsɔr/ *n* sore place on the skin, caused by lying too long in bed

bed·spread /'bɛdsprɛd/ *n* decorative cover for a bed

bed·stead /'bɛdstɛd/ *n* main framework of a bed

bed·time /'bɛdtaɪm/ *n* time for going to bed

bee /bi/ *n* 1 stinging insect that makes HONEY 2 **a bee in one's bonnet** fixed idea; OBSESSION 3 **the bee's knees** *infml* the best person or thing

beech /bitʃ/ *n* large forest tree with green or shiny brown leaves

beef¹ /bif/ *n* [U] meat of farm cattle ♦ ~**y** *adj* (of a person) big and strong

beef² *vi* complain

  beef up /ˌ· '·/ *phr vt* make stronger or more complete

bee·hive /'bihaɪv/ *n* HIVE

bee·line /'bilaɪn/ *n* **make a beeline for** go straight towards

been /bɪn/ *n* 1 *past participle of* BE 2 gone and come back: *Have you ever been to England?*

beep /bip/ *vi/t* 1 sound a car horn 2 attract attention using a small electronic machine (**beeper**) ♦ *n* 1 sound of a horn or beeper 2 short high sounding note, esp. as given on the radio to show the exact time

beer /bɪr/ *n* [U] alcoholic drink made from MALT ~**y** *adj*: *beery breath*

beet /bit/ *n* 1 root from which sugar is made 2 large red root vegetable

bee·tle /'bitl/ *n* insect with hard wing coverings

be·fall /bɪˈfɔl/ *vi/t* befell /-ˈfɛl/, befallen /-ˈfɔlən/ *fml* happen (to)

be·fit /bɪˈfɪt/ *vt* -**tt**- *fml* be suitable for: *befitting behavior*

be·fore /bɪˈfɔr, -ˈfoʊr/ *prep* 1 earlier than 2 ahead of; in front of ♦ *adv* already; formerly: *I've seen you before.* ♦ *conj* 1 before the time when 2 rather than

be·fore·hand /bɪˈfɔrˌhænd, -ˈfoʊr-/ *adv* before something else happens

be·friend /bɪˈfrɛnd/ *vt* be a friend to

beg /bɛg/ *v* -**gg**- 1 *vi/t* ask for (food, money, etc.) 2 *vt fml* request politely: *I beg to differ.* 3 **beg the question** to take as true something that is not yet proved

beg·ger /'bɛgə/ *n* person who lives by begging ~**ly** *adj* much too little

be·gin /bɪˈgɪn/ *vi/t* began /bɪˈgæn/, begun /bɪˈgʌn/ 1 start; take the first step 2 **to begin with** as the first reason ~**ner** *n* person starting to learn ~**ning** *n* [C;U] starting point

be·grudge /bɪˈgrʌdʒ/ *vt* to GRUDGE

be·guile /bɪˈgaɪl/ *vt fml* 1 charm 2 deceive; cheat

be·half /bɪˈhæf/ *n* **on behalf of** for; in the interests of: *I'm speaking on John's behalf.*

be·have /bɪˈheɪv/ *vi* 1 (of people or things) act in a particular way 2 show good manners

be·hav·ior /bɪˈheɪvjə/ *n* [U] way of behaving

be·head /bɪˈhɛd/ *vt* cut off the head of

be·hest /bɪˈhɛst/ *n fml* **at someone's behest** by someone's command

be·hind /bɪˈhaɪnd/ *prep* 1 at or to the back of: *hide behind the door* 2 less good than: *He's behind the others in mathematics.* 3 in support of ♦ *adv* 1 behind something 2 where something was before: *I've left the key behind!* 3 late; slow: *We're behind with the rent.* ♦ *n infml* BUTTOCKS

be·hold /bɪˈhoʊld/ *vt* beheld /bɪˈhɛld/ *lit* see

be·hold·en /bɪˈhoʊldn/ *adj* **be beholden to** owing something to

beige /beɪʒ/ *adj, n* pale brown

be·ing¹ /ˈbiː-ɪŋ/ n **1** [U] existence: *When did the club come into being?* **2** [C] living thing, esp. a person

being² v present participle of BE

be·lat·ed /bɪˈleɪtɪd/ adj delayed; too late ~**ly** adv

belch /bɛltʃ/ v **1** vi pass gas up from the stomach **2** vt send out (large amounts of smoke, etc.) **belch** n

be·lea·guered /bɪˈliːɡəʳ/ adj fml **1** surrounded by an army **2** worried continuously

be·lie /bɪˈlaɪ/ vt fml give a false idea of

be·lief /bəˈliːf/ n **1** [S;U] feeling that something is true, or can be trusted **2** [C] idea that is believed: *religious beliefs*

be·lieve /bəˈliːv/ v **1** vt consider to be true **2** vi have religious faith **believable** adj that can be believed **believer** n

believe in phr vt **1** think that (something exists): *believe in fairies* **2** feel sure of the value of: *believe in lots of exercise*

be·lit·tle /bɪˈlɪtl/ vt fml cause to seem unimportant: *Don't belittle your efforts.*

bell /bɛl/ n **1** metal object that makes a ringing sound: *church bells* | *a bicycle bell* **2** object shaped like a cup: *the bell of a flower* **3 ring a bell** remind one of something

bel·lig·er·ent /bəˈlɪdʒərənt/ n, adj **1** (country that is) at war **2** (person who is) ready to fight

bel·low /ˈbɛloʊ/ vi/t shout in a deep voice

bel·lows /ˈbɛloʊz/ n [P] –**lows** instrument for blowing air into a fire, etc.

bell pep·per /ˈ· ͵·–/ n PEPPER

bel·ly /ˈbɛli/ n **1** infml the part of the human body between the chest and legs **2** curved surface like this: *the belly of a plane* ~**ful** /-fʊl/ n infml too much

bel·ly·ache /ˈbɛliˌeɪk/ vi complain repeatedly

belly but·ton /ˈ·· ͵·–/ n infml NAVEL

be·long /bɪˈlɔŋ/ vi be in the right place: *This chair belongs upstairs.* ~**ings** n [P] one's property

belong to phr vt **1** be the property of **2** be a member of

be·lov·ed /bɪˈlʌvd, bɪˈlʌvɪd/ n, adj (person who is) dearly loved

be·low /bɪˈloʊ/ adv, prep in a lower place (than); under: *He saw the valley below.* | *below the knee* | *see page 85 below*

belt¹ /bɛlt/ n **1** band worn round the waist **2** circular piece of material that

drives a machine **3** area with a particular quality, crop, etc. **4** BELTWAY **5 below the belt** infml unfair or unfairly — see also BLACK BELT

belt² v **1** vt fasten with a belt **2** vt infml hit hard

belt out phr vt infml sing loudly

belt·way /ˈbɛltˌweɪ/ n road that goes around a town

be·moan /bɪˈmoʊn/ vt fml express sorrow for

be·mused /bɪˈmjuːzd/ adj unable to think clearly

bench /bɛntʃ/ n **1** [C] long seat **2** [C] long table for working on: *a carpenter's bench* **3 a** [the+s] place where a judge sits in court **b** judges as a group

bend /bɛnd/ vi/t bent /bɛnt/ (cause to) move into a curve or move away from an upright position: *bend the wire* | *bend down to kiss the child* ♦ n **1** curve: *a bend in the road* **2 round the bend** infml crazy **bends** [P] pain suffered by divers (DIVE) who come to the surface too quickly

be·neath /bɪˈniːθ/ adv, prep fml **1** below; under **2** not worthy of: *beneath contempt*

ben·e·dic·tion /ˌbɛnəˈdɪkʃən/ n religious blessing

ben·e·fac·tor /ˈbɛnəˌfæktəʳ/ **benefactress** /-trɪs/ fem. — n person who gives money, etc. **–tion** /ˌbɛnəˈfækʃən/ n **1** [U] giving of money **2** [C] money given

ben·e·fi·cial /ˌbɛnəˈfɪʃəl◄/ adj (of things) helpful; useful

ben·e·fi·cia·ry /ˌbɛnəˈfɪʃiˌɛri, -ˈfɪʃəri/ n receiver of a benefit

ben·e·fit /ˈbɛnɪfɪt/ n **1** [U] advantage; profit: *She's had the benefit of a very good education.* **2** [C;U] money or help given by an insurance agreement, the government, etc: *The company provides medical benefits* **3** [C] event to raise money for some person or special purpose **4 the benefit of the doubt** favorable consideration given because there is no proof of guilt or wrongness ♦ v **1** vt be helpful to **2** vi gain advantage

be·nev·o·lent /bəˈnɛvələnt/ adj wishing to do good; kind **–lence** n [U]

be·nign /bɪˈnaɪn/ adj kind and harmless

bent¹ /bɛnt/ v **1** past t. and p. of BEND **2 bent on** determined on: *She's bent on winning.*

bent² n special natural skill: *a natural bent for languages*

be·queath /bɪˈkwið, bɪˈkwiθ/ vt fml give to others after death

be·quest /bɪˈkwɛst/ n fml something bequeathed

be·rate /bɪˈreɪt/ vt fml speak angrily to

be·reaved /bəˈrivd/ adj fml having lost someone by death: a bereaved mother **bereavement** n [C;U]

be·reft /bəˈrɛft/ adj completely without: bereft of hope

be·ret /bəˈreɪ/ n round soft flat cap

ber·ry /ˈbɛri/ n small soft fruit with seeds

ber·serk /bəˈsɜk, -ˈzɜk/ adj violently angry

berth /bəθ/ n berths /bəðz/ 1 sleeping place in a ship or train 2 place where a ship can be tied up in a harbor 3 **give someone a wide berth** avoid someone ♦ vi/t tie up (a ship)

be·seech /bɪˈsitʃ/ vt besought /bɪˈsɔt/ or beseeched fml ask eagerly

be·set /bɪˈsɛt/ vt beset, present participle **besetting** attack continuously: beset by doubts

be·side /bɪˈsaɪd/ prep 1 at the side of 2 in comparison with 3 **beside oneself** almost crazy (with joy, etc.) 4 **beside the point** having nothing to do with the main question

be·sides /bɪˈsaɪdz/ adv also ♦ prep in addition to

be·siege /bɪˈsidʒ/ vt surround (a place) with armed forces: (fig.) They besieged her with questions.

be·sot·ted /bɪˈsɑtɪd/ adj made foolish or unable to behave sensibly

best[1] /bɛst/ adj (superlative of GOOD) 1 the highest in quality or skill: the best tennis player in America 2 **the best part of** most of see also SECOND BEST

best[2] adv (superlative of WELL) 1 in the best way: She did best. 2 to the greatest degree; most: He thinks he knows best.

best n [S] 1 the greatest degree of good: She wants the best for her children. 2 one's best effort: I did my best. 3 **All the best!** (used when saying goodbye) I wish you success! 4 **at its/one's best** in as good a state as possible 5 **at (the) best** if the best happens 6 **make the best of** do as well as one can with (something unsatisfactory)

bes·ti·al /ˈbɛstʃəl, ˈbis-/ adj (of human behavior) very cruel **~ity** /ˌbɛstʃiˈæləti, ˌbis-/ n [U]

best man /ˌ· ˈ·/ n man attending the BRIDEGROOM at a wedding

be·stow /bɪˈstoʊ/ vt fml give

best·sel·ler /ˌbɛstˈsɛlə/ n book, etc., that sells in very large numbers

bet /bɛt/ n 1 agreement to risk money on a future event 2 sum of money risked in this way ♦ vi/t bet or betted; pres. p. **betting** 1 risk (money) on a race, etc. 2 be sure: I bet he's angry!

be·tray /bɪˈtreɪ/ vt 1 be unfaithful to 2 make known (a secret): (fig.) Her face betrayed (= showed) her nervousness. **~er** n **~al** n [C;U]

be·trothed /bɪˈtroʊðd/ adj lit having promised to marry

bet·ter /ˈbɛtə/ adj 1 higher in quality; more good: a better way to do it 2 well again after illness ♦ adv 1 in a better way: It works better now. 2 **go one better (than)** do better (than) 3 **had better** ought to; should: I'd better not tell him. 4 **know better (than)** be sensible enough not to ♦ n **get the better of** defeat ♦ vi/t 1 improve 2 **bet·ter oneself: a** earn more **b** educate oneself **~ment** improvement **betters** n [P] people better than oneself

better off /ˌ· ˈ·/ adj 1 having more money 2 improved

be·tween /bɪˈtwin/ prep 1 in the space or time that separates: Stand between Sue and Brian. | Don't eat between meals. 2 (shows connection): an air service between Boston and Houston 3 (shows division or sharing): The difference between spaghetti and noodles. | Between us, we collected $17. ♦ adv 1 in the space or time between things 2 **few and far between** very rare

bev·el /ˈbɛvəl/ vt -l- make a sloping edge on **bevel** n

bev·er·age /ˈbɛvərɪdʒ, ˈbɛvrɪdʒ/ n fml liquid for drinking, esp. one that is not water or medicine

bev·y /ˈbɛvi/ n large group

be·wail /bɪˈweɪl/ vt fml express sorrow for

be·ware /bɪˈwɛr/ vi/t (used in giving orders) Be careful!: Beware of the dog.

be·wil·der /bɪˈwɪldə/ vt confuse: a bewildering mass of detail

be·witch /bɪˈwɪtʃ/ vt 1 use magic on 2 charm: a bewitching smile

be·yond /bɪˈyɑnd/ *prep* **1** on the further side of: *beyond the mountains* **2** outside the limits of; more than: *beyond belief* **3** **beyond me** too hard for me to understand ♦ *adv* further: *fly to Cairo and beyond*

bi·as /ˈbaɪəs/ *n* [C;U] fixed unfair opinion; PREJUDICE ♦ *vt* **-s-** cause to form fixed opinions: *a biased judgment*

bib /bɪb/ *n* **1** piece of cloth or plastic tied under a child's chin **2** top part of an APRON

Bi·ble /ˈbaɪbəl/ *n* holy book of the Christians and Jews: (fig.) *This dictionary is my bible.* **biblical** /ˈbɪblɪkəl/ *adj*

bib·li·og·ra·phy /ˌbɪbliˈɑgrəfi/ *n* list of writings on a subject **-pher** person who writes such a list

bi·cen·ten·ni·al /ˌbaɪsɛnˈtɛniəl/ *n* 200th ANNIVERSARY **bicentennial** *adj*

bi·ceps /ˈbaɪsɛps/ *n* **biceps** muscle of the upper arm

bick·er /ˈbɪkə/ *vi* quarrel about small matters

bi·cy·cle /ˈbaɪsɪkəl/ *n* vehicle with two wheels ridden by pushing its PEDALS **bicycle** *vi*

bid[1] /bɪd/ *vi/t* **bid 1** offer (a price) at a sale **2** (in card games) declare what one intends to win ♦ *n* **1** amount that is bid **2** attempt: *a rescue bid* **~der** *n*

bid[2] *vt* **bade** /bæd, beɪd/ *or* **bid, bidden** /ˈbɪdn/ *or* **bid;** *pres.* p. **bidding** *lit* order: *She bade him come.* **~ding** *n* [U]

bide /baɪd/ *vt* **bide one's time** wait till the right moment

bi·en·ni·al /baɪˈɛniəl/ *adj* happening once every 2 years ♦ *n* plant that makes flowers in its second year, then dies

bi·fo·cals /ˈbaɪˌfoʊkəlz, baɪˈfoʊkəlz/ *n* [P] galsses made in 2 parts, suitable both for looking at distant objects and for reading **bifocal** *adj*

big /bɪg/ *adj* **-gg- 1** of more than average size, importance, etc.: *big ears | a big decision* **2** generous: *big hearted* **3** *infml* very popular

big·a·my /ˈbɪgəmi/ *n* [U] being married to 2 people at the same time **-mist** *n* **-mous** *adj*

big busi·ness /ˌ· ˈ·ˌ/ *n* [U] very large, influential companies considered as a group

big deal /ˌ· ˈ·/ *n infml* **1** important event or situation **2** used to say that something is very important: *A two dollar tip? Big Deal!* **3** **no big deal** used to show one is not upset or angry: "*I'm really sorry!*" "*No big deal.*"

big-head·ed /ˌbɪgˈhɛdɪd◂/ *adj infml* CONCEITED

big name /ˌ· ˈ·/ *n* famous person, esp. an actor, musician etc.

big·ot /ˈbɪgət/ *n* person who will not change an unreasonable opinion **~ry** *n* [U] behavior typical of a bigot

big shot /ˈ· ·/ *also* **big noise** — *n* person of great importance or influence

big-tick·et /ˈ· ˌ··/ *adj* very expensive

big time /ˈ· ˌ·/ *n infml* **the big time** highest level of an activity: *He's not ready for the big time yet.* **big-time** *adj* — **big time** *adv* used to emphasize: *I got lucky, big time!*

big·wig /ˈbɪgwɪg/ *n infml* important person

bi·jou /ˈbiʒu/ *adj* (esp. of a building) small and pretty

bike /baɪk/ *n, vi* **1** BICYCLE **2** MOTORCYCLE

bi·ki·ni /bɪˈkini/ *n* clothing worn by a woman for swimming, consisting of two separate pieces

bi·lat·er·al /baɪˈlætərəl/ *adj* with 2 sides or 2 groups: *a bilateral agreement*

bile /baɪl/ *n* [U] **1** liquid formed in the LIVER **2** bad temper

bilge /bɪldʒ/ *n* [U] **1** ship's bottom, with dirty water in it **2** *infml* foolish talk

bi·lin·gual /baɪˈlɪŋgwəl/ *adj* using 2 languages

bil·ious /ˈbɪljəs/ *adj* sick because food is not DIGESTed properly

bill[1] /bɪl/ *n* **1** list of things that must be paid for **2** plan for a future law **3** piece of paper money **4** printed notice **5** **fill the bill** be suitable **6** **foot the bill** pay and take responsibility (for) ♦ *vt* **1** send a bill to **2** advertise in printed notices **3** arrange a performance

bill[2] *n* bird's beak

billboard /ˈbɪlbɔrd, -boʊrd/ *n* large board usu. outdoors on which advertisements are put

bil·let /ˈbɪlɪt/ *n* private home where soldiers are put to live ♦ *vt* put in billets

bill-fold /ˈbɪlfoʊld/ *n* WALLET

bil·liards /ˈbɪljədz/ *n* [U] game played on a table, with balls and long sticks

bil·lion /ˈbɪljən/ *determiner, n* **billion** *or* **billions** one thousand million **~th** *determiner, n, adv*

bil·low /ˈbɪloʊ/ n rolling mass of smoke, etc., like a large wave **billow** vi

bil·ly club /ˈbɪli ˌklʌb/ n short thick stick used as a weapon by a policeman

billy goat /ˈbɪli ˌɡoʊt/ n male goat

bim·bo /ˈbɪmboʊ/ n infml derog attractive but stupid woman

bin /bɪn/ n large container for storing things, or for waste

bi·na·ry /ˈbaɪnəri/ adj 1 double 2 using only 0 and 1 as a base: the binary scale

bind /baɪnd/ v **bound** /baʊnd/ 1 vt tie up: bind the prisoner's arms | bind up a wound | (fig.) bound together by friendship 2 vt fasten (a book) into its cover 3 vi/t (cause to) stick together in a mass 4 vt cause to obey, esp. by a law or a promise: a binding agreement | He felt bound to tell her. ~**er** n 1 person or thing that binds books 2 removable cover for holding sheets of papers, etc. ~**ing** n book cover

binge[1] /bɪndʒ/ n infml period of drinking and wild behavior

binge[2] vi eat a lot of food in a short time, esp. as a result of an EATING DISORDER

bin·go /ˈbɪŋɡoʊ/ n [U] 1 game played for money, by covering numbered squares on a card 2 infml (an expression of pleasure)

bi·noc·u·lars /bɪˈnɑkyələrz, baɪ-/ n [P] pair of glasses like short TELESCOPES for both eyes

bi·o·chem·is·try /ˌbaɪoʊˈkɛmɪstri/ n [U] chemistry of living things

bi·o·de·gra·da·ble /ˌbaɪoʊdɪˈɡreɪdəbəl/ adj able to be made harmless by the chemical action of bacteria, etc.

bi·og·ra·phy /baɪˈɑɡrəfi/ n written account of someone's life –**pher** n a person who writes this –**phical** /ˌbaɪəˈɡræfɪkəl◂/ adj

bi·o·logi·cal war·fare /ˌbaɪəˌlɑdʒɪkəl ˈwɔrfɛr/ n [U] way of fighting a war using BACTERIA to harm the enemy

bi·ol·o·gy /baɪˈɑlədʒi/ n [U] scientific study of living things –**gist** n –**gical** /ˌbaɪəˈlɑdʒɪkəl◂/ adj

bi·on·ic /baɪˈɑnɪk/ adj having more than human strength, speed, etc.

bi·o·pic /ˈbaɪoʊˌpɪk/ n biographical film

bi·op·sy /ˈbaɪˌɑpsi/ n removal of material from a living body to test it for possible disease

bi·o·tech·nol·o·gy /ˌbaɪoʊtɛkˈnɑlədʒi/ n [U] use of living cells, bacteria, etc., in industry

bi·ped /ˈbaɪpɛd/ n creature with two feet

bi·plane /ˈbaɪpleɪn/ n aircraft with 2 pairs of wings

birch /bɜrtʃ/ n 1 tree with smooth wood and thin branches 2 rod made from this wood, used for punishing

bird /bɜrd/ n 1 [C] creature with wings and feathers that can fly 2

birds of a feather /ˌ· · ˈ·◂/ people of the same kind — see also EARLY BIRD

bird's-eye view /ˌ· ˈ·◂/ n view seen from above, like a map

birth /bɜrθ/ n 1 [C;U] act, time, or process of being born: She gave birth to a fine baby. 2 [U] family origin: French by birth

birth con·trol /ˈ· ·ˌ·/ n [U] CONTRACEPTION

birth·day /ˈbɜrθdeɪ/ n ANNIVERSARY of the day one was born

birth·mark /ˈbɜrθmɑrk/ n mark on the skin at birth

birth·rate /ˈbɜrθreɪt/ n number of births during a particular time

birth·right /ˈbɜrθraɪt/ n something that belongs to someone because of the family or nation they were born into

bis·cuit /ˈbɪskɪt/ n small round bread-like cake often eaten with GRAVY

bi·sect /ˈbaɪsɛkt, baɪˈsɛkt/ vt divide into 2

bi·sex·u·al /baɪˈsɛkʃuəl/ adj sexually attracted to people of both sexes

bish·op /ˈbɪʃəp/ n 1 Christian priest of high rank 2 piece in CHESS ~**ric** /ˈbɪʃəprɪk/ n DIOCESE

bi·son /ˈbaɪsən, -zən/ n bisons or bison 1 large wild hairy cowlike animal 2 BUFFALO

bis·tro /ˈbistroʊ, ˈbɪ-/ n small BAR (4) or restaurant

bit[1] /bɪt/ v past t. of BITE

bit[2] n 1 small piece: bits of paper/of news 2 a short time: We walked around for a bit. 3 a bit rather: I'm a bit tired. 4 every bit as quite as; no less: She's every bit as good as you are. 5 not a bit not at all

bit[3] n single unit of computer information

bit[4] n part of a BRIDLE that goes inside the horse's mouth

bitch /bɪtʃ/ n 1 female dog 2 derog unpleasant woman ♦ vi sl 1 complain continually 2 make nasty or unpleasant remarks about others ~**y** *adj* making nasty remarks about people

bite /baɪt/ *v* **bit** /bɪt/, **bitten** /ˈbɪtˈn/ **1** *vi/t* cut with the teeth **2** *vi/t* (of snakes and insects) sting **3** *vi* (of fish) accept food on a hook **4** *vi* take firm hold: *This clamp won't bite the wood.* **5** accept an offer esp. one that is meant to deceive: *When they offered, I bit.* **6 bite off more than one can chew** attempt too much **7 bite the bullet** suffer bravely **bite the dust** *infml* be killed or defeated ♦ *n* **1** [C] piece removed by biting **2** [C;U] wound made by biting **3** [S] something to eat **4** [U;S] sharpness; bitterness **biting** *adj* painful: *biting wind/remarks*

bit·ter /ˈbɪtə/ *adj* **1** not sweet; tasting like beer or black coffee **2** very cold: *a bitter wind* **3** causing grief: *bitter disappointment* **4** full of hate: *bitter enemies* **5 to the bitter end** to the end in spite of all unpleasant difficulties ~**ly** *adv* ~**ness** *n* [U]

bit·ter·sweet /ˌbɪtəˈswiːt◁/ *adj* pleasant, but mixed with sadness

biv·ou·ac /ˈbɪvuæk, ˈbɪvwæk/ *n* camp without tents ♦ *vi* -**ck**- spend the night in a bivouac

bi·zarre /bɪˈzɑːr/ *adj* very strange ~**ly** *adv*

blab /blæb/ *vi* -**bb**- *sl* tell a secret

black /blæk/ *adj* **1** of the color of night: (fig.) *Your hands are black.* (= very dirty) **2** of a race of people with dark skin, esp. of the African race **3** (of coffee) without milk **4** very bad; hopeless **5** very angry: *a black look* **6** (of humor) funny about unpleasant or dangerous people or events: *black humor* ♦ *n* **1** [U] black color **2** [C] black person ♦ *vt* make black ~**ly** *adv* **1** angrily **2** sadly ~**ness** *n* [U]

black and blue /ˌ · · ˈ·/ *adj* bruised

black·ball /ˈblækbɔːl/ *vt* vote against (someone who wants to join a club)

black belt /ˌ· ˈ·/ *n* (person who holds) a high rank in judo, karate, etc.

black·board /ˈblækbɔːd, -boʊrd/ *n* board used in schools for writing on

black box /ˌ· ˈ·/ *n* apparatus fitted to an aircraft to record information about an accident

black·en /ˈblækən/ *vi/t* make or become black: (fig.) *They blackened his character by spreading lies.*

black eye /ˌ· ˈ·/ *n* dark skin around the eye, from being hit

black·head /ˈblækhed/ *n* spot on the skin with a black top

black hole /ˌ· ˈ·/ *n* area in outer space into which everything is pulled, even light itself

black·jack /ˈblækdʒæk/ *n* **1** [C] type of fighting weapon carried in the hand **2** [U] type of poker game

black·list /ˈblæklɪst/ *n* list of people to be avoided or punished **blacklist** *vt*

black mag·ic /ˌ· ˈ·/ *n* magic used for evil purposes

black·mail /ˈblækmeɪl/ *n* [U] **1** getting money by threatening to make known unpleasant facts **2** influencing of someone's actions by threats, causing anxiety, etc.: *He accused his mother of using emotional blackmail to stop him leaving home.* ♦

blackmail *vt* ~**er** *n*

black mar·ket /ˌ· ˈ·/ *n* [S] unlawful buying and selling of goods, etc.: *We bought our dollars on the black market.* ~**eer** /ˌ· ·ˈ·/ *n*

black·out /ˈblækaʊt/ *n* **1** darkness, caused by electrical failure **2** short loss of consciousness **3** intentional prevention of reporting: *a news blackout* **black out** *vi/t*

black sheep /ˌ· ˈ·/ *n* family member who brings shame on it

black·smith /ˈblæksmɪθ/ *n* person who works metal and makes iron things

blad·der /ˈblædə/ *n* **1** skin bag inside the body, where waste liquid collects **2** any bag that can be filled with air or liquid

blade /bleɪd/ *n* **1** sharp cutting part of a knife, etc. **2** flat part of an oar, propeller, or bat (1) **3** long narrow leaf: *blades of grass*

blame /bleɪm/ *vt* **1** responsible for something bad **2 be to blame** be guilty ♦ *n* [U] responsibility for something bad ~**less** *adj* free from guilt ~**worthy** *adj* guilty

blanch /blæntʃ/ *vi/t* **1** make or become white **2** cook a short time in boiling water

bland /blænd/ *adj* **1** (of food) without much taste **2** (of people or their behavior) showing no strong feelings or opinions, esp. so as to avoid giving offense ~**ly** *adv* ~**ness** *n* [U]

blan·dish·ments /ˈblændɪʃmənts/ *n* [P] flattery

blank[1] /blæŋk/ *adj* **1** without writing **2** empty or expressionless: *My mind went blank.* ~**ly** *adv*: *He looked at me blankly.* ~**ness** *n* [U]

blank[2] *n* **1** empty space **2** CARTRIDGE with no bullet in it **3 draw a blank** be unsuccessful

blank check /ˌ· ˈ·/ *n* **1** check that is signed, but with the amount left blank **2** complete freedom to do what one wants

blan·ket /ˈblæŋkɪt/ *n* thick bed covering: (fig.) *A blanket of snow covered the hills.* — see also WET BLANKET ♦ *vt* cover as if with a blanket ♦ *adj* including all cases: *a blanket rule*

blank verse /ˌ· ˈ·/ *n* [U] poetry that does not RHYME

blare /bleər/ *vi/t* make the loud noise of a horn **blare** *n* [S]

bla·sé /blɑˈzeɪ/ *adj* seeming not to be concerned or excited about something, or about things in general

blas·phe·my /ˈblæsfəmi/ *n* [C;U] bad language about God and holy things –**mous** *adj* **blaspheme** /blæsˈfim/, /ˈblæsfim/ *vi*

blast[1] /blæst/ *n* **1** strong air movement **2** rush of air from an explosion **3** sound of a brass wind instrument **4 at full blast** as hard as possible

blast[2] *v* **1** *vi/t* break up (rock, etc.) with explosives **2** *vt* DAMN

blast off *phr vi* (of a spacecraft) leave the ground **blast-off** /ˈ· ·/ *n* [U]

bla·tant /ˈbleɪtnt/ *adj* too noticeable; shameless ~**ly** *adv* –**tancy** *n* [U]

blaze /bleɪz/ *n* **1** [S] bright flame: (fig.) *a sudden blaze of anger* **2** [C] big dangerous fire ♦ *vi* **1** burn or shine brightly **2** spread news about: *The news was blazed across the front page.* **3 blaze a trail** lead the way

blaz·er /ˈbleɪzər/ *n* JACKET which fits loosely, sometimes with the sign of a school, etc., on it

bleach /blitʃ/ *vi/t* make or become white or pale ♦ *n* [U] chemical used for bleaching cloth

bleach·ers /ˈblitʃərz/ *n* [*the*+P] cheap seats, open to the air, for watching a game

bleak /blik/ *adj* cold and cheerless: *bleak weather* | (fig.) *bleak prospects* ~**ly** *adv* ~**ness** *n* [U]

blear·y /ˈblɪri/ *adj* (of eyes) red and tired –**ily** *adv* –**iness** *n* [U]

bleat /blit/ *vi*, *n* (make) the sound of a sheep or goat

bleed /blid/ *v* **bled** /blɛd/ **1** *vi* lose blood **2** *vt* draw blood from, as doctors once did **3** *vt* draw off liquid or air from **4 bleed for someone** feel pity

bleep /blip/ *n* repeated high sound made by a machine to attract attention ♦ *vi/t* make this sound

blem·ish /ˈblɛmɪʃ/ *n* mark, etc., that spoils perfection **blemish** *vt*

blend /blɛnd/ *vi/t* mix together ♦ *n* mixture ~**er** kitchen mixing machine

blend in *phr vi* go together well

bless /blɛs/ *vt* **blessed** or **blest** /blɛst/ **1** ask God's favor for **2** make holy **3 be blessed with** be lucky enough to have ~**ed** /ˈblɛsɪd/ *adj* **1** holy **2** desirable **3** *infml* (used to give force to expressions of annoyance)

bless·ing /ˈblɛsɪŋ/ *n* **1** [C] God's favor **2** [C] something one is glad of **3** [U] approval

blew /blu/ *past t.* of BLOW[1]

blight /blaɪt/ *n* **1** [U] disease of plants **2** [C] something that spoils **3** [U] condition of ugliness, disorder, and decay **blight** *vt*: *blighted hopes*

blind[1] /blaɪnd/ *adj* **1** unable to see **2** unwilling to recognize: *blind to her faults* **3** without reason or purpose: *blind panic* **4** drunk **5 turn a blind eye (to)** pretend not to see or notice (something, esp. something illegal) ♦ *vt* **1** make unable to see or understand **2 blind with science** confuse or fill with admiration by a show of detailed or specialist knowledge ~**ly** *adv* ~**ness** *n* [U]

blind[2] *n* place where one may watch animals, birds etc. without being seen

blind al·ley /ˌ· ˈ·/ *n* narrow street with no way out

blind drunk /ˌ· ˈ·/ *adj* extremely drunk

blind·ers /ˈblaɪndərz/ *n* [P] leather pieces fixed to prevent a horse from seeing sideways

blind·fold /ˈblaɪndfoʊld/ *vt* cover (the eyes) with a piece of cloth ♦ *n* piece of material to cover the eyes ♦ *adv* with the eyes covered: *I could do it blindfolded.*

blind spot /ˈ· ·/ **1** part of an area that cannot easily be seen **2** something one is never able to understand

blink /blɪŋk/ *vi/t* shut and open (the eyes) quickly: (fig.) *The lights blinked in the* *distance.* **blink** *n* **1** act of blinking **2 on the blink** not working properly

blink·ers /'blɪŋkəz/ *n* [P] **1** leather pieces fixed to prevent a horse from seeing sideways **2** flashing lights on a car showing which way it will turn **3** inability to see or understand

blinkered /-əd/ *adj*

bliss /blɪs/ *n* [U] complete happiness **~ful** *adj* **~fully** *adv*

blis·ter /'blɪstə/ *n* **1** watery swelling under the skin **2** swelling like this on a rubber tire, painted wood, etc. ♦ *vi/t* form blisters **~ing** *adj* **1** very hot **2** very angry and intended to hurt: *a blistering attack*

blithe /blaɪð, blaɪθ/ *adj* free from care **~ly** *adv*

blitz /blɪts/ *n* **1** sudden violent attack, esp. from the air **2** period of great activity for some special purpose: *an advertising blitz*

bliz·zard /'blɪzəd/ *n* severe snowstorm

bloat·ed /'bloʊtɪd/ *adj* unpleasantly swollen

blob /blɒb/ *n* drop of liquid or small round mass

bloc /blɒk/ *n* group of people, nations, etc., acting as a unit — see also EN BLOC

block /blɒk/ *n* **1** solid piece of material: *a block of wood/ice* **2** *sl* head: *I'll knock your block off!* **3** distance between one street and the next: *The store is 4 blocks away.* **4** group of things considered together: *a block of theater seats* **5** blockage ♦ *vt* **1** prevent movement through **2** shut off from view **3** prevent the success of: *to block legislation*

block·ade /blɒ'keɪd/ *n* surrounding of a place, by ships or soldiers, to stop people or goods from going in or out: *to raise/lift* (= end) *a blockade* ♦ *vt* surround in this way

block·age /'blɒkɪdʒ/ *n* something that stops movement; OBSTRUCTION: *a blockage in the pipe*

block·bust·er /'blɒkˌbʌstə/ *n* something very big, effective, or successful

blond /blɒnd/ *adj* **1** (of hair) light in color; yellow **2 blonde** /blɒnd/ *fem.* having blond hair **blonde** *n* blonde woman

blood /blʌd/ *n* **1** [U] red liquid that flows through the body: *blood donors* **2** [U] family relationship: *people of noble*

blood **3 in cold blood** cruelly and on purpose **4 make someone's blood boil** make someone very angry **5 make someone's blood run cold** frighten someone **~less** *adj* without fighting **~y** *adj* bleeding **~ily** *adv*

blood·bath /'blʌdbæθ/ *n* merciless killing; MASSACRE

blood broth·er /ˌ ˈ‑/ *n* one of two or more men who have promised complete loyalty to one another

blood·cur·dling /'blʌdˌkɜːdlɪŋ/ *adj* very frightening

blood group /ˈ ‑/ *n* class of human blood

blood·hound /'blʌdhaʊnd/ *n* large dog that tracks people and animals

blood poi·son·ing /ˈ ˌ‑‑/ *n* [U] condition in which an infection spreads from a part of the body through the BLOOD-STREAM

blood pres·sure /ˈ ˌ‑/ *n* [C;U] measurable force with which blood flows through the BLOODSTREAM

blood·shed /'blʌdʃed/ *n* [U] killing, usu. in fighting

blood·shot /'blʌdʃɒt/ *adj* (of the eyes) red

blood·stain /'blʌdsteɪn/ *n* spot of blood **~ed** *adj*

blood·stream /'blʌdstriːm/ *n* flow of blood through the body

blood·suck·er /'blʌdˌsʌkə/ *n* **1** creature that bites and then sucks blood from the wound **2** person who tries to get as much money as possible from other people

blood·thirst·y /'blʌdˌθɜːsti/ *adj* eager to kill; too interested in killing

blood·y mur·der /ˌ ˈ‑/ *n* **scream/ shout bloody murder** *infml* complain very loudly

bloom /bluːm/ *n* **1** flower **2 in the bloom of** at the best time of/for ♦ *vi* **1** produce flowers **2** show as healthy color **3** BLOSSOM (2)

blos·som /'blɒsəm/ *n* **1** flower of a tree or bush **2 in blossom** bearing flowers ♦ *vi* **1** produce blossoms **2** develop favorably

blot[1] /blɒt/ *n* **1** spot, esp. of ink **2** shameful fault: *a blot on her character* **3** something ugly: *a blot on the landscape*

blot[2] *vt* **-tt-** **1** make blots on **2** dry up (ink)

blot out *phr vt* cover; hide: *Clouds blotted out the sun.*

blotch /blɒtʃ/ n large spot or mark ~**y** adj

blot·ter /ˈblɒtə/ n large piece of BLOTTING PAPER

blotting pa·per /ˈ·· ˌ·/ n [U] thick soft paper used to dry wet ink after writing

blouse /blaʊs, blaʊz/ n woman's shirt

blow¹ /bləʊ/ v **blew** /bluː/, **blown** /bləʊn/ **1** vi/t send out air; move by the force of air: *The wind blew the tree down.* | *He blew the candle out.* **2** vi/t sound made by blowing: *to blow a trumpet* **3** vt clean (one's nose) by blowing through it **4** vi/t melt (an electrical FUSE) **5** vt sl lose (a favorable chance) as the result of foolishness **6** vt infml spend (money) freely **7** vi sl leave quickly **8 blow hot and cold (about)** be favorable (to) at one moment and unfavorable (to) at the next **9 blow one's own trumpet/horn** infml praise oneself **10 blow one's top/stack** sl explode with anger **11 blow someone a kiss** kiss one's hand, then wave or blow over it towards someone **12 blow someone's brains out** infml kill someone by a shot through the head **13 blow someone's mind** sl fill someone with wonder **14 blow the whistle on** sl cause something undesirable to stop, by bringing it to the attention of esp. the public

blow over phr vi (of a storm) stop blowing: (fig.) *The scandal will soon blow over.*

blow up phr v **1** vi/t explode **2** vt fill with air: *blow up the tires* **3** make (a photograph) larger: (fig.) *The affair was blown up by the newspapers.* **4** get angry suddenly **5** (of bad weather) start blowing: *There's a storm blowing up.*

blow² n act of blowing: *Give your nose a good blow.*

blow³ n **1** hard stroke with the hand or a weapon **2** sudden misfortune **3 come to blows** start to fight — see also BODY BLOW

blow-by-blow /ˌ· · ˈ·◂/ adj with full details, given in the order in which they happened

blow·er /ˈbləʊə/ n apparatus for producing a current of air or gas

blown /bləʊn/ past p. of BLOW¹

blow·out /ˈbləʊ-aʊt/ n **1** very big meal **2** bursting of a container (esp. a tire)

blow·torch /ˈbləʊtɔːtʃ/ n lamp that blows a flame (e.g. for burning off paint)

BLT n bacon, lettuce and tomato sandwich

blub·ber¹ /ˈblʌbə/ n [U] fat of sea creatures, esp. WHALES

blubber² vi weep noisily

blud·geon /ˈblʌdʒən/ vt **1** hit with something heavy **2** force to do something, by threats

blue /bluː/ adj **1** of the color of the clear sky **2** sad; DEPRESSED **3** concerned with sex; improper: *blue films* ◆ n [U] **1** blue color **2 out of the blue** unexpectedly

blues n **1** [S;U] slow sad song or music from the South **2** [U] sadness

blue·ber·ry /ˈbluːˌberi/ n garden bush with small blue berries

blue-blood·ed /ˌ· ˈ··◂/ adj of noble birth

blue book /ˈ· ˌ·/ n **1** book of paper used in colleges for writing answers to test questions **2** book of empty pages with a blue cover for writing college examinations

blue chip /ˌ· ˈ·/ n, adj (an industrial stock) that is expensive and in which people have confidence

blue-col·lar /ˌ· ˈ··◂/ adj of or concerning workers who do hard or dirty work with their hands

blue jay /ˈ· ·/ n bright blue bird from eastern North America

blue laws /ˈ· ˌ/ n laws forbidding drinking, dancing, etc.

blue moon /ˌ· ˈ·/ n [S] **once in a blue moon** infml almost never

blue·print /ˈbluːprɪnt/ n copy of a plan for making or building something: (fig.) *a blueprint for the reforms*

blue-sky /ˌ· ˈ·◂/ adj done in order to test ideas, rather than for any particular practical purpose

blue·stock·ing /ˈbluːˌstɒkɪŋ/ n woman thought to be too highly educated

blue tail fly /ˌ· · ˈ·/ n large bluegreen fly

bluff¹ /blʌf/ vi **1** deceive someone by pretending to be stronger or cleverer than one is: *They say they'll blow up the place, but they're only bluffing.* **2 bluff it out** escape trouble by continuing a deception **bluff** n [S;U] **1** action of bluffing **2 call someone's bluff** tell someone to do what they threaten to do

bluff² adj (of a person) rough and cheerful

blun·der /ˈblʌndə/ n stupid mistake ◆ vi **1** make a blunder **2** move awkwardly ~**er** n

blunt /blʌnt/ adj **1** not sharp: *a blunt pencil* **2** not trying to be polite ◆ vt make

less sharp ~**ly** adv roughly and plainly
~**ness** n [U]

blur /blə/ n [S] something whose shape is not clearly seen ♦ vt **-rr-** make hard to see: (fig.) to blur a distinction

blurb /blɜːb/ n short description of the contents of a book

blurt /blɜːt/ v

blurt out phr vt say suddenly without thinking

blush /blʌʃ/ vi become red in the face, from shame **blush** n ~**ingly** adv

blus·ter /ˈblʌstə/ vi 1 speak roughly and noisily 2 (of wind) blow roughly

bluster n [U] ~**y** adj windy

B-mov·ie /ˈbiː ˌmuːvi/ n cheaply made film not considered to be of very good quality

B.O. n [U] body odour; unpleasant smell from a person's body

boar /bɔː, bʊə/ n wild pig

board /bɔːd, bʊəd/ n 1 [C] flat piece of wood, etc.: floor boards | a notice board | a chessboard 2 BLACKBOARD 3 (cost of) meals: room and board 4 committee of people controlling something 5 **above board** completely open and honest 6 **across the board** including all groups or members, as in an industry: a raise of $10 a week across the board 7 **go by the board** (of plans) come to no result 8 **on board** on a ship or public vehicle ♦ v 1 vt cover with boards 2 vt go on board a ship, etc. 3 vi/t get or supply meals and a room for payment: to board with a friend ~**er** n person who pays to live and receive meals somewhere

board game /ˈ· ·/ n game played by moving pieces on a marked board

board·ing·house /ˈbɔːdɪŋhaʊs, ˈbʊəd-/ n private lodging house that supplies meals

boarding pass /ˈ·· ·/ n official card to be given up when one enters an aircraft

boarding school /ˈ·· ˌ·/ n [C;U] school at which children live instead of going there daily from home

board·walk /ˈbɔːdwɔːk, ˈbʊəd-/ n wide path along the coast in a tourist town

boast /bəʊst/ v 1 vi talk too proudly 2 vt have (a cause for pride): This computer boasts many ingenious features. ♦ n 1 act of boasting 2 cause for pride ~**ful** adj full of praise for oneself

boat /bəʊt/ n water vehicle, esp. smaller than a ship — see also **in the same boat** (SAME[1]) ♦ vi go in a boat, esp. for pleasure

boat·er /ˈbəʊtə/ n stiff hat made of STRAW

bob[1] /bɒb/ vi **-bb-** move quickly up and down: a boat bobbing on the water

bob[2] vt cut (a woman's hair) to the shoulder or shorter ♦ n a bobbed haircut

bob·bin /ˈbɒbɪn/ n small roller for thread

bob·ble /ˈbɒbəl/ vt to drop a BASEBALL vi to BOB[1]

bobby pin /ˈbɒbi ˌpɪn/ n flat pin for holding hair

bobby socks, bobby sox /ˈbɒbi ˌsɒks/ n [P] girl's socks reaching above the ankle

bob·sled /ˈbɒbsled/ vi, n (ride in) a small vehicle that runs on metal blades, used for sliding down snowy slopes

bode /bəʊd/ vi **bode well/ill** be a good/bad sign for the future

bod·ice /ˈbɒdɪs/ n top part of a woman's dress

bod·i·ly /ˈbɒdl-i/ adj of the human body; PHYSICAL ♦ adv taking hold of the whole body

bod·y /ˈbɒdi/ n 1 person or animal's whole physical structure, alive or dead 2 this without the head or limbs 3 main part of something: The important news in the body of the letter 4 group of people: an elected body 5 object; piece of matter: The sun is a heavenly body. 6 large amount: a body of water such as a lake 7 **keep body and soul together** remain alive (by getting money for food)

body blow /ˈ·· ·/ n 1 (in boxing (BOX[2])) blow that falls below the breast and above the waist 2 a serious SETBACK

bod·y·guard /ˈbɒdiˌgɑːd/ n man or group of men guarding someone important

bod·y·work /ˈbɒdiˌwɜːk/ n [U] outside parts of a motor vehicle

bog[1] /bɒg, bɔːg/ n [C;U] area of soft wet ground ~**gy** adj

bog[2] v **bog down** phr vi/t **-gg-** sink into a bog: (fig.) to get bogged down in one's work

bog·gle /ˈbɒgəl/ vi pause in shocked surprise

bo·gus /ˈbəʊgəs/ adj pretended; false

bo·gy /ˈbəʊgi/ n imaginary evil spirit

bo·he·mi·an /bəʊˈhiːmiən/ adj not following accepted social customs

boil¹ /bɔɪl/ *vi/t* **1** bring or come to the temperature at which a liquid changes to gas: *212°F is the boiling point of water.* **2** cook at this temperature: *to boil eggs* **3 boil down** boil till almost no water remains ♦ *n* [S]: *Bring the soup to a boil.*

boil away *phr vi* disappear by boiling

boil down to *phr vt* be no more than: *It all boils down to a question of money.*

boil over *phr vi* **1** (of a boiling liquid) flow over the sides of the container **2** get out of control (and develop into): *The conflict broke out into war.*

boil up *phr v* **1** *vt* make hot and cook **2** *vi* reach a dangerous level

boil² *n* painful infected swelling under the skin

boil·er /ˈbɔɪlə/ *n* large container for boiling water, e.g. to provide heating in a house

bois·ter·ous /ˈbɔɪstərəs/ *adj* noisily cheerful ~**ly** *adv*

bold /bəʊld/ *adj* **1** daring; courageous **2** without respect or shame **3** clearly marked: *a bold drawing* ~**ly** *adv* ~**ness** *n* [U]

bol·ster¹ /ˈbəʊlstə/ *n* long PILLOW

bolster² *v* **bolster up** *phr vt* encourage; support

bolt¹ /bəʊlt/ *n* **1** bar that fastens a door or window **2** screw used with a NUT (2) to hold things together ► THUNDERBOLT **4 a bolt from the blue** something unexpected and unpleasant — see also NUTS AND BOLTS

bolt² *v* **1** *vt* fasten with a BOLT¹ (1) **2** *vi* run away suddenly **3** *vt* swallow (food) hastily ♦ *n* [S] **1** act of running away **2 make a bolt for it** run away ♦ *adv* **bolt upright** straight and stiff

bomb /bɒm/ *n* **1** [C] container filled with explosive **2** [*the*+S] the NUCLEAR bomb **3** bad film **4 bombs away!** let's go! ♦ *v* **1** *vt* attack with bombs **2** *vi infml* move quickly **3** *vi infml* fail ~**er** *n* **1** aircraft that drops bombs **2** person who throws bombs

bom·bard /bɒmˈbɑːd/ *vt* attack heavily with gunfire: (fig.) *He was bombarded with questions.* ~**ment** *n* [C;U]

bom·bas·tic /bɒmˈbæstɪk/ *adj* using impressive but meaningless words ~**ically** *adj*

bomb·shell /ˈbɒmʃel/ *n* great shock

bo·na fi·de /ˌbəʊnə ˈfaɪd, ˈbɒnə-, ˌbəʊnə ˈfaɪdi/ *adj* real

bo·nan·za /bəˈnænzə, bəʊ-/ *n* something very profitable

bond /bɒnd/ *n* **1** something that unites: *a bond of friendship* **2** written promise, esp. to pay back money with interest **3** state of being stuck together ♦ *vt* unite; stick

bonds /bɒndz/ *n* [P] chains or ropes for tying someone up

bond·age /ˈbɒndɪdʒ/ *n* [U] *lit* slavery

bone /bəʊn/ *n* [C;U] **1** any of the various hard parts of the body which are surrounded by flesh and skin **2 cut to the bone** reduce as much as possible **3 feel in one's bones** believe strongly though without proof **4 have a bone to pick with someone** have something to complain about **5 make no bones about** feel no doubt or shame about — see also BARE BONES, FUNNY BONE ♦ *vt* take bones out of (fish, etc.) ~**less** *adj* **bony** *adj* **1** very thin, showing the bones **2** (of food) full of bones

bone-dry /ˌ ˈ ◂/ *adj* perfectly dry

bon·fire /ˈbɒnfaɪə/ *n* large outdoor fire

bonkers /ˈbɒŋkəz/ *adj* crazy

bon·net /ˈbɒnɪt/ *n* round hat tied under the chin worn esp. by babies

bo·nus /ˈbəʊnəs/ *n* **1** additional payment beyond what is usual **2** anything pleasant in addition to what is expected

boo /buː/ *interj, n* boos shout of disapproval ♦ *vi/t* shout "boo"

booby prize /ˈbuːbi ˌpraɪz/ *n* prize given for the worst performance in a competition

booby trap /ˈ ◂ ˌ ◂/ *n* thing which looks harmless, used for surprising people unpleasantly, such as a hidden bomb ♦ **booby-trap** *vt* -**pp**-

book¹ /bʊk/ *n* **1** set of sheets of paper fastened together, to be read or written in: *books on travel* | *a bookseller* | *bookshelves* | *a bookstore* **2** collection of matches, tickets, etc., fastened like a book **3** main division of the Bible or of a long poem **4 a closed book** subject about which one knows very little **5 by the book** according to the rules **6 in one's book** in one's opinion **7 throw the book at** (esp. of the police) make all possible charges against

books /bʊks/ *n* [P] business accounts

book² *vt* write down a legal charge against: *booked for speeding* ~**able** *adj*

book·case /ˈbʊk-keɪs/ *n* piece of furniture to hold books

book club /'· ·/ *n* club that offers books cheaply to its members

book·end /'bʊkɛnd/ *n* support for a row of books

book·ing /'bʊkɪŋ/ *n* planned performance of a professional entertainer

book·keep·ing /'bʊkˌkipɪŋ/ *n* [U] keeping business accounts –er *n*

book·let /'bʊklɪt/ *n* small thin book

book·mak·er /'bʊkˌmeɪkə/ also **bookie** /'bʊki/ *infml* — *n* person who takes BETS (2) on races

book·mark /'bʊkmɑrk/ *n* something put in a book to keep one's place

book·mo·bile /'bʊkmoʊˌbil/ *n* library kept in a motor vehicle that travels from town to town

book·worm /'bʊkwəm/ *n* person who loves reading

boom¹ /bum/ *vi* **1** make a deep hollow sound **2** grow rapidly: *Business is booming.* **boom** *n*: *a boom in exports*

boom² /bum/ *n* **1** long pole to which a sail is fastened **2** heavy chain across a river to stop logs floating down or to prevent ships sailing up **3** long pole on the end of which a camera or MICROPHONE can be moved about

boo·mer·ang /'buməˌræŋ/ *n* curved stick which makes a circle and comes back when thrown ♦ *vi* have the opposite effect to that intended

boon¹ /bun/ *n fml* comfort; help

boon·docks /'bʊndɑks/ *n [the+P] infml* rough country area where few people live

boor /bʊr/ *n* rude person ~ish *adj* ~ishly *adv*

boost /bust/ *vt* raise; increase **boost** *n* ~er **1** something that boosts **2** additional amount of a drug

boot¹ /but/ *n* **1** heavy shoe that comes up over the ankle **2** give/get the boot *infml* dismiss/be dismissed from a job **3** lick someone's boots work very hard to gain someone's favor **4** put the boot in *sl* kick someone **5** too big for one's boots too proud

boot² *vt infml* kick

boot out *phr vt infml* send away rudely and sometimes with force

boot³ *n* to boot in addition

booth /buθ/ *n* **1** tent, hut, etc., where goods are sold **2** small enclosed space: *a telephone/voting booth*

boot·leg /'butˌlɛg/ *vi/t* -gg- make, carry or sell (alcoholic drink) illegally **bootleg** *adj* ~ger *n*

booze /buz/ *vi sl* drink alcohol ♦ *n* [U] *sl* alcoholic drink **boozer** *sl* person who boozes

bor·der¹ /'bɔrdə/ *n* **1** edge **2** line between 2 countries

border *vt* put or be a border to

border on *phr vt* be very much like: *Your remarks border on rudeness!*

bor·der·line /'bɔrdəˌlaɪn/ *adj* that may or may not be something: *Anne will pass the exam, but Sue is a borderline case.* (= may pass or fail) ♦ *n* (line marking) a border

bore¹ /bɔr, boʊr/ *v past t. of* BEAR²

bore² *n* dull person or activity ♦ *vt* make (someone) tired or uninterested: *a boring job* ~dom *n* [U] state of being bored

bore³ *vi/t* make a round hole (in) ♦ *n* **1** hole made by boring **2** measurement of the hole inside a gun, pipe, etc.

born /bɔrn/ *adj* **1** be born come into existence by birth **2** being something by nature: *a born leader* **3** born and bred having grown up from birth in the stated place **4** born of owing existence to

born-a·gain /'· ·/ *adj* having accepted a particular religion, esp. EVANGELICAL Christianity, esp. through a deep experience of the spirit: *a born-again Christian* | (fig.) *a born-again jogger*

borne /bɔrn, boʊrn/ *v past p. of* BEAR²

bo·rough /'bɝoʊ, 'bʌroʊ/ *n* town, or division of a large town, esp. New York

bor·row /'bɑroʊ, 'bɔroʊ/ *v* **1** *vi/t* receive something that is lent, and will be returned **2** *vt* copy (ideas, words, etc.) ~er *n*

bos·om /'bʊzəm, 'bu-/ *n lit* **1** the front of the human chest, esp. the female breasts **2** place where one feels love, sorrow, etc. **3** a bosom buddy a very close friend **4** in the bosom of in a close relationship with

boss /bɔs/ *n infml* person who controls others; employer; etc. ♦ *vt* give orders to ~y *adj* too fond of giving orders

bot·a·ny /'bɑtⁿn-i/ *n* [U] scientific study of plants –**nist** *n* –**nical** /bə'tænɪkəl/ *adj*

botch /bɑtʃ/ *vt* do a repair (of something) badly

both /boʊθ/ *determiner, pron* this one and that one: *both of us* | *both New York and London*

both·er /'baðər/ *v* **1** *vt* cause inconvenience to; annoy in little ways: *Does the noise bother you?* **2** *vi* trouble oneself: *Don't bother to lock the door.* ♦ *n* [C;U] trouble; inconvenience ~**some** *adj* causing bother

bot·tle /'batl/ *n* **1** container with a narrow neck for liquids **2** container for holding a baby's milk **3 the bottle** alcoholic drink, esp. when drunk too much: *He's on/hitting the bottle again.* ♦ *vt* put into bottles

bottle up *phr vt* control (feelings) in an unhealthy way

bot·tle·neck /'batl,nɛk/ *n* narrow part of a road which slows down traffic: (fig.) *a bottleneck in production*

bot·tom¹ /'batəm/ *n* **1** [C] base; lowest part or level: *the bottom of the stairs* | *He was the bottom of the class.* **2** [C] part of the body that one sits on **3** [S] ground under the sea, a lake, etc. **4** last half of an INNING in baseball **5** [S] cause: *get to the bottom of the trouble* **6 at bottom** really **7 from the bottom of one's heart** truly **8 knock the bottom out of** take away the necessary support on which something rests ~**less** *adj* very deep

bottom² *v* **bottom out** *phr vi* reach the lowest point before rising again

bottom line /ˌ·· '·/ *n* [*the*+S] **1** the amount of money shown (as profit or loss) at the bottom of a set of accounts **2** the most important result in the end, esp. with regard to money

bot·u·lis·m /'batʃə,lɪzəm/ *n* [U] form of food poisoning

bou·doir /'budwɑr/ *n lit* woman's private room

bough /baʊ/ *n* large branch of a tree

bought /bɔt/ *v past t. and p. of* BUY

boul·der /'boʊldər/ *n* large rock

bounce /baʊns/ *v* **1** *vi* (of a ball) spring back again: *The ball bounced against the wall.* **2** *vi/t* move up and down quickly: *She bounced about the room.* **3** *vi* (of a check) be returned by the bank as worthless ♦ *n* **1** [C;U] act of bouncing **2** [U] behavior which is full of life **bouncer** *n* strong person employed (esp. at a club) to throw out unwelcome visitors **bouncing** *adj* (esp. of babies) strong and healthy

bound¹ /baʊnd/ *v past t. and p. of* BIND

bound² *adj* **bound to** sure to: *It's bound to rain.* **bound up in** busy with

bound³ *vi* jump; LEAP **bound** *n* — see also BOUNDS

bound⁴ *adj* going to (a place): *bound for home*

bound·a·ry /'baʊndəri, -dri/ *n* outer limit; border

bound·less /'baʊndlɪs/ *adj* unlimited

bounds /baʊndz/ *n* [P] **1** furthest limits **2 out of bounds a** forbidden to be visited **b** (of a ball in sports) outside the playing area

boun·ty /'baʊnti/ *n* **1** [C] something given out of kindness, or offered as a reward **2** [U] *fml* generosity –**tiful** *adj fml* generous

bou·quet¹ /boʊ'keɪ, bu-/ *n* bunch of flowers

bouquet² /bu'keɪ/ *n* smell of a wine

bour·geois /bʊr'ʒwɑ, 'bʊrʒwɑ/ *n, adj* **1** (person) of the MIDDLE CLASS **2** (person) too interested in material possessions ~**ie** /ˌbʊrʒwɑ'zi/ *n* [U] the MIDDLE CLASS

bout /baʊt/ *n* short period of activity or illness

bou·tique /bu'tik/ *n* small fashionable shop, esp. for clothes

bou·ton·niere /ˌbut'n'ɪr, -'yɛr/ *n* flower worn on a man's coat

bo·vine /'boʊvaɪn/ *adj* slow and dull, like a cow

bow¹ /baʊ/ *vi/t* bend forward, to show respect **bow** *n*

bow out *phr vi* give up a position or stop taking part in something

bow to *phr vt* obey; accept: *I bow to your judgment.*

bow² /boʊ/ *n* **1** piece of curved wood with a string, for shooting arrows **2** similar piece of wood for playing stringed musical instruments **3** knot formed by doubling a string into two curved pieces ♦ *vi/t* bend; curve **2** play (music) with a bow

bow³ /baʊ/ *n* front of a ship

bow·els /'baʊəlz/ *n* [P] **1** pipe that carries waste matter from the stomach **2** inside part: *the bowels of the Earth*

bowl¹ /boʊl/ *n* **1** deep round container for liquids, etc. **2** anything in the shape of a bowl

bowl² *v* **1** *vi/t* throw or roll (a ball) in a sport **2** *vi* play LAWN BOWLS or BOWLING

bowl over *phr vt* surprise greatly

bow·leg·ged /ˈboʊˌlɛgɪd, -ˌlɛgd/ *adj* having legs curving outwards at the knees

bowl·er /ˈboʊlə/ *n* person who bowls

bowl·ing /ˈboʊlɪŋ/ *n* [U] indoor game in which a big ball is rolled along a track (a **bowling alley**)

bow tie /ˌboʊ ˈtaɪ/ *n* TIE¹ (1) fastened at the front with a BOW² (3)

bow win·dow /ˌboʊ ˈwɪndoʊ/ *n* curved window

box¹ /baks/ *n* **1** [C] stiff container for solids: *a box of chocolates* **2** [C] small enclosed space: *a box at the theater* — see also BLACK BOX, PANDORA'S BOX ♦ *vt* put in boxes

box in *phr vt* enclose in a small space

box² /vi/t fight with the FISTS, for sport: *a boxing match* ~**er** *n* ~**ing** *n* [U]

box·er shorts /ˈ·· ˌ·/ *n* [pl.] loose UNDERWEAR for men

box num·ber /ˈ· ˌ·· / *n* number used as a mailing address, esp. in replying to newspaper advertisements

box of·fice /ˈ· ˌ·· / *n* place where tickets are sold in a theater, etc.: *The show was a box-office success.* (= made a large profit)

boy /bɔɪ/ *n* young male person ~**hood** *n* time of being a boy ~**ish** *adj* like a boy

boy·cott /ˈbɔɪkat/ *vt* refuse to trade with or take part in **boycott** *n*

boy·friend /ˈbɔɪfrɛnd/ *n* woman's male companion

bo·zo /ˈboʊzoʊ/ *n sl* stupid person

bra /bra/ *n* woman's undergarment supporting the breasts

brace¹ /breɪs/ *n* something that stiffens or supports **braces** *n* [P] wire worn to straighten the teeth

brace² *vt* **1** support **2** prepare (oneself) **bracing** *adj* (of weather) cold but usu. healthy

brace·let /ˈbreɪslɪt/ *n* decoration for the wrist

brack·en /ˈbrækən/ *n* [U] FERN which grows in forests

brack·et /ˈbrækɪt/ *n* **1** support for a shelf, etc. **2** either of various pairs of signs used for enclosing a piece of information, for example [ ] **3** group of people: *the 16–25 age bracket* ♦ *vt* put in brackets

brack·ish /ˈbrækɪʃ/ *adj* (of water) not pure; a little salty ~**ness** *n* [U]

brag /bræg/ *vi* **-gg-** talk too proudly; BOAST

braid /breɪd/ *n* **1** twisted length of hair **2** [U] threads of silk, gold, etc., twisted together to decorate the edges of material: *gold braid*

braille /breɪl/ *n* [U] type of raised printing that blind people can read

brain /breɪn/ *n* **1** the organ in the head that controls thought **2** mind; INTELLIGENCE **3** *infml* clever person **4 have something on the brain** think about something continually, or too much ♦ *vt infml* hit on the head ~**less** *adj* stupid ~**y** *adj* clever **brains** *n* [U] **1** material of which the brain consists **2** ability to think

brain·child /ˈbreɪntʃaɪld/ *n* [S] someone's successful idea

brain drain /ˈ· ·/ *n* movement of skilled people to other countries

brain·pow·er /ˈbreɪnˌpaʊə/ *n* [U] ability to reason

brain·storm /ˈbreɪnstɔrm/ *n* sudden clever idea ~**ing** *n* [U] rapid exchange of ideas among a group to find answers to problems ♦ *vi* practice brainstorming

brain·wash /ˈbreɪnwaʃ, -wɔʃ/ *vt* force someone to change their beliefs ~**ing** *n* [U]

braise /breɪz/ *vt* cook (meat or vegetables) slowly in a covered dish

brake /breɪk/ *n* apparatus for slowing or stopping a vehicle **brake** *vi/t*

bram·ble /ˈbræmbəl/ *n* common wild prickly bush

bran /bræn/ *n* [U] crushed skin of grain

branch¹ /bræntʃ/ *n* **1** stem growing from the trunk of a tree **2** division; part: *branch of a bank/of a family*

branch² *vi* form branches

branch out *phr vi* add to one's range

brand /brænd/ **1** product of a particular producer: *my favorite brand of soup* | (fig.) *his own brand* (= special kind) *of humor* **2** mark made, esp. by burning, to show ownership ♦ *vt* **1** give a lasting bad name to: *He was branded as a liar.* **2** mark with a BRAND (2): (fig.) *The experience branded her for life.*

bran·dish /ˈbrændɪʃ/ *vt* wave (e.g. a weapon) about

brand name /ˈ· ·/ *n* name a company gives to a product

brand-new /ˌbrænd ˈnuː◂/ adj just bought or made

bran·dy /ˈbrændi/ n [C;U] strong alcoholic drink made from wine

brash /bræʃ/ adj bold and disrespectful ~**ly** adv ~**ness** n [U]

brass /brɑːs/ n [U] 1 bright yellow metal 2 musical instruments made of this: a brass band — see also TOP BRASS

bras·siere /brəˈzɪr/ n fml BRA

brat /bræt/ n derog child, esp. one with bad manners

bra·va·do /brəˈvɑːdoʊ/ n [U] unnecessary show of boldness

brave /breɪv/ adj ready to meet pain or danger; fearless ♦ vt meet (danger, etc.) without showing fear ~**ly** adv ~**ry** /ˈbreɪvəri/ n [U]

bra·vo /ˈbrɑːvoʊ, brɑːˈvoʊ/ interj, n -**vos** (shout of) well done!

brawl /brɔːl/ n noisy quarrel brawl vi

brawn /brɔːn/ n [U] human muscle -**y** adj strong

bray /breɪ/ vi make the sound a DONKEY makes bray n

bra·zen /ˈbreɪzən/ adj without shame

bra·zier /ˈbreɪʒər/ n container for burning coals

breach /briːtʃ/ n 1 [C;U] act of breaking a law, promise, etc.: breach of contract 2 [C] hole (in a wall, etc.) 3 **breach of the peace** law fighting in public ♦ vt break through

bread /bred/ n [U] 1 food made of baked flour 2 food as a means of staying alive: earn one's daily bread 3 sl money 4 **bread and butter** one's way of earning money to live on 5 **know which side one's bread is buttered** know who or what will be of most gain to oneself

bread·crumb /ˈbredkrʌm/ n very small bit of bread

bread·line /ˈbredlaɪn/ n **on the bread-line** very poor

breadth /bredθ, bretθ/ n [U] 1 width 2 broad range; SCOPE

bread·win·ner /ˈbredˌwɪnər/ n person whose wages support a family

break¹ /breɪk/ v **broke** /broʊk/, **broken** /ˈbroʊkən/ 1 vi/t separate suddenly into parts: to break a window | The rope broke. 2 vi/t make or become by breaking: The box broke open. 3 vi/t make or become useless as a result of damage: a broken watch 4 vt disobey; not keep:

break a promise/an appointment 5 vi/t interrupt; stop: break the silence 6 vi/t (cause to) fail or be destroyed: The scandal could break him politically. 7 vi/t bring or come into notice: The news broke. 8 vt do better than (a record) 9 vi (of a voice) change suddenly 10 vt discover the secret of (a CODE) 11 **break new/fresh ground** do something new and different 12 **break one's back** make every possible effort 13 **break the back of** finish the main or worst part of 14 **break the ice** begin to be friendly with people one did not know before 15 **break wind** let out gases from the bowels

break away phr vi escape: (fig.) break away from old traditions

break down phr v 1 vi/t destroy; to be reduced to pieces: (fig.) They broke down her resistance. 2 vi (of machinery) stop working 3 vi fail: The peace talks have broken down. 4 vi (of a person) lose control of one's feelings 5 vi/t separate into kinds; divide: break the figures down into several lists

break even phr vi make neither a loss nor a profit

break in phr v 1 vi enter a building by force 2 vi interrupt 3 vt make (a person or animal) accustomed to something new

break into phr vt 1 enter by force 2 begin suddenly: to break into song 3 interrupt 4 use part of, esp. unwillingly: We'll have to break into our savings.

break of phr vt cure (someone) of (a bad habit)

break off phr vi/t 1 stop; end 2 separate from the main part: A branch broke off.

break out phr vi 1 (of something bad) start suddenly: War broke out. 2 show or express something suddenly: He broke out in a rash. 3 escape

break through phr vi/t 1 force a way through 2 make a new advance

break up phr v 1 vi/t divide into small pieces; separate 2 vi/t bring or come to an end: Their marriage broke up. 3 vi/t (cause to) suffer greatly 4 vi (of a crowd) cease to be together 5 vi amuse greatly

break with phr vt end one's connection with

break² n 1 act of breaking or a condition produced (as if) by breaking: a break in the clouds 2 pause for rest: a coffee break

3 change from the usual pattern or custom: *a break from the past* | *a break in the weather* **4** *infml* chance (esp. to make things better); piece of good luck **5 break of day** DAWN **6 make a break for it** try to escape

break·able /'breɪkəbəl/ *n, adj* (something) easily broken

break·age /'breɪkɪdʒ/ *n* [C;U] **1** example of breaking **2** something broken

break·a·way /'breɪkəˌweɪ/ *n* person or thing that escapes: *a breakaway group*

break·down /'breɪkdaʊn/ *n* **1** sudden failure in operation: *a breakdown in the peace talks* **2** sudden weakness or loss of power in body or mind: *a mental breakdown* **3** division into kinds; detailed explanation (of figures, etc.) — see also NERVOUS BREAKDOWN

break·er /'breɪkə/ *n* **1** large wave rolling onto the shore **2** person or thing that breaks something: *an icebreaker*

break·fast /'brɛkfəst/ *n* [C;U] first meal of the day

break-in /'· ·/ *n* entering of a building illegally and by force

break·out /'breɪkaʊt/ *n* violent or forceful escape from an enclosed space or a difficult situation, esp. an escape from prison

break·through /'breɪkθru/ *n* important advance or discovery

break·up /'breɪkʌp/ *n* **1** coming to an end **2** division into parts

breast /brɛst/ *n* **1** part of a woman's body which produces milk: *a breastfed baby* **2** upper front part of the body: *his breast pocket* | *a bird with a red breast* **3 make a clean breast of** tell the whole truth about ♦ *vt* push aside with one's chest: (fig.) *The ship breasted the waves.*

breath /brɛθ/ *n* **1** [U] air taken into and breathed out of the lungs **2** [C] single act of breathing air in and out once **3** sign or slight movement (of something): *There's a breath of spring in the air.* | *There wasn't a breath of wind.* **4** moment: *In one breath he said he loved me, in the next that he didn't.* **5 get one's breath (back)** also **catch one's breath** — return to one's usual rate of breathing **6 hold one's breath** stop breathing for a time **7 out of breath** breathing very fast, as after running **8 take one's breath away** surprise one greatly **9 under one's breath** in a whisper **10**

waste one's breath talk uselessly ~**less** *adj* ~**lessly** *adv*

Breatha·lyz·er /'brɛθəˌlaɪzə/ *n tdmk* piece of equipment used by police to check whether a driver is drunk — **breathalyze** *vt*

breathe /brið/ *v* **1** *vi/t* take (air, etc.) into the lungs and send it out again **2** *vt* say softly; whisper **3** *vt* send out (a smell, feeling, etc.) **4 breathe again** feel calm after feeling anxious **5 breathe down someone's neck** *infml* keep too close a watch on someone ~**er** *n* short rest

breath·tak·ing /'brɛθˌteɪkɪŋ/ *adj* very exciting or unusual

breed /brid/ *v* **bred** /brɛd/ **1** *vi* (of animals) produce young **2** *vt* keep (animals, etc.) for the purpose of producing young ones **3** *vt* produce; cause: *Flies breed disease.* ♦ *n* kind of animal or plant: *a new breed of rose* ~**er** *n* person who breeds animals or plants ~**ing** *n* [U] **1** business of breeding animals, etc. **2** polite manners

breeding-ground /'·· ·/ *n* **1** place where the young, esp. of wild creatures, are produced **2** place or point of origin: *a breeding-ground for disease*

breeze /briz/ *n* **1** light gentle wind **2** *sl* something easily done ♦ *vi* come and go quickly and without ceremony **breezy** *adj* **1** rather windy **2** cheerful in manner

breth·ren /'brɛðrən/ *n* [P] (used in church, etc.) brothers

brev·i·ty /'brɛvəti/ *n* [U] shortness

brew /bru/ *vi/t* prepare (beer, tea, coffee): (fig.) *Trouble is brewing.* ♦ *n* result of brewing: *a strong brew* ~**er** *n* person who makes beer ~**ery** *n* place where beer is made

bribe /braɪb/ *vt* influence unfairly by gifts ♦ *n* something offered in this way: *judges who take bribes* ~**ry** /'braɪbəri/ *n* [U] giving or taking bribes

bric-a-brac /'brɪk ə ˌbræk/ *n* [U] small decorations in a house

brick /brɪk/ *n* **1** [C;U] (piece of) baked clay for building: *brick walls* **2** something shaped like a brick **3 bang/beat one's head against a brick wall** waste one's efforts by trying to do something impossible ♦ *v* **brick in/up** *phr vt* fill or enclose with bricks

brick·lay·er /'brɪkˌleɪə/ *n* workman who puts bricks in place ~**ing** *n* [U]

brid·al /'braɪdl/ *adj* of a bride or wedding

bride /braɪd/ n woman about to be married, or just married

bride·groom /ˈbraɪdgrum, -grʊm/ n man about to be married, or just married

brides·maid /ˈbraɪdzmeɪd/ n girl attending the bride at a wedding

bridge[1] /brɪdʒ/ n **1** structure carrying a road or railroad over a river, etc. **2** raised part of a ship where the captain and officers stand **3** upper part of the nose **4** part of a musical instrument over which the strings are stretched **5** piece of metal that keeps false teeth in place ♦ vt build a bridge across

bridge[2] n [U] card game for 4 players

bri·dle /ˈbraɪdl/ n leather bands around a horse's head to control its movements ♦ v **1** vt put a bridle on **2** vi show displeasure

brief[1] /briːf/ adj **1** short: a brief visit **2** in brief in as few words as possible ~**ly** adv

brief[2] n short statement of facts or instructions — see also BRIEFS ♦ vt give necessary instructions or information

brief·case /ˈbriːfkeɪs/ n flat leather case for papers

briefs /briːfs/ n [P] short UNDERPANTS

bri·gade /brɪˈgeɪd/ n **1** army unit of about 5,000 soldiers **2** organization with certain duties

brig·a·dier /ˌbrɪgəˈdɪə◂/ also **brigadier general** n officer with rank just above a COLONEL and below a MAJOR GENERAL

bright /braɪt/ adj **1** giving out light; shining **2** (of a color) strong: bright red **3** cheerful; happy **4** clever **5** showing hope or signs of future success: a bright future ~**en** vi/t make or become bright ~**ly** adv ~**ness** n [U]

bril·liant /ˈbrɪljənt/ adj **1** very bright: brilliant blue **2** very clever: a brilliant idea **3** very hopeful; successful: a brilliant career ~**ly** adv –**liance**, –**liancy** n [U]

brim /brɪm/ n **1** edge of a cup, etc. **2** bottom part of a hat ♦ **brimming** adj

brine /braɪn/ n salty water

bring /brɪŋ/ vt **brought** /brɔːt/ **1** carry or lead towards someone: Bring him to the party. **2** cause to come: His letter brought many offers of help. **3** be sold for **4** law make (a charge) officially **5** bring home make very clear **6** bring to bear use **7** bring to light REVEAL **8** bring to mind cause to remember

bring about phr vt cause

bring around phr vt persuade into a change of opinion

bring back phr vt **1** return or cause to return: That song brings back memories. **2** obtain and return with

bring down phr vt **1** cause to fall or come down: bring down prices **2** reduce or lower: to bring someone down to your own level **3** DEPRESS

bring down on phr vt cause (something bad) to happen: bring trouble down on the family

bring forward phr vt **1** introduce; suggest: bring forward a plan **2** bring something in the future nearer to the present

bring in phr vt **1** cause to come; introduce **2** produce as profit; earn

bring off phr vt succeed in doing

bring on phr vt **1** cause to happen: bring on a fever **2** help to develop; improve

bring out phr vt **1** produce; cause to appear: Responsibility brings out the best in her. **2** encourage, esp. to talk

bring round/to phr vt cause to regain consciousness

bring through phr vt cause to come successfully through (illness, etc.)

bring together phr vt cause (esp. a man and a woman) to unite

bring up phr vt **1** educate and care for (children) **2** mention a suject **3** VOMIT (food)

brink /brɪŋk/ n edge; VERGE: on the brink of disaster

brink·man·ship /ˈbrɪŋkmənʃɪp/ n [U] infml art of trying to gain an advantage by going to the limit of safety, esp. in international politics, before stopping

brisk /brɪsk/ adj quick and active: a brisk walk ~**ly** adv ~**ness** n [U]

bris·tle /ˈbrɪsəl/ n [C;U] short stiff hair on a brush, etc. ♦ vi (of hair) stand up stiffly: (fig.) bristling with anger –**tly** /ˈbrɪsli/ adj

bristle with phr vt have plenty of: streets bristling with armed guards

brit·tle /ˈbrɪtl/ adj **1** hard but easily broken **2** lacking WARMTH or depth of feeling

broach /brəʊtʃ/ vt introduce (a subject) for conversation

broad /brɔd/ *adj* **1** large when measured from side to side; wide **2** not limited; respecting the ideas of others: *broad opinions* | *a* **broad-minded** *person* **3** not detailed: *in broad outline* **4** full; clear: *in broad daylight* **5** (of speech) showing clearly where the speaker comes from: *a broad Southern accent* **6** not acceptable in polite society: *broad humor* ~**en** *vi/t* make or become broader: *Travel broadens the mind.* ~**ly** *adv* more or less; mostly ~**ness** *n* [U]

broad·cast /ˈbrɔdkæst/ *n* radio or television program ♦ *v* **broadcast 1** *vi/t* send out (broadcasts) **2** *vt* make widely known: *He broadcast the news to his friends.* ~**er** *n* ~**ing** *n* [U]

broad jump /ˈ· ·/ *n* [S] sport of jumping as far as possible along the ground

broad·side /ˈbrɔdsaɪd/ *n* **1** large advertisement on a wall **2** firing of all the guns on one side of a ship

Broad·way /ˈbrɔdweɪ/ *n* part of New York City where theaters are

bro·cade /broʊˈkeɪd/ *n* [U] decorative cloth with a raised pattern

broc·co·li /ˈbrɑkəli/ *n* green vegetable similar to a CAULIFLOWER

bro·chure /broʊˈʃʊr/ *n* small book of instructions, or giving details of a service offered

brogue[1] /broʊg/ *n* strong thick shoe

brogue[2] *n* Irish ACCENT (1)

broil /brɔɪl/ *vi/t* cook under or over direct heat: (fig.) *broiling hot weather*

broke[1] /broʊk/ *v past t. of* BREAK[1]

broke[2] *adj* completely without money

bro·ken[1] /ˈbroʊkən/ *v past p. of* BREAK[1]

broken[2] *adj* **1** violently separated; damaged: *a broken window* | (fig.) *broken dreams* | (fig.) *a broken man* **2** not kept to; destroyed: *a broken promise* | *a broken home* (= where a child's parents do not live together) **3** imperfectly spoken or written: *broken English*

broken·heart·ed /ˌbroʊkənˈhɑrtɪd◂/ *adj* filled with grief

bro·ker[1] /ˈbroʊkə/ *n* person who buys and sells stock, etc., for others

broker[2] *vt* arrange the details of a business deal, plan, etc. so that everyone agrees

bro·ker·age /ˈbroʊkərɪdʒ/ *n* [U] **1** (place of) business of a broker **2** amount of money charged by a broker

bron·chi·al /ˈbrɑŋkiəl/ *adj* of the tubes of the WINDPIPE

bron·chi·tis /brɑŋˈkaɪtɪs/ *n* [U] illness of the bronchial tubes

bronze /brɑnz/ *n* [U] **1** (the redbrown color of) a metal that is a mixture of copper and tin **2** MEDAL made of bronze ♦ *vt* give this color to: *bronzed by the sun*

brooch /broʊtʃ, brutʃ/ *n* decoration pinned to a dress

brood /brud/ *n* family of birds, etc. ~**y** *adj* **1** (of a hen) wanting to sit on eggs **2** sad and silent ~**ily** *adv* ~**iness** *n* [U] ♦ *vi* think long and sadly about something

brook /brʊk/ *n* small stream

broom /brum, brʊm/ *n* sweeping brush with a long handle

broth /brɔθ/ *n* [U] thin soup

broth·el /ˈbrɑθəl, -ðəl, ˈbrɔ-/ *n* house of PROSTITUTES

broth·er /ˈbrʌðə/ *n* **1** male relative with the same parents **2** male member of the same profession, religious group, etc. ~**hood** *n* **1** [U] condition or feeling of friendliness and companionship **2** [C] all the people in a profession, etc. ~**ly** *adj* **1** like a brother **2** friendly

brother-in-law /ˈ·· · ·/ *n* **brothers-in-law** brother of one's husband or wife; one's sister's husband

brought /brɔt/ *v past t. and p. of* BRING

brow /braʊ/ *n* **1** EYEBROW **2** FOREHEAD **3** top of a hill

brow·beat /ˈbraʊbit/ *vt* -**beat**, -**beaten** /-bitʼn/ frighten into doing something

brown /braʊn/ *adj, n* (of) the color of earth or coffee ♦ *vi/t* make or become brown

brown·ie /ˈbraʊni/ *n* cake-like COOKIE made with chocolate

Brownie point /ˈ·· ·/ *n* [usu. pl.] mark of notice and approval for something good that one has done

brown-nose /ˈ· ·/ *vi sl* try to win approval dishonestly, esp. from a teacher

browse /braʊz/ *vi* **1** read without clear purpose **2** feed on young plants, grass, etc. **browse** *n* [S]

browser /ˈbraʊzə/ *n* computer program that lets one find and use information on the INTERNET

bruise /bruz/ *n* discolored place where the skin has been hurt ♦ *v* **1** *vt* cause a bruise on **2** *vi* show a bruise

brunch /brʌntʃ/ n [C;U] late morning meal that is both breakfast and LUNCH

bru·nette /bruˈnɛt/ n person of a race with fair skin and dark hair

brunt /brʌnt/ n **bear the brunt of** suffer the heaviest part of (an attack)

brush[1] /brʌʃ/ n **1** [C] instrument for sweeping, painting, etc., made of hair, nylon, etc.: *a toothbrush | a clothes brush* **2** [C] act of brushing **3** [C] short unpleasant meeting: *a brush with the police* **4** [U] (land covered by) small rough trees and bushes **5** [C] bushy tail

brush[2] v **1** vt clean with a brush **2** vi/t touch or move lightly

brush aside/away phr vt refuse to pay attention to

brush off /ˌ· ˈ·/ phr vt refuse to listen to or have a relationship with (someone)

brush-off /ˈ· ·/ n [the+S] clear refusal to be friendly: *She gave me the brush-off.*

brush up phr vt improve one's knowledge of (something known but partly forgotten) by study: *I must brush up (on) my French.*

brusque /brʌsk/ adj quick and rather impolite **~ly** adv **~ness** n [U]

brus·sels sprout /ˈbrʌsəl ˌspraʊt/ n vegetable like a very small CABBAGE

bru·tal /ˈbruːtl/ adj without tender feeling; cruel **~ly** adv **~ity** /bruˈtæləti/ n [C;U]

bru·tal·ize /ˈbruːtl-aɪz/ vt fml treat someone in a cruel and violent way

brute /bruːt/ n **1** rough cruel person **2** animal ♦ like (that of) an animal in being cruel or very strong: *brute force* **brutish** adj like animals rather than people

bub·ble /ˈbʌbəl/ n hollow ball of liquid containing air or gas ♦ vi **1** form, produce, or rise as bubbles: *She was bubbling (over) with happiness.* **2** make the sound of bubbles rising in liquid **bubbly** adj **1** full of bubbles **2** showing happy feelings freely

bubble gum /ˈ· ·/ n [U] CHEWING GUM that can make bubbles

buck[1] /bʌk/ n **1** [C] male of certain animals, esp. the deer, cat, and rabbit **2** [C] dollar **3** [the+S] responsibility: *to pass the buck*

buck[2] v **1** vi (of a horse) jump up with all 4 feet off the ground **2** vt throw off (a rider) by doing this

buck·et /ˈbʌkɪt/ n **1** (contents of) an open container with a handle, for liquids **2** large quantity: *The rain came down in buckets.* **~ful** /-fʊl/ n contents of a bucket

bucket shop /ˈ·· ·/ n dishonest BROKERAGE house

buck·le[1] /ˈbʌkəl/ n metal fastener for a belt, etc.

buck·le[2] vi/t **1** fasten with a buckle **2** bend; twist: *a buckled wheel* **3** begin to yield: *Her knees buckled.*

buckle down phr vi begin to work seriously

bud /bʌd/ n **1** flower or leaf before it opens **2** nip something in the bud do harm to (something), esp. so as to keep from succeeding — see also TASTE BUD ♦ vi **-dd-** produce buds **~ding** adj beginning to develop

Bud·dhis·m /ˈbudɪzəm, ˈbuː-/ n [U] eastern religion based on Buddha's teachings **Buddhist** n, adj

bud·dy /ˈbʌdi/ n **1** infml companion; friend **2** sl man (used as a form of address)

budge /bʌdʒ/ vi/t move a little

bud·get /ˈbʌdʒɪt/ n **1** plan of how to spend money, esp. public money taken in by taxation **2** amount of money stated in this ♦ vi plan one's spending ♦ adj cheap: *budget rentals*

buff[1] /bʌf/ n, adj [U] (of) a faded yellow color

buff[2] vt polish (metal) with something soft

buff[3] n person interested in a subject: *a film buff*

buf·fa·lo /ˈbʌfəloʊ/ n large wild cow-like animal; BISON

buff·er /ˈbʌfə/ n spring on a railroad car that takes the shock when it hits anything

buffer zone /ˈ·· ·/ n NEUTRAL area separating opposing forces or groups

buf·fet[1] /ˈbʌfeɪ, bʊ-/ n table, etc., where one can get food to be eaten nearby

buf·fet[2] /ˈbʌfɪt/ vt hit sharply: *buffeted by the wind*

buf·foon /bəˈfuːn/ n noisy fool

bug /bʌg/ n **1** any insect **2** GERM **3** apparatus for secret listening **4** eager interest in something: *the travel bug* **5** fault in a machine, esp. a computer ♦ vt **-gg-** **1** fit with a BUG (3) **2** trouble (someone) continually

bug·bear /ˈbʌgbeər/ n something feared

bug·ger /ˈbʌgə/ n friend or child: *a cute little bugger* —**y** n [U] SODOMY

bug·gy /ˈbʌgi/ n **1** light carriage **2** small chair on wheels for a child

bu·gle /ˈbjuːgəl/ n brass musical instrument **bugler** n

build[1] /bɪld/ vi/t built /bɪlt/ make by putting pieces together: *build houses/ ships* | (fig.) *Hard work builds character.* ~**er** n —**ing** n **1** thing with a roof and walls; house, etc. **2** work of a builder

build on phr vt **1** base on **2** depend on

build up phr v **1** vt increase; develop: *build up a business* **2** vi praise (something or someone) so as to influence the opinion of others

build[2] n shape and size of one's body

bulb /bʌlb/ n **1** round root of certain plants **2** glass part of an electric lamp ~**ous** adj fat and round

bulge /bʌldʒ/ n **1** swelling on a surface **2** sudden increase ♦ vi swell

bu·limia /buːˈlɪmiə/ n [U] mental illness that makes someone eat too much and then VOMIT so as not to gain weight —**mic** /buːˈlɪmɪk/ adj

bulk /bʌlk/ n **1** [U] great size or quantity **2 in bulk** in large quantities **3 the bulk of** most of ~**y** adj large and fat

bulk·head /ˈbʌlkhed/ n wall which divides a ship, etc., into several parts

bull /bʊl/ n **1** male of cattle and some other large animals **2 bull in a china shop** person who is rough where care is needed **3 take the bull by the horns** face difficulties with courage

bull·doze /ˈbʊldəʊz/ vt move (earth, etc.) with a powerful machine (a **bull-dozer**): (fig.) *bull-doze a bill through the House*

bul·let /ˈbʊlɪt/ n piece of shot fired from a small gun: *a bullet-proof car* — see also **bite the bullet** (BITE)

bul·le·tin /ˈbʊlətɪn, ˈbʊlətən/ n short official report

bulletin board /ˈ··· ˌ·/ n **1** board on a wall for putting information, pictures, etc. for everyone to see **2** place for leaving information for everyone to see on a computer system

bul·lion /ˈbʊljən/ n [U] bars of gold or silver

bul·lish /ˈbʊlɪʃ/ adj marked by, tending to cause, or hopeful of rising prices (as in a STOCK EXCHANGE)

bull mar·ket /ˌ· ˈ·./ n situation in which value of STOCK MARKET increases

bul·lock /ˈbʊlək/ n BULL that cannot breed

bull's-eye /ˈ· ·/ n center of a TARGET

bull·shit /ˈbʊlʃɪt/ n [U] sl nonsense ♦ vi/t -tt- sl talk nonsense, esp. confidently in order to deceive, persuade, or get admiration

bul·ly /ˈbʊli/ n person who hurts weaker people ♦ vt hurt in this way

bul·rush /ˈbʊlrʌʃ/ n tall grasslike waterside plant

bul·wark /ˈbʊlwək, ˈbʌl-/ n wall built for defense

bum /bʌm/ n sl TRAMP (1) or lazy person ♦ vt -mm- sl ask for; beg

bum out phr v DEPRESS

bum·med /bʌmd/, **bum·med out** adj sl upset or disappointed **bummer** /ˈbʌmə/ n [sing] sl something that upsets or disappoints

bump /bʌmp/ v **1** vi/t knock violently **2** vi move along in an uneven way ♦ n **1** (sound of) a sudden blow **2** swelling ~**y** adj uneven

bump into phr vt meet by chance

bump off phr vt infml kill

bump·er /ˈbʌmpə/ n protective bar on the front or back of a car ♦ adj very large: *a bumper harvest*

bun /bʌn/ n **1** small round sweet cake **2** bread in a particular shape: *hotdog bun* **3** hair twisted into a tight shape

bunch /bʌntʃ/ n **1** number of small things fastened together **2** group: *a bunch of girls* ♦ vi/t form into a bunch

bun·dle /ˈbʌndl/ n **1** number of articles fastened together: *a bundle of sticks/laundry* **2** a mass: *a bundle of nerves/laughs* ♦ vi/t hurry roughly **2** vt make into a bundle

bung /bʌŋ/ n round piece of material to close the hole in a container

bun·ga·low /ˈbʌŋgələʊ/ n small house all on one level

bun·gle /ˈbʌŋgəl/ vt do (work) badly —**gler** n

bunk /bʌŋk/ n bed above or below another

bun·ker /ˈbʌŋkə/ n **1** place to store things **2** shelter for soldiers

bun·kum /ˈbʌŋkəm/ n insincere talk

bun·ny /ˈbʌni/ n (child's word for) a rabbit

buns /bʌnz/ n sl BUTTOCKS

buoy[1] /ˈbui, bɔi/ n floating object fastened to the bed of the sea to show a danger, rocks, etc.

buoy[2] v **buoy up** phr vt **1** keep floating **2** keep high

buoy·an·cy /ˈbɔiənsi, ˈbuyənsi/ n [U] **1** tendency to float **2** cheerfulness **3** ability, e.g. of prices or business activity, to remain or return quickly to a high level after a period of difficulty –**ant** adj showing buoyancy

bur·den /ˈbɜdn/ n fml heavy load or duty ♦ vt fml load; trouble

bur·den·some /ˈbɜdnsəm/ adj being a burden: a burdensome task

bu·reau /ˈbyʊroʊ/ n **bureaus 1** CHEST OF DRAWERS , government department **3** business office

bu·reauc·ra·cy /byʊˈrɑkrəsi/ n **1** [U] group of government officials who are appointed, not elected **2** [C;U] government by such a group, usually supposed to be ineffective and full of unnecessary rules –**rat** /ˈbyʊrəˌkræt/ n appointed official –**ratic** /ˌbyʊrəˈkrætɪk◁/ adj –**ratically** adv

bur·geon /ˈbɜdʒən/ vi fml grow; develop

burg·er /ˈbɜgər/ n infml HAMBURGER

bur·glar /ˈbɜglər/ n thief who breaks into buildings ♦ –**glarize** /ˈbɜgləˌraɪz/ — vt break into (a building) to steal –**y** n [C;U] (example of) the crime of being a burglar

bur·i·al /ˈbɛriəl/ n [C;U] (ceremony of) burying

bur·ly /ˈbɜli/ adj (of a person) strong and heavy

burn[1] /bɜn/ v **burnt** /bɜnt/ or **burned 1** vi be on fire: a burning match/house **2** vt damage or destroy by fire or acid: burn old letters **3** vt use for heating or lighting: a woodburning stove **4** vi be very hot: burning sands **5** vi feel or wish very strongly: She's burning to tell you. **6 burn one's bridges** destroy all means of going back, so that one must go forward **7 burn one's fingers** also **get one's fingers burnt** infml — suffer the unpleasant results of a foolish action **8 burn the candle at both ends** infml use up all one's strength by doing too many different things **9 burn the midnight oil** work very late –**er** n part of a stove, etc. that produces flames ~**ing** adj **1** on fire **2** very strong and urgent

burn away phr vi disappear by burning

burn down phr vi destroy (a building) by fire

burn out phr v **1** vt make (a building) hollow by fire **2** vi stop burning because there is nothing left to burn **3** vi/t stop working through damage caused by heat: (fig.) He was burned out (= no longer active) at 38.

burn up phr vt **1** destroy completely by fire or great heat **2** become angry

burn[2] n mark or hurt place made by burning

burn·er /ˈbɜnər/ n **1** part of stove that produces heat or flame **2 put sth on the back burner** infml delay dealing with something until later

bur·nish /ˈbɜnɪʃ/ vt polish by rubbing

burn·out /ˈbɜnaʊt/ n [C;U] **1** moment when the engine of a ROCKET or JET uses up all its fuel and stops burning **2** state of not operating from overwork

burp /bɜp/ v, n BELCH

bur·row /ˈbɜroʊ, ˈbɑroʊ/ n hole where a rabbit, etc., lives ♦ vi/t make a hole; dig

bur·sar /ˈbɜsər, -sɑr/ n person in a college who has charge of money, buildings, etc.

bur·sa·ry /ˈbɜsəri/ n where the bursar works

burst[1] /bɜst/ vi/t **burst 1** break suddenly by pressure from inside: a burst pipe **2** (cause to) come into the stated condition suddenly, often with force: They burst open the door. **3** be filled to breaking point (with a substance or usu. pleasant feeling): I'm bursting (= very eager) to tell someone the news. | The river burst its banks.

burst in on phr vt interrupt noisily

burst into phr vt **1** enter quickly and suddenly **2** BREAK into (2)

burst out phr v **1** vi begin suddenly (to use the voice without speaking): They burst out laughing/crying. **2** say suddenly

burst[2] n sudden OUTBREAK or effort: a burst of speed

bur·y /ˈbɛri/ vt **1** put into a grave **2** hide away: buried treasure | (fig.) She buried her head in her hands.

bus /bʌs/ n large motor vehicle for carrying passengers ♦ vt -**ss**-, -**s**- take by bus

bus·boy /ˈbʌsbɔɪ/ n person who clears restaurant tables

bush /bʊʃ/ n 1 [C] low woody plant: *rose bush* 2 [U] wild land in Australia 3 **beat about the bush** avoid coming to the main point ~**y** adj (of hair) growing thickly

busi·ness /ˈbɪznɪs/ n 1 [U] trade; the getting of money 2 [C] activity which earns money; store, etc. 3 [C;U] one's employment; duty: *A teacher's business is to teach.* 4 [S] affair; matter 5 **have no business** to have no right to 6 **like nobody's business** very fast or well 7 **Mind your own business!** Don't ask about things that don't concern you. ~**like** adj doing things calmly and effectively

busi·ness·man /ˈbɪznɪsˌmæn/ n, **-woman** /-ˌwʊmən/ fem., **-men** /-mɛn/ person in a business firm

bus stop /ˈ· ·/ n place where buses stop for passengers

bust¹ /bʌst/ vt **busted** or **bust** infml 1 break, esp. with force 2 sl (of the police) take to a police station 3 sl (of the police) enter without warning to look for something illegal ♦ adj infml 1 broken 2 **go bust** (of a business) fail

bust² n 1 human head and shoulders as shown in a SCULPTURE 2 woman's breasts

bus·tle /ˈbʌsəl/ vi be busy, often noisily **bustle** n [S]

bus·y /ˈbɪzi/ adj 1 working; not free 2 full of work: *a busy morning* 3 (of telephones) in use ♦ vt keep (oneself) busy **busily** adv

busy·body /ˈbɪziˌbɑdi, -ˌbʌdi/ n annoying person who is too interested in people's private lives

but /bət; strong bʌt/ conj 1 rather; instead: *not one, but two* 2 yet at the same time; however: *I want to go, but I can't.* 3 (shows disagreement or surprise): *But I don't want to!* | *But that's wonderful!* ♦ prep 1 except: *nobody but me* 2 **but for** except for; without ♦ adv lit 1 only: *You can but try.* 2 **all but** almost ♦ n unwanted argument: *No buts! You're going!*

butch·er /ˈbʊtʃər/ n 1 person who kills animals for food, or sells meat 2 cruel killer ♦ vt kill and prepare for food 3 kill in a bloody way ~**y** n [U] cruel needless killing

but·ler /ˈbʌtˡlər/ n chief male servant

butt¹ /bʌt/ vi/t push with the head or horns

butt in phr vi interrupt

butt² n 1 person that people make fun of 2 end of something: *cigarette butt* 3 BOTTOM¹ (2)

but·ter /ˈbʌtər/ n [U] yellow fat made from cream ♦ vt spread butter on

butter up phr vt sl praise too much; FLATTER

but·ter·cup /ˈbʌtərˌkʌp/ n yellow wild flower

but·ter·fin·gers /ˈbʌtərˌfɪŋgərz/ n person likely to drop things

but·ter·fly /ˈbʌtərˌflaɪ/ n 1 insect with large colored wings 2 person who spends all his/her time running after pleasure: *a social butterfly* 3 **have butterflies in one's stomach** feel very nervous before doing something

but·ter·scotch /ˈbʌtərˌskɑtʃ/ n sweet food made from sugar and butter boiled together

but·tocks /ˈbʌtəks/ n [P] the fleshy parts on which a person sits

but·ton /ˈbʌtˡn/ n 1 small round object passed through a hole to fasten a garment, etc. 2 button-like object pressed to start a machine ♦ vi/t fasten with a button

but·ton·hole /ˈbʌtˡnˌhoʊl/ n hole for a button ♦ vt stop and force to listen

but·tress /ˈbʌtrɪs/ n support for a wall ♦ vt support; strengthen

bux·om /ˈbʌksəm/ adj (of a woman) fat and healthy, esp. having large breasts

buy /baɪ/ vi/t **bought** /bɔt/ 1 obtain by paying money 2 accept; believe ♦ n something bought ~**er** n person who buys, esp. professionally for a firm

buy·out /ˈbaɪaʊt/ n situation in which a person or group gains control of a company by buying all or most of its stock

buzz /bʌz/ v 1 vi make the noise that bees make: (fig.) *The room buzzed with excitement.* 2 vi/t call someone with an electrical signaling apparatus (a **buzzer**) 3 fly low and fast over: *Planes buzzed the crowd.* ♦ n 1 [C] noise of buzzing 2 infml telephone call: *Give me a buzz.* 3 sl pleasant feeling as if from a drug

buzz off phr vi infml go away

buzz·word /ˈbʌzˌwərd/ n word or phrase, esp. related to a specialized subject, which is thought to express something important but is often hard to understand

by /baɪ/ *prep, adv* **1** beside; near: *Sit by me.* **2** through; using: *enter by the door | travel by car | earn money by writing* **3** past: *He walked by (me) without speaking.* **4** before: *Do it by tomorrow.* **5** (shows who or what does something): *a play by Shakespeare | struck by lightning* **6** (shows amounts and measurements): *They overcharged me by $3. | a room 15 feet by 40 | pay by the hour* **7** (shows how or with what): *hold it by the handle* **8** (shows the size of groups following each other): *The animals went in two by two.* **9** during: *to sleep by day* **10 by and by** before long **11 by and large** on the whole; usually

bye /baɪ/ also **bye-bye** /ˌ· ˈ·, ˈ· ·/ — *interj infml* goodbye

by·gone /ˈbaɪgɒn, -gən/ *adj* past: *in bygone days* ♦ *n* [P] **let bygones be bygones** forgive past quarrels

by·law /ˈbaɪlɔ/ *n* rule governing a company or organization

ByoB *adj abbrev for*: bring your own bottle; used about a party to which people bring their own alcohol.

by·pass /ˈbaɪpæs/ *n* road that goes around a busy town, etc. ♦ *vt* avoid by going around

by·prod·uct /ˈ· ˌ··/ *n* something produced while making something else

by·stand·er /ˈbaɪˌstændə/ *n* person who watches without taking part

byte /baɪt/ *n* unit of computer information equal to eight BITS³

by·way /ˈbaɪˌweɪ/ *n* smaller road or path which is not much used or known

by·word /ˈbaɪˌwəd/ *n* (name of a) person, place, or thing thought to represent some quality: *a byword for cruelty/hospitality*

by·zan·tine /ˈbɪzənˌtin, -taɪn/ *adj* secret, indirect, and difficult to understand

C

C, c /si/ the 3rd letter of the English alphabet

c *written abbrev. for:* **1** cent(s) **2** CIRCA **3** CUBIC **4** centimeter(s) **5** COPYRIGHT

C *abbrev. for:* **1** CELSIUS **2** century

cab /kæb/ *n* **1** taxi **2** the part of a bus, train engine, etc., where the driver sits ♦ **–bbie** *n* cab driver

cab·a·ret /ˌkæbəˈreɪ◂/ *n* [C;U] performance of music and dancing in a restaurant, etc.

cab·bage /ˈkæbɪdʒ/ *n* [C;U] round vegetable with thick green leaves

cab·in /ˈkæbɪn/ *n* **1** small room on a ship **2** small roughly built house

cab·i·net /ˈkæbənɪt/ *n* **1** piece of furniture with shelves and drawers **2** chief officials of a government

ca·ble /ˈkeɪbəl/ *n* **1** [C;U] thick heavy rope used on ships etc.: *a cable trolley* **2** [C] wire carrying electricity, telephone messages, etc. **3** [C] TELEGRAM ♦ *vi/t* send or tell by TELEGRAM

cable car /ˈ·· ·/ *n* car driven by an underground cable, esp. in San Francisco

cable TV /ˌkeɪbəl ti ˈvi/ *n* special system for providing more programs on television

ca·boose /kəˈbus/ *n* last car on a train

cab·stand /ˈkæbstænd/ *n* place where taxis wait for passengers

cache /kæʃ/ *n* secret store of things

cack·le /ˈkækəl/ *vi* **1** make the noise a hen makes **2** laugh unpleasantly **cackle** *n*

ca·coph·o·ny /kəˈkɑfəni/ *n* [C;U] unpleasant mixture of loud noises **–nous** *adj*

cac·tus /ˈkæktəs/ *n* **-tuses** *or* **-ti** /-taɪ/ fleshy desert plant with PRICKLES

ca·det /kəˈdɛt/ *n* young person training in the armed forces or police

cadge /kædʒ/ *vi/t derog* get or try to get by taking advantage of a person's friendship or generosity

ca·dre /ˈkædri, ˈkɑdrə/ *n* (member of) an inner group of trained people

caf·e /kæˈfeɪ, kə-/ *n* small restaurant serving light meals and drinks

caf·e·te·ri·a /ˌkæfəˈtɪriə/ *n* restaurant where people collect their own food

caf·feine /ˈkæfin, kæˈfin/ *n* [U] chemical in coffee, etc. that makes one feel more active

cage /keɪdʒ/ *n* container with bars, for keeping birds or animals in ♦ *vt* put in cage

cag·ey /ˈkeɪdʒi/ *adj* secretive

ca·hoots /kəˈhuts/ *n* **in cahoots with** working secretly with, usu. to cause harm

Cain /keɪn/ *see* **raise Cain** (RAISE)

ca·jole /kəˈdʒoʊl/ *vt* persuade by praise or false promises

cake /keɪk/ *n* **1** [C;U] soft sweet food baked with flour, etc.: *a birthday cake* **2** [C] flat piece of something: *a cake of soap* **3** (sell) like hot cakes very quickly **4** have one's cake and eat it too have the advantages of something without the disadvantages that go with it — see also PIECE OF CAKE ♦ *vt* cover thickly: *shoes caked with mud*

CAL /ˌkæl, ˌsi eɪ ˈɛl/ *abbrev. for:* computer-assisted learning

ca·lam·i·ty /kəˈlæməti/ *n* terrible misfortune **–tous** *adj*

cal·ci·um /ˈkælsiəm/ *n* [U] metal substance found in bones and chalk

cal·cu·late /ˈkælkyəˌleɪt/ *vt* **1** find out by using numbers: *calculate the cost* **2** plan, intend: *take a calculated risk* **–lable** *adj* able to be measured **–lator** *n* small machine that calculates **–lation** /ˌkælkyəˈleɪʃən/ *n* [C;U]

cal·cu·lat·ing /ˈkælkyəˌleɪtɪŋ/ *adj* coldly SHREWD

cal·en·dar /ˈkæləndər/ *n* **1** list of the days and months of the year **2** system of naming and dividing the months, etc. **3** a daily record of events, meetings, etc. in one's life

calf [1] /kæf/ *n* **calves** /kævz/ **1** [C] young of cattle and some other large animals **2** [U] its leather: **calfskin** *boots*

calf [2] *n* **calves** back of the human leg, between knee and ankle

cal·i·ber /ˈkæləbər/ *n* **1** [S;U] quality: *work of (a) high caliber* **2** inside size of a tube or gun; bullet size

cal·i·co /ˈkælɪˌkoʊ/ *n* printed cotton cloth ♦ *adj* (of a cat) with three colors

call¹ /kɔl/ v 1 vi/t speak or say loudly 2 vt name: *We'll call the baby Jean.* 3 vt tell to come: *Call a doctor!* 4 vi/t telephone 5 vi fml make a short visit: *Let's call at Bob's.* 6 vt say publicly that something is to happen: *call a meeting/an election/a strike* 7 vt consider to be: *She called me a coward.* 8 vt waken: *Please call me at 7.* 9 **call it a day** quit 10 **call the shots** be in control

call back phr v 1 vt cause (someone) to return 2 vi/t return a telephone call

call for phr vt 1 demand 2 need; deserve 3 collect

call in phr vt ask to come: *call the doctor in*

call off phr vt 1 decide not to have (a planned event) 2 tell to keep away

call on/upon phr vt fml 1 visit 2 ask to do something

call out phr vt 1 order officially to help: *Call out the army!* 2 order to STRIKE

call up phr vt 1 telephone 2 order to join the armed forces

call² n 1 shout; cry 2 telephone conversation 3 short visit 4 demand; need: *There's no call for rudeness.* 5 command to meet, come, or do something 6 **on call** ready to work if needed

call·er /ˈkɔlə/ n person who visits or makes a telephone call

call girl /ˈ·ˌ·/ n woman PROSTITUTE who makes her arrangements by telephone

cal·lig·ra·phy /kəˈlɪɡrəfi/ n [U] (art of) beautiful writing

call·ing /ˈkɔlɪŋ/ n fml profession; trade

cal·lous /ˈkæləs/ adj unkind; without sympathy ~**ness** n [U]

cal·low /ˈkæloʊ/ adj young and inexperienced

call num·ber /ˈ· ˌ·· / n number on books in a library

cal·lus /ˈkæləs/ n an area of hard skin

calm /kɑm/ adj 1 not excited; quiet 2 (of weather) not windy 3 (of the sea) smooth **calm** n [S;U] **calm** vi/t make or become calm: *We tried to calm him down.* ~**ly** adv ~**ness** n [U]

cal·o·rie /ˈkæləri/ n unit of heat, or of ENERGY produced by a food

calves /kævz/ n pl. of CALF

ca·lyp·so /kəˈlɪpsoʊ/ n kind of West Indian song

cam·cord·er /ˈkæmˌkɔrdə/ n small camera, held in one hand, for recording moving pictures and sound

came /keɪm/ v past t. of COME

cam·el /ˈkæməl/ n large animal with a long neck and one or two large HUMPS on its back

cam·e·o /ˈkæmioʊ/ n -os 1 piece of jewelry consisting of a raised shape on a darker background 2 small part in a movie or play acted by a famous actor

cam·e·ra /ˈkæmrə/ n 1 apparatus for taking photographs or moving pictures 2 **in camera** in secret

cam·ou·flage /ˈkæməˌflɑʒ, -ˌflɑdʒ/ n [C;U] use of color, shape, etc. to hide an object ♦ **camouflage** vt

camp¹ /kæmp/ n 1 [C;U] place where people live in tents or huts for a short time 2 [C] group of people with the same esp. political ideas 3 **break/strike camp** take up and put away tents ♦ vi set up or live in a camp: *We go camping every summer.*

camp² adj infml 1 (of a man) behaving or looking like a woman, esp. intentionally

camp·er /ˈkæmpə/ n [C] 1 person who camps 2 motor vehicle big enough to live in on vacation, usu. having cooking equipment and beds

cam·paign /kæmˈpeɪn/ n connected set of military, political, or business actions intended to obtain a particular result ♦ vi lead, take part in or go on a campaign

camp ground /ˈ· ·/ n place for camping

camp·site /ˈkæmpsaɪt/ n place where one can camp

cam·pus /ˈkæmpəs/ n [C;U] grounds of a university, college or school: *campus* (= university) *life*

can¹ /kən; strong kæn/ v aux 1 be able to: *Can you swim? | I can't hear you.* 2 be allowed to; may: *You can go home now.* 3 (shows what is possible): *He can be very annoying. | It can't be true.*

can² /kæn/ n 1 metal container for foods or liquids: *a can of beans | a gas can* 2 **can it!** be quiet! ♦ vt -**nn**- preserve (food) in a can

ca·nal /kəˈnæl/ n watercourse dug for boats to travel along or to bring water

ca·nar·y /kəˈnɛri/ n small yellow bird which sings beautifully

can·cel /ˈkænsəl/ vt -l- also -ll- 1 decide not to have (a planned event): *cancel a trip* 2 destroy the value of (a check, etc.)

by stamping it ~**lation** /ˌkænsəˈleɪʃən/ n [C;U]

cancel out phr vi/t balance; equal: *The 2 debts cancel each other out.*

Can·cer /ˈkænsə/ n 1 [s] fourth sign of the ZODIAC, represented by a CRAB 2 someone born between June 21st and July 22nd

can·cer n [C;U] diseased growth in the body ~**ous** adj

can·did /ˈkændɪd/ adj honest; sincere ~**ly** adv

can·di·date /ˈkændədeɪt, -dɪt/ n 1 person to be chosen or elected for a position 2 person taking an examination ~**dacy** n [U] being a candidate

can·died /ˈkændid/ adj covered with shiny sugar

can·dle /ˈkændl/ n wax stick with string inside, which gives light when it burns: *We ate by candlelight.*

can·dle·stick /ˈkændlˌstɪk/ n holder for a candle

can·dor /ˈkændə/ n [U] being CANDID

can·dy /ˈkændi/ n [C;U] sweets, chocolate, etc.

candy bar /ˈ·· ˌ·/ n BAR of candy, nuts etc. covered with chocolate

candy cane /ˈ·· ˌ·/ n red and white curved stick of sugar candy eaten esp. at Christmas

candy strip·er /ˈkændi ˌstraɪpə/ n young woman who helps in a hospital without pay

cane /keɪn/ n stem of certain tall plants, used for making furniture, for punishing children, etc. ♦ vt hit with a cane

ca·nine /ˈkeɪnaɪn/ adj, n (of, for, typical of) a dog

can·is·ter /ˈkænəstə/ n metal box for holding a dry substance or a gas

can·ker /ˈkæŋkə/ n [C;U] disease of trees, and of animal and human flesh

can·ned /kænd/ adj 1 (of food) preserved in a CAN[2] 2 (of music, laughter, applause) recorded to be used on television or radio shows

can·ne·ry /ˈkænəri/ n factory where food is put in cans

can·ni·bal /ˈkænəbəl/ n 1 person who eats human flesh 2 animal that eats its own kind ~**ism** n [U]

can·non /ˈkænən/ n **cannons** or **cannon** big gun, fixed to a carriage or used on military aircraft

can·not /ˈkænɒt, kæˈnɒt, kə-/ v fml can not: *We cannot accept.*

can·ny /ˈkæni/ adj clever; not easily deceived

ca·noe /kəˈnuː/ n light boat moved by a PADDLE

can·on /ˈkænən/ n 1 religious law 2 accepted standard of behavior or thought 3 kind of Christian priest ~**ize** vt declare to be a SAINT ~**ical** /kəˈnɑnɪkəl/ adj according to religious law

can o·pen·er /ˈ· ˌ·-·/ n tool for opening cans

can·o·py /ˈkænəpi/ n 1 cloth roof over a bed, etc.: (fig.) *a canopy of leaves* 2 cover over the front of a plane

cant /kænt/ n [U] insincere talk

can't /kænt/ v short for: can not: *I can't come tonight.*

can·tan·ker·ous /kænˈtæŋkərəs/ adj quarrelsome

can·teen /kænˈtiːn/ n 1 small container used by soldiers for carrying water 2 place in a factory, office, etc., where food is served

can·ter /ˈkæntə/ n [S] horse's movement, slower than a GALLOP **canter** vi/t

can·ti·le·ver /ˈkæntlˌiːvə, -ˌɛvə/ n armlike beam sticking out from an upright support, esp. for a bridge

can·vas /ˈkænvəs/ n 1 [U] strong cloth used for tents, etc. 2 [C] oil painting done on this

can·vass /ˈkænvəs/ vi/t go through (a place) or to (people) to ask for votes or find out opinions ~**er** n

can·yon /ˈkænyən/ n deep narrow valley

cap /kæp/ n 1 soft flat covering for the head, with no BRIM 2 protective top of a bottle, tube, etc. 3 small quantity of explosive in paper for toy guns ♦ vt -pp- 1 cover the top of 2 do or say better than

ca·pa·ble /ˈkeɪpəbəl/ adj 1 skillful, intelligent: *a very capable doctor* 2 able to do or be: *That remark is capable of being misunderstood.* –**bly** adv –**bility** /ˌkeɪpəˈbɪləti/ n 1 [C;U] having skills and apparatus necessary for the stated type of war: *nuclear capability* 2 [P] undeveloped qualities and abilities

ca·pac·i·ty /kəˈpæsəti/ n 1 [S;U] amount that something can hold: *The seating capacity of this theater is 500.* 2 [C;U] ability; power 3 [C] position: *speaking in my capacity as mayor* 4 filled to capacity completely full

cape[1] /keɪp/ n loose outer garment without SLEEVES

cape[2] n piece of land sticking out into the sea

ca·pil·la·ry /ˈkæpəˌlɛri/ n very thin tube, esp. a blood vessel

cap·i·tal /ˈkæpətl/ n 1 [C] town where the center of government is 2 [S;U] wealth, esp. when used to produce more wealth or start a business 3 [C] letter in its large form; A, B, C, etc.: *write in capitals/in capital letters* 4 **make capital of** use to one's advantage ♦ adj punishable by death: *a capital offense*

cap·i·tal·is·m /ˈkæpətlˌɪzəm/ n [U] system based on the private ownership of wealth –ist n person who owns capital

cap·i·tal·ize /ˈkæpətlˌaɪz/ vt 1 write with a capital letter 2 supply money to (a firm)

capitalize on phr vt use to one's advantage

capital pun·ish·ment /ˌ··· ˈ···/ n [U] punishment by death according to law

Cap·i·tol /ˈkæpətl/ n [the] building in Washington D.C. where Congress meets

ca·pit·u·late /kəˈpɪtʃəˌleɪt/ vi accept defeat; stop opposing –**lation** /kəˌpɪtʃəˈleɪʃən/ n [C;U]

ca·price /kəˈpris/ n [C;U] sudden foolish change of behavior –**pricious** /kəˈprɪʃəs/ adj changing; untrustworthy

Ca·pricorn /ˈkæpriˌkɔrn/ n 1 [s] tenth sign of the ZODIAC, represented by a GOAT 2 someone born between December 22nd and January 19th

cap·size /ˈkæpsaɪz, kæpˈsaɪz/ vi/t (cause a boat to) turn over

cap·sule /ˈkæpsəl/ n 1 very small container of medicine to be swallowed whole –2 part of a spacecraft where the pilots live

cap·tain /ˈkæptən/ n 1 leader of a team 2 person in command of a ship or aircraft 3 officer of middle rank in the armed forces ♦ vt be the captain of

cap·tion /ˈkæpʃən/ n words written above or below a picture or newspaper article

cap·ti·vate /ˈkæptəˌveɪt/ vt charm; attract: *her captivating beauty*

cap·tive /ˈkæptɪv/ n prisoner, esp. taken in war ♦ adj: (fig.) *a captive audience* (= group not able or not allowed to stop watching or listening) –**tivity** /kæpˈtɪvəti/ n [U] state or condition of being a captive

cap·tor /ˈkæptɚ, -tɔr/ n person who captures someone

cap·ture /ˈkæptʃɚ/ vt 1 make a prisoner of; take control of by force 2 preserve on film, in words, etc. ♦ n 1 [U] capturing; being captured 2 [C] person or thing captured

car /kɑr/ n 1 vehicle with wheels and a motor, used for carrying people 2 vehicle that is pulled

car·a·mel /ˈkærəməl, -ˌmɛl, ˈkɑrməl/ n 1 [U] cooked sugar 2 [C] candy made of boiled sugar

car·at /ˈkærət/ n unit expressing the purity of gold, or the weight of a jewel

car·a·van /ˈkærəˌvæn/ n group of people with vehicles or animals crossing a desert, etc.

car·bo·hy·drate /ˌkɑrboʊˈhaɪdreɪt, -drɪt, -bə-/ n [C;U] food such as sugar which provides heat and ENERGY

car·bon /ˈkɑrbən/ n 1 [U] substance found in diamonds, coal, etc. 2 **carbon paper** [C;U] a paper with a coat of ink used for making copies **b** copy made with this

car·bon·ated /ˈkɑrbəˌneɪtɪd/ adj (of drinks) containing BUBBLES

carbon copy /ˌ·· ˈ··/ n 1 person or thing that is very similar to another 2 copy of something written using CARBON (2)

carbon di·ox·ide /ˌkɑrbən daɪˈɑksaɪd/ n [U] gas produced when animals breathe out, plants and animals DECAY, etc.

carbon mon·ox·ide /ˌkɑrbən məˈnɑksaɪd/ n [U] poisonous gas produced when engines burn gasoline

car·bu·re·tor /ˈkɑrbəˌreɪtɚ/ n apparatus that mixes the air and gas in a car engine

car·cass /ˈkɑrkəs/ n dead body, esp. of an animal

car·cin·o·genic /ˌkɑrsɪnəˈdʒɛnɪk◂/ adj causing CANCER

card /kɑrd/ n 1 **a** [C] one of 52 pieces of stiff paper used for various games **b** [P] games played with these 2 [C] piece of stiff paper with various uses: *a membership card* | *a birthday card* | *a postcard* 3 [U] cardboard 4 **lay/put one's cards on the table** say what one intends to do 5 **on the cards** probable: *They say war's on the cards.* 6 **play one's cards right** act in the most effective manner to get what one wants

card·board /ˈkɑrdbɔrd, -boʊrd/ n [U] thick stiff paper: *a cardboard box*

car·di·ac /ˈkɑrdiˌæk/ adj of the heart

car·di·gan /ˈkɑrdəgən/ n short knitted (KNIT) coat with SLEEVES, usu. fastened at the front

car·di·nal /ˈkɑrdn-əl, ˈkɑrd-nəl/ n **1** priest of the highest rank in the Roman Catholic church **2** red bird ♦ adj fml most important; main

cardinal num·ber /ˌ··· ˈ··/ n 1, 2, 3, etc.

care¹ /keʳ/ n **1** [C;U] worry; anxiety: free from care | her many cares **2** [U] protection; charge: under a nurse's care **3** [U] serious attention: Take care not to drop it. **4** care of also in care of abbrev. c/o (used when addressing letters to mean) at the address of **5** take care of be responsible for **~ful** adj attentive; CAUTIOUS **~fully** adv **~less** adj **1** not taking care; inattentive **2** free from care; not worried **~lessly** adv **~lessness** n [U]

care² vi **1** be worried; mind: I don't care where we go. **2** care to like to; want: Would you care to sit down?

   care for phr vt **1** look after; nurse **2** like to have: Would you care for a drink?

ca·reen /kəˈrin/ vi lean or move quickly to one side while in a vehicle

ca·reer /kəˈrɪr/ n **1** profession **2** general course of a person's life

care·free /ˈkerfri/ adj free from anxiety

care·giver /ˈkerˌgɪvə/, **carer** /ˈkerə/ n person who takes care of a child or an old or sick person

ca·ress /kəˈres/ n light loving touch ♦ vt give a caress to

care·tak·er /ˈkerˌteɪkə/ n person employed to look after a building

car·go /ˈkɑrgoʊ/ n **-goes** or **-gos** [C;U] goods carried by a ship, plane, or vehicle

car·i·ca·ture /ˈkærəkəˌtʃʊr, -tʃə/ n funny drawing (or written description) of someone to make them seem silly ♦ vt make a caricature of

car·jack·ing /ˈkɑrˌdʒækɪŋ/ n [C,U] crime of violently forcing a driver to drive somewhere or taking the car **–jacker** n

car·nage /ˈkɑrnɪdʒ/ n [U] killing of many people

car·nal /ˈkɑrnl/ adj physical, of the flesh, or esp. sexual: carnal desires

car·na·tion /kɑrˈneɪʃən/ n white, pink or red flower with a sweet smell

car·ni·val /ˈkɑrnəvəl/ n [C;U] **1** period of public rejoicing **2** traveling amusement park

car·ni·vore /ˈkɑrnəˌvɔr, -ˌvoʊr/ n animal that eats flesh **–vorous** /kɑrˈnɪvərəs/ adj

car·ol /ˈkærəl/ n religious song of joy, esp. sung (SING) at Christmas

carp¹ /kɑrp/ n carp or carps large FRESHWATER fish

carp² vi complain unnecessarily

car·pen·ter /ˈkɑrpəntə/ n person who makes wooden objects **–try** n [U] work of a carpenter

car·pet /ˈkɑrpɪt/ n [C;U] cloth for covering floors — see also RED CARPET ♦ vt cover (as if) with a carpet

car pool /ˈ· ·/ n agreement made by people to take turns driving each other to work, etc. ♦ vt take part in a car pool

car·riage /ˈkærɪdʒ/ n **1** [C] vehicle, esp. one pulled by a horse **2** [U] (cost of) moving goods **3** [C] movable part of a machine: the carriage of a typewriter **4** [S;U] fml way of walking

car·ri·er /ˈkæriə/ n **1** person or business that carries goods **2** person or animal that passes diseases to others without catching them **3** military vehicle or ship that carries soldiers, etc: aircraft carrier

car·ri·on /ˈkæriən/ n [U] dead or decaying flesh

car·rot /ˈkærət/ n long orange root vegetable

car·ry /ˈkæri/ v **1** vt move while supporting; have with one: carry a gun | carry a child on one's back **2** vt take from one place to another: Pipes carry oil across the desert. | Flies carry disease. **3** vt bear the weight of: This beam carries the whole roof. **4** vt have as a usual or necessary result: Such a crime carries a serious punishment. **5** vt contain; have: All the newspapers carried the story. **6** vt win by voting: The motion was carried. **7** vi reach a distance: Her voice doesn't carry very far. **8** be carried away get excited **9** carry a torch for be in love with

   carry off phr vt perform successfully

   carry on phr vi **1** continue: carry on talking **2** behave in a foolish excited manner **carry-on** /ˈ·· ·/ n piece of light LUGGAGE

   carry on with phr vt **1** have a love affair with (someone) **2** to carry/be carrying on with for the present time

   carry out phr vt fulfill; complete ♦ **car·ryout** /ˈkæriˌaʊt/ n (meal from) a restaurant that sells food to eat elsewhere

carry through phr vt **1** help to continue: *Her courage carried her through.* **2** fulfill; complete: *carry a plan through*

car·ry·all /ˈkæriˌɔl/ n large basket, bag, etc.

carrying charge /ˈ··· ˌ·/ n money added to the price of things bought by INSTALLMENT PLAN

car seat /ˈ· ˌ·/ n seat for babies or small children, attached to seat of the car

cart /kɑrt/ n **1** wheeled vehicle pulled by an animal, or pulled or pushed by hand: *shopping cart* **2 put the cart before the horse** do things in the wrong order ♦ vt **1** carry in a cart **2** carry; take: *carting these books around*

carte blanche /ˌkɑrt ˈblɑnʃ, -ˈblɑntʃ/ n [U] full freedom

car·tel /kɑrˈtɛl/ n combination of independent firms, to limit competition

car·ti·lage /ˈkɑrtl-ɪdʒ/ n [C;U] elastic substance found around the joints in animals

car·ton /ˈkɑrtⁿn/ n CARDBOARD box

car·toon /kɑrˈtun/ n **1** humorous drawing of something interesting in the news **2** film made by photographing a set of drawings ~**ist** n

car·tridge /ˈkɑrtrɪdʒ/ n **1** tube containing explosive and a bullet for a gun **2** part of a record player that holds the needle **3** container of MAGNETIC TAPE or photographic film

cart·wheel /ˈkɑrtˌwil, -ˌhwil/ n circular movement in which a person turns over by putting their hands on the ground and moving their legs sideways in the air

carve /kɑrv/ v **1** vt make by cutting wood, stone, etc.: *carve one's name on a tree* | (fig.) *She carved herself (out) a good position in business.* **2** vi/t cut (cooked meat) into pieces

carving /ˈkɑrvɪŋ/ n something carved from wood, etc.

car wash /ˈ· ˌ·/ n place with machines to wash one's car

cas·cade /kæˈskeɪd/ n waterfall ♦ vi pour like a waterfall

case¹ /keɪs/ n **1** [C] example; situation: *I'll make an exception in your case.* | *several cases of fever* | *police investigating a case of robbery* **2** [C] legal question to be decided; arguments supporting one side of a question: *to judge this case* | *the*

case for the defense **3** [C;U] gram form of word showing the part it plays in a sentence **4** [C] person having medical treatment **5 in any case** whatever happens **6 in case of: a** because of anxiety about: *insure the house in case of fire* **b** if (something) happens: *In case of fire, ring the bell.* **7 (just) in case** so as to be safe (if): *Take your coat in case it rains.*

case² n large box or container: *a packing case* | *a* **suitcase**

case·ment /ˈkeɪsmənt/ n lit window

cash /kæʃ/ n [U] **1** money in coins or notes **2** money in any form ♦ vt exchange (a check, etc.) for cash

cash in on phr vt take advantage of

cash cow /ˈ· ˌ·/ n infml business or product that can be depended on to make PROFIT

cash crop /ˈ· ˌ·/ n crop grown for sale

ca·shew /ˈkæʃu, kæˈʃu, kə-/ n (tropical American tree with) a small curved nut

cash flow /ˈ· ˌ·/ n [U] movement of money into and out of a company

cash·ier¹ /kæˈʃɪr/ n person who receives and pays out money in a bank, store, etc.

cash·ier² /kæˈʃɪr, kə-/ vt dismiss with dishonor from service in the armed forces

cashier's check /ˈ·· ˌ·/ n check from a bank signed by a cashier of that bank

cash·mere /ˈkæʒmɪr, ˈkæʃ-/ n [U] fine soft wool

cash reg·is·ter /ˈ· ˌ···/ n machine for recording the amount of sales

cas·ing /ˈkeɪsɪŋ/ n protective covering, as on a tire

ca·si·no /kəˈsinoʊ/ n –nos building where people play cards or other games for money

cask /kæsk/ n barrel for liquids

cas·ket /ˈkæskɪt/ n **1** COFFIN **2** box for jewels, letters, etc.

cas·se·role /ˈkæsəˌroʊl/ n deep dish for cooking and serving meat; food cooked in this

cas·sette /kəˈsɛt, kæ-/ n container of MAGNETIC TAPE, or photographic film

cas·sock /ˈkæsək/ n priest's long garment

cast¹ /kæst/ vt cast **1** fml throw: *cast a net* | *a snake casting off its skin* | *The sun casts long shadows.* **2** give (a vote) **3** make by pouring hot metal: *cast a statue* **4** choose as an actor; choose actors for (a play) ~**ing** n mass made by pouring metal

cast aside *phr vt* get rid of

cast off *phr vi/t* unloose (a boat)

cast² *n* **1** actors in a play, film, etc. **2** act of throwing a fishing line, etc. **3** hard covering to protect a broken bone **4** object made by casting metal **5** general shape or quality: *an inquiring cast of mind* **6** slight SQUINT (1)

cas·ta·nets /ˌkæstəˈnets/ *n* [P] musical instrument made of 2 hollow shells to be knocked together

cast·a·way /ˈkɑːstəˌweɪ/ *n* person cast up on shore from a wrecked ship

caste /kɑːst/ *n* [C;U] Hindu social class

cast·er /ˈkɑːstə/ *n* small wheel on a chair, etc.

cas·ti·gate /ˈkæstəˌgeɪt/ *vt fml* punish severely; criticize (CRITIC)

cast·ing vote /ˌ·· ˈ·/ *n* deciding vote when both sides have an equal number of votes

cast i·ron /ˌ· ˈ·· ◄/ *n* hard but easily breakable type of iron **cast-iron** /ˌ· ˈ·· ◄/ *adj* **1** made of cast iron **2** very strong; unbreakable: *a cast-iron stomach* | *a cast-iron excuse*

cas·tle /ˈkɑːsəl/ *n* large building that can be defended against attack

cast-off /ˈ· ·/ *n, adj* (piece of clothing) thrown away by the original owner

cast·or oil /ˌkɑːstə ˈɔɪl◄/ *n* [U] thick vegetable oil used as a LAXATIVE

cas·trate /ˈkæstreɪt/ *vt* remove the sex organs of (a male) **–tration** /kæˈstreɪʃən/ *n* [C;U]

cas·u·al /ˈkæʒuəl/ *adj* **1** informal: *casual clothes* **2** from chance: *casual meeting* **3** employed for a short time: *casual labor* **4** not serious or thorough: *the casual reader* **~ly** *adv*

cas·u·al·ty /ˈkæʒuəlti, ˈkæʒəlti/ *n* person killed or hurt in an accident or battle

cat /kæt/ *n* **1** small furry animal often kept as a pet **2** animal related to this; lion, tiger, etc. **3** *sl* man **4 let the cat out of the bag** tell a secret (usu. unintentionally) **5 rain cats and dogs** rain very heavily

cat·a·clys·m /ˈkætəˌklɪzəm/ *n fml* violent event, such as an EARTHQUAKE **~ic** /ˌkætəˈklɪzmɪk◄/ *adj*

cat·a·comb /ˈkætəˌkoʊm/ *n* underground burial place with many rooms

cat·a·log, -logue /ˈkætlˌɔg, -ˌɑg/ *n* list of places, goods for sale, etc., in order ♦ *vt* make a list of

cat·a·lyst /ˈkætl-ɪst/ *n* something that quickens activity without itself changing

cat·a·pult /ˈkætəpʌlt, -ˌpʊlt/ *n* ancient military machine for shooting stones ♦ *vt* fire (as if) from a catapult: (fig.) *He was catapulted to fame.*

cat·a·ract /ˈkætəˌrækt/ *n* **1** large waterfall **2** eye disease causing blindness

ca·tas·tro·phe /kəˈtæstrəfi/ *n* sudden terrible misfortune **–phic** /ˌkætəˈstrɑfɪk◄/ *adj*

cat·call /ˈkætˌkɔl/ *v, n* (make) a loud whistle or cry expressing disapproval, esp. at the theater, etc.

catch¹ /kætʃ/ *v* **caught** /kɔt/ **1** *vt* get hold of (a moving object) and stop it: *catch a ball* **2** *vt* make a prisoner; trap: *catch a fish/a thief* **3** *vt* discover doing something: *I caught him reading my diary.* **4** *vt* be in time for: *catch a train* **5** *vt* get (an illness) **6** *vi/t* get hooked or stuck: *My skirt caught in the door.* **7** *vt* hear; understand **8** *vt* to hit (a person or animal) **9 catch fire** start to burn **10 catch it** *infml* be in trouble for doing something wrong **11 catch one's breath a** stop breathing for a moment because of surprise or shock **b** rest for a short while after hard work **12 catch sight of** see for a moment **13 catch someone's eye** attract someone's attention by looking at them **~ing** *adj* infectious

catch on *phr vi* **1** become popular **2** understand

catch up *phr vi/t* **1** come up from behind; draw level **2 caught up in** completely interested in or involved

catch² *n* **1** getting and holding a ball **2** (amount of) something caught: *big catch of fish* **3** hook, etc. for fastening something **4** hidden difficulty; SNAG **~er** *n* position behind the BATTER in BASEBALL

catch-22 /ˌkætʃ twɛnti ˈtu/ *n* [U] situation from which one is prevented from escaping by something that is part of the situation itself: *I can't get a job unless I belong to the union, and I can't join the union until I have a job — it's a catch-22 situation!*

catch·phrase /ˈkætʃfreɪz/ *n* fashionable phrase that everyone uses

catch·y /ˈkætʃi/ adj (of a tune, etc.) easy to remember

cat·e·gor·i·cal /ˌkætəˈgɒrɪkəl, -ˈgɑr-/ adj (of a statement) unconditional; made without doubt ~**ly** adv

cat·e·go·ry /ˈkætəˌgɒri, -ˌgɔʊri/ n division in a system; class –**gorize** /-gəˌraɪz/ vt put in a category

ca·ter /ˈkeɪtə/ vi provide food and drinks at a party ~**er** n

    cater for phr vt provide what is necessary: magazines catering for all opinions

cat·er·pil·lar /ˈkætəˌpɪlə, ˈkætəˌpɪlə/ n 1 wormlike creature that eats leaves 2 (cap.) tdmk vehicle with endless chain of plates on the wheels

cat·fish /ˈkætˌfɪʃ/ n FRESHWATER fish used for food

ca·thar·sis /kəˈθɑrsɪs/ n -**ses** /-siz/ [C;U] getting rid of bad feelings by expressing them through art or by reliving them **cathartic** adj

ca·the·dral /kəˈθidrəl/ n chief church of a DIOCESE

cath·ode /ˈkæθoʊd/ n part of an electrical instrument from which ELECTRONS leave

cath·o·lic /ˈkæθəlɪk/ adj 1 fml general; broad: catholic tastes 2 (cap.) ROMAN CATHOLIC ♦ n (cap.) a ROMAN CATHOLIC

Cath·o·li·cism /kəˈθɒləˌsɪzəm/ n [U] teachings of the ROMAN CATHOLIC church

cat·nap /ˈkætˌnæp/ n short light sleep

cat·sup /ˈkɛtʃəp, ˈkæ-, ˈkætsəp/ n KETCHUP

cat·tle /ˈkætl/ n [P] cows and BULLS

cat·ty /ˈkæti/ adj indirectly SPITE*ful*

cat·walk /ˈkætˌwɔk/ n narrow raised PLATFORM (2)

cau·cus /ˈkɔkəs/ n political meeting to decide future plans

caught /kɔt/ v past t. and p. of CATCH

caul·dron /ˈkɔldrən/ n lit large pot for boiling things

cau·li·flow·er /ˈkɔlɪˌflaʊə, ˈkɑ-/ n [C;U] green vegetable with a large white head of flowers

cause /kɔz/ n 1 [C;U] thing that produces a result: the cause of the accident 2 [U] reason: no cause for complaint 3 [C] purpose strongly supported: good causes such as famine relief ♦ vt be the cause of: to cause trouble

cause·way /ˈkɔzweɪ/ n raised road across water, etc.

caus·tic /ˈkɔstɪk/ adj 1 able to burn by chemical action 2 (of remarks) bitter; nasty

cau·tion /ˈkɔʃən/ n 1 [U] great care 2 [C] spoken warning by a policeman, etc. — see also **throw caution to the wind** (THROW) ♦ vt warn ~**ary** adj giving a warning

cau·tious /ˈkɔʃəs/ adj with caution; careful ~**ly** adv

cav·al·cade /ˈkævəlˌkeɪd, ˌkævəlˈkeɪd/ n procession of riders, vehicles, etc.

cav·a·lier /ˌkævəˈlɪr◂/ adj thoughtless; OFFHAND

cav·al·ry /ˈkævəlri/ n [U] soldiers on horseback, or (now) with armored vehicles

cave[1] /keɪv/ n underground hollow place

cave[2] v cave in phr vi 1 (of a roof) fall down 2 give up opposition; YIELD

ca·ve·at /ˈkæviˌæt, ˈkɑviˌɑt/ n law warning

cav·ern /ˈkævən/ n large cave ~**ous** adj (of a hole) very large

cav·i·ar /ˈkæviˌɑr/ n [U] salty eggs (ROE) of a large fish

cav·i·ty /ˈkævəti/ n fml hole in a solid mass, such as a tooth

ca·vort /kəˈvɔrt/ vi infml (esp. of a person) jump or dance about noisily

CB n [U] Citizens' Band; radio by which people can speak to each other over short distances

cc abbrev. for: CUBIC centimeter

CD n COMPACT DISC

CD play·er /ˌ· ˈ·, ˌ· ˌ·/ n machine for playing music recorded on CDs

CD-ROM /ˌsi di ˈrɑm/ n COMPACT DISC on which very large quantities of information can be stored for use by a computer

cease /sis/ vi/t fml stop (an activity) ~**less** adj unending; continuous ~**lessly** adv

cease-fire /ˌ· ˈ·, ˈ· ˌ·/ n agreement to stop fighting; TRUCE

ce·dar /ˈsidə/ n [C;U] (wood of) a tall EVERGREEN tree

cede /sid/ vt fml give (esp. land, after losing a war)

ceil·ing /ˈsilɪŋ/ n 1 upper surface of a room 2 official upper limit on prices, etc.

cel·e·brate /ˈsɛləˌbreɪt/ v 1 vt/i mark (an event) by enjoying oneself 2 vt praise; honor –**brated** adj famous –**bration** /ˌsɛləˈbreɪʃən/ n [C;U] ce·leb·ri·ty /sə'lebrəti/ n 1 [C] famous person 2 [U] fame

cel·er·y /'seləri/ n [U] plant whose green-white stems are eaten as a vegetable

ce·les·tial /sə'lestʃəl/ adj fml of the sky or heaven

cel·i·bate /'seləbıt/ n, adj (person who is) unmarried and not sexually active, esp. for religious reasons –bacy n [U]

cell /sel/ n 1 small room: prison cell 2 small unit of living matter 3 apparatus for making electricity chemically 4 single group of people in a secret organization: Communist cells

cel·lar /'selə/ n underground room for storing things: wine cellar

cel·lo /'tʃeloʊ/ n -los kind of large VIOLIN held between the knees cellist n person who plays a cello

cel·lu·lar phone /ˌselyələ 'foʊn/, cell phone n telephone you carry with you, which works using radio signals

cel·lu·lite /'selyəlaıt/ n [U] fat that can be seen in lumps just under the skin

cel·lu·loid /'selyəlɔıd/ n [U] tdmk 1 strong plastic formerly made for making photographic film 2 on celluloid on cinema film

Cel·si·us /'selsiəs, -ʃəs/ adj , n (in) the temperature scale in which water freezes at 0° and boils at 100°

Cel·tic /'seltık, 'kel-/ adj of the Celts, a European people who include the Welsh and Bretons

ce·ment /sı'ment/ n [U] 1 grey powder that becomes hard like stone when mixed with water, and is used in building 2 any thick sticky glue used for filling holes or joining things ♦ vt join with cement: (fig.) to cement our friendship

cem·e·ter·y /'seməˌteri/ n piece of ground used for burials

cen·sor /'sensə/ n official who examines books, films, etc., to remove anything offensive ♦ vt examine or remove material as a censor: a censored book/film ~ship n [U] work of a censor; censoring

cen·so·ri·ous /sen'sɔriəs, -'soʊr-/ adj fml always looking for mistakes and faults; severely CRITICal

cen·sure /'senʃə/ n fml blame; disapproval ♦ vt express disapproval of

cen·sus /'sensəs/ n official counting, esp. of a country's population

cent /sent/ n (coin equal to) 0.01 of any of certain units of money, e.g. the dollar

cen·taur /'sentɔr/ n imaginary creature, half man and half horse

cen·ten·ni·al /sen'teniəl/ n 100th ANNIVERSARY

cen·ter /'sentə/ n 1 [C] middle point 2 [C] place for a particular activity: a shopping center 3 [the+S] a middle position, in politics, not supporting EXTREME (2) ideas ♦ vi/t gather to a center: His interests are centered on/around his family.

cen·ti·grade /'sentəˌgreıd/ adj, n CELSIUS

cen·ti·me·ter /'sentəˌmitə/ n (unit of length equal to) 1/100 of a meter

cen·ti·pede /'sentəˌpid/ n worm-like creature with many legs

cen·tral /'sentrəl/ adj 1 at the center 2 most important; main ~ly adv ~ize vt bring under central control ~ization n [U] /ˌsentrələ'zeıʃən/

central pro·ces·sing u·nit /ˌ·· '·· ·ˌ·/ also CPU — n the most important controlling part of a computer system

Central time /'·· ·ˌ·/ n time used in the Midwest and S Central part of the country, one hour behind Eastern time

cen·ter·piece /'sentəˌpis/ n thing in the central or most important position

cen·tri·fu·gal /sen'trıfyəgəl, -fə-/ adj tending to move out from the center

cen·trist /'sentrıst/ n, adj (of) a person who supports the CENTER (3)

cen·tu·ry /'sentʃəri/ n 1 100 years 2 period of 100 years counted forwards or backwards from Christ's birth

CEO n abbrev. for CHIEF EXECUTIVE OFFICER

ce·ram·ics /sə'ræmıks/ n [U;P] (making of) pots, bricks, etc. ceramic adj

ce·re·al /'sıriəl/ n 1 [C] food grain 2 [C;U] breakfast food such as CORNFLAKES

cer·e·bral /sə'ribrəl, 'serə-/ adj 1 relating to or connected with the brain 2 showing too much serious thinking

cer·e·mo·ni·al /ˌserə'moʊniəl/ adj for a ceremony: ceremonial banquet ♦ n [C;U] ceremony

cer·e·mo·ni·ous /ˌserə'moʊniəs/ adj formally polite

cer·e·mo·ny /'serəˌmoʊni/ n 1 [C] set of solemn actions to mark an important event: a wedding ceremony 2 [U] formal behavior

cer·tain¹ /ˈsət̩n/ adj 1 sure; without doubt: *I'm certain he saw me.* | *It's certain to rain.* 2 sure to happen: *facing certain death* 3 **make certain** do something to be sure: *Make certain he knows.* ~**ly** adv of course

cer·tain² determiner, pron 1 some, not named: *There are certain reasons against it.* 2 some, not a lot: *a certain amount of profit*

cer·tain·ty /ˈsət̩nti/ n 1 [C] established fact 2 [U] freedom from doubt

cer·tif·i·cate /səˈtɪfɪkɪt/ n official paper stating facts: *marriage certificate*

cer·tif·ied mail /ˌ··ˈ·/ n method of sending mail by which one gets official proof that it has been delivered

cer·ti·fy /ˈsət̩ɪfaɪ/ vt declare officially that something is true: *to certify the prisoner insane* **-fiable** adj

cer·ti·tude /ˈsət̩ɪtud/ n [U] fml state of being or feeling certain

cer·vi·cal /ˈsəvɪkəl, səˈvaɪkəl/ adj of the narrow opening (**cervix**) of the WOMB

Cesarian /sɪˈzɛriən/, **cesarian section** n operation to take a baby out by cutting, instead of by ordinary birth

ces·sa·tion /sɛˈseɪʃən/ n [C;U] fml short pause or stop

cess·pool /ˈsɛspul/ n underground hole where a house's SEWAGE is gathered

cf written abbrev. for: compare

CFC n gas that is damaging to the Earth's ATMOSPHERE

chafe /tʃeɪf/ v 1 vt rub; make sore by rubbing 2 vi become impatient: *chafe at the delay*

chaff /tʃæf/ n [U] outer covers of seeds, separated from the grain

chag·rin /ʃəˈgrɪn/ n [U] fml annoyance and disappointment

chain /tʃeɪn/ n 1 length of metal rings joined together 2 set of connected things: *chain of mountains/of events* ♦ vt fasten with a chain: *prisoners chained to the wall*

chain gang /ˈ··/ n group of prisoners chained together while working

chain re·ac·tion /ˌ· ·ˌ··, ˌ· ·ˌ·/ n set of events so related that each causes the next

chain-smoke /ˈ· ·/ vi/t smoke (cigarettes) continually **-smoker** n

chain store /ˈ· ·/ n group of stores under one ownership

chair /tʃɛr/ n 1 movable seat for one person 2 position of a chairperson 3 position of a PROFESSOR ♦ vt be chairperson of

chair·man /ˈtʃɛrmən/ **-woman** /-ˌwʊmən/ fem., **-men** /-mən, -ˌmɛn/ — n person in charge of a meeting, or directing the work of a group

chair·per·son /ˈtʃɛrˌpəsən/ n chairman or chairwoman

chal·et /ʃæˈleɪ, ˈʃæleɪ/ n 1 Swiss wooden house 2 small house or hut in mountains

chalk¹ /tʃɔk/ n 1 [U] kind of soft white rock 2 [C;U] this material used for writing or drawing ~**y** adj

chalk² vt write with chalk

chalk up phr vt 1 ATTRIBUTE 2 succeed in getting

chalk·board /ˈtʃɔkbɔrd, -bʊrd/ n board used in schools for writing on

chal·lenge /ˈtʃæləndʒ/ vt 1 invite to a fight, match, etc. 2 question the loyalty or rightness of ♦ n 1 invitation to compete 2 something exciting that needs a lot of effort **-lenging** adj difficult but exciting **-lenger** n

cham·ber /ˈtʃeɪmbə/ n 1 lit BEDROOM 2 a body that makes laws b room where it meets 3 enclosed space: *the 4 chambers of the heart*

cham·ber·maid /ˈtʃeɪmbəˌmeɪd/ n woman who cleans hotel BEDROOMS

chamber mu·sic /ˈ·· ˌ··/ n [U] music for a small group (a **chamber orchestra**)

cha·me·le·on /kəˈmilyən, -liən/ n small LIZARD that changes color to match its surroundings

champ¹ /tʃæmp/ vi 1 (of a horse) bite noisily 2 be impatient 3 **champ at the bit** be restless and difficult to control because of being impatient to do something

champ² n infml abbrev. for: CHAMPION (1)

cham·pagne /ʃæmˈpeɪn/ n [U] expensive white wine with BUBBLES

cham·pi·on /ˈtʃæmpiən/ n 1 person or animal that wins a competition 2 person who defends a principle or another person: *champion of justice* ♦ vt defend; support ~**ship** n 1 competition to find the champion 2 position of being the champion 3 act of championing

chance /tʃæns/ n 1 [U] good or bad luck 2 [C;U] likelihood: *no chance of winning* | *The chances are* (= it is likely) *he already knows.* 3 [C] favorable occasion; OPPORTUNITY: *a chance to travel* 4 [C;U] risk 5 **by chance** by accident 6 **on the (off) chance** in view of the (unlikely) possibility ♦ v 1 vt take a risk 2 vi fml happen accidentally: *We chanced to meet.* ♦ adj accidental –y adj risky

chan·cel·lor /ˈtʃænsələr/ n (often cap.) university or legal official of high rank

chan·de·lier /ˌʃændəˈlɪr/ n branched hanging holder for lights

change /tʃeɪndʒ/ v 1 vi/t make or become different: *change the subject* | *water changed into ice* 2 vt give and receive in return: *change a library book* | *change pounds into dollars* 3 vi/t put different clothes on 4 vi/t leave and enter (different vehicles): *change (trains) at Chicago* 5 **change one's mind** form a new opinion ♦ n 1 changing; something new: *a change of clothes* | *Let's have fish for a change.* 2 a money returned when something bought costs less than the amount paid b coins or notes of low value — see also SEA CHANGE ~**able** adj often changing

chan·nel /ˈtʃænl/ n 1 narrow sea passage 2 passage for liquids 3 television station 4 **channel hop** continually change television stations 5 way along which information passes: *go through the official channels* vt -l- also -ll- send through channels; direct: *channel my abilities into something useful*

chant /tʃænt/ vi/t sing (words) on one note ♦ **chant** n

cha·os /ˈkeɪɑs/ n [S;U] complete confusion –**otic** /keɪˈɑtɪk/ adj

chap /tʃæp/ vi/t -pp- (cause to) become sore, rough and cracked: *chapped lips*

chap·el /ˈtʃæpəl/ n small Christian church

chap·er·one /ˈʃæpəroʊn/ n older person who goes with a younger person and is responsible for their behavior ♦ **chaperon, -one** vt

chap·lain /ˈtʃæplɪn/ n priest in the armed forces, a hospital, etc.

chaps /tʃæps/ n [P] strong leather covering to protect COWBOYS' legs

chap·ter /ˈtʃæptər/ n 1 main division of a blook, usu. numbered 2 special period of history 3 local branch of a society, club, etc.

char /tʃɑr/ vi/t -rr- blacken by burning

char·ac·ter /ˈkærɪktər/ n 1 [C;U] qualities that make a person or thing different from others: *a man of good character* | *the character of the town* 2 [U] moral strength, honesty, etc. 3 [C] person in a book, etc. 4 [C] person, esp. an odd one 5 [C] written letter or sign: *Chinese characters* ~**less** adj ordinary; dull

char·ac·ter·is·tic /ˌkærɪktəˈrɪstɪk◂/ adj typical ♦ n special quality ~**ally** adv

char·ac·ter·ize /ˈkærɪktəˌraɪz/ vt 1 be typical of 2 describe the character of

cha·rade /ʃəˈreɪd/ n 1 [C] foolish unnecessary action 2 [P] game in which words are acted by players until guessed by other players

char·broil /ˈtʃɑrˌbrɔɪl/ vt BARBECUE ~**ed** adj: *charbroiled steak*

char·coal /ˈtʃɑrkoʊl/ n burned wood, used for drawing with, cooking fires, etc.

charge /tʃɑrdʒ/ v 1 vi/t ask in payment 2 vt record (something) to someone's debt 3 vi/t rush as if to attack 4 vt ACCUSE of a crime: *charged with stealing* 5 vt fml command; give as a duty 6 vt/i (cause to) take in electricity: *charge a battery* | (fig.) *a highly charged political question* (= causing strong feelings or much argument) ♦ n 1 [C] price asked or paid 2 [U] control; responsibility: *I'll take charge of the money.* 3 [C] statement blaming a person for wrongdoing: *a charge of murder* 4 [C] rushing attack by soldiers, animals, etc. 5 [C;U] electricity put into a BATTERY 6 **in charge (of)** responsible (for)

charge account /ˈ· ·ˌ/ n arrangement with a particular store that allows one to buy goods and pay for them later

charge card /ˈ· ·/ n plastic card which allows one to obtain goods at a particular store and pay later

char·gé d'af·faires /ˌʃɑrˌʒeɪ dəˈfer/ n official who represents his/her government where there is no AMBASSADOR

char·i·ot /ˈtʃæriət/ n ancient vehicle with 2 wheels, pulled by a horse

cha·ris·ma /kəˈrɪzmə/ n [U] fml great charm; power to win public admiration ~**tic** /ˌkærɪzˈmætɪk◂/ adj: *charismatic leader*

char·i·ty /'tʃærəti/ n 1 [U] generosity and help to the poor, etc. 2 [U] kindness shown in judging others 3 [C] organization for helping people –**table** adj –**tably** adv

char·la·tan /'ʃɑrlətən, -lət'n/ n person who falsely claims a special skill

char·ley horse /ˌtʃɑrli 'hɔrs/ n pain in a muscle

charm /tʃɑrm/ n 1 [C;U] power to delight people 2 [C] magic words; SPELL 3 [C] object worn to bring good luck 4 **work like a charm** happen or take place with complete success ♦ vt 1 please; delight: charming manners 2 control by magic ~**er** n person who charms ~**ing** adj very pleasing

chart /tʃɑrt/ n 1 information in the form of a picture or GRAPH: a sales chart 2 map, esp. of the sea ♦ vt make a chart of

char·ter /'tʃɑrtə/ n 1 [C] official statement of rights and freedoms 2 [U] hiring of buses, planes, etc.: charter flights ♦ vt hire (a bus, etc.)

charter mem·ber /ˌ·· '·· / n [C] original member of a society or organization

chase /tʃeɪs/ vi/t follow rapidly, in order to catch or drive away ♦ n 1 chasing something or someone 2 **give chase** chase someone

chas·m /'kæzəm/ n very deep crack in the earth

chas·sis /'ʃæsi, 'tʃæ-/ n **chassis** /-siz/ frame on which a vehicle is built

chaste /tʃeɪst/ adj avoiding wrong sexual activity

chas·ten /'tʃeɪsən/ vt improve by punishment or suffering

chas·tise /tʃæ'staɪz, 'tʃæstaɪz/ vt fml punish severely

chas·ti·ty /'tʃæstəti/ n [U] being chaste

chat /tʃæt/ vt -tt- talk informally **chat** n

châ·teau /'ʃætoʊ/ n -teaus or -teaux /ʃæ'toʊz, -'toʊ/ French castle

chat·ter /'tʃætə/ vi 1 talk rapidly about small things 2 (of the teeth) knock together from cold or fear ♦ n [U] 1 chattering talk 2 rapid speechlike sounds ~**er** n

chat·ter·box /'tʃætəˌbɑks/ n person who chatters

chauf·feur /'ʃoʊfə, ʃoʊ'fə/ **chauffeuse** /ʃoʊ'fʊz, -'fəz/ fem. — n paid driver of a private car **chauffeur** vi/t

chau·vin·is·m /'ʃoʊvəˌnɪzəm/ n proud belief that one's own country, or one's own sex, is the best –**ist** n, adj — see also MALE CHAUVINIST

cheap /tʃip/ adj 1 low in price 2 a of poor quality b offensively unpleasant 3 without serious feeling: cheap emotions 4 needing little effort: a cheap victory 5 infml STINGY 6 **feel cheap** feel ashamed ♦ adv at a low price: buy ~ly make or become cheaper ~**ly** adv ~**ness** n [U]

cheap·skate /'tʃipskeɪt/ n person who is unwilling to spend money

cheat /tʃit/ vi/t 1 act dishonestly; treat someone deceitfully: cheating at cards | cheat her out of her money 2 avoid or escape as if by deception: to cheat death ♦ n person who cheats

check /tʃɛk/ n 1 [C] examination to make sure something is correct 2 [S;U] stop; control: keep the disease in check 3 [C;U] pattern of squares 4 [C] restaurant bill 5 [C] written order to a bank to pay money 6 [C] mark (✓) put against an answer to show that it is correct or next to a name to show the person is present (2) 7 [U] (in CHESS) position of the king when under direct attack ♦ v 1 vi/t examine; make sure: check a letter for spelling mistakes 2 vt hold back; control: check the increase in crime 3 vt put somewhere to be looked after: check one's coat at the theater 4 vt mark with a check (6) see also BLANK CHECK, TRAVELER'S CHECK

check in phr vi report one's arrival at an airport, etc. **check-in** /'· ·/ n [C;U]

check out phr vi 1 leave a hotel after paying the bill 2 a find out if something is true by making inquiries b be found to be true after inquiries have been made 3 have the removal of (an article) recorded

check up on phr vt inquire thoroughly about

check·book /'tʃɛkbʊk/ n book of checks

checking ac·count /'·· ˌ·/ n person's main bank account which can be used for writing checks

check·ered /'tʃɛkəd/ adj partly bad and partly good: his checkered career

check·ers /'tʃɛkəz/ n [P] game played by two people on a board (**checkerboard**) with squares

check·list /'tʃɛkˌlɪst/ n complete list; INVENTORY

check·mate /ˈtʃɛkmeɪt/ n [C;U] 1 (in CHESS) position of a king when under direct attack so that escape is impossible 2 complete defeat ♦ vt 1 (in CHESS) win the game when a checkmate 2 stop; completely defeat

check·out /ˈtʃɛk-aʊt/, **checkout counter** n place where one pays in a store

check·point /ˈtʃɛkpɔɪnt/ n place where a CHECK (1) is made on people, traffic, etc.

check·room /ˈtʃɛk-rum, -rʊm/ n [C] place in a station where one can leave one's bags

checks and ba·lanc·es /ˌ· · ˈ···/ n system of limiting the power of the three branches of the US government

check·up /ˈtʃɛk-ʌp/ n general medical examination

cheek /tʃik/ n 1 [C] either side of the face below the eye 2 [U] rude behavior ~y adj rude

cheer /tʃɪr/ n 1 [C] shout of praise or joy 2 [U] happiness; good spirits ♦ vi/t 1 make or become happy: cheering news | Cheer up! 2 shout in approval; encourage by shouting ~ful adj happy ~fully adv ~less adj lacking cheerful qualities ~y adj merry

cheer·lead·er /ˈtʃɪrˌlidə/ n [C] person who calls for and directs cheering e.g. at a football game

cheese /tʃiz/ n [C;U] solid food made from milk

cheese·cake /ˈtʃizkeɪk/ n 1 [C] cake in a sweet pastry case which contains soft cheese 2 [U] pictures of women with few clothes on

cheesy /ˈtʃizi/ n infml 1 cheap and of low quality 2 not sincere: a cheesy smile

chee·tah /ˈtʃitə/ n spotted African animal of the cat family, able to run very fast

chef /ʃɛf/ n chief cook in a restaurant, etc.

chem·i·cal /ˈkɛmɪkəl/ adj of chemistry ♦ n chemical substance

chem·ist /ˈkɛmɪst/ n scientist specializing in chemistry

chem·is·try /ˈkɛməstri/ n [U] science of natural substances and how they combine and behave

chem·o·ther·a·py /ˌkimoʊˈθɛrəpi, ˌkɛ-/ n [U] use of chemical substances to treat and control diseases

cher·ish /ˈtʃɛrɪʃ/ vt fml 1 care for; love 2 keep (hope, etc.) in one's mind: cherish a memory

cher·ry /ˈtʃɛri/ n small round fruit with a pit

cher·ub /ˈtʃɛrəb/ n 1 pretty child, esp. one with wings in a painting 2 (pl. -ubim /-əbɪm/) kind of ANGEL ~ic /tʃəˈrubɪk/ adj

chess /tʃɛs/ n [U] board game for 2 players

chest /tʃɛst/ n 1 upper front part of the body 2 large strong box 3 get (something) off one's chest bring (a worry) out into the open by talking

chest·nut /ˈtʃɛsnʌt/ n 1 kind of smooth red-brown nut 2 joke or story so old and familiar that it is no longer funny or interesting ♦ adj red-brown

chest of drawers /ˌ· · ˈ·/ n piece of furniture with drawers

chew /tʃu/ vi/t 1 crush (food, etc.) with the teeth 2 bite off more than one can chew attempt more than one can deal with or succeed in finishing

chew over phr vt infml think about (a question, problem, etc.)

chew out phr vt speak to (someone) angrily esp. because they have done (something) wrong

chewing gum /ˈ·· ˌ·/ n sweet sticky substance to be chewed but not swallowed

chic /ʃik/ adj, n [U] (with) good style

Chi·ca·no /tʃɪˈkɑnoʊ/ n [C] US citizen from Mexico, or whose family comes from Mexico

chick /tʃɪk/ n baby bird

chick·en¹ /ˈtʃɪkən/ n 1 [C] common farmyard bird, esp. a young one 2 [U] its meat 3 count one's chickens before they're hatched make plans depending on something which has not yet happened ♦ adj sl cowardly

chicken² v chicken out phr vi sl decide not to do something because one is frightened

chicken pox /ˈtʃɪkən ˌpɑks/ n [U] infectious disease that causes spots

chide /tʃaɪd/ vi/t chided or chid /tʃɪd/, chid or chidden /ˈtʃɪdn/ fml or lit speak to (someone) angrily; REBUKE

chief /tʃif/ n leader; head of something: the chief of police ♦ adj 1 highest in rank 2 main 3 -in-chief of the highest rank: commander-in-chief ~ly adv mainly; specially

chief ex·ec·u·tive of·fi·cer /ˌ. .ˈ... ˌ.../ also **CEO** — n top director of a company

chief·tain /ˈtʃiftən/ n leader of a tribe, etc.

child /tʃaɪld/ n **children** /ˈtʃɪldrən/ 1 young human being 2 son or daughter 3 someone who behaves like a child ~**hood** n [C;U] time of being a child ~**ish** adj unsuitable for a grown person ~**less** adj having no children ~**like** adj simple; lovable

child·care /ˈtʃaɪldkɛr/ n [U] arrangement in which someone takes care of children while their parents are at work

child sup·port /ˈ. .ˌ./ n [U] money given to a woman for her children by their father who doesn't live with them

chill /tʃɪl/ vi/t 1 make or become cold 2 also **chill out** — infml relax: Chill out — everything will be O.K. 3 (cause to) have a feeling of cold as from fear: a chilling murder story ♦ n 1 [C] illness with coldness and shaking 2 [S] unpleasant coldness ~**y** adj 1 rather cold 2 unfriendly

chil·i /ˈtʃɪli/ n [C;U] 1 (powder made from) the red seed case of a kind of pepper which tastes very hot 2 dish with meat, beans, and chili

chime /tʃaɪm/ n sound of a set of bells ♦ vi/t 1 make this sound 2 infml be in agreement

chim·ney /ˈtʃɪmni/ n hollow passage to let out smoke from a fire

chim·pan·zee /ˌtʃɪmpænˈzi, tʃɪmˈpænzi/ also **chimp** /tʃɪmp/ n kind of African ape

chin /tʃɪn/ n the part of the face below the mouth

chi·na /ˈtʃaɪnə/ n [U] 1 baked clay 2 plates, cups, etc., made from this

Chi·na·town /ˈtʃaɪnətaʊn/ n [C;U] part of a city where there are Chinese restaurants, shops, etc.

chink /tʃɪŋk/ n narrow crack

chinos /ˈtʃinoʊz/ n [pl] loose pants made from heavy cotton

chip[1] /tʃɪp/ n 1 small piece broken off 2 place from which this was broken 3 thin piece of food: chocolate chip 4 small piece of material on which an INTEGRATED CIRCUIT is formed 5 flat plastic object used for representing money in certain games 6 **a chip off the old block** a person very like their father in character 7 **have a chip on one's shoulder** be quarrelsome or easily offended, as a result of feeling badly treated 8 **when the chips are down** when a very important point is reached — see also BLUE CHIP ~**per** adj happy; cheerful; active

chip[2] vi/t -pp- (cause to) lose a small piece from the edge

chip in phr vi/t infml add (one's share of money)

chi·rop·rac·tor /ˈkaɪrəpræktə/ n doctor who treats back problems and other illness by pressing on bones in the back

chirp /tʃɜrp/ vi make the short sharp sound of small birds ♦ n ~**y** adj (of people) cheerful

chis·el /ˈtʃɪzəl/ n metal tool for shaping wood or stone ♦ vt/i -l- cut with a chisel

chiv·al·ry /ˈʃɪvəlri/ n [U] 1 beliefs and practices of KNIGHTS in the MIDDLE AGES 2 good manners shown by a man towards women ~**rous** adj

chlo·rine /ˈklɔrin, ˈkloʊr-/ n [U] greenish yellow substance with a strong smell, used to DISINFECT places, esp. swimming pools

chlor·o·form /ˈklɔrəfɔrm, ˈkloʊr-/ n chemical used as an ANESTHETIC

chock-full /ˌtʃɑk ˈfʊl/ adj infml completely full

choc·o·late /ˈtʃɔklɪt, ˈtʃɑ-/ n 1 [U] solid brown substance eaten as candy 2 [C] small candy covered with this 3 [U] hot drink made from this ♦ adj dark brown

chocolate chips /ˈ. . ˌ/ n [pl] small pieces of chocolate used in baking

choice /tʃɔɪs/ n 1 [C] act of choosing 2 [U] power of choosing: have no choice but to obey 3 [U] variety to choose from: a big choice of stores ♦ adj 1 of high quality 2 well chosen

choir /kwaɪə/ n 1 group of singers 2 part of a church where they sit

choke /tʃoʊk/ v 1 vt/i stop breathing because the breathing passage is blocked 2 vt fill (a passage) completely: roads choked with traffic ♦ n apparatus that controls air going into a gas engine

choke back phr vt control (esp. violent or sad feelings) as if by holding in the throat: He choked back his tears.

chol·e·ra /ˈkɑlərə/ n [U] serious tropical disease of the stomach and bowels

cho·les·te·rol /kəˈlɛstərɔl, -ˌroʊl/ n [U] substance found in all cells of the body, which helps to carry fats

choose /tʃuːz/ *vi/t* **chose** /tʃoʊz/, **chosen** /ˈtʃoʊzən/ **1** pick out from many: *choose a cake* **2** decide: *choose where to go*

chop[1] /tʃɑp/ *vt* **-pp-** cut with a heavy tool: *chop wood/onions*

chop[2] *n* **1** quick cutting blow **2** piece of lamb or PORK with a bone in it

chop·per /ˈtʃɑpə/ *n* **1** heavy tool for chopping **2** *sl* HELICOPTER

chop·py /ˈtʃɑpi/ *adj* (of water) with short rough waves

chop·sticks /ˈtʃɑpstɪks/ *n* [P] pair of thin sticks used in East Asia for lifting food to the mouth

cho·ral /ˈkɔrəl, ˈkoʊrəl/ *adj* of a CHOIR

chord /kɔrd/ *n* **1 2** musical notes sounded together **2** straight line joining 2 points on a curve – see also **strike a chord** (STRIKE[1])

chore /tʃɔr, tʃoʊr/ *n* piece of regular or dull work

chor·e·og·ra·phy /ˌkɔriˈɑgrəfi, ˌkoʊr-/ *n* arranging dances for the stage –**pher** *n* **choreograph** /ˈkɔriəˌgræf, ˈkoʊr-/ *vt*

chor·is·ter /ˈkɔristə, ˈkoʊr-, ˈkɑr-/ *n* singer in a CHOIR

chor·tle /ˈtʃɔrtl/ *vi* give several laughs of pleasure and satisfaction **chortle** *n*

cho·rus /ˈkɔrəs, ˈkoʊrəs/ *n* [C] group of singers **2** [C] part of a song repeated after each VERSE **3** [S] something said by many people together: *a chorus of groans* ♦ *vt* sing or say together

chose /tʃoʊz/ *v past t. of* CHOOSE

cho·sen /ˈtʃoʊzən/ *v past p. of* CHOOSE

chow /tʃaʊ/ *n infml* food

chow·der /ˈtʃaʊdə/ *n* soup that uses milk as its base

Christ /kraɪst/ *n* man on whose teaching Christianity is based; Jesus

chris·ten /ˈkrɪsən/ *vt* **1** make into a member of the Christian church by giving of a name at BAPTISM **2** name (esp. a ship) at an official ceremony **3** use for the first time **~ing** *n* ceremony of BAPTISM

Chris·ten·dom /ˈkrɪsəndəm/ *n* [U] *lit* all Christian people or countries

Chris·tian /ˈkrɪstʃən/ *n* person who believes in the teachings of Christ ♦ *adj* **1** of Christianity **2** having qualities such as kindness, generosity, etc.

Chris·ti·an·i·ty /ˌkrɪstʃiˈænəti/ *n* [U] the religion based on the life and teachings of Christ

Christ·mas /ˈkrɪsməs/ *n* **1** also **Christmas Day** /ˌ·· ˈ·/ — holy day in honor of Christ's birth; December 25th **2** period before and after this

chrome /kroʊm/ *n* [U] hard metal used esp. as a shiny covering on car parts, etc.

chro·mo·some /ˈkroʊməˌsoʊm/ *n* extremely small thread in every living cell that controls the nature of a young animal or plant

chron·ic /ˈkrɑnɪk/ *adj* (of a disease) lasting a long time

chron·i·cle /ˈkrɑnɪkəl/ *n* record of historical events ♦ *vt* make a chronicle of

chro·nol·o·gy /krəˈnɑlədʒi/ *n* **1** [U] science that gives dates to events **2** [C] list of events in order –**ogical** /ˌkrɑnəˈlɑdʒɪkəl◁/ *adj* arranged in order of time

chro·nom·e·ter /krəˈnɑmətə/ *n* very exact clock

chrys·a·lis /ˈkrɪsəlɪs/ *n* shell-like form of an insect that will become a MOTH or BUTTERFLY

chry·san·the·mum /krɪˈsænθəməm/ also **mum** /mʌm/ — *n* garden plant with large flowers in bright colors

chub·by /ˈtʃʌbi/ *adj* pleasantly fat

chuck /tʃʌk/ *vt infml* **1** throw

chuck·le /ˈtʃʌkəl/ *vi* laugh quietly ♦ *n*

chump /tʃʌmp/ *n sl* fool

chunk /tʃʌŋk/ *n* thick lump **~y** *adj* thick

church /tʃɜːtʃ/ *n* **1** [C] building for public Christian worship: *a regular* **church-goer** /-ˌgoʊə/ **2** [S] profession of priests and ministers: *enter the church* **3** [C] (*usu. cap.*) branch of Christianity: *the Catholic Church*

church·yard /ˈtʃɜːtʃjard/ *n* church burial ground

churl·ish /ˈtʃɜːlɪʃ/ *adj* bad-tempered; rude **~ly** *adv*

churn[1] /tʃɜːn/ *n* container in which cream is shaken to make butter

churn[2] *vi/t* shake about violently

   churn out *phr vt* produce a large quantity of

chute /ʃut/ *n* sloped passage for something to slide down

chut·ney /ˈtʃʌtˈni/ *n* [U] mixture of fruits eaten with meat

chutz·pah /ˈhʊtspə/ *n* very high confidence in oneself

CIA *n* Central Intelligence Agency; US government department that collects information, esp. secretly

ci·der /ˈsaɪdə/ *n* [U] drink made from apples, either sweet cider (non-alcoholic) or hard cider (alcoholic)

ci·gar /sɪˈgɑr/ *n* roll of tobacco leaves for smoking

cig·a·rette /ˌsɪgəˈrɛt, ˈsɪgəˌrɛt/ *n* paper tube of cut tobacco for smoking

cinch /sɪntʃ/ *n* [S] *infml* **1** (something) done easily: *The exam was a cinch.* **2** (something) certain to happen: *It's a cinch that we'll win.*

cin·der /ˈsɪndə/ *n* piece of burned coal, etc.

cin·der·block /ˈsɪndəˌblɑk/ *n* building block made from cement and cinders

cin·e·ma /ˈsɪnəmə/ *n* **1** [C] theater where films are shown also **movie theater 2** [S] films as an art or industry

cin·na·mon /ˈsɪnəmən/ *n* [U] yellow-brown SPICE used in cooking

ci·pher /ˈsaɪfə/ *n* **1** system of secret writing **2** unimportant person

cir·ca /ˈsəkə/ *prep fml* (used with dates) about: *circa 1000 A.D.*

cir·cle /ˈsəkəl/ *n* **1** curved line on which every point is equally distant from the center **2** ring **3** group of people **4** upper floor in a theater ♦ *vi/t* **1** move around in a circle **2** draw a circle around

cir·cuit /ˈsəkɪt/ *n* **1** circular journey around an area **2** circular path of an electric current ~**ous** /səˈkyuətəs/ *adj* going a long way around: *a circuitous route*

cir·cu·lar /ˈsəkyələ/ *adj* **1** shaped like a circle **2** moving in a circle **3** not direct ♦ *n* printed notice given to many people

cir·cu·late /ˈsəkyəˌleɪt/ *vi/t* **1** move along a closed path **2** spread widely: *circulate rumors* **3** move about freely –**lation** /ˌsəkyəˈleɪʃən/ *n* **1** [U] flow around a closed system: *the circulation of the blood* **2** [U] passing of money among people: *the number of $5 bills in circulation* **3** [S] number of copies of a newspaper sold

cir·cum·cise /ˈsəkəmˌsaɪz/ *vt* cut off the skin at the end of the male sex organ or part of the sex organ (CLITORIS) of a woman –**cision** /ˌsəkəmˈsɪʒən/ *n* [C;U]

cir·cum·fer·ence /səˈkʌmfərəns/ *n* distance around: *the Earth's circumference*

cir·cum·nav·i·gate /ˌsəkəmˈnævəˌgeɪt/ *vt fml* sail right around

cir·cum·scribe /ˈsəkəmˌskraɪb/ *vt fml* limit

cir·cum·spect /ˈsəkəmˌspɛkt/ *adj fml* careful

cir·cum·stance /ˈsəkəmˌstæns/ *n* **1** (*usu. pl.*) conditions that influence a person or event **2 in/under no circumstances** never **3 in/under the circumstances** because of the conditions

cir·cum·stan·tial /ˌsəkəmˈstænʃəl/ *adj fml* **1** (of a description) detailed **2 circumstantial evidence** information worth knowing but not directly important

cir·cum·vent /ˌsəkəmˈvɛnt, ˈsəkəmˌvɛnt/ *vt* avoid by cleverness: *circumvent the tax laws*

cir·cus /ˈsəkəs/ *n* performance of skill and daring by a group of people and animals

cir·rho·sis /səˈroʊsɪs/ *n* [U] serious LIVER disease

cis·tern /ˈsɪstən/ *n* container for storing water

ci·ta·tion /saɪˈteɪʃən/ *n* **1** notice to appear in court **2** law traffic ticket

cite /saɪt/ *vt* **1** *fml* mention as an example **2** *law* call to appear in court

cit·i·zen /ˈsɪtəzən/ *n* **1** person living in a city or town **2** person with full membership of a country ~**ship** *n* [U]: *apply for French citizenship*

Cit·i·zens' Band /ˌ··· ˈ· ◁/ *n* [U] CB

cit·rus /ˈsɪtrəs/ *adj* (of fruit) of the orange family

cit·y /ˈsɪti/ *n* **1** [C] large important town **2** [C] its citizens **3** [S] (*cap.*) the center for money matters in London — see also INNER CITY

city hall /ˌ·· ˈ·/ *n often cap.* (public building used for) a city's local government

civ·ic /ˈsɪvɪk/ *adj* of a city or its citizens

civ·il /ˈsɪvəl/ *adj* **1** not military or religious **2** polite ~**ly** *adv* politely ~**ity** /səˈvɪləti/ *n* [C;U] politeness

civil en·gi·neer·ing /ˌ·· ··ˈ·· ◁/ *n* [U] building of public roads, bridges, etc.

ci·vil·ian /səˈvɪlyən/ *n, adj* (person) not of the armed forces

civ·i·li·za·tion /ˌsɪvələˈzeɪʃən/ *n* **1** [U] high level of human development and social organization **2** [C] particular civilized society: *ancient civilizations*

civ·i·lize /ˈsɪvəˌlaɪz/ vt **1** bring to civilization: *civilized nations* **2** improve in manners

civil rights /ˌ· ˈ·/ n [P] a citizen's rights to freedom and equality

civil ser·vant /ˌ· ˈ·-/ n person employed in the civil service

civil ser·vice /ˌ· ˈ·-/ n [the+S] **1** FEDERAL government departments, except the armed forces and law courts **2** people employed in this

civil war /ˌ· ˈ·/ n war between people from the same country

clad /klæd/ adj lit clothed; covered

claim /kleɪm/ v **1** vt/i demand (something) as one's right: *claim on the insurance* **2** vt declare to be true: *He claims to be rich.* ♦ n **1** demand for something as one's right; right to something **2** something claimed, esp. money under an insurance agreement **3** statement; declaration

clai·mant /ˈkleɪmənt/ n fml person who claims something

clair·voy·ant /kleərˈvɔɪənt/ adj, n (of a) person who can see what will happen in the future –ance n [U]

clam¹ /klæm/ n large SHELLFISH

clam² v clam up phr vi become silent

clam·bake /ˈklæmbeɪk/ n informal party by the sea, esp. where clams are cooked and eaten

clam·ber /ˈklæmbə/ vi climb with effort

clam·my /ˈklæmi/ adj unpleasantly wet and sticky

clam·or /ˈklæmə/ n [S;U] loud confused noise, esp. of complaint ♦ vi demand noisily: *a baby clamoring to be fed*

clamp¹ /klæmp/ n apparatus with a screw, for fastening things together

clamp² vt fasten with a clamp

clamp down on phr vt limit; prevent: *clamp down on drunk driving*

clampdown /ˈklæmpdaʊn/ n

clan /klæn/ n Scottish family group

clan·des·tine /klænˈdestɪn/ adj secret ~ly adv

clang /klæŋ/ vi/t make a loud ringing sound **clang** n [S]

clank /klæŋk/ vi/t make a sound like a heavy metal chain **clank** n [S]

clap /klæp/ v **-pp- 1** vi/t strike (one's hands) together: *The audience clapped loudly.* **2** vt strike lightly with the open hand: *clap him on the back* **3** vt infml put

quickly: *clapped her in jail* ♦ n **1** [C] loud explosive noise, esp. of thunder **2** [S] clapping: *Give him a clap!* **3** [S] sl GONORRHEA

clap·board /ˈklæpˌbɔrd, -ˌbʊərd/ n board covering the outer walls of a house

clap·trap /ˈklæptræp/ n [U] nonsense

clar·et /ˈklærət/ n [U] red wine from Bordeaux ♦ adj deep red

clar·i·fy /ˈklærəˌfaɪ/ vt fml make more easily understood –fication /ˌklærəfəˈkeɪʃən/ n [C;U]

clar·i·net /ˌklærəˈnɛt/ n kind of WOODWIND musical instrument ~tist n person who plays the clarinet

clar·i·ty /ˈklærəti/ n [U] clearness

clash /klæʃ/ v **1** vi come into opposition **2** vi (of colors) look wrong together **3** vi (of events) be planned for the same time **4** vi/t make a loud metallic noise ♦ n **1** [C] disagreement **2** [S] metallic noise

clasp /klæsp/ n **1** metal fastener **2** firm hold ♦ vt **1** seize firmly **2** fasten with a clasp

class /klæs/ n **1 a** [C] group of students taught together **b** [C;U] period of time they are taught for **2** [C] division; level: *a first-class carriage* **3** [U] high quality; elegance (ELEGANT) — see also FIRST CLASS ♦ vt put into a class; consider ~y adj fashionable and of high class **4** [C] social group of a particular rank: *the ruling class* **5** [U] system of dividing society into such groups

class ac·tion /ˌ· ˈ·-/ n legal action by a group of people similarly interested

clas·sic /ˈklæsɪk/ adj **1** of the highest rank **2** typical: *classic example* **3** having a long history; TRADITIONAL ♦ n piece of literature or art, a writer or artist of lasting importance **classics** n [P] ancient Greek and Roman literature

clas·si·cal /ˈklæsɪkəl/ adj **1** following ancient Greek or Roman models **2** (of music) with serious artistic intentions **3** TRADITIONAL

clas·si·fied ads /ˌklæsəfaɪd ˈædz/, **clas·si·fieds** /ˈklæsəfaɪdz/ n [pl.] small advertisements in the newspaper put in by people wanting to buy or sell something

clas·si·fy /ˈklæsəˌfaɪ/ vt arrange into classes –fied adj **1** divided into classes **2** officially secret –fication /ˌklæsəfəˈkeɪʃən/ n [C;U]

class·mate /ˈklæsmeɪt/ n child in the same class

class·room /ˈklæsrum, -rʊm/ n room in a school, etc., in which a class meets for a lesson

clat·ter /ˈklætə/ n [S;U] noise of hard objects hitting each other: a clatter of dishes ♦ vi/t make a clatter

clause /klɔz/ n 1 gram group of words containing a subject and verb 2 law separate division of a piece of legal writing

claus·tro·pho·bi·a /ˌklɔstrəˈfoʊbiə/ n [U] fear of being closed in

claw¹ /klɔ/ n 1 sharp nail on an animal's or bird's toe 2 limb of a CRAB, etc. 3 curved end of some tools

claw² /klɔ/ vi/t tear or pull with claws

clay /kleɪ/ n [U] earth from which bricks, pots, etc., are made

clean¹ /klin/ adj 1 not dirty 2 not yet used: clean piece of paper 3 morally pure: clean joke 4 smooth; regular: clean lines of a new car 5 **come clean** tell the unpleasant truth ~ly adv ~liness /ˈklɛnlɪnɪs/ n [U]

clean² /klin/ vt make clean ~er n person or thing that cleans –ners n 1 shop where clothes, etc., are cleaned with chemicals 2 **take someone to the cleaners** cause someone to lose all their money, etc.

clean out phr vt 1 make (the inside of a room, drawer, etc.) clean and tidy 2 take all someone's money

clean up phr vi/t 1 clean thoroughly 2 sl gain money as profit

clean³ /klin/ adv infml completely: "I clean forgot".

clean-cut /ˌ·ˈ·◁/ adj 1 well shaped 2 neat and clean in appearance

cleanse /klɛnz/ vt make pure **cleanser** n chemical, etc., used for cleaning

clean-shav·en /ˌ·ˈ··◁/ adj with no beard

clean sweep /ˌ·ˈ·/ n 1 complete change 2 complete victory

clear¹ /klɪr/ adj 1 easy to see through: clear glass 2 without marks, etc.: clear skin 1 (fig.) a clear conscience 3 easy to hear or understand 4 certain: I'm not clear where he lives. 1 a clear case of murder 5 open; empty: The road's clear of snow. 6 free; no longer touching: We're clear of danger now. 1 He swung clear of the wall. 7 (of wages or profit) remaining after all taxes, etc. have been paid ♦ n [U] **in the clear** free from guilt, debt, etc. ♦ adv 1 in a clear way: shout loud and clear 2 completely: The pris-

oner got clear away. 3 out of the way: jump clear of the train ~ly adv 1 in a clear way: speak clearly 2 undoubtedly: clearly wrong

clear² /klɪr/ v 1 vi/t become clear; remove something unwanted: The sky cleared. 1 clear snow from the road 2 vt get past without touching: clear a fence 3 vt give official approval to 4 vt free from blame 5 vt earn as CLEAR (7) profit or wages: She clears $10,000 a year.

clear away phr vt make an area tidy by removing

clear off phr vi go away

clear out phr v 1 vi go away 2 vt empty

clear up phr v 1 vt explain: clear up the mystery 2 vi/t tidy

clear·ance /ˈklɪrəns/ n 1 [U] official approval 2 [C;U] distance between objects 3 [U] also **security clearance** — official acceptance that one is in no way an enemy of one's country 4 [C] also **clearance sale** /ˈ·· ◁/ — time when a store sells goods cheaply so as to get rid of as many as possible

clear-cut /ˌ·ˈ·◁/ adj clear in meaning

clear·ing /ˈklɪrɪŋ/ n area cleared of trees

cleav·age /ˈklivɪdʒ/ n 1 division caused by splitting 2 space between a woman's breasts as seen when she is wearing a dress

cleave /kliv/ vt **cleaved** or **cleft** /klɛft/ or **clove** /kloʊv/, **cleaved** or **cleft** or **cloven** /ˈkloʊvən/ divide or make by a cutting blow ~–er n tool for cutting meat

cleave to phr vt lit remain loyal to

clef /klɛf/ n sign at the beginning of a line of written music to show the PITCH¹ (of) notes

cleft /klɛft/ v past t. of CLEAVE

clem·en·cy /ˈklɛmənsi/ n [U] fml mercy –ent adj fml (of weather) not severe

clench /klɛntʃ/ vt close tightly: clench one's fists

cler·gy /ˈklɜdʒi/ n [P] priests

cler·gy·man /ˈklɜdʒimən/ n –men /-mən/ Christian priest

cler·ic /ˈklɛrɪk/ n clergyman ~al adj 1 of priests 2 of clerks

clerk /klɑk/ n 1 office worker 2 official in charge of court records, etc.

clev·er /ˈklɛvə/ adj 1 quick at learning 2 intelligent but possibly deceitful: clever response 3 showing skill: clever idea ~ly adv ~ness n [U]

cli·ché /kliːˈʃeɪ/ n expression or idea used so often it has lost much of its force

click /klɪk/ n slight short sound, as of a camera ♦ v 1 vi/t make a click 2 vi understand an idea 3 vi like and understand someone: *We clicked immediately* 4 vi also **click on** vt press a button on a computer MOUSE to choose something from the screen that one wants the computer to do

cli·ent /ˈklaɪənt/ n 1 person who pays for advice from a professional person 2 customer

cli·en·tele /ˌklaɪənˈtɛl, ˌkliː-/ n clients; customers

cliff /klɪf/ n steep rock face, esp. on a coast

cliff·hang·er /ˈklɪfˌhæŋə/ n 1 competition, etc., whose result is in doubt until the very end 2 story told in parts, each of which ends at a moment of exciting doubt as to what will happen next

cli·mac·tic /klaɪˈmæktɪk/ adj forming a climax

cli·mate /ˈklaɪmɪt/ n 1 average weather conditions 2 condition of opinions: *political climate* **-matic** /klaɪˈmætɪk/ adj

cli·max /ˈklaɪmæks/ n 1 most powerful part of a story, usu. near the end 2 ORGASM ♦ vi/t bring or come to a climax

climb /klaɪm/ v 1 vi/t move, esp. using hands and feet: *climb a ladder* | *go climbing in the Rockies* 2 vi rise: *The road climbs steeply.* 3 vi (of a plant) grow upwards ♦ n 1 journey by climbing 2 place to climb **~er** n person or thing that climbs

clinch¹ /klɪntʃ/ vt settle (an agreement) firmly

clinch² n EMBRACE

cling /klɪŋ/ vi **clung** /klʌŋ/ hold tightly **~ing** adj 1 (of clothes) fitting tightly 2 (of a person) too dependent

clin·ic /ˈklɪnɪk/ n place for general or specialized medical treatment **~al** adj 1 of clinics or hospitals 2 coldly scientific

clink /klɪŋk/ vi/t (cause to) make a sound like pieces of glass knocking together **clink** n [S]

clip¹ /klɪp/ n small esp. metal object for holding things together: *paper clip* **clip** vt **-pp-**

clip² vt **-pp-** 1 cut with scissors, etc. 2 sl hit ♦ n 1 cutting 2 sl quick blow: *a clip on the ear* **~pers** n [P] tool with a scis-

sors action **~ping** n 1 piece cut off 2 piece cut from a newspaper

clique /kliːk, klɪk/ n derog closely united group of people

clit·o·ris /ˈklɪtərɪs/ n small front part of the female sex organ

cloak /kloʊk/ n loose outer garment without SLEEVES ♦ vt keep secret

cloak-and-dag·ger /ˌ· · ˈ·-/ adj (of stories, etc.) dealing with adventure and mystery

cloak·room /ˈkloʊk-rʊm, -rʊm/ n room where coats, etc., may be left

clob·ber /ˈklɒbə/ vt sl 1 attack severely 2 defeat completely

clock /klɒk/ n 1 instrument for measuring time 2 **around the clock** all day and all night 3 **put the clock back** return to old-fashioned ideas 4 **watch the clock** think continually of how soon work will end 5 **work against the clock** work very quickly in order to finish a job before a certain time ♦ vt record (time, speed, distance, etc.)

clock in/out phr vi record the time of arriving at/leaving work

clock up phr vt infml 1 record (a distance traveled, a speed reached, etc.) 2 succeed in getting

clock·wise /ˈklɒk-waɪz/ adv in the direction of the movement of a clock

clock·work /ˈklɒk-wɜːk/ n [U] 1 machinery wound up with a key 2 **like clockwork** without trouble

clod /klɒd/ n lump or mass of clay or earth

clog¹ /klɒg/ n wooden shoe

clog² vi/t **-gg-** (cause to) become blocked or filled

clois·ter /ˈklɔɪstə/ n covered passage usu. forming part of a college, MONASTERY, etc. **~ed** adj sheltered from the world

clone /kloʊn/ n descendant of a single plant or animal produced by non-sexual means ♦ **clone** vt

close¹ /kloʊz/ v 1 vt/i shut: *close one's eyes* | *When does the store close?* 2 vt bring to an end: *close a bank account* 3 **close a deal (with)** settle a business agreement ♦ n [S] fml end of a period of time: *at the close of day*

close down phr vi/t (of a factory, etc.) stop operating **closedown** /ˈkloʊzdaʊn/ n

close in _phr vi_ surround gradually

close² /kloʊs/ _adj_ **1** near: _close to the stores_ | _a close friend_ **2** thorough: _close inspection_ **3** without fresh air; too warm **4** decided by a small difference: _a close finish to the race_ ♦ _adv_ **1** near: _close behind/together_ **2** **close on** almost **3** **close to home** near the (the. unpleasant) truth **~ly** _adv_ **~ness** _n_ [U]

close call /ˌkloʊs ˈkɔl/ _n infml_ situation in which something dangerous or very unpleasant is only just avoided

closed cir·cuit tele·vi·sion /ˌkloʊs səkɪt ˈtɛləvɪʒən/ _n_ [U] system of cameras that watch a building, room etc. for crime

close-knit /ˌkloʊs ˈnɪt◄/ also

closely-knit /ˌ•• ˈ•◄/ — _adj_ tightly bound together by social, political, etc., beliefs and activities

close-set /ˌkloʊs ˈsɛt◄/ _adj_ set close together: _close-set eyes_

close shave /ˌkloʊs ˈʃeɪv/ _n infml_ situation in which something dangerous or very unpleasant is only just avoided — see also CLOSE CALL

clos·et /ˈklɑzɪt/ _n_ cupboard built into a wall ♦ _adj_ not publicly admitted; secret ♦ _vt_ enclose (esp. oneself) in a private room

close-up /ˈkloʊs ʌp/ _n_ photograph taken from very near

clo·sure /ˈkloʊʒər/ _n_ [C;U] closing: _bank closures_

clot /klɑt/ _n_ lump formed from liquid: _blood clot_ ♦ _vi/t_ -tt- form into clots

cloth /klɔθ/ _n_ [C;U] (piece of) material made by weaving

clothe /kloʊð/ _vt_ provide clothes for

clothes /kloʊz, kloʊðz/ _n_ [P] things to cover the body; garments

clothes·horse /ˈkloʊzhɔrs, ˈkloʊðz-/ _n infml_ person who is very interested in clothes and fashion

clothes·line /ˈkloʊzlaɪn, ˈkloʊðz-/ _n_ wire hung outdoors for drying clothes

clothes·pin /ˈkloʊzpɪn, ˈkloʊðz-/ _n_ wooden or plastic CLIP for hanging clothes on a clothesline

cloth·ing /ˈkloʊðɪŋ/ _n_ [U] clothes

cloud /klaʊd/ _n_ **1** [C;U] white or gray mass floating in the sky which is formed from very small drops of water **2** [C] similar floating mass: _clouds of smoke/mosquitoes_ **3** [C] something threatening: _the clouds of war_ **4** **have one's head in the clouds** be impractical **5** **under a cloud** out of favor ♦ _v_ **1** _vt/i_ cover with clouds **2** _vt_ confuse: _cloud the issue_ **~y** _adj_ **1** full of clouds **2** not clear

clout /klaʊt/ _n_ **1** [C] blow with the hand **2** [U] influence, esp. political ♦ _vt_ strike, esp. with the hand

clove¹ /kloʊv/ _n_ dried flower of a tropical tree used in cooking

clove² _n_ any of the smallest pieces into which the root of the GARLIC plant can be divided

clo·ven /ˈkloʊvən/ _v past p._ of CLEAVE

clo·ver /ˈkloʊvər/ _n_ [C;U] **1** plant with 3 leaves on each stem, often grown as food for cattle **2** **in clover** living in comfort

clown /klaʊn/ _n_ **1** performer in a CIRCUS who makes people laugh **2** person acting like this ♦ _vi_ behave foolishly

cloy /klɔɪ/ _vi/t_ (of food) become unpleasant because too sweet: (fig.) _cloying sentimentality_

club¹ /klʌb/ _n_ **1** society of people who meet for amusement or some purpose; building where they meet: _health/tennis club_ **2** NIGHTCLUB **3** heavy stick used as a weapon **4** stick for striking the ball in GOLF **5** playing card with one or more black figures shaped like clovers on it — see also BOOK CLUB

club² _vt_ -bb- hit someone hard with a club

club sand·wich /ˌ• ˈ••/ _n_ sandwich with three pieces of bread with meats and cheeses between them

cluck /klʌk/ _vi_ make the noise a hen makes **cluck** _n_

clue /klu/ _n_ **1** something that helps to find the answer to a problem **2** **not have a clue** know nothing; be unable to understand

clump¹ /klʌmp/ _n_ group of trees, etc.

clump² _vi_ walk heavily

clum·sy /ˈklʌmzi/ _adj_ **1** awkward in movement **2** TACTless **-sily** _adv_ **-siness** _n_ [U]

clung /klʌŋ/ _v past t. and p._ of CLING

clunk·er /ˈklʌŋkər/ _n_ old car or machine that doesn't work well

clus·ter /ˈklʌstər/ _n_ group of things close together ♦ _vi_ form a close group

clutch¹ /klʌtʃ/ _v_ **1** _vt_ hold tightly **2** _vi_ try to seize: _He clutched at a branch._ ♦ _n_ **1** act of clutching **2** apparatus connecting and disconnecting the working parts of a car engine **clutches** n [P] control: *in the clutches of the enemy*

clutch² n (chickens born from) a number of eggs laid by one bird: (fig.) *a whole clutch of new problems*

clut·ter /ˈklʌtə/ vt make untidy ♦ n [U] scattered disorderly things

cm written abbrev. for: centimeter(s)

Co. /koʊ/ abbrev. for: COMPANY (1)

C.O. n Commanding Officer; person in the armed forces in charge of others

coach /koʊtʃ/ n 1 person who trains people for sports, or gives private lessons ♦ vt train; teach 2 large carriage pulled by a horse or horses ♦ adj of a cheap travel ticket: *I flew back coach.*

co·ag·u·late /koʊˈægjəˌleɪt/ vi/t change from a liquid to a solid

coal /koʊl/ n [C;U] (piece of) black mineral that can be burned: *a coalmine*

co·a·lesce /ˌkoʊəˈles/ vi fml grow together; unite

coal·field /ˈkoʊlfild/ n area where there is coal under the ground

co·a·li·tion /ˌkoʊəˈlɪʃən/ n union of political parties or groups for a special purpose

coarse /kɔrs, koʊrs/ adj 1 not fine; lumpy 2 rough in manner; insensitive ~**ly** adv ~**ness** n [U] **coarsen** vi/t

coast /koʊst/ n 1 stretch of land by the ocean 2 **the coast is clear** all danger has gone ♦ vi 1 go DOWNHILL on a bicycle, etc., without effort or power 2 do something without effort ~**al** adj

coast·guard /ˈkoʊstgɑrd/ n 1 military organization responsible for the coast and ocean nearby 2 member of the coastguard

coast·line /ˈkoʊstlaɪn/ n shape of a coast

coat /koʊt/ n 1 outer garment with SLEEVES, fastened at the front 2 animal's fur, etc. 3 covering on a surface: *coat of paint* ♦ vt cover (a surface) ~**ing** n thin covering

coat hang·er /ˈ· ˌ·/ n a HANGER

coat·room /ˈkoʊt-rum, -rʊm/ n CLOAKROOM

coax /koʊks/ vt 1 persuade gently 2 obtain (something) by gently persuading

cob /kɑb/ n 1 long hard central part of an ear of corn 2 strong horse with short legs 3 male SWAN

cob·ble¹ /ˈkɑbəl/ also **cobble-stone** /ˈkɑbəlˌstoʊn/ — n rounded stone used for road surfaces –**bled** adj covered with cobbles

cobble² vt put together quickly and roughly

cob·bler /ˈkɑblə/ n shoe repairer

co·bra /ˈkoʊbrə/ n kind of poisonous snake

cob·web /ˈkɑbweb/ n a SPIDER's net of spun threads

co·caine /koʊˈkeɪn, ˈkoʊkeɪn/ n [U] drug used against pain, or for pleasure

cock /kɑk/ n 1 fully grown male bird, esp. a chicken 2 hammer of a gun 3 a TAP for controlling the flow of liquid in a pipe 4 sl PENIS ♦ 1 vt/i raise up: *The horse cocked its ears.* 2 vt set (the hammer of a gun) in the correct position for firing

cock·a·ma·mie /ˌkɑkəˈmeɪmi◁/ adj sl making no sense

cock·a·too /ˈkɑkəˌtu/ n -**toos** Australian bird with a large CREST (1) on its head

cock·eyed /ˈkɑkaɪd/ adj 1 stupid 2 CROOKed (1)

Cock·ney /ˈkɑkni/ n [C] person from the industrial parts of London

cock·pit /ˈkɑkpɪt/ n part of a plane where the pilot sits

cock·roach /ˈkɑk-roʊtʃ/ n large insect which lives esp. in dirty or old houses

cock·sure /ˌkɑkˈʃʊr/ adj having too much confidence in oneself

cock·tail /ˈkɑkteɪl/ n 1 mixed alcoholic drink 2 mixture of fruit or SEAFOOD — see also MOLOTOV COCKTAIL

cock·y /ˈkɑki/ adj sl too sure of oneself

co·coa /ˈkoʊkoʊ/ n [U] 1 brown powder tasting of chocolate 2 hot drink made from this

co·co·nut /ˈkoʊkəˌnʌt, -nət/ n [C;U] (flesh of) a very large tropical nut

co·coon /kəˈkun/ n silky covering that protects some insects in their inactive stage ♦ vt protect from hardship

cod /kɑd/ n **cod** or **cods** large sea fish

cod·dle /ˈkɑdl/ vt treat (someone) too tenderly

code /koʊd/ n 1 system of signs, or of secret writing: *computer code* 2 collection of laws or social customs ♦ vt translate into a code

co·ed /ˈkoʊed, ˌkoʊˈed/ n female student in a college open to both sexes ♦ /ˈkoʊed/ adj coeducational

co·ed·u·ca·tion /ˌkouɛdʒəˈkeɪʃən/ n [U] education of boys and girls together ~**al** adj

co·erce /kouˈəs/ vt fml force to do something –**ercive** adj –**ercion** /kouˈəʒən/ n [U]

co·ex·ist /ˌkouɪgˈzɪst/ vi exist at the same time –**ence** n [U] (esp. of countries) existing together peacefully

cof·fee /ˈkɔfi/ n [C;U] (drink made by pouring boiling water onto) the (crushed) berries of a tropical tree

coffee cake /ˈ·· ·/ n [C;U] sweet heavy cake, eaten with coffee

coffee shop /ˈ·· ·/ n small restaurant serving cheap meals

coffee ta·ble /ˈ·· ·/ n low table

cof·fers /ˈkɔfəz, ˈkɔ-/ n [pl.] supply of money

cof·fin /ˈkɔfɪn/ n box in which a dead person is buried

cog /kɑg/ n **1** tooth on the edge of a wheel that moves another wheel **2 cog in the machine** unimportant person in a very large organization

co·gent /ˈkoudʒənt/ adj fml forceful; convincing (CONVINCE): cogent arguments **cogency** n

co·gnac /ˈkounjæk, ˈkɑn-, ˈkɔn-/ n [U] kind of BRANDY

cog·nate /ˈkɑgneɪt/ adj fml related: cognate languages

co·hab·it /ˌkouˈhæbɪt/ vi fml live together as though married ~**ation** /kouˌhæbəˈteɪʃən/ n [U]

co·her·ent /kouˈhɪrənt, -ˈhɛr-/ adj (of speech, ideas, etc.) reasonably connected; clear –**ence** n [U] ~**ly** adv

co·he·sive /kouˈhisɪv, -zɪv/ adj sticking together –**sion** /-ˈhiʒən/ n [U]

coil /kɔɪl/ vi/t twist into a circle ♦ n **1** connected set of twists: coil of rope **2** twisted wire that carries an electric current

coin /kɔɪn/ n piece of metal money ♦ vt **1** make (coins) **2** invent (new words)

co·in·cide /ˌkouɪnˈsaɪd/ vi **1** happen at the same time **2** (of opinions, etc.) agree

co·in·ci·dence /kouˈɪnsədəns, -ˌdɛns/ n [C;U] accidental and surprising combination of events: By sheer coincidence, we have the same birthday. –**dental** /kouˌɪnsəˈdɛntl/ adj

coke /kouk/ n [U] **1** substance left after gas has been removed from coal **2** COCAINE

col·an·der /ˈkʌləndə, ˈkɑ-/ n bowl with holes, for separating liquid from food

cold¹ /kould/ adj **1** low in temperature: cold wind **2** unfriendly: a cold stare **3** (of cooked food) allowed to get cool **4** unconscious: I knocked him out cold. **5 get/have cold feet** lose courage **6 give/get the cold shoulder** treat/be treated unsympathetically ~**ly** adv ~**ness** n [U]

cold² n **1** [U] low temperature **2** [C;U] illness of the nose and throat **3 (out) in the cold** not noticed; unwanted

cold-blood·ed /ˌ· ˈ··◁/ adj **1** (of snakes, etc.) having a body temperature that varies with the surroundings **2** cruel; without feeling: cold-blooded murder

cold-cuts /ˌkouldˈkʌts/ n [P] thin pieces of cold cooked meat

cold-heart·ed /ˌ· ˈ··◁/ adj unkind

cold tur·key /ˌ· ˈ··/ n [U] sl (the unpleasant sick feeling caused by) the sudden stopping of the use of a drug by an ADDICT

cold war /ˌ· ˈ·/ n severe political struggle without actual fighting

cole·slaw /ˈkoul ˌslɔ/ n [U] SALAD made with thinly cut cabbage and carrots

col·ic /ˈkɑlɪk/ n [U] severe pain in the stomach and bowels

col·lab·o·rate /kəˈlæbəˌreɪt/ vi **1** work together **2** help the enemy –**rator** n –**ration** /kəˌlæbəˈreɪʃən/ n [U]

col·lage /kəˈlɑʒ, kou-/ n picture made by gluing various materials or objects onto a surface

col·lapse /kəˈlæps/ v **1** vi fall down suddenly; The bridge collapsed under the weight of the train. **2** vi fall helpless **3** vi/t fold flat ♦ n [C;U] collapsing: (fig.) the collapse of the peace talks –**lapsible** adj that can be folded for packing, etc.

col·lar /ˈkɑlə/ n **1** part of a garment that fits around the neck **2** band put around an animal's neck ♦ vt seize and hold

col·lar·bone /ˈkɑləˌboun/ n bone joining the RIBS to the shoulders

col·late /kəˈleɪt, kɑ-, ˈkouleɪt, ˈkɑ-/ vt fml **1** compare (copies of books, etc.) to find the differences **2** arrange (the sheets) of (esp. a book) in the proper order

col·lat·e·ral /kəˈlætərəl/ n [S;U] property promised as SECURITY for a debt

col·league /ˈkɑlig/ n fellow worker

col·lect[1] /kəˈlɛkt/ v 1 vt/i gather together: *collect taxes* | *A crowd collected in the street.* 2 vt save (stamps, etc.) as a HOBBY 3 vt regain control of (oneself, one's thoughts, etc.) 4 vt get: *collect one's skirt from the cleaners* **~ed** adj controlled; calm **~ive** adj shared by many people: *collective ownership* **~ive** n business owned and controlled by the people who work in it **~ively** adv: *collectively responsible* **~or** n person who collects something: *coin collector* **~ion** /kəˈlɛkʃən/ n 1 [U] collecting 2 [C] set of things, sum of money, etc., collected

col·lect[2] adj, adv to be paid for by the receiver: *Call me collect.*

collective bar·gain·ing /ˌ·ˈ·· ˈ··/ n [U] talks between unions and employers about working conditions, etc.

col·lege /ˈkɑlɪdʒ/ n 1 school for higher education; part of a university 2 group of people with a common profession or purpose: *the College of Arts and Sciences*

college boards /ˌ·· ˈ·/ n set of examinations demanded for a person to be admitted to many universities

col·lide /kəˈlaɪd/ vi 1 crash violently 2 be opposed: *The bosses collided with the unions.*

col·li·sion /kəˈlɪʒən/ n [C;U] colliding

col·lo·qui·al /kəˈloʊkwiəl/ adj (of words, style, etc.) suitable for informal conversation **~ly** adv **~ism** n colloquial expression

col·lude /kəˈlud/ vi fml act in collusion

col·lu·sion /kəˈluʒən/ n fml secret agreement to deceive

co·logne /kəˈloʊn/ n [C;U] liquid with a pleasant smell, put on the skin

co·lon[1] /ˈkoʊlən/ n lower part of the bowels

colon[2] n the mark (:)

colo·nel /ˈkɜrnl/ n army or airforce officer of middle rank

co·lo·ni·al /kəˈloʊniəl/ adj 1 of or about colonies (COLONY (1)) 2 of the period, etc., before 1776: *colonial furniture* ♦ n person living or having lived in a COLONY (1) **~ism** n [U] principle of having colonies

col·o·nize /ˈkɑləˌnaɪz/ vt make into a colony: *colonize Australia* **–nist** n person living in a new COLONY (1) **–nization** /ˌkɑlənəˈzeɪʃən/ n [U]

col·on·nade /ˌkɑləˈneɪd/ n row of PILLARS

col·o·ny /ˈkɑləni/ n 1 place lived in and controlled by people from a distant country 2 group of people of the same kind, living together

col·or /ˈkʌlə/ n 1 [C;U] red, blue, green, etc. 2 [C;U] paint or DYE 3 [U] appearance of the skin 4 [U] interesting details of a place, thing, or person — see also OFF COLOR ♦ v 1 vt give color to 2 vi BLUSH 3 vt change; influence **~ed** adj 1 having colors; not just white, or black and white 2 (of people) black or brown **~ful** adj 1 brightly colored 2 exciting **~ing** n [C;U] 1 substance giving color 2 skin color, showing health **~less** adj 1 without color 2 dull **colors** ♦ n [P] 1 official flag 2 something worn as the sign of a club, team, etc. 3 **show one's true colors** show one's real nature or character — see also FLYING COLORS

color-blind /ˈ·· ˌ·/ adj unable to see the difference between colors

color line /ˈ·· ˌ·/ n customs or laws that prevent people of different colors from mixing

co·los·sal /kəˈlɑsəl/ adj extremely large

co·los·sus /kəˈlɑsəs/ n **-suses** or **-si** /-saɪ/ very large person or thing

colt /koʊlt/ n young male horse

col·umn /ˈkɑləm/ n 1 PILLAR 2 something this shape: *a column of figures* | *a marching column of soldiers* 3 a division of a page 4 newspaper article — see also FIFTH COLUMN **~ist** /ˈkɑləmnɪst, -ləmɪst/ n writer of a newspaper column

co·ma /ˈkoʊmə/ n unnatural deep sleep

co·ma·tose /ˈkoʊməˌtoʊs, ˈkɑ-/ adj 1 in a coma 2 inactive and sleepy

comb /koʊm/ n 1 [C] toothed piece of plastic, etc., for tidying the hair or as an ornament 2 [S] act of combing 3 HONEYCOMB ♦ vt 1 tidy (hair) with a comb 2 search (a place) thoroughly

com·bat /ˈkɑmbæt/ n [C;U] struggle; fight **combat** /ˈkɑmbæt, ˈkʌmbæt/ vt **/ɪt/ -t-** or **-tt-**: *to combat inflation* **~ant** /kəmˈbætˌnt, ˈkɑmbəˌtɑnt/ n person who fights **~ive** /kəmˈbætɪv/ adj fond of fighting

com·bi·na·tion /ˌkɑmbəˈneɪʃən/ n 1 [U] combining: *We worked well in combination.* 2 [C] people or things combined 3 [C] numbers needed to open a special lock: *combination lock*

com·bine[1] /kəmˈbaɪn/ vi/t join together; unite

com·bine² /ˈkɒmbaɪn/ n **1** group of people, businesses, etc., acting together **2** also **combine harvester** /ˌ·· ˈ···/ machine that cuts and THRESHEs grain

com·bo /ˈkɒmbəʊ/ n infml **1** combination **2** group of musicians

com·bus·ti·ble /kəmˈbʌstəbəl/ adj burning easily

com·bus·tion /kəmˈbʌstʃən/ n [U] process of burning

come /kʌm/ vi came /keɪm/, **come 1** move towards the speaker; arrive **2** reach a particular point: The water came up to my neck. | We came to an agreement. | The bill comes to $18.50. **3** have a particular position: Monday comes after Sunday. **4** happen: How did you come to be invited? **5** begin: I came to realize the truth. **6** become: come apart | come undone | My dream came true. **7** be offered, produced, etc.: Shoes come in different sizes. | Milk comes from cows. **8** sl have an ORGASM **9** come and go pass or disappear **10** how come? why? **11** to come in the future **comer** n **1** person who appears likely to be successful in their job **2** all comers everyone who comes and tries **coming** n [S] arrival **coming** adj future: the coming winter

come about phr vi happen

come across/upon phr vt find by chance

come across phr vi be effective and well received

come along phr vi **1** improve; advance **2** arrive by chance **3** Come along! Hurry up!

come apart phr vi break into pieces without the need of force

come at phr vt advance towards in a threatening manner

come away phr vi become disconnected without being forced

come back phr vi return

come between phr vt cause trouble between

come by phr vt obtain; receive

come down phr vi **1** fall **2** come down in the world fall to a lower standard of living **3** come down in favor of/on the side of decide to support

come down on phr vt punish

come down to phr vt be no more than: It all comes down to a question of money.

come down with phr vt catch (an infectious illness)

come forward phr vi offer oneself to fill a position, give help to police, etc.

come from phr vt have (a place) as one's home

come in phr vi **1** become fashionable **2** come in handy/useful be useful

come in for phr vt receive (esp. blame)

come in on phr vt take part in

come into phr vt **1** INHERIT **2** begin to be in (a state or activity)

come of phr vt result from: No good will come of it.

come off phr v **1** vi happen as planned **2** vt **come off it!** stop lying or pretending

come on phr vi **1** improve; advance **2** (of weather, illness, etc.) begin **3** Come on! Hurry up!

come on to phr vt do or say something that shows sexual interest in someone **come-on** n something said to show this

come out phr vi **1** appear **2** become known **3** (of color, etc.) be removed **4** end up: How did everything come out? **5** (of a photograph) be successful **6** declare oneself to be HOMOSEXUAL

come out against phr vt declare one's opposition to

come out in phr vt be partly covered by (marks caused by an illness)

come out with phr vt say, esp. suddenly

come over phr v **1** vt (of feelings, etc.) influence suddenly: What's come over you? **2** vi make a short informal visit

come round phr vi **1** also **come to —** regain consciousness **2** change one's opinions **3** happen as usual

come through phr v **1** vi (of news, etc.) become known **2** vi/t SURVIVE

come to phr vt **1** enter the mind of: The idea came to me suddenly. **2** concern: He's ignorant when it comes to politics. **3** COME round

come under phr vt **1** be in (a particular class): Rabbits come under the heading of pets. **2** be governed or controlled by

come up phr vi **1** happen **2** come near

come up against phr vt meet (difficulties)

come up with phr vt think of (a plan, reply, etc.); produce

come·back /ˈkʌmbæk/ *n* return to strength or fame

co·me·di·an /kəˈmidiən/ *n* **1 comedienne** /kəˌmidiˈɛn/ *fem.* — actor who makes people laugh **2** amusing person

come·down /ˈkʌmdaʊn/ *n* fall in importance

com·e·dy /ˈkɑmədi/ *n* **1** [C;U] (type of) funny play, film, etc. **2** [U] amusing quality of something

com·et /ˈkɑmɪt/ *n* bright heavenly body with a tail

come-up·pance /ˌkʌm ˈʌpəns/ *n* punishment or misfortune that is richly deserved

com·fort /ˈkʌmfət/ *n* **1** [U] lack of pain or anxiety; physical satisfaction **2** [C] something that satisfies physical needs **3** [C;U] (person or thing that brings) help for an unhappy person ♦ *vt* make less unhappy

com·for·ta·ble /ˈkʌmftəbəl, ˈkʌmfətəbəl/ *adj* **1** giving comfort: *a comfortable chair* **2** feeling comfort; not suffering or anxious —**bly** *adv*

com·for·ta·bly off /ˌ···· ˈ·/ *adj* fairly rich

com·fort·er /ˈkʌmfətə/ *n* thick QUILTed bed cover

com·fy /ˈkʌmfi/ *adj infml* comfortable

com·ic /ˈkɑmɪk/ *adj* **1** funny **2** of COMEDY ♦ *n* **1 comic book** children's magazine with sets of funny drawings **2** COMEDIAN —**al** *adj* funny **comics** *n* [P] part of a newspaper with funny drawings

comic strip /ˈ·· ˌ·/ *n* set of drawings telling a short funny story

com·ma /ˈkɑmə/ *n* the sign (,)

com·mand /kəˈmænd/ *v* **1** *vt/i* order; direct: *command them to attack* | *your commanding officer* **2** *vt* deserve and get: *command respect* **3** *vt* control (a place) from above ♦ *n* **1** [C] order, instruction **2** [U] control: *take command of the army* **3** [C] division of an army, air force, etc. **4** [S;U] ability to use something: *a good command of spoken English* —**er** *n* **1** naval officer of middle rank **2** any officer in command

com·man·dant /ˈkɑmənˌdænt/ *n* officer in charge of a military organization

com·man·deer /ˌkɑmənˈdɪr/ *vt* seize (private property) for public use

com·mand·ment /kəˈmændmənt/ *n* law given by God

com·man·do /kəˈmændoʊ/ *n* **-dos** or **-does** (member of) a fighting force trained to make quick RAIDS

com·mem·o·rate /kəˈmɛməˌreɪt/ *vt* honor the memory of —**rative** /kəˈmɛmərətɪv/ *adj*: *commemorative stamps* —**ration** /kəˌmɛməˈreɪʃən/ *n* [U]

com·mence /kəˈmɛns/ *vi/t fml* begin; start ~**ment** *n* [U] ceremony when people finish school and are given DIPLOMAS

com·mend /kəˈmɛnd/ *vt fml* **1** praise **2** put into someone's care ~**able** *adj* worthy of praise ~**ation** /ˌkɑmənˈdeɪʃən/ *n* **1** [U] praise **2** [C] official prize

com·men·su·rate /kəˈmɛnsərɪt, -ʃərɪt/ *adj fml* equal; suitable: *a job commensurate with his abilities*

com·ment /ˈkɑmɛnt/ *n* [C;U] written or spoken opinion ♦ *vi/t* make a comment

com·men·ta·ry /ˈkɑmənˌtɛri/ *n* **1** [C] collection of opinions on a book, etc. **2** [C;U] description broadcast during an event: *football commentary*

com·men·tate /ˈkɑmənˌteɪt/ *vi* broadcast a description —**tator** *n*

com·merce /ˈkɑmɝs/ *n* [U] buying and selling; business

com·mer·cial /kəˈmɝʃəl/ *adj* **1** of or used in commerce: *commercial law/vehicles* **2** producing profit **3** (of television or radio) paid for by charges made for advertisements ♦ *n* television or radio advertisement ~**ly** *adv* ~**ize** *vt* make into a matter of profit rather than religion, art, etc.

com·mis·e·rate /kəˈmɪzəˌreɪt/ *v* **commiserate with** *phr vt* express sympathy for —**ration** /kəˌmɪzəˈreɪʃən/ *n* [C;U]

com·mis·sion /kəˈmɪʃən/ *n* **1** [C;U] payment for selling goods, made to the salesman **2** [C] job or duty given to someone **3** [C] group officially appointed to find out and report on facts **4** [C] paper appointing an officer in the armed forces **5 out of commission** not working ♦ *vt* **1** give a COMMISSION (2, 4) to **2** place an order for: *commission a portrait* ~**er** *n* **1** member of a COMMISSION (3) **2** government representative in certain countries

com·mit /kəˈmɪt/ *vt* -**tt**- **1** do (something wrong) **2** send (someone) to prison or a MENTAL hospital **3 commit oneself: a** make oneself responsible **b** give a firm opinion ~**ment** *n* responsibility to do something ~**tal** *n* [C;U] committing someone to prison, etc.

com·mit·tee /kəˈmɪti/ n group chosen to do special business

com·mod·i·ty /kəˈmɑdəti/ n article of trade; product

com·mo·dore /ˈkɑməˌdɔr, -ˌdoʊr/ n 1 naval officer of high rank 2 president of a sailing club

com·mon[1] /ˈkɑmən/ adj 1 ordinary; usual: common salt | the common cold 2 shared in a group: common knowledge ~ly adv

common[2] n 1 area of grassland with no fences which all people are free to use 2 **in common** in shared possession

common de·nom·i·na·tor /ˌ··ˈ····/ n quality or belief shared by all the members of a group

com·mon·er /ˈkɑmənə/ n ordinary person

com·mon·place /ˈkɑmənˌpleɪs/ adj ordinary; dull

common sense /ˌ·· ˈ·◄/ n [U] practical good sense gained from experience

com·mon·wealth /ˈkɑmənˌwɛlθ/ n 1 country which governs itself: Puerto Rico is a commonwealth. 2 official title of certain states, such as Massachusetts

com·mo·tion /kəˈmoʊʃən/ n [S;U] noisy confusion

com·mu·nal /kəˈmyunl, ˈkɑmyənl/ adj shared by a group

com·mune[1] /ˈkɑmyun, kəˈmyun/ n 1 group who live and work together and share their possessions 2 local government division in France, etc.

com·mune[2] /kəˈmyun/ vi exchange thoughts, ideas or feelings: commune with nature

com·mu·ni·ca·ble /kəˈmyunɪkəbəl/ adj fml (esp. of ideas, thoughts, illnesses, etc.) that can be (easily) passed from one person to another

com·mu·ni·cate /kəˈmyunəˌkeɪt/ v 1 vi/t make (opinions, etc.) known 2 vt pass on (a disease) 3 vi (of rooms) be connected –**cator** n person who communicates –**cation** /kəˌmyunəˈkeɪʃən/ n 1 [U] communicating 2 [C] fml message, letter, etc. –**cations** n [P] ways of traveling or sending messages

com·mu·ni·ca·tive /kəˈmyunɪkətɪv, -ˌkeɪtɪv/ adj willing to give information

com·mu·nion /kəˈmyunyən/ n [U] fml sharing of beliefs, feelings, etc. 2 (cap.) Christian ceremony of sharing bread and wine

com·mu·ni·qué /kəˌmyunəˈkeɪ, kəˈmyunəˌkeɪ/ n official report

com·mu·nism /ˈkɑmyəˌnɪzəm/ n [U] 1 social and political system by which the government owns the means of production 2 (cap.) system of government on this principle with only one political party –**nist** n, adj

com·mu·ni·ty /kəˈmyunəti/ n 1 [C] group of people with shared interests 2 [S] people in general; the public 3 [U] shared possession

community col·lege /ˌ···· ˈ··/ n college that people go to for 2 years to learn a skill or prepare for a university

com·mute /kəˈmyut/ v 1 vi travel regularly between home and work 2 vt make (a punishment) less severe –**muter** n person who commutes to work

com·pact[1] /kəmˈpækt, ˈkɑmpækt/ adj neatly packed into a small space

com·pact[2] /ˈkɑmpækt/ n 1 container for face powder 2 small car

compact disc /ˌkɑmpækt ˈdɪsk/ also **CD** — n small circular piece of plastic on which sound, information, etc., can be stored

com·pan·ion /kəmˈpænyən/ n person who spends time with another ~**able** adj friendly ~**ship** n [U] friendly company

com·pa·ny /ˈkʌmpəni/ n 1 [C] business; people working together: a bus/theater company 2 [C] group of about 120 soldiers 3 [U] a presence of companions: I was grateful for her company. b companions, esp. guests 4 **be good/bad company** be a good/bad person to be with 5 **part company (with/from)** finish a relationship

com·pa·ra·ble /ˈkɑmpərəbəl/ adj similar

com·par·a·tive /kəmˈpærətɪv/ adj 1 gram expressing an increase in quality or quantity: "Worse" is the comparative form of "bad." 2 measured or judged by a comparison that is not stated: She's a comparative newcomer to television. (= has not been on television often) 3 making a comparison: a comparative study of European languages ♦ n gram comparative form of an adjective or adverb ~**ly** adv

com·pare /kəmˈpɛr/ v 1 vt judge (one thing) against another thing, to show likeness or difference 2 vt show the likeness between (2 things) 3 vi be worthy of comparison

com·pa·ri·son /kəm'pærəsən/ n 1 [C;U] (statement of) comparing: *Boston is small in comparison with New York.* 2 [U] likeness: *There's no comparison between them.*

com·part·ment /kəm'part˺mənt/ n separate division of a space; small room in a railroad car, etc.

com·pass /'kʌmpəs/ n 1 instrument for showing direction, with a needle that points to the north 2 *fml* range; limit: *outside the compass of this department* also **pair of compasses** instrument for drawing circles

com·pas·sion /kəm'pæʃən/ n [U] sympathy; pity **~ate** adj **~ately** adv

com·pat·i·ble /kəm'pætəbəl/ adj able to exist or work together **–bly** adv **–bility** /kəm,pætə'bilət̬i/ n [U]

com·pat·ri·ot /kəm'peɪtriət/ n person of the same nationality as another

com·pel /kəm'pel/ vt **-ll-** force to do something **~ling** adj important; urgent: *compelling reasons*

com·pen·sate /'kampən,seɪt/ vt/i pay, or give something, to balance a loss **–sation** /,kampən'seɪʃən/ n [S;U] something given to compensate: *unemployment compensation* **–satory** /kəm'pɛnsə,tɔri, -,touri/ adj

com·pete /kəm'pit/ vi try to win in a competition

com·pe·tence /'kampət̬əns/ n [U] ability to do what is needed **–tent** adj **–tently** adv

com·pe·ti·tion /,kampə'tɪʃən/ n 1 [C] test of strength, skill, etc. 2 [U] trying to win: *tough competition between them* 3 [U] person or people against whom one competes

com·pet·i·tive /kəm'pɛt̬ət̬ɪv/ adj 1 decided by competition 2 liking to compete

com·pet·i·tor /kəm'pɛt̬ət̬ə/ n person, firm, etc., that competes

com·pile /kəm'paɪl/ vt make (a book, etc.) from collected facts **–piler** /-ə/ n **–pilation** /,kampə'leɪʃən/ n 1 [U] act of compiling 2 [C] something compiled

com·pla·cen·cy /kəm'pleɪsənsi/ n [U] unreasonable feeling of satisfaction **–cent** adj **–cently** adv

com·plain /kəm'pleɪn/ vi/t say that one is unhappy: *to complain that the room is too hot*

com·plaint /kəm'pleɪnt/ n 1 [C;U] (statement of) complaining 2 [C] illness: *a liver complaint*

com·ple·ment /'kampləmənt/ n 1 something that completes 2 full number needed 3 *gram* noun or adjective after a verb such as 'be' or 'become' ♦ /-,mɛnt/ vt make complete or perfect **~ary** /,kamplə-'mɛntəri/ adj supplying what is needed

com·plete /kəm'plit/ adj 1 having all necessary parts; whole 2 finished; ended 3 total; thorough: *complete silence* ♦ vt 1 make whole 2 finish **~ly** adv in every way **–pletion** /-'pliʃən/ n

com·plex¹ /kəm'plɛks, kam-, 'kamplɛks/ adj 1 difficult to understand 2 made of many connected parts **~ity** /kəm-'plɛksət̬i/ n [C;U]

com·plex² /'kamplɛks/ n 1 system of many connected parts: *new sports complex* 2 group of unconscious fears or feelings

com·plex·ion /kəm'plɛkʃən/ n 1 natural appearance of the skin: *good/dark complexion* 2 general character of a situation

com·pli·ance /kəm'plaɪəns/ n [U] *fml* complying (COMPLY) **–ant** adj

com·pli·cate /'kamplə,keɪt/ vt make difficult to deal with **–cated** adj COMPLEX **–cation** /,kamplə'keɪʃən/ n added difficulty

com·plic·i·ty /kəm'plɪsət̬i/ n [U] *fml* taking part with someone else in a crime

com·pli·ment¹ /'kampləmənt/ n expression of praise **compliments** n [P] good wishes

com·pli·ment² /'kamplə,mɛnt/ vt express admiration of **~ary** /,kamplə'mɛntəri, -'mɛntri/ adj 1 expressing admiration 2 given free: *complimentary tickets*

com·ply /kəm'plaɪ/ vi *fml* agree to do something; obey

com·po·nent /kəm'pounənt/ n any part of a whole machine or system

com·pose /kəm'pouz/ v 1 vi/t write (music, poetry, etc.) 2 vt get (oneself) under control 3 **be composed of** consist of **–posed** adj calm **–poser** n writer of music

com·pos·ite /kəm'pazɪt, kam-/ adj, n (something) made up of different parts

com·po·si·tion /,kampə'zɪʃən/ n 1 [U] act of writing music, poetry, etc. 2 [C] something written 3 [U] mixture or arrangement of parts

com·post /'kɒmpoʊst/ *n* [U] decayed plant matter, used to improve the soil

com·po·sure /kəm'poʊʒə/ *n* [U] calmness

com·pound¹ /'kɒmpaʊnd/ *adj* consisting of 2 or more parts ♦ *n*: *chemical compounds*

com·pound² /kəm'paʊnd/ *vt* **1** make by combining parts **2** make worse: *compound an error*

com·pound³ /'kɒmpaʊnd/ *n* enclosed area containing buildings

com·pre·hend /ˌkɒmprɪ'hend/ *vt fml* **1** understand **2** include

com·pre·hen·sion /ˌkɒmprɪ'henʃən/ *n* [U] *fml* power of understanding –**sible** /-səbəl/ *adj* understandable –**sibly** *adv*

com·pre·hen·sive /ˌkɒmprɪ'hensɪv◂/ *adj* thorough; including a lot

com·press /kəm'pres/ *vt* **1** force into less space **2** put (ideas, etc.) into fewer words **~ion** /-'preʃən/ *n* [U]

com·prise /kəm'praɪz/ *v* consist of; have as parts

com·pro·mise /'kɒmprəˌmaɪz/ *n* [C;U] agreement reached by each side agreeing to some of the other side's demands ♦ *v* **1** *vi* make a compromise **2** *vt* put into a dishonorable position

comp·trol·ler /kən'troʊlə/ *n* (state government) official who looks after income and spending

com·pul·sion /kəm'pʌlʃən/ *n* **1** [U] force that makes a person do something **2** [C] strong desire –**sive** /-sɪv/ *adj* caused by a compulsion: *compulsive drinking*

com·pul·so·ry /kəm'pʌlsəri/ *adj* that must be done by law, etc. –**rily** *adv*

com·punc·tion /kəm'pʌŋkʃən/ *n* [U] feeling of guilt

com·pute /kəm'pyut/ *vt* calculate

com·put·er /kəm'pyutə/ *n* ELECTRONIC machine that stores, recalls, and deals with information **~ize** *vt* use or begin to use a computer to control (an operation) **~ization** /kəmˌpyutərə'zeɪʃən/ *n* [U]

com·rade /'kɒmræd/ *n* **1** *fml* close companion **2** fellow member of a union or political party **3** communist (COMMU-NISM) **~ship** *n* [U]

con /kɒn/ *vt* -**nn**- trick (a trusting person) ♦ *n infml for* CON GAME

con·cave /ˌkɒn'keɪv◂/ *adj* curved inwards

con·ceal /kən'sil/ *vt* hide **~ment** *n* [U]

con·cede /kən'sid/ *vt* **1** admit as true **2** give as a right **3** end a game or match by admitting defeat

con·ceit /kən'sit/ *n* [U] too high an opinion of oneself **~ed** *adj*

con·ceive /kən'siv/ *v* **1** *vt* think of; imagine **2** *vi/t* become PREGNANT –**ceivable** *adj* imaginable; possible –**ceivably** *adv*

con·cen·trate /'kɒnsənˌtreɪt/ *v* **1** *vi* direct all one's attention: *concentrate on the problem* **2** *vt/i* bring or come together in one place **3** *vt* make (a liquid) stronger ♦ *n* [C;U] concentrated liquid

con·cen·tra·tion /ˌkɒnsən'treɪʃən/ *n* **1** [U] close attention **2** [C] close gathering

concentration camp /.ˈ.. ˌ./ *n* large prison for political prisoners

con·cen·tric /kən'sentrɪk/ *adj* (of circles) having the same center

con·cept /'kɒnsept/ *n* general idea; NOTION **~ual** /kən'septʃuəl/ *adj* of or based on (the formation of) concepts **~ualize** *vi/t* form a concept (of)

con·cep·tion /kən'sepʃən/ *n* **1** [C;U] understanding **2** [U] forming of an idea **3** [C;U] *fml* starting of a new life by the union of a male and female sex cell

con·cern /kən'sən/ *vt* **1** be about (a subject) **2** be of importance to: *problems which concern all of us* **3** worry: *I'm concerned about her.* ♦ *n* **1** [C] something that matters to someone **2** [U] worry: *no cause for concern* **3** [C] business; company: *a going concern* **~ing** *prep* about

con·cert /'kɒnsət/ *n* **1** musical performance **2 in concert: a** working together **b** playing at a concert

con·cert·ed /kən'sətɪd/ *adj* done together by agreement: *a concerted effort*

con·cer·ti·na /ˌkɒnsə'tinə/ *n* small ACCORDION ♦ *vi* (of a vehicle) become pressed together as the result of a crash

con·cer·to /kən'tʃertoʊ/ *n* -**tos** piece of music for one instrument supported by an ORCHESTRA

con·ces·sion /kən'seʃən/ *n* **1** something CONCEDEd after a disagreement **2** official permission to do something **3** also **concession stand** space for a small business within a larger one **~ary** given as a concession **~aire** /kənˌseʃə'ner/ *n* **-er** *n* holder of a CONCESSION (3)

con·cierge /ˌkɒnˈsyɛɾʒ, koʊn-/ n hotel official who looks after guests' needs

con·cil·i·ate /kənˈsɪlˌeɪt/ vt remove the anger of **-ation** /kənˌsɪliˈeɪʃən/ n [U] **-atory** /kənˈsɪliəˌtɔri, -ˌtoʊri/ adj trying to conciliate

con·cise /kənˈsaɪs/ adj expressing a lot in a few words **~ly** adv **~ness** n [U]

con·clude /kənˈklud/ v fml 1 vt/i bring or come to an end 2 vt come to believe 3 vt settle: *conclude an agreement*

con·clu·sion /kənˈkluʒən/ n 1 decision; settlement 2 end **-sive** /-sɪv, -zɪv/ adj ending all doubt: *conclusive proof*

con·coct /kənˈkɑkt, kɑn-/ vt 1 make by mixing parts 2 invent (something false) **~ion** /-ˈkɑkʃən/ n mixture

con·cord /ˈkɑŋkɔrd/ n [U] friendly agreement

con·course /ˈkɑŋkɔrs, -koʊrs/ n place where crowds can gather

con·crete /ˈkɑnˌkrit, ˈkɑŋkrit/ adj 1 real or solid; not ABSTRACT: *A car is a concrete object.* 2 clear; particular: *concrete proposals* ♦ n /ˈkɑŋkrit/ [U] building material made of sand, cement, etc. ♦ vt cover (a path, wall, etc.) with concrete

con·cur /kənˈkɚ/ vi -rr- fml 1 agree 2 happen at the same time **~rence** /kənˈkɚəns, -ˈkar-/ n [C;U] **~rent** adj **~rently** adv

con·cus·sion /kənˈkʌʃən/ n damage to the brain by a heavy blow

con·demn /kənˈdɛm/ vt 1 express disapproval of 2 state the punishment for: *condemn him to death* | (fig.) *She was condemned to life in a wheelchair.* 3 declare (a building, etc.) unfit for use **~ation** /ˌkɑndɛmˈneɪʃən, -dəm-/ n [C;U]

con·dense /kənˈdɛns/ vt/i 1 make (a gas) liquid 2 make (a liquid) thicker 3 put into fewer words **-denser** n **-densation** /ˌkɑndɛnˈseɪʃən, -dən-/ n [U] 1 act of condensing 2 drops of water formed when steam condenses

con·de·scend /ˌkɑndɪˈsɛnd/ vi 1 do something unsuited to one's social or professional position 2 derog behave as though one is grander than others **-scension** /-ˈsɛnʃən/ n [U]

con·di·ment /ˈkɑndəmənt/ n fml something used for giving taste to food

con·di·tion¹ /kənˈdɪʃən/ n 1 [U] state; way of being: *a car in poor condition* 2 [C] something necessary for something else: *I'll*

come on condition that John comes too. 3 [C] illness 4 **in/out of condition** thoroughly fit/not fit 5 **on no condition** never **conditions** n [P] surrounding facts: *better working conditions* **-tional** adj depending on conditions **-tionally** adv

condition² vt 1 control; DETERMINE 2 train to behave in a certain way **~ing** n [U]

con·di·tion·er /kənˈdɪʃənɚ/ n [C;U] special liquid put on hair after washing to make it softer

con·do /ˈkɑndoʊ/ n condos infml CONDOMINIUM

con·do·lence /kənˈdoʊləns/ n [C;U] expression of sympathy

con·dom /ˈkɑndəm, ˈkʌn-/ n usu. rubber covering worn over the male sex organ during SEXUAL INTERCOURSE, as a means of birth control and as a protection against disease

con·do·min·i·um /ˌkɑndəˈmɪniəm/ also **con·do** — n apartment which is owned by the people living in it

con·done /kənˈdoʊn/ vt forgive (wrong behavior)

con·du·cive /kənˈdusɪv/ adj fml likely to produce: *conducive to health*

con·duct¹ /kənˈdʌkt/ v 1 vt direct; lead 2 vt/i direct the playing of (musicians) 3 vt be the path for (electricity, etc.) 4 **conduct oneself** fml behave **~ive** adj able to conduct electricity, etc. **~ion** /-ˈdʌkʃən/ n [U] passage of electricity, etc.

con·duct² /ˈkɑndʌkt, -dəkt/ n [U] 1 fml behavior 2 management of something

con·duc·tor /kənˈdʌktɚ/ n 1 person who conducts musicians 2 person who collects payments on a train 3 substance that conducts electricity, etc.

con·duit /ˈkɑnduət/ n pipe for water, gas, etc.

cone /koʊn/ n 1 hollow or solid object with a round base and pointed top 2 fruit of a PINE or FIR tree

con·fec·tion·er·y /kənˈfɛkʃənɛri/ n [U] candies, cakes, etc. **~er** n person who sells these

con·fed·e·ra·cy /kənˈfɛdərəsi/ also **con·fed·e·ra·tion** /kənˌfɛdəˈreɪʃən/ — n 1 union of people, parties, or states 2 **the Confederacy** — see CONFEDERATE STATES

con·fed·e·rate /kənˈfɛdərɪt/ n 1 ACCOMPLICE 2 member of a confederacy

Confederate states /ˌ··· ˈ·/ n the 11 southern states that fought against the North in the CIVIL WAR

con·fer /kən'fɜː/ v –rr– fml 1 vi talk together 2 vt give (a title, etc.) to

con·fe·rence /'kɒnfərəns/ n meeting for the exchange of ideas

con·fess /kən'fes/ vi/t admit (one's faults) ~**or** n priest who hears one's confession –**ion** /-'feʃən/ n [C;U] telling of one's faults

con·fet·ti /kən'feti/ n [U] bits of colored paper thrown at parties

con·fi·dant /'kɒnfɪˌdænt, -ˌdɑnt, ˌkɒnfə'dænt, -'dɑnt/ **confidante** (same pronunciation) fem. — n person to whom one tells secrets

con·fide /kən'faɪd/ vt tell (a secret) trustingly
confide in phr vt talk freely to

con·fi·dence /'kɒnfədəns/ n 1 [U] faith; trust 2 [U] belief in one's own ability 3 [C] something told secretly 4 **in confidence** secretly –**dent** adj sure

con·fi·den·tial /ˌkɒnfə'denʃəl◂/ adj 1 told in secret 2 trusted with secrets: confidential secretary ~**ly** adv

con·fig·u·ra·tion /kənˌfɪgjə'reɪʃən/ n shape; arrangement

con·fine[1] /kən'faɪn/ vt 1 keep shut in: confined to bed 2 keep within the limits ~**ment** n 1 [U] being shut up 2 [C;U] giving birth to a child: her 3rd confinement

con·fine[2] /'kɒnfaɪn/ n [P] limits

con·firm /kən'fɜːm/ vt 1 support; give proof of: confirm a telephone message in writing 2 admit (a person) to membership of the Christian church ~**ed** adj firmly settled; unlikely to change: confirmed bachelor ~**ation** /ˌkɒnfə'meɪʃən/ n 1 proof 2 religious service in which someone is confirmed

con·fis·cate /'kɒnfəˌskeɪt/ vt seize (private property) officially, without payment –**cation** /ˌkɒnfə'skeɪʃən/ n [C;U]

con·flict[1] /'kɒnflɪkt/ n 1 disagreement; argument 2 fml war

con·flict[2] /kən'flɪkt/ vi be in opposition

con·form /kən'fɔːm/ vi obey established rules or customs ~**ist** n person who conforms ~**ity** n [U]

con·found /kən'faʊnd, kɒn-/ vt confuse and surprise

con·front /kən'frʌnt/ vt face; meet: confront problems –**ation** /ˌkɒnfrən'teɪʃən/ n [C;U] angry opposition

con·fuse /kən'fjuːz/ vt 1 cause to be mixed up in the mind: I'm confused. 2 be unable to tell the difference between: to confuse Jack and/with Paul 3 make less clear: confusing the issue –**fusion** /-'fjuːʒən/ n [U]

con·fus·ing /kən'fjuːzɪŋ/ adj difficult to understand because there is no clear order or pattern

con·fute /kən'fjuːt/ vt prove to be wrong

con·game /'kɒnˌgeɪm/ n trick played in order to cheat a trusting person of money

con·geal /kən'dʒiːl/ vi/t become solid: congealed blood

con·ge·nial /kən'dʒiːniəl/ adj pleasant; in agreement with one's tastes ~**ly** adv

con·gen·i·tal /kən'dʒenətl/ adj (of diseases) existing from one's birth

con·ges·ted /kən'dʒestɪd/ adj too full; blocked –**tion** /-'dʒestʃən/ n [U]

con·glom·e·rate /kən'glɒmərɪt/ n large business firm producing many kinds of goods –**ration** /kənˌglɒmə'reɪʃən/ n

con·grat·u·late /kən'grætʃəˌleɪt/ vt express pleasure at (someone's) success or good luck: I congratulated them on the birth of their daughter. –**lations** /kənˌgrætʃə'leɪʃənz/ interj, n [P] I congratulate you –**latory** /kən'grætʃələˌtɔri, -ˌtoʊri/ adj

con·gre·gate /'kɒŋgrəˌgeɪt/ vi gather together –**gation** /ˌkɒŋgrə'geɪʃən/ n group of people gathered together in church

con·gress /'kɒŋgrɪs/ n 1 (cap.) highest of the US bodies which make laws, consisting of the Senate and the House of Representatives: a congressman 2 formal meeting to exchange information ~**ional** /kən'greʃənəl/ adj

con·i·cal /'kɒnɪkəl/ adj like a CONE in shape

co·ni·fer /'kɒnəfə, 'koʊ-/ n tree that bears cones (CONE (2))

con·jec·ture /kən'dʒektʃə/ vi/t fml guess
♦ n [C;U] –**tural** adj

con·ju·gal /'kɒndʒəgəl/ adj fml of marriage

con·ju·gate /'kɒndʒəˌgeɪt/ vt gram give the forms of (a verb) –**gation** /ˌkɒndʒə'geɪʃən/ n class of verbs conjugated in the same way

con·junc·tion /kən'dʒʌŋkʃən/ n 1 gram word such as 'but' or 'while' 2 **in conjunction with** in combination with

con·junc·ti·vi·tis /kənˌdʒʌŋktɪ'vaɪtɪs/ n painful eye disease

con·jure /ˈkʌndʒə/ v **1** vi do clever tricks that seem magical **2** vt cause to appear as if by magic: (fig.) *conjure up memories of the past*

conk /kʌŋk/ vi sl **conk out 1** break or fail (esp. of a machine) **2** lose consciousness **3** die

con·nect /kəˈnekt/ v **1** vt/i join together: *connect 2 pipes* **2** vt think of as related

con·nec·tion /kəˈnekʃən/ n **1** [C;U] being connected; relationship **2** [C] plane, train, etc., planned to take passengers arriving by another one **3** [C] person connected to others by family or business **4 in connection with** fml with regard to

con·nive /kəˈnaɪv/ v **connive at** phr vt make no attempt to stop (something wrong) **–nivance** n [U]

con·nois·seur /ˌkɒnəˈsə, -ˈsɜr/ n person with special knowledge of art, wine, etc.

con·note /kəˈnəʊt/ vt fml (of a word) suggest something more than its ordinary meaning **–notation** /ˌkɒnəˈteɪʃən/ n: *"Skinny" has bad connotations.*

con·quer /ˈkɒŋkə/ vt **1** defeat (enemies): (fig.) *conquer one's fear* **2** take (a place) by force: *a conquered city* **–or** n

con·quest /ˈkɒŋkwest/ n **1** [U] conquering **2** [C] something conquered, esp. land gained in war

con·science /ˈkɒnʃəns/ n **1** [C;U] knowledge of right and wrong: *to have a guilty conscience* **2 on one's conscience** causing one to feel guilty

con·sci·en·tious /ˌkɒnʃiˈenʃəs◄/ adj careful and honest: *conscientious work/workers* **~ly** adv **~ness** n [U]

conscientious ob·jec·tor /ˌ···· ··ˈ··/ n person who refuses to serve in the armed forces because of moral or religious beliefs

con·scious /ˈkɒnʃəs/ adj **1** awake and able to think **2** knowing; AWARE **3** intentional: *conscious effort* **~ly** adv **~ness** n [S;U]

con·script¹ /kənˈskrɪpt/ vt make someone serve in the armed forces **~ion** /kənˈskrɪpʃən/ n [U] practice of conscripting people

con·script² /ˈkɒnskrɪpt/ n conscripted person

con·se·crate /ˈkɒnsəˌkreɪt/ vt **1** declare as holy: *consecrated wine* **2** set apart solemnly for a particular purpose: *con-* secrate one's life to helping the poor **–cration** /ˌkɒnsəˈkreɪʃən/ n [U]

con·sec·u·tive /kənˈsekjʊtɪv/ adj following in unbroken order **~ly** adv

con·sen·sus /kənˈsensəs/ n general agreement

con·sent /kənˈsent/ vi give permission ♦ n [U] permission

con·se·quence /ˈkɒnsəkwens, -kwəns/ n **1** [C] result **2** [U] fml importance: *It's of no consequence to me.*

con·se·quent /ˈkɒnsəkwent, -kwənt/ adj fml following as a result **~ly** adv

con·se·quen·tial /ˌkɒnsəˈkwenʃəl◄/ adj fml **1** consequent **2** important

con·ser·va·tion /ˌkɒnsəˈveɪʃən/ n [U] **1** protection of animals, plants, ancient buildings, etc. **2** careful use of a limited supply, to prevent waste **~ist** n **~ism** n [U]

con·ser·va·tive /kənˈsɜvətɪv/ adj **1** not liking change **2** rather low: *a conservative estimate* **3** of a political party opposed to sudden change ♦ n person who dislikes change **~ly** adv **–tism** n [U]

con·ser·va·to·ry /kənˈsɜvəˌtɔri, -ˌtoʊri/ n **1** GREENHOUSE connected to another building **2** school of music or acting

con·serve¹ /kənˈsɜv/ vt use carefully; preserve: *conserve one's energy*

con·serve² /ˈkɒnsɜv/ n fml fruit preserved by cooking in sugar; JAM

con·sid·er /kənˈsɪdə/ v **1** vi/t think about **2** vt take into account; remember: *you have to consider your wife* **3** vt believe to be: *consider him suitable* **~ed** adj reached after careful thought **~ing** prep if one takes into account: *She did well, considering her age.*

con·sid·er·a·ble /kənˈsɪdərəbəl/ adj fairly large **–bly** adv much

con·sid·er·ate /kənˈsɪdərɪt/ adj kind and thoughtful **~ly** adv

con·sid·er·a·tion /kənˌsɪdəˈreɪʃən/ n **1** [U] thoughtful attention **2** [C] fact to be remembered when deciding something **3** [C] payment; reward **4 take something into consideration** remember when making a judgment

con·sign /kənˈsaɪn/ vt **1** send (goods) for sale **2** fml give into someone's care **~ment** n **1** [C] goods consigned **2** [U] act of consigning

con·sist /kənˈsɪst/ v

consist in phr vt fml have as a base; depend on

consist of *phr vt* be made up of

con·sis·ten·cy /kən'sıstənsi/ *n* 1 [U] state of always behaving in the same way 2 [C] degree of thickness of a liquid –**tent** *adj* 1 not changing 2 in agreement –**tently** *adv*

con·sole[1] /kən'sool/ *vt* make less unhappy –**solation** /ˌkɑnsə'leıʃən/ *n* [C;U] (person or thing giving) comfort

con·sole[2] /'kɑnsool/ *n* surface containing the controls for a machine or system

con·sol·i·date /kən'sɑlədeıt/ *vi/t* 1 (cause to) become stronger 2 combine into one –**dation** /ˌkɑnsɑlə'deıʃən/ *n*

con·so·nant[1] /'kɑnsənənt/ *n* (letter representing) a speech sound such as b, m, s, made by stopping or RESTRICT*ing* the flow of air from the lungs

consonant[2] *adj fml* in agreement

con·sort[1] /'kɑnsort/ *n* wife or husband of a ruler

con·sort[2] /kən'sort/ *v* **consort with** *phr vi* spend time in company

con·sor·ti·um /kən'sortiəm, -'sortiəm/ *n* -**tiums** *or* -**tia** /-ʃiə, -tiə/ combination of a number of companies, banks, etc.

con·spic·u·ous /kən'spıkyuəs/ *adj* easily seen; noticeable ~**ly** *adv*

con·spir·a·cy /kən'spırəsi/ *n* [C;U] (plan made by) conspiring

con·spir·a·tor /kən'spırətə/ *n* person who conspires

con·spire /kən'spaıə/ *vi* 1 plan something bad together secretly 2 (of events) combine in a bad way

con·stant /'kɑnstənt/ *adj* 1 happening all the time 2 unchanging: *a constant speed* 3 continuous 4 loyal ♦ *n* something that never varies ~**ly** *adv* –**stancy** *n* [U] 1 freedom from change 2 *fml* loyalty

con·stel·la·tion /ˌkɑnstə'leıʃən/ *n* named group of stars

con·ster·na·tion /ˌkɑnstə'neıʃən/ *n* [U] great shock and fear

con·sti·pa·tion /ˌkɑnstə'peıʃən/ *n* [U] being unable to empty the bowels properly –**ted** /'kɑnstəˌpeıtɪd/ *adj*

con·stit·u·en·cy /kən'stıtʃuənsi/ *n* (voters in) an area that elects a representative

con·stit·u·ent /kən'stıtʃuənt/ *n* 1 necessary part: *the constituents of cement* 2 voter ♦ *adj* helping to make a whole

con·sti·tute /'kɑnstəˌtut/ *vt* 1 form when added together 2 establish

con·sti·tu·tion /ˌkɑnstə'tuʃən/ *n* 1 laws and principles by which a country is governed 2 (*cap.*) **the Constitution** of the United States 3 person's physical condition 4 structure of something ~**al** *adj* 1 by or of a political constitution 2 in agreement with the Constitution 3 of a person's constitution ~**ally** *adv*

con·strain /kən'streın/ *vt fml* force (someone) to do something

con·straint /kən'streınt/ *n* [C;U] something that limits freedom: *acted under constraint*

con·strict /kən'strıkt/ *vt* make narrower or tighter ~**ion** /-'strıkʃən/ *n* [C;U]

con·struct /kən'strʌkt/ *vt* make out of parts; build

con·struc·tion /kən'strʌkʃən/ *n* 1 [U] building; the building industry 2 [C] something built 3 [P] road repairing 4 [C] meaning given to something as of a law –**tive** /-tıv/ *adj* helpful: *constructive suggestions*

construction pa·per /·'·· ˌ·'·/ *n* [U] thick colored paper

con·strue /kən'stru/ *vt* place a certain meaning on

con·sul /'kɑnsəl/ *n* representative of a government in a foreign city ~**ar** *adj* ~**ate** /-lıt/ *n* consul's office

con·sult /kən'sʌlt/ *vt* go to (a person, book, etc.) for advice ~**ation** /ˌkɑnsəl'teıʃən/ *n* [C;U]

con·sul·tant /kən'sʌltənt/ *n* person who gives professional advice –**tancy** *n* –**tative** /-tətıv/ *adj* giving advice

con·sume /kən'sum/ *vt fml* 1 eat or drink 2 use up; destroy –**suming** *adj* main: *a consuming interest in trains* –**sumer** *n* person who buys goods

con·sum·mate[1] /kən'sʌmıt, 'kɑnsə-/ *adj* perfect; complete

con·sum·mate[2] /'kɑnsəˌmeıt/ *vt fml* 1 complete (a marriage) by having sex 2 make perfect –**mation** /ˌkɑnsə'meıʃən/ *n* [C;U]

con·sump·tion /kən'sʌmpʃən/ *n* 1 [S;U] consuming; amount consumed 2 [U] TUBERCULOSIS –**tive** /-tıv/ *adj* suffering from TUBERCULOSIS

con·tact /'kɑntækt/ *n* 1 [U] meeting; relationship: *Have you been in contact with the disease?* 2 [C] person one knows who can help one: *some useful contacts in*

Spain **3** [C] electrical part that touches another to carry electric current ♦ *vt* reach (someone) by telephone, etc.

contact lens /ˈ‥ ˌ‥/ *n* plastic LENS (1) shaped to fit over the eye to improve eyesight

con·ta·gious /kənˈteɪdʒəs/ *adj* (of disease) spreading by touch

con·tain /kənˈteɪn/ *v* **1** have within itself: *Beer contains alcohol.* **2** keep under control: *I can't contain myself.*

con·tain·er /kənˈteɪnə/ *n* **1** box, bottle, etc., used to contain something **2** large metal box in which goods are packed to be carried on ships, etc.

con·tam·i·nate /kənˈtæməˌneɪt/ *vt* make impure or dirty: *contaminated water* –**nation** /kənˌtæməˈneɪʃən/ *n* [U]

con·tem·plate /ˈkɒntəmˌpleɪt/ *vt* **1** think about; consider as possible **2** look solemnly at –**plation** /ˌkɒntəmˈpleɪʃən/ *n* [U] deep thought –**plative** /kənˈtemplətɪv, ˈkɒntəmpleɪtɪv/ *adj*

con·tem·po·ra·ry /kənˈtempəˌreri/ *adj* **1** modern; of the present **2** of the same time ♦ *n* person of the same age, or living at the same time

con·tempt /kənˈtempt/ *n* [U] complete lack of respect –**ible** *adj* deserving contempt ~**uous** *adj* showing contempt

contempt of court /‥ˌ‥ ˈ‥/ *n* [U] offense of disobeying a judge in court

con·tend /kənˈtend/ *v* **1** *vi* compete; struggle **2** *vt fml* claim; declare ~**er** *n* competitor

con·tent[1] /kənˈtent/ *adj* satisfied; happy ♦ *vt* make happy ~**ed** *adj* quietly happy ~**edly** *adv* ~**ment** *n* [U] quiet happiness

con·tent[2] /ˈkɒntent/ *n* **1** [U] subject matter of a book **2** [S] amount contained in something: *a high fat content* **contents** *n* [P] what something contains

con·ten·tion /kənˈtenʃən/ *n* **1** [C] claim; point of view **2** [U] struggle –**tious** *adj* **1** causing argument **2** quarrelsome

con·test[1] /ˈkɒntest/ *n* struggle; competition

con·test[2] /kənˈtest, ˈkɒntest/ *vt fml* **1** compete for **2** argue about the rightness of ~**ant** *n* competitor

con·text /ˈkɒntekst/ *n* **1** words that surround a word or phrase **2** surrounding conditions

con·ti·nent[1] /ˈkɒntənənt, ˈkɒntˌn-ənt/ *n* **1** [C] large land mass; Europe, Asia, etc. **2** [*the*] (*cap.*) Europe without Britain ~**al** /ˌkɒntəˈnentl◂/ *adj* (*cap.*) of the 13 American **colonies**: *Continental Congress*

con·ti·nen·tal break·fast /ˌ‥‥ ˈ‥/ *n* light breakfast usu. of bread, butter, JAM and coffee

con·tin·gen·cy /kənˈtɪndʒənsi/ *n* possible event that might cause problems

con·tin·gent[1] /kənˈtɪndʒənt/ *adj* **1** dependent on something uncertain **2** happening by chance

contingent[2] *n* **1** part of a larger force of soldiers, ships, etc. **2** part of a larger gathering of people

con·tin·u·al /kənˈtɪnyuəl/ *adj* regular; frequent ~**ly** *adv*

con·tin·ue /kənˈtɪnyu/ *vi/t* **1** go on doing something **2** start again after stopping –**uation** /kənˌtɪnyuˈeɪʃən/ *n* **1** [U] act of continuing **2** [C] something which continues from something else

con·ti·nu·i·ty /ˌkɒntəˈnuəti/ *n* [U] uninterrupted connection

con·tin·u·ous /kənˈtɪnyuəs/ *adj* continuing unbroken: *The brain needs a continuous supply of blood.* ~**ly** *adv*

con·tort /kənˈtɔrt/ *vt* twist out of shape ~**ion** /-ˈtɔrʃən/ *n* [C;U]

con·tour /ˈkɒntʊr/ *n* **1** shape of the edges of something, such as a coast **2** line on a map showing the edges of areas above a certain height

con·tra·band /ˈkɒntrəˌbænd/ *n* goods that cannot be brought legally into a country

con·tra·cep·tion /ˌkɒntrəˈsepʃən/ *n* [U] (methods for) preventing sex from resulting in pregnancy (PREGNANT) –**tive** /-ˈseptɪv◂/ *n*, *adj* (drug, etc.) used for contraception

con·tract[1] /ˈkɒntrækt/ *n* formal agreement to do something ~**ual** /kənˈtræktʃuəl/ *adj*

con·tract[2] /kənˈtrækt/ *v* **1** *vi/t* arrange by formal agreement **2** *vi/t* (cause to) become smaller **3** *vt fml* get (a disease) ~**ion** /-ˈtrækʃən/ *n* **1** [U] process of getting smaller **2** [C] shortened form of a word **3** [C] strong tightening of a muscle

con·trac·tor /ˈkɒntræktə, kənˈtræk-/ *n* firm that provides supplies and/or workers, esp. for building work

con·tra·dict /ˌkɒntrəˈdɪkt/ v **1** vt/i say the opposite of; declare to be wrong **2** vt (of a statement, fact, etc.) be opposite to (another) ~**ory** adj: *contradictory reports* ~**ion** /-ˈdɪkʃən/ n [C;U]

con·trap·tion /kənˈtræpʃən/ n apparatus with a strange appearance

con·tra·ry[1] /ˈkɒntrεri/ n [S] **1** opposite **2 on the contrary** no, not at all **3 to the contrary** to the opposite effect ◆ adj completely contrary; opposed

con·tra·ry[2] /ˈkɒntrεri, kənˈtrεri/ adj (of a person) unreasonable

con·trast[1] /kənˈtrɑːst, -ˈtræst, ˈkɒntræst/ v **1** vt compare so that differences are made clear **2** vi show a difference: *sharply contrasting attitudes*

con·trast[2] /ˈkɒntræst/ n [C;U] noticeable difference

con·tra·vene /ˌkɒntrəˈviːn/ vt fml break (a law) –**vention** /-ˈvenʃən/ n [C;U]

con·trib·ute /kənˈtrɪbjuːt, -jət/ v **1** vt/i join with others in giving something **2** vi help in causing: *contribute to good health* **3** vt write (an article) for a magazine –**utor** n person who contributes –**utory** adj –**ution** /ˌkɒntrəˈbjuːʃən/ n [C;U]

con·trite /kənˈtraɪt, ˈkɒntraɪt/ adj fml sorry for having done wrong ~**ly** adv –**trition** /kənˈtrɪʃən/ n [U]

con·trive /kənˈtraɪv/ vt succeed in doing something: *contrive to escape* – **trivance** n clever plan or invention –**trived** adj unnatural and forced

con·trol /kənˈtrəʊl/ vt -ll- **1** direct; have power over **2** hold back; RESTRAIN ◆ n **1** [U] power to control: *lose control of oneself* **2** [C;U] means of controlling: *wage control(s)* **3** [C] place where something is controlled: *controls of a plane* **4** [C] standard against which the results of a study are measured **5 out of control** in(to) a state of not being controlled **6 under control** working properly ~**ler** n person who directs something

con·tro·ver·sy /ˈkɒntrəvɜːsi/ n [C;U] fierce argument –**sial** /ˌkɒntrəˈvɜːʃəl◄/ adj causing controversy –**sially** adv

con·va·lesce /ˌkɒnvəˈles/ vi spend time getting well after an illness –**lescence** n [S;U] time spent getting well –**lescent** n, adj (person) spending time getting well

con·vene /kənˈviːn/ v **1** vi meet together **2** vt call (a group) to meet –**vener**, –**venor** n person who convenes meetings

con·ve·nience /kənˈviːnyəns/ n **1** [U] fitness; suitableness **2** [C] useful tool or apparatus **3** [U] personal comfort –**ent** adj **1** suited to one's needs **2** near –**ently** adv

convenience store /·'·· ˌ·/ n store that stays open longer than other stores and sells food, medicines, and things for the house

con·vent /ˈkɒnvεnt, -vənt/ n place where NUNS live

con·ven·tion /kənˈvεnʃən/ n **1** [C;U] accepted social custom **2** [C] meeting of a group with a shared purpose **3** [C] formal political agreement ~**al** adj following accepted customs ~**ally** adv

con·verge /kənˈvɜːdʒ/ vi come together and meet: *roads converging at the station* –**vergence** n [U]

con·ver·sant /kənˈvɜːsənt/ adj fml having knowledge or experience

con·ver·sa·tion /ˌkɒnvəˈseɪʃən/ n [C;U] informal talk ~**al** adj (of language) used in conversation

con·verse[1] /kənˈvɜːs/ vi fml talk informally

con·verse[2] /kənˈvɜːs, ˈkɒnvɜːs/ adj opposite: *the converse opinion* ~**ly** adv

con·ver·sion /kənˈvɜːʒən, -ʃən/ n [C;U] act of converting

con·vert[1] /kənˈvɜːt/ vt/i **1** change into another form: *convert dollars into pounds* **2** change to a particular religious belief, etc. ~**er** n apparatus that converts something, esp. information to be put into a computer ~**ible** adj (esp. of money) able to be converted ~**ible** n car with a roof that can be folded back

con·vert[2] /ˈkɒnvɜːt/ n person who has accepted a particular belief

con·vex /ˌkɒnˈvεks◄, kənˈvεks/ adj curved outwards

con·vey /kənˈveɪ/ vt **1** take; carry **2** make (feelings, etc.) known ~**er**, ~**or** n

conveyor belt /·'·· ˌ·/ n endless moving belt carrying objects from one place to another

con·vict[1] /kənˈvɪkt/ vt prove (someone) to be guilty of a crime

con·vict[2] /ˈkɒnvɪkt/ n convicted person who is sent to prison

con·vic·tion /kənˈvɪkʃən/ n [C;U] **1** being convicted of a crime **2** firm belief

con·vince /kənˈvɪns/ vt cause to feel sure of something –**vincing** adj: *a convincing argument* –**vincingly** adv

con·viv·i·al /kən'vɪvɪəl/ *adj* merry and friendly ~**ity** /kənˌvɪvɪ'ælətɪ/ *n* [U]

con·vo·lut·ed /'kɒnvəˌluːtɪd/ *adj fml* **1** twisted **2** difficult to understand –**lution** /ˌkɒnvə'luːʃən/ *n* twist

con·voy /'kɒnvɔɪ/ *n* **1** group of ships or vehicles traveling together, esp. for safety **2** protecting force of fighting ships, etc. ♦ *vt* go with and protect

con·vulse /kən'vʌls/ *vt* shake violently –**vulsive** *adj* –**vulsion** /-'vʌlʃən/ *n*

coo /kuː/ *vi* **1** make the soft cry of a DOVE **2** speak lovingly

cook /kʊk/ *v* **1** prepare (food) by using heat **2** *vi* (of food) be cooked **3** *vt* change (accounts, etc.) dishonestly ♦ *n* person who cooks food

cook·book /'kʊkbʊk/ *n* book with instructions for preparing and cooking food

cook·ie /'kʊkɪ/ *n* **1** small sweet cake **2** person: *a smart/tough cookie*

cool[1] /kuːl/ *adj* **1** pleasantly cold **2** fashionable; attractive: *a cool guy* **3** calm; unexcited: *a cool-headed decision* **4** not very friendly **5** (used to add force to an expression): *a cool $1,000 a month* ♦ *n* **1** cool temperature: *the cool of the evening* **2** calmness: *lose one's cool* ♦ *adv* **play it cool** act calmly ~**ness** *n* [U] ~**ly** /'kuːl-lɪ/ *adv*

cool[2] *vi/t* make or become cool

cool down/off/out *phr vi* become calmer

cool·er /'kuːlə/ *n* container for keeping food or drinks cool

coop[1] /kuːp/ *n* cage for small creatures

coop[2] *v*

coop up *phr vt* shut into a small space

co·op·e·rate /koʊ'ɒpəˌreɪt/ *vi* work together for a shared purpose –**rative** /-rətɪv/ *adj* helpful –**rative** *n* company, farm, etc., owned by its workers –**ration** /koʊˌɒpə'reɪʃən/ *n*

co-opt /koʊ'ɒpt/ *vt* (of an elected group) choose as a fellow member

co·or·di·nate /koʊ'ɔːdnˌeɪt/ *vt* cause to work together effectively: *coordinate our efforts* –**nation** /koʊˌɔːdn'eɪʃən/ *n* [U]

cop[1] /kɒp/ *n sl* policeman

cop[2] *v*

cop out *phr vi sl* avoid responsibility **cop-out** /'·ˌ·/ *n*

cope /koʊp/ *vi* deal with something successfully

cop·i·er /'kɒpɪə/ *n* machine for making paper copies (COPY (1))

co·pi·ous /'koʊpɪəs/ *adj* present in great quantity ~**ly** *adv*

cop·per[1] /'kɒpə/ *n* **1** [U] a soft redbrown metal **b** its color **2** [C] copper coin

copper[2] *n sl* policeman

cop·u·late /'kɒpjəˌleɪt/ *vi fml* have sex –**lation** /ˌkɒpjə'leɪʃən/ *n* [U]

cop·y /'kɒpɪ/ *n* **1** thing made to be like another **2** single example of a book, newspaper, etc. see also HARD COPY, SOFT COPY ♦ *v* **1** *vt* make a copy of **2** *vt* do the same as **3** *vi/t* cheat in an examination, etc., by copying

cop·y·cat /'kɒpɪˌkæt/ *n derog infml* person who copies other people's behavior, dress, work, etc.

cop·y·right /'kɒpɪˌraɪt/ *n* [C;U] legal right to be the only seller of a book, etc.

cor·al /'kɒrəl, 'kɑrəl/ *n* [U] white, pink, or red substance formed by small sea creatures

cord /kɔːd/ *n* [C;U] **1** thick string or thin rope **2** electric wire **3** quantity of wood for burning

cor·dial /'kɔːdʒəl/ *adj* warm and friendly ~**ly** *adv* in a cordial manner

cord·less /'kɔːdlɪs/ *adj* (of electric apparatus) with a BATTERY instead of a CORD: *a cordless phone*

cor·don /'kɔːdn/ *n* ring of police, etc., surrounding an area ♦ *v* **cordon off** *phr vt* protect with a cordon

cords /kɔːdz/ *n* [P] *infml* pants made from corduroy

cor·du·roy /'kɔːdəˌrɔɪ, ˌkɔːdə'rɔɪ/ *n* strong cotton cloth with raised lines

core /kɔː/ *n* **1** central part: *core of an apple* **2** **to the core** thoroughly ♦ *vt* remove the core of (a fruit)

cork /kɔːk/ *n* **1** [U] BARK of a tree (the **cork oak**) **2** [C] piece of this used for closing a bottle ♦ *vt* close with a cork

cork·screw /'kɔːkskruː/ *n* metal tool for removing a cork from a bottle

corn[1] /kɔːn/ *n* [U] (seed of) a tall food plant with long bunches of yellow seeds

corn[2] *n* painful lump of hard skin on the foot

cor·ne·a /'kɔːnɪə/ *n* protective covering on the front surface of the eye

corned beef /ˌkɔːnd 'biːf/ *n* [U] kind of cooked BEEF usu. sold in thin slices

cor·ner /ˈkɔrnə/ n **1** point where 2 lines, edges, or roads meet **2** part of the world: *remote corners of America* **3 around the corner** near **4 cut corners** use a shorter method **5 in a tight corner** in a difficult position **6 turn the corner** become better after a period of difficulties, etc. ♦ v **1** vt force into a difficult position **2** vt gain control of (by buying, selling, or production of goods) **3** vi (of a vehicle) turn a corner

corn meal /ˈ· ·/ n COARSE flour made of corn

cor·ner·stone /ˈkɔrnəstoʊn/ n **1** stone set at one bottom corner of a building **2** something of great importance, on which everything else is based

cor·net /kɔrˈnɛt/ n musical instrument like a TRUMPET

corn·flakes /ˈkɔrnfleɪks/ n [P] bits of crushed CORN[1] to be eaten with milk at breakfast

corn·y /ˈkɔrni/ adj sl too silly; old-fashioned

coronary /ˈkɔrənɛri ˈkɑr-/ n stopping of the blood supply to the heart; kind of HEART ATTACK ♦ adj related to the heart

cor·o·na·tion /ˌkɔrəˈneɪʃən, ˌkɑr-/ n ceremony of crowning a king or queen

cor·o·ner /ˈkɔrənə, ˈkɑr-/ n official who inquires into the cause of a person's death if it is not clearly known

cor·po·ral[1] /ˈkɔrpərəl/ adj fml of the human body: *corporal punishment*

corporal[2] /ˈkɔrprəl/ n person of low rank in an army or other military force

cor·po·rate /ˈkɔrpərɪt/ adj **1** shared by a whole group: *corporate responsibility* **2** of a CORPORATION

cor·po·ra·tion /ˌkɔrpəˈreɪʃən/ n large business organization

corps /kɔr, koʊr/ n **1 a** trained army group **b** branch of the army equal to 2 DIVISIONS **2** group with the same activity: *the press corps*

corpse /kɔrps/ n dead body

cor·pu·lent /ˈkɔrpyələnt/ adj very fat

cor·pus·cle /ˈkɔrpəsəl, -ˌpʌsəl/ n any of the red and white cells in the body

cor·ral /kəˈræl/ n enclosed area (esp. in the western states) for cattle and horses ♦ vt **-ll-** put in a corral

cor·rect[1] /kəˈrɛkt/ adj **1** without mistakes; true **2** proper: *correct behavior* ~**ly** adv ~**ness** n [U]

correct[2] vt make right; show the mistakes in ~**ive** adj, n ~**ion** /kəˈrɛkʃən/ n **1** [U] correcting **2** [C] change that improves something **3** [U] punishment

cor·re·late /ˈkɔrəleɪt, ˈkɑr-/ vi/t (show to) have a close connection –**ation** /ˌkɔrəˈleɪʃən, ˌkɑr-/ n close connection

cor·re·spond /ˌkɔrəˈspɑnd, ˌkɑr-/ vi **1** be equal; match **2** exchange letters ~**ing** adj matching; equal

cor·re·spon·dence /ˌkɔrəˈspɑndəns, ˌkɑr-/ n [S;U] **1** (of) writing letters **2** equality between things; likeness –**dent** n **1** person with whom one exchanges letters **2** someone employed by a newspaper, television or radio station, etc., to report news from a distant area

cor·ri·dor /ˈkɔrədə, -ˌdɔr, ˈkɑr-/ n passage between rows of rooms

cor·rob·o·rate /kəˈrɑbəˌreɪt/ vt support (an opinion, etc.) by proof –**ration** /kəˌrɑbəˈreɪʃən/ n [U]

cor·rode /kəˈroʊd/ vt/i destroy slowly, esp. by chemical action

cor·ro·sion /kəˈroʊʒən/ n [U] **1** corroding **2** RUST, etc., produced by corroding –**sive** /-sɪv, -zɪv/ adj

cor·ru·gated /ˈkɔrəˌgeɪtɪd, ˈkɑr-/ adj having wavelike folds –**gation** /ˌkɔrəˈgeɪʃən, ˌkɑr-/ n

cor·rupt /kəˈrʌpt/ adj **1** morally bad, esp. dishonest **2** containing mistakes ♦ vt/i make or become corrupt ~**ly** adv ~**ion** /-ˈrʌpʃən/ n [U]

cor·sage /kɔrˈsɑʒ, -ˈsɑdʒ/ n flowers worn on a woman's dress for a special occasion

cor·set /ˈkɔrsɪt/ also **corsets** pl. — n tightly fitting undergarment formerly worn by women

cos·met·ic /kazˈmɛtɪk/ n cream, powder, etc., for the skin or hair ♦ adj **1** of, related to, or causing increased beauty **2** dealing only with the outside appearance rather than the central part of something

cos·mic /ˈkazmɪk/ adj of the whole universe

cos·mo·naut /ˈkazməˌnɔt/ n a Soviet ASTRONAUT

cos·mo·pol·i·tan /ˌkazməˈpalətˈn/ adj **1** consisting of people from many parts of the world **2** not narrow in one's attitudes ♦ n cosmopolitan person

cos·mos /ˈkazməs, -moʊs/ n the whole universe

cost[1] /kɔst/ n 1 [C] price of something 2 [U] what is needed to gain something 3 **at all costs** whatever it may cost 4 **to one's cost** from one's own unpleasant experience ~**ly** adj expensive **costs** [P] cost of taking a matter to a court of law

cost[2] vt 1 (past t. and p. cost) have as a price: *It cost me $5.* | (fig.) *The mistake cost him his job.* 2 (past t. and p. **costed**) calculate the price to be charged for (a job)

co-star /ˈkoʊ stɑr/ n famous actor or actress who appears with another famous actor or actress in a film, etc. ♦ **co-star** vi

cost-ef-fec-tive /ˈ· ·ˌ·/ adj bringing the best possible profits or advantages for the lowest possible cost ~**ly** adv ~**ness** n [U]

cos-tume /ˈkɑstum/ n [C;U] clothes, esp. as worn in plays

costume jew-el-ry /ˈ·· ˌ···, ·· ˈ···/ n [U] jewelry which looks valuable but is made from cheap materials

cot /kɑt/ n light narrow bed which folds flat

cot-tage /ˈkɑtɪdʒ/ n small house, used esp. for vacation

cottage cheese /ˌ·· ˈ·/ n [U] type of soft wet white cheese

cot-ton[1] /ˈkɑtˀn/ n [U] 1 soft white hair of a southern crop plant 2 thread or cloth made from this 3 soft mass of cotton for cleaning wounds, etc.

cotton[2] v **cotton on** phr vi infml understand

couch[1] /kaʊtʃ/ n long seat like a bed

couch[2] vt fml express: *His refusal was couched in unfriendly terms.*

couch po-ta-to /ˈ· ·ˌ··/ n infml someone who spends a lot of time sitting and watching television

cou-gar /ˈkugər/ n large American wild cat; mountain lion

cough /kɔf/ v 1 vi push air out noisily from the lungs 2 vt produce by doing this: *cough up blood* ♦ n 1 [C] act of coughing 2 [S] illness that makes a person cough

cough up phr vt infml produce (money or information) unwillingly

could /kəd; strong kʊd/ v aux 1 (describes **can** in the past): *He could read when he was 4.* 2 (used to describe what someone has said): *She asked if she could smoke.*

3 (used to show what is possible): *I think the accident could have been prevented.* 4 (used to make a request): *Could you help me?*

could-n't /ˈkʊdnt/ v short for: could not

coun-cil /ˈkaʊnsəl/ n group of people appointed or elected to manage something ~**lor** n member of a council

coun-sel /ˈkaʊnsəl/ n **counsel** 1 [C] law legal advisor acting for someone 2 [C] fml advice ♦ v -l- fml advise ~**ing** n [U] advice ~**or** n advisor

count[1] /kaʊnt/ v 1 vi/t name (numbers) in order: *count (to) 20* 2 vt find the total of 3 vt include: *6 people, counting me* 4 vt consider to be: *count yourself lucky* 5 vi have value: *Every moment counts.* ♦ n 1 act of counting; total 2 one of a number of crimes of which a person is thought to be guilty: *guilty on all counts* 3 **be out for the count** (in BOXING) be counted out; be unconscious 4 **keep/lose count** know/no longer know the exact number ~**able** adj that can be counted: *Egg is a countable noun.* ~**less** adj very many

count down phr vt count backwards to zero, esp. before sending a spacecraft into space **countdown** /ˈkaʊntdaʊn/ n

count in phr vt include

count on/upon phr vt depend on; expect

count out phr vt 1 put down in turn while counting 2 not include 3 declare (a BOXER who fails to get up after 10 seconds) to be a loser of a fight

count[2] n European nobleman

count-a-ble /ˈkaʊntəbəl/ adj (of nouns) having a singular and plural form

coun-te-nance /ˈkaʊntənəns/ n fml 1 [C] face 2 [U] support; approval ♦ vt fml give approval to

coun-ter[1] /ˈkaʊntər/ n 1 table where people in a store, etc., are served 2 **over the counter** (when buying drugs) without a PRESCRIPTION 3 **under the counter** secretly and often unlawfully

counter[2] n 1 object used in some games instead of money 2 machine that counts

counter[3] vt/i meet an attack; oppose: *counter her proposal*

counter[4] adv, adj opposed; opposite: *act counter to all advice*

coun-ter-act /ˌkaʊntərˈækt/ vt reduce the effect of: *counteract a poison*

coun·ter·at·tack /ˈkaʊntərəˌtæk/ *vi/t, n* (make) an attack to oppose another

coun·ter·bal·ance /ˈkaʊntərˌbæləns/ *vt, n* (act as) a force that balances another

coun·ter·clock·wise /ˌkaʊntərˈklɑkwaɪz/ *adv* in the opposite direction to the movement of a clock

coun·ter·feit /ˈkaʊntərfɪt/ *n, adj* (thing) made as a copy of something else, to deceive: *counterfeit money* ♦ *vt* make a counterfeit of

coun·ter·part /ˈkaʊntərˌpɑrt/ *n* person or thing that matches another, but in a different system

coun·ter·pro·duc·tive /ˌkaʊntərprəˈdʌktɪv/ *adj* having an opposite effect from the one intended

coun·ter·sign /ˈkaʊntərˌsaɪn/ *vt* add another signature to (a paper already signed)

coun·tess /ˈkaʊntɪs/ *n* **a** woman who holds the rank of COUNT or EARL for herself **b** wife of a COUNT or EARL

coun·try /ˈkʌntri/ *n* **1** [C] nation, with its land and population **2** [S;U] also **coun·try·side** /ˈkʌntriˌsaɪd/ — land outside towns ♦ *adj* of, in or from the country

country and west·ern /ˌ·· ˈ··/ also **country mu·sic** /ˌ·· ˈ··/ — *n* [U] popular music in the style of the southern and western states

country club /ˈ·· ˌ·/ *n* club whose members can play GOLF, attend social activities, etc.

coun·try·man /ˈkʌntrimən/ **-woman** /-ˌwʊmən/ *fem.* — *n* **-men** /-mən/ person from the same country

coun·ty /ˈkaʊnti/ *n* area divided from others for purposes of local government

county clerk /ˌ·· ˈ·/ *n* elected official in most states who keeps records of property titles, etc.

coup /ku/ *n* **1** clever effective action **2** also **coup d'é·tat** /ˌku deɪˈtɑ, -dɑ-/ — sudden and violent seizure of state power by a small group

cou·pe /kup, kuˈpeɪ/ *n* closed car with 2 doors and a sloping back

cou·ple /ˈkʌpəl/ *n* **1** two things of the same kind **2** two people, esp. a husband and wife **3** a few ♦ *v* **1** *vt* join (two things) together **2** *vi* (of animals) MATE **–pling** *n* something that joins two things, esp. two railroad cars

cou·pon /ˈkupɑn, ˈkyu-/ *n* small piece of paper used to pay less money for something in a store

cour·age /ˈkɜrɪdʒ, ˈkʌr-/ *n* [U] ability to control fear; bravery **–ageous** /kəˈreɪdʒəs/ *adj* brave **–ageously** *adv*

cou·ri·er /ˈkʊriə, ˈkɜ-, ˈkʌr-/ *n* official messenger

course /kɔrs, koʊrs/ *n* **1** path along which something moves **2** area for races or certain sports: *a golf course* **3** plan of action **4** a set of lessons, treatments, etc. **b** university studies: *a 4 year course* **5** any of several parts of a meal **6 a matter of course** that which one expects to happen **7 in due course** at the right time **8 in the course of** during **9 of course** certainly **10 run/take its/their course** (of an illness, etc.) continue to its natural end **11 stay the course** continue something through to the end in spite of difficulty ♦ *vi* (of liquid) flow quickly

court¹ /kɔrt, koʊrt/ *n* **1 a** [C] room (**courtroom**) or building where law cases are judged **b** [U] people gathered there **2** [C] area for certain ball games such as BASKETBALL and tennis **3** [C] king or queen with the royal family, officials, etc. **4** [C] also **court·yard** /ˈkɔrtˈyard, ˈkoʊrt-/ — open space surrounded by buildings or in the middle of a building

court² *vt fml* **1** try to win the favor of **2** visit and pay attention to (a woman a man hopes to marry) **3** risk foolishly: *to court disaster*

court·house /ˈkɔrt·haʊs, ˈkoʊrt-/ *n* building with courtrooms and other offices

cour·te·ous /ˈkɜtiəs/ *adj fml* polite and kind **~ly** *adv*

cour·te·sy /ˈkɜtəsi/ *n* **1** [C;U] polite behavior **2 by courtesy of** with the permission of

court·mar·tial /ˈ·· ˌ··/ *n* (trial before) a court for offenses against military law ♦ *vt* **–l–** try (someone) in a court-martial

court·ship /ˈkɔrtˈʃɪp, ˈkoʊrt-/ *n* [U] (period of) trying to attract someone to oneself, esp. with the aim of marriage

cous·in /ˈkʌzən/ *n* **1** child of one's uncle or aunt **2** related person or thing — see also FIRST COUSIN, SECOND COUSIN

cove /koʊv/ *n* small BAY¹

cov·e·nant /ˈkʌvənənt/ *n* formal agreement

cov·er[1] /ˈkʌvə/ **1** vt spread something over; hide in this way: *cover the body with a sheet* **2** vt lie on the surface of; spread over (something): *furniture covered in dust* | *The town covers five square miles.* **3** vt travel (a distance) **4** vt include: *a talk covering the whole history of medicine* **5** vt report (an event) for a newspaper **6** vt be enough money for **7** vt protect from loss; insure **8** vt keep a gun aimed at **9** vi/t act in place of (someone who is absent)

cover up phr vt prevent (something) from being noticed **cover-up** /ˈ··ˌ·/ n

cover up for phr vt hide something wrong or shameful in order to save (someone else) from punishment, blame, etc.

cover[2] n **1** [C] anything that protects or hides by covering: *cushion covers* | (fig.) *The business is a cover for illegal activity.* **2** [C] outside of a book or magazine **3** [U] shelter; protection **4** [U] insurance against loss, etc. **5** **take cover** find a safe place to hide **6** **under plain/separate cover** in a plain/separate envelope ~**ing** n something that covers or hides

cov·er·age /ˈkʌvərɪdʒ/ n [U] time and space given to reporting an event

cov·er·alls /ˈkʌvərɔːlz/ n [P] garment for the whole body, to protect one's clothes

cover charge /ˈ·· ˌ·/ n charge made by a restaurant etc. in addition to the cost of the food and drinks or of the service

cover let·ter /ˈ·· ˌ··/ n letter or note containing an explanation or additional information, sent with a package or another letter

cov·ert /ˈkʌvət, ˈkoʊ-, koʊˈvɜːt/ adj hidden; secret ~**ly** adv

cov·et /ˈkʌvɪt/ vt desire (esp. someone else's possessions) eagerly ~**ous** adj

cow[1] /kaʊ/ n female of cattle and some other large animals

cow[2] vt frighten into obedience

cow·ard /ˈkaʊəd/ n person afraid of pain or danger ~**ly** adj

cow·ard·ice /ˈkaʊədɪs/ n [U] lack of courage

cow·boy /ˈkaʊbɔɪ/ also **cow·hand** /ˈkaʊhænd/ — n man who takes care of cattle on horseback

cow·er /ˈkaʊə/ vi bend low from fear or shame

co·work·er /ˈkoʊˌwɜːkə/ n someone who works with another person

coy /kɔɪ/ adj pretending not to be confident in one's own ability ~**ly** adv

coy·ote /kaɪˈoʊti, ˈkaɪ-oʊt/ n small WOLF

co·zy /ˈkoʊzi/ adj warm and comfortable –**zily** adv –**ziness** n [U]

CPU abbrev. for CENTRAL PROCESSING UNIT

crab /kræb/ n SHELLFISH with 10 legs, that can be eaten

crab·by /ˈkræbi/ adj bad-tempered

crack[1] /kræk/ v **1** vi/t break without dividing into pieces: *cracked cups* **2** vi/t make a sudden explosive sound: *crack a whip* **3** vi/t cause to break open: *crack a safe* **4** vi (of a voice) change suddenly in level **5** vi/t hit suddenly **6** vi lose strength or control: *crack (up) under the strain* **7** make (a joke) **8** discover the secret of (a CODE (1)) **9** (cause to) strike with a sudden blow **10 cracked up to be** believed to be **11 get cracking** be or become busy doing something in a hurried way

crack down phr vi take strong action against something

crack[2] n **1** thin line caused by breaking **2** explosive sound: *crack of thunder* **3** sudden sharp blow **4** sudden change in the level of the voice **5** quick joke; clever remark **6 at the crack of dawn** very early in the morning ♦ adj very skillful: *crack troops*

crack[3] n [U] sl extremely pure form of COCAINE, taken illegally for pleasure

crack·down /ˈkrækdaʊn/ n infml severe enforcement of laws or rules

crack·er /ˈkrækə/ n thin hard bread with salt

crack·le /ˈkrækəl/ vi make small sharp sounds: *The fire crackled.* **crackle** n [S;U]

crack·pot /ˈkrækpɒt/ adj strange; crazy ♦ n crackpot person

cra·dle /ˈkreɪdl/ n **1** small bed for a baby **2** origin of something: *the cradle of Western civilization* **3** frame to support something ♦ vt hold gently

craft[1] /krɑːft/ n trade needing skill, esp. with one's hands

craft[2] n craft boat, aircraft, or spacecraft

crafts·man /ˈkrɑːftsmən/ **crafts· wo·man** /-ˌwʊmən/ fem. — n **-men** /-mən/ skilled worker ~**ship** n [U]

craft·y /ˈkrɑːfti/ adj cleverly deceitful –**ily** adv –**iness** n [U]

crag /kræg/ n high steep rock ~**gy** adj **1** steep and rough **2** (esp. of a man's face) rough in appearance

cram /kræm/ v -**mm**- **1** vt force into a small space; fill too full: *box crammed with letters* **2** vi study hard for a short time: *cram for an examination*

cramp /kræmp/ n [C;U] sudden painful tightening of a muscle ♦ vt **1** cause to have a cramp **2** prevent natural growth or development **3 cramp someone's style** prevent someone from showing their abilities to the full ~**ed** adj limited in space

cran·ber·ry /ˈkrænɪbɛri/ n small sour red BERRY

crane /kreɪn/ n **1** machine with a movable arm for lifting heavy objects **2** tall waterbird with long legs ♦ vi/t stretch out (one's neck) to see better

cra·ni·um /ˈkreɪniəm/ n bony part of the head, covering the brain **cranial** adj

crank /kræŋk/ n **1** handle for turning, shaped like an L **2** person with strange ideas ♦ vt **1** move by turning a crank **2** use a CRANK (1) to start a car ~**y** adj **1** (of people or ideas) peculiar **2** bad-tempered

crank out phr vt produce rapidly

cran·ny /ˈkræni/ n small narrow opening in a wall, etc.

crap /kræp/ n [U] taboo sl **1** (act of passing) solid waste from the bowel **2** nonsense **crap** vi -**pp**-

crash /kræʃ/ v **1** vi/t fall or hit violently: *The car crashed into a tree.* **2** vi make a sudden loud noise **3** vi move violently and noisily: *The elephant crashed through the fence.* **4** vi (of computers) suddenly stop working **5** vi fail suddenly in business ♦ n **1** violent vehicle accident: *a car/plane crash* **2** sudden loud noise **3** sudden stopping of a computer **4** sudden business failure ♦ adj intended to get quick results: *a crash diet/course*

crash hel·met /ˈ· ˌ·/ n protective HELMET worn by those who ride motorcycles, etc.

crash-land /ˌ· ˈ·/ vi/t (cause a plane) to crash in a controlled way **crash landing** n

crass /kræs/ adj fml showing great stupidity and a complete lack of feeling or respect for others

crate /kreɪt/ n large wooden or plastic box for bottles, etc.

cra·ter /ˈkreɪtə/ n **1** mouth of a VOLCANO **2** hole made by a bomb, etc. **3** round hole with a flat bottom on the moon's surface

crave /kreɪv/ vi/t have a very strong desire for (something) **craving** n

craw·dad /ˈkrɔdæd/, **craw·fish** /ˈkrɔfɪʃ/ n CRAYFISH

crawl /krɔl/ vi **1** move slowly, esp. with the body close to the ground: *crawling babies*/(fig.) *traffic* **2** be covered by crawling insects, etc. **3** have an unpleasant sensation, as of insects, etc., moving slowly over one's skin: *The idea makes my skin crawl.* **4** infml try to win the favor of someone by being too nice to them ♦ n [S] **1** very slow movement **2** rapid way of swimming ~**er** n **1** something, esp. a vehicle, that goes slowly **2** person who CRAWLS (4)

cray·fish /ˈkreɪfɪʃ/ n [C;U] small animal similar to a LOBSTER living in rivers and streams, or its meat

cray·on /ˈkreɪən, -ən/ n pencil of colored chalk or wax **crayon** vi/t

craze /kreɪz/ n popular fashion that lasts a short time ♦ vt make excited or crazy

cra·zy /ˈkreɪzi/ adj **1** INSANE; foolish **2** wildly excited ~**zily** adv ~**ziness** n [U]

creak /krik/ vi, n make the sound of a badly oiled door ~**y** adj

cream /krim/ n [U] **1** thick liquid that rises to the top of milk **2** soft mixture like this: *face cream* **3** best part: *the cream of the students* ♦ adj yellow-white ♦ vt **1** make into a soft mixture: *creamed potatoes* **2** take cream from the surface of (milk) **3** sl defeat ~**y** adj **1** containing cream **2** like cream

crease /kris/ n line made by folding or pressing ♦ vi/t press into creases

cre·ate /kriˈeɪt/ vt **1** cause (something new) to exist; make **2** appoint to a rank; *create him a general* ~**ator** n **1** [C] a person who creates something **2** [the] (cap.) God ~**ation** /-ˈeɪʃən/ n **1** [U] act of creating **2** [C] something created **3** [U] the whole universe

cre·a·tive /kriˈeɪtɪv/ adj able to make new things; inventive ~**ly** adv ~**tivity** /ˌkriˈtɪvəti/ n [U]

crea·ture /ˈkritʃə/ n person, animal, or being

cre·dence /ˈkridns/ n fml acceptance as true; belief

cre·den·tials /krəˈdɛnʃəlz/ n [P] written proof of a person's ability and trustworthiness

cred·i·ble /ˈkrɛdəbəl/ *adj* that can be believed **–bly** *adv* **–bility** /ˌkrɛdəˈbɪləti/ *n* [U]

cred·it¹ /ˈkrɛdɪt/ *n* **1** [U] system of buying things and paying later: *buy on credit* **2** [U] quality of being likely to repay debts **3** [U] amount of money in someone's bank account **4** [U] belief; trust **5** [C;U] (cause of) public honor: *get credit for an invention* | *He's a credit to his team.* **6** [C] unit of a student's work **7 to someone's credit a** in someone's favor **b** to/in someone's name **~able** *adj* deserving approval **~ably** *adv* **credits** *n* [P] names of actors, etc., which appear at the beginning or end of a film or television show

credit² *vt* **1** believe **2** add to an account

credit card /ˈ·· ˌ·/ *n* plastic card allowing one to buy goods without paying in paper money or coin

cred·i·tor /ˈkrɛdətər/ *n* person to whom money is owed

cred·u·lous /ˈkrɛdʒələs/ *adj* too willing to believe **–lity** /krəˈdulɪti/ *n* [U]

creed /krid/ *n* system of (esp. religious) beliefs

creek /krik, krɪk/ *n* small stream **up the creek** *sl* in a difficult situation

creep¹ /krip/ *vi* **crept** /krɛpt/ **1** move slowly and quietly; CRAWL **2** (of a plant) grow along the ground or a surface **3** CRAWL (3) **~er** *n* creeping plant **~y** *adj* strange and frightening **creeps** *n* [P] feeling of fear and strangeness

creep² *n infml* unpleasant person

cre·mate /ˈkrimeɪt, krɪˈmeɪt/ *vt* burn (a dead person) **–mation** /krɪˈmeɪʃən/ *n* [C;U]

crem·a·to·ri·um /ˌkriməˈtɔriəm, -ˈtoʊr-, ˌkrɛ-/ *n* place where bodies are cremated

crepe /kreɪp/ *n* **1** [U] cloth, paper or rubber with a lined and folded surface **2** [C] very thin PANCAKE

crept /krɛpt/ *v past t. and p. of* CREEP

cre·scen·do /krəˈʃɛndoʊ/ *n* **–dos** gradual increase of force or loudness, esp. in music

cres·cent /ˈkrɛsənt/ *n* **1** curved shape of the new moon **2** something shaped like this, such as a curved street

crest /krɛst/ *n* **1** growth of feathers on a bird's head **2** decoration like this on a soldier's HELMET **3** top of a hill, wave, etc. **4** picture used as a personal mark on letters, etc.

crest·fal·len /ˈkrɛstˌfɔlən/ *adj* disappointed

cre·vasse /krəˈvæs/ *n* deep crack in ice

crev·ice /ˈkrɛvɪs/ *n* narrow crack in rock, etc.

crew /kru/ *n* **1 a** all the people working on a ship or plane **b** all of these except the officers **2** group working together: *a camera crew* ♦ *vi* act as ship's crew

crew cut /ˈ· ˌ·/ *n* very short hair style

crib /krɪb/ *n* **1** bed for a small child **2** book supplying a translation ♦ *vt* **-bb-** copy (someone's work) dishonestly

crib death /ˈ· ˌ·/ *n* [C;U] unexplained death of a healthy baby

crick /krɪk/ *n* painful stiffening of the muscles, esp. in the back or the neck **crick** *vt*

crick·et /ˈkrɪkɪt/ *n* **1** jumping insect that makes a loud noise

cried /kraɪd/ *v past t. and p. of* CRY

cries /kraɪz/ *v pres. t. of* CRY *n pl. of* CRY

crime /kraɪm/ *n* **1** [C;U] offense that is punishable by law **2** [S] a shame

crim·i·nal /ˈkrɪmənəl/ *adj* of crime ♦ *n* person who is guilty of crime **~ly** *adv*

crim·son /ˈkrɪmzən/ *n, adj* [U] deep red

cringe /krɪndʒ/ *vi* **1** bend low from fear; COWER **2** behave towards someone in a way that shows no respect for oneself

crin·kle /ˈkrɪŋkəl/ *n* fold made by crushing ♦ *vi/t* make or get crinkles

crip·ple /ˈkrɪpəl/ *n* person who cannot use the limbs, esp. the legs, well ♦ *vt* **1** make into a cripple **2** damage seriously: *crippling debts*

cri·sis /ˈkraɪsɪs/ *n* **-ses** /-siz/ moment of great danger or difficulty — see also MID-LIFE CRISIS

crisp /krɪsp/ *adj* **1** hard, dry, and easily broken: *crisp bacon* **2** (of weather) cold and dry **3** (of style, manners, etc.) quick and clear: *crisp reply* ♦ *vi/t* cook until crisp **~ly** *adv* **~ness** *n* [U] **~y** *adj*

criss·cross /ˈkrɪskrɔs/ *vi/t, n* (make) a network of crossed lines

cri·te·ri·on /kraɪˈtɪriən/ *n* **-ria** /-riə/ standard on which a judgment is based

crit·ic /ˈkrɪtɪk/ *n* **1** person who gives judgments about art, music, etc. **2** person who expresses disapproval **~al** *adj* **1** finding fault **2** of a critic's work **3** of or at a CRISIS: *critical decisions* **~ism** /ˈkrɪtəˌsɪzəm/ *n* [C;U] **1** work of a critic **2** disapproval **~ize** *vi/t* **1** make judgments **2** find fault

cri·tique /krɪˈtiːk/ n book or article criticizing the work of esp. a writer

crit·ter /ˈkrɪtər/ n infml CREATURE

croak /krouk/ vi/t, n 1 (make) the deep low noise a FROG makes 2 speak with a rough voice as if one has a sore throat 3 sl die

croc·o·dile /ˈkrɑkədaɪl/ n 1 [C] large tropical river REPTILE 2 [U] its skin, used as leather

crocodile tears /ˈkrɑkədaɪl ˌtɪrz/ n [P] insincere sorrow

cro·cus /ˈkroukəs/ n small spring plant with purple, yellow and white flowers

crois·sant /krwɑˈsɑnt/ n soft bread roll shaped in a curve

cro·ny /ˈkrouni/ n infml (old) friend or companion

crook /krʊk/ n 1 infml thief 2 bend or curve: the crook of her arm ♦ vi/t bend ~ed /ˈkrʊkɪd/ adj 1 not straight 2 dishonest

croon /krun/ vi/t sing gently in a low soft voice ~er n

crop[1] /krɑp/ n 1 plant grown by a farmer 2 amount gathered in a season: (fig.) this year's crop of students

crop[2] vt -pp- 1 (of animals) bite off the tops of (grass etc.) 2 cut (hair, etc.) short

crop up phr vi happen unexpectedly

cro·quet /krouˈkeɪ/ n [U] outdoor game in which players knock wooden balls through HOOPS

cross[1] /krɔs/ n 1 the mark + 2 a upright post with a bar across it, esp. that on which Christ died **b** this shape as a sign of the Christian faith 3 sorrow; pain 4 mixture of 2 things

cross[2] v 1 vi/t go or put across 2 vt oppose (someone's wishes, etc.) 3 vi (of letters) pass in opposite directions 4 vt mix different breeds of (animals or plants) **5 cross oneself** make the sign of the cross with the hand **6 cross one's mind** come into one's thoughts **7 cross swords** argue **8 keep one's fingers crossed** hope that nothing will happen to upset one's plans ~ing n 1 journey across the sea 2 place where a road, etc., may be crossed

cross off/out phr vt draw a line through (writing)

cross[3] adj angry ~ly adv ~ness n [U]

cross·bow /ˈkrɔsbou/ n weapon combining a BOW[2] (1) and a gun

cross·check /ˌkrɔsˈtʃek, ˈkrɔstʃek/ vt test (a calculation, etc.) by using a different method

cross-coun·try /ˌ·ˈ··◄/ adj, adv across the fields or open country

cross-dress·ing /·ˈ·-·/ n transvestism (TRANSVESTITE)

cross-ex·am·ine /ˌ·-·-·/ vt question (esp. a witness in court) closely, to test answers given before

cross-eyed /·ˈ·/ adj with the eyes looking in towards the nose

cross·fire /ˈkrɔsfaɪər/ n [U] gunfire across one's direction of movement

cross-leg·ged /ˌkrɔs ˈlegɪd◄, -ˈlegd◄/ adj having the knees wide apart and ankles crossed

cross-pur·pos·es /ˌ·ˈ···/ n be at cross-purposes misunderstand one another

cross-ref·er·ence /ˌ·ˈ···/ n note directing the reader to another place in the book

cross·roads /ˈkrɔsroudz/ n -roads 1 place where roads cross 2 point where a decision must be made

cross-sec·tion /·ˈ·-·/ n 1 (drawing of) a surface made by cutting across 2 typical example of a whole

cross·town /ˈkrɔstaun/ adj traveling in a direction in a place, or across a town or city: a crosstown bus

cross·walk /ˈkrɔswɔk/ n set of white lines across a street where people have a right to walk across

cross·word puz·zle /ˈkrɔswərd ˌpʌzəl/ n printed game in which words are fitted into numbered squares

crotch /krɑtʃ/ n place between the tops of a person's legs

crotch·et·y /ˈkrɑtʃəti/ adj infml bad-tempered

crouch /krautʃ/ vi lower the body by bending the knees

crow[1] /krou/ n 1 large shiny black bird 2 **as the crow flies** in a straight line 3 **eat crow** admit one is wrong

crow[2] vi 1 make the loud cry of a COCK 2 speak proudly

crow·bar /ˈkroubɑr/ n iron bar for raising heavy objects

crowd /kraud/ n 1 large number of people together 2 particular ~ social group: the college crowd ♦ v 1 vi come together in a crowd 2 vt (esp. of people) fill: a crowded bus

crown /kraʊn/ n 1 [C] circular head decoration, esp. for a king or queen 2 [the+S] royal power 3 [C] top of a head, hat, hill, etc. 4 artificial cap on a tooth ♦ vt 1 place a crown on the head of 2 cover the top of: *mountains crowned with snow* 3 complete worthily 4 **to crown it all** to complete good or bad luck ~**ing** adj above all things

crow's feet /'· ·/ n [P] line at the outer corner of a person's eye: WRINKLE

crow's nest /'· ·/ n small shelter near top of a ship's MAST from which a person can watch for danger, etc.

cru·cial /'kruːʃəl/ adj of the greatest importance ~**ly** adv

cru·ci·ble /'kruːsəbəl/ n pot for melting metals in

cru·ci·fix /'kruːsəfɪks/ n cross with a figure of Christ on it

cru·ci·fix·ion /ˌkruːsə'fɪkʃən/ n [C;U] death by nailing to a cross

cru·ci·fy /'kruːsəfaɪ/ vt 1 kill by crucifixion 2 be very cruel to, esp. publicly

crud /krʌd/ n 1 dirt 2 unspecific illness usu. of stomach

crude /kruːd/ adj 1 in a natural state; untreated 2 without sensitive feeling: *crude jokes* 3 badly made ♦ n [U] crude oil ~**ly** adv **crudity** n [C;U]

cru·el /'kruːəl/ adj -**ll**- 1 liking to cause suffering 2 causing suffering: *cruel disappointment* ~**ly** adv ~**ty** n [C;U]

cruise /kruːz/ v 1 vi sail slowly for pleasure 2 vi (of a car, etc.) move at a steady speed 3 vi/t look (in public places) for a sexual partner, esp. one of the same sex ♦ n sea voyage for pleasure **cruiser** n 1 fast fighting ship 2 motor boat with a CABIN

cruise mis·sile /ˌ· '··/ n GUIDED MISSILE that flies low and can examine the ground

crumb /krʌm/ n small piece of dry food, esp. bread: (fig.) *crumbs of information*

crum·ble /'krʌmbəl/ v 1 vi/t break into small pieces 2 vi come to ruin ~**bly** adj easily crumbled

crum·my /'krʌmi/ adj worthless

crum·ple /'krʌmpəl/ 1 vi/t crush into irregular folds 2 vi lose strength

crunch /krʌntʃ/ v 1 vt crush (food) noisily with the teeth 2 vi make a crushing noise ♦ n [S] 1 crunching sound 2 CRISIS: *when it comes to the crunch*

cru·sade /kruː'seɪd/ n 1 Christian war against the Muslims in the Middle Ages 2 any united struggle: *a crusade for women's rights* ♦ vi take part in a crusade –**sader** n

crush /krʌʃ/ v 1 vi/t break or spoil by pressure 2 vi press; push: *They crushed through the gates.* 3 vt destroy completely: (fig.) *He felt crushed by her cruel remark.* ♦ n 1 [S] crowd of people pressed together 2 [C] strong and foolish love for someone, but only temporary

crust /krʌst/ n [C;U] hard outer surface of something, esp. bread ~**y** adj 1 with a hard crust 2 bad-tempered

crus·ta·cean /krʌ'steɪʃən/ n SHELLFISH

crutch /krʌtʃ/ n 1 stick to help someone to walk 2 something that gives moral support: *He uses religion as a crutch.* 3 CROTCH

crux /krʌks/ n central part of a problem

cry¹ /kraɪ/ v 1 vi produce tears from the eyes 2 vi/t call out loudly: *'Help!' he cried.* 3 vi (of a bird or animal) make its natural sound 4 **cry one's eyes/heart out** cry very bitterly 5 **for crying out loud** sl (used to give strength to a demand, etc.): *Oh, for crying out loud, shut that door!*

cry out for phr vt need very badly

cry² n 1 [C] shout expressing something: *cries of joy* | *a war cry* | *a cry for help* 2 [S] period of crying 3 bird's or animal's natural sound 4 **a far cry from** a great deal different from (something)

cry·ba·by /'kraɪˌbeɪbi/ n [C] person who cries too readily with little cause

crypt /krɪpt/ n room under a church

cryp·tic /'krɪptɪk/ adj with a hidden meaning

crys·tal /'krɪstəl/ n 1 [C;U] (piece of) transparent ice-like mineral 2 [U] expensive colorless glass 3 [C] regular shape formed naturally by some substances such as sugar 4 [C] transparent cover of a clock or watch face ~**lize** v 1 vi/t form into crystals 2 vi/t make (ideas, etc.) fixed in form 3 vt preserve (fruit) with sugar

crystal ball /ˌ·· '·/ n ball used by FORTUNE TELLERS to look into the future

cub /kʌb/ n young lion, bear, etc.

cub·by·hole /'kʌbihoʊl/ n small room or cupboard

cube /kyub/ n 1 solid object with 6 equal square sides 2 result of multiplying a number by itself twice ♦ vt multiply a number by itself twice: *3 cubed is 27.*

cu·bic /ˈkyubɪk/ adj multiplying length by width and height: *a cubic foot*

cu·bi·cle /ˈkyubɪkəl/ n small division of a large room

cuck·oo /ˈkuku, ˈkʊ-/ n bird that lays its eggs in other birds' nests and makes a noise like its name

cu·cum·ber /ˈkyukʌmbə/ n long green vegetable eaten raw

cud /kʌd/ n 1 food swallowed and brought up again by cows, etc., for further eating 2 **chew the cud** think deeply before making a decision

cud·dle /ˈkʌdl/ n 1 vt hold lovingly in one's arms 2 vi lie close and comfortably ♦ n [S] cuddling; HUG **–dly** adj suitable for cuddling

cue¹ /kyu/ n 1 signal for the next actor to speak in a play 2 example of how to behave

cue² n stick for pushing the ball in BILLIARDS or POOL² (2)

cuff /kʌf/ n 1 end of a SLEEVE 2 **off the cuff** (of an answer, etc.) without preparation

cuff link /ˈ· ·/ n button-like object used for fastening cuffs

cui·sine /kwɪˈzin/ n [U] style of cooking

cul-de-sac /ˌkʌl də ˈsæk, ˌkʊl-/ n street closed at one end

cu·li·na·ry /ˈkʌləˌnɛri, ˈkyu-/ adj of, related to the kitchen or cooking

cull /kʌl/ 1 vt fml gather (information, etc.) 2 vi/t take the best parts from a group

cul·mi·nate /ˈkʌlməˌneɪt/ v

  culminate in phr vt fml reach the last and highest point: *The battle culminated in victory.* **–nation** /ˌkʌlməˈneɪʃən/ n [S]

cul·pa·ble /ˈkʌlpəbəl/ adj fml deserving blame **–bly** adv **–bility** /ˌkʌlpəˈbɪləti/ n [U]

cul·prit /ˈkʌlprɪt/ n guilty person

cult /kʌlt/ n 1 system of worship 2 popular fashion: *cult films*

cul·ti·vate /ˈkʌltəˌveɪt/ vt 1 a prepare (land) for crops b grow (crops) 2 improve or develop by careful attention, study, etc. 3 pay friendly attention to (people) **–vated** adj educated and having good manners **–vation** /ˌkʌltəˈveɪʃən/ n [U]

cul·ture /ˈkʌltʃə/ n 1 [C;U] art, thought, and customs of a society: *tribal cultures* 2 [U] high development in art and thought 3 [U] raising animals and growing plants **–tural** adj: *cultural activities* **–tured** adj 1 cultivated 2 produced by humans: *cultured pearls*

cum·ber·some /ˈkʌmbəsəm/ adj heavy and awkward to carry

cu·mu·la·tive /ˈkyumyəlɑtɪv, -ˌleɪ-/ adj increasing by one addition after another **~ly** adv

cun·ning /ˈkʌnɪŋ/ adj clever in deceiving ♦ n [U] quality of being cunning **~ly** adv

cunt /kʌnt/ n taboo VAGINA

cup /kʌp/ n 1 container, usu. with a handle, to drink from 2 thing shaped like a cup: *bra cups* 3 gold or silver container given as a prize in competitions 4 HOLE in GOLF ♦ vt **-pp-** form (one's hands) into a cup shape

cup·board /ˈkʌbəd/ n place to keep dishes, plates, etc. in a kitchen

cup·cake /ˈkʌpkeɪk/ n small cake for one person

cu·ra·ble /ˈkyʊrəbəl/ adj that can be cured

cu·ra·tor /kyʊˈreɪtə, ˈkyʊˌreɪtə, -ətə/ n person in charge of a MUSEUM, etc.

curb /kəb/ n 1 stone edge of a SIDEWALK 2 controlling influence; CHECK (2) ♦ vt hold back; control

curd /kəd/ n [C;U] thick soft substance that separates from milk when it becomes sour

cur·dle /ˈkədl/ vi/t (cause to) form into CURDS; (cause to) thicken

cure /kyʊr/ vt 1 a bring back to health: (fig.) *a plan to cure the economy* b make (a disease) go away 2 preserve (food, skin, tobacco) by drying, etc. ♦ n 1 something that cures a person or disease 2 a return to health after illness

cur·few /ˈkəfyu/ n [C;U] time or signal for people to stay indoors

cu·ri·o /ˈkyʊriˌoʊ/ n **–os** rare or beautiful small object

cu·ri·os·i·ty /ˌkyʊriˈɑsəti/ n 1 [S;U] desire to know 2 [C] interesting rare object

cu·ri·ous /ˈkyʊriəs/ adj 1 eager to learn 2 peculiar **~ly** adv

curl¹ /kəl/ n 1 hanging twist of hair 2 thing this shape: *curls of smoke* **~y** adj having curls

curl² /vi/t twist; wind

curl up phr vi/t (cause to) lie comfortably with the limbs drawn close to the body: curl up with a good book

cur·ren·cy /ˈkərənsi, ˈkʌr-/ n 1 [C;U] money in use in a country 2 [U] state of being generally believed

cur·rent¹ /ˈkərənt, ˈkʌr-/ adj 1 of the present time: current fashion 2 commonly accepted 3 (of money) used as currency

current² n 1 flow of liquid, gas, or electricity 2 general tendency or course of events

cur·ric·u·lum /kəˈrɪkyələm/ n -la /-lə/ or -lums course of study in a school, etc.

cur·ry¹ /ˈkəri, ˈkʌri/ n [C;U] Indian dish of meat, vegetables, etc. with a hot taste ◆ vt make into curry

curry² v **curry favor** try to win approval dishonestly

curse /kəs/ n 1 words calling for evil to come to someone 2 cause of misfortune: Foxes are a curse to farmers. 3 word or words used in swearing ◆ vi/t 1 call down evil upon 2 use violent language (against) 3 **be cursed with** suffer from

cursed /ˈkəsɪd/ adj hateful; annoying

cur·sor /ˈkəsə/ n mark which can move around a SCREEN connected to a computer to point to a particular position

cur·so·ry /ˈkəsəi/ adj (of work, reading, etc.) not thorough –**rily** adv

curt /kət/ adj (of speech) impolitely short –**ly** adv ~**ness** n [U]

cur·tail /kəˈteɪl/ vt fml shorten; reduce ~**ment** n [C;U]

cur·tain /ˈkətˈn/ n 1 cloth hung over a window, or in front of a theater stage: (fig.) curtain of smoke 2 [P] sl the end, esp. of a person's life

curt·sy /ˈkətsi/ vi, n (make) a woman's act of bending the knees and lowering the head to show respect

cur·va·ture /ˈkəvətʃə, -ıtʃʊr/ n [C;U] state of being curved

curve /kəv/ n line that is not straight and has no angles ◆ vi/t: The road curves to the right.

cush·ion /ˈkʊʃən/ n bag filled with something soft, for lying or sitting on: (fig.) a cushion of air ◆ vt 1 lessen the force of 2 protect from hardship

cush·y /ˈkʊʃi/ adj (of a job, style of life, etc.) easy

cuss /kʌs/ vi/t CURSE (2) ◆ n difficult person

cus·tard /ˈkʌstəd/ n [U] sweet yellow mixture of eggs and milk

cus·to·di·an /kʌˈstoʊdiən/ n person in charge of a public building

cus·to·dy /ˈkʌstədi/ n [U] 1 right to look after someone: give him custody of his child 2 being guarded or imprisoned: in police custody

cus·tom /ˈkʌstəm/ n 1 [C;U] established social behavior 2 [C] something someone does regularly **customs** n [P] 1 taxes on goods entering or leaving a country 2 place where these taxes are collected

cus·tom·a·ry /ˈkʌstəˌmɛri/ adj established by custom; usual

custom-built /ˌ·· ˈ·◀/ also **custom-made** /ˌ·· ˈ·◀/ adj made especially for one person or group of people

cus·tom·er /ˈkʌstəmə/ n person who buys things from a store

cus·tom·ized /ˈkʌstəˌmaɪzd/ adj changed to match the needs of one person or group of people

cut¹ /kʌt/ v **cut**, -**tt**- 1 vt/i use something sharp to divide, remove, shorten, make a hole, etc.: cut your fingers/your hair/the corn 2 vi a be able to be cut b (of a knife, etc.) be sharp 3 vt make shorter or smaller: cut a long speech 4 vt make (esp. a public service) less in size, amount, etc.: They're cutting postal deliveries/bus services. 5 vt stay away on purpose: cut a lecture 6 vt put (a film) into final form 7 vt hurt the feelings of someone: cutting remarks 8 vt (of a line, path, etc.) cross 9 vi stop filming a scene 10 **cut corners** do something quickly and cheaply but not perfectly 11 **cut it close** leave oneself too little time or money 12 **cut it out** stop doing something 13 **cut no/not much ice** have no/little influence 14 **cut one's losses** stop doing something before one loses any more money 15 **cut someone (dead)** refuse to recognize them

cut across phr vt 1 go across instead of around 2 make a different division in: cut across party lines

cut back phr v 1 vt PRUNE (a plant) 2 vi/t reduce **cutback** /ˈkʌtˌbæk/ n planned reduction

cut down phr vt 1 vt bring down by cutting 2 vi/t reduce: cut down (on) *smoking* **3** knock down or kill (someone) **4 cut down to size** reduce from too great importance to true or suitable importance

cut in *phr vi* **1** interrupt **2** drive between moving vehicles **3** *vt* include

cut off *phr vt* **1** separate by cutting **2** disconnect (telephone, gas, electricity, etc.) **3** separate from others: *cut off by floods* **4** end unexpectedly **5** DISINHERIT

cut out *phr v* **1** *vt* remove by cutting **2** *vt* make by cutting: *cut out a dress* **3** *vt/i* stop: *cut out smoking | The engine keeps cutting out.* **4 not cut out for** not suitable for

cut up *phr vt* **1** cut into little pieces **2** make unhappy **3** behave in a humorous way

cut² *n* **1** opening made by cutting **2** piece of meat, etc., cut off **3** reduction: *cuts in government spending* **4** way in which clothes, hair, etc., are shaped **5** *infml* someone's share of a profit **6 a** act of removing a part, to improve or shorten **b** part removed **7 a cut above** better

cut-and-dried /ˌ· · ˈ· ◄/ *adj* unlikely to change; fixed

cute /kyut/ *adj* **1** delightfully pretty **2** (too) clever

cu·ti·cle /ˈkyutɪkəl/ *n* skin at the base of one's nails

cut·ler·y /ˈkʌtləri/ *n* [U] *fml* sharp knives

cut·let /ˈkʌtˈlɪt/ *n* small piece of meat

cut·ter /ˈkʌtə/ *n* **1** person or tool that cuts **2** small fast boat

cut·throat /ˈkʌtˈθroʊt/ *adj* fierce; unprincipled: *cutthroat competition*

cut·ting /ˈkʌtɪŋ/ *n* piece cut from a plant to form a new one

cutting edge /ˌ·· ˈ· ◄/ *n* [*the*+S] most advanced stage or development: *the cutting edge of fashion* **cutting-edge** *adj*: *cutting-edge technology*

cy·a·nide /ˈsaɪəˌnaɪd/ *n* [U] strong poison

cy·ber·net·ics /ˌsaɪbəˈnɛtɪks/ *n* [U] science of how information is dealt with by machines and the brain

cy·ber·space /ˈsaɪbəˌspeɪs/ *n* [U] connections between computers in different places

cy·cle¹ /ˈsaɪkəl/ *n* (time needed for) a set of events in regularly repeated order: *a 50-minute cycle*

cycle² *v, n* bicycle **cyclist** *n*

cyclical /ˈsaɪklɪkəl, ˈsɪ-/ *adj fml* happening in cycles

cy·clone /ˈsaɪkloʊn/ *n* very violent wind moving rapidly in a circle

cyl·in·der /ˈsɪləndə/ *n* **1** object or container with a circular base and straight sides **2** tube for a PISTON in an engine

cym·bal /ˈsɪmbəl/ *n* one of a pair of metal plates struck together to make a noise in music

cyn·ic /ˈsɪnɪk/ *n* person who sees little good in anything and shows it by making unkind remarks ~**al** *adj* ~**ally** *adv* ~**ism** /ˈsɪnəˌsɪzəm/ *n* [U]

cy·press /ˈsaɪprəs/ *n* EVERGREEN tree with dark green leaves and hard wood

cyst /sɪst/ *n* hollow growth in the body, containing liquid

czar /zɑr/ *n* **1** (until 1917) male ruler of Russia **2** important government official responsible for a particular area: *the drug czar*

czarina /zɑˈrinə/ *n* (until 1917) **1** female ruler of Russia **2** wife of the czar

D

D, d /di/ the 4th letter of the English alphabet

D *written abbrev. for:* **1** died **2** DIAMETER **3** DEMOCRAT

DA *n* district attorney

dab /dæb/ *vi/t* **-bb-** touch or cover lightly ♦ *n* small quantity of paint, etc.

dab·ble /ˈdæbəl/ *v* **1** *vi* work at something not professionally: *dable in politics* **2** *vt* move (one's feet, etc.) playfully about in water

dachs·hund /ˈdɑks-hʊnt, -hʊnd/ *n* small dog with short legs and a long body

dad /dæd/ *n infml* father

dad·dy /ˈdædi/ *n* (child's word for) father

daf·fo·dil /ˈdæfədil/ *n* yellow spring flower shaped like a bell

daf·fy /ˈdæfi/ *adj* crazy

dag·ger /ˈdægə/ *n* **1** short knife used as a weapon **2** look daggers at look angrily at

dai·ly /ˈdeili/ *adj, adv* every day ♦ *n* newspaper sold every day but Sunday

dain·ty /ˈdeinti/ *adj* small, pretty, and delicate **–tily** *adv* **–tiness** *n* [U]

dair·y /ˈdɛri/ *n* place where milk, butter, cheese, etc., are produced or sold ♦ *adj*: *dairy cattle/products*

dai·sy /ˈdeizi/ *n* **1** common white flower with yellow center **2** as fresh as a daisy not tired

dal·ly /ˈdæli/ *vi* waste time

dally with *phr vt* play with (an idea)

Dal·ma·tian /dælˈmeiʃən/ *n* dog with white fur and small black spots

dam¹ /dæm/ *n* wall built to keep back water

dam² *vt* **-mm-** make a dam across

dam up *phr vt* control (a feeling, esp. of anger) in an unhealthy way

dam·age /ˈdæmɪdʒ/ *n* [U] harm; loss: *brain damage* ♦ *vt* cause damage to **damages** /ˈdæmɪdʒɪz/ *n* [P] money paid for damage done

dame /deim/ *n sl* woman

damn /dæm/ *vt* **1** (of God) punish **2** declare to be bad **3** ruin: *damning evi-*

dence **4 Well, I'll be damned!** *infml* I'm very surprised ♦ *n* **not give a damn** not care at all ♦ *interj* (used in curses): *Damn it!* **damn,** also **~ed** /dæmd/ *adj, adv* (used for giving force to an expression): *run damned* (= very) *fast | He's a damn fool.* **~able** /ˈdæmnəbəl/ *adj* very bad **~ation** /dæmˈneiʃən/ *n* [U] **1** act of damning **2 in damnation** (used for giving force to an expression of anger): *What in damnation do you mean?* **damnedest** /ˈdæmdist/ *n* **do one's damnedest** do everything possible

damp¹ /dæmp/ *adj* slightly wet ♦ *n* [U] slight wetness **~ness** *n* [U]

damp² also **dampen** /ˈdæmpən/ *vt* **1** wet slightly **2** reduce (eagerness, etc.): *damp their spirits*

damp down *phr vt* make (a fire) burn more slowly

damp·er /ˈdæmpə/ *n* **1** metal plate controlling the flow of air to a fire **2** influence reducing eagerness

dam·sel /ˈdæmzəl/ *n old lit* **1** young unmarried woman of noble birth; young girl **2 damsel in distress** *humor* girl in trouble

dance /dæns/ *n* **1** [C] (music for) a set of movements performed to music **2** [C] party with dances **3** [U] art of dancing — see also SONG AND DANCE ♦ *vi/t* do a dance **dancer** *n*

dan·de·li·on /ˈdændɪˌlaiən/ *n* common bright yellow flower

dan·druff /ˈdændrəf/ *n* bits of dead skin in the hair

dan·dy /ˈdændi/ *n* man who is almost too well dressed ♦ *adj* good: *fine and dandy*

dan·ger /ˈdeindʒə/ *n* **1** [U] possibility of harm **2** [C] cause of danger **~ous** *adj* not safe **~ously** *adv*

dan·gle /ˈdæŋgəl/ *vi/t* **1** hang loosely **2 keep someone dangling** keep someone waiting and not knowing what the result will be

dan·ish /ˈdeiniʃ/ *n* pastry with fruit center: *prune danish*

dank /dæŋk/ *adj* unpleasantly wet and cold

dap·per /ˈdæpə/ *adj* neatly dressed

dare /dɛr/ *v* **1** *vi* be brave enough (to): *He didn't dare (to) ask.* **2** *vt* CHALLENGE to do something: *I dared her to jump.* ♦ *n* CHALLENGE: *She jumped for a dare.*

dare·dev·il /ˈdɛrˌdɛvəl/ *n* person foolishly fond of adventure

dar·ing /'dɛrɪŋ/ n [U] bravery ♦ adj 1 brave 2 shocking ~ly adv

dark /dɑrk/ adj 1 without (much) light: darkroom 2 tending towards black: dark green 3 secret; hidden: dark mysteries 4 evil; sad ♦ n [U] 1 absence of light 2 after/before dark after/before night 3 in the dark not knowing something ~en vi/t make or become darker ~ly adv ~ness n [U]

Dark Ag·es /ˌ· ˈ·/ n [the+P] period in Europe about A.D. 476 to A.D. 1000

dark horse /ˌ· ˈ·/ n unknown competitor who may win

dark·room /'dɑrk-rum, -rʊm/ n room where photographs are developed and printed

dar·ling /'dɑrlɪŋ/ adj, n dearly loved (person)

darn¹ /dɑrn/ vt/i mend (holes in cloth) ♦ n darned hole

darn² n, adj, interj DAMN

dart /dɑrt/ n 1 pointed object to throw, esp. in a game called **darts** 2 quick movement ♦ vi/t move or send suddenly

dart·board /'dɑrt˺bord, -bourd/ n circular board at which darts are thrown

dash /dæʃ/ v 1 vi run quickly 2 vi/t strike violently: The waves dashed the boat against the rocks. 3 vt destroy (hopes, etc.) ♦ n 1 [C] sudden quick run or short race 2 [C] small amount added: a dash of pepper 3 [C] the mark (–) 4 [U] combination of bravery and style: I admire his dash. ~ing adj having a lot of DASH (4)

dash·board /'dæʃbord, -bourd/ n instrument board in a car

da·ta /'deɪtə, 'dætə, 'dɑtə/ n [P;U] facts; information, esp. as stored in a computer's **data bank** for **data processing**

da·ta·base /'deɪtəˌbeɪs/ n computer's collection of data

date¹ /deɪt/ n 1 day, month, or year of an event 2 arrangement to meet socially 3 person of the opposite sex whom one arranges to meet socially 4 out of date: a old-fashioned b no longer VALID 5 to date up till now 6 up to date modern

date² v 1 vt guess the date of 2 vt write the date on 3 vi become old-fashioned 4 vi/t make a social date with **dated** adj old fashioned

date from also **date back to** phr vt have lasted since

date³ n small tropical fruit with a long pit

date rape /ˈ· ˌ·/ n [C;U] RAPE that happens during a DATE¹ (2)

daub /dɔb/ vt cover with something sticky

daugh·ter /'dɔtə/ n someone's female child

daughter-in-law /ˈ·· · ˌ·/ n daughters-in-law son's wife

daunt /dɔnt, dɑnt/ vt discourage ~less adj not discouraged

daunt·ing /dɔnrɪŋ, dɑn-/ adj frightening; making one less confident: a daunting task

daw·dle /'dɔdl/ vi waste time; be slow

dawn¹ /dɔn/ n 1 [C;U] first light of morning 2 [S] first appearance: the dawn of civilization

dawn² vi begin to grow light

dawn on phr vt become known to: The truth dawned on me.

day /deɪ/ n 1 [C] period of 24 hours 2 [C;U] time between sunrise and sunset: the **daylight hours** | in the **daytime** 3 [C] hours that one works 4 [C] period; time: the present day 5 [S] period of success 6 **call it a day** finish working for the day 7 **day after day** also **day in, day out** continuously 8 **make someone's day** make someone very happy 9 **one day** at some time 10 **one's days** one's life 11 **the other day** recently 12 **these days** now

day·break /'deɪbreɪk/ n [U] DAWN (1)

day·care cen·ter /'deɪkɛr ˌsɛntə/ n public NURSERY for babies and children

day·dream /'deɪdrim/ vi, n (have pleasant dreamlike thoughts

day·light sav·ing time /ˌdeɪlaɪt 'seɪvɪŋ ˌtaɪm/ n time used in the summer when clocks move ahead one hour

day·lights /'deɪlaɪts/ n [P] beat/ knock/ scare the (living) daylights out of hit/frighten (someone) very severely

day-to-day /ˌ· ˈ· ˈ·/ adj 1 happening each day: We just live day-to-day. 2 planning for one day at a time

daze /deɪz/ vt make unable to think clearly ♦ n dazed condition

daz·zle /'dæzəl/ vt 1 make unable to see because of too strong light 2 cause wonder to: dazzled by success

dea·con /'dikən/ ~ess /-kənɪs/ fem. — n Christian church officer below a priest

dead¹ /dɛd/ adj 1 no longer alive 2 no longer used or usable: dead languages/battery | *The telephone went dead.* **3** complete: *dead silence* **4** without activity: *the place seems dead* **5** NUMB: *My fingers went dead.* **6** (of sound or color) dull ♦ *adv* **1** completely: *stop dead* **2** directly: *dead ahead* ~en *vt* cause to lose (strength, feeling, brightness): *deaden pain/noise*

dead[2] *n* **in the dead of** in the greatest or least active period of

dead-beat /'dɛdbiːt/ *n* lazy aimless person

dead end /ˌ· '·◁/ *n* end (of a street) with no way out: (fig.) *We've reached a dead end in our talks.*

dead let-ter /ˌ· '··/ *n* letter that can't be delivered because the address is wrong

dead-line /'dɛdlaɪn/ *n* fixed date for finishing something

dead-lock /'dɛdlɑk/ *n* disagreement that cannot be settled

dead-ly /'dɛdli/ *adj* **1** likely to cause death **2** total: *deadly enemies* **3** *infml* very dull ♦ *adv* **1** like death: *deadly pale* **2** very: *deadly dull*

dead-pan /'dɛdpæn/ *adj, adv* with no show of feeling, esp. when telling jokes

dead ring-er /ˌ· '·/ *n* someone who looks exactly like someone else

dead wood /'· ◁/ *n* [U] useless people or things

deaf /dɛf/ *adj* **1** unable to hear **2** deaf to unwilling to listen to ~en *vt* (of loud noises) make unable to hear: *The noise was deafening.* (= very loud) ~ness *n* [U]

deal[1] /diːl/ *vi/t* dealt /dɛlt/ **1** give out (esp. playing cards) as a share **2** strike: *deal someone a blow* ~er *n* **1** person who deals cards **2** person in business: *car dealer* ~ing *n* [U] methods of business or personal relations ~ings *n* [P] personal or business relations

deal in *phr vt* do business in; sell

deal with *phr vt* **1** do business with **2** take action about **3** be about: *a book dealing with Ireland*

deal[2] *n* **1** [C] business arrangement **2** [C] one's turn to deal cards **3 a good/great deal 1** [U] a fairly/very large amount: *work a good deal faster* **2** [C] something sold cheap

deal-er-ship /'diːlərʃɪp/ *n* business that sells a particular company's products, esp. cars

dean /diːn/ *n* important university official

dear /dɪr/ *adj* **1** loved; precious **2** (at the beginning of letters): *Dear Sir* ♦ **1** *n* loved person **2** (used when speaking to someone you love): *Yes, dear.* ♦ *interj* (expressing surprise, sorrow, etc.): *Oh dear!* ~**ly** *adv* **1** with much feeling **2** at terrible cost

dearth /dɜːθ/ *n* [S] *fml* lack

death /dɛθ/ *n* **1** [C;U] end of life: (fig.) *the death of our hopes* **2** [U] state of being dead **3** cause of death: *Drinking will be the death of him.* **4** at death's door in danger of dying; about to die **5** death warmed up/over *infml* very ill or tired **6** put to death kill, esp. officially **7** to death beyond proper limits: *sick/bored/worried to death* ~less *adj* unforgettable ~ly *adj, adv* like death

death row /ˌdɛθ 'roʊ/ *n* prison area for those waiting for the death sentence

death trap /'· ·/ *n* very dangerous thing or place

de-ba-cle /deɪ'bɑkəl, dɪ-/ *n* sudden complete failure

de-base /dɪ'beɪs/ *vt* make lower in value ~ment *n* [C;U]

de-bate /dɪ'beɪt/ *n* [C;U] (process of) discussion (DISCUSS) ♦ *vi/t* **1** hold a debate about **2** think about; wonder **debatable** *adj* doubtful: questionable

de-bauch-er-y /dɪ'bɔtʃəri/ *n* immoral behavior, esp. in relation to sex and alcohol

de-bil-i-tate /dɪ'bɪlɪˌteɪt/ *vt* make weak ~ty *n* [U] *fml* weakness

deb-it /'dɛbɪt/ *n* record of money owed ♦ *vt* charge against an account

deb-o-nair /ˌdɛbə'nɛr◁/ *adj* cheerful and fashionably dressed

de-brief /diː'briːf/ *vt* find out information from (someone on one's own side) by thorough questioning after an action

deb-ris /də'briː, deɪ-/ *n* [U] broken remains; ruins

debt /dɛt/ *n* [C;U] something owed; state of owing ~or *n* person who owes money

de-bug /ˌdiː'bʌg/ *vt infml* **1** remove the BUGS (3) from a room or building **2** search for and remove the BUGS (5) in (a computer PROGRAM)

de-bunk /diː'bʌŋk, dɪ-/ *vt* point out the truth about a wrong idea

de-but /deɪ'byu, dɪ-, 'deɪbyu/ *n* first public appearance

dec-ade /'dɛkeɪd, dɛ'keɪd/ *n* period of 10 years

dec·a·dent /ˈdɛkədənt/ adj falling to a lower level of morals –**dence** n [U]

de·caf·fein·at·ed /diˈkæfəˌneɪtɪd/ adj (of coffee, tea, COLA, etc.) from which CAFFEINE has been removed

de·cal /ˈdikæl, ˈdɛkəl/ n picture for sticking or printing onto a surface

de·cant /dɪˈkænt/ vt pour (liquid) from another container –**er** n glass container for liquid, esp. wine

de·cap·i·tate /dɪˈkæpəˌteɪt/ vt BEHEAD

de·cath·lon /dɪˈkæθlɑn, -lən/ n ATHLETIC competition with 10 separate events

de·cay /dɪˈkeɪ/ vi 1 go bad: decayed teeth 2 lose health, power, etc. ♦ n [U] process of decaying

de·ceased /dɪˈsist/ adj fml dead ♦ n fml the dead person

de·ceit /dɪˈsit/ n [U] dishonesty ~**ful** adj dishonest ~**fully** adv

de·ceive /dɪˈsiv/ vt cause to believe something false **deceiver** n

De·cem·ber /dɪˈsɛmbə/ n the 12th and last month of the year

de·cent /ˈdisənt/ adj 1 socially acceptable; proper 2 good enough: a decent meal 3 kind **decency** n [U] being DECENT (1)

de·cen·tral·ize /ˌdiˈsɛntrəˌlaɪz/ vi/t move (a business, etc.) from a central office or place to several smaller ones

de·cep·tion /dɪˈsɛpʃən/ n 1 [U] deceiving 2 [C] trick –**tive** /-tɪv/ adj misleading –**tively** adv

dec·i·bel /ˈdɛsəˌbɛl, -bəl/ n unit of loudness

de·cide /dɪˈsaɪd/ v 1 vi/t make a choice or judgment: She decided to go. 2 vt make (someone) decide 3 vi/t end uncertain state **decided** adj 1 easily seen: decided improvement 2 sure of oneself **decidedly** adv certainly

decide on phr v decide in favor of

de·cid·u·ous /dɪˈsɪdʒuəs/ adj (of trees) losing their leaves in autumn

dec·i·mal /ˈdɛsəməl/ adj based on the number 10 ♦ n number such as .5 or .06 ~**ize** vi/t change to a decimal system of money, etc.

dec·i·mate /ˈdɛsəˌmeɪt/ vt destroy a large part of

de·ci·pher /dɪˈsaɪfə/ vt read (something difficult, esp. a CODE)

de·ci·sion /dɪˈsɪʒən/ n 1 [C;U] deciding; choice: reach a decision 2 [U] firmness of judgment

de·ci·sive /dɪˈsaɪsɪv, -zɪv/ adj 1 firm in judgment 2 leading to a clear result ~**ly** adv ~**ness** n [U]

deck[1] /dɛk/ n 1 floor of a ship 2 PACK of playing cards 3 raised wooden floor outside the back of a house, for relaxing on

deck[2] vt 1 decorate 2 **decked out** dressed or decorated for a special occasion

dec·la·ra·tion /ˌdɛkləˈreɪʃən/ n [C;U] 1 declaring 2 official statement

de·clare /dɪˈklɛr/ vt 1 make known officially: declare war 2 state clearly 3 tell CUSTOMS officials about (taxable goods)

de·clas·si·fy /ˌdiˈklæsəˌfaɪ/ vt declare (esp. political and military information) no longer secret

de·cline /dɪˈklaɪn/ v 1 vi become worse or less 2 vt/i refuse (an invitation, etc.) politely ♦ n period of declining (DECLINE (1)): Interest in the arts is on the decline.

de·code /diˈkoʊd/ vt read (something written in CODE)

de·com·pose /ˌdikəmˈpoʊz/ vi go bad; DECAY –**position** /ˌdikɑmpəˈzɪʃən/ n [U]

de·con·tam·i·nate /ˌdikənˈtæməˌneɪt/ vt remove dangerous substances from –**nation** /-ˌtæməˈneɪʃən/ n [U]

de·cor /deɪˈkɔr, ˈdeɪkɔr/ n decoration and furnishings of a place

dec·o·rate /ˈdɛkəˌreɪt/ v 1 vt add something beautiful to 2 vi/t paint, put paper, etc., on room 3 vt give a mark of honor, such as a MEDAL, etc. to, –**rator** n person who decorates houses –**rative** /ˈdɛkərətɪv, ˈdɛkəreɪ-/ adj beautiful; attractive –**ration** /ˌdɛkəˈreɪʃən/ n 1 [U] decorating 2 [C] something that decorates 3 [C] mark of honor, MEDAL, etc.

dec·o·rous /ˈdɛkərəs/ adj (of appearance or behavior) correct

de·co·rum /dɪˈkɔrəm, -ˈkoʊr-/ n [U] fml correct behavior

de·coy /ˈdikɔɪ, dɪˈkɔɪ/ n something used for getting a person or bird into a trap **decoy** vt

de·crease[1] /dɪˈkris/ vi/t (cause to) become less

de·crease[2] /ˈdikris/ n 1 [U] process of decreasing 2 [C] amount by which something decreases

de·cree /dɪˈkri/ n official command or decision ♦ vt order officially

de·crep·it /dɪˈkrɛpɪt/ adj weak from old age

de·cry /dɪˈkraɪ/ vt fml speak disapprovingly of

ded·i·cate /ˈdɛdɪˌkeɪt/ vt **1** give to a serious purpose: *dedicate her life to medical research* | *a dedicated doctor* **2** declare (a book, etc.) to be in honor of someone, by printing their name at the front –**cation** /ˌdɛdəˈkeɪʃən/ n **1** [C;U] act of dedicating **2** [U] words used in dedicating a book

de·duce /dɪˈdjuːs/ vt reach (a piece of knowledge) by reasoning

de·duct /dɪˈdʌkt/ vt take away (part) from a total ~**ible** adj: *expenses deductible from tax*

de·duc·tion /dɪˈdʌkʃən/ n [C;U] **1** example of deducing; knowledge deduced: *a brilliant deduction* **2** process of deducting; something deducted: *a salary of $20,000 after all deductions*

deed /diːd/ n **1** lit something done; action **2** law signed agreement

deem /diːm/ vt fml consider; judge

deep /diːp/ adj **1** going far down from the top, or in from the outside: *deep river/wound* | *ankle-deep in mud* **2** (of color) dark **3** (of sound) low **4** strong; extreme: *deep sleep* | *deep distrust* | *in deep trouble* **5** difficult to understand **6** a wise: *a deep thinker* b mysterious: *a deep secret* **7** go off the deep end sl become confused **8** in/into deep water infml in/into serious trouble **9** thrown in at the deep end suddenly and unexpectedly faced with a difficult piece of work ♦ adv far down; far in ~**en** vi/t make or become deeper ~**ly** adv ~**ness** n [U]

deep freeze /ˌ · ˈ·/ vt freeze food quickly in order to preserve it ♦ /ˈ· ˌ·/ n FREEZER

deep fry /ˌ· ˈ·/ vt FRY completely under the surface of oil or fat

deep-root·ed /ˌ· ˈ··◄/ also **deep-seated** — adj strongly fixed: *deep-rooted habits*

deer /dɪr/ n large fast animal of which the males have ANTLERS

de·face /dɪˈfeɪs/ vt spoil the surface of ~**ment** n [U]

de fac·to /ˌdeɪ ˈfæktəʊ, dɪ-/ adj, adv fml in actual fact, though not by law

de·fame /dɪˈfeɪm/ vt fml attack the good REPUTATION of **defamation** /ˌdɛfəˈmeɪʃən/ n [U] **defamatory** /dɪˈfæməˌtɔːri, -ˌtoʊri/ adj

de·fault /dɪˈfɔːlt/ n [U] failure to fulfill a contract, pay a debt, etc. **default** vi ~**er** n

de·feat /dɪˈfiːt/ vt **1** win a victory over **2** cause to fail ♦ n [C;U] (example or act of) defeating ~**ism** n [U] practice of thinking or behaving in expectation of defeat ~**ist** n

def·e·cate /ˈdɛfəˌkeɪt/ vi fml pass waste matter from the bowels

de·fect¹ /ˈdiːfɛkt, dɪˈfɛkt/ n imperfection; fault ~**ive** /dɪˈfɛktɪv/ adj

de·fect² /dɪˈfɛkt/ vi desert one's political party, country, etc. ~**or** n ~**ion** /-ˈfɛkʃən/ n [C;U]

de·fend /dɪˈfɛnd/ vt **1** keep safe; protect **2** act as a lawyer for (someone charged with a crime) **3** argue in favor of

de·fen·dant /dɪˈfɛndənt/ n person against whom a legal charge or claim is brought

de·fense /dɪˈfɛns/ n **1** [U] act or process of defending **2** [C] something used in defending **3** [C;U] law a arguments used in defending someone in court b lawyers who defend someone **4** players or part of a game that stops the other team from making points ~**less** adj unable to defend oneself

de·fen·si·ble /dɪˈfɛnsəbəl/ adj that can be defended

de·fen·sive /dɪˈfɛnsɪv/ adj **1** used in defense **2** (of someone) who always seems to be expecting attack ♦ n on the defensive prepared for attack ~**ly** adv ~**ness** n [U]

de·fer /dɪˈfɜː/ vt -rr- POSTPONE ~**ment** n [C;U]

defer to phr vt fml accept the decision of

def·er·ence /ˈdɛfərəns/ n [U] fml respect for another's wishes

de·fi·ance /dɪˈfaɪəns/ n [U] open disobedience –**ant** adj –**antly** adv

de·fi·cien·cy /dɪˈfɪʃənsi/ n [C;U] lack: *vitamin deficiency* –**cient** adj

def·i·cit /ˈdɛfəsɪt/ n amount by which something, esp. money, is too little

de·file /dɪˈfaɪl/ vt fml make dirty

de·fine /dɪˈfaɪn/ vt **1** give the meaning of; explain exactly **2** set, mark or show the limits of: *a clearly-defined shape*

def·i·nite /ˈdɛfənɪt/ adj clear; ~**ly** adv **1** in a clear way **2** certainly

definite ar·ti·cle /ˌ··· ˈ···/ n (in English) the word THE

def·i·ni·tion /ˌdɛfəˈnɪʃən/ n **1** [C;U] (statement) defining something **2** [U] clearness of shape: *The photograph lacks definition.*

de·fin·i·tive /dɪˈfɪnətɪv/ adj that cannot be questioned; not needing change

de·flate /dɪˈfleɪt, diː-/ v 1 vt let air or gas out of (a tire, etc.) 2 vi/t reduce the supply of money in a country **deflation** /-ˈfleɪʃən/ n [U] **deflationary** adj

de·flect /dɪˈflɛkt/ vi/t turn aside from a straight course: (fig.) to deflect someone from their purpose ~**ion** /-ˈflɛkʃən/ n [C;U]

de·form /dɪˈfɔrm/ vt spoil the shape of ~**ity** n [C;U] imperfection of the body

de·fraud /dɪˈfrɔd/ vt deceive so as to get something: They defrauded him of $50.

de·frost /dɪˈfrɔst/ vt remove ice from; unfreeze

deft /dɛft/ adj effortlessly skillful ~**ly** adv

de·funct /dɪˈfʌŋkt/ adj dead

de·fuse /diˈfyuz/ vt 1 remove the FUSE from (a bomb, etc.) 2 make harmless

de·fy /dɪˈfaɪ/ vt 1 refuse to obey 2 CHALLENGE to do something impossible 3 remain unreachable by all efforts at or from: It defies description.

de·gen·er·ate /dɪˈdʒɛnərɪt/ adj having become worse than before ♦ n degenerate person ♦ vi /-nəˌreɪt/ become worse –**rative** /-nərətɪv/ adj –**ration** /dɪˌdʒɛnəˈreɪʃən/ n [U]

de·grade /dɪˈgreɪd/ vt 1 bring shame to 2 vi/t change to a simpler chemical form **degradation** /ˌdɛɡrəˈdeɪʃən/ n [C;U]

de·gree /dɪˈgri/ n 1 unit of measurement of angles, or of temperature 2 stage; level: getting better by degrees 3 title given to a university student – see also THIRD DEGREE

de·hy·drate /diˈhaɪdreɪt/ vt remove water from

deign /deɪn/ vt derog CONDESCEND

de·i·ty /ˈdiəti, ˈdeɪ-/ n god or goddess

de·ject·ed /dɪˈdʒɛktɪd/ adj low in spirits; sad –**tion** /-ˈdʒɛkʃən/ n [U]

de·lay /dɪˈleɪ/ v 1 vt make later 2 vi act slowly ♦ n 1 [U] delaying 2 [C] example or time of being delayed

de·lec·ta·ble /dɪˈlɛktəbəl/ adj delightful; DELICIOUS

del·e·gate[1] /ˈdɛləɡɪt/ n person chosen to act for others

del·e·gate[2] /ˈdɛləˌɡeɪt/ v 1 vi/t give (power, etc.) to someone else 2 vt appoint (someone) as a delegate –**gation** /ˌdɛləˈɡeɪʃən/ n 1 [U] act of delegating 2 [C] group of delegates

de·lete /dɪˈlit/ vt take out (written words) **deletion** /-ˈliʃən/ n [C;U]

de·li /ˈdɛli/ n, infml DELICATESSEN

de·lib·e·rate[1] /dɪˈlɪbrɪt/ adj 1 done on purpose 2 (of speech, movement, etc.) slow; unhurried ~**ly** adv

de·lib·e·rate[2] /dɪˈlɪbəˌreɪt/ vi/t fml consider carefully –**ration** /dɪˌlɪbəˈreɪʃən/ n fml 1 [C] (process of) deliberating 2 [U] being slow and unhurried

del·i·ca·cy /ˈdɛlɪkəsi/ n 1 [U] being delicate 2 [C] something good to eat

del·i·cate /ˈdɛlɪkɪt/ adj 1 easily damaged, hurt, or made ill 2 soft and fine: delicate silk 3 needing careful treatment: a delicate situation 4 pleasing but not easy to recognize: a delicate flavor 5 sensitive: delicate instruments ~**ly** adv

del·i·ca·tes·sen /ˌdɛlɪkəˈtɛsən/ also **deli** infml — n store that sells ready cooked foods and sandwiches

de·li·cious /dɪˈlɪʃəs/ adj (esp. of taste or smell) delightful ~**ly** adv

de·light /dɪˈlaɪt/ n 1 [U] great pleasure; joy 2 [C] cause of great pleasure ♦ v 1 vt give delight to 2 vi find delight: He delights in scandal. ~**ful** adj very pleasing ~**fully** adv

de·lin·e·ate /dɪˈlɪniˌeɪt/ vt fml show by drawing

de·lin·quent /dɪˈlɪŋkwənt/ n, adj (person) who breaks a law –**quency** n [U]

de·lir·i·ous /dɪˈlɪriəs/ adj excited and dreamy, esp. because of illness ~**ly** adv –**ium** /-riəm/ n [U] excited dreamy state

de·liv·er /dɪˈlɪvər/ vt 1 take (goods, letters, etc.) to people's houses 2 help in the birth of 3 give (a blow, kick, etc.) 4 say (a speech, etc.) 5 fml rescue ~**er** n fml rescuer ~**ance** n [U] saving; rescue ~**y** n 1 [C;U] delivering things; things delivered 2 [C] birth of a child 3 [C;U] style of public speaking

del·ta /ˈdɛltə/ n land in the shape of a TRIANGLE at the mouth of a river

de·lude /dɪˈlud/ vt mislead; deceive

del·uge /ˈdɛlyudʒ/ n heavy rain; flood **deluge** vt

de·lu·sion /dɪˈluʒən/ n 1 [U] deluding 2 [C] false belief

de·luxe /dɪˈlʌks, -ˈluks/ adj of very high quality

delve /dɛlv/ vi search deeply

Dem. /dɛm/ abbrev. for: DEMOCRAT

dem·a·gogue /ˈdɛməˌgɑg, -ˌgɔg/ n leader who gains power by exciting the crowds

de·mand /dɪˈmænd/ n 1 [C] demanding; claim 2 [S;U] desire for things that people can pay for: *a great demand for teachers* ♦ vt 1 ask for firmly; claim 2 need: *problems demanding your attention* ~**ing** adj needing a lot of attention or effort

de·mean /dɪˈmin/ vt fml bring shame to; DEGRADE

de·mea·nor /dɪˈminə/ n [U] fml behavior

de·ment·ed /dɪˈmɛntɪd/ adj crazy

de·mer·it /diˈmɛrɪt/ n fml fault

de·mil·i·ta·rize /diˈmɪlətəˌraɪz/ vt remove armed forces from (an area) –**rization** /ˌdimɪlətərəˈzeɪʃən/ n [U]

de·mise /dɪˈmaɪz/ n [U] law death

dem·o /ˈdɛmoʊ/ n infml demos DEMONSTRATION (2)

de·moc·ra·cy /dɪˈmɑkrəsi/ n 1 [U] government by elected representatives of the people 2 [C] country governed in this way 3 [U] social equality

dem·o·crat /ˈdɛməˌkræt/ n 1 person who believes in democracy 2 (cap.) member of the Democratic Party ~**ic** /ˌdɛməˈkrætɪk◄/ adj 1 of or favoring democracy 2 (cap.) of a US political party (the **Democratic Party**) ~**ically** adv

Democrat n member or supporter of the **Democratic Party** /ˌ·ˈ··◄, ˌ·◄/, one of the two largest political parties of the US ~**ic** adj

de·mog·ra·phy /dɪˈmɑgrəfi/ n [U] study of the numbers, types, habits and movement of human population –**phic** /ˌdɛməˈgræfɪk, ˌdi–/ adj

de·mol·ish /dɪˈmɑlɪʃ/ vt 1 pull down (buildings, etc.); destroy 2 infml eat up hungrily –**molition** /ˌdɛməˈlɪʃən/ n [C;U]

de·mon /ˈdimən/ n 1 evil spirit 2 very active skillful person ~**ic** /dɪˈmɑnɪk/ adj of, by or like a demon

dem·on·strate /ˈdɛmənˌstreɪt/ v 1 vt show clearly 2 vi take part in a public demonstration –**strator** n –**stration** /ˌdɛmənˈstreɪʃən/ n 1 [C;U] showing something 2 [C;U] also **demo** /ˈdɛmoʊ/ — a public show of opinion, by marching, etc. **b** showing of a product to attract buyers: *software demo*

de·mon·stra·tive /dɪˈmɑnstrətɪv/ adj showing feelings openly

de·mor·al·ize /dɪˈmɔrəˌlaɪz, -ˈmɑr-/ vt destroy the courage and confidence of –**ization** /dɪˌmɔrələˈzeɪʃən, dɪˌmɑr-/ n [U]

de·mote /dɪˈmoʊt/ vt reduce in rank **demotion** /dɪˈmoʊʃən/ n [C;U]

de·mure /dɪˈmyʊr/ adj quiet and MODEST ~**ly** adv

den /dɛn/ n 1 home of a wild animal 2 secret or private place 3 small, quiet room in a house

de·ni·al /dɪˈnaɪəl/ n 1 [U] denying (DENY) 2 [C] statement that something is false

den·i·grate /ˈdɛnəˌgreɪt/ vt declare to be worthless

den·im /ˈdɛnəm/ n [U] strong cotton cloth **denims** [P] JEANS

de·nom·i·na·tion /dɪˌnɑməˈneɪʃən/ n 1 religious group 2 unit of value

de·nom·i·na·tor /dɪˈnɑməˌneɪtə/ n see COMMON DENOMINATOR

de·note /dɪˈnoʊt/ vt be the name or sign of; mean

de·nounce /dɪˈnaʊns/ vt speak or write publicly against

dense /dɛns/ adj 1 closely packed 2 hard to see through: *dense fog* 3 stupid ~**ly** adv **density** n [C;U]

dent /dɛnt/ n 1 small hollow in a surface, made by a blow 2 **make a dent in** make a first step towards success in ♦ vt make a dent

den·tal /ˈdɛntəl/ adj of the teeth

dental floss /ˈ·· ˌ·/ n [U] thin string used for cleaning between the teeth

den·tist /ˈdɛntɪst/ n person trained to treat the teeth ~**ry** n [U]

den·tures /ˈdɛntʃəz/ n [P] false teeth

de·nun·ci·a·tion /dɪˌnʌnsiˈeɪʃən/ n [C;U] act or example of denouncing (DENOUNCE)

de·ny /dɪˈnaɪ/ vt 1 declare untrue 2 refuse to allow

de·o·do·rant /diˈoʊdərənt/ n [C;U] chemical that hides bad smells

de·part /dɪˈpɑrt/ vi fml 1 leave; go away 2 **depart this life** lit to die ~**ed** adj gone for ever

depart from phr vt turn or move away from

de·part·ment /dɪˈpɑrtˈmənt/ n 1 division of a government, business, college, etc. 2 infml activity or subject for which a person is responsible ~**al** /ˌdipɑrtˈmɛntəl, dɪˌpɑrt-/ adj

department store /ˈ··ˌ·/ n large store divided into departments

de·par·ture /dɪˈpɑːtʃə/ n [C;U] going away: (fig.) *a new departure* (= change from a usual course of action) *in television*

de·pend /dɪˈpɛnd/ v 1 [*it+vt*] vary according to; be decided by: *It depends how much you want to spend.* **2 That (all) depends/It all depends** That/It has not yet been decided

   depend on/upon *phr vt* 1 trust 2 be supported by 3 vary according to

de·pen·da·ble /dɪˈpɛndəbəl/ adj that can be trusted

de·pen·dence /dɪˈpɛndəns/ n [U] 1 being dependent: *our dependence on oil* 2 trust 3 need to have certain drugs regularly

de·pen·dent¹ /dɪˈpɛndənt/ adj that depends on

de·pen·dent² n person supported by another

de·pict /dɪˈpɪkt/ vt fml show in a picture, or in words

de·plete /dɪˈpliːt/ vt fml lessen (supplies, etc.) greatly **depletion** /-ˈpliːʃən/ n [U]

de·plore /dɪˈplɔː, dɪˈplʊə/ vt be very sorry about (and consider wrong) **deplorable** adj very bad

de·ploy /dɪˈplɔɪ/ vt arrange for effective action ~**ment** n [U]

de·pop·u·late /ˌdiːˈpɒpjʊˌleɪt/ vt reduce greatly the population

de·port /dɪˈpɔːt, dɪˈpʊərt/ vt send (an unwanted foreigner) out of the country ~**ation** /ˌdiːpɔːˈteɪʃən, -pʊər-/ n [C;U]

de·pose /dɪˈpəʊz/ vt remove (a ruler) from power

de·pos·it¹ /dɪˈpɒzɪt/ vt 1 put down 2 (of a river, etc.) leave (soil, etc.) lying 3 put in a bank, etc., to be safe ~**or** n person who deposits money

deposit² n 1 [C;U] material deposited by a natural process 2 first part of a payment for something, to show that an agreement will be kept

dep·ot /ˈdiːpəʊ/ n 1 building where goods are stored 2 bus garage 3 train station

de·praved /dɪˈpreɪvd/ adj wicked **depravity** /dɪˈprævəti/ n [C;U]

de·pre·ci·ate /dɪˈpriːʃiˌeɪt/ vi (esp. of money) fall in value ~**ation** /dɪˌpriːʃiˈeɪʃən/ n [U]

de·press /dɪˈprɛs/ vt 1 sadden: *depressing news* 2 make less active 3 fml press down

~**ed** adj 1 sad 2 suffering from low levels of business activity

de·pres·sion /dɪˈprɛʃən/ n 1 [C;U] sad feeling 2 [C] period of reduced business activity 3 [C] hollow in a surface 4 [C] area of low air pressure

de·prive /dɪˈpraɪv/ vt prevent from having something: *deprive us of our rights* **deprivation** /ˌdɛprəˈveɪʃən/ n [C;U]

dept. abbrev. for: DEPARTMENT

depth /dɛpθ/ n [C;U] 1 (degree of) being deep 2 in depth done thoroughly 3 out of one's depth: **a** in water deeper than one's height **b** beyond one's understanding **depths** n [the+P] deepest or most central part of: *the depths of winter/ despair*

dep·u·ty /ˈdɛpjəti/ n 1 person given power to act for another 2 person working under a public official –**tize** vi act as a deputy

de·rail /dɪˈreɪl, diː-/ vt cause (a train) to run off the line ~**ment** n [C;U]

de·ranged /dɪˈreɪndʒd/ adj unbalanced in the mind

derby /ˈdɜːbi/ n man's round hard hat

de·reg·u·late /diːˈrɛgjʊˌleɪt/ vt remove from control by law –**lation** /ˌdiːrɛgjʊˈleɪʃən/ n [U]

der·e·lict /ˈdɛrəlɪkt/ adj fallen into ruin ♦ n person, esp. an alcoholic (ALCOHOL), who has no home and no legal means of support ~**ion** /ˌdɛrəˈlɪkʃən/ n 1 state of being derelict 2 failure to do one's duty

de·ride /dɪˈraɪd/ vt fml laugh unkindly at

de·riv·a·tive¹ /dɪˈrɪvətɪv/ adj derog not original or new

de·riv·a·tive² n something coming or developed from something else: *petroleum derivatives*

de·rive /dɪˈraɪv/ v 1 vt obtain from somewhere: *derive pleasure from one's work* 2 vi have something as an origin: *words that derive from Latin* **derivation** /ˌdɛrəˈveɪʃən/ n [C;U]

der·ma·ti·tis /ˌdɜːməˈtaɪtɪs/ n [U] skin disease with redness and swelling

de·rog·a·to·ry /dɪˈrɒgətəri, -ˌtʊəri/ adj fml (of words) showing disapproval

der·rick /ˈdɛrɪk/ n 1 large CRANE (1) 2 tower over an oil well

de·scend /dɪˈsɛnd/ vi/t 1 go down 2 be **descended from** have as an ANCESTOR ~**ant** n person descended from another

   descend on/upon *phr vt* 1 arrive suddenly 2 attack suddenly

de·scent /dɪˈsɛnt/ n 1 [C;U] going down 2 [C] downward slope 3 [U] family origins: *of German descent*

de·scribe /dɪˈskraɪb/ vt 1 say what something is like 2 *fml* draw the shape of: *describe a circle*

de·scrip·tion /dɪˈskrɪpʃən/ n 1 [C;U] statement that describes 2 [C] sort: *birds of every description* **-tive** /-tɪv/ adj 1 that describes 2 saying how a language is used

des·e·crate /ˈdɛsəˌkreɪt/ vt spoil (a holy thing or place) **-cration** /ˌdɛsəˈkreɪʃən/ n [S;U]

de·seg·re·gate /diˈsɛgrɪˌgeɪt/ vt end racial segregation (SEGREGATE) in

des·ert¹ /ˈdɛzət/ n large area of dry sandy land

de·sert² /dɪˈzɜːt/ v 1 vt leave (a place) empty 2 vt leave (people) cruelly 3 vi leave military service without permission ~**er** n person who deserts (3) ~**ion** /-ˈzɜːʃən/ n [C;U]

de·serts /dɪˈzɜːts/ n [P] what someone deserves

de·serve /dɪˈzɜːv/ vt be worthy of: *She deserved to win.* **deservedly** /dɪˈzɜːvɪdli/ adj rightly **deserving** adj

de·sign /dɪˈzaɪn/ vt 1 draw a plan for (something to be made) 2 plan (something) for a purpose: *books designed for use in colleges* ♦ n 1 [C] plan drawn for making something 2 [U] art of designing things 3 [C] decorative pattern 4 [C] plan in the mind **designs** n [P] evil plans: *designs on your life*

des·ig·nate /ˈdɛzɪgˌneɪt/ vt choose for a particular job or purpose ♦ adj /-nət, -neɪt/ chosen for an office but not yet officially placed in it

de·sign·er¹ /dɪˈzaɪnə/ n person who makes plans or designs

designer² adj 1 made by a designer: *designer jeans* 2 *humor* or *derog* intended to make the user appear extremely fashionable: *designer stubble/drug*

de·sir·a·ble /dɪˈzaɪrəbəl/ adj worth having; attractive **-bly** adv **-bility** /dɪˌzaɪrəˈbɪləti/ n [U]

de·sire /dɪˈzaɪə/ vt wish for; want very much ♦ n 1 [C;U] strong wish 2 [C;U] strong wish for sexual relations with 3 [C] something desired **desirous** adj feeling or having a desire

de·sist /dɪˈzɪst, dɪˈsɪst/ vi stop doing

desk /dɛsk/ n table at which one writes or does business: *airport information desk*

desk·top /ˈdɛsktɒp/ adj being or using a small computer: *desktop publishing* ♦ n top surface of a desk

des·o·late /ˈdɛsəlɪt/ adj sad and lonely **-lation** /ˌdɛsəˈleɪʃən/ n [U]

de·spair /dɪˈspeə/ vi lose all hope ♦ n loss of hope ~**ingly** adv

des·per·ate /ˈdɛspərɪt, ˈdɛsprɪt/ adj 1 ready for any wild act because of despair 2 very dangerous and without much hope of success ~**ly** adv **-ation** /ˌdɛspəˈreɪʃən/ n [U]

des·pic·a·ble /dɪˈspɪkəbəl/ adj deserving to be despised

de·spise /dɪˈspaɪz/ vt regard as worthless

de·spite /dɪˈspaɪt/ prep in spite of

de·spon·dent /dɪˈspɒndənt/ adj without hope; discouraged **-dency** n [U]

des·pot /ˈdɛspɒt, -pət/ n ruler with total power who governs cruelly ~**ic** /dɛˈspɒtɪk, dɪ-/ adj

des·sert /dɪˈzɜːt/ n [C;U] sweet food served at the end of a meal

de·sta·bil·ize /diˈsteɪbəlaɪz/ vt make (a government, etc.) unsteady

des·ti·na·tion /ˌdɛstəˈneɪʃən/ n place to which someone or something is going

des·tined /ˈdɛstɪnd/ adj intended, esp. by fate: *He was destined to become famous.*

des·ti·ny /ˈdɛstɪni/ n [C;U] fate; what must happen

des·ti·tute /ˈdɛstətjuːt/ adj 1 without food, clothes, shelter, etc. 2 *fml* lacking in: *destitute of feeling* **-tution** /ˌdɛstəˈtjuːʃən/ n [U]

de·stroy /dɪˈstrɔɪ/ vt 1 make useless; ruin 2 kill (esp. an animal) ~**er** n 1 someone who destroys 2 small fast fighting ship

de·struc·tion /dɪˈstrʌkʃən/ n [U] destroying; ruin **-tive** /-tɪv/ adj 1 causing destruction 2 not helpful: *destructive criticism*

de·tach /dɪˈtætʃ/ vt separate from something larger ~**ed** adj 1 (of a house) not joined to others 2 not influenced by personal feelings ~**ment** n 1 [U] being detached (2) 2 [C] group of soldiers, etc.

de·tail /ˈdiːteɪl, dɪˈteɪl/ n 1 small fact about something 2 small working party of soldiers, etc. ♦ vt 1 describe fully: *a detailed account* 2 appoint (soldiers, etc.) for special work

de·tain /dɪˈteɪn/ vt prevent (someone) from leaving

de·tect /dɪˈtɛkt/ vt notice; discover ~**able** adj ~**ive** n person who catches criminals ~**or** n instrument for finding something: a metal detector ~**ion** /-ˈtɛkʃən/ n [U]

dé·tente /deɪˈtɑnt/ n [C;U] calmer political relations between unfriendly countries

de·ten·tion /dɪˈtɛnʃən/ n [U] act of preventing a person from leaving

de·ter /dɪˈtɜ/ vt -rr- discourage from doing something

de·ter·gent /dɪˈtɜdʒənt/ n [C;U] product for washing things, like soap

de·te·ri·o·rate /dɪˈtɪriəˌreɪt/ vi become worse -**ation** /dɪˌtɪriəˈreɪʃən/ n [U]

de·ter·mi·na·tion /dɪˌtɜməˈneɪʃən/ n [U] 1 strong will to succeed 2 firm intention 3 finding out

de·ter·mine /dɪˈtɜmɪn/ vt 1 form a firm intention 2 limit; fix 3 find out; calculate

de·ter·mined /dɪˈtɜmɪnd/ adj having a strong desire to continue doing something, even when it is difficult

de·ter·min·er /dɪˈtɜmənə/ n gram word (such as "his" in "his new car") that describes a noun and comes before any adjectives that describe the same noun

de·ter·rent /dɪˈtɛrənt, -ˈtɜ-/ n, adj (something) that DETERS

de·test /dɪˈtɛst/ vt hate very much ~**able** adj

det·o·nate /ˈdɛtʰnˌeɪt/ vi/t explode -**nator** n piece of equipment used for detonating -**nation** /ˌdɛtʰnˈeɪʃən/ n [C;U]

de·tour /ˈditʊr/ n way around something

de·tox /ˈditɑks/ n [U] infml special treatment to help someone stop drinking alcohol or taking drugs

de·tract /dɪˈtrækt/ v **detract from** phr vt lessen the value of

de·trac·tor /dɪˈtræktə/ n person who says bad things about another

det·ri·ment /ˈdɛtrəmənt/ n [U] fml harm; damage ~**al** /ˌdɛtrəˈmɛnʃl◂/ adj

deuce /dus/ n 1 playing card with number 2 or 2 spots 2 (in tennis) 40 points to each player

de·val·ue /diˈvælyu/ vi/t 1 reduce the exchange value of (money) 2 make (a person or action) seem less valuable or

important -**uation** /diˌvælyuˈeɪʃən/ n [C;U]

dev·a·state /ˈdɛvəˌsteɪt/ vt destroy completely -**station** /ˌdɛvəˈsteɪʃən/ n [U]

de·vel·op /dɪˈvɛləp/ v 1 vi/t (cause to) grow or become more advanced 2 vt use (land) for building on 3 vt begin to have: develop measles 4 vt cause (a photograph) to appear on paper ~**er** n person who develops land ~**ment** n 1 [U] developing 2 [C] new event 3 developed piece of land

de·vel·op·ing coun·try /ˌ···ˈ··/ n poor country that is trying to improve its industry and living conditions

de·vi·ant /ˈdiviənt/ adj different from an accepted standard ~**ce** n [U]

de·vi·ate /ˈdiviˌeɪt/ vi turn away from what is usual -**ation** /ˌdiviˈeɪʃən/ n [C;U] noticeable difference

de·vice /dɪˈvaɪs/ n 1 instrument or tool 2 plan; trick 3 **leave someone to their own devices** leave (someone) alone, without help

dev·il /ˈdɛvəl/ n 1 evil spirit 2 sl person: You lucky devil! ~**ish** adj evil; like the devil ~**ishly** adv very: devilishly hard work

devil's ad·vo·cate /ˌ·· ˈ···/ n person who opposes an idea or plan to test how good it is

devil's food cake /ˌ·· ˈ· ˌ·/ n chocolate cake with chocolate FROSTING

de·vi·ous /ˈdiviəs/ adj not direct; not very honest

de·vise /dɪˈvaɪz/ vt plan; invent

de·void /dɪˈvɔɪd/ adj **devoid of** fml empty of: a house devoid of furniture | devoid of human feeling

de·volve /dɪˈvɑlv/ v pass on work

de·vote /dɪˈvoʊt/ vt give completely to something **devoted** adj loyal; loving **devotion** /-ˈvoʊʃən/ n [U] 1 great love 2 devoutness **devotions** n [P] prayers

dev·o·tee /ˌdɛvəˈti, -ˈteɪ, -voʊ-/ n person who admires someone or something

de·vour /dɪˈvaʊə/ vt 1 eat up hungrily: (fig.) I devoured the book. 2 completely take up the attention of: devoured by hate

de·vout /dɪˈvaʊt/ adj 1 seriously religious 2 deeply felt: a devout hope ~**ly** adv

dew /du/ n [U] drops of water that form on cold surfaces in the night ~**y** adj wet as if with dew: a dewy-eyed look

dex·ter·i·ty /dɛkˈstɛrəti/ n [U] quick cleverness, esp. with one's hands –**terous**, –**trous** /ˈdɛkstrəs/ adj

di·a·be·tes /ˌdaɪəˈbitɪs, -ˈbitiz/ n [U] disease in which there is too much sugar in the blood –**tic** /-ˈbɛtɪk◂/ n, adj (person) suffering from this

di·a·bol·i·cal /ˌdaɪəˈbɑlɪkəl/ adj very cruel or bad ~**ly** adv

di·ag·nose /ˈdaɪəgˌnoʊs, ˌdaɪəgˈnoʊs/ vt discover the nature of (a disease)

di·ag·no·sis /ˌdaɪəgˈnoʊsɪs/ n -**ses** /-siz/ [C;U] (judgment made by) diagnosing –**nostic** /-ˈnɑstɪk◂/ adj

di·ag·o·nal /daɪˈægənəl/ adj (of a straight line) joining opposite corners of a square, etc. ~**ly** adv

di·a·gram /ˈdaɪəˌgræm/ n plan drawn to explain a machine, idea, etc. ~**matic** /ˌdaɪəgrəˈmætɪk/ adj

di·al /ˈdaɪəl/ n 1 marked face of a clock, etc. 2 wheel with holes on a telephone ♦ vi/t –l– make a telephone call

di·a·lect /ˈdaɪəˌlɛkt/ n [C;U] variety of a language, spoken in one part of a country

di·a·log, -logue /ˈdaɪəˌlɔg, -ˌlɑg/ n [C;U] 1 conversation in a book or play 2 exchange of opinion between leaders, etc.

di·am·e·ter /daɪˈæmətər/ n distance across a circle, measured through the center

di·a·met·ri·cal·ly /ˌdaɪəˈmɛtrɪkli/ adv completely: diametrically opposed/opposite

di·a·mond /ˈdaɪmənd, ˈdaɪəmənd/ n 1 [C] hard valuable precious stone 2 [C] figure with 4 equal sides, standing on one of its points 3 [C] red figure shaped like a diamond on a playing card 4 BASEBALL playing area 5 **diamond in the rough** person with qualities needing more development

di·a·per /ˈdaɪpər, ˈdaɪə-/ n cloth worn by a baby to take up waste matter from its body

di·a·phragm /ˈdaɪəˌfræm/ n 1 muscle separating the lungs from the stomach 2 thin plate in a telephone, camera, etc.

di·ar·rhe·a /ˌdaɪəˈriə/ n [U] illness in which the bowels are emptied too often

di·a·ry /ˈdaɪəri/ n (book for) a daily record of events in one's life –**rist** n writer of a diary

di·a·tribe /ˈdaɪəˌtraɪb/ n fml violent attack in words

dice /daɪs/ n small 6-sided block with spots on it, used in games [P] – see also DIE[2] ♦ vt 1 cut (food) into small squares 2 **dice with death** take a great risk ~**y** adj risky and uncertain

di·chot·o·my /daɪˈkɑtəmi/ n fml division into 2 opposite parts or groups

dick /dɪk/ n 1 sl DETECTIVE 2 taboo sl PENIS

dic·tate[1] /ˈdɪkteɪt, dɪkˈteɪt/ vi/t 1 say (words) for someone else to write down 2 give (orders)

dic·tate[2] /ˈdɪkteɪt/ n order (esp. from within ourselves): the dictates of your own conscience

dic·ta·tion /dɪkˈteɪʃən/ n 1 [U] dictating 2 [C] piece of writing dictated

dic·ta·tor /ˈdɪkteɪtər/ n ruler with complete power ~**ship** n [C;U] (country with) government by a dictator ~**ial** /ˌdɪktəˈtɔriəl, -ˈtoʊr-/ adj

dic·tion /ˈdɪkʃən/ n [U] way in which someone pronounces words

dic·tion·a·ry /ˈdɪkʃəˌnɛri/ n book giving a list of words in alphabetical order, with their meanings

did /dɪd, d; strong dɪd/ v past t. of DO

di·dac·tic /daɪˈdæktɪk/ adj fml intending to teach

did·n't /ˈdɪdnt/ v short for: did not

die[1] /daɪ/ vi **died**, pres p. **dying** /ˈdaɪ-ɪŋ/ 1 stop living; become dead: My love will never die. | His desires died with him. 2 **be dying for/to** want very badly 3 **die hard** (of beliefs customs, etc.) take a long time to disappear

die away phr vi fade and then cease

die down phr vi become less: The excitement soon died down.

die off phr vi die one by one

die out phr vi become EXTINCT

die[2] n 1 metal block for shaping coins, etc. 2 singular of DICE

die·hard /ˈdaɪhɑrd/ n person who strongly opposes change

die·sel /ˈdizəl/ n [U] heavy oil used instead of gas, esp. in buses and trains

di·et /ˈdaɪət/ n 1 food and drink usually taken 2 limited list of food and drink that someone is allowed for medical reasons 3 **(be/go) on a diet** (be/start) living on a limited list of food usu. in order to lose weight ♦ vi eat according to a DIET (2)

dif·fer /ˈdɪfər/ vi 1 be different 2 disagree

dif·fer·ence /ˈdɪfrəns/ n 1 [C;U] way or fact of being different 2 [C] slight disagreement **3 split the difference** agree on an amount exactly between

dif·fe·rent /ˈdɪfrənt/ *adj* **1** unlike **2** separate: *They go to different schools.* **3** various: *It comes in different colors.* **4** unusual –**ly** *adv*

dif·fe·ren·ti·ate /ˌdɪfəˈrenʃiˌeɪt, -tʃi-/ *vi/t* see a difference (between)

dif·fi·cult /ˈdɪfɪˌkʌlt/ *adj* **1** hard to do, understand, etc. **2** (of people) not easily pleased

dif·fi·cul·ty /ˈdɪfɪˌkʌlti/ *n* **1** [U] being difficult; trouble **2** [C] something difficult; problem

dif·fuse[1] /dɪˈfyuz/ *vi/t fml* spread freely in all directions –**fusion** /-ˈfyuʒən/ *n* [U]

dif·fuse[2] /dɪˈfyus/ *adj fml* **1** diffused[1] **2** using too many words

dig /dɪg/ *vi/t* **dug** /dʌg/, *pres p.* **digging 1** break up and move (earth) **2** make (a hole) in this way: *dig an underground tunnel* **3** *sl* like or understand **4 dig someone in the ribs** touch someone with one's elbow, as to share a joke ♦ *n* **1** quick push **2** place being uncovered by archaeologists (ARCHAEOLOGY) **3** unpleasant remark **digs** *n* [P] place to live

dig at *phr vt* speak to (someone) in an unpleasant way: *Stop digging at me!*

dig in *phr v* **1** *vi/t* dig a protective place for oneself; get firmly settled **2** *vi* start eating

dig out *phr vt* get out by digging

dig up *phr vt* find (something buried) by digging: (fig.) *dig up an old scandal*

di·gest[1] /daɪˈdʒɛst, dɪ-/ *vt* **1** change (food) so that the body can use it **2** arrange (facts) in one's mind ~**ible** /-əl/ *adj* ~**ive** *adj* of or helping in digesting food ~**ion** /-ˈdʒɛstʃən/ *n* ability to digest food

di·gest[2] /ˈdaɪdʒɛst/ *n* short SUMMARY

dig·it /ˈdɪdʒɪt/ *n* **1** any number from 0 to 9 **2** *fml* finger or toe ~**ize** *vt* use digits to express information

dig·i·tal /ˈdɪdʒɪtl/ *adj* **1** giving information in the form of numbers 0 to 9: *digital watch* **2** using a system in which information is represented by changing electrical signals: *digital recordings* –**ly** *adv*

dig·ni·fied /ˈdɪgnəˌfaɪd/ *adj* having dignity

dig·ni·ta·ry /ˈdɪgnəˌtɛri/ *n fml* person of high rank

dig·ni·ty /ˈdɪgnəti/ *n* [U] **1** nobleness of character **2** formal grand behavior **3 beneath one's dignity** below one's standard of moral or social behavior

di·gress /daɪˈgrɛs, dɪ-/ *vi fml* (of a writer or speaker) move away from the subject ~**ion** /-ˈgrɛʃən/ *n* [C;U]

dike /daɪk/ *n* **1** bank to hold back water **2** ditch

di·lap·i·dat·ed /dəˈlæpəˌdeɪtɪd/ *adj* falling to pieces

di·late /daɪˈleɪt, ˈdaɪleɪt/ *vi/t* (cause to) become wider by stretching: *eyes dilated with terror* **dilation** /-ˈleɪʃən/ *n* [U]

di·lem·ma /dəˈlɛmə/ *n* difficult choice between 2 things

dil·et·tante /ˌdɪləˈtɑnt/ *n, adj* (person) who enjoys art or branch of study but does not take it seriously

dil·i·gence /ˈdɪlədʒəns/ *n* [U] steady effort –**gent** *adj* –**gently** *adv*

dill /dɪl/ *n* [U] plant whose seeds and leaves are used in cooking

di·lute /daɪˈlut, dɪ-/ *vt* make (liquid) weaker and thinner **dilution** /-ˈluʃən/ *n* [C;U]

dim /dɪm/ *adj* -**mm**- **1** (of light) not bright **2** not easy to see **3** *sl* stupid **4 take a dim view of** think badly of ♦ *vi/t* -**mm**- make or become dim ~**ly** *adv* ~**ness** *n* [U]

dime /daɪm/ *n* **1** coin of US and Canada worth 10 cents **2 a dime a dozen** *sl* common

di·men·sion /dɪˈmɛnʃən, daɪ-/ *n* **1** measurement of breadth, length, or height **2** particular area or part of a problem, subject, etc. **3** –**dimensional** having (so many) dimensions: *2-dimensional* **dimensions** *n* [P] size

di·min·ish /dɪˈmɪnɪʃ/ *vi/t* make or become smaller

di·min·u·tive /dɪˈmɪnyətɪv/ *adj fml* very small

dim·ple /ˈdɪmpəl/ *n* small hollow in the cheek, etc.

dim·wit /ˈdɪmwɪt/ *n* stupid person ~**ted** /ˈdɪmˈwɪtɪd◂/ *adj*

din /dɪn/ *n* loud unpleasant noise

dine /daɪn/ *vi fml* eat dinner –**er** *n* **1** cheap restaurant with fast food **2** dining car

dine off *phr vt* eat for dinner

dine out *phr v* eat a meal in a restaurant, hotel, etc.

diner /ˈdaɪnə/ n **1** small restaurant serving inexpensive meals **2** someone eating in a restaurant

din·ghy /ˈdɪŋgi, ˈdɪŋi/ n small open boat

din·gy /ˈdɪndʒi/ adj dirty and faded

dining room /ˈ·· ˌ·/ n room in a house or hotel where meals are eaten

dining ta·ble /ˈ·· ˌ··/ n table for having meals on

dink·y /ˈdɪŋki/ n adj infml very small

din·ner /ˈdɪnə/ n [C;U] main meal of the day, eaten either at midday or in the evening

di·no·saur /ˈdaɪnəˌsɔr/ n **1** large REPTILE that no longer exists **2** something very large and old-fashioned that no longer works well

di·o·cese /ˈdaɪəsɪs, -ˌsɪs, -ˌsiz/ n area controlled by a BISHOP -**cesan** /daɪˈɑsəsən/ adj

dip¹ /dɪp/ v -**pp**- **1** vt put into a liquid for a moment **2** vi/t drop slightly: *temperatures dipped overnight*

dip into phr vt **1** use up (money) **2** read (a book) for a short time

dip² n **1** [C] quick swim **2** [C] downward slope **3** [U] liquid into which food is dipped at parties **4** [C] (liquid for) dipping animals: *cattle dip*

diph·the·ri·a /dɪfˈθɪriə, dɪp-/ n [U] serious infectious disease of the throat

diph·thong /ˈdɪfθɔŋ, -θɑŋ, ˈdɪp-/ n compound vowel sound

di·plo·ma /dɪˈploʊmə/ n official paper showing success in studying something: *high school diploma*

di·plo·ma·cy /dɪˈploʊməsi/ n [U] **1** management of relations between countries **2** skill at dealing with people

dip·lo·mat /ˈdɪpləˌmæt/ n person whose profession is DIPLOMACY (1) -**ic** /ˌdɪpləˈmætɪk◂/ adj of or having diplomacy ~**ically** /-kli/ adv

diplomatic re·la·tions /ˌ···· ·ˈ··/ n [P] connection between 2 countries that each keep an EMBASSY in the other country

dire /daɪə/ adj terrible

di·rect¹ /dəˈrɛkt, daɪ-/ vt **1** tell (someone) the way to a place **2** control; manage **3** fml command; order **4** aim

direct² adj **1** going straight: *direct route* **2** with nothing coming between: *direct result* **3** honest; clearly expressed: *direct answer* **4** exact: *direct opposite* ♦ adv without turning aside ~**ly** adv **1** in a direct way **2** at once ~**ness** n [U]

di·rec·tion /dəˈrɛkʃən, daɪ-/ n **1** [C] point towards which a person or thing moves or faces **2** [U] control; management **directions** n [P] instructions

di·rec·tive /dəˈrɛktɪv, daɪ-/ n official order

direct ob·ject /·ˌ· ˈ·ˌ·/ n the noun, noun phrase, or PRONOUN that is needed to complete the meaning of a TRANSITIVE verb: *In "I saw Mary," "Mary" is the direct object.*

di·rec·tor /dəˈrɛktə, daɪ-/ n **1** SENIOR manager of a firm **2** person who directs a play or movie ~**ship** n company director's position

di·rec·to·ry /dəˈrɛktəri, daɪ-/ n book or list of names, facts, etc.: *telephone directory*

direct speech /·ˌ· ˈ·/ n [U] gram actual words of a speaker

dirt /dət/ n [U] **1** unclean matter; mud, etc. **2** nasty talk **3 treat someone like dirt** treat someone as worthless ~**y** adj **1** not clean **2** unpleasantly concerned with sex: *dirty jokes* **3** unpleasant: *dirty looks* ~**y** vt make dirty ~**ily** adv

dirt cheap /ˌ· ˈ·◂/ adj extremely cheap

dis /dɪs/ vt -**ss**- sl make unfair and unkind remarks about

dis·a·bil·i·ty /ˌdɪsəˈbɪləti/ n **1** [U] being disabled **2** [C] HANDICAP (1)

dis·a·ble /dɪsˈeɪbəl/ vt make unable to use one's body properly -**abled** adj ~**ment** n [C;U]

dis·ad·van·tage /ˌdɪsədˈvæntɪdʒ/ n [C;U] unfavorable condition ~**ous** /ˌdɪsædvænˈteɪdʒəs, -vən-, dɪsˌæd-/ adj

dis·ad·van·taged /ˌdɪsədˈvæntɪdʒd/ adj suffering from a disadvantage with regard to one's social position, family background, etc.

dis·af·fect·ed /ˌdɪsəˈfɛktɪd/ adj lacking (esp. political) loyalty -**fection** /-ˈfɛkʃən/ n [U]

dis·a·gree /ˌdɪsəˈgri/ vi **1** have different opinions **2** be different ~**able** adj unpleasant ~**ably** adv ~**ment** n [C;U] difference of opinion

disagree with phr vt (of food, etc.) make ill

dis·ap·pear /ˌdɪsəˈpɪr/ vi **1** go out of sight **2** cease to exist ~**ance** n [C;U]

dis·ap·point /ˌdɪsəˈpɔɪnt/ vt fail to fulfill hopes ~**ed** adj sad at not seeing hopes fulfilled ~**ing** adj ~**ingly** adv ~**ment** n **1** [U] being disappointed **2** [C] something disappointing

dis·ap·prove /ˌdɪsəˈpruv/ vi have an unfavorable opinion –**proval** n [U]

dis·arm /dɪsˈarm/ v **1** vt take away weapons from **2** vi reduce a nation's military strength **3** vt drive away the anger of: a disarming smile ~**ingly** adv: smile disarmingly

dis·ar·ma·ment /dɪsˈarməmənt/ n [U] act or principle of DISARMING (2)

dis·ar·ray /ˌdɪsəˈreɪ/ n [U] fml disorder

di·sas·ter /dɪˈzæstər/ n [C;U] sudden serious misfortune –**trously** adj –**trously** adv

disaster a·re·a /·ˈ·· ˌ··/ n place which gets government help because of a disaster

dis·a·vow /ˌdɪsəˈvaʊ/ vt fml refuse to admit (knowledge, etc.)

dis·band /dɪsˈbænd/ vi/t break up (a group)

dis·be·lief /ˌdɪsbəˈlif/ n [U] lack of belief

dis·be·lieve /ˌdɪsbəˈliv/ vi/t refuse to believe

disc /dɪsk/ n DISK

dis·card /dɪsˈkard/ vt get rid of; throw away

di·scern /dɪˈsɜrn, dɪˈzɜrn/ vt see or understand esp. with difficulty –**ible** adj ~**ing** adj able to decide and judge; having good taste ~**ment** n [U]

dis·charge[1] /dɪsˈtʃardʒ, ˈdɪstʃardʒ/ v **1** vt send (a person) away **2** vt/i let out (gas, liquid, etc.) **3** vt perform (a duty or promise) **4** vt pay (a debt) **5** vt fire (a gun, etc.)

dis·charge[2] /ˈdɪstʃardʒ/ n **1** [U] discharging **2** [C;U] something discharged

dis·ci·ple /dɪˈsaɪpəl/ n follower of a (religious) leader

dis·ci·pli·nar·i·an /ˌdɪsəpləˈnɛriən/ n person who can make others obey and believes in firm discipline

dis·ci·pline /ˈdɪsəplɪn/ n **1** [U] training to produce obedience and self-control **2** [U] control gained by this training **3** [U] punishment **4** [C] branch of learning ♦ vt **1** train to be obedient **2** punish

dis·claim /dɪsˈkleɪm/ vt say one does not own: disclaim responsibility ~**er** n written statement which disclaims

dis·close /dɪsˈkloʊz/ vt make (a secret) known

dis·clo·sure /dɪsˈkloʊʒər/ n **1** [U] act of disclosing **2** [C] disclosed secret

dis·co /ˈdɪskoʊ/ n -**cos** club where people dance to recorded music

dis·col·or /dɪsˈkʌlər/ vi/t change color for the worse –**oration** /dɪsˌkʌləˈreɪʃən/ n [C;U]

dis·com·fort /dɪsˈkʌmfərt/ n [C;U] (cause of) being uncomfortable

dis·con·nect /ˌdɪskəˈnɛkt/ vt undo the connection of ~**ed** adj (of thoughts and ideas) badly arranged

dis·con·tent /ˌdɪskənˈtɛnt/ n [U] restless unhappiness ~**ed** adj

dis·con·tin·ue /ˌdɪskənˈtɪnju/ vi/t fml stop; end

dis·cord /ˈdɪskɔrd/ n **1** [U] fml disagreement between people **2** [C;U] lack of musical HARMONY ~**ant** /dɪsˈkɔrdənt/ adj

dis·count[1] /ˈdɪskaʊnt/ n reduction in cost

dis·count[2] /dɪsˈkaʊnt/ vt **1** reduce the price of **2** regard (information) as unimportant or untrue

discount store /ˈ·· ˌ·/ n department store that sells goods cheaper than other stores

dis·cour·age /dɪsˈkɜrɪdʒ, -ˈkʌr-/ vt **1** take away hope from **2** persuade not to do something ~**ment** n [C;U]

dis·course /ˈdɪskɔrs, -koʊrs/ n [C;U] fml serious conversation or speech

dis·cour·te·ous /dɪsˈkɜtiəs/ adj fml not polite ~**ly** adv

dis·cov·er /dɪsˈkʌvər/ vt find; find out ~**er** n ~**y** n **1** [U] discovering **2** [C] something found

dis·cred·it /dɪsˈkrɛdɪt/ vt stop people from believing in ~**able** adj bringing shame

di·screet /dɪˈskrit/ adj not saying too much; showing good sense and judgment: a discreet silence ~**ly** adv

dis·crep·an·cy /dɪsˈkrɛpənsi/ n difference between amounts, etc.

di·scre·tion /dɪsˈkrɛʃən/ n [U] **1** being discreet **2** ability to decide what to do: use your own discretions ~**ary** adj

dis·crim·i·nate /dɪsˈkrɪməˌneɪt/ v **1** vi/t recognize a difference **2** discriminate against/in favor of treat worse/better than others –**nating** adj (of a person) able to choose the best by seeing small differences –**natory** /-ˌnaˌtɔri, -ˌtɔʊri/ adj –**nation** /dɪsˌkrɪməˈneɪʃən/ n [U]

dis·cus /ˈdɪskəs/ n heavy plate to be thrown as a sport

di·scuss /dɪsˈkʌs/ vt talk about ~**ion** /-ˈkʌʃən/ n [C;U]

dis·dain /dɪsˈdeɪn/ n [U] fml CONTEMPT ♦ vt regard with contempt; be too proud for: She disdained to answer. ~**ful** adj

dis·ease /dɪˈziːz/ n [C;U] illness –**eased** adj: ill

dis·em·bark /ˌdɪsɪmˈbɑːk/ vi/t (cause to) leave a ship

dis·em·bod·ied /ˌdɪsɪmˈbɒdiːd◂/ adj existing with no body: a disembodied voice

dis·en·chant·ed /ˌdɪsɪnˈtʃɑːntɪd◂/ adj having lost belief in the value of something –**ment** n [U]

dis·en·gage /ˌdɪsɪnˈɡeɪdʒ/ vi/t 1 come loose and separate 2 stop fighting

dis·en·tan·gle /ˌdɪsɪnˈtæŋɡəl/ vt make free from knots: (fig.) disentangle truth from lies

dis·fa·vor /dɪsˈfeɪvə/ n [U] fml dislike; disapproval

dis·fig·ure /dɪsˈfɪɡjə/ vt spoil the beauty of ~**ment** n [C;U]

dis·grace /dɪsˈɡreɪs/ n [S;U] (cause of) shame or loss of respect ♦ vt bring disgrace to ~**ful** adj

dis·grun·tled /dɪsˈɡrʌntəld/ adj annoyed and disappointed

dis·guise /dɪsˈɡaɪz/ vt change the appearance of, to hide or deceive ♦ n 1 [C] something worn to disguise someone 2 [U] being disguised

dis·gust /dɪsˈɡʌst/ n [U] dislike caused esp. by a bad smell or taste or bad behavior ♦ vt cause disgust in ~**ingly** adv

dish¹ /dɪʃ/ n 1 large plate 2 cooked food of one kind

dish² v sl talk with friends

dish out phr vt 1 serve out to several people 2 **dish it out** punish or express disapproval of someone else, esp. thoughtlessly or unjustly

dish up phr vi/t put (a meal) onto dishes

di·shev·eled /dɪˈʃevəld/ adj (esp. of someone's hair) messy

dis·hon·est /dɪsˈɒnɪst/ adj not honest ~**ly** adv ~**y** n [U]

dis·hon·or /dɪsˈɒnə/ n [S;U] fml (person or thing bringing) loss of honor ♦ vt 1 bring dishonor to 2 cause (a check) to BOUNCE (3) ~**able** adj

dish tow·el /ˈ· ··/ n cloth for drying washed cups, plates, etc.

dish·wash·er /ˈdɪʃˌwɒʃə, -ˌwɔː-/ n machine that washes dishes

dis·il·lu·sion /ˌdɪsəˈluːʒən/ vt tell the unpleasant truth to ~**ed** adj ~**ment** n [U]

dis·in·fect /ˌdɪsɪnˈfekt/ vt make (things and places) free from infection ~**ant** n chemical that disinfects

dis·in·gen·u·ous /ˌdɪsɪnˈdʒenjuəs/ adj not sincere; slightly dishonest

dis·in·her·it /ˌdɪsɪnˈherɪt/ vt take away the right to INHERIT from

dis·in·te·grate /dɪsˈɪntəɡreɪt/ vi/t break up into small pieces –**gration** /dɪsˌɪntəˈɡreɪʃən/ n [U]

dis·in·ter·est·ed /dɪsˈɪntrəstɪd, -ˈɪntərestɪd, -ˈɪntərəstɪd/ adj not influenced by personal advantage

dis·joint·ed /dɪsˈdʒɔɪntɪd/ adj (of words, ideas, etc.) not well connected ~**ly** adv

disk /dɪsk/ n 1 anything round and flat, such as a plate or record 2 flat piece of CARTILAGE in one's back: a slipped disk 3 flat circular piece of plastic used for storing computer information

disk drive /ˈ· ·/ n piece of electrical equipment used for passing information to and from a DISK (3)

disk·ette /dɪsˈket/ n computer DISK (3)

disk jock·ey /ˈ· ·/ also **DJ** — n broadcaster who introduces records of popular music

dis·like /dɪsˈlaɪk/ vt not like ♦ n [C;U]: have a dislike of cats

dis·lo·cate /ˈdɪsləʊˌkeɪt, dɪsˈləʊkeɪt/ vt 1 put (a bone) out of place 2 put (traffic, plans, etc.) into disorder –**cation** /ˌdɪsləʊˈkeɪʃən/ n [C;U]

dis·lodge /dɪsˈlɒdʒ/ vt force out of a position

dis·loy·al /dɪsˈlɔɪəl/ adj not loyal ~**ly** adv ~**ty** n [C;U]

dis·mal /ˈdɪzməl/ adj sad; hopeless ~**ly** adv

dis·man·tle /dɪsˈmæntəl/ vt take to pieces

dis·may /dɪsˈmeɪ/ vt, n [U] (fill with) great fear and hopelessness

dis·mem·ber /dɪsˈmembə/ vt cut or tear (a body) apart

dis·miss /dɪsˈmɪs/ vt 1 fml remove from a job 2 send away 3 refuse to think seriously about 4 (of a judge) stop (a court case) ~**al** n [C;U] ~**ive** adj contemptuous (CONTEMPT)

dis·o·be·di·ent /ˌdɪsəˈbiːdiənt/ adj refusing to obey ~**ly** adv –**ence** n [U]

dis·o·bey /ˌdɪsəˈbeɪ/ vi/t not obey

dis·or·der /dɪsˈɔrdə/ n 1 [U] confusion 2 [C;U] public violence 3 [C;U] illness of the body or mind: *eating disorder* (= eating too much or too little) ♦ vt put into disorder ~**ly** adj

disorderly con·duct /ˌ···· ˈ·-/ n [U] small offenses: *He was charged with disorderly conduct.*

dis·or·gan·ize /dɪsˈɔrgənaɪz/ vt throw into confusion

dis·or·i·ent /dɪsˈɔriənt, -ˈoʊr-/ vt cause (someone) to lose sense of time, direction, etc.; confuse ~**ation** /dɪsˌɔriənˈteɪʃən, -ˌoʊri-/ n [C;U] confused

dis·own /dɪsˈoʊn/ vt say that one has no connection with

dis·par·age /dɪsˈpærɪdʒ/ vt speak without respect of –**agingly** adv

dis·pa·rate /ˈdɪspərɪt/ adj fml that cannot be compared; very different –**rity** /dɪsˈpærəti/ n [C;U] inequality

dis·pas·sion·ate /dɪsˈpæʃənɪt/ adj calm and fair; not taking sides ~**ly** adv

di·spatch /dɪsˈpætʃ/ vt 1 send: *dispatch invitations* 2 finish (work, etc.) quickly 3 kill officially ♦ n 1 [C] message sent 2 [U] sending 3 [U] speed and effectiveness

di·spel /dɪsˈpɛl/ vt -ll- drive away; scatter

dis·pen·sa·tion /ˌdɪspənˈseɪʃən, -pɛn-/ n 1 system of beliefs governing human affairs 2 [C;U] permission to disobey a rule 3 [U] fml dispensing

di·spense /dɪsˈpɛns/ vt 1 give out to people 2 prepare (medicines) **dispensary** n place where medicines are dispensed

dispense with phr vt do without

di·spens·er /dɪsˈpɛnsə/ n container for holding and dispensing things in small amounts: *a paper cup dispenser*

di·sperse /dɪsˈpɜrs/ vi/t scatter in different directions **dispersal** n [U]

di·spir·it·ed /dɪsˈpɪrɪtɪd/ adj lit discouraged

dis·place /dɪsˈpleɪs/ vt 1 force out of the right place 2 take the place of ~**ment** n [U]

di·splay /dɪsˈpleɪ/ vt show ♦ n [C;U]: *a display of skill*

dis·po·sa·ble /dɪsˈpoʊzəbəl/ adj 1 to be used once and then thrown away: *disposable plates* 2 able to be used: *disposable income*

dis·pos·al /dɪsˈpoʊzəl/ n [U] 1 removal 2 **at one's disposal** for one to use

dis·pose /dɪsˈpoʊz/ v **dispose of** phr vt get rid of

dis·posed /dɪsˈpoʊzd/ adj 1 willing: *I don't feel disposed to help.* 2 having a tendency

dis·po·si·tion /ˌdɪspəˈzɪʃən/ n fml person's natural character

dis·pos·sess /ˌdɪspəˈzɛs/ vt fml take property away from

dis·pro·por·tion·ate /ˌdɪsprəˈpɔrʃənɪt, -ˈpoʊr-/ adj too much or too little ~**ly** adv

dis·prove /dɪsˈpruv/ vt prove to be false

di·spute /dɪsˈpyut/ v 1 vi/t argue (about) 2 vt question the truth of 3 vt struggle over or about (esp. in defense): *disputed territory* ♦ n [C;U] argument

dis·qual·i·fy /dɪsˈkwɑləfaɪ/ vt make unfit to do something –**fication** /dɪsˌkwɑləfəˈkeɪʃən/ n [C;U]

dis·re·gard /ˌdɪsrɪˈgɑrd/ vt pay no attention to ♦ n [U] lack of attention

dis·re·pair /ˌdɪsrɪˈpɛr/ n [U] need for repair

dis·rep·u·ta·ble /dɪsˈrɛpyətəbəl/ adj having a bad REPUTATION

dis·re·pute /ˌdɪsrɪˈpyut/ n [U] loss of people's good opinion

dis·re·spect /ˌdɪsrɪˈspɛkt/ n [U] rudeness ~**ful** adj

dis·rupt /dɪsˈrʌpt/ vt throw into disorder ~**ive** adj: *disruptive influence* ~**ion** /-ˈrʌpʃən/ n [C;U]

dis·sat·is·fy /dɪsˈsætɪsˌfaɪ, dɪsˈsætɪs-/ vt fail to satisfy; displease: *a dissatisfied customer* –**faction** /dɪsˌsætɪsˈfækʃən, dɪsˌsæ-/ n [U]

dis·sect /dɪˈsɛkt, daɪ-/ vt cut up (a body) in order to study it ~**ion** /-ˈsɛkʃən/ n [C;U]

dis·sem·i·nate /dɪˈsɛməneɪt/ vt fml spread (ideas, etc.) widely –**nation** /dɪˌsɛməˈneɪʃən/ n [U]

dis·sen·sion /dɪˈsɛnʃən/ n [C;U] disagreement; argument

dis·sent /dɪˈsɛnt/ vi disagree with an opinion ♦ n [U] refusal to agree ~**er** n

dis·ser·ta·tion /ˌdɪsəˈteɪʃən/ n long (written) account of a subject

dis·ser·vice /dɪsˈsɜrvɪs, dɪsˈsə-/ n [U] harm or harmful action

dis·si·dent /ˈdɪsədənt/ n, adj (person) who disagrees: *political dissidents*

dis·sim·i·lar /dɪsˈsɪmələr, dɪsˈsɪ-/ adj not similar; different

dis·so·ci·ate /dɪˈsoʊʃiˌeɪt, -siː-/ also **disas-sociate** — n separate in one's mind –**ation** /dɪˌsoʊsiˈeɪʃən, -ʃiː-/ n [U]

dis·so·lute /ˈdɪsəˌluːt/ n, adj (person) who leads a bad or immoral life ~**ly** adv ~**ness** n [U]

dis·so·lu·tion /ˌdɪsəˈluːʃən/ n [U] breaking up of a group

dis·solve /dɪˈzɑlv/ vi/t 1 make (a solid) become liquid 2 cause (a group) to break up: *dissolve the socialist economy* 3 fade out or away gradually: *his strength/the clouds dissolved* 4 lose one's self-control under the influence of strong feeling: *dissolve into tears/laughter*

dis·suade /dɪˈsweɪd/ vt persuade not to –**suasion** /ˈsweɪʒən/ n [U]

dis·tance /ˈdɪstəns/ n 1 [C;U] separation in space between places 2 [S] distant place: *watch from a distance* 3 **go the dis-tance** (in sports) keep playing, etc. till the end of the match 4 **keep one's distance** stay far enough away 5 **keep someone at a distance** treat someone without much friendliness — see also MIDDLE DISTANCE ♦ vt separate (esp. oneself) esp. in the mind or feelings

dis·tant /ˈdɪstənt/ adj 1 far off 2 not close: *distant relations* 3 unfriendly ~**ly** adv

dis·taste /dɪsˈteɪst/ n [U] dislike ~**ful** adj unpleasant

dis·tend /dɪˈstend/ vi/t fml swell

dis·till /dɪˈstɪl/ v 1 make (a liquid) into gas and then make the gas into liquid, as when making alcoholic drinks 2 get or take the most important part(s) of (a book, an idea, etc.) ~**ery** n place where WHISKEY, etc., is distilled –**ation** /ˌdɪstəˈleɪʃən/ n [U]

dis·tinct /dɪˈstɪŋkt/ adj 1 different; sepa-rate 2 clearly noticed ~**ly** adv

dis·tinc·tion /dɪˈstɪŋkʃən/ n 1 [C;U] difference 2 [S;U] being unusually excel-lent 3 [C] mark of honor –**tive** /-tɪv/ adj showing a difference –**tively** adv

dis·tin·guish /dɪˈstɪŋgwɪʃ/ v 1 vi/t recog-nize a difference 2 vi/t see clearly 3 vt make different 4 **distinguish oneself** perform noticeably well ~**able** adj ~**ed** adj excellent; famous

dis·tort /dɪˈstɔrt/ vt 1 twist out of the natural shape 2 give a false account of ~**ion** /ˈstɔrʃən/ n [C;U]

dis·tract /dɪˈstrækt/ vt take (someone's attention) away ~**ed** adj anxious and

confused ~**ion** /-ˈstrækʃən/ n 1 [C] amuse-ment, etc., that distracts 2 [U] anxious confusion

dis·traught /dɪˈstrɔt/ adj very anxious and troubled

dis·tress /dɪˈstres/ n [U] 1 great suffering or sorrow 2 serious danger ♦ vt cause suffering to: *distressing news*

dis·trib·ute /dɪˈstrɪbyət/ vt 1 give out: *dis-tribute prizes* 2 scatter –**utor** n 1 person who distributes goods 2 instrument that distributes electric current in an engine –**ution** /ˌdɪstrəˈbyuːʃən/ n [C;U]

dis·trict /ˈdɪstrɪkt/ n area of a country or city

district at·tor·ney /ˌ·· ·ˈ··/ also **DA** — n lawyer from a particular area of a town or city, etc.

dis·trust /dɪsˈtrʌst/ vt have no trust in ♦ n [S;U] lack of trust –**ful** adv

dis·turb /dɪˈstɜrb/ vt 1 interrupt 2 worry: *disturbing news* ~**ance** n [C;U] 1 act of disturbing 2 noisy disorder ~**ed** adj having or showing signs of an illness of the mind

ditch /dɪtʃ/ n passage cut for water to flow through ♦ vt sl get rid of

dith·er /ˈdɪðər/ vi be unable to decide **dither** n [S]

dit·to /ˈdɪtoʊ/ n -**tos** the same

dit·ty /ˈdɪti/ n short simple song

dive /daɪv/ vi **dived** or **dove** /doʊv/ 1 jump head first into water 2 go under water 3 (of a plane or bird) go down steeply and swiftly 4 go down quickly: *dive under the table* 5 enter quickly into some matter or activity ♦ n 1 act of diving 2 not very respectable club, etc.

div·er n person who dives, or works on the sea bottom

di·verge /dəˈvɜrdʒ, daɪ-/ vi separate; get further apart **divergence** n [C;U]

di·verse /dəˈvɜrs, daɪ-/ adj of different kinds **diversity** n [S;U] variety

di·ver·si·fy /dəˈvɜrsəˌfaɪ, daɪ-/ vi/t make diverse: *diversify our range of products* –**fication** /dəˌvɜrsəfəˈkeɪʃən, daɪ-/ n [U]

di·ver·sion /dəˈvɜrʒən, daɪ-/ n 1 [C;U] diverting 2 [C] something that amuses people ~**ary** adj intended to DIVERT: *diversionary tactics*

di·vert /dəˈvɜrt, daɪ-/ vt turn to another direction: *divert a river/my attention*

di·vest /dəˈvest, daɪ-/ vt take away from someone

di·vide /dəˈvaɪd/ vi/t **1** separate into parts **2** find out how many times one number is contained in another **3** be an important cause of disagreement between ♦ n something that divides

div·i·dend /ˈdɪvədɛnd, -dənd/ n **1** part of profit that is divided among the owners of SHARES (2) **2 pay dividends** produce an advantage

di·vine[1] /dəˈvaɪn/ adj **1** of God or a god **2** excellent **divinity** /dəˈvɪnəti/ n **1** [U] quality or state of being divine **2** [C] god or goddess **3** [U] THEOLOGY

divine[2] vi/t fml find out; guess **2** find (water or minerals) underground using a stick shaped like a **Y diviner** n

div·ing board /ˈdaɪvɪŋ ˌbɔrd, -ˌboʊrd/ n high board off which people DIVE (1) into the water

di·vis·i·ble /dəˈvɪzəbəl/ adj that can be divided

di·vi·sion /dəˈvɪʒən/ n **1** [U] separation or sharing **2** [C] one of the parts into which a whole is divided: the company's export division **3** [C] something that separates **4** [U] disagreement **5** [U] process of dividing numbers ~**al** adj

di·vi·sive /dəˈvaɪsɪv, -ˈvɪ-/ adj causing disunity

di·vorce /dəˈvɔrs, -ˈvoʊrs/ n **1** [C;U] legal ending of a marriage **2** [C] separation ♦ v **1** vt/i end a marriage by law **2** vt separate completely **divorcée** fem., **divorcé** masc. /dəˌvɔrˈseɪ, -ˌvoʊr-, dəˈvɔrseɪ, -ˈvoʊr-/ — n divorced person

di·vulge /dəˈvʌldʒ, daɪ-/ vt fml tell (a secret)

diz·zy /ˈdɪzi/ adj **1** feeling as if things are going around and around **2** causing this feeling: dizzy heights **3** silly ~**zily** adv ~**ziness** n [U]

DJ n DISK JOCKEY

DNA n [U] acid which carries GENETIC information in a cell

do[1] /də/ strong du/ v aux **did** /dɪd/, **done** /dʌn/ **1** (used with another verb): Do you like it? | He doesn't know. **2** (used instead of another verb): He walks faster than I do. | She likes it, and so do I. | She sings, doesn't she?

do[2] v **1** vt perform (an action); work at or produce: do a chore/one's homework/the cooking/business/one's best/one's duty | do (= study) science in school | do 80 miles an hour | It'll do you good. **2** vi a advance: do well/badly **b** behave: Do as you're told!

3 vi/t be enough or suitable (for): Will $5 do (you)? | That will do! **4** vt tour: We did Europe in two weeks. **5 do well by** treat well **6 How do you do?** (used when one is introduced to someone) **7 make do** use (something) even though it may not be perfect or enough **8 nothing doing** sl no **9 That does it!** (expression showing that enough, or too much, has been done) **10 What do you do (for a living)?** What is your work?

do away with phr vt **1** cause to end **2** kill or murder (someone or oneself)

do for phr vt **1** kill or ruin **2 What will you do for (something)?** What arrangements will you make for (something)?: What will you do for food?

do in phr vt **1** kill **2** tire completely

do out of phr vt cause to lose, by cheating

do over phr vt do again

do up phr vt **1** fasten or wrap **2** repair; improve

do with phr vt **1** need; want **2** cause (oneself) to spend time doing: I don't know what to do with myself since you've gone. **3** (in questions with "what") to do with regard to: "What did you do with my pen?" (= where did you put it?) **4 have/be to do with** be connected with

do without vi/t succeed without

do[3] n infml **1** hair style **2 dos and don'ts** rules of behavior

do·cile /ˈdɑsəl/ adj quiet and easily taught

dock[1] /dɑk/ n **1** place where ships are loaded and unloaded, or repaired **2** wooden platform in a lake, river, etc. where boats can stop for people to get on and off ♦ vi/t **1** (cause to) sail into, or remain at, a dock (1) **2** (cause spacecraft) to join in space ~**er** n person who works at a dock, loading and unloading ships

dock[2] vt cut off the end of: (fig.) dock someone's wages

doc·tor /ˈdɑktər/ n **1** person trained in medicine **2** person holding one of the highest university degrees ♦ vt **1** change dishonestly: doctor the accounts **2** make (an animal) unable to breed

doc·tor·ate /ˈdɑktərət/ n degree of a DOCTOR (2)

doc·trine /ˈdɑktrɪn/ n [C;U] belief; set of teachings ~**trinal** /ˈdɑktrənəl/ adj

doc·u·ment /'dɑkyəmənt/ n 1 paper giving information, proof, etc. 2 piece of work written using a computer♦ /-mɛnt/ vt prove or support with documents ~ation /ˌdɑkyəmən'teɪʃən, -mən-/ n [U] documents used as proof

doc·u·men·ta·ry /ˌdɑkyə'mɛntəri◄/ adj 1 of documents 2 giving or teaching facts through art ♦ n film, broadcast, etc., dealing with facts

dodge /dɑdʒ/ v 1 vi/t avoid (something) by suddenly moving aside 2 vt avoid dishonestly ♦ n clever trick **dodger** n: tax dodger

doe /doʊ/ n female of esp. the deer, rat, and rabbit

does /dʌz; strong dʌz/ v 3rd pers. sing. pres. of DO

does·n't /'dʌzənt/ v short for: does not

dog /dɔg/ n 1 common animal with 4 legs, useful to humans 2 male of this and similar animals 3 **a dog's life** a very unhappy life 4 **go to the dogs** be ruined 5 **let sleeping dogs lie** leave something alone — see also TOP DOG ♦ vt -gg- follow closely; PURSUE: dogged by bad luck

dog-eared /'· ·/ adj (of pages) bent down with use

dog-eat-dog /ˌ· ·'·◄/ adj having, showing or marked by cruel self-interest

dog·ged /'dɔgɪd/ adj refusing to give up; determined ~**ly** adv

doggie bag /'dɔgi ˌbæg/ n bag to put food into from a restaurant

dog·gone /dɔ'gɔn, dɑ'gɑn◄/ adj euph DAMN

dog·house /'dɔghaʊs/ n **in the dog-house** in a state of disfavor or shame

dog·ma /'dɔgmə, 'dɑgmə/ n [C;U] (religious) belief to be accepted without reasoning ~**tic** /dɔg'mætɪk, dɑg-/ adj trying to force one's beliefs on other people ~**tically** adv

do-good·er /'· ˌ·◄/ n person who tries to do good things for others

dog-tired /ˌ· '·◄/ adj very tired

dol·drums /'doʊldrəmz, 'dɑl-/ n [P] **in the doldrums** sad and dull

dole /doʊl/ v **dole out** phr vt give in small shares

dole·ful /'doʊlfəl/ adj unhappy ~**ly** adv

doll[1] /dɑl/ n 1 small toy figure of a person 2 sl person that one likes

doll[2] v **doll up** phr vt dress prettily

dol·lar /'dɑlə/ n 1 unit of money, as used in the US, Canada, and other countries 2 piece of paper, coin, etc., of this value

dollar sign /'·· ˌ·/ n 1 the mark $ 2 **dollar signs in one's eyes** thinking about getting money

dol·lop /'dɑləp/ n shapeless mass, esp. of food

dol·phin /'dɑlfɪn, 'dɔl-/ n sea animal, two to three meters long, which swims in groups

do·main /doʊ'meɪn, də-/ n 1 area of interest or knowledge 2 land controlled by one ruler

dome /doʊm/ n rounded roof **domed** adj like or covered with a dome

do·mes·tic /də'mɛstɪk/ adj 1 of the house, home, or family 2 not foreign: domestic policies 3 (of animals) not wild ♦ n house servant ~**ally** adv

dom·i·cile /'dɑməˌsaɪl, -səl, 'doʊ-/ n fml place where one lives **domicile** vt

dom·i·nant /'dɑmənənt/ adj most noticeable or important; dominating ~**nance** n [U] controlling influence; importance

dom·i·nate /'dɑməˌneɪt/ vi/t 1 have power (over); control 2 have the most important place (in) 3 rise or be higher than: The cathedral dominated the whole town. ~**nation** /ˌdɑmə'neɪʃən/ n [U]

do·min·ion /də'mɪnyən/ n 1 [U] lit power to rule 2 [C] land under one government

dom·i·no /'dɑməˌnoʊ/ n -noes small flat piece of wood with spots on it, used with others in a game (**dominoes**)

domino ef·fect /'··· ˌ·/ n [S] situation in which one event causes similar ones to happen one after another

do·nate /'doʊneɪt, doʊ'neɪt/ vt give (money, etc.) esp. for a good purpose **donation** /doʊ'neɪʃən/ n [C;U]

done /dʌn/ v 1 past p. of DO 2 finished 3 socially acceptable

don·key /'dɑŋki, 'dʌŋ-, 'dɔŋ-/ n 1 animal like a small horse, with long ears 2 fool

do·nor /'doʊnə/ n person who gives or donates: blood donor

don't /doʊnt/ v short for: do not

donut /'doʊnʌt, -nət/ n a DOUGHNUT

doo·dle /'dudl/ vi/t draw lines, figures, etc., aimlessly while thinking of something else **doodle** n

doom /dum/ n 1 unavoidable destruction 2 **doom and gloom** hopelessness ~**ed** DESTINED to something bad

Dooms·day /'dumzdeɪ/ n end of the world

door /dɔr, doʊr/ n 1 thing that closes an entrance: *bedroom/cupboard/car door* 2 DOORWAY 3 (in some fixed phrases) house or building: *live next door/2 doors away* 4 **be on the door** have some duty at the door, such as collecting tickets 5 **by the back door** secretly or by a trick 6 **shut/close the door to/on** make impossible 7 **out of doors** OUTDOORS

door·bell /'dɔrbɛl, 'doʊr-/ n button near a door that you press to make a sound to let someone inside know you are there

door·knob /'dɔrnɑb, 'doʊr-/ n round handle for opening and closing a door

door·man /'dɔrmən, 'doʊr-/ n **-men** /-mən/ 1 man working at the door of a theater, hotel, etc. 2 bouncer (BOUNCE)

door·step /'dɔrstɛp, 'doʊr-/ n step in front of a door

door·way /'dɔrweɪ, 'doʊr-/ n opening for a door

dope /doʊp/ n 1 [U] harmful drug 2 [C] fool ♦ vt give dope to ~**y** adj 1 sleepy and unable to think clearly, (as if) caused by drugs 2 stupid

dork /dɔrk/ n sl boring, stupid, unfashionable person ~**y** adj

dorm /dɔrm/ n infml DORMITORY

dor·mant /'dɔrmənt/ adj inactive: *dormant volcano*

dor·mi·to·ry /'dɔrmətɔri, -ˌtoʊri/ n building belonging to a university where students live

dos·age /'doʊsɪdʒ/ n fml amount of a dose

dose /doʊs/ n measured amount of medicine to be taken at a time ♦ vt give medicine to

dos·si·er /'dɑsiˌeɪ, 'dɔ-/ n set of papers containing facts about a person or subject

dot /dɑt/ n 1 small spot 2 **on the dot** at the exact moment ♦ vt **-tt-** 1 mark with a dot 2 cover with dots 3 **dotted about** scattered 4 **sign on the dotted line** agree to something quickly and unconditionally ~**ty** adj slightly mad

dote /doʊt/ v **dote on** phr vt be too fond of

dou·ble¹ /'dʌbəl/ adj 1 with 2 parts or uses: *double doors* | *a double meaning* 2 for 2 people: *a double bed* ♦ adv, predeterminer twice: *cloth folded double* | *buy*

double the amount **doubly** adv twice as: *doubly careful*

double² n 1 [C;U] twice the amount: *I'll have a double (vodka) please.* 2 [C] person who looks just like another 3 **on the double** quickly **doubles** n [P] match between 2 pairs of players

double³ v 1 vi/t make or become twice as much 2 vt fold in half

double as phr vt have as a second use or job

double up phr vi/t bend (the body) at the waist: *doubled up with pain*

double bass /ˌdʌbəl 'beɪs/ n largest musical instrument of the VIOLIN family, with a very deep sound

double bill /ˌ·· '·/ n entertainment having two acts or performers

double-breast·ed /ˌ·· '··/ adj (of a coat) crossing over in front, with 2 rows of buttons

double-check /ˌ·· '·/ vi/t examine (something) twice for exactness or quality

double chin /ˌ·· '·/ n fold of loose skin between the face and neck

double-cross /ˌ·· '·/ vt cheat; BETRAY ~**er** n

double head·er /ˌ·· '··/ n two games between the same teams or 2 different pairs of teams played one after the other

double-joint·ed /ˌ·· '··/ adj having joints that move backwards as well as forwards

double take /'·· ˌ·/ n late reaction of surprise to something unusual: *He did a double take.*

doubt /daʊt/ vt 1 feel uncertain about 2 consider unlikely: *I doubt he'll come.* ♦ n 1 [C;U] (feeling of) being uncertain 2 **in doubt** in a condition of being uncertain 3 **no doubt** probably ~**ful** adj 1 uncertain 2 not likely ~**less** adv 1 without doubt 2 probably

dough /doʊ/ n [U] 1 mixture for making bread 2 sl money

dough·nut, donut /'doʊnʌt, -nət/ n circular cake cooked in hot oil

dour /daʊɚ, dʊɚ/ adj hard and cold in one's nature; unfriendly ~**ly** adv

douse /daʊs/ vt 1 throw water over 2 put out (a light)

dove¹ /dʌv/ n 1 kind of PIGEON 2 person in favor of peace

dove² /doʊv/ v past t. of DIVE

dow·dy /'daʊdi/ adj 1 dressed in a dull way 2 (of clothes) dull

down[1] /daʊn/ adv 1 to or at a lower level: The sun's going down. | Please sit down. 2 to the south: come down from Canada 3 on paper: write/copy it down 4 from the past: jewels handed down in the family 5 (shows reduction): Profits are down. 6 **Down with** . . . Let's get rid of . . . ♦ prep 1 to or at a lower level on: run down the hill | swim down the river 2 along: They live down the road. 3 to: I'm just going down to the store. ♦ adj 1 at a lower level, esp. lying on the ground: The telephone wires are down. | Prices are down. 2 directed down: the down escalator 3 finished: 8 down and 2 to go 4 sad 5 not working: The computer/ phone is down. 6 **down on** having a low opinion or dislike for ♦ vt 1 knock down; defeat 2 drink quickly ~**y** n **sl** 1 drug that reduces activity 2 experience or state of affairs which makes one sad

down[2] n [U] soft feathers or hair ~**y** adj

down-and-out /ˌ· · ˈ·◂/ adj, n (person who is) suffering from bad fortune, lack of money, etc.

down·cast /ˈdaʊnkæst/ adj 1 downhearted 2 (of eyes) looking down

down·fall /ˈdaʊnfɔl/ n sudden ruin

down·grade /ˈdaʊngreɪd/ vt reduce to a lower position

down·heart·ed /ˌdaʊnˈhɑrtɪd/ adj low in spirits; sad

down·hill /ˌdaʊnˈhɪl◂/ adj, adv 1 down a slope 2 **go downhill** become worse

down-home /ˈ· ·◂/ adj having nice, simple qualities: down-home cooking

down·load /ˌdaʊnloʊd/ vt move information from a large computer system to another computer

down pay·ment /ˌ· ˈ·◂/ n part of the full price paid at the time of buying, with the rest to be paid later

down·play /ˈdaʊnpleɪ/ vt make (something) seem less important than it really is

down·pour /ˈdaʊnpɔr, -poʊr/ n heavy fall of rain

down·right /ˈdaʊnraɪt/ adv completely: downright ugly

down·side /ˈdaʊnsaɪd/ n bad or negative side of something

down·size /ˈdaʊnsaɪz/ vi/t make a company smaller by reducing the number of people working there

Down's Syn·drome /ˈdaʊnz ˌsɪndroʊm/ n [U] condition present from birth, that stops someone from developing normally, both mentally and physically

down·stairs /ˌdaʊnˈsterz/ adv, adj on or to a lower floor

down·state /ˈdaʊnsteɪt/ adj, adv southern or country parts of a state: downstate Illinois

down·stream /ˌdaʊnˈstrim◂/ adv, adj moving with the current of a river

down·time /ˈdaʊntaɪm/ n [U] time during which a computer is not operating

down-to-earth /ˌ· · ˈ·◂/ adj practical; sensible

down·town /ˌdaʊnˈtaʊn◂/ adv, adj to or in the center of a city or town

down·trod·den /ˈdaʊnˌtrɑdn/ adj treated badly by those in power

down·turn /ˈdaʊntərn/ n time in which business activity is reduced and conditions become worse: economic downturn

down·ward /ˈdaʊnwəd/ adj going down -**wards** adv

down·wind /ˌdaʊnˈwɪnd◂/ adj, adv way the wind is blowing

dow·ry /ˈdaʊri/ n property that a woman's father gives to her husband when she marries

doze /doʊz/ vi sleep lightly **doze** n [S]

doz·en /ˈdʌzən/ determiner, n **dozen** or **dozens**

Dr. written abbrev. for: Doctor

drab /dræb/ adj dull ~**ness** n [U]

draft /dræft/ n 1 first rough plan of something 2 written order for money from a bank 3 current of air 4 depth of water a ship needs 5 practice of making someone serve in the armed forces ♦ vt 1 make a DRAFT (1) of 2 make someone serve in the armed forces

drafts·man /ˈdræftsmən/ -**woman** /-ˌwʊmən/ fem. — n -**men** /-mən/ 1 person who drafts new laws 2 **a** person who draws parts of a new machine or building **b** person who draws well

drag /dræg/ v 1 vt pull (something heavy) along 2 vi move too slowly: The meeting dragged on for hours. 3 vt cause to come or go unwillingly: They dragged me to a party. 4 vi move along while touching the ground: Her long dress dragged in the dust. 5 vt search the bottom of (water) with a net 6 **drag one's feet/heels** act intentionally in a slow or ineffective way ♦ n 1 [C] someone or something that makes it hard to advance 2 [S] **sl** dull event or person **3** [U] *sl* the clothing of one sex worn by the other **4** [C] *sl* act of breathing in cigarette smoke

drag on *phr vi* last an unnecessarily long time

drag out *phr v* **1** *vi/t* (cause to) last an unnecessarily long time **2** *vt* force (something) to be told

drag up *phr vt* raise (a subject) unnecessarily

drag·on /ˈdrægən/ *n* **1** imaginary animal that breathes fire **2** fierce old woman

drain /dreɪn/ *vi/t* **1** (cause to) flow away **2** make or become dry by removing liquid: *drain a field* **3** empty by drinking the contents of **4** make weak and tired ♦ *n* **1** ditch or pipe to carry water away **2** hole in a bath, etc. where a PLUG (1) fits **3** something that uses up money, etc. **4** **down the drain** used wastefully or brought to nothing **~age** *n* [U] system for draining

drake /dreɪk/ *n* male duck

dra·ma /ˈdrɑːmə, ˈdræmə/ *n* **1** [C] theatrical play **2** [U] plays as a group **3** [C;U] exciting situation **~tic** /drəˈmætɪk/ *adj* **1** of the theater **2** exciting **~tically** *adv* **~tist** /ˈdræmətɪst, ˈdrɑː-/ *n* writer of plays **~tize** *vt* **1** turn (a story, etc.) into a play **2** present (facts) in an exciting way

drank /dræŋk/ *v past t. of* DRINK

drape /dreɪp/ *vt* **1** hang (cloth) in folds **2** cause to hang or stretch out loosely or carelessly: *He draped his legs over the arm of the chair.* **~ry** /ˈdreɪpəri/ *also* **drapes** — *n* [U] (cloth for) curtains, etc.

dras·tic /ˈdræstɪk/ *adj* sudden and violent **~ally** *adv*

draw¹ /drɔː/ *v* **drew** /druː/, **drawn** /drɔːn/ **1** *vi/t* make (pictures) with a pen or pencil **2** *vt* cause to come, go, or move by pulling: *get drawn into an argument* | *horse-drawn cart* | *She drew me aside.* **3** *vt* take or pull out: *draw his sword* | *draw $100 from the bank* | *draw blood* (= cause to flow) | *draw a bath* (= put water in the bathtub) **4** *vt* attract: *The play drew big crowds.* **5** *vi* move steadily: *The car drew ahead.* **6** *vt* make or get by reasoning: *draw a comparison/lesson/conclusion* **7** *vi* end a game without either side winning **8** *vi/t* take (breath) in **9** **draw a blank** fail to find the information, etc. looked for **10** **draw the curtains/the blinds** close the curtains or blinds **11**

draw the line (at) refuse to do or accept

drawn *adj* stretched out of shape: *face drawn with sorrow* **drawing** *n* **1** [U] art of drawing pictures **2** [C] picture

draw away *phr v* **1** *vi/t* move (something) away **2** *vi* get further and further ahead

draw back *phr vi* be unwilling to join others

draw in *phr vi* **1** (of days) become shorter **2** arrive

draw into *phr vt* encourage (someone unwilling) to join in

draw on *phr vt* **1** make use of **2** come near in time

draw out *phr v* **1** *vi* (of days) become longer **2** *vt* persuade to talk

draw up *phr v* **1** *vt* DRAFT (a plan, check etc.) **2** *vi* (of a vehicle) arrive and stop

draw² *n* **1** result with neither side winning **2** LOTTERY **3** person or thing that attracts the public **4** money a SALESMAN gets before he sells anything

draw·back /ˈdrɔːbæk/ *n* disadvantage

drawer /drɔːr/ *n* sliding container in a piece of furniture

draw·ing board /ˈ·· ˌ·/ *n* **go back to the drawing board** start working again on a plan or idea after an earlier idea has failed

drawl /drɔːl/ *vi/t* speak or say slowly **drawl** *n*

drawn /drɔːn/ *v past p. of* DRAW

dread /dred/ *vt* fear greatly ♦ *n* [S;U] great fear **~ful** *adj* terrible **~fully** *adv*

dread·locks /ˈdredlɒks/ *n* [P] hair hanging in many thick pieces that look like rope

dream¹ /driːm/ *n* **1** image experienced during sleep **2** something hopefully desired **3** something very beautiful – see also WET DREAM **~less** *adj* (of sleep) peaceful

dream² *vi/t* **dreamed** *or* **dreamt** /dremt/ **1** have a dream **2** imagine (something) **3** **not dream of** refuse to consider **~er** *n* **1** person who dreams **2** impractical person **~y** *adj* **1** seeming half asleep **2** peaceful and beautiful

dream up *phr vt* invent (esp. something silly)

drear·y /ˈdrɪəri/ *adj* sad and dull **-ily** *adv* **-iness** *n* [U]

dredge /dredʒ/ *vi/t* bring up mud, etc. from the bottom of water

dredge up *phr vt* **1** bring to the surface of water **2** produce or bring up (usu. something unpleasant): *dredge up the past*

dregs /drɛgz/ *n* [P] **1** bits of matter that sink to the bottom of liquid **2** worthless part: *the dregs of society*

drench /drɛntʃ/ *vt* make thoroughly wet

dress /drɛs/ *vt* **1** put clothes on **2** *vi* put on formal evening clothes **3** *vt* clean and cover (a wound) **4** *vt* arrange; prepare: *dress a salad/a store window* **5 dressed to kill** dressed in one's best clothes ♦ *n* **1** [C] woman's outer garment made in one piece **2** [U] clothing — see also EVENING DRESS ~**ing** *n* **1** covering for a wound **2** SAUCE, etc. — see also WINDOW DRESSING ~**y** showy or too ornamental

dress up *phr v* **1** *vi/t* put special clothes on **2** *vt* make (something or someone) seem different or more attractive

dres·ser /ˈdrɛsə/ *n* chest of drawers

dress·ing room /ˈ··ˌ·/ *n* room where an actor gets ready to act on stage, on television, etc.

dress re·hears·al /ˈ· ··ˌ·/ *n* last time actors practice a play, using all the clothes and objects that will be used in the real performance

drew /dru/ *v past t. of* DRAW

drib·ble /ˈdrɪbəl/ *v* **1** *vi* let SALIVA flow out slowly from the mouth **2** *vi/t* let (liquid) flow slowly **3** *vi/t* move (a ball) by many short kicks or strokes **dribble** *n*

dried /draɪd/ *v past t. and p. of* DRY

drift /drɪft/ *n* **1** mass of something blown together: *snowdrifts* **2** aimless movement **3** general meaning: *the drift of his argument* ♦ *vi* **1** be driven by wind or water **2** move or live aimlessly ~**er** person who DRIFTS(2)

drill¹ /drɪl/ *n* tool for making holes ♦ *vi/t* use a drill (on)

drill² *n* [C;U] training by repeating and following orders: *army drill* ♦ *vi/t* do or give drill

dri·ly /ˈdraɪli/ *adv* in a DRY¹(4) manner

drink /drɪŋk/ *v* **drank** /dræŋk/, **drunk** /drʌŋk/ **1** *vi/t* swallow (liquid) **2** *vi* take in (too much) alcohol ♦ *n* **1** [C;U] liquid to drink **2** alcohol to drink ~**able** *adj* ~**er** *n* person who drinks too much alcohol

drink to *phr vt* wish (someone or something) good health or success

drip /drɪp/ *vi/t* **1** fall or let fall in drops **2** overflow with or as if with liquid: (fig.) *She was dripping with diamonds.* ♦ *n* **1** (sound of) liquid falling in drops **2** dull person ~**ping** *adj* very wet

drip-dry /ˌ· ˈ·/ *adj* (of clothes) that will dry smooth if hung while wet

drive¹ /draɪv/ *v* **drove** /droʊv/, **driven** /ˈdrɪvən/ **1** *vi/t* guide (a wheeled vehicle) **2** *vt* take (someone) in a vehicle **3** *vt* force (animals, etc.) to go **4** *vt* be the power for **5** *vt* send by hitting **6** *vt* force (someone) into a bad state: *The pain's driving me mad.* **7** *vi* (esp. of rain) move violently **8 be driving at** mean; HINT **driver** *n* person who drives vehicles or animals

drive² *n* **1** [C] journey in a vehicle **2** [C] a big road through a scenic area **3** [C] stroke in a ball game **4** [C] CAMPAIGN **5** [U] force of mind: *He lacks drive.* **6** [C] important natural need which must be fulfilled **7** journey for cows: *a cattle drive*

drive-by /ˈ· ·/ *adj* **drive-by shooting/ killing** act of shooting someone from a moving car

drive-in /ˈ· ·/ *n, adj* (place) that people can use while remaining in their cars: *a drive-in restaurant/movie/bank*

driv·el /ˈdrɪvəl/ *n* [U] nonsense

driz·zle /ˈdrɪzəl/ *n* [U] fine misty rain **drizzle** *vi*

droll /droʊl/ *adj* odd and amusing: *a droll person/expression*

drom·e·da·ry /ˈdrɑməˌdɛri/ *n* camel with one HUMP (1)

drone /droʊn/ *vi* make a continuous low dull sound **drone** *n* [S]

drone on *phr vi* speak for a long time in an uninteresting manner

drool /drul/ *vi* let liquid flow from the mouth: (fig.) *Stop drooling* (= show pleasure in a foolish way) *over that singer.*

droop /drup/ *vi* hang downwards **droop** *n* [S]

drop¹ /drɑp/ *n* **1** [C] small round mass of liquid **2** [C] small round piece of candy **3** [S] a distance or fall straight down **b** fall in quantity: *a drop in sales* **4 at the drop of a hat** suddenly **drops** *n* liquid medicine taken drop by drop

drop² *v* **-pp- 1** *vi/t* fall or let fall **2** *vi/t* (cause to) become less: *The temperature dropped.* **3** *vt* let (someone) get out of a vehicle **4** *vt* stop; give up: *drop a subject* **5** *vt* say or write informally: *drop a hint/a note* **6** *vt* leave out (from a team)

drop back/behind *phr vi* get further away by moving more slowly

drop in/by *phr vi* make an unexpected visit

drop off *phr vi* 1 get less 2 fall asleep

drop out *phr vi* stop taking part

dropout /'drɒp-aʊt/ *n* person who leaves high school, etc., without finishing

drop·pings /'drɒpɪŋz/ *n* [P] waste matter from the bowels of animals or birds

drought /draʊt/ *n* [C;U] long period of dry weather when there is not enough water

drove[1] /droʊv/ *v past t. of* DRIVE

drove[2] *n* group; crowd: *droves of tourists*

drown /draʊn/ *v* 1 *vi/t* die or kill by being under water 2 *vt* cover completely with water 3 *vt* cover up (a sound) with a louder one 4 **drown one's sorrows** drink alcohol in an attempt to forget one's troubles

drowsy /'draʊzi/ *adj* sleepy –**sily** *adv* –**siness** *n* [U]

drudge /drʌdʒ/ *vi* do hard dull work ♦ *n* person who drudges ~**ry** /'drʌdʒəri/ *n* [U] hard uninteresting work

drug /drʌg/ *n* 1 medicine 2 substance taken for pleasure: *a drug addict* ♦ *vt* -**gg**- 1 add harmful drugs to 2 give drugs to

drug·gist /'drʌgɪst/ *n* person who sells medicines

drug·store /'drʌgstɔr, -stoʊr/ *n* store that sells medicine, also paper products, food, etc.

drum[1] /drʌm/ *n* 1 musical instrument made of a skin stretched over a circular frame 2 container, etc., shaped like this: *oil drum*

drum[2] *vi* -**mm**- 1 beat a drum 2 make drumlike noises 3 **drum something into someone** make someone remember something by saying it often ~**mer** *n* person who plays a drum

drum out *phr vt* send away formally and disapprovingly

drum up *phr vt* obtain by continuous effort and esp. by advertising

drunk[1] /drʌŋk/ *v past p. of* DRINK

drunk[2] *adj* under the influence of alcohol

drunk[3] *n* also **drunkard** /'drʌŋkəd/ — person who drinks too much

drunk·en /'drʌŋkən/ *adj* 1 DRUNK[2] 2 resulting from or connected with too much

drinking: *a drunken sleep* ~**ly** *adv* ~**ness** *n* [U]

dry[1] /draɪ/ *adj* 1 not wet: *dry clothes/climate* 2 (of wine) not sweet 3 not allowing the sale of alcohol 4 amusing without appearing to be so; quietly IRONIC: *dry wit* 5 uninteresting ~**ly**, **drily** *adv* ~**ness** *n* [U]

dry[2] *v* 1 *vi/t* make or become dry 2 *vt* preserve (food) by removing liquid ~**er**, **drier** *n* machine that dries

dry out *phr vi/t* 1 (cause to) give up dependence on alcohol 2 (cause to) become completely dry

dry up /ˌ·'·/ *phr vi* 1 (of a supply) stop coming 2 *sl* SHUT UP (1)

dry-clean /ˈ· ·, ˌ· '·/ *vt* clean (clothes) with chemicals instead of water ~**ers** *n* cleaners (CLEAN) ~**ing** *n* [U] 1 action or industry of dry-cleaning clothes 2 clothes that need to be or have just been dry-cleaned

dry rot /ˌ· '·/ *n* [U] disease that turns wood into powder

dry run /ˌ· '·/ *n* practice attempt made before the real thing

du·al /'duəl/ *adj* having 2 parts; double: *dual citizenship* (= of 2 countries) ~**ity** /duˈælɪti/ *n* [U]

dub /dʌb/ *vt* -**bb**- 1 give (a name) to 2 change the spoken language of (a film)

du·bi·ous /'dubiəs/ *adj* feeling or causing doubt ~**ly** *adv*

duch·ess /'dʌtʃɪs/ *n* **a** wife of a DUKE **b** woman who holds the rank of DUKE in her own right

duck /dʌk/ *n* 1 [C] common swimming bird 2 [U] its meat 3 **take to something like a duck to water** learn or get used to something very easily ♦ *v* 1 *vi/t* lower (one's head) quickly 2 *vt* push (someone) under water 3 *vt* try to avoid responsibility — see also LAME DUCK, SITTING DUCK

duck·ling /'dʌklɪŋ/ *n* young duck — see also UGLY DUCKLING

duct /dʌkt/ *n* tube that carries liquids, air, etc.

dud /dʌd/ *n sl* useless thing or person: *a dud check*

dude /dud/ *n infml* man

due /du/ *adj* 1 owed 2 *fml* suitable; proper 3 expected: *The train is due any minute.* 4 **due to** because of ♦ *adv* (before **north, south, east, west**) exactly ♦ *n* something that rightfully

belongs to one: *give him his due* **dues** *n*
[P] official payments

du·el /ˈduəl/ *n* fight arranged between 2
people **duel** *vi*

du·et /duˈet/ *n* piece of music for 2 performers

duf·fel bag /ˈdʌfəl ˌbæg/ *n* large cloth
bag used (by soldiers) to carry clothes,
etc.

dug /dʌg/ *v past t. and p. of* DIG

dug·out /ˈdʌgaʊt/ *n* 1 boat made of a
hollow log 2 shelter for baseball team

duke /duk/ *n* British nobleman of the
highest rank ~**dom** *n* rank or lands of a
duke

dull /dʌl/ *adj* 1 not bright or shining 2
slow in thinking 3 not sharp: *a dull pain*
4 uninteresting ♦ *vt* make dull ~**ness** *n*
[U]

du·ly /ˈduli/ *adv* properly; as expected

dumb /dʌm/ *adj* 1 unable to speak 2
unwilling to speak; silent 3 *sl* stupid ~**ly**
adv ~**ness** *n* [U]

dumb·found /dʌmˈfaʊnd, ˈdʌmfaʊnd/ *vt*
make dumb from surprise

dum·my /ˈdʌmi/ *n* 1 object made to look
like a real thing or person 2 *sl* stupid
person

dump /dʌmp/ *vt* 1 drop carelessly 2 sell
(goods) abroad more cheaply than at
home ♦ *n* 1 place for dumping waste 2
stored rubbish 3 *sl* dirty untidy place 4 **in
the dumps** sad ~**truck** *n* large vehicle
for carrying earth and stones ~**y** *adj*
short and fat

dump·ling /ˈdʌmplɪŋ/ *n* ball of boiled
DOUGH

dump·ster /ˈdʌmpstə/ *n* large container
for carrying away unwanted things

dunce /dʌns/ *n* slow learner

dune /dun/ *n* long low sandhill piled up
by the wind

dung /dʌŋ/ *n* [U] animal MANURE

dun·geon /ˈdʌndʒən/ *n* underground
prison

dunk /dʌŋk/ *vt* dip (esp. food) into liquid
while eating

du·o /ˈdu-oo/ *n* a pair, esp. of musicians

dupe /dup/ *vt* trick; deceive ♦ *n fml*
person who is duped

du·plex /ˈdupleks/ *n* pair of joined
houses

du·pli·cate[1] /ˈdupləkət/ *n, adj* (something
that is) exactly like another

du·pli·cate[2] /ˈdupləkeɪt/ *vt* copy exactly
~**cator** *n* machine that copies ~**cation**
/ˌdupləˈkeɪʃən/ *n* [U]

du·plic·i·ty /duˈplɪsəti/ *n* [U] *fml*
dishonesty

dur·a·ble /ˈdʊrəbəl/ *adj* lasting for a long
time **durables** *n* [P] goods expected to
last for years

du·ra·tion /dʊˈreɪʃən/ *n* [U] *fml* 1 time
during which something lasts 2 **for the
duration** as long as something lasts

du·ress /dʊˈres/ *n* [U] *fml* threats:
promise under duress

dur·ing /ˈdʊrɪŋ/ *prep* 1 all through (a
length of time) 2 at some moment in: *die
during the night*

dusk /dʌsk/ *n* [U] time when the light of
day fades

dust[1] /dʌst/ *n* [U] powder made of earth
or other matter ~**y** *adj* covered with dust

dust[2] *vt* 1 clean the dust from: *dust books*
2 cover with powder: *dust crops* ~**er** *n*
cloth, etc. for removing dust

dust off *phr vt* begin to use or practice
again, after a period of not doing so

dust jack·et /ˈ. ˌ../ *n* loose paper cover on
a hard cover book

dust·pan /ˈdʌstpæn/ *n* flat container into
which house dust is swept

Dutch /dʌtʃ/ *adj* 1 of the Netherlands
(Holland) 2 **go dutch (with someone)**
share costs 3 **dutch treat** meal or entertainment where costs are shared

du·ty /ˈduti/ *n* [C;U] 1 something one must
do 2 tax: *customs duties* 3 **heavy duty** (of
machines, etc.) able to do hard work 4
on/off duty having/not having to work
dutiful *adj* showing respect and obedience **dutifully** *adv*

duty-free /ˌ.. ˈ.◂/ *adj, adv* (of goods)
allowed to enter a country without tax

dwarf /dwɔrf/ *n* **dwarfs** or **dwarves**
/dwɔrvz/ very small person, animal, or
plant ♦ *vt* cause to look small

dwell /dwel/ *vi* dwelled or dwelt /dwelt/
lit live (in a place) ~**er** *n* person or
animal that lives somewhere: *city-
dwellers* ~**ing** *n fml* home

dwell on *phr vt* think or speak a lot
about

dwin·dle /ˈdwɪndl/ *vi* become gradually
fewer or smaller

dye /daɪ/ *n* [C;U] substance used to color
cloth, etc. ♦ *vi/t* dyes, dyed, dyeing
color with dye

dyed-in-the-wool /ˌ· · ·ˈ·◂/ *adj* impossible to change (as to the stated or known quality): *a dyed-in-the-wool Republican*

dy·ing /ˈdaɪ-ɪŋ/ *v present p. of* DIE

dyke /daɪk/ *n sl* LESBIAN

dy·nam·ic /daɪˈnæmɪk/ *adj* **1** powerful and active **2** of force that causes movement ~**ally** *adv* **dynamics** *n* [U] **1** science that deals with matter in movement **2** way in which systems or people behave, react, and affect each other: *dynamics of power in business* –**ism** /ˈdaɪnəˌmɪzəm/ *n* [U] being DYNAMIC (1)

dy·na·mite /ˈdaɪnəˌmaɪt/ *n* [U] **1** powerful explosive **2** something or someone that will cause great shock, admiration, etc. ♦ *vt* blow up with dynamite

dy·na·mo /ˈdaɪnəˌmoʊ/ *n* -**mos 1** machine that turns movement into electricity **2** person with a lot of energy

dyn·a·sty /ˈdaɪnəsti/ *n* line of rulers of the same family

dys·en·te·ry /ˈdɪsənˌtɛri/ *n* [U] painful bowel disease

dys·func·tion·al /dɪsˈfʌŋkʃənl/ *adj* not working normally, or not showing normal social behavior: *dysfunctional families*

dys·lex·i·a /dɪsˈlɛksiə/ *n* [U] inability to read, from difficulty in recognizing letter shapes –**ic** *adj*

E

E, e /iː/ the 5th letter of the English alphabet

E. written abbrev. for: east(ern)

each /iːtʃ/ determiner, pron every one separately: *each child* | *each of the children* ♦ adv for or to each: *They cost fifty cents each.*

each oth·er /ˌ· ·ˈ·/ pron with each doing something to the other: *kiss each other* | *hold each other's hands*

ea·ger /ˈiːgə/ adj keen; wanting very much **~ly** adv **~ness** n [U]

ea·gle /ˈiːgəl/ n large bird with a hooked beak, that eats meat **~-eyed** /ˌ· ·ˈ·/ adj having very good eyesight

ear[1] /ɪr/ n **1** [C] either of the 2 parts of the head with which we hear **2** [S] good recognition of sounds: *an ear for music* **3 all ears** listening eagerly **4 play by ear** play music without written notes **5 up to one's ears in** deep in; very busy with

ear[2] n head of a plant that produces grain: *ear of corn*

ear·ache /ˈɪreɪk/ n [U] pain inside the ear

ear·drum /ˈɪrdrʌm/ n tight skin inside the ear which allows one to hear sound

earl /ɜːl/ n British nobleman of high rank

ear·lobe /ˈɪrloʊb/ n soft piece of flesh at the bottom of the ear

ear·ly /ˈɜːli/ adv, adj **1** sooner than usual or expected: *The train arrived early.* | *an early supper* **2** near the beginning: *It happened early in the morning/in the early morning.* **3 at the earliest** and not sooner

early bird /ˌ· ·ˈ·/ n person who gets up or arrives early

ear·mark /ˈɪrmɑːrk/ vt set aside (money, time, etc.) for a particular purpose

ear·muffs /ˈɪrmʌfs/ n [P] 2 pieces of material attached to ends of a band worn over the head to keep the ears warm

earn /ɜːn/ v **1** vi/t get (money) by working **2** vt deserve (what one has worked for) **~er** n **~ings** n [P] money earned

ear·nest /ˈɜːnɪst/ adj determined and serious ♦ n **in earnest: a** in a determined way **b** not joking **~ly** adv **~ness** n [U]

ear·phones /ˈɪrfoʊnz/ n [P] apparatus put in ears to listen to the radio, a CD, etc.

ear·plug /ˈɪrplʌg/ n soft thing put into the ear to keep out noise, etc.

ear·ring /ˈɪrɪŋ, ˈɪrˌrɪŋ/ n decoration for the ear

ear·shot /ˈɪrʃɑt/ n **within/out of earshot** within/beyond the distance at which a sound can be heard

earth /ɜːθ/ n **1** [S;U] (often cap.) the world we live on: *the planet Earth* **2** [U] its surface, as opposed to the sky: *The rocket fell to earth.* **3** [U] soil: *hard earth* **~ly** adj **1** of this world, not heaven **2** possible: *no earthly reason* **~y** adj **1** like soil **2** concerned with the body, not the mind

earth·quake /ˈɜːθkweɪk/ n sudden violent shaking of the earth's surface

earth·worm /ˈɜːθwɜːm/ n WORM

ease[1] /iːz/ n [U] **1** ability to do something easily **2** state of being comfortable **3 ill at ease** uncomfortable

ease[2] v **1** vi/t make or become less painful or difficult **2** vt make less anxious **3** vt move slowly and carefully into a different position

ease off/up phr vi become less active or severe

ea·sel /ˈiːzəl/ n wooden frame to support a picture or BLACKBOARD

east /iːst/ n **1** [the+S] (often cap.) direction from which the sun rises **2** area of the US east of the Mississippi River ♦ adj **1** in the east **2** (of wind) from the east ♦ adv to the east **~ward** adj, adv

Eas·ter /ˈiːstər/ n Christian holy day in memory of Christ's death

Easter Bun·ny /ˌ·· ˈ··/ n [the+S] imaginary rabbit that children believe brings colored eggs and chocolate at Easter

eas·ter·ly /ˈiːstəli/ adj east

east·ern /ˈiːstən/ adj of the east part of the world or of a country

Eastern time /ˌ·· ˈ·/ n time used in the eastern states of the US

eas·y /ˈiːzi/ adj **1** not difficult **2** comfortable; without worry ♦ adv **go easy on: a** be less severe with **b** not use too much of **–ily** adv **1** without difficulty **2** without doubt: *easily the best*

easy chair /ˌ·· ˈ·/ n an ARMCHAIR

eas·y·go·ing /ˌizi'gouɪŋ◂/ adj pleasantly calm and unhurried

easy lis·ten·ing /ˌ·· '···/ n [U] music that is relaxing to listen to

eat /it/ v ate /eɪt/, **eaten** /'it'n/ **1** vi/t take in (food) through the mouth **2** vt [(away, into)] destroy by chemical action **3 be eaten up with** be full of (violent feeling) **4 eat one's words** admit that one was wrong **5 eat your heart out** infml be very jealous — see also CROW[1] (3) ~**able** adj ~**er** n

eating dis·or·der /'·· ·ˌ··/ n medical condition in which you do not eat normal amounts of food or do not eat regularly

eaves /ivz/ n [P] edges of a roof, beyond the walls

eaves·drop /'ivzdrɑp/ vi -**pp**- listen secretly to conversation ~**per** n

ebb /ɛb/ vi grow less or lower: *His courage ebbed away.* ♦ n [S] at a **low ebb** in a bad state

eb·o·ny /'ɛbəni/ adj, n [U] (of the color of) hard black wood

e·bul·lient /ɪ'bʌliənt, ɪ'bʊl-/ adj fml full of happy excitement –**lience** n [U]

ec·cen·tric /ɪk'sɛntrɪk/ adj **1** (of people) unusual; peculiar **2** (of circles) not having the same center ~**ity** /ˌɛksən-'trɪsəti, -sən-/ n [C;U]

ec·cle·si·as·ti·cal /ɪˌklizi'æstɪkəl/ adj of the Christian church

ech·o /'ɛkou/ n -**oes** sound sent back from a surface ♦ v **1** vi come back as an echo **2** vt copy or repeat (words, ideas, etc.)

é·clair /eɪ'klɛr, ɪ-, 'eɪklɛr/ n cake shaped like a finger, with cream inside

e·clec·tic /ɪ'klɛktɪk/ adj fml using ideas from many different systems ~**ism** /-təˌsɪzəm/ n [U]

e·clipse /ɪ'klɪps/ n disappearance of the sun's light (cut off by the moon) or of the moon's light (cut off by the Earth) ♦ vt **1** cause an eclipse of **2** make (something) less important by comparison

e·col·o·gy /ɪ'kɑlədʒi/ n [U] relations of living things to their surroundings -**gist** n -**gical** /ˌikə'lɑdʒɪkəl◂, ˌɛk-/ adj

ec·o·nom·ic /ˌɛkə'nɑmɪk◂, ˌi-/ adj **1** connected with business, industry, and wealth **2** profitable ~**al** adj not wasteful ~**ally** adv

ec·o·nom·ics /ˌɛkə'nɑmɪks, ˌi-/ n [U] study of the way in which wealth is produced and used -**nomist** /ɪ'kɑnəmɪst/ n

e·con·o·mize /ɪ'kɑnəˌmaɪz/ vi avoid waste

e·con·o·my /ɪ'kɑnəmi/ n **1** [C] economic system of a country **2** [C;U] avoidance of waste — see also MIXED ECONOMY ♦ adj cheap: *an economy class air ticket*

e·co·sys·tem /'ikouˌsɪstəm/ n all the living things in an area and the relationship between them

ec·sta·sy /'ɛkstəsi/ n [C;U] great joy **ecstatic** /ɪk'stætɪk, ɛk-/ adj **ecstatically** adv

e·cu·men·i·cal /ˌɛkyə'mɛnɪkəl◂/ adj favoring Christian unity

ec·ze·ma /'ɛksəmə, ˌɛgzəmə, ɪg'zimə/ n [U] red swollen condition of the skin

ed. abbr. for: EDITOR, EDITION

ed·dy /'ɛdi/ n circular movement of water, smoke, etc. ♦ vi move in eddies

edge /ɛdʒ/ n **1** cutting part of a knife, etc. **2** narrowest part along the outside of an object: *the edge of a coin* **3** place where something begins or ends: *the water's edge* **4 have the edge on** be better than **5 on edge** nervous **6 set someone's teeth on edge** infml give an unpleasant feeling to someone **7 take the edge off** infml make less severe ♦ v **1** vt put a border on **2** vi/t move gradually, esp. sideways **edging** n [C;U] border **edgy** adj nervous

ed·i·ble /'ɛdəbəl/ adj that can be eaten

e·dict /'idɪkt/ n official public command

ed·i·fice /'ɛdəfɪs/ n fml large fine building

ed·it /'ɛdɪt/ vt prepare (a newspaper, film, etc.) for printing or showing ~**or** n person who edits

e·di·tion /ɪ'dɪʃən/ n **1** one printing, esp. of a book **2** form in which a book is printed: *a paper back edition*

ed·i·to·ri·al /ˌɛdə'tɔriəl, -'tour-/ adj of an editor ♦ n newspaper article giving the paper's opinion

ed·u·cate /'ɛdʒəˌkeɪt/ vt teach; train ♦ -**or** n person who educates

ed·u·ca·tion /ˌɛdʒə'keɪʃən/ n [S;U] (knowledge resulting from) teaching or training ~**al** adj

ed·u·tain·ment /ˌɛdʒu'teɪnmənt/ n [U] movies, television programs, or computer SOFTWARE that educate and entertain children

eel /il/ n long snake-like fish

ee·rie /'ɪri/ adj frightening because of being strange: *an eerie silence* **eerily** adv

ef·fect /ɪˈfekt/ n [C;U] **1** result; what happens because of a cause **2 in effect: a** in operation **b** in fact **3 take effect** come into operation — see also SIDE EFFECT ♦ vt fml produce; cause **effects** n [P] **1** sounds, etc., produced in a film or play **2** fml personal belongings

ef·fec·tive /ɪˈfektɪv/ adj **1** producing the desired result: very effective new laws **2** fml actual: the effective strength of our army ~**ly** adv ~**ness** n [U]

ef·fem·i·nate /ɪˈfemənɪt/ adj (of a man) too like a woman -**nacy** n [U]

ef·fi·cient /ɪˈfɪʃənt/ adj working well; an efficient secretary/machine ~**ly** adv -**ciency** n [U]

ef·fi·gy /ˈefədʒi/ n fml wooden, stone, etc., likeness of someone

ef·flu·ent /ˈefluənt/ n [C;U] flowing out of liquid chemical or human waste

ef·fort /ˈefət/ n **1** [U] use of strength **2** [C] attempt: a good effort ~**less** adj successful without effort ~**lessly** adv

ef·fu·sive /ɪˈfjuːsɪv/ adj showing too much feeling ~**ly** adv

EFL abbrev. for: English as a foreign language

e.g. /ˌiː ˈdʒiː/ abbrev. for: for example

e·gal·i·tar·i·an /ɪˌɡæləˈteəriən/ adj believing in social equality ~**ism** n [U]

egg¹ /eɡ/ n **1** [C] round object with a shell, containing a baby bird, snake, etc. **2** [C;U] (the contents of) an egg when used as food: a boiled egg **3** [C] female cell producing young **4 have egg on one's face** remain silent

egg² v **egg on** phr vt encourage someone, esp. to do wrong

egg·head /ˈeɡhed/ n derog a HIGHBROW

egg·plant /ˈeɡplænt/ n large purple vegetable

e·go /ˈiːɡoʊ/ n **egos 1** one's opinion of oneself: an enormous ego **2** tech one's conscious self — see also ALTER EGO

e·go·cen·tric /ˌiːɡoʊˈsentrɪk◂/ adj thinking only about oneself; selfish

e·go·is·m /ˈiːɡoʊˌɪzəm/ n [U] selfishness -**ist** n

e·go·tis·m /ˈiːɡəˌtɪzəm/ n [U] believing that one is more important than other people -**tist** n -**tistic** /ˌiːɡəˈtɪstɪk◂/, -**tisti·cal** adj

ego trip /ˈ·· ˌ·/ n act or set of acts done mainly because it makes one feel proud of oneself

e·gre·gious /ɪˈɡriːdʒəs/ adj fml noticeably bad

eight /eɪt/ det, n, pron **8 eighth** det, adv, n, pron 8th

eigh·teen /ˌeɪˈtiːn◂/ det, n, pron **18 ~th** det, adv, n, pron 18th

eigh·ty /ˈeɪti/ det, n, pron **80 -tieth** det, adv, n, pron 80th

ei·ther¹ /ˈiːðə, ˈaɪ-/ det, pron, conj **1** one or the other: I haven't seen either John or Sam. | I haven't met either (of them). | He either drives or walks. **2** each of two: houses on either side of the road

either² adv (used with negative expressions) also: I haven't been to France, or Germany either.

e·jac·u·late /ɪˈdʒækjəˌleɪt/ vi/t **1** throw out (SPERM) suddenly from the body **2** fml cry out suddenly -**lation** /ɪˌdʒækjəˈleɪʃən/ n [C;U]

e·ject /ɪˈdʒekt/ vt fml throw out ~**ion** /ɪˈdʒekʃən/ n [U]

ejection seat /·ˈ·· ˌ·/ n seat that throws one out of a plane that is burning, etc.

eke /iːk/ v **eke out** phr vt **1** make (supplies) last as long as possible **2** work hard to earn little money: eke out a living

e·lab·o·rate¹ /ɪˈlæbrɪt/ adj full of detail ~**ly** adv

e·lab·o·rate² /ɪˈlæbəˌreɪt/ vi add more detail -**ration** /ɪˌlæbəˈreɪʃən/ n [C;U]

e·lapse /ɪˈlæps/ vi fml (of time) pass

e·las·tic /ɪˈlæstɪk/ adj able to spring back into shape after stretching or bending ♦ n elastic material ~**ity** /ˌiːlæˈstɪsəti, ɪlæ-/ n [U]

e·lat·ed /ɪˈleɪtɪd/ adj proud and happy -**ion** /ɪˈleɪʃən/ n [U]

el·bow /ˈelboʊ/ n joint where the arm bends ♦ vt push with the elbows

elbow grease /ˈ·· ˌ·/ n [U] hard work with the hands

elbow room /ˈ·· ˌ·/ n [U] space to move freely

el·der /ˈeldə/ adj (of a family member) older: my elder sister ♦ n person in a respected official position ~**ly** adj rather old

elder states·man /ˌ·· ˈ·ˌ·/ n old and respected person who is asked for advice because of his or her experience

el·dest /ˈeldɪst/ n, adj (person who is) the oldest of 3 or more

e·lect /ɪˈlɛkt/ vt **1** choose by voting **2** fml decide: *She elected to go.* ♦ adj fml chosen, but not yet at work: *president elect* ~**or** n **1** person with the right to vote **2** member of the electoral college ~**oral** adj ~**orally** adv

e·lec·tion /ɪˈlɛkʃən/ n [C;U] (occasion of) choosing representatives by voting

electoral col·lege /ˌ···ˈ··/ n group of representatives who elect the president

e·lec·to·rate /ɪˈlɛktərɪt/ n all the electors (1)

e·lec·tric /ɪˈlɛktrɪk/ adj **1** worked by or producing electricity: *an electric razor* **2** *infml* very exciting ~**al** adj concerned with or using electricity: *an electrical fault* ~**ally** adv **electric chair** /ˌ··ˈ·/ n [the+S] punishment of electrocuting (ELECTROCUTE) a criminal

e·lec·tri·cian /ɪˌlɛkˈtrɪʃən, ˌiːlɛk-/ n person who fits and repairs electrical equipment

e·lec·tri·ci·ty /ɪˌlɛkˈtrɪsəti, ˌiːlɛk-/ n [U] power supply, carried usu. by wires, for heating, lighting, etc.

e·lec·tri·fy /ɪˈlɛktrəˌfaɪ/ vt **1** use electric power for **2** excite greatly

e·lec·tro·cute /ɪˈlɛktrəˌkyut/ vt kill by passing electric current through the body ~**cution** /ɪˌlɛktrəˈkyuʃən/ n [C;U]

e·lec·trode /ɪˈlɛktroʊd/ n point at which current enters or leaves a BATTERY (1)

e·lec·trol·y·sis /ɪˌlɛkˈtrɑləsɪs/ n [U] the use of electricity **a** for separation of a liquid into its chemical parts or **b** for destruction of hair roots

e·lec·tron /ɪˈlɛktrɑn/ n small piece of matter that moves around the NUCLEUS of an atom

e·lec·tron·ic /ɪˌlɛkˈtrɑnɪk, ˌiːlɛk-/ adj of, using, or produced by equipment that works by means of an electric current passing through CHIPS[1] (4), TRANSISTORS, etc. (for example, televisions, computers, etc.): *electronic music/mail* ~**ally** adv **electronics** n [U] study or making of such equipment

el·e·gant /ˈɛləgənt/ adj graceful; stylish ~**ly** adv **-gance** n [U]

el·e·ment /ˈɛləmənt/ n **1** [C] simple substance consisting of only one kind of atom **2** [S] small amount: *an element of truth in what you say* **3** [C] part of a whole: *Honesty is an important element in his character.* **4** [C] heating part of a piece of electric equipment **5 in/out of one's element** doing/not doing what one is best at **elements** n [the+P] **1** (bad) weather **2** first things to study in a subject **elemental** /ˌɛləˈmɛntəl◀/ adj of the forces of nature

el·e·men·ta·ry /ˌɛləˈmɛntəri◀/ adj **1** easy: *elementary questions* **2** concerned with the beginning of something: *elementary arithmetic* **3** concerned with elementary school

elementary school /···ˈ·· ˌ·/ n school for the first 6 to 8 years of a child's education

el·e·phant /ˈɛləfənt/ n very large animal with TUSKS and a long round nose (TRUNK) — see also WHITE ELEPHANT ~**ine** /ˌɛləˈfæntin, -taɪn/ adj heavy and awkward

el·e·vate /ˈɛləˌveɪt/ vt fml **1** raise **2** improve (the mind)

el·e·va·tion /ˌɛləˈveɪʃən/ n **1** [U] fml act of elevating **2** [S] height above sea level **3** [C] drawing of one side of a building

el·e·va·tor /ˈɛləˌveɪtə/ n **1** apparatus in a building for taking people and things from one floor to another **2** machine for raising grain, etc.

e·lev·en /ɪˈlɛvən/ det, n, pron 11 ~**th** det, adv, n, pron 11th

eleventh hour /ˌ··· ˈ·/ n [the+S] the very last moment

elf /ɛlf/ n **elves** /ɛlvz/ small usu. male fairy ~**in** adj

e·li·cit /ɪˈlɪsɪt/ vt fml get (information, etc.) from someone

e·lide /ɪˈlaɪd/ vt leave out (a sound) in pronunciation

el·i·gi·ble /ˈɛlədʒəbəl/ adj fulfilling the conditions; suitable ~**bility** /ˌɛlədʒəˈbɪləti/ n [U]

e·lim·i·nate /ɪˈlɪməˌneɪt/ vt remove; get rid of ~**nation** /ɪˌlɪməˈneɪʃən/ n [U]

e·lite /ɪˈlit, eɪ-/ n favored powerful group in society **elitism** n [U]

elk /ɛlk/ n very large animal like a DEER

el·lipse /ɪˈlɪps/ n OVAL shape

el·lip·ti·cal /ɪˈlɪptɪkəl/ adj **1** OVAL **2** (of speech) with hidden meaning

elm /ɛlm/ n large tree with broad leaves

e·lon·gate /ˈiːlɔŋgeɪt, ˈɪlɔŋˌgeɪt/ vt make longer

e·lope /ɪˈloʊp/ vi run away to get married ~**ment** n [C;U]

el·o·quent /ˈɛləkwənt/ adj **1** able to influence people by using language well **2** fml showing something very strongly: an eloquent reminder of the horrors of wars –**quence** n [U]

else /ɛls/ adv **1** more; as well: What else can I say? **2** apart from (what is mentioned): He's here. Everyone else has gone home. **3** otherwise: You must pay or else go to prison.

else·where /ˈɛlswɛr, -hwɛr/ adv at, in, from, or to another place

e·lu·ci·date /ɪˈlusəˌdeɪt/ vt fml explain -**dation** /ɪˌlusəˈdeɪʃən/ n [U]

e·lude /ɪˈlud/ vt escape from

e·lu·sive /ɪˈlusɪv, -zɪv/ adj hard to find or remember

elves /ɛlvz/ pl. of ELF

e·ma·ci·at·ed /ɪˈmeɪʃiˌeɪtɪd/ adj extremely thin –**ation** /ɪˌmeɪʃiˈeɪʃən, -si-/ n [U]

e·mail, e-mail /ˈiˌmeɪl/ n **1** [U] system by which letters, information, etc. can be sent quickly from one computer to another **2** [C] message sent by this system

em·a·nate /ˈɛməˌneɪt/ v **emanate from** phr vi fml come out (from somewhere) -**nation** /ˌɛməˈneɪʃən/ n [U]

e·man·ci·pate /ɪˈmænsəˌpeɪt/ vt make (slaves, etc.) free -**pation** /ɪˌmænsəˈpeɪʃən/ n [U]

em·balm /ɪmˈbɑm/ vt preserve (a dead body) with chemicals, etc. ~**er** n

em·bank·ment /ɪmˈbæŋkmənt/ n wall that holds back water or carries a road or railroad

em·bar·go /ɪmˈbɑrgoʊ/ n -**goes** official order forbidding trade ♦ vt put an embargo on

em·bark /ɪmˈbɑrk/ vi/t go or put onto a ship ~**ation** /ˌɛmbɑrˈkeɪʃən/ n [C;U]

embark on/upon phr vt start (something new)

em·bar·rass /ɪmˈbærəs/ vt make ashamed or socially uncomfortable: an embarrassing question/silence ~**ingly** adv ~**ment** n [C;U]

em·bas·sy /ˈɛmbəsi/ n offices of an AMBASSADOR

em·bat·tled /ɪmˈbætld/ adj surrounded by enemies or difficulties

em·bed /ɪmˈbɛd/ vt -**dd**- fix firmly in surrounding material

em·bel·lish /ɪmˈbɛlɪʃ/ vt **1** decorate **2** add (esp. untrue) details to ~**ment** n [C;U]

em·ber /ˈɛmbər/ n [usu. pl.] piece of very hot coal, etc., in a dying fire

em·bez·zle /ɪmˈbɛzəl/ vi/t steal (money placed in one's care) ~**ment** n [U] –**zler** n

em·bla·zon /ɪmˈbleɪzən/ vt show (a decoration, etc.) noticeably

em·blem /ˈɛmbləm/ n sign representing something: The school's emblem is a knight.

em·bod·y /ɪmˈbɑdi/ vt fml give physical expression to -**iment** n: She's the embodiment of evil.

em·boss /ɪmˈbɔs, ɪmˈbɑs/ vt decorate with a raised pattern

em·brace /ɪmˈbreɪs/ v **1** vi/t take (someone) lovingly in one's arms **2** vt fml include **3** vt fml become a believer in: embrace the Muslim faith ♦ n: a warm embrace

em·broi·der /ɪmˈbrɔɪdər/ vi/t **1** decorate (cloth) by sewing in colored thread **2** EMBELLISH ~**y** n [U]

em·bry·o /ˈɛmbriˌoʊ/ n -**os** creature or baby in its first state before birth ~**nic** /ˌɛmbriˈɑnɪk◂/ adj

em·cee /ˌɛmˈsi/ n MASTER OF CEREMONIES

em·er·ald /ˈɛmərəld/ n [C;U] (color of) a bright green precious stone

e·merge /ɪˈmɜrdʒ/ vi **1** come out **2** (of facts) become known **emergence** n [U]

emergent adj beginning to develop: emergent nations

e·mer·gen·cy /ɪˈmɜrdʒənsi/ n dangerous happening which must be dealt with at once

emergency room /·ˈ··· ˌ·/ n part of hospital that immediately treats people who are badly hurt or very sick

em·i·grant /ˈɛməgrənt/ n person who emigrates

em·i·grate /ˈɛməˌgreɪt/ vi leave one's own country to live in another –**gration** /ˌɛməˈgreɪʃən/ n [C;U]

ém·i·gré /ˈɛməˌgreɪ/ n fml a REFUGEE

em·i·nence /ˈɛmənəns/ n [U] great importance

em·i·nent /ˈɛmənənt/ adj (of a person) famous and admired ~**ly** adv fml extremely

e·mir /əˈmɪr/ n Muslim ruler ~**ate** /ˈɛmərɪt, əˈmɪrət, -reɪt/ n lands, etc., of an emir

em·is·sa·ry /ˈɛməˌsɛri/ n fml person sent with a message or to do special work

e·mis·sion /ɪˈmɪʃən/ n fml 1 [U] act of emitting 2 [C] something emitted

e·mit /ɪˈmɪt/ vt -tt- fml send out: to emit smoke/a humming sound

e·mo·tion /ɪˈmoʊʃən/ n 1 [C] strong feeling, such as love, sorrow, etc. 2 [U] strength of feeling: a voice shaking with emotion ~**al** adj 1 concerning the emotions 2 having feelings that are (too) strong ~**ally** adv

e·mo·tive /ɪˈmoʊtɪv/ adj causing strong feeling

em·pa·thy /ˈɛmpəθi/ n [S;U] ability to imagine oneself in the position of another person –**thize** vi

em·per·or /ˈɛmpərə/ n ruler of an empire

em·pha·sis /ˈɛmfəsɪs/ n -ses /-siz/ [C;U] special force or attention given to something important

em·pha·size /ˈɛmfəˌsaɪz/ vt place emphasis on

em·phat·ic /ɪmˈfætɪk/ adj strongly emphasized ~**ally** adv

em·phy·se·ma /ˌɛmfəˈsimə, -ˈzi-/ n serious lung illness, often resulting from smoking

em·pire /ˈɛmpaɪə/ n group of countries under one government

em·ploy /ɪmˈplɔɪ/ vt 1 give paid work to 2 fml use ~**able** adj suitable as a worker ~**er** n person who employs others ~**ment** n 1 [U] paid work 2 [C] fml useful activity

em·ploy·ee /ɪmˈplɔɪ-i, ˌɛmplɔɪˈi, ˌɪm-/ n employed person

em·pow·er /ɪmˈpaʊə/ vt fml give power to ~**ment** n

em·press /ˈɛmprɪs/ n female ruler of an empire

emp·ty /ˈɛmpti/ adj 1 containing nothing 2 insincere: empty promises ◆ n [usu. pl.] empty container ◆ vt/i make or become empty –**tiness** n [U]

empty-hand·ed /ˌ·· ˈ··◂/ adj having gained nothing

em·u·late /ˈɛmyəˌleɪt/ vt try to do as well as or better than –**lation** /ˌɛmyəˈleɪʃən/ n [U]

en·a·ble /ɪˈneɪbəl/ vt make able: to enable them to walk again

en·act /ɪˈnækt/ vt make (a law)

e·nam·el /ɪˈnæməl/ n [U] 1 glassy covering on metal, etc. 2 hard surface of the teeth ◆ vt -l- cover with enamel

en·am·ored /ɪˈnæmə d/ adj very fond (of an idea, etc.)

en·cap·su·late /ɪnˈkæpsəˌleɪt/ vt express in a short form

en·case /ɪnˈkeɪs/ vt cover completely

en·chant /ɪnˈtʃænt/ vt 1 delight 2 use magic on ~**ing** adj delightful ~**ingly** adv ~**ment** n [C;U]

en·chi·la·da /ˌɛntʃəˈlɑdə/ n Mexican dish of meat, etc. inside a TORTILLA

en·clave /ˈɛnkleɪv, ˈɑŋ-/ n part of a country, etc. surrounded by another: ethnic enclaves in Chicago

en·close /ɪnˈkloʊz/ vt 1 surround with a fence, etc. 2 put (something else) into an envelope

en·clo·sure /ɪnˈkloʊʒə/ n 1 enclosed place 2 something put in with a letter 3 act of enclosing

en·com·pass /ɪnˈkʌmpəs/ vt include; be concerned with

en·core /ˈɑŋkɔr, ˈɑŋkoʊr, ˈɑn-/ interj, n (word calling for) a repeated performance

en·coun·ter /ɪnˈkaʊntə/ vt fml meet (something dangerous or unexpected) ◆ n sudden (esp. unpleasant) meeting

en·cour·age /ɪnˈkɜɪdʒ, -ˈkʌr-/ vt give approval to; urge: He encouraged her to try. ~**ment** n [C;U]

en·cour·ag·ing /ɪnˈkɜɪdʒɪŋ, -ˈkʌr-/ adj causing feelings of hope and confidence: encouraging words

en·croach /ɪnˈkroʊtʃ/ vi go beyond what is right or usual: encroach on their territory ~**ment** n [C;U]

en·crust·ed /ɪnˈkrʌstɪd/ adj thickly covered: encrusted with jewels/mud

en·cum·ber /ɪnˈkʌmbə/ vt load; BURDEN –**brance** n

en·cy·clo·pe·di·a /ɪnˌsaɪkləˈpidiə/ n book of many facts in alphabetical order –**dic** adj wide and full

end¹ /ɛnd/ n 1 point where something stops or finishes: the end of the road/of August 2 little piece remaining: Throw away the ends. 3 fml aim; purpose 4 **at a loose end** having nothing to do 5 **in the end** at last 6 **make ends meet** get just enough money 7 **on end** of an endless amount of 8 **on end** a continuously: for hours on end b upright 9 **put an end to** stop — see also SHARP END ~**less** adj never finishing ~**lessly** adv

end² /ˈ··/ vi/t finish ~**ing** n end (of a story, etc.)

end up *phr vi* finish (one's trip, etc.): *Where did you end up staying last night?*

en·dan·ger /ɪnˈdeɪndʒə/ *vt* cause danger to

en·dear /ɪnˈdɪr/ *vt* **endear oneself to** make oneself loved by ~**ment** *n* expression of love

en·deav·or /ɪnˈdɛvə/ *vi fml* try ♦ *n* [C;U] *fml* effort

en·dem·ic /ɛnˈdɛmɪk, ɪn-/ *adj* (esp. of something bad) often happening in a place

en·dive /ˈɛndaɪv/ *n* [U] plant with leaves which are eaten as a vegetable

en·dorse /ɪnˈdɔrs/ *vt* **1** express approval of (opinions, etc.) **2** write one's name on (a check) ~**ment** *n* [C;U]

en·dow /ɪnˈdaʊ/ *vt* **1** give a continuing income to (a school, etc.) **2** be endowed with *fml* have (a good quality) from birth ~**ment** *n* [C;U]

en·dur·ance /ɪnˈdʊrəns/ *n* [U] power of enduring

en·dure /ɪnˈdʊr/ *v* **1** *vt* suffer (pain, etc.) patiently **2** *vi* continue to exist

end zone /ˈ· ·/ *n* end of a football field where the ball must be carried or caught to win points

en·e·ma /ˈɛnəmə/ *n* putting of a liquid, esp. a medicine, into the bowels through the RECTUM

en·e·my /ˈɛnəmi/ *n* **1** person who hates or opposes another person **2** country with which one is at war

en·er·get·ic /ˌɛnəˈdʒɛtɪk◂/ *adj* very active ~**ally** *adv*

en·er·gy /ˈɛnədʒi/ *n* [U] **1** ability to be active and work hard **2** power that drives machines, etc.: *nuclear energy*

en·fant ter·ri·ble /ˌɑnfɑn tɛˈriblə/ *n* shocking but also often interesting and amusing person

en·force /ɪnˈfɔrs, ɪnˈfoʊrs/ *vt* cause (a law etc.) to be obeyed ~**able** *adj* ~**ment** *n* [U]

en·fran·chise /ɪnˈfræntʃaɪz/ *vt* give the right to vote to ~**ment** *n* [U]

en·gage /ɪnˈɡeɪdʒ/ *v fml* **1** arrange to employ **2** *vi/t* lock (machine parts) together **engaged** *adj* **1** having agreed to marry **2** *fml* busy or in use ~**ment** *n* **1** agreement to marry **2** *fml* arrangement to meet someone **3** *fml* battle

engage in *phr vt fml* make (someone) busy in

en·gag·ing /ɪnˈɡeɪdʒɪŋ/ *adj* charming ~**ly** *adv*

en·gen·der /ɪnˈdʒɛndə/ *vt fml* cause; produce

en·gine /ˈɛndʒən/ *n* **1** machine that turns power into movement **2** machine that pulls a train

en·gi·neer /ˌɛndʒəˈnɪr/ *n* **1** person who plans machines, roads, bridges, etc. **2** person who controls engines ♦ *vt* cause by secret planning ~**ing** *n* [U] profession of an ENGINEER (1)

en·grave /ɪnˈɡreɪv/ *vt* cut (words, etc.) on a hard surface **engraver** *n* –**engraving** *n* **1** [C] picture printed from an engraved piece of metal **2** [U] work of an engraver

en·grossed /ɪnˈɡroʊst/ *adj* paying complete attention: *engrossed in a book*

en·gulf /ɪnˈɡʌlf/ *vt* swallow up: *a house engulfed in flames*

en·hance /ɪnˈhæns/ *vt* increase (something good) ~**ment** *n* [C;U]

e·nig·ma /ɪˈnɪɡmə/ *n* mystery ~**tic** /ˌɛnɪɡˈmætɪk◂/ *adj* ~**tically** *adv*

en·joy /ɪnˈdʒɔɪ/ *vt* **1** get pleasure from **2** *fml* possess (something good) **3** **enjoy oneself** be happy ~**able** *adj* nice ~**ably** *adv* ~**ment** *n* [C;U]

en·large /ɪnˈlɑrdʒ/ *vt/i* (cause to) become larger ~**ment** *n* [C;U]

enlarge on/upon *phr vt* say more about

en·light·en /ɪnˈlaɪtˈn/ *vt* make free from false beliefs ~**ment** *n* [U]

en·list /ɪnˈlɪst/ *v* **1** *vi/t* (cause to) join the armed forces **2** *vt* obtain (help, etc.) ~**ment** *n* [C;U]

en·liv·en /ɪnˈlaɪvən/ *vt* to make more active or cheerful

en masse /ˌɑn ˈmæs/ *adv* all together

en·mi·ty /ˈɛnməti/ *n* [C;U] *fml* hatred

e·nor·mi·ty /ɪˈnɔrməti/ *n* **1** [U] enormous size **2** [C;U] *fml* great wickedness

e·nor·mous /ɪˈnɔrməs/ *adj* very large ~**ly** *adv* extremely

e·nough /ɪˈnʌf/ *determiner, pron, adv* **1** as much or as many as is needed: *enough food/chairs | not big enough* **2** fair enough *infml* all right **3** oddly/strangely enough . . . and this is strange, but . . . **4** sure enough as expected

en·rage /ɪnˈreɪdʒ/ *vt* make very angry

en·rich /ɪnˈrɪtʃ/ *vt* **1** make rich **2** improve by adding something ~**ment** *n* [U]

en·roll /ɪn'rool/ vi/t **1** (cause to) join a group officially ~**ment** n [C;U]

en route /ɑn 'rut, ɛn-/ adv on the way; traveling

en·sem·ble /ɑn'sɑmbəl/ n **1** small group of musicians **2** fml set of things

en·shrine /ɪn'ʃraɪn/ vt fml preserve as if holy

en·sign /'ɛnsən, -saɪn/ n **1** ship's flag **2** US naval officer of low rank

en·slave /ɪn'sleɪv/ vt make into a slave ~**ment** n [U]

en·sue /ɪn'su/ vi fml happen afterwards or as a result

en·sure /ɪn'ʃʊr/ also **insure** — vt make (something) certain to happen

en·tail /ɪn'teɪl/ vt make necessary

en·tan·gle /ɪn'tæŋgəl/ vt cause to become twisted with something else ~**ment** n [C;U]

en·ter /'ɛntə/ v **1** vi/t come or go in or into **2** vt become a member of **3** vt put into a book, list, etc.

  enter into phr vt take part in

  enter on/upon phr vt fml begin

en·ter·prise /'ɛntəˌpraɪz/ n **1** [C] plan that needs courage **2** [U] willingness to take risks **3** [U] type of business organization: private enterprise — see also FREE ENTERPRISE –**prising** adj having ENTERPRISE (2)

en·ter·tain /ˌɛntə'teɪn/ v **1** vi/t amuse and interest **2** vt/i provide food and drink for (guests) **3** vt fml be willing to consider (ideas) ~**er** person who amuses people professionally ~**ment** n **1** [U] act of entertaining **2** [C] public amusement

en·thuse /ɪn'θuz/ vi speak with enthusiasm

en·thu·si·as·m /ɪn'θuziˌæzəm/ n [C;U] great interest and admiration –**ast** n person who is very interested in something –**astic** /ɪnˌθuzi'æstɪk◂/ adj full of enthusiasm –**astically** adv

en·tice /ɪn'taɪs/ vt persuade, esp. to do wrong ~**ment** n [C;U]

en·tire /ɪn'taɪə/ adj complete ~**ly** adv ~**ty** /ɪn'taɪəti, -'taɪrəti/ n [U] fml

en·ti·tle /ɪn'taɪtl/ vt **1** give a right (to) **2** give a title to (a book, etc.) ~**ment** n [U]

en·ti·ty /'ɛnəti/ n thing with separate existence

en·tou·rage /ˌɑntu'rɑʒ/ n people who surround someone important

en·trails /'ɛntreɪlz/ n bowels

en·trance¹ /'ɛntrəns/ n **1** [C] door, etc., by which one enters **2** [C] act of entering **3** [U] right to enter

en·trance² /ɪn'træns/ vt fill with delight

en·trant /'ɛntrənt/ n person who enters a race, profession, etc.

en·treat /ɪn'trit/ vt fml beg; IMPLORE ~**y** n [C;U] act of entreating

en·trée /'ɑntreɪ/ n main dish of a meal

en·trenched /ɪn'trɛntʃt/ adj (of beliefs, etc.) firmly established

en·tre·pre·neur /ˌɑntrəprə'nɜ, -'nʊr, -'nyʊr/ n person who starts a business, etc., and takes business risks ~**ial** adj

en·trust /ɪn'trʌst/ vt give to someone to take care of

en·try /'ɛntri/ n **1** [C;U] act of coming or going in **2** place where one enters **3** [C] something written in a list

en·twine /ɪn'twaɪn/ vt twist together or around

e·nu·me·rate /ɪ'numəˌreɪt/ vt fml name one by one –**ration** /ɪˌnumə'reɪʃən/ n [C;U]

e·nun·ci·ate /ɪ'nʌnsiˌeɪt/ vt/i pronounce (words) clearly –**ation** /ɪˌnʌnsi'eɪʃən/ n [U]

en·vel·op /ɪn'vɛləp/ vt cover completely: enveloped in flames ~**ment** n [U]

en·ve·lope /'ɛnvəˌloup, 'ɑn-/ n paper container for a letter

en·vi·a·ble /'ɛnviəbəl/ adj very desirable -**bly** adv

en·vi·ous /'ɛnviəs/ adj feeling ENVY ~**ly** adv

en·vi·ron·ment /ɪn'vaɪrənmənt, -'vaɪən-/ n conditions in which people, animals, etc., live ~**al** /ɪnˌvaɪrən'mɛntl◂, -ˌvaɪən-/ adj ~**ally** adv ~**alist** n person who tries to keep our natural surroundings from being spoiled

en·vi·sion /ɪn'vɪʒən/ vt — see in the mind; expect

en·voy /'ɛnvɔɪ, 'ɑn-/ n messenger; representative

en·vy /'ɛnvi/ n [U] **1** bad feeling one has towards someone who has better luck than oneself **2 the envy of (someone)** something which other people want to have or to be: Her house is the envy of all her friends. ♦ vt feel envy towards or because of

en·zyme /'ɛnzaɪm/ n substance produced by living cells that causes chemical change

e·on /ˈiːən/ n very long time

e·phem·er·al /ɪˈfɛmərəl/ adj lasting only a short time

ep·ic /ˈɛpɪk/ n **1** long poem, film, etc., about the deeds of gods or great men **2** derog event needing a lot of time and effort ♦ adj (of stories) full of bravery and excitement

ep·i·dem·ic /ˌɛpəˈdɛmɪk◂/ n many cases of an infectious disease at the same time

ep·i·gram /ˈɛpəˌgræm/ n short amusing poem or saying

ep·i·lep·sy /ˈɛpəˌlɛpsi/ n disease of the brain causing sudden unconsciousness –leptic /ˌɛpəˈlɛptɪk◂/ adj, n

ep·i·logue /ˈɛpəˌlɔg, -ˌlɑg/ n last part of a play or book

E·pis·co·pal·i·an /ɪˌpɪskəˈpeɪliən/ also **E·pis·co·pal** /ɪˈpɪskəpəl/ — n, adj (of or being a) member of the Protestant Episcopal Church

ep·i·sode /ˈɛpəˌsoʊd/ n one separate event or period of time

ep·ist·le /ɪˈpɪsəl/ n fml LETTER (1)

ep·i·taph /ˈɛpəˌtæf/ n words written above a grave

ep·i·thet /ˈɛpəˌθɛt/ adj adjective, esp. used of a person

e·pit·o·me /ɪˈpɪtəmi/ n something that perfectly shows a particular quality: My son is the epitome of laziness. –mize vt be typical of

e·poch /ˈɛpək, ˈɛpɑk/ n period of historical time, esp. one in which some very important event happened ~-making adj extremely important

e·qual /ˈikwəl/ adj **1** the same in size, value, etc. **2 equal to** having enough ability, etc., for ♦ n person equal to another ♦ vt -l- be the same as ~ize vt make equal —ly adv: equally fit | to share the work equally ~ity /ɪˈkwɑləti/ n [U]: the equality of women

equal sign /ˈ·· ·/ n the mark =

eq·ua·nim·i·ty /ˌikwəˈnɪməti, ˌɛ-/ n [U] fml calmness of mind

e·quate /ɪˈkweɪt/ vt consider as equal

e·qua·tion /ɪˈkweɪʒən/ n statement that 2 quantities are equal: $2x + 1 = 7$ is an equation.

e·qua·tor /ɪˈkweɪtə/ n [the+S] imaginary line around the world, equally distant from the North and South POLES ~ial /ˌikwəˈtɔriəl◂, -ˈtoʊr-, ˌɛ-/ adj

e·ques·tri·an /ɪˈkwɛstriən/ adj fml concerned with riding horses

e·qui·lib·ri·um /ˌikwəˈlɪbriəm/ n [U] fml BALANCE (1)

e·quine /ˈikwaɪn, ˈɛ-/ adj fml related to horses

e·qui·nox /ˈikwəˌnɑks, ˈɛ-/ n time of year when day and night are of equal length

e·quip /ɪˈkwɪp/ vt -pp- provide with what is necessary ~ment n [U] things needed for an activity

eq·ui·ta·ble /ˈɛkwɪtəbəl/ adj fair and just: an equitable division of the money –bly adv

eq·ui·ties /ˈɛkwətiz/ n [P] tech business's ordinary stock, on which no fixed amount of interest is paid

eq·ui·ty /ˈɛkwəti/ n [U] fml fairness

e·quiv·a·lent /ɪˈkwɪvələnt/ n, adj (something) the same in value

e·quiv·o·cal /ɪˈkwɪvəkəl/ adj doubtful in meaning; questionable -cate /-ˌkeɪt/ vi fml speak in an equivocal way on purpose

ER abbr. for: EMERGENCY ROOM

e·ra /ˈɪrə, ˈɛrə/ n period of historical time, marked esp. by particular developments

e·rad·i·cate /ɪˈrædəˌkeɪt/ vt put an end to (something bad) –cation /ɪˌrædəˈkeɪʃən/ n [U]

e·rase /ɪˈreɪs/ vt fml remove (pencil marks) from paper

e·ras·er /ɪˈreɪsə/ n piece of rubber for removing pencil marks

e·rect /ɪˈrɛkt/ adj upright ♦ vt **1** put upright: erect a tent **2** fml build: erect a monument ~ly adv ~ness n [U] ~ion /ɪˈrɛkʃən/ n **1** [U] the act of erecting something **2** [C] fml a building **3** [C;U] (an example of) the state of the PENIS when upright

er·go·nom·ics /ˌɚgəˈnɑmɪks/ n [U] study of how people work best with machines –ic adj –ically adv

e·rode /ɪˈroʊd/ vt (of acids, water, etc.) wear away; reduce erosion /ɪˈroʊʒən/ n [U]

e·rot·ic /ɪˈrɑtɪk/ adj of sexual love ~ism /-ˌtəˌsɪzəm/ n [U]

err /ɚ, ɛr/ vi fml make a mistake

er·rand /ˈɛrənd/ n short journey to do or esp. buy something

er·rant /ˈɛrənt/ adj fml wandering away and misbehaving

er·rat·ic /ɪˈrætɪk/ adj changeable; not regular ~ally adv

er·ro·ne·ous /ɪˈrəʊniəs/ *adj fml* (of a belief) incorrect ~**ly** *adv*

er·ror /ˈerə/ *n* **1** [C] mistake **2** [U] state of being mistaken

er·u·dite /ˈeruˌdaɪt, ˈerə-/ *adj fml* full of learning

e·rupt /ɪˈrʌpt/ *vi* (of a VOLCANO) explode suddenly ~**ion** /ɪˈrʌpʃən/ *n* [C;U]

es·ca·late /ˈeskəˌleɪt/ *vi/t* (cause to) grow greater or more serious -**lation** /ˌeskəˈleɪʃən/ *n* [U]

es·ca·la·tor /ˈeskəˌleɪtə/ *n* set of moving stairs

es·ca·pade /ˈeskəˌpeɪd/ *n* wild dangerous act

es·cape /ɪˈskeɪp/ *v* **1** *vi/t* get out; get free (from) **2** *vt* avoid (something dangerous): *to escape death* **3** *vt* be forgotten by: *His name escapes me.* ♦ *n* [C;U] (act of) getting free

es·cap·is·m /ɪˈskeɪpˌɪzəm/ *n* [U] activity providing escape from dull reality -**ist** *adj, n*

es·chew /ɪsˈtʃuː/ *vt fml* avoid

es·cort¹ /ˈeskɔːt/ *n* **1** person or people who go with another as a protection or honor **2** social companion, esp. a man

es·cort² /ɪˈskɔːt/ *vt* go with as an escort

Es·ki·mo /ˈeskəməʊ/ *n* member of a race of people living in the icy far north of N. America

ESL *n, adj abbrev. for:* English as a second language

ESOL /ˈiːsɒl/ *n, adj abbrev. for:* English for speakers of other languages

e·soph·a·gus /ɪˈsɒfəgəs/ *n med* food tube from the mouth to the stomach

es·o·ter·ic /ˌesəˈterɪk◂/ *adj* having deep and secret meanings understood only by a few people ~**ally** *adv*

ESP *n* [U] extrasensory perception; knowledge obtained without using one's ordinary 5 senses

es·pe·cial·ly /ɪˈspeʃəli/ *adv* **1** to a particularly great degree: *not especially hot* **2** in particular: *I like fruit, especially apples.*

es·pi·o·nage /ˈespiəˌnɑːʒ/ *n* [U] spying (SPY)

es·pouse /ɪˈspaʊz/ *vt fml* support (an aim, etc.) **espousal** *n* [C;U]

es·pres·so /eˈspresəʊ/ *n* [C;U] very strong coffee served in small cups

es·say /ˈeseɪ/ *n* short piece of writing on a subject ~**ist** *n* writer of essays

es·sence /ˈesəns/ *n* **1** [U] most important quality of something **2** [C;U] liquid, etc., with some particular strong taste or smell: *vanilla essence* **3** of the essence extremely important

es·sen·tial /ɪˈsenʃəl/ *adj* **1** necessary **2** FUNDAMENTAL: *the essential difference between us* ♦ *n* [*usu. pl.*] something necessary ~**ly** *adv* deep down, at base: *She's essentially kind.*

es·tab·lish /ɪˈstæblɪʃ/ *vt* **1** begin; CREATE (an organization, set of rules, etc.) **2** settle (esp. oneself) firmly in a particular state or position: *the film which established her reputation as a director* **3** make certain of (a fact, etc.) ~**ment** *n* **1** [U] of establishing **2** [C] *fml* place run as a business **3** [*the*+S] (*cap.*) *often derog* the powerful people who control public life

es·tate /ɪˈsteɪt/ *n* **1** piece of land in the country, with one owner **2** *law* whole of a person's property, esp. as left after death — see also REAL ESTATE

es·teem /ɪˈstiːm/ *n fml* respect: *I hold him in high esteem.* ♦ *vt* **1** respect greatly **2** *fml* consider to be estimable /ˈestəməbəl/ *adj* worthy of respect

es·thet·ics /esˈθetɪks, ɪs-/ *n* [U] science of beauty, esp. in art **esthetic** *adj* –**ically** *adv*

es·ti·mate¹ /ˈestɪˌmeɪt/ *vt/i* calculate; form an opinion about (cost, etc.) –**mation** /ˌestɪˈmeɪʃən/ *n* [U] judgment; opinion

es·ti·mate² /ˈestɪmɪt/ *n* calculation of cost, number, etc.

es·tranged /ɪˈstreɪndʒd/ *adj* unfriendly: *estranged wife* (= not living with her husband)

es·tro·gen /ˈestrədʒən/ *n* [U] substance in females that makes the body ready to produce young

es·tu·a·ry /ˈestʃuˌeri/ *n* mouth of a river, into which the sea flows

etc., etcetera /ɪt ˈsetərə, -trə/ *adv* and the rest; and other things

etch /etʃ/ *vi/t* draw with a needle and acid on metal ~**ing** *n* [C;U]

e·ter·nal /ɪˈtɜːnəl/ *adj* lasting forever ~**ly** *adv*

e·ter·ni·ty /ɪˈtɜːnəti/ *n* **1** [U] endless time after death **2** [C] an extremely long time

e·ther /ˈiːθə/ *n* **1** [U] liquid that easily changes to a gas **2** upper levels of the air

e·the·re·al /ɪˈθɪəriəl/ *adj* extremely light and delicate

eth·ic /'ɛθɪk/ n system of moral behavior: *the Christian ethic* ~**al** *adj* **1** of morals **2** morally good ~**ally** *adv* **ethics** n **1** [U] science of morals **2** [P] moral rules

eth·nic /'ɛθnɪk/ *adj* of or related to a racial, national, or tribal group ~**ally** *adv*

ethnic cleans·ing /ˌ‧‧ '‧‧/ n [U] forced removal of members of particular races, religions etc. from an area

e·thos /'iːθɒs/ n [S] characteristic moral beliefs of a person or group

et·i·quette /'ɛtɪkɪt, -ˌkɛt/ n [U] formal rules of manners

et·y·mol·o·gy /ˌɛtəˈmɒlədʒi/ n [U] study of the origins of words

eu·ca·lyp·tus /ˌjuːkəˈlɪptəs/ n tree whose oil is used as medicine for colds

eu·lo·gy /'juːlədʒi/ n *fml* speech in praise of someone –**gize** *vt* praise highly –**gistic** /ˌjuːləˈdʒɪstɪk◄/ *adj* full of praise

eu·nuch /'juːnək/ n man who has been castrated (CASTRATE)

eu·phe·mis·m /'juːfəˌmɪzəm/ n [C;U] (use of) a pleasanter, less direct word for something unpleasant –**mistic** /ˌjuːfəˈmɪstɪk◄/ *adj*

eu·pho·ri·a /juˈfɔːriə, -ˈfoʊr-/ n [U] state of happiness and cheerful excitement –**ric** /juˈfɔːrɪk, -ˈfɑːr-/ *adj*

eu·tha·na·si·a /ˌjuːθəˈneɪʒə/ n [U] painless killing of very sick or very old people

e·vac·u·ate /ɪˈvækjuˌeɪt/ *vt* take all the people away from (a dangerous place) –**ation** /ɪˌvækjuˈeɪʃən/ n [C;U] -**ee**- /-kjuˈiː/ n person who has been evacuated

e·vade /ɪˈveɪd/ *vt* avoid; escape from

e·val·u·ate /ɪˈvæljuˌeɪt/ *vt* calculate the value of –**ation** /ɪˌvæljuˈeɪʃən/ n [C;U]

e·van·gel·i·cal /ˌiːvænˈdʒɛlɪkəl, ˌɛvæn-/ n, *adj* (*often cap.*) **1** (member) of those Christian churches that believe in studying the Bible rather than in ceremonies **2** (person) showing very great eagerness in spreading certain beliefs

e·van·ge·list /ɪˈvændʒəlɪst/ n traveling Christian religious teacher –**lism** n [U] ~**ic** /ɪˌvændʒəˈlɪstɪk◄/ *adj*

e·vap·o·rate /ɪˈvæpəˌreɪt/ *vi/t* change into steam and disappear –**ration** /ɪˌvæpəˈreɪʃən/ n [U]

e·va·sion /ɪˈveɪʒən/ n [C;U] the act of evading (EVADE): *tax evasion* –**sive** /-sɪv, -zɪv/ *adj*

eve /iːv/ n [S] **1** (*usu. cap.*) day before a (religious) holiday **2** time just before any event: *on the eve of the election*

e·ven¹ /'iːvən/ *adv* **1** (shows that something is unexpected and surprising): *John's a very good swimmer, but even he doesn't swim in the river.* (= so certainly nobody else does) **2** (makes comparisons stronger): *It's even colder than yesterday.* **3 even if** it does not matter if **4 even now/so/then** in spite of that: *I explained, but even then he didn't understand.* **5 even though** though

e·ven² *adj* **1** smooth and regular: *an even surface/temperature* **2** (of things that can be compared) equal: *an even chance* **3** (of numbers) that can be divided by two ~**ly** *adv* ~**ness** n [U]

e·ven³ *v* **even out** *phr vi/t* (cause to) become level or equal

even-hand·ed /ˌ‧‧ '‧‧◄/ *adj* giving fair and equal treatment to all sides

eve·ning /'iːvnɪŋ/ n time between afternoon and when most people go to bed

evening dress /'‧‧ ˌ‧/ n **1** [U] formal clothes for the evening **2** [C] woman's formal long dress

eve·nings /'iːvnɪŋz/ *adv* regularly in the evening: *Tom works evenings.*

e·vent /ɪˈvɛnt/ n **1** (important) happening **2** one race, etc., in a day's sports **3 at all events** in spite of everything **4 in the event of . . . if** (something) happens ~**ful** *adj* full of important events

e·ven·tu·al /ɪˈvɛntʃuəl/ *adj* happening at last ~**ly** *adv* in the end: *They eventually succeeded.* ~**ity** /ɪˌvɛntʃuˈæləti/ n *fml* possible event

ev·er /'ɛvər/ *adv* **1** at any time: *Does it ever snow?* | *Nothing ever annoys him.* | *colder than ever* **2** always: *ever since Christmas* | *the ever-increasing population* **3** (gives force to a question): *What ever is that?* **4** (gives force to an EXCLAMATION): *Was she ever mad!*

ev·er·glade /'ɛvərˌgleɪd/ n low wet land with tall grass and branching WATERWAYS

ev·er·green /'ɛvərˌgriːn/ n, *adj* (tree) that does not lose its leaves in winter

ev·er·last·ing /ˌɛvərˈlæstɪŋ◄/ *adj* lasting forever

ev·er·y /'ɛvri/ *determiner* **1** each: *I enjoy every minute of it.* **2** (of things that can be counted) once in each: *I go every 3 days.* **3** as much as is possible: *I have* *every reason to trust him.* **4 every other** the 1st, 3rd, 5th, etc., or the 2nd, 4th, 6th, etc.: *Take the pills every other day.* **5 every now and then** also **every so often** — sometimes, but not often

ev·ery·bod·y /ˈɛvrɪˌbɑdɪ, -ˌbʌdɪ/ *pron* everyone

ev·ery·day /ˈɛvrɪˌdeɪ/ *adj* ordinary; common

ev·ery·one /ˈɛvrɪˌwʌn, -wən/ *pron* **1** every person: *Everyone was pleased.* **2** all the people usually here: *Where is everyone?*

ev·ery·thing /ˈɛvrɪˌθɪŋ/ *pron* **1** each thing: *They've eaten everything.* **2** all that matters: *Money isn't everything.*

ev·ery·where /ˈɛvrɪˌwɛr, -ˌhwɛr/ also **ev·ery·place** /-ˌpleɪs/ — *adv* at or to every place

every which way /ˌ· · ˈ·/ *adv* in every direction

e·vict /ɪˈvɪkt/ *vt* force to leave a house, etc., by law **~ion** /ɪˈvɪkʃən/ *n* [C;U]

ev·i·dence /ˈɛvədəns/ *n* [U] **1** proof **2** answers given in a court of law **3 in evidence** present and easily seen

ev·i·dent /ˈɛvədənt, -ˌdɛnt/ *adj* plain and clear **~ly** *adv*

e·vil /ˈivəl/ *adj* harmful; wicked ♦ *n* [C;U] *fml* wickedness or misfortune **~ly** *adv*

e·voc·a·tive /ɪˈvɑkətɪv/ *adj* bringing memories: *an evocative smell*

e·voke /ɪˈvoʊk/ *vt fml* produce (a memory)

ev·o·lu·tion /ˌɛvəˈluʃən/ *n* [U] gradual development, esp. of living things from earlier and simpler forms

e·volve /ɪˈvɑlv/ *vi/t* develop gradually

ewe /yu/ *n* female sheep

ex·a·cer·bate /ɪgˈzæsəˌbeɪt/ *vt fml* make (something bad) worse

ex·act[1] /ɪgˈzækt/ *adj* correctly measured; PRECISE: *the exact time* **~ly** *adv* **1** correctly **2** (as a reply) I agree! **3 not exactly** not really **~ness**, also **~itude** *n* [U]

exact[2] *vt fml* demand and obtain by force **~ing** *adj* demanding great effort

ex·ag·ge·rate /ɪgˈzædʒəˌreɪt/ *vi/t* make (something) seem larger, etc., than it is **-ration** /ɪgˌzædʒəˈreɪʃən/ *n* [C;U]

ex·al·ta·tion /ˌɛgzɔlˈteɪʃən, ˌɛksɔl-/ *n* great joy because of success

ex·alt·ed /ɪgˈzɔltɪd/ *adj, fml* of high rank

ex·am /ɪgˈzæm/ *n* test of knowledge

ex·am·i·na·tion /ɪgˌzæməˈneɪʃən/ *n* **1** [C] *fml* exam **2** [C;U] act of examining

ex·am·ine /ɪgˈzæmɪn/ *vt* **1** look carefully at: *Has the doctor examined you yet?* **2** ask questions, to find out something or to test knowledge **-iner** *n*

ex·am·ple /ɪgˈzæmpəl/ *n* **1** something that shows a general rule: *a typical example* **2** something to be copied: *Her courage is an example to us all.* **3 for example** (*abbrev.* **e.g.**) here is one of the things just spoken of **4 make an example of someone** punish someone to frighten others

ex·as·pe·rate /ɪgˈzæspəˌreɪt/ *vt* annoy very much **-ratedly** *adv* **-ratingly** *adv* **-ration** /ɪgˌzæspəˈreɪʃən/ *n* [U]

ex·ca·vate /ˈɛkskəˌveɪt/ *vt* **1** dig (a hole) **2** uncover by digging **-vator** *n* person or machine that excavates **-vation** /ˌɛkskəˈveɪʃən/ *n* [C;U]

ex·ceed /ɪkˈsid/ *vt* **1** be greater than **2** do more than: *to exceed the speed limit* **~ingly** *adv fml* extremely

ex·cel /ɪkˈsɛl/ *vi* **-ll-** *fml* be extremely good (at something)

ex·cel·lent /ˈɛksələnt/ *adj* very good **-lence** *n* [U]

ex·cept /ɪkˈsɛpt/ *prep* not including; but not: *Everyone except John was tired.* ♦ *vt fml* leave out; not include

ex·cep·tion /ɪkˈsɛpʃən/ *n* **1** [C;U] (a case of) leaving out or being left out: *Everyone, without exception, must attend.* | *I don't usually see people after 5:00, but I'll make an exception in your case.* **2 take exception to** be made angry by **~al** *adj* unusual, esp. because very good **~ally** *adv*

ex·cerpt /ˈɛksəpt/ *n* piece taken from a book, etc.

ex·cess /ɪkˈsɛs, ˈɛksɛs/ *n, adj* [S;U] (an amount that is) greater than is usual or allowed: *an excess of violence in the film* **~ive** *adj* too much **~ively** *adv* **excesses** *n* [P] extremely bad, cruel, etc., behavior

ex·change /ɪksˈtʃeɪndʒ/ *vt* give and receive in return: *I exchanged my pounds for dollars.* ♦ *n* **1** [C;U] act of exchanging **2** [U] changing of money: *the rate of exchange* **3** [C] place where **a** telephone wires meet **b** business people meet: *a stock exchange* **4** [C] short period of fighting or talking — see also FOREIGN EXCHANGE

ex·cise[1] /'ɛksaɪz/ n [U] tax on goods produced inside a country

ex·cise[2] /ɪk'saɪz/ vt fml remove by cutting

ex·cite /ɪk'saɪt/ vt 1 cause to have strong (pleasant) feelings: an excited little boy 2 fml suggest (feelings): to excite interest ~**ment** n [C;U] **excitable** adj easily excited **exciting** adj: exciting films

ex·claim /ɪk'skleɪm/ vi/t speak or say suddenly

ex·cla·ma·tion /ˌɛksklə'meɪʃən/ n word(s) exclaimed

exclamation point /·'··· ˌ·/ n PUNCTUATION MARK (!) written after an exclamation

ex·clude /ɪk'sklud/ vt 1 keep out or leave out 2 shut out from the mind: Don't exclude that possibility. **excluding** prep not including **exclusion** /ɪk'skluʒən/ n [C;U]

ex·clu·sive /ɪk'sklusɪv, -zɪv/ adj 1 keeping out unsuitable people 2 not shared ♦ n story appearing in only one newspaper ~**ly** adv only: exclusively for women

ex·com·mu·ni·cate /ˌɛkskə'myunəˌkeɪt/ vt exclude from the Christian Church –**cation** /ˌɛkskəˌmyunə'keɪʃən/ n [C;U]

ex·cre·ment /'ɛkskrəmənt/ n [U] fml solid waste from the bowels

ex·crete /ɪk'skrit/ vt pass out (waste matter)

ex·cru·ci·at·ing /ɪk'skruʃiˌeɪtɪŋ/ adj (of pain) very bad ~**ly** adv

ex·cur·sion /ɪk'skɜʒən/ n short trip for pleasure

ex·cuse[1] /ɪk'skyuz/ vt 1 forgive: Please excuse my bad handwriting. 2 make (bad behavior) seem less bad 3 free from a duty 4 **Excuse me** (said when starting to speak to a stranger, or when one wants to get past a person, or to APOLOGIZE for something) 5 **excuse oneself** ask permission to be absent **excusable** adj that can be forgiven

ex·cuse[2] /ɪk'skyus/ n reason given when asking to be excused

ex·e·cute /'ɛksɪˌkyut/ vt 1 kill as a legal punishment 2 fml carry out; perform: execute a plan –**cution** /ˌɛksɪ'kyuʃən/ n 1 [C;U] legal killing 2 [U] fml carrying out; performance –**cutioner** n official who executes criminals

ex·ec·u·tive /ɪg'zɛkyətɪv/ adj concerned with managing, or carrying out decisions ♦ n 1 [C] person in an executive position in business 2 [the+S] branch of government that carries out the law

ex·ec·u·tor /ɪg'zɛkyətər/ n person who carries out the orders in a WILL[2] (5)

ex·em·pla·ry /ɪg'zɛmpləri/ adj fml suitable to be copied

ex·em·pli·fy /ɪg'zɛmpləˌfaɪ/ vt be or give an example of –**fication** /ɪgˌzɛmpləfə'keɪʃən/ n [C;U]

ex·empt /ɪg'zɛmpt/ adj freed from a duty, etc. ♦ vt make exempt ~**ion** /ɪg'zɛmpʃən/ n [C;U]

ex·er·cise /'ɛksərˌsaɪz/ n 1 [U] use of the powers of the body to improve it: go swimming for exercise 2 [C] something done for training: naval exercises 3 [C] written school work 4 [S;U] use (of a power or right) ♦ 1 vi/t take or give EXERCISE (1) 2 vt use (a power or right)

ex·ert /ɪg'zɜt/ vt 1 use (strength, etc.) 2 **exert oneself** make an effort ~**ion** /ɪg'zɜʃən/ n [C;U]

ex·hale /ɛks'heɪl, ɛk'seɪl/ vi/t breathe out **exhalation** /ˌɛks-hə'leɪʃən, ˌɛksə-/ n [U]

ex·haust /ɪg'zɔst/ vt 1 tire out 2 use up completely ♦ n 1 pipe by which gases escape from an engine 2 [U] these gases ~**ive** adj thorough ~**ively** adv ~**ion** /ɪg'zɔstʃən/ n [U]

ex·hib·it /ɪg'zɪbɪt/ vt 1 show publicly for sale, etc. 2 fml show that one has (a quality) ♦ n something shown in a MUSEUM, etc. ~**or** n person showing exhibits

ex·hi·bi·tion /ˌɛksə'bɪʃən/ n 1 public show of objects 2 act of exhibiting ~**ism** n behavior of someone who wants to be looked at ~**ist** n

ex·hil·a·rat·ing /ɪg'zɪləˌreɪt/ adj exciting, making you feel happy –**ration** /ɪgˌzɪlə'reɪʃən/ n [U]

ex·hort /ɪg'zɔrt/ vt fml urge strongly ~**ation** /ˌɛksɔr'teɪʃən, ˌɛgzɔr-/ n [C;U]

ex·hume /ɪg'zum, ɛks'hyum/ vt dig up (a dead body) **exhumation** /ˌɛksyu'meɪʃən/ n [C;U]

ex·ile /'ɛksaɪl, 'ɛgzaɪl/ n 1 [U] unwanted absence from one's country 2 [C] someone forced into this ♦ vt send into exile

ex·ist /ɪg'zɪst/ vi have life; be real: The problems she talks about simply don't exist. ~**ence** n 1 [U] state of being real 2 [S] way of living: lead a miserable existence ~**ent** adj existing; present

ex·is·ten·tial /ˌegzɪˈstɛnʃəl◂/ adj related to existence

ex·it /ˈegzɪt, ˈɛksɪt/ n 1 way out of a building 2 act of leaving ♦ vi (used as a stage direction) he/she/it goes out

exit ramp /ˈ·· ·/ n road for driving onto or off a FREEWAY

ex·o·dus /ˈɛksədəs/ n [S] going away of many people

ex·on·er·ate /ɪgˈzɑnəˌreɪt/ vt fml free (someone) from blame –ration /ɪgˌzɑnəˈreɪʃən/ n [U]

ex·or·bi·tant /ɪgˈzɔrbətənt/ adj (of cost) too much –ly adv

ex·or·cize /ˈɛksɔrˌsaɪz, -sə-/ vt drive out (an evil spirit, etc.) by prayers –cism /ˈɛksɔrˌsɪzəm, -sə-/ n act or art of exorcizing –cist n

ex·ot·ic /ɪgˈzɑtɪk/ adj pleasantly strange: exotic flowers/food ~ally adv

ex·pand /ɪkˈspænd/ vi/t (cause to) grow larger or more detailed

    expand on/upon phr vt make more detailed

ex·panse /ɪkˈspæns/ n wide open space

ex·pan·sion /ɪkˈspænʃən/ n [C;U] act of expanding ~ism n intention of expanding one's land, etc. ~ist n, adj

ex·pan·sive /ɪkˈspænsɪv/ adj friendly and willing to talk ~ly adv

ex·pat·ri·ate /ɛksˈpeɪtri-ɪt/ n, adj (person) living abroad

ex·pect /ɪkˈspɛkt/ vt think or believe that something will happen ~ing adj infml PREGNANT ~ation /ˌɛkspɛkˈteɪʃən/ n 1 [U] state of expecting 2 [C] something expected

ex·pec·tant /ɪkˈspɛktənt/ adj 1 waiting hopefully 2 PREGNANT ~ly adv –tancy n [U] hope

ex·pe·di·ent /ɪkˈspidiənt/ adj (of an action) useful, esp. for one's own purposes ♦ n useful plan, esp. one thought of in a hurry because of urgent need –ency n [U], adj

ex·pe·dite /ˈɛkspəˌdaɪt/ vt fml make (a plan) go faster

ex·pe·di·tion /ˌɛkspəˈdɪʃən/ n (people making) a journey for a purpose: an expedition to the North Pole ~ary adj (of an army) sent abroad to fight

ex·pel /ɪkˈspɛl/ vt -ll- 1 dismiss officially from a school, etc. 2 fml force out from a container

ex·pend /ɪkˈspɛnd/ vt spend; use up ~able adj that can be used up without worrying

ex·pen·di·ture /ɪkˈspɛndətʃɚ, -ˌtʃʊr/ n [S;U] fml spending

ex·pense /ɪkˈspɛns/ n [U] 1 cost 2 at someone's expense: a with someone paying b (of a joke) against someone **expenses** n [P] money for a purpose: We'll pay his traveling expenses.

ex·pen·sive /ɪkˈspɛnsɪv, -zɪv/ adj costing a lot ~ly adv

ex·pe·ri·ence /ɪkˈspɪriəns/ n 1 [U] knowledge gained by practice 2 [C] something that happens to: a fascinating experience ♦ vt suffer or learn by experience: to experience defeat –enced adj having EXPERIENCE (1)

ex·per·i·ment /ɪkˈspɛrəmənt/ n [C;U] test carried out to learn something ♦ /-ˌmɛnt, -mənt/ vi perform experiments ~al /ɪkˌspɛrəˈmɛntəl◂/ adj used for or based on experiments ~ation /ɪkˌspɛrəmɛnˈteɪʃən/ n [U]

ex·pert /ˈɛkspɚt/ n, adj (person) with special skill or training ~ly adv

ex·per·tise /ˌɛkspɚˈtiz/ n [U] skill in a particular field

ex·pire /ɪkˈspaɪɚ/ vi 1 (of something that lasts for a time) come to an end 2 lit die **expiry**, also **expiration** /ˌɛkspəˈreɪʃən/ n [U]

ex·plain /ɪkˈspleɪn/ v 1 vi/t make (a meaning) clear 2 vt be the reason for

    explain away phr vt give an excuse for (something) in order to avoid blame

ex·pla·na·tion /ˌɛkspləˈneɪʃən/ n 1 [U] act of explaining 2 [C] something that explains **explanatory** /ɪkˈsplænəˌtɔri, -ˌtoʊri/ adj (of a statement) explaining

ex·ple·tive /ˈɛksplətɪv, ɪkˈsplitɪv/ n fml word used for swearing

ex·pli·ca·ble /ɪkˈsplɪkəbəl, ˈɛksplɪ-/ adj fml (of behavior, etc.) understandable

ex·plic·it /ɪkˈsplɪsɪt/ adj (of a statement, etc.) clearly and fully expressed ~ly adv ~ness n [U]

ex·plode /ɪkˈsploʊd/ v 1 vi/t blow up; burst 2 vi show violent feeling

ex·ploit[1] /ɪkˈsplɔɪt/ vt 1 use (people) unfairly for profit 2 use (things) fully for profit ~er n ~ation /ˌɛksplɔɪˈteɪʃən/ n [U] ~ative /ɪkˈsplɔɪtətɪv/ adj tending to exploit

ex·ploit[2] /ˈɛksplɔɪt/ n brave successful act

ex·plore /ɪkˈsplɔr, ɪkˈsploʊr/ vt 1 travel through (a place) for discovery 2 examine (a subject) carefully **explorer** n

ex·plo·ra·tion /ˌeksplə'reɪʃən/ n [C;U]
ex·plor·a·to·ry /ɪk'splɔrətɔri, ɪk'splouə-ˌtɔri/ adj
ex·plo·sion /ɪk'splouʒən/ n 1 (noise of) exploding 2 sudden increase: *the population explosion*
ex·plo·sive /ɪk'splousɪv, -zɪv/ n, adj (substance) that explodes ~ly adv
ex·po·nent /ɪk'spounənt/ n someone who expresses or supports a belief
ex·port¹ /ɪk'spɔrt, ɪk'spourt, 'eks.pɔrt, 'ekspourt/ vi/t send (goods) abroad for sale ~er n
ex·port² /'eks.pɔrt, 'ekspourt/ n 1 [U] (business of) exporting 2 [C] something exported
ex·pose /ɪk'spouz/ vt 1 uncover; leave without protection 2 make known (a secret crime, etc.) 3 uncover (photographic film) to the light 4 **expose oneself** show one's sexual parts on purpose, in the hope of shocking people **exposure** /ɪk'spouʒər/ n [C;U]
ex·po·sé /ˌekspou'zeɪ, -spə-/ n public statement of something shameful
ex·po·si·tion /ˌekspə'zɪʃən/ n [C;U] fml explaining; explanation
ex·press¹ /ɪk'spres/ vt 1 make known by words or looks: *She expressed surprise at his decision.* 2 **express oneself** speak or write one's thoughts or feelings
express² adj 1 going quickly 2 clearly stated: *her express wish* ♦ n express train ♦ adv by an express method ~ly adv 1 clearly 2 on purpose
ex·pres·sion /ɪk'spreʃən/ n 1 [C;U] act of expressing: *political expression* 2 [C] word or phrase: *an odd expression to use* 3 [C] look on someone's face: *a surprised expression* 4 [U] quality of showing feeling: *singing without much expression* ~less adj without EXPRESSION (4)
ex·pres·sive /ɪk'spresɪv/ adj showing feelings ~ly adv
ex·press·way /ɪk'spres.weɪ/ n wide road for fast travel over long distances
ex·pro·pri·ate /eks'prouprieɪt/ vt fml take away for public use –ation /ɪkˌsprou-pri'eɪʃən/ n [C;U]
ex·pul·sion /ɪk'spʌlʃən/ n [C;U] act of expelling (EXPEL)
ex·qui·site /ɪk'skwɪzɪt, 'ekskwɪ-/ adj beautifully made or done ~ly adv
ex·tend /ɪk'stend/ v 1 vt make longer or larger: *extend the parking lot* 2 vt stretch

out (part of one's body) to the limit 3 vt fml offer, give: *extend a welcome* 4 vi [(to)] (of land) reach
ex·ten·sion /ɪk'stenʃən/ n 1 [U] act of extending 2 [C] part added 3 [C] telephone line inside a set of offices, etc.
extension cord /·'·· ˌ·/ n additional piece of electric wire attached to another wire to make it longer
ex·ten·sive /ɪk'stensɪv, -zɪv/ adj large in amount or area ~ly adv
ex·tent /ɪk'stent/ n 1 [U] amount or length: *the extent of the damage* 2 [S] degree: *to a large extent*
ex·te·ri·or /ɪk'stɪriər/ n outside of something **exterior** adj
ex·ter·mi·nate /ɪk'stɜrməˌneɪt/ vt kill all of –nation /ɪkˌstɜrmə'neɪʃən/ n [U]
ex·ter·nal /ɪk'stɜrnl/ adj outside ~ly adv
ex·tinct /ɪk'stɪŋkt/ adj 1 (of a kind of animal) no longer existing 2 (of a VOLCANO) no longer active ~ion /ɪk'stɪŋkʃən/ n [U] state of being or becoming extinct
ex·tin·guish /ɪk'stɪŋgwɪʃ/ vt fml 1 put out (a fire, etc.) 2 destroy (hope, etc.) ~er n apparatus for putting out fires
ex·tol /ɪk'stoul/ vt -ll- praise highly
ex·tort /ɪk'stɔrt/ vt obtain by force or threats ~ion /ɪk'stɔrʃən/ n [C;U] ~ionist n
ex·tor·tion·ate /ɪk'stɔrʃənɪt/ adj EXORBITANT
ex·tra /'ekstrə/ adj, adv beyond what is usual or necessary: *extra money* | *pay extra* ♦ n 1 extra thing 2 film actor in a crowd scene 3 special EDITION (1) of a newspaper
ex·tract¹ /ɪk'strækt/ vt 1 pull out, esp. with difficulty 2 get (a substance) from another substance ~ion /ɪk'strækʃən/ n 1 [C;U] act or example of extracting 2 [U] family origin: *of Russian extraction*
ex·tract² /'ekstrækt/ n 1 piece of writing taken from a book, etc. 2 product obtained by extracting: *almond extract*
ex·tra·cur·ric·u·lar /ˌekstrəkə'rɪkyələ-◂/ adj outside the ordinary course of work in a school or college
ex·tra·dite /'ekstrəˌdaɪt/ vt send (a foreign criminal) home for trial –dition /ˌekstrə'dɪʃən/ n [C;U]
ex·tra·mar·i·tal /ˌekstrə'mærətl-◂/ adj (of sexual relationships) outside marriage

ex·tra·mu·ral /ˌɛkstrəˈmyʊrəl◂/ *adj* 1 connected with but outside an organization 2 involving representatives from more than one school

ex·tra·ne·ous /ɪkˈstreɪniəs/ *adj* not directly connected

extra·or·di·na·ry /ɪkˈstrɔrdnˌɛri/ *adj* 1 very strange 2 beyond what is ordinary: *a man of extraordinary ability* –**narily** *adv*

ex·trap·o·late /ɪkˈstræpəˌleɪt/ *vi/t* guess from facts already known

ex·tra·sen·so·ry per·cep·tion /ˌɛkstrəˌsɛnsəri pəˈsɛpʃən/ *n* [U] see ESP

ex·tra·ter·res·tri·al /ˌɛkstrətəˈrɛstriəl/ *adj* (from) outside the Earth

ex·trav·a·gant /ɪkˈstrævəgənt/ *adj* 1 wasteful of money, etc. 2 (of ideas, behavior, etc.) beyond what is reasonable –**gance** *n* [C;U]

ex·trav·a·gan·za /ɪkˌstrævəˈgænzə/ *n* very grand and expensive piece of entertainment

ex·treme /ɪkˈstrim/ *adj* 1 furthest or greatest possible: *extreme cold* | *the extreme south of the country* 2 *often derog* beyond the usual limits: *extreme opinions* ♦ *n* furthest possible degree: *He's gone from one extreme to the other.* ~**ly** *adv* very

ex·trem·is·m /ɪkˈstrimɪzəm/ *n* [U] *derog* holding of (politically) extreme opinions –**ist** *n, adj*

ex·trem·i·ty /ɪkˈstrɛməti/ *n* [S;U] highest degree **extremities** *n* [P] hands and feet

ex·tri·cate /ˈɛkstrəˌkeɪt/ *vt* set free from something that is hard to escape from

ex·tro·vert /ˈɛkstrəˌvɜt/ *n* cheerful person who likes to be with others

ex·u·be·rant /ɪgˈzubərənt/ *adj* overflowing with life and excitement ~**ly** *adv* –**rance** *n* [U]

ex·ude /ɪgˈzud, ɪkˈsud/ *vi/t* (cause to) flow out slowly in all directions

ex·ult /ɪgˈzʌlt/ *vi fml* show great delight ~**ant** *adj* ~**antly** *adv* ~**ation** /ˌɛgzʌlˈteɪʃən, ˌɛksʌl-/ *n* [U]

eye /aɪ/ *n* 1 either of the 2 parts of the head with which we see 2 way of seeing: *an experienced eye* 3 hole in a needle 4 ring into which a hook fits 5 **be in the public eye** be often seen by the public 6 **have an eye for** be able to judge 7 **in one's mind's eye** in one's imagination 8 **in the eyes of** in the opinion of 9 **keep an eye on** watch carefully 10 **lay eyes on** *infml* catch sight of 11 **see eye to eye** agree completely 12 **up to one's eyes in** *infml* very busy with ♦ *vt* look at closely

eye·ball /ˈaɪbɔl/ *n* the whole of the EYE (1), including the part inside the head ♦ *v* look at closely

eye·brow /ˈaɪbraʊ/ *n* line of hairs above each eye

eye-catch·ing /ˈ· ˌ·◂/ *adj* unusual and attractive to look at

eye·lash /ˈaɪlæʃ/ *n* hair on the edge of the eyelid

eye·lid /ˈaɪˌlɪd/ *n* piece of skin that moves to close the eye

eye-o·pen·er /ˈ· ˌ·◂/ *n* something surprising that changes one's ideas about something

eye shad·ow /ˈ· ˌ·/ *n* [U] colored powder to decorate eyelids

eye·sight /ˈaɪsaɪt/ *n* [U] power of seeing

eye·sore /ˈaɪsɔr, -soʊr/ *n* something ugly to look at

eye·wit·ness /ˈaɪˌwɪtˈnɪs/ *n* person who sees something happen and can describe it

F

F, f /ɛf/ the 6th letter of the English alphabet

F *abbrev. for:* FAHRENHEIT

fa·ble /ˈfeɪbəl/ n short story that teaches a lesson **fabled** *adj* spoken of as true; famous

fab·ric /ˈfæbrɪk/ n [C;U] **1** woven cloth **2** structure of a building, etc.

fab·ri·cate /ˈfæbrəˌkeɪt/ vt invent (something false) **–cation** /ˌfæbrəˈkeɪʃən/ n [C;U]

fab·u·lous /ˈfæbyələs/ adj **1** existing in fables **2** unbelievable: *fabulous wealth* **3** excellent **~ly** adv very: *fabulously rich*

fa·cade /fəˈsɑd/ n **1** front of a building **2** false appearance

face¹ /feɪs/ n **1** [C] front part of the head **2** [C] expression on the face **3** [C] front; surface: *face of a cliff* **4** [U] position of respect: *afraid of losing face* **5 face to face** in someone's direct presence **6 in the face of** in opposition to **7 on the face of it** APPARENT*ly* **8 make a face/faces** make an expression with the face **9 to someone's face** openly in their presence **~less** adj with no clear character

face² v **1** vi/t turn the face towards **2** vt meet and oppose: *face danger* **3** vt cover the front of: *a building faced with stone*

face up to phr vt be brave enough to deal with

face·lift /ˈfeɪsˌlɪft/ n medical operation to make the face look younger

fac·et /ˈfæsɪt/ n **1** one of the flat sides of a cut jewel **2** ASPECT of a subject

fa·ce·tious /fəˈsiʃəs/ adj using silly jokes **~ly** adv

face val·ue /ˌ ˈˌ/ n **1** [C;U] value shown on a postage stamp, etc. **2** [U] value of something as it first appears

fa·cial /ˈfeɪʃəl/ adj of the face ♦ n facial beauty treatment

fa·cile /ˈfæsəl/ adj (of words) too easy; not deep

fa·cil·i·tate /fəˈsɪləˌteɪt/ vt fml make easy

fa·cil·i·ty /fəˈsɪləti/ n [U] ability to do things easily **–ties** n [P] useful things: *shopping/sporting facilities*

fac·sim·i·le /fækˈsɪməli/ n exact copy of a picture, etc. **facsimile machine** n fml FAX

fact /fækt/ n **1** [C] something known to be true **2** [U] truth **3 in fact** really

fac·tion /ˈfækʃən/ n group within a larger (political) one

fac·tor /ˈfæktər/ n influence that helps to produce a result

fac·to·ry /ˈfæktəri/ n place where goods are made by machinery

facts of life /ˌ ˈ ˌ/ n [P] the details of sex and birth

fac·tu·al /ˈfæktʃuəl/ adj based on fact **~ly** adv

fac·ul·ty /ˈfækəlti/ n **1** natural power of the mind or body: *the faculty of hearing* **2 a** teachers in a school, university, etc. **b** university department

fad /fæd/ n temporary interest in something

fade /feɪd/ v **1** vi/t (cause to) lose color or freshness **2** vi disappear gradually

fade in/out phr (in film making and broadcasting) (cause to) appear/disappear slowly

fag /fæg/ n derog sl for HOMOSEXUAL

Fah·ren·heit /ˈfærənˌhaɪt/ n scale of temperature in which water freezes at 32° and boils at 212°

fail /feɪl/ v **1** vi/t be unsuccessful or unable **2** vi not do what is wanted: *The crops/business failed.* **3** vt judge to be unsuccessful in a test **4** vt disappoint or leave (someone) at a bad time: *My courage failed me.* **5** vi lose strength: *His health is failing.* ♦ n **without fail** certainly

fail·ing /ˈfeɪlɪŋ/ n fault; weakness ♦ prep in the absence of

fail-safe /ˌ ˈ ˌ/ adj **1** made so that any failure will stop the machine **2** certain to succeed: *a fail-safe plan*

fail·ure /ˈfeɪlyər/ n **1** [U] lack of success **2** [C] person or thing that fails **3** [C;U] non-performance; inability: *heart failure*

faint /feɪnt/ adj **1** likely to lose consciousness **2** lacking strength or courage **3** not clear or bright **4** slight: *faint chance* ♦ vi lose consciousness ♦ n act of fainting **~ly** adv **~ness** n [U]

faint-heart·ed /ˌ ˈ ˌ/ adj cowardly

fair¹ /fɛr/ adj **1** just and honest: *fair play* **2** between poor and good: *a fair knowledge of French* **3** having a good, clean appearance: *a fair copy of the report* **4** (of skin or hair) not dark **5** (of weather) not stormy ♦ *adv* **1** honestly: *play fair* **2 fair and square: a** honestly **b** directly **3 fair enough** *infml* all right **~ly** *adv* **1** honestly **2** fairly warm

fair² *n* **1** competition for showing farm products, animals, etc., with amusements **2** large show of goods: *book fair*

fair game /ˌ· ˈ·/ *n* [U] **a** something that it is reasonable to attack **b** person, idea, etc., which can easily be laughed at or CRITICized

fair·ground /ˈfɛrɡraʊnd/ *n* open space for a FAIR²(1)

fair·way /ˈfɛrweɪ/ *n* part of a GOLF course along which one hits the ball

fair-weath·er friend /ˌ· ·· ˈ·/ *n* friend who is absent in times of trouble

fai·ry /ˈfɛri/ *n* **1** small imaginary person with magical powers **2** *derog* HOMOSEXUAL man

fairy god·moth·er /ˌ·· ˈ··· / *n* person who helps, and esp. saves, someone who is in trouble

fairy tale /ˈ·· ·/ *n* **1** story about magic **2** untrue story **fairy-tale** *adj* magically wonderful

fait ac·com·pli /ˌfeɪt ækəmˈpli, ˌfɛt ækəmˈpli/ *n* **faits accomplis** /ˌfeɪt ækəmˈpliz, ˌfɛz ɑkəmˈpli/ something that has happened and cannot now be changed

faith /feɪθ/ *n* **1** [U] confident trust **2** [C;U] religious belief **3** [U] loyalty to a promise: *keep faith with them* **~ful** *adj* **1** loyal **2** true to the facts: *faithful copy* ♦ *n* [*the*+P] religious people **~fully** *adv* **~less** *adj fml* disloyal

faith heal·ing /ˈ· ˌ·· / *n* [U] method of treating diseases by prayer, etc.

fake /feɪk/ *n* person or thing that is not what he/she/it looks like or pretends to be ♦ *vi/t* make or copy (e.g. a work of art) to deceive

fal·con /ˈfælkən, ˈfɔl-/ *n* bird that can be trained to hunt **~er** *n* person who trains falcons **~ry** *n* [U] hunting with falcons

fall¹ /fɔl/ *vi* **fell** /fel/, **fallen** /ˈfɔlən/ **1** come or go down freely: *She fell into the lake.* | *The house fell down.* **2** hang loosely: *Her hair falls over her shoulders.* **3** become lower: *The temperature fell.* **4** (of land) slope down **5** happen: *Christmas falls on a Friday.* **6** become: *fall asleep/in love* **7** be wounded or killed in battle **8** be defeated **9** (of the face) take on a look of sadness, etc. **10 fall flat** produce no result **11 fall into line** obey or CONFORM **12 fall short** fail to reach a standard

fall back *phr vi* RETREAT

fall back on *phr vt* use when there is failure or lack of other means

fall behind *phr vi/t* not keep level (with)

fall for *phr vt* **1** be attracted by **2** accept and be cheated by

fall off *phr vi* become less

fall on *phr vt* attack eagerly

fall out *phr vi* argue: *fell out with his boss*

fall through *phr vi* (of a plan) fail

fall² *n* **1** act of falling **2** something that has fallen: *a heavy fall of snow* **3** AUTUMN

falls *n* [P] WATERFALL

fal·la·cy /ˈfæləsi/ *n* [C;U] false belief or reasoning **–lacious** /fəˈleɪʃəs/ *adj fml* based on fallacy

fall guy /ˈ· ·/ *n infml for* SCAPEGOAT

fal·li·ble /ˈfæləbəl/ *adj* able to make mistakes **–bility** /ˌfæləˈbɪləti/ *n* [U]

fall·out /ˈfɔlaʊt/ *n* [U] dangerous dust left in the air after a NUCLEAR explosion

false /fɔls/ *adj* **1** not true or correct **2** disloyal: *false friend* **3** not real: *a false eye* **4** careless; unwise: *One false move and I'll shoot you!* **~ly** *adv* **~ness** *n* [U] **~hood** *n* [C;U] lying; lie

false a·larm /ˌ· ·ˈ·/ *n* warning of something bad that does not happen

false pre·tens·es /ˌ· ˈ···/ *n* [P] behavior intended to deceive

fal·set·to /fɔlˈsɛtoʊ/ *n* [C;U] **-tos** (man with an) unnaturally high voice

fal·si·fy /ˈfɔlsəˌfaɪ/ *vt* make false **–fication** /ˌfɔlsəfəˈkeɪʃən/ *n* [C;U]

fal·ter /ˈfɔltər/ *vi* **1** move or behave uncertainly **2** speak in an unsteady manner **~ingly** *adv*

fame /feɪm/ *n* [U] condition of being well known **famed** *adj* famous

fa·mil·iar /fəˈmɪlyər/ *adj* **1** often seen; common **2** too friendly **3 familiar with** knowing thoroughly **~ly** *adv* **~ity** /fəˌmɪliˈærəti/ *n* [C;U]

fa·mil·iar·ize /fəˈmɪlyəˌraɪz/ *vt* make well informed

fam·i·ly /ˈfæməli/ *n* **1** one's parents, children, aunts, etc. **2** one's children **3** people descended from the same ANCES-

TOR **4** division of living creatures or languages: *the cat family* ♦ *adj* suitable for children: *a family film*

family plan·ning /ˌ··· ˈ·· ·/ *n* [U] controlling of the number of children in a family by CONTRACEPTION

family room /ˈ··· ˌ·/ *n* room in a house where a family can watch television, play games, etc.

family tree /ˌ··· ˈ·/ *n* drawing showing the relationship of family members

fam·ine /ˈfæmɪn/ *n* [C;U] serious lack of food

fam·ished /ˈfæmɪʃt/ *adj* very hungry

fa·mous /ˈfeɪməs/ *adj* very well known **~ly** *adv* very well

fan[1] /fæn/ *n* instrument for making a flow of air ♦ *v* **-nn- 1** *vt* send cool air onto **2** *vi* spread in a half circle

fan[2] *n* enthusiastic supporter: *football fans*

fa·nat·ic /fəˈnætɪk/ *n* person who is too enthusiastic about something: *religious fanatics* **~al** *adj* **~ally** *adv* **~ism** /-təˌsɪzəm/ *n* [U]

fan·ci·ful /ˈfænsɪfəl/ *adj* showing imagination rather than reason **~ly** *adv*

fan club /ˈ· ˌ·/ *n* organization for FANS of a particular sports team, famous person, etc.

fan·cy /ˈfænsi/ *n* **1** [C] opinion not based on fact **2** *lit* [U] imagination **3** **take a fancy** to become fond of ♦ *adj* **1** decorative and unusual **2** higher than the usual or reasonable price

fan·fare /ˈfænfer/ *n* short loud piece of TRUMPET music to introduce a person or event

fang /fæŋ/ *n* long sharp tooth

fan mail /ˈ· ·/ *n* [U] letters to a famous person from FANS[2]

fan·ny /ˈfæni/ *n sl* BOTTOM[1] (2)

fan·tas·tic /fænˈtæstɪk/ *adj* **1** wonderful **2** (of ideas) not practical **3** wild and strange **~ally** *adv*

fan·ta·size /ˈfæntəˌsaɪz/ *vi* have fantasies about

fan·ta·sy /ˈfæntəsi, -zi/ *n* [C;U] (something made by) imagination: *sexual fantasies*

FAQ *n* frequently asked questions; list of questions commonly asked

far /far/ *adv, adj* **farther** /ˈfarðər/ or **further** /ˈfərðər/, **farthest** /ˈfarðɪst/ or **furthest** /ˈfərðɪst/ **1** a long way: *too far to walk* | *the far distance* **2** very much: *far*

better **3** (of a political position) very much to the LEFT or RIGHT: *the far left* **4** **as/so far as** to the degree that: *So far as I know, he's coming.* **5** **far and away** by a great deal or amount: *She's far and away the best actress.* **6** **far from: a** very much not: *I'm far from pleased.* **b** instead of: *Far from being angry, he's delighted.* **7** **how far** to what degree **8** **so far** until now **9** **So far, so good** Things are satisfactory up to this point, at least

far·a·way /ˈfarəˌweɪ/ *adj* **1** distant **2** (of a look in someone's eyes) dreamy

farce /fars/ *n* **1** light funny play **2** set of silly events **farcical** *adj*

fare /fer/ *n* **1** [C] money charged for a trip **2** [U] *fml* food ♦ *vi* get on; succeed: *fare badly*

Far East /ˌ· ˈ·◂/ *n* [S] countries east of India

fare·well /ˌferˈwel/ *interj, n fml* goodbye

far-fetched /ˌfarˈfetʃt◂/ *adj* hard to believe

far-flung /ˌ· ˈ·◂/ *adj* spread over a great distance

farm /farm/ *n* area of land and buildings where crops are grown and animals raised ♦ *vi/t* use (land) as a farm

  farm out *phr vt* send (work) for other people to do

farm·er /ˈfarmər/ *n* person who owns or manages a farm

farm·hand /ˈfarmhænd/ *n* worker on a farm

farm·house /ˈfarmhaʊs/ *n* main house on a farm

farm·yard /ˈfarmyard/ *n* yard surrounded by farm buildings

far-off /ˌ· ˈ·/ *adj* distant

far-reach·ing /ˌ· ˈ··◂/ *adj* having a wide influence

far·sight·ed /ˌfarˈsaɪtɪd◂, ˈfarˌsaɪtɪd/ *adj* **1** able to judge future effects **2** able to see things only when they are far away

fart /fart/ *vi taboo* send out air from the bowels **fart** *n taboo* **1** escape of air from the bowels **2** *sl* extremely unpleasant person

far·ther /ˈfarðər/ *adv, adj* FURTHER

far·thest /ˈfarðɪst/ *adv, adj* FURTHEST

fas·ci·nate /ˈfæsəˌneɪt/ *vt* attract and interest strongly **–nating** *adj* **–nation** /ˌfæsəˈneɪʃən/ *n* [S;U]

fas·cis·m /ˈfæʃɪzəm/ *n* [U] political system marked by total state control under a single leader, and support of one's own nation and race **fascist** n, adj

fash·ion /ˈfæʃən/ n 1 [C;U] way of dressing or behaving that is popular at a certain time 2 [S] fml manner of doing something: in an orderly fashion 3 after a fashion not very well ♦ vt fml make; shape ~**able** according to the latest fashion ~**ably** adv

fast[1] /fæst/ adj 1 quick: fast cars 2 firmly fixed: fast colors 3 (of a clock) showing time later than the right time ♦ adv 1 quickly 2 firmly 3 fast asleep sleeping deeply 4 pull a fast one (on) infml deceive (someone) with a trick

fast[2] vi eat no food, esp. for religious reasons ♦ n period of fasting

fas·ten /ˈfæsən/ vi/t make or become firmly fixed ~**er** n thing that fastens things together ~**ing** n something that holds things shut

fasten on phr vt take eagerly and use

fast food /ˌ· ˈ·/ n [U] restaurant food that is cooked and ready before being ordered

fas·tid·i·ous /fæˈstɪdiəs, fə-/ adj difficult to please; disliking anything dirty or nasty ~**ly** adv ~**ness** n [U]

fat /fæt/ n [U] 1 material under the skins of animals and human beings which helps keep them warm 2 this substance used in cooking ♦ adj 1 having a lot of FAT (1) on the body 2 thick or tightly packed: fat book ~**ness** n [U]

fa·tal /ˈfeɪtl/ adj causing death or ruin ~**ly** adv

fa·tal·is·m /ˈfeɪtlˌɪzəm/ n [U] belief that events are controlled by FATE (1) ~**ist** n

fa·tal·i·ty /feɪˈtæləti, fə-/ n 1 [C] violent death 2 [U] being fatal

fat cat /ˌ· ˈ·/ n derog sl wealthy person with a bad influence or way of life

fate /feɪt/ n 1 [U] power beyond human control that decides events 2 [C] end, esp. death 3 [S] the future ~**ful** adj important (esp. in a bad way) for the future: fateful decision ~**fully** adv **fated** adj 1 caused by fate 2 infml very unlucky

fat-free /ˌ· ˈ·/ adj (of food) containing no fat: fat-free yogurt

fa·ther /ˈfɑːðər/ n 1 male parent 2 (usu. cap.) priest ♦ vt become the father of ~**hood** n [U] ~**less** adj ~**ly** adj like a good father **fathers** n [P] FOREFATHERS

father-in-law /ˈ·· ˌ· ˌ/ n **fathers-in-law** father of one's wife or husband

fa·ther·land /ˈfɑːðərˌlænd/ n one's native land

Father's Day /ˈ·· ˌ/ n third Sunday in June, when fathers are given presents and cards

fath·om /ˈfæðəm/ n unit of measurement (6 feet) for the depth of water ♦ vt understand fully

fa·tigue /fəˈtiːg/ n 1 [U] tiredness 2 [U] weakness in metals caused by repeated bending 3 [C] (in the army) a job of cleaning or cooking — see also **fatigues** ♦ vt fml make tired

fa·tigues /fəˈtiːgz/ n [P] military clothes

fat·ten /ˈfætn/ vt make fatter

fat·ty /ˈfæti/ adj containing fat ♦ n sl fat person

fat·u·ous /ˈfætʃuəs/ adj silly: fatuous remarks ~**ly** adv

fau·cet /ˈfɔːsɪt/ n apparatus with a handle for controlling the flow of water, etc. from a pipe, barrel, etc.

fault /fɔːlt/ n 1 mistake or imperfection 2 crack in the Earth's surface 3 **at fault** in the wrong 4 **find fault with** complain about 5 **one's fault** something one can be blamed for 6 **to a fault** (of good qualities) too; too much ♦ vt find mistakes in ~**less** adj perfect ~**y** adj

fau·na /ˈfɔːnə/ n [U] animals of a particular area or period

faux pas /ˌfoʊ ˈpɑː/ n **faux pas** /ˌfoʊ ˈpɑːz/ social mistake

fa·vor /ˈfeɪvər/ n 1 [U] approval: gain widespread favor 2 [C] kind act: do me a favor 3 **in favor of**: in support of 4 **in one's favor** to one's advantage ♦ vt 1 approve of 2 be unfairly fond of; treat with favor ~**able** adj 1 showing or winning approval 2 advantageous ~**ably** adv

fa·vo·rite /ˈfeɪvrɪt, -vərɪt/ n 1 person or thing loved above all others 2 horse expected to win a race ♦ adj most loved ~**ritism** n [U] unfairly generous treatment of one person

fawn[1] /fɔːn/ n 1 [C] young deer 2 [U] light yellow-brown color

fawn[2] v **fawn over** phr vt try to gain the favor of, by being too attentive

fax /fæks/ vt send (copies of printed material) in ELECTRONIC form along a telephone line ♦ n 1 also **fax machine** — apparatus that does this 2 paper sent by fax

faze /feɪz/ vt shock into silence

FBI *n* Federal Bureau of Investigation; US police department under central control for crimes involving more than one state

fear /fɪr/ *n* **1** [C;U] feeling that danger is near **2** [U] danger **3** No fear! Certainly not! ♦ *vi/t fml* be afraid (of) ~ful *adj* **1** terrible; shocking **2** *fml* afraid ~less *adj* not afraid ~lessly *adv* ~some *adj lit* frightening

fea·si·ble /ˈfizəbəl/ *adj* able to be done; possible –bility /ˌfizəˈbɪləti/ *n* [U]

feast /fist/ *n* **1** special large meal **2** religious FESTIVAL ♦ *vi* eat and drink very well **2** feast one's eyes on look at with delight

feat /fit/ *n* difficult action successfully done

fea·ther /ˈfɛðə/ *n* **1** one of a bird's many light skin coverings **2** a feather in one's cap honor to be proud of ♦ *vt* **1** put feathers on or in **2** feather one's nest make oneself dishonestly rich while in a trusted position ~y *adj* soft and light

fea·ture /ˈfitʃə/ *n* **1** noticeable quality **2** part of the face **3** long newspaper piece **4** film being shown at a theater ♦ *v* **1** *vt* include as a performer **2** *vi* play an important part ~less *adj* uninteresting **features** *n* [P] face

Feb·ru·a·ry /ˈfɛbruˌɛri, ˈfɛbyuˌɛri/ *n* the 2nd month of the year

fe·ces /ˈfisiz/ *n* [P] solid waste from the bowels

fec·und /ˈfɛkənd, ˈfi-/ *adj fml* FERTILE

fed /fɛd/ *v past t. and p. of* FEED

fed·e·ral /ˈfɛdərəl/ *adj* **1** of or being a federation **2** of the US government as opposed to the states

fed·e·ra·tion /ˌfɛdəˈreɪʃən/ *n* **1** [C] united group of states, organizations, etc. **2** [U] action or result of uniting in this way

fed up /ˌ · ˈ·/ *adj sl* tired and discontented

fee /fi/ *n* money paid for professional services, to join a club, etc.

fee·ble /ˈfibəl/ *adj* weak **feebly** *adv*

feed /fid/ *v* fed /fɛd/ **1** *vt* give food to **2** *vi* (esp. of animals) eat **3** *vt* supply; provide: *feed information into a computer* ♦ *n* **1** animal's meal **2** [U] food for animals **3** [C] pipe, etc., through which a machine is fed

feed·back /ˈfidbæk/ *n* information about the results of an action, passed back to the person in charge

feel¹ /fil/ *v* felt /fɛlt/ **1** *vt* touch with the fingers **2** *vt* experience (the touch of something): *feel the wind* **3** *vi* search with the fingers: *feel for a pencil* **4** be consciously: *feel hungry/happy* **5** *vt* suffer because of: *feel the cold* **6** give a sensation: *This sheet feels wet.* **7** *vt* believe without reasoning: *I feel they won't come.* **8** feel like want: *I feel like a drink.*

feel for *phr vt* be sorry for

feel² *n* [S] **1** sensation caused by touching **2** act of feeling **3** get the feel of become used to and skilled at

feel·er /ˈfilə/ *n* **1** thread-like part of an insect's head, with which it touches things **2** suggestion made to test opinion

feel·ing /ˈfilɪŋ/ *n* **1** [S] consciousness of something felt **2** [S] belief not based on reason **3** [U] power to feel **4** [U] excitement of mind: *cause ill feeling* **5** [U] sympathy **feelings** *n* [P] EMOTIONS

feet /fit/ *n pl. of* FOOT

feign /feɪn/ *vt fml* pretend to have or be

feint /feɪnt/ *n* false attack or blow ♦ *vi* make a feint

feist·y /ˈfaɪsti/ *adj* excited and quarrelsome

fe·line /ˈfilaɪn/ *adj* of or like a cat

fell¹ /fɛl/ *v past t. of* FALL

fell² *vt* cut or knock down: *fell a tree/a man*

fel·low /ˈfɛloʊ/ *n* **1** man **2** member of a learned society or college ♦ *adj* another of the same group: *fellow prisoners/students* ~ship *n* **1** [C] group or society **2** [U] companionship **3** [C] position of a college fellow

fel·o·ny /ˈfɛləni/ *n* [C;U] serious crime (e.g. murder) **felon** *n* person guilty of felony

felt¹ /fɛlt/ *v past t. and p. of* FEEL

felt² *n* [U] thick cloth made of pressed wool

felt-tip pen /ˌ · ˈ·/ *n* pen with felt point at the end

fe·male /ˈfimeɪl/ *adj* **1** of the sex that produces babies **2** (of plants) producing fruits **3** having a hole into which something fits: *female plug* ♦ *n* woman or female animal

fem·i·nine /ˈfɛmənɪn/ *adj* **1** suitable for a woman **2** *gram* of the class of words for females –ninity /ˌfɛməˈnɪnəti/ *n* [U] being feminine (1)

fem·i·nis·m /ˈfɛmə͵nɪzəm/ n [U] principle that women should have the same rights as men –**nist** n, adj

fence¹ /fɛns/ n 1 wall made of wood or wire 2 someone who buys and sells stolen goods 3 **sit on the fence** avoid taking sides in an argument ♦ vt surround or separate with a fence

fence² vi 1 fight with a long thin sword as a sport 2 avoid giving an honest answer **fencer** n

fenc·ing /ˈfɛnsɪŋ/ n [U] 1 fighting with a sword as a sport 2 material for making fences

fend /fɛnd/ vi
  fend for oneself take care of oneself
  fend off phr vt push away

fend·er /ˈfɛndə/ n 1 side part of a car that covers the wheels 2 protective cover over a cycle wheel

fender-ben·der /ˈfɛndə ͵bɛndə/ n car accident with little damage

fer·ment¹ /fəˈmɛnt/ vi/t 1 change chemically so that sugar becomes alcohol 2 make or become excited ~**ation** /͵fɜmənˈteɪʃən, -mɛn-/ n [U]

fer·ment² /ˈfɜmənt/ n [U] trouble and excitement

fern /fɜn/ n plant with feathery green leaves

fe·ro·cious /fəˈroʊʃəs/ adj fierce; violent ~**ly** adv

fe·ro·ci·ty /fəˈrɑsəti/ n [U] ferociousness

fer·ret /ˈfɛrɪt/ n small fierce animal that hunts rats and rabbits ♦ vi/t search; find by searching

Ferris wheel /ˈfɛrɪs ͵wil, -͵hwil/ n very large wheel with seats for people to ride on at a FAIR, etc.

fer·rous /ˈfɛrəs/ adj of or containing iron

fer·ry /ˈfɛri/ also **fer·ry·boat** /ˈfɛribout/ — n boat that carries people and things across a narrow piece of water ♦ vt carry (as if) on a ferry

fer·tile /ˈfɜtl/ adj 1 producing young, crops, etc. 2 (of a person's mind) inventive –**tility** /fəˈtɪləti/ n [U]

fer·ti·lize /ˈfɜtl͵aɪz/ vt make fertile –**lizer** plant food –**lization** /͵fɜtl-əˈzeɪʃən/ n [U]

fer·vent /ˈfɜvənt/ adj feeling strongly: fervent hope/believer ~**ly** adv

fer·vor /ˈfɜvə/ n [U] strong feeling or belief

fes·ter /ˈfɛstə/ vi 1 (of a wound) become infected 2 feel anger without expressing it

fes·ti·val /ˈfɛstəvəl/ n 1 time for public happiness: Christmas is a festival of the church. 2 group of musical, etc., performances held regularly

fes·tive /ˈfɛstɪv/ adj joyful

fes·tiv·i·ty /fɛˈstɪvəti/ n [C;U] festive activity

fes·toon /fɛˈstun/ vt decorate with chains of flowers, RIBBONS, etc.

fetch /fɛtʃ/ vt 1 go and get and bring back 2 be sold for: The house fetched $30,000. 3 **fetch and carry** do the small duties of a servant

fete /feɪt/ n day of public amusement held esp. to collect money ♦ vt honor publicly

fet·id /ˈfɛtɪd, ˈfi-/ adj smelling bad

fet·ish /ˈfɛtɪʃ/ n something to which one pays too much attention

fet·ter /ˈfɛtə/ n chain for a prisoner's foot: (fig.) the fetters of an unhappy marriage ♦ vt tie; prevent from moving

fe·tus /ˈfitəs/ n creature or baby before birth, at a later stage than an EMBRYO

feud /fyud/ n violent continuing argument ♦ vi have a feud

fe·ver /ˈfivə/ n [S;U] 1 (disease causing) high body temperature — see also YELLOW FEVER 2 excited state ~**ish** adj 1 of or having fever 2 unnaturally fast ~**ishly** adv

few /fyu/ determiner, pron, n [P] 1 (with a) some: Let's invite a few friends. 2 (without a) not many: She has few friends.

fi·an·cé /͵fiɑnˈseɪ, fiˈɑnseɪ/ **fiancée** (same pronunciation) fem. — n person one is ENGAGED to

fi·as·co /fiˈæskoʊ/ n –**cos** complete failure

fib /fɪb/ n, vi, n -bb- (tell) a small lie ~**ber** n

fi·ber /ˈfaɪbə/ n 1 [C] thin threadlike plant or animal growth 2 [U] mass of threads 3 [U] person's inner character 4 substance in fruits and vegetables necessary for health: high-fiber diet **fibrous** /ˈfaɪbrəs/ adj

fi·ber·glass /ˈfaɪbə͵glæs/ n [U] material of glass fibers used for making boats, etc.

fiber op·tics /͵faɪbə ˈɑptɪks/ n [U] use of long thin glass threads to carry information in the form of light, esp. on telephone lines

fick·le /ˈfɪkəl/ adj not loyal; often changing

fic·tion /ˈfɪkʃən/ n 1 [U] stories 2 [S;U] untrue story ~al adj

fic·ti·tious /fɪkˈtɪʃəs/ adj untrue: invented

fid·dle /ˈfɪdl/ n 1 VIOLIN 2 dishonest practice 3 (as) fit as a fiddle perfectly healthy 4 play second fiddle (to) play a less important part (than) ♦ v 1 vi move things aimlessly 2 vi play the VIOLIN –dler n

fi·del·i·ty /fəˈdɛləti, faɪ-/ n [U] 1 faithfulness 2 closeness to an original

fid·get /ˈfɪdʒɪt/ vi move one's body around restlessly ~y adj

field[1] /fiːld/ n 1 [C] piece of farming land 2 [C] open area: a football field | an oilfield | a battlefield 3 [C] branch of knowledge 4 [S] place where practical operations actually happen: study tribal languages in the field 5 [C] area where a force is felt: gravitational field

field[2] v 1 vi/t (in baseball, etc.) catch or stop (the ball) 2 vt produce (a team or army) ~er n

field day /ˈ· ·/ n 1 day for outdoor activities with a school, club, etc. 2 have a field day enjoy oneself very much

field e·vent /ˈ· ·̩·/ n sports event with competitions, such as throwing weights or jumping

field glass·es /ˈ· ̩·/ n [P] BINOCULARS

field·work /ˈfiːldwɜːk/ n [U] study done in the FIELD[1] (4)

fiend /fiːnd/ n 1 devil 2 infml someone very enthusiastic about something ~ish adj ~ishly adv

fierce /fɪəs/ adj 1 angry, violent, and cruel 2 severe: fierce heat/competition ~ly adv ~ness n [U]

fi·er·y /ˈfaɪəri/ adj 1 like fire 2 violent: fiery temper

fi·es·ta /fiˈestə/ n religious holiday with public dancing, etc.

fif·teen /ˌfɪfˈtiːn/ det, n, pron 15 ~th det, adv, n, pron 15th

fifth /fɪθ, fɪfθ/ det, n, pron, adv 5th

fif·ty /ˈfɪfti/ det, n, pron 50 ~tieth /ˈfɪftiəθ/ det, adv, n, pron 50th

fifty-fif·ty /ˌ· ·̩·/ adj, adv (of a division or chances) equal(ly)

fig /fɪg/ n (tree that bears) a soft sweet fruit with many seeds

fig· written abbrev. for: 1 FIGURATIVE 2 FIGURE[1] (5)

fight[1] /faɪt/ vi/t/ fought /fɔt/ 1 use violence (against); struggle 2 argue ~er n 1

person who fights professionally: (fig.) a tireless fighter against racism 2 small military aircraft

fight back 1 recover from a bad or losing position 2 defend oneself by fighting

fight off phr vt keep away with an effort

fight out phr vt settle (a quarrel) by fighting

fight[2] n 1 [C] battle 2 [U] power or wish to fight 3 [C] boxing (BOX[2]) match

fighting chance /ˌ· ·̩·/ n small but real chance if great effort is made

fig·ment /ˈfɪgmənt/ n something not real: a figment of his imagination

fig·u·ra·tive /ˈfɪgjərətɪv/ adj (of words, phrases, etc.) used in some way other than the main or usual meaning, to suggest a picture in the mind or make a comparison ~ly adv: She's up to her eyes in paperwork — figuratively speaking, of course!

fig·ure[1] /ˈfɪgjə/ n 1 (shape of) a human body: a good figure 2 person: a leading political figure 3 (sign for) a number 4 price 5 DIAGRAM

figure[2] v 1 vi take a part 2 vt believe 3 That figures infml That seems reasonable

figure on phr vt plan on; include in one's plans

figure out phr vt discover by thinking

fig·ure·head /ˈfɪgjəˌhɛd/ n someone who is the chief in name only

figure of speech /ˌ· · ·̩·/ n figurative expression

fil·a·ment /ˈfɪləmənt/ n thin thread, esp. in an electric light BULB (2)

filch /fɪltʃ/ vt steal secretly (something of small value)

file[1] /faɪl/ n steel tool for rubbing or cutting hard surfaces ♦ vt rub or cut with a file: file one's nails

file[2] n 1 arrangement for storing papers 2 store of papers on one subject 3 unit of collected information in a computer

file[3] vt put in a file

file for phr vt law request officially

file[4] n line of people one behind the other ♦ vi walk in a file

filet /fiˈleɪ, ˈfɪleɪ/ n FILLET

fil·i·bus·ter /ˈfɪləˌbʌstə/ vi delay Congressional action by making long speeches filibuster n

fil·i·gree /ˈfɪləˌgriː/ n [U] decorative wire work

filing cab·i·net /ˈ·· ˌ···/ n piece of office furniture for storing papers

fil·ings /ˈfaɪlɪŋz/ n [P] very small sharp bits that have been rubbed off a metal surface with a FILE¹

fill /fɪl/ v 1 vt/i make or become full 2 vt go or be put into: *fill a vacancy* 3 fulfill ♦ n full supply ~**er** n substance added to increase size ~**ing** n 1 material to fill a hole, esp. in a tooth 2 food mixture folded inside pastry, SANDWICHes, etc.

fill in phr vt 1 tell (what is necessary): *He filled me in about the accident.* 2 supply the most recent information 3 take someone's place

fill out phr v 1 vi get fatter 2 vt put in (what is necessary): *fill out a form*

fill up phr v make or become full

fil·let /ˈfɪˈleɪ, ˈfɪleɪ/ n piece of meat or fish without bones ♦ vt remove bones from

fil·ly /ˈfɪliː/ n young female horse

film /fɪlm/ n 1 [C;U] (roll of) thin material used in photography 2 [C] *fml* cinema picture; MOVIE 3 [S;U] thin covering: *film of oil* ♦ vi/t make a FILM (2) (of) ~**y** adj very thin: *filmy silk*

film·strip /ˈfɪlmˌstrɪp/ n [C;U] length of photographic film that shows drawings, etc., separately as still pictures

fil·ter /ˈfɪltə/ n 1 apparatus through which liquids are passed to clean or change them: *coffee filter* 2 glass that changes the color or amount of light ♦ vi/t go or send (as if) through a filter: *People filtered out of the gym.*

filth /fɪlθ/ n [U] 1 very nasty dirt 2 something rude or unpleasant ~**y** adj

fin /fɪn/ n winglike part of a fish 2 thing shaped like this on a car, etc.

fi·nal /ˈfaɪnl/ adj 1 last 2 (of a decision, etc.) that cannot be changed ♦ also **finals** pl. n 1 last of a set of matches 2 last and most important examinations in a college course ~**ly** adv 1 at last 2 allowing no further change ~**ist** n player in a final match or competition ~**ize** vt give final form to

fi·na·le /fɪˈnæli, -ˈnɑ-/ n last division of a piece of music, etc.

fi·nance /ˈfaɪnæns, fɪˈnæns/ n [U] 1 management of (public) money 2 money, esp. provided by a bank, to help run an organization or buy something ♦ vt provide money for **finances** n [P] money owned or provided **financial** /fɪˈnænʃəl, faɪ-/ adj **financially** adv

financial aid /ˌ·· ˈ·/ n [U] money given or lent to students to pay for college education

fi·nan·cier /ˌfɪnənˈsɪr, fəˌnæn-, ˌfaɪnæn-/ n someone who controls large sums of money

finch /fɪntʃ/ n small bird with an attractive song

find /faɪnd/ vt **found** /faʊnd/ 1 get (something lost or not known) by searching 2 learn by chance or effort: *find (out) where he lives* 3 obtain by effort: *find time to study* 4 (of a thing) arrive at: *Water finds its own level.* 5 know to exist: *Elephants are found in Africa.* 6 *law* decide to be: *find someone guilty* 7 **find fault with** criticize or blame ♦ n something good or valuable that is found ~**er** n ~**ing** n 1 what is learned by inquiry 2 *law* decision made in court 3 something learned as the result of an official inquiry

fine¹ /faɪn/ adj 1 good; beautiful 2 very thin or small: *fine thread/dust* | (fig.) *fine distinction* 3 (of weather) bright; not wet 4 healthy ♦ adv 1 very well 2 very thin ~**ly** adv 1 into small bits 2 delicately: *finely tuned*

fine² n money paid as a punishment ♦ vt take a fine from

fine arts /ˌ· ˈ·/ n [P] painting, music, etc.

fine print /ˌ· ˈ·/ n [U] small but important writing on a contract, etc.

fi·nesse /fɪˈnɛs/ n [U] delicate skill

fin·ger /ˈfɪŋgə/ n 1 any of the 5 end parts of the hand 2 part of a covering for the hand, covering a finger 3 object shaped like a finger 4 **(have) a finger in every pie** (have) a part in everything that is going on 5 **keep one's fingers crossed** hope for the best 6 **lay a finger on** harm 7 **not lift a finger** make no effort to help 8 **put one's finger on** find 9 **twist around one's little finger** successfully influence ♦ vt feel with one's fingers ~**ing** n [U] use of the fingers when playing music

finger·nail /ˈfɪŋgəˌneɪl/ n one of the hard flat pieces at the ends of the fingers

fin·ger·print /ˈfɪŋgəˌprɪnt/ n mark made by a finger pressed onto a surface ♦ vt take (someone's) fingerprints

fin·ger·tip /ˈfɪŋgəˌtɪp/ n 1 end of a finger 2 **have something at one's fingertips** know it well

fin·i·cky /ˈfɪnɪki/ adj disliking many things

fin·ish /ˈfɪnɪʃ/ v 1 vi/t come or bring to an end 2 vt eat or drink the rest of 3 take all one's powers, hopes of success, etc. ♦ n 1 [C] last part 2 [S;U] appearance or condition of having been properly polished, painted, etc.

finish off phr vt kill

finish with phr vt have no more use for

fi·nite /ˈfaɪnaɪt/ adj 1 limited 2 gram (of a verb) changing according to tense and subject ~**ly** adv

fir /fɜ/ n straight tree with leaves like needles

fire¹ /faɪə/ n 1 [U] condition of burning: afraid of fire 2 [C] something burning, on purpose or by accident: light a fire | forest fires 3 heat used for cooking: Put the pan on the fire. 4 [U] destruction by fire 5 [U] shooting from guns 6 **catch fire** start to burn 7 **on fire** burning 8 **open/cease fire** start/stop shooting 9 **set fire to** cause to burn 10 **under fire** being shot at — see also **hang fire** (HANG¹)

fire² v 1 vi/t shoot off (bullets or arrows) 2 vt dismiss from a job 3 vt excite: fire one's imagination 4 vt bake (clay things) in a KILN

fire a·larm /ˈ. .,./ n signal that warns people of fire

fire·arm /ˈfaɪəɑrm/ n gun

fire·bomb /ˈfaɪəbɑm/ n bomb that causes fire

fire·brand /ˈfaɪəbrænd/ n person who causes trouble; agitator (AGITATE)

fire department /ˈ. .,../ n company of people that put out fires

fire drill /ˈ. ./ n [C;U] practice in leaving a burning building safely

fire en·gine /ˈ. ,../ n vehicle that carries fire fighters and their equipment

fire es·cape /ˈ. .,./ n outside stairs for leaving a burning building

fire ex·tin·guish·er /ˈ. .,..,/ n apparatus containing water or chemicals for stopping small fires

fire·fight·er /ˈfaɪəˌfaɪtə/ n person who puts out fires

fire·fight·ing /ˈfaɪəˌfaɪtɪŋ/ n [U] 1 action to put out large fires 2 actions taken to discover and remove causes of sudden trouble in organizations, etc.

fire hy·drant /ˈ. .,./ n water pipe near a street, for getting water to stop fires

fire·place /ˈfaɪəpleɪs/ n opening for a fire in a room

fire·pow·er /ˈfaɪəˌpaʊə/ n [U] ability to deliver gunfire

fire·proof /ˈfaɪəpruf/ adj unable to be damaged by fire **fireproof** vt

fire·side /ˈfaɪəsaɪd/ n area around the fireplace

fire sta·tion /ˈ. .,./ n building for a FIRE DEPARTMENT

fire·wood /ˈfaɪəwʊd/ n [U] wood cut to be used on fires

fire·work /ˈfaɪəwɜk/ n container of explosive powder, burned to make colored lights **fireworks** n [P] 1 show of FIREWORKS 2 show of anger

firing line /ˈ.. ./ n [S] position of being the object of attack

firing squad /ˈ.. ,./ n group of soldiers ordered to shoot an offender

firm¹ /fɜm/ adj, adv 1 solidly fastened 2 not likely to change 3 determined; RESOLUTE ~**ly** adv ~**ness** n [U]

firm² n business company

first /fɜst/ determiner, adv 1 before the others 2 for the first time: my first visit 3 rather than do something else 4 **first thing** at the earliest time in the morning ♦ n, pron [S] 1 person or thing before others: the first to arrive 2 **at first** at the beginning ~**ly** adv before anything else

first aid /ˌ. ./ n [U] treatment given by an ordinary person to someone hurt in an accident, etc.

first base /ˌ. ./ n [U] first step of a course of action

first class /ˌ. ./ n [U] best traveling conditions on a plane, etc. **firstclass** adj of the best quality

first cous·in /ˌ. .,./ n child of one's aunt or uncle

first de·gree /ˌ. .,./ adj of the highest level of seriousness: first degree murder

first fam·i·ly /ˌ. .,../ n [the] President, his wife and children

first floor /ˌ. ./ n part of a building at ground level

first·hand /ˌfɜstˈhænd/ adj, adv (of information) directly from its origin

first la·dy /ˌ. .,./ n [the] wife of the President

first name /ˈ. ./ n name that stands before one's family name

first-rate /ˌ. ./ adj of the best quality

fis·cal /ˈfɪskəl/ adj fml of public money, taxes, etc.

fiscal year /ˌ·· ˈ·/ n yearly period over which accounts are calculated

fish /fɪʃ/ n fishes or fishes 1 [C] creature that has cold blood and lives in water 2 [U] its flesh as food 3 **drink like a fish** drink too much alcohol ♦ v 1 vi try to catch fish 2 vi search indirectly: fish for compliments 3 vt bring out or up: He fished a key from his pocket. ~y adj 1 like fish 2 seeming false: a fishy story

fish·er·man /ˈfɪʃəmən/ n -men /-mən/ man who catches fish, esp. as a job

fish·ing /ˈfɪʃɪŋ/ n [U] sport or job of catching fish

fis·sion /ˈfɪʃən/ n [U] splitting of a cell or atom

fis·sure /ˈfɪʃə/ n deep crack in rock

fist /fɪst/ n hand when closed tightly: holding a **fistful** of coins

fit¹ /fɪt/ v -tt- 1 vi/t be the right size and shape (for): The lid doesn't fit. 2 vt put in place: fit a new lock 3 vt make suitable for ♦ n [S] 1 quality of fitting well 2 way that something fits: a tight fit ~ted adj

fit in phr v 1 vi match; HARMONIZE 2 vt make room or time for

fit out phr vt supply; FURNISH

fit² adj 1 suitable, right: fit to eat | Do as you think fit. 2 physically healthy 3 ready to: laugh fit to burst 4 **fit to be tied** very angry ~ness n [U]

fit³ n 1 short attack of illness, etc.: fit of coughing 2 sudden loss of consciousness 3 **by fits and starts** not regularly 4 **have a fit** be very angry

fit·ful /ˈfɪtfəl/ adj restlessly irregular ~ly adv

fit·ting /ˈfɪtɪŋ/ adj fml suitable ♦ n 1 something fixed into a building 2 occasion of trying whether clothes fit

five /faɪv/ det, n, pron 1 5 2 $5 bill

fix¹ /fɪks/ vt 1 fasten firmly 2 arrange; decide on: fix a price 3 repair 4 tidy: I must fix my hair. 5 prepare (food or drink) 6 arrange the result of (something) dishonestly ~ative /-ətɪv/ n chemical for sticking things in position ~ation /fɪkˈseɪʃən/ n OBSESSION

fix on phr vt choose

fix up phr vt 1 provide 2 repair, change or improve

fix² n 1 awkward situation 2 sl INJECTION of a drug 3 position calculated by looking at the stars, etc.

fix·ture /ˈfɪkstʃə/ n 1 something fixed into a building 2 person long established in the same place

fizz /fɪz/ vi, n [S] (make) a sound of BUBBLES in a liquid ~y adj

fiz·zle out /ˈfɪzəl/ v fizzle out phr vi end disappointingly

fjord /fjɔrd, fyɔrd/ n narrow arm of the sea between steep cliffs, esp. in Norway

flab /flæb/ n [U] infml soft loose flesh

flab·ber·gast·ed /ˈflæbəˌgæstɪd/ adj surprised and shocked

flab·by /ˈflæbi/ adj 1 (of muscles) too soft 2 lacking force or effectiveness –biness n [U]

flac·cid /ˈflæksɪd, ˈflæsɪd/ adj not firm enough

flag¹ /flæg/ n piece of cloth used as the sign of a country, etc., or to make signals — see also WHITE FLAG ♦ vt -gg- put a flag on

flag down phr vt signal (a vehicle) to stop

flag² vi -gg- become weak

flag·pole /ˈflægpoʊl/ n long pole to raise a flag on

fla·grant /ˈfleɪgrənt/ adj openly bad ~ly adv

flag·ship /ˈflægˌʃɪp/ n 1 most important business, product, etc. 2 chief naval ship in a group

flag·stone /ˈflægstoʊn/ n flat stone for a floor or path

flail /fleɪl/ vi wave violently but aimlessly about

flair /flɛr/ n [S] natural ability to do something

flak /flæk/ n 1 gunfire directed at enemy aircraft 2 severe opposition

flake¹ /fleɪk/ n small leaf-like bit: soap flakes **flaky** adj 1 made up of flakes or tending to flake 2 infml ECCENTRIC **flakiness** n [U]

flake² vi fall off in flakes

flake out phr vi become crazy

flam·boy·ant /flæmˈbɔɪənt/ adj 1 brightly colored 2 (of a person) showy and bold

flame /fleɪm/ n [C;U] 1 (tongue of) burning gas 2 **in flames** burning — see also OLD FLAME ♦ v 1 vi burn brightly 2 vi break out with sudden violence: (fig.) in a flaming temper 3 vt send (someone) an angry EMAIL message

flam·ma·ble /ˈflæməbəl/ also **inflamma-ble** /ɪnˈflæm-/ — *adj* easily set on fire and quick to burn

flank /flæŋk/ *n* side of an animal, person, or moving army ♦ *vt* be placed beside

flan·nel /ˈflænl/ *n* [U] soft loosely woven cloth

flap /flæp/ *n* 1 [C] flat part of anything that covers an opening 2 [S] sound of flapping ♦ *vi/t* 1 wave slowly up and down: *flap its wings* 2 get excited and anxious

flap·jack /ˈflæpˌdʒæk/ *n* thin round cake cooked in a pan

flare¹ /fleər/ *vi* burn brightly but in an unsteady way ♦ *n* 1 [S] flaring light 2 [C] bright light used as a signal

flare up *phr vi* become suddenly hotter, more violent, etc. **flare-up** /ˈ-ˌ-/ *n*

flare² *vi/t* widen towards the bottom: *flared skirt* **flare** *n*

flash¹ /flæʃ/ *vi* 1 *vi/t* shine for a moment 2 *vi* move very fast 3 *vt* send by radio, etc.: *flash news to L.A.*

flash² *n* 1 sudden bright light: (fig.) *a flash of inspiration* 2 short news report 3 FLASHLIGHT (1) 4 **in a flash** at once ♦ *adj* 1 sudden: *flash flood* 2 modern and expensive in appearance **~y** *adj* unpleasantly big, bright, etc.

flash·back /ˈflæʃbæk/ *n* [C;U] scene in a film, etc., that goes back in time

flash·light /ˈflæʃlaɪt/ *n* 1 small electric light carried in the hand 2 apparatus for taking photographs in the dark

flask /flæsk/ *n* flat bottle for carrying drinks in one's pocket

flat¹ /flæt/ *n* 1 low level plain 2 flat part or side (of) 3 (in music) flat note 4 flat piece of stage scenery 5 a flat tire

flat² *adj* -tt- 1 smooth and level 2 spread out fully: *lie down flat* 3 not very thick: *flat cakes* 4 (of a tire) without enough air in it 5 (of beer, etc.) having lost its gas 6 dull and lifeless 7 (in music) below the right note 8 firm; with no more argument: *a flat refusal*

flat³ *adv* 1 into a flat or level position 2 below the right note: *sing flat* 3 and no more: *3 minutes flat* 4 **flat broke** with no money at all 5 **flat out** directly: *He refused her flat out.*

flat rate /ˈ-ˌ-/ *n* one charge including everything

flat·ten /ˈflætn/ *vi/t* make or become flat

flat·ter /ˈflætər/ *vt/i* 1 praise too much or insincerely 2 give pleasure to 3 (of a picture) show (a person) as more beautiful **~er** *n* **~y** *n* [U] flattering remarks

flat·u·lence /ˈflætʃələns/ *n* [U] *fml* GAS (4)

flat·ware /ˈflætˌweər/ *n* — see SILVERWARE

flaunt /flɔnt, flɑnt/ *vt derog* show for admiration: *flaunt her wealth*

fla·vor /ˈfleɪvər/ *n* 1 [C;U] taste: *6 popular flavors | not much flavor* 2 [S] particular feeling or character ♦ *vt* give taste to **~ing** *n* [C;U] something added to improve the taste **~less** *adj*

flaw /flɔ/ *n* fault or weakness **~less** *adj* **~lessly** *adv* ♦ *vt* make a flaw in

flea /fli/ *n* wingless jumping insect that feeds on blood

flea-bag /ˈflibæg/ *n* cheap, dirty hotel

flea mar·ket /ˈ-ˌ-/ *n* street market where used goods are sold

fleck /flek/ *n* small spot or grain ♦ *vt* mark with flecks

fledg·ling /ˈfledʒlɪŋ/ *n* 1 young bird learning to fly 2 inexperienced person

flee /fli/ *vi/t* fled /fled/ *fml* hurry away (from); escape

fleece /flis/ *n* sheep's woolly coat ♦ *vt* rob by a trick; charge too much

fleet /flit/ *n* 1 number of ships under one command 2 group of buses, etc., under one control

fleet·ing /ˈflitɪŋ/ *adj* not lasting long: *fleeting glimpse*

flesh /fleʃ/ *n* 1 [U] soft part of a person or animal that covers the bones 2 [U] soft part of a fruit 3 [S] the body as opposed to the soul 4 **flesh and blood a** human beings **b** one's relatives 5 **in the flesh** in real life **~y** *adj* fat

flew /flu/ *past t. of* FLY

flex /fleks/ *vt* bend or stretch (one's muscles)

flex·i·ble /ˈfleksəbəl/ *adj* 1 easily bent 2 easily changed: *flexible plans* **–bility** /ˌfleksəˈbɪləti/ *n* [U]

flick /flɪk/ *n* light sudden blow or movement ♦ *vt* touch or strike lightly

flick·er /ˈflɪkər/ *vi* 1 burn in an unsteady way 2 move backwards and forwards ♦ *n* [S] 1 flickering 2 temporary feeling: *flicker of interest*

fli·er, flyer /ˈflaɪər/ *n* 1 person (esp. a pilot) or thing that flies 2 LEAFLET

flight[1] /flaɪt/ n 1 [C;U] flying: *birds in flight* | (fig.) *His account contained some amazing flights of fancy.* 2 [C] journey by air 3 [C] aircraft making a journey: *Flight Number 347 to Geneva* 4 [C] group of birds or aircraft 5 [C] set of stairs ~**less** *adj* unable to fly

flight[2] n [C;U] (an example of) the act of running away; escape

flight attendant /'· ·ˌ··/ n person on an aircraft who serves passengers

flight deck /'· ˌ·/ n place where a pilot sits to control an airplane

flight·y /'flaɪti/ *adj* (of a person) too influenced by sudden desires or ideas

flim·sy /'flɪmzi/ *adj* light and thin; easily destroyed –**sily** *adv*

flinch /flɪntʃ/ *vi* move back in pain or fear

fling /flɪŋ/ *vt* **flung** /flʌŋ/ throw violently ♦ *n* [S] short time of enjoyment, often with no sense of responsibility

flint /flɪnt/ n 1 [C;U] hard stone that makes SPARKS (1) 2 bit of metal in a cigarette lighter that lights the gas

flip /flɪp/ 1 *vt* send spinning into the air 2 *vi* become mad or very angry ♦ *n* quick light blow

flip·pant /'flɪpənt/ *adj* disrespectful about serious subjects –**ly** *adv* –**pancy** *n* [U]

flip·per /'flɪpə/ n 1 flat limb of a SEAL[2], etc. 2 rubber shoe shaped like this, for swimming

flip side /'· ·/ n less interesting side of a record

flirt /flɜt/ *vi* behave as if sexually attracted ~*s* person who flirts ~**ation** /flə'teɪʃən/ n [C;U] ~**atious** /flə'teɪʃəs/ *adj* liking to flirt

flirt with *phr vt* 1 consider, but not seriously 2 risk, esp. needlessly or lightly

flit /flɪt/ *vi* –**tt**– fly or move quickly and lightly

float /fləʊt/ v 1 *vi/t* (cause to) stay on the surface of liquid or be held up in air 2 *vt* establish (a business) by selling STOCK 3 *vi/t* (allow to) vary in exchange value: *float the $4* suggest ♦ *n* 1 light object that floats 2 flat decorated vehicle drawn in a PARADE 3 money kept for use if an unexpected need arises ~**ing** *adj* not fixed

flock /flɒk/ n 1 group of sheep, goats, or birds 2 crowd 3 priest's congregation (CONGREGATE) ♦ *vi* move in large group

flog /flɒg/ *vt* –**gg**– 1 beat severely 2 **flog a dead horse** waste time with useless efforts

flood /flʌd/ also **floods** *pl.* — n 1 water covering a place that is usu. dry 2 large quantity: *floods of tears* ♦ *vi/t* 1 fill or cover with water 2 overflow 3 arrive in large numbers

flood·gate /'flʌdgeɪt/ n 1 gate for controlling water 2 **open the floodgates** suddenly let loose something that held back

flood·light /'flʌdlaɪt/ n powerful light thrown on the outside of buildings, etc. ♦ *vt* –**lit**/ -lɪt/ light with floodlights

floor /flɔr, floʊr/ n 1 [C] surface one stands on indoors: *dance floor* 2 [C] level of a building — see also FIRST FLOOR 3 [S] members of a body which makes laws 4 **go through the floor** *infml* (of a price) sink to a very low level 5 **take the floor**: a speak in a DEBATE b start dancing at a party, etc. ♦ *vt* 1 provide with a floor 2 knock down; defeat 3 confuse

floor·board /'flɔrbord, 'floʊrbord/ n board in a wooden floor

floor lamp /'· ·/ n lamp on a tall base which stands on the floor

flop /flɒp/ *vi* –**pp**– 1 fall awkwardly 2 fail ♦ *n* 1 [S] awkward fall 2 [C] failure ~**py** *adj* soft and loose: *floppy hat* –**piness** n [U]

flop·house /'flɒphaʊs/ n cheap hotel

flop·py disk /ˌ·· '·/ n plastic circle on which computer information is stored

flo·ra /'flɔrə, 'floʊrə/ n [U] plants of a particular area or period

flo·ral /'flɔrəl, 'floʊrəl/ *adj* of flowers

flor·id /'flɒrɪd, 'flɑrɪd/ *adj* 1 too highly decorated 2 having a red face

flor·ist /'flɒrɪst, 'flɔr-, 'flɑr-/ n person who sells flowers

floss /flɒs, flɑs/ *vi/t* clean between the teeth with DENTAL FLOSS ♦ *n* [U] DENTAL FLOSS

flo·til·la /floʊ'tɪlə, flə-/ n group of small ships

flounce /flaʊns/ *vi* move violently to express anger or attract attention

floun·der /'flaʊndə/ *vi* 1 make wild movements, esp. in water 2 lose control when speaking, etc. ♦ *n* flat fish used for food

flour /flaʊə/ n [U] powder of crushed grain, used for making bread, etc.

flour·ish /'flɜrɪʃ, 'flʌrɪʃ/ v 1 *vi* grow in a healthy manner: (fig.) *Business is flourishing.* 2 *vt* BRANDISH ♦ *n* noticeable fancy movement

flout /flaʊt/ *vt* treat (rules, etc.) without respect

flow /fləʊ/ vi (of liquid) move smoothly: (fig.) *traffic flowed past* ♦ n [S;U] steady stream or supply ~**ing** adj curving or hanging gracefully

flow chart /'· ˌ·/ n drawing showing how the parts of a process are connected

flow·er /'flaʊə/ n 1 [C] part of a plant that produces seeds 2 [S] *lit* best part: *the flower of the nation's youth* ~**less** adj ~**y** adj 1 decorated with flowers 2 (of language) FLORID (1) ♦ vi produce flowers

flow·er·bed /'flaʊəˌbɛd/ n small piece of ground where flowers are grown

flow·er·pot /'flaʊəˌpɒt/ n pot in which a plant is grown

flown /fləʊn/ v past p. of FLY

flu /flu/ also **influenza** fml — n [U] infectious disease like a bad cold but more serious

fluc·tu·ate /'flʌktʃuˌeɪt/ vi fml (of levels, etc.) change continually –**ation** /ˌflʌktʃu-'eɪʃən/ n [C;U]

flue /flu/ n pipe through which smoke or heat passes

flu·ent /'fluːənt/ adj 1 able to speak easily 2 (of speech) coming easily ~**ly** adv –**ency** n [U]

fluff /flʌf/ n [U] 1 soft light pieces from woolly material 2 soft fur or hair on a young animal or bird ♦ vt 1 shake or brush out: *fluff out its feathers* 2 do (something) badly or unsuccessfully ~**y** adv covered with fluff: *fluffy kitten* ~compare FUZZ

flu·id /'fluːɪd/ adj 1 able to flow 2 unsettled: *Our ideas on the subject are still fluid.* ♦ n [C;U] liquid

fluid ounce /ˌ· '·/ n unit for measuring liquid, ¹/₁₆ of a PINT or .0296 liter

fluke /fluːk/ n [S] piece of accidental good luck

flung /flʌŋ/ v past t. and p. of FLING

flunk /flʌŋk/ vt 1 fail (an examination, etc.) 2 GRADE as unsatisfactory someone's examination answers

  flunk out phr vi/t (cause to) leave school because of low GRADES

flunk·y, flunk·ey /'flʌŋki/ n infml someone always with an important person, treating him/her with too much respect

flu·o·res·cent /fluːˈrɛsənt, flɔ-, floʊ-/ adj giving out bright light when certain waves have passed through

flu·o·ride /'flɔraɪd, 'flʊ-/ n [U] chemical compound said to protect teeth against decay –**ridate** /'flʊrəˌdeɪt, 'flɔ-, 'floʊ-/ vt add fluoride to –**ridation** /ˌflʊrə'deɪʃən, ˌflɔ-, ˌfloʊ-/ n [U]

flur·ry /'flʌri, 'flɑri/ n 1 [C] sudden rush of rain, snow, etc. 2 [S] nervous excitement ♦ vt make nervous

flush /flʌʃ/ n 1 [C] (cleaning with) a rush of water 2 [S] redness of the face 3 [S] feeling of eager excitement ♦ v 1 vt clean with a rush of water 2 vi BLUSH 3 vt make (someone) leave a hiding place ♦ adj 1 level 2 sl having plenty of money ~**ed** adj proud and excited

flute /fluːt/ n WOODWIND musical instrument played by blowing sideways across it

flut·ist /'fluːtɪst/ n person who plays the flute

flut·ter /'flʌtə/ vi/t 1 a move (wings) quickly and lightly b fly by doing this 2 move in a quick irregular way: *flags fluttering* ♦ n 1 [S;U] fluttering or shaking movement 2 [S] state of excitement

flux /flʌks/ n [U] fml continual change

fly[1] /flaɪ/ v **flew** /flu/, **flown** /fləʊn/ 1 vi move through the air as a bird or aircraft does 2 vt control (an aircraft) 3 raise (a flag) 4 FLEE 5 vi go fast: *Time flies. | I have to fly.* (= I have to leave in a hurry) 6 **fly in the face of** DEFY 7 **fly into a rage/temper** become suddenly angry 8 **fly off the handle** infml become suddenly and unexpectedly angry 9 **let fly** attack with words, bullets or blows

fly[2] n 1 winged insect 2 hook that is made to look like a fly, used in fishing 3 **fly in the ointment** infml something that spoils the perfection of something 4 **like flies** infml in very large numbers

fly[3] /flaɪ/ n covered front opening on pants

fly-by-night /'· · ˌ·/ adj (of an organization) unable to be trusted and unlikely to exist very long

fly·er /'flaɪə/ n FLIER

flying col·ors /ˌ· '·ˌ·/ n [P] **with flying colors** very successfully; very well

flying sau·cer /ˌ· '·/ n spacecraft believed to come from another world

flying start /ˌ· '·/ n very good beginning: *We got off to a flying start.*

fly swat·ter /'· ˌ·/ n instrument for hitting and killing flies

FM n, adj abbrev. for: frequency modulation, a band of radio stations

foal /fəʊl/ n young horse

foam /fəʊm/ n [U] 1 mass of BUBBLES 2 infml FOAM RUBBER ♦ vi produce foam ~**y** adj

foam rub·ber /ˌ ˈ··/ n [U] soft rubber full of BUBBLES

fo·cus /ˈfəʊkəs/ n -**cuses** or -**ci** /-kaɪ, -saɪ/ 1 [C] point at which beams of light, etc., meet 2 [S] center of attention 3 **in/out of focus** (not) giving a clear picture because the LENS is not correctly placed ♦ vi/t -**s**- or -**ss**- 1 come or bring to a focus 2 direct (attention) **focal** adj

fod·der /ˈfɒdə/ n [U] 1 food for farm animals 2 anything that supplies a continuous demand

foe /fəʊ/ n lit enemy

fog /fɒg, fɔg/ n [C;U] (period of) thick mist ♦ vi/t -**gg**- (cause to) become covered with fog ~**gy** adj 1 misty 2 not clear: I haven't the foggiest idea.

fog·bound /ˈfɒgbaʊnd, ˈfɔg-/ adj prevented by fog from traveling

fog·horn /ˈfɒghɔːn, ˈfɔg-/ n horn used for warning ships in fog

foi·ble /ˈfɔɪbəl/ n foolish little personal habit

foil[1] /fɔɪl/ vt prevent (someone) from succeeding in a plan

foil[2] n 1 [U] thin sheet metal 2 [C] person or thing that provides a CONTRAST to another

foil[3] n thin sword for fencing (FENCE[2] (1))

foist /fɔɪst/ vt force someone to accept: He tried to foist his company on them.

fold[1] /fəʊld/ v 1 vt bend back on itself 2 vi be able to be folded: folding table 3 vt cross (the arms) 4 vi (of a business) fail 5 vi stop taking part in a game of POKER ♦ n line made by folding ~**er** n cardboard holder for papers

fold[2] n enclosure for sheep

fo·li·age /ˈfəʊliɪdʒ/ n [U] fml leaves

folk /fəʊk/ n 1 [P] people 2 [U] folk music ♦ adj of music, etc. that has grown up among ordinary people: folk singer/ concert/dancing **folks** n [P] one's relatives or parents

folk·lore /ˈfəʊklɔː, -lʊə/ n [U] beliefs long preserved among a tribe or nation

fol·low /ˈfɒləʊ/ v 1 vi/t come or go after 2 vt go along: follow the river 3 vt attend or listen to carefully 4 vi/t understand: I don't quite follow (you). 5 vt act according to: follow instructions 6 vi be a necessary result 7 **as follows** as now to be told 8 **follow suit** do what someone else has done ~**er** n someone who follows or supports ~**ing** adj 1 next: the following day 2 to be mentioned now ~**ing** n group of supporters

follow through phr vt carry out to the end

follow up phr vt take action to continue or add to the effect of something done before **follow-up** /ˈ··/ n: The paper's doing a follow-up next week.

fol·ly /ˈfɒli/ n [C;U] fml foolishness

fo·ment /fəʊˈmɛnt/ vt fml help (something bad) to develop

fond /fɒnd/ adj 1 loving 2 foolishly hopeful: fond belief 3 having a great liking or love (for) ~**ly** adv ~**ness** n [C;U]

fon·dle /ˈfɒndl/ vt touch lovingly

font /fɒnt/ n 1 container for water for BAPTISM 2 style of letters and numbers

food /fuːd/ n [C;U] 1 something, esp. solid, that creatures eat 2 **food for thought** something to think about carefully

food poi·son·ing /ˈ· ˌ···/ n [U] illness caused by eating food containing harmful BACTERIA

food pro·ces·sor /ˈ· ˌ···/ n kitchen apparatus for cutting or mixing food quickly

food stamps /ˈ· ·/ n [P] notes supplied by the government that can be exchanged for food

fool /fuːl/ n 1 silly person 2 **make a fool of oneself** behave in a silly way ♦ v 1 vt deceive 2 vi behave in a silly way 3 vi joke ~**ish** adj silly ~**ishly** adv ~**ishness** n [U]

fool·har·dy /ˈfuːlˌhɑːdi/ adj taking unwise risks

fool·proof /ˈfuːlpruːf/ adj that cannot fail

foot[1] /fʊt/ n **feet** /fiːt/ 1 [C] end part of the leg 2 [S] bottom: foot of the stairs 3 [C] (measure of length equal to) 12 inches (INCH) 4 **a foot in the door** favorable position from which to advance, gain influence, etc. 5 **on foot** walking 6 **put one's feet up** rest 7 **put one's foot down** speak firmly 8 **put one's foot in one's mouth** infml say the wrong thing 9 **set foot in/on** enter; visit ~**age** n [U] length of news or movie film ~**ing** n 1 firm placing of the feet: lose one's footing 2 position in relation to others: on an equal footing

foot² *vt* **foot the bill** *infml* pay the bill

foot·ball /'fʊt'bɔːl/ *n* **1** [U] game played between 2 teams of 11 players using an OVAL ball that can be handled or kicked **2** [C] ball used in this game

foot·bridge /'fʊt¡brɪdʒ/ *n* narrow bridge to be used only by people walking

foot·hill /'fʊt¡hɪl/ *n* low hill at the foot of a mountain

foot·hold /'fʊt¡hoʊld/ *n* **1** place where a foot can stand **2** position from which to advance

foot·lights /'fʊtlaɪts/ *n* [P] lights along the front of a stage floor

foot·loose /'fʊtluːs/ *adj* free to go wherever one wants and do what one likes: *footloose and fancy-free*

foot·note /'fʊt¡noʊt/ *n* note at the bottom of a page

foot·path /'fʊt¡pæθ/ *n* –paths /-pædz/ narrow path for walking on

foot·print /'fʊt¡prɪnt/ *n* mark made by a foot

foot·step /'fʊtstep/ *n* **1** sound of a person's step **2 follow in someone's footsteps** follow an example set by someone else in the past

foot·wear /'fʊt¡wer/ *n* [U] shoes, etc.

foot·work /'fʊt¡wɜːk/ *n* [U] use of the feet in sports, etc.

for¹ /fər, *strong* fɔr/ *prep* **1** intended to be given to, used by, or used for: *a present for you* | *cake for the party* **2** to help: *lift it for you* | *medicine for a cold* **3** (shows purpose): *What's this knife for?* **4** in support of: *play football for Miami* **5** towards: *set off for school* **6** so as to get: *wait for the bus* | *no demand for wheat* **7** (shows price or amount): *buy it for $1* **8** meaning: *Red is for danger.* **9** (shows distance or time): *stay for a week* **10** because of: *rewarded for his bravery* **11** in regard to: *an ear for music* | *good for his health* **12** considering: *tall for his age* **13** (introducing phrases): *no need for you to go*

for² *conj fml* and the reason is that

for·age /'fɒrɪdʒ, 'fɑr-/ *n* [U] food for horses and cattle ♦ *vi* search about

for·ay /'fɒreɪ, 'fɑreɪ/ *n* sudden rush into enemy country: (fig.) *his unsuccessful foray into politics*

for·bear¹ /fɔr'ber, fə-/ *vi* -bore /-'bɔr, -'boʊr/, -borne /-'bɔrn, -'boʊrn/ *fml* hold oneself back from doing something ~ance *n* [U] patient forgiveness

for·bear² /'fɔrber, 'foʊr-/ FOREBEAR

for·bid /fə'bɪd, fɔr-/ *vt* -bade /-'bæd, -'beɪd/ *or* -bad /-'bæd/, -bidden /-'bɪdn/ **1** refuse to allow **2 God forbid (that)** I very much hope it will not happen (that) ~ding *adj* looking dangerous

force /fɔrs, foʊrs/ *n* **1** [U] strength; violence **2** [C;U] influence **3** [C] power that produces change: *the force of gravity* **4** [C] group of soldiers, police, etc. — see also FORCES **5 in force** in large numbers **6 in(to) force** into/in operation **7 join forces (with)** unite (with) for a purpose ♦ *vt* **1** use (physical) force on **2** produce with effort: *forced laughter* **3** hasten the growth of (plants) **4 force someone's hand** make someone act as someone wishes or before they are ready ~ful *adj* (of people, words, etc.) powerful ~fully *adv* **forcible** *adj* done by physical force **forcibly** *adv*

for·ceps /'fɔrseps, -seps/ *n* [P] medical instrument for holding objects

ford /fɔrd, foʊrd/ *vt* cross a river without a bridge

fore /fɔr, foʊr/ *adj* front ♦ *n* **come to the fore** become well known; noticeable

fore·arm /'fɔrɑrm, 'foʊr-/ *n* arm between the hand and elbow

fore·bod·ing /fɔr'boʊdɪŋ, foʊr-/ *n* [C;U] feeling of coming evil

fore·cast /'fɔrkæst, 'foʊr-/ *vt* -cast *or* -casted say in advance (what will happen in future) ♦ *n* statement of future events: *weather forecast*

fore·close /fɔr'kloʊz, foʊr-/ *vi/t* take back property because a MORTGAGE has not been repaid

fore·fa·thers /'fɔr¡fɑðəz, 'foʊr-/ *n* [P] ANCESTORS

fore·fin·ger /'fɔr¡fɪŋgə, 'foʊr-/ *also* **index finger** — *n* finger next to the thumb

fore·front /'fɔrfrʌnt, 'foʊr-/ *n* [S] leading position

fore·go /fɔr'goʊ, foʊr-/ *vt* FORGO

foregone con·clu·sion /¡·· ·'··/ *n* result that is certain from the start

fore·ground /'fɔrgraʊnd, 'foʊr-/ *n* nearest part of a view

fore·hand /'fɔrhænd, 'foʊr-/ *n, adj* (tennis stroke) with the inner part of hand and arm turned forward

fore·head /'fɒrɪd, 'fɑrɪd, 'fɔrhed, 'fɑr-/ *n* face above the eyes

for·eign /'fɒrɪn, 'fɑrɪn/ *adj* **1** of a country that is not one's own **2** coming or brought

in from outside: *a foreign body in her eye*
3 foreign to not natural in ~**er** *n* foreign
person

foreign af·fairs /ˌ··ˈ··ˈ/ *n* [P] matters
concerning international relations and
the interests of one's own country in
foreign countries

foreign ex·change /ˌ·· ··ˈ/ *n* [U] (practice
of buying and selling) foreign money

foreign serv·ice /ˌ·· ˈ··/ *n* [U] work in
embassies (EMBASSY) abroad

fore·man /ˈfɔrmən, ˈfoʊr-/ **forewoman**
/-ˌwʊmən/ *fem.* — *n* -**men** /-mən/ **1** worker
in charge of others **2** leader of a JURY

fore·most /ˈfɔrmoʊst, ˈfoʊr-/ *adj* most
important

fo·ren·sic /fəˈrɛnsɪk, -zɪk/ *adj* used in the
law and the tracking of criminals: *foren-
sic medicine*

fore·run·ner /ˈfɔrˌrʌnə, ˈfoʊr-/ *n* person or
thing that prepares the way for another

fore·see /fɔrˈsi, foʊr-/ *vt* -**saw** /-ˈsɔ/, -**seen**
/-ˈsin/ see in advance ~**able** *adj* that can
be foreseen **2 in the foreseeable future**
soon

fore·shad·ow /fɔrˈʃædoʊ, foʊr-/ *vt* be a
sign of (what will happen)

fore·sight /ˈfɔrsaɪt, ˈfoʊr-/ *n* [U] ability to
imagine the future; wise planning

for·est /ˈfɔrɪst, ˈfar-/ *n* [C;U] **1** area
covered with trees **2 not see the forest
for the trees** miss what is clear by
looking too closely ~**er** *n* person who
works in a forest ~**ry** *n* [U] work of plant-
ing and caring for trees

fore·stall /fɔrˈstɔl, foʊr-/ *vt* prevent (a
person or plan) by acting first

forest rang·er /ˈ·· ˌ··/ *n* person who
protects or manages a public forest

fore·taste /ˈfɔrteɪst, ˈfoʊr-/ *n* [S] first
experience of something that will come
later

fore·tell /fɔrˈtɛl, foʊr-/ *vt* -**told** /-ˈtoʊld/
PROPHESY

fore·thought /ˈfɔrθɔt, ˈfoʊr-/ *n* [U] wise
planning for the future

for·ev·er /fəˈrɛvə, fɔ-/ *adv* **1** for all future
time **2** continually **3 take forever** take
an extremely long time

fore·warn /fɔrˈwɔrn, foʊr-/ *vt* warn of
coming danger

fore·went /fɔrˈwɛnt, foʊr-/ *past t. of*
FOREGO

fore·word /ˈfɔrwəd, ˈfoʊr-/ *n* short introduction to a book

for·feit /ˈfɔrfɪt/ *vt* lose as a punishment ♦
n something forfeited

for·gave /fəˈgeɪv/ *v past t. of* FORGIVE

forge¹ /fɔrdʒ, foʊrdʒ/ *vt* **1** copy in order to
deceive: *a forged passport* **2** form (metal)
by heating and hammering: (fig.) *forge a
new agreement*

forge ahead *phr vi* move with a sudden
increase of speed and power

forge² *n* place where metal is forged

forg·er /ˈfɔrdʒə, ˈfoʊr-/ *n* person who
forges papers, etc. ~**ry** /ˈfɔrdʒəri, ˈfoʊr-/ *n*
1 [U] forging of papers, etc. **2** [C] forged
paper, etc.

for·get /fəˈgɛt/ *vi/t* -**got** /-ˈgɑt/, -**gotten**
/-ˈgɑtˈn/ **1** fail to remember: *Don't forget
to lock the door.* **2** stop thinking about:
Let's just forget it. ~**ful** *adj* in the habit
of forgetting

for·give /fəˈgɪv/ *vi/t* -**gave** /-ˈgeɪv/, -**given**
/-ˈgɪvən/ stop blaming (someone for some-
thing) -**givable** *adj*: *forgivable mistake*
-**giving** *adj* willing to forgive ~**ness** *n*
[U] act of forgiving

for·go, **fore-** /fɔrˈgoʊ, foʊr-/ *vt* -**went**
/-ˈwɛnt/, -**gone** /-ˈgɔn/ *fml* go without

fork¹ /fɔrk/ *n* **1** instrument with points,
for lifting food to the mouth **2** farm or gardening tool like this **3** place where a road,
etc., divides; one of the divisions **4** main
branch of a river

fork² *v* **1** *vt* lift, etc., with a fork **2** *vi*
divide into branches ~**ed** *adj* that
divides into 2 or more points at the end

fork out *phr vi/t* pay (money) unwillingly

fork·lift¹ /ˈfɔrklɪft/ *n* small vehicle with a
movable apparatus for lifting goods

for·lorn /fəˈlɔrn, fɔr-/ *adj lit* alone and
unhappy ~**ly** *adv*

form¹ /fɔrm/ *n* **1** [C;U] shape **2** [C] plan;
kind: *forms of government* **3** [U] way in
which a work of art is put together **4** [C]
official paper with spaces for answering
questions **5** [U] degree of skill, fitness,
etc.: *to be in form* **6** [U] correct practice:
a matter of form ~**less** *adj* shapeless

form² *v* **1** *vi* begin to exist: *A cloud
formed.* **2** *vt* make from parts: *form a
committee* **3** *vt* have the shape or substance of: *The buildings form a square.*

form·al /ˈfɔrməl/ *adj* **1** suitable for official
occasions: *formal dress/language* **2**
regular in shape: *formal garden* **3** stiff
in manner and behavior ~**ly** *adv* ~**ize** *vt*

make formal ~**ity** /fɔrˈmæləti/ n **1** [U] attention to rules **2** [C] act in accordance with custom: *legal formalities*

for·mat /ˈfɔrmæt/ n size, shape, or arrangement of something ♦ vt -tt- arrange (a book, computer information, etc.) in a particular format

for·ma·tion /fɔrˈmeɪʃən/ n **1** [U] shaping of something **2** [C;U] arrangement; structure

for·ma·tive /ˈfɔrmətɪv/ adj giving shape: *a child's formative years*

for·mer /ˈfɔrmə/ adj of an earlier period: *her former husband* ♦ n fml first of **2** things mentioned —**ly** adv in earlier time

for·mi·da·ble /ˈfɔrmədəbəl, fɔrˈmɪdə-/ adj **1** large and frightening **2** hard to defeat —**bly** adv

for·mu·la /ˈfɔrmyələ/ n -**las** or -**lae** /-li/ **1** rule expressed in a short form by letters, numbers, etc.: *chemical formulae* **2** list of substances used in making something: (fig.) *a formula for trouble* **3** combination of suggestions, plans, etc.: *a peace formula* **4** milk food for very young babies

for·mu·late /ˈfɔrmyəˌleɪt/ vt **1** express exactly (a plan) —**lation** /ˌfɔrmyə-ˈleɪʃən/ n [C;U]

for·ni·cate /ˈfɔrnəˌkeɪt/ vi esp. law have sex outside marriage —**cation** /ˌfɔrnə-ˈkeɪʃən/ n [U]

for·sake /fəˈseɪk, fɔr-/ vt -**sook** /-ˈsʊk/, -**saken** /-ˈseɪkən/ lit DESERT[2] (2)

fort /fɔrt, foʊrt/ n **1** building for military defense **2 hold the fort** look after everything while someone is away

forte /fɔrt, foʊrt, ˈfɔrteɪ/ n something someone does particularly well

forth /fɔrθ, foʊrθ/ adv lit **1** forward **2 and (so on and) so forth** etc.

forth·com·ing /ˌfɔrθˈkʌmɪŋ◂, ˌfoʊrθ-/ adj **1** happening soon **2** supplied when needed: *No answer was forthcoming.* **3** ready to be helpful

forth·right /ˈfɔrθraɪt, ˈfoʊrθ-/ adj speaking plainly; direct

for·ti·eth /ˈfɔrti-ɪθ/ det, n, pron, adv 40th

for·ti·fy /ˈfɔrtəˌfaɪ/ vt **1** strengthen against attack **2** make stronger: *fortified milk* (= with VITAMINS added) —**fication** /ˌfɔrtəfəˈkeɪʃən/ n **1** [C] towers, etc., for defense **2** [U] act of fortifying

for·ti·tude /ˈfɔrtəˌtud/ n [U] uncomplaining courage

for·tress /ˈfɔrtrɪs/ n large fort

for·tu·i·tous /fɔrˈtuətəs/ adj fml accidental

for·tu·nate /ˈfɔrtʃənɪt/ adj lucky ~**ly** adv

for·tune /ˈfɔrtʃən/ n **1** [C;U] good or bad luck **2** [C] that which will happen to a person in the future: *tell someone's fortune* **3** [C] great sum of money: *diamonds worth a fortune* **4 a small fortune** a lot of money

fortune cook·ie /ˈ·· ˌ·/ n cookie served in Chinese restaurants with a piece of paper inside telling what will happen in your future

for·tune tell·er /ˈfɔrtʃən ˌtelə/ n person who claims to be able to tell people their future

for·ty /ˈfɔrti/ det, n, pron 40

for·um /ˈfɔrəm, ˈfoʊrəm/ n place for public argument

for·ward¹ /ˈfɔrwəd/ adj **1** toward the front or future **2** advanced in development **3** too bold often in sexual matters ♦ vt **1** send (letters, etc.) to a new address **2** fml send (goods) ♦ n player in BASKETBALL, etc. ~**ness** n [U] being FORWARD¹ (2, 3)

forward² also **forwards** — adv toward the front or future

for·went /fɔrˈwent, foʊr-/ past t. of FORGO

fos·sil /ˈfɑsəl/ n **1** part or print of an ancient animal or plant, preserved in rock, ice, etc. **2** old person with unchanging ideas —**ize** /-aɪz/ vi/t **1** change into a fossil **2** (cause to) become very fixed (in ideas, etc.)

fossil fuel /ˌ·· ˈ··/ n [C;U] FUEL such as gas or oil formed from plants and animals living millions of years ago

fos·ter /ˈfɑstə, ˈfɑ-/ vt fml **1** encourage to develop **2** take (a child) into one's home for a while

fought /fɔt/ v past t. and p. of FIGHT

foul¹ /faʊl/ adj **1** very unpleasant: *foul smell/language/weather* **2 fall foul of** get into trouble with ~**ly** adv

foul² n act that is against the rules

foul³ vi/t **1** make dirty **2** be guilty of a FOUL².

foul out phv v stop playing BASKETBALL, etc., because of too many fouls

foul up phr vt infml spoil (an occasion, etc.) **foul-up** /ˈ· ·/ n

foul play /ˌ· ˈ·/ n [U] **1** (in sports) unfair play **2** criminal violence, esp. murder

found[1] /faʊnd/ v past t. and p. of FIND

found[2] vt 1 establish; build 2 base: *stories founded on fact* ~**er** n person who establishes something

foun·da·tion /faʊnˈdeɪʃən/ n 1 [U] founding of an organization 2 [U] BASIS: *rumors without foundation* 3 [C] organization that gives out money **foundations** n [P] base that supports a building: (fig.) *the foundations of her success*

found·er /ˈfaʊndə/ vi lit (of a ship) fill with water and sink

foun·dry /ˈfaʊndri/ n place where metal is melted and poured into shapes

foun·tain /ˈfaʊntˈn/ n 1 decorative structure from which water springs up 2 flow of liquid

fountain pen /ˈ·· ·/ n refillable ink pen

four /fɔr, foʊr/ det, n, pron 4

four·teen /ˌfɔrˈtin◂, ˌfoʊr-/ det, n, pron 14 ~**th** det, adv, n, pron 14th

fourth /fɔrθ, foʊrθ/ det, adv, n, pron 4th

fowl /faʊl/ n **fowls** or **fowl** 1 farmyard bird, esp. a hen 2 any bird

fox /faks/ n doglike wild animal, said to be clever ♦ vt confuse; deceive

fox·y /ˈfaksi/ adj 1 like a fox (e.g. clever, etc.) 2 attractive

foy·er /ˈfɔɪə/ n entrance hall of a theater, etc.

frac·as /ˈfreɪkəs, ˈfræ-/ n fml noisy argument

frac·tion /ˈfrækʃən/ n 1 division of a whole number (e.g. ⅓) 2 small part: *a fraction of the cost* ~**al** adj so small as to be unimportant

frac·tious /ˈfrækʃəs/ adj restless and complaining

frac·ture /ˈfræktʃə/ n [C;U] fml breaking of a bone, etc. ♦ vi/t fml break

frag·ile /ˈfrædʒəl, -dʒaɪl/ adj 1 easily broken 2 having a small thin body or weak in health –**gility** /frəˈdʒɪləti/ n [U]

frag·ment[1] /ˈfrægmənt/ n piece broken off ~**ary** /ˈfrægməntəri, -mɛntɛri/ adj incomplete

frag·ment[2] /ˈfrægmɛnt, frægˈmɛnt/ vi/t break into pieces ~**ation** /ˌfrægmənˈteɪʃən, -mɛn-/ n [U]

fra·grant /ˈfreɪgrənt/ adj smelling sweet ~**ly** adv –**grance** n [C;U]

frail /freɪl/ adj weak, esp. in body ~**ty** n 1 [U] quality of being frail 2 [C] fault of character

frame /freɪm/ n 1 border into which something fits: *a window frame* 2 structure on which something is built 3 human or animal body 4 single photograph in a film 5 **frame of mind** state of mind at a particular time ♦ vt 1 put in a frame (1) 2 give shape to; express: *frame a question* 3 infml make (a guiltless person) seem guilty of a crime

frame·work /ˈfreɪmwɜrk/ n supporting structure

fran·chise /ˈfræntʃaɪz/ n 1 [S] the right to vote 2 [C] the right to sell a product

frank /fræŋk/ adj open and honest ~**ly** adv ~**ness** n [U]

frank·fur·ter /ˈfræŋkfətə/ n also **frank** red SAUSAGE; HOT DOG

fran·tic /ˈfræntɪk/ adj wildly anxious, afraid, happy, etc. ~**ally** adv

fra·ter·nal /frəˈtɜrnl/ adj BROTHERly

fra·ter·ni·ty /frəˈtɜrnəti/ n 1 [C] people joined by common interests 2 [C] university club for men 3 [U] fml brotherly feeling

frat·er·nize /ˈfrætərnaɪz/ vi meet and be friendly (with someone) –**nization** /ˌfrætərnaˈzeɪʃən/ n [U]

fraud /frɔd/ n 1 [C;U] criminal deceit to make money 2 [C] person who falsely claims to be something

fraud·u·lent /ˈfrɔdʒələnt/ adj deceitful; got or done by fraud ~**ly** adv

fraught /frɔt/ adj 1 full of: *fraught with danger* 2 infml **a** (of a person) worried **b** (of conditions) difficult

fray[1] /freɪ/ vi/t develop loose threads by rubbing: *frayed collar* | (fig.) *frayed nerves*

fray[2] n [S] lit battle

freak /frik/ n 1 strange unnatural creature or event 2 person who takes a special interest in the stated thing: *a film freak* ~**ish** adj unreasonable; unusual

freck·le /ˈfrɛkəl/ n small brown spot on the skin **freckled** adj

free /fri/ adj 1 able to act as one wants; not in prison or controlled by rules: *free speech* | *You are free to go.* 2 not busy or being used: *Is this seat free?* | *free time* 3 without payment: *free tickets* 4 (of a way or passage) not blocked 5 not fixed; loose 6 **free and easy** unworried 7 **free from/of** untroubled by; without: *free from dirt* | *tax free* 8 **free with** ready to give ♦ adv 1 without payment 2 without control 3 in a loose position ♦ vt **freed** /frid/ set free ~**ly** adv 1 readily; openly 2 in great amounts

free-base /ˈ· ˌ/ *vi sl* smoke a specially prepared mixture of COCAINE

free-bie /ˈfribi/ *n infml* something that is given or received without payment

free-dom /ˈfridəm/ *n* [U] **1** state of being free **2** [*the*+S] certain rights, often given as a favor: *freedom to use the car*

freedom of speech /ˌ·· · ˈ·/ *n* [U] FREE SPEECH

free en-ter-prise /ˌ· ˈ···/ *n* [U] social system in which private trade, business, etc., is carried on without much government control

free-for-all /ˈ· · ˌ/ *n* argument, etc., in which many people join

free-hand /ˈfrihænd/ *adj, adv* drawn without instruments

free-lance /ˈfrilæns/ *adj, adv, n* (done by) a writer, etc., who works for many employers **freelance** *vi* **-lancer** *n*

free-load /ˈfrilod/ *vi* live on another person's money ~**er** *n*

free speech /ˌ· ˈ·/ *n* [U] right to express one's ideas in public

free trade /ˌ· ˈ·/ *n* [U] system of allowing foreign goods freely into a country

free verse /ˌ· ˈ·/ *n* [U] poetry that does not follow the usual rules

free-way /ˈfriweɪ/ *n* EXPRESSWAY

free will /ˌ· ˈ·/ *n* [U] **1** ability to decide freely what to do **2** belief that human effort can influence events, and they are not fixed in advance by God

freeze /friz/ *v* **froze** /frooz/, **frozen** /ˈfroozən/ **1** *vi/t* harden into ice **2** *vi* (of weather) be at the temperature at which ice forms **3** *vi/t* stop working properly because of cold **4** *vi* feel very cold **5** *vt* preserve (food) at low temperatures **6** *vi/t* stop moving **7** *vt* fix (prices, wages, etc.) ♦ *n* [U] **1** period of freezing weather **2** fixing of prices or wages ~**er** *n* machine that freezes food

freeze out *phr vt infml* prevent from being included

freeze over *phr vi/t* (cause to) turn to ice on the surface

freight /freɪt/ *n* [U] goods carried by ship, plane, etc. ~**er** *n* ship or plane that carries goods

French fries /ˈfrentʃ fraɪz/ *n* [P] thin pieces of potato cooked in hot oil

fre-net-ic /frəˈnɛtɪk/ *adj* too excited; feverish

fren-zy /ˈfrenzi/ *n* [S;U] violent excitement

fre-quen-cy /ˈfrikwənsi/ *n* **1** [U] the happening of something a large number of times **2** [C;U] rate at which something happens or is repeated **3** [C] particular number of radio waves per second

fre-quent[1] /ˈfrikwənt/ *adj* happening often ~**ly** *adv*

fre-quent[2] /friˈkwɛnt, ˈfrikwənt/ *vt fml* go to (a place) often .

fresh /frɛʃ/ *adj* **1** recently made, found, etc.; not STALE: *fresh flowers* **2** (of food) not frozen or canned **3** (of water) not salt **4** new and different: *Make a fresh start.* **5 a** (of wind) fairly strong **b** (of weather) cool and windy **6** not tired **7** too bold with someone of the opposite sex ♦ *adv* **1** just; newly **2 fresh out of** *infml*, having just used up one's supplies of ~**ly** *adv* ~**ness** *n* [U]

fresh-en /ˈfrɛʃən/ *vi/t* **1** make or become fresh **2** (of wind) become stronger

freshen up *phr vi/t* **1** (cause to) feel less tired, look more attractive, etc. **2** (of a drink) add more liquid, esp. alcohol, to it

fresh-man /ˈfrɛʃmən/ *n* **-men** /-mən/ student in the first year at high school, college or university

fresh-wa-ter /ˈfrɛʃˌwɔtə, ˌˈwɑtə/ *adj* of a river or lake, not the sea

fret /frɛt/ *vi/t* **-tt-** worry about small things ~**ful** *adj* anxious and complaining ~**fully** *adv*

fri-ar /ˈfraɪə/ *n* man belonging to a Christian religious group

fric-tion /ˈfrɪkʃən/ *n* [U] **1** rubbing of one surface against another **2** disagreement within a group

Fri-day /ˈfraɪdi, -deɪ/ *n* the 6th day of the week, between Thursday and Saturday — see also GOOD FRIDAY

fridge /frɪdʒ/ *n infml* REFRIGERATOR

friend /frɛnd/ *n* **1** person whom one likes but who is not related **2** helper; supporter **3 make friends** form a friendship ~**less** *adj* without friends ~**ly** *adj* **1** acting as a friend **2** not causing unpleasant feelings in competitions, etc.: *a friendly game* ~**liness** *n* [U] ~**ship** *n* [C;U] friendly relationship

fries /fraɪz/ *n* see FRENCH FRIES

frig-ate /ˈfrɪgɪt/ *n* small fast fighting ship

fright /fraɪt/ *n* [C;U] feeling of fear

fright·en /ˈfraɪtᵊn/ vt fill with fear **~ed** adj **~ingly** adv

fri·gid /ˈfrɪdʒɪd/ adj **1** (of a woman) disliking sex **2** very cold **~ly** adv **–gidity** /frɪˈdʒɪdəti/ n [U]

frill /frɪl/ n **1** decorative wavy edge on cloth **2** unnecessary decoration **~y** adj

fringe /frɪndʒ/ n **1** decorative edge of hanging threads on a curtain, etc. **2** edge: the fringe(s) of the crowd **3** not official; not CONVENTIONAL: fringe politics ♦ vt be the border of

fringe ben·e·fit /ˈ· ˌ···/ n something given with a job, besides wages

frisk /frɪsk/ v **1** vi jump about playfully **2** vt search (someone) with the hands, for hidden weapons **~y** adj joyfully playful

frit·ter[1] /ˈfrɪtə/ n piece of cooked BATTER[2] with fruit, meat, etc., inside

fritter[2] v **fritter away** phr vt waste: He fritters away his money.

fri·vol·i·ty /frɪˈvɒləti/ n **1** [U] quality of being frivolous **2** [C] frivolous act or remark

friv·o·lous /ˈfrɪvələs/ adj not serious enough; silly **~ly** adv

frizz·y /ˈfrɪzi/ adj (of hair) very curly, like wool

fro /frəʊ/ adv — see TO AND FRO

frog /frɒg, frag/ n **1** small jumping creature that lives on land and in water **2 a frog in the/one's throat** difficulty in speaking because of roughness in the throat or emotion

frol·ic /ˈfrɒlɪk/ vi **-ck-** jump about happily **frolic** n **~some** adj playful

from /frəm; strong frʌm, fram/ prep **1** starting at (a place or time): fly from New York to Paris | work from Monday till Friday **2** given or sent by: a letter from John **3** away: subtract 10 from 15 **4** using: Bread is made from flour. **5** because of: suffer from heart disease **6** out of: He took a knife from his pocket. **7** in a state of protection or prevention with regard to: She saved the child from drowning. **8** judging by: From what John tells me, they're very rich.

frond /frɒnd/ n leaf of a FERN or PALM[1]

front /frʌnt/ n **1** [C] part in the direction that something moves or faces: the front of the aircraft/of the house | his front teeth **2** [C] line where fighting takes place in war **3** [the+S] road beside the sea in a tourist town **4** [C] line dividing cold from warmer air **5** [C] (often false) outward appearance: present a smiling front **6** [C] combined effort or movement against opposing forces: present a united front **7** [C] particular area of activity: They have made little progress on the jobs front. **8** [C] infml person, group or thing used for hiding the real nature of a secret or unlawful activity: front for a gang of car thieves **9 in front: a** ahead **b** in the most forward position **10 in front of: a** ahead of **b** in the presence of **11 up front** infml as payment in advance ♦ vi/t face (towards): The hotel fronts onto the lake. **~al** adj at, of, or from the front

front·age /ˈfrʌntɪdʒ/ n front width of a building or piece of land

fron·tier /frʌnˈtɪə/ n **1** edge of a country **2** part of a country that marks furthest point where people have settled **frontiers** n [P] furthest limit: the frontiers of knowledge

front line /ˌ· ˈ·◂/ n [S] **1** military FRONT (2) **2** most advanced position **front-line** adj

front man /ˈ· ·/ n someone who explains the views or future plans of esp. a large company to the public

front-page /ˌ· ˈ·◂/ adj very interesting; worthy of being on the front page of a newspaper: front-page news

front room /ˌ· ˈ·/ n LIVING ROOM

front-run·ner /ˌ· ˈ·◂/ n person who has the best chance of success in competing for something

frost /frɒst/ n **1** [U] white powder that forms on things below freezing point **2** [C;U] (period of) freezing weather ♦ v **1** vi/t (cause to) become covered with frost **2** vt **a** roughen the surface of (glass) **b** cover with frosting **~y** adj **1** very cold **2** unfriendly: a frosty greeting

frost·bite /ˈfrɒstbaɪt/ n [U] harmful swelling, etc., of the limbs, caused by cold **–bitten** /ˈfrɒstˌbɪtᵊn/ adj

frosting /ˈfrɒstɪŋ/ n mixture of powdery sugar with liquid, used to decorate cakes

froth /frɒθ/ n [U] **1** mass of small BUBBLES on beer, etc. **2** derog light empty show of talk or ideas ♦ vi produce froth **~y** adj covered with froth

frown /fraʊn/ vi draw the EYEBROWS together in anger or effort **frown** n

froze /frəʊz/ v past t. of FREEZE

fro·zen /ˈfrəʊzᵊn/ v past p. of FREEZE

fru·gal /ˈfruːgəl/ adj **1** not wasteful **2** small and cheap: frugal supper

fruit /frut/ n **1** [C;U] part of a plant containing the seed, often eatable **2** [C] also **fruits** pl. result or reward **3** male HOMOSEXUAL ♦ vi bear fruit ~**ful** adj useful; successful ~**fully** adv ~**less** adj unsuccessful ~**lessly** adv ~**y** adj **1** like fruit **2** (of a voice) rich and deep **3** crazy

fruit·cake /ˈfrutˌkeɪk/ n **1** [C;U] cake containing small dried fruits, nuts, etc. **2** [C] infml a crazy, silly person **3 as nutty as a fruitcake** completely crazy

fru·i·tion /fruˈɪʃən/ n [U] fml fulfillment of plans, etc.

frump·y /ˈfrʌmpi/ adj (of a woman) unattractive and wearing old-fashioned clothes

frus·trate /ˈfrʌstreɪt/ vt **1** disappoint and annoy **2** prevent the fulfillment of (plans) –**tration** /frʌˈstreɪʃən/ n [C;U]

fry /fraɪ/ vi/t cook in hot fat or oil **fry** n see FRENCH FRIES, SMALL FRY

frying pan /ˈ·· ·/ n **1** flat pan for frying **2 out of the frying pan into the fire** out of a bad position into an even worse one

ft. written abbrev. for: FOOT¹ (3)

fuck /fʌk/ vi/t taboo have sex (with) ♦ n taboo sl **1** act of having sex **2 not give a fuck** not care at all

    fuck off phr vi taboo sl go away
    fuck over phr vt taboo sl treat badly
    fuck up phr vt taboo sl spoil; ruin ♦
    fuck-up /ˈ· ·/ n

fudge¹ /fʌdʒ/ n [U] creamy brown candy made of sugar, milk, butter, etc.

fudge² v **1** vt put together roughly and dishonestly **2** vi/t avoid taking firm action (on)

fu·el /ˈfyuəl/ n [C;U] material (e.g. coal) that produces heat or power ♦ v -**l**- **1** vt provide with fuel **2** vt take in fuel

fu·gi·tive /ˈfyudʒətɪv/ n person escaping from something

ful·crum /ˈfʊlkrəm, ˈfʌl-/ n -**crums** or -**cra** /-krə/ point on which a LEVER turns

ful·fill /fʊlˈfɪl/ vt **1** perform (a promise, duty, etc.) **2** develop fully the character and abilities of (oneself) ~**ment** n [U]

full /fʊl/ adj **1** holding as much or as many as possible: full bottle/bus **2** well fed **3** complete: your full name **4** highest possible: full speed **5** (of a garment) loose: full skirt **6** rounded; PLUMP **7 full of** thinking only of ♦ n **1 in full** completely **2 to the full** thoroughly ♦ adv **1** straight; directly: The sun shone full on her face. **2** very: They knew full well he

wouldn't keep his promise. ~**ly** adv **1** least: It's fully an hour since he left. **2** completely ~**ness**, **fulness** n [U]

full-blown /ˌ· ˈ·◄/ adj **1** (of a flower) completely open **2** fully developed: a full-blown war

full-fledged /ˌfʊl ˈflɛdʒd◄/ adj **1** (of a bird) having grown all its feathers **2** completely trained

full-grown /ˌ· ˈ·◄/ adj completely developed

full-length /ˌ· ˈ·◄/ adj **1** (of a painting, etc.) showing someone from head to foot **2** not shorter than usual

full moon /ˌ· ˈ·/ n the moon when seen as a circle

full-scale /ˌ· ˈ·◄/ adj **1** (of a model, etc.) as big as the object represented **2** (of an activity) not lessened: full-scale war

full-time /ˌ· ˈ·◄/ adj working or studying all the usual hours

fum·ble /ˈfʌmbəl/ vi **1** use the hands awkwardly **2** vi/t drop (a football) ♦ n

fume /fyum/ vi show great anger

fumes /fyumz/ n [P] gas or smoke with a strong smell

fu·mi·gate /ˈfyuməˌgeɪt/ vt disinfect by means of smoke or gas

fun /fʌn/ n [U] **1** playfulness **2** (cause of) amusement; enjoyment **3 for fun** also **for the fun of it** — for pleasure **4 in fun** not seriously **5 make fun of** laugh unkindly at

func·tion /ˈfʌŋkʃən/ n **1** natural purpose of something or someone **2** important social gathering ♦ vi be in action; work ~**al** adj **1** made for use, not decoration **2** functioning

fund /fʌnd/ n supply of money for a purpose ♦ vt provide money for

fun·da·men·tal /ˌfʌndəˈmɛntəl◄/ adj central; very important: fundamental difference ♦ n important rule ~**ly** adv ~**ism** n [U] belief in the exact truth of the Bible ~**ist** n, adj

fu·ne·ral /ˈfyunərəl/ n ceremony of burying or burning a dead person

funeral par·lor /ˈ··· ˌ·/ n — see MORTUARY

fun·gus /ˈfʌŋgəs/ n -**gi** /-dʒaɪ, -gaɪ/ or -**guses** [C;U] leafless plant that grows on wood, etc.

funk·y /ˈfʌŋki/ adj infml (of JAZZ or similar music) having a simple direct style and feeling

fun·nel /ˈfʌnl/ n tube with a wide mouth for pouring liquids through ♦ vi/t -l- pass (as if) through a FUNNEL (1)

fun·ny /ˈfʌni/ adj 1 amusing 2 strange –**nily** adv

funny bone /ˈ·· ·/ also **crazy bone** — n tender part of the elbow

fur /fɜː/ n 1 [U] soft thick hair of a cat, rabbit, etc. 2 [C] (garment made of) the skin of an animal and the attached fur ~**ry** adj

fu·ri·ous /ˈfyʊəriəs/ adj 1 very angry 2 wild; uncontrolled –**ly** adv

fur·long /ˈfɜːlɔŋ/ n a measure of length equal to 220 yards (201 meters)

fur·nace /ˈfɜːnɪs/ n 1 enclosed space where metals, etc., are heated 2 enclosed fire to heat a house

fur·nish /ˈfɜːnɪʃ/ vt 1 put furniture in 2 fml supply ~**ings** n [P] furniture, etc., for a room

fur·ni·ture /ˈfɜːnɪtʃə/ n [U] beds, chairs, etc.

fu·ror /ˈfyʊərɔːr/ n [S] sudden burst of public interest

fur·row /ˈfɜːoʊ, ˈfʌroʊ/ n 1 track cut by a PLOW 2 WRINKLE ♦ vt make furrows in

fur·ther /ˈfɜːðə/ adv, adj 1 (comparative of FAR) at or to a greater distance or more distant point: too tired to walk any further 2 more: any further questions 3 **further to** continuing the subject of 4 **go further** give, do, or say more ♦ vt help to advance ~**ance** n [U] fml advancement ~**most** adj farthest

fur·ther·more /ˈfɜːðəˌmɔːr, -ˌmoʊr/ adv fml also

fur·thest /ˈfɜːðɪst/ adv, adj (superlative of FAR) at or to the greatest distance or degree

fur·tive /ˈfɜːtɪv/ adj trying to escape notice ~**ly** adv ~**ness** n [U]

fu·ry /ˈfyʊəri/ n 1 [S;U] great anger 2 [U] wild force

fuse¹ /fyuːz/ n wire that melts to break an electric connection ♦ vi/t 1 join by melting 2 stop working because a fuse has melted

fuse² n 1 pipe, etc., that carries fire to an explosive article 2 part of a bomb, etc., that makes it explode

fu·se·lage /ˈfyuːsəˌlɑːʒ, -lɪdʒ, -zə-/ n body of an aircraft

fu·sion /ˈfyuːʒən/ n [C;U] join together by melting: (fig.) a fusion of different styles of music

fuss /fʌs/ n [S;U] 1 unnecessary show of excitement or annoyance 2 **make a fuss of** pay loving attention to ♦ vi show unnecessary anxiety ~**y** adj 1 too concerned about details 2 (of dress, etc.) too highly decorated

fu·tile /ˈfyuːtl, -taɪl/ adj unsuccessful; useless: futile attempts **futility** /fyuːˈtɪləti/ n [U]

fu·ton /ˈfuːtɑːn/ n soft flat MATTRESS for use as a bed, or folded as a chair

fu·ture /ˈfyuːtʃə/ n 1 [S] time after the present: in the future 2 [C] what will happen to someone or something: an uncertain future 3 [U] likelihood of success 4 **in the future** from now on **future** adj: his future wife | the future tense

fu·tur·is·tic /ˌfyuːtʃəˈrɪstɪk/ adj of strange modern appearance

fuzz /fʌz/ n [U] FLUFF ~**y** adj 1 (of hair) standing up in a light short mass 2 not clear in shape 3 (of cloth, etc.) having a raised soft hairy surface –**ily** adv –**iness** n [U]

FYI abbrev. for: for your information

G

G, g /dʒiː/ the 7th letter of the English alphabet

g *written abbrev. for*: GRAM(s)

gab /gæb/ *vi* talk informally ♦ *n* — see **the gift of the gab** (GIFT)

ga·ble /ˈgeɪbəl/ *n* top of a wall with 3 corners, between sloping roofs

gad·get /ˈgædʒɪt/ *n* small useful machine or tool **~ry** *n* [U] gadgets

gaffe /gæf/ *n* social mistake

gag /gæg/ *n* **1** something put over someone's mouth to stop them from talking **2** joke ♦ *vt* **-gg-** put a GAG(1) on **gag on** *phr v* fail to swallow

gag·gle /ˈgægəl/ *n* [S] **1** group of GEESE **2** group of noisy people: *gaggle of reporters*

gai·e·ty /ˈgeɪəti/ *n* [U] cheerfulness

gai·ly /ˈgeɪli/ *adv* cheerfully

gain¹ /geɪn/ *v* **1** *vi/t* obtain (something useful) **2** *vi* (of a clock) go too fast **3** *vt fml* reach (a place) with effort

gain on *phr vt* get close to (someone ahead in a race)

gain² *n* [C;U] increase in wealth or amount **~ful** *adj* paid for: *gainful employment* **~fully** *adv*

gait /geɪt/ *n* way of walking

gal /gæl/ *n infml* woman

ga·la /ˈgɑːlə, ˈgeɪlə, ˈgælə/ *n* special public entertainment

gal·ax·y /ˈgæləksi/ *n* large group of stars **–actic** /gəˈlæktɪk/ *adj*

gale /geɪl/ *n* **1** strong wind **2** noisy burst of laughter, etc.

gall¹ /gɒl/ *n* [U] daring rudeness

gall² *vt* cause to feel annoyed disappointment or anger

gall blad·der /ˈ·ˌ·/ *n* baglike organ in which BILE is stored

gal·le·ry /ˈgæləri/ *n* **1** place where works of art are shown **2** upper floor of a hall or church **3** passage in a mine **4** top floor in a theater

gal·ley /ˈgæli/ *n* **1** ancient ship rowed by slaves **2** ship's kitchen

gal·lon /ˈgælən/ *n* (a measure for liquids equal to) 231 CUBIC inches or 4 QUARTS

gal·lop /ˈgæləp/ *n* [S] movement of a horse at its fastest speed **gallop** *vi/t*

gal·lows /ˈgæloʊz/ *n* **gallows** wooden frame on which criminals were once killed by hanging

gall·stone /ˈgɒlstoʊn/ *n* hard stone or grain that forms in the GALL BLADDER

ga·lore /gəˈlɔːr, gəˈloʊr/ *adj* in plenty: *bargains galore*

gal·va·nize /ˈgælvənaɪz/ *vt* **1** cover (another metal) with ZINC **2** shock into action

gam·ble /ˈgæmbəl/ *v* **1** *vi/t* BET (1) **2** *vi* take a risk ♦ *n* [S] risky matter **–bler** *n*

game /geɪm/ *n* **1** [C] form of play or sport **2** [C] single part of a match in tennis, etc. **3** [U] wild animals and birds hunted for food and sport **4** [C] *infml* secret trick: *give the game away* (= let a secret plan be known) **5** [C] *infml* profession or activity: *the advertising game* — see also BIG GAME, FAIR GAME ♦ *adj* brave and willing **–ly** *adv* **games** *n* [P] sport competitions

game show /ˈ· ˌ·/ *n* television program in which people play games or answer questions to win prizes or money

game war·den /ˈ· ˌ·/ *n* person in charge of public land and wild animals there

gam·ut /ˈgæmət/ *n* [S] whole range of a subject

gan·der /ˈgændə/ *n* male GOOSE

gang¹ /gæŋ/ *n* **1** group of people working together, esp. criminals **2** group of friends

gang² *v* **gang up** *phr vi* work together (against someone); CONSPIRE

gang·plank /ˈgæŋplæŋk/ *n* movable bridge for getting into or out of a ship

gan·grene /ˈgæŋgriːn, gæŋˈgriːn/ *n* [U] decay of a body part because blood has stopped flowing there **–grenous** /-grənəs/ *adj*

gang·ster /ˈgæŋstə/ *n* member of a criminal GANG (1)

gang·way /ˈgæŋweɪ/ *n* large gangplank ♦ *interj* (said to make people clear a path)

gap /gæp/ *n* empty space between 2 things: (fig.) *gaps in my knowledge*

gape /geɪp/ *vi* **1** look hard in surprise **2** come apart: *gaping hole*

gar·age /gəˈrɑːʒ, gəˈrɑːdʒ/ *n* **1** building in which motor vehicles are kept **2** place that repairs them, and sells gas and oil

garage sale /ˈ· ·/ n sale of personal belongings from a family's garage

gar·bage /ˈgɑrbɪdʒ/ n [U] **1** waste material to be thrown away **2** nonsense

garbage can /ˈ·· ·/ n container for waste materials

garbage dis·pos·al /ˈ·· ··/ n apparatus under a kitchen SINK that cuts food waste into small pieces

garbage man /ˈ·· ·/ n person employed to empty garbage cans

garbage truck /ˈ·· ·/ n vehicle that collects the contents of garbage cans

gar·den /ˈgɑrdn/ n **1** piece of land for growing flowers and vegetables **2** also **gardens** pl. — public park ♦ vi work in a garden ~**er** n

gar·gan·tu·an /gɑrˈgæntʃuən/ adj extremely large

gar·gle /ˈgɑrgəl/ vi wash the throat by blowing through liquid

gar·goyle /ˈgɑrgɔɪl/ n figure of an ugly creature on a church roof, etc.

gar·ish /ˈgɛrɪʃ, ˈgærɪʃ/ adj unpleasantly bright ~**ly** adv

gar·land /ˈgɑrlənd/ n circle of flowers for decoration ♦ vt put garlands on

gar·lic /ˈgɑrlɪk/ n [U] plant like an onion, used in cooking

gar·ment /ˈgɑrmənt/ n fml piece of clothing

gar·net /ˈgɑrnɪt/ n red jewel

gar·nish /ˈgɑrnɪʃ/ vt decorate (food) ♦ n something used to garnish

gar·ret /ˈgærɪt/ n lit small usu. unpleasant room at the top of a house

gar·ri·son /ˈgærəsən/ n **1** soldiers living in a town or fort **2** fort or camp where such soldiers live ♦ vt (send a group of soldiers to) guard (a place)

gar·ter /ˈgɑrtə/ n elastic band to keep a STOCKING up

garter snake /ˈ·· ·/ n small harmless snake

gas /gæs/ n -s- or -ss- **1** [C;U] substance like air **2** [U] substance used for heating, cooking, etc. **3** [U] liquid obtained from PETROLEUM and used for producing power in engines **4** [U] (condition of having) gas in the stomach ♦ v **1** vt kill with gas **2** vi infml talk a long time ~**eous** /ˈgæsiəs, ˈgæʃəs/ adj of or like gas

  gas up phr vi fill a vehicle with gas

gash /gæʃ/ vt, n (wound with) a long deep cut

gas·ket /ˈgæskɪt/ n flat piece of material placed between surfaces to prevent oil, etc., from escaping

gas mask /ˈ· ·/ n breathing equipment that protects the wearer against poisonous gas

gas·o·line /ˌgæsəˈlin, ˈgæsəˌlin/ n [U] GAS (3)

gasp /gæsp/ v **1** vi breathe quickly and with effort **2** vt say while gasping **gasp** n

gas sta·tion /ˈ· ··/ n place that sells gas and oil and may also do repairs

gas tank /ˈ· ·/ n container inside a car that holds gas (3)

gas·tric /ˈgæstrɪk/ adj of the stomach: gastric juices

gas·tro·nom·ic /ˌgæstrəˈnɑmɪk/ adj related to good food: gastronomic delights of the city

gate /geɪt/ n **1** frame closing an opening in a wall, fence, etc. **2** way in or out at an airport **3** (money paid by) the number of people attending a match, etc.

gate·crash /ˈgeɪtˌkræʃ/ vi/t go to (a party, public event, etc.) uninvited or without a ticket ~**er** n

gate·way /ˈgeɪtˌweɪ/ n **1** [C] opening for a gate **2** [S] way of finding: the gateway to success

gath·er /ˈgæðə/ v **1** vi/t come or bring together **2** vt obtain gradually: gather facts/speed **3** vt collect (flowers, crops, etc.) **4** vt understand: I gather she's ill. **5** vt draw (cloth) into small folds: gathered skirt ~**ing** n meeting

gauche /gouʃ/ adj socially awkward

gau·dy /ˈgɔdi/ adj too bright; too highly decorated –**dily** adv

gauge /geɪdʒ/ n **1** instrument for measuring **2** thickness or width of e.g. a gun barrel **3** distance between the RAILS of a railway ♦ vt **1** measure **2** make a judgment about

gaunt /gɔnt, gɑnt/ adj **1** thin, as if ill or hungry **2** (of a place) bare and unattractive ~**ness** n [U]

gaunt·let /ˈgɔntˈlɪt, ˈgɑntˈ-/ n long GLOVE protecting the wrist

gauze /gɔz/ n [U] thin net-like cloth

gave /geɪv/ v past t. of GIVE

gav·el /ˈgævəl/ n small hammer used by a chairman, etc., to get attention

gawk /gɔk/ vi look at something in a foolish way

gaw·ky /ˈgɔːki/ adj awkward in movement –**kiness** n [U]

gay /geɪ/ adj 1 HOMOSEXUAL 2 bright: gay colors 3 cheerful ♦ n GAY (1) person

gaze /geɪz/ vi look steadily ♦ n [S] steady fixed look

ga·ze·bo /gəˈziːbou/ n small outdoor shelter in a park or yard

ga·zelle /gəˈzel/ n small deerlike animal that runs quickly

GDP n [the+S] Gross Domestic Product; the total value of everything produced in a country, usu. in a single year, except for income received from abroad

gear¹ /gɪr/ n 1 [C;U] set of toothed wheels in a machine 2 [U] equipment: football gear 3 [U] apparatus of wheels, etc.: the landing gear of an aircraft

gear² v

gear to phr vt allow (an activity or action) to be influenced by (a particular fact): education geared to the needs of industry

gear up phr vt infml put (esp. oneself) into a state of excited or anxious expectation

gear·box /ˈgɪrbɑks/ n case containing the gears of a vehicle

gear shift /ˈ·ˌ·/ n rod that controls the gears of a vehicle

GED n General Equivalency Diploma; official qualification that people who did not finish high school can study for

geek /giːk/ n sl boring unfashionable person –**y** adj

geese /giːs/ n pl. of GOOSE

Gei·ger count·er /ˈgaɪgə ˌkaʊntə/ n instrument that measures RADIOACTIVITY

gei·sha /ˈgeɪʃə, ˈgiːʃə/ n Japanese woman trained to dance, play music, and entertain men

gel¹ /dʒel/ n [C;U] thick wet substance used in beauty and cleaning products

gel² v -l- 1 (of liquid) become thicker 2 (of idea, plan, etc.) become more definite

gel·a·tin /ˈdʒelətən, -lətˈn/ n [U] soft material used in making food and medicine

gem /dʒem/ n 1 jewel 2 very valuable thing or person

Gem·i·ni /ˈdʒeməˌnaɪ/ n 1 [S] 3rd sign of the ZODIAC, represented by TWINS 2 someone born between May 21 and June 21

gen·der /ˈdʒendə/ n [C;U] 1 (in grammar) (division into) MASCULINE, FEMININE, or NEUTER 2 division into male and female; sex

gene /dʒiːn/ n material in a cell controlling HEREDITY

ge·ne·al·o·gy /ˌdʒiːniˈɑlədʒi, -ˈæl-, ˌdʒɛ-/ n [C;U] (study of) the history of a family, often shown in a drawing like a tree –**gical** /ˌdʒiːniəˈlɑdʒɪkəl, ˌdʒɛ-/ adj

gen·e·ral /ˈdʒenərəl/ adj 1 concerning all: the general feeling 2 not detailed: a general idea 3 (in titles) chief: Attorney General ♦ n 1 army or airforce officer of very high rank 2 **in general** usually ~ly adv 1 usually 2 by most people 3 without considering details –**rality** /ˌdʒenəˈræləti/ n 1 [C] general statement 2 [U] being general

gen·e·ral·ize /ˈdʒenərəˌlaɪz/ vi make a general statement –**ization** /ˌdʒenərələˈzeɪʃən/ n [C;U] (statement formed by) generalizing

gen·e·rate /ˈdʒenəˌreɪt/ vt produce: generate heat –**rator** n machine that generates esp. electricity –**rative** /ˈdʒenərətɪv/ adj able to produce

gen·e·ra·tion /ˌdʒenəˈreɪʃən/ n 1 [C] length of time in which a child grows up and has children 2 [C] people of about the same age 3 [U] act of generating

generation gap /ˌ···ˈ·ˌ·/ n [the+S] lack of understanding between GENERATIONS (2) because of different attitudes

ge·ner·ic /dʒəˈnerɪk/ adj not having a TRADEMARK (1) ~**ally** adv

gen·e·ros·i·ty /ˌdʒenəˈrɑsəti/ n 1 [U] quality of being generous 2 [C] generous act

gen·e·rous /ˈdʒenərəs/ adj 1 giving freely 2 more than enough ~**ly** adv

gen·e·sis /ˈdʒenəsɪs/ n [S] origin

ge·net·ic /dʒəˈnetɪk/ adj related to GENES –**ally** adv

genetic en·gi·neer·ing /ˌ·ˌ·· ···ˈ·ˌ·/ n science of changing GENES in animals or plants to make them stronger or healthier

ge·net·ics /dʒəˈnetɪks/ n [U] study of HEREDITY

ge·nial /ˈdʒiːnyəl, ˈdʒiːniəl/ adj cheerful and kind ~**ly** adv

gen·i·tals /ˈdʒenətlz/ n [P] outer sex organs **genital** adj

ge·nius /ˈdʒiːnyəs/ n 1 [U] great and rare powers of thought, skill, or imagination 2 [C] person with this ability 3 [S] special ability or skill: She has a genius for saying the wrong thing.

gen·o·cide /ˈdʒenəˌsaɪd/ n [U] killing of a whole race of people

gen·re /ˈʒɒnrə/ n fml class; kind

gent /dʒent/ n sl gentleman

gen·teel /dʒenˈtiːl/ adj unnaturally polite

gen·tile /ˈdʒentaɪl/ n, adj (sometimes cap.) (person who is) not Jewish

gen·til·i·ty /dʒenˈtɪləti/ n [U] being genteel

gen·tle /ˈdʒentəl/ adj not rough or violent ~**ness** n [U] **-tly** adv

gen·tle·man /ˈdʒentəlmən/ n **-men** /-mən/ **1** man who behaves well and can be trusted **2** any man **3** lit man of good family ~**ly** adj like a GENTLEMAN (1)

gen·try /ˈdʒentri/ n [S] wealthy people who live in the country: the local gentry

gen·u·ine /ˈdʒenyuɪn/ adj real; true ~**ly** adv ~**ness** n [U]

ge·nus /ˈdʒiːnəs/ n **genera** /ˈdʒenərə/ division of plants or animals

ge·og·ra·phy /dʒiˈɒgrəfi/ n [U] study of the countries of the world and of seas, towns, etc. **-pher** n **-phical** /ˌdʒiəˈgræfɪkəl◂/ adj **-phically** adv

ge·ol·o·gy /dʒiˈɒlədʒi/ n [U] study of the Earth's history as recorded in rocks **-gist** n **-gical** /ˌdʒiəˈlɒdʒɪkəl◂/ adj **-gically** adv

ge·om·e·try /dʒiˈɒmətri/ n [U] study of lines, angles, and surfaces and their relationships **geometric** /ˌdʒiəˈmetrɪk◂/ adj **geometrically** adv

ge·ri·at·rics /ˌdʒeriˈætrɪks, ˌdʒɪr-/ n [U] medical care of old people **geriatric** adj

germ /dʒɜːm/ n **1** BACTERIUM carrying disease **2** beginning of an idea, etc.

Ger·man shep·herd /ˌdʒɜːmən ˈʃepəd/ n large WOLF-like dog

ger·mi·nate /ˈdʒɜːməˌneɪt/ vi/t cause (a seed) to start growing **-nation** /ˌdʒɜːməˈneɪʃən/ n [U]

ger·und /ˈdʒerənd/ n VERBAL NOUN

ges·ta·tion /dʒeˈsteɪʃən/ n [S;U] carrying of a young creature inside the mother's body

ges·tic·u·late /dʒeˈstɪkyəˌleɪt/ vi wave the hands and arms about to express something **-lation** /dʒeˌstɪkyəˈleɪʃən/ n [C;U]

ges·ture /ˈdʒestʃə/ n **1** [C;U] movement of the body to express something **2** [C] action done to show one's feelings

get /get/ v **got** /gɒt/, **gotten** /ˈgɒtn/ pres. p. **getting 1** vt receive; obtain: get a letter |

get permission **2** vt collect; bring **3** vt catch (an illness) **4** vi/t (cause to) go or arrive: get home | get my boots off **5** [+adj] become: get sick/married **6** vi come or bring to the stated degree of success: Now we're getting somewhere. **7** vt succeed in or be allowed: It's nice when you get to know him. | I never get to drive the car. **8** vt prepare (a meal) **9** vt hear or understand: I don't get you. **10** vt confuse; PUZZLE: It's got me! **11** vt annoy: It's his attitude that gets me. **12** vt infml **a** punish or harm (someone) in return for harm they have done you: I'll get you for this! **b** catch or attack: The crocodiles will get them. **13** get (something) done: **a** cause something to be done: I must get these shoes mended. **b** experience something that happens to one: I got my hand caught in the door. **14** have got have: He's got red hair.

get around phr v **1** vi be able to move again after an illness **2** vi travel **3** vt avoid; CIRCUMVENT **4** vi persuade to do something (of news, etc., spread)

get across/over phr vi/t (cause to) be understood

get along phr vi **1** make progress; manage **2** progress **3** be friendly: They don't get along very well.

get around to phr vt find time for; do at last

get at phr vt **1** reach **2** mean; IMPLY **3** say unkind things

get away phr vi escape

get away with phr vt escape punishment for

get back phr vi **1** return **2** return to power after having lost it **3** speak or write to a person at a later time: I can't tell you now, but I'll get back to you tomorrow. **4** get back at someone also get one's own back on someone — punish someone in return for a wrong done to oneself

get by phr vi **1** continue to live; SURVIVE **2** be acceptable; be good enough but not very good

get down phr **1** vt swallow: get the medicine down **2** vt write down **3** vt DEPRESS: This weather gets me down. **4** vi enjoy oneself at a party

get down to phr vt begin to work at

get in phr v **1** vi arrive: The plane got in late. **2** vt call (someone) to help **3** vt collect a supply of **4** vt enter (a vehicle)

5 vt say (something), esp. by interrupting a conversation

get into phr vt **1** develop (a bad condition): *get into trouble* **2** become accustomed to

get off phr v **1** vi leave; start **2** vi/t (cause to) escape punishment **3** vt leave (a public vehicle) **4** vt DISMOUNT (1)

get onto phr vt **1** CONTACT **2** begin to talk about (something): *How did we get onto that subject?*

get out phr v **1** vi/t (cause to) escape **2** vi become known

get over phr vt **1** get better from (illness, etc.) **2** manage to deal with **3** reach the end of (usu. something unpleasant) **4** make clear; cause to be understood **5 I can't/couldn't get over** I am/was very much surprised at

get through phr v **1** vi/t pass (an examination, etc.) **2** vi reach someone by telephone **3** vi finish **4** vi/t (cause to) be understood by someone

get together phr vi have a meeting or party

get up phr vi rise from bed

get up to phr vt **1** do (something bad) **2** reach

get·a·way /ˈgɛtəˌweɪ/ n [S] escape

get-to·geth·er /ˈ· ·ˌ·ˌ·/ n friendly informal meeting for enjoyment

get-up /ˈgɛtʌp/ n set of clothes

get-up-and-go /ˌ· · ·ˈ·/ n [U] infml forceful active quality of mind

gey·ser /ˈgaɪzə/ n natural spring of hot water

ghast·ly /ˈgæsfli/ adj **1** very bad; terrible **2** pale and looking very ill

ghet·to /ˈgɛtoʊ/ n –tos or -toes part of city where poor people live

ghost /goʊst/ **1** (spirit of) a dead person who appears again **2** show **ghost writer** /ˈ· ˌ·/ — person who writes material which another person gives out as their own **3 give up the ghost** die **4 the ghost of** a the slightest ~**ly** adj like a ghost ♦ vt write (something) as a GHOST (2)

ghost town /ˈ· ·/ n empty town that was once busy

ghoul /guːl/ n GHOST (1) ~**ish** adj frightening because relating to dead bodies, etc.

GI n US soldier ♦ adj military: *GI haircut*

gi·ant /ˈdʒaɪənt/ **giantess** /-tɛs/ fem. — n big strong person or creature ♦ adj very large

gib·ber·ish /ˈdʒɪbərɪʃ, ˈgɪ-/ n [U] meaningless talk

gib·lets /ˈdʒɪblɪts/ n [P] bird's heart, etc., taken out before cooking

gid·dy /ˈgɪdi/ adj **1** (causing a) feeling of unsteady movement **2** (of a person) not serious ~**diness** n [U]

gift /gɪft/ n **1** something given freely **2** TALENT: *a gift for music* **3 the gift of the gab** infml the ability to speak well continuously, and esp. to persuade people ~**ed** adj TALENTED

gift cer·tif·i·cate /ˈ· ·ˌ·ˌ·/ n official piece of paper worth a certain amount of money, to be exchanged in a store for something

gift horse /ˈ· ·/ n **look a gift horse in the mouth** complain about a gift

gig /gɪg/ n popular musician's performance

gi·gan·tic /dʒaɪˈgæntɪk/ adj very large

gig·gle /ˈgɪgəl/ vi laugh in a silly way **giggle** n [C] act of giggling

gild /gɪld/ vt **1** cover with gold or gold paint **2 gild the lily** to try to improve something that is already good enough, so spoiling the effect

gill¹ /gɪl/ n organ through which a fish breathes

gill² /dʒɪl/ n small measure of liquid

gilt /gɪlt/ n [U] material with which things are gilded

gim·mick /ˈgɪmɪk/ n trick, phrase, etc., used to draw attention ~**y** adv

gin /dʒɪn/ n [U] colorless alcoholic drink

gin·ger /ˈdʒɪndʒə/ n [U] **1** plant whose root tastes hot and is used in cooking **2** orange-brown color: *ginger hair*

ginger ale /ˌ·· ·/ n [C;U] non-alcoholic drink with BUBBLES

gin·ger·bread /ˈdʒɪndʒəˌbrɛd/ n [U] cake with ginger in it

gin·ger·ly /ˈdʒɪndʒəli/ adv carefully

ging·ham /ˈgɪŋəm/ n [U] cotton cloth with a pattern of squares

gi·raffe /dʒəˈræf/ n African animal with a long neck

gir·der /ˈgədə/ n metal beam supporting a roof, bridge, etc.

gir·dle /ˈgədl/ n **1** woman's UNDERWEAR that fits tightly around the stomach **2** lit something that surrounds something: *a girdle of islands* ♦ vt lit go all around

girl /gɜːl/ n young female person **~hood** n time of being a girl **~ish** adj like a girl

girl·friend /ˈgɜːlfrend/ n **1** man's female companion **2** woman's female friend

Girl Scouts /ˌ· ·/ n organization for girls that teaches them practical skills

girth /gɜːθ/ n **1** [C] band around a horse's middle to hold the SADDLE firm **2** [U] fml thickness measured around something: *the girth of a tree*

gist /dʒɪst/ n [S] main points of something

give¹ /gɪv/ v **gave** /geɪv/, **given** /ˈgɪvən/ **1** vt cause or allow someone to have: *give him a present/a job* | *Give me time.* **2** vt pay in exchange: *I'll give $3000 for the car.* **3** vi supply money: *give generously to charity* **4** vt provide: *Cows give milk.* **5** vt perform (an action): *give an order/a sign* **6** vt offer (an amusement, etc.): *give a party* **7** vi bend or stretch under pressure **8** vt fml cause to believe, esp. wrongly: *I was given to understand that he was ill.* **9** vt call on (people present) to drink a TOAST (2) to: *I give you the President!* **10 give or take (a certain amount)** more or less (a certain amount) **11 give rise to** cause to happen **12 give way (to): a** admit defeat in an argument or fight **b** break **c** become less useful or important than **d** allow oneself to show (esp. a feeling) **giver** n

give away phr vt **1** give freely **2** show the truth about

give back phr vt return (something) to the owner

give in phr v **1** vi SURRENDER **2** vt deliver

give off phr vt send out (a smell, etc.)

give out phr vt **1** DISTRIBUTE **2** vi come to an end: *My strength gave out.*

give up phr v **1** vi/t stop: *give up smoking* **2** vi stop trying to guess, etc. **3** vt regard as lost or hopeless **4** vt offer as a prisoner **5** vt deliver to someone: *give up one's seat in the train*

give² n [U] quality of bending or stretching under pressure

give-and-take /ˌ· · ˈ·/ n [U] willingness to COMPROMISE (= give way to another's wishes)

give·a·way /ˈgɪvəweɪ/ n [S] something unintentional that makes a secret known ♦ adj (of a price) very low

giv·en /ˈgɪvən/ adj **1** fixed and stated: *a given time* **2 be given to** have a tendency to ♦ prep if one takes into account:

Given her inexperience, she's done a good job.

giz·mo /ˈgɪzmoʊ/ n GADGET

gla·cial /ˈgleɪʃəl/ adj of ice or an ICE AGE

gla·cier /ˈgleɪʃə/ n mass of ice that flows slowly down a valley

glad /glæd/ adj **1** pleased **2** lit causing happiness **~ly** adv willingly **~ness** n [U]

glade /gleɪd/ n lit open space in a forest

glad·i·a·tor /ˈglædɪeɪtə/ n (in ancient Rome) man who fought in public as an entertainment

glam·o·rize /ˈglæməraɪz/ vt make (something) appear more attractive than it really is

glam·our /ˈglæmə/ n **1** the charm of something unusual or expensive **2** sexual attraction **glamorous** adj

glance /glɑːns/ vi give a rapid look ♦ n **1** rapid look **2 at a glance** at once

glance off phr vt (of a blow, etc.) hit and move off at an angle

gland /glænd/ n body organ that treats materials in the blood to produce various liquid substances

glare /gleə/ vi **1** look fiercely **2** shine too strongly **glare** n [S] **glaring** adj **1** too bright **2** noticeably bad: *glaring injustice*

glass /glɑːs/ n **1** [U] hard transparent material used in windows, etc. **2** [C] something made of this, esp. a container for drinking from **3** [C] amount held by such a container — see also GLASSES **~y** adj like glass: *a glassy stare*

glass ceil·ing /ˌ· ˈ·/ n [the+S] attitudes and practices preventing women or people from other races from getting high-level jobs

glass·es /ˈglɑːsɪz/ n [P] two pieces of specially cut glass in a frame, worn in front of the eyes for improving a person's ability to see

glass·ware /ˈglɑːsweə/ n [U] glass objects generally

glau·co·ma /glaʊˈkoʊmə, glɔː-/ n [U] eye disease marked by increased pressure within the center part of the eye

glaze /gleɪz/ v **1** vt put a shiny surface on (pots, etc.) **2** vt fit (a window, etc.) with glass **3** vi (of the eyes) become dull ♦ n [U] shiny surface

gleam /gliːm/ n **1** a gentle light **2** sudden sign of something: *a gleam of interest* ♦ vi send out a gleam

glean /gliːn/ vt gather (facts, etc.) in small amounts

glee /gliː/ n [U] joyful satisfaction ~**ful** adj ~**fully** adv

glen /glɛn/ n lit narrow valley

glib /glɪb/ adj **-bb-** speaking or spoken too easily: *glib excuses* ~**ly** adv ~**ness** n [U]

glide /glaɪd/ vi **1** move smoothly and noiselessly **2** fly in a glider ♦ n gliding movement **glider** n plane with no engine

glim·mer /ˈglɪmə/ vi shine faintly ♦ n **1** faint light **2** small uncertain sign: *a glimmer of hope*

glimpse /glɪmps/ n quick incomplete view of something ♦ vt see for a moment

glint /glɪnt/ vi, n (give out) a small flash of light

glis·ten /ˈglɪsən/ vi shine as if wet

glitch /glɪtʃ/ n small fault in the operation of something

glit·ter /ˈglɪtə/ vi flash brightly: *glittering diamonds* ♦ n [S;U] brightness

gloat /gloʊt/ vi look at something with selfish satisfaction ~**ingly** adv

glob /glɒb/ n infml small amount of thick liquid or soft substance: *glob of tooth paste*

glo·bal /ˈgloʊbəl/ adj **1** of the whole world **2** taking account of all considerations ~**ly** adv

global warm·ing /ˌ· ˈ··/ n [U] increase in Earth's temperature caused by increase of gases around the Earth

globe /gloʊb/ n **1** [C] object in the shape of a ball; esp. one with a map of the Earth painted on it **2** [*the*+S] the Earth

glob·u·lar /ˈglɒbyələ/ adj shaped like a ball

glob·ule /ˈglɒbyʊl/ n drop of liquid

gloom /gluːm/ n **1** [U] darkness **2** [S;U] sadness; hopelessness ~**y** adj ~**ily** adv

glo·ri·fy /ˈglɔrəˌfaɪ, ˈgloʊr-/ vt **1** praise; worship **2** cause to seem more important: *Her cabin is just a glorified hut.* -**fication** /ˌglɔrəfəˈkeɪʃən, ˌgloʊr-/ n [U]

glo·ri·ous /ˈglɔriəs, ˈgloʊr-/ adj **1** having great honor: *glorious victory* **2** splendid ~**ly** adv

glo·ry¹ /ˈglɔri, ˈgloʊri/ n [U] **1** great honor **2** splendid beauty

glory² v **glory in** phr vt enjoy, often selfishly

gloss /glɒs, glɑs/ n [S;U] **1** shiny brightness **2** pleasant but deceiving outer appearance **3** explanation of a piece of writing ♦ vt write an explanation of ~**y** adj shiny

  gloss over phr vt hide (faults)

glos·sa·ry /ˈglɒsəri, ˈglɔ-/ n list of explanations of words

glove /glʌv/ n **1** covering for the hand **2** **fit like a glove** fit perfectly — see also KID GLOVES

glove com·part·ment /ˈ· ·ˌ··/ n small space in front of a car's passenger seat, for storing things

glow /gloʊ/ vi **1** give out heat or light without flames **2** be warm and red in the face ♦ n [S] glowing light ~**ing** adj strongly approving: *a glowing account*

glow·er /ˈglaʊə/ vi look with an angry expression ~**ingly** adv

glow-worm /ˈgloʊˌwɜːm/ n insect that gives out a greenish light

glu·cose /ˈgluːkoʊs/ n [U] sugar found in fruit

glue /gluː/ n [U] sticky substance for joining things ♦ vt pres. p. **gluing** or **glueing 1** join with glue **2 glued to** close to: *children glued to the television* ~**y** adj

glum /glʌm/ adj **-mm-** sad; GLOOMY ~**ly** adv

glut /glʌt/ vt **-tt-** supply with too much: *stores glutted with imports* ♦ n [S] too large a supply

glu·ti·nous /ˈgluːtˈn-əs/ adj fml sticky

glut·ton /ˈglʌtˈn/ n **1** person who eats too much **2** person who is always ready to do more of something hard or unpleasant: *a glutton for punishment* ~**ous** adj GREEDY ~**y** n [U] fml habit of eating too much

gly·ce·rin /ˈglɪsərɪn/ n [U] colorless liquid used in making soap, medicines, and explosives

gnarled /nɑrld/ adj rough and twisted: *gnarled tree trunks*

gnash /næʃ/ n strike (one's teeth) together

gnat /næt/ n small flying insect that stings

gnaw /nɔ/ vi/t bite steadily (at): (fig.) *gnawing anxiety*

gnome /noʊm/ n (in stories) little (old) man who lives under the ground

GNP n [*the*+S] Gross National Product; total value of everything produced in a country, usu. in a single year

go¹ /goʊ/ v **went** /wɛnt/, **gone** /gɒn, gɑn/ **1** vi leave a place: *I have to go now.* **2** vi move; travel: *go by bus* | *go shopping* **3** *vi* lead; reach: *This road goes to the West Coast.* **4** *vi* start an action: *Ready, set, go!* **5 a** become: *go crazy* | *This milk's gone bad.* **b** be or remain: *Her protests went unnoticed.* **6** *vi* match; fit: *Blue and green don't go (together).* | *4 into 3 won't go.* | *Your dress goes with your eyes.* **7** *vi* belong: *The knives go in this drawer.* **8** *vi* (of machines) work: *This clock doesn't go.* **9** *vi* be sold: *The house is going cheap.* **10** *vt* have (certain words or sounds): *Ducks go "quack."* **11** *vi* become weak or worn out: *My voice is going.* **12** *vi* lose one's usual powers of control: *let oneself go* | *He's pretty far gone.* **13** *vi* state or do up to or beyond a limit: *go too far* **14** *vi* be accepted or acceptable: *What she says goes.* **15** *vi* happen or develop in the stated way: *The party went well.* **16 as someone/something goes** compared with the average person or thing of that type: *He's not a bad cook, as cooks go, but he's no expert.* **17 be going to** (shows the future): *Is it going to rain?* **18 go all out for** be very enthusiastic about or **19 go a long way** also **go far: a** (of money) buy a lot **b** (of a person) succeed **20 go and: a** go in order to: *go and get it* **b** (shows surprise): *She went and bought it!* **21 go for it** *infml* make every effort to succeed at something **22 go it alone** act independently **23 to go** left; remaining: *only 3 more days to go* **24 -goer** person who goes somewhere regularly: *churchgoers*

go about *phr vt* perform; work at: *go about one's business*

go after *phr vt* try to get; chase

go against *phr vt* **1** oppose **2** be unfavorable to: *The case may go against you.*

go ahead *phr vi* **1** begin **2** continue

go along *phr vi* continue

go along with *phr vt* agree with

go around *phr vi* **1** (of an illness) spread **2** be enough for everyone: *not enough chairs to go around* **3** be often out in public (with someone)

go at *phr vt* attack; TACKLE

go back *phr vi* **1** return **2** stretch back in time

go back on *phr vt* break (a promise, etc.)

go by *phr v* **1** *vi* pass (in place or time): *A year went by.* **2** *vt* act according to **3** *vt* judge by **4 go by the name of** be called

go down *phr vi* **1** become lower **2** sink: *The sun/The ship went down.* **3** become less swollen **4** (of food) be swallowed **5** be accepted: *His speech went down well with the crowd.* **6** be recorded: *This day will go down in history.*

go for *phr vt* **1** attack **2** go after **3** like or be attracted by **4 go for nothing** be wasted

go in *phr vi* **1** (of the sun, etc.) become covered by clouds **2** join

go in for *phr vt* **1** enter (a competition) **2** have a habit of: *go in for football*

go into *phr vt* **1** enter (a profession) **2** explain or examine thoroughly

go off *phr v* **1** *vi* **a** explode **b** ring or sound loudly **2** *vi* succeed or fail: *The conference went off well.* **3** *vi* stop operating

go off with *phr vt* take away without permission

go on *phr v* **1** *vi* happen: *What's going on?* **2** *vi* (of time) pass **3** *vi* **a** continue: *go on with your work* **b** talk, complain, or behave in a certain way continually **4** *vi* be put into operation **5** *vt* use as proof, etc.: *I'm going on what you told me.* **6 go on!** *infml* I don't believe you!

go out *phr vi* **1** leave the house **2** spend time with someone **3** stop burning or shining: *The light went out.* **4** become unfashionable **5** (of the sea) go back to its low level **6** take part: *go out for football*

go over *phr vt* **1** examine **2** repeat

go through *phr v* **1** *vi* be approved officially **2** *vt* suffer or experience **3** *vt* finish; spend **4** *vt* search

go through with *phr vt* complete

go to *phr vt* make oneself have: *go to a lot of trouble*

go under *phr vi* **1** (of a ship) sink **2** fail

go up *phr vi* **1** rise **2** be built **3** be destroyed in fire, etc.

go with *phr vt* **1** match **2** be often found with

go without *phr vi/t* **1** DO without **2 it goes without saying** it is clear without needing to be stated

go² *n* **1** [U] quality of being very active **2** [C] attempt **3 from the word go** from the beginning **4 no go** *infml* useless **5 It's all go.** it's very busy **6 make a go of** *infml* make a success of **7 on the go** very busy

goad /goʊd/ vt urge by continuous annoyance ♦ n stick for driving cattle

go·a·head¹ /'· ·ˌ·/ n [(the) S] permission to take action

go-ahead² adj active in using new methods

goal /goʊl/ n 1 one's aim or purpose 2 a place where the ball must go to gain points in some games b point(s) gained by sending the ball there

goal·keep·er /'goʊlˌkipə/ n player responsible for keeping the ball out of a team's goal

goal·post /'goʊlpoʊst/ n one of the 2 posts between which the ball must go to gain a goal

goat /goʊt/ n 1 horned animal like a sheep 2 get one's goat annoy one

goa·tee /goʊ'ti/ n small pointed beard

gob·ble /'gabəl/ vi/t eat quickly and often noisily

gob·ble·dy·gook /'gabəldiˌgʊk, -ˌguk/ n [U] meaningless official language

go-be·tween /'· ·ˌ·/ n person who takes messages, etc., from one person or side to another

gob·let /'gablɪt/ n glass or metal drinking cup with a stem and no handle

gob·lin /'gablɪn/ n unkind fairy that plays tricks on people

go-cart /'goʊ kart/ n small low racing car

god /gad/ **god·dess** /'gadɪs/ fem. — n 1 [C] being who is worshipped 2 (cap.) (in the Christian, Jewish, and Muslim religions) the maker and ruler of the world ~less adj fml wicked; not showing respect or belief in God ~like adj like a god: godlike beauty ~ly adj fml religious; leading a good life

god·child /'gadtʃaɪld/ n boy (godson) or girl (goddaughter) for whom someone makes promises at BAPTISM

god·fa·ther /'gadˌfaðə/ n male GODPARENT

god-fear·ing /'· ˌ·ˌ·/ adj fml good and well behaved

god-for·sak·en /'gadfəˌseɪkən, ˌgadfə-'seɪ-/ adj (of places) sad and empty

god·moth·er /'gadˌmʌðə/ n female godparent

god·pa·rent /'gadˌpɛrənt/ n person who takes responsibility for a new Christian at BAPTISM

god·send /'gadsɛnd/ n unexpected lucky chance or thing

goes /goʊz/ v 3rd person sing. present tense of GO

go·fer, gopher /'goʊfə/ n person whose job is to bring or take things for other people

go-get·ter /'· ·ˌ·/ n someone who is forceful and determined, and likely to succeed

gog·gle /'gagəl/ vi STARE with the eyes wide open **goggles** n [P] glasses to protect the eyes

go·ing /'goʊɪŋ/ n [U] speed or condition of travel: fast/rough going ♦ adj operating at present: the going rate | a going concern

goings-on /ˌ·· '·/ n [P] undesirable activities

gold /goʊld/ n 1 [U] valuable yellow metal 2 [U] gold coins 3 [U] the color of gold: gold paint 4 [C] adj MEDAL 5 as good as gold very well behaved

gold·en /'goʊldən/ adj 1 of or like gold 2 very favorable: a golden opportunity

golden par·a·chute /ˌ·· '··/ n large amount of money given to someone leaving a company

golden rule /ˌ·· '·/ n [S] very important rule of behavior

gold·fish /'goʊldˌfɪʃ/ n **goldfish** small orange fish kept as a pet

gold leaf /ˌ· '·/ n [U] thin sheets of gold

gold·mine /'goʊldmaɪn/ n 1 mine where gold is found 2 profitable business

gold rush /'· ·/ n rush to newly discovered gold mines

gold·smith /'goʊldˌsmɪθ/ n person who makes things out of gold

golf /galf, gɔlf/ n game in which people hit a ball into holes with GOLF CLUBS ~er n

golf ball /'· ·/ n small hard ball used in golf

golf club /'· ·/ n 1 stick with a long handle for hitting the ball in golf 2 club for golfers with buildings and land they can use

golf course /'· ·/ n area of land for playing golf

gone /gɔn, gan/ v past p. of GO: George has gone to Iowa. (= he is there now)

gong /gɔŋ, gaŋ/ n round piece of metal that makes a ringing sound when struck

gon·na /'gɔnə, gənə/ v nonstandard way of writing "going to" as spoken informally

gon·or·rhe·a /ˌgɑnəˈriə/ n [U] disease passed on during sexual activity

goo /gu/ n [U] sticky substance

good¹ /gʊd/ adj **better** /ˈbɛtər/, **best** /bɛst/ **1** satisfactory: good food/ brakes **2** pleasant: good news **| have a good time 3** useful; suitable: Milk is good for you. **4** smart: good at math **5** well-behaved **6** morally right: good deeds **7** fml kind: Be good enough to hold this. **8** thorough: have a good cry **9** a good: **a** at least: a good 3 hours **b** large in size, amount: a good distance **10** **a good deal a** quite a lot **b** something sold cheaply **11** all in good time (it will happen) at a suitable later time; be patient **12** as good as almost the same as **13** Good! I agree, I'm glad, etc. **14** good and . . . infml completely: I'll do it when I'm good and ready. **15** good for: **a** effective in use: The ticket is good for a month. **b** likely to produce: She's always good for a few dollars/a laugh. **16** in good time early **17** make good be successful

good² n [U] **1** something that is good **2** something that causes gain or improvement: It'll do you good. **|** It's no good. (= it's useless) **|** What's the good of/What good is it having a car if you don't drive? **3** for good forever **4** Good for you! (used to express approval and pleasure at someone's success, etc.) **5** up to no good doing or intending doing something bad — see also GOODS

good af·ter·noon /ˌ· ˌ·ˈ·/ interj (used when meeting someone in the afternoon)

good·bye /gʊdˈbaɪ/ interj (used when leaving someone)

good eve·ning /ˌ· ˈ·-/ interj (used when meeting someone in the evening)

good-for-noth·ing /ˌ· ·ˈ··, ˌ· ·ˌ·/ adj, n useless (person)

Good Fri·day /ˌ· ˈ·-/ n the Friday before EASTER

good-hu·mored /ˌ· ˈ··◁/ adj cheerful and friendly

good-look·ing /ˌ· ˈ··◁/ adj attractive; beautiful

good mor·ning /ˌ· ˈ·-/ interj (used when meeting someone in the morning)

good-na·tured /ˌ· ˈ··◁/ adj kind

good·ness /ˈgʊdnɪs/ n [U] **1** quality of being good **2** the best part of food, etc. **3** (used in expressions of surprise and annoyance): Goodness me! **|** for goodness' sake

good night /· ˈ·/ interj (used when leaving someone at night, or going to sleep)

goods /gʊdz/ n [P] **1** things for sale **2** proof of guilt: I've got the goods on him. **3** possessions **4** come up with/deliver the goods produce in full what is expected

good Sam·ar·i·tan /ˌ· ·ˈ···/ n nice person who helps others in trouble

good·will /ˌgʊdˈwɪl/ n [U] **1** kind feelings **2** popularity of a business, as part of its value

good·y /ˈgʊdi/ n something very pleasant, esp. to eat

goo·ey /ˈgui/ adj **1** sticky and sweet **2** SENTIMENTAL

goof /guf/ n infml **1** foolish person **2** silly mistake ♦ vi infml make a silly mistake ~**y** adj

goof off phr vi infml waste time or avoid work

goose /gus/ n geese /gis/ **1** bird like a large duck **2** silly person

goose bumps /ˈ· ·/ n [U] condition in which the skin rises up in small points

GOP n [the] the Republican Party

go·pher /ˈgoʊfər/ n **1** rat-like animal that lives in a hole **2** GOFER

gore¹ /gɔr, goʊr/ vt wound with horns or TUSKS

gore² n [U] lit (esp. thick) blood **gory** adj

gorge¹ /gɔrdʒ/ n **1** steep narrow valley **2** make someone's gorge rise make someone feel sickened

gorge² vi/t eat or feed eagerly

gor·geous /ˈgɔrdʒəs/ adj wonderful; beautiful ~**ly** adv

go·ril·la /gəˈrɪlə/ n the largest of the APES

gosh /gɑʃ/ interj (expressing surprise)

gos·pel /ˈgɑspəl/ n **1** something completely true **2** [C] (cap.) any of 4 accounts of Christ's life in the Bible

gos·sip /ˈgɑsəp/ n **1** [S;U] talk about other people's private lives **2** [C] person who likes this kind of talk ♦ vi spend time in gossip

got /gɑt/ v past t. and p. of GET

got·ta /ˈgɑtə/ v nonstandard way of writing "got to" as spoken informally

got·ten /ˈgɑtˈn/ v past p. of GET

gouge /gaʊdʒ/ v get too much money for: They gouged me on these tickets. **gouge out** phr vt push or dig out violently

gourd /gɔrd, goʊrd, gʊrd/ n hard outer shell of a fruit

gour·met /gʊrˈmeɪ, ˈgʊrmeɪ/ n person who knows a lot about food and drink ♦ adj: gourmet food

gout /gaʊt/ n [U] disease that makes the toes and fingers swell painfully

gov·ern /ˈgʌvən/ v 1 vi/t rule (a country, etc.) 2 vt control: The price is governed by the quantity produced. ~ance n [U] fml governing

gov·ern·ess /ˈgʌvənɪs/ n woman who teaches children in their home

gov·ern·ment /ˈgʌvəmənt, ˈgʌvənmənt/ n 1 [C] group of people who govern: the Swiss government 2 [U] act or process of governing: the art of government 3 [U] form or method of governing: a return to democratic government ~al /ˌgʌvənˈmentəl, -vəˈmen-/ adj

gov·er·nor /ˈgʌvənə, -və-/ n elected official head of a state in the US: the governor of California ~ship n [U]

gown /gaʊn/ n 1 woman's dress 2 outer garment worn by judges, members of universities, etc. 3 loose garment worn for some special purpose: a nightgown/dressing gown

GPA n grade-point average; average of all a student's grades

grab /græb/ vt/i -bb- seize suddenly and roughly ♦ n 1 sudden attempt to seize something 2 up for grabs ready for anyone to take or win

grace /greɪs/ n [U] 1 beauty of movement or shape 2 delay allowed as a favor: give them a week's grace 3 prayer of thanks before or after meals 4 God's favor towards people 5 a saving grace pleasing quality for which the person's faults are forgiven him 6 with (a) good/bad grace willingly/unwillingly ♦ vt fml give honor or beauty to ~ful adj 1 having GRACE (1) 2 suitably expressed ~fully adv ~less adj awkward

gra·cious /ˈgreɪʃəs/ adj 1 polite and pleasant 2 having those qualities made possible by wealth: gracious living ~ly adv ~ness n [U]

gra·da·tion /greɪˈdeɪʃən, grə-/ n fml stage; degree: gradations of color

grade /greɪd/ n 1 level of quality 2 a class in an American school: She's in third grade. b mark given for school work c gradient 3 make the grade succeed;

reach the necessary standard ♦ vt separate into levels of quality

grade school /ˈ· ·/ n ELEMENTARY SCHOOL

gra·di·ent /ˈgreɪdiənt/ n degree of slope, as on a road

grad school /ˈgræd ˌskuːl/ n [C;U] university for people with a first college degree

grad·u·al /ˈgrædʒuəl/ adj happening slowly; not sudden ~ly adv ~ness n [U]

grad·u·ate¹ /ˈgrædʒuɪt/ n person who has completed a school or college course

grad·u·ate² /ˈgrædʒuˌeɪt/ v 1 vi become a graduate 2 vt GRADE 3 vt mark with degrees for measurement –ation /ˌgrædʒuˈeɪʃən/ n 1 [U] (ceremony of) becoming a graduate 2 [C] mark of measurement

graduate school /ˈ··· ·/ n GRAD SCHOOL

graf·fi·ti /grəˈfiːti/ n [P;U] drawings or writings on a wall

graft /græft/ n 1 [C] piece from one plant fixed inside another to grow there 2 [C] piece of skin or bone similarly fixed into the body 3 [U] practice of obtaining money or advantage by the dishonest use of esp. political influence ♦ vt put onto as a graft

grain /greɪn/ n 1 [C] single seed of rice, wheat, etc. 2 [U] crops from food plants like these 3 [C] small hard piece: grains of sand | (fig.) a grain of truth 4 [U] natural arrangement of threads or FIBERS in wood, cloth, etc. 5 be/go against the grain it is not what one wishes (to do, know, etc.)

gram /græm/ n (measure of weight equal to) 1/1000 of a kilogram

gram·mar /ˈgræmə/ n [C;U] (book that teaches) rules for the use of words

grammar school /ˈ·· ··/ n ELEMENTARY SCHOOL

gram·mat·i·cal /grəˈmætɪkəl/ adj 1 concerning grammar 2 correct according to the rules of grammar

grand /grænd/ adj 1 splendid; IMPRESSIVE 2 (of people) important 3 pleasant; delightful ♦ n 1 GRAND PIANO 2 (pl. grand) sl 1,000 dollars

grand·child /ˈgræntʃaɪld/ n grandchildren /-ˌtʃɪldrən/ boy or girl who is the child of the stated person's son or daughter

grand·daugh·ter /ˈgrænˌdɔtə/ n girl who is the child of the stated person's son or daughter

gran·deur /ˈgrændʒə, -dʒʊr/ n [U] quality of being grand; magnificence (MAGNIFICENT)

grand·fa·ther /ˈgrændˌfɑðə/ n male GRANDPARENT

grandfather clock /ˈ··· ˌ·/ n tall clock that stands on the floor

gran·di·ose /ˈgrændiˌoʊs, ˌgrændiˈoʊs/ adj intended to seem splendid and important

grand jur·y /ˌ· ˈ·/ n group of people who decide whether there should be a TRIAL in a court of law

grand·ma /ˈgrændmɑ, ˈgræmɑ/ n infml grandmother

grand·moth·er /ˈgrændˌmʌðə/ n female grandparent

grand·pa /ˈgrændpɑ, ˈgræmpɑ/ n infml grandfather

grand·par·ent /ˈgrændˌpɛrənt, -ˌpær-/ n parent of someone's father or mother

grand pi·an·o /ˌ· ·ˈ··/ n large piano with strings set parallel to the ground

grand slam /ˌ· ˈ·/ n 1 the winning of all of a set of important sports competitions 2 baseball HOME RUN when there is a player on every base

grand·son /ˈgrændsʌn/ n boy who is the child of the stated person's son or daughter

grand·stand /ˈgrændstænd/ n seats arranged in rising rows, for people watching races, etc.

grand to·tal /ˌ· ˈ··/ n complete amount

gran·ite /ˈgrænɪt/ n [U] hard usu. grey rock

gran·ny, -nie /ˈgræni/ n infml grandmother ♦ adj for old people: a granny flat

gra·no·la /grəˈnoʊlə/ n [U] breakfast dish of grain, nuts, fruit, etc., eaten with milk

grant /grænt/ vt 1 fml give: grant permission 2 admit the truth of 3 **take something for granted** accept it without question ♦ n money granted esp. officially

gran·u·lat·ed /ˈgrænyəˌleɪtɪd/ adj (of sugar) in the form of not very fine powder

gran·ule /ˈgrænyul/ n small grain

grape /greɪp/ n green or purple fruit from which wine is made — see also SOUR GRAPES

grape·fruit /ˈgreɪpfrut/ n large yellow fruit like a sour orange

grape·vine /ˈgreɪpvaɪn/ n [S] unofficial way of spreading news: hear about it through the office grapevine

graph /græf/ n drawing showing the relationship between 2 changing values

graph·ic /ˈgræfɪk/ adj 1 clear and detailed: a graphic description 2 of drawing, printing, etc. ~ally adv 1 clearly 2 using graphs **graphics** n [P] drawings, etc.

graph·ite /ˈgræfaɪt/ n [U] black substance used in pencils, etc.

grap·ple /ˈgræpəl/ v grapple with phr vt seize and struggle with: (fig.) grapple with a problem

grasp /græsp/ vt 1 take firm hold of 2 succeed in understanding ♦ n 1 firm hold 2 understanding ~ing adj too eager for money

grass /græs/ n 1 [U] common wild green plants that cows, etc., eat 2 [C] one of these plants: tall grasses

grass·hop·per /ˈgræsˌhɑpə/ n insect which can jump high and makes a sharp noise by rubbing parts of its body together

grass roots /ˌ· ˈ·/ n [P] ordinary people, not those with political power ♦ adj: grass roots protest

grate[1] /greɪt/ n metal frame in a fireplace or covering a hole

grate[2] v 1 vt rub into pieces on a rough surface: grated cheese 2 vi make a sharp unpleasant sound **grater** n tool for grating food, etc.

grate·ful /ˈgreɪtfəl/ adj feeling or showing thanks ~ly adv ~ness n [U]

grat·i·fy /ˈgrætɪˌfaɪ/ vt please; satisfy ~ing adj pleasing –fication /ˌgrætəfəˈkeɪʃən/ n [C;U]

grat·ing /ˈgreɪtɪŋ/ n network of bars to protect an opening

grat·i·tude /ˈgrætɪˌtud/ n [U] gratefulness

gra·tu·i·tous /grəˈtuətəs/ adj fml not deserved or necessary: gratuitous insults ~ly adv

gra·tu·i·ty /grəˈtuəti/ n fml TIP[3] for a service done

grave[1] /greɪv/ n hole where a dead person is buried

grave[2] adj serious; solemn ~ly adv

grav·el /ˈgrævəl/ n [U] small stones used for making paths, etc. ~ly adj 1 covered with gravel 2 having a low rough hard sound

grave·stone /ˈgreɪvstoʊn/ n stone over a grave

grave·yard /ˈgreɪvjɑrd/ n CEMETERY

graveyard shift /ˈ·· ˌ·/ n night working hours

grav·i·tate /ˈgrævəteɪt/ vi be attracted (as if) by gravity –**tation** /ˌgrævəˈteɪʃən/ n [U]

grav·i·ty /ˈgrævəti/ n [U] 1 force by which objects are drawn towards each other and to the earth 2 seriousness: *the gravity of his illness*

gra·vy /ˈgreɪvi/ n [U] juice that comes out of meat in cooking

gravy train /ˈ·· ˌ·/ n [the+S] something from which many people can make money or profit without much effort

gray, grey /greɪ/ adj 1 of the color of black mixed with white 2 having gray hair ♦ n [U] gray color ♦ vi become gray

gray mat·ter /ˈ· ˌ··/ n [U] 1 the brain 2 infml power of thought

graze[1] /greɪz/ vi (of animals) eat growing grass

graze[2] vt 1 rub the skin from 2 rub lightly while passing ♦ n surface wound

grease /gris/ n [U] soft fat or oil ♦ vt 1 put grease on 2 **grease someone's palm** BRIBE someone 3 **like greased lightning** infml extremely fast **greasy** /ˈgrisi, -zi/ adj

great /greɪt/ adj 1 excellent and important: *great writers* 2 large: *great pleasure | a great many people* 3 enthusiastic; active: *a great filmgoer* 4 to an extreme degree: *great friends* 5 very good: *a great film* 6 **great-:** a parent of someone's GRANDPARENT: *his great-grandfather* is child of someone's GRANDCHILD: *his great-granddaughter* –**ly** adv very much ~**ness** n [U]

Great Plains /ˌ· ˈ·/ n dry, flat area of land in North America

greed /grid/ n [U] desire for too much food, money, etc. ~**y** adj ~**ily** adv

green /grin/ adj 1 of a color between yellow and blue; the color of leaves and grass 2 pale and unhealthy in the face 3 (of fruit, plants, etc.) young or unripe 4 inexperienced and easily deceived 5 very jealous: *green with envy* ♦ n 1 [U] green color 2 [C] smooth area with grass: *village green* ~**ness** n [U] **greens** n [P] green leafy vegetables

green·back /ˈgrinbæk/ n dollar

green card /ˈ· ˌ·/ n official document giving permission to live and work in the US

green·er·y /ˈgrinəri/ n [U] green leaves and plants

green·house /ˈgrinhaʊs/ n glass building for growing plants in

green thumb /ˌ· ˈ·/ n [S] natural skill in making plants grow

greet /grit/ vt 1 welcome 2 be suddenly seen or heard ~**ing** n 1 words used on meeting or writing to someone 2 a good wish: *Christmas greetings*

greet·ing card /ˈ·· ˌ·/ n card sent to someone on his/her BIRTHDAY, at Christmas, etc.

gre·gar·i·ous /grɪˈgɛriəs/ adj fond of companionship

gre·nade /grəˈneɪd/ n small bomb to be thrown by hand

grew /gru/ v past t. of GROW

grey·hound /ˈgreɪhaʊnd/ n thin dog with long legs, which can run quickly

grid /grɪd/ n 1 GRATING 2 system of numbered squares on a map

grid·i·ron /ˈgrɪdaɪərn/ n field marked for football

grid·lock /ˈgrɪdlɑk/ n [U] 1 situation in which streets are so full of cars that traffic cannot move 2 situation in which people are unwilling to COMPROMISE, so that no progress is made

grief /grif/ n [U] 1 (cause of) great sorrow 2 **come to grief** suffer harm; fail 3 **Good grief!** (expression of surprise and some dislike)

griev·ance /ˈgrivəns/ n cause for complaint

grieve /griv/ v 1 vi suffer grief 2 vt make unhappy

grill /grɪl/ v 1 vi/t cook over direct heat outside 2 vt question severely ♦ n BARBECUE

grille /grɪl/ n bars filling a space, esp. for safety

grim /grɪm/ adj -**mm**- 1 serious; terrible: *grim news* 2 showing determination: *grim smile* ~**ly** adv ~**ness** n [U]

gri·mace /ˈgrɪməs, grɪˈmeɪs/ vi twist the face to express pain, etc. **grimace** n

grime /graɪm/ n [U] black dirt on a surface **grimy** adj

grin /grɪn/ vi -**nn**- 1 smile widely 2 **grin and bear it** suffer without complaint **grin** n

grind /graɪnd/ vt **ground** /graʊnd/ 1 crush into powder: *grind coffee beans* 2 rub (the teeth) together **3** make smooth or sharp by rubbing: *grind knives* **4** press upon with a strong twisting movement **5** **grind to a halt** stop noisily ♦ *n infml* [S] hard dull work ~**er** *n* person or machine that grinds

grind away *phr v* study hard

grind down *phr vt* keep in a state of suffering and hopelessness

grind out *phr vt derog* produce (esp. writing or music) continually, but like a machine

grind·stone /'graɪndstəʊn/ *n* **1** round stone that is turned to sharpen tools **2** **one's nose to the grindstone** in a state of continuous hard work

grin·go /'grɪŋgəʊ/ *n often derog.* white American or European, esp. when in countries where the people speak Spanish

grip /grɪp/ *vi/t* -**pp**- **1** seize tightly **2** hold someone's attention: *a gripping story* ♦ *n* **1** tight hold **2** thing that grips **3** **come/get to grips with** deal seriously with

gripe /graɪp/ *vi sl* complain continuously ♦ **gripe** *n*

gris·ly /'grɪzli/ *adj* shocking and sickening

gris·tle /'grɪsəl/ *n* [U] CARTILAGE in cooked meat

grit /grɪt/ *n* [U] **1** small stones and sand **2** lasting courage: determination ♦ *vt* -**tt**- **1** put grit on (esp. a road) **2** **grit one's teeth** show determination ~**ty** *adj*

griz·zly bear /'grɪzli beər/ *n* large strong bear

groan /grəʊn/ *vi, n* (make) a loud deep sound of suffering

gro·cer /'grəʊsər/ *n* storekeeper who sells foods and other things for the home

gro·cer·ies /'grəʊsəriz, 'grəʊʃriz/ *n* [P] goods sold by a grocer

gro·cery store /'grəʊsri ˌstɔr, -ʃri-/ *n* store selling foods and other things for the home

grog·gy /'grɒgi/ *adj* weak and unsteady from illness, etc. –**giness** *n* [U]

groin /grɔɪn/ *n* place where the legs meet the front of the body

groom /grum/ *n* **1** person who looks after horses **2** man about to be married, or just married ♦ *vt* **1** brush and clean (horses) **2** make (oneself) neat and tidy **3** prepare (someone) for special work

groove /gruv/ *n* long hollow in a surface

grope /grəʊp/ *v* **1** *vi* search about with the hands as in the dark **2** *vt sl* (try to) feel the body of (a person) to get sexual pleasure **grope** *n*

gross¹ /grəʊs/ *adj* **1** bad; unpleasant **2** rough; rude **3** clearly wrong: *gross negligence* **4** total: *gross income* ♦ *vt* gain as total profit ~**ly** *adv* ~**ness** *n* [U]

gross² *determiner, n* **gross** or **grosses** 144

gro·tesque /grəʊˈtɛsk/ *adj* strange and ugly ~**ly** *adv*

grot·to /'grɒtəʊ/ *n* -**toes** *or* -**tos** cave

grouch /graʊtʃ/ *n* person who always complains ♦ *vi* complain angrily ~**y** *adj*

ground¹ /graʊnd/ *v past t. and p. of* GRIND

ground² *n* **1** [S;U] surface of the earth **2** [U] soil **3** [C] piece of land used for a particular purpose: *a playground* **4** [U] a base for argument: *You're on safe ground as long as you avoid the subject of politics.* **b** area of knowledge or experience: *It was absurd to try to cover so much ground in such a short course.* **5** [U] position of advantage to be won or defended: *The army has lost ground.* | *The idea is gaining ground.* (= becoming more popular) **6** [C] safety wire carrying electricity to the ground **7** **get off the ground** make a successful start **8** **into the ground** more or further than is necessary — see also GROUNDS ~**less** *adj* without reason: *groundless fears* ~**lessly** *adv*

ground³ *v* **1** *vi* (of a boat) strike against the bottom of the sea, a river, etc. **2** *vt* cause (a plane or pilot) to stay on the ground **3** *vt* base: *arguments grounded on experience* ~**ing** *n* [S] first necessary training in something

ground floor /ˌ ˈ ◂/ *n* **1** part of a building at ground level **2** **get/be in on the ground floor** be part of an activity, business operation, etc., from the time it starts

ground·hog /'graʊndˌhɒg/ *n* small brown furry animal that lives in holes in the ground

grounds /graʊndz/ *n* [P] **1** solid bits at the bottom of a liquid **2** gardens, etc., around a building **3** reason: *grounds for divorce*

ground·work /'graʊndwɜrk/ *n* [U] work on which further study, etc., is based

group /grup/ *n* connected set of people or things ♦ *vi/t* form into groups

grouse¹ /graʊs/ *vi, n* GRUMBLE

grouse[2] *n* **grouse** small fat bird which is shot for food and sport

grove /grəʊv/ *n lit* small group of trees

grov·el /ˈgrɒvəl, ˈgrʌ-/ *vi* -l- **1** lie flat in fear or obedience **2** be shamefully humble and eager to please ~**ler** *n*

grow /grəʊ/ *v* **grew** /gruː/, **grown** /grəʊn/ **1** *vi* get bigger **2** *vi* (of plants) live and develop **3** *vt* cause (plants, etc.) to grow **4** *fml* become: *grow old* **grown** *adj* ADULT: *grown men*

  grow on *phr vt* become more pleasing to: *This music will grow on you.*

  grow out of *phr vt* get too big or old for

  grow up *phr vi* **1** develop from child to man or woman **2** start to exist: *customs that have grown up*

growl /graʊl/ *vi, n* (make) the threatening noise of an angry dog

grown-up /ˌ· ˈ·◂/ *adj, n* ADULT

growth /grəʊθ/ *n* **1** [S;U] process of growing; increase **2** [C] something that has grown, esp. an unnatural lump in the body

grub[1] /grʌb/ *n* **1** [C] insect in the worm-like stage **2** [U] *sl* food

grub[2] *vi/t* -bb- dig with the hands or PAWS

grub·by /ˈgrʌbi/ *adj* rather dirty –**biness** *n* [U]

grudge /grʌdʒ/ *n* continuing feeling of anger against someone **grudgingly** *adv*

gru·el·ing /ˈgruəlɪŋ/ *adj* very tiring

grue·some /ˈgruːsəm/ *adj* very shocking and sickening –**ly** *adv*

gruff /grʌf/ *adj* (of the voice) deep and rough ~**ly** *adv* ~**ness** *n* [U]

grum·ble /ˈgrʌmbəl/ *vi* complain ♦ *n* complaint

grump·y /ˈgrʌmpi/ *adj* bad-tempered –**ily** *adv* –**iness** *n* [U]

grunt /grʌnt/ *vi, n* (make) the short rough sound that pigs make

guar·an·tee /ˌgærənˈtiː/ *n* **1** written promise to replace an article if it is found to be imperfect **2** agreement to be responsible for a debt ♦ *vt* **1** give a guarantee about **2** promise: *I guarantee you'll enjoy it.*

guar·an·tor /ˈgærəntɔr, -tə/ *n law* person who agrees to be responsible for a debt

guard /gɑrd/ *n* **1** [U] state of watching against attack: *soldiers on guard* **2 a** [C] person keeping guard **b** [S] group of these people **3** [C] protective apparatus or person: *a bodyguard* — see also OLD GUARD ♦ *vt* **1** defend **2** watch (prisoners) to prevent escape ~**ed** *adj* not saying too much

  guard against *phr vt* prevent by care: *guard against infection*

guard·i·an /ˈgɑrdiən/ *n* person responsible for a child ~**ship** *n* [U]

gu·ber·na·to·ri·al /ˌguːbənəˈtɔːriəl, -ˈtʊər-, ˌgjuː-/ *adj* of a governor

guer·ril·la /gəˈrɪlə/ *n* member of an unofficial army which attacks in small groups

guess /ges/ *v* **1** *vi/t* form an opinion (on) without knowing all the facts **2** *vt infml* suppose; consider likely ♦ *n* **1** opinion formed by guessing **2** attempt to guess

guess·work /ˈgeswɜrk/ *n* [U] guessing

guest /gest/ *n* **1** person invited to someone's home, or staying in a hotel **2** person, esp. an entertainer, invited to take part in a show, etc. **3 be my guest!** please feel free to do so ♦ *vi* take part as a guest performer

guest·house /ˈgesthaʊs/ *n* -**houses** /-ˌhaʊzɪz/ small house for guests

guf·faw /gəˈfɔː/ *vi* laugh loudly and esp. rudely **guffaw** *n*

guid·ance /ˈgaɪdns/ *n* [U] help; advice

guidance coun·sel·or /ˈ··· ˌ·-·/ *n* person whose job is to give students advice

guide /gaɪd/ *n* **1** person who shows the way **2** something that influences behavior **3** also **guidebook** /ˈgaɪdbʊk/ — book describing a place **4** instruction book ♦ *vt* act as a guide to

guide·lines /ˈgaɪdlaɪnz/ *n* [P] main points on how to deal with something

guild /gɪld/ *n* association of people with the same interests

guil·lo·tine /ˈgɪlətiːn, ˈgiə-, gɪləˈtiːn, ˌgiə-/ *n* machine for cutting off the heads of criminals

guilt /gɪlt/ *n* [U] **1** fact of having done wrong; blame **2** shame ~**y** *adj* having done wrong

guinea pig /ˈgɪni ˌpɪg/ *n* **1** small tailless furry animal sometimes used in scientific tests **2** person on whom something is tested

guise /gaɪz/ *n fml* outer appearance

gui·tar /gɪˈtɑr/ *n* stringed musical instrument played with the fingers

gulch /gʌltʃ/ *n* narrow stony valley with steep sides made by a rushing stream

gulf /gʌlf/ n **1** piece of sea partly surrounded by land **2** division, esp. between opinions

gull /gʌl/ n any of several kinds of large birds that live on or near the sea

gul·let /ˈgʌlɪt/ n food pipe in the throat

gul·li·ble /ˈgʌləbəl/ adj easily tricked ~**bility** /ˌgʌləˈbɪləti/ n [U]

gulp /gʌlp/ vi/t swallow hastily **gulp** n

gum¹ /gʌm/ n flesh in which the teeth are fastened

gum² n **1** [U] sticky plant substance **2** [U] CHEWING GUM ♦ vt -**mm**- stick with GUM (1) ~**my** adj sticky

gump·tion /ˈgʌmpʃən/ n [U] **1** practical good sense **2** courage

gum·shoe /ˈgʌmʃuː/ n DETECTIVE

gun¹ /gʌn/ n weapon that fires bullets or SHELLs through a tube — see also **stick to one's guns** (STICK²)

gun² v

gun down phr vt shoot, causing to fall to the ground dead or wounded

gun for phr vt **1** aim at **2** search for in order to attack

gun·boat /ˈgʌnbəʊt/ n small heavily armed warship

gun·fire /ˈgʌnfaɪə/ n [U] (sound of) shooting

gung-ho /ˌgʌŋ ˈhəʊ◄/ adj showing extreme, often foolish, eagerness, esp. to attack an enemy

gun·man /ˈgʌnmən/ n -**men** /-mən/ armed criminal

gun·ner /ˈgʌnə/ n soldier who uses heavy guns

gun·ny·sack /ˈgʌniˌsæk/ n cloth bag for storing potatoes, coal, etc.

gun·point /ˈgʌnpɔɪnt/ n **at gunpoint** under a threat of death by shooting

gun·pow·der /ˈgʌnˌpaʊdə/ n [U] explosive powder

gun·shot /ˈgʌnʃɒt/ n sound or act of firing a gun

gur·gle /ˈgɜːgəl/ vi, n (make) the sound of water flowing unevenly

gu·ru /ˈguru, ˈguəru, guˈru/ n **gurus 1** Eastern religious teacher **2** greatly respected person whose ideas are followed

gush /gʌʃ/ v **1** vi flow out: oil gushing from a pipe **2** vt send out (liquid) in large quantities **3** vi express admiration foolishly ♦ n [S] sudden flow

gust /gʌst/ n sudden rush of wind ~**y** adj

gus·to /ˈgʌstəʊ/ n [U] eager enjoyment

gut /gʌt/ vt **1** take out the inner organs of: gut a fish **2** destroy the inside of (a building) ♦ adj coming from feelings rather than thought: gut reactions **guts** n [P] **1** bowels **2** bravery and determination **gutsy** n brave

gut·ter /ˈgʌtə/ n **1** [C] ditch or pipe that carries away rainwater **2** [the+S] the lowest level of society

guy /gaɪ/ n sl a man b person, male or female: Come on, you guys!

guz·zle /ˈgʌzəl/ vi/t eat or drink eagerly

gym /dʒɪm/ n **1** [C] gymnasium **2** [U] gymnastics

gym·na·si·um /dʒɪmˈneɪziəm/ n hall with apparatus for indoor exercise

gym·nas·tics /dʒɪmˈnæstɪks/ n [U] training of the body by physical exercises –**tic** adj

gy·ne·col·o·gy /ˌgaɪnəˈkɒlədʒi/ n [U] medical study and treatment of the female sex organs –**gist** n –**gical** /ˌgaɪnəkəˈlɒdʒɪkəl/ adj –**gically** adv

gyp·sy /ˈdʒɪpsi/ n person with no fixed home who travels with others, working in CARNIVALs, etc.

gy·rate /dʒaɪˈreɪt, dʒaɪˈreɪt/ vi fml swing around and around **gyration** /dʒaɪˈreɪʃən/ n [C;U]

gy·ro·scope /ˈdʒaɪrəˌskəʊp/ n wheel that spins inside a frame, used for keeping ships, etc., steady

H, h /eɪtʃ/ the 8th letter of the English alphabet

hab·it /ˈhæbɪt/ n **1** [C;U] person's usual behavior **2** [C] clothes worn by a MONK or NUN

hab·it·a·ble /ˈhæbətəbəl/ adj fit to be lived in

hab·i·tat /ˈhæbəˌtæt/ n natural home of an animal or plant

hab·i·ta·tion /ˌhæbəˈteɪʃən/ n fml [U] living in: houses fit for habitation

ha·bit·u·al /həˈbɪtʃuəl/ adj **1** usual **2** (done) by habit ~**ly** adv

hack[1] /hæk/ vi/t cut roughly **hack into** phr vt use a computer to enter another computer system, usu. dishonestly

hack[2] n writer who does a lot of poor quality work

hack·er /ˈhækə/ n someone who is able to use or change information in a computer system without permission

hack·neyed /ˈhæknid/ adj (of a saying) meaningless because used too often

hack·saw /ˈhæksɔ/ n tool with a blade with fine teeth, used esp. for cutting metal

had /d, əd, hæd/ strong hæd/ v past t. and p. of HAVE

had·dock /ˈhædək/ n haddock common fish, used as food

had·n't /ˈhædnt/ v short for: had not

hag /hæg/ n derog ugly old woman

hag·gard /ˈhægəd/ adj (of the face) lined and hollow from tiredness

hag·gle /ˈhægəl/ vi argue over a price

hail[1] /heɪl/ n [U] frozen rain drops: (fig.) a hail of bullets ♦ vi (of hail) fall

hail[2] vi call out to: hail a taxi **2** recognize (someone) as important: They hailed him king.

    hail from phr vt come from: She hails from New Orleans.

hail·stone /ˈheɪlstoʊn/ n single piece of hail

hair /hɛr/ n **1** [C] threadlike growth from the skin **2** [U] mass of these growths **3** **let one's hair down** behave as one likes

after being formal **4** **make someone's hair curl** infml shock someone **5** **make one's hair stand on end** frighten one badly **6** **tear one's hair out** show extreme grief or anger ~**y** adj **1** covered with hair **2** infml exciting in a way that causes fear; dangerous ~**iness** n [U]

hair·brush /ˈhɛrbrʌʃ/ n brush used to make one's hair neat

hair·cut /ˈhɛrkʌt/ n **1** act of getting one's hair cut by someone **2** style one's hair is cut into

hair·do /ˈhɛrdu/ n -dos style a person's hair is shaped into

hair·dress·er /ˈhɛrˌdrɛsə/ n person who cuts and shapes hair

hair·piece /ˈhɛrpis/ n piece of false hair used to make one's own hair seem thicker

hair·pin curve /ˌhɛrpɪn ˈkəv/ n curve on a road in the shape of a U

hair·rais·ing /ˈ· ˌ·/ adj very frightening

hair·split·ting /ˈ· ˌ·/ n [U] derog act or habit of paying too much attention to unimportant differences and details

hair spray /ˈ· ·/ n [U] sticky liquid put on the hair to make it stay in place

hair·style /ˈhɛrstaɪl/ n style a person's hair is shaped into

hale /heɪl/ adj **hale and hearty** very healthy

half[1] /hæf/ n halves /hævz/ **1** either of 2 equal parts; ½: Half of 50 is 25. **2** either of 2 parts into which something is divided: He's in the bottom half of the class. **3** coin, ticket, drink, etc., of ½ the value or amount: Just a half, please. **4** **by halves** incompletely **5** **go halves** share something equally **6** **my/your/his/her better half** one's husband or wife

half[2] predeterminer, adj ½ in amount: She bought half a pound of rice.

half[3] adv **1** partly: half cooked | half French **2** **half and half** ½ one and ½ the other **3** **not half** not at all: This food's not half bad. **4** **not half as** not nearly as

half-and-half /ˌ· · ˈ·/ n [U] mixture of milk and cream, used in coffee, etc.

half-baked /ˌ· ˈ·◂/ adj (esp. of ideas) not sensible

half-broth·er /ˈ· ˌ·/ n brother related through only one parent

half-heart·ed /ˌ· ˈ···◂/ adj showing not much interest

half-life /ˈ· ˌ·/ n time it takes for half the atoms in a radioactive (RADIOACTIVE) substance to decay

half-mast /ˌ· ˈ·/ n point near the middle of a FLAGPOLE where the flag flies as a sign of sorrow

half-sis·ter /ˈ· ˌ·/ n sister related through only one parent

half-time /ˌhæfˈtaɪm◂/ n [U] period of rest between 2 parts of a sports game

half-way /ˌhæfˈweɪ◂/ adj, adv 1 at the middle point between 2 things 2 meet someone halfway make an agreement with someone which partly meets the demands of both sides

halfway house /ˌ· · ˈ·/ n home for people getting over criminal or drug problems

half-wit /ˈ· ·/ n stupid person or one with a weak mind ~ted /ˌ· ˈ·◂/ adj

hall /hɔl/ n 1 passage inside the entrance of a house 2 large room for meetings, etc.

hal·le·lu·ja /ˌhælɪˈluːjə/ interj (expression of praise to God)

hall·mark /ˈhɔlmɑrk/ n mark proving that something is really silver or gold: (fig.) Clear expression is the hallmark of a good writer.

hall of fame /ˌ· · ˈ·/ n [S] list of famous sports players, or the building where their uniforms, equipment, etc. can be seen

hal·lowed /ˈhæloʊd/ adj fml holy

Hal·low·een /ˌhæləˈwin, ˌhɑ-/ n October 31, when children play tricks and dress in strange clothes

hal·lu·ci·nate /həˈlusəˌneɪt/ vi see things that are not there ~**natory** /-sənəˌtɔri, -ˌtʊuri/ adj fml **~nation** /həˌlusəˈneɪʃən/ n [C;U] (experience of seeing) something which is not really there, because of illness or drugs

hall·way /ˈhɔlweɪ/ n HALL (1)

ha·lo /ˈheɪloʊ/ n -loes or -los 1 circle representing light around the heads of holy people in pictures 2 circle of light around the sun or moon

halt /hɔlt/ vi/t fml stop **halt** n [S]

hal·ter /ˈhɔltər/ n 1 rope for leading a horse 2 woman's shirt with an open back

halt·ing /ˈhɔltɪŋ/ adj stopping and starting uncertainly

halve /hæv/ v 1 reduce by half: halve the time 2 divide into halves

halves /hævz/ n pl. of HALF

ham /hæm/ n 1 [C;U] (preserved meat from) the upper part of a pig's leg 2 [C] actor whose performance is unnatural 3 [C] non-professional radio operator ♦ vi/t perform like a HAM (2)

ham·burg·er /ˈhæmˌbɜrgər/ n 1 flat round cake of small bits of meat, eaten in a BUN (2) 2 GROUND BEEF

ham·mer[1] /ˈhæmər/ n 1 tool with a metal head for driving nails into wood 2 part of a piano, etc., that hits another part 3 **come under the hammer** be offered for sale at an AUCTION 4 **throwing the hammer** sport in which a heavy metal ball on a chain is thrown

hammer[2] v 1 vi/t hit with a hammer 2 vt defeat thoroughly 3 vi work continuously: hammer away at the problem 4 vt force: hammer the facts into their heads

    hammer out phr vt talk about in detail and come to a decision about

ham·mock /ˈhæmək/ n cloth or net hung up to sleep in

ham·per[1] /ˈhæmpər/ vt cause difficulty in movement

hamper[2] n large basket with a lid

ham·ster /ˈhæmstər/ n small mouselike animal often kept as a pet

ham·string /ˈhæmˌstrɪŋ/ n cordlike TENDON at the back of the leg ♦ vt **-strung** /-ˌstrʌŋ/ make powerless

hand[1] /hænd/ n 1 [C] movable part at the end of the arm 2 [C] pointer on a clock, etc. 3 [C] set of playing cards held by one player 4 [C] writing by hand 5 [C] worker; someone with a skill: farm hands — see also OLD HAND 6 [S] help: give/lend a hand 7 [C;U] control: get out of hand | have the matter in hand | in the hands of the police 8 [S] APPLAUSE: Give the singer a big hand. 9 **at first hand** by direct experience 10 **at hand** near in time or place 11 **at second/third/fourth hand** as information passed on through 1, 2, or 3 people 12 **by hand**: a not typed (TYPE) or printed b delivered directly, not by mail 13 **change hands** go from the possession of one person to that of another 14 **get/keep one's hand in** get/stay used to an activity 15 **get the upper hand (of)** get control or power (over something/somebody difficult) 16 **give someone a free hand** let them do things in their own way 17 **hand in glove (with)** closely connected (with someone), esp. in something bad 18 **hand in hand**: a holding each other's hands b in close connection 19 **hand over fist** very quickly and successfully 20 **have a hand in** be partly responsible for **21 have one's hands full** be very busy **22 in hand** ready for use **23 live from hand to mouth** have just enough money, food, etc., to live **24 on hand** ready for use or to take part **25 on the one/other hand** (used for comparing 2 things) **26 (out of/off) one's hands** (no longer) one's responsibility **27 play into someone's hands** do something which gives (one's opponent) an advantage **28 raise one's hand to/against** (make a movement) to hit **29 show one's hand** make one's power or intentions clear, esp. after keeping them secret **30 throw in one's hand** accept defeat **31 to hand** within reach **32 try one's hand (at)** attempt (an activity) **33 turn one's hand to** begin to practice (a skill) **34 wait on (someone) hand and foot** do every little thing for (someone) **35 with a heavy hand** in a firm manner

hand² vt **1** give with one's hand(s) **2 (have to) hand it to someone** (have to) admit the high quality or success of someone

hand down phr vt give (clothes) to a younger or smaller person

hand in phr vt deliver

hand on phr vt give to someone else

hand out phr vt **1** give out to several people **2** give freely: *He's always ready to hand out advice.*

hand over phr vt give control of: *We handed him over to the police.*

hand·bag /ˈhændbæg/ n woman's small bag for money and personal things

hand·book /ˈhændbʊk/ n book of instructions

hand·cuffs /ˈhændkʌfs/ n [P] pair of metal rings for fastening a criminal's wrists **handcuff** vt put handcuffs on

hand·ful /ˈhændfʊl/ n **1** as much as can be held in one hand **2** small number (of people) **3** *infml* person or animal that is hard to control

handgun /ˈhændgʌn/ n small gun – see PISTOL

hand·i·cap /ˈhændɪˌkæp/ n **1** disability of the body or mind **2** disadvantage given to the stronger competitors in a sport ♦ vt **-pp- 1** give a disadvantage to **2** (of a disability of body or mind) prevent (someone) from acting or living as most people do

hand·i·work /ˈhændɪˌwɜːk/ n [U] **1** work demanding the skillful use of the hands **2** result of someone's action

hand·ker·chief /ˈhæŋkətʃɪf, -ˌtʃiːf/ n cloth or paper for drying the nose, etc.

han·dle¹ /ˈhændl/ n part of a door, cup, etc., that one holds

handle² vt **1** touch or move with the hands **2** control; deal with: *handle the accounts* **3** (of a car, boat, etc.) obey controlling movements in the stated way –**dler** n person who controls an animal

han·dle·bars /ˈhændlˌbɑːz/ n [P] curved bar above front wheel of a bicycle, etc., which controls the direction it goes in

hand·made /ˌhændˈmeɪd◂/ adj made by a person, not by a machine

hand-me-down /ˈ· · ˌ/ n piece of clothing worn by someone and then given to his/her younger relative

hand·out /ˈhændaʊt/ n **1** something given free **2** printed sheet of information given out

hand·picked /ˌhændˈpɪkt◂/ adj carefully chosen

hand·shake /ˈhændʃeɪk/ n act of taking each other's hand as a greeting

hand·some /ˈhænsəm/ adj **1** of good appearance: *a handsome boy* **2** more than large enough: *a handsome reward* **~ly** adv

hand·stand /ˈhændstænd/ n position in which the body is supported upside down on the hands

hand·writ·ing /ˈhændˌraɪtɪŋ/ n [U] (style of) writing done by hand –**written** /ˈhændˌrɪtⁿ/ adj written by hand

hand·y /ˈhændi/ adj **1** useful **2** skillful with one's hands **3** easily reached **4 come in handy** be useful –**ily** adv

hand·y·man /ˈhændiˌmæn/ n **-men** /-mɛn/ person who does small repairs

hang¹ /hæŋ/ v **hung** /hʌŋ/ **1** vi/t fix or be fixed from above so that the lower part is free **2** vi/t (of certain kinds of meat) be kept in this position until ready to eat **3** vt stick (WALLPAPER) on a wall **4** vt (past t. and p. **hanged**) kill by dropping with a rope around the neck **5 hang fire** be delayed **6 hang one's head** appear ashamed

hang around phr vi **1** wait without purpose **2** delay **3** spend time: *hang around with friends*

hang back phr vi be unwilling to move

hang on *phr vi* **1** keep hold of something **2** wait **3** pay close attention to **4** depend on

hang onto *phr vt* try to keep

hang out *phr vi infml* **1** live or spend a lot of time **2** let it all hang out *sl* behave exactly as you want to

hang up *phr vi* **1** finish a telephone conversation **2** put something on a hook **3** be hung up on/about *sl* be anxious or have a fixed idea about

hang² *n* get/have the hang of something understand how a machine, etc., works

han·gar /ˈhæŋə, ˈhæŋgə/ *n* building where aircraft are kept

hang·er /ˈhæŋə/ *n* hook and bar to hang a garment from

hanger-on /ˌ· ˈ·/ *n* **hangers-on** person who tries to be friendly in the hope of advantage

hang glid·ing /ˈ· ˌ··/ *n* [U] the sport of gliding (GLIDE (2)) using a large KITE (1) instead of a plane

hang·man /ˈhæŋmən/ *n* **-men** /-mən/ man whose work is hanging criminals

hang·out /ˈhæŋaʊt/ *n infml* place one likes to go often, such as a BAR

hang·o·ver /ˈhæŋˌoʊvə/ *n* **1** feeling of sickness, etc., the day after drinking too much alcohol **2** condition or effect resulting from an earlier event or state

hang·up /ˈhæŋʌp/ *n sl* something about which a person gets unusually worried

han·ker /ˈhæŋkə/ *v* **hanker after/for** *phr vt* desire strongly **hankering** *n* [S]

han·kie /ˈhæŋki/ *n* handkerchief

hank·y-pank·y /ˌhæŋki ˈpæŋki/ *n* [U] improper behavior, esp. deceit or sexual activity of a not very serious kind

Ha·nuk·kah /ˈhɑnəkə/ *n* [U] eight-day Jewish festival in December

hap·haz·ard /ˌhæpˈhæzəd/ *adj* unplanned; disorderly

hap·less /ˈhæpləs/ *adj lit* unlucky

hap·pen /ˈhæpən/ *vi* **1** (of an event) take place: *When did the accident happen?* **2** be or do by chance: *We happened to meet.* **3** be true by or as if by chance: *As it happens, we do know each other.* ~**ing** *n* event

happen on *phr vt* find by chance

hap·py /ˈhæpi/ *adj* **1** pleased; contented **2** causing pleasure: *a happy occasion* **3** (of thoughts, etc.) suitable: *a happy remark*

4 (used in good wishes): *Happy Birthday!* –**pily** *adv* –**piness** *n* [U]

happy-go-luck·y /ˌ··· ˈ·· ◂/ *adj* unworried; CAREFREE

happy hour /ˈ·· ˌ/ *n* limited period in the day when alcoholic drinks are sold at lower than usual prices in a bar, etc.

ha·rangue /həˈræŋ/ *vt* attack or try to persuade with a long angry speech **harangue** *n*

har·ass /həˈræs, ˈhærəs/ *vt* worry repeatedly ~**ment** *n* [U]

har·bor /ˈhɑrbə/ *n* sheltered area where ships are safe ♦ *vt* **1** give protection to **2** keep (thoughts or feelings) in the mind

hard¹ /hɑrd/ *adj* **1** firm and stiff: *hard skin* **2** difficult: *hard question* **3** needing or using effort: *hard work/worker* **4** unpleasant; severe: *hard winter* | *Don't be too hard on him.* **5** (of water) containing minerals that stop soap from forming LATHER easily **6** (of drugs) dangerous and ADDICTive ~**ness** *n* [U]

hard² *adv* **1** with great effort: *push hard* **2** heavily: *raining hard* **3 hard at it** working hard **4 hard by** *fml* near **5 hard done by** unfairly treated **6 hard hit** suffering loss **7 hard put (to it)** having great difficulty **8 hard up** *infml* not having enough (esp. money) **9 take (it) hard** suffer deeply

hard-and-fast /ˌ·· ˈ· ◂/ *adj* (of rules) fixed

hard·back /ˈhɑrdbæk/ *n* book with a stiff cover

hard·ball /ˈhɑrdbɔl/ *n* [U] **1** baseball **2 play hardball** use methods that are not gentle, and may be unfair

hard·board /ˈhɑrdbɔrd, -boʊrd/ *n* [U] stiff cardboard, used like wood

hard-boiled /ˌ· ˈ· ◂/ *adj* **1** (of eggs) boiled until the yellow part is hard **2** (of people) not showing feeling

hard cop·y /ˈ· ˌ··/ *n* [U] readable information from a computer, esp. printed on paper

hard-core /ˌhɑrdˈkɔr◂, -ˈkoʊr◂/ *n* [U] small unchanging group within an organization ♦ *adj* **1** very strongly following a particular belief or activity **2** showing or describing sexual activity in a very detailed way: *hardcore pornography*

hard cur·ren·cy /ˌ· ˈ···/ *n* [C;U] money that can be freely exchanged

hard·en /ˈhɑrdn/ *vi/t* make or become hard or firm

harden to phr vt make (someone) less sensitive to (something or doing something)

hard-heart·ed /ˌ ˈ··◂/ adj not kind or gentle

hard la·bor /ˌ ˈ·· / n [U] (punishment which consists of) hard physical work such as digging, etc.

hard-line /ˌ ˈ·◂/ adj having a firm unchanging opinion or attitude **hard-liner** n

hard luck /ˌ ˈ·/ n [U] bad luck

hard·ly /ˈhɑrdli/ adv 1 almost not: I can hardly wait. 2 not at all: You can hardly blame me.

hard-nosed /ˌ ˈ·◂/ adj infml determined to get what one wants

hard of hear·ing /ˌ ˈ··◂/ adj partly DEAF

hard-pressed /ˌ ˈ·◂/ adj experiencing severe or continual difficulties

hard sell /ˌ ˈ·◂/ n [U] method of selling by putting pressure on buyers

hard·ship /ˈhɑrdˌʃɪp/ n [C;U] difficult conditions of life, such as lack of money, food, etc.

hard·ware /ˈhɑrdwɛr/ n [U] 1 pans, tools, etc., for the home 2 machinery which makes up a COMPUTER 3 machinery used in war

hardware store /ˈ·· ˌ/ n store that sells HARDWARE (1)

hard·wood /ˈhɑrdwʊd/ n [U] strong wood from trees that lose their leaves in the fall

har·dy /ˈhɑrdi/ adj able to bear cold, hard work, etc. **–diness** n [U]

hare /hɛr/ n animal like a large rabbit that can run quickly

hare·brained /ˈhɛrbreɪnd/ adj impractical; foolish

hare·lip /ˈhɛrˌlɪp/ n top lip divided into 2 parts

har·em /ˈhɛrəm, ˈhærəm/ n (women living in) the women's part of a Muslim house

hark /hɑrk/ vi lit listen

hark back phr vi talk about the past

harm /hɑrm/ n [U] 1 damage; injury (INJURE) 2 out of harm's way safe ♦ vt cause harm to **–ful** adj **~less** adj not dangerous

har·mon·i·ca /hɑrˈmɑnɪkə/ n musical instrument played by moving the mouth up and down it and blowing

har·mo·nize /ˈhɑrməˌnaɪz/ vi/t 1 (cause to) be in agreement, esp. in style, color, etc. 2 sing or play in musical HARMONY

har·mo·ny /ˈhɑrməni/ n 1 [C;U] musical notes pleasantly combined 2 [U] peaceful agreement 3 [C;U] pleasant combination of colors, etc.

har·ness /ˈhɑrnɪs/ n [C;U] 1 leather bands, etc., that fasten a horse to a cart 2 similar arrangement for tying someone to something: safety harness ♦ vt 1 fasten with a harness 2 use (wind, water, etc.) to produce esp. electrical power

harp[1] /hɑrp/ n large musical instrument with strings played with the fingers **~ist** n

harp[2] v **harp on** phr vt talk a lot about (one's misfortunes)

har·poon /hɑrˈpun/ vt, n (strike with) a spear on a rope, for hunting WHALES, etc.

harp·si·chord /ˈhɑrpsiˌkɔrd/ n kind of old-fashioned piano

har·row·ing /ˈhæroʊɪŋ/ adj causing painful feelings

harsh /hɑrʃ/ adj 1 painful to the senses: harsh light 2 cruel **~ly** adv **~ness** n [U]

har·vest /ˈhɑrvɪst/ n 1 (time of) gathering the crops 2 amount of crops gathered ♦ vt gather (crops)

has /s, z, əz, həz; strong hæz/ v 3rd pers. sing. pres. t. of HAVE

has-been /ˈ· ˌ/ n derog person or thing no longer popular or respected

hash /hæʃ/ n [U] 1 meal of (recooked) cut up meat and potatoes 2 make a hash of something do something badly 3 infml HASHISH

hash browns /ˌhæʃˈbraʊnz/ n [P] potatoes cut in very small thin pieces, cooked until brown

hash·ish /ˈhæʃiʃ, hæˈʃiʃ/ n [U] strongest form of the drug CANNABIS

has·n't /ˈhæzənt/ v short for: has not

has·sle /ˈhæsəl/ n infml a lot of trouble ♦ vi/t cause trouble or difficulties for

haste /heɪst/ n [U] quick movement, or action

has·ten /ˈheɪsən/ vi/t 1 fml hurry 2 be quick to (say): I hasten to add that no one was hurt.

hast·y /ˈheɪsti/ adj 1 done (too) quickly 2 (of people) too quick in acting or deciding **–ily** adv

hat /hæt/ n 1 covering for the head 2 **keep (something) under one's hat** keep (something) secret 3 **take one's hat off** to show admiration for 4 **talking through one's hat** saying something stupid – see also OLD HAT ~**ter** n maker of hats

hatch[1] /hætʃ/ v 1 vi/t (cause to) be born from an egg 2 vt form (a plan)

hatch[2] n (cover over) a hole in a wall or floor

hatch·back /'hætʃbæk/ n car with a door at the back that opens upwards

hatch·et /'hætʃɪt/ n 1 small AX 2 **bury the hatchet** become friends again after a bad argument

hatchet job /'·· ˌ·/ n cruel attack in speech or writing

hate /heɪt/ vt 1 dislike very much 2 be sorry: I hate to tell you. ♦ n [C;U] strong dislike ~**ful** adj very unpleasant ~**fully** adv

ha·tred /'heɪtrɪd/ n [S;U] hate

haugh·ty /'hɔːti/ adj too proud; ARROGANT –**tily** adv –**tiness** n [U]

haul /hɔːl/ vi/t 1 pull with effort 2 pull with a vehicle ♦ n 1 **a** amount of fish caught **b** amount of something gained, esp. stolen goods 2 distance that something travels or is carried: the long haul home

haul off phr v 1 prepare to strike: He hauled off and punched him. 2 take away

haunt /hɔːnt/ vt 1 (of a spirit) appear in 2 visit regularly 3 remain in the thoughts of: haunted by the memory | haunting tune ♦ n place often visited

have[1] /v, əv, hæv; strong hæv/ v aux, pres. t. I/you/we/they **have**, he/she/it **has** /z, əz, həz; strong hæz/; past t. **had** /d, əd, həd; strong hæd/ 1 **a** (forms perfect tenses): I've/I have finished. **b** Had (I, he, etc.) if (I, he, etc.) had: Had I known, I would have stayed. 2 **had better (do/not do)** ought (not) to: You'd better tell him about it. 3 **have (got) to** be forced to; must; I'll have to wash it. 4 **have had it** infml have experienced, worked, etc., all one can: I've had it! Let's go home.

have[2] vt 1 also **have got** — possess: She has/has got two sisters. 2 experience or enjoy: to have a party/a vacation 3 receive: I had some good news today. 4 eat, drink, or smoke: I had a cigarette. 5 ask (someone) to one's home: We're having some people around/over for drinks. 6 allow: I won't have all this noise. 7 cause to be done: You should have your hair cut. 8 give birth to: to have twins 9 **have done with** finish 10 **have it in for** be as unkind as possible to 11 **have one's eyes on** watch continuously 12 **have to do with** have a connection with

have on phr vt 1 be wearing 2 have arranged to do 3 have (unfavorable information) recorded against (someone) 4 **have nothing on** be not nearly as good as

have out phr vt 1 get (a tooth or organ) removed 2 settle by argument: have the whole thing out with Bill

ha·ven /'heɪvən/ n calm safe place

have·n't /'hævənt/ v short for: have not

hav·oc /'hævək/ n [U] widespread damage

hawk[1] /hɔːk/ n 1 bird that catches creatures for food 2 person who believes in use of force, esp. military

hawk[2] vt sell (goods) on the street or at the doors of houses

hay /heɪ/ n [U] dried grass for animal food

hay fe·ver /'· ˌ·/ n [U] illness like a bad cold, caused by breathing in POLLEN from the air

hay·stack /'heɪstæk/ n large pile of stored hay

hay·wire /'heɪwaɪə/ adj **go haywire** (of plans, etc.) become badly disordered

haz·ard /'hæzəd/ n danger; risk ♦ vt 1 offer (a guess or suggestion) 2 put in danger ~**ous** adj dangerous

haze /heɪz/ n [S;U] light mist **hazy** adj 1 misty 2 uncertain: I'm hazy about the details. ♦ vt play tricks on (a FRESHMAN)

ha·zel /'heɪzəl/ n, adj light greenish brown: hazel eyes

H-bomb /'eɪtʃ bɑm/ n HYDROGEN BOMB

he /i, strong hi/ pron (used for the male subject of a sentence)

head[1] /hɛd/ n 1 [C] part of the body containing the eyes, mouth, and brain 2 [the S] end where this rests: the head of the bed 3 [C] mind: Don't put ideas into his head. 4 [S] **a** ability: no head for figures **b** the power to be in control of oneself: to keep/lose one's head in a crisis 5 ruler; chief: heads of state 6 [(the)S] **a** top: head *of a hammer/a page/the stairs* **b** front: *head of a procession* **7** [S] pressure of steam or water **8 a/per head** for each person: *cost $5 a head* **9 above/over one's head** too hard to understand **10 bring/come to a head** reach a point where something must be done **11 eat/shout, etc., one's head off** *infml* eat/ shout, etc., too much, loudly, etc. **12 go to one's head: a** make one too drunk **b** make one (or someone) too excited **c** make someone too proud **13 head and shoulders above** very much better than **14 head over heels: a** turning over headfirst **b** completely: *head over heels in love* **15 make head or tail of** manage to understand **16 out of one's head** *infml* crazy **17 put your/our/their heads together** think out a plan with other people **18 turn someone's head: a** make someone too proud **b** make someone fall in love **heads** *n* [U] front of a coin

head² *v* **1** *vt* be at the top or front of: *head a procession* **2** *vt* be the best at something **3** *vi* go somewhere: *head north/towards Rome/for the bar* **4** be the chief, director, etc.: *to head the department*

head off *phr vt* **1** cause to change direction **2** prevent

head·ache /ˈhɛdeɪk/ *n* **1** pain in the head **2** problem

head·dress /ˈhɛd-drɛs/ *n* decorative head covering

head·first /ˌhɛdˈfɜːst/ *adj, adv* with the rest of the body following the head

head·gear /ˈhɛdɡɪr/ *n* [U] covering for the head

head·hunt·er /ˈhɛdˌhʌntə/ *n* person who tries to find suitable people for important jobs

head·ing /ˈhɛdɪŋ/ *n* words written as a title at the top of a page

head·light /ˈhɛdlaɪt/ *n* strong light on the front of a vehicle

head·line /ˈhɛdlaɪn/ *n* **1** heading above a newspaper story **2** main point of the news on radio or TV

head·long /ˈhɛdlɒŋ, ˌhɛdˈlɒŋ◂/ *adj, adv* **1** HEADFIRST **2** in foolish haste

head·on /ˌ▪ ˈ▪◂/ *adv, adj* with the front parts meeting, usu. violently: *a head-on collision*

head·phones /ˈhɛdfəʊnz/ *n* [P] listening apparatus that fits over the ears

head·quar·ters /ˈhɛdˌkwɔːtəz/ *n* -ters also HQ central office of an organization

head·rest /ˈhɛdrɛst/ *n* support for the head

head·room /ˈhɛd-rum, -rʊm/ *n* [U] space to stand or move under something

head start /ˌ▪ ˈ▪/ *n* [S] advantage in a race or competition

head·stone /ˈhɛdstəʊn/ *n* stone marking the top end of a grave

head·strong /ˈhɛdstrɒŋ/ *adj* uncontrollable; impatient

head·way /ˈhɛdweɪ/ *n* **make headway** advance; make PROGRESS

heal /hiːl/ *vi/t* make or become healthy again ~**er** *n*

health /hɛlθ/ *n* [U] **1** state of being well, without disease **2** condition of body or mind: *in poor health* **3** TOAST (2): *to drink someone's health* ~**y** *adj* **1** physically strong **2** producing good health **3** showing good health: (fig.) *healthy profits*

health care /ˈ▪ ˌ▪/ *n* [U] service and business of taking care of people's health, giving medical treatment, etc.

health club /ˈ▪ ˌ▪/ *n* place where people who have paid to be members go to exercise

health food /ˈ▪ ˌ▪/ *n* [C;U] food that contains only natural substances

heap /hiːp/ *n* untidy pile ♦ *vt* pile up: *heap food on the plate* **heaps** *n* [P] *infml* lots: *heaps of time*

hear /hɪr/ *v* **heard** /hɜːd/ **1** *vi/t* receive (sounds) with the ears **2** *vt* be told or informed: *I hear they're married.* **3** *vt* listen to with attention: *A priest heard my confession.* **4** *vt* consider (a case) officially as a judge **5 won't/wouldn't hear of** refuse(s) to allow

hear from *phr vt* receive news from, esp. by letter

hear of *phr vt* know about: *I've never heard of him.*

hear out *phr vt* listen to, till the end

hear·ing /ˈhɪrɪŋ/ *n* **1** [U] ability to hear sound **2** [U] distance at which one can hear **3** [C;U] act or experience of hearing **4** [C] chance to explain **5** [C] *law* trial of a case

hearing aid /ˈ▪▪ ▪/ *n* small electric apparatus to improve hearing

hearing-im·paired /ˌ▪▪ ▪ˈ▪/ *adj* unable to hear well, or at all

hear·say /ˈhɪrseɪ/ *n* [U] things heard but unproved

hearse /hɜːs/ n car for carrying a body to a funeral

heart /hɑːt/ n **1** [C] organ that pumps blood around the body **2** [C] center of a person's feelings: *a kind heart* | *My heart bled* (= I was very sorry) *for him.* **3** [C] something shaped like a heart **4** [C] center: *heart of a lettuce/of the city/of the matter* **5** [C] red figure in the shape of a heart, on a playing card **6** [U] courage: *take/lose heart* **7 after one's own heart** of the kind that one likes **8 break someone's/one's heart** make/become very unhappy **9 by heart** from memory **10 eat one's heart out** be very troubled **11 from the (bottom of one's) heart** with real feeling **12 have one's heart in the right place** be a kind person **13 lost one's heart to** fall in love with **14 set one's heart on** want very much **15 take something to heart** feel it deeply

heart·ache /ˈhɑːteɪk/ n [U] deep sorrow

heart at·tack /ˈ· ·ˌ·/ n dangerous condition in which the heart beats irregularly and painfully

heart·beat /ˈhɑːtbiːt/ n [C;U] pumping movement of the heart

heart·break /ˈhɑːtbreɪk/ n terrible sorrow ~**ing** adj causing heartbreak

heart·brok·en /ˈhɑːtˌbrəʊkən/ adj BROKEN-HEARTED

heart·burn /ˈhɑːtbɜːn/ n [U] unpleasant feeling of burning in the chest, caused by INDIGESTION

heart di·sease /ˈ· ·ˌ·/ n [U] condition in which the heart has difficulty pumping blood

heart·en /ˈhɑːtn/ vt encourage

heart·felt /ˈhɑːtfelt/ adj sincere

hearth /hɑːθ/ n area around the fire in a home

heart·land /ˈhɑːtlænd/ n **1** central and most important area **2** the MIDWEST

heart·less /ˈhɑːtlɪs/ adj cruel ~**ly** adv ~**ness** n [U]

heart·rend·ing /ˈhɑːtˌrendɪŋ/ adj causing great pity

heart·strings /ˈhɑːtstrɪŋz/ n [P] deepest feelings of love and pity

heart·throb /ˈhɑːtθrɒb/ n infml **1** person who is very attractive and with whom others fall in love **2** person whom one loves: *his latest heartthrob*

heart-to-heart /ˌ· ·ˈ· ·/ n open talk about personal details **heart-to-heart** adj

heart·warm·ing /ˈhɑːtˌwɔːmɪŋ/ adj causing pleasant feelings: *heartwarming response*

heart·y /ˈhɑːti/ adj **1** friendly and cheerful **2** healthy **3** (of meals) large —**ily** adv in a hearty way

heat[1] /hiːt/ n **1** [U] (degree of) hotness **2** [U] hot weather: *I don't like the heat much.* **3** [U] great excitement **4** [C] part of a race, those who win then racing against others **5 in heat** (of female dogs, etc.) in a state of sexual excitement — see also WHITE HEAT

heat[2] vi/t make or become hot ~**ed** adj excited and angry ~**er** n machine for heating air or water ~**ing** n [U] system for keeping rooms warm

hea·then /ˈhiːðən/ n, adj (person) not belonging to one of the large established religions

heat·stroke /ˈhiːtstrəʊk/ n [U] SUNSTROKE

heat wave /ˈ· ·/ n period of unusually hot weather

heave /hiːv/ v **1** vi/t pull or lift with effort **2** vt throw (something heavy) **3** vi rise and fall regularly **4** vi VOMIT **5 heave a sigh** SIGH

heav·en /ˈhevən/ n **1** [U] home of God or the gods **2** (usu. cap.) God: *Heaven help you!* | *Good heavens!* **3** [C usu. pl.] the sky **4** [U] wonderful place or state **5 move heaven and earth** do everything possible (to cause or prevent something) — see also SEVENTH HEAVEN

heav·en·ly /ˈhevənli/ adj **1** of heaven: *The moon is a* **heavenly** *body.* **2** wonderful

heav·y[1] /ˈhevi/ adj **1** of great weight **2** of unusual amount: *heavy rain/traffic* | *a heavy smoker* (= someone who smokes a lot) **3** needing effort: *heavy work* **4** serious and dull: *heavy reading* **5** (of food) too solid **6** (of the sea) with big waves **7 find it heavy going** find it very difficult **8 make heavy weather of something** make a job or problem seem more difficult than it really is ♦ adv in a troublesome, dull way —**ily** adv —**iness** n [U]

heav·y[2] n serious usu. male part in a play, etc., esp. a bad character

heavy-du·ty /ˌ· ·ˈ· ·◂/ adj (of clothes, machines, etc.) strong enough for rough treatment

heavy-hand·ed /ˌ· ·ˈ· ·◂/ adj **1** severe; awkward; not careful

heavy in·dus·try /ˌ‿ ˈ‿‿/ n [U] industry that produces large goods, or materials such as coal, steel, etc., that are used in the production of other goods

heavy met·al /ˌ‿ ˈ‿‿/ n [U] type of ROCK music with a loud beat, played on electric GUITARS

heav·y·weight /ˈhevɪˌweɪt/ n, adj 1 (a FIGHTER) of the heaviest class in boxing (BOX²) 2 (a person or thing) a of more than average weight b having great importance or influence

He·brew /ˈhibru/ n [U] language of the ancient Jews and of modern Israel

heck·le /ˈhekəl/ vi/t interrupt (a speaker) disapprovingly at a meeting –ler n

hec·tare /ˈhekter/ n (a measure of area of land equal to) 10,000 square meters

hec·tic /ˈhektɪk/ adj full of hurry and excitement

he'd /ɪd; strong hid/ short for: 1 he would 2 he had

hedge /hedʒ/ n 1 row of bushes dividing gardens or fields 2 protection: a hedge against inflation ♦ v 1 vt make a hedge around 2 vi refuse to answer directly 3 **hedge one's bets** protect oneself against loss by favoring or supporting more than one side in a competition, etc.

he·don·is·m /ˈhidnˌɪzəm/ n [U] idea that pleasure is the only important thing in life –ist n –istic /ˌhidnˈɪstɪk◂/ adj

heed /hid/ vt fml give attention to ♦ n [U] fml attention ~less adj

heel /hil/ n 1 back of the foot 2 part of a shoe, sock, etc., which covers this, esp. the raised part of a shoe under the foot 3 unpleasant person, who treats others badly 4 **at/on one's heels** close behind one 5 **cool one's heels** rest 6 **down at heel** (of people) untidy and looking poor 7 **kick one's heels** not have anything particular to do ♦ v 1 vt put a heel on (a shoe) 2 vi (of a dog) follow closely

hef·ty /ˈhefti/ adj big and heavy

heif·er /ˈhefər/ n young cow

height /haɪt/ n 1 [C;U] (degree of) being high 2 [C] measurement from top to bottom 3 [C] also **heights** pl. — high place 4 [S] a highest degree: the height of fashion b the main or most active point: the height of the storm

height·en /ˈhaɪtˈn/ vi/t make or become greater in degree

hei·nous /ˈheɪnəs/ adj fml (of wickedness) extreme

heir /er/ **heiress** /ˈerɪs/ fem. — n person with the legal right to receive property, etc., when the owner dies

heir·loom /ˈerlum/ n valuable object given by older members of a family to younger ones over many years

held /held/ v past t. and p. of HOLD

hel·i·cop·ter /ˈhelɪˌkɑptər/ n aircraft that flies by means of blades on top, which turn quickly

he·li·um /ˈhiliəm/ n [U] very light gas used in AIRSHIPS, etc.

hell /hel/ n 1 [U] place where the wicked are said to be punished after death 2 [C] terrible place 3 [U] sl (used in anger or to give force): What the hell's that? | That's a hell of a good car. 4 **for the hell of it** for fun 5 **give someone hell** treat them roughly 6 **hell to pay** sl serious trouble or punishment 7 **like hell**: a very much: I worked like hell all week. b not at all: "He paid, didn't he?" "Like hell he did." 8 **play hell with** cause damage to ♦ interj (an expression of) anger or disappointment ~ish adj terrible

he'll /ɪl, il, hil; strong hil/ short for: he will

hel·lo /həˈlou, heˈlou, ˈhelou/ interj, n -los (used in greeting and answering a telephone)

helm /helm/ n 1 wheel or TILLER that guides a ship 2 **at the helm** in control

hel·met /ˈhelmɪt/ n protective head covering

help¹ /help/ v 1 vi/t make it possible for (someone) to do something; be useful (to) 2 vt avoid; prevent: I can't help laughing. | It can't be helped. (= these things happen) 3 vt give food, etc., to: Help yourself to sugar. | He just helped himself to the money. (= took) ~er n person who helps ~ing n serving of food

    help out phr vi/t give help (to someone) at a time of need

help² n 1 [U] act of helping; AID 2 [C] someone or something that helps 3 **so help me** I am speaking the truth 4 **Help!** Please bring help. ~ful adj useful ~fully adv ~less adj unable to look after oneself ~lessly adv

help·ing verb /ˈ‿‿ ˌ‿/ n verb used with another verb to show tense, person, etc.

hem¹ /hem/ n edge of a skirt, etc., turned under and sewn

hem² *vt* **-mm-** put a hem on

hem in *phr vt* surround closely

hem·i·sphere /ˈhɛməˌsfɪr/ *n* **1** half a SPHERE **2** half of the Earth: *the southern hemisphere*

hem·line /ˈhɛmlaɪn/ *n* length of a skirt or dress

he·mo·phil·i·a /ˌhiːməˈfɪliə, -ˈfɪlyə/ *n* [U] disease that makes the sufferer bleed badly after only a small cut **-iac** /-iˌæk/ *n* person suffering from hemophilia

hem·or·rhage /ˈhɛmərɪdʒ/ *n* [C;U] flow of blood, esp. long and unexpected

hem·or·rhoid /ˈhɛməˌrɔɪd/ *n* swollen blood vessel at the lower end of the bowel

hemp /hɛmp/ *n* [U] plant used for making rope, rough cloth, and the drug MARI-JUANA

hen /hɛn/ *n* female bird, esp. the kind kept for its eggs on farms

hence /hɛns/ *adv fml* **1** for this reason **2** from here or now

hence·forth /ˈhɛnsfɔrθ, -fourθ, ˌhɛnsˈfɔrθ, -ˈfourθ/ **–forward** /ˌhɛnsˈfɔrwəd/ *adv fml* from now on

hench·man /ˈhɛntʃmən/ *n* **-men** /-mən/ faithful supporter who may use violent methods

hep·a·ti·tis /ˌhɛpəˈtaɪtɪs/ *n* [U] serious disease of the LIVER

her /ə, hə/ *strong* hɜ/ *pron* (used for the female object of a sentence) ♦ *determiner* of her: *her car* **hers** /hɜz/ *pron* of her; her one(s): *It's hers.*

her·ald /ˈhɛrəld/ *n* (in former times) person who brought important news ♦ *vt fml* be a sign of (something coming)

herb /əb, hɜb/ *n* any plant used in medicine or to improve the taste of food **~al** *adj* of herbs **~alist** *n* person who uses herbs, esp. to treat disease

her·biv·o·rous /həˈbɪvərəs, ə-/ *adj* (of animals) which eat grass or plants

herd /hɜd/ *n* **1** group of animals together **2** people generally, thought of as acting all alike ♦ *vt* drive in a herd: (fig.) *to herd tourists into a bus*

here /hɪr/ *adv* **1** at, in, or to this place: *"It's Professor Worth here."* (= speaking on the telephone) **2** at this point: *Here we agree.* **3 here and there** scattered about **4 Here goes!** Now I'm going to have a try. **5 Here's to** (said when drinking a TOAST (2)) **6 neither here nor there** not connected with the matter being talked about

here·a·bouts /ˈhɪrəˌbaʊts/ *adv* somewhere near here

here·af·ter /hɪrˈæftə/ *adv fml* in the future ♦ *n* [S] life after death

here·by /hɪrˈbaɪ, ˈhɪrbaɪ/ *adv fml* by this means

he·red·i·ta·ry /həˈrɛdəˌtɛri/ *adj* passed down from parent to child

he·red·i·ty /həˈrɛdəti/ *n* [U] fact that qualities are passed on from parent to child

here·in /hɪrˈɪn/ *adv fml* in this

her·e·sy /ˈhɛrəsi/ *n* [C;U] belief that goes against what is officially accepted

her·e·tic /ˈhɛrətɪk/ *n* person guilty of heresy **~al** /həˈrɛtɪkəl/ *adj*

here·with /ˌhɪrˈwɪθ, -ˈwɪð/ *adv fml* with this

her·i·tage /ˈhɛrətɪdʒ/ *n* something passed down within a family or nation

her·mit /ˈhɜmɪt/ *n* person who lives alone, esp. for religious reasons

her·ni·a /ˈhɜniə/ *n* [C;U] conditions in which an organ, esp. the bowel, pushes through its covering wall

he·ro /ˈhɪroʊ/ *n* **-roes 1** someone admired for bravery, etc. **2** most important character in a story **~ic** /hɪˈroʊɪk/ *adj* very brave **~ically** *adv* **~ics** *n* [P] grand speech or actions that mean nothing **~ism** /ˈhɛroʊˌɪzəm/ *n* [U] courage

her·o·in /ˈhɛroʊɪn/ *n* [U] drug made from MORPHINE

her·o·ine /ˈhɛroʊɪn/ *n* female HERO

her·pes /ˈhɜpiz/ *n* [U] very infectious sexual disease

her·ring /ˈhɛrɪŋ/ *n* sea fish used for food — see also RED HERRING

her·self /əˈsɛlf; *strong* həˈsɛlf/ *pron* **1** (*reflexive form of* she): *She hurt herself.* **2** (*strong form of* she): *She ate it herself.* **3** (all) by herself: **a** alone **b** without help **4** to herself not shared

he's /iz; *strong* hiz/ *short for*: **1** he is **2** has

hes·i·tant /ˈhɛzətənt/ *adj* tending to hesitate **–tancy** *n* [U]

hes·i·tate /ˈhɛzəˌteɪt/ *vi* **1** pause because one is uncertain **2** be unwilling **–tation** /ˌhɛzəˈteɪʃən/ *n* [C;U]

het·e·ro·ge·ne·ous /ˌhetərəˈdʒiːniəs, -ˈdʒiːnyəs/ adj fml of many different kinds

het·e·ro·sex·u·al /ˌhetərəˈsekʃuəl◂/ adj attracted to people of the other sex ~ity /ˌhetərəˌsekʃuˈæləti/ n [U]

hew /hyuː/ vi/t **hewed**, **hewed** or **hewn** /hyuːn/ fml cut with a heavy tool

hex·a·gon /ˈheksəˌgɒn/ n figure with 6 sides ~al /hekˈsægənəl/ adj

hey·day /ˈheɪdeɪ/ n [S] time of greatest success

hi /haɪ/ interj infml HELLO (= informal greeting)

hi·a·tus /haɪˈeɪtəs/ n fml space where something is missing

hi·ber·nate /ˈhaɪbəˌneɪt/ vi (of some animals) sleep during the winter ~nation /ˌhaɪbəˈneɪʃən/ n [U]

hic·cup /ˈhɪkəp/ n 1 sudden stopping of the breath with a sharp sound 2 small problem or delay **hiccup** vi have HICCUPS (1)

hick /hɪk/ n infml foolish person from the country

hide¹ /haɪd/ v **hid** /hɪd/, **hidden** /ˈhɪdn/ 1 vt put out of sight 2 vi keep oneself from being seen

hide² n 1 animal's skin 2 **hide or/nor hair** of infml any sign of

hide-and-seek /ˌ· · ˈ·/ n [U] children's game in which one child closes his/her eyes while the others hide, then tries to find them

hid·e·ous /ˈhɪdiəs/ adj very ugly; very unpleasant to look at ~ly adv

hide·out /ˈhaɪdaʊt/ also **hide·a·way** /ˈhaɪdəˌweɪ/ — n place where one can go to avoid people

hid·ing¹ /ˈhaɪdɪŋ/ n beating

hiding² n [U] state of being hidden: go into hiding

hi·er·ar·chy /ˈhaɪəˌrɑːrki/ n [C;U] organization with higher and lower ranks

hi·e·ro·glyph·ics /ˌhaɪərəˈglɪfɪks/ n [P] writing that uses pictures, as in ancient Egypt

high¹ /haɪ/ adj 1 far above the ground: a high mountain | 20 feet high 2 great: high cost 3 good: high standards 4 (of a musical note) not deep 5 (of time) as the middle point: high summer | It's high time we were going. (= We should go at once.) 6 infml under the influence of drink or drugs ♦ n 1 high point or level: Sales are at an all-time high. 2 state of

great excitement: on a high ~ly adv 1 very: highly amused 2 very well: highly paid

high² adv 1 to or at a high level: aim high 2 feelings ran high people got excited and angry 3 **high and dry** deserted 4 **high and low** everywhere

high and might·y /ˌ· ˈ·· ◂/ adj infml too proud and certain of one's own importance

high·brow /ˈhaɪbraʊ/ n, adj (person) knowing a lot about art, books, etc.

high chair /ˈhaɪ ˌtʃer/ n seat for eeding a small child

high-class /ˌ· ˈ· ◂/ adj 1 of good quality 2 of high social position

higher ed·u·ca·tion /ˌ·· ···ˈ·/ n [U] education at a university or college

high-fli·er, -flyer /ˌ· ˈ·/ n 1 clever person who has high aims 2 stock of high value

high-grade /ˌ· ˈ· ◂/ adj of high quality

high-hand·ed /ˌ· ˈ· ◂/ adj using power too forcefully

high horse /ˈ· ·, ·ˈ ·/ n **on one's high horse** infml derog behaving as if one knows best, or more than others

high jump /ˈ· ·/ n [S] sport of jumping over a bar

high-lev·el /ˌ· ˈ·· ◂/ adj in or at a position of high importance

high life /ˈ· ·/ n [S] enjoyable life of the rich and fashionable

high·light /ˈhaɪlaɪt/ n 1 most important detail 2 lightest area on a picture, or in the hair ♦ vt throw attention onto

high·light·er /ˈhaɪlaɪtə/ n pen used to mark words so they are noticed more easily

high point /ˈ· ·/ n [S] most remembered part of an activity, esp. because pleasant

high-mind·ed /ˌ· ˈ·· ◂/ adj having high principles

High·ness /ˈhaɪnɪs/ n (title of some royal persons)

high-pow·ered /ˌ· ˈ·· ◂/ adj having great force or ability

high-pro·file /ˌ· ˈ·/ adj attracting a lot of attention from the public

high-rise /ˈ· ·/ adj, n (building) with many floors

high school /ˈ· ·/ n school for children in GRADES 9–12

high-spir·it·ed /ˌ· ˈ··· ◂/ adj active and fond of adventure

high-strung /ˌ· ˈ· ◂/ adj nervous; excitable

high tech·nol·o·gy /ˌ· ·ˈ···◂/ n [U] use of the most modern machines, processes, etc., in business or industry **high tech**, **hi-tech** /ˌhaɪ ˈtɛk◂/ adj

high·way /ˈhaɪweɪ/ n wide main road for fast traffic

hi·jack /ˈhaɪdʒæk/ vt **1** take control of (esp. an aircraft) by force **2** stop and rob (a train, etc.) ~**er** n

hike /haɪk/ vi, n (go for) a long country walk ♦ vt increase: *They've hiked the prices.* **hiker** n

hi·lar·i·ous /hɪˈlɛəriəs, -ˈlær-/ adj full of or causing laughter ~**ly** adv

hill /hɪl/ n **1** raised piece of land, not as high as a mountain **2** slope on a road, etc. ~**y** adj

hill·bil·ly /ˈhɪlˌbɪli/ n derog someone from a mountain area

hilt /hɪlt/ n **1** handle of a sword **2** (**up) to the hilt** completely

him /ɪm; strong hɪm/ pron (used for the male object of a sentence)

him·self /ɪmˈsɛlf; strong hɪmˈsɛlf/ pron **1** (reflexive form of **he**): *He shot himself.* **2** (strong form of **he**): *He made it himself.* **3** (**all) by himself: a** alone **b** without help **4 to himself** not shared

hind /haɪnd/ adj (of animals' legs) back

hin·der /ˈhɪndə/ vt delay the PROGRESS of –**drance** /ˈhɪndrəns/ n [C;U]

hind·quar·ters /ˈhaɪndˌkwɔːtəz/ n [P] animal's back legs

hind·sight /ˈhaɪndsaɪt/ n [U] ability to understand the past, and esp. what went wrong

Hin·du /ˈhɪndu/ n **-dus** person whose religion is Hinduism **Hindu** adj

Hin·du·is·m /ˈhɪnduˌɪzəm/ n [U] chief religion of India, noted for its CASTE system and belief in reincarnation (REINCARNATE)

hinge¹ /hɪndʒ/ n metal joint on which a door, etc., swings

hinge² vt fix on hinges

hinge on/upon phr vt depend on

hint /hɪnt/ n **1** small or indirect suggestion: (fig.) *There's a hint of summer in the air.* **2** useful advice ♦ vi/t suggest indirectly

hin·ter·land /ˈhɪntəˌlænd/ n [S] inner part of a country

hip¹ /hɪp/ n fleshy part where the legs join the body

hip² adj sl modern and fashionable

hip·pie /ˈhɪpi/ n (young) person with long hair who is against the standards of ordinary society

hip·po·pot·a·mus /ˌhɪpəˈpɒtəməs/ also **hip·po** /ˈhɪpoʊ/ — n **-muses** or **-mi** /-maɪ/ large African river animal

hire /haɪə/ vt get the use or services of something or someone for wages or payment: *hire a teacher* ♦ n person or thing hired: *new hires*

his /ɪz; strong hɪz/ determiner of him: *his shoes* ♦ pron of him; his one(s): *It's his.*

hiss /hɪs/ vi t make a sound like "s", esp. to show disapproval **hiss** n

his·to·ri·an /hɪˈstɔːriən, -ˈstoʊr-/ n person who studies history

his·tor·ic /hɪˈstɒrɪk, -ˈstɑːr-/ adj important in history: *a historic event*

his·tor·i·cal /hɪˈstɒrɪkəl, -ˈstɑːr-/ adj about history: *historical research/novels* ~**ly** adv

his·to·ry /ˈhɪstəri/ n **1** [U] study of past events **2** [C] account of past events **3** [C] record of someone's past: *her medical history* **4 make history** do something important which will be remembered — see also HISTORIAN

hit¹ /hɪt/ vt hit, pres. p. hitting **1** come, or bring something, hard against: *He hit the ball with the bat.* | *The car hit the wall.* **2** reach: *hit the main road* **3** have a bad effect on **4 hit it off** have a good relationship **5 hit the bottle** infml drink too much alcohol **6 hit the nail on the head** say or do the right thing **7 hit the road** infml start on a journey **8 hit the roof** show or express great anger **9 hit the spot** satisfy completely

hit back phr vi reply forcefully to an attack on oneself

hit on/upon phr vt find by chance

hit out at/against phr vt attack in words

hit up phr vt infml (ask to) borrow: *He hit me up for $10.*

hit² n **1** blow **2** successful performance

hit-and-run /ˌ· · ˈ·/ n accident in which a driver hits someone with his/her car, then drives away without stopping to help ♦ adj

hitch /hɪtʃ/ v **1** vt fasten by hooking a rope or metal part on something **2** vi hitch-

hike 3 get hitched get married ♦ *n* **1** difficulty or delay **2** kind of knot

hitch up *phr vt* pull up into place

hitch·hike /ˈhɪtʃhaɪk/ *vi* travel by getting rides in other people's cars **hitchhiker** *n*

hi-tech /ˌhaɪ ˈtɛk/ *adj* of or using HIGH TECHNOLOGY

hith·er·to /ˌhɪðəˈtu, ˈhɪðəˌtu/ *adv fml* until now

hit list /ˈ· ·/ *n infml* list of people or organizations against whom some (bad) action is planned

hit man /ˈ· ·/ *n infml* criminal who is employed to kill someone

hit-or-miss /ˌ· · ˈ·/ *adj* depending on chance

HIV *n* [U] VIRUS carried in the blood that often develops into the disease AIDS: *He's HIV positive.* (= He has HIV.)

hive /haɪv/ *n* **1** box, etc., where bees are kept **2** very busy place

HMO *n* health maintenance organization, a kind of health care like insurance

hoard /hɔrd, hoʊrd/ *n* (secret) store of something valuable ♦ *vt* save; store, esp. secretly

hoarse /hɔrs, hoʊrs/ *adj* (of a voice) sounding rough ~**ly** *adv* ~**ness** *n* [U]

hoax /hoʊks/ *n* trick to deceive someone **hoax** *vt*

hob·ble /ˈhɑbəl/ *n* **1** *vi* walk with difficulty **2** *vt* tie 2 legs of (a horse)

hob·by /ˈhɑbi/ *n* pleasant activity for one's free time

ho·bo /ˈhoʊboʊ/ *n* person who has no home or work

hock[1] /hɑk/ *n* lower part of leg of a pig, horse, cow, etc.

hock[2] *vt sl for* PAWN[2]

hock·ey /ˈhɑki/ *n* [U] game played on ice by two teams of 11 players each, with sticks and a PUCK

hodgepodge /ˈhɑdʒpɑdʒ/ *n* confused mixture

hoe /hoʊ/ *n* garden tool for breaking up the soil **hoe** *vi/t*

hog /hɔg, hɑg/ *n* **1** pig **2** person who eats too much **3 go the whole hog** *infml* do something thoroughly — see also ROAD HOG ♦ *vt* take and keep (all of something) for oneself

hoist /hɔɪst/ *vt* pull up on a rope ♦ *n* **1** upward push **2** apparatus for lifting heavy goods

hold[1] /hoʊld/ *v* **held** /hɛld/ **1** *vt* keep in the hands, etc. **2** *vt* keep in a particular position: *hold one's head up* | *Hold it!* (= don't move) **3** *vt* support: *The branch won't hold me.* **4** *vt* not allow to leave: *The police held 2 men.* **5** *vt* not use: *hold one's breath* **6** *vt* defend against attack **7** *vi* remain unchanged: *What I said still holds.* **8** *vt* have room for: *The theater holds 500.* **9** *vt* possess: *hold the office of chairman* **10** *vt* believe **11** *vt* cause to happen: *hold an election* **12** *vt* keep (the interest or attention) of (someone) **13 hold court** receive admirers in a group **14 hold good** be true **15 Hold it!** *infml* Don't move. **16 hold one's own** keep one's (strong) position **17 hold one's tongue** not talk **18 hold the line** keep a telephone connection **19 hold water** seem to be true

hold against *phr vt* allow (something bad) to influence one's feelings about (someone)

hold back *phr v* **1** *vt* control **2** *vt* keep secret **3** *vi* be unwilling to act

hold down *phr vt* **1** keep in a low position **2** keep (a job)

hold forth *phr vi* talk at length

hold off *phr v* **1** *vt* keep at a distance **2** *vi/t* delay

hold on *phr vi* **1** wait (esp. on the telephone) **2** continue in spite of difficulties

hold onto *phr vt* keep possession of

hold out *phr vi* **1** continue to exist; last **2** offer

hold out for *phr vt* demand firmly and wait in order to get

hold over *phr vt* POSTPONE

hold to *phr vt* keep to: *I'll hold you to your promise.*

hold up *phr vt* **1** delay **2** rob by force

hold[2] *n* **1** [U] holding **2** [C] something to hold, esp. in climbing **3** [C] influence

hold[3] *n* bottom of a ship, where goods are stored

hold·er /ˈhoʊldə/ *n* **1** person who possesses something **2** container

hold·ings /ˈhoʊldɪŋz/ *n* [P] land, etc., that one possesses

hold·up /ˈhoʊldʌp/ *n* **1** delay, as in traffic **2** attempt at armed robbery

hole[1] /hoʊl/ n **1** empty space in something solid **2 a** home of a small animal **b** small ugly space to live in **3** infml difficult position **4** (in GOLF) hollow place in the ground into which the ball must be hit: *an 18-hole golf course* **5 make a hole** in infml use up a large part of **6 pick holes in** find faults in — see also BLACK HOLE

hole[2]

hole up phr vi sl hide as a means of escape

hol·i·day /ˈhɑləˌdeɪ/ n day set by law or custom when people don't go to work because they are celebrating something

hol·i·ness /ˈhoʊlinɪs/ n [U] **1** being holy **2** (cap.) (title of the Pope)

ho·lis·tic /hoʊˈlɪstɪk/ adj concerning the whole of something or someone, not just its parts: *holistic medicine*

hol·ler /ˈhɑlə/ vi shout

hol·low /ˈhɑloʊ/ adj **1** having an empty space inside **2** lacking flesh: *hollow cheeks* **3** (of sounds) as if made by striking an empty container **4** insincere ♦ n **1** wide hole **2** small valley ♦ vt make hollow

hol·ly /ˈhɑli/ n [C;U] tree whose red berries are used for Christmas decoration

hol·o·caust /ˈhɑləˌkɔst, ˈhoʊ-/ n great destruction and the loss of many lives, esp. by burning

hol·o·gram /ˈhoʊləˌgræm, ˈhɑ-/ n picture made with LASER light so that it appears to be solid rather than flat

hol·ster /ˈhoʊlstə/ n leather holder for a PISTOL

ho·ly /ˈhoʊli/ adj **1** connected with, or serving, religion **2** leading a pure and blameless life

hom·age /ˈhɑmɪdʒ, ˈɑ-/ n [U] fml signs of great respect

home[1] /hoʊm/ n **1** [C] place where one lives **2** [C;U] one's house and family: *She came from a poor home.* **3** [S] **a** place where a plant or animal is found **b** place where something was originally discovered, made, or developed **4** [C] place for the care of people or animals: *an old people's home* **5** [U] (in sports) place which a player must try to reach **6 be/feel at home** feel comfortable **7 make oneself at home** behave freely **8 nothing to write home about** nothing special

home[2] adv **1** to or at one's home: *go home* **2** to the right place: *strike a nail home* **3 bring/come home to one** make/become clearly understood **4 home free** infml having safely or successfully completed something

home[3] adj **1** of or related to one's home or origin **2** not foreign **3** prepared or made in the home: *home grown* **4** (of a sports match) played at the place, sports field, etc., of one's home area

home[4] v **home in on** phr vt aim exactly towards — see also HOMING

home·boy /ˈhoʊmbɔɪ/ n sl friend or person who comes from one's neighborhood

home·com·ing /ˈhoʊmˌkʌmɪŋ/ n **1** arrival home, esp. after a long absence **2** yearly event at a school or university

home·land /ˈhoʊmlænd/ n country where one was born

home·less /ˈhoʊmlɪs/ adj without a home

home·ly /ˈhoʊmli/ adj not attractive

home·made /ˌhoʊmˈmeɪd◄/ adj made at home, not bought from a store: *home-made cookies*

home·mak·er /ˈhoʊmˌmeɪkə/ n woman who looks after her children and home; HOUSEWIFE

ho·me·op·a·thy /ˌhoʊmiˈɑpəθi/ n [U] system of treating disease with small amounts of substances that in larger amounts would produce a similar illness –**opathic** /ˌhoʊmiəˈpæθɪk◄/ adj

home·page /ˌhoʊmˈpeɪdʒ/ n place on the INTERNET where one can find information on a particular person, company, etc.

home·room /ˈhoʊmrum, -rʊm/ n room in a school where students in the same GRADE meet at certain times of the day

home run /ˌ· ˈ·/ also **hom·er** /ˈhoʊmə/ — n a point in BASEBALL, made by hitting the ball so far that it is possible to run to each base

home·sick /ˈhoʊmˌsɪk/ adj unhappy because away from home ~**ness** n [U]

home·stead /ˈhoʊmstɛd/ n land and its buildings given to a farmer (in former times)

home·work /ˈhoʊmwɚk/ n [C] **1** school work done outside the school **2** preparations done before taking part in an important activity

hom·ey /ˈhoʊmi/ adj infml nice and comfortable, home

hom·i·cide /ˈhɑməˌsaɪd/ n [C;U] fml murder –**cidal** /ˌhɑməˈsaɪdl◄/ adj

hom·ing /'hoʊmɪŋ/ adj of or having the ability to a guide oneself home b (of machines) guide themselves towards the place they are aimed at

ho·mo·ge·ne·ous /ˌhoʊmə'dʒiːniəs, -dʒiːnjəs, ˌhɑ-/ adj formed of parts of the same kind

ho·mo·ge·nize /hə'mɑdʒəˌnaɪz/ vt make (the parts of a whole, esp. a mixture) become evenly spread

hom·o·nym /'hɑmənɪm/ n word with the same sound and spelling as another word, but with a different meaning, e.g. "bear" (verb) and "bear" (animal)

ho·mo·pho·bi·a /ˌhoʊmə'foʊbiə/ n [U] hatred and fear of HOMOSEXUALs **–phobic** adj

ho·mo·sex·u·al /ˌhoʊmə'sɛkʃuəl/ n, adj (person) sexually attracted to people of the same sex **–ity** /ˌhoʊməˌsɛkʃu'æləti/ n [U]

hon·cho /'hɑntʃoʊ/ n infml important person who controls something: the record company's head honcho

hon·est /'ɑnɪst/ adj 1 not likely to lie or cheat 2 (of actions, etc.) showing these qualities **–ly** adv 1 in an honest way 2 really

hon·es·ty /'ɑnəsti/ n [U] quality of being honest

hon·ey /'hʌni/ n 1 [U] sweet substance that bees make 2 [C] dearly loved person

hon·ey·comb /'hʌniˌkoʊm/ n wax structure that bees make to store honey

hon·ey·moon /'hʌniˌmun/ n 1 vacation taken by 2 people who have just gotten married 2 short period of good relations, etc., at the beginning of a period in office, etc. ◆ vi spend one's honeymoon **honeymooner** n

honk /hɑŋk, hɔŋk/ vi, n (make) the sound of a car horn

hon·or·ar·y /'ɑnəˌrɛri/ adj 1 (of a rank, etc.) given as an honor 2 unpaid: honorary chairman

hon·or /'ɑnə/ n 1 [U] great public respect 2 [U] high standards of behavior: men of honor 3 [S] person or thing that brings pride: He's an honor to his parents. 4 [C] (cap.) (used as a title for a judge) ◆ vt 1 bring honor to 2 keep (an agreement) **honors** n [P] 1 marks of respect: full military honors 2 a university degree

hon·or·a·ble /'ɑnərəbəl/ adj 1 bringing or showing honor 2 (cap.) (title for certain high officials, judges, etc.) **–bly** adv

honor roll /'·· ˌ·/ n list of students with high grades

hood /hʊd/ n 1 covering for the head and neck a except the face, so that it can be pushed back b including the face, to avoid recognition 2 folding cover over a BUGGY², etc. 3 lid over the front of a car 4 young male who makes trouble

hood·lum /'hʌdləm, 'hʊd-/ n young person who does bad or illegal things

hoof /hʊf/ n hoofs or hooves /hʊvz, huvz/ horny foot of a horse, etc.

hook /hʊk/ n 1 curved piece of metal or plastic for catching, hanging, or fastening things 2 (in boxing (BOX²)) blow given with the elbow bent 3 by hook or by crook by any means possible 4 off the hook no longer in a difficult situation ◆ vt catch, hang, or fasten with a hook **~ed** adj 1 shaped like a hook 2 dependent (on drugs, etc.)

hook·er /'hʊkə/ n infml PROSTITUTE

hook·y /'hʊki/ n infml play hooky stay away from school without permission

hoo·li·gan /'huligən/ n noisy violent person who breaks things, etc. **~ism** n [U]

hoop /hup/ n circular band of wood or metal

hoo·ray /hʊ'reɪ, hə'reɪ/ interj, n (shout of joy or approval)

hoot /hut/ n 1 sound made by an OWL 2 shout of dislike 3 not care/give a hoot/two hoots not care at all 4 very funny situation ◆ vi/t (cause to) make a hoot

hooves /hʊvz, huvz/ pl. of HOOF

hop /hɑp/ vi -pp- 1 (of people) jump on one leg 2 (of small creatures) jump 3 get into or onto a vehicle ◆ n 1 jump 2 distance flown by a plane without landing

hope /hoʊp/ n 1 [C;U] expectation that something good will happen 2 [C] person or thing that may bring success 3 beyond/past hope with no chance of success 4 hold out hope give encouragement ◆ vi/t wish and expect **~ful** adj feeling or giving hope **~fully** adv 1 in a hopeful way 2 if our hopes succeed **~less** adj 1 feeling or giving no hope 2 not skilled: hopeless at math **~lessly** adv

hop·per /'hɑpə/ n large FUNNEL for grain or coal

hops /hɒps/ n [U] climbing plant used for giving taste to beer

horde /hɔrd, hoʊrd/ n large moving crowd

ho·ri·zon /həˈraɪzən/ n **1** line where the sky seems to meet the earth or sea **2 broaden one's horizons** increase the range of one's experience

hor·i·zon·tal /ˌhɔrəˈzɑntəl◂, ˌhɑr-/ adj flat; level ♦ n a horizontal line, surface or position ~ly adv

hor·mone /ˈhɔrmoʊn/ n substance produced in the body that influences growth, etc.

horn /hɔrn/ n **1** [C] pointed growth on an animal's head **2** [U] material that this is made of: **horn-rimmed** glasses **3** [C] apparatus, e.g. in a car, that makes a warning sound **4** [C] musical instrument played by blowing **5 blow one's own horn** praise oneself ~y adj **1** taboo sl sexually excited **2** hard and rough

hor·net /ˈhɔrnɪt/ n large stinging insect

hor·o·scope /ˈhɔrəˌskoʊp, ˈhɑr-/ n set of ideas about someone's character, life and future gained by knowing the position of the stars or PLANETS at the time of their birth

hor·ren·dous /həˈrɛndəs, hɔ-, hɑ-/ adj really terrible ~ly adv

hor·ri·ble /ˈhɔrəbəl, ˈhɑr-/ adj **1** causing HORROR **2** very unpleasant –**bly** adv

hor·rif·ic /hɔˈrɪfɪk, hɑ-, hə-/ adj horrifying ~**ly** adv

hor·ri·fy /ˈhɔrəˌfaɪ, ˈhɑr-/ vt fill with horror: horrifying news

hor·ror /ˈhɔrɚ, ˈhɑrɚ/ n **1** [C;U] (something causing) great shock and fear **2** [U] unpleasant person, usu. a child **3 have a horror of** hate ♦ adj frightening: horror films –s n infml [the+P] state of great fear, worry or sadness

hors d'oeu·vre /ɔr ˈdɚv/ n -d'oeuvres /-ˈdɚvz/ small things served at the beginning of a meal

horse[1] /hɔrs/ n **1** large animal with four legs, that people ride on, etc. **2** apparatus for jumping over **3 eat like a horse** eat a lot **4 (straight) from the horse's mouth** (of information) directly from the person concerned — see also DARK HORSE, HIGH HORSE, TROJAN HORSE

horse[2] v **horse around** phr vi infml play roughly or waste time in rough play

horse·back /ˈhɔrsbæk/ n **on horseback** riding a horse ♦ adj, adv on the back of a horse: horseback riding

horse·play /ˈhɔrsˌpleɪ/ n [U] rough noisy behavior

horse·pow·er /ˈhɔrsˌpaʊɚ/ n **horsepower** unit measuring the power of an engine

horse·shoe /ˈhɔrʃˌʃu, ˈhɔrs-/ n shoe in the shape of a U for a horse, believed to bring good luck

hor·ti·cul·ture /ˈhɔrtəˌkʌltʃɚ/ n [U] science of growing fruit, flowers, and vegetables –**tural** /ˌhɔrtəˈkʌltʃərəl/ adj

hose[1] /hoʊz/ n tube used for watering gardens, etc. ♦ vt use a hose on

hose[2] n [U] socks and STOCKINGS

ho·sier·y /ˈhoʊʒəri/ n [U] socks, stockings, etc.

hos·pice /ˈhɑspɪs/ n hospital for people with incurable illnesses

hos·pi·ta·ble /ˈhɑspɪtəbəl, hɑˈspɪ-/ adj offering a friendly welcome to guests –**bly** adv

hos·pi·tal /ˈhɑspɪtl/ n place where people who are sick or injured (INJURE) are treated –**ize** vt put into a hospital

hos·pi·tal·i·ty /ˌhɑspəˈtæləti/ n [U] being hospitable

host[1] /hoʊst/ n **1** man who receives guests **2** person who introduces performers, e.g. on a television show ♦ vt act as a host

host[2] n large number: a host of difficulties

hos·tage /ˈhɑstɪdʒ/ n prisoner kept by an enemy so that the other side will obey demands, etc.

hos·tel /ˈhɑstl/ n building where students, etc., can live and eat

host·ess /ˈhoʊstɪs/ n **1** female host **2** young woman who acts as companion, dancing partner, etc., in a social club

hos·tile /ˈhɑstl, ˈhɑstaɪl/ adj **1** unfriendly **2** belonging to an enemy

hos·til·i·ty /hɑˈstɪləti/ n [U] unfriendliness –**ties** n [P] war

hot[1] /hɑt/ adj -**tt- 1** having a high temperature **2** having a burning taste: hot pepper **3** fierce; excitable: hot temper **4** (of news) very recent **5** knowledgeable about and interested in: She's very hot on jazz. **6 hot and bothered** a worried by a feeling that things are going wrong **b** sexually excited **7 hot on someone's trail** following someone closely **8 not so hot** infml not very good ~**ly** adv **1** angrily **2** eagerly: hotly pursued

hot[2] v -**tt- hot up** phr vi become more exciting or dangerous

hot air /ˌ· ˈ·/ n [U] meaningless talk

hot·bed /ˈhɒtˌbed/ n place where something bad can develop: *a hotbed of crime*

hot-blood·ed /ˌ· ˈ··◂/ adj PASSIONATE

hot dog /ˈ· ·/ n 1 FRANKFURTER in a long BUN (2) 2 person too confident of his abilities

ho·tel /hoʊˈtel/ n building where people can stay in return for payment

hot·line /ˈhɒtˌlaɪn/ n 1 direct telephone line between heads of government 2 telephone line for a special purpose

hot po·ta·to /ˌ· ·ˈ··/ n subject or problem that no one wants to deal with

hot seat /ˈ· ·/ n *infml* position of difficulty from which one must make important decisions

hot·shot /ˈhɒtˌʃɒt/ n person who is very successful and confident

hot spot /ˈ· ·/ place where there is likely to be unrest and perhaps war

hot-tem·pered /ˌ· ˈ··◂/ adj easily made angry

hot wa·ter /ˌ· ˈ··/ n [U] trouble: *get into hot water*

hot-wa·ter bot·tle /ˌ· ˈ·· ˌ··/ n rubber container for hot water to reduce aches and pain

hound /haʊnd/ n hunting dog ♦ vt chase and worry

hour /aʊə/ n 1 period of 60 minutes 2 time when a new hour starts: *arrive on the hour* 3 distance one can travel in this period of time: *It's only an hour away.* 4 period of time: *my lunch hour* 5 **after hours** later than the usual times of work or business 6 **at all hours** (at any time) during the whole day and night — see also ELEVENTH HOUR, HAPPY HOUR ~ly adj, adv once every hour

hour·glass /ˈaʊəˌɡlæs/ n container in which sand drops through a narrow passage, formerly used to measure time

house¹ /haʊs/ n **houses** /ˈhaʊzɪz/ 1 a building for people to live in, esp. on more than one level b people in such a building: *You'll wake the whole house.* 2 building for a stated purpose: *a hen house* | *the House of Representatives* 3 *(often cap.)* noble or royal family 4 a division of a school b business firm: *the house magazine* 5 theater, or the people in it 6 **bring the house down** cause loud admiration 7 **get on like a house on fire** be very friendly 8 **keep house** do

or control the cleaning, cooking, etc. 9 **on the house** (of drinks) paid for by the people in charge

house² /haʊz/ vt provide a home, or space, for

house·boat /ˈhaʊsboʊt/ n boat for living in

house·bound /ˈhaʊsbaʊnd/ adj unable to leave one's home

house·bro·ken /ˈhaʊsˌbroʊkən/ adj (of pets) trained to empty the bowels and BLADDER outside the house

house·hold /ˈhaʊsˌhoʊld, ˈhaʊsoʊld/ n all the people living in a house ♦ adj concerned with the management of a house: *household expenses* ~er n person who owns or is in charge of a house

household name /ˌ·· ˈ·/ n person or thing that is very well known or talked about by almost everyone

house hus·band /ˈ· ˌ··/ n married man who works at home for his family, cleaning, cooking, etc.

house·keep·er /ˈhaʊsˌkipə/ n person paid to run a house

house·keep·ing /ˈhaʊsˌkipɪŋ/ n 1 work of running a house 2 money set aside for food, etc.

House of Rep·re·sen·ta·tives /ˌ· · ··ˈ··/ n [the] the larger and lower of the 2 parts of the central body that makes the laws in such countries as the US and Australia

house·warm·ing /ˈhaʊsˌwɔrmɪŋ/ n party given for friends when one has moved into a new house

house·wife /ˈhaʊswaɪf/ n -**wives** /-waɪvz/ married woman who works at home for her family, cleaning, cooking, etc.

house·work /ˈhaʊswɜrk/ n [U] cleaning, etc., in a house

hous·ing /ˈhaʊzɪŋ/ n 1 [U] places to live 2 [C] protective cover for a machine

housing de·vel·op·ment /ˈ·· ·ˌ··/ n group of houses built in the same area, usu. at the same time by 1 company

housing proj·ect /ˈ·· ˌ··/ n group of apartments built by the government for poor people

hov·el /ˈhʌvəl, ˈhɑ-/ n dirty little house

hov·er /ˈhʌvə, ˈhɑ-/ vi 1 (of birds, etc.) stay in the air in one place 2 (of people) wait around

how /haʊ/ adv 1 (used in questions) a in what way: *How do you spell it?* b in what state of health: *How are you*? **c** (in questions about number, size, etc.): *How big is it*? **2** (showing surprise): *How kind of you!* **3 How come . . .**? *infml* Why is it that . . .? **4 How do you do?** (used when formally introduced to someone; this person replies with the same phrase) ♦ *conj* the way in which: the fact that: *I remember how they laughed.*

how·dy /ˈhaʊdi/ *interj infml* (used to greet people) HELLO

how·ev·er /haʊˈevə/ *adv* **1** in whatever degree or way: *We'll go, however cold it is.* **2** in spite of this **3** in what way (showing surprise): *However did you get here*?

howl /haʊl/ *vi/t, n* (make) a long loud cry ~**er** *n* silly mistake that makes people laugh

HQ *n* [C;U] HEADQUARTERS

hr., hrs. *written abbrev. for*: hour(s)

hub /hʌb/ *n* **1** center of a wheel **2** center of activity

hub·bub /ˈhʌbʌb/ *n* [S] mixture of loud noises

hub·cap /ˈhʌbkæp/ *n* metal covering for the center of a wheel on a car

hud·dle /ˈhʌdl/ *vi/t* get or come together in a crowd ♦ *n* crowd

hue /hjuː/ *n fml* color

huff /hʌf/ *n* [S] bad temper ~**y** *adj*

hug /hʌg/ *vt* -**gg**- **1** hold tightly in one's arms **2** travel along beside: *The boat hugged the coast.* **hug** *n*

huge /hjuːdʒ, juːdʒ/ *adj* very big ~**ly** *adv* very much

huh /hʌ/ *interj* (used for asking a question or expressing surprise or disapproval)

hu·la /ˈhuːlə/ *n* Hawaiian dance

hulk /hʌlk/ *n* **1** old broken ship **2** heavy, awkward person or creature

hull /hʌl/ *n* body of a ship or aircraft

hum /hʌm/ *v* -**mm**- **1** *vi* BUZZ (1) **2** *vi/t* sing with closed lips **3** *vi* be full of activity ♦ *n* [U]

hu·man /ˈhjuːmən, ˈjuː-/ *adj* **1** of people **2** kind, etc., as people should be: *He's really very human.* ♦ *n* person ~**ism** *n* [U] system of belief based on people's needs, and not on religion ~**ize** *vt* make human or humane ~**ly** *adv* according to human powers: *not humanly possible*

hu·mane /hjuːˈmeɪn, juː-/ *adj* **1** showing human kindness and the qualities of a

civilized person **2** trying not to cause pain: *a humane method of killing animals* ~**ly** *adv*

hu·man·i·tar·i·an /hjuːˌmænəˈtɛrɪən, juː-/ *n, adj* (person) trying to improve life for human beings by improving living conditions, etc. ~**ism** *n* [U]

hu·man·i·ty /hjuːˈmænəti, juː-/ *n* [U] **1** being human or humane **2** people in general

human re·sourc·es /ˌ··· ·ˈ··/ *n* [U] department in a company that deals with employing, training, and helping people

human rights /ˌ·· ˈ·/ *n* [P] basic rights every person has, esp. to be treated fairly and equally without cruelty

hum·ble /ˈhʌmbəl/ *adj* **1** low in rank; unimportant **2** having a low opinion of oneself and a high opinion of others: not proud ♦ *vt* make humble –**bly** *adv*

hum·drum /ˈhʌmdrʌm/ *adj* dull and ordinary

hu·mid /ˈhjuːmɪd, ˈjuː-/ *adj* (of air) DAMP ~**ify** /hjuːˈmɪdəfaɪ, juː-/ *vt* make humid ~**ity** *n* [U]

hu·mil·i·ate /hjuːˈmɪliˌeɪt, juː-/ *vt* cause to feel ashamed –**ation** /hjuːˌmɪliˈeɪʃən, juː-/ *n* [C;U]

hu·mil·i·ty /hjuːˈmɪləti, juː-/ *n* [U] quality of being HUMBLE (2)

hu·mor /ˈhjuːmə, ˈjuː-/ *n* [U] ability to be amused or cause amusement ♦ *vt* keep (someone) happy by acceptance of their foolish wishes, behavior, etc. **humor along** *phr vt* encourage in a joking or friendly way

hu·mor·ist /ˈhjuːmərɪst, ˈjuː-/ *n* person who makes jokes in speech or writing

hu·mor·ous /ˈhjuːmərəs, ˈjuː-/ *adj* funny ~**ly** *adv*

hump /hʌmp/ *n* **1** [C] round lump, esp. on a CAMEL's back **2 over the hump** *infml* past the worst part of the work ♦ *v* **1** *vt infml* carry (something heavy), esp. with difficulty **2** *vi/t taboo sl* have sex with

hunch¹ /hʌntʃ/ *n* idea based on feeling rather than reason

hunch² *vt* pull (part of the body) into a rounded shape: *hunched shoulders*

hunch·back /ˈhʌntʃbæk/ *n* (person with) a back misshaped by a round lump ~**ed** *adj*

hun·dred /ˈhʌndrɪd/ *det, n, pron* -**dred** or -**dreds** 100 ~**th** /ˈhʌndrɪdθ/ *det, adv, n, pron* 100th

hun·dred·weight /ˈhʌndrɪdˌweɪt/ *n* -**weight** (a measure of weight equal to) 100 pounds

hung /hʌŋ/ v past t. and p. of HANG — see also **be hung up on** (HANG **up**)

hun·ger /'hʌŋgə/ n 1 [U] need for food 2 [S] strong wish ♦ vi feel hunger –**gry** adj feeling hunger

hunger strike /'·· ˌ·/ n refusal to eat as a sign of strong dissatisfaction

hung ju·ry /ˌ· '·ˌ·/ n jury that can not agree on a VERDICT

hung over /ˌ· '··◄/ adj sick because one drank too much alcohol the previous day

hunk /hʌŋk/ n 1 thick piece of food, etc. 2 infml physically attractive man

hunt /hʌnt/ vi/t 1 chase (animals) for food or sport 2 search (for) ♦ n 1 chasing or searching 2 people hunting animals: a bear hunt ~**er** n

hunt down/out/up phr vt find by searching

hur·dle /'hɜdl/ n 1 frame to jump over in a race 2 difficulty to be dealt with

hurl /hɜl/ vt throw violently: (fig.) He hurled abuse at the other driver.

hur·ri·cane /'hɜrəˌkeɪn, 'hʌr-/ n violent storm from the ocean with a strong fast circular wind

hur·ry /'hɜri, 'hʌri/ vi/t (cause to) go or do something (too) quickly: Hurry up! (= Be quick!) ♦ n [S;U] 1 quick activity 2 need to hurry –**ried** adj done (too) quickly –**riedly** adv

hurt /hɜt/ v hurt 1 vt cause pain or damage to 2 vt cause pain (to the feelings of (a person) 3 vi feel pain 4 vi/t matter (to): It won't hurt (you) to wait. ♦ n [C;U] harm; damage ~**ful** adj –**fully** adv

hur·tle /'hɜtl/ vi move or rush with great force

hus·band /'hʌzbənd/ n man to whom a woman is married

hush /hʌʃ/ vi/t (cause to) be silent ♦ n [S;U] silence

hush up phr vt keep secret

husk /hʌsk/ n dry outer covering of some vegetables, fruits, and seeds

hus·ky /'hʌski/ adj 1 (of a voice) HOARSE 2 (of a person) big and strong –**kily** adv

hus·tle /'hʌsəl/ vt 1 push or drive as if one is in a hurry 2 persuade someone forcefully, esp. to buy something ♦ n [U] hurried activity **hustler** /'hʌslə/ n 1 infml busy, active person, esp. one who tries to persuade people to buy things, etc. 2 sl male PROSTITUTE

hut /hʌt/ n small simple building

hutch /hʌtʃ/ n cage for rabbits, etc.

hy·brid /'haɪbrɪd/ n animal or plant of mixed breed

hy·drant /'haɪdrənt/ n water pipe in the street, used to put out fires

hy·drau·lic /haɪ'drɒlɪk/ adj using water pressure

hy·dro·e·lec·tric /ˌhaɪdroʊɪ'lɛktrɪk◄/ adj producing electricity by water power

hy·dro·gen /'haɪdrədʒən/ n [U] light gas that burns easily

hydrogen bomb /'··· ˌ·/ n bomb made using hydrogen which explodes when the central parts of the atoms join together

hy·giene /'haɪdʒin/ n [U] cleanness, to prevent the spreading of disease **hygienist** /haɪ'dʒinɪst, 'haɪdʒin-/ person who knows a lot about hygiene **hygienic** /haɪ'dʒenɪk, -'dʒinɪk/ adj

hymn /hɪm/ n song of praise to God

hype /haɪp/ vt infml try to get a lot of public attention for, esp. more than is deserved **hype** n [U] attempts to do this

hyped up /ˌ· '·◄/ adj infml very excited and anxious

hy·per·ac·tive /ˌhaɪpə'æktɪv◄/ adj also **hyper** unable to rest or be quiet

hy·per·bo·le /haɪ'pɜbəli/ n exaggeration (EXAGGERATE)

hy·phen /'haɪfən/ n the mark (-) joining words or word parts ~**ate** vt join with a hyphen

hyp·no·sis /hɪp'noʊsɪs/ n [U] state similar to sleep in which a person can be influenced by the person who produced the state –**notic** /-'nɑtɪk/ adj –**tism** /'hɪpnəˌtɪzəm/ n [U] production of hypnosis –**tist** n –**tize** vt produce hypnosis in

hy·po·chon·dri·ac /ˌhaɪpə'kɑndriˌæk/ n someone who worries unnecessarily about their health

hy·poc·ri·sy /hɪ'pɑkrəsi/ n [U] pretending to be different from and usu. better than one is

hyp·o·crite /'hɪpəˌkrɪt/ n person who practices hypocrisy –**critical** /ˌhɪpə-'krɪtɪkəl◄/ adj

hy·po·der·mic /ˌhaɪpə'dɜmɪk◄/ adj, n (of) a needle for putting drugs into the body

hy·pot·e·nuse /haɪ'pɑt'nˌjus, -ˌuz/ n longest side of a TRIANGLE with a 90-degree angle

hy·poth·e·sis /haɪˈpɒθəsɪs/ *n* idea that may explain facts –**etical** /ˌhaɪpəˈθɛtɪkəl/ *adj* not yet proved

hys·ter·ec·to·my /ˌhɪstəˈrɛktəmi/ *n* medical operation to remove a woman's UTERUS

hys·te·ri·a /hɪˈstɛriə, -ˈstɪr-/ *n* [U] uncontrolled nervous excitement –**rical** /hɪˈstɛrɪkəl/ *adj* –**rics** *n* [P] attack(s) of hysteria

I

I, i[1] /aɪ/ the 9th letter of the English alphabet

I[2] *pron* (used for the person speaking, as the subject of a sentence)

ice[1] /aɪs/ *n* 1 [U] frozen water 2 **skating on thin ice** taking risks 3 **keep something on ice** take no immediate action about something

ice[2] *vt* 1 make cold with ice 2 cover with FROSTING

ice over/up *phr vi* become covered with ice

ice age /ˈ· ˌ·/ *n* period when ice covered many northern countries

ice·berg /ˈaɪsbɜːg/ *n* 1 mass of floating ice in the ocean 2 **the tip of the iceberg** a small sign of a much larger situation, problem, etc.

ice·box /ˈaɪsbɒks/ *old-fash. for* REFRIGERATOR

ice·break·er /ˈaɪsˌbreɪkə/ *n* 1 ship that cuts through floating ice 2 action which makes people who have just met more relaxed

ice cap /ˈ· ˌ·/ *n* lasting covering of ice, e.g. at the POLES[2] (1)

ice cream /ˈ· ˌ·/ *n* [C;U] frozen creamy food

ice pack /ˈ· ˌ·/ *n* bag of ice to put on the body

ice pick /ˈ· ˌ·/ *n* tool for breaking ice

ice skate /ˈ· ˌ·/ *n* SKATE (1) **ice-skate** *vi*

i·ci·cle /ˈaɪsɪkəl/ *n* pointed stick of ice, formed when water freezes as it runs down

ic·ing /ˈaɪsɪŋ/ *n* [U] FROSTING

i·con /ˈaɪkɒn/ *n* 1 small picture on a computer screen that you CLICK on to make the computer do something 2 famous person or thing, that people think represents an important idea 3 picture of a holy person

ic·y /ˈaɪsi/ *adj* 1 very cold 2 covered with ice **icily** *adv*

I'd /aɪd, aɪd/ *short for:* 1 I would 2 I had

ID card /ˌaɪ ˈdiː kɑːd/ *n* card that gives a person's name, address, age, etc., as proof of their IDENTITY

i·de·a /aɪˈdɪə/ *n* 1 [C] plan, thought, or suggestion for a possible course of action 2 [C;U] picture in the mind; CONCEPTION 3 [C] opinion or belief: *strange ideas* 4 understanding: *They have no idea how to run a company.* 5 [C] guess; feeling of probability: *I've an idea she doesn't like him.*

i·de·al /aɪˈdɪəl/ *adj* 1 perfect 2 too good to exist ♦ *n* 1 [*often pl.*] (belief in) high principles or perfect standards 2 perfect example ~**ist** *n* ~**ize** *vt* imagine as perfect ~**ly** *adv* 1 in an ideal way: *ideally suited* 2 if things were perfect

i·de·al·ism /aɪˈdɪəˌlɪzəm/ *n* [U] quality or habit of living according to one's ideals, or the belief that such a way of life is possible –**ist** *n* –**istic** *adj* /ˌaɪdɪəˈlɪstɪk◂, aɪˌdɪə-/ –**istically** *adv*

i·den·ti·cal /aɪˈdentɪkəl, ɪ-/ *adj* 1 exactly alike 2 the same ~**ly** *adv*

i·den·ti·fy /aɪˈdentɪˌfaɪ, ɪ-/ *vt* show the identity of –**fication** /aɪˌdentəfəˈkeɪʃən, ɪ-/ *n* [U] 1 identifying 2 also **ID card**, etc., that proves who one is

identify with *phr vt* 1 consider (someone) to be connected with 2 feel sympathy for

i·den·ti·ty /aɪˈdentəti, ɪ-/ *n* 1 [C;U] who or what a person or thing is 2 [U] sameness

i·de·ol·o·gy /ˌaɪdiˈɒlədʒi, ˌɪdi-/ *n* [C;U] set of (political or social) ideas –**ogical** /ˌaɪdiəˈlɒdʒɪkəl, ˌɪdi-/ *adj*

id·i·o·cy /ˈɪdiəsi/ *n* 1 [U] stupidity 2 [C] stupid act

id·i·om /ˈɪdiəm/ *n* phrase that means something different from the meanings of its separate words: *"Kick the bucket" is an idiom meaning "die."*

id·i·o·mat·ic /ˌɪdiəˈmætɪk◂/ *adj* typical of natural speech ~**ally** *adv*

id·i·o·syn·cra·sy /ˌɪdiəˈsɪŋkrəsi/ *n* personal peculiarity –**tic** /ˌɪdiəsɪnˈkrætɪk/ *adj* –**tically** *adv*

id·i·ot /ˈɪdiət/ *n* foolish, stupid person ~**ic** /ˌɪdiˈɒtɪk◂/ *adj*

i·dle[1] /ˈaɪdl/ *adj* 1 not working 2 lazy 3 useless: *idle threats* ~**ness** *n* [U] **idly** *adv*

idle[2] *vi* 1 waste time 2 (of an engine) run slowly because it is disconnected **idler** *n*

i·dol /ˈaɪdl/ *n* 1 image worshiped as a god 2 someone greatly admired ~**ize** *vt* worship as an idol

i·dyll·ic /aɪˈdɪlɪk/ *adj* simple and happy

i.e. /ˌaɪ ˈiː/ *that is; by which is meant: open to adults, i.e. people over 18*

if /ɪf/ *conj* **1** on condition that: *I'll come if I can.* **2** even though: *It was nice, if expensive.* **3** whether: *I don't know if he'll come.* **4 if anything** perhaps even **5 if I were you** (used when giving advice): *If I were you, I'd burn it.* **6 it isn't/it's not as if** it's not true that ♦ *n* **ifs and buts** reasons given for delay ♦

iffy /'ɪfi/ *adj* doubtful

ig·loo /'ɪɡluː/ *n* round house made from blocks of hard snow and ice

ig·nite /ɪɡ'naɪt/ *vi fml* start to burn

ig·ni·tion /ɪɡ'nɪʃən/ *n* **1** [C] electrical apparatus that starts an engine **2** [U] *fml* action of igniting

ig·no·ra·mus /ˌɪɡnə'reɪməs, -'ræ-/ *n* stupid person

ig·no·rant /'ɪɡnərənt/ *adj* **1** without knowledge of **2** rude, esp. because of lack of social training **–rance** *n* [U]

ig·nore /ɪɡ'nɔr, ɪɡ'nɔʊr/ *vt* refuse to notice

ill /ɪl/ *adj* **worse** /wɜrs/, **worst** /wɜrst/ **1** sick **2** bad: *ill fortune* ♦ *adv* **1** badly: *The child was ill-treated.* **2** not enough: *ill fed* ♦ *n* bad thing: *the social ills of poverty and unemployment*

I'll /aɪl, aɪl/ *short for:* I will or I shall

ill-ad·vised /ˌ·· '·◂/ *adj* unwise

il·le·gal /ɪ'liːɡəl/ *adj* against the law **–ly** *adv* **–ity** /ˌɪlɪ'ɡæləti/ *n* [C;U]

il·le·gi·ble /ɪ'lɛdʒəbəl/ *adj* impossible to read

il·le·git·i·mate /ˌɪlɪ'dʒɪtəmɪt/ *adj* **1** born to unmarried parents **2** against the rules **–ly** *adv*

il·lic·it /ɪ'lɪsɪt/ *adj* against the law or the rules **–ly** *adv*

il·lit·e·rate /ɪ'lɪtərɪt/ *adj* unable to read or write **–racy** *n* [U]

ill·ness /'ɪlnɪs/ *n* [C;U] sickness; DISEASE

il·lo·gi·cal /ɪ'lɑdʒɪkəl/ *adj* against LOGIC; not sensible **–ly** *adv*

il·lu·mi·nate /ɪ'luːməneɪt/ *vt* **1** give light to **2** decorate with lights **3** (esp. in former times) decorate with gold and bright colors **–nating** *adj* helping to explain: *illuminating remark* **–nation** /ɪˌluːmə'neɪʃən/ *n* [U] act of illuminating or state of being illuminated

il·lu·sion /ɪ'luːʒən/ *n* something seen wrongly; false idea **–sory** /ɪ'luːsəri, -zəri/ *adj fml* unreal

il·lus·trate /'ɪləˌstreɪt/ *vt* **1** add pictures to **2** explain by giving examples **–trator** *n* person who draws pictures for a book, etc. **–tration** /ˌɪlə'streɪʃən/ *n* **1** [C] picture

2 [C] example **3** [U] act of illustrating **–trative** /ɪ'lʌstrətɪv, 'ɪlə,streɪtɪv/ *adj* used as an example

il·lus·tri·ous /ɪ'lʌstriəs/ *adj* famous

I'm /ɑm, aɪm/ *short for:* I am

im·age /'ɪmɪdʒ/ *n* **1** picture in the mind, or seen in a mirror **2** general opinion about a person, etc., that has been formed or intentionally planted in people's minds **3** copy; likeness: *He's the image of his father.* **4** IDOL (1) **–ry** *n* [U] METAPHORs, etc., in literature

i·ma·gi·na·ry /ɪ'mædʒəˌnɛri/ *adj* unreal

i·ma·gine /ɪ'mædʒɪn/ *vt* **1** form (an idea) in the mind: *imagine a world without cars* **2** believe; suppose: *I imagine they've forgotten.* **–ginable** *adj* that can be imagined **–ginative** *adj* good at imagining **–gina·tion** /ɪˌmædʒə'neɪʃən/ *n* **1** [C;U] ability to imagine **2** [U] something only imagined

im·bal·ance /ɪm'bæləns/ *n* lack of balance or equality

im·be·cile /'ɪmbəsəl, -ˌsɪl/ *n* IDIOT **–cility** /ˌɪmbə'sɪləti/ *n* **1** [U] being an imbecile **2** [C] foolish act

im·i·tate /'ɪmɪteɪt/ *vt* **1** copy (behavior) **2** take as an example **–tator** *n* **–tative** *adj* following an example; not inventive **–tation** /ˌɪmə'teɪʃən◂/ *n* **1** [C;U] act or act of imitating **2** [C] copy of the real thing

im·mac·u·late /ɪ'mækjəlɪt/ *adj* clean; pure **–ly** *adv*

im·ma·te·ri·al /ˌɪmə'tɪriəl/ *adj* **1** unimportant **2** without physical substance

im·ma·ture /ˌɪmə'tʃʊr, -'tʊr/ *adj* not fully formed or developed **–turity** *n* [U]

im·me·di·ate /ɪ'miːdi-ɪt/ *adj* **1** done or needed at once: *an immediate reply* **2** nearest: *the immediate future* **–ly** *adv* **1** at once **2** with nothing between: *immediately in front* **–acy** *n* [U] nearness or urgent presence of something

im·mense /ɪ'mɛns/ *adj* very large **–ly** *adv* very much **immensity** *n* [U]

im·merse /ɪ'mɜrs/ *vt* put deep into liquid: (fig.) *immersed in my work* **immersion** /ɪ'mɜrʒən, -ʃən/ *n* [U]

im·mi·grate /'ɪməˌɡreɪt/ *vi* come to live in a country **–grant** *n* person who does this **–gration** /ˌɪmə'ɡreɪʃən/ *n* [U]

im·mi·nent /'ɪmənənt/ *adj* going to happen soon **–ly** *adv*

im·mo·bile /ɪ'moʊbəl, -ˌbɪl/ *adj* unmoving; unable to move **–bility** /ˌɪmoʊ'bɪləti/

n [U] –**bilize** /ɪˈmoʊbəˌlaɪz/ *vt* make immobile

im·mor·al /ɪˈmɒrəl, ɪˈmɑr-/ *adj* **1** not good or right **2** sexually improper ~**ity** /ˌɪməˈrælɪti/ *n* [C;U]

im·mor·tal /ɪˈmɔrtl/ *adj* living or remembered for ever ♦ *n* immortal being ~**ize** *vt* give endless life or fame to ~**ity** /ˌɪmɔrˈtælɪti/ *n* endless life

im·mune /ɪˈmyun/ *adj* unable to be harmed; protected **immunity** *n* [U] **immunize** /ˈɪmyəˌnaɪz/ *vt* protect from disease

immune sys·tem /ˈ·ˌ·/ *n* system in the body that fights substances that cause disease

im·pact /ˈɪmpækt/ *n* **1** force of one object hitting another **2** influence; effect **3 on impact** at the moment of hitting ♦ *vi/t* /ɪmˈpækt, ˈɪmpækt/ hit

impact on /·ˈ· ·, ·ˈ· ·/ *phr vt* affect, usu. negatively

im·pair /ɪmˈpɛr/ *vt* spoil; weaken

im·pale /ɪmˈpeɪl/ *vt* run something sharp through: *impaled on the spikes*

im·part /ɪmˈpɑrt/ *vt fml* give (knowledge, etc.)

im·par·tial /ɪmˈpɑrʃəl/ *adj* fair; just ~**ly** *adv* ~**ity** /ˌɪmpɑrʃiˈælɪti/ *n* [U]

im·pass·a·ble /ɪmˈpæsəbəl/ *adj* (of roads, etc.) impossible to travel over

im·passe /ˈɪmpæs, ɪmˈpæs/ *n* point where further movement is blocked

im·pas·sioned /ɪmˈpæʃənd/ *adj* full of deep feelings: *impassioned speech*

im·pas·sive /ɪmˈpæsɪv/ *adj* showing no feelings; calm ~**ly** *adv*

im·pa·tient /ɪmˈpeɪʃənt/ *adj* **1** not patient **2** eager: *impatient to go* ~**ly** *adv* –**tience** *n* [U]

im·peach /ɪmˈpitʃ/ *vt* charge (a public official) with a crime against the country ~**ment** *n* [C;U]

im·pec·ca·ble /ɪmˈpɛkəbəl/ *adj* faultless –**bly** *adv*

im·pede /ɪmˈpid/ *vt* get in the way of

im·ped·i·ment /ɪmˈpɛdəmənt/ *n* something that makes action difficult or impossible: *a speech impediment*

im·pel /ɪmˈpɛl/ *vt* -**ll**- (of an idea, etc.) cause (someone) to act

im·pend·ing /ɪmˈpɛndɪŋ/ *adj* (esp. of something bad) about to happen

im·pen·e·tra·ble /ɪmˈpɛnɪtrəbəl/ *adj* **1** that cannot be gone through **2** impossible to understand

im·per·a·tive /ɪmˈpɛrətɪv/ *adj* urgent; that must be done ♦ *n gram* verb form expressing a command (e.g. "Come!") ~**ly** *adv*

im·per·fect /ɪmˈpɜrfɪkt/ *adj* not perfect ♦ *n gram* verb form showing incomplete action ~**ly** *adv* ~**ion** /ˌɪmpɜrˈfɛkʃən/ *n* [C;U] **1** [U] imperfect state **2** [C] fault

im·pe·ri·al /ɪmˈpɪriəl/ *adj* of an EMPIRE or its ruler ~**ly** *adv* ~**ism** *n* [U] (belief in) the making of an EMPIRE ~**ist** *n, adj*

im·per·il /ɪmˈpɛrəl/ *vt* -**l**- put in danger

im·per·son·al /ɪmˈpɜrsənəl/ *adj* without personal feelings: *large impersonal organizations* ~**ly** *adv*

im·per·so·nate /ɪmˈpɜrsəˌneɪt/ *vt* pretend to be (another person) –**nation** /ɪmˌpɜrsəˈneɪʃən/ *n* [C;U]

im·per·vi·ous /ɪmˈpɜrviəs/ *adj* **1** not letting water, etc., through **2** not easily influenced: *impervious to criticism*

im·pet·u·ous /ɪmˈpɛtʃuəs/ *adj* acting quickly but without thought ~**ly** *adv* –**osity** /ɪmˌpɛtʃuˈɑsɪti/ *n* [U]

im·pe·tus /ˈɪmpətəs/ *n* **1** [U] force of something moving **2** [S;U] STIMULUS: *a fresh impetus to the negotiations*

im·pinge /ɪmˈpɪndʒ/ *v* **impinge on/upon** *phr vt* have an effect on

im·plant /ɪmˈplænt/ *vt* fasten or put deeply into ♦ /ˈɪmplænt/ *n* object put into the body in a medical operation

im·plau·si·ble /ɪmˈplɔzəbəl/ *adj* seeming to be untrue or unlikely

im·ple·ment[1] /ˈɪmpləmənt/ *n* tool or instrument

im·ple·ment[2] /ˈɪmpləˌmɛnt/ *vt* carry out (plans, etc.)

im·pli·cate /ˈɪmplɪˌkeɪt/ *vt fml* show (someone) to be concerned: *a letter implicating him in the crime*

im·pli·ca·tion /ˌɪmplɪˈkeɪʃən/ *n* **1** [C;U] (example of) the act of implying **2** [C] possible later effect of something **3** [U] act of implicating

im·pli·cit /ɪmˈplɪsɪt/ *adj* **1** meant though not expressed **2** unquestioning: *implicit trust* ~**ly** *adv*

im·plore /ɪmˈplɔr, ɪmˈploʊr/ *vt* beg; request strongly: *implore them to go*

im·ply /ɪmˈplaɪ/ *vt* **1** express indirectly: *He implied that he had not yet made a decision* **2** make necessary

im·po·lite /ˌɪmpəˈlaɪt/ *adj* not polite; rude

im·port¹ /ɪmˈpɔrt, -ˈpoʊrt, ˈɪmpɔrt, -poʊrt/ *vt* bring in (goods) from abroad ~**er** *n* ~**ation** /ˌɪmpɔrˈteɪʃən, -poʊrt/ *n* [C;U]

im·port² /ˈɪmpɔrt, -poʊrt/ *n* 1 [C] something imported 2 [U] *fml* importance

im·por·tant /ɪmˈpɔrtnt, -ˈpoʊrtnt/ *adj* mattering very much ~**ly** *adv* –**tance** *n* [U]

im·pose /ɪmˈpoʊz/ *v* 1 *vt* establish (a tax, etc.) 2 *vt* force the acceptance of 3 *vi* take unfair advantage **imposing** *adj* large and IMPRESS*ive* **imposition** /ˌɪmpəˈzɪʃən/ *n* [C;U] act of imposing

im·pos·si·ble /ɪmˈpɑsəbəl/ *adj* 1 not possible 2 hard to bear: *make life impossible* –**bly** *adv* –**bility** /ˌɪmpɑsəˈbɪləti/ *n*

im·pos·tor /ɪmˈpɑstər/ *n* someone who deceives by pretending to be someone else

im·po·tent /ˈɪmpətənt/ *adj* 1 powerless 2 (of a man) unable to perform the sex act ~**ly** *adv* –**tence** *n* [U]

im·pound /ɪmˈpaʊnd/ *vt* take away officially

im·pov·e·rished /ɪmˈpɑvərɪʃt/ *adj* extremely poor

im·prac·ti·cal /ɪmˈpræktɪkəl/ *adj* not practical; not sensible or reasonable

im·preg·na·ble /ɪmˈprɛgnəbəl/ *adj* impossible to enter by attack

im·preg·nate /ɪmˈprɛgneɪt/ *vt* 1 make wet; SATURATE: *cloth impregnated with polish* 2 *fml* make PREGNANT

im·press /ɪmˈprɛs/ *vt* 1 fill with admiration 2 tell (someone) that something matters: *impress on them that they must work* ~**ive** *adj* causing admiration ~**ively** *adv* ~**ion** /-ˈprɛʃən/ *n* 1 effect produced on the mind 2 mark left by pressing 3 attempt to copy a person's appearance or behavior, esp. in theater, etc. ~**ionable** *adj* easily influenced

im·print¹ /ɪmˈprɪnt/ *vt* press (a mark) on

im·print² /ˈɪmprɪnt/ *n* mark left on or in something

im·pris·on /ɪmˈprɪzən/ *vt* put in prison ~**ment** *n* [U]

im·prob·a·ble /ɪmˈprɑbəbəl/ *adj* unlikely –**bly** *adv* –**bility** /ɪmˌprɑbəˈbɪləti/ *n* [C;U]

im·promp·tu /ɪmˈprɑmptu/ *adj, adv* without preparation

im·prop·er /ɪmˈprɑpər/ *adj* 1 not suitable or correct 2 socially unacceptable ~**ly** *adv*

im·prove /ɪmˈpruv/ *vi/t* make or become better ~**ment** *n* [C;U] (sign of) improving

im·pro·vise /ˈɪmprəˌvaɪz/ *vi/t* 1 do (something one has not prepared for) 2 invent (music) while one plays –**visation** /ˌɪmprɑvəˈzeɪʃən, ˌɪmprəvə-/ *n* [C;U]

im·pulse /ˈɪmpʌls/ *n* 1 [C;U] sudden urge 2 sudden force: *nerve impulse* **impulsive** /ɪmˈpʌlsɪv/ *adj* acting on IMPULSE (1)

im·pu·ni·ty /ɪmˈpyunəti/ *n* [U] **with impunity** without being punished

im·pure /ɪmˈpyʊr/ *adj* 1 mixed with something else 2 morally bad

impurity /ɪmˈpyʊrəti/ *n* [C;U]

in¹ /ɪn/ *prep* 1 contained or surrounded by: *in a box* | *in a field* | *in France* 2 (of time) **a** during: *in the summer* **b** at the end of: *finish in 5 minutes* 3 included as part of: *people in a story* 4 wearing: *the girl in red* 5 using: *write in pencil* | *pay in cash* 6 (shows an area of employment): *a job in insurance* 7 (shows direction): *the sun in my eyes* 8 (shows the way something is done or happens): *in public* | *in a hurry* | *in danger* 9 into or arranged: *in rows* 10 for each: *a 1 in 10 chance* 11 with regard to: *weak in judgment* 12 as a/an: *What did you give him in return?* 13 **in all** as the total

in² *adv* 1 (in order to be) contained or surrounded; away from the outside: *Open the bag and put the money in.* 2 towards or at home or the usual place: *Let's stay in tonight.* 3 into a surface: *hammer a nail in* 4 available or complete: *Results aren't in yet.* 5 so as to be added: *Fill in your name.* 6 (in sport) **a** having completed a run **b** (of a ball) inside the line 7 fashionable: *Long hair is in again.* 8 so as to have a position of power: *The Democrats are sure to get in.* 9 **be in for** be about to have (esp. something bad) 10 **be in on** take part in 11 **be in with** *infml* be friendly with

in³ *adj* 1 directed inwards: *a letter in my in tray* 2 *infml* fashionable: *the in place to go* 3 shared by only a few favored people: *an in joke*

in⁴ *n* **the ins and outs (of something)** *infml* the details (of a difficult situation, etc.)

in·a·bil·i·ty /ˌɪnəˈbɪləti/ *n* [S;U] lack of power or skill

in·ac·ces·si·ble /ˌɪnəkˈsɛsəbəl/ *adj* impossible to reach

in·ac·cu·rate /ɪnˈækyərɪt/ *adj* not correct ~**ly** *adv* –**racy** *n* [C;U]

in·ad·e·quate /ɪnˈædəkwɪt/ adj not good enough ~**ly** adv

in·a·li·en·a·ble /ɪnˈeɪlyənəbəl/ adj fml (of rights, etc.) that cannot be taken away

i·nane /ɪˈneɪn/ adj stupid ~**ly** adv **inanity** /ɪˈnænəti/ n [C;U]

in·an·i·mate /ɪnˈænəmɪt/ adj not living: Stones are inanimate.

in·ap·pro·pri·ate /ˌɪnəˈprouˈpri-ɪt◂/ adj not suitable ~**ly** adv ~**ness** n [U]

in·ar·tic·u·late /ˌɪnɑrˈtɪkyəlɪt/ adj 1 (of speech) not clear 2 (of people) not speaking clearly ~**ly** adv

in·as·much as /ˌɪnəzˈmʌtʃ əz/ conj fml to the degree that: because

in·au·gu·rate /ɪˈnɔgyəˌreɪt, -gə-/ vt 1 start or introduce formally with a special ceremony 2 be the beginning of (a period of time) –**ral** adj: his inaugural speech –**ration** /ɪˌnɔgyəˈreɪʃən, -gə-/ n [C;U]

Inauguration Day /-ˌ··ˈ·· ˌ·/ the 20th of January following the election of a new president

in·born /ˌɪnˈbɔrn◂/ adj present from one's birth

in·bred /ˌɪnˈbrɛd◂/ adj 1 inborn 2 produced by breeding between closely related family members

Inc. /ɪŋk, ɪnˈkɔrpəˌreɪtɪd/ adj incorporated; (of a business) formed into a legal CORPORATION

in·cal·cu·la·ble /ɪnˈkælkyələbəl/ adj too great to be counted –**bly** adv

in·can·des·cent /ˌɪnkənˈdɛsənt◂, -kæn-/ adj shining brightly when heated –**cence** n [U]

in·can·ta·tion /ˌɪnkænˈteɪʃən/ n [C;U] words used in magic

in·ca·pac·i·tate /ˌɪnkəˈpæsəˌteɪt/ vt make unable (to do something) –**ty** n [S;U] lack of ability

in·car·ce·rate /ɪnˈkɑrsəˌreɪt/ vt fml put in prison –**ration** /ɪnˌkɑrsəˈreɪʃən/ n [U]

in·car·nate /ɪnˈkɑrnɪt, -ˌneɪt/ adj in human form: the devil incarnate –**nation** /ˌɪnkɑrˈneɪʃən/ n 1 [U] state of being incarnate 2 [C] any of a person's many lives: (fig.) in her former incarnation as mayor 3 [the] (cap.) the coming of God to Earth in the body of Jesus Christ

in·cen·di·a·ry /ɪnˈsɛndiˌɛri/ adj 1 causing fires: incendiary bomb 2 causing violence: incendiary speech

in·cense /ˈɪnsɛns/ n [U] substance burned to make a sweet smell

in·cen·tive /ɪnˈsɛntɪv/ n [C;U] encouragement to get things done

in·cep·tion /ɪnˈsɛpʃən/ n fml beginning

in·ces·sant /ɪnˈsɛsənt/ adj (of something bad) never stopping ~**ly** adv

in·cest /ˈɪnsɛst/ n [U] sexual relationship between close relatives ~**uous** /ɪnˈsɛstʃuəs/ adj

inch /ɪntʃ/ n 1 a measure of length equal to $\frac{1}{12}$ of a foot or 2.54 centimeters 2 small amount 3 **every inch** completely 4 **within an inch of** very near ♦ vi/t move slowly

in·ci·dence /ˈɪnsədəns/ n [S] rate of happening: a high incidence of disease

in·ci·dent /ˈɪnsədənt/ n 1 event, esp. one that is unusual 2 event that includes or leads to violence, danger, or serious disagreement: The spy scandal caused a diplomatic incident.

in·ci·dent·al /ˌɪnsəˈdɛntl◂/ adj 1 happening in connection with something else: incidental expenses 2 something (esp. a fact or detail) that is unimportant ~**ally** adv (used to introduce a new subject in talking)

in·cin·e·rate /ɪnˈsɪnəˌreɪt/ vt fml burn (unwanted things) –**rator** n machine for burning things

in·cip·i·ent /ɪnˈsɪpiənt/ adj fml at an early stage

incision /ɪnˈsɪʒən/ n [C;U] (act of making) a cut, done with a special tool

in·cite /ɪnˈsaɪt/ vt encourage (violence, or people to be violent) ~**ment** n [U]

in·cline¹ /ɪnˈklaɪn/ v 1 vt encourage to feel or think 2 vi tend: I incline to take the opposite view. 3 vi/t slope 4 vt fml (cause to) move downward: He inclined his head (in greeting). **inclined** adj tending: The handle is inclined to stick. **inclination** /ˌɪnkləˈneɪʃən/ n 1 [C;U] liking 2 [C] tendency 3 [C] act of inclining

in·cline² /ˈɪnklaɪn/ n slope

in·clude /ɪnˈklud/ vt 1 have as a part 2 put in with something else **inclusion** /ɪnˈkluʒən/ n [U] **inclusive** /-ˈklusɪv, -zɪv/ adj including everything

in·clud·ing /ɪnˈkludɪŋ/ prep having the thing mentioned as a part of a group or set: There were 20 people, including the teacher.

in·cog·ni·to /ˌɪnkɑgˈnitoʊ, ɪnˈkɑgnəˌtoʊ/ adj, adv taking another name

in·co·her·ent /ˌɪnkoʊˈhɪrənt/ adj not clearly expressed ~**ly** adv –**ence** n [U]

in·come /ˈɪnkʌm, ˈɪŋ-/ n money received regularly

income tax /ˈ·· ˌ·/ n tax on one's income

in·com·ing /ˈɪnˌkʌmɪŋ/ adj coming in, starting a period in office

in·com·mu·ni·ca·do /ˌɪnkəˌmyunɪˈkɑdou/ adv (of people) prevented from giving or receiving messages

in·com·pa·ra·ble /ɪnˈkɑmpərəbəl/ adj unequaled; very great –**bly** adv

in·com·pat·i·ble /ˌɪnkəmˈpætəbəl/ adj not suitable to be together –**bility** /ˌɪnkəmˌpætəˈbɪləti/ n [U]

in·com·pe·tent /ɪnˈkɑmpətənt/ adj not skillful –**tence** n [U]

in·com·plete /ˌɪnkəmˈplit/ adj not finished or not having all parts

in·com·pre·hen·si·ble /ˌɪnkɑmprɪˈhɛnsəbəl, ɪnˌkɑm-/ adj impossible to understand –**sion** /-ˈhɛnʃən/ n [U] failure to understand –**bility** /ˌɪnkɑmprɪˌhɛnsəˈbɪləti, ɪnˌkɑm-/ n [U]

in·con·cei·va·ble /ˌɪnkənˈsivəbəl/ adj impossible to imagine

in·con·gru·ous /ɪnˈkɑŋgruəs/ adj out of place –**ity** /ˌɪnkɑŋˈgruəti, -kən-/ n [C;U]

in·con·se·quen·tial /ˌɪnkɑnsəˈkwɛnʃəl, ɪnˌkɑn-/ adj 1 unimportant 2 not RELEVANT –**ly** adv

in·con·sid·er·ate /ˌɪnkənˈsɪdərɪt/ adj not thinking of other people ~**ly** adv

in·con·so·la·ble /ˌɪnkənˈsoʊləbəl/ adj too sad to be comforted –**bly** adv

in·con·ti·nent /ɪnˈkɑntˀn·ənt, -tənən/ adj unable to control one's bowels and BLADDER –**nence** n [U]

in·con·ve·nience /ˌɪnkənˈvinyəns/ n (cause of) state of difficulty when things do not suit one ♦ vt cause inconvenience to –**ent** adj causing inconvenience –**ently** adv

in·cor·po·rate /ɪnˈkɔrpəˌreɪt/ vt 1 form into a CORPORATION 2 include in something larger –**ration** /ɪnˌkɔrpəˈreɪʃən/ n [U]

in·cor·rect /ˌɪnkəˈrɛktˀ/ adj not correct; wrong ~**ly** adv

in·cor·ri·gi·ble /ɪnˈkɔrədʒəbəl, -ˈkɑr-/ adj bad, and impossible to improve –**bly** adv

in·crease /ɪnˈkris/ vi/t (cause to) become larger **increasingly** adv more and more **increase** /ˈɪŋkris/ n rise in amount, numbers, or degree

in·cred·i·ble /ɪnˈkrɛdəbəl/ adj 1 unbelievable 2 infml wonderful –**bly** adv

in·cred·u·lous /ɪnˈkrɛdʒələs/ adj not believing ~**ly** adv –**lity** /ˌɪnkrəˈduləti/ n [U] disbelief

in·cre·ment /ˈɪnkrəmənt, ˈɪŋ-/ n increase in money or value

in·crim·i·nate /ɪnˈkrɪməˌneɪt/ vt cause (someone) to seem guilty of a crime or fault

in·cu·bate /ˈɪŋkyəˌbeɪt, ˈɪn-/ vt keep (eggs) warm until they HATCH –**bator** n apparatus for keeping eggs warm, or for keeping PREMATURE babies alive –**bation** /ˌɪŋkyəˈbeɪʃən/ n [U] 1 act of incubating 2 period between infection and the appearance of a disease

in·cum·bent /ɪnˈkʌmbənt/ adj **be incumbent on** fml be the moral duty of ♦ n person holding a (political) office

in·cur /ɪnˈkər/ vt -**rr**- bring (esp. something bad) on oneself: incur expenses

in·cur·a·ble /ɪnˈkyʊrəbəl/ adj that cannot be cured –**bly** adv

in·cur·sion /ɪnˈkəʒən/ n fml sudden entrance; invasion (INVADE)

in·debt·ed /ɪnˈdɛtɪd/ adj grateful ~**ness** n [U]

in·de·cent /ɪnˈdisənt/ adj 1 sexually offensive 2 unsuitable ~**ly** adv –**cency** n [U]

in·de·ci·sion /ˌɪndɪˈsɪʒən/ n [U] inability to decide

in·deed /ɪnˈdid/ adv fml certainly; really: "Did you see him?" "I did indeed."

in·de·fen·si·ble /ˌɪndɪˈfɛnsəbəl/ adj that cannot be defended: indefensible behavior

in·de·fin·a·ble /ˌɪndɪˈfaɪnəbəl/ adj impossible to describe –**bly** adv

in·def·i·nite /ɪnˈdɛfənɪt/ adj not clear or fixed ~**ly** adv for an unlimited period **indefinite ar·ti·cle** /ˌ···· ˈ···/ (in English) A or AN

in·del·i·ble /ɪnˈdɛləbəl/ adj that cannot be removed or washed out –**bly** adv

in·del·i·cate /ɪnˈdɛlɪkɪt/ adj not polite or modest ~**ly** adv –**cacy** n [U]

in·dent /ɪnˈdɛnt/ vi/t start (a line of writing) further into the page than the others ♦ /ˈɪndɛnt/ n: a half-inch indent ~**ation** /ˌɪndɛnˈteɪʃən/ n 1 [C;U] (act of making) a space at the beginning of a line of writing 2 space pointing inwards: the indentations of a coastline

In·de·pend·ence Day /ˌɪndɪˈpɛndəns ˌdeɪ/ n US national holiday to celebrate its beginning as an independent nation

in·de·pen·dent /ˌɪndɪˈpɛndənt◁/ *adj* **1** governing itself **2** not depending on advice, money, etc., from others ♦ *n* (*often cap.*) person who does not belong to an established political party **~ly** *adv* **–dence** *n* [U]

in-depth /ˈ· ˈ·◁/ *adj* very thorough

in·de·scri·ba·ble /ˌɪndɪˈskraɪbəbəl/ *adj* that cannot be described **–bly** *adv*

in·de·struc·ti·ble /ˌɪndɪˈstrʌktəbəl/ *adj* too strong to be destroyed

in·de·ter·mi·nate /ˌɪndɪˈtɜːmənɪt/ *adj* not fixed as one thing or another

in·dex /ˈɪndɛks/ *n* **-dexes** or **-dices** /-dəˌsiz/ **1** alphabetical list of subjects mentioned in a book **2 a** sign by which something can be measured **b** system of comparing prices with their former level: *the cost of living index* ♦ *vt* make, include in, or provide with an INDEX (1)

index fin·ger /ˈ· ˌ·/ *n* FOREFINGER

In·di·an /ˈɪndiən/ *n, adj* **1** Native American **2** (person) from India

Indian sum·mer /ˌ·· ˈ·/ *n* period of warm weather in fall

in·di·cate /ˈɪndɪˌkeɪt/ *vt* **1** point at; show **2** show (the direction in which one is turning in a vehicle) by hand signals, lights, etc. **–cator** *n* needle or dial showing measurement **–cation** /ˌɪndəˈkeɪʃən/ *n* [C;U] sign or suggestion indicating something

in·dic·a·tive /ɪnˈdɪkətɪv/ *adj* showing ♦ *n gram* verb form expressing a fact or action

in·di·ces /ˈɪndəˌsiz/ *n pl. of* INDEX

in·dict /ɪnˈdaɪt/ *vt* charge officially with a crime **~able** *adj* for which one can be indicted: *indictable offense* **~ment** *n* [C;U] *under indictment for murder*

in·dif·fer·ent /ɪnˈdɪfrənt/ *adj* **1** not interested **2** not very good **~ly** *adv* **–ence** *n* [U]

in·di·ge·nous /ɪnˈdɪdʒənəs/ *adj* NATIVE to a place: *indigenous flowers*

in·di·ges·tion /ˌɪndɪˈdʒɛstʃən, -daɪ-/ *n* [U] illness from not being able to DIGEST food

in·dig·nant /ɪnˈdɪɡnənt/ *adj* angry, esp. at something unjust **~ly** *adv* **–nation** /ˌɪndɪɡˈneɪʃən/ *n* [U] indignant feeling

in·dig·ni·ty /ɪnˈdɪɡnəti/ *n* [C;U] treatment that makes one feel ashamed

in·di·rect /ˌɪndəˈrɛkt◁, -daɪ-/ *adj* **1** not straight; not directly connected to: *indirect route | indirect result* **2** (of taxes) paid by increasing the cost of goods or services **3** meaning something which is not directly mentioned: *an indirect answer* **~ly** *adv*

indirect ob·ject /ˌ··· ˈ··/ *n* person or thing that the DIRECT OBJECT is given to, made for, done to, etc.: *In "I asked him a question," "him" is the indirect object.*

indirect speech /ˌ··· ˈ/ *n* [U] *gram* speech reported without repeating the actual words (e.g. *She said, "I'm coming."* becomes *She said she was coming.*)

in·dis·creet /ˌɪndɪˈskrit/ *adj* not acting carefully or politely **~ly** *adv* **–cretion** /-ˈskrɛʃən/ *n* **1** [U] state or quality of being indiscreet **2** [C] indiscreet act: *youthful indiscretions*

in·dis·crim·i·nate /ˌɪndɪˈskrɪmənɪt/ *adj* not choosing or chosen carefully **~ly** *adv*

in·di·spen·sa·ble /ˌɪndɪˈspɛnsəbəl/ *adj* necessary

in·dis·pu·ta·ble /ˌɪndɪˈspyutəbəl/ *adj* beyond doubt: *indisputable proof* **–bly** *adv*

in·dis·tin·guish·a·ble /ˌɪndɪˈstɪŋɡwɪʃəbəl/ *adj* impossible to tell apart: *indistinguishable from silk*

in·di·vid·u·al /ˌɪndəˈvɪdʒuəl/ *adj* **1** single; separate **2** (of a manner, style, or way of doing things) particular to a person, thing, etc. ♦ *n* single person (in a group) **~ly** *adv* separately **~ism** *n* [U] belief in the rights of each person in society **~ist** *n, adj* (person) independent and unlike other people **~istic** /ˌɪndəˌvɪdʒuˈlɪstɪk/ *adj* **~ity** /ˌɪndəˌvɪdʒuˈæləti/ *n* [U] qualities that make a person unusual

in·doc·tri·nate /ɪnˈdɑktrəˌneɪt/ *vt* train to accept ideas without question **–nation** /ɪnˌdɑktrəˈneɪʃən/ *n* [U]

in·do·lent /ˈɪndələnt/ *adj fml* lazy **–lence** *n* [U]

in·dom·i·ta·ble /ɪnˈdɑmətəbəl/ *adj* too strong to be discouraged or controlled

in·door /ˈɪndɔr, ˈɪndoʊr/ *adj* inside a building **indoors** *adv*

in·duce /ɪnˈdus/ *vt* **1** persuade **2** cause; produce **~ment** *n* [C;U] (something, esp. money, which provides) encouragement to do something

in·duct /ɪnˈdʌkt/ *vt* introduce someone officially into an organization, esp. the army

in·duc·tion /ɪnˈdʌkʃən/ *n* **1** [U] act or ceremony of introducing a person to a new job, organization, etc. **2** [C;U] (action of causing) birth of a child which has been hastened by the use of drugs **3** [U] way of reasoning using known facts to produce general laws

in·dulge /ɪnˈdʌldʒ/ v **1** vt allow to do or have something nice **2** vi allow oneself pleasure: *indulge in a cigar* **indulgence** n **1** [U] indulging **2** [C] something in which one indulges **indulgent** adj (too) kind

in·dus·tri·al /ɪnˈdʌstriəl/ adj of or having INDUSTRY (1) ~**ly** adv ~**ism** n [U] system in which industries are important ~**ist** n owner or manager of an industry ~**ize** vi/t (cause) to become industrially developed

industrial park /ˌ·ˌ·· ˈ·/ n area with many factories

in·dus·tri·ous /ɪnˈdʌstriəs/ adj working hard ~**ly** adv

in·dus·try /ˈɪndəstri/ n **1** [C;U] (branch of) the production of goods for sale: *the clothing industry* **2** [U] continual hard work

i·ne·bri·at·ed /ɪˈnibriˌeɪtɪd/ adj fml drunk

in·ed·i·ble /ɪnˈɛdəbəl/ adj unsuitable for eating

in·ef·fec·tive /ˌɪnəˈfɛktɪv/ adj unable to produce the right results ~**ly** adv ~**ness** n [U]

in·ef·fec·tu·al /ˌɪnəˈfɛktʃuəl/ adj which does not give a good enough effect, or who is not able to get things done ~**ly** adv

in·ef·fi·cient /ˌɪnəˈfɪʃənt/ adj not working well ~**ly** adv –**ciency** n [U]

in·el·i·gi·ble /ɪnˈɛlədʒəbəl/ adj not fulfilling the conditions –**bility** /ɪnˌɛlədʒəˈbɪləti/ n [U]

in·ept /ɪˈnɛpt/ adj **1** foolishly unsuitable **2** totally unable to do things ~**ly** adv ~**itude** n [C;U]

in·e·qual·i·ty /ˌɪnɪˈkwɑləti/ n [C;U] lack of fairness or equality

in·ert /ɪˈnɜrt/ adj **1** unable to move **2** not acting chemically: *inert gases*

in·er·tia /ɪˈnɜrʃə/ n [U] **1** force that keeps a thing in the same state until pushed **2** laziness

in·es·ca·pa·ble /ˌɪnəˈskeɪpəbəl/ adj unavoidable

in·ev·i·ta·ble /ɪˈnɛvətəbəl/ adj **1** unavoidable **2** infml expected and familiar: *The principal made her inevitable joke about the school food.* –**bly** adv –**bility** /ɪnˌɛvətəˈbɪləti/ n [U]

in·ex·cu·sa·ble /ˌɪnɪkˈskyuzəbəl/ adj unforgivable –**bly** adv

in·ex·pli·ca·ble /ˌɪnɪkˈsplɪkəbəl, ɪnˈɛksplɪkə-/ adj too strange to be explained –**bly** adv

in·ex·pen·sive /ˌɪnɪkˈspɛnsɪv, -zɪv/ adj low in price –**ly** adv

in·fal·li·ble /ɪnˈfæləbəl/ adj **1** never making mistakes **2** always effective: *infallible cure* –**bility** /ɪnˌfæləˈbɪləti/ n [U]

in·fa·mous /ˈɪnfəməs/ adj famous for something bad –**my** n [C;U]

in·fan·cy /ˈɪnfənsi/ n [S;U] early childhood

in·fant /ˈɪnfənt/ n fml baby

in·fan·tile /ˈɪnfənˌtaɪl, -tɪl/ adj childish

in·fan·try /ˈɪnfəntri/ n [U] foot soldiers

in·fat·u·at·ed /ɪnˈfætʃuˌeɪtɪd/ adj foolishly loving –**ation** /ɪnˌfætʃuˈeɪʃən/ n [C;U]

in·fect /ɪnˈfɛkt/ vt give disease to: (fig.) *She infected the whole class with her laughter.* (= everyone laughed) ~**ion** /-ˈfɛkʃən/ n [C;U] (disease spread by) infecting ~**ious** adj able to infect: (fig.) *infectious laughter*

in·fer /ɪnˈfɜr/ vt -rr- draw (meaning) from facts: *I inferred from his letter that he had not made a decision.* ~**ence** /ˈɪnfərəns/ n [C;U]

in·fe·ri·or /ɪnˈfɪriər/ adj less good; low(er) in rank ♦ n [C] inferior person ~**ity** /ɪnˌfɪriˈɔrəti, -ˈɑrə-/ n [U]

in·fer·no /ɪnˈfɜrnoʊ/ n -**nos** place of very great heat and large uncontrollable flames

in·fer·tile /ɪnˈfɜrtl/ adj not FERTILE: *infertile eggs*

in·fest /ɪnˈfɛst/ vt (of something bad) be present in large numbers ~**ation** n

in·fi·del·i·ty /ˌɪnfəˈdɛləti/ n [C;U] **1** (act of) disloyalty **2** (act of) sex with someone other than one's marriage partner

in·fight·ing /ˈɪnˌfaɪtɪŋ/ n [U] disagreement between members of a group

in·fil·trate /ɪnˈfɪlˌtreɪt, ˈɪnfɪl-/ vt enter secretly, with an unfriendly purpose –**tration** /ˌɪnfɪlˈtreɪʃən/ n [U]

in·fi·nite /ˈɪnfənɪt/ adj without limits; endless ~**ly** adv

in·fin·i·tive /ɪnˈfɪnətɪv/ n main verb form that can follow other verbs and be used with **to** (e.g. "go" in *I can go* and *I want to go*)

in·fin·i·ty /ɪnˈfɪnəti/ n [U] endless space or quantity

in·firm /ɪnˈfɜːm/ adj fml weak in body or mind ~**ity** n [C;U]

in·fir·ma·ry /ɪnˈfɜːməri/ n room where sick people are given treatment

in·flame /ɪnˈfleɪm/ vt make violent **inflamed** red and swollen: inflamed eye

in·flam·ma·ble /ɪnˈflæməbəl/ adj **1** which can easily be set on fire and which burns quickly **2** easily excited or made angry

in·flam·ma·tion /ˌɪnfləˈmeɪʃən/ n [C;U] inflamed condition

in·flam·ma·to·ry /ɪnˈflæmətəri, -ˌtʊəri/ adj likely to inflame: inflammatory speeches

in·flate /ɪnˈfleɪt/ v **1** vt blow up (a tire, etc.) with air **2** vi/t increase the supply of money in a country **inflated** adj **1** full of air **2** too big: inflated prices | an inflated opinion of oneself

in·fla·tion /ɪnˈfleɪʃən/ n [U] **1** act of inflating or state of being inflated **2** rise in prices caused by increased production costs or an increase in money supply ~**ary** adj likely to cause INFLATION (2)

in·flec·tion /ɪnˈflekʃən/ n [C;U] **a** gram change in the form of a word to show difference in its use **b** movement up or down of the voice

in·flex·i·ble /ɪnˈfleksəbəl/ adj impossible to bend or change –**bly** adv –**bility** /ɪnˌfleksəˈbɪləti/ n [U]

in·flict /ɪnˈflɪkt/ vt force (punishment, etc.) on ~**ion** /-ˈflɪkʃən/ n [C;U]

in·flu·ence /ˈɪnfluəns/ n [C;U] **1** (power to have) an effect **2** someone with this power: She's a bad influence on you. **3** under the influence drunk ♦ vt have an influence on

in·flu·en·tial /ˌɪnfluˈenʃəl/ adj having great influence

in·flu·en·za /ˌɪnfluˈenzə/ n [U] fml FLU

in·flux /ˈɪnflʌks/ n [C;U] arrival in large numbers or quantities

in·fo /ˈɪnfəʊ/ n infml for: information

in·fo·mer·cial /ˌɪnfəˈmɜːʃəl/ n long television advertisement made to seem like a regular program

in·form /ɪnˈfɔːm/ vt fml give information to ~**ant** n person who gives information ~**ed** adj **1** knowing things: well-informed **2** having and using suitable knowledge: an informed guess ~**er** n person who tells the police about someone

inform against/on phr vt tell the police that (someone) is guilty

in·for·mal /ɪnˈfɔːməl/ adj not formal; without ceremony: an informal meeting | informal clothes ~**ly** adv ~**ity** /ˌɪnfɔːˈmæləti/ n [U]

in·for·ma·tion /ˌɪnfəˈmeɪʃən/ n [U] **1** knowledge given; facts **2** service that provides telephone numbers: I got your number from information.

information tech·nol·o·gy /ˌ···· ·ˈ···/ n [U] science of collecting and using information by means of computer systems

in·for·ma·tive /ɪnˈfɔːmətɪv/ adj telling one useful things

in·fra·red /ˌɪnfrəˈred◀/ adj of the light RAYS of longer WAVELENGTH than those we can see

in·fra·struc·ture /ˈɪnfrəˌstrʌktʃə/ n necessary BASIC systems (e.g. of power, roads, laws, banks) needed to keep a country going

in·fringe /ɪnˈfrɪndʒ/ vt/i fml go against (a law, or someone's rights) ~**ment** n [C;U]

in·fu·ri·ate /ɪnˈfjʊərieɪt/ vt make very angry

in·fuse /ɪnˈfjuːz/ vt **1** fill (someone) with a quality **2** put (tea, etc.) into hot water to make a drink **infusion** /-ˈfjuːʒən/ n [C;U] (liquid made by) infusing

in·ge·ni·ous /ɪnˈdʒiːnjəs/ adj clever at making or inventing: ingenious person/ excuse ~**ly** adv –**nuity** /ˌɪndʒəˈnuːəti/ n [U]

in·grained /ɪnˈɡreɪnd, ˈɪnɡreɪnd/ adj deeply fixed: ingrained dirt/habits

in·grat·i·tude /ɪnˈɡrætəˌtuːd/ n [U] ungratefulness

in·gre·di·ent /ɪnˈɡriːdiənt/ n one of a mixture of things, esp. in baking

in·hab·it /ɪnˈhæbɪt/ vt fml live in (a place) ~**ant** n person living in a place

in·hale /ɪnˈheɪl/ vi/t breathe in **inhaler** n apparatus for inhaling medicine to make breathing easier **inhalation** /ˌɪnhəˈleɪʃən/ n [C;U]

in·her·ent /ɪnˈhɪərənt, -ˈher-/ adj necessarily present: problems inherent in the system ~**ly** adv

in·her·it /ɪnˈherɪt/ vi/t receive (property, etc.) from someone who has died: (fig.) He's inherited his father's meanness. ~**ance** n **1** [C] something inherited **2** [U] inheriting ~**or** n person who inherits

in·hib·it /ɪnˈhɪbɪt/ vt prevent; HINDER ~**ion** /ˌɪnhɪˈbɪʃən/ n feeling of being unable to do what one really wants to ~**ed** adj not confident or relaxed enough to do what one really wants to

in·house /ˈ·ˌ·/ *adj, adv* within a company or organization rather than outside: *an in-house design team*

in·hu·man /ɪnˈhyumən, ɪnˈyu-/ *adj* cruel ~**ity** /ˌɪnhyuˈmænəti, ˌɪnyu-/ *n* [C;U]

in·hu·mane /ˌɪnhyuˈmeɪn, ˌɪnyu-/ *adj* unkind; not HUMANE ♦ *n* [C;U] ~**ly** *adv*

in·im·i·ta·ble /ɪˈnɪmətəbəl/ *adj* too good or unusual to be copied –**bly** *adv*

i·ni·tial /ɪˈnɪʃəl/ *adj* at the beginning ♦ *n* first letter of someone's name ♦ *vt* **-l-** write one's initials on ~**ly** *adv* at first

i·ni·ti·ate[1] /ɪˈnɪʃiˌeɪt/ *vt* **1** start (something) working **2** introduce (someone) into a group, etc. –**ation** /ɪˌnɪʃiˈeɪʃən/ *n* [C;U]

i·ni·ti·ate[2] /ɪˈnɪʃi-ɪt/ *n* person instructed or skilled in some special field

i·ni·tia·tive /ɪˈnɪʃətɪv, -ʃiə-/ *n* **1** [U] ability to act without help or advice: *on his own initiative* **2** [C] first step: *initiatives to encourage investment*

in·ject /ɪnˈdʒɛkt/ *vt* put (a drug, etc.) into someone with a needle: (fig.) *inject new life, interest, etc., into something* ~**ion** /-ˈdʒɛkʃən/ *n* [C;U]

in·junc·tion /ɪnˈdʒʌŋkʃən/ *n fml* official order

in·jure /ˈɪndʒər/ *vt* hurt; damage **injured** *adj, n* hurt (people) **injury** *n* **1** [U] harm; damage **2** [C] wound, etc.

in·jus·tice /ɪnˈdʒʌstɪs/ *n* [C;U] (act of) unfairness

ink /ɪŋk/ *n* [C;U] colored liquid for writing, printing, etc. ~**y** *adj* black

ink·ling /ˈɪŋklɪŋ/ *n* [S;U] slight idea

in·laid /ˈɪnleɪd, ɪnˈleɪd/ *adj* set ornamentally into another substance: *inlaid gold*

in·land /ˈɪnlənd, ɪnˈlænd/ *adj, adv* inside or into a country *travel inland*

in·laws /ˈ·ˌ·/ *n* [P] relatives by marriage

in·let /ˈɪnlɛt, ˈɪnlɪt/ *n* narrow piece of water reaching into the land

in·mate /ˈɪnmeɪt/ *n* person living in a prison, hospital, etc.

inn /ɪn/ *n* small hotel

in·nards /ˈɪnərdz/ *n* [P] inside parts, esp. of the stomach

in·nate /ɪˈneɪt/ *adj* (of a quality) present from birth ~**ly** *adv*

in·ner /ˈɪnər/ *adj* **1** on the inside; close to the middle **2** secret, esp. if of the spirit: *inner meaning/life*

inner ci·ty /ˌ·· ˈ··/ *n* center of an old city where many poor people live

in·ning /ˈɪnɪŋ/ *n* period of play in BASEBALL: *He scored a home run in the second inning.*

inn·keep·er /ˈɪnˌkipər/ *n* manager of an INN

in·no·cent /ˈɪnəsənt/ *adj* **1** not guilty **2** harmless **3** unable to recognize evil; simple ~**ly** *adv* –**cence** *n* [U]

in·noc·u·ous /ɪˈnɑkyuəs/ *adj* harmless

in·no·va·tion /ˌɪnəˈveɪʃən/ *n* **1** [C] new idea **2** [U] introducing new things –**vate** /ˈɪnəˌveɪt/ *vi* make changes –**tor** *n* –**tive** also –**tory** /ˈɪnəvəˌtɔri, -ˌtoʊri/ *adj*

in·nu·en·do /ˌɪnyuˈɛndoʊ/ *n* -**does** *or* -**dos** [C;U] unpleasant indirect remark(s)

in·nu·mer·a·ble /ɪˈnumərəbəl/ *adj* too many to count

i·noc·u·late /ɪˈnɑkyəˌleɪt/ *vt* introduce a weak form of a disease into (someone) as a protection –**lation** /ɪˌnɑkyəˈleɪʃən/ *n* [C;U]

in·of·fen·sive /ˌɪnəˈfɛnsɪv◂/ *adj* not causing dislike; not rude ~**ly** *adv*

in·or·di·nate /ɪnˈɔrdn-ɪt/ *adj fml* beyond reasonable limits ~**ly** *adv*

in·put /ˈɪnpʊt/ *n* [S;U] something put in for use, esp. information into a computer ♦ *vt* -**tt**-; *past t. & p.* **input** put (information) into a computer

in·quire /ɪnˈkwaɪər/ *vi/t* ask for information (about) **inquiring** *adj* that shows an interest in knowing

inquiry /ɪnˈkwaɪəri, ˈɪnkwaɪ-, ˈɪŋkwəri/ *n* **1** [C;U] (act of) inquiring **2** [C] set of meetings, etc., to find out why something happened

inquire into *phr vt* look for information about

in·qui·si·tion /ˌɪnkwəˈzɪʃən/ *n* thorough and esp. cruel inquiry

in·quis·i·tive /ɪnˈkwɪzətɪv/ *adj* asking too many questions ~**ly** *adv*

in·roads /ˈɪnroʊdz/ *n* **1** attack upon or advance into a new area **2** effort or activity that lessens the quantity or difficulty of what remains afterwards: *inroads in fighting a disease*

ins and outs /ˌ· ən ˈ·/ *n* [*the*+P] details (of a situation, procedure, etc.)

in·sane /ɪnˈseɪn/ *adj* crazy ~**ly** *adv*

insanity /ɪnˈsænəti/ *n* [U]

in·sa·tia·ble /ɪnˈseɪʃəbəl, -ʃiə-/ adj impossible to satisfy **–bly** adv

in·scribe /ɪnˈskraɪb/ vt fml write (words) on **inscription** /ɪnˈskrɪpʃən/ n piece of writing inscribed, esp. on stone

in·sect /ˈɪnsekt/ n small creature with 6 legs

in·sec·ti·cide /ɪnˈsektɪˌsaɪd/ n [C;U] chemical used to kill insects

in·se·cure /ˌɪnsɪˈkyʊr/ adj 1 not safe 2 not sure of oneself **–ly** adv **–curity** n [U]

in·sem·i·na·tion /ɪnˌseməˈneɪʃən/ n [U] putting of male seed into a female

in·sen·si·tive /ɪnˈsensətɪv/ adj not SENSITIVE **~ly** adv **–tivity** /ɪnˌsensəˈtɪvəti/ n [S;U]

in·sep·a·ra·ble /ɪnˈsepərəbəl/ adj impossible to separate

in·sert[1] /ɪnˈsɜːt/ vt put into something: *insert a key in a lock* ♦ /ˈɪnsɜːt/ n written or printed material put in between pages of a book **~ion** /ɪnˈsɜːʃən/ n [C;U]

in·ser·vice /ˌ·ˈ··◂/ adj (taking place) during one's work: *in-service training*

in·set /ˈɪnset/ n picture, etc., in the corner of a larger one

in·side /ɪnˈsaɪd, ˈɪnsaɪd/ n 1 [the+S] a part nearest to the middle, or that faces away from the open air **b** *infml* position in which one is able to know special or secret information 2 [C] also **insides** pl. — *infml* one's stomach 3 **inside out: a** with the inside parts on the outside **b** thoroughly: *know it inside out* ♦ /ˈɪnsaɪd/ adj 1 facing or at the inside: *the inside pages of a newspaper* 2 from someone closely concerned: *inside information* ♦ /ɪnˈsaɪd/ adv to or in the inside, esp. indoors: *The children are playing inside.* ♦ prep 1 to or on the inside of: *inside the car* 2 in less time than: *inside an hour*

insider /ɪnˈsaɪdə/ n person accepted in a social group, esp. someone with special information or influence

insider trad·ing /ˌ·ˈ··/ n [U] illegal practice of buying and selling stock by people who use their knowledge of the business affairs of the companies they work for

in·sight /ˈɪnsaɪt/ n [C;U] understanding: *insight into their lives*

in·sig·ni·a /ɪnˈsɪgniə/ n object worn as a sign of rank

in·sig·nif·i·cant /ˌɪnsɪgˈnɪfəkənt/ adj not important **~ly** adv **–cance** n [U]

in·sin·u·ate /ɪnˈsɪnyuˌeɪt/ vt 1 suggest (something unpleasant) indirectly 2 gain acceptance for (esp. oneself) by secret means **–ation** /ɪnˌsɪnyuˈeɪʃən/ n [C;U]

in·sip·id /ɪnˈsɪpɪd/ adj derog lacking a strong character, taste, or effect

in·sist /ɪnˈsɪst/ vi/t 1 order: *insist that he should go* 2 declare firmly: *He insists he wasn't there.* **~ent** adj repeatedly insisting **~ence** n [U]

in so far as /ˌ·· ˈ· ·/ conj to the degree that

in·so·lent /ˈɪnsələnt/ adj fml disrespectful; rude **–lence** n [U]

in·sol·u·ble /ɪnˈsɑlyəbəl/ adj 1 impossible to answer 2 impossible to DISSOLVE

in·sol·vent /ɪnˈsɑlvənt/ n, adj (someone) unable to pay debts **–vency** n [U]

in·som·ni·a /ɪnˈsɑmniə/ n [U] inability to sleep **insomniac** /-niˌæk/ n, adj (someone) who habitually cannot sleep

in·spect /ɪnˈspekt/ vt examine closely **~or** n 1 official who inspects something 2 police officer of high rank **~ion** /ɪˈspekʃən/ n [C;U]

in·spire /ɪnˈspaɪə/ vt 1 encourage to act 2 fill with a feeling: *inspire them with confidence* **inspiration** /ˌɪnspəˈreɪʃən/ n 1 [U] act of inspiring or state of being inspired 2 [C] something that inspires 3 [C] sudden good idea **inspired** /ɪnˈspaɪəd/ adj very clever

in·sta·bil·i·ty /ˌɪnstəˈbɪləti/ n [U] 1 state of being unsteady 2 (of people) tendency to act in changeable ways

in·stall /ɪnˈstɔl/ vt 1 put (a machine, etc.) somewhere 2 settle (someone) in a position **~ation** /ˌɪnstəˈleɪʃən/ n 1[U] installing 2 [C] equipment, etc., installed

in·stall·ment /ɪnˈstɔlmənt/ n 1 single part of a story, etc., that appears in regular parts 2 single regular payment

in·stance /ˈɪnstəns/ n 1 EXAMPLE (1) 2 **for instance** for example ♦ vt give as an example

in·stant /ˈɪnstənt/ n moment of time ♦ adj happening or produced at once **~ly** adv at once

instant re·play /ˌ·· ˈ··/ n second showing of a sports event immediately after it happens

in·stan·ta·ne·ous /ˌɪnstənˈteɪniəs/ adj happening at once **~ly** adv

in·stead /ɪnˈstɛd/ adv **1** in place of that **2** **instead of** in place of: *You go instead of me.*

in·step /ˈɪnstɛp/ n upper surface of the foot

in·sti·gate /ˈɪnstɪˌgeɪt/ vt fml cause to do or happen **–gator** n **–gation** /ˌɪnstəˈgeɪʃən/ n [U]

in·still /ɪnˈstɪl/ vt put (ideas) into someone's mind

in·stinct /ˈɪnstɪŋkt/ n [C;U] natural tendency to act in a certain way **~ive** /ɪnˈstɪŋktɪv/ adj: *instinctive fear of snakes* **~ively** adv

in·sti·tute /ˈɪnstɪˌtuːt/ n society formed for a special purpose ♦ vt fml start; establish

in·sti·tu·tion /ˌɪnstɪˈtuːʃən/ n **1** [C] (building for) a hospital, school, prison, etc., where people are taken care of **2** [C] established custom **3** [U] act of instituting **–al** adj ~make into an INSTITUTION (2) **2** (of people) put into an INSTITUTION (1)

in·struct /ɪnˈstrʌkt/ vt **1** give orders to **2** teach **3** law inform officially **~ive** adj teaching something useful

in·struc·tor /ɪnˈstrʌktə/ n university teacher who does not have a Ph.D. (= highest degree)

in·struc·tion /ɪnˈstrʌkʃən/ n **1** [C] order **2** [U] act of instructing; teaching **instructions** n [P] advice on how to do something: *Follow the instructions on the packet.*

in·stru·ment /ˈɪnstrəmənt/ n **1** thing that helps in work **2** apparatus for playing music **~al** /ˌɪnstrəˈmɛntl/ adj **1** for musical instruments **2** helpful; causing: *His information was instrumental in catching the thief.* **~alist** n player of a musical instrument

in·sub·or·di·nate /ˌɪnsəˈbɔːdn-ɪt/ adj disobedient **–nation** /ˌɪnsəˌbɔːdnˈeɪʃən/ n [C;U]

in·sub·stan·tial /ˌɪnsəbˈstænʃəl/ adj not firm or solid

in·suf·fe·ra·ble /ɪnˈsʌfərəbəl/ adj unbearable

in·suf·fi·cient /ˌɪnsəˈfɪʃənt◄/ adj not enough **~ly** adv **–ciency** n [S;U]

in·su·lar /ˈɪnsələ/ adj **1** having narrow attitudes; concerned mainly with oneself **2** of an island **~ity** /ˌɪnsəˈlærəti/ n [U]

in·su·late /ˈɪnsəˌleɪt/ vt **1** cover, to prevent the escape of heat, electricity, etc. **2** protect from experiences **–lator** n thing that insulates **–lation** /ˌɪnsəˈleɪʃən/ n [U] (material for) insulating

in·su·lin /ˈɪnsəlɪn/ n [U] substance produced by the body to allow sugar to be used for energy

in·sult[1] /ɪnˈsʌlt/ vt be rude to

in·sult[2] /ˈɪnsʌlt/ n **1** rude remark or action **2** **add insult to injury** do or say something more against someone when one has already harmed them enough

in·sur·ance /ɪnˈʃʊərəns/ n **1** [U] agreement to pay money in case of misfortune **2** [U] money paid by or to an insurance company for this **3** [S;U] protection against anything

in·sure /ɪnˈʃʊə/ vt **1** protect by insurance: *insured against fire* — see also ENSURE

in·sur·gent /ɪnˈsɜːdʒənt/ n, adj REBEL **–gency** n [C;U]

in·sur·moun·ta·ble /ˌɪnsəˈmaʊntəbəl/ adj too large, difficult, etc., to be dealt with

in·sur·rec·tion /ˌɪnsəˈrɛkʃən/ n [C;U] REBELLION

in·tact /ɪnˈtækt/ adj undamaged

in·take /ˈɪnteɪk/ n **1** [S] amount or number taken in **2** [C] pipe to let in gas, water, etc.

in·tan·gi·ble /ɪnˈtændʒəbəl/ adj **1** which cannot be known by the senses or described: *an intangible quality* **2** which is hidden or not material, but known to be real: *intangible assets of the business, such as the loyalty of its customers* **–bly** adv **–bility** /ɪnˌtændʒəˈbɪləti/ n [U]

in·te·ger /ˈɪntɪdʒə/ n a whole number

in·te·gral /ˈɪntɪgrəl, ɪnˈtɛgrəl/ adj necessary to complete something: *an integral part of the argument*

in·te·grate /ˈɪntɪˌgreɪt/ vi/t (cause to) mix with other races or people **–gration** /ˌɪntɪˈgreɪʃən/ n [U] **–grationist** n believer in integration

in·teg·ri·ty /ɪnˈtɛgrəti/ n [U] **1** honesty; trustworthiness **2** wholeness

in·tel·lect /ˈɪntɪˌlɛkt/ n [C;U] ability to think **~ual** /ˌɪntəˈlɛktʃuəl/ adj **1** of the intellect **2** clever and well-educated **~ual** n intellectual person **~ually** adv

in·tel·li·gence /ɪnˈtɛlədʒəns/ n [U] **1** ability to learn and understand **2** (people who gather) information about enemies **–gent** adj clever **–gently** adv

in·tel·li·gent·si·a /ɪnˌtelə'dʒentsiə/ n [P] intellectuals as a social group

in·tel·li·gi·ble /ɪn'telədʒəbəl/ adj understandable **–bly** adv **–bility** /ɪnˌtelədʒə-'bɪləti/ n [U]

in·tend /ɪn'tend/ vt have as one's purpose; mean

in·tense /ɪn'tens/ adj strong (in quality or feeling) **~ly** adv **intensity** n [U] quality or appearance of being intense

in·ten·si·fy /ɪn'tensəfaɪ/ vi/t make or become more intense **–fication** /ɪnˌtensəfə'keɪʃən/ n [U]

in·ten·sive /ɪn'tensɪv, -zɪv/ adj giving a lot of attention **~ly** adv

intensive care /ˌ·· '·/ n [U] hospital department that treats seriously injured or very sick people

in·tent¹ /ɪn'tent/ n [U] **1** purpose: *enter with intent to steal* **2 to all intents and purposes** in almost every way

in·tent² adj **1** with fixed attention **2** determined

in·ten·tion /ɪn'tenʃən/ n **1** [C;U] plan; purpose **2 good intentions** wish to bring about a good result **~al** adj done on purpose **~ally** adv

in·ter /ɪn'tɜːr/ vt **-rr-** fml bury

in·ter·act /ˌɪntər'ækt/ vi have an effect on each other **~ion** /-'ækʃən/ n [C;U]

in·ter·act·ive /ˌɪntər'æktɪv/ adj **1** that interacts **2** allowing the exchange of information between a computer and a user while a program is in operation

in·ter·cede /ˌɪntər'siːd/ vi speak in favor of someone

in·ter·cept /ˌɪntər'sept/ vt stop (someone or something moving between 2 places) **~ion** /-'sepʃən/ n [C;U]

in·ter·change /ˌɪntər'tʃeɪndʒ/ vi/t exchange **~able** adj ♦ /'ɪntərtʃeɪndʒ/ n **1** [C;U] (act of) interchanging **2** [C] system of smaller roads connecting main roads

in·ter·com /'ɪntərˌkɑm/ n system for talking through a machine to people fairly near

in·ter·con·ti·nen·tal /ˌɪntərˌkɑntə'nentl, -ˌkɑnt'n'entl/ adj between CONTINENTS

in·ter·course /'ɪntərkɔrs/ n [U] **1** SEXUAL INTERCOURSE **2** fml conversation, etc., between people

in·terest /'ɪntrɪst, 'ɪntərest/ n **1** [S;U] willingness to give attention: *take an inter-*
est **2** [U] quality that makes people give attention: *That's of no interest to her.* **3** [C] activity or subject that one likes to give time to **4** [C] also **interests** pl. — **advantage**: *It's in your interest to go.* **5** [U] money paid for the use of money: *10% interest* **6** [C] share in a business ♦ vt cause to feel INTEREST (1) **~ed** /'ɪntrɪstɪd, 'ɪntərestɪd/ adj **1** feeling INTEREST (1) **2** personally concerned **~ing** adj having INTEREST (2)

in·ter·face /'ɪntərfeɪs/ n point where 2 systems meet and act on each other ♦ vi/t connect or be connected by means of an interface

in·ter·fere /ˌɪntər'fɪr/ vi **1** enter into a matter that does not concern one and in which one is not wanted **2** prevent something from working properly **–ference** n [U] **1** act of interfering **2** noises, etc., that stop radio or television from working properly

  interfere with phr vt **1** get in the way of **2** touch or move (something) in a way that is not allowed **3** annoy or touch sexually

in·ter·im /'ɪntərɪm/ adj done as part of something to follow later: *interim report*

in·te·ri·or /ɪn'tɪriər/ n inside of something **interior** adj

interior de·sign /ˌ··· ·'·/ n [U] job or skill of choosing and arranging furniture, paint, art, etc., for the inside of houses and buildings **~er** n

in·ter·ject /ˌɪntər'dʒekt/ vi/t fml make (a sudden remark) between others **~ion** /-'dʒekʃən/ n **1** [C] word or phrase, such as *"Good heavens!"* interjected **2** [U] act of interjecting

in·ter·lude /'ɪntərlud/ n period of time between 2 parts or activities

in·ter·mar·ry /ˌɪntər'mæri/ vi (of groups of people) become connected by marriage **–marriage** /-'mærɪdʒ/ n [U]

in·ter·me·di·a·ry /ˌɪntər'midiˌeri/ n person who persuades opposing sides to agree

in·ter·me·di·ate /ˌɪntər'midi-ɪt/ adj between 2 others; HALFWAY

in·ter·mi·na·ble /ɪn'tɜːmənəbəl/ adj long and dull; (seeming) endless **–bly** adv

in·ter·mis·sion /ˌɪntər'mɪʃən/ n time between the parts of a play, etc.

in·ter·mit·tent /ˌɪntər'mɪt'nt/ adj not continuous **~ly** adv

in·tern¹ /ɪn'tɜːn/ vt put in prison, esp. in time of war **~ment** n [U]

in·tern² /ˈɪntən/ n 1 person, esp. a student, who is gaining practical experience for a short time in a job 2 person who is almost finished training to be a doctor and is gaining practical experience in a hospital ~**ship** n [U] time of being an intern

in·ter·nal /ɪnˈtənl/ adj 1 inside 2 not foreign: *internal trade* ~**ly** adv

Internal Rev·e·nue Ser·vice /ˌ·,·· ˈ··· ,·ˈ·/ n [the] government department that collects taxes also **IRS**

in·ter·na·tion·al /ˌɪntəˈnæʃənəl◄/ adj between nations ~**ly** adv ~**ism** n [U] principle that nations should work together

In·ter·net /ˈɪntəˌnɛt/ n [the] system of connected computers allowing computer users around the world to exchange information

in·ter·play /ˈɪntəˌpleɪ/ n [U] INTERACTion

in·ter·pret /ɪnˈtəprɪt/ v 1 vt understand or explain the meaning of 2 vi/t turn (spoken words) into another language ~**er** n person who INTERPRETS (2) ~**ation** /ɪnˌtəprəˈteɪʃən/ n [C;U] 1 explanation (example) of a performance of music, theater, etc., by someone giving their own idea of the COMPOSER's, writer's, etc., intentions

in·ter·ro·gate /ɪnˈtɛrəˌgeɪt/ vt 1 question formally esp. for a long time and often with the use of threats or violence 2 (try to) get direct information from: *to interrogate a computer* –**gation** /ɪnˌtɛrəˈgeɪʃən/ n [C;U] –**gative** /ˌɪntəˈrɑgətɪv/ adj asking a question

in·ter·rupt /ˌɪntəˈrʌpt/ vi/t break the flow of (speech, etc.) ~**ion** /-ˈrʌpʃən/ n [C;U]

in·ter·sect /ˌɪntəˈsɛkt/ vi/t cut across: *intersecting paths* ~**ion** /-ˈsɛkʃən, ˈɪntəˌsɛkʃən/ n 1 [U] act of intersecting 2 [C] place where two or more roads meet

in·ter·sperse /ˌɪntəˈspəs/ vt put here and there among other things

in·ter·state /ˈɪntəˌsteɪt/ adj between states: *interstate crime/highway*

in·ter·val /ˈɪntəvəl/ n 1 time between events 2 distance between things

in·ter·vene /ˌɪntəˈvin/ vi 1 interrupt so as to stop something 2 (of time) happen between events –**vention** /-ˈvɛnʃən/ n [C;U]

in·ter·view /ˈɪntəˌvyu/ n meeting where a person is asked questions ♦ vt ask

(someone) questions in an interview ~**ee** /ˌɪntəˈvyuˈi/ n person who is being or is to be interviewed, esp. for a job ~**er** n person who interviews

in·tes·tine /ɪnˈtɛstɪn/ also -**tines** pl n bowels –**tinal** adj

in·ti·ma·cy /ˈɪntəməsi/ n 1 [U] state of being intimate 2 [C] remark or action of a kind that happens only between people who know each other very well 3 euph [U] the act of sex

in·ti·mate¹ /ˈɪntəmɪt/ adj 1 having a close relationship: *intimate friends* 2 private: *her intimate thoughts* 3 resulting from close study: *intimate knowledge* ~**ly** adv

in·ti·mate² /ˈɪntəˌmeɪt/ vt fml make known; suggest –**mation** /ˌɪntəˈmeɪʃən/ n [C;U]

in·tim·i·date /ɪnˈtɪməˌdeɪt/ vt frighten by threats –**dation** /ɪnˌtɪməˈdeɪʃən/ n [U]

in·to /ˈɪntə; *before vowels* ˈɪntu; *strong* ˈɪntu/ prep 1 so as to be in: *jump into the water* | *get into trouble* 2 so as to be: *translate it into French* 3 against: *bump into a tree* 4 (used when dividing): *7 into 11 won't go.*

in·tol·e·ra·ble /ɪnˈtɑlərəbəl/ adj unbearable –**bly** adv

in·tol·e·rant /ɪnˈtɑlərənt/ adj not tolerant (TOLERATE) –**rance** /-əns/ n [U]

in·to·na·tion /ˌɪntəˈneɪʃən, -tou-/ n [C;U] rise and fall of the voice in speech

in·tox·i·cat·ed /ɪnˈtɑksəˌkeɪtɪd/ adj drunk: (fig.) *intoxicated by success* –**cation** /ɪnˌtɑksəˈkeɪʃən/ n [U]

in·tra·mu·ral /ˌɪntrəˈmyorəl◄/ n happening within one school or college: *intramural sports*

in·tran·si·tive /ɪnˈtrænsətɪv, -zə-/ adj (of a verb) having a subject but no object: "*Break*" *is intransitive in the sentence* "*My cup fell and broke*" *but transitive in* "*I broke my cup.*"

in·tra·ve·nous /ˌɪntrəˈvinəs◄/ adj into a VEIN: *intravenous injection*

in·trep·id /ɪnˈtrɛpɪd/ adj fml fearless ~**ly** adv

in·tri·ca·cy /ˈɪntrɪkəsi/ n 1 [U] being intricate 2 [C] something intricate

in·tri·cate /ˈɪntrɪkɪt/ adj having many details; COMPLICATEd ~**ly** adv

in·trigue /ɪnˈtrig/ v 1 vt interest greatly 2 vi make PLOTs ♦ /ˈɪntrig, ɪnˈtrig/ n 1 [U] act or practice of secret planning 2 [C] PLOTs **intriguing** /ɪnˈtrigɪŋ/ adj very interesting, esp. because of some strange quality

in·trin·sic /ɪnˈtrɪnsɪk, -zɪk/ adj belonging naturally; INHERENT **~ally** adv

in·tro /ˈɪntroʊ/ n infml INTRODUCTION

in·tro·duce /ˌɪntrəˈdus/ vt **1** make (people) known to each other **2** bring or put in **–duction** /-ˈdʌkʃən/ n **1** [U] act of introducing **2** [C] occasion of telling people each other's names **3** [C] explanation at the beginning of a book, etc. **4** [C] simple book about a subject **–ductory** /-ˈdʌktəri/ adj happening or said at the beginning

in·tro·vert /ˈɪntrəˌvɜrt/ n quiet introspective person **~ed** adj

in·trude /ɪnˈtrud/ vi come in when not wanted **intruder** n person who intrudes, esp. intending to steal **intru·sive** /-ˈtrusɪv, -zɪv/ adj intruding **intru·sion** /-ˈtruʒən/ n [C;U]

in·tu·i·tion /ˌɪntuˈɪʃən/ n **1** [U] power of knowing something without reasoning or learned skill **2** [C] something known in this way **–tive** /ɪnˈtuətɪv/ adj **–tively** adv

in·un·date /ˈɪnənˌdeɪt/ vt flood; (fig.) inundated with letters **–dation** /ˌɪnənˈdeɪʃən/ n [C;U]

in·vade /ɪnˈveɪd/ vt **1** attack and take control of (a country) **2** crowd into **invader** n **invasion** /-ˈveɪʒən/ n [C;U]

in·val·id¹ /ɪnˈvælɪd/ adj not VALID: invalid argument/ticket **~ate** vt make invalid **~ation** /ɪnˌvæləˈdeɪʃən/ n [U]

in·va·lid² /ˈɪnvəlɪd/ n person weakened by illness

in·val·u·a·ble /ɪnˈvælyəbəl, -yuəbəl/ adj too valuable for the worth to be measured

in·vent /ɪnˈvɛnt/ vt **1** produce for the first time **2** think of (something untrue) **~ive** adj able to invent **~or** n **~ion** /-ˈvɛnʃən/ n **1** [U] act of inventing **2** [C] something invented

in·ven·to·ry /ˈɪnvənˌtɔri, -ˌtoori/ n list, esp. one of all the goods in a place ♦ v make such a list

in·verse /ɪnˈvɜrs◄, ˈɪnvɜrs/ n, adj opposite

in·vert /ɪnˈvɜrt/ vt fml turn upside down **inversion** /-ˈvɜrʒən, -ʃən/ n [C;U]

in·ver·te·brate /ɪnˈvɜrtəbrɪt, -ˌbreɪt/ n animal without a BACKBONE

in·vest /ɪnˈvɛst/ vt use (money) to make more money **~ment** n **1** [U] act of invest-

ing **2** [C] (something bought with) money invested **~or** n

invest in phr v buy

in·ves·ti·gate /ɪnˈvɛstəˌgeɪt/ vi/t inquire carefully (about): investigate a crime **–gator** n **–gative** adj **–gation** /ɪnˌvɛstəˈgeɪʃən/ n [C;U]

in·vet·e·rate /ɪnˈvɛtərɪt/ adj fixed in a bad habit: inveterate liar

in·vig·o·rat·ing /ɪnˈvɪgəˌreɪt/ adj giving health and strength: an invigorating swim

in·vin·ci·ble /ɪnˈvɪnsəbəl/ adj too strong to be defeated **–bly** adv

in·vis·i·ble /ɪnˈvɪzəbəl/ adj that cannot be seen **–bly** adv **–bility** /ɪnˌvɪzəˈbɪləti/ n [U]

in·vite /ɪnˈvaɪt/ vt **1** ask to come **2** ask politely for: invite questions **inviting** adj attractive **invitingly** adv **invitation** /ˌɪnvəˈteɪʃən/ n **1** [C] request to come: invitations to a wedding **2** [U] act of inviting: entrance by invitation only **3** [C] encouragement to an action

in·voice /ˈɪnvɔɪs/ vt, n (send) a bill for goods received

in·voke /ɪnˈvoʊk/ vt fml **1** call to (God, the law) for help **2** beg for **3** cause to appear by magic

in·vol·un·ta·ry /ɪnˈvɑlənˌtɛri/ adj done without intention: an involuntary smile **–rily** /ɪnˌvɑlənˈtɛrəli/ adv

in·volve /ɪnˈvɑlv/ vt **1** have as a necessary result **2** cause to become concerned **involved** adj **1** COMPLICATED **2** (of a person) closely concerned in relationships and activities with others, esp. in a personal or sexual way **~ment** n [C;U]

in·ward /ˈɪnwərd/ adj, adv **1** on or towards the inside **2** of the mind or spirit: inward peace **~ly** adv **inwards** adv

i·o·dine /ˈaɪəˌdaɪn, -dɪn/ n [U] chemical used to prevent infection in wounds

i·on /ˈaɪən, ˈaɪɑn/ n atom with an electrical CHARGE **~izer** /ˈaɪəˌnaɪzər/ n machine that produces negative ions, believed to make the air more healthy

i·o·ta /aɪˈoʊtə/ n [S] very small amount

IOU n "I owe you"; signed piece of paper saying one owes money

IQ n intelligence quotient; measure of INTELLIGENCE

IRA /ˈaɪɑr/ n Individual Retirement Account, a PENSION for one person using their own money

i·ras·ci·ble /ɪˈræsəbəl, aɪ-/ adj fml easily made angry

i·rate /ˌaɪˈreɪt◂/ adj angry ~**ly** adv

ir·i·des·cent /ˌɪrəˈdesənt◂/ adj changing color as light falls on it –**cence** n [U]

i·ris /ˈaɪrɪs/ n 1 tall yellow or purple flower 2 colored part of the eye

irk /ɜːk/ vt annoy ~**some** adj annoying

i·ron /ˈaɪən/ n 1 [U] common hard metal used in making steel, etc. 2 [C] heavy object for making cloth smooth 3 **have several irons in the fire** have various different interests, activities, or plans at the same time ♦ adj very firm: iron will

iron² vt make smooth with an iron

iron out phr vt remove (difficulties, etc.)

Iron Age /ˈ·· ·/ n [the] time in the history of mankind when iron was used for tools, etc.

Iron Cur·tain /ˌ· ˈ··/ n division preventing the flow of ideas between western Europe and the Communist (COMMUNISM) countries after the Second World War

i·ron·ic /aɪˈrɑnɪk/ also —**al** — adj expressing IRONY ~**ally** adv

ironing board /ˈ··· ·/ n narrow table for ironing clothes on

i·ron·y /ˈaɪrəni/ n 1 [U] intentional use of words which are opposite to one's real meaning, in order to be amusing or to show annoyance 2 [C;U] event or situation which is the opposite of what one expected

ir·ra·tion·al /ɪˈræʃənəl/ adj not reasonable ~**ly** adv

ir·rec·on·ci·la·ble /ɪˌrekənˈsaɪləbəl, ɪˈrekənˌsaɪ-/ adj impossible to bring into agreement –**bly** adv

ir·re·fu·ta·ble /ɪˈrefjətəbəl, ˌɪrɪˈfjutə-/ adj fml too strong to be disproved

ir·reg·u·lar /ɪˈregjələr/ adj 1 uneven 2 fml against the usual rules 3 gram not following the usual pattern ~**ly** adv –**ity** /ˌɪˌregjəˈlærəti/ n [C;U]

ir·rel·e·vant /ɪˈreləvənt/ adj not RELEVANT –**vance** n

ir·rep·a·ra·ble /ɪˈrepərəbəl/ adj too bad to be put right –**bly** adv

ir·re·place·a·ble /ˌɪrɪˈpleɪsəbəl/ adj too special for anything else to REPLACE it

ir·re·proa·cha·ble /ˌɪrɪˈproʊtʃəbəl/ adj fml faultless –**bly** adv

ir·re·sis·ti·ble /ˌɪrɪˈzɪstəbəl/ adj so nice, powerful, etc., that one cannot RESIST it –**bly** adv

ir·re·spec·tive /ˌɪrɪˈspektɪv/ adv **irrespective of** without regard to

ir·re·spon·si·ble /ˌɪrɪˈspɑnsəbəl/ adj not trustworthy; careless –**bly** adv –**bility** /ˌɪrɪˌspɑnsəˈbɪləti/ n [U]

ir·re·trie·va·ble /ˌɪrɪˈtrivəbəl/ adj impossible to get back or put right –**bly** adv

ir·rev·e·rent /ɪˈrevərənt/ adj not respectful, esp. of holy things ~**ly** adv –**rence** n [U]

ir·rev·o·ca·ble /ɪˈrevəkəbəl/ adj unchangeable once made or started: irrevocable decision –**bly** adv

ir·ri·gate /ˈɪrəˌgeɪt/ vt supply water to (land) –**gation** /ˌɪrəˈgeɪʃən/ n [U]

ir·ri·ta·ble /ˈɪrətəbəl/ adj easily annoyed –**bly** adv –**bility** /ˌɪrətəˈbɪləti/ n [U]

ir·ri·tate /ˈɪrəˌteɪt/ vt 1 annoy 2 make sore –**tation** /ˌɪrəˈteɪʃən/ n [C;U]

IRS n [the] INTERNAL REVENUE SERVICE

is /s, z, əz; strong ɪz/ v 3rd person sing. present tense of BE

Is·lam /ɪsˈlɑm, ˈɪslɑm, -ləm, ˈɪz-/ n (people and countries that practice) the Muslim religion ~**ic** /ɪsˈlɑmɪk, ˈlæ-, ɪz-/ adj

is·land /ˈaɪlənd/ n 1 piece of land surrounded by water 2 raised place where people can wait in the middle of a road for traffic to pass ~**er** n person living on an island

isle /aɪl/ n lit island

is·n't /ˈɪzənt/ v short for: is not

i·so·late /ˈaɪsəˌleɪt/ vt keep separate from others –**lated** adj alone; only: an isolated case –**lation** /ˌaɪsəˈleɪʃən/ n [U]

is·sue /ˈɪʃu/ n 1 [C] subject to be talked about or argued about — see also SIDE ISSUE 2 [C] printing at one time of a magazine, etc. 3 [U] law children ♦ vt produce or provide officially: issue a statement/new uniforms

it /ɪt/ pron 1 that thing already mentioned: "Where's my dinner?" "The cat ate it." 2 that person: "Who's that?" "It's me." 3 (used in statements about weather, time, or distance): It's raining. | It's Thursday. | It's not far to Paris. 4 (used when the real subject comes later): It's too bad you forgot. 5 (making part of a sentence more important): It was Jane who told me. ♦ n 1 infml a very important person: He thinks he's it. b the important point: This is it, I have to decide. 2 **That's it: a** That's complete;

there's nothing more to come. **b** That's right.

i·tal·ics /ɪˈtælɪks, aɪ-/ n [P] sloping printed letters **–icize** /-ləˌsaɪz/ vt print in italics

itch /ɪtʃ/ vi **1** have the feeling of wanting to SCRATCH the skin **2** be itching to/for want very much ♦ n **1** itching feeling **2** strong desire — see also SEVEN-YEAR ITCH **~y** adj

it'd /ˈɪtəd/ short for: **1** it would **2** it had

i·tem /ˈaɪtəm/ n **1** single thing on a list, etc. **2** piece of news **~ize** vt make a detailed list of

i·tin·e·rant /aɪˈtɪnərənt/ adj traveling from place to place

i·tin·e·ra·ry /aɪˈtɪnəˌrɛri/ n plan for a trip

it'll /ˈɪtl/ short for: it will

its /ɪts/ determiner of it: its ears

it's /ɪts/ short for: **1** it is **2** it has

it·self /ɪtˈsɛlf/ pron **1** (reflexive form of **it**): The cat washed itself. **2** (strong form of **it**): I had the copy, but the letter itself was missing. **3** (all) by itself: **a** alone **b** without help **4** in itself without considering the rest **5** to itself not shared

IV n medical apparatus used for putting liquid directly into the body

I've /aɪv, əv/ short for: I have

i·vo·ry /ˈaɪvəri/ n [U] **1** hard white substance of which the TUSKS of ELEPHANTS are made **2** creamy white color of this

i·vy /ˈaɪvi/ n [U] climbing plant with shiny leaves **ivied** adj covered with ivy

Ivy League /ˌ·· ˈ·◂/ n [S] a group of old and respected east coast universities

J

J, j /dʒeɪ/ the 10th letter of the English alphabet

jab /dʒæb/ *vi/t* **-bb-** push with force (something pointed) ♦ *n* sharp forceful push

jab·ber /ˈdʒæbə/ *vi/t* talk or say quickly **jabber** *n* [S;U]

jack¹ /dʒæk/ *n* **1** apparatus for lifting a car, etc. **2** playing card between the 10 and the queen

jack² *v*

> **jack off** *phr vt taboo sl for* MASTURBATE
> **jack up** *phr vt* lift with a JACK (1)

jack·al /ˈdʒækəl, -kɔl/ *n* kind of wild dog

jack·et /ˈdʒækɪt/ *n* **1** short coat with SLEEVES **2** cover for a machine, pipe, etc. **3** loose paper book cover

jack·ham·mer /ˈdʒækˌhæmə/ *n* power tool held in the hands, for digging up streets

jack·knife /ˈdʒæknaɪf/ *n* large pocket knife, the blade of which folds into the handle

jack·knife /ˈ· ·/ *vi* (of a vehicle) bend suddenly in the middle

jack-o'-lan·tern /ˈdʒæk ə ˌlæntən/ *n* PUMPKIN with a face cut into it, used as a decoration at HALLOWEEN

jack·pot /ˈdʒækpɑt/ *n* biggest money prize to be won in a game

Ja·cuz·zi /dʒəˈkuzi/ *n tdmk* bath fitted with a system of hot water currents

jade /dʒeɪd/ *n* [U] (color of) a green precious stone

ja·ded /ˈdʒeɪdɪd/ *adj* tired because of having had too much of something, esp. experience

jag·ged /ˈdʒægɪd/ *adj* with a rough uneven edge

jag·uar /ˈdʒægwɑr, ˈdʒægyuˌɑr/ *n* large spotted wild cat of S. America

jail /dʒeɪl/ *n* [C;U] prison ♦ *vt* put in jail **~er** *n* person in charge of prisoners

jam¹ /dʒæm/ *n* [U] fruit boiled in sugar, for spreading on bread

jam² *v* **-mm-** **1** *vt* crush or press tightly: *jam clothes into a bag* | *jam the brakes on* **2** *vi* get stuck: *The door jammed.* **3** *vt* block (radio messages) ♦ *n* **1** closely jammed mass: *traffic jam* **2 in a jam** in a difficult situation

jam·bo·ree /ˌdʒæmbəˈri/ *n* large party or gathering

jam-packed /ˌ· ˈ· ◂/ *adj* with many people or things very close together

jan·gle /ˈdʒæŋgəl/ *vi/t* (cause to) make the noise of metal striking metal

jan·i·tor /ˈdʒænətə/ *n* person who cleans a building

Jan·u·a·ry /ˈdʒænyuˌeri/ *n* the 1st month of the year

jar¹ /dʒɑr/ *n* short wide bottle

jar² *vi/t* **-rr-** **1** *vi* make a nasty sound **2** *vt* give a nasty shock to **3** *vi* go badly together: *jarring colors*

jar·gon /ˈdʒɑrgən/ *n* [U] language used by a particular group: *computer jargon*

jaun·dice /ˈdʒɔndɪs, ˈdʒɑn-/ *n* [U] disease that makes the skin yellow **jaundiced** *adj* mistrustful and CYNICAL: *jaundiced opinions*

jaunt /dʒɔnt, dʒɑnt/ *n* short pleasure trip **~y** *adj* cheerful and confident

jav·e·lin /ˈdʒævəlɪn/ *n* light spear for throwing

jaw /dʒɔ/ *n* one of the 2 bony structures where the teeth are fixed ♦ *vi/t infml* talk (to) for a long time

jaws /dʒɔz/ *n* [P] **1** animal's mouth **2** two parts of a tool, etc., that hold things tightly: (fig.) *the jaws of death*

jay·walk /ˈdʒeɪwɔk/ *vi* cross streets carelessly

jazz¹ /dʒæz/ *n* [U] music with a strong beat, originated by black Americans **~y** *adj* brightly coloured

jazz² *v* **jazz up** *phr vt* make brighter or more interesting

jeal·ous /ˈdʒɛləs/ *adj* **1** unhappy at not being liked as much as someone else: *jealous husband* **2** very ENVIOUS **3** wanting to keep what one has **~ly** *adv*

jeal·ous·y /ˈdʒɛləsi/ *n* [C;U] jealous feeling

jeans /dʒinz/ *n* [P] strong cotton pants

Jeep /dʒip/ *n tdmk* (military) car for traveling on rough ground

jeer /dʒɪr/ *vi/t* laugh rudely (at) **jeer** *n* **~ingly** *adv*

Jell-O /ˈdʒɛloʊ/ *n* [U] *tdmk* soft sweet food made with GELATIN

jel·ly /ˈdʒɛli/ *n* **1** [C;U] fruit juice boiled with sugar to spread on bread **2** [S;U] any material between a liquid and a solid state

jeop·ar·dize /ˈdʒɛpəˌdaɪz/ *vt fml* put in danger

jeop·ar·dy /ˈdʒɛpədi/ *n* [U] *fml* danger: *put one's future in jeopardy*

jerk[1] /dʒɜːk/ *n* sudden quick pull or movement ♦ *vi/t* pull or move with a jerk **~y** *adj* not smooth in movement

jerk[2] *n sl* person who is stupid and has bad manners

jer·sey /ˈdʒɜːzi/ *n* 1 [U] smooth material used in clothing 2 [C] shirt worn in sports

jest /dʒɛst/ *vi fml* joke **jest** *n* [C;U] **~er** *n* man kept in past times to amuse a ruler

jet[1] /dʒɛt/ *n* 1 narrow stream of gas or liquid forced out of a hole 2 hole from which this comes 3 aircraft whose engine (**jet engine**) works on this principle ♦ *vi* 1 come in a JET (1) 2 travel by JET[2]

jet[2] *n* [U] hard shiny black mineral: (fig.) **jet-black** /ˈ· ·/ *hair*

jet lag /ˈ· ·/ *n* [U] tiredness after flying to a place where the time is different

jet set /ˈ· ·/ *n* [S] international social group of rich fashionable people

jet·ti·son /ˈdʒɛtɪsən, -zən/ *vt* throw away

Jew /dʒuː/ *n* person descended from the people of ancient Israel whose history is told in the Bible **~ish** *adj*

jew·el /ˈdʒuəl/ *n* 1 (real or artificial) precious stone 2 very valuable person or thing **~er** *n* person who sells jewels **~ry** [U] jewels worn as decoration

jif·fy /ˈdʒɪfi/ *n* [S] moment: *I'll come in a jiffy.*

jig /dʒɪg/ *n* (music for) a quick merry dance ♦ *vi* jump up and down

jig·gle /ˈdʒɪgəl/ *vi/t* shake from side to side

jig·saw /ˈdʒɪgsɔː/ also **jigsaw puz·zle** /ˈ·· ·/ — *n* picture cut into pieces to be put together for fun

jilt /dʒɪlt/ *vt* unexpectedly refuse (an accepted lover)

jin·gle /ˈdʒɪŋgəl/ *n* 1 sound as of small bells ringing 2 simple poem used esp. for advertisement ♦ *vi/t* (cause to) sound with a jingle

jinx /dʒɪŋks/ *n* something that brings bad luck

jit·ters /ˈdʒɪtəz/ *n* [P] anxiety before an event **–tery** *adj*

jive /dʒaɪv/ *n* [U] 1 informal speech of black Americans 2 (dance performed to) a kind of popular music with a strong beat ♦ *vi* dance to jive music

job /dʒɒb/ *n* 1 [C] regular paid employment: *out of a job* (= unemployed) 2 [C] piece of work 3 [C] *sl* crime, esp. a robbery 4 [S] something hard to do: *You'll have a job getting it open.* 5 [S] one's affair; duty: *It's not my job to interfere.* 6 [C] *infml* example of a certain type: *His new car is quite a job.* 7 [C] *infml* a PLASTIC SURGERY operation: *a nose job* 8 **make the best of a bad job** do as much or as well as possible in unfavorable conditions 9 **on the job** while working; at work **~ber** *n* person who sells WHOLESALE **~less** *adj* unemployed

jock /dʒɒk/ *n infml* ATHLETE

jock·ey /ˈdʒɒki/ *n* professional rider in horse races ♦ *vi/t* try by all possible means to get into a good position: *jockey for position*

jock·strap /ˈdʒɒkstræp/ *n* supporter for male sex organs worn esp. while playing sports

joc·u·lar /ˈdʒɒkjələ/ *adj fml* joking; not serious **~ly** *adv*

jog /dʒɒg/ *v* **-gg-** 1 *vt* knock slightly 2 *vi* run slowly for exercise 3 **jog someone's memory** make someone remember ♦ *n* **~ger** *n* someone who JOGS (2)

jog along *phr vi* move slowly and uneventfully

join /dʒɔɪn/ *v* 1 *vt* fasten; connect: *join 2 ropes* 2 *vi/t* come together (with); meet: *join me for a drink* | *The stream joins the river.* 3 *vt* become a member of: *join the army* ♦ *n* place where 2 things are joined

join in *phr vi* take part in an activity

join up *phr vi* offer oneself for military service

joint[1] /dʒɔɪnt/ *n* 1 place where things (esp. bones) join 2 *sl* public place for drinking, etc. 3 *sl* cigarette containing MARIJUANA

joint[2] *adj* shared: *joint bank account* **~ly** *adv*

joint ven·ture /ˌ· ˈ·/ *n* business arrangement in which 2 or more companies work together

joist /dʒɔɪst/ *n* beam supporting a floor

joke /dʒəʊk/ *n* 1 something said or done to amuse people 2 **play a joke on someone** do something to make other people laugh at someone ♦ *vi* tell jokes

joker *n* 1 person who makes jokes 2

additional playing card with no fixed value

jol·ly /ˈdʒɑli/ *adj* happy; pleasant

jolt /dʒoʊlt/ *vi/t* shake or shock **jolt** *n*

jos·tle /ˈdʒɑsəl/ *vi/t* knock or push (against)

jot /dʒɑt/ *n* [S] very small bit: *not a jot of truth* ♦ *vt* **-tt-** write quickly **~ter** *n* notebook **~ting** *n* rough note

jour·nal /ˈdʒɜnl/ *n* **1** magazine **2** DIARY **~ism** *n* profession of writing for newspapers **~ist** *n* person whose profession is journalism

jour·ney /ˈdʒɜni/ *n* long trip, esp. by land ♦ *vi lit* travel

jo·vi·al /ˈdʒoʊviəl/ *adj* friendly and cheerful **~ly** *adv*

jowls /dʒaʊlz/ *n* lower part of the face, hanging down

joy /dʒɔɪ/ *n* **1** [U] great happiness **2** [C] something that causes joy **~ful** *adj fml* full of or causing joy **~fully** *adv* **~ous** *adj lit* joyful

joy·ride /ˈdʒɔɪraɪd/ *n* ride for pleasure in a (stolen) car

Jr. *written abbrev. for:* JUNIOR

ju·bi·lant /ˈdʒubələnt/ *adj fml* joyful; delighted **–lation** /ˌdʒubəˈleɪʃən/ *n* [U] rejoicing

Ju·da·ism /ˈdʒudiˌɪzəm, -deɪ-, -də-/ *n* [U] religion and civilization of the Jews

judge /dʒʌdʒ/ *n* **1** public official who decides legal cases **2** person who decides in a competition, etc. **3** person who can give a valuable opinion: *I'm no judge of music.* ♦ *vi/t* act as a judge (in); form an opinion (about)

judg·ment /ˈdʒʌdʒmənt/ *n* **1** [U] ability to decide correctly: *a man of sound judgment* **2** [C] opinion **3** [C;U] decision of a judge or court of law: *She passed* (= gave) *judgment on the accused man.*

ju·di·cial /dʒuˈdɪʃəl/ *adj* of law courts and judges **~ly** *adv*

ju·di·cia·ry /dʒuˈdɪʃiˌɛri, -ʃəri/ *n* **1** all the judges, as a group **2** branch of government that includes the courts

ju·di·cious /dʒuˈdɪʃəs/ *adj fml* sensible **~ly** *adv*

ju·do /ˈdʒudoʊ/ *n* [U] type of unarmed fighting for defense, from Asia

jug /dʒʌg/ *n esp.* container for liquids, with a handle and a lip for pouring

jug·gle /ˈdʒʌgəl/ *vi/t* **1** keep (objects) in the air by throwing and catching them **2** play tricks (with), esp. to deceive: *juggling the figures* **juggler** *n*

juice /dʒus/ *n* [C;U] liquid from fruit, vegetables, or meat **juicy** *adj* **1** having a lot of juice **2** *infml* interesting esp. because providing details about improper behavior

juke·box /ˈdʒukbɑks/ *n* music machine operated by coins

Ju·ly /dʒʊˈlaɪ, dʒə-/ *n* the 7th month of the year

jum·ble /ˈdʒʌmbəl/ *vi/t* mix in disorder ♦ *n* [S] disorderly mixture

jum·bo /ˈdʒʌmboʊ/ *adj* very large: *jumbo jet*

jump[1] /dʒʌmp/ *v* **1** *vi* push oneself off the ground with one's leg muscles **2** *vt* cross in this way: *jump a stream* **3** *vi* move suddenly: *The noise made me jump.* **4** *vi* rise sharply: *Oil prices have jumped.* **5** *vt* attack suddenly **6** *vt* leave, pass, or escape from (something) illegally **7** **jump down someone's throat** *infml* attack someone in words, strongly and unexpectedly **8** **jump the gun** start something too soon **9** **jump all over someone** express disapproval firmly

jump at *phr vt* accept eagerly: *She jumped at the chance to go.*

jump[2] *n* **1** act of jumping **2** thing to jump over **3** **be/stay one jump ahead** do the right thing because one knows or guesses what one's competitors are going to do **~y** *adj* nervously excited

jump·er /ˈdʒʌmpə/ *n* **1** dress with no SLEEVES **2** horse or person that jumps

jump-start /ˈ. ./ *vt* **1** help a process or activity work better or more quickly **2** start a car by connecting it to the BATTERY of a car that works

jump·suit /ˈdʒʌmpsut/ *n* a garment combining top and pants in one piece

junc·tion /ˈdʒʌŋkʃən/ *n* place of joining: *railroad junction*

junc·ture /ˈdʒʌŋktʃə/ *n fml* point in time

June /dʒun/ *n* the 6th month of the year

jun·gle /ˈdʒʌŋgəl/ *n* [C;U] thick tropical forest

ju·nior /ˈdʒunyə/ *n, adj* **1** (someone) younger **2** (someone) of low or lower rank **3** third year student in a college or high school

Junior *adj* the younger (of two men in the same family with the same name)

junior college /ˌ. ˈ.ˌ./ *n* two-year college

junk /dʒʌŋk/ n [U] **1** old useless things **2** sl dangerous drug, esp. HEROIN ♦ vt infml get rid of as worthless

junk food /ˈ· ·/ n [U] infml unhealthy food

junk·ie /ˈdʒʌŋki/ n sl person who takes HEROIN: (fig.) I'm a real sugar junkie.

junk mail /ˈ· ·/ n [U] mail, usu. for advertising, sent to people although they have not asked for it

jun·ta /ˈhʊntə, ˈdʒʌntə/ n (military) government that has seized power by armed force

Ju·pi·ter /ˈdʒupətər/ n the largest PLANET, 5th in order from the sun

jur·is·dic·tion /ˌdʒʊrəsˈdɪkʃən/ n [U] legal power

ju·ror /ˈdʒʊrə/ n member of a jury

ju·ry /ˈdʒʊri/ n **1** group of people chosen to decide questions of fact in a court of law **2** group of people chosen to judge a competition of any kind

just[1] /dʒəst/ adv **1** exactly: That's just right. **2** completely: It's just perfect! **3** at this moment: I'm just coming. **4** only a short time (ago): just after breakfast | I just finished it. **5** almost not: She arrived just in time. **6** only: no dinner, just coffee **7** just about very nearly **8** just as well: **a** a lucky or suitable: It's just as well I brought my coat—it's freezing! **b** with good reason, considering the situation: Since there's no more work to do, we might just as well go home. **9** just now: **a** at this moment: We're having dinner just now—come back later. **b** a moment ago: Paul telephoned just now to say he'll be late. **10** just yet quite yet

just[2] /dʒʌst/ adj fair; according to what is deserved ~**ly** adv

jus·tice /ˈdʒʌstɪs/ n **1** [U] quality of being just; fairness **2** [U] the law: court of justice **3** [C] JUDGE (1) esp. of the SUPREME COURT **4** do justice to someone also do someone justice — treat someone in a fair way

Justice of the Peace /ˌ·· · · ·/ n official who judges cases in the lowest law courts

jus·ti·fy /ˈdʒʌstəˌfaɪ/ vt give or be a good reason for –**fiable** /ˈdʒʌstəˌfaɪəbəl, ˌdʒʌstəˈfaɪ-/ adj –**fiably** adv –**fication** /ˌdʒʌstəfəˈkeɪʃən/ n [U] good reason

jut /dʒʌt/ vi -tt- stick out or up further than the things around it

ju·ve·nile /ˈdʒuvəˌnaɪl, -nl/ n **1** young person **2** actor or actress who plays such a person ♦ adj **1** of or for juveniles **2** childish or foolish

juvenile de·lin·quen·cy /ˌ··· ·ˈ···/ n [U] crimes by JUVENILES (1) –**quent** n

jux·ta·pose /ˈdʒʌkstəˌpoʊz, ˌdʒʌkstəˈpoʊz/ vt fml put side by side –**position** /ˌdʒʌkstəpəˈzɪʃən/ n [U]

K

K, k /keɪ/ the 11th letter of the English alphabet

K *written abbrev. for*: **1** 1024 BYTES of computer DATA **2** *infml* one thousand: a *$30K salary* **3** KARAT: *14K gold*

ka·bob /kəˈbab/ *n* small pieces of meat cooked on a stick

ka·lei·do·scope /kəˈlaɪdəˌskoʊp/ *n* tube containing mirrors, and often bits of colored glass, turned to produce changing patterns **–scopic** /kəˌlaɪdəˈskapɪk/ *adj* changing quickly and often

kan·ga·roo /ˌkæŋgəˈru/ *n* Australian animal that jumps along on its large back legs, and carries its baby in a pocket

kar·at /ˈkærət/ *n* unit for measuring how pure gold is

ka·ra·te /kəˈrati/ *n* [U] Asian style of fighting using the hands and feet

kay·ak /ˈkaɪæk/ *n* light covered CANOE

ka·zoo /kəˈzu/ *n* simple musical instrument that uses the voice

keel¹ /kil/ *n* **1** bar along the bottom of a boat **2 on an even keel** steady

keel² *v* **keel over** *phr vi* fall over sideways

keen /kin/ *adj* **1** (of the 5 senses) good, strong, quick, etc.: *keen eyesight* **2** (of edges) sharp; cutting: (fig.) *keen wind* **~ly** *adv* **~ness** *n* [U]

keep¹ /kip/ *v* **kept** /kɛpt/ **1** *vt* continue to have; not lose or give back **2** *vi/t* (cause to) continue being: *keep them warm* | *Keep off the grass!* **3** *vi* continually do something: *He keeps complaining.* **4** *vt* fulfill (a promise) **5** *vt* prevent: *keep them from knowing* **6** *vt* not tell (a secret) **7** *vt* make records of or in: *keep accounts/a diary* **8** *vt* support with money, etc. **9** *vt* own or manage: *keep chickens/a store* **10** *vi* remain fresh: *This fish won't keep.* **11** *vt* take suitable notice of (a holiday, etc): *keep Christmas* **12 keep (oneself) to oneself** not mix with or talk to other people very much **13 keep one's head** remain calm **14 keep one's shirt on** *infml* to remain calm; not to become

upset or angry **15 keep someone company** remain with someone

keep at *phr vt* continue working at (something)

keep back *phr vt* not tell or give; WITHHOLD

keep down *phr vt* **1** prevent from increasing **2** OPPRESS

keep from *phr vt* **1** not to tell (someone) about something **2** prevent oneself from (doing something)

keep on *phr v* **1** *vi* continue talking **2** *vt* continue to employ (someone) **3** *vi* continue to have (something)

keep out *phr vi/t* (cause to) stay away or not enter

keep to *phr vt* **1** stay in: *keep to the left* **2** limit oneself to: *keep to the point* **3** keep (something) private to (oneself): *Keep this to yourself.*

keep up *phr v* **1** *vi* stay level **2** *vt* continue doing: *Keep up the good work!* **3** *vt* prevent from going to bed **4** *vt* prevent from falling or dropping: *a belt to keep my pants up* | (fig.) *Keep your spirits up!* (= remain cheerful)

keep² *n* **1** [U] (cost of) necessary food, etc: *earn one's keep* **2** [C] central tower of a castle **3 for keeps** *infml* forever

keep·ing /ˈkipɪŋ/ *n* [U] **1** care; charge: *leave my jewels in my keeping* **2 in/out of keeping with** suitable/not suitable for

keep·sake /ˈkipseɪk/ *n* thing kept to remind one of the giver

keg /kɛg/ *n* small barrel

ken·nel /ˈkɛnl/ *n* place where dogs are bred (BREED (2)) or kept for a while

kept /kɛpt/ *v past t. and p. of* KEEP¹

ker·nel /ˈkɜrnl/ *n* **1** center of a nut, seed, etc. **2** important part of a subject

kerosene /ˈkɛrəˌsin, ˌkɛrəˈsin/ *n* sort of oil burned for lighting and heating

ketch·up /ˈkɛtʃəp, ˈkæ-/ *also* **catsup** — *n* [U] thick liquid made from TOMATO juice

ket·tle /ˈkɛtl/ *n* pot with a SPOUT, for boiling water

key¹ /ki/ *n* **1** shaped piece of metal for locking a door, etc.: *car keys* **2** something that explains or helps one to understand **3** any of the parts of a piano, etc., to be pressed to produce the desired sound or effect: *typewriter keys* **4** musical notes starting at a particular base note: *the key of C* ♦ *adj* very important; necessary:

key industries | *a key position in the company*

key² /ˈkiːbərd/ *vt* **1** make suitable: *factories keyed to military needs* **2** keyboard (information) **3** keyed up excited and nervous

key·board /ˈkiːbərd, -boʊrd/ *n* row of KEYs (3) ♦ *vt* put (information) into a machine by working a keyboard

key·hole /ˈkiːhoʊl/ *n* hole for a KEY (1)

key·note /ˈkiːnoʊt/ *n* central idea (of a speech, etc.)

kg *written abbrev. for:* KILOGRAM(s)

kha·ki /ˈkæki, ˈkɑ-/ *n* [U] **1** yellow-brown color **2** cloth of this color, esp. as worn by soldiers **khakis** [P] pants made of light brown cloth

kib·butz /kɪˈbʊts/ *n* -**zim** /ˌkɪbʊtˈsim/ *or* -**zes** farm or other place in Israel where many families live and work together

kick¹ /kɪk/ *v* **1** *vt* hit with the foot **2** *vi* move the feet as if to kick **3** *vi* (of a gun) move violently when fired **4** *vt sl* stop or give up (a harmful activity) **5** **kick someone in the teeth** *infml* discourage or disappoint someone very much **6** **kick the bucket** *sl* die

kick around *phr v* **1** *vi/t* (of ideas) discuss **2** *vi* lie unnoticed in (a place) **3** *vt* beat roughly

kick in *phr v* **1** contribute one's share of money **2** take effect

kick off *phr vi* begin

kick out *phr vt* remove or dismiss (someone), esp. violently

kick up *phr vt* make (trouble): *kick up a fuss*

kick² *n* **1** [C] act of kicking **2** [C] *sl* excitement: *drive fast for kicks* **3** [S;U] *infml* strength **4** [C] extremely strong new interest: *She's on a health food kick.*

kick·back /ˈkɪkbæk/ *n* BRIBE paid to government officials in exchange for a contract

kick·off /ˈkɪk-ɔf/ *n* first kick in football

kid¹ /kɪd/ *n* **1** [C] child or young person **2** [C;U] (leather from) a young goat

kid² *vi/t* -**dd**- *sl* pretend; deceive

kid gloves /ˌ· ˈ·/ *n* [P] gentle methods of dealing with people

kid·nap /ˈkɪdnæp/ *vt* -**pp**- take (someone) away by force, so as to demand money, etc. ~**per** *n*

kid·ney /ˈkɪdni/ *n* organ that separates waste liquid from the blood

kill /kɪl/ *vt* **1** cause to die: (fig.) *My feet are killing me.* (= hurting very much) | (fig.) *The boss will kill me* (= be very angry) *when she finds out.* **2** destroy; spoil **3** **kill time** make time pass quickly **4** **kill two birds with one stone** get two good results from one action ♦ *n* [S] **1** bird or animal killed **2** act or moment of killing ~**er** *n* ~**ing** *n* **1** murder **2** **make a killing** make a lot of money suddenly

kiln /kɪln/ *n* oven for baking pots, bricks, etc.

kil·o·byte /ˈkɪləˌbaɪt/ *n* 1024 BYTEs of computer information

kil·o·gram /ˈkɪləˌgræm/ *n* (a measure of weight equal to) 2.2 pounds

kil·o·me·ter /kɪˈlɑmətər, ˈkɪləˌmitər/ *n* (a measure of length equal to) 0.62 of a mile

kil·o·watt /ˈkɪləˌwɑt/ *n* 1000 WATTs

kilt /kɪlt/ *n* short skirt worn esp. by Scotsmen

ki·mo·no /kəˈmoʊnoʊ/ *n* -**nos** **1** long loose Japanese garment **2** loose DRESSING GOWN

kin /kɪn/ *n* [P] **next of kin** one's closest relative(s) — see also KITH AND KIN

kind¹ /kaɪnd/ *n* **1** type; sort: *all kinds of people* **2** **a kind of** unclear or unusual sort of: *I had a kind of feeling she'd phone.* **3** **in kind** (of payment) in goods, not money **4** **kind of** *infml* in a certain way; rather **5** **of a kind: a** of the same kind: *They're two of a kind.* **b** of a not very good kind: *It was coffee of a kind, but we couldn't drink it.*

kind² *adj* helpful and friendly ~**ness** *n* **1** [U] quality of being kind **2** [C] kind act

kin·der·gar·ten /ˈkɪndərˌgɑrtⁿn, -ˌgɑrdn/ *n* school for young children, usu. five-year olds

kind-heart·ed /ˌ· ˈ·◄/ *adj* having a kind nature ~**ly** *adv* ~**ness** *n* [U]

kin·dle /ˈkɪndl/ *vt/i* (cause to) start burning -**dling** *n* [U] materials for starting a fire

kind·ly /ˈkaɪndli/ *adv* **1** in a kind way **2** (showing annoyance) please **3** **take kindly to** accept willingly ♦ *adj fml* kind

kin·dred /ˈkɪndrɪd/ *adj* **1** related **2** **kindred spirit** person with almost the same habits, interests, etc.

king /kɪŋ/ *n* **1** (title of) the male ruler of a country **2** most important man or animal **3** playing card with a picture of a king

king·dom /ˈkɪŋdəm/ n **1** country governed by a king or queen **2** any of the three divisions of natural objects: *the animal/plant/mineral kingdom*

king·pin /ˈkɪŋˌpɪn/ n most important person in a group

king-size /ˈ· ·/ adj larger than the standard size

kink /kɪŋk/ n **1** twist in hair, a pipe, etc. **2** strangeness of character ~**y** adj sexually unnatural

kiss /kɪs/ vi/t touch with the lips as a sign of love or a greeting **kiss** n act of kissing

kit /kɪt/ n **1** necessary clothes, tools, etc.: *a sailor's/carpenter's kit* **2** set of pieces to be put together: *model airplane kit*

kitch·en /ˈkɪtʃən/ n room for cooking in

kitch·en·ette /ˌkɪtʃəˈnɛt/ n very small kitchen

kite /kaɪt/ n frame covered with paper or cloth, for flying in the air

kitsch /kɪtʃ/ n objects, works of literature which pretend to be art but are considered silly, funny, or worthless

kit·ten /ˈkɪtn/ n young cat

kit·ty /ˈkɪti/ n **1** money collected by several people for an agreed purpose **2** *infml* cat

kitty-cor·ner /ˈ· ˌ·-/ adv across a street diagonally (DIAGONAL)

ki·wi /ˈkiwi/ n **1** flightless New Zealand bird **2** *infml* New Zealander

KKK — see KU KLUX KLAN

Kleen·ex /ˈklinɛks/ n [C;U] *tdmk* paper handkerchief

klep·to·ma·ni·a /ˌklɛptəˈmeɪniə/ n [U] disease of the mind that makes one steal ~**ac** /-niˌæk/ n person with kleptomania

klutz /klʌts/ n CLUMSY, stupid person

km *written abbrev. for:* KILOMETER(s)

knack /næk/ n *infml* special skill

knap·sack /ˈnæpsæk/ n bag carried on the back containing clothes, etc.

knead /nid/ vt mix (flour and water, etc.) by pressing with the hands **2** press and rub (muscles) to cure pain, stiffness, etc.

knee /ni/ n **1** middle joint of the leg **2** part of a pair of pants, etc., that covers the knee **3** bring someone to his knees defeat someone completely ♦ vt hit with the knee

knee-cap /ˈnikæp/ n bone at the front of the knee

knee-deep /ˌ· ˈ·◄/ adj deep enough to reach the knees: (fig.) *knee-deep in debt* (= in trouble over debt)

knee-jerk /ˈ· ·/ adj *derog* (of opinion) held without thought

kneel /nil/ vi **knelt** /nɛlt/ *or* **kneeled** go down on one's knees

knew /nu/ v *past t. of* KNOW[1]

knick·ers /ˈnɪkəz/ n [P] short pants fitting tightly below the knees

knick-knack /ˈnɪknæk/ n small decorative object

knife /naɪf/ n **knives** /naɪvz/ blade with a handle, for cutting ♦ vt wound with a knife

knight /naɪt/ n **1** (in former times) noble soldier **2** piece in CHESS ~**hood** n [C;U] rank of a knight ♦ vt make (someone) a KNIGHT (2)

knit /nɪt/ vi/t **knitted** *or* **knit 1** make (clothes, etc.) by forming a network of threads with long needles (**knitting needles**) **2** join closely; grow together ~**ting** n something being knitted

knives /naɪvz/ n *pl. of* KNIFE

knob /nɑb/ n round handle or control button

knock[1] /nɑk/ v **1** vt/t hit: *knock on the door* **2** vt *sl* say bad things about **3** (of a car engine) make a noise like hitting **4** **knock someone's block off** *infml* hit someone very severely **5** **knock on wood** knock on something wooden to keep away bad luck

knock around phr v **1** vi/t be present or active (in) **2** vt treat roughly **3** *infml* travel continuously

knock back phr vt **1** drink quickly **2** shock

knock down phr vt **1** destroy (a building) with blows **2** strike to the ground: *knocked down by a bus* **3** reduce (a price)

knock off phr v **1** vi/t stop (work) **2** vt take from a total payment: *knock $2 off the price* **3** vt *sl* rob **4** vt finish quickly **5** vt *sl* murder

knock out phr vt **1** make unconscious by hitting **2** (of a drug) make (someone) go to sleep **3** cause someone to be dismissed from a competition **4** *sl* fill with great admiration

knock up phr vt *sl* make PREGNANT

knock[2] n **1** sound of knocking **2** *infml* piece of bad luck

knock·er /ˈnɑkə/ n instrument fixed to a door, for knocking

knock-kneed /ˌ˖ ˈ˖/ adj with knees that touch when walking

knock·out /ˈnɑk-aʊt/ n 1 also KO — act of knocking a BOXer unconscious 2 person or thing causing admiration ♦ adj infml causing great admiration

knoll /noʊl/ n small round hill

knot /nɑt/ n 1 fastening made by tying rope, etc. 2 hard lump in wood, etc. 3 small group of people 4 a measure of the speed of a ship, about 1853 meters per hour 4 get tied (up) into knots (over) become confused (about) ♦ vt -tt- make a knot in; join with a knot ~ty adj 1 (of wood) with KNOTS (2) 2 difficult: knotty problem

know[1] /noʊ/ v knew /nu/, known /noʊn/ 1 vi/t have (information) in the mind 2 vt have learned 3 vt be familiar with: Do you know Paris well? 4 vt be able to recognize: You'll know him by his red hair. 5 [only in past and perfect tenses] see, hear, etc.: I've known him to run 10 miles before breakfast. — see also let someone know (LET)

    know backwards phr vt know or understand perfectly

    know of phr vt have heard of or about: I know of him, but I've never met him.

know[2] n in the know having knowledge or information (about a certain thing)

know-how /ˈ˖ ˌ˖/ n [U] practical ability

know·ing /ˈnoʊɪŋ/ adj having secret understanding ~ly adv 1 in a knowing way 2 intentionally

know-it-all /ˈ˖ ˖ ˌ˖/ n person who behaves as if he/she knew everything

knowl·edge /ˈnɑlɪdʒ/ n [S;U] 1 understanding 2 learning 3 information about something 4 to the best of one's

knowledge so far as one knows — see also WORKING KNOWLEDGE

knowl·edge·a·ble /ˈnɑlɪdʒəbəl/ adj having a lot of knowledge or information

known[1] /noʊn/ past p. of KNOW[1]

known[2] adj 1 publicly recognized: known criminals 2 known as: a generally recognized as b also publicly called

knuck·le[1] /ˈnʌkəl/ n finger joint

knuckle[2] v

    knuckle down phr vi start working hard

    knuckle under phr vi be forced to accept the orders of someone more powerful

KO n infml for KNOCKOUT (1)

ko·a·la /koʊˈɑlə/ n type of small Australian animal like a bear

kook /kuk/ n sl 1 unusual person 2 crazy person

kook·y /ˈkuki/ adj infml behaving in a silly unusual manner

Ko·ran /kɔˈræn, -ˈrɑn, koʊ-, kə-/ n [the] the holy book of the Muslims

ko·sher /ˈkoʊʃə/ adj 1 (of food) prepared according to Jewish law 2 infml honest and trustworthy

kow·tow /ˌkaʊˈtaʊ, ˈkaʊtaʊ/ vi obey without question

Krem·lin /ˈkremlɪn/ n (buildings containing) the government of the former Soviet Union

ku·dos /ˈkudɑs, -doʊs/ n [U] public admiration and glory (for something done)

Ku Klux Klan /ˌku klʌks ˈklæn/ also **KKK** — n [U] secret organization in the American south that hates black people

kung fu /ˌkʌŋ ˈfu, ˌkʊŋ-/ n [U] Chinese style of fighting, like KARATE

kw written abbrev. for: KILOWATT(s)

L

L, l /ɛl/ the 12th letter of the English alphabet

l *written abbrev. for:* **1** (*often cap.*) lake **2** line **3** liter(s)

lab /læb/ *n* laboratory

la·bel /ˈleɪbəl/ *n* piece of paper, etc., fixed to something to say what it is, who owns it, etc. ♦ *vt* -**l**- **1** fix a label on **2** describe as: *They labeled him a thief.*

la·bor·a·to·ry /ˈlæbrəˌtɔri, -ˌtoʊri/ *n* building or room where a scientist works

la·bo·ri·ous /ləˈbɔriəs, -ˈboʊr-/ *adj* needing great effort ~**ly** *adv*

la·bor¹ /ˈleɪbər/ *n* **1** [U] hard work **2** [U] workers as a group **3** [S;U] act of giving birth ♦ *adj* of the workers

  labor under *phr vt* suffer from: *labor under a delusion*

labor² *v* **1** *vi* work hard **2** *vt* work something out in too great detail: *labor the point*

Labor Day /ˈ·· ˌ·/ *n* holiday on the first Monday in September celebrating labor

labor u·nion /ˈ·· ˌ·-/ *n* workers' organization to represent their interests and deal with employers

lab·y·rinth /ˈlæbəˌrɪnθ/ *n* MAZE

lace /leɪs/ *n* **1** [U] netlike decorative cloth **2** [C] cord for fastening shoes, etc. ♦ *vt* **1** fasten with a lace **2** make (a drink) stronger by adding alcohol **lacy** *adj* like LACE (1)

la·ce·rate /ˈlæsəˌreɪt/ *vt fml* cut; wound ~**ration** /ˌlæsəˈreɪʃən/ *n* [C;U]

lack /læk/ *vt* be without (enough of) ♦ *n* [S;U] absence; need ~**ing** *adj* **1** missing **2** **be lacking in** without the usual or needed amount of

lack·lus·ter /ˈlækˌlʌstər/ *adj* lifeless; dull

la·con·ic /ləˈkɑnɪk/ *adj fml* using few words ~**ally** *adv*

lac·quer /ˈlækər/ *n* [U] transparent substance that makes a hard shiny surface, or keeps hair in place ♦ *vt* cover with lacquer

la·crosse /ləˈkrɔs/ *n* [U] field game for 2 teams, using sticks with nets at the end

lad /læd/ *n lit* boy; youth

lad·der /ˈlædər/ *n* bars joined to each other by steps, for climbing: (fig.) *the promotion ladder*

la·den /ˈleɪdn/ *adj* heavily loaded: (fig.) *laden with sorrow*

la·dle /ˈleɪdl/ *n* large spoon for serving liquids ♦ *vt* serve with a ladle

  ladle out *phr vt* give out freely

ladies' room /ˈ·· ˌ·/ *n* room in a public building with toilets for women

la·dy /ˈleɪdi/ *n* **1** woman **2** woman of good manners or high social rank **3** (*cap.*) (title for) a woman of noble rank ~**like** *adj* (of a woman) behaving like a LADY (2)

la·dy·bug /ˈleɪdiˌbʌg/ *n* small round redorange insect with black spots

lag /læg/ *vi* -**gg**- move too slowly: *lag behind the others*

la·goon /ləˈgun/ *n* lake of sea water, (partly) separated from the sea

laid /leɪd/ *v past t. and p. of* LAY²

laid-back /ˌ· ˈ·◂/ *adj infml* cheerfully informal and unworried

lain /leɪn/ *v past p. of* LIE²

lair /lɛr/ *n* home of a wild animal

lake /leɪk/ *n* large mass of water surrounded by land

lamb /læm/ *n* **1** [C] young sheep **2** [U] its meat **3** [C] harmless gentle person ♦ *vi* give birth to lambs

lam·bast /læmˈbeɪst, ˈlæmbeɪst/ *vt infml* beat or attack fiercely (in words)

lame /leɪm/ *adj* **1** unable to walk properly **2** (of excuses, etc.) weak ♦ *vt* make lame ~**ly** *adv* ~**ness** *n* [U]

lame duck /ˌ· ˈ·/ *n* political official whose period in office will soon end

la·ment /ləˈmɛnt/ *vi/t* **1** express grief or sorrow (for) **2** **the late lamented** the recently dead (person) ♦ *n* song, etc., expressing sorrow ~**able** /ləˈmɛntəbəl/ *adj fml* **1** unsatisfactory **2** worthy of blame ~**ation** /ˌlæmənˈteɪʃən/ *n* [C;U] *fml*

lamp /læmp/ *n* **1** apparatus for giving light **2** apparatus for producing sorts of heat that improve health

lam·poon /læmˈpun/ *n* written attack that makes someone look foolish **lampoon** *vt*

lamp·shade /ˈlæmpʃeɪd/ *n* cover for a lamp

lance /læns/ *n* long spearlike weapon

land¹ /lænd/ *n* **1** [U] solid dry part of the Earth's surface **2** [C] country; nation

3 [U] earth for farming **4** [U] also **lands** *pl.* — ground owned as property **5 see how the land lies** try to discover the present state of affairs before taking action ~**ed** *adj* owning a lot of land

land² /lænd/ *v* **1** *vi/t* come or bring to land **2** *vt* succeed in getting: *land the top job*

land in *phr vt* bring (someone) into (an undesirable state or position): *Her resignation landed us in a real mess.*

land with *phr vt* give (someone) (something unwanted): *I got landed with organizing the Christmas party.*

land·fill /ˈlændˌfɪl/ *n* area filled in by buried waste materials

land·ing /ˈlændɪŋ/ *n* **1** level space at the top of a set of stairs **2** arrival on land: *crash landing* **3** place where people and goods are loaded, esp. from a ship

landing gear /ˈ·· ·/ *n* [U] wheels and UNDERCARRIAGE of an aircraft

land·la·dy /ˈlændˌleɪdi/ *n* a female LANDLORD

land·locked /ˈlændlɒkt/ *adj* surrounded by dry land

land·lord /ˈlændlɔrd/ *n* person from whom one rents land or buildings

land·mark /ˈlændmɑrk/ *n* **1** recognizable object from which one can tell one's position **2** important event, discovery, etc.

land·mine /ˈlændmaɪn/ *n* bomb hidden below the surface of the ground

land·scape /ˈlændskeɪp/ *n* (picture of) country scenery ♦ *vt* make (land) into a garden

land·slide /ˈlændslaɪd/ *n* **1** sudden fall of earth and rocks **2** great success in an election

lane /leɪn/ *n* **1** narrow road **2** division of a wide road, to keep fast and slow vehicles apart **3** path used regularly by ships or aircraft **4** path marked for each competitor in a race

lan·guage /ˈlæŋgwɪdʒ/ *n* [C;U] **1** system of human expression by means of words: *the origins of language* **2** particular system as used by a people or nation: *the English language* **3** system of signs: *computer languages* **4** particular style or manner of expression: *poetic language* **5** words and phrases considered shocking: *bad language*

language la·bora·tory /ˈ·· ˌ····/ *n* room where foreign languages are taught using TAPE RECORDERS, etc.

lan·guid /ˈlæŋgwɪd/ *adj* lacking strength, will ~**ly** *adv*

lan·guish /ˈlæŋgwɪʃ/ *vi fml* **1** experience long suffering **2** become weak

lank·y /ˈlæŋki/ *adj* ungracefully tall and thin

lan·tern /ˈlæntən/ *n* container around the flame of a light

lap¹ /læp/ *n* front of a seated person between the waist and the knees

lap² *v* -**pp**- **1** *vt* drink as a cat does **2** *vi* (of water) move with soft sounds ♦ *n* act or sound of lapping

lap³ *n* single journey around a racing track ♦ *vt* -**pp**- pass (another racer) so as to be one lap ahead

la·pel /ləˈpel/ *n* part of the front of a coat that is joined to the collar and folded back

lapse /læps/ *n* **1** small fault or mistake **2** failure in correct behavior, belief, etc. **3** passing away of time ♦ *vi* **1** sink gradually: *lapse into silence* **2** (of time) pass **3** (of business agreements, etc.) come to an end **lapsed** *adj* **1** no longer practicing, esp. one's religion **2** *law* no longer in use

lap·top /ˈlæptɒp/ *n* small computer that can be carried around

lar·ce·ny /ˈlɑrsəni/ *n* [C;U] *law* (an act of) stealing

lard /lɑrd/ *n* [U] pig's fat used in cooking ♦ *vt* **1** put lard on **2** use lots of noticeable phrases in one's speech or writing

large /lɑrdʒ/ *adj* **1** big **2** *at large*: **a** free **b** as a whole: *the country at large* ~**ly** *adv* mostly

lark /lɑrk/ *n* **1** kind of bird **2** fun activity

lar·va /ˈlɑrvə/ *n* -**vae** /-vi/ wormlike young of an insect

lar·yn·gi·tis /ˌlærənˈdʒaɪtɪs/ *n* [U] painful swelling of the larynx

lar·ynx /ˈlærɪŋks/ *n* hollow boxlike part in the throat, where voice is produced by the VOCAL CORDS

las·civ·i·ous /ləˈsɪviəs/ *adj* causing, showing, or feeling uncontrolled sexual desire ~**ly** *adv*

la·ser /ˈleɪzər/ *n* apparatus producing a strong narrow beam of light

lash¹ /læʃ/ *v* **1** *vi/t* whip **2** *vi/t* move about violently **3** *vt* tie tightly

lash out *phr vi* attack violently

lash² *n* **1** (a hit with) the thin striking part of a whip: (fig.) *the lash of the waves* **2** EYELASH

las·so /ˈlæsoʊ, læˈsuː/ n -s rope for catching horses and cattle ♦ vt catch with a lasso

last¹ /læst/ determiner, adv 1 after the others 2 only remaining: my last $5 3 most recent(ly): When did we last meet? 4 least suitable or likely: He's the last person I'd have expected to see here. 5 every last every, not leaving out any ♦ n, pron [(the) S] 1 person or thing after all others: the last to leave 2 the only remaining: the last of the wine 3 the one or ones before the present one: the week before last (= 2 weeks ago) 4 at (long) last in the end ~ly adv in the end

last² v 1 vi continue 2 vi/t be enough (for): The food will last (us) a week. ~ing adj continuing for a long time

last-ditch /ˌ· ˈ·◂/ adj done as one last effort before accepting defeat

last name /ˈ· ·/ n person's family name; SURNAME

last straw /ˌ· ˈ·/ n [the+S] the difficulty, etc., that makes the total unbearable when it is added to one's present difficulties

last word /ˌ· ˈ·/ n [the+S] 1 remark that ends an argument 2 most modern example of something

latch¹ /lætʃ/ n 1 small bar for fastening a door, gate, window, etc. 2 spring lock for a house door which can be opened from outside with a key

latch² vt

latch on phr vi understand

latch onto phr vt 1 latch on 2 refuse to leave (someone)

late /leɪt/ adj, adv 1 after the usual time: The train was late. 2 near the end: in late September 3 recently dead: his late wife 4 recent: the latest fashions | Have you heard the latest? (= most recent news) 5 at the latest and not later 6 of late lately ~ly adv not long ago

la·tent /ˈleɪtn̩t/ adj existing but not yet noticeable or developed: latent talent **latency** n [U]

lat·er·al /ˈlætərəl/ adj of, from, or to the side ~ly adv

lateral think·ing /ˌ··· ˈ··/ n [U] making of unusual connections in the mind to find a new and clever answer to a problem

la·tex /ˈleɪteks/ n [U] liquid from which natural rubber is made

la·ther /ˈlæðər/ n [S;U] 1 FROTH made with soap and water 2 in a lather infml worried ♦ v 1 vi make a lather 2 vt cover with lather

Lat·in /ˈlætn̩/ n, adj (of) the language of the ancient Romans

Latin A·mer·i·can /ˌ·· ·ˈ···◂/ adj of the Spanish- or Portuguese-speaking countries of N., Central, and S. America

La·ti·no /ləˈtiːnoʊ/ **Latina** /ləˈtiːnə/ fem. — n, adj (person) having family members originally from Latin America

lat·i·tude /ˈlætəˌtuːd/ n [S;U] 1 distance north or south of the EQUATOR, measured in degrees 2 freedom of choice **latitudes** n [P] area at a particular latitude

la·trine /ləˈtriːn/ n outdoor TOILET in a camp, etc.

lat·ter /ˈlætər/ adj of a later period: his latter years ♦ n fml second of 2 things mentioned ~ly adv recently

lat·tice /ˈlætɪs/ n wooden or metal frame with a network of crossing bars used as a fence, etc.

laugh /læf/ vi 1 express amusement, happiness, etc., by breathing out forcefully so that one makes sounds with the voice, usu. while smiling 2 no laughing matter serious ♦ n 1 act or sound of laughing 2 something done for a joke 3 have the last laugh win after earlier defeats ~able adj foolish

laughing stock /ˈ·· ·/ n someone or something regarded as foolish

laugh·ter /ˈlæftər/ n [U] laughing

launch /lɔntʃ, lantʃ/ vt 1 send (a newly built boat) into the water 2 send (a ROCKET, etc.) into the sky 3 begin (an activity): launch an attack/a company ♦ n 1 act of launching 2 large boat with a motor ~er n

launch into phr vt begin with eagerness, force, etc.

launch·ing pad /ˈ·· ·/ n base from which spacecraft, etc., are launched

laun·der /ˈlɔndər, ˈlɑn-/ vt 1 wash and iron (clothes) 2 hide (origins of money made from crime)

laun·dro·mat /ˈlɔndrəˌmæt, ˈlɑn-/ n place where the public pay to wash their clothes in machines

laun·dry /ˈlɔndri, ˈlɑn-/ n 1 [C] place where clothes are laundered 2 [U] clothes (needing to be) laundered

laur·e·ate /ˈlɔri-ɪt, ˈlɑr-/ *adj* see POET LAUREATE

laur·el /ˈlɔrəl, ˈlɑrəl/ *n* EVERGREEN bush with shiny leaves **laurels** *n* [P] 1 honor gained for something done 2 **rest on one's laurels** be satisfied with what one has done already, and not do any more

la·va /ˈlavə, ˈlævə/ *n* [U] melted rock that flows from a VOLCANO

la·va·to·ry /ˈlævətɔri, -ˌtoʊri/ *n* TOILET

lav·en·der /ˈlævəndər/ *n* [U] (pale purple color of) a plant having flowers with a strong smell

lav·ish /ˈlævɪʃ/ *adj* 1 generous 2 given or produced in (too) great quantity: *lavish praise* ♦ *vt* give freely: *She lavishes money on them.* **~ly** *adv*

law /lɔ/ *n* 1 [C] rule made by a government 2 [U] all these rules: *Stealing is against the law.* 3 [C] statement of what always happens in certain conditions: *the laws of physics* 4 [*the*+S] *infml* police or a policeman 5 **be a law unto oneself** do exactly what one wishes 6 **law and order** respect for the law 7 **lay down the law** give an opinion in an unpleasant commanding manner **~ful** *adj* allowed or recognized by law **~fully** *adv* **~less** *adj* not governed by laws **~lessness** *n* [U]

law·a·bid·ing /ˈ· ·ˌ··/ *adj* obeying the law

lawn /lɔn/ *n* area of closely cut grass

lawn·mow·er /ˈlɔnˌmoʊər/ *n* machine that cuts grass

law·suit /ˈlɔsut/ *n* non-criminal case in a law court

lax /læks/ *adj* careless and uncontrolled **~ity** *n* [C;U]

lax·a·tive /ˈlæksətɪv/ *n, adj* (medicine) helping the bowels to empty

lay[1] /leɪ/ *v past t. of* LIE[2]

lay[2] /leɪ/ *v* **laid** /leɪd/ 1 *vt* a put, esp. carefully, in a flat position: *She laid his coat on the bed.* **b** set in proper order or position: *to lay bricks* 2 *vt* arrange for use: *lay the table for dinner* 3 *vt* cause to settle or disappear: *lay his fears to rest* 4 *vi/t* (of a bird, insect, etc.) produce (eggs) 5 *vt* make (a statement, claim, etc.) in a serious or official way: *lay charges against someone* 6 *vt sl* have sex with: *He only goes to parties to get laid.* 7 **lay hold of** catch and hold firmly 8 **lay waste** destroy completely

lay down *phr vt* 1 state firmly: *lay down the law* 2 give up (one's life) 3 store (esp. wine) for the future

lay in *phr vt* get and store a supply of

lay into *phr vt* attack with words or blows

lay low *phr vt* 1 knock down 2 make sick

lay off *phr vt* 1 stop employing 2 give up

lay on *phr vt* **lay it on** tell something in a way that goes beyond the truth

lay out *phr vt* 1 arrange or plan: *lay out a garden* 2 knock (someone) down 3 spend (money) 4 prepare a dead person for the funeral

lay up *phr vt* 1 keep in bed with an illness: *laid up with the flu* 2 collect and store for future use

lay[3] *adj* 1 of or by people who are not priests 2 not professional

lay·er /ˈleɪər/ *n* 1 thickness of some substance laid over a surface: *layers of rock* 2 bird that lays eggs

lay·man /ˈleɪmən/ *n* **-men** /-mən/ LAY[3] person

lay·off /ˈleɪɔf/ *n* stopping of a worker's employment

lay·out /ˈleɪaʊt/ *n* (planned) arrangement: *the layout of the room*

laze /leɪz/ *vi* rest lazily

la·zy /ˈleɪzi/ *adj* 1 avoiding work 2 spent in inactivity **lazily** *adv* **laziness** *n* [U]

la·zy·bones /ˈleɪziˌboʊnz/ *n* lazy person

lb. *written abbrev. for:* POUND[1] (1)

lead[1] /lid/ *v* **led** /lɛd/ 1 *vi/t* guide, esp. by going first 2 *vi* (of a road, etc.) go somewhere: (fig.) *The plan led to trouble.* 3 *vt* influence: *What led you to do it?* 4 *vt* control or govern: *lead an army* 5 *vi/t* be ahead (of) in sports 6 *vt* experience (a kind of life) 7 *vi* (of a newspaper) have as a main story **~ing** *adj* most important; chief

lead on *phr vt* influence (someone) to do something wrong or believe something untrue

lead up to *phr vt* be a preparation for

lead[2] /lid/ *n* 1 [C] guiding suggestion 2 [S] a chief or front position **b** distance by which one competitor is ahead 3 [C] (person playing) the chief acting part in a play or film 4 [C] main or most important article in a newspaper 5 [C] wire carrying electrical power

lead[3] /lɛd/ *n* 1 [U] heavy grayish metal used for water pipes, etc. 2 [C;U] (stick of) GRAPHITE used in pencils

lead·en /ˈlɛdn/ adj 1 dull gray 2 heavy and sad

lead·er /ˈlidə/ n person who leads ~**ship** n [U] position or qualities of a leader

leading light /ˌlidɪŋ ˈlaɪt/ n person of importance

leaf[1] /lif/ n **leaves** /livz/ 1 flat green part of a plant, joined to its stem 2 sheet of paper or metal 3 part of a table top that can be slid or folded out 4 **turn over a new leaf** begin a new course of improved behavior, habits, etc. ~**y** adj

leaf[2] v **leaf through** phr vt turn the pages (of a book, etc.) quickly without reading much

leaf·let /ˈliflɪt/ n small sheet of printed matter ♦ v give out (political) leaflets

league /lig/ n 1 group of people, countries, etc., joined together for a shared aim 2 group of sports clubs that play against each other 3 level of quality: *They're not in the same league.* 4 **in league (with)** working together secretly

leak /lik/ n 1 accidental hole through which something flows 2 spreading of secret news: *security leak* ♦ v 1 vi/t (allow to) pass through a leak 2 vt make (secrets) publicly known ~**y** adj

leak·age /ˈlikɪdʒ/ n [C;U] process or amount of leaking

lean[1] /lin/ v **leaned** 1 vi bend from an upright position 2 vi/t support or rest in a sloping position: *lean a ladder against a tree* 3 **lean over backwards** make every possible effort (to) ~**ing** n tendency: *have artistic leanings*

lean on/upon phr vt 1 depend on 2 infml influence (someone) by threats

lean towards phr vt favor (a plan or opinion)

lean[2] adj 1 not fat 2 producing little profit: *a lean year for business*

leap /lip/ v **leapt** /lɛpt/ or **leaped** 1 jump 2 sudden increase in number, quantity, etc. 3 **by leaps and bounds** very quickly 4 **a leap in the dark** action or risk taken without knowing what will happen ♦ n sudden jump

leap·frog /ˈlipfrɔg, -frɑg/ n [U] game in which players jump over each other ♦ vi/t go ahead of (each other) in turn

leap year /ˈ· ·/ n a year, every 4th year, in which February has 29 days

learn /lən/ vi/t **learned** or **learnt** /lənt/ 1 gain (knowledge or skill): *learn French* |

learn to swim 2 fix in the memory: *learn a poem* 3 become informed (of): *learn of his success* ~**er** n ~**ing** n [U] knowledge gained by study ~**ed** /ˈlənɪd/ adj having great knowledge

learn·ing dis·a·bil·i·ty /ˈ· · ·ˌ· · ·/ n mental problem that affects one's ability to learn

lease /lis/ n 1 contract for the use of a place in return for rent 2 **a new lease on life** new strength or desire to be happy, etc. ♦ vt give or take (a place) on a lease

leash /liʃ/ n chain, etc., for leading a dog

least[1] /list/ determiner, pron 1 smallest number, amount, etc.: *Buy the one that costs (the) least.* 2 **at least: a** not less than: *at least $100* **b** if nothing else: *At least it's legal.* 3 **in the least** at all

least[2] adv (superlative of LITTLE) 1 less than anything else or than any others 2 **not least** partly, and quite importantly

leath·er /ˈlɛðə/ n preserved animal skin used for making shoes, etc. ~**y** adj stiff like leather

leave[1] /liv/ v **left** /lɛft/ 1 vi/t go away (from) 2 vt allow to remain: *leave the door open* | *Is there any coffee left?* 3 vt fail to take or bring: *I've left my coat behind.* 4 vt give by a WILL[2] (5) 5 vt allow something to be the responsibility of (someone) *I'll leave you to buy the tickets.* 6 vt have remaining in a sum: *2 from 8 leaves 6.* 7 **leave go/hold of** stop holding 8 **leave it at that** do or say no more 9 **leave someone/something alone** stop behaving annoyingly in someone's presence or touching something 10 **leave someone/something standing** infml be much better than someone or something 11 **leave something up to someone** let someone decide

leave off phr vi/t stop (doing something)

leave out phr vt not include

leave[2] n 1 [C;U] time spent away from work 2 [U] fml permission 3 **take leave of** say goodbye to: *She must have taken leave of her senses.* (= gone crazy)

leaves /livz/ n pl. of LEAF[1]

lech·er·ous /ˈlɛtʃərəs/ adj derog wanting continual sexual pleasure ~**ly** adv

lec·tern /ˈlɛktən/ n sloping table to hold a book

lec·ture /ˈlɛktʃə/ n 1 speech given as a method of teaching 2 long solemn scold-

ing or warning ♦ *vi/t* give a lecture (to)
~turer *n* person who gives (university)
lectures

led /led/ *v past t. and p. of* LEAD¹

ledge /ledʒ/ *n* shelf sticking out from a
wall, rock, etc.

led·ger /ˈledʒə/ *n* account book of a
business

leech /liːtʃ/ *n* **1** wormlike creature that
sucks blood **2** person who makes profit
from others

leek /liːk/ *n* vegetable with long fleshy
stem and broad leaves that tastes
slightly like onions

leer /lɪr/ *vi, n* (look with) an unpleasant
smile

lee·way /ˈliːweɪ/ *n* additional time,
money, etc., allowing the chance of
success

left¹ /left/ *v past t. and p. of* LEAVE¹

left² *adj* **1** on the side of the body that contains the heart **2** in the direction of one's
left side **3** belonging to or favoring the
LEFT³ (2) in politics

left³ *n* [U] **1** left side or direction **2** political parties that favor more change
and more state control ♦ *adv* towards
the left **~ist** *n, adj* (a supporter) of the
political left

left field /ˌ· ˈ·/ *n* **1** position in baseball **2**
(way) out in left field impractical, not
REALISTIC

left-hand /ˌ· ˈ·◄/ *adj* on the left side **~ed**
adj using the left hand for most actions
~er left-handed person

left·o·vers /ˈleftˌoʊvəz/ *n* [P] food
remaining uneaten after a meal

left wing /ˌ· ˈ·/ *n* [U] LEFT³ (2) ♦ *adj*

leg /leg/ *n* **1** limb that includes the foot,
used for walking **2** part of a garment
that covers this **3** support of a table, etc.
4 single stage of a journey **5** **not have a
leg to stand on** have no good reason or
excuse **6** **on one's/its last legs: a** very
tired **b** nearly worn out **c** nearly dead **7**
pull someone's leg make fun of a
person in a playful way

leg·a·cy /ˈlegəsi/ *n* **1** money, etc., left in
someone's WILL **2** something left behind:
Disease is often a legacy of war.

le·gal /ˈliːgəl/ *adj* of, allowed, or
demanded by the law **~ly** *adv* **~ize** *vt*
make legal **~ity** /lɪˈgæləti/ *n* [U]

legal ten·der /ˌ·· ˈ·/ *n fml* money that
must by law be accepted in payment

le·gend /ˈledʒənd/ *n* **1** [C] old story which
may not be true **2** [U] such stories col-
lectively **3** [C] famous person or act **4** [C]
words that explain a picture, etc., in a
book **~ary** *adj* famous in legends

leg·gings /ˈlegɪnz/ *n* [P] outer coverings
to protect the legs

le·gi·ble /ˈledʒəbəl/ *adj* that can be read
easily **–bly** *adv* **–bility** /ˌledʒəˈbɪləti/ *n*
[U]

le·gion /ˈliːdʒən/ *n* **1** division of an army,
esp. in ancient Rome **2** large group of
people ♦ *adj fml* very many **~ary** *n*
member of a legion (1)

le·gis·late /ˈledʒəˌsleɪt/ *vi* make laws
–lator *n* **–lation** /ˌledʒəˈsleɪʃən/ *n* [U] **1**
law or set of laws **2** act of making laws

le·gis·la·tive /ˈledʒəˌsleɪtɪv/ *adj* having
the power and duty to make laws: *a leg-
islative assembly* ♦ *n* [U] the branch of
government that does this

le·gis·la·tor /ˈledʒəˌsleɪtə/ *n* person who
makes laws

le·gis·la·ture /ˈledʒəˌsleɪtʃə/ *n* body of
people who make the laws

le·git·i·mate /ləˈdʒɪtəmət/ *adj* **1** legally
correct **2** born of parents married to
each other **3** reasonable: *legitimate con-
clusion* **~ly** *adv* **–macy** *n* [U]

leg·ume /ˈlegyuːm, ləˈgyuːm/ *n* (seeds of)
beans, PEAS etc., used as food

lei·sure /ˈliːʒə, ˈlɛ-/ *n* [U] **1** free time **2**
at one's leisure at a convenient time
leisured *adj* having leisure **2** leisurely

lei·sure·ly /ˈliːʒəli, ˈlɛ-/ *adj* unhurried

lem·on /ˈlemən/ *n* **1** [C] sour fruit with
a hard yellow skin **2** [U] light bright
yellow **3** [C] *sl* something unsatisfactory
or worthless, esp. a car

lem·on·ade /ˌleməˈneɪd◄/ *n* [U] drink
made of lemons, sugar, and water

lend /lend/ *v* **lent** /lent/ **1** *vt/i* give something for a limited time: *lend him $10
until tomorrow* **2** *vt* give; add: *The flags
lent color to the streets.* **3** **lend a hand**
give help **4** **lend itself to** be suitable for
~er *n*

length /leŋkθ, leŋθ, leŋθ/ *n* **1** [C;U] measurement of something from one end to
the other or of its longest side **2** [U]
quality or condition of being long: *the
length of the exam paper* **3** [C] distance
from front to back of a horse or boat in a
race: *win by 3 lengths* **4** [C] amount of
time from beginning to end **5** [C] piece of

something: *a length of string* **6 at length:** **a** in many words **b** *fml* finally **7 go to any/great lengths** be prepared to do anything ~y *adj* (too) long

length·en /ˈlɛŋkθən, ˈlɛŋθən, ˈlɛnθən/ *vi/t* make or become longer

length·wise /ˈlɛŋkθwaɪz, ˈlɛŋθ-, ˈlɛnθ-/ also **length·ways** /-weɪz/ — *adv* in the direction of the longest side

le·ni·ent /ˈliniənt, ˈlinyənt/ *adj* not severe in judgment ~ly *adv* –ence, –ency n [U]

lens /lɛnz/ *n* **1** curved piece of glass in a camera, microscope, etc. **2** part of the eye that can FOCUS light **3** CONTACT LENS

lent /lɛnt/ *v past t. and p. of* LEND

Lent *n* the 40 days before EASTER

len·til /ˈlɛntəl/ *n* small beanlike seed used for food

Le·o /ˈlioʊ/ *n* **1** [S] 5th sign of the ZODIAC, represented by a lion **2** someone born between July 23 and August 22

leop·ard /ˈlɛpəd/ **leopardess** /ˈlɛpədɪs/ *fem. n* large spotted catlike animal

le·o·tard /ˈliəˌtɑrd/ *n* close fitting garment made in one piece worn by dancers, etc.

lep·er /ˈlɛpə/ *n* **1** person with leprosy **2** person avoided by other people for social or moral reasons

lep·ro·sy /ˈlɛprəsi/ *n* [U] disease in which the skin becomes rough, flesh and nerves are destroyed, and fingers, toes, etc., drop off –rous *adj*

les·bi·an /ˈlɛzbiən/ *adj, n* (of or being) a woman HOMOSEXUAL ~ism *n* [U]

le·sion /ˈliʒən/ *n fml* wound

less¹ /lɛs/ *determiner, pron,* (*comparative of* LITTLE) *n* **1** smaller amount: *less noise* | *less than a mile* **2 less and less** (an amount) that continues to become smaller **3 less than no time** a very short time **4 none the less** but in spite of everything **5 think (the) less of** have a lower opinion of

less² *adv* **1** not so; to a smaller degree (than): *less cold* **2** not so much: *to work less* **3 less and less** increasingly rarely **4 much/still less** and certainly not

less³ *prep* but we subtract; MINUS: *I earned $100, less tax.*

less·en /ˈlɛsən/ *vi/t* make or become less

less·er /ˈlɛsə/ *adj, adv* smaller: *the lesser of 2 evils*

les·son /ˈlɛsən/ *n* **1** (period of) teaching something in school, etc. **2** experience from which to learn: *The accident taught him a lesson.*

let /lɛt/ *vt* let *pres. p.* letting **1** allow (to do or happen): *He let his beard grow.* **2** (the named person) must, should, or can: *Let each man decide for himself.* | (when suggesting a plan) "*Let's have a party!*" **3** give the use of (a place) for rent **4 let alone** and certainly not: *He can't walk, let alone run.* **5 let go** stop holding **6 let oneself go: a** behave freely **b** stop taking care of one's appearance **7 let someone go: a** set someone free **b** dismiss someone from a job **8 let someone know** tell someone, esp. at a later date

let down *phr vt* **1** make (clothes) longer **2** disappoint

let in for *phr vt* cause (esp. oneself) to have (something unwanted)

let into/in on *phr vt* allow to share (a secret)

let off *phr vt* **1** excuse from punishment **2** explode: *let off fireworks*

let on *phr vi* **1** tell a secret **2** pretend

let out *phr v* **1** *vt* give (a sound, etc.) **2** *vt* make (clothes) wider **3** *vi* finish: *School lets out at 3 o'clock*

let up *phr vi* lessen or stop

let·down /ˈlɛtdaʊn/ *n* disappointment

le·thal /ˈliθəl/ *adj* causing death

let·ter /ˈlɛtə/ *n* **1** [C] written message sent to someone **2** [C] sign representing a sound **3** [(*the*) S] actual words of something: *the letter of the law* ~ing *n* [U] style and size of written letters **letters** *n* [U] *fml* literature

let·ter·head /ˈlɛtəˌhɛd/ *n* name and address printed at the top of the owner's writing paper

let·tuce /ˈlɛtɪs/ *n* [C;U] green leafy vegetable, eaten raw

let·up /ˈlɛtʌp/ *n* [C;U] lessening of activity

leu·ke·mi·a /luˈkimiə/ *n* [U] serious disease in which the blood has too many white cells

lev·el¹ /ˈlɛvəl/ *adj* **1** flat; HORIZONTAL **2** equal: *Pete and Dan are level in math.* **3 one's level best** all that one can do

level² *n* [C;U] **1** line or surface parallel with the ground; position of height in relation to a flat surface: *The garden is on*

2 levels. | (fig.) *The decision was made at the presidential level.* **2** standard of quality or quantity: *increase production levels* **3** apparatus for testing whether a surface is level[1] (1) **4 on the level** honest(ly)
level[3] *vt/i* make or become level
level at/against *phr vt* **1** aim (a weapon) at **2** bring (a charge) against (someone)
level off/out *phr vi* stop rising or falling
level with *phr vt infml* speak truthfully to
level[4] *adv* so as to be level: *a missile flying level with the ground*
level-head·ed /ˌ·· ˈ··◂/ *adj* calm and sensible
le·ver /ˈlɛvɚ, ˈli-/ *n* **1** bar that turns on its middle point, to lift things **2** rod that works a machine **3** something which may be used for influencing ♦ *vt* move with a lever: *Lever it into position.*
le·ver·age /ˈlɛvərɪdʒ, ˈli-/ *n* [U] power of a lever: (fig.) *use political leverage*
lev·i·tate /ˈlɛvəˌteɪt/ *vi* rise into the air as if by magic –**tation** /ˌlɛvəˈteɪʃən/ *n* [U]
lev·i·ty /ˈlɛvət̬i/ *n* [U] *fml* lack of proper seriousness
lev·y /ˈlɛvi/ *vt* demand and collect (esp. taxes) officially
lewd /lud/ *adj* sexually dirty: *lewd songs* ~**ly** *adv* ~**ness** *n* [U]
lex·i·cog·ra·phy /ˌlɛksəˈkɑgrəfi/ *n* [U] writing of dictionaries –**pher** *n*
lex·i·con /ˈlɛksɪˌkɑn, -kən/ *n* dictionary or word list
li·a·bil·i·ty /ˌlaɪəˈbɪlət̬i/ *n* **1** [U] condition of being liable **2** [C] debt that must be paid **3** [C] someone or something that limits one's activities or freedom
li·a·ble /ˈlaɪəbəl/ *adj* **1** responsible in law **2 liable to** have a tendency to
li·aise /liˈeɪz/ *vi* exchange information with another person, department, etc.
li·ai·son /liˈeɪzɑn/ *n* **1** [S;U] working association between groups **2** [C] sexual relationship between an unmarried man and woman
li·ar /ˈlaɪɚ/ *n* person who tells lies
lib /lɪb/ *n* [U] liberation (LIBERATE)
li·bel /ˈlaɪbəl/ *n* [C;U] damaging written statement about someone ♦ *vt* -**l**- make a libel against ~**ous** *adj*: *a libelous remark*
lib·e·ral /ˈlɪbrəl, ˈlɪbərəl/ *adj* **1** willing to respect the opinions of others **2** (of education) leading to wide general knowledge **3** given freely: *liberal supplies* ~**ism** *n* [U] LIBERAL (1) opinions ~**ize** *vt* remove limits on freedom: *liberalize the divorce laws* ~**ization** /ˌlɪbrələˈzeɪʃən/ *n* [U]
liberal arts /ˌ··· ˈ·/ *n* subjects taught at a college or university related to social and human studies
lib·e·rate /ˈlɪbəˌreɪt/ *vt fml* set free –**rated** *adj* socially and sexually free –**rator** *n* –**ration** /ˌlɪbəˈreɪʃən/ *n* [U]
lib·er·tar·i·an /ˌlɪbɚˈtɛriən/ *n* believer in freedom of thought ~**ism** *n* [U]
lib·er·ty /ˈlɪbɚt̬i/ *n* [U] **1** personal or political freedom **2** chance or permission to do or use something **3 at liberty** free **4 take liberties** behave too freely
li·bi·do /lɪˈbidoʊ/ *n* -**dos** *tech* the sexual urge
Li·bra /ˈlibrə/ *n* **1** [S] 7th sign of the ZODIAC, represented by a SCALE **2** someone born between September 23 and October 23
li·brar·i·an /laɪˈbrɛriən/ *n* person in charge of a library ~**ship** *n* [U]
li·bra·ry /ˈlaɪˌbrɛri/ *n* (room or building with) a collection of books, records, etc.
lice /laɪs/ *n pl. of* LOUSE
li·cense /ˈlaɪsəns/ *n* **1** [C;U] (paper showing) official permission to do something **2** [U] *fml* uncontrolled freedom
license *vt* give a LICENSE (1) to
license plate /ˈ·· ˌ·/ *n* official number shown on a vehicle
lick /lɪk/ *vt* **1** move the tongue across **2** (of flames or waves) pass lightly over **3** *infml* defeat ♦ *n* **1** [C] act of licking **2** [C] small amount (of work, etc.) **3** [S] *infml* speed
lic·o·rice /ˈlɪkərɪʃ/ *n* [U] black substance used in medicine and candy
lid /lɪd/ *n* **1** movable cover of a container **2** EYELID
lie[1] /laɪ/ *vi, n* **lied**, *pres. p.* **lying** (make) a false statement — see also WHITE LIE
lie[2] *vi* **lay** /leɪ/, **lain** /leɪn/, *pres. p.* **lying** /ˈlaɪ-ɪŋ/ **1** be or remain in a flat position on a surface **2** be or remain in a particular position or state: *The town lies 2 miles to the east.* | *The machinery was lying idle.* **3** be the responsibility of: *The decision lies with you.* **4 lie low** be in hiding or avoid being noticed ♦ *n* [S] way something lies

lie around *phr vi* be lazy; do nothing

lie behind *phr vt* be the reason for

lie down *phr vi* **1 lie down on the job** do work that is not good enough in quantity or quality **2 take something lying down** suffer something bad without complaining or trying to stop it

lie over *phr vi* be POSTPONEd

lie·de·tec·tor /ˈ· ·ˌ·/ *n* instrument that is said to show when someone is telling LIES[1]

lieu /luː/ *n* **in lieu (of)** instead of

lieu·ten·ant /luːˈtɛnənt/ *n* officer of low rank in the armed forces

life /laɪf/ *n* **lives** /laɪvz/ **1** [U] active force that makes animals and plants different from stones or machines **2** [U] living things: *There is no life on the moon.* **3** [U] human existence: *Life is full of surprises.* **4** [C] period or way of being alive: *their busy lives* | (fig.) *during the life of this company* | (fig.) *The machine has a life of 10 years.* **5** [C] person: *No lives were lost.* **6** [U] activity; movement; strength: *full of life* **7** [U] existence as a collection of widely different experiences: *You see life in the navy.* **8** [U] also **life im·pris·on·ment** /ˌ· ·ˈ··/ — punishment of being put in prison for a long time **9** [C] BIOGRAPHY **10** [*the*+S] person or thing that is the cause of enjoyment in a group: *the life and soul of the party* **11** [U] using a living person as the subject of a painting, etc.: *painted from life* **12 as large as life** unexpectedly, without any possibility of mistake, but the real person **13 come to life: a** regain one's senses after fainting **b** show or develop interest, excitement, etc. **14 for dear life** with the greatest effort **15 Not on your life!** Certainly not! **16 take one's life** kill oneself **17 take one's life in one's (own) hands** be in continual danger **18 take someone's life** kill them ~**less** *adj* **1** dead **2** not active; dull ~**lessly** *adv* ~**like** *adj* like a real person

life·blood /ˈlaɪfblʌd/ *n* [U] something that gives continuing strength

life·boat /ˈlaɪfboʊt/ *n* boat for saving people in danger at sea

life cy·cle /ˈ· ˌ·/ *n* all the stages of development through which a creature passes during its life

life·guard /ˈlaɪfgɑrd/ *n* swimmer employed to help other swimmers in danger

life in·sur·ance /ˈ· ·ˌ·/ *n* [U] insurance that provides money to one's family after one's death

life jack·et /ˈ· ˌ·/ *n* garment worn to support a person in water

life·line /ˈlaɪflaɪn/ *n* **1** rope for saving life **2** something on which one's life depends

life·long /ˈlaɪflɔŋ/ *adj* lasting all one's life

life-size — *adj* (of a work of art) as big as what it represents

life·style /ˈlaɪfstaɪl/ *n* way of living

life-threat·en·ing /ˈ· ˌ···/ *adj* (of illness, etc.) that could kill

life·time /ˈlaɪftaɪm/ *n* time during which someone is alive

lift[1] /lɪft/ *v* **1** *vt* raise to a higher level **2** *vt* improve: *lift my spirits* **3** *vi* (of clouds, etc.) disappear **4** *vt* bring to an end: *lift a ban* **5** *vt* steal

lift off *phr vi* (of an aircraft or spacecraft) leave the ground **lift-off** /ˈ· ·/ *n*

lift[2] *n* **1** act of lifting **2** free ride in a vehicle **3** feeling of increased strength, higher spirits, etc.

lig·a·ment /ˈlɪgəmənt/ *n* band that joins bones together

light[1] /laɪt/ *n* **1** [U] force by which we see things: *sunlight* **2** [C] lamp, etc., that gives light **3** [C] (something that will make) a flame **4** [C] bright part of a painting, etc. **5** [S;U] brightness in the eyes **6** [C] way in which something is regarded: *see it in a different light* **7 bring/come to light** make or become known **8 in a good/bad light** in a favorable/unfavorable way **9 in light of** taking into account **10 see the light: a** be born **b** be made public **c** understand or accept an idea or truth **11 throw/shed light on** explain

light[2] *v* **lit** /lɪt/ *or* **lighted 1** *vi/t* (cause to) start burning **2** *vt* give light to: *lighted streets* ~**ing** *n* system or quality of lights in a place

light up *phr v* **1** *vi/t* make or become bright **2** *vi* start smoking

light[3] *adj* **1** not dark: *a light room* **2** pale: *light green*

light[4] *adj* **1** not heavy **2** small in amount: *light lunch/traffic* **3** easy to bear or do: *light duties* **4** gentle: *light touch* **5** quick and graceful **6** (of wine, etc.) not very strong **7** not serious: *light reading* **8** (of sleep) not deep **9 make light of** treat as of little importance ♦ *adv* with few trav-

eling cases or possessions: *to travel light*
~**ly** *adv* **1** gently **2** slightly **3** not seriously ~**ness** *n* [U]

light⁵ *vt* **lit** /lɪt/ *or* **lighted** come down from flight and settle: (fig.) *I finally lit on the idea of going to Paris.*

light into *phr vt* attack strongly

light bulb /'· ·/ *n* BULB (2)

light·en /'laɪtn/ *vi/t* make or become a brighter **b** less heavy, or **c** (also **lighten up**) more cheerful

light·er /'laɪtə/ *n* instrument for lighting cigarettes, etc.

light-head·ed /ˌ· '··◂/ *adj* **1** unable to think clearly **2** not sensible

light-heart·ed /ˌ· '··◂/ *adj* cheerful

light·house /'laɪthaʊs/ *n* tower with a powerful light to guide ships

light·ning /'laɪtnɪŋ/ *n* [U] **1** electric flash of light in the sky **2** very quick, short, or sudden: *a lightning visit*

light·weight /'laɪtweɪt/ *n* **1** person or thing of less than average weight **2** someone who does not think deeply or seriously **lightweight** *adj*

light year /'· ·/ *n* **1** distance that light travels in a year **2** *infml* a very long time

li·ka·ble /'laɪkəbəl/ *adj* (esp. of people) nice; attractive

like¹ /laɪk/ *vt* **1** regard with pleasure or fondness **2** be willing (to): *I don't like to ask.* **3** (with **would**) wish or choose (to have): *I'd like a boiled egg.* | *Would you like to read it?* **4 How do you like ...?** (used when asking for an opinion) **5 I'd like to ...** I would be surprised/interested to **6 I like that!** That's very annoying! **7 if you like** if that is what you want **liking** *n* [S] **1** fondness **2 to one's liking** which suits one's ideas or expectations **likes** *n* [P] things that one likes

like² *prep* **1** in the same way as; similar to: *Do it like this.* **2** typical of: *It's not like her to be late.* **3** such as: *Houses like that are expensive.* **4 something like** about ♦ *n* **1** something of the same kind: *running, swimming, and the like* **2 the likes of** people or things of the stated type ♦ *adj fml* similar ♦ *conj* as: *Make it like you make tea.*

like·li·hood /'laɪklɪˌhʊd/ *n* [U] probability

like·ly /'laɪkli/ *adj* **1** probable **2 (That's) a likely story!** *infml* (said to show that one disbelieves what someone has said) ♦

adv **1** most/very likely probably **2 Not likely!** *infml* Certainly not!

like-mind·ed /ˌ· '··◂/ *adj* having the same ideas, interests, etc.

lik·en /'laɪkən/ *v* **liken to** *phr vt* to compare to

like·ness /'laɪknɪs/ *n* [C;U] sameness in appearance: *a family likeness*

like·wise /'laɪkwaɪz/ *adv* similarly; also

li·lac /'laɪlək, -lɑk, -læk/ *n* **1** [C] bush with pinkish purple or white flowers **2** [U] pinkish purple

lilt /lɪlt/ *n* [S] pleasant pattern of rising and falling sound ~**ing** *adj*

lil·y /'lɪli/ *n* plant with large esp. white flowers: *her lily-white skin*

limb /lɪm/ *n* **1** leg, arm, or wing **2** branch of a tree **3 out on a limb** alone without support **4 tear limb from limb** tear (a person) apart

lim·ber /'lɪmbə/ *v* **limber up** *phr vi* exercise the muscles before a game, etc.

lim·bo /'lɪmboʊ/ *n* [U] state of being uncertain

lime¹ /laɪm/ *n* [U] white substance used in making cement

lime² *n* sour green fruit like a LEMON

lime·light /'laɪmlaɪt/ *n* [*the*+S] the center of public attention

lim·e·rick /'lɪmərɪk/ *n* funny poem with 5 lines

lim·it /'lɪmɪt/ *n* **1** farthest point or edge **2** *infml* someone or something too bad to bear **3 off limits** where one is not allowed to go **4 within limits** up to a reasonable amount — see also TIME LIMIT ♦ *vt* keep below a limit ~**ed** *adj* **1** small; having limits **2** (*abbrev.* **Ltd**) (of a British company) having a reduced duty to pay back debts: *a limited company* ~**less** *adj* endless

lim·i·ta·tion /ˌlɪmɪˈteɪʃən/ *n* **1** [U] limiting **2** [C] condition that limits

lim·ou·sine /'lɪməˌzin, ˌlɪməˈzin/ also **limo** /'lɪmoʊ/ *infml* — *n* long expensive car with the driver's seat separated from the back

limp¹ /lɪmp/ *vi, n* [S] (walk with) an uneven step

limp² *adj* lacking firmness; not stiff ~**ly** *adv*

linch·pin /'lɪntʃˌpɪn/ *n* person or thing that keeps something together

line¹ /laɪn/ *n* **1** long narrow mark on a surface: *a line drawing* (= done with pen or pencil) **2** limit; border: *the finishing* *line in a race* — see also BOTTOMLINE **3 a** row: *boys standing in (a) line* **b** row of words on a printed page: *The actor forgot his lines.* **4** row of military defenses **5** a direction followed: *the line of fire* **6** piece of string, wire, etc.: *fishing line* **7** telephone connection: *Hold the line, please.* **8** railroad **9** system of travel: *airline* **10** method of action: *new line of approach* | *You're on the right lines.* (= following the right method) **11** an official POLICY (1): *the party line* **12** trade or profession **13** family following one another: *line of politicians* **14** a short letter **15** area of interest **16** type of goods: *a new line in hats* **17 in line for** being considered for **18 in line with** in accordance with **19 (step) out of line** (act) differently from others or from what is expected **20 (reach) the end of the line** (reach) the last stages, esp. a point of failure **21 read between the lines** find hidden meanings

line² *vt* **1** mark with lines or WRINKLES: *lined paper* | *His face is very lined.* **2** form rows along: *crowds lining the streets*

line up *phr v* **1** *vi/t* form into a row, esp. to wait for something **2** *vt* arrange (an event)

line³ *vt* **1** cover the inside of (something) with material: *lined boots* **2 line one's pocket(s)/purse** make money for oneself *lining* n [C;U]: *brake linings*

lin·e·age /ˈlɪni·ɪdʒ/ n [C;U] *fml* line of relationship from one person to another down through a family

lin·e·ar /ˈlɪniə/ *adj* **1** in lines **2** of length: *linear measurements*

line·back·er /ˈlaɪnˌbækə/ n player (in football) close behind the line of scrimmage

lin·en /ˈlɪnən/ n [U] **1** cloth made from grasslike plant **2** sheets, TABLECLOTHS, *etc.*

lin·er /ˈlaɪnə/ n **1** large passenger ship **2** something used to LINE³

line·up /ˈlaɪnʌp/ n **1** collection of people, esp. side by side in a line looking forward **2** competitors in a race or game **3** set of events

lin·ger /ˈlɪŋgə/ *vi* be slow to disappear: *lingering illness*

lin·ge·rie /ˌlɒnʒəˈreɪ, ˈlænʒəri/ n [U] *fml* women's underwear

lin·go /ˈlɪŋgəʊ/ n *-goes sl* language

lin·guist /ˈlɪŋgwɪst/ n **1** person who studies and is good at foreign languages **2** person who studies language in

general ~**ic** /lɪŋˈgwɪstɪk/ *adj* of language ~**ics** n [U] study of language

link /lɪŋk/ n **1** connection **2** one ring of a chain — see also LINKS ♦ *vt/i* join; connect

link·age /ˈlɪŋkɪdʒ/ n [C;U] system or way of connection

li·no·le·um /lɪˈnəʊliəm/ n [U] smooth hard covering for floors

lint /lɪnt/ n [U] bits of cotton, FUZZ

li·on /ˈlaɪən/ **lioness** /ˈlaɪənɪs/ *fem.* — n **1** large yellow catlike animal **2** famous and important person: *a literary lion* **3 the lion's share** the biggest part ~**ize** *vt* treat (someone) as important

lip /lɪp/ n **1** edge of the mouth **2** edge of a cup, etc. **3 lick/smack one's lips** think of or remember something (esp. food) with enjoyment — see also STIFF UPPER LIP

lip-read /ˈlɪp riːd/ *vi/t* understand speech by watching lip movements

lip ser·vice /ˈ·ˌ·/ n [U] **pay lip service** to support in words, but not in fact

lip·stick /ˈlɪpˌstɪk/ n [C;U] (stick of) colored substance put on the lips

liq·ue·fy /ˈlɪkwəˌfaɪ/ *vi/t fml* make or become liquid –**faction** /ˌlɪkwəˈfækʃən/ n [U]

li·queur /lɪˈkə, lɪˈkɜːr/ n [C;U] strong sweet alcoholic drink

liq·uid /ˈlɪkwɪd/ n [C;U] a substance which is not a solid or a gas, which flows freely and is wet ♦ *adj* **1** in the form of a liquid **2** clear and looking wet **3** (of sounds) pure and flowing **4** easily exchanged for money: *liquid assets* ~**ize** *vt* crush into juice

liq·ui·date /ˈlɪkwəˌdeɪt/ v **1** *vt* kill **2** *vi/t* arrange the end of (an unsuccessful company) –**dation** /ˌlɪkwəˈdeɪʃən/ n [U]

liq·uor /ˈlɪkə/ n [U] strong alcohol

liquor store /ˈ·· ˌ·/ n store that sells alcohol to take home

lisp /lɪsp/ *vi* pronounce /s/ to sound like /θ/ **lisp** n [S]

list /lɪst/ n set of things written in order: *shopping list* — see also HIT LIST ♦ *vt* put into a list

lis·ten /ˈlɪsən/ *vi* **1** give attention in hearing **2 Don't listen to someone** Don't believe or do what someone says ~**er** n

listen in *phr vt* **1** listen to (a broadcast on) the radio **2** listen to other people's conversation when one should not

list·less /ˈlɪstlɪs/ adj tired and not interested ~**ly** adv ~**ness** n [U]

list price /ˈ· ·/ n price suggested for an article by the makers

lit /lɪt/ v past t. and p. of LIGHT² or LIGHT⁵

lit·a·ny /ˈlɪtⁿn-i/ n form of long Christian prayer: (fig.) a long litany of complaints

li·ter /ˈliːtə/ n metric measure of liquid slightly larger than a QUART

lit·er·a·cy /ˈlɪtərəsi/ n [U] state or condition of being literate

lit·er·al /ˈlɪtərəl/ adj 1 giving one word for each word: a literal translation 2 following the usual meaning of words ~**ly** adv 1 really 2 word by word

lit·er·a·ry /ˈlɪtəˌreri/ adj of literature or writers

lit·er·ate /ˈlɪtərɪt/ adj 1 able to read and write 2 well educated

lit·er·a·ture /ˈlɪtərətʃə, -ɪtʃʊr, ˈlɪtrə-/ n [U] 1 written works of artistic value 2 printed material giving information: sales literature

lithe /laɪð/ adj (of people or animals) able to bend easily

lit·i·ga·tion /ˌlɪtɪˈɡeɪʃən/ n [U] fml process of taking action in law, in non-criminal matters

lit·ter /ˈlɪtə/ n 1 [U] paper, etc., scattered messily: a litter basket 2 [C] family of young animals ♦ vt scatter litter on

lit·tle¹ /ˈlɪtl/ adj 1 small: little birds 2 short: a little while 3 young 4 unimportant ♦ adv 1 not much: little-known facts 2 fml not at all: They little knew that I was watching.

little² det, pron, n **less, least** 1 [U] (without a or only) not much: I have very little (money) left. 2 [S] (with a or the) a small amount, but at least some: a little milk | stay a little longer 3 little by little gradually

little fin·ger /ˌ· ˈ·/ also **pinkie** /ˈpɪŋki/ — n smallest finger on the hand

lit·ur·gy /ˈlɪtədʒi/ n form of Christian worship –**gical** /lɪˈtɜːdʒɪkəl/ adj

live¹ /lɪv/ v 1 vi be alive: The doctor says he'll live. 3 vi have one's home: live in Paris 4 vt lead (a kind of life) 5 **live and let live** be tolerant (TOLERATE) 6 **live it up** infml have a lot of fun

    live down phr vt cause (a bad action) to be forgotten, by later good behavior

    live off phr vt 1 produce one's food or income from 2 get money for one's needs from

    live on phr v 1 vt have as one's food or income 2 vi continue in life or use

    live out phr v 1 vt live till the end of 2 vt experience in reality: live out one's fantasies

    live through phr vt remain alive during: live through 2 world wars

    live together phr vi live as if married

    live up to phr vt keep to the high standards of

    live with phr vt 1 live as if married with 2 accept (an unpleasant thing)

live² /laɪv/ adj 1 alive 2 able to explode or shock: live bomb/wire 3 (of broadcasting) seen or heard as it happens

live·li·hood /ˈlaɪvliːhʊd/ n way one earns one's money

live·ly /ˈlaɪvli/ adj 1 full of quick movement and thought 2 bright: lively colors –**liness** n [U]

liv·en /laɪvən/ v **liven up** phr vi/t make or become lively

liv·er /ˈlɪvə/ n 1 [C] organ in the body that cleans the blood 2 [U] animal's liver as food

lives /laɪvz/ n pl. of LIFE

live·stock /ˈlaɪvstɑk/ n [P] farm animals

live wire /ˌlaɪv ˈwaɪə/ n very active person

liv·id /ˈlɪvɪd/ adj 1 bluish gray 2 very angry

liv·ing¹ /ˈlɪvɪŋ/ adj 1 alive 2 still in use: living language

living² n 1 [S] LIVELIHOOD 2 [U] manner of life

living room /ˈ·· ˌ·/ n main room for general use in a house

living will /ˌ·· ˈ·/ n official document stating what legal and medical decisions should be made if one is too sick to decide for oneself

liz·ard /ˈlɪzəd/ n REPTILE with 4 legs and a long tail

load /loʊd/ n 1 something being carried 2 **a** the stated vehicle can carry **b** weight borne by the frame of a building 3 amount of work to be done 4 **a load off someone's mind** the removing of a great worry 5 **loads** of infml a lot of ♦ v 1 vt/i put a load on or in 2 vt put a bullet, etc., into (a gun) or film into (a camera) ~**ed** adj 1 containing a hidden trap: a loaded question 2 sl very rich 3 sl drunk

loaf¹ /loʊf/ n **loaves** /loʊvz/ 1 [C] single mass of baked bread 2 [C;U] food prepared in a solid piece: meat loaf

loaf[2] /vi/ waste time **~er** n **1** someone who loafs **2** men's shoe without LACES: *pair of loafers*

loan /loʊn/ n **1** something lent **2** amount of money lent **3 on loan** being borrowed ◆ vt lend

loan shark /ˈ· ·/ n person who lends money at very high interest

loathe /loʊð/ vt hate very much **loathing** n [S;U]

loath·some /ˈloʊðsəm, ˈloʊθ-/ adj DISGUSTing

loaves /loʊvz/ n pl. of LOAF

lob /lab/ vt **-bb-** send (a ball) in a high curve ◆ n lobbed ball

lob·by /ˈlabi/ n **1** hall or passage in a public building **2** group of people who try to influence those in power: *the gun lobby* ◆ vi/t **1** meet (a LEGISLATOR) in order to persuade him/her to support one's actions, etc. **2** be publicly active in trying to bring about change **~ist** n

lobe /loʊb/ n **1** lower fleshy part of the ear **2** division of the brain or lungs

lob·ster /ˈlabstə/ n [C] sea animal with CLAWS and 8 legs **2** [U] its meat as food

lo·cal /ˈloʊkəl/ adj **1** of a certain place: *our local doctor* **2** limited to one part: *local anesthetic* ◆ n **1** person living in a place **2** local train, bus, etc. **~ly** adv

lo·cal·i·ty /loʊˈkæləti/ n fml place; area

lo·cal·ize /ˈloʊkəlaɪz/ vt keep inside a small area

lo·cate /ˈloʊkeɪt, loʊˈkeɪt/ vt fml **1** learn the position of **2** fix in a particular place: *offices located in the town center* **location** /loʊˈkeɪʃən/ n **1** [C] position **2** [U] act of locating **3 on location** in a town, country, etc., to make a film

lock[1] /lak/ n **1** apparatus for fastening a door, etc. **2** piece of water closed off by gates, so that the level can be raised or lowered **3 lock, stock, and barrel** completely

lock[2] v **1** vi/t fasten with a lock **2** vi become fixed or blocked

lock away phr vt keep safe or secret, as by putting in a locked place

lock in/out phr vt keep (a person or criminal) inside/outside a place by locking the door

lock onto phr vt (esp. of a MISSILE) find and follow (the object to be attacked) closely

lock up phr v **1** vi/t make (a building) safe by locking the doors **2** vt put in a safe place and lock the door: *He should be locked up!* (= in prison)

lock[3] n small piece of hair: *his curly locks*

lock·er /ˈlakə/ n small cupboard for clothes, etc., esp. at school, in a sports building, etc.

lock·et /ˈlakɪt/ n case for a small picture, etc., worn on a chain round the neck

lo·co·mo·tive /ˌloʊkəˈmoʊtɪv/ n fml train engine

lo·cust /ˈloʊkəst/ n large flying insect that destroys crops

lodge[1] /ladʒ/ v **1** vi stay somewhere and pay rent **2** vi/t (cause to) become fixed: *The chicken bone lodged in his throat.* **3** vt make (a report, etc.) officially: *lodge a complaint*

lodge[2] n **1** small house on the land of a larger one **2** house in wild country for hunters, etc.: *ski lodge* **3** Native American house **4** meeting place for an organization

lodg·ing /ˈladʒɪŋ/ n [S;U] place to stay

loft /lɔft/ n **1** raised area above the main part of a room **2** an apartment made from this **loft·y** /ˈlɔfti/ adj **1** (of ideas, etc.) noble **2** proud **3** lit high **–ily** adv

log[1] /lɔg, lɑg/ n **1** thick piece of wood from a tree **2** official record of a journey **3 sleep like a log** sleep deeply without moving

log[2] vt **-gg-** record in a LOG[1] (2)

log in/on phr vi begin a period of using a computer system by performing a fixed set of operations

log off/out phr vi finish a period of using a computer system by performing a fixed set of operations

log·ger·heads /ˈlɔgəˌhɛdz, ˈlɑ-/ n **at loggerheads** always disagreeing

lo·gic /ˈladʒɪk/ n [U] **1** science of formal reasoning **2** good sense **~al** adj **~ally** adv

lo·gis·tics /loʊˈdʒɪstɪks, lə-/ n [P] detailed planning of an operation

log·o /ˈloʊgoʊ/ n **-os** sign, pattern, etc., representing a business or organization

loin /lɔɪn/ n [C;U] (piece of) meat from the lower part of an animal

loi·ter /ˈlɔɪtə/ vi stand somewhere for no clear reason **~er** n

loll /lal/ vi lie lazily

lol·li·pop /ˈlɑliˌpɑp/ n hard candy on a stick

lone /loʊn/ adj fml alone; single

lone·ly /ˈloʊnli/ adj **1** alone and unhappy **2** (of places) without people **–liness** n [U]

lone·some /ˈloʊnsəm/ adj LONELY (1)

long¹ /lɔŋ/ adj **1** large when measured from beginning to end: long hair | a long time | 2 miles long **2 long on** with a lot of

long² adv **1** (for) a long time: long ago | Will you be long? **2 as/so long as** on condition that **3 no longer/(not) any longer** (not) any more **4 so long** goodbye for now ♦ n **1** a long time: It won't take long. **2 before long** soon **3 the long and (the) short of it** infml the general result, expressed in a few words

long³ vi wish very much: longing to go **~ing** adj, n [C;U] (showing) a strong wish **~ingly** adv

   long for phr vt want very much

long-dis·tance /ˌ ˈ·· ◄/ adj covering a long distance ♦ adv to or from a distant point

lon·gev·i·ty /lɑnˈdʒɛvəti, lɔn-/ n [U] fml long life

long·hand /ˈlɔŋhænd/ n [U] ordinary writing by hand

lon·gi·tude /ˈlɑndʒəˌtud/ n [C;U] distance east or west of Greenwich, England, measured in degrees **–tudinal** /ˌlɑndʒəˈtudn-əl/ adj going along, not across

long-range /ˌ ˈ· ◄/ adj covering a long distance or time

long·shore·man /ˌlɔŋˈʃɔrmən, -ˈʃoʊr-, ˈlɔŋˌʃɔrmən, -ˌʃoʊr-/ n man whose job is to load and unload ships

long shot /ˈ· ˌ/ n something not likely to happen

long-stand·ing /ˌlɔŋ ˈstændɪŋ◄/ adj having existed for a long time: longstanding rivalry

long-suf·fer·ing /ˌlɔŋ ˈsʌfərɪŋ◄/ adj patient under continued difficulties

long-term /ˌ ˈ· ◄/ adj for or in the distant future

long-wind·ed /ˌlɔŋ ˈwɪndɪd◄/ adj saying too much; dull

look¹ /lʊk/ v **1** vi use the eyes to see something **2** seem; appear: You look tired. **3** vi face: The window looks east. **4 look as if/like** seem probable: It looks as if he's gone.

look after phr vt take care of

look ahead phr vi plan for the future

look around phr vi search

look at phr vt **1** watch **2** consider; examine **3 not much to look at** not attractive in appearance

look back phr vi **1** remember **2 never look back** continue to succeed

look down on phr vt DESPISE

look for phr vt try to find

look forward to phr vt expect to enjoy

look into phr vt examine; INVESTIGATE

look on phr v **1** vi watch **2** vt regard as

look out phr vi take care; keep watching

look over phr vt examine quickly

look through phr vt examine for points to be noted

look to phr vt **1** depend on: I look to you for support. **2** pay attention to

look up phr v **1** vi improve **2** vt find (information) in a book **3** vt find and visit

look up to phr vt respect

look² n **1** act of looking **2** appearance **3 I don't like the look of it/the looks of this.** (This state of affairs, etc.) suggests something bad to me. **looks** n [P] person's (attractive) appearance

look·ing glass /ˈ·· ˌ/ n mirror

look·out /ˈlʊk-aʊt/ n [S] **1** state of watching **2** person who keeps watch **3** place from where one keeps watch

loom¹ /lum/ n machine for weaving cloth

loom² vi appear in a threatening way: Fear of failure loomed large in his life.

loon·y /ˈluni/ n, adj sl LUNATIC

loop /lup/ n (shape of) a piece of string, etc., curved back on itself ♦ vi/t make (into) a loop

loop·hole /ˈluphoʊl/ n way of escape: loopholes in the tax laws

loose /lus/ adj **1** not firmly fastened: a loose tooth **2** free from control: loose cattle **3** not packed together: loose crackers **4** (of clothes) too wide **5** not exact: a loose translation **6** without sexual morals: loose living **7 cut loose** break away from a group or situation **8 hang loose** keep calm **~ly** adv

loose end /ˌ ˈ·/ n [usu. pl.] **1** part not fully completed **2 at loose ends** having nothing to do

loos·en /ˈluːsən/ *vi/t* make or become looser **loosen up** *phr v* relax

loot /luːt/ *n* [U] 1 goods taken illegally by soldiers, etc. 2 money ♦ *vi/t* take loot (from) ~**er** *n*

lop /lɒp/ *vt* -**pp**- cut (branches) from a tree

lop·sid·ed /ˌlɒpˈsaɪdɪd/ *adj* with one side lower than the other

lord /lɔːd/ *n* 1 ruler; master 2 nobleman: 3 (*cap.*) God

lose /luːz/ *v* **lost** /lɒst/ 1 *vt* be unable to find: *lose a book/one's way* 2 *vt* have taken away: *lose one's job* 3 *vi/t* fail to win: *lose a battle* 4 *vt* have less of: *lose weight/money* 5 *vi* (of a clock) go too slowly 6 *vt* (cause to) fail to hear, see, or understand: *You've lost me; could you explain that again?* 7 **lose oneself in something** give all one's attention to something so as not to notice anything else 8 **lose sight of** forget

lose out *phr vi* 1 make a loss 2 be defeated

los·er /ˈluːzə/ *n* 1 person who loses 2 *sl* person who is never successful in life, work, or relationships

loss /lɒs/ *n* 1 [U] act of losing; failure to keep 2 [C] person, thing, or amount lost: *The army suffered heavy losses.* 3 [C] failure to make a profit 4 **at a loss** uncertain what to do or say 5 **be a dead loss** *infml* have no worth or value

lost /lɒst/ *v* past t. and p. of LOSE

lost cause /ˌ· ˈ·/ *n* something which has no chance of success

lot¹ /lɒt/ *n* 1 a great number or amount: *a lot of people* | *lots (and lots) of money* 2 group or amount: *a new lot of students* 3 **a lot** much: *a lot better* 4 **a fat lot** *infml* none at all

lot² *n* 1 [C] piece of land 2 [C;U] (use of) different objects to make a decision by chance: *choose the winner by lot* 3 [S] *fml* one's fate 4 [C] thing sold at an AUCTION 5 **a bad lot** a bad person

lo·tion /ˈloʊʃən/ *n* [C;U] liquid mixture for the skin to make it clean and healthy

lot·te·ry /ˈlɒtəri/ *n* system of giving prizes to people who bought numbered tickets, chosen by chance

loud /laʊd/ *adj* 1 producing a lot of sound 2 unpleasantly colorful ♦ *adv* in a loud way ~**ly** *adv* ~**ness** *n* [U]

loud·speak·er /ˈlaʊdˌspiːkə/ *n* part of a radio or record player from which the sound comes out

lounge /laʊndʒ/ *vi* stand or sit lazily ♦ *n* comfortable room to sit in

louse /laʊs/ *n* **lice** /laɪs/ 1 insect that lives on people's and animals' bodies 2 worthless person

lou·sy /ˈlaʊzi/ *adj* 1 very bad: *lousy weather* 2 covered with lice

lov·a·ble /ˈlʌvəbəl/ *adj* deserving, causing, or worthy of love

love /lʌv/ *n* 1 [U] great fondness for someone 2 [S;U] warm interest: *a love of music* 3 [C] loved person or thing 4 [U] (in tennis) ZERO 5 **give/send someone's love** send friendly greetings 6 **make love (to)** have sex (with) 7 **not for love or/nor money** *infml* not at any price ♦ *v* 1 *vi/t* feel love (for) 2 *vt* like very much: *I'd love a drink.* **loving** *adj* fond

love af·fair /ˈ· ·ˌ·/ *n* sexual relationship: (fig.) *a love affair with Russian literature* (= a great interest and liking)

love·ly /ˈlʌvli/ *adj* 1 beautiful: *lovely girl/view* 2 very pleasant: *lovely dinner*

lov·er /ˈlʌvə/ *n* 1 person who has a sexual relationship with another person outside marriage 2 person who is fond of the stated thing: *art lovers*

love·sick /ˈlʌvˌsɪk/ *adj* sad because of unreturned love

low /loʊ/ *adj* 1 not high: *low wall/cost/standards* 2 (of a supply) nearly finished 3 (of sounds) **a** deep **b** not loud 4 unhappy 5 not fair or honest: *a low trick* 6 for a slow speed: *a low gear* ♦ *adv* to or at a low level: *bend low* ♦ *n* low point or level

low·brow /ˈloʊbraʊ/ *adj* not interested in art, books, etc.

low·down /ˈloʊdaʊn/ *n* [*the*+S] *sl* plain facts

low·down /ˌ· ˈ·/ *adj* worthless; dishonorable

low·er¹ /ˈloʊə/ *adj* at or nearer the bottom: *the lower leg*

lower² *vt* 1 make less high 2 **lower oneself** bring oneself down in people's opinion

low·er³ /ˈlaʊə/ *vi* 1 be dark and threatening 2 FROWN severely

low-key /ˌ· ˈ·/ *adj* quiet and controlled

low·ly /ˈloʊli/ *adj* low in rank; HUMBLE –**liness** *n* [U]

loy·al /ˈlɔɪəl/ adj faithful to one's friends, country, etc. ~**ist** n person who remains loyal to a ruler ~**ly** adv

loy·al·ty /ˈlɔɪəlti/ n 1 [U] being loyal 2 [C] connection that binds one to someone or something to which one is loyal

loz·enge /ˈlɒzəndʒ/ n medical sweet: cough lozenge

LP n record that plays for about 20 minutes each side

LSD n [U] illegal drug that causes hallucinations (HALLUCINATE)

lu·bri·cant /ˈluːbrəkənt/ n [C;U] substance that lubricates; oil, etc.

lu·bri·cate /ˈluːbrəˌkeɪt/ vt make (machine parts) work without rubbing

lu·cid /ˈluːsɪd/ adj 1 easy to understand 2 able to think clearly ~**ly** adv ~**ity** /luˈsɪdəti/ n [U]

luck /lʌk/ n [U] 1 what happens to someone by chance 2 success: wish them luck 3 be down on one's luck have bad luck, esp. be without money 4 be in/out of luck have/not have good fortune ~**y** adj having or bringing good luck ♦ v **luck out** phr vi have an experience of good luck ~**ily** adv

lu·cra·tive /ˈluːkrətɪv/ adj profitable

lu·di·crous /ˈluːdɪkrəs/ adj causing laughter; foolish ~**ly** adv

lug /lʌg/ vt **-gg-** pull or carry with difficulty ♦ n rough stupid person

lug·gage /ˈlʌgɪdʒ/ also **baggage** — n [U] bags, etc., of a traveler

lu·gu·bri·ous /ləˈguːbriəs/ adj fml sorrowful ~**ly** adv

luke·warm /ˌluːkˈwɔːm◄/ adj 1 (of liquid) neither warm nor cold 2 not eager

lull /lʌl/ vt cause to rest ♦ n [S] calm period

lul·la·by /ˈlʌləˌbaɪ/ n song to make a child go to sleep

lum·ber¹ /ˈlʌmbə/ v 1 vi move heavily and awkwardly 2 vt give (someone) an unwanted object or job

lumber² n 1 wood for building 2 useless articles stored away

lum·ber·jack /ˈlʌmbəˌdʒæk/ n man whose job is cutting down trees to make lumber

lu·mi·na·ry /ˈluːməˌnɛri/ n fml famous respected person

lu·mi·nous /ˈluːmənəs/ adj shining in the dark –**nosity** /ˌluːməˈnɒsəti/ n [U]

lump /lʌmp/ n 1 solid mass: lump of coal/sugar 2 hard swelling 3 **lump in the throat** tight sensation in the throat caused by unexpressed pity, sorrow, etc. ♦ v **lump it** accept bad conditions without complaint ~**y** adj: lumpy gravy

lump together phr vt consider (2 or more things) as a single unit

lump sum /ˌ· ˈ·/ n money given as a single payment rather than in parts

lu·na·cy /ˈluːnəsi/ n insanity (INSANE)

lu·nar /ˈluːnə/ adj of the moon

lu·na·tic /ˈluːnəˌtɪk/ adj, n crazy or foolish (person)

lunch /lʌntʃ/ also **lunch·eon** /ˈlʌntʃən/ fml — n [C;U] meal eaten at about noon **lunch** vi

lung /lʌŋ/ n either of the 2 breathing organs in the chest

lunge /lʌndʒ/ vi, n (make) a sudden forward movement

lurch¹ /lɜːtʃ/ vi move irregularly

lurch² n 1 lurching movement 2 **leave someone in the lurch** leave them when they are in difficulty

lure /lʊə/ n something that attracts: the lure of wealth ♦ vt attract into trouble

lu·rid /ˈlʊərɪd/ adj 1 unnaturally bright: lurid colors 2 shocking; unpleasant

lurk /lɜːk/ vi wait in hiding, esp. for a bad purpose

lus·cious /ˈlʌʃəs/ adj 1 having a ripe sweet taste 2 sexually attractive

lush¹ /lʌʃ/ adj (of plants) growing thickly

lush² n sl, esp. alcoholic (ALCOHOL)

lust /lʌst/ n [C;U] strong (sexual) desire: lust for power **lust** vi ~**ful** adj

lus·ter /ˈlʌstə/ n [S;U] 1 brightness of a polished surface 2 glory

lust·y /ˈlʌsti/ adj strong and healthy

lux·u·ri·ant /lʌgˈʒʊriənt, lʌkˈʃʊr-/ adj growing well and thickly ~**ly** adv –**ance** n [U]

lux·u·ri·ate /lʌgˈʒʊriˌeɪt, lʌkˈʃʊr-/ v **luxuriate in** phr vt enjoy oneself lazily in

lux·u·ri·ous /lʌgˈʒʊriəs, lʌkˈʃʊr-/ adj comfortable and esp. expensive

lux·u·ry /ˈlʌkʃəri, ˈlʌgʒəri/ n 1 [U] great comfort, as provided by wealth 2 [C] something pleasant, but not necessary and not often had or done

Ly·cra /ˈlaɪkrə/ n [U] tdmk stretchy cloth used esp. in sports clothes

ly·ing /ˈlaɪ-ɪŋ/ v pres. p. of LIE¹ and LIE²

lynch /lɪntʃ/ vt (esp. of a crowd) kill without a legal trial

lyr·ic /ˈlɪrɪk/ n, adj (short poem) expressing strong feelings in songlike form ~**al** adj fml full of joyful feeling **lyrics** n [P] words of a popular song

M

M, m /ɛm/ the 13th letter of the English alphabet

m *written abbrev. for:* **1** mile(s) **2** meter(s) **3** million **4** married **5** male

ma /mɑ, mɔ/ *n sl* mother

ma'am /mæm/ *n* (polite way of addressing a woman)

ma·ca·bre /məˈkɑbrə, məˈkɑb, məˈkɑbə/ *adj* causing fear, esp. because connected with death

mac·a·ro·ni /mækəˈroʊni/ *n* (U) small tube-shaped PASTA

mace /meɪs/ *n* liquid used as a defensive weapon that causes tears and discomfort

Mach /mɑk/ *n* speed of an aircraft in relation to the speed of sound: *Mach 2* (= twice the speed of sound)

ma·chet·e /məˈʃɛti, -ˈtʃɛ-/ *n* large heavy knife

ma·chine /məˈʃin/ *n* **1** instrument or apparatus that uses power to work **2** group that controls and plans activities of a political party ♦ *vt* make or produce by machine

ma·chine gun /·'· ¡·/ *n* gun that fires continuously

ma·chin·e·ry /məˈʃinəri/ *n* (U) **1** machines: *farm machinery* **2** working parts of a machine or engine **3** operation of a system or organization

ma·cho /ˈmɑtʃoʊ/ *adj often derog* (trying to seem) strong and brave

mack·e·rel /ˈmækərəl/ *n* mackerel or mackerels sea fish, often eaten

mad /mæd/ *adj* -dd- **1** angry **2** very foolish **3** ill in the mind **4** filled with strong interest: *She's mad about politics.* **5** like mad very hard, fast, loud, etc. ~ly *adv*: madly (= very much) *in love* ~ness *n* (U) ~den *vt* annoy extremely

mad·am /ˈmædəm/ *n* (often cap.) **1** (polite way of addressing a woman) **2** woman who manages a house of PROSTITUTES

made /meɪd/ *v past t. and p. of* MAKE

mael·strom /ˈmeɪlstrəm/ *n lit* **1** violent WHIRLPOOL **2** destroying force of events

maes·tro /ˈmaɪstroʊ/ *n* -tros great or famous musician

maf·i·a /ˈmɑfiə/ *n* **1** (*usu. cap.*) large US and Italian organization of criminals **2** influential group who support each other without any concern for people outside the group: *the medical mafia*

mag·a·zine /ˌmægəˈzin, ˈmægəˌzin/ *n* **1** sort of book with a paper cover, which contains writing, photographs, and advertisements, that is printed every week or month and is of interest to a particular group of people **2** part of a gun in which bullets are stored

ma·gen·ta /məˈdʒɛntə/ *adj* dark purplish red

mag·got /ˈmægət/ *n* wormlike young of flies and other insects

mag·ic /ˈmædʒɪk/ *n* **1** use of strange unseen forces, or of tricks, to produce effects **2** special wonderful quality: *the magic of the theater* — see also BLACK MAGIC ♦ *adj* caused by or used in magic: *a magic trick/ring* ~al *adj* strange and wonderful ~ally *adv*

ma·gi·cian /məˈdʒɪʃən/ *n* person who practices or entertains with magic

ma·gis·trate /ˈmædʒɪˌstreɪt, -strɪt/ *n* JUSTICE OF THE PEACE

mag·nan·i·mous /mægˈnænəməs/ *adj fml* very generous ~ly *adv* -mity /ˌmægnəˈnɪməti/ *n* (U)

mag·nate /ˈmægneɪt, -nɪt/ *n* wealthy and powerful person

mag·ne·si·um /mægˈniziəm, -ʒiəm/ *n* silver-white metal

mag·net /ˈmægnɪt/ *n* **1** piece of iron or steel that draws other metal objects towards it **2** person or thing that attracts or interests people greatly ~ism *n* (U) magnetic force ~ize *vt* ~ic /mægˈnɛtɪk/ *adj*: *a magnetic personality* ~ically *adv*

mag·nif·i·cent /mægˈnɪfəsənt/ *adj* extremely fine or good -cence *n* (U) ~ly *adv*

mag·ni·fy /ˈmægnəˌfaɪ/ *vt* cause to look or seem larger -fication /ˌmægnəfəˈkeɪʃən/ *n* (U)

magnifying glass /'···· ¡·/ *n* curved LENS (1) for magnifying things

mag·ni·tude /ˈmægnəˌtud/ *n* (U) *fml* degree of size or importance

ma·hog·a·ny /məˈhɑgəni/ *n* (U) dark reddish wood used for furniture

maid /meɪd/ *n* **1** female worker in a house or hotel **2** maiden — see also OLD MAID

maid·en /'meɪdn/ n lit young unmarried woman ♦ adj 1 first: *the ship's maiden voyage* 2 unmarried: *my maiden aunts*

maiden name /'·· ·/ n family name a woman had before marriage

maid of hon·or /ˌ· '·/ n main BRIDESMAID in a wedding

mail¹ /meɪl/ n [U] 1 the official system for carrying letters, parcels, etc. 2 letters, etc., that one sends or receives ♦ vt send through this system

mail² n [U] soldiers' protective clothing in former times, made of small metal rings

mail·box /'meɪlbɑks/ n box into which people put letters for mailing

mail·man /'meɪlmæn, -mən/ n **mailmen** /-mɛn, -mən/ man who delivers mail

mail or·der /ˌ· '··/ n [U] method of selling in which goods are sent by mail

maim /meɪm/ vt wound very seriously and usu. lastingly

main¹ /meɪn/ adj chief; most important: *its main function* ~**ly** adv: *His money comes mainly from investments.*

main² n 1 large pipe or wire supplying water, gas, or electricity 2 **in the main** mainly; mostly

main·frame /'meɪnfreɪm/ n the largest and most powerful kind of computer

main·land /'meɪnlænd, -lənd/ n a land mass, considered without its islands **mainland** adj

main·stay /'meɪnsteɪ/ n someone or something which provides the chief means of support

main·stream /'meɪnstrim/ n main or usual way of thinking or acting in relation to a subject

main·tain /meɪn'teɪn/ vt 1 keep in good condition 2 support with money 3 continue to have or do 4 continue to say, believe, or argue

main·te·nance /'meɪntˀn-əns/ n [U] keeping in good condition

ma·jes·ty /'mædʒəsti/ n 1 (cap.) (used as a title for kings and queens) 2 [U] fml grandness –**tic** /mə'dʒɛstɪk/ adj: *majestic scenery* –**tically** adv

major¹ /'meɪdʒɚ/ adj of great importance or seriousness: *a major problem* | *major surgery*

major² n 1 army officer, above CAPTAIN 2 university student in a particular field of study: *an English major* — see also SERGEANT MAJOR

major³ v **major in** phr vt study as the chief subject(s) for a college degree

ma·jor·i·ty /mə'dʒɔrəti, mə'dʒɑ-/ n 1 [(the) S] most 2 [C] difference in number between a large and small group: *win by a majority of 300 votes*

make¹ /meɪk/ vt **made** /meɪd/ 1 produce: *make a cake/a noise/a decision* | *a bag made of leather* | *wine made from local grapes* 2 cause to be: *It made me happy.* 3 force; cause: *I can't make him understand.* 4 earn (money) 5 calculate or be counted as: *That makes the fourth glass you've had!* 6 add up to: *2 and 2 make 4* 7 tidy (a bed that has been slept in) 8 have the qualities of: *That story makes good reading.* 9 reach: *We made harbor by night fall.* 10 complete: *That picture really makes the room.* 11 **make believe** pretend 12 **make do** use something for lack of any better: *We had to make do with water.* 13 **make it: a** arrive in time **b** succeed 14 **make one's way** go: *I made my way home.* 15 **make or break** which will cause success or complete failure 16 **make a play for** try to get 17 **make the most of** take advantage 18 **make time** travel quickly 19 **make tracks** leave quickly **maker** n 1 person who makes something: *a watchmaker* 2 (usu. cap.) God **making** n 1 be the **making of** cause to improve greatly 2 **have the makings of** have the possibility of developing into

make for phr vt 1 move in the direction of: *I made for the exit.* 2 result in: *Large print makes for easy reading.*

make into phr vt use in making: *He made the bottle into an interesting ornament.*

make of phr vt 1 understand by: *I don't know what to make of the situation.* 2 give (the usu. stated importance) to: *She makes too much of her problems.*

make off phr vi leave in a hurry

make off with phr vt steal

make out phr v 1 vt write (a check, etc.) in complete form 2 vt see, hear, or understand properly 3 vt claim; pretend 4 vi succeed 5 vt argue as proof: *make out a case* (= give good reasons) 6 vi kiss, etc.: *making out in the backseat of a car*

make over phr vt 1 remake 2 pass over to someone else, esp. legally

make up phr v 1 vt invent (a story, etc.), esp. to deceive 2 vi/t use special paint and powder on the face to look beautiful or change the appearance **3** *vt* prepare for use: *A pharmacist made up the doctor's prescriptions.* **4** *vt* form as a whole: *Oil makes up half of our exports.* **5** *vi* become friends again after a quarrel

make up for *phr vt* give something good to take away disappointment: *I bought him a present to make up for my bad behavior.*

make² *n* **1** type of product **2 on the make** searching for personal gain

make·be·lieve /ˈ· ·ˌ·/ *n* pretending

make·shift /ˈmeɪkˌʃɪft/ *adj* used because there is nothing better

make·up /ˈmeɪk·ʌp/ *n* [C;U] **1** colored powder, etc., worn on the face **2** combination of members or qualities

ma·laise /mæˈleɪz/ *n* [C;U] **1** failure to be active and successful **2** feeling of not being well

ma·lar·i·a /məˈlɛriə/ *n* [U] tropical disease spread by MOSQUITOes

male /meɪl/ *n, adj* (person or animal) of the sex that does not give birth

male chau·vin·ist /ˌ· ·····◂/ *n derog* man who behaves unreasonably towards women because he thinks they are less able, strong, etc., than men

ma·lev·o·lent /məˈlɛvələnt/ *adj lit* wishing to do evil to others **~ly** *adv* **–lence** *n* [U]

mal·func·tion /mælˈfʌŋkʃən/ *n* fault in operation **malfunction** *vi*

mal·ice /ˈmælɪs/ *n* [U] desire to hurt or harm **–icious** /məˈlɪʃəs/ *adj: a malicious attack* **–iciously** *adv*

ma·lign /məˈlaɪn/ *adj fml* bad; causing harm ♦ *vt* say bad things about

ma·lig·nant /məˈlɪgnənt/ *adj* **1** (of disease) likely to kill **2** *fml* malign **~ly** *adv*

mall /mɔl/ *n* also **shopping mall** — very large building with many stores inside

mal·le·a·ble /ˈmæliəbəl/ *adj* (of metal) easy to shape; soft: (fig.) *a malleable personality*

mal·let /ˈmælɪt/ *n* wooden hammer

mal·nour·ished /ˌmælˈnɔrɪʃt, -ˈnʌrɪʃt/ *adj* sick or weak because of lack of (proper) food

mal·nu·tri·tion /ˌmælnuˈtrɪʃən/ *n* [U] lack of (proper) food

mal·prac·tice /ˌmælˈpræktɪs/ *n* [C;U] failure to do one's professional duty well or honestly

malt /mɔlt/ *n* [U] partly grown grain used esp. for making beer and WHISKEY

mal·treat /mælˈtrit/ *vt fml* treat roughly and/or cruelly **~ment** *n* [U]

ma·ma /ˈmɑmə/ *n infml* mother

mam·mal /ˈmæməl/ *n* animal of the sort fed on the mother's milk when young

mam·moth /ˈmæməθ/ *adj* extremely large

man /mæn/ *n* **men** /mɛn/ **1** [C] adult male person **2** [U] the human race: *Man must change in a changing world.* **3** [C] person: *All men must die.* **4** [C] male of low rank: *officers and men* **5** [C] male member of a team **6** [C] object used in board games: *chess men* **7** *sl* term of address for a man (or woman) **8 a man of the world** man with a lot of experience **9 man and wife** *fml* married **10 one's own man** independent in action **11 the man in the street** the average person **12 to a man** every person: *They agreed, to a man.* — see also BEST MAN, FRONT MAN ♦ *vt* **-nn-** provide with people for operation **~hood** *n* [U] quality or time of being a (brave) man

man·a·cle /ˈmænəkəl/ *n* metal ring for fastening a prisoner's hands or feet

man·age /ˈmænɪdʒ/ *v* **1** *vt* be in charge of; run **2** *vi/t* succeed in doing: *I barely managed to get out of the way.* **3** *vi* succeed in living, esp. on a small amount of money: *We don't earn much, but we manage.* **~able** *adj* easy or possible to deal with **~ment** *n* [U] **1** managing **2** the people in charge **manager** *n* person who runs a business, hotel, sports team, etc. **~agerial** /ˌmænəˈdʒɪriəl◂/ *adj: managerial responsibilities*

man·date /ˈmændeɪt/ *n* government's right or duty to act according to the wishes of the electors

man·da·to·ry /ˈmændəˌtɔri, -ˌtoʊri/ *adj fml* which must be done

mane /meɪn/ *n* long hair on a horse's or lion's neck

ma·neu·ver /məˈnuvər/ *n* **1** skillful movement **2** secret trick to gain a purpose **3 on maneuvers** doing battle training ♦ *vt* move or turn, esp. skillfully or deceivingly: *The car maneuvers well in wet weather.* **–verable** *adj*

man·ger /ˈmeɪndʒər/ *n* long open container for animals' food

man·gle /ˈmæŋgəl/ *vt* crush and tear so as to ruin

man·go /ˈmæŋgoʊ/ n -goes or -gos tropical fruit with sweet yellow flesh

man·han·dle /ˈmænˌhændl/ vt hold or move forcefully or roughly

man·hole /ˈmænhoʊl/ n opening in the road leading to underground pipes, wires, etc.

ma·ni·a /ˈmeɪniə/ n [C;U] 1 madness 2 extreme interest or desire: a mania for collecting matchboxes | soccer mania **maniac** /-niæk/ n ~cal /məˈnaɪəkəl/ adj: maniacal laughter

man·i·cure /ˈmænɪˌkyʊr/ vt, n (give) treatment for the hands, esp. the nails, including cleaning, cutting, etc. –**curist** n

man·i·fest[1] /ˈmænəˌfest/ adj fml plain to see or understand; OBVIOUS ~ly adv

manifest[2] vt show plainly ~**ation** /ˌmænəfeˈsteɪʃən, -fə-/ n [C;U]

man·i·fes·to /ˌmænəˈfestoʊ/ n -tos or -toes statement of intentions or opinions, esp. as made by a political party before an election

man·i·fold /ˈmænəˌfoʊld/ adj many in number or kind

ma·nip·u·late /məˈnɪpyəˌleɪt/ vt 1 fml handle skillfully 2 control and influence for one's own purposes –**lative** /-lətɪv, -ˌleɪtɪv/ adj –**lation** /məˌnɪpyəˈleɪʃən/ n [U]

man·kind /ˌmænˈkaɪnd/ n [U] human beings

man·ly /ˈmænli/ adj having qualities (believed to be) suitable to a man –**liness** n [U]

man-made /ˌ-ˈ-◂/ adj 1 produced by people 2 (of materials) not made from natural substances

man·ner /ˈmænər/ n 1 fml way: a meal prepared in the Japanese manner 2 way of behaving towards people: a rude manner 3 all manner of fml every sort of 4 -**mannered** /-mænərd/ having the stated way of behaving: bad-mannered 5 (as) to the manner born as if one is used to (something, esp. social position) from birth **manners** n [U] (polite) social practices: It's bad manners to make a noise while you eat.

man·ner·is·m /ˈmænəˌrɪzəm/ n (bad or strange) way of behaving that has become a habit

man·or /ˈmænər/ n area of land owned by the local lord in former times

man·pow·er /ˈmænˌpaʊər/ n [U] number of workers needed

man·sion /ˈmænʃən/ n large grand house

man·slaugh·ter /ˈmænˌslɔtər/ n [U] crime of killing someone unintentionally

man·tel /ˈmæntl/ n shelf above a fireplace

mantle /ˈmæntl/ n 1 covering: a mantle of snow 2 (sign of) general or official recognition: He took over the mantle of world heavyweight champion

man·u·al[1] /ˈmænyuəl/ adj of or using the hands ~**ly** adv

manual[2] n book giving information or instructions

man·u·fac·ture /ˌmænyəˈfæktʃər/ vt make in large quantities using machinery ♦ n [U] manufacturing: goods of foreign manufacture ~**turer** n

ma·nure /məˈnʊr/ n [U] animal waste matter put on land to make crops grow ♦ vt put manure on

man·u·script /ˈmænyəˌskrɪpt/ n 1 first copy of a book, etc., written by hand or on a machine 2 old book written by hand

man·y /ˈmeni/ determiner, pron 1 a large number (of): I don't have as many as you. | many people 2 a good/great many 3 one too many infml too much (alcohol) to drink

map /mæp/ n 1 representation of (part of) the Earth's surface as if seen from above: a map of France 2 (put something) on the map (cause something to be) considered important ♦ vt -**pp**- make a map of **map out** phr vt plan carefully

mar /mar/ vt fml spoil

mar·a·thon /ˈmærəˌθɑn/ n 1 running race of about 26 miles (42 kilometers) 2 (hard) activity that lasts a long time ♦ adj lasting a long time: a marathon speech of 6 hours

ma·raud·ing /məˈrɔdɪŋ/ adj moving around looking for things or people to attack –**er** n

mar·ble /ˈmɑrbəl/ n [U] 1 hard smooth usu. white stone used for STATUES or buildings 2 small glass ball rolled against others in a game (**marbles**)

march /mɑrtʃ/ v 1 vi walk with regular forceful steps like a soldier 2 vt force to go: They marched him off to prison. ♦ n act of marching: (fig.) the march (= steady advance) of history

March n the 3rd month of the year

mare /mɛr/ n female horse

mar·ga·rine /ˈmɑrdʒərɪn/ n food substance like butter

mar·gin /ˈmɑrdʒɪn/ n **1** space down the edge of a page, with no writing or printing in it **2** amount by which one thing is greater than another: *We won by a decisive margin.* **3** area on the outside edge of a larger area: *the margin of the stream*

mar·gin·al /ˈmɑrdʒənl/ adj **1** small in importance or amount: *a marginal difference* **2** on the border ~**ly** adv

mar·i·jua·na /ˌmærəˈwɑnə/ n [U] illegal drug from a plant, smoked in cigarettes

ma·ri·na /məˈrinə/ n small harbor for pleasure boats

mar·i·nade /ˌmærəˈneɪd, ˈmærəˌneɪd/ n [C;U] mixture of oil, wine, etc., into which food is put for a time before being cooked –**nate** /ˈmærəˌneɪt/ vt keep in a marinade

ma·rine /məˈrin/ adj **1** of the ocean **2** of ships and sailing ♦ n soldier who serves in one of the main branches of the US armed forces (the **Marine Corps**)

mar·i·ner /ˈmærənə/ n sailor

mar·i·o·nette /ˌmæriəˈnɛt/ n PUPPET with strings

mar·i·tal /ˈmærətl/ adj of marriage

mar·i·time /ˈmærəˌtaɪm/ adj **1** MARINE **2** near the ocean

mark¹ /mɑrk/ n **1** something on or put onto a surface: *dirty marks on the wall* | *tire marks in the snow* **2** something that shows a quality: *They all stood as a mark of respect.* **3** a number that represents a judgment of quality: *The top mark in the test was 8 out of 10.* **4** printed or written sign: *punctuation mark* **5** particular type of machine: *the new Mark 4 gun* **6 make one's mark (on)** gain success, fame, etc., (in) **7 short of the mark** *infml* **a** slow in understanding or acting **b** not good enough **8 up to the mark: a** of an acceptable standard **b** in good health **9 wide of the mark** not correct or close to the subject

mark² /mɑrk/ vi/t **1** spoil with marks: *Hot cups have marked the table.* | *The table marks easily.* **2** vt give MARKS¹ (3) to **3** vt stay close to (an opposing player) to spoil their play **4** vt be a sign of: *A cross marks his grave.* | *The election marks a turning point in our affairs.* **5 mark time** spend time on work, etc., without making any

advance **6 (You) mark my words!** You will see later that I am right. ~**ed** adj noticeable ~**edly** /ˈmɑrkɪdli/ adv

  mark down/up phr vt lower/raise the price of

  mark out phr vt **1** also **mark off** — draw lines around (an area) **2** [(for)] show or choose as likely to become (successful) or gain (success)

mark³ n German unit of money

mark·er /ˈmɑrkə/ n **1** tool for making marks **2** object for marking a place

mar·ket¹ /ˈmɑrkɪt/ n **1** (place for) a gathering of people to buy and sell goods **2** desire to buy; demand: *There's no market for coats at this time of year.* **3** area where goods are sold: *the foreign/domestic market* **4** trade: *the coffee market* **5 in the market for** wishing to buy **6 on the market** (of goods) for sale **7 play the market** buy and sell stock to try to make a profit — see also BLACK MARKET

market² vt present and offer for sale ~**ing** n [U] skills of advertising, supplying, and selling goods ~**able** adj: (fig.) *marketable skills* ~**ability** /ˈmɑrkətəˈbɪləti/ n [U]

mar·ket·place /ˈmɑrkɪtˌpleɪs/ n **1** place where a market is held **2** activities of buying and selling

market re·search /ˌˈ·· ·ˈ·, ˌ·· ˈ·/ n [U] study of what people buy and why

mark·ing /ˈmɑrkɪŋ/ n [U] (any of a set of) colored marks on an animal's fur or feathers

marks·man /ˈmɑrksmən/, **markswoman** /ˌ·ˌwʊmən/ fem. — n -**men** /-mən/ person who can shoot well ~**ship** n [U]

mark·up /ˈmɑrk-ʌp/ n price increase by a seller

mar·ma·lade /ˈmɑrməˌleɪd/ n [U] JAM made from oranges

ma·roon¹ /məˈrun/ vt put or leave in a lonely or dangerous place, without help

maroon² adj dark red

mar·quee /mɑrˈki/ n sign above the entrance to a theater

mar·riage /ˈmærɪdʒ/ n [C;U] **1** ceremony to marry people **2** state of being husband and wife ~**able** adj suitable for marriage

mar·ried /ˈmærid/ adj **1** having a husband or wife: *They're getting married Friday.* | *He's married to a doctor.* **2** of MARRIAGE (2): *married life*

mar·row /ˈmæroʊ/ n [U] soft fatty substance inside bones

mar·ry /ˈmæri/ v **1** vi/t take (as) a husband or wife: *He never married.* | *She married a soldier.* **2** vt join in marriage: *The priest married them.* **3** vt [(off)] cause to get married: *They married their daughter (off) to a young diplomat.*

Mars /marz/ n the PLANET 4th in order from the sun

marsh /marʃ/ n [C;U] (area of) soft wet land –y adj

mar·shal¹ /ˈmarʃəl/ n **1** law official, like a SHERIFF **2** military officer of very high rank **3** organizer (ORGANIZE) of an event, such as a ceremony or race

marshal² vt -l- **1** arrange (esp. facts) in good order **2** lead (people) carefully

marsh·mal·low /ˈmarʃˌmɛloʊ, -ˌmæloʊ/ n type of soft round candy

mar·su·pi·al /marˈsupiəl/ n animal, esp. Australian, that carries its young in a pocket of skin

mar·tial /ˈmarʃəl/ adj fml of war, soldiers, etc.

martial art /ˌ·· ˈ·/ n Eastern fighting sport: *Judo is a martial art.*

martial law /ˌ·· ˈ·/ n [U] government by the army under special laws

Mar·tian /ˈmarʃən/ n, adj (creature) from MARS

mar·ti·ni /marˈtini/ n alcoholic drink of GIN and VERMOUTH

mar·tyr /ˈmartər/ n **1** someone who dies or suffers for their (religious) beliefs **2 make a martyr of oneself** give up one's own wishes to help others, or in the hope of being praised ♦ vt kill as a martyr

mar·vel /ˈmarvəl/ n wonderful thing or example: *the marvels of modern science* ♦ vi -l- fml be filled with surprise and admiration ~ous adj very pleasing or good ~lously adv

Marx·is·m /ˈmarkˌsɪzəm/ n [U] teaching of Karl Marx on which COMMUNISM is based –ist n, adj

mas·ca·ra /mæˈskærə/ n [U] dark substance for coloring the EYELASHes

mas·cot /ˈmæskat/ n object, animal, or person thought to bring good luck, used to represent a sports team

mas·cu·line /ˈmæskyəlɪn/ adj **1** (in grammar) having to do with males **2** of or like a man –linity /ˌmæskyəˈlɪnəti/ n [U]

mash /mæʃ/ vt [(UP)] crush into a soft substance ♦ n [U] boiled grains fed to horses, cows, etc.

mask /mæsk/ n covering for the face, to hide or protect it ♦ vt hide ~ed adj wearing a mask

mask·ing tape /ˈ·· ˌ·/ n [U] special type of sticky TAPE, made of brown paper

mas·o·chis·m /ˈmæsəˌkɪzəm/ n [U] **1** gaining pleasure from being hurt **2** wish to be hurt so as to gain sexual pleasure –chist n –chistic /ˌmæsəˈkɪstɪk/ adj

Ma·son /ˈmeɪsən/ n man belonging to an ancient society whose members help each other ~ic /məˈsanɪk/ adj

ma·son n person who builds things with bricks or stone

ma·son·ry /ˈmeɪsənri/ n [U] stone building blocks

mas·que·rade /ˌmæskəˈreɪd/ vi pretend: *thieves masquerading as bank employees* ♦ n **1** hiding of the truth **2** party where people wear MASKs

mass /mæs/ n **1** [C] large lump, heap, or quantity: *a mass of clouds* **2** [C] also **masses** pl. — infml lots: *masses of work to do* **3** [U] (in science) amount of matter in a body ♦ vi/t gather in large numbers or quantity –**masses** n [the+P] ordinary people in society

Mass n (in the Catholic and Orthodox churches) important religious ceremony

mas·sa·cre /ˈmæsəkər/ n killing of large numbers of people ♦ **massacre** vt

mas·sage /məˈsɑʒ, məˈsɑdʒ/ n [C;U] (act of) pressing and rubbing someone's body, esp. to cure pain or stiffness ♦ vt **1** give a massage to **2** change (facts, figures, etc.) usu. in a dishonest way

mas·seur /məˈsər, mæˈ-/ **masseuse** /mæˈsuz, mə-/ fem. — n person who gives massages

mas·sive /ˈmæsɪv/ adj extremely big ~ly adv ~ness n

mass me·di·a /ˌ· ˈ···/ n [the+S] the MEDIA

mass-pro·duce /ˌ· ·ˈ·/ vt produce (goods) in large numbers to the same pattern **mass production** n [U]

mast /mæst/ n long upright pole for carrying sails — see also HALF-MAST

mas·tec·to·my /mæˈstɛktəmi/ n operation for the removal of a breast

mas·ter¹ /ˈmæstər/ n **1 mistress** /ˈmɪstrɪs/ fem. — person in control of people, animals, or things **2** great artist, writer, etc. — see also OLD MASTER **3** captain of a ship **4** something from which copies are made: *a master tape* ~**ful** *adj* able or eager to control others ~**fully** *adv* ~**ly** *adj* showing great skill.

master² *vt* **1** learn or gain as a skill: *master the art of public speaking* **2** control and defeat: *He mastered his fear of heights.*

mas·ter·mind /ˈmæstəˌmaɪnd/ *vt* plan cleverly: *mastermind a crime* ♦ *n* very smart person

master of ce·re·mo·nies /ˌ·· ·ˈ····/ also emcee, MC — *n* person who introduces speakers or performers at a public event

mas·ter·piece /ˈmæstəˌpiːs/ *n* piece of work, esp. of art, done with extreme skill

master's de·gree /ˈ·· ·ˌ·/ *n* higher university degree

mas·ter·y /ˈmæstəri/ *n* [U] **1** power to control **2** great skill or knowledge

mas·tur·bate /ˈmæstəˌbeɪt/ *vi/t* excite the sex organs (of) by handling, rubbing, etc. **–bation** /ˌmæstəˈbeɪʃən/ *n* [U]

mat /mæt/ *n* **1** piece of strong material for covering part of a floor **2** small piece of material for putting under objects on a table

match¹ /mætʃ/ *n* **1** sports or other competition between two people or sides; game: *a tennis match* **2** one who is equal to or better than another: *I'm no match for her at math.* **3** good combination: *The hat and shoes are a perfect match.* **4** marriage: *Both her daughters made good matches.* ♦ *v* **1** *vi/t* be similar (to) or combine well (with): *The curtains and carpets don't match.* **2** *vt* be equal to or find an equal for: *a restaurant that can't be matched for service*

match² *n* short thin stick that burns when its end is rubbed against a rough surface

match·box /ˈmætʃbɒks/ *n* box for holding matches

match·mak·er /ˈmætʃˌmeɪkə/ *n* person who tries to arrange others' love affairs

mate¹ /meɪt/ *n* **1** friend, or person one works or lives with: *We're mates/school-mates/roommates.* **2** either one of a male and female pair **3** officer on a non-navy ship

mate² *vi* (esp. of animals) join sexually to produce young

mate³ *n, v* CHECKMATE

ma·te·ri·al /məˈtɪriəl/ *n* **1** [C;U] substance of which things are or can be made **2** [U] cloth **3** [U] knowledge of facts from which a (written) work may be produced: *She's collecting material for a book.* ♦ *adj* **1** of matter or substance, not spirit **2** *fml* important or necessary ~**ly** *adv*

ma·te·ri·al·is·m /məˈtɪriəˌlɪzəm/ *n* [U] (too) great interest in the pleasures of the world, money, etc. **–ist** *n* ~**istic** /məˌtɪriəˈlɪstɪk◄/ *adj*

ma·te·ri·al·ize /məˈtɪriəˌlaɪz/ *vi* **1** become able to be seen **2** become real or actual: *Her hopes never materialized.* **3** come; arrive **–ization** /məˌtɪriələˈzeɪʃən/ *n* [U]

ma·ter·nal /məˈtɜːnl/ *adj* **1** of or like a mother **2** related through the mother's part of the family: *my maternal grandmother*

ma·ter·ni·ty /məˈtɜːnəti/ *n* [U] motherhood ♦ *adj* for women who are going to give birth: *a maternity hospital/dress*

math·e·mat·ics /ˌmæθəˈmætɪks/ also **math** /mæθ/ — *n* [U] science of numbers **–ical** *adj* **–ically** *adv* **–ician** /ˌmæθəməˈtɪʃən/ *n*

mat·i·née /ˈmætˈneɪ/ *n* afternoon performance of a play, movie, etc.

ma·tri·arch /ˈmeɪtriˌɑːk/ *n* woman who controls a (family) group ~**al** /ˌmeɪtriˈɑːkəl◄/ *adj* ruled by women

ma·tric·u·late /məˈtrɪkjəleɪt/ *vi* become a member of a university **–ation** /məˌtrɪkjəˈleɪʃən/ *n* [U]

mat·ri·mo·ny /ˈmætrɪˌməʊni/ *n* [U] being married **–nial** /ˌmætrɪˈməʊniəl◄/ *adj*

ma·tron /ˈmeɪtrən/ *n* **1** woman in charge of living arrangements in a school, prison, or other institution for girls or women **2** *lit* older married woman, esp. of quiet behavior ~**ly** *adj* 1 *euph* (of a woman) fat: *a matronly figure* **2** with the DIGNITY of a MATRON (3)

matte, matt /mæt/ *adj* not shiny

mat·ted /ˈmætɪd/ *adj* twisted in a thick mass

mat·ter¹ /ˈmætə/ *n* **1** [C] subject; affair: *several important matters to discuss* **2** [*the+*S] trouble; cause of pain, illness, etc.: *Is anything the matter?* **3** [U] substance of which things are made: *all the matter in the universe* — see also GRAY MATTER **4** [U] things of a particular kind or for a particular purpose: *reading matter* (= magazines, books, etc.) **5 a matter of: a** a little more or less than: *It's only a matter of hours before the doctor arrives.* **b** needing as a part: *Learning is a matter of concentration.* **6 a matter of course** a usual event **7 as a matter of fact** in fact; really **8 for that matter** (used when mentioning another possibility) **9 no matter ... it** makes no difference: *No matter how hard I tried, I couldn't move it.* **10 That's a matter of opinion.** My opinion is different from yours.

matter² *vi* be important

matter-of-fact /ˌ…ˈ…◂/ *adj* without feelings or imagination

mat·ting /ˈmætɪŋ/ *n* [U] rough woven material, esp. for the floor

mat·tress /ˈmætrɪs/ *n* large filled cloth case for sleeping on

ma·ture /məˈtʃʊr, məˈtʊr/ *adj* **1** fully developed **2** sensible, like a mature person **3** *fml* carefully thought about ♦ *vi/t* become or make mature **–turity** *n* [U]

maud·lin /ˈmɔdlɪn/ *adj* stupidly sad, esp. when drunk

maul /mɔl/ *vt* hurt by handling roughly: *mauled by a lion*

mau·so·le·um /ˌmɔsəˈliəm, -zə-/ *n* grand building containing one or more graves

mauve /moʊv/ *adj* pale purple

mav·e·rick /ˈmævərɪk/ *n* person who acts differently from the rest of a group

mawk·ish /ˈmɔkɪʃ/ *adj* expressing love and admiration in a silly way

max·im /ˈmæksɪm/ *n* rule for sensible behavior

max·i·mize /ˈmæksəˌmaɪz/ *vt* make as big as possible

max·i·mum /ˈmæksəməm/ *n, adj* **-ma** /-mə/ or **-mums** largest (amount, number, etc.): *our maximum offer* | *He smokes a maximum of 10 cigarettes a day.* **-mal** *adj*

may /meɪ/ *v aux* **1** (shows a possibility): *He may come and he may not.* | *She may have missed the train.* (= perhaps she has missed it) **2** have permission to; be allowed to: *You may come in now.* | *May we go home, please?* **3** (used when expressing a wish): *May you live happily ever after!* **4 may as well** have no strong reason not to: *It's late, so I may as well go to bed.*

May *n* the 5th month of the year

may·be /ˈmeɪbi/ *adv* perhaps

may·hem /ˈmeɪhɛm/ *n* [U] violent disorder and confusion

may·on·naise /ˌmeɪəˈneɪz, ˈmeɪəˌneɪz/ *n* [U] thick liquid made from eggs and oil, added to food

may·or /ˈmeɪər, mɛr/ *n* person elected to be head of a city or town

maze /meɪz/ *n* arrangement of twisting paths in which one becomes lost

M.B.A. *n* Master of Business Administration; higher degree related to being in charge of a business

MC *n* MASTER OF CEREMONIES — see also EMCEE

M.D. *abbrev. for*: Doctor of Medicine

me /mi/ *pron* (object form of I)

mead·ow /ˈmɛdoʊ/ *n* field of grass

mea·ger /ˈmigər/ *adj* not big enough **~ly** *adv* **~ness** *n* [U]

meal¹ /mil/ *n* (food eaten at) an occasion for eating

meal² /mil/ *n* [U] crushed grain

mealy-mouthed /ˌmili ˈmaʊðd/ *adj* expressing (unpleasant) things too indirectly

mean¹ /min/ *vt* meant /mɛnt/ **1** (of words, signs, etc.) represent an idea: *"Melancholy" means "sad."* | *The red light means "stop."* **2** intend: *He said Tuesday, but meant Thursday.* | *I said I'd help and I meant it.* (= I am determined to do so) **3** be a sign of: *This could mean war.* **4** be of importance to the stated degree: *Her work means a lot/everything to her.* **5 be meant to** be supposed to **6 mean business** act with serious intentions **7 mean well** act with good intentions **~ing** *n* [C;U] **1** idea intended to be understood, esp. from words: *"Measure" has several meanings.* **2** importance or value: *His life lost its meaning when his wife died.* **~ing** *adj* suggesting a hidden thought: *a meaning look* **~ingful** *adj*: *a meaningful look* **~ingless** *adj*

mean² *adj* **1** unkind; nasty **2** bad-tempered **3** ungenerous **4 no mean** very good: *He's no mean cook.*

mean³ *n, adj* average

me·an·der /miˈændər/ *vi* **1** wander **2** (of a stream) flow slowly and twistingly

means /minz/ *n* **means** **1** [C] method; way **2** [P] money, esp. enough to live on **3 by all means** (a polite way of giving permission) **4 by means of** using; with **5 by no means** *fml* not at all **6 live beyond/within one's means** spend more than/not more than one can afford

meant /mɛnt/ *v past t. and p. of* MEAN¹

mean·time /'miːntaɪm/ *n* **in the meantime** MEANWHILE (1)

mean·while /'miːnwaɪl, -hwaɪl/ *adv* **1** in the time between 2 events **2** during the same period of time

mea·sles /'miːzəlz/ *n* [U] infectious disease in which the sufferer has small red spots on the skin

meas·ly /'miːzli/ *adj sl* too small

mea·sure¹ /'mɛʒə/ *vt* **1** find or show the size, amount, degree, etc., of: *Measure the (height of the) cupboard first.* | *A clock measures time.* **2** be of the stated size: *The river measured 200 yards from side to side.* **–surable** *adj* **–surably** *adv*

measure off/out *phr vt* take from a longer length or larger quantity

measure up *phr vi* show good enough qualities (for)

mea·sure² *n* **1** [U] measuring system **2** [C] unit in such a system **3** [S;U] *fml* amount: *She's had a certain measure of success.* **4** [C] act to bring about an effect: *The police were forced to take strong measures.* **5 for good measure** in addition **6 take someone's measure/get the measure of someone** judge what someone is like **–sured** *adj* careful and steady **~ment** *n* **1** [U] act of measuring **2** [C] length, height, etc., measured

meat /miːt/ *n* [U] **1** flesh of animals (not fish) for eating **2** valuable matter, ideas, etc.: *It was a clever speech, but there was no real meat to it.* **~y** *adj*

mec·ca /'mɛkə/ *n* place that many people wish to reach

me·chan·ic /mɪ'kænɪk/ *n* person skilled in using or repairing machinery

me·chan·i·cal /mɪ'kænɪkəl/ *adj* **1** of or worked on or produced by machinery **2** without new thought or strong feeling **~ly** *adv*

me·chan·ics /mɪ'kænɪks/ *n* **1** [U] science of the action of forces on objects **2** [U] science of machinery **3** [P] way in which something works

mech·a·nis·m /'mɛkənɪzəm/ *n* machine or the way it works: (fig.) *the mechanism of the brain*

mech·a·nize /'mɛkənaɪz/ *vt* (start to) use machines for or in **–ization** /ˌmɛkənə-ˈzeɪʃən/ *n* [U]

med·al /'mɛdl/ *n* usu. coinlike object given as a mark of honor, esp. for bravery **~ist** *n* person who has won a medal, esp. in sports

me·dal·lion /mə'dæljən/ *n* large medal, or piece of jewelry like a medal

med·dle /'mɛdl/ *vi* take action in a matter which does not concern one **~dler** *n*

me·di·a /'miːdiə/ *n* [U;P] television, radio, newspapers, etc. — see also MEDIUM²

me·di·ate /'miːdieɪt/ *vi* act so as to bring agreement after a quarrel **–ator** *n* **–ation** /ˌmiːdi'eɪʃən/ *n* [U]

Med·ic·aid /'mɛdɪkeɪd/ *n* [U] system by which the government helps to pay the medical costs of people on low incomes

med·i·cal /'mɛdɪkəl/ *adj* of or for the treatment of illness, esp. with medicine rather than operations ♦ *n* medical examination of the body **~ly** *adv*

Med·i·care /'mɛdɪkeər/ *n* [U] system of medical care provided by the government, esp. for old people

med·i·ca·tion /ˌmɛdɪ'keɪʃən/ *n* [C;U] medicine, esp. a drug

me·di·ci·nal /mə'dɪsənəl/ *adj* as medicine; curing **~ly** *adv*

med·i·cine /'mɛdəsən/ *n* **1** [C;U] substance for treating illness **2** [U] science of treating illness **3 a taste/dose of one's own medicine** deserved punishment

medicine man /'··· ·/ *n* (in certain tribes) man with magical powers, esp. for curing people

med·i·e·val /ˌmiːdi'iːvəl, ˌmɛ-, ˌmɪ-/ *adj* of the MIDDLE AGES

me·di·o·cre /ˌmiːdi'oʊkə/ *adj* ordinary quality **–crity** /ˌmiːdi'ɑkrəti/ *n* [U]

med·i·tate /'mɛdəteɪt/ *v* **1** *vi* make the mind quiet, esp. to gain calmness or understanding **2** *vt* plan or consider carefully **–tation** /ˌmɛdə'teɪʃən/ *n* [C;U]

me·di·um¹ /'miːdiəm/ *adj* of middle size, amount, quality, etc.

medium² *n* **-dia** /-diə/ *or* **-diums** **1** method of artistic expression or of giving information **2** condition or surroundings in which things exist **3** middle position: *a happy medium between eating all the time and not eating at all*

medium³ n -**diums** person who claims to receive messages from the spirits of the dead

med·ley /ˈmɛdli/ n mass of different types mixed together

meek /miːk/ adj gentle and uncomplaining ~**ly** adv ~**ness** n [U]

meet¹ /miːt/ v **met** /mɛt/ **1** vi/t come together (with): *I met an old friend in the street.* | *Our lips met (in a kiss).* **2** vi/t be introduced (to) **3** vt fml find or experience: *She met her death in a plane crash.* **4** vt follow (as if) in answer: *His speech was met with boos.* **5** vt satisfy: *Their offer meets all our needs.* **6** vt pay: *Have you enough money to meet your debts?* **7 meet someone halfway** make an agreement which partly satisfies both sides **8 more (in/to something) than meets the eye** hidden facts or reasons (in or for something) ~**ing** n occasion of coming together, esp. to talk

meet up phr vi infml meet, esp. by informal arrangements

meet with phr vt **1** experience: *I met with an accident.* **2** have a meeting with

meet² n gathering of people for sports events: *a track meet*

meg·a·bucks /ˈmɛɡəˌbʌks/ n infml [P] lots of money

meg·a·byte /ˈmɛɡəˌbaɪt/ n unit for measuring computer information, equal to 1,000,000 BYTES

meg·a·lo·ma·ni·a /ˌmɛɡəloʊˈmeɪniə/ [U] belief that one is more important, powerful, etc., than one really is –**niac** /-niæk/ n

meg·a·phone /ˈmɛɡəˌfoʊn/ n instrument shaped like a horn, for making the voice louder

mel·an·chol·y /ˈmɛlənˌkɑli/ adj, n [U] sad(ness) –**ic** /ˌmɛlənˈkɑlɪk◂/ adj

mel·ee /ˈmeɪleɪ, meɪˈleɪ/ n struggling or disorderly crowd

mel·low /ˈmɛloʊ/ adj **1** suggesting gentle ripeness (of color) soft and warm **3** (of people) relaxed and agreeable ♦ vi/t become or make mellow ~**ness** n [U]

mel·o·dra·mat·ic /ˌmɛlədrəˈmætɪk◂/ adj too full of excited feeling ~**ally** adv

mel·o·dy /ˈmɛlədi/ n **1** tune **2** song –**dic** /məˈlɑdɪk/ adj of or having melody –**dious** /məˈloʊdiəs/ adj tuneful

mel·on /ˈmɛlən/ n large round juicy fruit

melt /mɛlt/ v **1** vi/t become or make liquid: *The sun melted the ice.* **2** vi go away: disappear **3** vi become more sympathetic

melt down phr vt make (a metal object) liquid by heating

melt·down /ˈmɛltdaʊn/ n dangerous situation in which material burns through the bottom of an atomic RE-ACTOR

melting pot /ˈ·· ˌ·/ n place where many different CULTURES are mixed together

mem·ber /ˈmɛmbə/ n **1** someone who belongs to a club, group, etc. **2** part of the body, such as an organ or limb ~**ship** n **1** [U] state of being a member (1) **2** [C] all the members of a club, society, etc.

mem·brane /ˈmɛmbreɪn/ n [C;U] soft thin skin

me·men·to /məˈmɛntoʊ/ n -**tos** object that brings back pleasant memories

mem·o /ˈmɛmoʊ/ also **memorandum** — n -**os** note from one person or office to another within an organization

mem·oirs /ˈmɛmwɑrz/ n [P] AUTO-BIOGRAPHY

mem·o·ra·bil·i·a /ˌmɛmərəˈbɪliə, -ˈbɪl-/ n [P] interesting things connected with a famous person or event

mem·o·ra·ble /ˈmɛmrəbəl/ adj worth remembering, esp. because good –**bly** adv

mem·o·ran·dum /ˌmɛməˈrændəm/ n -**da** /-də/ fml MEMO

me·mo·ri·al /məˈmɔriəl, -ˈmoʊr-/ n something, esp. a stone MONUMENT, in memory of a person, event, etc.

Memorial Day /·ˈ·· ˌ·/ n day for remembering all those who died fighting in wars; celebrated on the last Monday in May

mem·o·rize /ˈmɛməˌraɪz/ vt learn and remember, on purpose

mem·o·ry /ˈmɛmri, -məri/ n **1** [C;U] ability to remember: *She's got a good memory.* **2** [C] example of remembering: *one of my earliest memories* **3** [U] time during which things happened which can be remembered: *within living memory* **4** [U] opinion held of someone after their death: *to praise his memory* **5** [C] part of a computer in which information is stored **6 in memory of** as a way of remembering or being reminded of

men /mɛn/ n pl. of MAN

men·ace /ˈmɛnɪs/ n 1 [C;U] threat; danger 2 [C] troublesome person or thing ♦ vt threaten

me·na·ge·rie /məˈnædʒəri, -ʒə-/ n collection of wild animals kept privately or for the public to see

mend /mɛnd/ v 1 vt repair 2 vi regain one's health 3 **mend one's ways** improve one's behavior ♦ n 1 repaired place 2 **on the mend** regaining one's health ~**er** n

me·ni·al /ˈminiəl, ˈminyəl/ adj (of a job) humble and not interesting or important ♦ n someone who does menial work

men·in·gi·tis /ˌmɛnənˈdʒaɪtɪs/ n [U] serious brain illness

men·o·pause /ˈmɛnəˌpɔz/ n [S] time of life when a woman's PERIOD¹ (3) stops

men·stru·al /ˈmɛnstruəl, -strəl/ adj of a woman's PERIOD

men·stru·ate /ˈmɛnstruˌeɪt/ vi have a PERIOD –**ation** /ˌmɛnstruˈeɪʃən/ n [U]

men·tal /ˈmɛntəl/ adj 1 of or in the mind: mental illness | a mental picture 2 of or for illness of the mind: a mental hospital 3 infml crazy ~**ly** adv

men·tal·i·ty /mɛnˈtæləti/ n 1 [U] abilities and powers of the mind 2 [C] person's character and way of thought

men·thol /ˈmɛnθɔl, -θɑl, -θoʊl/ n [U] substance which smells and tastes of MINT¹ ~**ated** /-θəˌleɪtɪd/ adj

men·tion /ˈmɛnʃən/ vt 1 tell of or about, esp. in a few words 2 **Don't mention it.** (polite reply to thanks) 3 **not to mention** and in addition there's . . . ♦ n 1 short remark about 2 naming of someone, esp. to honor them

men·tor /ˈmɛntɔr, -tɚ/ n person who habitually advises another

men·u /ˈmɛnyu/ n 1 list of food one can order in a restaurant 2 list of programs on computer SOFTWARE

meow /miˈaʊ/ vi, n (make) the crying sound a cat makes

mer·ce·na·ry /ˈmɚsəˌnɛri/ adj influenced by the wish for money ♦ n soldier who fights for whoever will pay him

mer·chan·dise /ˈmɚtʃənˌdaɪz, -ˌdaɪs/ n [U] things for sale

mer·chant /ˈmɚtʃənt/ n person who buys and sells goods in large amounts ♦ adj used in trade, not war: the merchant navy

mer·cu·ry /ˈmɚkyəri/ n [U] 1 silvery liquid metal 2 (cap.) the PLANET nearest the sun –**rial** /mɚˈkyʊriəl/ adj quick, active, and often changing

mer·cy /ˈmɚsi/ n [U] 1 willingness to forgive, not to punish; kindness and pity 2 fortunate event 3 **at the mercy of** defenseless against **merciful** adj **merciless** adj

mere /mɪr/ adj only; nothing more than: a mere child ~**ly** adv only

merge /mɚdʒ/ v 1 vi combine, esp. gradually, so as to become a single thing 2 vi/t join together: The two companies merged. **merger** n joining together of 2 or more companies

me·rid·i·an /məˈrɪdiən/ n 1 imaginary line over the Earth's surface from the top to the bottom, used on maps 2 highest point, esp. of a star

me·ringue /məˈræŋ/ n [C;U] a mixture of sugar and the white part of eggs which is cooked for a short time

mer·it /ˈmɛrɪt/ n [C;U] good quality ♦ vt fml deserve

mer·maid /ˈmɚmeɪd/ n (in stories) woman with a fish's tail

mer·ry /ˈmɛri/ adj full of or causing laughter and fun –**rily** adv –**riment** n [U]

merry-go-round /ˈ·· · ·ˌ·/ n machine with large model animals on which children ride around and around

mesh¹ /mɛʃ/ n [C;U] 1 net, esp. with small holes 2 threads in such a net

mesh² vi (of the teeth of GEARS) to connect: (fig.) Their characters just don't mesh. (= fit together suitably)

mes·mer·ize /ˈmɛzməˌraɪz/ vt hold the complete attention of, as if by a strong force

mess¹ /mɛs/ n 1 [S;U] (state of) untidiness or dirt 2 [S] bad situation; trouble 3 [C] room where soldiers, etc., eat 4 **make a mess of** ruin; spoil ~**y** adj

mess² v

   mess around phr v 1 vi act or speak stupidly 2 vi spend time with no particular plan or purpose 3 **mess around with** euph have sexual relations with

   mess up phr vt ruin; spoil

mes·sage /ˈmɛsɪdʒ/ n 1 piece of information passed from one person to another 2 main moral idea of a story, picture, etc. 3 **get the message** understand what is meant

mes·sen·ger /ˈmɛsəndʒə/ n person who brings a message

mes·si·ah /məˈsaɪə/ n **1** new leader in a religion **2** (*cap.*) Jesus Christ

met /mɛt/ v past t. and p. of MEET¹

me·tab·o·lis·m /məˈtæbəˌlɪzəm/ n process by which a body lives, esp. by changing food into ENERGY —**lic** /ˌmɛtəˈbɑlɪk/ adj

met·al /ˈmɛtl/ n [C;U] usu. solid shiny material, such as iron, copper, or silver ~**lic** /məˈtælɪk/ adj

met·al·lur·gy /ˈmɛtlˌədʒi/ n [U] scientific study of metals —**gist** n —**gical** /ˌmɛtlˈədʒɪkəl/ adj

met·a·mor·pho·sis /ˌmɛtəˈmɔrfəsɪs/ n -**ses** /-sɪz/ complete change from one form to another

met·a·phor /ˈmɛtəˌfɔr/ n [C;U] (use of) a phrase which describes one thing by stating another thing with which it can be compared (as in *the roses in her cheeks*) — see also MIXED METAPHOR ~**ical** /ˌmɛtəˈfɔrkəl, -ˈfɑr-/ adj ~**ically** adv

met·a·phys·i·cal /ˌmɛtəˈfɪzɪkəl/ adj **1** concerned with the science of being and knowing **2** (of ideas) at a high level and difficult to understand

mete /mit/ v

mete out phr vt fml or lit give (esp. punishment)

me·te·or /ˈmitiə/ n small piece of matter that flies through space and can be seen burning if it comes near the Earth ~**ic** /ˌmitiˈɔrɪk/, -ˈɑrɪk/ adj very fast: *a meteoric rise to fame* ~**ically** adv

me·te·or·ite /ˈmitiəˌraɪt/ n meteor that lands on the Earth

me·te·o·rol·o·gy /ˌmitiəˈrɑlədʒi/ n [U] scientific study of weather —**gist** n —**gical** /ˌmitiərəˈlɑdʒɪkəl/ adj

me·ter¹ /ˈmitə/ n machine that measures something: *a gas meter*

meter² n **1** a measure of length equal to 39.37 inches

meter³ n [C;U] arrangement of beats in poetry

me·thane /ˈmɛθeɪn/ n [U] gas that burns easily

meth·od /ˈmɛθəd/ n **1** [C] way of doing something **2** [U] proper planning and arrangement **3 method to one's madness** good reason for doing something that appears strange ~**ical** /məˈθɑdɪkəl/ adj careful; using an ordered system ~**ically** adv

meth·od·ol·o·gy /ˌmɛθəˈdɑlədʒi/ n set of methods

me·tic·u·lous /məˈtɪkyələs/ adj very careful, with great attention to detail ~**ly** adv

met·ric /ˈmɛtrɪk/ adj using a measured system (**metric system**) based on the meter and kilogram

met·ro /ˈmɛtroʊ/ adj related to a large city: *the metro area*

me·trop·o·lis /məˈtrɑpəlɪs/ n main or capital city —**litan** /ˌmɛtrəˈpɑlətˈn/ adj

met·tle /ˈmɛtl/ n fml will to continue bravely in spite of difficulties

mez·za·nine /ˈmɛzəˌnin/ n **1** floor that comes between 2 other floors of a building **2** lowest BALCONY in a theater

mg written abbrev. for: MILLIGRAM(s)

mice /maɪs/ pl. of MOUSE

mi·crobe /ˈmaɪkroʊb/ n bacterium

mi·cro·bi·ol·o·gy /ˌmaɪkroʊbaɪˈɑlədʒi/ n [U] scientific study of very small living creatures —**gist** n

mi·cro·chip /ˈmaɪkroʊˌtʃɪp/ n CHIP¹ (4)

mi·cro·cosm /ˈmaɪkrəˌkɑzəm/ n something small that represents all the qualities, activities, etc., of something larger

mi·cro·film /ˈmaɪkroʊˌfɪlm/ n [C;U] film for photographing something in a very small size ♦ vt photograph on microfilm

mi·cro·or·gan·is·m /ˌmaɪkroʊˈɔrgəˌnɪzəm/ n bacterium

mi·cro·phone /ˈmaɪkrəˌfoʊn/ n electrical instrument for collecting sound, so as to make it louder or broadcast it

mi·cro·pro·ces·sor /ˌmaɪkroʊˈprɑsɛsə/ n central controlling CHIP¹ (4) in a small computer

mi·cro·scope /ˈmaɪkrəˌskoʊp/ n scientific instrument that makes things look larger, used for studying extremely small things —**scopic** /ˌmaɪkrəˈskɑpɪk/ adj **1** very small **2** using a microscope —**scopically** adv

mi·cro·wave /ˈmaɪkrəˌweɪv/ also **microwave oven** — n box that cooks food using very short electric waves **microwave** vt cook (food) in a microwave

mid·air /ˌmɪdˈɛr/ n [U] point up in the sky

mid·dle /ˈmɪdl/ adj, n [S;U] (in or at) the center or a point half of the distance between 2 ends

middle age /ˌ· ·ˈ·◁/ n [U] period between youth and old age **middle-aged** adj

Middle Ag·es /ˌ· ·ˈ·/ n [the+P] period between about A.D. 1100 and 1500 in Europe

middle class /ˌ· ·ˈ·◁/ n social class of business and professional people, office workers, etc. **middle-class** adj

Middle East /ˌ· ·ˈ·+S/ countries in Asia west of India ~**ern** adj

mid·dle·man /ˈmɪdlˌmæn/ n -**men** /-mɛn/ someone who buys from a producer and sells to a customer

middle name /ˌ· ·ˈ·/ n 1 name coming between the FIRST NAME and the LAST NAME 2 infml something for which a person is well known: Generosity's my middle name.

middle-of-the-road /ˌ· · · ˈ·◁/ adj favoring a course of action that most people would agree with

middle school /ˈ·· ·/ n school for children 11–14 years old

midge /mɪdʒ/ n small winged insect that bites

midg·et /ˈmɪdʒɪt/ adj, n very small (person)

mid-life cri·sis /ˌ· · ˈ··/ n continuing feeling of unhappiness, lack of confidence, etc., suffered by someone in the middle years of life

mid·night /ˈmɪdnaɪt/ n [U] 12 o'clock at night

midst /mɪdst/ n **in the midst of** in the middle of; among

mid·term /ˈmɪdtɜrm/ n examination taken in the middle of a SEMESTER ♦ adj

mid·way /ˌmɪdˈweɪ◁/ adj, adv (at a point) half the distance between 2 ends or places

Mid·west /ˌmɪdˈwɛst/ n [the+S] part of the US east and west of the Mississippi River

mid·wife /ˈmɪdwaɪf/ n -**wives** /-waɪvz/ nurse who helps women giving birth ~**wifery** /ˈmɪdˌwaɪfəri/ n [U]

miffed /mɪft/ adj infml slightly angry

might[1] /maɪt/ v aux 1 (used for expressing slight possibility): He might come, but it's unlikely. 2 past t. of MAY: I thought it might rain. 3 ought; should: You might have offered to help! 4 **might as well** have no strong reason not to 5 **might well** be likely to

might[2] n [U] power; strength ~**y** adj very great: a mighty blow

mi·graine /ˈmaɪɡreɪn/ n [C;U] very severe headache

mi·grant /ˈmaɪɡrənt/ n migrating person or bird: migrant workers

mi·grate /ˈmaɪɡreɪt/ vi 1 (of birds or fish) travel regularly from one part of the world to another, according to the season 2 move from one place to another, esp. for a limited period –**gration** /maɪˈɡreɪʃən/ n [C;U] –**gratory** /ˈmaɪɡrəˌtɔri, -ˌtoʊri/ adj

mike /maɪk/ n sl for MICROPHONE

mild /maɪld/ adj not strong, forceful, or severe; gentle ~**ly** adv ~**ness** n [U]

mil·dew /ˈmɪldu/ n [U] gray or whitish growth on plants and on things kept a long time in slightly wet conditions ~**ed** adj

mile /maɪl/ n a measure of length equal to 1.609 kilometres or 5280 feet

mile·age /ˈmaɪlɪdʒ/ n [C;U] 1 distance traveled, measured in miles 2 fixed amount of money paid for each mile traveled 3 amount of use: The newspapers are getting a lot of mileage out of the inauguration.

mile·stone /ˈmaɪlstoʊn/ n 1 stone beside the road, saying how far to the next town 2 important event

mi·lieu /mɪlˈyu, -ˈyɜ, mil-/ n -s or -x (same pronunciation) [usu. sing] person's social surroundings

mil·i·tant /ˈmɪlətənt/ n, adj (person) taking a strong active part in a struggle ~**ly** adv –**tancy** n [U]

mil·i·ta·ris·m /ˈmɪlətəˌrɪzəm/ n [U] derog belief in the use of armed force –**rist** n –**ristic** /ˌmɪlətəˈrɪstɪk◁/ adj

mil·i·ta·ry /ˈmɪləˌtɛri/ adj of, for, or by soldiers, armies, or war ♦ n [the+P] the army

mil·i·tate /ˈmɪləˌteɪt/ v **militate against** phr v act, serve, or have importance as a reason against

mi·li·tia /məˈlɪʃə/ n force trained to be soldiers in time of special need

milk /mɪlk/ n [U] 1 white liquid produced by human or animal females to feed their young 2 white liquid produced by certain plants: coconut milk ♦ v 1 vt take milk from (a cow, etc.) 2 vi (of a cow, etc.) give milk 3 vt get money, knowledge of a secret, etc., from (someone or something) by clever or dishonest means 4 vt get poison from (a snake) ~**y** adj

milk·shake /'mɪlk‚ʃeɪk/ n drink of milk and ice cream with an added taste of fruit, chocolate, etc.

mill[1] /mɪl/ n **1** (building containing) a machine for crushing grain to flour **2** factory: *a cotton mill* **3** small machine for crushing: *a coffee mill* **4** put someone through/go through the mill (cause someone to) pass through (a time of) hard training, hard experience, etc. ♦ vt crush or produce in a mill ~er person who owns or works a flour mill

mill[2] v mill around phr vi move purposelessly in large numbers

mill[3] n 1/10 of a CENT (1/1000 of a dollar), used to fix levels of tax

mil·len·ni·um /mɪ'lenɪəm/ n -nia /-nɪə/ **1** [C] 1,000 years **2** the millennium future age in which everyone will be happy

mil·li·gram /'mɪləɡræm/ n a measure of weight equal to 0.001 GRAMS

mil·li·me·ter /'mɪləˌmitə/ n a measure of length equal to 0.001 METERS (2)

mil·lion /'mɪlyən/ determiner, n, pron **million** *or* **millions 1** 1,000,000 **2** also **millions of** — very large number ~th det, n, pron, adv

mil·lion·aire /ˌmɪlyə'nɛr/ — **millionairess** /-rɪs/ fem. — n person who has a million or more dollars; very wealthy person

mime /maɪm/ n [C;U] use of actions without language to show meaning, esp. as a performance ♦ n actor who does this ♦ vi/t act in mime

mim·ic /'mɪmɪk/ vt -ck- **1** copy (someone or something) amusingly **2** appear very like (something else) ♦ n person who mimics others ♦ adj not real

mince /mɪns/ vi/t **1** vt cut into very small pieces **2** not to mince one's words speak of something sad or bad using plain direct language

mince·meat /'mɪnsmit/ n [U] **1** mixture of dried fruit used as a filling for pastry **2** make mincemeat of defeat or destroy (a person, belief, etc.) completely

mind[1] /maɪnd/ n **1** [C;U] person's (way of) thinking or feeling; thoughts: *She has a very quick mind.* **2** [U] memory: *I'll bear/keep it in mind.* (= not forget it) | *I can't call it to mind.* (= remember it) **3** [C] attention: *Keep your mind on your work.* | *You need something to take your mind off the problem.* **4** [C;U] intention: *Nothing was further from my mind.* | *I've*

got a good mind to (= I think I may) *report you.* **5** [C;U] opinion: *We are of one/of the same mind on this matter.* | **To my mind** (= in my opinion) *you're quite wrong.* **6** [C] person considered for his/her ability to think well: *She's one of the finest minds in the country.* **7** be in two minds (about something) be unable to reach a decision **8** change one's mind change one's intentions or opinions **9** have half a mind have a desire or intention that is not firmly formed **10** in one's right mind not crazy **11** know one's own mind know what one wants **12** make up one's mind reach a decision **13** mind over matter control over events or material objects by the power of the mind **14** on one's mind causing anxiety **15** out of one's mind crazy **16** speak one's mind express plainly one's thoughts and opinions ~ful adj giving attention ~less adj not needing or using thought; stupid ~lessly adv ~lessness n [U]

mind[2] v **1** vi/t be opposed to (a particular thing): *"Coffee or tea?" "I don't mind."* (= I'd like either) | *Would you mind opening* (= please open) *the window?* **2** vi/t be careful (of): *Mind your manners!* **3** vt take care of; look after **4** Do you mind! I am offended and annoyed. **5** mind one's own business not INTERFERE **6** mind you also mind — take this into account also **7** never mind: a don't worry b it doesn't matter **8** never you mind it is not your business

mind-bog·gling /'·ˌ‚·/ adj sl very surprising

mind's eye /ˌ· '·/ n [U] imagination; memory

mine[1] /maɪn/ pron of me; my one(s): *This pen's mine, not yours.*

mine[2] n **1** place where coal or metal are dug from the ground: *a goldmine* | (fig.) *He's a mine of information.* (= can tell you a lot) **2** sort of bomb placed just under the ground or in the sea ♦ v **1** vi/t dig or get from a MINE[2] (2) **2** vt put MINES[2] (2) in or under **3** vt destroy by MINES[2] (2) **miner** n worker in a MINE[2] (1)

mine·field /'maɪnfild/ n **1** place where MINES[2] (2) have been put **2** something full of hidden dangers

min·e·ral /'mɪnərəl/ n substance formed naturally in the earth, such as stone, metal, coal, salt, or oil

min·e·ral·o·gy /ˌmɪnəˈrælədʒi, -ˈræ-/ n [U] scientific study of minerals –**gist** n

mineral wa·ter /ˈ··· ˌ·-/ n [U] water from a spring, containing minerals

min·gle /ˈmɪŋgəl/ 1 vi/t mix so as to form an undivided whole 2 vi infml talk to different people at a party

min·i /ˈmɪni/ n anything that is smaller than other things of the same kind: a miniskirt

min·i·a·ture /ˈmɪniətʃə, ˈmɪnɪtʃə, -ˌtʃʊr/ adj, n very small (thing, esp. a copy of a bigger one) –**turize** vt

min·i·mal /ˈmɪnɪməl/ adj as little as possible ~**ly** adv

min·i·mize /ˈmɪnəˌmaɪz/ vt 1 reduce as much as possible 2 treat as if not serious

min·i·mum /ˈmɪnəməm/ n, adj smallest (amount, number, etc.)

minimum wage /ˌ··· ˈ·/ n [C;U] lowest amount of money that can legally be paid per hour to workers

min·ing /ˈmaɪnɪŋ/ n [U] digging minerals out of the earth

min·is·cule /ˈmɪnəsˌkjul/ adj extremely small

min·is·ter¹ /ˈmɪnɪstə/ n 1 Christian priest 2 politician in charge of a foreign government department: the Minister of Defense ~**ial** /ˌmɪnɪˈstɪriəl◄/ adj

minister² v minister to phr vt fml help: ministering to the sick

min·is·try /ˈmɪnɪstri/ n 1 [The+S] job of being a priest: to enter the ministry (= become a priest) 2 [C] foreign government department

min·i·van /ˈmɪniˌvæn/ n large vehicle with seats for 6–7 people

mink /mɪŋk/ n mink [C;U] (valuable brown fur of) a small fierce animal

mi·nor¹ /ˈmaɪnə/ adj of small importance or seriousness: a minor problem | minor surgery

minor² n law person too young to be held responsible

mi·nor·i·ty /məˈnɔrəti/ n 1 [C] less than half: A minority of people favor it. 2 [C] small part of a population different from the rest: minority rights | minority interest (= supported by a small number of people) 3 [U] law state or time of being a minor

mint¹ /mɪnt/ n 1 [C] PEPPERMINT 2 [U] plant with leaves that smell fresh, used in food ~**y** adj

mint² n 1 place where coins are made 2 **make a mint** earn a lot of money ♦ vt make (a coin) ♦ adj (of a stamp, coin, etc.) unused and in perfect condition

mi·nus /ˈmaɪnəs/ prep 1 made less by: 10 minus 4 is 6. 2 below freezing point: It was minus 10 today. (= –10°) 3 infml without ♦ n also **minus sign** /ˈ·· ˌ·/ — a sign (–) showing a number less than zero, or that one number is to be taken away from another ♦ adj less than zero

min·us·cule /ˈmɪnəˌskjul/ adj extremely small

min·ute¹ /ˈmɪnɪt/ n 1 60th part of an hour 2 short time: Wait a minute! 3 60th part of a degree of angle 4 short note of an official matter, such as on a report — see also MINUTES 5 **the minute (that)** as soon as

mi·nute² /maɪˈnut/ adj very small ~**ness** [U]

min·utes /ˈmɪnɪts/ n [(the)P] written record of a meeting

mir·a·cle /ˈmɪrəkəl/ n 1 unexplainable but wonderful act or event, esp. as done by a holy person: (fig.) It's a miracle the explosion didn't kill her. 2 wonderful example (of a quality, ability, etc.): a miracle of modern science –**culous** /mɪˈrækyələs/ adj

mi·rage /mɪˈrɑʒ/ n something seen that is not really there, esp. as caused by the hot desert air

mire /maɪə/ n [U] esp. lit deep mud

mir·ror /ˈmɪrə/ n piece of glass in which one can see oneself ♦ vt show truly (as if) in a mirror

mirror im·age /ˈ·· ˌ·/ n image in which the right side appears on the left, and the left side on the right

mis·an·throp·ic /ˌmɪsənˈθrɑpɪk/ adj disliking everyone ~**ally** adv –**ist** /mɪsˈænθrəpɪst/ n

mis·be·have /ˌmɪsbɪˈheɪv/ vi/t behave (oneself) badly

misc. written abbrev. for: MISCELLANEOUS

mis·cal·cu·late /ˌmɪsˈkælkyəˌleɪt/ vi/t calculate wrongly; form a wrong judgment of something –**lation** /ˌmɪsˌkælkyəˈleɪʃən/ n

mis·car·riage /ˈmɪsˌkærɪdʒ, ˌmɪsˈkærɪdʒ/ n giving birth to a child too early for it to live

miscarriage of jus·tice /ˌ·ˌ·· ˈ·ˌ, ˌ··· ˈ·ˌ/ n unfair legal decision

mis·car·ry /ˌmɪsˈkæri/ vi 1 have a miscarriage 2 fml (of a plan) go wrong

mis·cel·la·ne·ous /ˌmɪsəˈleɪniəs◄/ adj of many different kinds

mis·chief /ˈmɪstʃɪf/ n 1 slightly bad behavior, esp. by children 2 damage; harm

mis·chie·vous /ˈmɪstʃəvəs/ adj 1 playfully troublesome 2 causing harm, esp. intentionally ~ly adv

mis·con·cep·tion /ˌmɪskənˈsɛpʃən/ n case of wrong understanding

mis·con·duct /ˌmɪsˈkɑndʌkt/ n [U] fml bad behavior, esp. sexual

mis·deed /ˈmɪsˈdiːd/ n fml wrong act

mis·de·mea·nor /ˌmɪsdɪˈminə/ n crime or wrong act which is not very serious

mi·ser /ˈmaɪzə/ n person who loves money and hates spending it ~**liness** [U] ~**ly** adj

mis·er·a·ble /ˈmɪzərəbəl/ adj 1 very unhappy 2 causing lack of cheerfulness: *miserable weather* 3 very low in quality or very small in amount: *a few miserable pennies* –**bly** adv

mis·er·y /ˈmɪzəri/ n [C;U] great unhappiness or suffering

mis·fit /ˈmɪsˌfɪt/ n someone who cannot live or work happily in their surroundings

mis·for·tune /mɪsˈfɔrtʃən/ n [C;U] 1 bad luck, esp. of a serious nature 2 very unfortunate event, condition, etc.

mis·giv·ing /mɪsˈɡɪvɪŋ/ n [C;U] feeling that it might be better not to do a thing

mis·guid·ed /mɪsˈɡaɪdɪd/ adj showing bad judgment; foolish ~**ly** adv

mis·hap /ˈmɪs-hæp/ n slight unfortunate happening

mis·judge /ˌmɪsˈdʒʌdʒ/ vt judge wrongly, esp. form a wrong or unfairly bad opinion –**judgment** n [C;U]

mis·lay /mɪsˈleɪ/ vt -**laid** /-ˈleɪd/ misplace (2)

mis·lead /mɪsˈlid/ vt -**led** /-ˈlɛd/ cause to think or act mistakenly

mis·man·age /ˌmɪsˈmænɪdʒ/ vt control or deal with (private, public or business affairs) badly –**ment** n [U]

mis·no·mer /ˌmɪsˈnoʊmə/ n unsuitable name

mi·so·gy·nist /mɪˈsɑdʒənɪst/ n person who hates women

mis·place /ˌmɪsˈpleɪs/ vt 1 put in the wrong place: (fig.) *misplaced trust* 2 lose for a short time

mis·print /ˈmɪsˌprɪnt/ n mistake in printing

mis·rep·re·sent /ˌmɪsrɛprɪˈzɛnt/ vt give an intentionally untrue account or explanation of ~**ation** /ˌmɪsrɛprɪzenˈteɪʃən/ n [C;U]

miss[1] /mɪs/ v 1 vi/t fail to hit, catch, meet, see, hear, etc.: *He shot at me, but missed.* | *I missed the train.* | *She narrowly missed being killed.* 2 vt feel unhappy at the absence or loss of ♦ n failure to hit, etc. — see also NEAR MISS ~**ing** adj not in the proper place; lost

miss out phr vi lose a chance to gain advantage or enjoyment

miss[2] n (usu. cap.) (title of a girl or unmarried woman) *Miss Brown*

mis·sile /ˈmɪsəl/ n 1 explosive flying weapon 2 object or weapon thrown: *They threw bottles and other missiles at the police.*

mis·sion /ˈmɪʃən/ n 1 special job, duty, or purpose: *He felt his mission in life was to help others.* | *They were sent on a secret mission.* 2 group of people sent abroad: *a peace mission* 3 place where missionaries work

mis·sion·a·ry /ˈmɪʃəˌnɛri/ n person sent abroad to teach and spread religion

mis·spell /ˌmɪsˈspɛl/ vt spell wrongly

mist /mɪst/ n [C;U] thin FOG: (fig.) *lost in the mists of time* ~**y**: (fig.) *misty memories*

mis·take /mɪˈsteɪk/ vt -**took** /mɪˈstʊk/, -**taken** /mɪˈsteɪkən/ 1 have a wrong idea about: *He mistook my meaning.* 2 fail to recognize ♦ n [C;U] something done through carelessness, lack of knowledge or skill, etc.: *I made a terrible mistake.* | *I did it by mistake.*

mistake for phr vt think wrongly that (a person or thing) is (someone or something else): *I mistook him for his brother.*

mis·tak·en /mɪˈsteɪkən/ adj wrong; incorrect ~**ly** adv

mis·tle·toe /ˈmɪsəlˌtoʊ/ n [U] plant with white berries, used for Christmas decorations

mis·took /mɪˈstʊk/ past t. of MISTAKE

mis·tress /ˈmɪstrɪs/ n 1 woman in control 2 man's unmarried female sexual partner

mis·trust /mɪsˈtrʌst/ vt not trust ♦ n [U] lack of trust ~**ful** adj

mis·un·der·stand /ˌmɪsʌndəˈstænd/ vi/t -stood /-ˈstʊd/ understand wrongly ~ing n [C;U] lack of correct understanding, esp. with slight disagreement

mit·i·gate /ˈmɪtəˌgeɪt/ vt fml lessen the severity of –gation /ˌmɪtəˈgeɪʃən/ n [U]

mitt /mɪt/ n type of protective mitten

mit·ten /ˈmɪtˈn/ n GLOVE without separate finger parts

mix /mɪks/ v 1 vi/t combine so that the parts no longer have a separate shape, appearance, etc.: Oil and water don't mix. | Mix blue and yellow to make green. | She mixed herself a cocktail. 2 vi be or enjoy being in the company of others ~ed adj 1 of different kinds 2 for both sexes 3 mixed up in connected with (something bad) ~er n ♦ n [C;U] MIXTURE (1): cake mix

mixed bag /ˌ· ˈ·/ n [S] collection of things of many different kinds (and qualities)

mixed bles·sing /ˌ· ˈ··/ n [S] something that is bad as well as good

mixed met·a·phor /ˌ· ˈ···/ n use of 2 METAPHORS together with a foolish or funny effect

mix·ture /ˈmɪkstʃə/ n 1 [C;U] set of substances (to be) mixed together 2 [S] combination: a mixture of amusement and disbelief 3 [U] act of mixing

mix-up /ˈ· ·/ n state of disorder and confusion

mm written abbrev. for: MILLIMETERS

MO 1 medical officer 2 MODUS OPERANDI

moan /moʊn/ vi, n (make a) a low sound of pain b discontented complaint

moat /moʊt/ n long deep hole around esp. a castle usu. filled with water

mob /mɑb/ n 1 noisy (violent) crowd 2 group of criminals ♦ vt -bb- gather around a to attack b because of interest or admiration

mo·bile /ˈmoʊbəl/ adj (easily) movable; not fixed –bility /moʊˈbɪləti/ n [U]

mobile home /ˌ· ˈ·/ n long, narrow house on wheels

mo·bi·lize /ˈmoʊbəˌlaɪz/ vt bring into action, esp. ready for war –ization /ˌmoʊbələˈzeɪʃən/ n [U]

moc·ca·sin /ˈmɑkəsən/ n simple soft leather shoe

mock¹ /mɑk/ vt laugh at unkindly or unfairly

mock² adj not real; pretended: a mock battle

mock·e·ry /ˈmɑkəri/ n 1 [U] mocking 2 [S] something unworthy of respect 3 make a mockery of show to be foolish or untrue

mock·ing·bird /ˈmɑkɪŋˌbəd/ n bird that copies the songs of other birds

mo·dal verb /ˌmoʊdl ˈvəb/ n verb that goes in front of another, such as can, may or would

mode /moʊd/ n way of doing something

mod·el /ˈmɑdl/ n 1 small copy: a model airplane 2 person who models clothes 3 person to be painted or photographed 4 person or thing of the highest quality: a model student 5 type of vehicle, machine, weapon, etc.: His car is the latest model. ♦ v -l- 1 vt make a small copy 2 vi/t wear (clothes) to show them to possible buyers

  model after phr vt form as a copy of: She modeled herself after her mother.

mo·dem /ˈmoʊdɛm/ n electronic apparatus for changing information from a form which a computer understands into a form which can be sent along a telephone line, etc., to another computer

mod·e·rate¹ /ˈmɑdərɪt/ adj 1 neither too much nor too little; middle 2 not politically extreme ~ly adv not very –ration /ˌmɑdəˈreɪʃən/ n [U] 1 self-control 2 reduction in force or degree 3 in moderation within sensible limits

mod·e·rate² /ˈmɑdəˌreɪt/ vi/t lessen in force, degree, etc.

mod·e·rate³ /ˈmɑdərɪt/ n person whose opinions are MODERATE¹(2)

mod·ern /ˈmɑdən/ adj 1 of the present time 2 new and different from the past ~ize v 1 vt make suitable for modern use 2 vi start using more modern methods ~ization /ˌmɑdənəˈzeɪʃən/ n [C;U]

mod·est /ˈmɑdɪst/ adj 1 not too proud 2 not large 3 not sexually improper ~ly adv ~y n [U]

mod·i·cum /ˈmɑdɪkəm/ n small amount

mod·i·fy /ˈmɑdəˌfaɪ/ vt 1 change, esp. slightly 2 make (a claim, condition, etc.) less hard to accept or bear 3 (esp. of an adjective or adverb) go with and describe (another word) –fication /ˌmɑdəfəˈkeɪʃən/ n [C;U]

mod·u·late /ˈmɑdʒəˌleɪt/ vt vary the strength, nature, etc., of (a sound) –lation /ˌmɑdʒəˈleɪʃən/ n [C;U]

mod·ule /ˈmɑdʒul/ n **1** standard part used in building, making furniture, etc. **2** part of a spacecraft for independent use –**ular** /ˈmɑdʒələr/ adj

mo·gul /ˈmoʊɡəl/ n person of very great power and wealth, esp. in the film industry

mo·hair /ˈmoʊhɛr/ n [U] (cloth from) the long silky hair of a sort of goat

moist /mɔɪst/ adj slightly wet ~**en** /ˈmɔɪsən/ vi/t make or become moist ~**ure** /ˈmɔɪstʃər/ n [U] liquid in or on something ~**urize** vt remove the dryness from ~**urizer** n [C;U] cream or liquid for making the skin soft

mo·lar /ˈmoʊlər/ n large back tooth

mo·las·ses /məˈlæsɪz/ n [U] any of the sweet substances produced during the refining (REFINE) of sugar

mold[1] /moʊld/ n container into which a soft substance is poured, to take on the shape of the container when it sets ♦ vt shape or form (something solid): (fig.) influences that molded her character ~**ing** n [C;U] decorative stone, plastic, or wood band(s)

mold[2] n [U] soft often greenish growth on old food, etc. ~**y** adj: moldy cheese

mole[1] /moʊl/ n small furry animal that lives underground

mole[2] n small, dark brown mark on the skin

mol·e·cule /ˈmɑləˌkyul/ n very small piece of matter, made of 2 or more atoms –**cular** /məˈlɛkyələr/ adj

mole·hill /ˈmoʊlˌhɪl/ n small pile of earth thrown up by a mole — see also **make a mountain out of a molehill** (MOUNTAIN)

mo·lest /məˈlɛst/ vt **1** attack; harm **2** attack (esp. a woman or child) sexually

mol·li·fy /ˈmɑləˌfaɪ/ vt make less angry

mol·lusk /ˈmɑləsk/ n any of a class of limbless animals with soft bodies, usu. with a shell

molt /moʊlt/ vi (of a bird or animal) lose most of its feathers, fur, etc.

mol·ten /ˈmoʊltn̩/ adj (of metal or rock) melted

mom /mɑm/ n mother

mo·ment /ˈmoʊmənt/ n **1** very short period of time **2** particular point in time **3** /ˈmoʊmɛnt, -mənt/ fml importance: a matter of great moment **4** /ˈmoʊmənt/ **the moment (that)** as soon as ~**ary** adj lasting a moment ~**arily** /ˌmoʊmənˈtɛrəli/ adv **1** for just a very short time **2** very soon; in a moment

moment of truth /ˌ·· · ˈ·/ n moment when something important will happen

mo·men·tous /moʊˈmɛntəs, mə-/ adj extremely important ~**ness** n [U]

mo·men·tum /moʊˈmɛntəm, mə-/ n [U] measurable quantity of movement in a body: (fig.) The campaign had lost its momentum.

mom·my /ˈmɑmi/ n (child's word for) mother

mon·arch /ˈmɑnək, ˈmɑnɑrk/ n non-elected ruler; king, queen, etc. ~**y** /ˈmɑnəki/ n **1** [U] rule by a monarch **2** [C] country ruled by a monarch

mon·as·te·ry /ˈmɑnəsˌtɛri/ n building in which MONKS live

mo·nas·tic /məˈnæstɪk/ adj of MONKS or monasteries

Mon·day /ˈmʌndi, -deɪ/ n day of the week between Sunday and Tuesday

mon·e·ta·ry /ˈmɑnəˌtɛri/ adj of or about money

mon·ey /ˈmʌni/ n [U] **1** something used for paying, esp. coins or paper notes **2** wealth: We're in the money. (= rich) **3 for my money** in my opinion **4** one's **money's worth** full value for the money one has spent

money-grub·bing /ˈmʌni ˌɡrʌbɪŋ/ adj determined to gain money, even dishonestly

money order /ˈ·· ˌ·/ n check available at post offices that can be used as money

mon·grel /ˈmɑŋɡrəl, ˈmʌŋ-/ n **1** dog of mixed breed; MUTT **2** person or thing of mixed race or origin

mon·i·tor /ˈmɑnətər/ vt watch or listen to carefully for a special purpose ♦ n **1** television used to show the view seen by a television camera **2** instrument for monitoring a physical condition: a heart monitor **3 a** SCREEN for use with a computer **b** parts of a computer operation that make sure that the computer system is working properly **4** person who listens to foreign radio news, etc., and reports on its content

monk /mʌŋk/ n member of a male religious group that lives together

mon·key[1] /ˈmʌŋki/ n **1** small animal with a long tail, that climbs trees **2** infml child full of playful tricks **3 make a monkey (out) of someone** infml make someone appear foolish

monkey² v **monkey around** *phr vi* play foolishly

monkey busi·ness /'·· ·,·/ n [U] *infml* secret behavior which causes trouble

mon·o /'manoʊ/ n MONONUCLEOSIS

mon·o·chrome /'manə,kroʊm/ *adj* **1** in only one color **2** in black and white only

mo·nog·a·my /mə'nagəmi/ n [U] having only one husband or wife at a time **–mous** *adj*

mon·o·gram /'manə,græm/ n combined letters, esp. someone's INITIALS **~med** *adj*

mon·o·lith·ic /,manə'lɪθɪk◂/ *adj* **1** like a large stone pillar **2** *often derog* forming a large unchangeable whole

mon·o·logue /'manə,lɔg, -,lag/ n long speech by one person

mon·o·nu·cle·o·sis /,manoʊ,nukli'oʊsɪs/ n infectious illness causing sleeping and fever

mo·nop·o·ly /mə'napəli/ n unshared control or right to do or produce something: (fig.) *He thinks he's got a monopoly on brains.* (= that he alone is clever) **–lize** *vt* keep unshared control of

mon·o·rail /'manə,reɪl/ n railroad with one RAIL

mon·o·tone /'manə,toʊn/ n [S] way of speaking or singing in which the voice continues on the same note: *to speak in a monotone*

mo·not·o·ny /mə'natʰni/ n [U] dull sameness **–onous** *adj* dull; boring (BORE²) **–onously** *adv*

mon·soon /man'sun/ n (time of) very heavy rains in and near India

mon·ster /'manstə/ n **1** strange usu. large and frightening creature ♦ *adj* **2** very evil person ♦ *adj* unusually large: *a monster potato* — see also GREEN-EYED MONSTER

mon·stros·i·ty /man'strasəti/ n something very ugly and usu. large

mon·strous /'manstrəs/ *adj* **1** extremely bad; shocking **2** unnaturally large, strange, etc. **~ly** *adv*

mon·tage /man'taʒ/ n [C;U] picture made from separate parts combined

Mon·te·rey Jack /,mantəreɪ 'dʒæk/ n white slightly soft cheese used esp. for Mexican food

month /mʌnθ/ n 12th part of a year; **~ly** *adj*

mon·u·ment /'manyəmənt/ n **1** something built in honor of a person or event

2 historical old building or place **3** work, esp. a book, worthy of lasting fame **~al** /,manyə'mɛntl◂/ *adj* **1** intended as a monument **2** very large **3** (esp. of something bad) very great in degree **~ally** *adv* extremely

moo /mu/ *vi, n* (make) the sound of a cow

mooch /mutʃ/ *vt sl* get by asking

mooch off *phr vt* get from someone by asking

mood¹ /mud/ n **1** state of feeling: *in a cheerful mood* **2** state of feeling in which one is bad-tempered or angry **~y** *adj* often having bad moods **~ily** *adv*

mood² n (in English) any of the three sets of verb forms that express a fact or action (INDICATIVE), **b** a command (IMPERATIVE), or **c** a doubt, wish, etc. (SUBJUNCTIVE)

moon¹ /mun/ n **1** large body that moves around the Earth and shines at night **2** body that moves around a PLANET other than the Earth — see also BLUE MOON

moon·beam /'munbim/ n beam of light from the moon

moon·light¹ /'munlaɪt/ [U] light of the moon

moonlight² *vi* **-ed** have a second job in addition to a regular one

moon·shine /'munʃaɪn/ n WHISKEY made and sold secretly

moonshine n alcohol made illegally

moor /mʊr/ *vi/t* fasten (a boat) to land, etc., by means of ropes, etc. **~ings** n [P] **1** ropes, ANCHORS, etc., for mooring **2** also **mooring** — place where a boat is moored

moose /mus/ n **moose** large North American animal like a deer

moot point /,mut 'pɔɪnt/ n **1** matter which is no longer important **2** undecided matter, on which people have different opinions

mop¹ /map/ n **1** long stick with thick string or a SPONGE at one end, for washing floors **2** thick untidy mass of hair

mop² *vt* **-pp-** wash or dry (as if) with a mop: *She mopped her brow.*

mop up *phr vt* **1** remove liquid, dirt, etc., with a mop **2** finish dealing with: *mop up small enemy groups*

mope /moʊp/ *vi* be continuously sad

mo·ped /'moʊpɛd/ n small motorcycle

mor·al /ˈmɔrəl, ˈmarəl/ adj **1** of or based on the difference between good and evil or right and wrong: She has high moral principles. **2** pure and honest in character and behavior ♦ n lesson that can be learned from a story or event ~**ize** vi give one's opinions on right and wrong, esp. when unwelcome **morals** n [P] standards of (sexual) behavior ~**ity** /məˈræləti/ n [U] rightness or pureness of behavior or of an action

mo·rale /məˈræl/ n [U] pride and confidence, esp. in relation to a job to be done

moral sup·port /ˌ·· ·ˈ·/ n [U] encouragement

mo·rass /məˈræs/ n [C] a situation that is difficult or impossible to escape from

mor·a·to·ri·um /ˌmɔrəˈtɔriəm, -ˈtoʊr-, ˌmar-/ n -ria /-riə/ official period during which a particular thing is not done

mor·bid /ˈmɔrbɪd/ adj interested in death in an unhealthy way ~**ly** adv ~**ity** /mɔrˈbɪdəti/ n [U]

more[1] /mɔr, moʊr/ adj **1** (forms COMPARATIVES): more difficult **2** to a greater degree: He likes this one more than that one. **3** again: Do it just once more.

more[2] determiner, pron (comparative of **many, much**) **1** a greater or additional number or quantity (of): He wants more food. | I can't eat any more. **2 more and more** increasingly **3 more or less: a** nearly **b** about

more·o·ver /mɔrˈoʊvə, moʊr-/ adv fml in addition; besides

mo·res /ˈmɔreɪz/ n [P] fml fixed moral customs in a social group

morgue /mɔrg/ n place where dead bodies are kept until a funeral

morn·ing /ˈmɔrnɪŋ/ n **1** time between sunrise and noon **2 in the morning** tomorrow morning **3 mornings** [P] in the morning: She works mornings.

morning-af·ter pill /ˌ·· ·ˈ· ˌ·/ n drug taken by mouth by a woman within 72 hours of having sex, to prevent her from having a baby

mo·ron /ˈmɔran, ˈmoʊran/ n derog very stupid person ~**ic** /məˈranɪk/ adj

mo·rose /məˈroʊs/ adj angry and silent ~**ly** adv

mor·phine /ˈmɔrfin/ n [U] powerful drug for stopping pain

Morse code /ˌmɔrs ˈkoʊd/ n [U] system of sending messages with letters represented by combinations of long and short signals

mor·sel /ˈmɔrsəl/ n small piece, esp. of food

mor·tal /ˈmɔrtl/ adj **1** that will die **2** of human beings **3** causing death: a mortal wound ♦ n human being ~**ly** adv **1** so as to cause death **2** very much: mortally offended ~**ity** /mɔrˈtæləti/ n [U] **1** rate or number of deaths **2** state of being mortal

mor·tar[1] /ˈmɔrtə/ n [U] mixture of LIME, sand, and water, used in building

mortar[2] n **1** apparatus for firing small bombs **2** thick bowl in which things are crushed

mor·tar·board /ˈmɔrtəˌbɔrd, -ˌboʊrd/ n cap with a flat square top, worn at GRADUATION ceremonies

mort·gage /ˈmɔrgɪdʒ/ n **1** agreement to borrow money to buy esp. a house, which belongs to the lender until the money is repaid **2** the amount borrowed ♦ vt give up the ownership of (a house, etc.) for a time in return for money lent

mor·ti·cian /mɔrˈtɪʃən/ n UNDERTAKER

mor·ti·fy /ˈmɔrtəˌfaɪ/ vt make ashamed –**fication** /ˌmɔrtəfəˈkeɪʃən/ n [U]

mor·tu·a·ry /ˈmɔrtʃuˌɛri/ n **1** FUNERAL PARLOR **2** MORGUE

mo·sa·ic /moʊˈzeɪ·ɪk/ n pattern or picture formed by small pieces of colored stone or glass

Mos·lem /ˈmazləm, ˈmas-/ n, adj Muslim

mosque /mask/ n building in which Muslims worship

mos·qui·to /məˈskitoʊ/ n -tos or -toes small flying insect that sucks blood from whatever it bites

moss /mɔs/ n [U] (thick flat mass of) a small usu. green plant of wet places

most[1] /moʊst/ adv **1** (forms SUPERLATIVES): the most difficult question **2** more than anything else: He likes bananas most of all. **3** fml very: I was most upset.

most[2] determiner, pron (superlative of **many, much**) **1** nearly all: Most people dislike him. **2 at (the) most** not more than **3 for the most part** mainly **4 make the most of** get the best advantage from ~**ly** adv mainly

mo·tel /moʊˈtɛl/ n hotel specially built for people traveling by car

moth /mɔθ/ n moths /mɔðz, mɔθs/ insect with large wings that flies mainly at night

moth·ball /'mɒθbɔl/ n 1 ball of chemical with a strong smell for keeping moths away from clothes 2 **in mothballs** stored and not used

moth-eat·en /'··ˌ·-/ adj 1 (of clothes) eaten by the young of moths 2 very worn out

moth·er /'mʌðə/ n 1 female parent 2 (usu. cap.) female head of a CONVENT: mother superior ♦ vt care for or protect (too) lovingly ~**hood** n [U] ~**ly** adj like a good mother

mother-in-law /'··· ˌ·/ n **mothers-in-law** wife's or husband's mother

mother-of-pearl /ˌ··· ˈ·/ n [U] shiny substance from inside certain shells, used for decoration

Mother's Day /'·· ˌ·/ n second Sunday in May, when mothers are celebrated

mo·tif /moʊ'tif/ n (repeated) artistic or musical pattern

mo·tion /'moʊʃən/ n 1 [U] act, way, or process of moving: the ship's rolling motion 2 [C] single movement 3 [C] suggestion formally made at a meeting 4 **go through the motions** do something without care or interest 5 **put/set in motion** start (a machine or process) ♦ vi/t signal or direct by a movement of esp. the hand ~**less** adj unmoving

motion pic·ture /ˌ·· ˈ·-/ n fml FILM (2): the motion picture industry

mo·ti·vate /'moʊtəˌveɪt/ vt 1 give (someone) a (strong) reason for doing something; encourage 2 be the reason why (something) was done –**vation** /ˌmoʊtə'veɪʃən/ n [U]

mo·tive /'moʊtɪv/ n reason for action

mot·ley /'mɒtli/ adj usu. derog. of many different kinds and qualities

mo·tor /'moʊtə/ n machine that changes power into movement: an electric motor ♦ adj 1 driven by an engine: a motor boat 2 of cars, etc.: a motor mechanic 3 of movement: motor control ~**ist** n car driver

mo·tor·cy·cle /'moʊtəˌsaɪkəl/ n also **motorbike** /-ˌbaɪk/ infml — large heavy bicycle driven by an engine

motor home /'·· ˌ·/ n large vehicle with beds, a kitchen, etc., in it, used for traveling

mo·tor·ist /'moʊtərɪst/ n person who drives a car

motor scoot·er /'·· ˌ·-/ n SCOOTER (2)

mot·tled /'mɒtld/ adj irregularly marked with colors and/or shapes

mot·to /'mɒtoʊ/ n **-toes** or **-tos** phrase or short sentence used as a guiding principle

mound /maʊnd/ n 1 pile 2 small hill

mount[1] /maʊnt/ v 1 vi rise: Costs mounted. 2 vt get on (a horse, bicycle, etc.) 3 vt provide with a horse, etc.: the mounted police 4 vt prepare and produce: mount an exhibition/an attack 5 vt fix on a support or in a frame 6 vt go up; climb ♦ n animal for riding

mount[2] n (usu. cap.) (used before names of mountains): Mount Everest

moun·tain /'maʊnt'n/ n 1 very high rocky hill 2 very large amount 3 **make a mountain out of a molehill** make a problem seem more difficult than it is ~**ous** adj 1 full of mountains 2 extremely large

moun·tain·eer /ˌmaʊnt'n'ɪr/ n mountain climber ~**ing** n [U]

Mountain time /'·· ˌ·/ n [U] the time used in the Rocky Mountain area of the US, two hours earlier than Eastern time

mourn /mɔrn, moʊrn/ vi/t feel or express grief (for), esp. when someone dies ~**er** n ~**ful** adj (too) sad ~**ing** n [U] 1 grief 2 funeral clothes, usu. black

mouse /maʊs/ n **mice** /maɪs/ 1 furry animal with a long tail, like a rat but smaller 2 quiet nervous person 3 small box connected to a computer by a wire which, when moved by hand, causes a CURSOR to move around on a MONITOR (3) so that choices can be made within the PROGRAM in use **mousy** adj 1 (of a person) unattractively plain and quiet 2 (of hair) dull brown

mousse /mus/ n [C;U] 1 sweet dish made from cream and eggs 2 FOAM used in hair to hold a style

mous·tache /'mʌstæʃ, mə'stæʃ/ n MUSTACHE

mouth[1] /maʊθ/ n **mouths** /maʊðz/ 1 opening in the face for eating and speaking 2 opening; entrance: the mouth of the cave 3 **down in the mouth** not cheerful 4 **keep one's mouth shut** keep silent

mouth[2] /maʊð/ vt 1 say by moving the lips soundlessly 2 repeat without understanding or sincerity

mouth·ful /'maʊθfʊl/ n 1 amount put into the mouth 2 long word or phrase, difficult to say

mouth·piece /'maʊθpis/ n 1 part of a musical instrument, telephone, etc., held in or near the mouth **2** person, newspaper, etc., that only expresses the opinions of others

mouth·wa·ter·ing /ˈ. ˌ.../ *adj* (of food) very attractive

move¹ /muːv/ *v* **1** *vi/t* (cause to) change place or position: *Sit still and don't move!* **2** *vi* act: *I had to move fast to clinch the deal.* **3** *vi* change one's home **4** *vt* cause to have strong feelings, esp. of pity: *a very moving story* **5** *vi/t* make (a formal suggestion) at a meeting ~**ment** *n* **1** [C;U] (act of) moving: *Police are watching his movements.* (= activities) **2** [C] group of people in a united effort: *a religious movement* — see also WOMEN'S MOVEMENT **3** [C] separate part of a large piece of music

move in *phr v* **1** take possession of a new home **2** (prepare to) take control, attack, etc.

move on *phr v* **1** change (to something new) **2** *vi/t* go away to another place or position

move out *phr vi* leave one's former home

move over *phr vi* change position in order to make room for someone or something else

move² *n* **1** change of position or place, esp. in games like CHESS **2** set of actions to bring about a result: *new moves to settle the dispute* **3** get a move on *infml* hurry up **4** make a move: **a** (start to) leave **b** begin to take action **5** on the move: **a** traveling around **b** having started to move or happen

mov·ie /ˈmuːviː/ *n* FILM (2) **movies** *n* [the+P] CINEMA: *What's on at the movies?/ Let's go to the movies.*

movie star /ˈ.. ˌ/ *n* popular actor or actress often seen in films

mow /moʊ/ *vt* mowed, mowed *or* mown /moʊn/ cut (grass, corn, etc.) ~**er** *n*

mow down *phr vt* knock down or kill, esp. in large numbers

mpg *written abbrev. for:* miles per GALLON

mph *written abbrev. for:* miles per hour

Mr. /ˈmɪstə/ *n* (ordinary man's title): *Mr. Smith*

Mrs. /ˈmɪsɪz/ *n* (married woman's title)

Ms. /mɪz/ *n* (unmarried or married woman's title)

Mt. *written abbrev. for:* MOUNT²

much¹ /mʌtʃ/ *adv* **1** a lot: *much better* | *much too small* **2** to the stated degree: *I liked it very much.* | *She would so much like to go.* **3** in most ways: *much the same as usual*

much² *determiner, pron* **more, most 1** large amount or part (of): *He gave me too much cake.* | *How much is it?* (= What does it cost?) | *I didn't get much.* | (fig.) *I don't think much of that.* (= I have a low opinion of it) **2** I thought as much I had expected that the stated usu. bad thing would happen **3** make much of: **a** treat as important **b** understand **4** much as although **5** not much of a not a very good **6** not up to much not very good **7** so much for that is the end of **8** too much for too difficult for

muck /mʌk/ *n* [U] **1** dirt **2** worthless or improper material

mu·cus /ˈmyuːkəs/ *n* [U] slippery body liquid, as produced in the nose

mud /mʌd/ *n* [U] **1** very wet earth **2** one's name is mud one is spoken badly of after causing trouble ~**dy** *adj*

mud·dle¹ /ˈmʌdl/ *n* state of confusion and disorder

muddle² *vt* **1** put into disorder **2** confuse the mind of

muddle along *phr vi* continue confusedly, with no plan

muddle through *phr vi* succeed in spite of having no plan or good method

mud·sling·ing /ˈmʌdˌslɪŋɪŋ/ *n* attempt to persuade voters not to vote for an opponent by saying bad things about that person

muff¹ /mʌf/ *n* fur or cloth cover to keep the hands or ears warm

muff² *vt* spoil a chance to do (something) well

muffin /ˈmʌfɪn/ *n* type of small cake, often made with fruit, etc.

muf·fle /ˈmʌfəl/ *vt* make (sound) less easily heard

muf·fler /ˈmʌflə/ *n* **1** wool piece of clothing worn to keep one's neck warm **2** (a car) apparatus for reducing noise

mug¹ /mʌg/ *n* **1 a** large drinking cup with straight sides and a handle **b** the contents of this: *a mug of coffee* **2** *sl* face

mug² *vt* -gg- rob violently ~**ger** *n*

mug·gy /ˈmʌgi/ *adj* (of weather) unpleasantly warm with heavy wet air

mule /myuːl/ *n* animal that is the young of a donkey and a horse

mull /mʌl/ vt heat (wine) with sugar, SPICES, etc.

mull over phr vt consider carefully

mul·ti·cul·tur·al /ˌmʌltiˈkʌltʃərəl◁/ adj involving people or ideas from many different countries, races, religions, etc. ~**ism** n [U]

mul·ti·lat·er·al /ˌmʌltiˈlætərəl◁/ adj including more than 2 groups, countries, etc. ~**ly** adv

mul·ti·me·di·a /ˌmʌltiˈmidiə/ adj using a mixture of sounds, words, pictures, etc., to give information, esp. on computer ♦ n [U]

mul·ti·na·tion·al /ˌmʌltiˈnæʃənəl◁/ adj having factories, offices, etc., in many different countries **multinational** n

mul·ti·ple /ˈmʌltəpəl/ adj of many different types or parts ♦ n number which contains a smaller number an exact number of times: Please order in multiples of 10.

multiple scle·ro·sis /ˌ··· ·ˈ··/ n [U] serious nerve disease in which one can no longer control one's physical movements and actions

mul·ti·plic·i·ty /ˌmʌltəˈplɪsəti/ n [S;U] large number or great variety

mul·ti·ply /ˈmʌltəplaɪ/ v 1 vt add (a number) to itself the stated number of times: 2 multiplied by 3 is 6. 2 vi/t increase in number or amount 3 vi breed –**plication** /ˌmʌltəpləˈkeɪʃən/ n [C;U]

mul·ti·ra·cial /ˌmʌltiˈreɪʃəl◁/ adj including or involving people of many different races

mul·ti·tude /ˈmʌltəˌtud/ n 1 large number 2 large crowd

mum¹ /mʌm/ n infml CHRYSANTHEMUM

mum² adj infml not saying or telling anything: Mum's the word. (= silence must/will be kept about this)

mum·ble /ˈmʌmbəl/ vi/t speak or say unclearly

mum·bo jum·bo /ˌmʌmboʊ ˈdʒʌmboʊ/ n [U] derog meaningless talk or actions

mum·mi·fy /ˈmʌməˌfaɪ/ vt preserve as a MUMMY

mum·my /ˈmʌmi/ n dead body preserved from decay, esp. in ancient Egypt

mumps /mʌmps/ n [U] infectious illness with swelling in the throat

munch /mʌntʃ/ vi/t eat (something hard) with a strong jaw movement

munch·ies /ˈmʌntʃiz/ n [P] 1 small pieces of food eaten between meals 2 feeling of hunger for these

mun·dane /mʌnˈdeɪn/ adj ordinary; with nothing exciting or interesting in it

mu·ni·ci·pal /myuˈnɪsəpəl/ adj of a town or its local government

mu·ni·ci·pal·i·ty /myuˌnɪsəˈpæləti/ n town, city, etc., with its own local government

mu·ni·tions /myuˈnɪʃənz/ n [P] bombs, guns, etc.; war supplies

mu·ral /ˈmyʊrəl/ n painting done directly on a wall

mur·der /ˈmɜrdər/ n [C;U] 1 crime of killing someone intentionally 2 very difficult or tiring experience — see also BLOODY MURDER ♦ vt kill illegally and intentionally ~**er** n ~**ous** adj 1 intending or likely to cause murder 2 violent (in appearance)

murk·y /ˈmɜrki/ adj unpleasantly dark

mur·mur /ˈmɜrmər/ n 1 [C] soft low continuous sound 2 [S] complaint ♦ vi/t make or express in a murmur: She murmured her approval.

Mur·phy's Law /ˌmɜrfiz ˈlɔ/ n [S] idea that anything that can go wrong will go wrong

mus·cle /ˈmʌsəl/ n 1 [C;U] (one of) the pieces of elastic material in the body which can tighten to produce movement 2 [U] strength 3 not move a muscle stay very still

muscle² v **muscle in** phr vi force one's way into (esp.) a group activity, so as to gain a share in what is produced

mus·cu·lar /ˈmʌskyələr/ adj 1 of muscles 2 with large muscles; strong

muse¹ /myuz/ vi think deeply

muse² n 1 (often cap.) any of 9 ancient Greek goddesses representing an art or science 2 force or person that seems to help someone write, paint, etc.

mu·se·um /myuˈziəm/ n building where objects of historical, scientific, or artistic interest are kept and shown

mush /mʌʃ/ n [U] soft mass of half liquid, half solid material ~**y** adj

mush·room /ˈmʌʃrum, -rʊm/ n type of FUNGUS that is often eaten ♦ vi grow and develop fast

mu·sic /ˈmyuzɪk/ n [U] 1 sounds arranged in patterns, usu. with tunes 2 art of making music 3 printed representation of music 4 **face the music** admit to blame, responsibility, etc., and accept the results, esp. punishment or difficulty ~**ian** /myuˈzɪʃən/ n

mu·sic·al /ˈmyuːzɪkəl/ adj 1 of music 2 skilled at music ♦ n play or film with songs and usu. dances ~**ly** adv

musical chairs /ˌ··· ˌ·/ n [U] party game in which people have to find seats when the music stops

musk /mʌsk/ n [U] substance with a strong smell used in PERFUMES ~**y** adj

mus·ket /ˈmʌskɪt/ n early type of gun with a long BARREL

Mus·lim /ˈmʌzləm, ˈmʊz-, ˈmʊs-/ n, adj (follower) of the religion started by Mohammed

mus·sel /ˈmʌsəl/ n sea animal with a black shell, often eaten

must /məst; strong mʌst/ vi 3rd person sing. **must** 1 (shows what is necessary): It's an order; you must obey. 2 (shows what is likely): You must be cold. ♦ /mʌst/ n something that should be done, seen, etc.

mus·tache /ˈmʌstæʃ, məˈstæʃ/ n hair on the upper lip

mus·tang /ˈmʌstæŋ/ n wild horse

mus·tard /ˈmʌstəd/ n [U] yellow or brown substance with a hot taste, made from a plant and usu. eaten with meat

mus·ter /ˈmʌstə/ vt gather; collect

must·n't /ˈmʌsənt/ short for: must not

must·y /ˈmʌsti/ adj with an unpleasant smell as if old –**iness** n [U]

mu·tant /ˈmyuːtʰnt/ n creature having a strange, ABNORMAL shape

mu·ta·tion /myuˈteɪʃən/ n [C;U] (example or result of) a process of change in living cells, causing a new part or type **mutate** vi/t

mute /myuːt/ adj not speaking or spoken; silent ♦ n 1 person who cannot speak 2 object put on or in a musical instrument to make it sound softer ~**ly** adv **muted** adj (of sound or color) softer than usual

mu·ti·late /ˈmyuːtʰleɪt/ vt wound and make ugly or useless –**lation** /ˌmyuːtʰleɪʃən/ n [C;U]

mu·ti·ny /ˈmyuːtʰn-i/ n [C;U] (an example of) the act of taking power from the person in charge, esp. on a ship –**nous** adj 1 taking part in a mutiny 2 angrily disobedient –**nously** adv ♦ vi take part in a mutiny

mutt /mʌt/ n dog of no particular breed

mut·ter /ˈmʌtə/ vi/t speak or say quietly and unclearly

mut·ton /ˈmʌtʰn/ n [U] meat from a sheep

mu·tu·al /ˈmyuːtʃuəl/ adj 1 equal for both sides: their mutual dislike (= they dislike each other) 2 shared by both: mutual interests/friends ~**ly** adv

mutual fund /ˈ··· ˌ/ n company through which one can buy STOCK in various other companies

muz·zle /ˈmʌzəl/ n 1 animal's nose and mouth 2 covering for an animal's muzzle, to stop it biting 3 front end of a gun barrel ♦ vt 1 put a muzzle on (an animal) 2 force to keep silent

my /maɪ/ determiner of me: my parents ♦ interj (expresses surprise)

myr·i·ad /ˈmɪriəd/ n, adj large and varied number (of)

my·self /maɪˈsɛlf/ pron 1 (reflexive form of I): I hurt myself. 2 (strong form of I): I'll do it myself. 3 (in) my usual state of mind or body: I'm not myself today. (= I feel ill) 4 (all) by myself a alone b without help 5 to myself not shared

mys·te·ry /ˈmɪstəri/ n 1 [C] something which cannot be explained or understood 2 [U] strange secret quality –**rious** /mɪˈstɪriəs/ adj 1 unexplainable: his mysterious disappearance 2 hiding one's intentions –**riously** adv –**riousness** n [U]

mys·tic /ˈmɪstɪk/ n person who practices mysticism

mys·ti·cis·m /ˈmɪstɪˌsɪzəm/ n gaining of secret religious knowledge **mystical** /ˈmɪstɪkəl/, **mystic** adj **mystically** adv

mys·ti·fy /ˈmɪstɪˌfaɪ/ vt cause (someone) to wonder or be unsure: her mystifying disappearance

mys·tique /mɪˈstiːk/ n special quality that makes a person or thing seem mysterious and different, esp. causing admiration

myth /mɪθ/ 1 story from ancient times 2 widely believed false story or idea ~**ical** adj 1 of myths 2 not real

my·thol·o·gy /mɪˈθɑlədʒi/ n [U] myths: heroes of Greek mythology –**gical** /ˌmɪθəˈlɑdʒɪkəl◄/ adj

N

N, n /ɛn/ the 14th letter of the English alphabet

N. *written abbrev. for:* north(ern)

nab /næb/ *vt* **-bb-** *sl* **1** ARREST **2** get; take

nag¹ /næg/ *vi/t* **-gg-** continuously complain (at) or worrying: *a nagging hurting or worrying:* *a nagging headache*

nag² *n* old horse

nail¹ /neɪl/ *n* **1** thin pointed piece of metal for hammering into a piece of wood **2** hard flat piece at the end of each finger and toe **3 hard as nails** without any tender feelings **4 hit the nail on the head** do or say exactly the right thing

nail² *vt* **1** fasten with a nail **2** *sl* catch; trap

nail down *phr vt* force to tell plans or wishes clearly

nail pol·ish /ˈ· ˌ·/ *n* [U] liquid for giving a hard shiny surface on finger and toe nails

na·ive /naˈiːv/ *adj* **1** without experience of life **2** too willing to believe without proof ~**ly** *adv* ~**ty** /naˈiːvəti/ *n* [U] quality of being naive

na·ked /ˈneɪkɪd/ *adj* **1** with no clothes on **2** uncovered: *a naked light* | (fig.) *the naked truth* **3 with the naked eye** without a microscope, TELESCOPE, etc. ~**ness** *n* [U]

name /neɪm/ *n* **1** [C] what someone (or something) is called: *Her name is Mary.* **2** [C] usu. offensive title for someone: *to call someone names* **3** [S;C] opinion others have of one; REPUTATION: *The restaurant has a good name.* | *He made a name for himself* (= became famous) *in show business.* **4** [C] *sl* famous or important person: *There were several big names* (= famous people) *at the party.* **5 in name only** in appearance or by title but not in fact **6 in the name of** by the right or power of: *Open up, in the name of the law!* **7 the name of the game** quality or object which is most necessary or important **8 to one's name** (esp. of money) as one's property: *He hasn't a penny to his name.* ♦ *vt* **1** give a name to: *They named their daughter Mary.* **2** say what the name of (someone or something) is: *Can you name this plant?* **3** appoint; choose ~**less** *adj* **1** whose name is not known or told **2** too terrible to mention ~**ly** *adv* and that is/they are: *There are two factors, namely cost and availability.*

name-drop /ˈneɪmdrɒp/ *vi* **-pp-** mention famous people as if one knew them well ~**per** *n*

name·sake /ˈneɪmseɪk/ *n* person with the same name

name tag /ˈ· ˌ·/ *n* small sign with one's name on it, worn at a party, meeting, etc.

nan·ny /ˈnæni/ *n* woman employed to take care of children

nap¹ /næp/ *n* short sleep ♦ *vi* **1** take a nap **2 catch someone napping** find or take advantage of someone unprepared

nap² *n* soft furry surface of cloth

na·palm /ˈneɪpɑːm/ *n* [U] fiercely burning gasoline jelly, used in bombs

nape /neɪp/ *n* back (of the neck)

nap·kin /ˈnæpkɪn/ *n* piece of cloth or paper used at meals for protecting clothes and cleaning the lips and fingers

nar·cis·sis·m /ˈnɑːsəˌsɪzəm/ *n* [U] too great love for one's own appearance or abilities –**sist** *n* –**sistic** /ˌnɑːsəˈsɪstɪk/ *adj*

nar·cot·ic /nɑːˈkɒtɪk/ *n* drug that produces sleep, harmful in large amounts

nar·rate /næˈreɪt, næˈreɪt/ *vt* tell (a story) or describe (events) –**rator** *n* –**ration** /næˈreɪʃən/ *n* [C;U]

nar·ra·tive /ˈnærətɪv/ *n* **1** [C;U] *fml* story **2** [U] art of narrating

nar·row¹ /ˈnærəʊ/ *adj* **1** small from one side to the other **2** limited **3** just barely successful: *a narrow escape* **4** not open to new ideas: *a narrow mind* — see also STRAIGHT AND NARROW ~**ly** *adv* only just ~**ness** *n* [U]

narrow² *vi/t* become or make narrower

narrow down *phr vt* reduce, limit

narrow-mind·ed /ˌ· ˈ·· ◂/ *adj* unwilling to respect the opinions of others when different from one's own ~**ness** *n* [U]

na·sal /ˈneɪzəl/ *adj* of the nose

nas·ty /ˈnɑːsti/ *adj* **1** not nice; unpleasant **2** dangerous or painful: *a nasty cut* –**tily** *adv* –**tiness** *n* [U]

na·tion /ˈneɪʃən/ *n* (all the people belonging to) a country

na·tion·al /ˈnæʃənəl/ adj 1 of or being a nation, esp. as opposed to a any of its parts: a national newspaper (= one read everywhere in the country) b another nation or other nations: The national news comes after the international news. 2 owned or controlled by the central government of a country: a national bank | the National Weather Service ♦ n person from a usu. stated country ~ly adv ~ism n [U] love of and pride in one's country 2 desire to become a separate independent country ~ist adj, n ~istic /ˌnæʃənəˈlɪstɪk◂/ adj showing too great nationalism ~ity /ˌnæʃəˈnæləti/ n [U] being from a particular country: a man of Italian nationality

National Guard /ˌ··· ◂/ n [the] state military forces that become part of the army in time of war

na·tion·al·ize /ˈnæʃənəˌlaɪz/ vt take (a business or industry) into government control –ization /ˌnæʃənələˈzeɪʃən/ n [U]

national park /ˌ··· ◂/ n large area of beautiful land protected by the government for people to visit

na·tion·wide /ˌneɪʃənˈwaɪd◂/ adj, adv happening over the whole country

na·tive /ˈneɪtɪv/ adj 1 of or being one's place of birth 2 found naturally in a place: native species 3 not learned: native ability ♦ n 1 person born in a place 2 local person 3 native animal or plant

Native A·mer·i·can /ˌ··· ·ʹ···/ n member of the peoples living in the Americas before European settlers came

Na·tiv·i·ty /nəˈtɪvəti/ n the birth of Christ

NATO /ˈneɪtoʊ/ n the North Atlantic Treaty Organization; a group of countries which give military help to each other

nat·u·ral /ˈnætʃərəl/ adj 1 existing in or happening ordinarily in the world, esp. not made by people: death from natural causes 2 usual; to be expected: It's natural to feel nervous. 3 existing from birth; not learned: a natural talent 4 having natural skill: a natural musician 5 ordinary; not AFFECTED ♦ n person with natural skill ~ly adv 1 as a natural skill: Swimming comes naturally to her. 2 in an ordinary way 3 of course ~ist n person who studies animals and plants ~istic /ˌnætʃərəˈlɪstɪk◂/ adj showing

things exactly as they are: a naturalistic painting ~istically adv

natural gas /ˌ·· ◂/ n [U] gas used for cooking or heating, taken from under the earth or ocean

nat·u·ral·ize /ˈnætʃərəˌlaɪz/ vt make (someone born elsewhere) a citizen of a country –ization /ˌnætʃərələˈzeɪʃən/ n [U]

natural his·to·ry /ˌ··· ·ʹ··/ n [U] study of animals and plants

natural re·sourc·es /ˌ··· ·ʹ··/ n [P] land, minerals, energy, etc., existing in a country

natural se·lec·tion /ˌ··· ·ʹ··/ n [U] process by which creatures well suited to their conditions live and those less well suited die

na·ture /ˈneɪtʃər/ n 1 [U] everything that exists in the world independently of people, such as animals and plants, the land, and the weather 2 [C;U] character: She has a very kind nature. — see also SECOND NATURE 3 [S] fml kind; sort

naugh·ty /ˈnɔti/ adj 1 (esp. of a child) behaving badly 2 sexually improper –tily adv –tiness n [U]

nau·se·a /ˈnɔziə, ˈnɔʒə, ˈnɔsiə, ˈnɔʃə/ n [U] feeling of sickness and desire to VOMIT –ous adj –ate /ˈnɔziˌeɪt, -ʒi-, -si-, -ʃi-/ vt cause to feel nausea: (fig.) nauseating hypocrisy

nau·ti·cal /ˈnɔtɪkəl/ adj of ships or sailing

na·val /ˈneɪvəl/ adj of a navy or fighting ships

na·vel /ˈneɪvəl/ n small sunken place in the middle of the stomach

nav·i·ga·ble /ˈnævɪgəbəl/ adj (of a river, etc.) deep and wide enough to let ships pass

nav·i·gate /ˈnævəˌgeɪt/ vi/t direct the course of (a ship, aircraft, etc., or a car) –gator n –gation /ˌnævəˈgeɪʃən/ n [U]

na·vy /ˈneɪvi/ n ships and sailors for fighting

navy blue /ˌ·· ·◂/ n [U] dark blue

near /nɪr/ adj 1 at a short distance; close: Christmas/My office is near. 2 nearest and dearest one's family ♦ adv, prep not far (from): Don't go near the edge. ♦ vi/t come closer (to) ~ly adv 1 almost 2 not nearly not at all ~ness n [U]

near·by /ˌnɪrˈbaɪ◂/ adj, adv near

near·sight·ed /ˌnɪrˈsaɪtɪd◂, ˈnɪrˌsaɪtɪd/ adj unable to see distant things clearly –ness n [U]

neat /nit/ *adj* **1** tidy **2** simple and effective: *a neat trick* **3** pleasing: *a really neat new car* **4** (of an alcoholic drink) with no water, etc., added ~**ly** *adv* ~**ness** *n* [U]

ne·ces·sa·ry /ˈnɛsəˌsɛri/ *adj* that is needed or must be done –**rily** /ˌnɛsəˈsɛrəli/ *adv* in a way that must be so: *Food that looks good doesn't necessarily taste good.*

ne·ces·si·tate /nəˈsɛsəˌteɪt/ *vt fml* make necessary

ne·ces·si·ty /nəˈsɛsəti/ *n* **1** [S;U] condition of being necessary; need: *There's no necessity to stay.* **2** [C] something necessary, esp. for life

neck¹ /nɛk/ *n* **1** part of the body joining the head to the shoulders **2** part of a garment that goes around this **3** narrow part sticking out from a broader part: *the neck of a bottle* **4** neck and neck doing equally well in a competition **5** neck of the woods *infml* area or part of the country **6** up to one's neck (in) deeply concerned (with or by): *He's up to his neck in debt.* (= he owes a lot of money)

neck² *vi infml* kiss and CUDDLE

neck·lace /ˈnɛk-lɪs/ *n* decorative chain or string of jewels, worn around the neck

neck·tie /ˈnɛktaɪ/ *n* TIE¹ (1)

nec·tar /ˈnɛktər/ *n* [U] **1** sweet liquid collected by bees from flowers **2** sweet drink

nec·ta·rine /ˌnɛktəˈrin/ *n* round juicy yellow-red fruit with one large seed and smooth skin

need¹ /nid/ *n* **1** [S;U] condition in which something necessary or desirable is missing: *a need for better medical services* **2** [S;U] necessary duty: *There's no need for you to come.* **3** [C] something one must have **4** [U] state of lacking food, money, etc.: *children in need* **5** if need be if necessary ~**less** *adj* unnecessary **2** needless to say of course ~**lessly** *adv*

need² *vt* have a need for; want: *To survive, plants need water.*

need³ *v* have to; must: *Do you think I need to go to the meeting?*

nee·dle /ˈnidl/ *n* **1** thin pointed pin or rod used in sewing or knitting (KNIT) **2** something long, thin, and sharp, such as a leaf, a pointer on a compass, or the part of a HYPODERMIC which is pushed into someone's skin **3** STYLUS ♦ *vt* annoy

nee·dle·work /ˈnidlˌwərk/ *n* [U] decorative sewing

need·y /ˈnidi/ *adj* poor

ne·gate /nɪˈgeɪt/ *vt* cause to have no effect **negation** /nɪˈgeɪʃən/ *n* [U]

neg·a·tive /ˈnɛgətɪv/ *adj* **1** saying or meaning "no": *a negative reply* **2** not useful or encouraging: *negative advice* **3** less than zero **4** (of electricity) of the type carried by ELECTRONS ♦ *n* **1** word, expression, or statement saying or meaning "no": *The answer was in the negative.* **2** film showing dark areas as light and light as dark

ne·glect /nɪˈglɛkt/ *vt* **1** give too little attention or care to **2** fail (to do something) esp. because of carelessness ♦ *n* [U] neglecting or being neglected ~**ful** *adj* tending to neglect things ~**fully** *adv* ~**fulness** *n* [U]

neg·li·gent /ˈnɛglɪdʒənt/ *adj* not taking enough care ~**ly** *adv* –**gence** *n* [U]

neg·li·gi·ble /ˈnɛglɪdʒəbəl/ *adj* too slight or unimportant to worry about

ne·go·ti·a·ble /nɪˈgoʊʃiəbəl, -ʃəbəl/ *adj* **1** that can be settled or changed by being negotiated **2** *infml* that can be traveled through, along, etc.

ne·go·ti·ate /nɪˈgoʊʃiˌeɪt/ *v* **1** *vi/t* talk to someone in order to try to get (an agreement) **2** *vt* travel safely along or through –**ator** *n* –**ation** /nɪˌgoʊʃiˈeɪʃən/ *n* [C;U]

neigh /neɪ/ *vi, n* (make) the sound of a horse

neigh·bor /ˈneɪbər/ *n* someone who lives next door, or near ~**hood** *n* **1** area in a town **2** the area around a point or place: (fig.) *a price in the neighborhood of* (= about) *$500* ~**ing** *adj* (of a place) near ~**ly** *adj* friendly

nei·ther /ˈniðər, ˈnaɪ-/ *determiner, pron, conj* not one and not the other: *Neither book/Neither of the books is very good.* ♦ *adv* also not: *I can't swim and neither can my brother.*

ne·on /ˈniɑn/ *n* [U] gas used in making bright electric lights

neph·ew /ˈnɛfyu/ *n* son of one's brother or sister

nep·o·tism /ˈnɛpəˌtɪzəm/ *n* [U] giving unfair favor and advantages to one's relatives

Nep·tune /ˈnɛptun/ *n* the PLANET 8th in order from the sun

nerd /nərd/ *n infml* boring unfashionable person

nerve /nərv/ *n* **1** [C] threadlike part in the body that carries feelings and messages to and from the brain **2** [U] courage: *I meant to do it, but I lost my nerve.* **3** [U] disrespectful rudeness: *He had the nerve to say I was a fool!* ♦ *vt* give courage to (someone, esp. oneself)

nerves *n* [P] **1** great nervousness **2 get on someone's nerves** make someone annoyed or bad-tempered **nervous** *adj* **1 a** rather frightened **b** easily excited and worried **2** of the nerves: *The brain is at the center of the* **nervous system. nervously** *adv* **nervousness** *n* [U]

nerve-rack·ing /ˈ. ˌ.·/ *adj* that causes great worry or fear

nervous break·down /ˌ. ˈ.·/ *n* serious medical condition of deep worrying, anxiety, and tiredness which stops one working

nest /nɛst/ *n* **1** hollow place built or used by a bird as a home and a place to keep its eggs **2** quiet place where one can go to rest ♦ *vi* build or use a nest

nest egg /ˈ. ·/ *n* amount of money saved for special future use

nes·tle /ˈnɛsəl/ *vi/t* settle, lie, or put in a close comfortable position: *She nestled down (into the big chair) and began to read.*

Net /nɛt/ *n* [the] INTERNET

net¹ *n* [C;U] (piece of) material made of strings, wires, etc., tied together with regular spaces between them: *the fisherman's nets* ♦ *vt* **-tt-** catch in a net **~ting** *n* string, wire, etc., made into a net

net² *adj* left after nothing further is to be taken away: *a net profit* ♦ *vt* **-tt-** gain as a profit

net·work¹ /ˈnɛt"wərk/ *n* **1** large system of lines, wires, etc., that cross or meet each other **2** group of radio or television stations **3** set of connected computers that can share information **4** group of people, organizations, etc., that are connected or work together

network² *vi/t* **1** connect (computers) to form a NETWORK¹ (1), to share information **2** form new relationships with people for personal or professional advantage

net·work·ing /ˈnɛt"wərkɪŋ/ *n* [U] meeting other people who do the same type of work, in order to share information, help each other, etc.

neu·rol·o·gy /nʊˈrɑlədʒi/ *n* [U] scientific study of nerves and their diseases **–gist** *n*

neu·ro·sis /nʊˈroʊsɪs/ *n* **-ses** /-siz/ a disorder of the mind in which one suffers from strong unreasonable fears and has troubled relations with other people **–rotic** /nʊˈrɑtɪk/ *adj* of or suffering from a neurosis

neu·ter /ˈnutər/ *adj* (in grammar) belonging to the class of words that mainly includes things rather than males or females ♦ *vt* remove part of the sex organs of (an animal)

neu·tral¹ /ˈnutrəl/ *adj* **1** not supporting either side in a war, argument, etc. **2** having no strong or noticeable qualities: *a neutral color* **~ize** *vt* cause to have no effect **~ity** /nuˈtrælət̮i/ *n* [U]

neutral² *n* **1** [U] the position of a car's GEARS in which the engine is not connected with the wheels **2** [C] a neutral person or country

neu·tron /ˈnutrɑn/ *n* a very small piece of matter that is part of an atom and carries no electricity

nev·er /ˈnɛvər/ *adv* not ever: *It never snows in the desert.*

nev·er·the·less /ˌnɛvərðəˈlɛs◂/ *adv* in spite of that; yet: *It was a cold day but nevertheless very pleasant.*

new /nu/ *adj* **1** only recently made or begun: *a new film* **2** different from the one before: *She's looking for a new job.* **3** having only recently arrived or started: *I'm new here.* **4 new-** newly; recently: *newmowed lawn* **5 new to** just beginning to know about or do; unfamiliar with **~ly** *adv* that has just happened or been done; recently: *a newly-built house* **~ness** *n* [U]

New Age /ˌ. ˈ.◂/ *n* set of beliefs about religion, medicine, and ways of life that are not part of traditional Western religions ♦ *adj*

new blood /ˌ. ˈ./ *n* [U] new members of a group, bringing new ideas, ENERGY, etc.

new·born /ˈnubɔrn/ *n* baby that has just recently been born ♦ *adj*

new·com·er /ˈnuˌkʌmər/ *n* someone who has just arrived

new·fan·gled /ˌnuˈfæŋgəld◂/ *adj* new but neither necessary nor better

new·ly·wed /ˈnuliˌwɛd/ *n* recently married person ♦ *adj*

new moon /ˌ. ˈ./ *n* time once every month when the moon doesn't appear

news /nuz/ n 1 [U] facts that are reported about a recent event: *a piece of news* 2 [the+S] regular report of recent events on radio or television

news·cast /ˈnuzkæst/ n news program on radio or television ~**er** n person who reads the news on television

news·let·ter /ˈnuzˌlɛtər/ n short written report about a club, organization, or subject sent regularly to people

news·pa·per /ˈnuzˌpeɪpər/ n paper printed with news, notices, advertisements, etc., that comes out every day or every week

news·print /ˈnuzˌprɪnt/ n [U] paper on which newspapers are printed

news·stand /ˈnuzstænd/ n place on a street where newspapers and magazines are sold

news·wor·thy /ˈnuzˌwɜði/ adj important or interesting enough to be reported as news

new year /ˌ· ˈ·/ n (often caps.) a year which has just begun or will soon begin

next /nɛkst/ adj 1 with nothing before or between; nearest: *the house next to mine* 2 the one following or after: *I'm coming next week.* ♦ adv 1 just afterwards: *First, heat the oil; next, add the onions.* 2 the next time: *when next we meet* 3 **next to** almost: *next to impossible*

next door /ˌ· ˈ·/ adv 1 in the next building: *She lives next door.* 2 **next door to** almost the same as

next of kin /ˌ· · ˈ·/ n person or people most closely related to one

nib·ble /ˈnɪbəl/ vi/t eat with small bites ♦ n small bite

nice /naɪs/ adj 1 good; pleasant: *have a nice day* 2 showing or needing careful understanding; SUBTLE: *a nice distinction* 3 *infml* bad: *He got us into a nice mess.* 4 **nice and** pleasantly; as was wanted: *The soup was nice and hot.* ~**ly** adv ~**ness** n [U]

niche /nɪtʃ/ n 1 hollow place in a wall, where something is put 2 suitable place, job, etc.

nick[1] /nɪk/ n 1 small cut 2 **in the nick of time** only just in time; almost too late ♦ vt make a small cut in

nick·el /ˈnɪkəl/ n 1 [C] US coin worth 5 cents 2 [U] hard silver-white metal

nickel-and-dime /ˌ· · ˈ·/ adj 1 not important 2 (of a business or operation) small

nick·name /ˈnɪknem/ n informal name used instead of someone's real name ♦ vt: *They nicknamed him "Baldy."*

nic·o·tine /ˈnɪkətin/ n [U] poisonous chemical found in tobacco

niece /nis/ n daughter of one's brother or sister

nif·ty /ˈnɪfti/ adj *infml* very good, attractive, or effective

nigh /naɪ/ adj *lit* near ♦ adv *lit* nearly

night /naɪt/ n 1 [C;U] dark part of the day, between sunset and sunrise 2 **at night: a** during the night **b** at the end of the day 3 **by night** during the night 4 **make a night of it** spend all or most of the night in enjoyment 5 **night after night** every night 6 **night and day** also **day and night** — all the time 7 **nights** every night: *I work nights.*

night·club /ˈnaɪtˌklʌb/ n restaurant open late at night where people may drink, dance, and see a show

night·fall /ˈnaɪtfɔl/ n [U] beginning of night

night·gown /ˈnaɪtˌgaʊn/ also **night·ie** /ˈnaɪti/ — n woman's garment worn in bed

nigh·tin·gale /ˈnaɪtnˌgeɪl, ˈnaɪtɪŋ-/ n bird with a beautiful song

night·life /ˈnaɪtˌlaɪf/ n [U] evening entertainment or social activity

night·ly /ˈnaɪtˈli/ adj, adv (happening, done, etc.) every night

night·mare /ˈnaɪtˌmɛr/ n 1 frightening dream 2 terrible experience or event

night·owl /ˈnaɪtˌaʊl/ n person who likes to be awake at night

night school /ˈ· ˌ·/ n [U] classes taught in the evenings, for people who work during the day

night·shirt /ˈnaɪtˌʃɜt/ n man's long loose shirt worn in bed

night·stand /ˈnaɪtstænd/ n small table beside a bed

nil /nɪl/ n nothing; zero

nim·ble /ˈnɪmbəl/ adj 1 quick, light, and neat in movement 2 quick in thought or understanding –**bly** adv ~**ness** n [U]

nine /naɪn/ det, n, pron 9 **ninth** det, adv, n, pron 9th

nine·teen /ˌnaɪnˈtin/ det, n, pron 19 ~**th** det, adv, n, pron 19th

nine-to-five /ˌ· · ˈ·/ adj, adv from 9:00 a.m. to 5:00 p.m., when most people work in an office

nine·ty /ˈnaɪnti/ *det, n, pron* 90 **–tieth** *det, adv, n, pron* 90th

nip /nɪp/ *v* **-pp-** 1 *vt* catch in a sharp tight usu. painful hold 2 **nip something in the bud** stop something before it has properly started ♦ *n* [S] 1 sharp tight hold or bite 2 coldness: *a nip in the air*

nip·ple /ˈnɪpəl/ *n* 1 round pointed area of dark skin on a breast 2 rubber object through which a baby sucks milk, etc., from a bottle

nip·py /ˈnɪpi/ *adj* cold

nir·va·na /nɪəˈvɑːnə, nɜː-/ *n* [U] (*usu. cap.*) (in Buddhism and Hinduism) state of complete escape from suffering

nit·pick·ing /ˈnɪtˌpɪkɪŋ/ *n* [U] habit of paying too much attention to small unimportant details **nitpicking** *adj*

ni·trate /ˈnaɪtreɪt/ *n* chemical used esp. to improve the soil for growing crops

ni·tro·gen /ˈnaɪtrədʒən/ *n* [U] gas that forms most of the Earth's air

nit·ty-grit·ty /ˌnɪti ˈɡrɪti/ *n* **get down to the nitty-gritty** *sl* deal with the difficult, practical, and important part of a matter

nit·wit /ˈnɪtˌwɪt/ *n* silly person

no /nəʊ/ *adv* 1 (used for refusing or disagreeing): *"Do you like it?" "No!"* 2 not any: *He felt no better.* ♦ *determiner* 1 not a; not any: *She felt no fear.* | *I'm no fool!* 2 (shows what is not allowed): *No smoking* (on a sign) ♦ *n* answer or decision of no: *a clear no*

no. *written abbrev. for:* number

no·bil·i·ty /nəʊˈbɪləti/ *n* [U] 1 people of high social rank with titles 2 state of being noble

no·ble /ˈnəʊbəl/ *adj* 1 of high moral quality; fine and unselfish 2 grand 3 of high social rank ♦ *n* lord in former times **–bly** *adv*

no·bod·y /ˈnəʊˌbɒdi/ *pron* no one ♦ *n* unimportant person

noc·tur·nal /nɒkˈtɜːnl/ *adj* happening or active at night

nod /nɒd/ *vi/t* **-dd-** bend (one's head) forward and down, esp. to show agreement or give a sign ♦ *n* act of nodding

nod off *phr vi* fall asleep unintentionally

no-frills /ˌ ˈ ◂/ *adj* without unnecessary features; BASIC

noise /nɔɪz/ *n* [C;U] sound, esp. loud and unpleasant **noisy** *adj* making a lot of noise **noisily** *adv* **noisiness** *n* [U]

no·mad /ˈnəʊmæd/ *n* member of a tribe that does not settle long in one place **~ic** /nəʊˈmædɪk/ *adj*

no-man's-land /ˈ· ·ˌ·/ *n* [S;U] 1 land no one owns or controls, esp. between two armies or borders 2 any place far away where there are no people

no·men·cla·ture /nəʊˈmenˌkleɪtʃə/ *n* [C;U] system of naming things

nom·i·nal /ˈnɒmənəl/ *adj* 1 not really what the name suggests: *He's only the nominal head of the business; his son really runs it.* 2 (of an amount of money) very small 3 of or being a noun **–ly** *adv*

nom·i·nate /ˈnɒməˌneɪt/ *vt* to suggest officially that (someone) should be chosen or elected **–nation** /ˌnɒməˈneɪʃən/ *n* [C;U]

nom·i·nee /ˌnɒməˈniː/ *n* person who has been nominated

non·cha·lant /ˈnɒnʃəˌlɑːnt, -tʃə-◂/ *adj* calm and usu. uninterested **~ly** *adv* **–lance** *n* [U]

non·con·form·ist /ˌnɒnkənˈfɔːmɪst◂/ *n, adj* (person) not following customary ways of living, thinking, etc.

non·de·script /ˌnɒndɪˈskrɪpt◂/ *adj* looking very ordinary and dull

none /nʌn/ *pron* not any: *She has several, but I have none.* | *None of the wine was drinkable.* ♦ *adv* 1 **none the** not at all: *My car is none the worse for* (= not damaged by) *the accident.* 2 **none too** not very

non·en·ti·ty /nɒnˈentəti/ *n* person without much ability, character, or importance

none·the·less /ˌnʌnðəˈles◂/ *adv* in spite of that; NEVERTHELESS

non·e·vent /ˌnɒn ɪˈvent/ *n* something much less important, interesting, etc., than expected

non-fat /ˌnɒnˈfæt◂/ *adj* (of milk, foods, etc.) containing no fat

non-fic·tion /ˌnɒnˈfɪkʃən/ *n* [U] writing about facts, not stories

no-no /ˈnəʊ nəʊ/ *n infml* something not allowed or not socially acceptable

no-non·sense /ˌ· ˈ·◂/ *adj* practical and direct

non-prof·it /ˌnɒnˈprɒfɪt/ *adj* (of organizations) using money earned to help people instead of making a profit, and paying no taxes

non·sense /ˈnɒnsens, -səns/ *n* [U] 1 meaningless words 2 foolish words, ideas, or

actions –**sensical** /nɑnˈsɛnsɪkəl/ *adj*
foolish

non seq·ui·tur /ˌnɑn ˈsɛkwɪtə/ *n* statement that does not follow by correct reasoning from what has been said before

non-smok·ing /ˌnɑnˈsmoʊkɪŋ◂/ *adj* (of buildings, areas, etc.) where smoking is not allowed **nonsmoker** *n*

non-stick /ˌnɑnˈstɪk◂/ *adj* with a special surface that food will not stick to when cooked

non-stop /ˌnɑnˈstɑp◂/ *adj, adv* without a pause or interruption

non-vio·lent /ˌnɑnˈvaɪələnt/ *adj* not using or not involving violence

noo·dle /ˈnudl/ *n* long thin piece of PASTA made from flour, cooked in soup or boiling water

nook /nʊk/ *n* **1** sheltered private place **2** **nooks and crannies** places that are hidden or that few people know

noon /nun/ *n* [U] 12 o'clock in the middle of the day

no one /ˈ. ˌ./ *pron* not anyone; no person

noose /nus/ *n* ring formed by the end of a rope, which closes tighter as it is pulled

nope /noʊp/ *adv infml* no

no-place /ˈnoʊpleɪs/ *adv infml* NOWHERE

nor /nə; *strong* nɔr/ *conj* **1** (used after **neither** or **not**) also not; or: *neither hot nor cold — just warm* **2** and also not: *She didn't call, nor she write.*

norm /nɔrm/ *n* usual or average way of happening or behaving

nor·mal /ˈnɔrməl/ *adj* according to what is usual, expected, or average ~**ly** *adv*: *Normally I go to bed at 11 o'clock.* ~**ity** /nɔrˈmæləti/ also ~**cy** /ˈnɔrməlsi/ *n* [U]

nor·mal·ize /ˈnɔrməˌlaɪz/ *vi/t* (cause to) become normal, esp. to bring or come back to a good or friendly state –**ization** /ˌnɔrmələˈzeɪʃən/ *n* [U]

north /nɔrθ/ *n* (*often cap.*) direction which is on the left of a person facing the rising sun ♦ *adj* **1** in the north **2** (of wind) from the north ♦ *adv* **1** towards the north **2 up north** to or in the north ~**ward** *adj, adv*

north·east /ˌnɔrθˈist◂/ *n, adj, adv* (direction) exactly between north and east ~**ern** *adj*

nor·ther·ly /ˈnɔrðəli/ *adj* towards or in the north

nor·thern /ˈnɔrðən/ *adj* of the north part of the world or of a country ~**er** *n* person who lives in or comes from the northern part of a country

Northern Lights /ˌ. ˈ./ *n* [*the*+P] bands of colored lights seen in the night sky in northern parts of the world

north·west /ˌnɔrθˈwɛst◂/ *n, adj, adv* (direction) exactly between north and west ~**ern** *adj*

nos. *written abbrev. for:* numbers

nose /noʊz/ *n* **1** [C] the part of the face above the mouth that is used for breathing and smelling **2** [C] (pointed) front end: *the nose of the rocket* **3** [S] ability to find out: *I have a nose for trouble.* | *Just follow your nose.* (= use this ability) **4** [C] too great an interest in things which do not concern you: *Stop poking your nose into my affairs!* **5 keep one's nose clean** keep out of trouble **6 pay through the nose (for)** pay a great deal too much money (for) **7 put someone's nose out of joint** make someone jealous by taking their place as the center of attention **8 turn one's nose up at** consider (something) not good enough to enjoy **9 under someone's (very) nose** quite openly in front of someone ♦ *vi* **1** move ahead slowly and carefully **2** try to find out about things that do not concern you

nose·bleed /ˈnoʊzblid/ *n* case of bleeding from the nose

nose·cone /ˈnoʊzkoʊn/ *n* pointed front part of a spacecraft or MISSILE

nose-dive /ˈnoʊzdaɪv/ *vi* **1** (of a plane) drop suddenly, front end first **2** fall suddenly and greatly: *Prices nosedived.* **nosedive** *n*

nose job /ˈnoʊz dʒɑb/ *n infml* medical operation on the nose to improve its appearance

no-show /ˌ. ˈ./ *n* expected person who doesn't appear

nos·tal·gia /nɑˈstældʒə, nə-/ *n* [U] fondness for past things –**gic** *adj*

nos·tril /ˈnɑstrəl/ *n* either of the 2 openings in the nose

nos·y /ˈnoʊzi/ *adj* interested in things that do not concern you

not /nɑt/ *adv* **1** (used for showing the opposite meaning): *He's happy, but I'm not.* | *It's a cat, not a dog!* | *Will he come, or not?* | *Not one* (=none) *remained.* **2 not at all** (a polite answer to thanks) **3 not**

that I don't mean that: *Not that it matters, but where were you last night?*

no·ta·ble /ˈnoʊtəbəl/ *adj* unusual or good enough to be especially noticed **-bly** *adv* particularly

no·ta·ry /ˈnoʊtəri/ also **Notary Pub·lic** /ˌ··· ˈ·-/ — *n* public official who watches the signing of written statements and makes them official **-rize** *vt* have a notary watch and sign (a document)

no·ta·tion /noʊˈteɪʃən/ *n* [C;U] system of signs for writing something down: *musical notation*

notch /nɑtʃ/ *n* cut in the shape of a V ♦ *vt* make a notch in

note /noʊt/ *n* **1** [C] short written record to remind one of something **2** [C] short piece of additional information in a look **3** [C] short informal letter **4** [C] (in some countries) piece of paper money **5** [C] (sign representing) a musical sound **6** [S] stated quality or feeling: *a note of anger in his voice* **7** [U] *fml* fame; importance: *a composer of some note* **8 compare notes** tell one's experiences and opinions of something to **9 take note of** pay attention to ♦ *vt* **1** record in writing: *The policeman noted down his address.* **2** notice and remember **noted** *adj* famous

note·book /ˈnoʊtbʊk/ *n* book of plain paper in which one writes NOTES[1] (1)

note·pa·per /ˈnoʊtˌpeɪpə/ *n* [U] paper for writing letters on

note·wor·thy /ˈnoʊtˌwɜːði/ *adj* NOTABLE

noth·ing /ˈnʌθɪŋ/ *pron* **1** not any thing: *There's nothing in this box — it's empty.* **2** something of no importance: *My debts are nothing to* (= much less than) *his.* **3 for nothing: a** free **b** with no good result **4 nothing but** nothing other than: *He's nothing but a criminal.* **5 nothing doing: a** I won't! **b** no result, interest, etc. **6 nothing for it** no other way **7 nothing like** not nearly: *It's nothing like as cold as yesterday.* **8 think nothing of** treat as easy or unimportant

no·tice /ˈnoʊtɪs/ *n* **1** [C] written or printed sign giving information **2** [U] information that something is going to happen; warning: *The rules may be changed without notice.* **3** [U] attention: *Don't take any notice of* (= pay no attention to) *him.* ♦ *vi/t* see, hear, etc., so as to be conscious and remember: *She was wearing a new dress, but he didn't even*

notice *(it).* **~able** *adj* big enough to be noticed **~ably** *adv*

no·ti·fy /ˈnoʊtɪfaɪ/ *vt* tell (someone), esp. formally **-fication** /ˌnoʊtəfəˈkeɪʃən/ *n* [U]

no·tion /ˈnoʊʃən/ *n* idea; opinion

no·to·ri·e·ty /ˌnoʊtəˈraɪəti/ *n* [U] state of being notorious

no·to·ri·ous /noʊˈtɔːriəs, -ˈtoʊr-/ *adj* famous for something bad: *a notorious liar* **~ly** *adv*

not·with·stand·ing /ˌnɑtwɪθˈstændɪŋ, -wɪð-/ *adv fml* in spite of that

noun /naʊn/ *n* word that is the name of a thing, quality, action, etc., and can be used as the subject or object of a verb

nour·ish /ˈnɜːɪʃ, ˈnʌrɪʃ/ *vt* **1** keep alive and healthy by giving food **2** keep (a feeling, plan, etc.) alive **~ing** *adj* **~ment** *n* [U] food

nov·el¹ /ˈnɑvəl/ *n* long written story **~ist** *n* novel writer

nov·el² *adj* new and interesting

nov·el·ty /ˈnɑvəlti/ *n* **1** [U] interesting newness **2** [C] something new and unusual **3** [C] small cheap object, usu. not very useful

No·vem·ber /noʊˈvɛmbə, nə-/ *n* the 11th month of the year

nov·ice /ˈnɑvɪs/ *n* person who has just begun and has no experience

now /naʊ/ *adv* **1** at this present time: *He used to be fat, but now he's slim.* **2** next; at once: *Now for* (= now we will have) *the next question.* **3** (used for attracting attention or giving a warning): *Now then, what's all this?* **4** (**every**) **now and again/then** at times; sometimes **5 from now on** starting now and continuing ♦ *conj* because: *Now that you've arrived, we can begin.*

now·a·days /ˈnaʊəˌdeɪz/ *adv* in these modern times

no way /ˌ· ˈ·/ *adv, interj sl* no; certainly not

no·where /ˈnoʊwɛr, ˈnoʊhwɛr/ *adv* **1** not anywhere **2 nowhere near** not at all near or nearly

nox·ious /ˈnɑkʃəs/ *adj* harmful; poisonous

noz·zle /ˈnɑzəl/ *n* short tube at the end of a pipe for controlling the flow of a liquid

nth /ɛnθ/ *adj* **to the nth degree** to the highest, greatest, furthest, etc., degree or form: *dull to the nth degree*

nu·ance /'nuɑns, nu'ɑns/ n slight delicate difference in meaning, color, etc.

nu·cle·ar /'nukliə/ adj being, using, or producing the great power got by breaking up atoms: *nuclear energy* | *nuclear warfare* (= with nuclear bombs)

nuclear fam·i·ly /ˌ··· ˈ··ˌ/ n family unit that consists only of husband, wife, and children, without grandmothers, uncles, etc.

nu·cle·us /'nukliəs/ n -clei /-kliaɪ/ **1** central part of **a** an atom **b** a CELL (2) **2** original part around which the rest is built

nude /nud/ adj with no clothes on ◆ n **1** (piece of art showing a) nude person **2 in the nude** with no clothes on

nudge /nʌdʒ/ vt push gently, esp. with the elbow **nudge** n

nu·di·ty /'nudəti/ n [U] state of being nude

nug·get /'nʌgɪt/ n small rough lump: *gold nuggets* | (fig.) *a nugget of information*

nui·sance /'nusəns/ n annoying person, animal, thing, or situation

nuke /nuk/ vt infml **1** attack with NUCLEAR weapons **2** cook in a MICROWAVE oven

null and void /ˌnʌl ən 'vɔɪd/ adj having no legal effect

nul·li·fy /'nʌləˌfaɪ/ vt cause to have no effect

numb /nʌm/ adj unable to feel: *fingers numb with cold* **numb** n [U]

num·ber /'nʌmbə/ n **1** [C] (written sign for) a member of the system used in counting and measuring: *1, 2, and 3 are numbers.* **2** [C;U] quantity; amount: *A large number of people came.* **3** [C] piece of music **4 have someone's number** have knowledge useful in annoying or defeating someone ◆ vt **1** give a number to: *numbered pages* **2** reach as a total: *The audience numbered over 5000.* **3** fml include: *I number him among my friends.* **4 someone's days are numbered** someone cannot continue or live much longer ~**less** adj too many to count

number one /ˌ·· ˈ·/ n **1** chief person or thing **2** oneself and no one else: *Look out for number one.*

nu·mer·al /'numərəl/ n sign that represents a number — see also ROMAN NUMERAL

nu·mer·i·cal /nu'mɛrɪkəl/ adj of or using numbers ~**ly** adv

nu·mer·ous /'numərəs/ adj many

nun /nʌn/ n member of a female religious group that lives together ~**nery** building where whey live

nurse /nɚs/ n person who takes care of sick, hurt, or old people, esp. in a hospital ◆ vt **1** take care of as or like a nurse **2** hold in the mind: *nurse a grudge* **3** handle carefully or lovingly: *He nursed the battered plane home.* **4** feed (a baby) with breast milk **nursing** n [U] job of being a nurse

nur·se·ry /'nɚsəri/ n **1** place where young children are taken care of **2** place where garden plants are grown to be sold

nursery rhyme /'··· ˌ·/ n song or poem for young children

nursery school /'··· ˌ·/ n school for young children of 2 to 4 years of age

nursing home /'·· ˌ·/ n place where old or sick people can live and be taken care of

nur·ture /'nɚtʃə/ vt lit give care and food to, so as to help development

nut /nʌt/ n **1** fruit with a hard shell and a softer dry inside which is eaten **2** small piece of metal with a hole through it for screwing onto a BOLT (2) **3** sl crazy person **4 a hard/tough nut to crack** a difficult question, person, etc., to deal with **nuts** adj sl crazy ◆ n [P] taboo sl TESTICLES ~**ty** adj **1** like or full of nuts **2** sl crazy

nut·case /'nʌtˌkeɪs/ n sl crazy person

nut·crack·er /'nʌtˌkrækə/ n tool for cracking the shell of a nut

nu·tri·ent /'nutriənt/ n, adj (a chemical or food) providing for life or growth

nu·tri·tion /nu'trɪʃən/ n [U] process of giving or getting food –**tious** adj valuable to the body as food

nuts and bolts /ˌ· ˈ·/ n [(the) P] the simple facts or skills of a subject or job

nut·shell /'nʌtˌʃɛl/ n **in a nutshell** described in as few words as possible

nuz·zle /ˈnʌzəl/ *vi/t* press closely, esp. with the nose

ny·lon /ˈnaɪlɒn/ *n* [U] strong artificial material made into cloth, plastic, etc.

ny·lons /ˈnaɪlɒnz/ *n* [P] very close fitting garment covering the legs and lower body

nymph /nɪmf/ *n* (in Greek and Roman literature) goddess of nature living in trees, streams, mountains, etc.

O

O, o /oʊ/ **1** the 15th letter of the English alphabet **2** (in speech) zero

oaf /oʊf/ *n* rough stupid awkward person

oak /oʊk/ *n* large broad tree with hard wood and curly leaves

oar /ɔr, oʊr/ *n* long pole with a flat blade, used for rowing a boat

o·a·sis /oʊˈeɪsɪs/ *n* **-ses** /-siz/ place with water and trees in a desert

oath /oʊθ/ *n* **oaths** /oʊðz/ **1** solemn promise **2** use of bad angry words; curse **3 be on/under oath** have promised to tell the truth

oat·meal /ˈoʊtˀmil/ *n* [U] raw or cooked crushed oats

oats /oʊts/ *n* [P] sort of grain used as food — see also WILD OATS

o·be·di·ent /əˈbidiənt, oʊ-/ *adj* doing what one is told to do ~**ly** *adv* –**ence** *n* [U]

o·bese /oʊˈbis/ *adj fml* fat to an unhealthy degree **obesity** *n* [U]

o·bey /əˈbeɪ, oʊ-/ *vi/t* do what one is told to do (by someone in a position of power)

o·bit·u·a·ry /əˈbɪtʃuˌɛri, oʊ-/ *n* report in a newspaper, etc., of someone's death

ob·ject[1] /ˈɑbdʒɪkt, -dʒɛkt/ *n* **1** thing that can be seen or felt **2** purpose **3** *gram* word or words that represent **a** the person or thing (the **direct object**) that something is done to (such as *door* in *She closed the door.*) or **b** the person (the **indirect object**) who is concerned in the result of an action (such as *her* in *I gave her the book.*) **4** person or thing that produces the stated feeling: *She has become an object of pity.* **5 be no object** not be a difficulty

ob·ject[2] /əbˈdʒɛkt/ *vi* be against something or someone: *I object to paying so much.*

ob·jec·tion /əbˈdʒɛkʃən/ *n* **1** statement or feeling of dislike or opposition **2** reason or argument against

ob·jec·tio·na·ble /əbˈdʒɛkʃənəbəl/ *adj* unpleasant –**bly** *adv*

ob·jec·tive[1] /əbˈdʒɛktɪv/ *adj* **1** not influenced by personal feelings; fair **2** existing outside the mind; real –**tivity** /ˌɑbdʒɛkˈtɪvət̬i/ *n* [U]

objective[2] *n* purpose of a plan

object les·son /ˈ·· ˌ··/ *n* event or story from which one can learn how or how not to behave

ob·jet d'art /ˌɔbʒeɪ ˈdɑr, ˌɑb-/ *n* **objets d'art** (*same pronunciation*) small object of some value as art

ob·li·ga·tion /ˌɑbləˈgeɪʃən/ *n* [C;U] duty: *You're under* **no obligation** *to buy.* (= you don't have to) –**tory** /əˈblɪgəˌtɔri, -ˌtoʊri/ *adj*

o·blige /əˈblaɪdʒ/ *vt fml* **1** make it necessary for (someone) to do something: *We were obliged to* (= had to) *leave.* **2** do a favor for **3 (I'm) much obliged (to you)** (used for thanking someone politely)

o·blig·ing /əˈblaɪdʒɪŋ/ *adj* kind and eager to help ~**ly** *adv*

o·blique /əˈblik, oʊ-/ *adj* **1** indirect: *an oblique hint* **2** sloping

o·blit·er·ate /əˈblɪt̬əˌreɪt/ *vt* remove all signs of; destroy –**ation** /əˌblɪt̬əˈreɪʃən/ *n* [U]

o·bliv·i·on /əˈblɪviən/ *n* [U] **1** state of being completely forgotten **2** state of being unconscious or not noticing one's surroundings

o·bliv·i·ous /əˈblɪviəs/ *adj* not noticing: *He was oblivious of/to the danger.*

ob·long /ˈɑblɔŋ/ *n* figure with 4 angles of 90 degrees, and 4 sides, 2 long and 2 shorter ones; RECTANGLE **oblong** *adj*

ob·nox·ious /əbˈnɑkʃəs/ *adj* extremely unpleasant ~**ly** *adv*

o·boe /ˈoʊboʊ/ *n* musical instrument made of a black wooden tube, played by blowing **oboist** *n* player of an oboe

ob·scene /əbˈsin, ɑb-/ *adj* very offensive or shocking, esp. sexually

obscenity /əbˈsɛnət̬i/ *n* [C;U] obscene word or behavior

ob·scure /əbˈskyʊr/ *adj* **1** hard to understand; not clear **2** not well known ♦ *vt* hide **obscurity** *n* [U] state of being obscure

ob·ser·vance /əbˈzɚvəns/ *n fml* **1** [U] doing something in accordance with a law, custom, etc. **2** [C] part of a religious ceremony

ob·ser·vant /əbˈzɚvənt/ *adj* quick at noticing things

ob·ser·va·tion /ˌɑbzɚˈveɪʃən, -sɚ-/ *n* **1** [C;U] action of noticing **2** [U] ability to notice things **3** [C] *fml* remark, esp. about something noticed **4 under observation** being carefully watched during a period of time

ob·ser·va·to·ry /əbˈzɜːvətəri, -ˌtʊəri/ *n* place where scientists look at and study the stars, moon, etc.

ob·serve /əbˈzɜːv/ *vt* **1** watch carefully **2** *fml* act in accordance with (a law, custom, etc.) **3** *fml* say **observer** *n* **1** someone who observes **2** someone who attends meetings, etc., only to listen, not take part

ob·sess /əbˈsɛs/ *v* **1** *vt* completely fill (someone's) mind, so they cannot think about anything else: *She was obsessed by the fear of failure.* **2** think about (something) all the time: *He's always obsessing about his marriage. She was an obsession* ~**ion** /-ˈsɛʃən/ *n* fixed and often unreasonable idea or pattern of behavior

ob·so·lete /ˌɒbsəˈliːt, ˈɒbsəliːt/ *adj* no longer used; out of date

ob·sta·cle /ˈɒbstəkəl/ *n* something that prevents action, movement, or success

obstacle course /ˈ··· ˌ/ *n* area of land on which soldiers train by climbing or jumping over objects in order to develop their fitness and courage

ob·ste·tri·cian /ˌɒbstəˈtrɪʃən/ *n* doctor concerned with obstetrics

ob·stet·rics /əbˈstɛtrɪks/ *n* [U] branch of medicine concerned with the birth of children

ob·sti·nate /ˈɒbstənət/ *adj* **1** not willing to obey or change one's opinion **2** difficult to control or defeat: *obstinate resistance* ~**ly** *adv* ~**nacy** *n* [U]

ob·struct /əbˈstrʌkt/ *vt* **1** block **2** put difficulties in the way of ~**ive** *adj* intentionally obstructing ~**ion** /əbˈstrʌkʃən/ *n* **1** [C] act of obstructing **2** [U] something that obstructs

ob·tain /əbˈteɪn/ *vt fml* get: *How did you obtain this information?* ~**able** *adj*

ob·tru·sive /əbˈtruːsɪv, -zɪv/ *adj fml* unpleasantly noticeable ~**ly** *adv*

ob·tuse /əbˈtjuːs, ɑb-/ *adj* **1** *fml* annoyingly slow to understand **2** (of an angle) more than 90° ~**ly** *adv* ~**ness** *n* [U]

ob·vi·ous /ˈɒbviəs/ *adj* easy to see and understand; clear: *an obvious lie* ~**ly** *adv*

oc·ca·sion /əˈkeɪʒən/ *n* **1** [C] time when something happens: *May I take this occa-*

sion (= this chance) *to thank you for your help.* **2** [U] *fml* reason: *He had no occasion to be so rude.* **3** [C] special event or ceremony **4 on occasion** *fml* occasionally — see also SENSE OF OCCASION ♦ *vt fml* cause

oc·ca·sion·al /əˈkeɪʒənəl/ *adj* happening sometimes; not regular ~**ly** *adv*

oc·cult /əˈkʌlt, ɑ-, ˈɑkʌlt/ *adj* magical and mysterious ♦ *n* [*the*+S]

oc·cu·pant /ˈɒkjəpənt/ *n* person who is living in a house, room, etc. ~**pancy** *n* [U] (period of) being an occupant

oc·cu·pa·tion /ˌɒkjəˈpeɪʃən/ *n* **1** [C] job **2** [C] something done to pass time **3** [U] taking possession of ~**al** *adj* of one's job

oc·cu·py /ˈɒkjəpaɪ/ *vt* **1** be in: *The seat was occupied.* (= someone was sitting in it) **2** fill (space or time): *Writing occupies most of my spare time.* **3** take possession of: *an occupied country* **4** keep busy ~**pant** *n*

oc·cur /əˈkɜː/ *vi* **-rr-** **1** happen **2** be found; exist: *a disease that occurs in children* ~**rence** /əˈkʌrəns, əˈkʌr-/ *n* **1** [C] event **2** [U] process of occurring

occur to *phr vt* (of an idea) come to (someone's) mind

o·cean /ˈoʊʃən/ *n* **1** [U] great mass of salt water that covers most of the Earth **2** [C] any of the large areas into which this is divided: *the Atlantic Ocean* ~**ic** /ˌoʊʃiˈænɪk/ *adj*

o'clock /əˈklɒk/ *adv* (used in telling the time when it is exactly a numbered hour): *at 5 o'clock*

oc·ta·gon /ˈɒktəɡən/ *n* flat figure with 8 sides and 8 angles

oc·tane /ˈɒkteɪn/ *n* substance added to increase the power and quality of gasoline: *high-octane fuel*

oc·tave /ˈɒktɪv/ *n* space of 8 degrees between musical notes

Oc·to·ber /ɑkˈtoʊbə/ *n* the 10th month of the year

oc·to·ge·nar·ian /ˌɒktədʒəˈneəriən/ *n* a person who is between 80 and 90 years old

oc·to·pus /ˈɒktəpəs/ *n* creature with 8 limbs that lives deep under the sea

OD *vi sl* take too much of a dangerous drug; OVERDOSE

odd /ɒd/ *adj* **1** strange; unusual **2** (of a number) that cannot be exactly divided by two **3** separated from its pair or set: *an odd shoe* **4** not regular: *doing odd jobs*

5 rather more than the stated number: *20-odd years ago* ~**ly** *adv* strangely ~**ity** *n* **1** [C] strange thing, person, etc. **2** [U] strangeness

odd·ball /'ɑdbɔl/ *n* strange person

odds /adz/ *n* [P] **1** probability of something happening: *The odds are* (= it is likely) *that she will fail.* **2 at odds** in disagreement

odds and ends /ˌ · ·ˈ·/ *n* [P] small articles of various kinds

ode /oʊd/ *n* long poem

o·di·ous /'oʊdiəs/ *adj fml* very unpleasant

o·dom·e·ter /oʊˈdɑmətər/ *n* instrument that tells how far a car, etc. has traveled

o·dor /'oʊdər/ *n fml* smell

of /əv, ə; *strong* ʌv, ɑv/ *prep* **1** belonging to: *the wheels of the car* **2** made from: *a crown of gold* **3** containing: *a bag of potatoes* **4** (shows a part or amount): *2 pounds of sugar* **5 a** that is/are: *a friend of mine | some fool of a boy* (= some foolish boy) **b** happening in or on: *the Battle of Bunker Hill* **6** in relation to; in connection with: *a teacher of English | fond of swimming* **7 a** done by: *the plays of Shakespeare* **b** done about: *a picture of Shakespeare* **8** with; having: *a matter of no importance* **9** (shows what someone or something is or does): *the laughter of the children | How kind of you!* **10** (used in dates): *the 27th of February* **11** during: *We often go there of an evening.*

off[1] /ɔf/ *adv, adj* **1** disconnected; removed: *The handle fell off.* **2** (esp. of electrical apparatus) not lit or working: *The TV is off.* **3** away: *She drove off.* **4** away or free from work: *She's taken this week off.* **5** so as to be finished or destroyed: *They were all killed off.* **6** not going to happen after all: *The party's off!* **7** incorrect: *off in his calculations* **8** provided with what you need: *They're not well off.* (= have not got much money) | *You'd be better off with a bike than that old car!* **9** not as usual: **a** *having an off day* **b** quiet and dull: *the off season* **10 off and on** sometimes **11 on the off chance** just in case **12 right/straight off** at once

off[2] *prep* **1** away from: *I jumped off the bus. | I cut a piece off the loaf. | The ship was blown off course.* **2** in the sea near: *an island off the coast*

off·beat /ˌɔfˈbit◄/ *adj* not conventional (CONVENTION)

off-col·or /ˌ ·ˈ·· ◄/ *adj* sexually improper: *off-color jokes*

of·fend /əˈfɛnd/ *v* **1** *vt* hurt the feelings of; upset **2** *vt* displease greatly **3** *vi* do wrong: *to offend against good manners* ~**er** *n* person who offends, esp. a criminal: *a first offender* (= someone found guilty of a crime for the first time) ~**ing** *adj* causing displeasure, discomfort, or inconvenience

of·fense /əˈfɛns/ *n* **1** [C] wrong act, esp. a crime **2** [U] cause for hurt feelings: *Don't take offense.* (= feel offended) **3** /'ɔfɛns/ [S] concerned with making points in a game: *a good offense*

of·fen·sive /əˈfɛnsɪv, -zɪv/ *adj* **1** extremely unpleasant **2** for attacking or making points in a game: *an offensive player* ♦ *n* **1** continued military attack **2 on the offensive** attacking ~**ly** *adv* ~**ness** *n* [U]

of·fer /'ɔfər, 'ɑfər/ *v* **1** *vt/i* say one will give or do: *The police are offering a big reward. | She offered to drive me there.* **2** *vt* provide; give: *The situation doesn't offer much hope. | He offered no resistance.* **3** give (to God): *She offered (up) a prayer.* ♦ *n* **1** statement offering something **2** what is offered ~**ing** *n* something offered

off·hand /ˌɔfˈhænd◄/ *adv, adj* **1** careless; disrespectful **2** without time to think or prepare

of·fice /'ɔfɪs, 'ɑ-/ *n* **1** [C] room or building where written work is done **2** [C] place where a particular service is provided: *a ticket office* **3** [C] government department: *the Office of Management and Budget* **4** [C;U] important job or position of power: *the office of president*

of·fi·cer /'ɔfəsər, 'ɑ-/ *n* **1** person in command in the army, navy, etc. **2** person in a government job: *a probation officer* **3** policeman

of·fi·cial /əˈfɪʃəl/ *adj* of, from, or decided by someone in a position of power and responsibility: *official permission* ♦ *n* person who holds an OFFICE (4) ~**ly** *adv* **1** formally by an official **2** as stated publicly (but perhaps not really) ~**dom** *n* [U] officials as a group ~**ese** /ˌɔfɪʃəˈliz/ *n* [U] *infml* language of government officials, considered unnecessarily hard to understand

of·fi·ci·ate /əˈfɪʃiˌeɪt/ vi perform official duties

of·fi·cious /əˈfɪʃəs/ adj too eager to give orders ~**ly** adv ~**ness** n [U]

off·ing /ˈɔfɪŋ/ n **in the offing** coming soon

off-ramp /ˈ. ./ n road for driving off a FREEWAY

off·set /ˈɔfsɛt, ˌɔfˈsɛt/ vt -**set**; present p. -**setting** make up for; balance: They offset the cost by charging higher prices.

off·shoot /ˈɔfʃut/ n new stem or branch: (fig.) an offshoot of a large company

off·shore /ˌɔfˈʃɔr, -ˈʃour/ adv, adj **1** in the sea near the coast: offshore islands **2** away from the coast: offshore winds

off·spring /ˈɔfsprɪŋ/ n **offspring** fml someone's child or children

off·stage /ˌɔfˈsteɪdʒ/ adv behind or away from the stage in a theater

off-the-rec·ord /ˌ. . ˈ. ./ adj, adv unofficial and not to be formally recorded

off-the-wall /ˌ. . ˈ./ adj amusingly foolish

off-white /ˌ. ˈ. ◁/ adj grayish or yellowish white

of·ten /ˈɔfən, ˈɔftən/ adv **1** many times: He was often ill. **2** in many cases: Very fat people are often unhealthy. **3** as often as not at least half of the time **4** every so often sometimes **5** more often than not more than half of the time

o·gle /ˈoʊɡəl/ vi/t look (at) with great sexual interest

o·gre /ˈoʊɡər/ n **1** fierce creature in fairy stories, like a very large person **2** frightening person

oh /oʊ/ interj (expresses surprise, fear, etc.)

oil /ɔɪl/ n [U] thick fatty liquid that burns easily, esp. PETROLEUM ♦ vt put oil on or into ~**y** adj **1** like or covered with oil **2** too polite **oils** n [P] paints containing oil

oil·field /ˈɔɪlfild/ n area with oil underneath it

oil paint·ing /ˈ. ˌ. ./ n [C;U] painting done using paint made with oil

oil rig /ˈɔɪlˌrɪɡ/ n large apparatus for getting oil up from under the ocean

oil well /ˈ. ./ n hole made in the ground to get oil

oink /ɔɪŋk/ n sound made by a pig ♦ vi

oint·ment /ˈɔɪntˌmənt/ n **1** [C;U] oily usu. medicinal substance rubbed on the skin

2 **a/the fly in the ointment** one small unwanted thing that spoils the happiness of an occasion

o·kay, OK /oʊˈkeɪ/ adj, adv **1** all right; satisfactory **2** (expresses agreement or permission) ♦ n approval; permission ♦ vt give permission for

old /oʊld/ adj **1** having lived or existed a long time **2** of a particular age: The baby is 2 years old. **3** having been so a long time: an old friend **4** former: He got his old job back. | an old boyfriend/girlfriend **5 of old: a** in the past **b** for a long time ♦ n [the+S] old people

old age /ˌ. ˈ. ◁/ n [U] part of one's life when one is old

old·en /ˈoʊldən/ adj lit past; long ago: in olden times

old-fash·ioned /ˌ. ˈ. . ◁/ adj once usual or fashionable but now less common

old flame /ˌ. ˈ./ n someone with whom one used to be in love

Old Glo·ry /ˌ. ˈ. ./ n US flag

old guard /ˈ. ˌ./ n [the+S] group of people with old-fashioned ideas who are against change

old hand /ˌ. ˈ./ n very experienced person

old hat /ˌ. ˈ./ adj old-fashioned

old·ie /ˈoʊldi/ n infml old thing or person

old maid /ˌ. ˈ./ n old unmarried woman

old-tim·er /ˈoʊldˈtaɪmər/ n **1** person who has somewhere or done something for a long time **2** old man

old wives' tale /ˌ. ˈ. ./ n ancient and not necessarily true belief

ol·i·gar·chy /ˈɑləˌɡɑrki/ n **1** [U] government by a small usu. unrepresentative group **2** [C] state governed in this way

ol·ive /ˈɑlɪv/ n **1** [C] small fruit of the **olive tree**, grown in Mediterranean countries and eaten raw or made into **olive oil** for cooking **2** [U] dull pale green

om·buds·man /ˈɑmbʊdzmən/ n -**men** /-mən/ person who deals with complaints about an organization

ome·lette /ˈɑmələt/ n flat round mass of eggs beaten together and cooked

o·men /ˈoʊmən/ n sign of something that will happen

om·i·nous /ˈɑmənəs/ adj seeming to show that something bad will happen ~**ly** adv

o·mis·sion /oʊˈmɪʃən, ə-/ n **1** [U] act of omitting **2** [C] something left out

o·mit /oʊ'mɪt, ə-/ vt 1 not include: An important detail was omitted. 2 fml not do; fail: They omitted to tell me.

om·nip·o·tent /ɑm'nɪpətənt/ adj fml having unlimited power –**tence** n [U]

om·nis·ci·ent /ɑm'nɪʃənt/ adj knowing everything –**ence** n [U]

om·niv·o·rous /ɑm'nɪvərəs/ adj (esp. of an animal) eating everything

on¹ /ɑn, ɔn// prep 1 touching, supported by, hanging from, or connected with: a lamp on the table 2 towards; in the direction of 3 directed towards: a tax on beer 4 in (a large vehicle): on a train 5 (shows when something happens): She's coming on Tuesday. 6 about: a book on golf 7 by means of: A car runs on gas. 8 in a state of: on fire | on vacation 9 working for; belonging to: She's on the committee. 10 directly after and because of: I acted on your advice. 11 paid for by: The drinks are on me!

on² adv, adj 1 continuously, instead of stopping: He kept on talking. 2 further; forward: We walked on to the next one. 3 (so as to be) wearing: He put his coat on. | He had nothing on. 4 with the stated part in front: They crashed head on. 5 in(to) a vehicle: The bus stopped and we got on. 6 (esp. of electrical apparatus) lit or working: The TV was on. 7 (of something arranged) happening or going to happen: What's on at the theater? | I've got nothing on on Tuesday. (= I'm not doing anything) 8 with the stated part forward: Look at it head on. 9 and so on etc. 10 on the hour every hour exactly at 3:00, 4:00, etc. 11 on and off from time to time 12 on and on without stopping

once /wʌns/ adv 1 one time: We've only met once. 2 formerly: He was once a famous singer. 3 all at once suddenly 4 at once: a now; without delay: Come at once! b together: Don't all speak at once! 5 for once for this one time only: Just for once he was telling the truth. 6 once and for all now, so as to be settled, with no further change 7 once in a while sometimes, but not often 8 once more again ♦ conj from the moment that: Once he's arrived, we can start.

once-o·ver /ˈ· ˌ·-/ n infml a quick look or examination

on·com·ing /ˈɑn,kʌmɪŋ, ˈɔn-/ adj coming towards one: oncoming traffic

one¹ /wʌn/ determiner, n 1 (the number) 1 2 a certain: They'll come back one day. | The victim was one Roy Malkin. 3 the same: They all ran in one direction. 4 particular type or example (of): He can't tell one tree from another. 5 at one fml in agreement 6 be one up (on) have the advantage (over) 7 for one as one (person, thing, reason, etc.) out of several: I for one, see no reason to continue. 8 in one combined: It's a table and desk all in one. 9 one and all every one 10 one and the same exactly the same 11 one of a member of: Our dog's like one of the family. 12 one or two a few

one² pron 1 single thing or person of the sort mentioned: Have you any books on gardening? I'd like to borrow one. 2 fml any person; you: One should do one's duty.

one an·oth·er /ˌ· ·ˈ·/ pron EACH OTHER: They hit one another.

one-man band /ˌ· ·ˈ·/ n 1 a street musician who plays different instruments all at one time 2 activity which someone does all on their own

one-night stand /ˌ· ·ˈ·/ n 1 performance (of music or a play) given only once in each of a number of places by a (group of) performers 2 sexual relationship which lasts only one night

one-of-a-kind /ˌ· · · ·ˈ·/ adj special because unlike any other

one-off /ˌ· ·ˈ·/ adj 1 happening or done only once 2 made as a single example

one-on-one /ˌ· ·ˈ·/ adj, adv between only two people: one-on-one discussion

one-piece /ˈ· ·/ adj made in one piece only

o·ner·ous /ˈɑnərəs, ˈoʊ-/ adj fml difficult; hard to bear: an onerous duty

one·self /wʌnˈsɛlf/ pron fml 1 (reflexive form of ONE² (2)): to wash oneself 2 (strong form of ONE² (2)): One shouldn't try and do everything oneself. 3 (all) by oneself: a alone b without help 4 to oneself not shared

one-shot /ˈ· ·/ adj 1 happening or done only once 2 made as a single example

one-sid·ed /ˌ· ·ˈ·◂/ adj with one side stronger or more favored than the other: a one-sided football game

one-time /ˈwʌntaɪm/ adj former

one-to-one /ˌ· · ·ˈ·◂/ adj, adv 1 matching one another exactly 2 between only two people

one-up-man-ship /ˌwʌnˈʌpmənˌʃɪp/ also -**ups** — n [U] art of getting an advantage without actually cheating

one-way /ˌ· ˈ·◄/ adj moving or allowing movement in one direction only: a one-way street

on-go-ing /ˈɑnˌgoʊɪŋ, ˈɔn-/ adj continuing: an ongoing problem

on-ion /ˈʌnyən/ n round white vegetable with a strong smell

on-line /ˈɑnlaɪn, ˈɔn-/ adj 1 connected to a large computer system, esp. the INTERNET 2 directly connected to and/or controlled by a computer **online** /ɑnˈlaɪn, ɔn-/ adv

on-look-er /ˈɑnˌlʊkɚ, ˈɔn-/ n person watching something happen

on-ly¹ /ˈoʊnli/ adj 1 with no others in the same group: my only friend | an only child (= with no brothers or sisters) 2 best: She's the only person for this job.

only² adv 1 and no one or nothing else: There were only 5 left. 2 **if only** (expresses a strong wish): If only she were here! 3 only too very; completely: I'm afraid it's only too true.

only³ conj except that; but: She wants to go, only she doesn't have enough money.

on-ramp /ˈ· ·/ n road for driving onto a FREEWAY

on-rush /ˈɑnrʌʃ, ˈɔn-/ n strong movement forward

on-set /ˈɑnsɛt, ˈɔn-/ n start, esp. of something bad

on-shore /ˌɑnˈʃɔr◄, -ˈʃoʊr◄, ˌɔn-/ adv, adj towards the coast: onshore winds

on-slaught /ˈɑnslɔt, ˈɔn-/ n fierce attack

on-to /ˈɑntə, ˈɔn-; before vowels -tu; strong -tu/ prep 1 to a position or point on: He jumped onto the train. 2 **be onto** have found out about (someone or something wrong or illegal)

o-nus /ˈoʊnəs/ n [S] duty; responsibility: The onus is on you to do it.

on-ward /ˈɑnwɚd, ˈɔn-/ adj, adv forward in space or time

oo-dles /ˈudlz/ n [P] infml lots

ooze /uz/ v 1 vi (of thick liquid) pass or flow slowly 2 vt have (liquid) oozing out: (fig.) He oozes charm. ◆ n [U] mud or thick liquid

o-pal /ˈoʊpəl/ n white precious stone with colors in it

o-paque /oʊˈpeɪk/ adj which you cannot see through ~**ness** n [U]

o-pen¹ /ˈoʊpən/ adj 1 not shut: an open window/book | (fig.) an open mind (= not closed to new ideas) 2 not surrounded by anything: open country 3 without a roof: an open boat 4 not fastened or folded: with his shirt open 5 not completely decided or answered: an open question 6 that one can go into as a visitor or customer: Is the bank open yet? 7 (of a job) not filled 8 not hiding or hidden; honest 9 that anyone can enter: an open competition 10 spread out: The flowers are open. 11 **open to: a** not safe from: open to criticism **b** willing to receive: open to suggestions 12 **with open arms** in a very friendly way ~**ly** adv not secretly ~**ness** n [U]

open² vi/t 1 make or become open: Open your mouth! 2 spread; unfold: open a map 3 (cause to) start: The story opens in a country village. 4 (cause to) begin business: The stores open at 9 o'clock. 5 **open fire** start shooting 6 **open someone's eyes (to something)** make someone know or understand something ~**er** n

open into/onto phr vt provide a means of entering or reaching

open out phr vi speak more freely

open up phr v 1 vt make possible the development of 2 vi open the door 3 vi speak more freely

open³ n [the+S] 1 the outdoors 2 **in(to) the open** (of opinions, secrets, etc.) in(to) the consciousness of the people around one

open-air /ˌ· ˈ·◄/ adj of or in the outdoors: an open-air theater

open-and-shut /ˌ· · ˈ·◄/ adj easy to prove

open-end-ed /ˌ· ˈ·◄/ adj with no limit set in advance

open-hand-ed /ˌ· ˈ·◄/ adj generous

open house /ˌ· ˈ·/ n occasion when a school, business, etc., allows the public to come in and see work done there

o-pen-ing /ˈoʊpənɪŋ/ n 1 hole or clear space 2 favorable set of conditions 3 unfilled job ◆ adj first; beginning

open-mind-ed /ˌ· ˈ·◄/ adj willing to consider and accept new ideas, opinions, etc.

op-e-ra /ˈɑprə/ n musical play in which (most of) the words are sung ~**tic** /ˌɑpəˈrætɪk◄/ adj

op-e-ra-ble /ˈɑpərəbəl/ adj (of a disease, etc.) that can be cured by an operation

op-e-rate /ˈɑpəˌreɪt/ v 1 vi/t (cause to) work: learning to operate the controls 2 vi carry on business: *We operate through-out Europe.* **3** *vi* cut the body to cure or remove diseased parts **4** *vi* produce effects: *The new law operates in our favor.*

operating room /ˈ···ˌ·/ *n* room in a hospital where medical treatments involving cutting the body are done

operating sys·tem /ˈ···ˌ·/ *n* set of PROGRAMS inside a computer that controls the way it works and helps it to handle other programs

op·e·ra·tion /ˌɑpəˈreɪʃən/ *n* **1** [U] condition or process of working **2** [C] thing (to be) done; activity **3** [C] cutting of the body to cure or remove a diseased part **4** [C] planned military movement **–al** *adj* **1** of operations: *operational costs* **2** ready for use

op·e·ra·tive /ˈɑpərətɪv, ˈɑpəˌreɪ-/ *adj* **1** (of a plan, law, etc.) working; producing effects **2** most important: *"Fast" is the operative word.* ♦ *n fml* worker

op·e·ra·tor /ˈɑpəˌreɪtə/ *n* person who works a machine, apparatus, or esp. telephone SWITCHBOARD

o·pin·ion /əˈpɪnyən/ *n* **1** [C] what someone thinks about something, based on personal judgment rather than facts: *In my opinion, its crazy.* **2** [U] what people in general think about something **3** [C] professional judgment or advice **~ated** *adj* too sure that what one thinks is right

o·pi·um /ˈoupiəm/ *n* [U] addictive (ADDICT) drug that produces sleep

op·po·nent /əˈpoʊnənt/ *n* **1** person who takes the opposite side in a competition or fight **2** person who opposes someone or something

op·por·tune /ˌɑpəˈtun/ *adj fml* **1** (of time) right for a purpose **2** coming at the right time **~ly** *adv*

op·por·tun·is·m /ˌɑpəˈtuˌnɪzəm/ *n* [U] taking advantage of every chance for success, sometimes to other people's disadvantage **–ist** *n*

op·por·tu·ni·ty /ˌɑpəˈtunəti/ *n* [C;U] favorable moment; chance

op·pose /əˈpoʊz/ *vt* be or act against

op·posed /əˈpoʊzd/ *adj* **1** against : *I'm opposed to abortion.* **2 as opposed to** and not

op·po·site /ˈɑpəzɪt, -sɪt/ *adj* **1** as different as possible from: *at opposite ends of the room* **2** facing: *the houses opposite* ♦ *n*

opposite thing or person: *Black and white are opposites.* ♦ *prep* facing: *She sat opposite me.*

op·po·si·tion /ˌɑpəˈzɪʃən/ *n* **1** [U] act or state of opposing **2** [U] people who are against one

op·press /əˈprɛs/ *vt* **1** rule in a hard cruel way **2** cause to feel ill or sad **~ive** *adj* **1** cruel; unjust **2** causing feelings of illness and unhappiness: *oppressive heat* **~or** *n* **~ion** /əˈprɛʃən/ *n* [U]

opt /ɑpt/ *vi* make a choice: *I opted for the smaller one.*

opt out *phr vi* decide not to take part

op·tic /ˈɑptɪk/ *adj* of the eyes: *the optic nerve*

op·ti·cal /ˈɑptɪkəl/ *adj* **1** of or about the sense of sight: *She thought she saw it, but it was an* **optical illusion.** (= something that deceives the sense of sight) **2** of or using light: *optical character recognition*

op·ti·mist /ˈɑptəˌmɪst/ *n* person who expects good things to happen **–mism** *n* [U] **~ic** /ˌɑptəˈmɪstɪk/ *adj*

op·ti·mize /ˈɑptəˌmaɪz/ *vt* make as perfect or effective as possible

op·ti·mum /ˈɑptəməm/ also **optimal** /ˈɑptəməl/—*adj* most favorable: *optimum conditions for growing rice*

op·tion /ˈɑpʃən/ *n* **1** [U] freedom to choose: *I had to do it; I had no option.* **2** [C] possible course of action that can be chosen **3** [C] right to buy or sell something at a stated time in the future — see also SOFT OPTION **~al** *adj* which you can choose to have or not to have

op·tom·e·trist /ɑpˈtɑmətrɪst/ *n* person who makes and sells glasses, etc., for people's eyes

op·u·lent /ˈɑpyələnt/ *adj* **1** showing great wealth **2** in good supply **–lence** *n* [U]

OR *abbrev. for:* OPERATING ROOM

or /ər/ *strong* ɔr/ *conj* **1** (shows different possibilities): *Will you have tea or coffee?* **2** if not: *Wear your coat or you'll be cold.* **3** (describes the same thing in a different way): *a yard, or three feet* **4** or **else** *infml* (used as a threat) or something bad will happen **5** or **so** about: *We waited for 5 minutes or so.*

o·ral /ˈɔrəl, ˈoʊrəl/ *adj* **1** spoken, not written: *an oral exam* **2** *med* of the mouth **~ly** *adv*

or·ange /ˈɔrɪndʒ, ˈɑr-/ n common round red-yellow fruit ♦ adj of the color of an orange

o·rang·u·tan /əˈræŋəˌtæn/ n large monkey with reddish hair and no tail

or·a·tor /ˈɔrətə, ˈɑr-/ n public speaker

or·bit /ˈɔrbɪt/ n 1 path of something going around something else, esp. in space 2 area of power or influence ♦ vi/t go around in an orbit: The satellite orbits the Earth. ~al adj

or·chard /ˈɔrtʃəd/ n place where fruit trees are grown

or·ches·tra /ˈɔrkɪstrə, ˈɔrˌkɛstrə/ n large group of musicians playing different instruments **orchestral** /ɔrˈkɛstrəl/ adj

or·ches·trate /ˈɔrkəˌstreɪt/ vt 1 arrange (music) to be played by an orchestra 2 plan (something with many parts) for best effect –**tration** /ˌɔrkəˈstreɪʃən/ n [C;U]

or·chid /ˈɔrkɪd/ n plant with bright flowers that have strange shapes

or·dain /ɔrˈdeɪn/ vt 1 make (someone) a priest 2 fml (of God, the law, etc.) order

or·deal /ɔrˈdil, ˈɔrdil/ n difficult or painful experience

or·der¹ /ˈɔrdə/ n 1 [U] way in which things are arranged: in alphabetical order | in order of importance | Leave everything in good order. (= neatly) 2 [U] fitness for use: The phone's out of order. (= doesn't work) 3 [U] condition in which laws and rules are obeyed: That new teacher can't keep order in his class. | Your papers are in order. (= acceptable according to the rules) 4 [C] command: An officer gives orders. 5 [C] request to supply goods: The waiter took our order. 6 [C] religious or social organization: The Benedictine order 7 [C] fml kind; sort: courage of the highest order 8 [P] state of being a priest, etc.: to take (holy) orders 9 **in order that** fml so that 10 **in order to** with the purpose of 11 **in the order of** about 12 **on order** asked for but not yet supplied — see also TALL ORDER

order² v 1 vt command: He ordered them to attack. 2 vt/i ask for (something) to be supplied: I ordered chicken soup. 3 vt arrange

order about phr vt give many commands to, unpleasantly

or·der·ly /ˈɔrdəli/ adj 1 well arranged 2 liking tidy arrangement 3 peaceful and well behaved: an orderly crowd ♦ n helper in a hospital –**liness** n [U]

or·di·nal num·ber /ˌɔrdn-əl ˈnʌmbə/ n one of the numbers (1st, 2nd, 3rd, etc.) that show order rather than quantity

or·di·nance /ˈɔrdn-əns/ n city or town law that forbids or restricts an activity

or·di·nary /ˈɔrdnˌɛri, ˈɔrdnˌɛri/ adj 1 not unusual; common 2 **out of the ordinary** unusual –**narily** /ˌɔrdnˈɛrəli/ adv usually

or·di·na·tion /ˌɔrdnˈeɪʃən/ n [U;C] act of ORDAINing a priest

ore /ɔr, oʊr/ n [U] rock from which metal is obtained

or·gan /ˈɔrgən/ n 1 part of an animal or plant that has a special purpose, such as the heart 2 organization with a special purpose within a larger one: Congress is an organ of government. 3 large musical instrument played by blowing air through pipes ~**ist** n ORGAN (2) player

or·gan·ic /ɔrˈgænɪk/ adj 1 of living things or physical organs 2 made of parts with related purposes 3 (of food) grown without chemicals ~**ally** adv

or·gan·is·m /ˈɔrgəˌnɪzəm/ n 1 living creature 2 whole made of related parts

or·gan·i·za·tion /ˌɔrgənəˈzeɪʃən/ n 1 [C] group of people with a special purpose, such as a business or club 2 [U] organizing; arrangement

or·gan·ize /ˈɔrgəˌnaɪz/ vt 1 arrange into a good system: a well-organized office 2 make necessary arrangements for: to organize a party –**izer** n

organized crime /ˌ··· ˈ·/ n [U] (activities of) a large powerful organization of criminals

or·gas·m /ˈɔrgæzəm/ n [C;U] highest point of sexual pleasure

or·gy /ˈɔrdʒi/ n 1 wild party where people get drunk and have sex 2 infml a set (of usu. pleasant activities) close together in time

O·ri·ent /ˈɔriənt, -ˌɛnt, ˈoʊr-/ n esp. lit [the] the eastern part of the world; Asia

o·ri·ent /ˈɔriˌɛnt, -ənt, ˈoʊr-/ vt 1 arrange or direct with a particular purpose: an export-oriented company 2 find out where you are

O·ri·en·tal /ˌɔriˈɛntl, ˌoʊr-/ adj of or from the Orient

o·ri·en·ta·tion /ˌɔriənˈteɪt, ˈoʊr-/ n 1 [C;U] beliefs, aims, or interests chosen by a person or group: political orientation 2 [U] training and preparation for a new job or activity **3 sexual orientation** fact of being HETEROSEXUAL or HOMOSEXUAL

or·i·gin /ˈɒrədʒɪn, ˈɑr-/ n 1 [C;U] starting point 2 [U] also **origins** pl. — parents and conditions of early life: a woman of humble origin

o·rig·i·nal /əˈrɪdʒənəl/ adj 1 first; earliest 2 new and different 3 not copied ♦ n the one from which copies have been made ~**ly** adv 1 in the beginning, before changing 2 in a new and different way ~**ity** /əˌrɪdʒəˈnæləti/ n [U] quality of being ORIGINAL (2)

o·rig·i·nate /əˈrɪdʒəˌneɪt/ vi/t (cause to) begin –**nator** n

o·ri·ole /ˈɔriˌoʊl, ˈɔriəl/ n black bird with red and yellow stripes on its wings

or·na·ment /ˈɔrnəmənt/ n [C;U] decorative object(s) ♦ vt /-ˌmɛnt/ decorate ~**al** /ˌɔrnəˈmɛntl◄/ adj ~**ation** /ˌɔrnəmɛnˈteɪʃən/ n [U]

or·nate /ɔrˈneɪt/ adj having (too) much ornament

or·ne·ry /ˈɔrnəri/ adj bad-tempered

or·ni·thol·o·gy /ˌɔrnəˈθɑlədʒi/ n [U] scientific study of birds –**gist** n

or·phan /ˈɔrfən/ n child with no parents ♦ vt cause to be an orphan ~**age** n place where orphans live

or·tho·don·tist /ˌɔrθəˈdɒntɪst/ n DENTIST who makes teeth straight

or·tho·dox /ˈɔrθəˌdɑks/ adj 1 generally or officially accepted or used: orthodox methods 2 holding orthodox opinions ~**y** n [U]

or·tho·pe·dic /ˌɔrθəˈpidɪk◄/ adj of the branch of medicine (**orthopedics**) that puts bones straight

Os·car /ˈɑskɚ/ n yearly prize for best work in films

os·cil·late /ˈɑsəˌleɪt/ vi 1 move regularly from side to side 2 vary between opposing choices –**lation** /ˌɑsəˈleɪʃən/ n [C;U]

os·ten·ta·tion /ˌɑstənˈteɪʃən, -tɛn-/ n [U] unnecessary show of wealth, knowledge, etc. –**tious** adj

os·tra·cize /ˈɑstrəˌsaɪz/ vt stop accepting (someone) into one's group –**cism** n [U]

os·trich /ˈɔstrɪtʃ, ˈɑ-/ n extremely large African bird with long legs that cannot fly

oth·er /ˈʌðɚ/ determiner, pron 1 the remaining one of a set; what is left as well as that mentioned: She held on with one hand and waved with the other. 2

additional: Do you have any other questions? 3 not this, not oneself, not one's own, etc.: He likes spending other people's money. 4 **one after the other** first one, then the next, etc. 5 **other than: a** except: no one other than me **b** anything but: I can't be other than grateful. 6 **the other day/night/afternoon/evening** on a recent day/night/afternoon/evening

oth·er·wise /ˈʌðɚˌwaɪz/ adv 1 differently 2 apart from that: The soup was cold, but otherwise the meal was excellent. 3 if not: Go faster, otherwise we'll be late.

ouch /aʊtʃ/ interj (expresses sudden pain)

ought /ɔt/ v aux 1 have a (moral) duty: You ought to look after them better. 2 (shows what is right or sensible): You ought to see a doctor. 3 will probably: Prices ought to come down soon.

ounce /aʊns/ n 1 [C] a measure of weight equal to 28.35 grams or 1/16 of a pound 2 [S] a small amount

our /aʊɚ, ɑr/ determiner of us: our house

ours /aʊɚz, ɑrz/ pron of us; our one(s)

our·selves /aʊɚˈsɛlvz, ɑr-/ pron 1 (reflexive form of **we**): We saw ourselves on TV. 2 (strong form of **we**): We built the house ourselves. 3 **(all) by ourselves: a** alone **b** without help 4 **to ourselves** not shared

oust /aʊst/ vt force (someone) out ~**er** n action of doing this

out¹ /aʊt/ adv 1 away from the inside: Open the bag and take the money out. 2 away from home or the usual place: Let's go out tonight. 3 away from a surface: The nail stuck out. 4 to lots of people or places: Hand out the drinks. 5 (of a fire or light) no longer burning 6 completely: I'm tired out. 7 aloud: Call the names out. 8 so as to be clearly seen, understood, etc.: Their secret is out. 9 in flower: Are the daffodils out (= in flower) yet? 9 wrong in guessing, etc.: I was 2 years out in my estimation. 10 (of the ball in a game, e.g. tennis) outside the line 11 no longer fashionable 12 (of the TIDE) away from the coast 13 **out of: a** from inside; away from: I jumped out of bed. | (fig.) We're out of danger (= safe) now. | (fig.) It's out of sight. (= can't be seen) **b** from among: 4 out of 5 people preferred it. **c** not having; without: We're out of gas. **d** because of: I came out of interest. **e** (shows what some-

thing is made from): *made out of wood.*
14 out of it: a lonely and unhappy because one is not included in something **b** *infml* not thinking clearly **15 out to** trying to: *He's out to get my job.*

out² *adj* **1** directed outward **2** openly HOMOSEXUAL **3 out-and-out** /ˌ · · ˈ· ◂/ complete; total

out³ *vt* make known as a HOMOSEXUAL

out·age /ˈaʊtɪdʒ/ *n* period of time when there is no supply of electricity: *power outage*

out·board mo·tor /ˌaʊtˈbɔːd ˈmoʊtəˌ, -boʊrd-/ *n* motor fixed to the back end of a small boat

out·break /ˈaʊtˈbreɪk/ *n* sudden appearance or start of something bad

out·burst /ˈaʊtˈbɜːst/ *n* sudden powerful expression of feeling

out·cast /ˈaʊtˈkæst/ *n* someone forced from their home or friendless

out·class /aʊtˈklæs/ *vt* be very much better than

out·come /ˈaʊtˈkʌm/ *n* effect; result

out·cry /ˈaʊtˈkraɪ/ *n* public show of anger

out·dat·ed /ˌaʊtˈdeɪtɪd/ *adj* no longer in general use

out·do /aʊtˈduː/ *vt* **-did** /-ˈdɪd/, **-done** /-ˈdʌn/, *3rd person sing. pres. t.* **-does** /-ˈdʌz/ do or be better than

out·door /ˈaʊtdɔː, -dɔːr-/ *adj* existing, happening, or used outside **outdoors** /ˌaʊtˈdɔːz, -ˈdɔːrz/ *adv*

out·er /ˈaʊtə/ *adj* on the outside; furthest from the middle

outer space /ˌ· · ˈ·/ *n* [U] area where the stars and other PLANETS, etc., are

out·field /ˈaʊtfiːld/ *n* area of a baseball field farthest from the BATTER

out·fit /ˈaʊtfɪt/ *n* **1** set of things esp. clothes for a particular purpose **2** group of people working together ♦ *vt* **-tt-** provide with a set of esp. clothes **~ter** *n*

out·go·ing /ˈaʊtˌɡoʊɪŋ/ *adj* **1** finishing a period in office **2** friendly

out·grow /ˈaʊtˈɡroʊ/ *vt* **-grew** /-ˈɡruː/, **-grown** /-ˈɡroʊn/ grow too big, too old, or too fast for

out·house /ˈaʊthaʊs/ *n* **-houses** /-haʊzɪz/ **1** small building near a larger main building **2** outdoor TOILET

out·ing /ˈaʊtɪŋ/ *n* **1** [C] short trip for pleasure, esp. by a group **2** [U;C] practice of making secret HOMOSEXUALS known

out·land·ish /aʊtˈlændɪʃ/ *adj* strange and unpleasing **~ly** *adv* **~ness** *n* [U]

out·last /aʊtˈlæst/ *vt* last longer than

out·law /ˈaʊtlɔː/ *n* (in former times) criminal being hunted ♦ *vt* declare (something) illegal

out·lay /ˈaʊtleɪ/ *n* money spent on something

out·let /ˈaʊtlɛt, -lɪt/ *n* **1** way out for liquid or gas: (fig.) *an outlet for his energy* **2** electrical SOCKET **3** store which sells goods cheaply: *a factory outlet*

out·line /ˈaʊtlaɪn/ *n* **1** line showing the shape of something **2** main ideas or facts, without details ♦ *vt: She outlined her plans.*

out·live /aʊtˈlɪv/ *vt* line longer than

out·look /ˈaʊtlʊk/ *n* **1** view from a place **2** future probabilities **3** one's general point of view

out·ly·ing /ˈaʊtˌlaɪ·ɪŋ/ *adj* distant; far from a city, etc.

out·mod·ed /aʊtˈmoʊdɪd/ *adj* no longer in fashion or use

out·num·ber /aʊtˈnʌmbəˌ/ *vt* be more in numbers than: *outnumbered by the enemy*

out-of-bounds /ˌ· · ˈ· ◂/ *adj* **1** (in sports) outside the playing area **2** (of behavior) unacceptable

out-of-date /ˌ· · ˈ· ◂/ *adj* no longer in use or in fashion

out-of-state /ˌ· · ˈ· ◂/ *adj, adv* from, to, or in another state

out-of-the-way /ˌ· · · ˈ· ◂/ *adj* **1** distant **2** unusual

out·pa·tient /ˈaʊtˌpeɪʃənt/ *n* person treated at a hospital but not staying there

out·post /ˈaʊtpoʊst/ *n* group of people or settlement far from the main group or settlement

out·put /ˈaʊtpʊt/ *n* **1** [C;U] production: *The factory's output is 200 cars a day.* **2** information produced by a computer

out·rage /ˈaʊtreɪdʒ/ *n* **1** [C] very wrong or cruel act **2** [U] anger caused by such an act ♦ *vt* offend greatly **~ous** /aʊtˈreɪdʒəs/ *adj* **1** very offensive **2** wildly unexpected and unusual

out·right /ˌaʊtˈraɪt◂/ *adv* **1** completely: *she won outright.* **2** without delay: *He was killed outright.* **3** openly: *Tell him outright what you think.* ♦ *adj* complete and clear: *an outright lie*

out·set /ˈaʊtsɛt/ *n* beginning: *There was trouble from/at the outset.*

out·shine /aʊtˈʃaɪn/ vt **-shone** /-ˈʃɒn/ **1** shine more brightly than **2** be much better than

out·side /ˌaʊtˈsaɪd◂, ˈaʊtsaɪd/ n **1** [(the)] the part furthest from the middle, or that faces away from one or towards the open air: *to paint the outside of a house* **2 at the outside** at the most ♦ adj **1** facing or at the outside: *the outside wall* **2** from elsewhere: *an outside broadcast* **3** (of a chance or possibility) slight ♦ adv **1** to or on the outside, esp. in the open air: *go outside* ♦ prep **1** to or on the outside of: *Wait just outside the door.* **2** beyond the limits of: *outside my experience*

out·sid·er /aʊtˈsaɪdə/ n **1** person not accepted in a social group **2** person or animal not expected to win

out·sized /ˈaʊtsaɪzd/ adj larger than the standard sizes

out·skirts /ˈaʊtskɜːts/ n [P] outer areas or limits of a town

out·smart /aʊtˈsmɑːt/ vt defeat by being more clever

out·spo·ken /aʊtˈspəʊkən/ adj expressing thoughts or feelings openly ~**ly** adv ~**ness** n [U]

out·stand·ing /aʊtˈstændɪŋ/ adj **1** much better than others **2** not yet done or paid ~**ly** adv

out·stay /aʊtˈsteɪ/ vt stay longer than: *to outstay one's welcome* (= stay too long as a guest so as to be no longer welcome)

out·strip /aʊtˈstrɪp/ vt **-pp-** do better than: *to outstrip one's competitors*

out·ward /ˈaʊtwəd/ adj, adv **1** away: *the outward journey* **2** on the outside but perhaps not really: *outward cheerfulness* ~**ly** adv **outwards** adv

out·weigh /aʊtˈweɪ/ vt be more important than

out·wit /aʊtˈwɪt/ vt **-tt-** defeat by being more clever

o·val /ˈəʊvəl/ n, adj (something) shaped like an egg

o·va·ry /ˈəʊvəri/ n part of a female that produces eggs

o·va·tion /əʊˈveɪʃən/ n joyful expression of public approval

ov·en /ˈʌvən/ n closed box for cooking, baking clay, etc.: (fig.) *It's like an oven in here.* (= uncomfortably hot)

over¹ /ˈəʊvə/ prep **1** higher than but not touching: *the clock over the fireplace* **2** so as to cover: *Put a cloth over the jug.* **3** from side to side of, esp. by going up and down: *to climb over a wall | a bridge over the river* **4** down across the edge of: *It fell over the cliff.* **5** in; through: *There's snow over most of the Rockies.* **6** in control of: *I don't want anyone over me, telling me what to do.* **7** more than: *over 10 years ago* **8** while doing, eating, etc.: *We held a meeting over lunch.* **9** by means of: *I heard it over the radio.* **10** about: *an argument over money* **11 over and above** as well as

over² adv **1** downwards from an upright position: *I fell over.* **2** across an edge or distance: *The milk boiled over. | We flew over to Europe.* **3** so that another side is seen: *Turn the page over.* **4** beyond: *children of 7 and over* (= older) **5** so as to be covered: *The windows are boarded over.* **6** remaining: *Was there any money left over?* **7** (shows something is repeated): *I had to do it (all) over again.* **8** in all details: *Think it over carefully.* ♦ adj ended: *The party's over.*

o·ver·all¹ /ˌəʊvərˈɔːl◂/ adj, adv including everything: *overall costs*

o·ver·alls /ˈəʊvərɔːlz/ n [P] heavy cotton pants with a piece that covers the chest, held up by 2 bands over the shoulders

o·ver·bear·ing /ˌəʊvəˈbeərɪŋ/ adj forcefully trying to tell others what to do

o·ver·board /ˈəʊvəbɔːd, -bʊəd/ adv **1** over the side of a boat into the water **2 go overboard** become very or too enthusiastic

o·ver·cast /ˌəʊvəˈkɑːst◂/ adj dark with clouds

o·ver·coat /ˈəʊvəˌkəʊt/ n long warm coat

o·ver·come /ˌəʊvəˈkʌm/ vt **-came** /-ˈkeɪm/, **-come 1** defeat **2** make helpless: *overcome with grief*

o·ver·crowd·ed /ˌəʊvəˈkraʊdɪd/ adj with too many people or things in (one place)

o·ver·do /ˌəʊvəˈduː/ vt **-did** /-ˈdɪd/, **-done** /-ˈdʌn/, 3rd person sing. pres. t. **-does** /-ˈdʌz/ do, decorate, perform, etc., too much: *I've been overdoing it* (= working too hard) *lately.*

o·ver·dose /ˈəʊvəˌdəʊs/ n too much of a drug

o·ver·drawn /ˌəʊvəˈdrɔːn◂/ adj having taken more money from your bank account than it contains

o·ver·due /ˌəʊvəˈdjuː◂/ adj late

o·ver·eat /ˌəʊvərˈiːt/ vi eat too much or more than is healthy

o·ver·flow /ˌoʊvəˈfloʊ/ vi/t 1 flow over the edge (of): The water's/The bathtub's overflowing. 2 go beyond the limits (of): The crowd overflowed into the street. ♦ /ˈoʊvəˌfloʊ/ n (pipe for carrying away) something that overflows

o·ver·grown /ˌoʊvəˈgroʊn/ adj 1 covered with plants growing uncontrolled 2 grown too large

o·ver·hang /ˌoʊvəˈhæŋ/ vi/t -hung /-ˈhʌŋ/ hang or stick out over (something) ♦ /ˈoʊvəˌhæŋ/ n overhanging rock, roof, etc.

o·ver·haul /ˌoʊvəˈhɔl/ n thorough examination: The car needs an overhaul.

o·ver·head /ˌoʊvəˈhɛd◄, ˈoʊvəˌhɛd/ adj, adv above one's head: overhead cables ♦ n /ˈoʊvəˌhɛd/ money spent regularly to keep a business running

o·ver·hear /ˌoʊvəˈhɪr/ vi/t -heard /-ˈhəd/ hear (what others are saying) without them knowing

o·ver·joyed /ˌoʊvəˈdʒɔɪd/ adj extremely pleased

o·ver·kill /ˈoʊvəˌkɪl/ n [U] something that goes beyond the desirable or safe limits

o·ver·land /ˈoʊvəˌlænd/ adj, adv across land and not by sea or air

o·ver·lap /ˌoʊvəˈlæp/ vi/t -pp- cover (something) partly and go beyond it: (fig.) Our interests overlap. (= are partly the same) ♦ /ˈoʊvəˌlæp/ n part that overlaps

o·ver·load /ˌoʊvəˈloʊd/ vt 1 load too heavily 2 put too much electricity through ♦ /ˈoʊvəˌloʊd/ n

o·ver·look /ˌoʊvəˈlʊk/ vt 1 give a view of from above 2 not notice; miss 3 forgive

o·ver·ly /ˈoʊvəli/ adv too much; very: We weren't overly impressed.

o·ver·night /ˌoʊvəˈnaɪt◄/ adj, adv 1 for or during the night 2 sudden(ly): an overnight success

o·ver·pass /ˈoʊvəˌpæs/ n place where two roads cross at different levels

o·ver·pow·er /ˌoʊvəˈpaʊə/ vt defeat by greater power ~ing very strong: an overpowering desire

o·ver·ran /ˌoʊvəˈræn/ past tense of OVERRUN

o·ver·rat·ed /ˌoʊvəˈreɪtɪd◄/ adj not as good or important as some people think

o·ver·re·act /ˌoʊvəriˈækt/ vi act too strongly as a result of (something)

o·ver·ride /ˌoʊvəˈraɪd/ vt -rode /-ˈroʊd/, -ridden /-ˈrɪdn/ forbid obedience to or acceptance of (and take the place of): My orders were overridden. –riding adj greater than anything else: of overriding importance

o·ver·rule /ˌoʊvəˈrul/ vt decide against (something already decided) by official power

o·ver·run /ˌoʊvəˈrʌn/ v -ran /-ˈræn/, -run 1 vt spread over and cause harm 2 vi/t continue beyond (a time limit)

o·ver·seas /ˌoʊvəˈsiz◄/ adv, adj in, to, or from a foreign country across the sea

o·ver·see /ˌoʊvəˈsi/ vt -saw /-ˈsɔ/, -seen /-ˈsin/ watch to see that work is properly done –seer /ˈoʊvəˌsiə/ n

o·ver·shad·ow /ˌoʊvəˈʃædoʊ/ vt 1 make worried and sadder 2 make appear less important

o·ver·shoot /ˌoʊvəˈʃut/ vi/t -shot /-ˈʃɑt/ go too far or beyond, and miss

o·ver·sight /ˈoʊvəˌsaɪt/ n unintended failure to notice or do something

o·ver·sleep /ˌoʊvəˈslip/ vi -slept /-ˈslɛpt/ wake up too late

o·ver·step /ˌoʊvəˈstɛp/ vt -pp- go beyond (the limits of what is proper or allowed)

o·vert /oʊˈvət, ˈoʊvət/ adj not hidden; open: overt resistance ~ly adv

o·ver·take /ˌoʊvəˈteɪk/ v -took /-ˈtʊk/, -taken /-ˈteɪkən/ vt (of something unpleasant) reach suddenly and unexpectedly

over-the-coun·ter /ˌ· · ˈ· · ·◄/ adj (of medicines) that can be bought without a PRESCRIPTION (=written order) from a doctor

over-the-hill /ˌ· · · ˈ·◄/ adj (too) old

o·ver·throw /ˌoʊvəˈθroʊ/ vt -threw /-ˈθru/, -thrown /-ˈθroʊn/ remove from power ♦ /ˈoʊvəˌθroʊ/ n the violent overthrow of the government

o·ver·time /ˈoʊvəˌtaɪm/ n, adv [U] (money paid for or time spent working) beyond the usual working time: to work overtime to do something (= use much effort)

o·ver·tones /ˈoʊvəˌtoʊnz/ n [P] things suggested but not stated clearly

o·ver·took /ˌoʊvəˈtʊk/ past tense of OVERTAKE

o·ver·ture /ˈoʊvətʃə, -ˌtʃʊr/ n musical introduction, esp. to an OPERA overtures n [P] offer to begin talks

o·ver·turn /ˌoʊvəˈtən/ v 1 vi/t turn over 2 vt bring to an end suddenly

o·ver·view /ˈoʊvəˌvyu/ n usu. short account (of something) which gives a general picture but no details

o·ver·weight /ˌoʊvəˈweɪt/ adj weighing too much

o·ver·whelm /ˌoʊvəˈwɛlm, -ˈhwɛlm/ vt 1 defeat or make powerless by much greater numbers 2 (of feelings) make completely helpless

o·ver·wrought /ˌoʊvəˈrɔt/ adj too nervous and excited

ow /aʊ/ interj (expresses sudden slight pain)

owe /oʊ/ vt 1 have to pay: I owed her $5. 2 feel grateful for: We owe a lot to our parents.

ow·ing /ˈoʊɪŋ/ adj 1 still to be paid 2 **owing to** /ˈ·· ·/ because of

owl /aʊl/ n night bird with large eyes

own¹ /oʊn/ determiner, pron 1 belonging to the stated person and no one else: At last I had my own room/a room of my own. 2 **come into one's own** begin to be properly respected for one's qualities 3 **have/get one's own back (on someone)** succeed in doing harm (to someone) in return for harm done to oneself 4 **hold one's own (against)** avoid defeat (by) 5 **on one's own: a** alone **b** without help

own² vt possess, esp. by legal right ~er n ~ership n [U]

own to phr vt admit

own up phr vi admit a fault or crime

ox /aks/ n oxen /ˈaksən/ large animal of the cattle type, esp. male

ox·y·gen /ˈaksədʒən/ n [U] gas present in the air, necessary for life

oy·ster /ˈɔɪstə/ n 1 flat shellfish, often eaten 2 **the world is one's/someone's oyster** there are no limits on where one/someone can go, etc.

oz. written abbrev. for: OUNCE(s)

o·zone /ˈoʊzoʊn/ n [U] type of oxygen in a LAYER high above the earth

P

P, p /piː/ **1** the 16th letter of the English alphabet **2 mind one's p's and q's** be careful in what one says so as to avoid displeasing others

p. *abbrev. for:* page

PA *n* public address system; apparatus for making one's voice heard in a large room or building

PAC *n* political action committee; organization that tries to influence politicians

pace /peɪs/ *n* **1** speed, esp. of walking or running: *She works so fast I can't keep pace with* (= go as fast as) *her.* **2** (distance moved in) a single step **3 put someone through his/her paces** make someone do something in order to show his/her abilities, qualities, etc. **4 set the pace** fix the speed for others to copy **5 show one's paces** show one's abilities/qualities ♦ *v* **1** *vi/t* walk (across) with slow regular steps **2** *vt* set the speed of movement for

pace out/off *phr vt* measure by taking steps

pace·mak·er /ˈpeɪsˌmeɪkə/ *n* **1** person who sets a speed or example for others to follow **2** machine used to make weak or irregular HEARTBEATS regular

Pa·cif·ic time /pəˈsɪfɪk ˌtaɪm/ *n* [U] time used on the West Coast of the US, 3 hours earlier than Eastern time

pa·ci·fi·er /ˈpæsəˌfaɪə/ *n* baby's rubber NIPPLE for sucking

pac·i·fist /ˈpæsəfɪst/ *n* person who believes war is wrong and refuses to fight **–fism** *n* [U]

pac·i·fy /ˈpæsəˌfaɪ/ *vt* make calm and quiet, esp. less angry **–fication** /ˌpæsəfəˈkeɪʃən/ *n* [U]

pack¹ /pæk/ *n* **1** number of things wrapped or tied together or put in a case **2** package **3** group of hunting animals **4** collection; group: *a pack of lies/thieves*

pack² *v* **1** *vi/t* put (things) into cases, boxes, etc., for taking somewhere or storing **2** *vi/t* fit or push into a space: *Crowds of people packed into the hall.* **3** *vt* cover, fill, or surround closely with pro-

tective material **4 pack a (hard) punch** *infml* **a** (of a fighter) able to give a strong hard blow **b** use very forceful language in an argument **5 send someone packing** *infml* cause someone undesirable to leave quickly **~ed** *adj* full of people

pack in *phr vt infml* attract in large numbers: *That film is really packing them in.*

pack off *phr vt infml* BUNDLE off

pack up *phr vt infml* **1** finish work **2** gather one's possessions: *pack up and leave*

pack·age /ˈpækɪdʒ/ *n* **1** number of things packed together in a container **2** set of related things offered as a unit ♦ *vt* **1** make into a package **2** put in a special container for selling

package tour /ˈ·· ˌ·/ *n* vacation where all travel, hotels, food, etc., are paid for together

pack·et /ˈpækɪt/ *n* small container or package: *a packet of sugar*

pack·ing /ˈpækɪŋ/ *n* [U] **1** putting things in cases or boxes **2** protective material for packing things

pack·rat /ˈpæk-ræt/ *n* person who saves things that appear useless

pact /pækt/ *n* solemn agreement

pad¹ /pæd/ *n* **1** something made or filled with soft material, for protection or to give shape **2** many sheets of paper fastened together: *a writing pad* **3** LAUNCHING PAD **4** *sl* one's house or home **5** bottom part of foot, usu. with thick skin, of some animals that have 4 feet ♦ *vt* **-dd-** **1** protect, shape, or make more comfortable with a pad or pads **2** make longer by adding unnecessary words **~ding** *n* [U] **1** material used to pad something **2** unnecessary words or sentences

pad² *vi* **-dd-** walk steadily and usu. softly

pad·dle /ˈpædl/ *n* short pole with a wide blade at one end or both ends, for rowing a small boat ♦ *v* **1** *vi/t* row with a paddle **2** *vi* swim, moving the arms and legs like a dog **3 paddle one's own canoe** *infml* depend on oneself and no one else

pad·dock /ˈpædək/ *n* small field where horses are kept

pad·dy /ˈpædi/ *n* field where rice is grown in water

pad·lock /ˈpædlɒk/ *n* lock that can be removed, fastened with a bar in the shape of a U, for locking gates, bicycles, etc. ♦ *vi/t* fasten or lock with a padlock

pa·gan /'peɪgən/ *n* person who does not believe in one's religion, or in any of the main religions ♦ *adj: pagan tribes* **~ism** *n* [U]

page[1] /peɪdʒ/ *n* one or both sides of a sheet of paper in a book, newspaper, etc.

page[2] *n* **1** boy servant at a hotel, club, etc. **2** boy attendant at a wedding

pag·eant /'pædʒənt/ *n* splendid public show or ceremony **~ry** *n* [U] splendid show of ceremonial grandness

pag·er /'peɪdʒə/ *n* small apparatus carried around that makes a sound to tell you to telephone someone

pa·go·da /pə'goudə/ *n* temple (esp. Buddhist or Hindu) built on several floors

paid /peɪd/ *past t. and p. of* PAY — see also **put paid to** (PUT)

paid-up /ˌ· '◁/ *adj* having paid in full (esp. so as to continue being a member)

pail /peɪl/ *n* bucket

pain /peɪn/ *n* **1** [U] suffering in body or mind; hurting: *Are you in pain?* **2** [C] case of such suffering in a particular part: *a pain in my stomach* **3** [S] also **pain in the neck** /ˌ· · '◁/ — *sl* person, thing, or happening that makes one angry or tired **4 on/under pain of** *fml* at the risk of suffering (a punishment) if something is not done ♦ *vt fml* cause pain to **~ed** *adj* displeased or hurt in one's feelings **~ful** *adj: a painful cut* **~less** *adj* **pains** *n* [P] effort; trouble: *I went to great pains to get the one you wanted.*

pain·kill·er /'peɪnˌkɪlə/ *n* medicine for reducing or removing pain

painstaking /'peɪnzˌteɪkɪŋ/ *adj* very careful and thorough

paint /peɪnt/ *n* [U] liquid coloring matter for decorating surfaces or making pictures ♦ *vi/t* **1** put paint on (a surface) **2** make a picture (of) with paint **3** describe in clear, carefully chosen words **4 paint the town red** go out and have a good time **~ing** *n* **1** [U] act or art of painting **2** [C] painted picture — see also OIL PAINTING **paints** *n* [P] set of small containers of paints of different colors, for painting pictures

paint·brush /'peɪntˌbrʌʃ/ *n* brush used for painting pictures or for painting rooms, houses etc.

paint·er /'peɪntə/ *n* person who paints pictures, or houses, rooms, etc.

pair /peər/ *n* **1** two of the same kind: *a pair of gloves* **2** something made of two similar parts: *a pair of scissors* **3** two people closely connected ♦ *vi/t* form into one or more pairs: *Jane and David paired off at the party.*

pair up *phr vi/t* (cause to) join in pairs, esp. for work or sport

pa·ja·mas /pə'dʒɑːməz, -'dʒæ-/ *n* [P] trousers and shirt that fit loosely, worn in bed

pal /pæl/ *n infml* friend

pal·ace /'pælɪs/ *n* large grand house, esp. where a king or president lives

pal·a·ta·ble /'pælətəbəl/ *adj fml* **1** good to taste **2** acceptable; pleasant: *not a palatable suggestion*

pal·ate /'pælɪt/ *n* **1** the top inside part of the mouth **2** ability to judge good food or wine

pa·la·tial /pə'leɪʃəl/ *adj* (of a building) large and splendid

pale[1] /peɪl/ *adj* **1** not bright or dark: *pale blue* **2** (of a face) rather white ♦ *vi* **1** become pale **2** seem less important, clever, etc., when compared with

pale[2] *n* limit of proper behavior: *beyond the pale*

pal·e·on·tol·o·gy /ˌpeɪliən'tɑlədʒi, -lɪən-/ *n* [U] study of FOSSILs **-gist** *n*

pal·ette /'pælɪt/ *n* board on which a painter mixes colors

pall[1] /pɔl/ *vi* become uninteresting or dull

pall[2] *n* **1** [S] heavy or dark covering: *a pall of smoke* **2** [C] cloth spread over a COFFIN

pall·bear·er /'pɔlˌbeərə/ *n* person who walks beside or helps carry a COFFIN

pal·let /'pælɪt/ *n* large flat frame used with a FORKLIFT TRUCK for lifting heavy goods

pal·lid /'pælɪd/ *adj* (of skin) pale to an unhealthy degree **~ness** *n* [U]

pal·lor /'pælə/ *n* [S] pallidness

palm[1] /pɑm/ *n* tall tropical tree with no branches and a mass of large leaves at the top

palm[2] *n* inside surface of the hand

palm[3] *v* **palm off** *phr vt* **1** get rid of by deception **2** deceive into accepting

pal·pa·ble /'pælpəbəl/ *adj fml* easily and clearly known: *a palpable lie* **-bly** *adv*

pal·try /ˈpɔltri/ adj worthlessly small or unimportant

pam·pas /ˈpæmpəz, -pəs/ n [U] wide treeless plains in South America

pam·per /ˈpæmpə/ vt treat too kindly

pam·phlet /ˈpæmflɪt/ n small book with paper covers

pan[1] /pæn/ n 1 round metal container for cooking, usu. with a long handle 2 container with holes in the bottom used for separating precious metals from other material

pan[2] v **-nn-** 1 vt infml CRITICIZE very severely 2 vi/t move (a camera) in order to follow the action being recorded on film or television 3 vi/t use a pan (2) to search for valuable metals: pan for gold

pan out phr vi happen in a particular way

pan·a·ce·a /ˌpænəˈsiə/ n something that will put right all troubles

pa·nache /pəˈnæʃ, pəˈnɑʃ/ n [U] showy splendid way of doing things

pan·cake /ˈpænkeɪk/ n flat cake cooked in a pan

pan·cre·as /ˈpæŋkriəs/ n bodily organ that helps in changing food chemically for use by the body

pan·da /ˈpændə/ n black and white bear-like animal from China

pan·de·mo·ni·um /ˌpændəˈmoʊniəm/ n [U] wild and noisy disorder

pan·der /ˈpændə/ v **pander to** phr vt satisfy in an unworthy way: The newspapers pander to people's interest in sex scandals.

Pan·do·ra's box /pænˈdɔrəz ˈbɑks, -ˌdoʊr-/ n **open Pandora's box** unintentionally cause, by taking some action, a large number of problems that did not exist or were not known about before

pane /peɪn/ n sheet of glass in a window

pan·el /ˈpænl/ n 1 flat piece of wood in a door or on a wall 2 board with instruments fixed in it: an aircraft's control panel 3 small group of people who answer questions on esp. a radio or television show 4 piece of cloth of a different color or material, set in a dress — see also SOLAR PANEL ♦ vt **-l-** decorate with PANELS (1): oak-paneled walls **~ing** n [U] PANELS (1)

pang /pæŋ/ n sudden sharp feeling of pain

pan·han·dle /ˈpænˌhændl/ vi beg on the street **~r** n

pan·ic /ˈpænɪk/ n [C;U] sudden uncontrollable fear or terror which spreads quickly ♦ vi/t **-ck-** (cause to) feel panic **~ky** adj suddenly afraid

panic-strick·en /ˈ·· ˌ·/ adj filled with panic

pan·o·ra·ma /ˌpænəˈræmə, -ˈrɑ-/ n 1 complete view of a wide stretch of land 2 general representation in words or pictures **–ramic** /-ˈræmɪk/ adj

pan·sy /ˈpænzi/ n 1 small garden plant with flowers 2 infml derog **a** EFFEMINATE young man **b** male HOMOSEXUAL

pant /pænt/ vi breathe quickly, with short breaths ♦ n quick short breath

pan·the·ism /ˈpænθiˌɪzəm/ n [U] religious idea that God and the universe are the same thing **–ist** n

pan·ther /ˈpænθə/ n LEOPARD, esp. a black one

pan·ties /ˈpæntiz/ n [P] women's short undergarment worn below the waist

pan·to·mime /ˈpæntəˌmaɪm/ n MIME

pan·try /ˈpæntri/ n small room with shelves where food is kept

pants /pænts/ n [P] 1 outer garment with 2 legs, covering the body from the waist downwards 2 **with one's pants down** sl awkwardly unprepared 3 **by the seat of one's pants** infml guided by one's experience rather than by a formal plan

pan·ty·hose /ˈpæntiˌhoʊz/ n [P] very thin piece of women's clothing covering feet, legs, and waist, usu. worn with dresses or skirts

pap·a /ˈpɑpə/ n father

pa·pa·cy /ˈpeɪpəsi/ n power and office of the POPE

pa·pal /ˈpeɪpəl/ adj of the POPE

pap·a·raz·zo /ˌpæpəˈrætsoʊ/ n **-zi** /-tsi/ newspaper writer or photographer who follows famous people about hoping to find out interesting or shocking stories about them

pa·per /ˈpeɪpə/ n 1 [U] material in thin sheets for writing or printing on, wrapping things in, etc. 2 [C] newspaper 3 [C] set of questions to be answered in an examination 4 [C] piece of writing for specialists, often read aloud 5 **on paper** as written down, but not yet tried out in reality ♦ vt cover with WALLPAPER

papers n [P] pieces of paper written on or printed, esp. used for official purposes

pa·per·back /ˈpeɪpərˌbæk/ n book with a thin cardboard cover

paper clip /ˈ·· ˌ·, ˌ·· ˈ·/ n piece of curved wire for holding papers together

pa·per·weight /ˈpeɪpərˌweɪt/ n heavy object put on papers to stop them being scattered

pa·per·work /ˈpeɪpərˌwɜːk/ n [U] writing reports and letters, keeping records, etc.

pap·ri·ka /pæˈpriːkə, ˈpæprɪkə/ n [U] red powder with a hot taste, from a plant and used in cooking

Pap smear /ˈpæp ˌsmɪr/ n medical test that takes cells from a woman's CERVIX to examine them for signs of disease

par /pɑr/ n **1** [S] (nearly) equal level: *Her skill is on a par with mine.* **2** [U] average number of hits in GOLF **3 under par** *infml* not in the usual or average condition of health

par·a·ble /ˈpærəbəl/ n short simple story which teaches a moral lesson

par·a·chute /ˈpærəʃut/ n piece of cloth on long ropes, fastened to someone to allow them to fall slowly and safely from an aircraft ♦ vi/t drop by means of a parachute

pa·rade /pəˈreɪd/ n **1** informal procession **2** ceremonial gathering of soldiers to be officially looked at — see also HIT PARADE ♦ v **1** vi walk or gather in a parade **2** vi walk showily **3** vt show in order to be admired: *parading her knowledge*

par·a·digm /ˈpærəˌdaɪm/ n fml model or typical example of something

par·a·dise /ˈpærəˌdaɪs, -ˌdaɪz/ n **1** [U] (usu. cap.) Heaven **2** [S;U] place or state of perfect happiness — see also FOOL'S PARADISE

par·a·dox /ˈpærəˌdɑks/ n **1** statement that says 2 opposite things but has some truth in it **2** strange combination of opposing qualities, ideas, etc. **~ical** /ˌpærəˈdɑksɪkəl/ adj **1** in a paradoxical way **2** it is a paradox that

par·af·fin /ˈpærəfɪn/ n [U] type of wax used to make CANDLES

par·a·gon /ˈpærəˌgɑn, -gən/ n person who is or seems to be a perfect model to copy

par·a·graph /ˈpærəˌgræf/ n division of a piece of writing that begins a new line

par·a·keet /ˈpærəˌkit/ n small brightly colored Australian bird

par·a·le·gal /ˌpærəˈligəl/ n person who helps a lawyer do his/her work

par·al·lel /ˈpærəˌlɛl/ adj **1** (of lines) always the same distance apart **2** comparable ♦ n **1** [C] comparable person or thing **2** [C] similarity (point of) **3** [C] line of LATITUDE ♦ vt **1**· be similar to

pa·ral·y·sis /pəˈræləsəs/ n [U] loss of movement in (some of) the body muscles **paralytic** /ˌpærəˈlɪtɪk◂/ adj suffering from paralysis

par·a·lyze /ˈpærəˌlaɪz/ vt **1** cause paralysis in **2** cause to stop working: *The strike paralyzed the industry.*

par·a·med·ic /ˌpærəˈmɛdɪk/ n someone, such as an AMBULANCE driver, who helps in the care of sick people but is not a doctor or nurse

pa·ram·e·ter /pəˈræmətər/ n (usu. pl.) any of the established limits within which something must operate

par·a·mil·i·tary /ˌpærəˈmɪləˌtɛri/ adj acting like an army, esp. illegally

par·a·mount /ˈpærəˌmaʊnt/ adj fml greater than all others in importance

par·a·noi·a /ˌpærəˈnɔɪə/ n [U] disease of the mind in which you think esp. that other people are trying to harm you **–noid** /ˈpærəˌnɔɪd/ adj (as if) suffering from paranoia

par·a·pher·na·lia /ˌpærəfəˈneɪlyə, -fə-ˈneɪl-/ n [U] small articles of various kinds

par·a·phrase /ˈpærəˌfreɪz/ vt, n (make) a re-expression of (something written or said) in different words

par·a·site /ˈpærəˌsaɪt/ n **1** animal or plant that lives and feeds on another **2** useless person supported by others' efforts **–sitic** /ˌpærəˈsɪtɪk◂/ adj

par·a·sol /ˈpærəˌsɔl, -ˌsɑl/ n SUNSHADE

par·a·troop·er /ˈpærəˌtrupər/ n soldier who drops from an aircraft using a PARACHUTE

par·cel¹ /ˈpɑrsəl/ n **1** something wrapped up in paper and fastened **2 part and parcel of** a most important part that cannot be separated from the whole of

parcel² v **1**· **parcel out** phr vt divide into parts or shares

parched /pɑrtʃt/ adj hot and dry

parch·ment /ˈpɑrtʃmənt/ n [C;U] treated animal skin, used formerly for writing on

par·don /ˈpɑrdn/ n **1** [C;U] (act of) forgiving, esp. of a guilty person, so they will no longer be punished **2 I beg your pardon**, also **pardon me** — a "Please excuse me for having accidentally touched/pushed you." **b** "Please repeat what you said." ♦ *vt* give pardon to ♦ *interj* (ask for something not fully heard to be repeated) ~**able** *adj* that can be forgiven

pare /pɛr/ *vt* cut off the edge or thin covering of: (fig.) *We must pare down* (= reduce) *costs.*

par·ent /ˈpɛrənt, ˈpær-/ *n* father or mother ~**al** /pəˈrɛntl/ *adj* ~**hood** *n* [U] state of being a parent

pa·ren·the·sis /pəˈrɛnθəsɪs/ *n* -**ses** /-ˌsɪz/ *fml* 1 (*usu. pl.*) either of the marks (or) used to enclose a piece of information **2** words introduced as an added explanation or thought

pa·ri·ah /pəˈraɪə/ *n fml* person not accepted by society

par·ish /ˈpærɪʃ/ *n* area for which a priest has responsibility: *the parish church*

par·i·ty /ˈpærəti/ *n* [U] *fml* being equal

park[1] /pɑrk/ *n* large usu. grassy enclosed piece of land in a town, used by the public for pleasure and rest

park[2] *vi/t* put (a vehicle) for a time: (fig.) *He just came in and parked himself on the sofa.*

par·ka /ˈpɑrkə/ *n* short coat with a HOOD

parking ga·rage /ˈ·· ˌ·/ *n* building with many levels for parking cars in

parking lot /ˈ·· ˌ·/ *n* open or enclosed place where cars and other vehicles may be left

parking me·ter /ˈ·· ˌ·/ *n* apparatus into which one puts one's money, allowing one to park near it for a time

park·way /ˈpɑrkweɪ/ *n* large road through a park

par·lance /ˈpɑrləns/ *n* [U] *fml* particular way of speaking or use of words

par·lia·ment /ˈpɑrləmənt/ *n* body of people elected or appointed to make laws in Britain and Commonwealth countries ~**ary** /ˌpɑrləˈmɛntri, ˈmɛntəri/◁ *adj*

par·lor /ˈpɑrlə/ *n* **1** LIVING ROOM **2** business place: *an ice-cream parlor*

pa·ro·chi·al /pəˈroʊkiəl/ *adj* **1** only interested in one's own affairs **2** of a PARISH: *parochial school*

par·o·dy /ˈpærədi/ *n* [C;U] copy of a writer's or musician's style, made to amuse ♦ *vt* make a parody of

pa·role /pəˈroʊl/ *n* [U] letting someone out of prison before their official period

in prison has ended ♦ *vt* let out of prison on parole

par·quet /pɑrˈkeɪ/ *n* [U] small wooden blocks making a floor

par·rot /ˈpærət/ *n* tropical bird with a curved beak and colored feathers ♦ *vt* repeat (someone else's words or actions) without thought or understanding

par·si·mo·ni·ous /ˌpɑrsəˈmoʊniəs/ *adj* unwilling to spend money; STINGY ~**ly** *adv* ~**ness** *n* [U]

pars·ley /ˈpɑrsli/ *n* [U] small plant used in cooking

pars·nip /ˈpɑrsnɪp/ *n* plant with a long white root used as a vegetable

part[1] /pɑrt/ *n* **1** [C] any of the pieces into which something is divided: *an engine with 100 moving parts* | *The travel is the best part of my trip.* **2** [S;U] share in an activity: *Did you take part in the fighting?* **3** [U] side; position: *He took my part* (= supported me) *in the quarrel.* **4** [C] (words of) a character acted in a play or film **5** [C] line on the head when the hair is parted **6 for my part** as far as I am concerned **7 for the most part: a** mostly **b** in most cases **8 part** partly **9 on the part of** of or by (someone) **10 play a part in** have an influence on **11 in good part** without being offended ♦ *adv* partly: *The exams are part written, part practical.* **parts** *n* [P] area of a country: *We don't have much rain in these parts.*

part[2] *v* **1** *vi/t* separate: *They parted as friends.* | *She parted the curtains.* **2** *vi* separate (hair on the head) along a line **3 part company (with): a** end a relationship (with) **b** no longer be together (with) **c** disagree (with) ~**ing** *n* [U] leaving

part with *phr vt* give away; stop having

par·take /pɑrˈteɪk/ *vi* -**took** /-ˈtʊk/, -**taken** /-ˈteɪkən/ *fml* eat or drink something offered

par·tial /ˈpɑrʃəl/ *adj* **1** not complete **2** (unfairly) favoring one more than another **3 partial to** very fond of ~**ly** *adv* ~**ity** /ˌpɑrʃiˈæləti/ *n* **1** [U] being PARTIAL (2) **2** [S] fondness: *a partiality for cream cakes*

par·tic·i·pant /pɑrˈtɪsəpənt, pə-/ *n* person who participates

par·tic·i·pate /pɑrˈtɪsəpeɪt, pə-/ *vi* separate take part or have a share in an activity –**pation** /pɑrˌtɪsəˈpeɪʃən, pə-/ *n* [U]

par·ti·ci·ple /ˈpɑːtəˌsɪpəl, -səpəl/ n PAST PARTICIPLE or PRESENT PARTICIPLE

par·ti·cle /ˈpɑːtɪkəl/ n very small piece

par·tic·u·lar /pəˈtɪkjələ/ adj 1 special; unusual: of no particular importance 2 single and different from others: this particular case 3 showing (too) much care over small matters 4 **in particular** especially ♦ n small single part of a whole; detail ~ly adv especially

parting shot /ˌ· ˈ·/ n remark or action made when leaving

par·ti·san /ˈpɑːtəzən, -sən/ n, adj 1 (person) giving strong unconditioned support to one side 2 member of an armed group that fights in secret against an enemy that has conquered its country

par·ti·tion /pɑːˈtɪʃən, pə-/ n 1 [C] thin wall indoors 2 [U] division, esp. of a country ♦ vt divide up

partition off phr vt separate with a partition

part·ly /ˈpɑːtli/ adv 1 not completely 2 in some degree

part·ner /ˈpɑːtnə/ n person you are with, doing something together: a dancing /business/marriage partner ♦ vt act as a partner to ~**ship** n 1 [U] being a partner 2 [C] business owned by 2 or more partners

part of speech /ˌ· · ˈ·/ n class of word, such as "noun" or "verb"

part-time /ˌ· ˈ·◂/ adj, adv (working) during only part of the regular working time

par·ty /ˈpɑːti/ n 1 gathering of people for food and amusement: a birthday party 2 association of people with the same political aims: the Democratic party 3 group of people doing something together: a search party 4 esp. law person or group concerned in a matter 5 **be (a) party to** take part in or know about (some action or activity) 6 **(follow) the party line** act according to the official opinion of a political party — see also THIRD PARTY ♦ vi infml enjoy oneself, esp. at a party or parties

pass¹ /pɑːs/ v 1 vi/t reach and move beyond: Several cars passed (us). 2 vi/t go through or across: A cloud passed across the sun. 3 vi/t (cause to) go: I passed a rope around the tree. 4 vi come to an end: Summer is passing. 5 vt give: Please pass me the salt. 6 vt (in sports) kick, throw,

etc., (esp. a ball) to a member of one's own side 7 a vi (of time) go by b vt spend (time) 8 vt accept officially: Congress passed a new law. 9 vi/t succeed in (an examination) 10 vt give (a judgment, opinion, etc.): The judge passed a heavy sentence on him. 11 **let something pass** leave (a wrong statement, mistake, etc.) without putting it right 12 **pass the hat** collect money for a cause 13 **pass the time of day (with)** give a greeting (to), and/or have a short conversation (with)

pass away phr vi die

pass by phr vt disregard

pass for phr vt be (mistakenly) accepted or considered as

pass off phr vt present falsely: passing herself off as a doctor

pass on phr vi 1 pass away 2 move on

pass out phr vi faint

pass over phr vt fail to choose

pass up phr vt fail to take advantage of; miss

pass² n 1 successful result in an examination 2 official paper showing that one is allowed to do something: a travel pass 3 act of giving the ball to someone else in sports 4 way by which one can travel through or over a place, esp. a range of mountains 5 act of trying to interest someone sexually: He made a pass at me.

pass·a·ble /ˈpɑːsəbəl/ adj 1 (just) good enough 2 a (of a road) fit to be used b (of a river) fit to be crossed –**bly** adv

pas·sage /ˈpæsɪdʒ/ n 1 [C] long narrow connecting way, esp. a CORRIDOR 2 [C] way through: We forced a passage through the crowd. 3 [U] fml going across, through, etc.: the bill's passage through the House 4 [U] onward flow (of time) 5 [S] (cost of) a journey by sea or air 6 [C] short part of a speech, piece of music, etc.

pas·sé /pæˈseɪ/ adj old-fashioned

pas·sen·ger /ˈpæsəndʒə/ n person being taken in a vehicle

pass·er·by /ˌpæsəˈbaɪ/ n **passersby** person who is going past a place

pass·ing /ˈpɑːsɪŋ/ n [U] 1 going by 2 ending; disappearance 3 death 4 **in passing** while talking about something else ♦ adj 1 moving or going by: passing traffic 2 not lasting long: I didn't give it a passing thought.

pas·sion /ˈpæʃən/ n 1 [C;U] strong deep feeling, esp. of love or anger 2 [S] a strong liking: *a passion for tennis* **3 the Passion** the suffering and death of Christ

pas·sion·ate /ˈpæʃənɪt/ *adj* filled with passion ~**ly** *adv*

pas·sive¹ /ˈpæsɪv/ *adj* **1** suffering something bad without (enough) opposition **2** (of verbs or sentences) expressing an action which is done to the subject of a sentence ~**ly** *adv* ~**ness** also –**sivity** /pæˈsɪvəti/ *n* [U]

passive² *n* [*the*+S] passive form of a verb

pass·port /ˈpæspɔːt, -poʊrt/ *n* **1** small official book allowing one to enter foreign countries **2** something that lets one get something else easily: *Is money a passport to happiness?*

pass·word /ˈpæswɜːd/ *n* secret word which one has to know to be allowed into a building, etc.

past¹ /pɑːst/ *adj* **1** (of time) earlier than the present: *the past few days* **2** ended: *Winter is past.* **3** *gram* expressing past time: *the past tense* **4** former: *a past president of our club* ♦ *n* [S] **1** (what happened in) the time before the present: *It happened in the past.* | *our country's glorious past* **2** *derog* secret former life containing wrongs of some kind: *a woman with a past*

past² *prep* **1** up to and beyond: *They rushed past us.* **2** beyond in time or age: *It's 10 minutes past four.* **3** beyond the possibility of: *I'm past caring.* (= no longer care) **4** *past it infml* no longer able to do the things one could formerly do ♦ *adv* by: *The children ran past.*

pas·ta /ˈpɑːstə/ *n* [U] food made in different shapes from flour paste

paste /peɪst/ *n* **1** soft mixture of powder and liquid **2** liquid mixture, usu. with flour, for sticking paper together ♦ *vt* fasten with paste

pas·tel /pæˈstɛl/ *adj* soft and light in color

pas·teur·ize /ˈpæstʃəraɪz, -stə-/ *vt* heat (a liquid) to destroy bacteria –**ization** /ˌpæstʃərəˈzeɪʃən, -stə-/ *n* [U]

pas·tiche /pæˈstiːʃ/ *n* work of art made of, or in the style of, other works of art

pas·time /ˈpæs-taɪm/ *n* something done to pass one's time pleasantly

past mas·ter /ˌ ˈ ˌ / *n* very skilled person

pas·tor /ˈpæstər/ *n* Christian priest in charge of a church

pas·tor·al /ˈpæstərəl/ *adj* **1** of a priest's duties amongst his religious group **2** of simple country life

past par·ti·ci·ple /ˌ ˈ ˌ / *n* form of a verb used in compounds to show the passive or the PERFECT[5] tenses (such as *broken* in *The cup was broken.*)

past per·fect /ˌ ˈ ˌ / *n* verb tense that expresses action completed before a particular time, formed in English with *had*

pas·try /ˈpeɪstri/ *n* **1** [U] a mixture of flour, fat, and liquid, eaten when baked **2** [C] article of food made from this

pas·ture /ˈpæstʃər/ *n* [C;U] (piece of) grassy land where farm animals feed ♦ *vt* put in a pasture to feed

past·y /ˈpeɪsti/ *adj* (of the face) white to an unhealthy degree

PA sys·tem /ˌpiː ˈeɪ ˌsɪstəm/ *n* way of talking to a large group of people at once or to people in many different places or rooms

pat¹ /pæt/ *vt* -**tt**- strike gently and repeatedly with a flat hand ♦ *n* **1** light friendly stroke with the hand **2** small shaped mass of butter **3 a pat on the back** expression of praise or satisfaction for something done

pat² *adj, adv* (too) easily or quickly answered or known

patch /pætʃ/ *n* **1** irregularly shaped part of a surface different from the rest: *damp patches on the wall* **2** small piece of material to cover a hole **3** small piece of ground: *a cabbage patch* **4** piece of material worn to protect a damaged eye ♦ *vt* put a PATCH (2) on

patch up *phr vt* **1** repair **2** become friends again after (a quarrel)

patch·work /ˈpætʃwɜːk/ *n* [C;U] (piece of) sewn work made by joining small bits of different materials: (fig.) *the patchwork of fields seen from an airplane*

patch·y /ˈpætʃi/ *adj* **1** in or having patches (PATCH (1)): *patchy fog* **2** incomplete or only good in parts –**ily** *adv* –**iness** *n* [U]

pât·é /ˈpɑːteɪ, pæ-/ *n* [U] food made by crushing meat, esp. LIVER, into a soft mass

pa·tent /ˈpeɪtˌnt/ *n* (official paper giving someone) the unshared right to make or sell a new invention ♦ *adj* **1** protected by a patent **2** *fml* clear to see: *his patent annoyance* ♦ *vt* obtain a patent for ~**ly** *adv fml* clearly

patent leath·er /ˌ· ˈ·· / n [U] very shiny leather, usu. black

pa·ter·nal /pəˈtɜːnl/ adj 1 of or like a father 2 protecting people like a father but allowing them no freedom 3 related to a person through the father's side of the family ~ly adv

pa·ter·nal·ism /pəˈtɜːnlˌɪzəm/ n [U] PATERNAL (2) way of controlling people –istic /pəˌtɜːnlˈɪstɪk/ adj ~istically adv

pa·ter·ni·ty /pəˈtɜːnəti/ n [U] esp. law origin from the male parent

path /pɑːθ/ n paths /pɑːðz/ 1 track or way where you can walk 2 line along which something moves: the path of an arrow

pa·thet·ic /pəˈθetɪk/ adj 1 causing pity or sorrow 2 derog hopelessly unsuccessful ~ally adv

pa·thol·o·gy /pəˈθɒlədʒi, pæ-/ n [U] study of disease –gist n specialist in pathology, esp. one who examines a dead body to find out how the person died –gical /ˌpæθəˈlɒdʒɪkəl◄/ adj 1 of pathology 2 caused by disease, esp. of the mind 3 great and unreasonable; pathological jealousy –gically adv

pa·thos /ˈpeɪθɒs, -θoʊs ˈpæ-/ n [U] quality that causes pity and sorrow

path·way /ˈpɑːθweɪ/ n PATH (1)

pa·tience /ˈpeɪʃəns/ n [U] ability to wait calmly, to control oneself when angered, or to accept unpleasant things without complaining

pa·tient¹ /ˈpeɪʃənt/ adj showing patience ~ly adv

patient² n person being treated medically

pat·i·o /ˈpætioʊ/ n –os space with a stone floor next to a house, for sitting out on in nice weather

pa·tri·arch /ˈpeɪtriɑːk/ n 1 old man who is much respected BISHOP of the Eastern Churches –al /ˌpeɪtriˈɑːkəl◄/ adj 1 ruled only by men 2 of a patriarch

pat·ri·cide /ˈpætrəˌsaɪd/ n [U] 1 murder of one's father 2 person guilty of this

pat·ri·ot /ˈpeɪtriət, -ˌɒt/ n someone who loves their country ~ism n [U] ~ic /ˌpeɪtriˈætɪk◄/ adj –ically adv

pa·trol /pəˈtroʊl/ n 1 [U] (period of) patrolling: warships on patrol in the Atlantic 2 [C] small group on patrol ♦ vi/t 1 go around (an area, building, etc.) repeatedly to see that there is no trouble

pa·tron /ˈpeɪtrən/ n 1 person who gives money for support: a patron of the arts 2 fml customer in a store, bar, etc., esp. regularly ~age /ˈpeɪtrənɪdʒ, ˈpæ-/ n [U] 1 support given by a PATRON (1) 2 right to appoint people to important positions 3 [U] regular support given to a business by its customers

pat·ron·ize /ˈpeɪtrəˌnaɪz, ˈpæ-/ vt 1 act towards (someone) as if you were better or more important than them 2 fml be a PATRON (2) of

patron saint /ˌ·· ˈ·/ n SAINT giving special protection to a particular place, activity, etc.

pat·ter¹ /ˈpætə/ vi, n (run with or make) the sound of something striking lightly, quickly, and repeatedly

patter² n [U] fast continuous amusing talk

pat·tern /ˈpætən/ n 1 regularly repeated arrangement, esp. with a decorative effect: cloth with a pattern of red and white squares 2 way in which something develops: the usual pattern of the illness 3 shape used as a guide for making something: a dress pattern ♦ vt 1 make a decorative pattern on 2 make according to a PATTERN (3)

pat·ty /ˈpæti/ n small flat piece of food or candy: hamburger patties

pau·ci·ty /ˈpɔːsəti/ n [S] fml less than is needed; lack

paunch /pɔːntʃ, pɑːntʃ/ n fat stomach ~y adj

pau·per /ˈpɔːpə/ n very poor person

pause /pɔːz/ n short but noticeable break in activity, speech, etc. ♦ vi make a pause

pave /peɪv/ vt 1 cover with a hard level surface 2 pave the way (for/to) prepare for or make possible

pave·ment /ˈpeɪvmənt/ n hard flat road surface

pa·vil·ion /pəˈvɪlyən/ n large public building, usu. put up for only a short time, used for EXHIBITIONs, etc.

paw /pɔː/ n 1 animal's foot with CLAWS 2 infml human hand: Keep your paws off me! ♦ vi/t 1 (of an animal) touch or strike with the foot 2 handle rudely or roughly

pawn¹ /pɔːn/ n 1 least valuable piece in CHESS 2 unimportant person used for someone else's advantage

pawn² *vt* leave with a pawnbroker in return for money lent ♦ *n* [U]: *My watch is in pawn.*

pawn·bro·ker /ˈpɔnˌbroukə/ *n* person who lends money in return for things one brings, which he keeps if one does not repay the money

pay /peɪ/ *v* **paid** /peɪd/ **1** *vi/t* give (money) to (someone) in return for goods bought, work done, etc. **2** *vt* settle (a bill, debt, etc.) **3** *vi/t* be profitable (to); be worth the trouble (to): *It doesn't pay (you) to argue with him.* **4** *vt* give, offer, or make: *Pay attention to what I say.* | *We paid them a visit.* **5 pay one's way** pay money for things a one buys them so as not to get into debt **6 pay through the nose (for)** *infml* pay far too much (for) ♦ *n* [U] **1** money received for work **2 in the pay of** employed by **~er** *n*

pay back *phr vt* **1** return (what is owing) to (someone) **2** return bad treatment, rudeness, etc., to

pay for *phr vt* receive suffering or punishment for

pay off *phr v* **1** *vt* pay all of (a debt) **2** *vt* pay and dismiss **3** *vt* pay (someone) to keep silent about a wrong act **4** *vi* be successful

pay out *phr v* make (a large payment)

pay up *phr vi* pay a debt in full, esp. unwillingly or late

pay·a·ble /ˈpeɪəbəl/ *adj* that must or can be paid

pay·check /ˈpeɪtʃɛk/ *n* weekly or monthly pay in check form

pay·day /ˈpeɪdeɪ/ *n* day on which one receives one's pay

pay dirt /ˈ· ·/ *n* [U] valuable discovery

pay·ee /peɪˈi/ *n tech* person to whom money is or should be paid

pay·load /ˈpeɪloʊd/ *n* amount carried in a vehicle, esp. a spacecraft

pay·ment /ˈpeɪmənt/ *n* **1** [U] act of paying **2** [C] amount of money (to be) paid — see also BALANCE OF PAYMENTS, DOWN PAYMENT

pay·off /ˈpeɪɔf/ *n* **1** payment made to settle matters **2** ending to something, when everything is explained

pay phone /ˈ· ·/ *n* telephone that works when money is put in it

pay·roll /ˈpeɪroʊl/ *n* **1** list of workers employed **2** total amount of wages paid in a particular company

PC *n* personal computer, for use at home or in businesses: *an IBM PC/PC-based software* ♦ *adj* politically correct

PE *n* [U] physical education; development of the body by games, exercises, etc.

pea /pi/ *n* large round green seed used as food

peace /pis/ *n* [U] **1** period free of war **2** calmness; quietness **3** good order in a country: *The job of the police is to keep the peace.* **4** lack of anxiety: *peace of mind* **5 hold one's peace** remain silent **6 make one's peace with** settle a quarrel with **~ful** *adj* **1** quiet; untroubled **2** without war **~fully** *adv* **~fulness** *n* [U]

peace·time /ˈpistaɪm/ *n* [S] time when a nation is not at war

peach /pitʃ/ *n* round soft juicy yellow-red fruit

pea·cock /ˈpikɑk/ *n* large bird with long beautifully colored tail feathers

peak /pik/ *n* **1** highest point, level, etc. **2** sharply pointed mountain top ♦ *adj* highest; greatest: *at peak fitness* ♦ *vi* reach a PEAK (1)

peal /pil/ *n* **1** loud, long sound: *peals of laughter* **2** sound of bells ringing ♦ *vi* (of a bell) ring loudly

pea·nut /ˈpinʌt/ *n* nut that grows in a shell underground **peanuts** *n* [P] *sl* very little money

peanut but·ter /ˈ·· ·ˌ·/ *n* [U] spreadable food made from crushed peanuts: *peanut butter and jelly*

pear /pɛr/ *n* sweet, juicy fruit, narrow at the stem end and wide at the other

pearl /pəl/ *n* round silver-white jewel formed in the shell of OYSTERS

pearly gates /ˌ·· ˈ·/ *n* [the+P] gates of Heaven

peas·ant /ˈpɛzənt/ *n* **1** person who works on the land in a poor country or in former times **2** *infml derog* person who is uneducated or has bad manners

peat /pit/ *n* [U] partly decayed plant material in the earth, used for growing things or burning **~y** *adj*

peb·ble /ˈpɛbəl/ *n* small stone **–bly** *adj*

pe·can /pɪˈkæn, ˈkɑn, ˈpikæn/ *n* kind of nut with a hard shell: *pecan pie*

peck /pɛk/ *v* **1** *vi/t* (of a bird) strike with the beak **2** *vt* kiss hurriedly ♦ *n* **1** stroke or mark made by pecking **2** hurried kiss

peck·ing or·der /ˈ.. ˌ.-/ n social order, showing who is more and less important

pe·cu·liar /pɪˈkjulyə/ adj 1 strange, esp. in a displeasing way 2 belonging only to a particular place, time, etc.: *a plant peculiar to these islands* 3 crazy 4 a little ill ~**ly** adv 1 especially 2 strangely ~**ity** /pɪˌkyuliˈærəti/ n 1 [U] being peculiar 2 [C] something PECULIAR (2) 3 [C] strange or unusual habit, etc.

ped·a·gog·i·cal /ˌpɛdəˈgadʒɪkəl, -ˈgou-/ adj of teaching or the study of teaching methods ~**ly** adv

ped·al /ˈpɛdl/ n part pushed with the foot to drive or control a machine: *a bicycle pedal* ♦ v -l- 1 vi work pedals 2 vi/t ride (a bicycle)

ped·ant /ˈpɛdnt/ n person who gives too much value to small details and formal rules ~**ic** /pəˈdæntɪk/ adj ~**ically** adv

ped·dle /ˈpɛdl/ vt try to sell by going from place to place

ped·dler /ˈpɛdlə/ n 1 person who peddles illegal drugs 2 person who peddles small articles

ped·es·tal /ˈpɛdəstl/ n 1 base on which a pillar or STATUE stands 2 **put someone on a pedestal** treat someone as better or nobler than anyone else

pe·des·tri·an¹ /pəˈdɛstriən/ n walker

pedestrian² adj 1 dull and ordinary 2 for pedestrians: *a pedestrian crossing*

pe·di·at·rics /ˌpidiˈætrɪks/ n [U] branch of medicine concerned with children –**rician** /ˌpidiəˈtrɪʃən/ n children's doctor

ped·i·gree /ˈpɛdəˌgri/ n [C;U] (an official description of) the set of people or animals from whom a person or animal is descended ♦ adj (of an animal) specially bred from a family of animals of high quality

pee /pi/ vi infml for: urinate (URINE) ♦ n infml 1 [S] act of peeing 2 [U] URINE

peek /pik/ vi, n (take) a quick look

peel /pil/ v 1 vt remove (the outer covering) from (esp. a fruit or vegetable): (fig.) *They peeled off their clothes and jumped in the water.* 2 vi come off in small pieces: *My skin is peeling.* 3 **keep one's eyes peeled** keep careful watch ♦ n [U] outer covering of fruits and vegetables

peep¹ /pip/ vi, n (take) a quick often secret look

peep² n 1 [C] short weak high sound 2 [S] sound, esp. something spoken

peer¹ /pɪr/ n fml one's equal in rank, quality, etc.

peer² vi look very carefully or hard: *peering through the mist*

peer·less /ˈpɪrlɪs/ adj fml better than any other

peer pres·sure /ˈ. ˌ.-/ n [U] strong feeling among young people that they should do the same thing their PEERS are doing

peg¹ /pɛg/ n short piece of wood, metal, etc., for hanging things on, etc.

peg² vt -gg- 1 decide or think that someone is as stated: *She had him pegged as a cheater.* 2 fasten with a peg: (fig.) *Prices have been pegged at this year's levels.*

pe·jo·ra·tive /pəˈdʒɔrətɪv, -ˈdʒɑr-/ adj (of a word or expression) saying that something is bad or worthless

pel·i·can /ˈpɛlɪkən/ n large water bird with a large beak in which it stores fish to eat

pel·let /ˈpɛlɪt/ n 1 small ball of soft material 2 small metal ball fired from a gun

pelt¹ /pɛlt/ v 1 vt attack by throwing things 2 vi (of rain) fall very heavily

pelt² n animal's skin with its fur

pel·vis /ˈpɛlvɪs/ n frame of bones in a bowl shape at the base of the SPINE –**vic** adj

pen¹ /pɛn/ n instrument for writing with ink

pen² n enclosed piece of land for keeping animals in ♦ vt -nn- shut in a pen or small space

pe·nal /ˈpinl/ adj of or being legal punishment, esp. in prison

pe·nal·ize /ˈpinlˌaɪz, ˈpɛn-/ vt put in an unfavorable or unfair situation

pen·al·ty /ˈpɛnlti/ n 1 punishment or disadvantage suffered, esp. for doing wrong 2 (in sports) disadvantage suffered by a player or team for breaking a rule

pen·ance /ˈpɛnəns/ n [U] willing punishment of oneself, to show one is sorry for doing wrong

pen·chant /ˈpɛntʃənt/ n liking for something

pen·cil¹ /ˈpɛnsəl/ n narrow pointed writing instrument containing a thin stick of black material

pencil² *v* -l- **pencil in** *phr vi* include for now, with the possibility of being changed later

pen·dant /ˈpɛndənt/ *n* hanging piece of jewelry, esp. around the neck

pend·ing /ˈpɛndɪŋ/ *adj* waiting to be decided ♦ *prep* until

pen·du·lum /ˈpɛndʒələm, -dʒə-/ *n* weight hanging so as to swing freely, esp. as used to control a clock

pen·e·trate /ˈpɛnətreɪt/ *v* **1** *vi/t* go (into or through): *The knife didn't penetrate his skin.* **2** *vt* see into or through –**trating** *adj* **1** (of sight, a question, etc.) sharp and searching **2** able to understand clearly and deeply –**tration** /ˌpɛnəˈtreɪʃən/ *n* [U] **1** act of penetrating **2** ability to understand clearly and deeply

pen·guin /ˈpɛŋgwɪn, ˈpɛn-/ *n* black and white sea bird of the ANTARCTIC that cannot fly

pen·i·cil·lin /ˌpɛnəˈsɪlɪn/ *n* [U] medicine that kills bacteria

pe·nin·su·la /pəˈnɪnsələ, -sjə-/ *n* piece of land almost surrounded by water

pe·nis /ˈpinɪs/ *n* male sex organ

pen·i·tent /ˈpɛnətənt/ *adj* feeling sorry and intending not to do wrong again –**tence** *n* [U]

pen·i·ten·tia·ry /ˌpɛnəˈtɛnʃəri/ *n* prison

pen·knife /ˈpɛn-naɪf/ *n* -**knives** /-naɪvz/ small knife with a folding blade

pen·man·ship /ˈpɛnmənˌʃɪp/ *n* practice of HANDWRITING

pen name /ˈ· ·/ *n* false name used by a writer instead of his/her real name

pen·nant /ˈpɛnənt/ *n* **1** long narrow pointed flag **2** CHAMPIONship in a sports division

pen·ni·less /ˈpɛnilɪs/ *adj* having no money

pen·ny /ˈpɛni/ *n* **pennies 1** unit of money equal to 1/100th of a dollar **2** a **pretty penny** a fairly large amount of money

pen pal /ˈ· ·/ *n* usu. foreign friend that you write to but never have usu. never met

pen·sion /ˈpɛnʃən/ *n* money paid regularly to someone who can no longer earn (enough) money by working esp. because of old age or illness

pension plan /ˈ·· ·/ *n* system for organizing the type of PENSION a company will give its workers

pen·sive /ˈpɛnsɪv/ *adj* deeply or sadly thoughtful ~**ly** *adv* ~**ness** *n* [U]

pen·ta·gon /ˈpɛntəˌgɑn/ *n* **1** [*cap.*] US government building from which the army, navy, etc., are controlled **2** flat five-sided shape

pent·house /ˈpɛnt-haʊs/ *n* set of rooms built on top of a tall building

pent-up /ˌpɛnt ˈʌp/ *adj* not allowed to be free or freely expressed: *pent-up emotions*

pe·nul·ti·mate /pɪˈnʌltəmət/ *adj* next to the last

peo·ple /ˈpipəl/ *n* **1** [P] persons other than oneself; persons in general: *How many people were at the meeting?* | *That sort of thing annoys people.* **2** [(*the*) P] all the ordinary members of a nation **3** [C] race; nation: *the peoples of Africa* **4** [P] persons from whom one is descended ♦ *vt* **1** live in (a place) **2** fill with PEOPLE (1)

pep¹ /pɛp/ *n* [U] *infml* enthusiastic activity and forcefulness

pep² *v* -**pp- pep up** *sl* make more active or interesting

pep·per¹ /ˈpɛpə/ *n* **1** [U] powder that tastes hot, made from the fruit of a tropical plant **2** [C] hollow vegetable that tastes slightly hot: *green peppers*

pepper² *vt* hit repeatedly with shots

pep·per·mint /ˈpɛpəˌmɪnt/ *n* **1** [U] MINT¹ (2) plant with a special strong taste **2** [C] candy with this taste

pep·pe·ro·ni /ˌpɛpəˈroʊni/ *n* [U] SAUSAGE with a hot taste used esp. for PIZZA

pep pill /ˈ· ·/ *n* PILL (1) taken to make one quicker or happier for a short time

pep ral·ly /ˈ· ˌ·/ *n* meeting at a school with speeches, music, and shouting to support a sports team

pep talk /ˈ· ·/ *n* talk intended to make people work harder, more quickly, etc.

per /pə/ *prep* **1** for each: *apples at 90 cents per pound* **2** *infml* according to: *as per your instructions*

per an·num /pə ˈænəm/ *adv* each year

per·ceive /pəˈsiv/ *vt fml* (come to) have knowledge of, esp. by seeing or understanding

per·cent /pəˈsɛnt/ *n, adj, adv* (one part) in or for each 100: *a 10 percent pay raise*

per·cen·tage /pəˈsɛntɪdʒ/ *n* **1** [C] number stated as if it is part of a whole which is 100: *a high percentage of babies* **2** [U] *infml* advantage; profit

per·cep·ti·ble /pə'sɛptəbəl/ *adj fml* noticeable **-bly** *adv*

per·cep·tion /pə'sɛpʃən/ *n* [U] *fml* 1 action of perceiving (PERCEIVE) 2 keen natural understanding

per·cep·tive /pə'sɛptɪv/ *adj* having or showing PERCEPTION (2) **-ly** *adv*

perch /pɜːtʃ/ *n* 1 branch, rod, etc., where a bird sits 2 high position or place ♦ *v* 1 *vi* (of a bird) sit 2 *vi/t* put or be in a high or unsafe place: *a house perched on top of the cliff*

per·co·late /'pɜːkəˌleɪt/ *vi* pass slowly through a material with small holes: (fig.) *The news gradually percolated through to us.* **-lator** *n* pot in which coffee is made by hot water percolating through the crushed beans

per·cus·sion /pə'kʌʃən/ *n* [U] musical instruments played by being struck: *The drum is a percussion instrument.*

pe·remp·to·ry /pə'rɛmptəri/ *adj fml* 1 impolitely quick and unfriendly 2 (of a command) that must be obeyed **-rily** /pə'rɛmptərəli, -rɛmp'tɔːrəli/ *adv*

pe·ren·ni·al /pə'rɛniəl/ *adj* 1 lasting forever or for a long time 2 (of a plant) living for more than 2 years ♦ *n* perennial plant **~ly** *adv*

per·fect¹ /'pɜːfɪkt/ *adj* 1 of the very best possible kind, standard, etc. 2 as good or suitable as possible: *Your English is almost perfect.* 3 with nothing missing; full: *a perfect set of teeth* 4 complete: *a perfect fool* 5 *gram* expressing an action that has happened and finished: *The perfect tense is formed with "have" in English.* **~ly** *adv*

per·fect² /pə'fɛkt/ *vt* make perfect **~ible** *adj*

per·fec·tion /pə'fɛkʃən/ *n* [U] 1 being perfect 2 making perfect 3 perfect example: *His performance was sheer perfection.*

per·fec·tion·ist /pə'fɛkʃənɪst/ *n* someone not satisfied with anything not perfect

per·fo·rat·ed /'pɜːfəˌreɪtɪd/ *adj* (of paper) with a line of holes to make it easier to tear **-ration** /ˌpɜːfə'reɪʃən/ *n* [C;U]

per·form /pə'fɔːm/ *v* 1 *vt* do (a piece of work, ceremony, etc.): *to perform an operation* 2 *vi/t* act or show (a play, piece of music, etc.), esp. in public 3 *vi* work or carry out an activity (in the stated way): *a car that performs well in the mountains*

~ance *n* 1 [U] action or manner of performing 2 [C] (public) show of music, a play, etc. **~er** *n* actor, musician, etc.

per·fume /'pɜːfjuːm, pə'fjuːm/ *n* [C;U] (liquid having) a pleasant smell ♦ *vt* /pə'fjuːm, 'pɜːfjuːm/ cause to smell pleasant

per·func·to·ry /pə'fʌŋktəri/ *adj fml* done hastily and without interest or care

per·haps /pə'hæps/ *adv* it may be; possibly

per·il /'pɛrəl/ *n* [C;U] (something that causes) great danger **~ous** *adj* possibly

pe·rim·e·ter /pə'rɪmətə/ *n* (length of) the border around an enclosed space, esp. a camp or AIRFIELD

pe·ri·od¹ /'pɪəriəd/ *n* 1 stretch of time 2 division of a school day 3 monthly flow of blood from a woman's body 4 a mark (.) showing esp. the end of a sentence **~ic** /ˌpɪəri'ɒdɪk◄/ *adj* repeated and regular **~ical** *n* magazine that comes out regularly **~ically** *adv*

period² *adv infml* (used at end of a sentence) and that is all I'm going to say on the matter: *I'm not going, period.*

pe·riph·e·ral /pə'rɪfərəl/ *adj* 1 on the periphery 2 slight: *of peripheral interest*

peripheral² *n* apparatus connected to a computer

pe·riph·e·ry /pə'rɪfəri/ *n* outside edge

per·i·scope /'pɛrəˌskəʊp/ *n* long tube with mirrors so that people lower down can see what is above them, esp. in SUBMARINES

per·ish /'pɛrɪʃ/ *vi fml* 1 die 2 (cause to) decay or lose natural qualities **~able** *adj* (of food) that will decay quickly **~ing**, **~ed** *adj* very cold

per·jure /'pɜːdʒə/ *vt* perjure oneself tell lies in a court of law **-jury** *n* [U] lying in court

perk¹ /pɜːk/ *n* money, goods, etc., that one gets from an employer in addition to one's pay: *Having Tuesdays free is one of the perks of the job.*

perk² *v* perk up *phr vi/t* make or become more cheerful

perk·y /'pɜːki/ *adj* confidently cheerful **-iness** *n* [U]

perm /pɜːm/ *n* act of putting artificial curls into hair ♦ *vt* give a perm to

per·ma·nent /'pɜːmənənt/ *adj* lasting a long time or forever **~ly** *adv* **-ence** *n* [U]

per·me·ate /'pɜːmiˌeɪt/ *vt* spread or pass through or into every part of

per·mis·si·ble /pə'mɪsəbəl/ *adj fml* allowed **–bly** *adv*

per·mis·sion /pə'mɪʃən/ *n* [U] act of allowing

per·mis·sive /pə'mɪsɪv/ *adj* allowing (too) much freedom, esp. in sexual matters **~ly** *adv* **~ness** *n* [U]

per·mit¹ /pə'mɪt/ *vi/t* **-tt-** allow

per·mit² /'pɜːmɪt/ *n* official paper allowing something

per·ni·cious /pə'nɪʃəs/ *adj fml* very harmful **–ly** *adv* **~ness** *n* [U]

per·pen·dic·u·lar /ˌpɜːpən'dɪkjələ/ *adj* **1** exactly upright **2** at an angle of 90° to another line or surface ♦ *n* [C;U] perpendicular line or position

per·pe·trate /'pɜːpəˌtreɪt/ *vt fml* be guilty of **–trator** *n*

per·pet·u·al /pə'petʃuəl/ *adj* lasting (as if) forever **~ly** *adv*

per·pet·u·ate /pə'petʃueɪt/ *vt fml* make (something) continue to exist for a long time **–ation** /pəˌpetʃu'eɪʃən/ *n* [U]

per·pe·tu·i·ty /ˌpɜːpə'tuəti/ *n* **in perpetuity** *fml* forever

per·plex /pə'pleks/ *vt* make (someone) feel confused by being difficult to understand: *a perplexing problem* **~ity** *n* [U]

per se /ˌpɜː 'seɪ/ *adv* considered alone and not in connection with other things

per·se·cute /'pɜːsɪˌkjuːt/ *vt* **1** cause to suffer, esp. for religious beliefs **2** trouble or harm continually **–cutor** *n* **–cution** /ˌpɜːsɪ'kjuːʃən/ *n* [C;U]

per·se·vere /ˌpɜːsɪ'vɪə/ *vi* continue firmly in spite of difficulties **–verance** *n* [U]

per·sist /pə'sɪst, -'zɪst/ *vi* **1** continue firmly in spite of opposition or warning: *Do not persist in this unwise action.* **2** continue to exist **~ent** *adj* persisting: *persistent rudeness/coughing* **~ently** *adv* **~ence** *n* [U]

per·son /'pɜːsən/ *n* **1** single human being **2** *gram* form of verb or PRONOUN, showing the speaker (**first person**), the one spoken to (**second person**), or the one spoken about (**third person**) **3 in person** personally; oneself **4 on one's person** carried around with one

per·so·na /pə'səunə/ *n* outward character a person takes on

per·son·a·ble /'pɜːsənəbəl/ *adj fml* attractive and friendly

per·son·al /'pɜːsənəl/ *adj* **1** of, for, or by a particular person: *It's a personal* (= *private*) *matter.* **2** rude **3** *fml* of the body: *personal cleanliness* **~ly** *adv* **1** directly and not through a representative **2** giving one's own opinion **3** privately

personal ad /'... .,/ *n* advertisement in a newspaper that gives or asks for messages, news, etc., about particular people

per·son·al·i·ty /ˌpɜːsə'næləti/ *n* **1** [C;U] whole nature or character of a person **2** [U] unusual, strong, exciting character: *She's got lots of personality.* **3** [C] person who is well known

personality cult /..'.... ./ *n* practice of giving too great admiration to a particular person, esp. a political or religious leader

per·son·al·ize /'pɜːsənəˌlaɪz/ *vt* **1** put one's name or INITIALS on **2** decorate in a way one likes **3** make suitable for a particular person's needs

personal pro·noun /ˌ... '../ *n* PRONOUN showing the PERSON (2), such as *I* or *you*

personal ster·e·o /ˌ... '.../ *n* small machine for playing CASSETTES, which has HEADPHONES and is carried around with the user

per·son·i·fy /pə'sɒnəfaɪ/ *vt* **1** be a good example of (a quality) **2** represent as being human **–fication** /pəˌsɒnəfə'keɪʃən/ *n* [C;U]

per·son·nel /ˌpɜːsə'nel/ *n* **1** [P] all employed people in a company, army, etc. **2** [U] department that deals with these people and their problems

per·spec·tive /pə'spektɪv/ *n* **1** [U] effect of depth, distance, and solidity in drawing and painting **2** [C;U] proper relationship of each part of a matter: *We must get the problem in perspective; it's not really that serious.*

per·spire /pə'spaɪə/ *vi fml* for SWEAT **–spiration** /ˌpɜːspə'reɪʃən/ *n* [U] *fml* **1** sweat **2** act of sweating

per·suade /pə'sweɪd/ *vt* make (someone) do something by reasoning, arguing, begging, etc.

per·sua·sion /pə'sweɪʒən/ *n* **1** [U] (skill in) persuading **2** [C] particular belief: *her political persuasions*

per·sua·sive /pə'sweɪsɪv, -zɪv/ *adj* able to persuade others **~ly** *adv* **~ness** *n* [U]

pert /pɜːt/ *adj* amusingly disrespectful **~ly** *adv* **~ness** *n* [U]

per·tain /pə'teɪn/ v **pertain to** phr vt fml be about or connected with

per·ti·nent /'pɜːtɪn·ənt/ adj fml directly connected; RELEVANT **~ly** adv **–nence** n [U]

per·turb /pə'tɜːb/ vt fml worry **~ation** /ˌpɜːtə'beɪʃən/ n [U]

pe·ruse /pə'ruːz/ vt fml read carefully **perusal** n [C;U]

per·vade /pə'veɪd/ vt fml spread all through

per·va·sive /pə'veɪsɪv, -zɪv/ adj pervading; widespread **~ly** adv **~ness** n [U]

per·verse /pə'vɜːs/ adj **1** purposely doing wrong or unreasonable things **2** awkward and annoying **~ly** adv

per·ver·sion /pə'vɜːʃən/ n **1** [C] perverted form of what is true, reasonable, etc. **2** [C] unnatural sexual act **3** [U] act of perverting

per·ver·si·ty /pə'vɜːsəti/ n **1** [U] being perverse **2** [C] perverse act

per·vert¹ /pə'vɜːt/ vt **1** lead into wrong or unnatural (sexual) behavior **2** use for a bad purpose

per·vert² /'pɜːvət/ n person who does unnatural sexual acts

pes·ky /'peski/ adj infml annoying; causing trouble

pes·si·mist /'pesəmɪst/ n person who expects bad things to happen **–mism** n [U] **–mistic** /ˌpesə'mɪstɪk/ adj

pest /pest/ n **1** animal or insect that harms food products **2** annoying person

pes·ter /'pestə/ vt annoy continually, esp. with demands

pes·ti·cide /'pestəsaɪd/ n [C;U] chemical to kill PESTS (1)

pes·tle /'pesəl, 'pestl/ n instrument for crushing things in a thick bowl

pet /pet/ n **1** animal kept as a companion: my pet cat **2** person especially favored ♦ v -tt- **1** vt touch lovingly **2** vi kiss and touch sexually

pet·al /'petl/ n colored leaflike part of a flower

pet·er /'piːtə/ v **peter out** phr vi gradually end

pe·tite /pə'tiːt/ adj (esp. of a woman) having a small and neat figure

pe·ti·tion /pə'tɪʃən/ n request or demand to a government, etc., signed by many people ♦ vi/t make or send a petition **~er** n

pet name /ˌ· '·/ n name for someone you like, instead of their real name

pet peeve /ˌpet 'piːv/ n small thing that one complains about often

pet·ri·fy /'petrəfaɪ/ vt **1** frighten very much **2** turn into stone

pe·tro·le·um /pə'trəʊliəm/ n [U] mineral oil obtained from below the ground

pet·ty /'peti/ adj **1** unimportant (by comparison) **2** showing a narrow and ungenerous mind **–tiness** n [U]

petty cash /ˌ·· '·/ n [U] money kept for small payments

petty of·fi·cer /ˌ·· '··◂/ n person of middle rank in the navy

pet·u·lant /'petʃələnt/ adj showing childish bad temper **~ly** adv **–lance** n [U]

pew /pjuː/ n seat in a church: (fig.) Take a pew. (= Sit down.)

pew·ter /'pjuːtə/ n [U] grayish metal made from lead and tin

PG abbrev. for: parental guidance; (of a film) which may in parts be unsuitable for children under 15

phal·lus /'fæləs/ n image of the male sex organ **–lic** adj

phan·tom /'fæntəm/ n **1** GHOST **2** something that is not really there

pha·raoh /'feərəʊ, 'færəʊ/ n ruler of ancient Egypt

phar·ma·ceu·ti·cal /ˌfɑːmə'sjuːtɪkəl/ adj of (the making of) medicine

phar·ma·cist /'fɑːməsɪst/ n **1** person who makes medicines **2** DRUGGIST

phar·ma·col·o·gy /ˌfɑːmə'kɒlədʒi/ n [U] study of medicine and drugs **–gist** n

phar·ma·cy /'fɑːməsi/ n **1** [C] DRUGSTORE **2** [U] making or giving out of medicines

phase /feɪz/ n **1** stage of development **2** way the moon looks at a particular time ♦ vt arrange in separate phases

phase in/out phr vt introduce/remove gradually

Ph.D. /ˌpiː eɪtʃ 'diː/ n doctor of philosophy; the highest university degree, or someone with this degree

pheas·ant /'fezənt/ n large bird often shot for food

phe·nom·e·nal /fɪ'nɒmənl/ adj very unusual **~ly** adv: phenomenally strong

phe·nom·e·non /fɪ'nɒmənɒn, -nən/ n **-na** /-nə/ **1** fact or event in the world as it appears or is experienced by the senses, esp. an unusual one **2** very unusual person, thing, etc.

phi·lan·thro·pist /fɪˈlænθrəpɪst/ n kind person who gives money to those who are poor or in trouble **–py** n [U] **–pic** /ˌfɪlənˈθrəpɪk◁/ adj

phil·is·tine /ˈfɪləˌstin/ n person who does not understand and actively dislikes art, music, beautiful things, etc.

phi·los·o·pher /fɪˈlɒsəfə/ n 1 person who studies philosophy 2 philosophical (2) person

phi·los·o·phize /fɪˈlɒsəˌfaɪz/ vi talk or write like a philosopher

phi·los·o·phy /fɪˈlɒsəfi/ n 1 [U] study of the nature and meaning of existence, reality, morals, etc. 2 [C] system of thought **–ophical** /ˌfɪləˈsɒfɪkəl◁/ adj 1 of philosophy 2 accepting things with calm courage **–ophically** adv

phlegm /flɛm/ n 1 [U] thick liquid produced in the nose and throat 2 fml calmness

phleg·mat·ic /flɛɡˈmætɪk/ adj calm and difficult to excite **~ally** adv

pho·bi·a /ˈfoʊbiə/ n strong (unreasonable) fear and dislike

phoe·nix /ˈfiːnɪks/ n imaginary bird that burned itself up and was born again from its ashes

phone /foʊn/ n, vi/t telephone

phone book /ˈ· ·/ n book with a list of all telephone numbers in an area

phone booth /ˈ· ·/ n hut containing a public telephone

phone-tap·ping /ˈ· ˌ··/ n [U] listening secretly to other people's telephone conversations by means of special electronic equipment

pho·net·ic /fəˈnɛtɪk/ adj 1 of the sounds of human speech 2 (of a language) with all the sounds spelled very much as they sound **~ally** adv

pho·net·ics /fəˈnɛtɪks/ n [U] study and science of speech sounds **–ician** /ˌfoʊnəˈtɪʃən/ n person

pho·no·graph /ˈfoʊnəˌɡræf/ n old-fash RECORD PLAYER

pho·ny /ˈfoʊni/ n, adj sl (someone or something) pretended or false

phos·phate /ˈfɒsfeɪt/ n [C;U] chemical found naturally or made from phosphoric acid, esp. as used for making plants grow better

phos·pho·res·cent /ˌfɒsfəˈrɛsənt/ adj shining faintly in the dark by a natural process **–cence** n [U]

phos·pho·rus /ˈfɒsfərəs/ n [U] yellowish waxlike chemical that burns when brought into the air **–phoric** /fɒsˈfɒrɪk, fɒsˈfɑ-, ˈfɒsfɔrɪk/ adj

pho·to /ˈfoʊtoʊ/ n **-tos** photograph

pho·to·cop·y /ˈfoʊtəˌkɒpi, ˈfoʊtoʊ-/ vi/t, n (make) a copy of a piece of paper **–ier** machine that does this

photo fin·ish /ˌ·· ˈ·-/ n very close finish to a race, etc., where a photograph is needed to show which competitor won

pho·to·gen·ic /ˌfoʊtəˈdʒɛnɪk◁/ adj that looks good when photographed

pho·to·graph /ˈfoʊtəɡræf/ n picture taken with a camera and film ♦ vt take a photograph of **~er** /fəˈtɒɡrəfə/ n **~y** n [U] art or business of producing photographs or films **–ic** /ˌfoʊtəˈɡræfɪk◁/ adj

pho·to·syn·the·sis /ˌfoʊtoʊˈsɪnθəsɪs/ n [U] process by which plants make food using sunlight

phras·al /ˈfreɪzəl/ adj of or being a phrase

phrasal verb /ˌ·· ˈ·/ n group of words that acts like a verb and consists usu. of a verb with an adverb and/or a PREPOSITION: "Set off" and "put up with" are phrasal verbs.

phrase /freɪz/ n 1 group of words without a FINITE verb 2 short (suitable) expression ♦ vt express in the stated way

phrase-book /ˈfreɪzbʊk/ n book explaining foreign phrases, for use abroad

phys·i·cal /ˈfɪzɪkəl/ adj 1 of or being matter or material things (not the mind, etc.) 2 of the body: physical strength **~ly** adv 1 with regard to the body 2 according to the laws of nature: physically impossible

phy·si·cian /fɪˈzɪʃən/ n fml doctor

phys·i·cist /ˈfɪzəsɪst/ n person who studies or works in physics

phys·ics /ˈfɪzɪks/ n [U] science dealing with matter and natural forces

phys·i·ol·o·gy /ˌfɪziˈɒlədʒi/ n [U] science of how living bodies work **–gist** n **–gical** /ˌfɪziəˈlɒdʒɪkəl◁/ adj

phys·i·o·ther·a·py /ˌfɪzioʊˈθɛrəpi/ n [U] exercises, rubbing, etc., to treat sick people **–pist** n

phy·sique /fɪˈziːk/ n shape and quality of a person's body

pi·an·o /pɪˈænəʊ/ n -os large musical instrument with wire strings, played by pressing black and white bars

pianist /ˈpiːənɪst, ˈpɪənɪst/ n someone who plays the piano

pic·co·lo /ˈpɪkələʊ/ n -los small FLUTE

pick[1] /pɪk/ vt 1 choose 2 pull off from a plant: picking fruit 3 take up with the fingers, a beak, or a pointed instrument 4 remove unwanted pieces from: picking her teeth 5 steal from: I had my pocket picked. 6 open (a lock) without a key 7 cause (a fight, etc.) intentionally 8 **pick and choose** choose very carefully 9 **pick holes in** find the weak points in 10 **pick one's way** walk carefully 11 **pick someone's brains** make use of someone's knowledge ~er n ~ings n [P] additional money or profits

pick at phr vt eat (a meal) with little interest

pick off phr vt shoot one by one

pick on phr vt choose unfairly for punishment or blame

pick out phr vt 1 choose specially 2 see among others, esp. with difficulty

pick up phr v 1 vt take hold of and lift up 2 vt gather together: Pick up your toys. 3 vi/t (cause to) start again 4 vt get: I picked up a cold last week. 5 vt go and meet or collect: I'll pick you up at the station. 6 vi improve, esp. in health 7 vt become friendly with for sexual purposes 8 vt catch: The police picked up the criminals at the airport. 9 vt be able to hear or receive (on a radio)

pick[2] n [U] 1 choice: Take your pick! 2 best: It's the pick of the new films.

pick[3] n 1 PICKAXE 2 sharp, pointed, usu. small instrument 3 small piece of metal, plastic, etc., for picking the strings of a GUITAR etc.

pick·ax /ˈpɪkæks/ n large tool with 2 sharp points, for digging up roads, etc.

pick·et /ˈpɪkɪt/ n 1 person or group outside a place of work trying to persuade others not to work there during a quarrel with employers 2 soldier guarding a camp 3 strong pointed stick fixed in the ground ♦ vt surround with or as PICKETS (1)

pick·le /ˈpɪkəl/ n 1 [C;U] CUCUMBER preserved in VINEGAR or salt water 2 [S] dirty, difficult, or confused condition: in a pickle ♦ vt preserve in VINEGAR –led adj infml drunk

pick-me-up /ˈ· · ˌ·/ n infml something, esp. a drink or medicine, that makes one feel stronger, happier, etc.

pick·pock·et /ˈpɪkˌpɒkɪt/ n person who steals from people's pockets

pick-up /ˈpɪk-ʌp/ n 1 light truck having an open body with low sides 2 person of the opposite sex who one meets informally, esp. for sexual relations

pick·y /ˈpɪki/ adj infml (of a person) difficult to please, because only liking a few things

pic·nic /ˈpɪknɪk/ n 1 informal outdoor meal 2 enjoyable experience ♦ vi -ck- have a picnic

pic·ture /ˈpɪktʃə/ n 1 [C] representation made by painting, drawing, or photography 2 [C] what is seen on a television: We don't get a very good picture. 3 old-fash [C] movie 4 [C] image in the mind 5 [S] person or thing that is beautiful 6 [S] perfect example: He's the picture of health. (= very healthy) 7 **in the picture:** a knowing all the facts b receiving much attention ♦ vt 1 imagine: Just picture the frightful scene. 2 paint or draw **pictures** n [P] 1 the movies 2 the film industry

pic·tur·esque /ˌpɪktʃəˈresk◂/ adj 1 charming to look at 2 (of language) unusually forceful and descriptive

pid·dling /ˈpɪdlɪŋ/ adj infml small and unimportant

pid·gin /ˈpɪdʒən/ n language which is a mixture of other languages

pie /paɪ/ n 1 baked dish of pastry filled with fruit 2 **as easy as pie** infml very easy 3 **piece/share/slice of the pie** share of money, profit, etc.: She wants a bigger slice of the pie.

piece[1] /piːs/ n 1 separate part or bit: pieces of broken glass 2 single object that is an example of its kind or class: a piece of paper/music/(fig.) advice 3 small object used in board games: a chess piece 4 sl small gun 5 **give someone a piece of one's mind** infml tell someone angrily what you think of them 6 **go to pieces** infml lose the ability to think or act clearly 7 **in one piece** unharmed 8 **piece of cake** infml something very easy to do 9 **say one's piece** say what one wants to or has planned to, esp. in a way that is annoying or unwelcome to others

piece[2] v **piece together** phr vt complete by finding all the bits and putting them together

pi·èce de ré·sis·tance /piˌɛs də rəziˈstɑns, -reɪ-/ n **pièces de résistance** (same pronunciation) the best or most important thing or event

piece·meal /ˈpiːsmiːl/ adj, adv (done) only one part at a time

piece·work /ˈpiːswɜːk/ n [U] work paid for by the amount done rather than by the hours worked

pie chart /ˈ· ˌ/ n circle divided into several parts showing the way in which something, e.g. money or population, is divided up

pier /pɪr/ n **1** long structure built out into the sea **2** supporting pillar

pierce /pɪrs/ vt make a hole in or through with a point: (fig.) A cry of fear pierced the silence. **piercing** adj **1** (of wind) very strong and cold **2** (of sound) unpleasantly sharp and clear **3** searching: a piercing look

pi·e·ty /ˈpaɪəti/ n [U] fml deep respect for God and religion

pig /pɪg/ n **1** fat animal with short legs and no fur, kept on farms for food **2** infml person who is dirty or rude or eats too much **3 make a pig of oneself** infml eat (or drink) too much

   pig out phr v infml eat too much at one meal

pi·geon /ˈpɪdʒən/ n **1** fairly large, light gray bird **2** sl person who is easily deceived

pi·geon·hole /ˈpɪdʒənhoʊl/ n **1** boxlike division for putting papers in **2** neat division which separates things to put simply ♦ vt **1** put aside and do nothing about **2** put in a PIGEONHOLE (2)

pigeon-toed /ˈ·· ˌ/ adj having feet that point inwards

piggy·back /ˈpɪgiˌbæk/ adv on the back and shoulders: He carried his son piggyback. | riding piggyback

pig·gy bank /ˈpɪgi ˌbæŋk/ n small container, usu. shaped like a pig, used by children for saving coins

pig·head·ed /ˈpɪgˌhɛdɪd/ adj very unwilling to agree or obey

pig·let /ˈpɪglɪt/ n young pig

pig·ment /ˈpɪgmənt/ n **1** [C;U] dry colored powder for making paint **2** [U] natural coloring matter in plants and animals **~ation** /ˌpɪgmənˈteɪʃən/ n [U]

pig·pen /ˈpɪgpɛn/ n **1** place where pigs are kept **2** infml very dirty room or house

pig·sty /ˈpɪgstaɪ/ n **1** small building for pigs **2** infml very dirty room or house

pig·tail /ˈpɪgteɪl/ n length of hair gathered together at the side of the head

pike[1] /paɪk/ n **pikes** or **pike** large river fish that eats smaller fish

pike[2] n spear with a long handle

pile[1] /paɪl/ n **1** tidy heap: a pile of books **2** also **piles** pl. — infml lots: I've got piles of work to do. **3** infml very large amount of money **4** large tall building — see also PILES ♦ v **1** vt make a pile of **2** vi come or go in a (disorderly) crowd: The children piled into the car.

   pile up phr vi form into a mass or large quantity

pile[2] n [C;U] soft surface of short threads on CARPETS or cloth

pile[3] n heavy supporting post hammered into the ground

pile-up /ˈpaɪlʌp/ n traffic accident with many vehicles

pil·fer /ˈpɪlfər/ vi/t steal (small things)

pil·grim /ˈpɪlgrəm/ n person on a journey to a holy place **~age** n [C;U] pilgrim's journey

pill /pɪl/ n **1** [C] small ball of medicine **2** [the+S] (often cap.) pill taken for birth control

pil·lage /ˈpɪlɪdʒ/ vi/t fml steal things violently from (a place taken in war)

pil·lar /ˈpɪlə/ n **1** tall upright round post, usu. of stone, used esp. as a support for a roof **2** important member and active supporter: a pillar of the church

pil·low /ˈpɪloʊ/ n filled cloth bag for supporting the head in bed

pil·low·case /ˈpɪloʊkeɪs/ n cloth cover for a pillow

pi·lot /ˈpaɪlət/ n **1** person who flies a plane **2** person who guides ships into a HARBOR, etc. ♦ adj intended to try something out: a pilot survey ♦ vt act as the pilot of

pilot light /ˈ·· ˌ/ n **1** small gas flame to light a main flame **2** small electric light to show an apparatus is turned on

pimp /pɪmp/ n man who controls and gets money from PROSTITUTES

pim·ple /ˈpɪmpəl/ n small raised red spot on the skin, esp. the face

PIN /pɪn/ n personal identification number; secret number one must give when using services such as bank machines, etc.

pin /pɪn/ n **1** short thin pointed piece of metal for fastening things **2** BROOCH ♦ vt

-nn- **1** fasten with a pin **2** keep in one position, esp. by weight from above **3 pin one's hopes on someone** depend on someone for help, etc.

pin down /phr vt/ **1** force to give clear details, make a firm decision, etc. **2** prevent from moving

pin·cer /'pɪnsə/ n footlike part of a CRAB, LOBSTER, etc., for seizing things **pincers** n [P] tool for holding things tightly

pinch /pɪntʃ/ v **1** vt press tightly between 2 surfaces or between finger and thumb **2** vi hurt by being too tight **3** vt infml steal **pinch pennies** not spend money ♦ n **1** [C] act of pinching **2** [C] amount picked up with finger and thumb: a pinch of salt **3** [the+S] suffering through not having enough esp. of money: We're beginning to feel the pinch. **4 in a pinch** if necessary **5 with a pinch of salt** as being untrue or not dependable: Take everything he says with a pinch of salt.

pinch-hit /'pɪntʃˌhɪt/ vi **1** hit the ball for another player in baseball **2** do something for someone else because they are suddenly unable to do it

pin·cush·ion /'pɪnˌkuʃən/ n small filled bag for sticking pins into until needed

pine[1] /paɪn/ n tall tree with thin sharp leaves that do not drop off in winter

pine[2] vi **1** lose strength and health through grief **2** have a strong desire, esp. that is impossible to fulfill

pine·ap·ple /'paɪnˌæpəl/ n [C;U] large tropical fruit with sweet juicy yellow flesh

ping /pɪŋ/ vi, n (make) a short sharp ringing sound

ping-pong /'pɪŋ pɒŋ, -pɔŋ/ n [U] TABLE TENNIS

pin·ion /'pɪnyən/ n small wheel fitting against a larger one for turning

pink /pɪŋk/ adj pale red ♦ n **in the pink** in perfect health

pink·eye /'pɪŋk-aɪ/ n [S] CONJUNCTIVITIS

pink·ie /'pɪŋki/ n smallest finger

pink slip /ˌ· ˈ·/ n notice of being fired from a job

pin·na·cle /'pɪnəkəl/ n highest point or degree: the pinnacle of success

pin·point /'pɪnpɔɪnt/ vt find or describe exactly

pins and nee·dles /ˌ· · ˈ·· / n [P] slight pricking pains in a limb

pin·stripe /'pɪnstraɪp/ n **1** [C] any of a pattern of parallel pale lines on dark cloth **2** [P] also **pinstripe suit** /ˌ· ˈ·/ — suit made of cloth with a pattern of pinstripes

pint /paɪnt/ n a measure of liquids equal to 16 fluid OUNCEs

pin-up /'pɪnʌp/ n picture of an attractive or admired person such as a popular singer, esp. as stuck up on a wall

pi·o·neer /ˌpaɪə'nɪr/ n person who does something first, preparing the way for others, esp. one who helped settle the western US ♦ vt act as a pioneer in

pi·ous /'paɪəs/ adj **1** having deep respect for God and religion **2** unlikely to be fulfilled: a pious hope –**ly** adv

pipe[1] /paɪp/ n **1** tube carrying liquid or gas **2** small tube with a bowllike container, for smoking tobacco **3** simple tubelike musical instrument **pipes** n [P] BAGPIPES

pipe[2] vt **1** carry in pipes **2** play music on a PIPE (3) or PIPEs **piper** n player of BAGPIPES

pipe down /phr vi/ infml stop talking or being noisy

pipe up /phr vi/ suddenly start to speak

pipe dream /'· ·/ n impossible hope, plan, or idea

pipe·line /'paɪp-laɪn/ n **1** line of joined pipes, esp. for carrying oil or gas **2 in the pipeline** about to arrive or appear; being prepared

pip·ing[1] /'paɪpɪŋ/ n [U] PIPEs[1] (1)

piping[2] adv **piping hot** very hot

pi·quant /'pɪkənt, 'pɪkɑnt, pɪ'kɑnt/ adj **1** having a pleasant sharp taste **2** interesting and exciting to the mind –**quancy** /'pikənsi/ n [U]

pique /pik/ n [U] annoyance and displeasure because of hurt pride ♦ vt offend

pi·ra·cy /'paɪrəsi/ n [U] robbery by pirates

pi·ra·nha /pɪ'rɑnyə, -'ræn-, -'rɑnə/ n fierce S. American river fish that eats flesh

pi·rate /'paɪrɪt/ n **1** person who sails around robbing ships **2** person who pirates things ♦ vt make and sell (a book, record, etc., by someone else) without permission or payment

pir·ou·ette /ˌpɪru'ɛt/ n very fast turn on one foot by a dancer **pirouette** vi

Pis·ces /ˈpaɪsiːz/ *n* 1 [S] 12th sign of the ZODIAC, represented by 2 fish 2 someone born between February 19 and March 20

piss¹ /pɪs/ *vi taboo sl* urinate (URINE)

piss off *phr v taboo sl* annoy

pissed off *adj* angry

piss² *n* [U] *taboo sl* URINE

pis·tol /ˈpɪstl/ *n* small gun held in one hand

pis·ton /ˈpɪstən/ *n* short part of an engine shaped like a pipe, that goes up and down inside a tube and sends power to the engine

pit¹ /pɪt/ *n* 1 hole in the ground 2 coal mine 3 small hollow mark on a surface 4 space in front of a stage where musicians sit 5 hard central part of certain fruit 6 **pit of the stomach** place where fear is thought to be felt **pits** *n* [P] 1 place beside the track where cars are repaired during a race 2 *infml* the worst possible example of something

pit² *vt* -tt- mark with PITS¹ (3)

pit against *phr vt* set against in competition or fight

pitch¹ /pɪtʃ/ *v* 1 *vt* set up (a camp or tent) 2 *vi* (of a ship or aircraft) move along with the front and back going up and down 3 *vt* set the PITCH² (2) of (a sound, music, etc.) 4 *vt* throw 5 *vi/t* (cause to) fall suddenly forwards 6 *vi* play the position of PITCHER² in baseball

pitch in *phr vi* 1 start eagerly 2 add one's help or support

pitch² *n* 1 degree of highness and lowness of a (musical) sound 2 level; degree: *a high pitch of excitement* 3 *infml* seller's special way of talking about goods he/she is trying to sell: *a good sales pitch* 4 action of pitching (pitch¹(6)): *a slow/fast pitch*

pitch³ *n* [U] black substance used for keeping out water: (fig.) *a* **pitch-black** /ˌ· ˈ·◂/ (= very dark) *night*

pitch·er¹ /ˈpɪtʃə/ *n* container for holding and pouring liquids

pitcher² *n* (in baseball) player who throws the ball towards the BATTER³

pitch·fork /ˈpɪtʃfɔːk/ *n* fork with a long handle for lifting dried grass on a farm

pit·e·ous /ˈpɪtiəs/ *adj fml* causing pity ~**ly** *adv*

pit·fall /ˈpɪtfɔːl/ *n* unexpected difficulty or danger

pit·i·ful /ˈpɪtɪfəl/ *adj* 1 causing or deserving pity 2 worthless; weak ~**ly** *adv*

pit·i·less /ˈpɪtɪlɪs/ *adj* merciless; cruel ~**ly** *adv*

pit stop /ˈ· ·/ *n* 1 stop at pits (PIT¹) 2 stop for food, etc. while traveling

pit·tance /ˈpɪtns/ *n* very small amount of pay or money

pit·y /ˈpɪti/ *n* 1 [U] sympathy and sorrow for others' suffering or unhappiness: *We took pity on* (= felt pity for and helped) *the homeless family.* 2 [S] unfortunate state of affairs: *It's a pity you have to go now.* 3 **for pity's sake** (used to add force to a request) please 4 **more's the pity** unfortunately ◆ *vt* feel pity for

piv·ot /ˈpɪvət/ *n* central point on which something turns ◆ *vi/t* turn on or provide with a pivot ~**al** *adj*

pix·el /ˈpɪksəl, -ˌsel/ *n tech* one small dot of light on a television or computer SCREEN

pix·ie /ˈpɪksi/ *n* small fairy that plays tricks

piz·za /ˈpiːtsə/ *n* [C;U] flat round pastry baked with cheese, TOMATOes, etc., on top

pizz·azz /pəˈzæz/ *n* [U] *sl* exciting, forceful quality

plac·ard /ˈplækɑːd, -kəd/ *n* board put up or carried around publicly, with information on it

pla·cate /ˈpleɪkeɪt, ˈplæ-/ *vt* cause to stop feeling angry

place¹ /pleɪs/ *n* 1 [C] particular position in space: *the place where the accident happened* | (fig.) *Sports never had a place in his life.* 2 [C] particular town, building, etc.: *Is San Diego a nice place to live in?* 3 [C] usual or proper position: *Put it back in its place.* 4 position in the result of a competition, race, etc.: *I got first place in the exam.* 5 [C] position of employment, in a team, etc.: *She got a place on the Board of Directors.* 6 [S] numbered point in an argument, etc.: *In the first place, I can't afford it.* 7 [S] *infml: It's not my place to tell them what to do.* 8 [C] space or seat for a person: *save our places; we'll be right back.* 9 [S] *infml* home: *Come back to my place.* 10 **go places** *infml* be increasingly successful 11 **in/out of place:** a in/out in the usual or proper position b suitable/unsuitable 12 **in place of** instead of 13 **know one's place** consider oneself of low rank and behave respectfully 14 **set a place** put knives, forks, spoons, etc., in position on the dinner table (for one person) **15 put someone in his/her place** show someone that he/she is not as important as he/she would like to be **16 take place** happen **17 take the place of** act or be used instead of; REPLACE

place² /vt **1** put in the stated place **2** make (an order for goods one wants to buy) **3** remember fully who (someone) is ~**ment** n [U] act or example of placing someone or something in a position

pla·ce·bo /plə'si:bou/ n -**bos** or -**boes** substance given instead of real medicine, without the person who takes it knowing that it is not real

pla·cen·ta /plə'sentə/ n -**tas** or -**tae** /-ti/ thick mass inside the WOMB joining the unborn child to its mother

plac·id /'plæsɪd/ adj not easily angered or excited ~**ly** adv

pla·gia·rize /'pleɪdʒə,raɪz/ vt take (words, ideas, etc.) from (someone else's work) and use them in one's own writings without admitting that one has done so –**rism** n [U]

plague /pleɪg/ n **1** [C;U] quickly spreading disease that kills many people **2** [C] widespread uncontrollable mass or number: a plague of locusts ♦ vt trouble or annoy continually

plaid /plæd/ adj (of cloth) having a pattern of colored squares

plain¹ /pleɪn/ adj **1** without decoration or pattern; simple **2** easy to see, hear, or understand **3** expressing thoughts clearly, honestly, and exactly **4** fairly ugly ♦ adv completely: plain stupid ~**ly** adv ~**ness** n [U]

plain² n large stretch of flat land

plain·clothes /ˌpleɪn'klouz◂, -'klouðz◂/ adj wearing ordinary clothes and not a uniform: a plainclothes policeman

plain sail·ing /ˌ· '··/ n [U] something easy to do

plain-spo·ken /ˌ· '··◂/ adj (too) direct and honest in speech

plain·tiff /'pleɪntɪf/ n person who brings a legal charge or claim

plain·tive /'pleɪntɪv/ adj sounding sad ~**ly** adv

plan /plæn/ n **1** arrangement for carrying out a (future) activity **2** (maplike drawing showing) an arrangement of parts in a system ♦ vi/t -**nn**- make a plan (for) ~**ner** n

plane¹ /pleɪn/ n **1** aircraft **2** level; standard: Let's keep the conversation on a friendly plane. **3** math flat surface ♦ adj math completely flat

plane² n tool with a sharp blade for making wood smooth ♦ vt use a plane on

plan·et /'plænɪt/ n large body in space that moves around a star, esp. the sun ~**ary** adj

plank /plæŋk/ n **1** long narrow wooden board **2** main principle of a political party's stated aims ~**ing** n [U] (floor) planks

plank·ton /'plæŋktən/ n [U] extremely small sea animals and plants

plant¹ /plænt/ n **1** [C] living thing with leaves and roots **2** [C] factory or other industrial building **3** [U] industrial machinery **4** [C] infml **a** person placed secretly in a group in order to discover facts about them **b** thing hidden on a person to make them seem guilty

plant² vt **1** put (plants or seeds) in the ground **2** infml hide (illegal goods) on someone to make them seem guilty **3** infml put (a person) secretly in a group **4** place firmly or forcefully ~**er** n

plan·ta·tion /plæn'teɪʃən/ n area where large plants are grown as a business, esp. in the old South: a cotton plantation

plaque /plæk/ n **1** flat metal or stone plate with writing on it, usu. fixed to a wall

plas·ma /'plæzmə/ n [U] liquid part of blood, containing the cells

plas·ter¹ /'plæstə/ n **1** [U] mixture of lime, water, sand, etc., which hardens when dry

plaster² vt **1** put plaster on (a wall, etc.) **2** cover too thickly ~**ed** adj infml drunk ~**er** n

plas·tic /'plæstɪk/ n [C;U] light artificial material used for making various things ♦ adj fml **1** easily formed into various shapes **2** connected with the art of shaping forms in clay, wood, etc. **3** infml not sincere ~**ity** /plæs'tɪsəti/ n [U]

plastic sur·ge·ry /ˌ· '···/ n [U] changing the shape of body parts, esp. the face, to look younger or after an accident

plate /pleɪt/ n **1** [C] a flat dish from which food is eaten or served **b** also **plate·ful** /-fʊl/ — amount of food this will hold **2** [C] flat, thin, usu. large piece of something hard **3** [U] metal covered with gold or silver **4** [C] picture in a book, usu. colored **5 on a plate** with too little effort

♦ *vt* cover (a metal article) thinly with gold, silver, or tin

plat·eau /ˈplætoʊ/ *n* -eaus *or* -eaux /-ˈtoʊz/ **1** large area of level high land **2** steady unchanging level, period, or condition

plate glass /ˌ· ˈ·◄/ *n* [U] clear glass in large thick sheets

plat·form /ˈplætfɔrm/ *n* **1** raised area beside the track at a train station **2** raised floor for speakers or performers **3** main ideas and aims of a political party, esp. as stated before an election

plat·i·num /ˈplætᵊn-əm, ˈplætᵊnəm/ *n* [U] very valuable gray-white metal

plat·i·tude /ˈplætətud/ *n* statement that is true but not new or interesting

pla·ton·ic /pləˈtɑnɪk/ *adj* (of friendship, esp. between a man and woman) not sexual

pla·toon /pləˈtun/ *n* small group of soldiers

plat·ter /ˈplætᵊ/ *n* large dish for serving food

plat·y·pus /ˈplætəpəs/ *n* small Australian animal that has a beak and lays eggs

plau·si·ble /ˈplɔzəbəl/ *adj* seeming true; believable ~**bly** *adv*

play¹ /pleɪ/ *n* **1** [U] activity for fun, esp. by children **2** [C] story written to be acted **3** [U] action in a sport: *Rain stopped play.* **4** [U] action; effect: *He had to* **bring** *all his experience* **into play.** (= use it)

play² *v* **1** *vi* amuse oneself with a game, toys, etc. **2** *vi/t* produce sounds or music (from) **3** *vi/t* take part in (a sport or game) **4** *vi/t* perform (in): *Who played the part of Hamlet?* **5** *vt* plan and carry out: *They played a trick on me.* **6** pretend to be: *Stop playing the fool!* (= being foolish) **7** *vt* strike and send (a ball) **8** *vt* place (a playing card) face upwards on the table **9** *vt* aim; direct: *The firemen played their hoses on the blaze.* **10** *vi* move lightly and irregularly: *A smile played across her lips.* **11 play ball** *infml* COOPERATE **12 play for time** delay in order to gain time **13 play into someone's hands** behave in a way that gives someone an advantage over one **14 play it by ear** act according to changing conditions, rather than making fixed plans in advance **15 play (it) safe** act so as to avoid trouble **16 play**

possum pretend to sleep **17 play the field** have many love affairs **18 play the game** do what others expect ~**er** *n* person playing a sport or a musical instrument

   play along *phr vi* pretend to agree, esp. to avoid trouble

   play at *phr vt* **1** PLAY⟨6⟩ **2** do in a way that is not serious

   play back *phr vt* listen to or look at (something just recorded) **playback** /ˈpleɪbæk/ *n* playing of something just recorded, esp. on television

   play down *phr vt* cause to seem less important

   play off *phr v* **1** *vt* set (people or things) in opposition, esp. for one's own advantage **2** *vi* play another game in order to decide who wins **play-off** /ˈ·· / *n* second game played to decide who wins

   play on *phr vt* try to use or encourage (others' feelings) for one's own advantage

   play up *phr v* **1** *vi/t* cause trouble or suffering (to) **2** *vt* give special importance to

   play up to *phr vt* act so as to win the favor of

   play with *phr vt* **1** consider (an idea) not very seriously **2 play with oneself** MASTURBATE **3 to play with** that one can use; AVAILABLE

play·boy /ˈpleɪbɔɪ/ *n* wealthy (young) man who lives for pleasure

play·ful /ˈpleɪfəl/ *adj* **1** full of fun **2** not intended seriously ~**ly** *adv* ~**ness** *n* [U]

play·ground /ˈpleɪgraʊnd/ *n* piece of ground for children to play on

playing card /ˈ·· ·/ *n fml for* CARD⟨1a⟩

play·mate /ˈpleɪmeɪt/ *n* child's friend who shares in games

play·off /ˈpleɪɔf/ *n* (series of) games played by the best sports teams or players, to decide the winner of a competition

play·pen /ˈpleɪpɛn/ *n* enclosed frame for a baby to play in

play·thing /ˈpleɪθɪŋ/ *n* **1** toy **2** person treated without consideration

play·wright /ˈpleɪraɪt/ *n* writer of plays

pla·za /ˈplɑzə, ˈplæzə/ *n* **1** public square or market place **2** small group of stores with one parking lot

plea /pli/ *n* **1** *fml* urgent or serious request **2** *law* statement by someone in a court saying whether they are guilty or not

plea bar·gain·ing /ˈ· ˌ··/ n [U] practice of agreeing to say in a court of law that one is guilty of a small crime in exchange for not being charged with a greater one
plea-bargain vi

plead /pliːd/ v 1 vi make continual and deeply felt requests 2 vt law say officially in court that one is (guilty or not guilty) 3 vt offer as an excuse: He pleaded ignorance.

pleas·ant /ˈplɛzənt/ adj pleasing; nice ~**ly** adv

pleas·ant·ry /ˈplɛzəntri/ n fml politely amusing remark

please /pliːz/ v 1 vi/t make (someone) happy or satisfied 2 vi want; like: They can appoint whoever they please. ♦ interj (used when asking politely for something) **pleased** adj happy; satisfied: Are you pleased with your new car?

plea·sur·a·ble /ˈplɛʒərəbəl/ adj fml enjoyable –**bly** adv

plea·sure /ˈplɛʒə/ n 1 [U] happy feeling; enjoyment 2 [C] something that gives one pleasure 3 [S] something that is not inconvenient and that one is pleased to do: "Thank you for helping me." "My pleasure."

pleat /pliːt/ n flat narrow fold in cloth ♦ vt make pleats in

pledge /plɛdʒ/ n 1 solemn promise 2 something valuable left with someone as a sign that one will fulfill an agreement 3 something given as a sign of love ♦ vt make a solemn promise of

ple·na·ry /ˈpliːnəri, ˈplɛ-/ adj fml 1 (of powers or rights) full; limitless 2 attended by all members: a plenary session of Congress

plen·ti·ful /ˈplɛntɪfəl/ adj in large enough quantities: plentiful supplies ~**ly** adv

plen·ty /ˈplɛnti/ pron as much as or more than is needed: There's plenty (of food) for everyone.

pleth·o·ra /ˈplɛθərə/ n [S] fml too much

Plex·i·glas /ˈplɛksiˌglæs/ n tdmk [U] strong glasslike plastic

pli·a·ble /ˈplaɪəbəl/ adj 1 easily bent 2 able and willing to change; ADAPT able 3 PLIANT (1) –**bility** /ˌplaɪəˈbɪləti/ n [U]

pli·ers /ˈplaɪəz/ n [P] small tool for holding small things or cutting wire

plight /plaɪt/ n bad or serious condition or situation

plod /plɑd/ vi -**dd**- 1 walk slowly and with effort 2 work steadily, esp. at something dull ~**der** n slow, steady, not very clever worker

plop /plɑp/ vi, n -**pp**- [S] (make or fall with) a sound like something falling smoothly into liquid

plot¹ /plɑt/ n 1 set of connected events on which a story is based 2 secret plan to do something bad 3 small piece of ground for building or growing things

plot² v -**tt**- 1 vi/t plan together secretly (something bad) 2 vt mark (the course of a ship or aircraft) on a map 3 vt mark (a line showing facts) on special paper with squares ~**ter** n

plow /plaʊ/ n farming tool for breaking up earth and turning it over ♦ v 1 vi/t break up and turn over (earth) with a plow 2 vi go forcefully or roughly

plow back phr vt put (money earned) back into a business

ploy /plɔɪ/ n something done to gain an advantage, sometimes deceivingly

pluck¹ /plʌk/ vt 1 pull the feathers off (a bird to be cooked) 2 pull out or pick up sharply 3 play an instrument by pulling (its strings) 4 esp. lit pick (a flower)

pluck up phr vt show (courage) in spite of fear

pluck² n [U] courage ~**y** adj brave

plug /plʌg/ n 1 small usu. round thing for blocking a hole, esp. in a BATHTUB, etc. 2 small object for connecting an apparatus with a supply of electricity 3 publicly stated favorable opinion about a product on radio, television, etc., intended to make people want to buy it ♦ vt -**gg**- 1 block or fill with a PLUG (1) 2 give a PLUG (3) to

plug in phr vt connect to a supply of electricity

plum /plʌm/ n roundish usu. dark red fruit with a hard seed in the middle ♦ adj very desirable: a plum job

plum·age /ˈpluːmɪdʒ/ n [U] feathers on a bird

plumb¹ /plʌm/ vt 1 (try to) find the meaning of 2 put in plumbing 3 **plumb the depths** reach the lowest point

plumb² adv exactly: plumb in the center

plumb·er /ˈplʌmə/ n person who fits and repairs water pipes

plumb·ing /ˈplʌmɪŋ/ n [U] 1 all the water pipes and containers in a building 2 work of a plumber

plume /plum/ n **1** (large or showy) feather **2** rising feathery shape: *a plume of smoke* **plumed** *adj*

plummet /ˈplʌmɪt/ vi fall steeply or suddenly

plump /plʌmp/ *adj* pleasantly fat ~**ness** n [U]

plump up *phr vt* make rounded and soft by shaking

plun·der /ˈplʌndə/ vi/t steal or rob in time of war ♦ n [U] (goods seized by) plundering ~**er** n

plunge /plʌndʒ/ vi/t **1** move suddenly forwards and/or downwards **2** (of the neck of a woman's garment) have a low front or in a V shape showing a large area of chest: *a plunging neckline* ♦ n **1** act of plunging **2 take the plunge** at last do something one had delayed **plunger** n **1** tool for clearing a stopped TOILET or DRAIN **2** part of a machine that moves up and down

plu·per·fect /ˌpluːˈpɜːfɪkt/ n PAST PERFECT

plu·ral /ˈplʊərəl/ n, *adj* (word or form) that expresses more than one

plus /plʌs/ *prep* with the addition of: *3 plus 2 is 5.* ♦ *adj* **1** greater than zero **2** additional and desirable ♦ n **1** sign (+) for adding **2** *infml* welcome or favorable addition

plush /plʌʃ/ *adj* looking very splendid and expensive

Plu·to /ˈpluːtoʊ/ n the PLANET 9th in order from the sun

plu·to·ni·um /pluˈtoʊniəm/ n [U] substance used in producing atomic power

ply[1] /plaɪ/ n [U] measure of the number of threads in wool, rope, etc., or the number of sheets in plywood

ply[2] v **1** vi travel regularly for hire or other business **2** vt work at (a trade)

ply with *phr vt* keep giving (esp. food) to

ply·wood /ˈplaɪwʊd/ n [U] material made of thin sheets of wood stuck together

p.m., PM *abbrev. for:* post meridiem = (*Latin*) after noon (used after numbers expressing time)

PMS n [U] premenstrual syndrome; anger or sadness and pain experienced by many women before each PERIOD

pneu·mat·ic /nuˈmætɪk/ *adj* **1** worked by air pressure **2** filled with air: *a pneumatic tire*

pneu·mo·nia /nuˈmoʊnyə/ n [U] serious lung disease

P.O. *abbrev. for:* POST OFFICE

poach[1] /poʊtʃ/ vi/t catch or kill (animals) illegally on someone else's land: (fig.) *poaching* (= stealing) *my ideas* ~**er** n

poach[2] vt cook in gently boiling water

P.O. box /ˌpiː ˈoʊ ˌbɑks/ n post office box; a box in a post office with a number on it, to which mail can be sent

pock·et /ˈpɑkɪt/ n **1** small baglike part in or on a garment **2** container for thin things in a case, inside a car door, etc. **3** small separate area or group: *pockets of mist* **4** (supply of) money: *beyond my pocket* (= too expensive) **5 in one's pocket** in one's control **6 out of pocket** having spent money without any good result ♦ *adj* small enough to put into one's pocket: *a pocket camera* ♦ vt **1** put into one's pocket **2** take (money) dishonestly

pock·et·book /ˈpɑkɪtˌbʊk/ n **1** small notebook **2** HANDBAG

pock·mark /ˈpɑkmɑrk/ n hollow mark on the skin where a diseased spot has been ~**ed** *adj*

pod /pɑd/ n long narrow seed container of PEAS and beans

po·di·um /ˈpoʊdiəm/ n -**ums** or -**dia** /-diə/ raised part for a speaker or performer to stand on

po·em /ˈpoʊɪm/ n piece of writing in patterns of lines and sounds

po·et /ˈpoʊɪt/ n writer of poetry ~**ic** /poʊˈɛtɪk/ *adj* **1** of poetry **2** graceful ~**ical** *adj* **1** written as poetry **2** poetic ~**ically** *adv*

poetic jus·tice /ˌ·· ˈ·/ n [U] something suitably bad happening to a person who does something wrong

poetic li·cense /ˌ·· ˈ·/ n [U] poet's freedom to change facts, not to obey the usual rules of grammar, etc.

po·e·try /ˈpoʊətri/ n [U] **1** art of a poet **2** poems **3** graceful quality

pog·rom /ˈpoʊgrəm, pəˈgrɑm/ n planned killing of large numbers of people

poi·gnant /ˈpɔɪnyənt/ *adj* sharply sad ~**ly** *adv* **poignancy** n [U]

poin·set·ti·a /pɔɪnˈsɛtiə/ n plant with red flowers, having associations with Christmas

point[1] /pɔɪnt/ n **1** [C] sharp end: *the point of a needle* **2** [C] particular place or moment: *a weak point in the plan* | *At that point I left.* **3** [C] unit for recording the SCORE in a game **4** [C] single particular idea or part of an argument or statement: *You've made* (= expressed) *an important point.* **5** [C] main idea, which gives meaning to the whole: *That's beside the point.* (= is unimportant) **6** [U] purpose; advantage: *There's no point in waiting any longer.* **7** [C] place on a measuring system: *the boiling point of water* | *the 32 points of the compass* **8** [C] particular quality or ability: *Spelling isn't her strong point.* **9** [C] sign (.) to the left of decimals: *4.2 is read as "4 point 2."* **10** case in point something that proves or is an example of the subject under consideration **11** in point of fact actually **12** make a point of take particular care to **13** on the point of just about to **14** to the point of so as to be almost **15** when it comes/came to the point when the moment for action or decision comes/came

point² *v* **1** *vi* show or draw attention to something by holding out a finger, stick, etc., in its direction **2** *vi/t* aim or be aimed: *The gun was pointed/pointing at his head.* **3** *vt* fill in and make smooth the spaces between bricks (of a wall, etc.) with CEMENT ~**ed** *adj* **1** having a sharp end **2** directed against a particular person: *a pointed remark* ~**edly** *adv*

point out *phr vt* draw attention to

point-blank /ˌ·ˈ·◄/ *adj*, *adv* **1** fired from a very close position **2** forceful and direct: *a point-blank refusal*

point·er /ˈpɔɪntə/ *n* **1** stick for pointing at things **2** thin piece that points to numbers on a measuring apparatus **3** piece of helpful advice **4** type of hunting dog

point·less /ˈpɔɪntlɪs/ *adj* meaningless; useless ~**ly** *adv* ~**ness** *n* [U]

point man /ˈ· ·/ *n* someone, esp. a soldier, who goes ahead of a group to see if there is any danger

point of view /ˌ· · ˈ·/ *n* particular way of considering something

point·y /ˈpɔɪnti/ *adj infml* having a sharp end

poise /pɔɪz/ *n* [U] **1** quiet confidence and self-control **2** balanced way of moving ♦ *vt* put lightly in a place where it is hard to be steady **poised** *adj* ready: *poised to attack* **2** showing poise

poi·son /ˈpɔɪzən/ *n* [C;U] substance that can kill or cause illness ♦ *vt* **1** give poison to or put poison in **2** have a damaging or evil effect on ~**ous** *adj*

poison ivy /ˌ·· ˈ··/ *n* [U] plant with an oily substance on its leaves that makes the skin itch if touched

poke /pəʊk/ *vi/t* **1** push out sharply: *She poked her head around the corner.* **2** push a pointed thing (into) **3** poke fun at cause (unkind) laughter at **4** poke one's nose into something inquire into something which does not concern one ♦ *n* act of poking

pok·er¹ /ˈpəʊkə/ *n* thin metal rod for poking a fire to make it burn better

po·ker² *n* [U] card game played for money

pok·y /ˈpəʊki/ *adj* too slow

po·lar /ˈpəʊlə/ *adj* of or near the North or South Poles

polar bear /ˌ·· ·/ *n* large white bear that lives near the North Pole

po·lar·i·ty /pəʊˈlærəti, pə-/ *n* [C;U] *fml* having or developing 2 opposite qualities

po·lar·ize /ˈpəʊləraɪz/ *vi/t* form into groups based on 2 directly opposite principles –**ization** /ˌpəʊlərəˈzeɪʃən/ *n* [U]

Po·lar·oid /ˈpəʊlərɔɪd/ *n tdmk* [C] camera that produces finished photographs in seconds

pole¹ /pəʊl/ *n* long straight thin stick or post

pole² *n* **1** (*often cap.*) point furthest north and south on the Earth: *the North Pole* **2** either end of a MAGNET **3** either of the points on a BATTERY where wires are fixed **4** either of 2 positions that are as far apart as they can be **5** poles apart widely separated in opinion, etc.

pole vault /ˈ· ·/ *n* jump over a high bar using a long pole

po·lice /pəˈliːs/ *n* [P] official body for making people obey the law, catching criminals, etc. ♦ *vt* control or keep a watch on with policemen: (fig.) *a new committee to police the nuclear industry*

police of·fi·cer /·ˈ· ˌ···/ also **po·lice·man** /pəˈliːsmən/ *masc* **police·wom·an** /pə-ˈliːsˌwʊmən/ *fem* — *n* member of the police

police state /·ˈ· ·/ *n* country where people are controlled by (secret) political police

pol·i·cy /ˈpɒləsi/ n **1** what a government, company, political party, etc., intends to do about a particular matter **2** insurance contract

po·li·o /ˈpəʊliəʊ/ n[U] serious infectious nerve disease, esp. of the SPINE, which often prevents movement

pol·ish¹ /ˈpɒlɪʃ/ vt **1** make smooth and shiny by rubbing **2** make as perfect as possible: *a polished performance* ♦ n **1** [U] liquid, paste, etc., for polishing **2** [S] act of polishing **3** [U] fine quality ~**ed** adj **1** (of a piece of artistic work, a performance, etc.) done with great skill and control **2** polite and graceful ~**er** n

polish off phr vt finish (food, work, etc.) quickly or easily

polish up phr vt improve by practicing

po·lite /pəˈlaɪt/ adj having good manners ~**ly** adv ~**ness** n [U]

po·lit·i·cal /pəˈlɪtɪkəl/ adj **1** of or concerning government and public affairs **2** of (party) politics **3** very interested or active in politics ~**ly** adv

political a·sy·lum /ˌˌˌ ˌˌˈˌˌ/ n [U] official protection given to someone who has left their country because they oppose its government

politically cor·rect /ˌˌˌˌ ˌˈˌ/ adj (of language, behavior, etc.) considered acceptable because not offensive to women, people of a particular race, DISABLED people, etc. **political correctness** n [U]

pol·i·ti·cian /ˌpɒləˈtɪʃən/ n person whose business is politics

pol·i·tics /ˈpɒlətɪks/ n **1** [U] the activity of winning and using government power, in competition with other parties: *active in local politics* **2** [U] art and science of government: *studying politics at university* **3** [P] political opinions **4** [U] activity within a group by which some members try to gain an advantage: *office politics*

pol·ka /ˈpəʊlkə, ˈpəʊkə/ n quick simple dance for people dancing in pairs

polka dot /ˈˌˌ ˌ/ n (one of a) pattern of round spots on a background of a different color: *a polka dot dress*

poll /pəʊl/ n **1** [C] also **opinion poll** — attempt to find out the general opinion about something by questioning a number of people chosen by chance **2** [C;U] election **3** [S] number of votes given ♦ vt **1** receive (a stated number of votes) **2** question in a POLL (1)

pol·len /ˈpɒlən/ n [U] yellow dust that makes plants produce seeds

pol·li·nate /ˈpɒləneɪt/ vt bring pollen to (a flower) –**nation** /ˌpɒləˈneɪʃən/ n [U]

poll·ster /ˈpəʊlstə/ n person who carries out POLLS (1)

pol·lute /pəˈluːt/ vt make dangerously impure or unfit for use: *polluted rivers* –**lution** /pəˈluːʃən/ n [U] **1** act of polluting **2** polluting substance –**lutant** n polluting substance

po·lo /ˈpəʊləʊ/ n [U] game played on horses by hitting a ball with a hammer that has a long handle — see also WATER POLO

pol·ter·geist /ˈpəʊltəˌɡaɪst/ n spirit that makes noises and throws things around

pol·y·es·ter /ˌpɒliˈestə, ˈpɒliˌestə/ n [U] artificial material used for cloth

po·lyg·a·my /pəˈlɪɡəmi/ n [U] having 2 or more wives at one time –**mist** n –**mous** adj

pol·y·glot /ˈpɒliˌɡlɒt/ adj fml speaking or including many languages

pol·y·gon /ˈpɒliˌɡən/ n figure with 5 or more straight sides

pol·y·graph /ˈpɒliˌɡræf/ n LIE DETECTOR

pol·y·mer /ˈpɒləmə/ n simple chemical compound with large MOLECULES

pol·yp /ˈpɒlɪp/ n **1** very simple small water animal **2** small diseased growth in the body

pol·y·un·sat·u·ra·ted /ˌpɒliʌnˈsætʃəreɪtɪd/ adj (of fat or oil) having chemicals combined in a way that is thought to be good for one's health when eaten

pom·e·gran·ate /ˈpɒməˌɡrænɪt, ˈpɒmə-/ n fruit with small red seeds inside

pomp /pɒmp/ n [U] grand solemn ceremonial show

pom·pom /ˈpɒmpɒm/ n **1** small decorative wool ball **2** large decoration made from colored paper, used by CHEERleaders

pom·pous /ˈpɒmpəs/ adj foolishly solemn and thinking oneself important ~**ly** adv ~**ness**, –**posity** /pɒmˈpɒsəti/ n [U]

pon·cho /ˈpɒntʃəʊ/ n -**chos** cloth worn over the shoulders, with a hole for the head

pond /pɒnd/ n small area of still water

pon·der /ˈpɒndə/ vi/t spend time considering

pon·der·ous /'pɑndərəs/ adj 1 heavy, slow, and awkward 2 dull and solemn

pon·tiff /'pɑntɪf/ n POPE

pon·tif·i·cate /pɑn'tɪfəˌkeɪt/ vi give one's opinion as if it were the only right one

pon·toon /pɑn'tun/ n floating hollow container connected with others to support a floating bridge

po·ny /'pouni/ n small horse

po·ny·tail /'pouniˌteɪl/ n hair tied in a bunch at the back of the head

pooch /putʃ/ n infml dog

poo·dle /'pudl/ n dog with curling hair, often cut in shapes

pooh-pooh /ˌpu'pu/ vt infml treat as not worth considering

pool¹ /pul/ n 1 small area of water in a hollow place 2 small amount of liquid on a surface 3 SWIMMING POOL

pool² n 1 [C] shared supply of money, goods, workers, etc. — see also CAR POOL 2 [U] game played with 15 balls on a table with holes in corners and sides ♦ vt put esp. money into a common pot to share

poop¹ /pup/ n [U] infml solid waste from the BOWELS

poop² vi infml pass solid waste from the BOWELS

poop out phr vi/t infml (cause to) become tired and stop trying to do something

pooped /pupt/ adj infml very tired

poor /pur/ adj 1 having very little money 2 less or worse than usual or than expected: a poor harvest/essay | poor weather/health 3 unlucky; deserving pity: Poor David failed his exams. ~ness n [U] low quality

poor·ly /'purli/ adv not well; badly: poorly paid

pop¹ /pɑp/ vi/t -pp- 1 (cause to) make a small explosive sound 2 come, go, or put quickly: A button popped off his shirt. 3 **pop the question** infml make an offer of marriage

pop up phr vi happen or appear suddenly

pop² n 1 [C] small explosive sound 2 [U] sweet FIZZY drink

pop³ n [U] modern popular music with a strong beat: a pop group/concert

pop⁴ n 1 father 2 (used as a form of address to an old man)

pop. abbrev. for: population

pop art /ˌ¹· '· ◄/ n [U] modern art showing objects from daily life

pop·corn /'pɑpkɔrn/ n [U] special CORN seeds heated so that they swell

pope /poup/ n (often cap.) the head of the Roman Catholic Church

pop·lar /'pɑplə/ n tall, straight, thin tree

pop·lin /'pɑplɪn/ n [U] strong cotton cloth

pop·py /'pɑpi/ n plant with bright flowers, usu. red

pop quiz /ˌ· '·/ n short test given without warning

Pop·si·cle /'pɑpsɪkəl/ n tdmk piece of ICE (2) on a stick

pop·u·lace /'pɑpyələs/ n fml [U] all the (ordinary) people of a country

pop·u·lar /'pɑpyələ/ adj 1 liked by many people: a popular restaurant 2 common; widespread: a popular name 3 of the general public: popular opinion ~ly adv by most people ~ize, -ise vt ~ity /ˌpɑpyə'lærəti/ n [U]

pop·u·late /'pɑpyəˌleɪt/ vt live in as a population

pop·u·la·tion /ˌpɑpyə'leɪʃən/ n (number of) people (or animals) living in a particular area or country

pop·u·list /'pɑpyəlɪst/ n person who claims to support the aims of ordinary people in politics

pop·u·lous /'pɑpyələs/ adj fml having a large population

porce·lain /'pɔrsəlɪn, 'pɔur-/ n [U] (cups, plates, etc., made from) fine, hard, thin, claylike substance

porch /pɔrtʃ, pɔurtʃ/ n roofed structure built out from a house

por·cu·pine /'pɔrkyəˌpaɪn/ n animal with long needle-like hairs on its back that are used in defense

pore¹ /pɔr/ n small hole in the skin, through which SWEAT passes

pore² v **pore over** phr vt read with close attention

pork /pɔrk, pɔurk/ n [U] meat from pigs

porn /pɔrn/ n [U] infml pornography

por·nog·ra·phy /pɔr'nɑgrəfi/ n [U] law or derog (books, films, etc.) showing or describing sexually exciting scenes –**graphic** /ˌpɔrnə'græfɪk◄/ adj

po·rous /'pɔrəs, 'pourəs/ adj allowing liquid to pass slowly through

por·poise /'pɔrpəs/ n large fishlike sea animal

port¹ /pɔrt/ n waterside city where ocean ships come and go

port² n [U] left side of a ship or aircraft

port³ n [U] strong, sweet red wine from Portugal

por·ta·ble /ˈpɔrtəbəl, ˈpoʊr-/ adj that can be carried

por·tend /pɔrˈtɛnd, poʊr-/ vt fml be a sign of (a future undesirable event)

por·ter /ˈpɔrtə, ˈpoʊr-/ n 1 person who carries loads, esp. travelers' bags, or goods in a train station 2 person in charge of the entrance to a hotel, hospital, etc.

port·fo·li·o /pɔrtˈfoʊliˌoʊ, poʊrt-/ n 1 a flat case for carrying drawings, etc. b drawings, etc., carried in this 2 collection of business shares owned

port·hole /ˈpɔrt-hoʊl, ˈpoʊrt-/ n window in a ship or aircraft

por·ti·co /ˈpɔrtɪˌkoʊ, ˈpoʊr-/ n -coes or -cos grand pillared (PILLAR) entrance to a building

por·tion¹ /ˈpɔrʃən/ n 1 part: the front portion of the train 2 share 3 quantity of food for one person

portion² v portion out phr vt share

port·ly /ˈpɔrtli, ˈpoʊr-/ adj (of a person) fat

por·trait /ˈpɔrtrɪt, -treɪt, ˈpoʊr-/ n 1 picture of a person 2 lifelike description in words

por·tray /pɔrˈtreɪ, poʊr-/ vt 1 represent, describe 2 act the part of ~al n [C;U]

pose /poʊz/ v 1 vi stand or sit in a particular position to be drawn, photographed, etc. 2 vt cause (a problem) 3 vt ask (a question) ♦ n 1 position when posing (POSE (1)) 2 pretended way of behaving

    pose as phr vt pretend to be

pos·er /ˈpoʊzə/ n person who behaves unnaturally to produce an effect

posh /pɑʃ/ adj fashionable and splendid

po·si·tion /pəˈzɪʃən/ n 1 place where something is 2 [U] proper place: Is everyone in position? 3 [C] way in which something is placed or stands, sits, etc. 4 [C] situation; state: the company's current financial position 5 [C] place in a rank or group: He finished in second position. 6 [C] fml job 7 [C] fml opinion ♦ vt place

pos·i·tive /ˈpɑzətɪv/ adj 1 leaving no possibility of doubt: positive proof 2 having

no doubt; sure 3 effective; actually helpful 4 more than zero 5 (of electricity) of the type carried by PROTONS 6 complete; real: a positive delight ~ly adv 1 in a POSITIVE (1,2) way 2 really; indeed

pos·se /ˈpɑsi/ n group of people gathered together to help find a criminal

pos·sess /pəˈzɛs/ vt 1 fml have; own 2 (of a feeling or idea) seem to control all (someone's) actions ~ed adj wildly mad ~or n

pos·ses·sion /pəˈzɛʃən/ n 1 [U] state of possessing; ownership 2 [C] something one owns 3 [U] control by an evil spirit

pos·ses·sive /pəˈzɛsɪv/ adj 1 unwilling to share one's own things 2 gram showing ownership: "My" is a possessive adjective. ~ly adv ~ness n [U]

pos·si·bil·i·ty /ˌpɑsəˈbɪlɪti/ n 1 [S;U] (degree of) likelihood 2 [U] fact of being possible 3 [C] something possible: The house is in bad condition but it has possibilities. (= can be improved)

pos·si·ble /ˈpɑsəbəl/ adj 1 that can exist, happen, or be done 2 acceptable; suitable ♦ n 1 [the+S] that which can exist, happen, or be done 2 [C] person or thing that might be suitable —bly adv 1 in accordance with what is possible: I'll do all I possibly can. 2 perhaps

pos·sum /ˈpɑsəm/ n small animal that climbs trees

post¹ /poʊst/ n 1 strong thick upright pole fixed in position 2 finishing place in a race ♦ vt 1 put up a notice about 2 report as being: The ship was posted missing.

post² v send by MAIL¹

post³ n 1 job 2 special place of duty, esp. of a soldier 3 military base ♦ vt 1 place (soldiers, policemen, etc.) on duty 2 send to a job, esp. abroad

post·age /ˈpoʊstɪdʒ/ n [U] charge for carrying a letter, parcel, etc., by post

postage stamp /ˈ·· ˌ/ n fml for STAMP

post·al /ˈpoʊstl/ adj 1 of the POST OFFICE 2 sent by mail

post·card /ˈpoʊstkɑrd/ n card for sending messages by mail without an envelope

post·date /ˌpoʊstˈdeɪt/ vt write a date later than the actual date of writing on (esp. a check)

post·er /ˈpoʊstə/ n large printed notice or picture

pos·te·ri·or /pɒˈstɪəriə, pəʊ-/ *adj fml* nearer the back ♦ *n* BOTTOM[1] (2)

pos·ter·i·ty /pɒˈsterəti/ *n* [U] people or times after one's death

post·grad·u·ate /ˌpəʊstˈgrædʒuɪt/ *adj* after getting a BACHELOR'S DEGREE

post·hu·mous /ˈpɒstjʊməs/ *adj* after death **~ly** *adv*

Post-It /ˈpəʊst ˌɪt/ *n tdmk* small sticky piece of paper, used for leaving notes

post·mark /ˈpəʊstmɑːk/ *n* official mark on a letter, etc., showing where and when it was posted **postmark** *vt*

post·mas·ter /ˈpəʊstˌmɑːstə/ *n* director of a post office

post·mor·tem /ˌpəʊstˈmɔːtəm/ *n* **1** tests to find out why someone died **2** finding out why something failed

post of·fice /ˈ· ˌ·/ *n* place where stamps are sold, letters can be mailed, and various sorts of government business are done

post·pone /pəʊstˈpəʊn/ *vt* move to a later time **~ment** *n* [C;U]

post·script /ˈpəʊstˌskrɪpt/ *n* remark(s) added at the end of a letter

pos·tu·late /ˈpɒstʃəˌleɪt/ *vt fml* accept as true, as a base for reasoning

pos·ture /ˈpɒstʃə/ *n* **1** physical position **2** manner of behaving or thinking on some occasion *vi* **1** place oneself in fixed physical positions, esp. in order to make other people admire one **2** pretend to be something one is not

po·sy /ˈpəʊzi/ *n* small bunch of flowers

pot[1] /pɒt/ *n* [C] large round container esp. for cooking and serving: *a soup pot/pots and pans* **2** [U] *sl for* MARIJUANA **3 go to pot** *infml* become ruined or worthless

pot[2] *v* **-tt-** *vt* plant in a pot **~ted** *adj* **1** (of meat, fish, etc.) made into a paste **2** (of a book) in short simple form

po·tas·si·um /pəˈtæsiəm/ *n* [U] soft silverwhite metal common in nature and necessary for life

po·ta·to /pəˈteɪtəʊ, -tə/ *n* **-toes** common brown or yellowish vegetable that grows underground

potato chip /·ˈ·· ˌ·/ *n* thin piece of dry cooked potato

pot·bel·ly /ˈpɒtˌbeli/ *n infml* fat stomach

po·tent /ˈpəʊtˀnt/ *adj* powerful: *a potent drug* **~ly** *adv* **potency** *n* [U]

po·ten·tial /pəˈtenʃəl/ *adj* that may become so; not (yet) actual: *potential danger* ♦ *n* [U] possibility for developing **~ly** *adv* **~ity** /pəˌtenʃiˈæləti/ *n* [C;U]

pot·hole /ˈpɒtˌhəʊl/ *n* **1** deep hole going far underground **2** unwanted hole in the road

po·tion /ˈpəʊʃən/ *n* liquid mixture intended as a medicine, poison, or magic charm

pot·luck /ˌpɒtˈlʌk◂/ *adj* (of a meal) to which everyone brings a dish: *potluck dinner* ♦ *n* **take potluck** choose without enough information; take a chance

potted plant /ˌ· ˈ·/ *n* plant grown (indoors) in a pot

pot·ter /ˈpɒtə/ *n* person who makes pottery

pot·ter·y /ˈpɒtəri/ *n* [U] (pots, dishes, etc., made of) baked clay

pot·ty /ˈpɒti/ *n* small toilet for children

pouch /paʊtʃ/ *n* **1** small leather bag **2** baglike part of an animal

poul·try /ˈpəʊltri/ *n* [U] (meat from) farmyard birds such as hens, ducks, etc.

pounce /paʊns/ *vi* fly down or jump suddenly to seize

pounce on *phr vt* seize or accept eagerly

pound[1] /paʊnd/ *n* **1** a measure of weight equal to 0.4536 kilograms or 16 OUNCES **2** standard unit of money in Britain

pound[2] *v* **1** *vt* crush **2** *vi/t* strike repeatedly and heavily **3** *vi* move with quick heavy steps

pound into *phr vi/t* repeat (something) forcefully over and over again to (someone)

pound[3] *n* place where lost animals and cats are kept until their owners take them back

pour /pɔː, pʊə/ *v* **1** *vi/t* (cause to) flow fast and steadily **2** *vi* rush together in large numbers **3** *vi* (of rain) fall hard

pour out *phr vt* tell freely and with feeling

pout /paʊt/ *vi* push the lips forwards, esp. to show displeasure **pout** *n*

pov·er·ty /ˈpɒvəti/ *n* [U] **1** being poor **2** *fml* lack

poverty line /ˈ··· ˌ·/ *n* [S] level of income for deciding who is poor, determined by the government: *living below the poverty line*

poverty-strick·en /'··· ͵··/ adj extremely poor

POW n PRISONER OF WAR

pow·der /'paʊdə/ n 1 [C;U] very fine dry grains 2 [U] substance like this with a pleasant smell, used on the skin 3 [U] gunpowder ♦ vt put POWDER (2) on ~**ed** adj produced in the form of powder: *powdered sugar* ~**y** adj

powder room /'·· ͵·/ n women's public TOILET

pow·er /'paʊə/ n 1 [U] strength 2 [U] force used for driving machines, producing electricity, etc.: *nuclear power* 3 [S;U] control over others; influence 4 [U] what one can do; (natural) ability: *the power of speech* 5 [C;U] right to act: *The police now have the power to search people in the street.* 6 [C] person, nation, etc., that has influence or control 7 **the powers that be** *infml* the unknown people in important positions who make decisions that have an effect on one's life — see also BLACK POWER ♦ vt supply power to (a machine)

pow·er·boat /'paʊəˌbəʊt/ n fast boat for racing

pow·er·ful /'paʊəfəl/ adj 1 full of force: *a powerful engine* 2 great in degree: *a powerful smell* 3 having much control or influence 4 having a strong effect: *powerful drugs* ~**ly** adv

pow·er·house /'paʊəˌhaʊs/ n infml person who is very enthusiastic and able

pow·er·less /'paʊəlɪs/ adj lacking strength or ability: *powerless to help*

power of at·tor·ney /͵·· ·ˌ·/ n [U] right to act for someone else in business or law

power plant /'·· ͵·/ n building where electricity is made

pow·wow /'paʊˌwaʊ/ n important meeting esp. of Native Americans

pp. *abbrev. for:* pages

PR n [U] PUBLIC RELATIONS

prac·ti·ca·ble /'præktɪkəbəl/ adj that can be done –**bility** /ˌpræktɪkə'bɪləti/ n [U]

prac·ti·cal /'præktɪkəl/ adj 1 concerned with action or actual conditions, rather than ideas 2 effective or convenient in actual use: *a practical uniform* 3 clever at doing things and dealing with difficulties; sensible ~**ly** adv 1 usefully; suitably 2 almost ~**ity** /ˌpræktɪ'kæləti/ n [C;U]

practical joke /͵·· ·/ n trick played on someone to amuse others

prac·tice /'præktɪs/ n 1 [C;U] regular or repeated doing of something, to gain skill 2 [U] experience gained by this 3 [U] actual doing of something: *to put a plan into practice* 4 [C] business of a doctor or lawyer 5 [C;U] something regularly done 6 **in/out of practice** having/not having practiced enough ♦ v 1 vi/t do (an action) or perform on (esp. a musical instrument) repeatedly to gain skill 2 vi/t do (the work of a doctor, lawyer, etc.) 3 vt act in accordance with (a religion): *a practicing Jew* 4 vt fml do (habitually) 5 **practice what one preaches** do what you advise others to do –**ticed** adj skilled through practice

prac·ti·tion·er /præk'tɪʃənə/ n person who works in a profession, esp. a doctor — see also GENERAL PRACTITIONER

prag·mat·ic /præg'mætɪk/ adj concerned with actual effects rather than general principles ~**ally** adv

prai·rie /'preəri/ n wide grassy plain

praise /preɪz/ vt 1 speak of with admiration 2 worship ♦ n [U] expression of admiration

praise·wor·thy /'preɪzˌwɜːði/ adj deserving praise

prance /prɑːns/ vi 1 (of an animal) jump on the back legs 2 move happily or showily

prank /præŋk/ n playful but foolish trick

prat·tle /'prætl/ vi talk continually about unimportant things ♦ n [U] foolish or unimportant talk

pray /preɪ/ vi 1 speak to God or a god, often silently, often asking for something 2 wish or hope strongly: *We're praying for fine weather.*

prayer /preə/ n 1 [C] (form of words used in) a solemn request to God or a god 2 [U] praying

preach /priːtʃ/ v 1 vi/t make (a religious speech) in public 2 vt urge others to accept: *preaching revolution* 3 vi offer unwanted advice on matters of right and wrong ~**er** n

pre·am·ble /'priːæmbəl, priːˈæmbəl/ n something said or written before getting to the main part

pre·car·i·ous /prɪ'keəriəs/ adj not firm or steady; full of danger ~**ly** adv

pre·cau·tion /prɪ'kɔːʃən/ n action done to avoid possible trouble ~**ary** adj

pre·cede /prɪˈsid/ vt come (just) before –**ceding** adj: the preceding day

pre·ce·dence /ˈprɛsədəns, prɪˈsidns/ n [U] (right to) a particular place before others, esp. because of importance

pre·ce·dent /ˈprɛsədənt/ n 1 [U] what has usu. been done before 2 [C] earlier act which shows what may be done now

pre·cept /ˈprisɛpt/ n fml guiding rule of behavior

pre·cinct /ˈprisɪŋkt/ n division of a town for election or police purposes

pre·cious /ˈprɛʃəs/ adj 1 of great value 2 fml (of words, manners, etc.) unnaturally fine or perfect ♦ adv very: precious few ~**ness** n [U]

pre·ci·pice /ˈprɛsəpɪs/ n very steep side of a mountain or cliff

pre·cip·i·tate[1] /prɪˈsɪpɪˌteɪt/ vt 1 fml make (an unwanted event) happen sooner 2 fml throw down suddenly 3 separate (solid matter) from liquid chemically ♦ n [C;U] precipitated matter –**tation** /prɪˌsɪpəˈteɪʃən/ n [U] fml 1 precipitating 2 rain, snow, etc. 3 unwise speed

pre·cip·i·tate[2] /prɪˈsɪpətɪt/ adj fml too hasty ~**ly** adv

pre·cip·i·tous /prɪˈsɪpətəs/ adj fml 1 dangerously steep 2 precipitate ~**ly** adv ~**ness** n [U]

pre·cise /prɪˈsaɪs/ adj 1 exact 2 (too) careful and correct about small details ~**ly** adv 1 exactly 2 yes, that is correct

pre·ci·sion /prɪˈsɪʒən/ n [U] exactness ♦ adj 1 done with exactness: precision bombing 2 giving exact results: precision instruments

pre·clude /prɪˈklud/ vt fml prevent

pre·co·cious /prɪˈkoʊʃəs/ adj developing unusually early ~**ly** adv ~**ness** n [U]

pre·con·cep·tion /ˌprikənˈsɛpʃən/ n opinion formed in advance without (enough) knowledge –**ceived** /-kənˈsivd◂/ adj: preconceived notions

pre·con·di·tion /ˌprikənˈdɪʃən/ n thing that must be agreed to if something is to be done

pre·cur·sor /prɪˈkɜsə, ˈpriˌkɜsə/ n one that came before and led to a later thing

pred·a·to·ry /ˈprɛdəˌtɔri, -ˌtoʊri/ adj 1 killing and eating other animals 2 living by attacking and robbing **predator** n predatory animal

pre·de·ces·sor /ˈprɛdəˌsɛsə/ n one that came before: my predecessor as principal

pre·des·ti·na·tion /ˌpridɛstəˈneɪʃən, priˌdɛs-/ n [U] belief that everything in the world has been decided by God, and that no human effort can change it

pre·des·tined /priˈdɛstɪn/ adj settled in advance, esp. as if by fate or the will of God

pre·de·ter·mined /ˌpridɪˈtɜmɪn/ adj 1 unchangeable from the beginning 2 arranged in advance

pre·dic·a·ment /prɪˈdɪkəmənt/ n difficult situation

pred·i·cate /ˈprɛdɪkɪt/ n part of a sentence which makes a statement about the subject

pre·dic·a·tive /ˈprɛdɪˌkeɪtɪv, -kətɪv/ adj coming after a verb

pre·dict /prɪˈdɪkt/ vt say in advance (what will happen) ~**able** adj 1 that can be predicted 2 not doing anything unexpected ~**ably** adv –**ion** /prɪˈdɪkʃən/ n [C;U] predicting or something predicted

pre·di·lec·tion /ˌprɛdlˈɛkʃən, ˌpri-/ n special liking for something

pre·dis·posed /ˌpridɪˈspoʊz/ adj likely to do or have something ~**position** /ˌpridɪspəˈzɪʃən/ n

pre·dom·i·nant /prɪˈdɑmənənt/ adj most powerful, noticeable, important, etc. ~**ly** adv ~**nance** n [U]

pre·dom·i·nate /prɪˈdɑməˌneɪt/ vi 1 have the main power or influence 2 be greatest in numbers

pre·em·i·nent /priˈɛmənənt/ adj better than any others ~**ly** adv –**nence** n [U]

pre·empt /priˈɛmpt/ vt prevent by taking action in advance ~**ive** adj

preen /prin/ vi/t (of a bird) clean (itself or its feathers) with its beak

pre·fab·ri·cate /priˈfæbrəˌkeɪt/ vt make (the parts of a building, ship, etc.) in advance in a factory and put them together later

pref·ace /ˈprɛfɪs/ n introduction to a book ♦ vt introduce (speech or writing) in the stated way

pref·a·to·ry /ˈprɛfəˌtɔri, -ˌtoʊri/ adj fml acting as a preface

pre·fer /prɪˈfɜ/ vt -rr- 1 like better; choose rather: I prefer wine to beer. 2 law make (a charge) officially ~**erable** /ˈprɛfərəbəl/ adj better, esp. because more suitable ~**ably** adv

pref·er·ence /ˈprɛfərəns, -frəns/ n [C;U] 1 liking for one thing rather than another

2 special favor shown to one person, group, etc.

pref·e·ren·tial /ˌprɛfəˈrɛnʃəl◂/ adj giving or showing PREFERENCE (2) ~ly adv

pre·fix /ˈpriˌfɪks/ n wordlike part added at the beginning of a word to change its meaning (as in *untie*) ♦ vt **1** add a prefix to **2** add (something) to the beginning (of)

preg·nant /ˈprɛgnənt/ adj **1** having an unborn child or young in the body **2** full of hidden meaning –**nancy** n

pre·heat /ˌpriˈhit/ vt heat an oven to a particular temperature before cooking food

pre·his·tor·ic /ˌprihɪˈstɔrɪk, -ˈstar-/ adj of times before recorded history ~**ally** adv

pre·judge /ˌpriˈdʒʌdʒ/ vt form an opinion about before knowing all the facts

prej·u·dice /ˈprɛdʒədɪs/ n **1** [C;U] unfair feeling against something **2** [U] fml damage; harm ♦ vt **1** cause to have a prejudice **2** weaken; harm: *It may prejudice your chances of success.*

prej·u·di·cial /ˌprɛdʒəˈdɪʃəl◂/ adj fml harmful

pre·lim·i·na·ry /prɪˈlɪməˌnɛri/ adj coming before (and preparing for) esp. the main one ♦ n preliminary act or arrangement

prel·ude /ˈprɛljud, ˈpreɪlud, ˈprilud/ n **1** something that is followed by something larger or more important **2** short piece of music introducing a large musical work

pre·mar·i·tal /ˌpriˈmærətl◂/ adj happening before marriage

pre·ma·ture /ˌpriməˈtʃʊr◂, -ˈtʊr◂/ adj happening before the proper time ~**ly** adv

pre·med /ˈpriˌmɛd/ also **premedical** /priˈmɛdɪkəl/ — adj of university courses for those planning to be doctors: *a premed student*

pre·med·i·tat·ed /priˈmɛdəˌteɪtɪd/ adj planned in advance –**tation** /priˌmɛdəˈteɪʃən/ n [U]

pre·men·stru·al /priˈmɛnstruəl◂/ adj happening before a woman's PERIOD

premenstrual syn·drome /ˌ··· ˈ·◂/ n [U] PMS

prem·ier /prɪˈmɪr, -ˈmyɪr, ˈprɪmɪr/ n PRIME MINISTER ♦ adj fml first in importance

pre·miere /prɪˈmɪr, -ˈmyɪr, -ˈmyɛr/ n first public performance of a film or play ♦ vt give a premiere of (a play or film)

prem·ise /ˈprɛmɪs/ n fml statement or idea on which reasoning is based

prem·is·es /ˈprɛmɪsɪz/ n [P] building and its land, considered as a piece of property

pre·mi·um /ˈprimiəm/ n **1** money paid for insurance **2** additional charge **3 at a premium** rare or difficult to obtain **4 put a premium on** cause to be an advantage ♦ adj best: *premium quality*

pre·mo·ni·tion /ˌpriməˈnɪʃən, ˌprɛ-/ n feeling that something is going to happen

pre·na·tal /ˌpriˈneɪtl◂/ adj existing or happening before birth: *prenatal care*

pre·oc·cu·pa·tion /priˌakyəˈpeɪʃən, ˌpriak-/ n **1** [U] being preoccupied **2** [C] something that takes up all one's attention

pre·oc·cu·pied /priˈakyəˌpaɪd/ adj thinking or worrying about something a lot, so that one does not pay attention to other things

pre·oc·cu·py /priˈakyəˌpaɪ/ vt fill (someone's) thoughts, taking attention away from other things

pre·or·dained /ˌpriɔrˈdeɪnd/ adj fml certain to happen because already decided by God or FATE

prep·a·ra·tion /ˌprɛpəˈreɪʃən/ n **1** [U] act or process of preparing **2** [C] arrangement for a future event **3** [C] fml (chemical) mixture for a certain purpose

pre·par·a·to·ry /prɪˈpærəˌtɔri, -ˌtoʊri, -ˈpɛr-, ˈprɛprə-/ adj done to get ready

pre·pare /prɪˈpɛr/ vi/t **1** get or make ready **2** put (oneself) into a suitable state of mind –**pared** adj willing: *not prepared to help*

pre·pon·der·ance /prɪˈpandərəns/ n [S] fml larger number; state of being more than

prep·o·si·tion /ˌprɛpəˈzɪʃən/ n word (such as *in* or *by*) used with a noun or PRONOUN to show its connection with another word ~**al** adj

pre·pos·ter·ous /prɪˈpastərəs/ adj foolishly unreasonable or improbable ~**ly** adv

prep school /ˈprɛp skul/ n private school that makes students ready for college

pre·req·ui·site /priˈrɛkwəzɪt/ n fml something needed before something else can happen

pre·rog·a·tive /prɪˈragətɪv/ n special right belonging to someone

pres·age /ˈprɛsɪdʒ, prɪˈseɪdʒ/ vt fml be a warning or sign of (a future event)

Pres·by·te·ri·an /ˌprɛzbəˈtɪriən, ˌprɛs-/ n, adj (member) of a Protestant church governed by a body of officials of equal rank

pre·school /ˈpriskul/ n school for very young children ♦ adj: preschool children

pre·sci·ent /ˈprɛʃiənt, -ʃənt/ adj fml seeming to know in advance –ence n [U]

pre·scribe /prɪˈskraɪb/ vt 1 order as a medicine or treatment 2 fml state (what must be done)

pre·scrip·tion /prɪˈskrɪpʃən/ n 1 [C] (doctor's written order for) a particular medicine or treatment 2 [U] act of prescribing

pre·scrip·tive /prɪˈskrɪptɪv/ adj saying how a language ought to be used

pres·ence /ˈprɛzəns/ n [U] 1 fact of being present 2 fml personal appearance and manner, as having a strong effect on others

presence of mind /ˌ·· · ˈ·/ n [U] ability to act quickly, calmly, and wisely when necessary

pres·ent¹ /ˈprɛzənt/ n gift

pre·sent² /prɪˈzɛnt/ vt 1 give, esp. as part of a ceremony 2 be the cause of: That presents no difficulties. 3 offer for consideration: to present a report 4 provide for the public to see in a theater, etc. 5 introduce and take part in (a radio or television show) 6 introduce (someone) esp. to someone of higher rank 7 **present itself** (of something possible) happen ~er n

pres·ent³ /ˈprɛzənt/ adj 1 here/there: I was not present at the meeting. 2 existing or being considered now: my present address 3 gram expressing an existing state or action: the present tense

pres·ent⁴ n 1 [the+S] the PRESENT³ (2) time 2 **at present** at this time 3 **for the present** now, but not necessarily in the future

pre·sen·ta·ble /prɪˈzɛntəbəl/ adj fit to be seen publicly –bly adv

pre·sen·ta·tion /ˌprɛzənˈteɪʃən, ˌpri-/ n 1 [C;U] act of presenting 2 [U] way something is shown, explained, etc., to others

present-day /ˌ·· ˈ·◂/ adj existing now; modern

pres·ent·ly /ˈprɛzəntli/ adv 1 now: I'm presently working for IBM. 2 soon

present par·ti·ci·ple /ˌ·· ˈ···/ n (in grammar) a participle that is formed in English by adding –ing to the verb and can be used in compound forms of the verb to show PROGRESSIVE tenses, or sometimes as an ADJECTIVE

pres·er·va·tion /ˌprɛzəˈveɪʃən/ n [U] 1 act of preserving 2 condition after a long time

pre·ser·va·tive /prɪˈzɜːvətɪv/ n, adj [C;U] (substance) used to PRESERVE (2) food

pre·serve /prɪˈzɜːv/ vt 1 keep from decaying or being destroyed or lost: preserving old customs/one's health 2 treat (food) so it can be kept a long time ♦ n 1 [P] JAM (1) 2 [C] something limited to one person or group

pre·side /prɪˈzaɪd/ vi be in charge, esp. at a meeting

pres·i·den·cy /ˈprɛzədənsi/ n office of president

pres·i·dent /ˈprɛzədənt/ n 1 head of state (and government) in countries that do not have a king or queen 2 head of a business firm, government department, club, etc. ~ial /ˌprɛzəˈdɛnʃəl◂/ adj

press¹ /prɛs/ v 1 vt push firmly and steadily 2 vt hold firmly as a sign of friendship, etc.: He pressed my hand warmly. 3 vt direct weight onto to make flat, shape, get liquid out, etc. 4 vi move strongly, esp. in a mass 5 vt give (clothes) a smooth surface and a sharp fold by using a hot iron 6 vt urge strongly: She pressed her guests to stay a little longer. 7 vi make quick action necessary 8 **press the flesh** shake hands with many people, esp. to win votes ~ed adj not having enough: pressed for time ~ing adj urgent

  press for phr vt demand urgently

  press on phr vi continue with determination

press² n 1 [U] (writers for) the newspapers 2 [U] treatment given in the newspapers: The play got good press. 3 [S] act of pushing steadily 4 [C] printing machine 5 [C] business for printing (and sometimes also selling) books, etc. 6 [C] apparatus for pressing something 7 [C] act of making a garment smooth with a hot iron 8 **go to press** (of a newspaper, etc.) start being printed

press con·fer·ence /ˈ· ˌ···/ n meeting where someone answers reporters' questions

press re·lease /'· ·ˌ·/ n official statement giving information to newspapers, radio, television, etc.

pres·sure /'preʃə/ n 1 [C;U] (force produced by) pressing: *Water pressure burst the dam.* 2 [C;U] (force of) the weight of the air 3 [U] forcible influence; strong persuading 4 [C;U] conditions of anxiety in life or work ♦ vt (try to) make (someone) do something by forceful demands

pressure cook·er /'·· ˌ·/ n closed metal pot in which food is cooked quickly in hot steam

pres·sur·ize /'preʃəˌraɪz/ vt control the air pressure inside

pres·tige /preˈstiʒ, -ˈstidʒ/ n [U] quality of being widely admired, esp. because of being the best or connected with high rank –**tigious** /preˈstidʒəs, -ˈsti-/ adj having or bringing prestige

pre·su·ma·bly /prɪˈzuːməblɪ/ adv it may reasonably be supposed that

pre·sume /prɪˈzuːm/ v 1 vt take as true without proof 2 vi fml be disrespectful enough; dare: *I wouldn't presume to argue.*

pre·sump·tion /prɪˈzʌmpʃən/ n [U] 1 act of supposing 2 fml disrespectful behavior

pre·sup·pose /ˌpriːsəˈpəʊz/ vt 1 accept as true in advance without proof 2 need according to reason: *A child presupposes a mother.* –**position** /ˌpriːsʌpəˈzɪʃən/ n [C;U]

pre·tend /prɪˈtend/ v 1 vi/t give an appearance of (something untrue), to deceive or as a game 2 vi attempt; dare

pre·tense /'pritɛns, prɪˈtɛns/ n 1 [S;U] false appearance or reason [U] claim to possess: *little pretense to fairness*

pre·ten·sion /prɪˈtɛnʃən/ n fml claim to possess a skill, quality, etc.

pre·ten·tious /prɪˈtɛnʃəs/ adj claiming importance, rank, or artistic value one does not have ~**ly** adv ~**ness** n [U]

pre·text /'pritɛkst/ n false reason

pret·ty /'prɪtɪ/ adj pleasing to look at ♦ adv 1 fairly; quite 2 **pretty well** almost: *pretty well finished* –**tily** adv — see also **a pretty penny** (PENNY)

pret·zel /'prɛtsl/ n salty bread baked in the shape of a loose knot

pre·vail /prɪˈveɪl/ vi fml 1 win 2 exist; be widespread ~**ing** adj 1 (of wind) that

usu. blows 2 common or general (in some place or time)

prevail upon phr vt fml persuade

prev·a·lent /'prevələnt/ adj fml common in a place or at a time ~**ly** adv –**lence** n [U]

pre·vent /prɪˈvent/ vt stop (something) happening or (someone) doing something ~**ion** /prɪˈvenʃən/ n [U]

pre·ven·tive /prɪˈventɪv/ adj that prevents esp. illness

pre·view /'priːvjuː/ n private showing or short description of film, show, etc., before it is publicly seen ♦ vt give a preview of

pre·vi·ous /'priːvɪəs/ adj before this one: *my previous employer* ~**ly** adv

prey¹ /preɪ/ n 1 animal hunted and eaten by another 2 such hunting and eating: *The eagle is a bird of prey.*

prey² v **prey on** phr vt 1 hunt and eat as prey 2 trouble greatly

price /praɪs/ n 1 money (to be) paid for something: (fig.) *the price of freedom* 2 **at a price** at a high price 3 **not at any price** not at all ♦ vt fix the price of

price·less /'praɪslɪs/ adj 1 extremely valuable 2 infml very funny

price tag /'· ·/ n 1 small ticket showing the price of an article 2 a (fixed or stated) price: *The government has not yet put a price tag on the plan.*

pric·ey /'praɪsɪ/ adj infml expensive

prick¹ /prɪk/ v 1 vt make a small hole in with something with a sharp point 2 vi/t (cause to) feel a light sharp pain on the skin 3 **prick up one's ears** start to listen carefully

prick² n 1 small sharp pain 2 mark made by pricking 3 taboo PENIS 4 taboo sl foolish, worthless man

prick·le /'prɪkəl/ n 1 [C] small sharp point on an animal or plant 2 [S] pricking sensation on the skin ♦ vi/t **prick·ly** adj 1 covered with prickles 2 that gives you a prickling sensation 3 difficult to deal with

pride¹ /praɪd/ n 1 [S;U] pleasure in what you (or someone connected with you) can do or have done well 2 [U] reasonable respect for oneself 3 [U] too high an opinion of yourself 4 [S] most valuable one: *the pride of my collection* 5 **pride of place** highest or best position

pride² *v* **pride oneself on** *phr vt* be proud of (oneself) because of

priest /priːst/ *n* **1** (in the Christian Church, esp. in the ROMAN CATHOLIC Church) specially trained person who performs religious ceremonies and other religious duties **2 priestess** /ˈpriːstes/ *fem.* — specially trained person in certain non-Christian religions **~hood** /-hʊd/ *n* [U] **1** position of being a priest **2** all the priests

prim /prɪm/ *adj* **-mm-** easily shocked by rude things **~ly** *adv*

pri·ma·cy /ˈpraɪməsi/ *n* [U] *fml* being first in importance, rank, etc.

prima don·na /ˌpriːmə ˈdɒnə, ˌprɪmə-/ *n* **1** main female OPERA singer **2** someone who thinks they are very important and often gets excited and angry

pri·mal /ˈpraɪməl/ *adj* belonging to the earliest times

pri·ma·ri·ly /ˈpraɪmerəli/ *adv* mainly

pri·ma·ry¹ /ˈpraɪmeri, -məri/ *adj* **1** chief; main: *the primary purpose of his visit* **2** earliest in time or order of development: *primary education*

primary² *n* election in which the members of a political party in a particular area vote for the person they would like to see as their party's CANDIDATE for a political office

primary care /ˌ··· ˈ·/ *n* [U] main medical help given, if no doctor with special skills in a particular area is needed

primary col·or /ˌ··· ˈ··/ *n* red, yellow, or blue

primary school /ˈ··· ˌ·/ *n* ELEMENTARY SCHOOL

pri·mate /ˈpraɪmeɪt/ *n* member of the most highly developed group of MAMMALS which includes human beings, monkeys, and related animals

prime¹ /praɪm/ *n* [S] time when someone is at their best

prime² *adj* **1** main **2** best

prime³ *vt* **1** put PRIMER¹ (1) on **2** instruct in advance **3** put explosive powder into (a gun)

prime min·is·ter /ˌ· ˈ···/ *n* chief minister and government leader in some countries

prime num·ber /ˌ· ˈ··/ *n* number that can only be divided by itself and 1

prim·er¹ /ˈpraɪmə/ *n* **1** [U] paint put on before the main painting **2** [C] tube containing explosive, esp. to set off a bomb

prim·er² /ˈprɪmə/ *n* simple book for beginners

prime rate /ˌ· ˈ·/ *n* lowest interest rate a bank charges, on which it bases other rates

prime time /ˌ· ˈ·/ *n* [U] time in the evening when most people watch television

pri·me·val /praɪˈmiːvəl/ *adj* very ancient

prim·i·tive /ˈprɪmətɪv/ *adj* **1** of the earliest stage of development **2** roughly made or done **3** old-fashioned and inconvenient ♦ *n* member of a PRIMITIVE (1) race or tribe **~ly** *adv*

pri·mor·di·al /praɪˈmɔːdiəl/ *adj* existing from or at the beginning of time

prim·rose /ˈprɪmrəʊz/ *n* pale yellow spring flower

prince /prɪns/ *n* **1** king's son **2** royal ruler of a small country **~ly** *adj* **1** of a prince **2** splendid; generous

Prince Charm·ing /ˌ· ˈ··/ *n* [S] wonderful male lover

prin·cess /prɪnˈsɪs, -ses/ *n* **1** king's daughter **2** prince's wife

prin·ci·pal /ˈprɪnsəpəl/ *adj* main ♦ *n* **1** [C] head of a school **2** [S] money lent, on which interest is paid **~ly** *adv*

prin·ci·pal·i·ty /ˌprɪnsəˈpælɪti/ *n* country ruled by a prince

prin·ci·ple /ˈprɪnsəpəl/ *n* **1** [C] general truth or belief: *the principle of free speech* **2** [C;U] moral rule which guides behavior: *She resigned on a matter of principle.* **3** [U] high personal standard of right and wrong: *a man of principle* **4** [P] general rules on which a skill, etc., is based: *Archimedes' principle* **5** **in principle** as an idea, if not in fact **6 on principle** because it would be morally wrong to do otherwise

print¹ /prɪnt/ *n* **1** [U] printed letters, words, etc. **2** [C] mark made on a surface: *a thumbprint* **3** [C] photography printed on paper **4** [C] picture printed from a metal sheet **5** **in/out of print** (of a book) that can still/no longer be obtained — see also SMALL PRINT

print² *v* **1** *vt/i* press (letters or pictures) on (esp. paper) with shapes covered with ink or paint **2** *vt* make (a book, magazine, etc.) by doing this **3** *vt* cause to be included in or produced as a newspaper, etc. **4** *vt* copy (a photograph) from film onto paper **5** *vt/i* write without joining the letters **~able** *adj* suitable for reading by anyone ~**er** *n* **1** person who prints books, etc. **2** copying machine

print·out /'prɪntˌaʊt/ *n* [C;U] printed record produced by a computer

pri·or /'praɪə/ *adj* **1** earlier **2** more important **3** prior to before

pri·o·ri·tize /praɪ'ɒrətaɪz/ *vt* give (something) priority

pri·or·i·ty /praɪ'ɒrəti/ *n* **1** [U] (right of) being first in position or earlier in time **2** [C] something that needs attention before others

pris·m /'prɪzəm/ *n* transparent block with 3 sides that breaks up light into different colors

pris·on /'prɪzən/ *n* [C;U] large building where criminals are kept for punishment

prison camp /'·· ·/ *n* guarded camp for prisoners of war

pris·on·er /'prɪzənə/ *n* person kept in prison

prisoner of war /ˌ··· '·/ also **POW** — *n* soldier, etc., caught by the enemy in war

pris·sy /'prɪsi/ *adj infml* annoyingly exact or proper

pris·tine /'prɪstiːn, prɪ'stiːn/ *adj fml* fresh and clean

priv·a·cy /'praɪvəsi/ *n* [U] **1** the (desirable) state of being away from other people **2** secrecy

pri·vate /'praɪvɪt/ *adj* **1** not (to be) shared with others; secret **2** just for one person or a small group, not everyone **3** not connected with or paid for by government: *private school* **4** not connected with one's work or rank; unofficial **5** quiet; without lots of people ♦ *n* soldier of the lowest rank ~**ly** *adv*

private de·tec·tive /ˌ·· ·'··/ *n* person, not a policeman, hired to follow people, report on their actions, etc.

private en·ter·prise /ˌ·· '···/ *n* [U] CAPITALISM

private eye /ˌ·· '·/ *n infml* private DETECTIVE

private parts /ˌ·· '·/ *n* [P] outer sexual organs

private sec·tor /ˌ·· '·· ·/ *n* [*the*+S] those industries and services that are owned and run by private companies, not by the state

pri·va·tion /praɪ'veɪʃən/ *n* [C;U] *fml* lack of things necessary for life

pri·vat·ize /'praɪvəˌtaɪz/ *vt* sell (an industry or organization owned by the government) into private ownership –**ization** /ˌpraɪvətə'zeɪʃən/ *n* [U]: *the privatization of public services*

priv·i·lege /'prɪvəlɪdʒ/ *n* **1** [C] special advantage limited to a particular person or group **2** [U] (unfair) possession of such advantages because of wealth, social rank, etc. –**leged** *adj* having (a) privilege

priv·y /'prɪvi/ *adj fml* sharing secret knowledge (of)

prize /praɪz/ *n* something you are given for winning, doing well, etc. ♦ *vt* value highly ♦ *adj* **1** that has gained or is worthy of a prize: *a prize hen* **2** given as a prize: *prize money*

prize·fight /'praɪzfaɪt/ *n* professional BOXING match ~**er** *n*

pro[1] /proʊ/ *n* **pros** *infml* a PROFESSIONAL

pro[2] *n* argument or reason in favor (of something)

pro·ac·tive /proʊ'æktɪv/ *adj* taking action to change events and make things happen, rather than reacting to them

prob·a·bil·i·ty /ˌprɒbə'bɪləti/ *n* **1** [S;U] likelihood **2** [C] probable event or result

prob·a·ble /'prɒbəbəl/ *adj* that has a good chance of happening or being true; likely –**bly** *adv*

pro·bate /'proʊbeɪt/ *n* [U] legal process of declaring someone's WILL (5) properly made

pro·ba·tion /proʊ'beɪʃən/ *n* [U] **1** (period of) testing someone's suitability **2** system of not sending criminals to prison if they behave well for a time

probation of·fi·cer /ˌ··· '··· ·/ *n* person who watches and advises criminals on probation (2)

probe /proʊb/ *vi/t* search or examine carefully (as if) with a long thin instrument ♦ *n* **1** metal tool for probing **2** spacecraft for searching through space **3** thorough inquiry

prob·lem /'prɒbləm/ *n* difficulty that needs attention and thought

prob·lem·at·ic /ˌprɒblə'mætɪk/ *adj* full of problems or causing problems

pro·ce·dure /prə'siːdʒə/ *n* **1** [C] set of actions for doing something **2** [U] way a meeting, trial, etc., is (to be) run –**dural** *adj*

pro·ceed /prəˈsid, proʊ-/ vi fml 1 begin or continue in a course of action 2 walk or travel in a particular direction

pro·ceed·ings /prəˈsidɪŋz, proʊ-/ n [P] legal action taken against someone

pro·ceeds /ˈproʊsidz/ n [P] money gained from the sale of something

pro·cess /ˈprasɛs, ˈproʊ-/ n 1 set of actions that produce continuation, change, or something new 2 method, esp. for producing goods 3 **in the process of** actually doing (the stated thing) at the time ♦ vt 1 treat and preserve (food): processed cheese 2 print a photograph from (film) 3 deal with; examine

pro·ces·sion /prəˈsɛʃən/ n [C;U] line of people or vehicles moving along, esp. during a ceremony

pro·ces·sor /ˈprasɛsə, ˈproʊ-/ n MICRO-PROCESSOR — see also WORD PROCESSOR

pro·claim /proʊˈkleɪm, prə-/ vt declare publicly and officially

proc·la·ma·tion /ˌprakləˈmeɪʃən/ n 1 [C] official public statement 2 [U] act of proclaiming

pro·cras·ti·nate /proʊˈkræstəneɪt, prə-/ vi fml delay (annoyingly) –**nation** /proʊˌkræstəˈneɪʃən, prə-/ n [U]

pro·cre·ate /ˈproʊkrieɪt/ vi fml produce young –**ation** /ˌproʊkriˈeɪʃən/ n [U]

proc·tor /ˈpraktə/ n teacher who watches over students during an examination ♦ vi to do this

pro·cure /proʊˈkyʊr, prə-/ v 1 vt fml obtain 2 vi/t provide (a woman) for sexual pleasure –**curer** n

prod /prad/ v -dd- 1 vi/t push with a pointed object 2 vt urge sharply **prod** n

prod·i·gal /ˈpradɪgəl/ adj fml 1 carelessly wasteful, esp. of money 2 giving or producing (something) freely and in large amounts –**ation** /ˌpradɪˈgæləti/ n [U]

pro·di·gious /prəˈdɪdʒəs/ adj wonderfully large, powerful, etc. –**ly** adv

prod·i·gy /ˈpradədʒi/ n person with wonderful abilities: child prodigy

pro·duce¹ /prəˈdus/ vt 1 bring into existence; give: These trees produce rubber. | Poverty produces ill health. 2 make (goods for sale) 3 give birth to 4 bring out and show 5 prepare and bring before the public

prod·uce² /ˈpradus, ˈproʊ-/ n [U] something produced, esp. on a farm

pro·duc·er /prəˈdusə/ n 1 person, company, etc., that produces goods 2 person in charge of the business of putting on a play, film, etc.

prod·uct /ˈpradʌkt, -dəkt/ n 1 something made or produced 2 result

pro·duc·tion /prəˈdʌkʃən/ n 1 [U] act of producing 2 [U] process of making products 3 [U] amount produced: a cut in production 4 [C] play, film, or broadcast that is produced

production line /ˈ··· ˌ·/ n arrangement of factory workers and machines for producing goods

pro·duc·tive /prəˈdʌktɪv/ adj 1 that produces a lot 2 causing or producing (a result) ~**ly** adv

pro·duc·tiv·i·ty /ˌproʊdʌkˈtɪvəti, ˌpradək-/ n [U] rate of producing goods, crops, etc.

prof /praf/ n infml for PROFESSOR

Prof. abbrev. for PROFESSOR

pro·fane /proʊˈfeɪn, prə-/ adj 1 showing disrespect, esp. for holy things 2 (esp. of language) socially shocking 3 fml concerned with human life in this world; SECULAR: profane art ♦ vt treat disrespectfully ~**ly** adv

pro·fan·i·ty /prəˈfænəti/ n [C;U] profane behavior or speech

pro·fess /prəˈfɛs, proʊ-/ vt fml 1 declare openly 2 claim, usu. falsely 3 have as one's religion ~**ed** adj 1 declared by oneself to be (the stated thing) 2 pretended

pro·fes·sion /prəˈfɛʃən/ n 1 form of employment, esp. a socially respected one like law or medicine 2 people in a particular profession 3 fml open declaration

pro·fes·sion·al /prəˈfɛʃənəl/ adj 1 working in a profession 2 doing for payment what others do for fun 3 showing high standards of work ♦ n professional person ~**ism** n [U] skill or quality of professionals

pro·fes·sor /prəˈfɛsə/ n university teacher of highest rank ~**ial** /ˌproʊfəˈsɔriəl, ˌprɑ-, -ˈsoʊr-/ adj

prof·fer /ˈprafə/ vt fml offer

pro·fi·cient /prəˈfɪʃənt/ adj very good at doing something ~**ly** adv –**ciency** n [U]

pro·file /ˈproʊfaɪl/ n 1 side view, esp. of someone's head 2 state of being noticed by other people around me: The management is trying to keep a **low profile** on this

issue. | a **high** *political* **profile** 3 short
description ♦ *vt* draw or write a profile of

prof·it[1] /ˈprɒfɪt/ *n* 1 [C;U] money gained 2
[U] advantage gained from some action

profit[2] *v* **profit by/from** *phr vt* gain
advantage or learn from

prof·it·a·bil·i·ty /ˌprɒfɪtəˈbɪləti/ *n* [U]
state of being profitable or the degree to
which a business is profitable

prof·it·a·ble /ˈprɒfɪtəbəl/ *adj* producing
profit **–bly** *adv*

prof·i·teer /ˌprɒfəˈtɪr/ *n* person who
makes unfairly large profits **profiteer** *vi*

profit mar·gin /ˈ·· ˌ·/ *n* difference
between production cost and selling
price

profit shar·ing /ˈ·· ˌ·/ *n* [U] workers
sharing the profits of a business

prof·li·gate /ˈprɒfləɡɪt, -ˌɡeɪt/ *adj fml* 1
foolishly wasteful 2 shamelessly
immoral

pro·found /prəˈfaʊnd/ *adj* 1 very strongly
felt; deep 2 having thorough knowledge
and understanding **~ly** *adv* **–fundity**
/prəˈfʌndəti/ *n* [C;U]

pro·fuse /prəˈfjus/ *adj* produced in great
quantity **~ly** *adv* **–fusion** /prəˈfjuʒən/ *n*
[S;U] (too) great amount

prog·e·ny /ˈprɒdʒəni/ *n* [U] *fml* 1 descend-
ants (DESCEND) 2 children

prog·no·sis /prɒɡˈnoʊsɪs/ *n* **-ses** /-siz/ 1
doctor's opinion of how an illness will
develop 2 description of the future

prog·nos·ti·cate /prɒɡˈnɒstəˌkeɪt/ *vt fml*
say (what is going to happen) **–cation**
/prɒɡˌnɒstəˈkeɪʃən/ *n* [C;U]

pro·gram[1] /ˈproʊɡræm, -ɡrəm/ *n* 1 television or radio show 2 set of instructions
for making a computer do something 3
plan for future action 4 list of performers or things to be performed

program[2] *vt* **-mm-** supply (a computer)
with a program **~able** *adj* controllable
by means of a program **~mer** *n*

pro·gress[1] /ˈprɒɡrɛs, -ɡrəs/ *n* [U] 1 continual improvement or development 2
forward movement in space 3 **in
progress** happening or being done

pro·gress[2] /prəˈɡrɛs/ *vi* make progress

pro·gres·sion /prəˈɡrɛʃən/ *n* 1 [S;U] pro-
gressing 2 [C] set of numbers that vary
in a particular way

pro·gres·sive /prəˈɡrɛsɪv/ *adj* 1 developing continuously or by stages 2 favoring
change or new ideas 3 (of a verb form)

showing action that is continuing ♦ *n*
person with progressive ideas, esp. about
social change **~ly** *adv*

pro·hib·it /proʊˈhɪbɪt, prə-/ *vt fml* 1 forbid
by law or rule 2 prevent

pro·hi·bi·tion /ˌproʊəˈbɪʃən/ *n* 1 [U] act of
prohibiting something, esp. the sale of
alcohol 2 [C] *fml* order forbidding something 3 (*cap*) period from 1920 to 1933
when sale of alcohol was forbidden in
the US

pro·hib·i·tive /proʊˈhɪbətɪv, prə-/ *adj* preventing or tending to discourage: *pro-
hibitive prices* (= too high) **~ly** *adv*

proj·ect[1] /ˈprɒdʒɛkt, -dʒɪkt/ *n* long piece of
planned work

pro·ject[2] /prəˈdʒɛkt/ *v* 1 *vi/t* stick out
beyond a surface 2 *vt fml* aim and throw
through the air 3 *vt* direct (sound or
light) into space or onto a surface 4 *vt*
make plans for: *our projected visit to
Mexico* 5 *vt* judge or calculate using the
information one has: *projected sales
figures* 6 *vi/t* express (oneself or one's
beliefs, etc.) outwardly, esp. to have a
favorable effect on others

pro·jec·tile /prəˈdʒɛktəl, -ˌtaɪl/ *n fml* object
or weapon thrown or fired

pro·jec·tion /prəˈdʒɛkʃən/ *n* 1 [U] act of
projecting 2 [C] something that sticks out
3 [C] guess of future possibilities based
on known facts

pro·jec·tion·ist /prəˈdʒɛkʃənɪst/ *n* person
who works a PROJECTOR, esp. in a movie
theater

pro·jec·tor /prəˈdʒɛktər/ *n* apparatus for
projecting films, etc.

pro·le·tar·i·at /ˌproʊləˈtɛriət/ *n fml* class
of unskilled workers who earn wages

pro-life /ˌ· ˈ· ◁/ *adj* opposed to ABORTION
–lifer *n*

pro·lif·e·rate /prəˈlɪfəˌreɪt, proʊ-/ *vi*
increase rapidly in numbers **–ration**
/prəˌlɪfəˈreɪʃən, proʊ-/ *n* [S;U]

pro·lif·ic /prəˈlɪfɪk, proʊ-/ *adj* producing a
lot **~ally** *adv*

pro·logue, -log /ˈproʊlɒɡ, -lɑɡ/ *n* 1 introduction to a play, long poem, etc. 2 event
that leads up to another, bigger one

pro·long /prəˈlɒŋ/ *vt* lengthen **~ed** *adv*
long

prom /prɒm/ *n* formal dance at a school
or college

prom·e·nade /ˌprɒməˈneɪd, -ˈnɑd/ *n fml*
unhurried walk ♦ *vi* walk slowly up and
down

prom·i·nent /ˈprɒmənənt/ *adj* **1** sticking out **2** noticeable **3** famous ~**ly** *adv* –**nence** *n* **1** [U] fact or quality of being prominent **2** [C] *fml* part that sticks out

pro·mis·cu·ous /prəˈmɪskyuəs/ *adj* not limited to one sexual partner –**cuity** /ˌprɑmə'skyuəti/ *n* [U]

prom·ise /ˈprɑmɪs/ *n* **1** [C] statement, which one wishes to be believed, of what one will do **2** [U] signs of future success, good results, etc. ◆ *v* **1** [I/T] make a promise: *I promise I won't tell them.* **2** *vt* cause one to expect or hope for –**ising** *adj* showing PROMISE (2)

prom·on·to·ry /ˈprɑmənˌtori, -ˌtoori/ *n* point of land stretching out into the sea

pro·mote /prəˈmoʊt/ *vt* **1** raise to a higher position or rank **2** help to arrange (a business, concert, etc.) **3** advertise **4** *fml* help to bring about –**moter** *n* person whose job is to promote events, activities, etc.

pro·mo·tion /prəˈmoʊʃən/ *n* [C;U] **1** raising of rank or position **2** advertising activity

prompt¹ /prɑmpt/ *vt* **1** cause; urge **2** remind (an actor) of forgotten words ~**er** *n* person who prompts actors

prompt² *adj* acting or done quickly or at the right time ~**ly** *adv* ~**ness** *n* [U]

prone /proʊn/ *adj* **1** likely to suffer: *prone to colds | accident-prone* **2** lying face downwards

prong /prɒŋ, prɑŋ/ *n* pointed part of a fork: (fig.) *a 3-pronged attack* (= from 3 directions)

pro·noun /ˈproʊnaʊn/ *n* word used instead of a noun, such as *he* or *it*

pro·nounce /prəˈnaʊns/ *vt* **1** make the sound of (a letter, word, etc.) **2** *fml* declare officially ~**ment** *n* solemn declaration –**nounced** *adj* very strong or noticeable

pron·to /ˈprɑntoʊ/ *adv infml* quickly; immediately: *Get in here pronto!*

pro·nun·ci·a·tion /prəˌnʌnsiˈeɪʃən/ *n* [C;U] way in which a language or word is pronounced

proof¹ /pruf/ *n* **1** [C;U] way of showing that something is true **2** [C] a test or trial **3** [C] test copy of something to be printed **4** [U] standard of strength for certain alcoholic drinks

proof² *adj* having or giving protection: *proof against temptation | waterproof*

proof·read /ˈprufˌrid/ *vi/t* read and correct mistakes in ~**er** *n*

prop¹ /prɑp/ *n* support for something heavy ◆ *vt* -**pp**- support or keep in a leaning position

prop² *n* small article used on stage

prop·a·gan·da /ˌprɑpəˈgændə/ *n* [U] information spread to influence public opinion

prop·a·gate /ˈprɑpəˌgeɪt/ *v* **1** *vi/t* (cause to) increase in number by producing young **2** *vt fml* spread (ideas, etc.) –**gation** /ˌprɑpəˈgeɪʃən/ *n* [U]

pro·pel /prəˈpɛl/ *vt* -**ll**- move or push forward

pro·pel·ler /prəˈpɛlə/ *n* 2 or more blades on a central bar that turns to drive an aircraft or ship

pro·pen·si·ty /prəˈpɛnsəti/ *n fml* natural tendency

prop·er /ˈprɑpə/ *adj* **1** right; suitable; correct **2** socially acceptable ~**ly** *adv*

proper noun /ˌ· ·ˈ·/ *n* name of a particular thing or person, spelled with a CAPITAL letter

prop·er·ty /ˈprɑpəti/ *n* **1** [U] something owned; possession(s) **2** [C;U] (area of) land and/or building(s) **3** [C] natural quality or power

proph·e·cy /ˈprɑfəsi/ *n* [C;U] (statement) telling what will happen in the future

proph·e·sy /ˈprɑfəˌsaɪ/ *vi/t* say (what will happen in the future)

proph·et /ˈprɑfɪt/ *n* **1** person who makes known and explains God's will **2** person who tells about the future ~**ic** /prəˈfɛtɪk/ *adj*

pro·pi·tious /prəˈpɪʃəs/ *adj fml* favorable; offering advantage

pro·po·nent /prəˈpoʊnənt/ *n fml* person who advises the use of something

pro·por·tion /prəˈpɔrʃən, -ˈpoʊr-/ *n* **1** [C;U] relationship between one thing or part and another in size, importance, etc. **2** [C] part of a whole **3** **in/out of proportion** according/not according to real importance ◆ *vt fml* make in or put into suitable proportion ~**al** *adj* in correct proportion **proportions** *n* [P] size and shape

pro·pos·al /prəˈpoʊzəl/ *n* **1** plan; suggestion **2** offer of marriage

pro·pose /prəˈpoʊz/ *v* **1** *vt* suggest **2** *vt* intend **3** *vi/t* make an offer of (marriage)

prop·o·si·tion /ˌprɑpə'zɪʃən/ n 1 statement giving an unproved judgment 2 suggested offer or arrangement 3 person or situation to be dealt with 4 suggested offer to have sex with someone ♦ vt infml make a PROPOSITION (esp. 4) to (someone)

pro·pri·e·ta·ry /prə'praɪəˌteri/ adj 1 privately owned: a proprietary brand name 2 of or like an owner

pro·pri·e·tor /prə'praɪətə/ n owner of a business

pro·pri·e·ty /prə'praɪəti/ n [U] fml 1 social or moral correctness 2 rightness or reasonableness

pro·pul·sion /prə'pʌlʃən/ n [U] force that PROPELs –sive /-sɪv, -zɪv/ adj

pro·sa·ic /prou'zeɪ·ɪk/ adj dull ~ally adv

pros and cons /ˌprouz ən 'kɑnz/ n [P] reasons for and against

pro·scribe /prou'skraɪb/ vt fml forbid, esp. by law

prose /prouz/ n [U] ordinary written language (not poetry)

pros·e·cute /'prɑsəˌkyut/ vi/t bring a criminal charge (against) in court –cutor n –cution /ˌprɑsə'kyuʃən/ n 1 [C;U] prosecuting 2 [the+S] group of people prosecuting someone in court 3 [U] fml the carrying out of something that needs to be done

pros·e·lyt·ize /'prɑsələˌtaɪz/ vi fml try to persuade people to become new members of a religion

pros·pect¹ /'prɑspɛkt/ n 1 [C;U] reasonable hope of something happening 2 [S;U] something which is likely soon 3 [C] wide or distant view

prospect² vi try to find gold, oil, etc. ~or n

pro·spec·tive /prə'spɛktɪv/ adj likely to become

pro·spec·tus /prə'spɛktəs/ n small book advertising a product, college, new business, etc.

pros·per /'prɑspə/ vi 1 become successful and esp. rich 2 grow well ~ous adj successful and rich ~ity /prɑ'spɛrəti/ n [U] success and wealth

pros·tate /'prɑsteɪt/ n organ in the male body producing a liquid that carries SPERM

pros·the·sis /prɑs'θisɪs/ n artificial body part

pros·ti·tute /'prɑstəˌtut/ n someone who has sex with people for money ♦ vt fml use dishonorably for money –tution /ˌprɑstə'tuʃən/ n [U]

pros·trate /'prɑstreɪt/ adj 1 lying face downwards, esp. in worship 2 without any strength or courage ♦ vt make prostrate

pro·tag·o·nist /prou'tægənɪst/ n 1 main supporter of a new idea 2 someone taking part

pro·tect /prə'tɛkt/ vt keep safe ~or n ~ion /prə'tɛkʃən/ n 1 [U] act of protecting or state of being protected 2 [C] something that protects

pro·tec·tion·is·m /prə'tɛkʃəˌnɪzəm/ n [U] helping one's own country's trade by taxing foreign goods

pro·tec·tive /prə'tɛktɪv/ adj 1 that protects 2 wishing to protect ~ly adv

pro·tec·tor·ate /prə'tɛktərɪt/ n country controlled and protected by another country

prot·é·gé /'proutəˌʒeɪ, ˌproutə'ʒeɪ/ n person guided and helped by another

pro·tein /'proutin/ n [C;U] food substance that builds up the body and keeps it healthy

pro·test¹ /'proutest/ n [C;U] 1 strong expression of disapproval, opposition, etc. 2 under protest unwillingly

pro·test² /prə'tɛst, prou-, 'proutest/ v 1 vi make a protest 2 vt declare strongly against opposition ~er n

Prot·es·tant /'prɑtɪstənt/ n, adj (member) of a branch of the Christian church that separated from the Roman Catholic Church in the 16th century

pro·to·col /'proutəˌkɔl, -ˌkɑl/ n [U] fixed rules of behavior

pro·ton /'proutɑn/ n very small piece of matter that is part of an atom and carries POSITIVE (5) electricity

pro·to·type /'proutəˌtaɪp/ n first form of a machine, afterwards developed

pro·tract·ed /prou'træktɪd, prə-/ adj lasting an (unnecessarily) long time

pro·trac·tor /prou'træktə, prə-/ n instrument for measuring and drawing angles

pro·trude /prou'trud/ vi fml stick out –trusion /prou'truʒən/ n [C;U]

proud /praʊd/ adj 1 showing proper and reasonable respect for oneself 2 having too high an opinion of oneself 3 having or expressing personal pleasure in something connected with oneself: *proud of her new car* **4** splendid; glorious ♦ *adv*: **do someone proud** make someone feel proud ~**ly** *adv*

prove /pruːv/ *v* **1** *vt* show to be true **2** be (later) found to be: *These revelations could prove highly embarrassing.*

prov·en /ˈpruːvən/ *adj* tested and shown to be true

prov·erb /ˈprɒvɜːb/ *n* short wise saying that is often heard ~**ial** /prəˈvɜːbiəl/ *adj* **1** widely known and spoken of **2** of, concerning, or like a proverb

pro·vide /prəˈvaɪd/ *vt* arrange for someone to get; supply –**vided** *conj* on condition that –**viding** *conj* provided

  provide for *phr vt* **1** supply with necessary things **2** (of the law) make possible

prov·i·dence /ˈprɒvədəns/ *n* [U] the kindness of fate

prov·i·den·tial /ˌprɒvəˈdɛnʃəl◂/ *adj fml* lucky

prov·ince /ˈprɒvɪns/ *n* **1** main division of a country **2** area of knowledge, activity, etc. –**incial** /prəˈvɪnʃəl/ *adj* **1** of a province **2** narrow or old-fashioned in interest, customs, etc. **provinces** /ˈprɒvɪnsɪz/ *n* [*the*+P] parts of a country far from the main city

pro·vi·sion /prəˈvɪʒən/ *n* **1** [U] act of providing **2** [U] preparation against future risks or future needs **3** [C] condition in an agreement or law

provisions /prəˈvɪʒənz/ *n* [P] food supplies

pro·vi·sion·al /prəˈvɪʒənl/ *adj* for use now, but likely to be changed ~**ly** *adv*

prov·o·ca·tion /ˌprɒvəˈkeɪʃən/ *n* **1** [U] act of provoking **2** [C] something annoying

pro·voc·a·tive /prəˈvɒkətɪv/ *adj* likely to cause **a** anger **b** sexual interest ~**ly** *adv*

pro·voke /prəˈvəʊk/ *vt* **1** make angry **2** cause (a feeling or action)

prow /praʊ/ *n* front part of a ship

prow·ess /ˈpraʊɪs/ *n* [U] *fml* great ability or courage

prowl /praʊl/ *vi/t* move about quietly and threateningly **prowl** *n* [S] ~**er** *n*

prox·im·i·ty /prɒkˈsɪməti/ *n* *fml* nearness

prox·y /ˈprɒksi/ *n* **1** [U] right to act for another person, esp. as a voter **2** [C] person given this right

Pro·zac /ˈprəʊzæk/ *n* [U] *tdmk* widely used drug for DEPRESSION

prude /pruːd/ *n* person easily offended by rude things, esp. connected with sex **prudish** *adj*

pru·dent /ˈpruːdnt/ *adj* sensible and careful ~**ly** *adv* –**dence** *n* [U]

prune[1] /pruːn/ *n* dried PLUM

prune[2] *vt* **1** cut off parts of (a tree or bush) to improve shape and growth **2** remove unwanted parts of

pru·ri·ent /ˈprʊəriənt/ *adj fml* interested in an unhealthy way in sex –**ence** *n* [U]

pry[1] /praɪ/ *vi* try to find out about someone's private affairs

pry[2] *vt* lift or force with a tool or metal bar

P.S. *n* note added at the end of a letter

psalm /sɑːm/ *n* religious song or poem, esp. as in the Bible

pseu·do·nym /ˈsuːdnɪm, ˈsuːdənɪm/ *n* invented name, esp. of a writer

psst /ps/ *interj* (used for quietly gaining someone's attention)

psych /saɪk/ *v sl*

  psych out *phr vt* **1** understand by INTUITION **2** frighten

  psych up *phr vt* make (esp. oneself) enthusiastic and ready

psy·che /ˈsaɪki/ *n fml* human mind or spirit

psyched /saɪkt/ *adj sl* mentally prepared and excited about an event or activity

psy·che·del·ic /ˌsaɪkəˈdɛlɪk◂/ *adj* **1** (of a drug) causing strange and powerful feelings **2** having strong patterns of color, lines, moving lights, noise, etc.

psy·chi·a·try /saɪˈkaɪətri, sɪ–/ *n* [U] study and treatment of diseases of the mind –**trist** *n* –**tric** /ˌsaɪkiˈætrɪk◂/ *adj*

psy·chic /ˈsaɪkɪk/ *adj* **1** having strange powers, such as the ability to see into the future **2** of the mind **3** connected with the spirits of the dead ♦ *n* someone with strange powers, e.g. ability to know what will happen in the future ~**ally** *adv*

psy·cho /ˈsaɪkəʊ/ *adj sl* behaving in a crazy, violent way ♦ *n sl* someone likely to behave in a crazy, violent way

psy·cho·a·nal·y·sis /ˌsaɪkəʊəˈnæləsɪs/ *n* [U] way of treating disorders of the mind by finding their causes in the patient's past life –**analyze** /ˌsaɪkəʊˈænlaɪz/ *vt* –**analyst** /–ˈænl-ɪst/ *n*

psy·cho·log·i·cal /ˌsaɪkəˈlɒdʒɪkəl/ *adj* **1** of or connected with the way the mind works **2** *infml* not real

psy·chol·o·gy /saɪˈkɒlədʒi/ *n* [U] study of how the mind works –**gist** *n*

psy·cho·path /ˈsaɪkəpæθ/ *n* crazy person who may be violent ~**ic** /ˌsaɪkəˈpæθɪk◂/ *adj*

psy·cho·sis /saɪˈkoʊsɪs/ *n* -**ses** /-siz/ serious disorder of the mind –**chotic** /saɪˈkɑtɪk/ *n, adj*

psy·cho·so·mat·ic /ˌsaɪkoʊsəˈmætɪk/ *adj* (of an illness) caused by anxiety, not a real disorder of the body

psy·cho·ther·a·py /ˌsaɪkoʊˈθerəpi/ *n* [U] treatment of mind disorders by psychological methods (not drugs, etc.) –**pist** *n*

pt. *written abbrev. for:* **1** part **2** PINT(s) **3** point **4** port

PTA *n* Parent Teacher Association, local organization to involve parents in their children's schools

pu·ber·ty /ˈpyubəti/ *n* period of change from childhood to the adult state in which one can produce children

pu·bic /ˈpyubɪk/ *adj* of or near the sexual organs

pub·lic /ˈpʌblɪk/ *adj* **1** of or for people in general or everyone; not private: *public opinion* **2** of the government: *public money* **3** not secret **4 go public** (of a company) offer stock for sale to the public **5 in the public eye** often seen in public or on television, or mentioned in newspapers ♦ *n* [S] **1** people in general **2** people interested in the stated thing **3 in public** openly ~**ly** *adv*

pub·li·ca·tion /ˌpʌbləˈkeɪʃən/ *n* **1** [U] act of publishing (PUBLISH) **2** [C] book, magazine, etc.

public de·fend·er /ˌ·· ·ˈ··/ *n* lawyer paid by the state to defend poor people in court

pub·li·cist /ˈpʌbləsɪst/ *n* person who publicizes something, esp. products

pub·lic·i·ty /pʌˈblɪsəti/ *n* [U] **1** public notice or attention: *unwelcome publicity* **2** business of publicizing things; advertising

pub·li·cize /ˈpʌbləsaɪz/ *vt* bring to public notice

public re·la·tions /ˌ·· ·ˈ··/ *n* also **PR** — **1** [U] forming of a favorable public opinion of an organization **2** [P] good relations between an organization and the public

public school /ˈ·· ˌ·/ *n* school run by the government

public sec·tor /ˌ·· ˈ··/ *n* [the+S] those industries and services that are owned and run by the state

pub·lish /ˈpʌblɪʃ/ *vt* **1** bring out (a book, newspaper, etc.) **2** make known generally: *publishing the victim's name* ~**er** *n*

puck /pʌk/ *n* hard flat piece of rubber used in HOCKEY

puck·er /ˈpʌkə/ *vi/t* tighten into folds

pud·ding /ˈpʊdɪŋ/ *n* [C;U] thick soft sweet food made from flour, milk, eggs, etc.

pud·dle /ˈpʌdl/ *n* small amount of water, esp. rain, lying in a hollow place in the ground

pudg·y /ˈpʌdʒi/ *adj* short and fat

pu·er·ile /ˈpyʊrəl, -raɪl/ *adj fml* childish; silly

puff¹ /pʌf/ *v* **1** *vi* breathe rapidly and with effort **2** *vi/t* send out or come out as little clouds of smoke or steam

  puff out/up *phr vi/t* swell

puff² *n* **1** sudden light rush of air, smoke, etc. **2** hollow piece of light pastry filled with a soft, sweet mixture **3** *infml* piece of writing praising a person or entertainment ~**y** *adj* rather swollen

puf·fin /ˈpʌfɪn/ *n* seabird with a large brightly colored beak

pug·na·cious /pʌɡˈneɪʃəs/ *adj fml* fond of quarreling and fighting

puke /pyuk/ *vi infml for:* VOMIT

pull¹ /pʊl/ *v* **1** *vi/t* bring (something) along behind one: *The horses pulled the plow.* **2** *vi/t* move (someone or something) towards oneself: *She pulled the door open.* **3** *vt* take with force: *He had a tooth pulled (out).* **4** *vt* stretch and damage: *pull a muscle* **5** *vi* move in or as a vehicle: *The train pulled out.* (= left) **6** *vt* attract **7 pull someone's leg** tell someone something that is not true as a joke **8 pull a fast one (on)** get the advantage (over) by a trick **9 pull a gun** take out a gun and aim it (at someone) **10 pull the rug from under** stop supporting

  pull away *phr vi* (esp. of a road vehicle) start to move off

  pull down *phr vt* destroy (a building, etc.)

pull in *phr vi* (of a train) arrive at a station

pull off *phr vt* succeed in doing (something difficult)

pull out *phr vi/t* **1** (cause to) stop taking part **2** (of a train) leave a station

pull over *phr vi/t* (of a vehicle) move to one side (and stop)

pull through *phr vi/t* **1** live in spite of illness or wounds **2** (help to) succeed in spite of difficulties

pull together *phr v* **1** work together to help a shared effort **2** *vt* control the feelings of (oneself)

pull up *phr vi* (of a vehicle) stop

pull² *n* **1** [C;U] (act of) pulling **2** [C] rope, handle, etc. for pulling something **3** [S] difficult steep climb **4** [U] special (unfair) influence

pul·ley /ˈpʊli/ *n* apparatus for lifting things with a rope

pull·o·ver /ˈpʊlˌoʊvə/ *n* article of clothing, esp. a SWEATER pulled on over the head

pul·mo·na·ry /ˈpʊlmənˌɛri, ˈpʌl-/ *adj* of the lungs

pulp /pʌlp/ *n* **1** [S;U] soft almost liquid mass, esp. of plant material **2** [U] book, magazine, etc., cheaply produced and containing matter of bad quality ♦ *vt* make into pulp

pul·pit /ˈpʊlpɪt, ˈpʌl-/ *n* raised platform from which a priest speaks in church

pul·sate /ˈpʌlseɪt/ *vi* **1** shake very rapidly and regularly **2** pulse –**sation** /pʌlˈseɪʃən/ *n* [C;U]

pulse /pʌls/ *n* **1** regular beating of blood in the body's blood tubes **2** strong regular beat **3** short sound or electrical charge ♦ *vi* move or flow with a strong beat

pul·ver·ize /ˈpʌlvəˌraɪz/ *vi* **1** crush to a powder **2** defeat thoroughly

pu·ma /ˈpyumə, ˈpumə/ *n* -mas *or* -ma large fierce wild cat

pum·mel /ˈpʌməl/ *vt* -l- hit repeatedly

pump¹ /pʌmp/ *n* machine for forcing liquid or gas into or out of something ♦ **1** *vt* empty or fill with a pump **2** *vt* put in or remove with a pump **3** *vi* **a** work a pump **b** work like a pump: *My heart was pumping fast.* **4** *vt* try to get information from with questions

pump² *n* light shoe for dancing, etc.

pump·kin /ˈpʌmpkɪn, ˈpʌŋkɪn/ *n* [C;U] extremely large, round, orange vegetable

pun /pʌn/ *n* amusing use of a word or phrase with 2 meanings

punch¹ /pʌntʃ/ *vt* **1** hit hard with the closed hand **2** cut a hole in with a special tool: *The inspector punched my ticket.* ♦ **1** [C] hard blow with the closed hand **2** [U] forcefulness **3** **pull one's punches** express an unfavorable opinion of someone or something less strongly than is deserved

punch² *n* [U] mixed sweet fruit drink usu. made with alcohol

punch³ *n* [C] steel tool for cutting holes

punch line /ˈ· ˌ/ *n* funny part at the end of a joke

punc·tu·al /ˈpʌŋktʃuəl/ *adj* coming, happening, etc., at exactly the right time ~**ly** *adv* –**ality** /ˌpʌŋktʃuˈæləti/ *n* [U]

punc·tu·ate /ˈpʌŋktʃuˌeɪt/ *vt* **1** divide into sentences, phrases, etc., with punctuation marks **2** repeatedly break the flow of –**ation** /ˌpʌŋktʃuˈeɪʃən/ *n* [U] **1** act or system of punctuating **2** punctuation marks

punctuation mark /··ˈ·· ˌ·/ *n* sign used in punctuating, e.g. a PERIOD¹ (4), or a COMMA

punc·ture /ˈpʌŋktʃə/ *n* small hole, esp. in a tire ♦ *vi/t* (cause to) get a puncture

pun·dit /ˈpʌndɪt/ *n* EXPERT who is often asked to give an opinion

pun·gent /ˈpʌndʒənt/ *adj* (of a taste or smell) strong and sharp

pun·ish /ˈpʌnɪʃ/ *vt* **1** cause (someone) to suffer for (a crime or fault) **2** deal roughly with ~**ment** *n* **1** [U] act of punishing **2** [C] way in which someone is punished

pun·ish·ing /ˈpʌnɪʃɪŋ/ *adj* that makes one thoroughly tired and weak

pu·ni·tive /ˈpyunətɪv/ *adj* **1** intended as punishment **2** very severe

punk /pʌŋk/ *n* (since the 1970s) young person with strange clothes and often colored hair who likes loud violent music

punt /pʌnt/ *n* kick used in football when the ball is dropped towards the foot –**er** person who punts

pu·ny /ˈpyuni/ *adj* small and weak

pup /pʌp/ *n* PUPPY

pu·pil¹ /ˈpyupəl/ *n* child being taught

pupil² *n* small, round black opening in the middle of the eye

pup·pet /ˈpʌpɪt/ n **1** toylike figure of a person or animal that is made to move as if it were alive **2** person or group that is controlled by someone else: *a puppet government*

pup·py /ˈpʌpi/ n young dog

puppy love /ˈ·· ·/ n [U] young boy's or girl's love that doesn't last long

pur·chase /ˈpɜtʃəs/ vt fml buy ♦ n fml **1** [U] act of buying **2** [C] something bought **3** [U] firm hold on a surface

pure /pyʊr/ adj **1** not mixed with anything else **2** clean **3** free from evil **4** complete; thorough: *by pure chance* ~**ly** adv wholly; only

pu·ree /pyʊˈreɪ/ n [C;U] soft partly liquid mass of food ♦ vt make (fruit or vegetable) into a puree

pur·ga·to·ry /ˈpɜgə₁tɔri, -₁toʊri/ n [U] **1** (in the Roman Catholic Church) place where the soul of a dead person is made pure and fit to enter heaven **2** situation of great suffering

purge /pɜdʒ/ vt **1** get rid of (an unwanted person) from (a state, group, etc.) by driving out, killing, etc. **2** make clean and free from (something evil) **3** empty the bowels with medicine ♦ n act of purging (PURGE (1))

pu·ri·fy /ˈpyʊrə₁faɪ/ vt make pure -**fication** /₁pyʊrəfəˈkeɪʃən/ n [U]

pur·ist /ˈpyʊrɪst/ n someone who tries to make sure things are always done correctly and not changed, esp. in matters of grammar

pu·ri·tan /ˈpyʊrət̬n̩, -rət̬ən/ n **1** person with hard fixed standards of behavior who thinks pleasure is wrong **2** (cap.) member of a former Christian group that wanted to make religion simpler and less ceremonial ~**ical** /₁pyʊrəˈtænɪkəl/ adj

pu·ri·ty /ˈpyʊrət̬i/ n [U] being pure

purl /pɜl/ n [U] knitting (KNIT) stitch done backwards ♦ vi/t use a purl stitch (on)

pur·ple /ˈpɜpəl/ adj of a color that is a mixture of red and blue

pur·port /ˈpɜpɔrt, -poʊrt/ n [U] fml meaning ♦ /pəˈpɔrt, -ˈpoʊrt/ vt have an intended appearance of being

pur·pose /ˈpɜpəs/ n **1** [C] reason for doing something **2** [C] use; effect; result: *It has served its purpose.* (= done what is needed) **3** [U] determined quality; power

of will **4 on purpose** intentionally ~**ful** adj determined ~**ly** adv intentionally

purr /pɜ/ vi make the low continuous sound of a pleased cat

purse[1] /pɜs/ n **1** small bag for carrying coins **2** woman's HANDBAG **3** amount of money offered, esp. as a prize

purse[2] vt draw (esp. the lips) together in little folds

purs·er /ˈpɜsə/ n ship's officer responsible for money and travelers' arrangements

purse strings /ˈ· ·/ n hold the purse strings control the spending of money

pur·sue /pəˈsu/ vt **1** follow in order to catch **2** fml continue steadily with: *pursuing a policy of neutrality* -**suer** n

pur·suit /pəˈsut/ n **1** [U] act of pursuing **2** [C] fml activity, esp. for pleasure

pus /pʌs/ n [U] thick yellowish liquid produced in an infected part of the body

push[1] /pʊʃ/ v **1** vi/t use sudden or steady pressure to move (someone or something) forward, away from oneself, or to a different position: *He pushed the drawer shut.* **2** vt try to force (someone) by continual urging **3** vt sell (illegal drugs) **4 be pushing** infml be nearly (a stated age) **5 push one's luck** take a risk ~**ed** adj not having enough: *pushed for time* ~**er** n seller of illegal drugs

push around phr vt treat roughly and unfairly

push for phr vt demand urgently and forcefully

push off phr vi infml go away

push[2] n **1** act of pushing **2** large planned attack and advance **3 at a push** if necessary **4 if/when push comes to shove** if action must be taken **5 give/get the push** infml dismiss/be dismissed from a job

push-but·ton /ˈ· ₁··/ n small button pressed to operate something

push·o·ver /ˈpʊʃˌoʊvə/ n [S] infml **1** something very easy to do or win **2** someone easily influenced or deceived

push-up /ˈ· ·/ n form of exercise where one lies face down and pushes with one's arms

push·y /ˈpʊʃi/ adj too forceful in getting things done, esp. for one's own advantage

pus·sy[1] /ˈpʊsi/ also **puss** /pʊs/, **pus·sy·cat** /ˈpʊsiˌkæt/ — n (child's name for) a cat

pussy[2] n taboo sl the female sex organ

pus·sy·foot /ˈpʊsiˌfʊt/ vi act too carefully

put /pʊt/ v put, pres. p. -tt- **1** move, place, or fix to, on, or in the stated place **2** cause to be: *She put her books in order.* | *Put your mistakes right at once.* **3** express in words **4** express officially for judgment: *I'll put your suggestions to the committee.* **5** write down

put around phr vt spread (bad or false news)

put across phr vt cause to be understood

put aside phr vt save (money)

put away phr vt **1** return to its usual storing place **2** infml eat (usu. large quantities of food) **3** place (someone) in prison or a hospital for crazy people

put back phr vt delay

put by phr vt PUT aside

put down phr vt **1** control; defeat: *put down a rebellion* **2** record in writing **3** embarrass: *He really put her down.* **4** kill (an old or sick animal) **5** cause to feel unimportant **6** pay (an amount) as part of the cost of something with a promise to pay the rest over a period of time ♦ n

put down to phr vt state that (something) is caused by

put forward phr vt suggest

put in phr vt **1** do (work) or spend (time) on work **2** interrupt by saying **3** (of a ship) enter a port

put in for phr vt make a formal request for

put into phr vt add (something) to (something): *Put more effort into your work!*

put off phr vt **1** delay **2** discourage **3** cause to dislike

put on phr vt **1** cover (part of) the body with (esp. clothing) **2** operate (a radio, light, etc.) by pressing or turning a button **3** increase: *She's put on weight.* **4** provide: *They're putting on another train.* **5** perform (a play, show, etc.) on stage **6** pretend to have (a feeling, quality, etc.) **7** deceive playfully

put onto phr vt give information about

put out phr vt **1** cause to stop burning **2** trouble or annoy **3** broadcast or print **4** put oneself out take trouble

put over phr vt put across

put over on phr vt put one over on deceive

put through phr vt **1** connect (a telephone caller) **2** cause to suffer or experience

put to phr vt **1** ask (a question) of or make (an offer) to **2** suggest to (someone) that **3 be hard put to** find it difficult to

put up phr vt **1** raise **2** put in a public place: *put up a notice* **3** provide food and a bed for **4** make; offer: *He didn't put up much of a fight.* **5** offer for sale **6** supply (money needed)

put up to phr vt give the idea of doing (esp. something bad)

put up with phr vt suffer without complaining

put-down /ˈ· ·/ n infml words that make someone feel unimportant or hurt

pu·tre·fy /ˈpyutrəˌfaɪ/ vi fml decay **–faction** /ˌpyutrəˈfækʃən/ n [U]

pu·trid /ˈpyutrɪd/ adj **1** very decayed and smelling bad **2** worthless; greatly disliked

putt /pʌt/ vi/t (in GOLF) hit (the ball) along the ground towards or into the hole ~**er** n **1** CLUB[1] (3) for putting **2** person who putts

put·ty /ˈpʌti/ n [U] soft oily paste, esp. for fixing glass to window frames

puz·zle /ˈpʌzəl/ v **1** vt cause (someone) difficulty in the effort to understand **2** vi try hard to find the answer ♦ n **1** picture cut into pieces to be put together for fun **2** game or toy to exercise the mind **3** something that puzzles one

puzzle out phr vt find the answer to by thinking hard

PVC n [U] type of plastic

pyg·my /ˈpɪgmi/ n **1** (usu. cap.) member of an African race of very small people **2** very small person

pyr·a·mid /ˈpɪrəmɪd/ n **1** solid figure with 4 sides, each having 3 angles, that slope up to meet at a point **2** large stone building in this shape, used as the burial place of kings, etc., in ancient Egypt

pyramid sell·ing /ˈ··· ˌ··/ n [U] system of selling in which someone buys the right to sell goods and then sells the goods to others, who sell them to others, etc.

pyre /paɪə/ n high mass of wood for burning a dead body

Py·rex /ˈpaɪreks/ n [U] tdmk strong glass used in making cooking containers

py·ro·tech·nics /ˌpaɪrəˈtekniks/ fml [P] a splendid show of FIREWORKS

py·thon /ˈpaɪθɒn, -θən/ n large tropical snake that crushes the animals it eats

Q

Q, q /kyu/ *n* the 17th letter of the English alphabet

QED there is the proof of my argument

Q-Tip /'kyu tɪp/ *n tdmk* small thin stick with cotton at each end, used for cleaning the ears or other small places

quack¹ /kwæk/ *vi, n* (make) the sound ducks make

quack² *n* person dishonestly claiming to be a doctor

quad¹ /kwɑd/ *n* square open space with four buildings around it as on a CAMPUS

quad² *n* QUADRUPLET

quad·ran·gle /'kwɑdræŋgəl/ *n fml* for QUAD¹

quad·rant /'kwɑdrənt/ *n* 1 quarter of a circle 2 instrument for measuring angles

quad·ri·lat·er·al /ˌkwɑdrə'lætərəl◂/ *n, adj* (flat figure) with 4 straight sides

quad·ri·ple·gic /ˌkwɑdrə'plidʒɪk/ *n* someone who has lost the use of both arms and both legs ♦ *adj*

quad·ru·ped /'kwɑdrəˌpɛd/ *n* creature with 4 legs

quad·ru·ple /kwɑ'drupəl, 'kwɑdrupəl/ *vi/t* multiply by 4 ♦ *adj, adv* 4 times as big

quad·ru·plet /kwɑ'drʌplɪt, 'dru-, 'kwɑdruplɪt/ *n* any of 4 children born at the same time

quag·mire /'kwæɡmaɪə, 'kwɑg-/ *n* 1 soft wet ground 2 bad situation that is difficult to escape from

quail /kweɪl/ *n* quail *or* quails (meat of) a type of small bird

quaint /kweɪnt/ *adj* attractively old-fashioned ~**ly** *adv*

quake /kweɪk/ *vi* shake; tremble

Quak·er /'kweɪkə/ *n* member of a Christian religious group that opposes violence

qual·i·fi·ca·tion /ˌkwɑləfə'keɪʃən/ *n* 1 [C] something that limits the force of a statement 2 [U] act of qualifying 3 [C *often pl.*] proof that one has passed an examination **qualifications** *n* [P] (proof of

having) the necessary ability, experience, or knowledge, esp. for a job

qual·i·fy /'kwɑləˌfaɪ/ *v* 1 *vi/t* (cause to) reach a necessary standard 2 *vt* limit the force or meaning of (a statement) –**fied** *adj* 1 having suitable qualifications 2 limited: *qualified approval*

qual·i·ta·tive /'kwɑləˌteɪtɪv/ *adj* of or about quality

qual·i·ty /'kwɑləti/ *n* 1 [C;U] (high) degree of goodness 2 [C] something typical of a person or thing ♦ *adj* of a high degree of goodness: *quality products*

quality con·trol /'··· ·ˌ·/ *n* [U] practice of checking goods as they are produced, to make sure their quality is good enough

quality time /'··· ·ˌ·/ *n* [U] time spent giving someone, esp. family members, one's full attention

qualm /kwɑm, kwɔm/ *n* uncomfortable feeling of unsureness

quan·da·ry /'kwɑndri, -dəri/ *n* feeling of not knowing what to do

quan·ti·fi·er /'kwɑntəˌfaɪə/ *n* (in grammar) a word or phrase that is used with a noun to show quantity, such as *much*, *few*, and *a lot of*

quan·ti·fy /'kwɑntəˌfaɪ/ *vt fml* measure –**fiable** /ˌkwɑntə'faɪəbəl◂/ *adj*

quan·ti·ta·tive /'kwɑntəˌteɪtɪv/ *adj* of or about quantity

quan·ti·ty /'kwɑntəti/ *n* 1 [U] the fact of being measurable, amount 2 [C] amount; number — see also UNKNOWN QUANTITY

quantum leap /ˌkwɑntəm 'lip/ *n* very large and important advance or improvement

quantum the·o·ry /'·· ·ˌ··/ *n* [U] idea that ENERGY travels in fixed amounts

quar·an·tine /'kwɔrənˌtin, 'kwɑr-/ *n* [U] period when a sick person or animal is kept away from others so the disease cannot spread ♦ *vt* put in quarantine

quark /kwork, kwɑrk/ *n* smallest possible piece of material forming the substances of which atoms are made

quar·rel¹ /'kwɔrəl, 'kwɑ-/ *n* 1 angry argument 2 cause for or point of disagreement

quarrel² *vi* -l- have an ARGUMENT (1) ~**some** *adj* likely to argue

quarrel with *phr vt* disagree with

quar·ry¹ /'kwɔri, 'kwɑ-/ *n* place where stone, sand, etc., are dug out ♦ *vt* dig from a quarry

quarry² n person or animal being hunted

quart /kwɔrt/ n a measure of amount equal to two pints

quar·ter /'kwɔrtər/ n 1 [C] a 4th part of a whole: *a quarter of a mile* 2 [C] 15 minutes: *quarter to 10* 3 [C] coin equal to one 4th of a dollar; 25 cents 4 [C] 3 months of the year 5 [C] part of a town: *the student quarter* 6 [C] person or place from which something comes: *no help from that quarter* 7 [U] *fml* giving of life to a defeated enemy ♦ vt 1 divide into 4 parts 2 provide lodgings for **quarters** n [P] 1 accommodation (ACCOMMODATE) 2 **at close quarters** near together

quar·ter·back /'kwɔrtərˌbæk/ n football player who directs the offense

quar·ter·fi·nal /ˌkwɔrtər'faɪnl/ n any of 4 matches where those that win play in SEMIFINALS

quar·ter·ly /'kwɔrtərli/ adj, adv (happening) 4 times a year ♦ n quarterly magazine

quar·tet /kwɔr'tɛt/ n (music for) 4 musicians

quartz /kwɔrts/ n [U] hard mineral used in making very exact clocks

qua·sar /'kweɪzɑr/ n very bright, very distant starlike object

quash /kwɑʃ/ vt 1 officially refuse to accept 2 put an end to: *quash a rebellion*

quat·rain /'kwɑt'reɪn/ n 4 lines of poetry

qua·ver /'kweɪvər/ vi (of a voice or music) shake ♦ n a shaking in the voice ~**y** adj

quay /ki, keɪ/ n place in a HARBOR by which ships stop and unload

quea·sy /'kwizi/ adj 1 feeling one is going to be sick 2 uncertain about the rightness of doing something

queen /kwin/ n 1 a female ruler b king's wife 2 leading female: *a beauty queen* 3 leading female insect in a group: *a queen bee* 4 sl male HOMOSEXUAL ~**ly** adj like, or suitable for, a queen

queen-size /'· ·/ adj larger than the standard size

queer /kwɪr/ adj 1 strange 2 *infml derog for*: HOMOSEXUAL ♦ n *infml derog* male HOMOSEXUAL

quell /kwɛl/ vt defeat; crush

quench /kwɛntʃ/ vt 1 satisfy (thirst) by drinking 2 put out (flames)

que·ry /'kwɪri/ n question or doubt ♦ vt express doubt or unsureness about

quest /kwɛst/ n *fml* long search

ques·tion¹ /'kwɛstʃən/ n 1 [C] sentence or phrase asking for information 2 [C] matter to be settled; problem 3 [C;U] doubt: *His honesty is beyond question.* 5 **in question** being talked about 5 **out of the question** impossible 6 **there's no question** of there's no possibility of

question² vt 1 ask (someone) questions 2 have doubts about ~**able** adj 1 uncertain 2 perhaps not true or honest ~**er** n

question mark /'·· ·/ n mark (?) written at the end of a question

ques·tion·naire /ˌkwɛstʃə'nɛr/ n set of questions asked to obtain information

quib·ble /'kwɪbəl/ vi argue about small unimportant points **quibble** n

quiche /kiʃ/ n flat pastry case filled with eggs, cheese, vegetables, etc.

quick¹ /kwɪk/ adj 1 fast 2 easily showing anger: *a quick temper* ♦ adv fast ~**ly** adv ~**en** vi/t make or become quicker ~**ness** n [U]

quick² n 1 [U] flesh to which the nails of fingers and toes are joined 2 **cut (a person) to the quick** hurt a person's feelings deeply

quick·ie /'kwɪki/ n something made or done in a hurry

quick·sand /'kwɪksænd/ n [U] wet sand which sucks things down

quick-wit·ted /ˌ· '··◂/ adj swift to understand and act

quid pro quo /ˌkwɪd prou 'kwou/ n something given in fair exchange

qui·et /'kwaɪət/ adj 1 with little noise 2 calm; untroubled: *a quiet life* ♦ n [U] 1 quietness 2 **keep something quiet** keep something a secret ♦ vi/t make or become quiet ~**ly** adv ~**ness** n [U]

quill /kwɪl/ n 1 long feather 2 pen made from this 3 sharp prickle on some animals, esp. the PORCUPINE

quilt /kwɪlt/ n cloth covering for a bed, filled with feathers, etc. ~**ed** made with cloth containing soft material with stitching across it

quin·tes·sence /kwɪn'tɛsəns/ n *fml* perfect type or example –**tessential** /ˌkwɪntə'sɛnʃəl/ adj

quint /kwɪnt/ n QUINTUPLET

quin·tet /kwɪn'tɛt/ n (music for) 5 musicians

quin·tu·plet /kwɪnˈtʌplɪt, -ˈtu-, ˈkwɪntʊplɪt/ *n* any of 5 children born at the same time

quip[1] /kwɪp/ *n* clever amusing remark ♦ *vi* -pp- make a quip

quirk /kwɜːk/ *n* **1** strange happening or accident **2** strange habit or way of behaving ~y *adj*

quit /kwɪt/ *vi/t* **quitted** *or* **quit**, *pres. p.* -tt- stop (doing something) and leave ~ter *n* person who lacks the courage to finish things when he/she meets difficulties

quite /kwaɪt/ *predeterminer*, *adv* **1** completely; perfectly: *not quite right* **2** very; rather: *quite cold* **3** **quite a/an** unusual: *quite a party* | *It's quite something to be a senator at 30.*

quits /kwɪts/ *adj* back on an equal level with someone after an argument, repaying money, etc.

quiv·er[1] /ˈkwɪvə/ *vi/t* (cause to) tremble a little **quiver** *n*

quiver[2] *n* container for ARROWS

quix·ot·ic /kwɪkˈsɒtɪk/ *adj* doing foolishly brave things in order to be helpful

quiz /kwɪz/ *n* -zz- **1** short examination

2 game where questions are asked ♦ *vt* -zz- ask questions of (someone), esp. repeatedly

quiz·zi·cal /ˈkwɪzɪkəl/ *adj* (of a smile or look) suggesting a question or secret knowledge ~ly *adv*

quo·rum /ˈkwɔːrəm, ˈkwoʊrəm/ *n* number of people who must be present for a meeting to be held

quo·ta /ˈkwoʊtə/ *n* amount officially to be produced, received, etc., as one's share

quo·ta·tion /kwoʊˈteɪʃən/ *n* **1** [C] words QUOTED (1) **2** [U] act of quoting **3** [C] amount QUOTED (2)

quotation marks /ˈ·· ˌ/ *n* marks (" or ") showing the start or end of a QUOTATION (1)

quote /kwoʊt/ *v* **1** *vi/t* repeat the words of (a person, book, etc.) in speech or writing **2** *vt* offer as a price for work to be done ♦ *n* **1** *infml* QUOTATION (1, 3) **2** in **quotes** in QUOTATION MARKS

quo·tient /ˈkwoʊʃənt/ *n* number gotten by dividing

R

R, r /ɑr/ the 18th letter of the English alphabet — see also THREE R's

R written abbrev. for: **1** river **2** (of a film) restricted; that can only be seen by persons under 17 if an adult comes with them

rab·bi /'ræbaɪ/ n Jewish priest

rab·bit /'ræbɪt/ n common small animal with long ears, often kept as a pet or eaten

rab·id /'ræbɪd/ adj **1** suffering from rabies **2** (of feelings or opinions) unreasoningly violent

ra·bies /'reɪbiz/ n [U] disease passed on by the bite of an infected animal and causing madness and death

rac·coon /ræ'kun/ n small North American animal with a tail with black and white rings around it

race¹ /reɪs/ n competition in speed: a horse race | (fig.) a race against time ♦ vi/t **1** compete in a race (against) **2** (cause to) go very fast

race² n **1** [C;U] (any of) the main divisions of human beings, each of a different physical type **2** [C] group of people with the same history, language, etc.: the German race **3** [C] breed or type of animal or plant

race·course /'reɪs-kɔrs, -koʊrs/ n RACE-TRACK

race·track /'reɪs-træk/ n track around which horses, runners, cars, etc., race

ra·cial /'reɪʃəl/ adj **1** of a RACE² **2** between RACES²: racial tension **~ly** adv

ra·cis·m /'reɪsɪzəm/ n [U] **1** belief that one's own RACE² is best **2** dislike or unfair treatment of other races **racist** adj, n

rack¹ /ræk/ n **1** frame or shelf with bars, hooks, etc., for holding things **2** instrument for hurting people by stretching their bodies **3** bar with teeth, moved along by a wheel with similar teeth

rack² vt **1** cause great pain or anxiety to **2 rack one's brains** think very hard

rack³ n **rack and ruin** ruined condition, esp. of a building

rack·et¹, racquet /'rækɪt/ n instrument with a netlike part for hitting the ball in games like tennis

racket² n **1** [S] loud noise **2** [C] dishonest business

rack·e·teer /ˌrækə'tɪr/ n someone who works a RACKET² (2) **~ing** n [U]

rac·y /'reɪsi/ adj (of a story, etc.) amusing, full of life, and perhaps dealing with sex

ra·dar /'reɪdɑr/ n [U] apparatus or method of finding solid objects by receiving and measuring the speed of radio waves seen as a SCREEN

ra·di·al¹ /'reɪdiəl/ adj like a wheel

radial² also **radial tire** /ˌ··· ˈ/ — n car tire with cords inside the rubber that go across the edge of the wheel rather than along it, so as to give better driving control

ra·di·ant /'reɪdiənt/ adj **1** sending out light or heat in all directions **2** (of a person) showing love and happiness **~ly** adv **–ance** n [U]

ra·di·ate /'reɪdieɪt/ vi/t send out light, heat, etc.: (fig.) She radiates happiness.

ra·di·a·tion /ˌreɪdi'eɪʃən/ n [U] **1** (act of) radiating **2** RADIOACTIVITY

ra·di·a·tor /'reɪdiˌeɪtər/ n **1** apparatus, esp. of hot water pipes, for heating a building **2** apparatus that keeps a car's engine cool

rad·i·cal /'rædɪkəl/ adj **1** (of a change) thorough and complete **2** in favor of complete political change ♦ n RADICAL (2) person **~ly** adv

rad·i·i /'reɪdiˌaɪ/ pl. of RADIUS

ra·di·o /'reɪdiˌoʊ/ n **1** [U] sending or receiving sounds through the air by electrical waves **2** [C] apparatus to receive such sounds **3** [U] radio broadcasting industry **4 on the radio: a** (of a sound) broadcast **b** (of a person) broadcast on the radio

ra·di·o·ac·tiv·i·ty /ˌreɪdioʊæk'tɪvəti/ n [U] **1** quality, harmful in large amounts to living things, that some ELEMENTS have of giving out ENERGY by the breaking up of atoms **2** the energy given out in this way: exposed to radioactivity **–tive** /ˌreɪdioʊ'æktɪv◂/ adj

ra·di·og·ra·phy /ˌreɪdi'ɑgrəfi/ n [U] taking of photographs made with X-RAYS, usu. for medical reasons **–pher** n [C] person who practices radiography

ra·di·ol·o·gy /ˌreɪdiˈɑlədʒi/ n [U] study and medical use of radioactivity –**gist** n [C]

radio tel·e·scope /ˌ··· ˈ···/ n radio receiver for following the movements of stars and other objects in space

rad·ish /ˈrædɪʃ/ n small plant with a round red root, eaten raw

ra·di·us /ˈreɪdiəs/ n -**dii** /-diˌaɪ/ 1 (length of) a straight line from the center of a circle to its side 2 stated circular area measured from its center point: *houses within a ten-mile radius of the town*

raf·fle /ˈræfəl/ n way of getting money by selling chances to win prizes ♦ vt offer as a raffle prize

raft /ræft/ n flat, usu. wooden, floating structure, used esp. as a boat

raf·ter /ˈræftər/ n large sloping beam that holds up a roof

rag /ræg/ n 1 small piece of old cloth 2 old worn article of clothing 3 *infml derog* newspaper

rage /reɪdʒ/ n [C;U] 1 (sudden feeling of) extreme anger 2 **all the rage** very fashionable ♦ vi 1 be in a rage 2 (of bad weather, pain, etc.) be very violent

rag·ged /ˈrægɪd/ adj 1 old and torn 2 dressed in old torn clothes 3 rough; uneven: *a ragged beard* | (fig.) *a ragged performance* ~**ly** adv

rag·time /ˈrægtaɪm/ n [U] popular music of the 1920s, in which the strong notes of the tune come just before the main beats

raid /reɪd/ n 1 quick attack on an enemy position 2 unexpected visit by the police in search of crime ♦ vi/t make a raid (on): (fig.) *The children raided the kitchen for food.* ~**er** n

rail¹ /reɪl/ n 1 [C] fixed bar, esp. to hang things on or for protection 2 [C] line of metal bars which a train runs on 3 [U] railroad ♦ vt enclose or separate with rails ~**ing** n rail in a fence

rail² vi *fml* curse or complain angrily

rail·road /ˈreɪlroʊd/ n 1 track for trains 2 system of such tracks ♦ vt 1 hurry (someone) unfairly 2 pass (a law) or carry out (a plan) quickly in spite of opposition

rain¹ /reɪn/ n 1 [U] water falling from the clouds 2 [S] thick fall of anything: *a rain of questions* 3 **as right as rain** in perfect health 4 **(come) rain or shine** whatever happens ~**y** adj 1 with lots of rain 2 **for**

a rainy day for a time when money may be needed

rain² v 1 vi (of rain) fall 2 vi/t (cause to) fall thickly, like rain 3 **rain cats and dogs** rain very heavily

rain out /ˌ· ˈ·/ phr v stop because of rain: *The game was rained out.*

rain·bow /ˈreɪnboʊ/ n arch of different colors that appears in the sky after rain

rain check /ˈ· ·/ n request to claim later something offered now

rain·coat /ˈreɪnkoʊt/ n coat worn to protect one from the rain

rain·drop /ˈreɪndrɑp/ n single drop of rain

rain·fall /ˈreɪnfɔl/ n [C;U] amount of rain that falls in a certain time

rain·for·est /ˈreɪnˌfɔrɪst, -ˌfɑr-/ n wet tropical forest

rain·storm /ˈreɪnstɔrm/ n storm with a lot of rain and strong wind

rain·wa·ter /ˈreɪnˌwɔtər, -ˌwɑ-/ n [U] water that has fallen as rain

raise /reɪz/ vt 1 lift 2 make higher in amount, size, etc. 3 collect together: *raise an army* 4 produce and look after (children, animals, or crops) 5 mention or introduce (a subject) for consideration 6 a make a (noise) b cause people to make (a noise) or have feelings: *raise a laugh/raise doubts* 7 bring to an end (something that controls or forbids): *raise a siege* 8 **raise Cain/hell/the roof** *infml* become very angry ♦ n wage increase

rai·sin /ˈreɪzən/ n dried GRAPE

rake¹ /reɪk/ n gardening tool with a row of points at the end of a long handle

rake² vt 1 gather, loosen, or level with a rake 2 examine or shoot in a continuous sweeping movement

rake in phr vt *infml* earn or gain a lot of (money)

rake up phr vt 1 produce with difficulty by searching 2 remember and talk about (something that should be forgotten)

rake³ n man who leads a wild life with regard to drink and women

ral·ly¹ /ˈræli/ n 1 large esp. political public meeting 2 motor race over public roads 3 long exchange of hits in tennis

ral·ly² v 1 vi/t come or bring together (again) for a shared purpose 2 vi recover

rally around phr vi help in time of trouble

ram /ræm/ n 1 adult male sheep that can be the father of young 2 any machine that repeatedly drops or pushes a weight onto or into something ♦ vt -mm- 1 run into (something) very hard 2 force into place with heavy pressure: (fig.) *My father keeps ramming his ideas down my throat.*

RAM /ræm/ n [U] Random-Access Memory; computer memory holding information that is needed by the computer for a limited period, and can be searched in any order one likes

Ram·a·dan /ˈræməˌdæn/ n [U] ninth month of the Muslim year, when no food may be eaten during daylight hours

ram·ble /ˈræmbəl/ n (long) country walk for pleasure

ramble² vi 1 go on a ramble 2 talk or write in a disordered wandering way –bler n –bling adj 1 (of speech or writing) disordered and wandering 2 (of a street, house, etc.) of irregular shape; winding 3 (of a plant) growing loosely in all directions

ram·bunc·tious /ræmˈbʌŋkʃəs/ adj too eager or active

ram·i·fi·ca·tion /ˌræməfəˈkeɪʃən/ n 1 branch of a system with many parts 2 any of the results that may follow from an action or decision

ramp /ræmp/ n 1 artificial slope connecting 2 levels 2 way onto or off a FREEWAY

ram·page /ˈræmpeɪdʒ, ræmˈpeɪdʒ/ vi rush about wildly or angrily ♦ /ˈræmpeɪdʒ/ n **on the rampage** rampaging

ram·pant /ˈræmpənt/ adj (of crime, disease, etc.) widespread and uncontrollable

ram·shack·le /ˈræmˌʃækəl/ adj (of a building or vehicle) falling to pieces

ran /ræn/ past t. of RUN

ranch /ræntʃ/ n 1 large farm where animals are raised 2 style of house all on one floor ♦ **-er** someone who owns or works on a RANCH (1)

ran·cid /ˈrænsɪd/ adj (of butter, cream, etc.) unpleasant because not fresh

R and D /ˌɑr ən ˈdi/ n [U] research and development; part of a business concerned with studying new ideas, planning new products, etc.

ran·dom /ˈrændəm/ adj without any fixed plan ♦ n **at random** in a random way ~**ly** adv ~**ness** n [U]

random ac·cess mem·ory /ˌ•• •• ˈ•••/ n [U] RAM

rang /ræŋ/ past t. of RING

range¹ /reɪndʒ/ n 1 [S;U] distance over which something has an effect or limits between which it varies: *He shot her at close range.* | *a wide range of temperature* 2 [C] area where shooting is practiced or MISSILES are tested 3 [C] connected line of mountains or hills 4 [the+S] stretch of grassy land where cattle feed 5 [C] set of different objects of the same kind, esp. for sale 6 large STOVE: *a gas range*

range² v 1 vi vary between limits 2 vi wander freely: *The conversation ranged over many topics.* 3 vt put in position

rang·er /ˈreɪndʒər/ n forest or park guard

rank¹ /ræŋk/ n 1 [C;U] position in the army, navy, etc.: *the rank of colonel* 2 [C;U] (high) social position 3 [C] line of people or things 4 **keep/break rank(s)** (of soldiers) stay in line/fail to stay in line 5 **of the first rank** among the best 6 **pull rank (on someone)** use unfairly the advantage of one's higher position ♦ v 1 vi/t be or put in a certain class 2 vt arrange in regular order **ranks** n [P] ordinary soldiers below the rank of SERGEANT

rank² adj 1 (of smell or taste) very strong and unpleasant 2 (of something bad) complete: *a rank beginner at the job* 3 (of a plant) too thick and widespread

rank and file /ˌ• • ˈ•/ n [S] ordinary people in an organization, not the leaders

ran·sack /ˈrænsæk/ vt 1 search thoroughly and roughly 2 search and rob

ran·som /ˈrænsəm/ n money paid to free a prisoner ♦ vt free by paying a ransom

rant /rænt/ vi talk wildly and loudly ♦ n [U]

rap¹ /ræp/ n 1 quick light blow 2 **take the rap (for)** infml receive the punishment (for someone else's crime) 3 **beat the rap** avoid punishment ♦ v -pp- 1 vi/t strike quickly and lightly 2 vt say sharply and suddenly

rap² n [C;U] type of popular music in which the words are spoken to music with a steady beat ♦ vi ~**per** n

ra·pa·cious /rəˈpeɪʃəs/ adj fml taking all one can, esp. by force ~**ness**, –**pacity** /rəˈpæsəti/ n [U]

rape¹ /reɪp/ vt have sex with (someone) against their will ♦ n [C;U] 1 act of raping 2 spoiling **rapist** n

rape² n [U] plant grown for the oil produced from its seeds

rap·id /'ræpɪd/ adj fast ~ly adv ~ity /rə'pɪdəti/ n [U]

rapid-fire /ˌ··/ adj (of a gun) able to fire shots quickly one after the other: (fig.) rapid-fire jokes/questions

rap·ids /'ræpɪdz/ n [P] quickly flowing rocky part of a river

rap·port /ræ'pɔr, ræ'poor, rə-/ n [U] close agreement and understanding

rapt /ræpt/ adj giving one's whole mind: rapt attention

rap·ture /'ræptʃər/ n [U] fml great joy and delight **-turous** adj

rare¹ /rer/ adj uncommon ~ly adv not often ~ness n [U]

rare² adj (of meat) lightly cooked

rar·ing /'rerɪŋ/ adj very eager: We're raring to go.

rar·i·ty /'rerəti/ n 1 [U] being uncommon 2 [C] something uncommon

ras·cal /'ræskəl/ n 1 misbehaving child 2 dishonest person

rash¹ /ræʃ/ adj without thinking enough of the (possibly bad) results ~ly adv ~ness n [U]

rash² n red spots on the skin, caused by illness: He broke out in (= became covered in) a rash. | (fig.) a rash (= sudden large number) of complaints

rasp·ber·ry /'ræzˌbɛri/ n 1 red berry, often eaten 2 rude sound made by putting one's tongue out and blowing

rasp·y /'ræspi/ adj making a rough unpleasant sound: a raspy voice

ras·ta·fa·ri·an /ˌræstə'ferɪən◂/ also **ras·ta** /'ræstə/ — n (often cap.) follower of a religion from Jamaica ~**ism** n

rat /ræt/ n 1 animal like a large mouse 2 worthless disloyal person ♦ v **-tt-**

rat on phr vt infml act disloyally; BETRAY

ratch·et /'rætʃɪt/ n toothed wheel or bar that allows a part of a machine to move past it in one direction only

rate¹ /reɪt/ n 1 amount measured in relation to another: a death rate of 500 a year 2 payment fixed according to a standard scale 3 of the (numbered) quality: a first-rate performer 4 at any rate in any case 5 at this/that rate if events continue in the same way — see also FLAT RATE

rate² vt 1 have the stated opinion about 2 deserve 3 infml have a good opinion of: I really rate her as a singer.

rath·er /'ræðər/ predeterminer, adv 1 fml to some degree: a rather cold day 2 more willingly: I'd rather have tea than coffee. 3 more exactly: He's done it, or rather he says he has.

rat·i·fy /'rætəˌfaɪ/ vt approve (a formal agreement) and make it official **-fica·tion** /ˌrætəfə'keɪʃən/ n [U]

rat·ing /'reɪtɪŋ/ n statement of the quality of a thing in comparison to others of its kind: Buyers gave the new model a high rating. **ratings** n [P] list of the positions of popularity given to television shows

ra·ti·o /'reɪʃioʊ, 'reɪʃoʊ/ n **-os** way one amount is related to another: The ratio of adults to children was 4 to 1.

ra·tion /'ræʃən, 'reɪ-/ n amount of something allowed to one person for a period ♦ vt 1 limit (someone) to a fixed ration 2 limit and control (supplies) **rations** n [P] supplies of food

ra·tion·al /'ræʃənl/ adj 1 (of ideas and behavior) sensible 2 (of a person) able to reason ~ly adv ~ity /ˌræʃə'næləti/ n [U]

ra·tio·nale /ˌræʃə'næl/ n [C;U] reasons and principles on which a practice is based

ra·tion·al·ize /'ræʃənlˌaɪz, -nəˌlaɪz/ vi/t 1 give or claim a rational explanation for (esp. strange behavior) **-ization** /ˌræʃnələ'zeɪʃən/ n [C;U]

rat race /ˈ· ·/ n endless competition for success in business

rat·tle /'rætl/ v 1 vi/t (cause to) make continuous quick hard noises 2 vi move quickly while making these noises 3 vt make anxious or afraid ♦ n 1 [C] toy or other instrument that rattles 2 [S] rattling noise

rattle off phr vt repeat quickly and easily from memory

rattle on/away phr vi talk quickly and continuously

rattle through phr vt perform quickly

rattle·snake /'rætlˌsneɪk/ n poisonous North American snake that rattles its tail

rat·ty /'ræti/ adj untidy or in bad condition

rau·cous /'rɔkəs/ adj unpleasantly loud and rough ~ly adv ~ness n [U]

raunch·y /'rɔntʃi, 'rɑn-/ adj infml OBSCENE **-ily** adv **-iness** n [U]

rav·age /ˈrævɪdʒ/ vt **1** ruin and destroy **2** rob (an area) violently **ravages** n [P] destroying effects

rave¹ /reɪv/ vi **1** talk wildly as if crazy **2** talk with extreme admiration ♦ adj full of very eager praise: rave reviews in the papers **raving** adj, adv wildly (crazy)

rave² n event at which young people dance all night to loud music with a strong beat

ra·ven /ˈreɪvən/ n large black bird of the CROW family

rav·e·nous /ˈrævənəs/ adj very hungry ~**ly** adv

ra·vine /rəˈviːn/ n deep narrow valley with steep sides

rav·ish /ˈrævɪʃ/ vt fml **1** lit RAPE¹ **2** fill with delight ~**ing** adj very beautiful

raw /rɔː/ adj **1** not cooked **2** not yet treated for use: raw materials **3** not yet trained or experienced **4** (of skin) painful; sore **5** (of weather) cold and wet ~**ness** n [U]

raw deal /ˌ· ˈ·/ n unfair treatment

ray /reɪ/ n narrow beam of light or other force: (fig.) a ray (= small bit) of hope

ray·on /ˈreɪɒn/ n [U] silk-like material made from plant substances

raze /reɪz/ vt fml make (buildings, cities, etc.) flat

ra·zor /ˈreɪzə/ n sharp instrument for removing hair, esp. from a man's face

razz·ma·tazz /ˌræzməˈtæz◂/ n [U] infml noisy showy activity

Rd. written abbrev. for: Road

re /riː/ prep fml on the subject of; with regard to

-'re /ə/ short for: are: We're ready.

reach /riːtʃ/ v **1** vt arrive at **2** vi stretch out an arm or hand for some purpose **3** vi/t touch by doing this: It's too high; I can't reach it. **4** vt say by doing this: Reach me my hat. **5** vi/t stretch (as far as): The garden reaches down to the lake. **6** vt get a message to ♦ n **1** [S;U] distance one can reach **2** [C] part of a river

re·act /riˈækt/ vi **1** act or behave as a result **2** change when mixed with another substance

re·ac·tion /riˈækʃən/ n **1** [C;U] (way of) reacting **2** [S;U] change back to a former condition **3** [U] quality of being reactionary

re·ac·tion·a·ry /riˈækʃənˌeri/ n, adj (person) strongly opposed to change

re·ac·tor /riˈæktə/ n large machine that produces ENERGY from atoms

read /riːd/ v read /red/ **1** vi/t look at and understand (something printed or written): read a newspaper **2** vi/t say (written words) to others: Read me a story. **3** vi (of something written) have (the stated form or meaning) or give (the stated idea): The letter reads as follows . . . | Her letters always read well. **4** vt (of a measuring instrument) show **5** vt understand from things seen or felt: I can't read his moods very well. **6 read between the lines** find hidden meanings **7 take something as read** accept something as true without any need to consider it further ~**able** adj interesting or easy to read

read·er /ˈriːdə/ n **1** someone who reads **2** schoolbook for beginners ~**ship** n [S] number or type of READERS (1)

read·ing /ˈriːdɪŋ/ n **1** [U] act or practice of reading **2** [C] opinion about the meaning of something **3** [C] figure shown by a measuring instrument **4** [U] something to be read: It makes (= is) interesting reading. **5** [U] knowledge gained through books

read-only memory /ˌ· ˈ·· ˌ··/ n [U] ROM

read-out /ˈriːd-aʊt/ n [U] information produced from a computer in readable form

read·y /ˈredi/ adj **1** prepared and fit for use **2** willing **3** (of thoughts or other expressions) quick: a ready wit ♦ adv in advance: ready-made clothes ~**ily** adv **1** willingly **2** easily ~**iness** n [U]

ready-made /ˌ·· ˈ·◂/ adj ready to be used immediately: ready-made pie crust

re·a·gent /riˈeɪdʒənt/ n chemical that shows the presence of a particular substance

re·al /riːl/ adj **1** actually existing **2** complete: a real idiot **3 for real** serious(ly) ♦ adv very ~**ly** adv **1** in fact; truly **2** very **3** (shows interest, doubt, or displeasure)

real es·tate /ˈ·· ˌ·/ n [U] houses or land to be bought

re·a·lis·m /ˈriːəlɪzəm/ n [U] **1** accepting the way things really are in life **2** (in art and literature) showing things as they really are ~**list** n ~**listic** /ˌriːəˈlɪstɪk◂/ adj

re·al·i·ty /riˈæləti/ n **1** [U] real existence **2** [C;U] something or everything real **3 in reality** in fact

re·a·lize /ˈriːəlaɪz/ v **1** vi/t (come to) have full knowledge and understanding (of) **2**

vt make (a purpose, fear, etc.) real **3** *vt* be sold for –**lization** /ˌrɪələˈzeɪʃən/ *n* [U]

realm /relm/ *n* **1** *fml* kingdom **2** area of activity; world

real-time /ˈ· ·/ *adj* of or being very quick information handling by a computer

Real-tor /ˈrɪltə/ *n tdmk* person in the REAL ESTATE business who is a member of the National Association of Realtors

real-ty /ˈrɪlti/ *n* [U] REAL ESTATE

ream /rim/ *n* 500 pieces of paper

reams /rimz/ *n* [P] a lot of writing

reap /rip/ *vi/t* cut and gather (a crop of grain); (fig.) *He reaped* (= gained) *the benefit of all his hard work.* ~**er** *n* — see also GRIM REAPER

rear¹ /rɪr/ *n, adj* [U] **1** back (part) **2** bring up the rear be last

rear² *v* **1** *vt* care for until fully grown **2** *vi* rise upright on the back legs **3** *vt* raise (the head)

rear-end /ˌ· ˈ·◁/ *vt infml* hit the back of someone's car with another car

re·ar·range /ˌriəˈreɪndʒ/ *vt* change the position or order of

rear-view mir·ror /ˌrɪrvyu ˈmɪrə/ *n* mirror in a car used to see what is behind

rea·son¹ /ˈrizən/ *n* **1** [C;U] why something is or was done; cause **2** [U] power to think, understand, and form opinions **3** [U] healthy mind that is not crazy: *to lose one's reason* (= go crazy) **4** [U] good sense **5 stand to reason** be clear to all sensible people **6 within reason** not beyond sensible limits

reason² *v* **1** *vt* use one's REASON¹ (2) **2** *vt* give as an opinion based on REASON¹ (2) ~**ing** *n* [U] steps in thinking about or understanding something

reason with *phr vt* try to persuade by fair argument

rea·so·na·ble /ˈriznəbəl, -zən-/ *adj* **1** showing fairness or good sense **2** not expensive –**bly** *adv* **1** sensibly **2** quite: *in reasonably good health*

re·as·sure /ˌriəˈʃʊr/ *vt* comfort and make free from worry –**surance** *n* [C;U] –**suring** *adj*

re·bate /ˈribeɪt/ *n* official return of part of a payment

reb·el¹ /ˈrɛbəl/ *n* person who rebels

re·bel² /rɪˈbɛl/ *vi* -**ll**- oppose or fight against someone in control

re·bel·lion /rɪˈbɛlyən/ *n* [C;U] (act of) rebelling –**lious** *adj*

re·birth /ˌriˈbɝθ, ˈribɝθ/ *n* [S] *fml* renewal (RENEW) of life; change of spirit

re·bound /rɪˈbaʊnd/ *vi* fly back after hitting something ♦ /ˈribaʊnd/ *n* **on the rebound: a** while rebounding **b** while in an unsettled state of mind as a result of failure in a relationship

rebound on *phr vt* (of a bad action) harm (the doer)

re·buff /rɪˈbʌf/ *n* rough or cruel answer or refusal ♦ *vt*

re·buke /rɪˈbyuk/ *vi fml* speak to angrily and giving blame to ♦ *n*

re·but /rɪˈbʌt/ *vt fml* prove the falseness of ~**tal** *n* [C;U]

re·call /rɪˈkɔl/ *vt* **1** remember **2** send for or take back ♦ /rɪˈkɔl, ˈrikɔl/ *n* **1** [U] ability to remember **2** [S;U] call to return

re·cant /rɪˈkænt/ *vi/t fml* say publicly that one no longer holds (a religious or political opinion) ~**ation** /ˌrikænˈteɪʃən/ *n* [C;U]

re·cap /ˈrikæp, riˈkæp/ *vi/t* -**pp**- repeat (the chief points of something said) ♦ /ˈrikæp/

re·ca·pit·u·late /ˌrikəˈpɪtʃəleɪt/ *vi/t fml* recap –**lation** /ˌrikəpɪtʃəˈleɪʃən/ *n* [C;U]

re·cede /rɪˈsid/ *vi* move back or away

re·ceipt /rɪˈsit/ *n* **1** [C] written statement that one has received money **2** [U] *fml* receiving **receipts** *n* [P] money received from a business

re·ceive /rɪˈsiv/ *vt* **1** get; be given: *receive a letter/a nasty shock* **2** accept as a visitor or member **3** turn (radio waves) into sound or pictures –**ceived** *adj* generally accepted –**ceiver** *n* **1** part of a telephone that is held to the ear **2** radio or television set **3** official who looks after the affairs of a BANKRUPT person **4** person who buys and sells stolen property **5** football player in a position to catch a pass

re·cent /ˈrisənt/ *adj* that happened or started only a short time ago ~**ly** *adv* not long ago

re·cep·ta·cle /rɪˈsɛptəkəl/ *n fml* container

re·cep·tion /rɪˈsɛpʃən/ *n* **1** [C] welcome: *a friendly reception* **2** [C] large formal party **3** [U] place where visitors to a hotel or other large building are welcomed **4** [U] quality of radio or television signals ~**ist** *n* person who welcomes and deals with visitors to a hotel, office, etc.

re·cep·tive /rɪˈsɛptɪv/ *adj* willing to consider new ideas ~**ness**, –**tivity** /ˌrisɛpˈtɪvəti/ *n* [U]

re·cess /ˈriːsɛs, rɪˈsɛs/ n 1 pause for rest during a working period, esp. for school children 2 space in an inside wall for shelves, cupboards, etc. 3 secret inner place ♦ /rɪˈsɛs/ vt make or put into a RECESS (2)

re·ces·sion /rɪˈsɛʃən/ n 1 period of reduced business activity 2 act of receding (RECEDE)

re·charge /riːˈtʃɑːdʒ/ vt put a new supply of electricity into (a BATTERY) –able adj

re·ci·pe /ˈrɛsəpi/ n set of cooking instructions

re·cip·i·ent /rɪˈsɪpiənt/ n fml person who receives something

re·cip·ro·cal /rɪˈsɪprəkəl/ adj fml given and received in return; MUTUAL ~ly adv

re·cip·ro·cate /rɪˈsɪprəˌkeɪt/ vi/t fml give or do (something) in return –cation /rɪˌsɪprəˈkeɪʃən/ n [U]

re·cit·al /rɪˈsaɪtl/ n performance of music or poetry by one person or a small group

re·cite /rɪˈsaɪt/ v 1 vi/t say (something learned) aloud in public 2 vt fml give a detailed account or list of recitation /ˌrɛsəˈteɪʃən/ n [C;U]

reck·less /ˈrɛkləs/ adj not caring about danger ~ly adv ~ness n [U]

reck·on /ˈrɛkən/ vt 1 calculate; add up 2 consider; regard 3 guess; suppose ~ing n [U] 1 calculation 2 punishment: a day of reckoning

reckon with phr vt 1 take account of in one's plans 2 have to deal with 3 to be reckoned with to be taken seriously as a possible opponent, competitor, etc.

re·claim /rɪˈkleɪm/ vt 1 ask for the return of 2 make (land) fit for use reclamation /ˌrɛkləˈmeɪʃən/ n [U]

re·cline /rɪˈklaɪn/ vi fml lie back or down; rest recliner n chair that folds back

re·cluse /ˈrɛkluːs, rɪˈkluːs/ n someone who lives alone on purpose

rec·og·nize /ˈrɛkəɡnaɪz/ vt 1 know again (as someone or something one has met before) 2 accept as being legal or real 3 be prepared to admit 4 show official gratefulness for –nizable /ˈrɛkəɡnaɪzəbəl, ˌrɛkəɡˈnaɪ-/ adj –nition /ˌrɛkəɡˈnɪʃən/ n [U]

re·coil /rɪˈkɔɪl/ vi 1 move back suddenly in fear or dislike 2 (of a gun) spring back when fired ♦ /ˈriːkɔɪl, rɪˈkɔɪl/ n [S;U]

rec·ol·lect /ˌrɛkəˈlɛkt/ vi/t remember ~ion /-ˈlɛkʃən/ n [C;U] memory

rec·om·mend /ˌrɛkəˈmɛnd/ vt 1 praise as being good for a purpose 2 advise: I'd recommend caution. 3 (of a quality) to make (someone or something) attractive: A hotel with little to recommend it. ~ation /ˌrɛkəmənˈdeɪʃən, -mɛn-/ n [C;U]

rec·om·pense /ˈrɛkəmˌpɛns/ n [S;U] fml reward or payment for trouble or suffering ♦ vt fml give recompense to

rec·on·cile /ˈrɛkənˌsaɪl/ vt 1 make friendly again 2 find agreement between (2 opposing things) –ciliation /ˌrɛkənˌsɪliˈeɪʃən/ n [U]

reconcile to phr vt cause (someone) to accept (something unpleasant)

re·con·di·tion /ˌriːkənˈdɪʃən/ vt repair and bring back into working order: a reconditioned engine

re·con·nais·sance /rɪˈkɒnəsəns, -zəns/ n [C;U] (act of) reconnoitering

re·con·noi·ter /ˌriːkəˈnɔɪtə, ˌrɛ-/ vi/t go near (the place where an enemy is) to find out information

re·con·sid·er /ˌriːkənˈsɪdə/ vi/t think again and change one's mind (about)

re·con·struc·tion /ˌriːkənˈstrʌkʃən/ n 1 [C] repeating of events in a crime, etc., to find new information 2 [U] (cap.) period in American history after the Civil War

re·cord¹ /rɪˈkɔːd/ v 1 vt write down so that it will be known 2 vi/t preserve (sound or a television show) so that it can be heard or seen again 3 vt (of an instrument) show by measuring

rec·ord² /ˈrɛkəd/ n 1 written statement of facts, events, etc. 2 known facts about past behavior: his criminal record 3 best yet done: the world record for the long jump 4 circular piece of plastic on which sound is stored for playing back 5 for the record to be reported as official 6 off the record unofficial(ly) 7 on the record: a (of facts or events) (ever) recorded: the coldest winter on record b (of a person) having publicly said, as if for written records ♦ adj better, faster, etc., than ever before: finished in record time

re·cord·er /rɪˈkɔːdə/ n 1 simple musical instrument played by blowing 2 TAPE RECORDER

re·cord·ing /rɪˈkɔːdɪŋ/ n recorded performance, speech, or piece of music

record play·er /ˈ·· ˌ·/ n machine for producing sounds from RECORDS² (4)

re·count[1] /ˌriːˈkaʊnt/ vt count (esp. votes) again ♦ /ˈriːkaʊnt/ n

re·count[2] /rɪˈkaʊnt/ vt fml tell

re·coup /rɪˈkuːp/ vt get back (something lost, esp. money)

re·course /ˈriːkɔːrs, -koʊrs, rɪˈkɔːrs, rɪˈkoʊrs/ n **have recourse to** fml make use of

re·cov·er /rɪˈkʌvər/ v **1** vt get back (something lost or taken away) **2** vi return to the proper state of health, strength, ability, etc. ~**able** adj ~**y** n [U]

rec·re·a·tion /ˌrekriˈeɪʃən/ n [C;U] (form of) amusement; way of spending free time ~**al** adj

recreation room /ˌ···ˈ·ˌ·/ n also **rec room** — room in the house esp. for games

recreation ve·hi·cle /ˌ···ˈ·ˌ···/ n RV

re·crim·i·na·tion /rɪˌkrɪməˈneɪʃən/ n [C;U] (act of) quarreling and blaming one another

re·cruit /rɪˈkruːt/ n new member of an organization, esp. the army, navy, etc. ♦ vi/t get recruits ~**ment** n [U]

rec·tan·gle /ˈrektɪˌtæŋɡəl/ n flat shape with four straight sides forming four 90° angles –**gular** /rekˈtæŋɡyələr/ adj

rec·ti·fy /ˈrektɪˌfaɪ/ vt fml put right

rec·tum /ˈrektəm/ n med lowest end of the bowel, where food waste passes out

re·cu·per·ate /rɪˈkuːpəˌreɪt/ vi get well again after illness –**rating** adj helping one to recuperate –**ration** /rɪˌkuːpəˈreɪʃən/ n [U]

re·cur /rɪˈkər/ vi **-rr-** happen again –**currence** /rɪˈkərəns, -ˈkɑːr-/ n [C;U]: frequent recurrence of the fever –**current** adj

re·cy·cle /ˌriːˈsaɪkəl/ vt treat (a used substance) so that it is fit to use again –**clable** adj

red /red/ adj **-dd-** **1** of the color of blood **2** (of hair) brownish orange **3** (of skin) pink **4** (cap.) infml COMMUNIST **5** **see red** become angry suddenly and lose control of oneself ♦ n **1** [C;U] red color **2** [U] red clothes **3** **in the red** in debt **4** infml a COMMUNIST ~**den** vi/t make or become red

red car·pet /ˌ· ˈ··/ n [S] special ceremonial welcome to a guest

Red Cres·cent /ˌ· ˈ··/ n [the] part of the RED CROSS working in Muslim countries

Red Cross /ˌ· ˈ·/ n [the] international organization that looks after the sick and wounded

re·deem /rɪˈdiːm/ vt **1** buy back (something given for money lent) **2** fml make (something bad) slightly less bad **3** fml fulfill (a promise, etc.)

re·demp·tion /rɪˈdempʃən/ n [U] redeeming

re·de·ploy /ˌriːdɪˈplɔɪ/ vt rearrange (soldiers, workers in industry, etc.) in a more effective way ~**ment** n

re·de·vel·op /ˌriːdɪˈveləp/ vt make an area more modern by replacing or repairing buildings ~**ment** n [U]

red-eye /ˈ· ˌ/ n [S] airplane flight that starts late at night and arrives early in the morning

red-hand·ed /ˌ· ˈ··◂/ adj in the act of doing wrong

red·head /ˈredhed/ n person with RED (2) hair

red her·ring /ˌ· ˈ··/ n something introduced to draw people's attention away from the main point

red-hot /ˌ· ˈ·◂/ adj so hot that it shines red: (fig.) red-hot enthusiasm

re·di·rect /ˌriːdɪˈrekt, -daɪ-/ vt send something in a different direction, or use something for a different purpose

red-let·ter day /ˌ· ˈ··ˌ·/ n specially good day

red-light dis·trict /ˌ· ˈ· ˌ··/ n area where PROSTITUTES work

red meat /ˌ· ˈ·/ n [U] dark-colored meat, e.g. BEEF

red·neck /ˈrednek/ n derog person who lives in the country, esp. one who is uneducated and has strong, unreasonable opinions

re·doub·le /rɪˈdʌbəl/ vi/t increase greatly

re·doubt /rɪˈdaʊt/ n fml small fort

re·doub·ta·ble /rɪˈdaʊtəbəl/ adj greatly respected and feared

re·dress /rɪˈdres/ vt fml **1** put right (a wrong, injustice, etc.) **2** **redress the balance** make things equal again ♦ /ˈrɪdres, rɪˈdres/ n [U] something, such as money, that puts right a wrong

red tape /ˌ· ˈ·/ n [U] silly, detailed unnecessary rules

re·duce /rɪˈduːs/ vt **1** make less **2** (of a person) lose weight on purpose –**duction** /rɪˈdʌkʃən/ n [C;U]: price reductions

reduce to phr vt **1** bring to (a less favorable state): The child was reduced to

refrigerate

tears. (= made to cry) **2** bring (something) to (a smaller number or amount)

re·dun·dant /rɪˈdʌndənt/ *adj* **1** unnecessarily repeating **2** no longer needed **–dancy** *n* [C;U]

red·wood /ˈredwʊd/ *n* extremely tall American CONIFEROUS tree

reed /riːd/ *n* **1** grasslike plant growing in wet places **2** thin piece of wood or metal in certain musical instruments, blown across to produce sound **~y** *adj* **1** full of reeds **2** (of a sound) thin and high

reef /riːf/ *n* line of sharp rocks or CORAL at or near the surface of the sea

reek /riːk/ *vi, n* (have) a strong unpleasant smell

reel[1] /riːl/ *n* **1** round object on which film, fishing line, etc., can be wound **2** length of time it takes to show this amount of film ♦ *vt* bring, take, etc., by winding

   reel off *phr vt* say quickly and easily from memory

reel[2] *vi* **1** walk in an unsteady way as if drunk **2** be shocked or confused **3** seem to go around and around

re·e·lect /ˌriːɪˈlekt/ *vt* elect again **~tion** /-ˈlekʃən/ *n* [U]

re·en·act /ˌriːɪˈnækt/ *vt* perform actions of a drama, crime, etc., that happened in the past **~ment** *n*

re·en·try /riːˈentri/ *n* [C;U] entering again, esp. into the Earth's ATMOSPHERE

ref /ref/ *n infml for* REFEREE (1)

re·fer /rɪˈfɜː/ *v* **-rr-**

   refer to *phr vt* **1** mention; speak about **2** be about or directed towards **3** look at for information **4** send to (a person or place) for information, a decision, etc.

ref·er·ee /ˌrefəˈriː/ *n* **1** person in charge of a game **2** person who gives a REFERENCE (3)

ref·er·ence /ˈrefrəns/ *n* **1** [C;U] (act of) mentioning **2** [C;U] (act of) looking at something for information **3** [C] **a** information about someone's character and ability, esp. when they are looking for a job **b** person who gives such information **4 in/with reference to** *fml* about **reference book** /ˈ···· ·/ *n* book for finding information

ref·e·ren·dum /ˌrefəˈrendəm/ *n* **-da** /-də/ *or* **-dums** direct vote by all the people to decide something

re·fill /riːˈfɪl/ *vt* fill again ♦ /ˈriːfɪl/ *n* **1** container filled with a substance to REFILL something **2** another drink to REFILL one's glass

re·fine /rɪˈfaɪn/ *vt* make pure **–refined** *adj* **1** made pure **2** showing education, delicateness of feeling, and good manners **~ment** *n* **1** [C] clever addition or improvement **2** [U] act of refining **3** [U] quality of being refined

re·fin·e·ry /rɪˈfaɪnəri/ *n* place where oil, sugar, etc., is refined

re·fi·nance /ˌriːˈfaɪnæns, -fɪˈnæns/ *vt* borrow or lend money so as to change the way a debt is paid

re·flect /rɪˈflekt/ *v* **1** *vt* throw back (heat, sound, or an image) **2** *vt* give an idea of; express **3** *vi* think carefully **~ive** *adj* thoughtful **~or** *n*

   reflect on *phr vt* **1** consider carefully **2** cause to be considered in a particular way

re·flec·tion /rɪˈflekʃən/ *n* **1** [C] reflected image **2** [U] reflecting of heat, sound, etc. **3** [C;U] deep and careful thought

re·flex /ˈriːfleks/ *n* unintentional movement made in reply to an outside influence: *quick/slow reflexes*

re·flex·ive /rɪˈfleksɪv/ *n, adj* (word) showing effect on oneself: *In "I enjoyed myself," "enjoy" is a reflexive verb.*

re·form /rɪˈfɔːm/ *vi/t* make or become (morally) right; improve ♦ *n* [C;U] action to improve conditions, remove unfairness, etc. **~er** *n*

re-form /ˌriːˈfɔːm/ *vi/t* (cause to) form again, esp. into ranks

ref·or·ma·tion /ˌrefəˈmeɪʃən/ *n* [U] **1** (moral) improvement **2** (*cap.*) religious movement of the 16th century leading to the establishment of Protestant churches

reform school /·ˈ· ·/ *also* **reformatory** /rɪˈfɔːmətəri, -ˌtɔːri/ — *n* special school for children who have broken the law

re·fract /rɪˈfrækt/ *vt* bend (light passing through) **~ion** /-ˈfrækʃən/ *n* [U]

re·frain[1] /rɪˈfreɪn/ *vi fml* not do something: *refrain from smoking*

refrain[2] *n* part of a song that is repeated

re·fresh /rɪˈfreʃ/ *vt* **1** cause to feel fresh or active again **2 refresh one's memory** help oneself to remember again **~ing** *adj* **1** producing comfort and new strength **2** pleasingly new and interesting **~ment** *n* [U] **~ments** *n* [P] food and drink

re·fri·ge·rate /rɪˈfrɪdʒəreɪt/ *vt* make (food, drink, etc.) cold to preserve it **–ration** /rɪˌfrɪdʒəˈreɪʃən/ *n* [U]

re·fri·ge·ra·tor /rɪˈfrɪdʒəˌreɪtə/ n electric box where food is kept cold

re·fuel /riˈfjuːl/ vi/t fill (a vehicle, plane, etc.) with more fuel before continuing on a trip

ref·uge /ˈrɛfjuːdʒ/ n [C;U] (place providing) protection or shelter

ref·u·gee /ˌrɛfjʊˈdʒiː◂, ˈrɛfjʊˌdʒiː/ n person forced to leave their country because of (political) danger

re·fund /ˈriːfʌnd/ n repayment ♦ /rɪˈfʌnd/ vt pay (money) back

re·fur·bish /ˌriːˈfɜːbɪʃ/ vt make fit for use again

re·fus·al /rɪˈfjuːzəl/ n [C;U] (a case of) refusing

re·fuse¹ /rɪˈfjuːz/ vi/t not accept, do, or give: *She refused my offer.*

ref·use² /ˈrɛfjuːs/ n [U] waste material; GARBAGE

re·fute /rɪˈfjuːt/ vt fml prove that (someone or something) is mistaken **refutation** /ˌrɛfjʊˈteɪʃən/ n [C;U]

re·gain /rɪˈɡeɪn/ vt get or win back

re·gal /ˈriːɡəl/ adj fml like a king or queen; very splendid **~ly** adv

re·gale /rɪˈɡeɪl/ v **regale with** phr vt entertain with

re·ga·lia /rɪˈɡeɪliə/ n [U] ceremonial clothes and decorations

re·gard¹ /rɪˈɡɑːd/ vt 1 look at or consider in the stated way: *I regard him as the finest lawyer in the country.* 2 fml pay respectful attention to **~ing** prep fml in connection with

regard² n [U] 1 respect 2 respectful attention; concern 3 **in/with regard to** in connection with **~less** adv 1 whatever may happen 2 expressing disregard for: *without worrying about* **regards** n [P] good wishes

re·gat·ta /rɪˈɡætə, -ˈɡæ-/ n meeting for boat races

re·gen·e·rate /rɪˈdʒɛnəˌreɪt/ vi/t grow again **–ration** /rɪˌdʒɛnəˈreɪʃən/ n [U]

re·gent /ˈriːdʒənt/ n member of a governing board of a state university

reg·gae /ˈrɛɡeɪ/ n [U] Jamaican popular dance and music

re·gime /reɪˈʒiːm, rɪ-/ n 1 (system of) government 2 regimen

re·gi·men /ˈrɛdʒəmən/ n fml fixed plan of food, exercise, etc., to improve health

re·gi·ment /ˈrɛdʒəmənt/ n large military group ♦ /-mɛnt/ vt control too firmly **~al** /ˌrɛdʒəˈmɛntl◂/ adj

re·gion /ˈriːdʒən/ n 1 quite large area or part 2 **in the region of** about **~al** adj

re·gis·ter¹ /ˈrɛdʒəstə/ n 1 (book containing) a record or list 2 range of the voice or a musical instrument 3 words, style, etc., used by speakers and writers in particular conditions

register² v 1 vt put into a REGISTER¹ (1) 2 vi put one's name on a list, esp. of those who will take part 3 vt (of a measuring instrument) show 4 vt (of a person or face) express 5 vt send by registered mail 6 vi have an effect (on a person)

registered mail /ˌ··· ˈ·/ n [U] system for mailing valuable things, which protects the sender against loss

re·gis·trar /ˈrɛdʒəˌstrɑː/ n 1 keeper of official records 2 official at a college who keeps student records and sends out GRADES and official papers

re·gis·tra·tion /ˌrɛdʒəˈstreɪʃən/ n [U] registering (REGISTER² (2))

re·gress /rɪˈɡrɛs/ vi fml go back to a former and usu. worse condition, way of behaving, etc. **~ion** /-ˈɡrɛʃən/ n [U]

re·gret¹ /rɪˈɡrɛt/ v -tt- be sorry about: *I've never regretted my decision to leave.* **~table** adj that one should regret **~tably** adv

regret² n [C;U] unhappiness at the loss of something, because of something one has done or not done, etc. **~ful** adj

re·group /ˌriːˈɡruːp/ vi/t form into new groups

reg·u·lar /ˈrɛɡjələ/ adj 1 usual or customary 2 not varying: *a regular pulse* | *a regular customer* 3 happening (almost) every time: *regular church attendance* 4 correct or usual 5 evenly shaped 6 employed continuously: *a regular soldier* 7 gram following the standard pattern: *regular verbs* 8 infml complete; thorough 9 pleasant and honest: *a regular guy* ♦ n regular visitor, customer, etc. **~ly** adv at regular times **~ize** vt make lawful **–larity** /ˌrɛɡjəˈlærəti/ n [U]

reg·u·late /ˈrɛɡjəˌleɪt/ vt 1 control, esp. by rules 2 make (a machine) work in a certain way **–latory** /-ləˌtɔːri, -ˌtoʊri/ adj fml having the purpose of regulating

reg·u·la·tion /ˌrɛɡjəˈleɪʃən/ n 1 [C] (official) rule 2 [U] control

re·gur·gi·tate /rɪˈɡɜːdʒəˌteɪt/ vt fml 1 bring back (swallowed food) through the mouth 2 repeat (something heard or read) in one's own work, without thought or change

re·hab /ˈriːhæb/ *vt infml* rehabilitate (1)

re·ha·bil·i·tate /ˌriːhəˈbɪləteɪt, ˌriːə-/ *vt* **1** make able to live an ordinary life again **2** put back into good condition **3** put back to a former high rank, position, etc. –**tation** /ˌriːhəˌbɪləˈteɪʃən, ˌriːə-/ *n* [U]

re·hash /ˈriːhæʃ/ *vt* use (old ideas) again **rehash** /ˈriːhæʃ/ *n*

re·hearse /rɪˈhɜːs/ *vi/t* practice for later performance **rehearsal** *n* [C;U]

reign /reɪn/ *n* period of reigning ♦ *vi* **1** be the king or queen **2** exist (noticeably): *Silence reigned.*

reign of ter·ror /ˌ· ·ˈ··/ *n* period of widespread official killing

re·im·burse /ˌriːɪmˈbɜːs/ *vt* pay (money) back to ~**ment** *n* [C;U]

rein /reɪn/ *n* **1** also **reins** *pl.* — long narrow (leather) band for controlling a horse **2** give (free) rein to give freedom to (feelings or desires) **3** keep a tight rein on control firmly — see also FREE REIN **reins** *n* [P] means of control: *take the reins* (= become the leader)

re·in·car·nate /ˌriːɪnˈkɑːneɪt/ *vt* cause to return to life in a new form after death –**nation** /ˌriːɪnkɑːˈneɪʃən/ *n* [C;U]

rein·deer /ˈreɪndɪr/ *n* reindeer large deer from northern parts of the world

re·in·force /ˌriːɪnˈfɔːs, -ˈfoəs/ *vt* strengthen with additions ~**ment** *n* [U] ~**ments** *n* [P] more soldiers sent to reinforce an army

reinforced con·crete /ˌ··· ·ˈ··/ *n* [U] CONCRETE strengthened by metal bars

re·in·state /ˌriːɪnˈsteɪt/ *vt* put back into a position formerly held ~**ment** *n* [C;U]

re·in·vent /ˌriːɪnˈvent/ **1** *vt* produce an idea, method, etc., based on something that existed in the past, but is slightly different **2 reinvent the wheel** waste time trying to find a way of doing something, when someone else has already discovered the best way to do it

re·it·er·ate /riˈɪtəreɪt/ *vt fml* repeat several times –**ration** /riˌɪtəˈreɪʃən/ *n* [C;U]

re·ject /rɪˈdʒekt/ *vt* refuse to accept ♦ /ˈriːdʒekt/ *n* something thrown away as useless or imperfect ~**ion** /rɪˈdʒekʃən/ *n* [C;U]

re·joice /rɪˈdʒɔɪs/ *vi* feel or show great joy **rejoicing** *n* [C;U] (public) show of joy

re·join[1] /ˌriːˈdʒɔɪn/ *vi/t* join again

re·join[2] /rɪˈdʒɔɪn/ *vt* answer, esp. angrily

re·join·der /rɪˈdʒɔɪndə/ *n* (rude) answer

re·ju·ve·nate /rɪˈdʒuːvəneɪt/ *vt* make young again –**nation** /rɪˌdʒuːvəˈneɪʃən/ *n* [U]

re·kin·dle /riːˈkɪndl/ *vt* make someone have a particular feeling, thought, etc., again: *rekindle an old romance*

re·lapse /rɪˈlæps/ *vi* return to a bad state of health or way of life **relapse** /rɪˈlæps, ˈriːlæps/

re·late /rɪˈleɪt/ *vt* **1** see or show a connection between **2** *fml* tell (a story) **related** *adj* of the same family or kind; connected

relate to *phr vt* **1** connect (one thing) with (another) **2** *infml* understand and accept

re·la·tion /rɪˈleɪʃən/ *n* **1** [C] member of one's family **2** [C;U] connection **3 in/with relation to** *fml* with regard to ~**ship** *n* [C] friendship or connection between people **2** [C;U] connection **relations** *n* [P] dealings between (and feelings towards) each other

rel·a·tive /ˈrelətɪv/ *n* RELATION (1) ♦ *adj* compared to each other or something else: *now living in relative comfort* ~**ly** *adv* quite

relative clause /ˌ··· ·ˈ·/ *n* CLAUSE joined on by a RELATIVE PRONOUN

relative pro·noun /ˌ··· ·ˈ··/ *n* PRONOUN which joins a CLAUSE to the rest of a sentence, such as *who*, *which*, or *that*

rel·a·tiv·i·ty /ˌreləˈtɪvəti/ *n* [U] relationship between time, ENERGY, and mass, said to change with increased speed

re·lax /rɪˈlæks/ *vi/t* make or become a less active and worried **b** less stiff, tight, or severe ~**ation** /ˌriːlækˈseɪʃən/ *n* **1** [C;U] (something done for) rest and amusement **2** [U] act of making or becoming less severe

re·lay /ˈriːleɪ/ *n* [C;U] **1** group that takes the place of another to keep work going continuously: *In a **relay (race)**, each member of each team runs part of the distance.* **2** (broadcast sent out by) an electrical connection for receiving and passing on signals

re·lease /rɪˈliːs/ *vt* **1** set free **2** allow to be seen or read publicly **3** press (a handle) so as to let something go ♦ *n* **1** [S;U] setting free **2** [C] new film, record, or piece of information that has been released

re·lent /rɪ'lɛnt/ *vi* become less cruel or severe **~less** *adj* continuously cruel or severe

rel·e·vant /'rɛləvənt/ *adj* directly connected with the subject **~ly** *adv* **–vance** *n* [U]

re·li·a·ble /rɪ'laɪəbəl/ *adj* that may be trusted **–ably** *adv* **–ability** /rɪ,laɪə'bɪləti/ *n* [U]

re·li·ant /rɪ'laɪənt/ *adj* dependent (on) **–ance** *n* [U] **1** dependence **2** trust

rel·ic /'rɛlɪk/ *n* **1** something old that reminds us of the past **2** part of something that belonged to a dead holy person

re·lief /rɪ'liːf/ *n* **1** [S;U] comfort at the ending of anxiety, pain, or dullness **2** [U] help for people in trouble **3** [C] person who takes over another's duty **4** [C;U] decoration that stands out above the rest of the surface it is on **5** [U] part of one's income on which one does not have to pay tax **6** **light relief** pleasant and amusing change

relief map /·' ·/ *n* map showing the height of land

re·lieve /rɪ'liːv/ *vt* **1** lessen (pain or trouble) **2** take over duties from **3** give variety or interest to **4** **relieve oneself** urinate (URINE) or empty the bowels **relieved** *adj* no longer worried

relieve of *phr vt* free from

re·li·gion /rɪ'lɪdʒən/ *n* [C;U] (system of) belief in and worship of one or more gods

re·li·gious /rɪ'lɪdʒəs/ *adj* **1** of religion **2** obeying the rules of a religion **3** performing the stated duties very carefully **~ly** *adv* regularly

re·lin·quish /rɪ'lɪŋkwɪʃ/ *vt fml for*: GIVE UP (5)

rel·ish /'rɛlɪʃ/ *n* [U] **1** great enjoyment **2** substance eaten with meat, to add taste ♦ *vt* enjoy

re·live /,riː'lɪv/ *vt* experience again in the imagination

re·lo·cate /,riː'ləʊˌkeɪt, ,riːləʊ'keɪt/ *vi/t* move to a new place

re·luc·tant /rɪ'lʌktənt/ *adj* unwilling **~ly** *adv* **–tance** *n* [U]

re·ly /rɪ'laɪ/ *v* **rely on** *phr vt* **1** trust **2** depend on

re·main /rɪ'meɪn/ *v* **1** *vi* stay or be left behind after others have gone **2** continue to be: *remain calm* ♦ *a prisoner* **remains** *n* [P] **1** parts which are left **2** *fml* dead body

re·main·der /rɪ'meɪndə/ *n* what is left over

re·mark /rɪ'mɑːk/ *n* spoken or written opinion ♦ *vt* say

remark on *phr vt fml* mention

re·mar·ka·ble /rɪ'mɑːkəbəl/ *adj* unusual or noticeable **–bly** *adv*

re·mar·ry /rɪ'mæri/ *vi/t* marry again, or marry a different person

re·me·di·al /rɪ'miːdiəl/ *adj* **1** providing a remedy **2** intended to improve one's skill in a particular field: *remedial math*

rem·e·dy /'rɛmədi/ *n* [C;U] way of curing something ♦ *vt* put (something bad) right

re·mem·ber /rɪ'mɛmbə/ *v* **1** *vt* call back into the mind **2** *vi/t* take care not to forget **3** *vt* give money or a present to

remember to *phr vt* send greetings from (someone) to: *Remember me to your wife.*

re·mem·brance /rɪ'mɛmbrəns/ *n* [U] **1** act of remembering **2** something given or kept to remind one

re·mind /rɪ'maɪnd/ *vt* cause to remember **~er** *n* something to make one remember

remind of *phr vt* cause to remember by seeing the same

rem·i·nisce /,rɛmə'nɪs/ *vi* talk pleasantly about the past **–niscence** *n* [U] **–niscences** *n* [P] written or spoken account of one's past life **–niscent** *adj* that reminds one (of); like

re·miss /rɪ'mɪs/ *adj fml* careless about a duty

re·mis·sion /rɪ'mɪʃən/ *n* [C;U] **1** lessening of the time someone has to stay in prison **2** *fml* period when an illness is less severe

re·mit /rɪ'mɪt/ *vt* **-tt-** *fml* **1** send (money) by mail **2** free someone from (a debt or punishment) **~tance** *n* **1** [C] money remitted **2** [U] *fml* act of remitting money

rem·nant /'rɛmnənt/ *n* **1** part that remains **2** end of a roll of cloth, sold cheaply

re·mod·el /,riː'mɒdl/ *vt* repair, improve (esp. a house)

rem·on·strate /'rɛmənˌstreɪt, rɪ'mɒnˌstreɪt/ *vi fml* express disapproval

re·morse /rɪˈmɔːs/ n [U] sorrow for having done wrong ~**ful** adj ~**less** adj 1 showing no remorse 2 threatening and not able to be stopped

re·mote /rɪˈməʊt/ adj 1 far distant in space or time 2 quiet and lonely: *a remote village* 3 widely separated; not close: *a remote connection* 4 slight: *a remote chance of success* 5 not showing interest in others ~**ly** adv at all: *not remotely interested* ~**ness** n [U]

remote con·trol /ˌ·· ·ˈ·/ n 1 *also* **remote** — [C] apparatus used to control a television, STEREO, etc., from a distance 2 controlling machinery by radio signals

re·move /rɪˈmuːv/ vt 1 take away; get rid of 2 move ♦ n stage; degree: *Their action was only (at) one removed from* (= was nearly) *revolution.* **removable** adj **removal** n [C;U] ~**mover** n [C;U]

re·mu·ne·rate /rɪˈmjuːnəreɪt/ vt fml pay ~**rative** /-ˈreɪtɪv, -rətɪv/ adj well paid ~**ration** /rɪˌmjuːnəˈreɪʃən/ n [S;U]

re·nais·sance /ˌrenəˈsɑːns◄, -ˈzɑːns◄/ n rebirth of interest in art, literature, etc., esp. (*cap.*) in Europe between the 14th and 17th centuries

Renaissance man /ˌ··· ˈ·/ n man with many skills and deep knowledge

rename /rɪˈneɪm/ vt change the name of

ren·der /ˈrendə/ vt fml 1 cause to be 2 give 3 perform ~**ing** *also* **rendition** /renˈdɪʃən/ — n performance

ren·dez·vous /ˈrɒndeɪvuː, -deɪ-/ n ~**vous** /-ˌvuːz/ 1 (arrangement for) a meeting 2 meeting place ♦ vi meet by arrangement

ren·e·gade /ˈrenəgeɪd/ n person who disloyally leaves one country or belief to join another

re·nege /rɪˈniːg, rɪˈneg/ vi fml break a promise

re·new /rɪˈnuː/ vt 1 repeat: *They renewed their attack.* 2 give new life and freshness to 3 get something new of the same kind to take the place of: *renew a driver's license* ~**al** n [C;U]

re·new·a·ble /rɪˈnuːəbəl/ adj 1 able to be replaced by natural processes: *renewable resources* 2 (of contracts, tickets, etc.) able to be made to continue after the date when it is supposed to end

re·nounce /rɪˈnaʊns/ vt say formally that one does not own or has no more connection with

ren·o·vate /ˈrenəveɪt/ vt put back into good condition ~**vation** /ˌrenəˈveɪʃən/ n [C;U]

re·nown /rɪˈnaʊn/ n [U] fame ~**ed** adj famous

rent[1] /rent/ n [C;U] money paid regularly for the use of a house, garage, etc. ♦ vt 1 pay rent for the use of 2 allow to be used in return for rent ~**al** sum of money fixed to be paid as rent

rent[2] n large tear

rent con·trol /ˈ· ·ˌ·/ n [U] use of laws to limit the price of rented apartments

re·nun·ci·a·tion /rɪˌnʌnsiˈeɪʃən/ n [C;U] (act of) renouncing (RENOUNCE) something

re·or·gan·ize /riːˈɔːgənaɪz/ vi/t ORGANIZE in a new and better way ~**ization** /riːˌɔːgənəˈzeɪʃən/ n [C;U]

rep[1] /rep/ n infml for SALES REPRESENTATIVE

rep[2] n [C;U] REPERTORY (company)

Rep. written abbrev. for: REPUBLICAN

re·pair /rɪˈpeə/ vt mend ♦ n 1 [C;U] (act or result of) mending 2 [U] condition: *in good repair* **repairs** n [P] work done on roads to make them smoother

rep·a·ra·tion /ˌrepəˈreɪʃən/ n [C;U] fml repayment for loss or damage

rep·ar·tee /ˌrepɑːˈtiː, -ˈteɪ, ˌrepɑː-/ n [U] quick amusing talk

re·pat·ri·ate /riːˈpætrieɪt/ vt send (someone) back to their own country ~**ation** /riːˌpætriˈeɪʃən/ n [U]

re·pay /rɪˈpeɪ/ vt repaid /-ˈpeɪd/ 1 pay (money) back to (someone) 2 reward ~**ment** n [C;U]

re·peal /rɪˈpiːl/ vt end (a law)

re·peat /rɪˈpiːt/ vt 1 say or do again 2 repeat oneself keep saying the same thing ♦ n 1 musical passage played a second time 2 performance broadcast a second time ~**ed** adj done again and again ~**edly** adv

re·pel /rɪˈpel/ vt -ll- 1 drive away (as if) by force 2 cause feelings of extreme dislike in ~**lent** adj extremely nasty ~**lent** n [C;U] substance that repels esp. insects

re·pent /rɪˈpent/ vi/t fml be sorry for (wrongdoing) ~**ant** adj ~**ance** n [U]

re·per·cus·sion /ˌriːpəˈkʌʃən/ n effect felt over a wide area

rep·er·toire /ˈrepətwɑː/ n set of things one can perform

rep·er·to·ry /ˈrepətɔːri, -ˌtoʊri/ n [U] performing several plays one after the other on different days with the same actors

rep·e·ti·tion /ˌrepəˈtɪʃən/ n [C;U] repeating **-tious, -tive** /rɪˈpetətɪv/ adj containing parts that are repeated too much

re·phrase /riːˈfreɪz/ vt put into different (clearer) words

re·place /rɪˈpleɪs/ vt 1 put back in the right place 2 take the place of 3 get another (better) one instead of **~ment** n 1 [U] act of replacing 2 [C] that which replaces someone or something

re·play /ˈriːpleɪ/ n [C;U] action in a sports game shown again immediately on television

re·plen·ish /rɪˈplenɪʃ/ vt fill up again

re·plete /rɪˈpliːt/ adj fml very full **-pletion** /-ˈpliːʃən/ n [U]

rep·li·ca /ˈreplɪkə/ n close copy

rep·li·cate /ˈreplɪkeɪt/ vt fml copy exactly

re·ply /rɪˈplaɪ/ vi, n answer

re·port[1] /rɪˈpɔːt/ n 1 [C] account of events, business affairs, etc. 2 [C;U] what is said generally but unofficially 3 [C] noise of an explosion

report[2] v 1 vi/t provide information (about); give an account of, esp. for a newspaper or radio or television 2 vi go somewhere and say that one is there (and ready for work) 3 vt make a complaint about **~er** n person who reports news

report card /ˈ· ˌ·/ n periodic written report of a child's behavior and work at school

re·port·ed·ly /rɪˈpɔːtɪdli/ adv according to what is said

reported speech /·ˌ· ˈ·/ n [U] INDIRECT SPEECH

re·pos·i·to·ry /rɪˈpɑzəˌtɔri, -ˌtoʊri/ n place where things are stored

re·pos·sess /ˌriːpəˈzes/ vt take back, esp. when rent has not been paid **~ion** /-ˈzeʃən/ n [C;U]

rep·re·hen·si·ble /ˌreprɪˈhensəbəl/ adj fml deserving blame; bad **-bly** adv

rep·re·sent /ˌreprɪˈzent/ v 1 vt act or speak officially for (someone else) 2 vt be a picture or STATUE of; show 3 vt be a sign of; stand for 4 be: This represents a considerable improvement. **~ation** /ˌreprɪzenˈteɪʃən, -zən-/ n 1 [U] act of representing or state of being represented 2 [C] something that REPRESENTS (2,3) something else

rep·re·sen·ta·tive /ˌreprɪˈzentətɪv/ adj 1 typical 2 (of government) in which the people and their opinions are represented ♦ n person who REPRESENTS (1) others, esp. in Congress — see also HOUSE OF REPRESENTATIVES

re·press /rɪˈpres/ vt control; hold back **~ive** adj hard and cruel **~ion** /-ˈpreʃən/ n [U] pushing unwelcome feelings into one's unconscious mind, with odd effects on behavior

re·prieve /rɪˈpriːv/ vt give a reprieve to ♦ n official order not to carry out the punishment of death (yet)

rep·ri·mand /ˈreprəˌmænd/ vt express severe official disapproval of **reprimand** n

re·pri·sal /rɪˈpraɪzəl/ n [C;U] (act of) punishing others for harm done to oneself

re·prise /rɪˈpriːz/ n repeating of a piece of music

re·proach /rɪˈprəʊtʃ/ n [C;U] 1 (word of) blame 2 **above/beyond reproach** perfect ♦ vt blame, not angrily but sadly **~ful** adj

re·pro·duce /ˌriːprəˈduːs/ vi/t 1 produce the young of (oneself or one's kind) 2 produce a copy (of) **-duction** /-ˈdʌkʃən/ n [C;U] **-ductive** /-ˈdʌktɪv/ adj concerned with producing young

rep·tile /ˈreptəl, ˈreptaɪl/ n animal, such as a snake, with blood that changes temperature **-tilian** /repˈtɪliən/ adj

re·pub·lic /rɪˈpʌblɪk/ n state ruled by a president and usu. an elected government, not by a king

re·pub·li·can[1] /rɪˈpʌblɪkən/ adj 1 belonging to or supporting a republic

republican[2] n person who favors republics **~ism** n [U] beliefs or practices of republicans

Republican n member or supporter of the **Republican Party**, one of the two largest political parties of the US

re·pu·di·ate /rɪˈpjuːdiˌeɪt/ vt fml 1 state that (something) is untrue 2 refuse to accept **-ation** /rɪˌpjuːdiˈeɪʃən/ n [U]

re·pug·nant /rɪˈpʌgnənt/ adj fml causing extreme dislike; nasty **-nance** n [U]

re·pulse /rɪˈpʌls/ vt 1 refuse coldly 2 drive back (an attack) **-pulsive** adj extremely unpleasant **-pulsion** /-ˈpʌlʃən/ n [U] 1 extreme dislike 2 natural force by which one body drives another away from it

rep·u·ta·ble /ˈrɛpyətəbəl/ adj having a good reputation –**bly** adv

rep·u·ta·tion /ˌrɛpyəˈteɪʃən/ n [C;U] opinion which people in general have about someone or something

re·pute /rɪˈpyut/ n [U] fml 1 reputation 2 good reputation **reputed** adj generally supposed, but with some doubt **reputedly** adv

re·quest /rɪˈkwɛst/ n 1 [C;U] polite demand 2 [C] something asked for ♦ vt demand politely

req·ui·em /ˈrɛkwiəm/ n (music for) a Christian ceremony for a dead person

re·quire /rɪˈkwaɪər/ vt 1 need 2 fml order, expecting obedience: *You are required to* (= must) *do it.* ~**ment** n something needed or demanded

re·run /ˈrirʌn/ n performance or television program broadcast more than once

re·scind /rɪˈsɪnd/ vt end (a law) or take back (a decision, order, etc.)

res·cue /ˈrɛskyu/ vt save or set free from harm or danger **rescue** n –**cuer** n

re·search /ˈrisərtʃ, rɪˈsərtʃ/ n [C;U] advanced and detailed study, to find out (new) facts ♦ vi/t do research (on or for) ~**er** n

re·sem·ble /rɪˈzɛmbəl/ vt look or be like –**blance** n [C;U] likeness

re·sent /rɪˈzɛnt/ vt feel hurt and angry because of ~**ful** adj ~**ment** n [U]

res·er·va·tion /ˌrɛzərˈveɪʃən/ n 1 [C;U] limiting condition(s): *I accepted every point, without reservation.* 2 [C] private doubt in one's mind 3 [C] arrangement to have or use something: *a hotel reservation* 4 [C] area set apart for particular people to live in

re·serve /rɪˈzərv/ vt 1 keep apart for a special purpose 2 arrange to have or use: *reserve hotel rooms* ♦ n 1 [C] quantity kept for future use 2 [C] piece of land kept for the stated purpose 3 [C] player who will play if another cannot 4 [U] being reserved 5 [the+S] also **reserves** pl. — military forces kept for use if needed 6 **in reserve** for future use 7 **without reserve** fml completely **reserved** adj not liking to show one's feelings or talk about oneself

reserve bank /ˈ· ·ˌ·/ n any of the 12 Federal Reserve Banks that hold the money of other banks

Reserve Of·fic·ers Train·ing Corps /ˌ· ˌ··· ˈ·· ˌ·/ also **ROTC** — n special course of study to prepare college students for the military

res·er·voir /ˈrɛzərvwɑr, -ˌvwɔr/ n 1 artificial lake for storing water 2 large supply (still unused)

re·side /rɪˈzaɪd/ vi fml have one's home

res·i·dence /ˈrɛzədəns/ n fml 1 [C] house 2 [U] state of residing 3 **in residence** actually living in a place

res·i·dent /ˈrɛzədənt/ n, adj 1 (person) who lives in a place 2 doctor employed by a hospital while receiving training ~**ial** /ˌrɛzəˈdɛnʃəl◂/ adj 1 consisting of private houses 2 for which one must live in a place: *a residential course*

re·sid·u·al /rɪˈzɪdʒuəl/ adj left over; remaining

res·i·due /ˈrɛzədu/ n what is left over

re·sign /rɪˈzaɪn/ vi/t leave (one's job or position) ~**ed** adj calmly suffering without complaint ~**edly** /rɪˈzaɪnədli/ adv

resign to phr vt cause (oneself) to accept calmly (something which cannot be avoided)

res·ig·na·tion /ˌrɛzɪgˈneɪʃən/ n 1 [C;U] (act or written statement of) resigning 2 [U] state of being resigned

re·sil·ient /rɪˈzɪlyənt/ adj 1 able to spring back to its former shape 2 able to recover quickly from misfortune –**ence** n [U]

res·in /ˈrɛzən/ n 1 [U] thick sticky liquid from trees 2 [C] artificial plastic substance

re·sist /rɪˈzɪst/ vt 1 oppose; fight against 2 remain unharmed by 3 force oneself not to succumb

re·sist·ance /rɪˈzɪstəns/ n [S;U] 1 act of resisting or ability to resist 2 [U] force opposed to movement: *wind resistance* 3 [(the)U] secret army fighting against an enemy in control of its country 4 **the line/path of least resistance** the easiest way –**ant** adj showing resistance

res·o·lute /ˈrɛzəlut/ adj firm; determined in purpose ~**ly** adv

res·o·lu·tion /ˌrɛzəˈluʃən/ n 1 [C] formal decision at a meeting 2 [C] firm decision: *a New Year's resolution to stop drinking* 3 [U] quality of being resolute 4 [U] action of resolving (RESOLVE (1))

re·solve /rɪˈzɒlv/ vt **1** find a way of dealing with (a problem); settle **2** decide firmly **3** make a RESOLUTION (1, 2) ♦ n [C;U] fml for RESOLUTION (2, 3)

res·o·nant /ˈrezənənt/ adj **1** (of a sound) full, clear, and continuing **2** producing resonance (2) –**nance** n [U] **1** quality of being resonant **2** sound produced in a body by sound waves from another

res·o·nate /ˈrezəneɪt/ vi **1** produce resonance (2) **2** be resonant

re·sort¹ /rɪˈzɔːt/ n **1** vacation place **2** as a/in the last resort if everything else fails

resort² v resort to phr vt make use of, esp. when there is nothing else

re·sound /rɪˈzaʊnd/ vi **1** be loud and clearly heard **2** be filled (with sound) ~**ing** adj very great: a resounding victory

re·source /rɪˈzɔːs, -sɔːs, rɪˈsɔːs, -ˈsɔːs/ n **1** [C] something that one can use or possess **2** [U] resourcefulness **3** leave someone to his own resources leave someone alone to pass the time as he wishes ♦ vt provide RESOURCES (1) for ~**ful** adj able to find a way around difficulties ~**fully** adv

re·spect /rɪˈspekt/ n **1** [U] great admiration and honor **2** [U] attention; care **3** [C] detail; point: In some respects it is worse. **4** with respect to with regard to; about ♦ vt feel or show respect for ~**ing** prep in connection with respects n [P] polite formal greetings

re·spec·ta·ble /rɪˈspektəbəl/ adj **1** socially acceptable **2** quite good; large: a respectable income –**bly** adv –**bility** /rɪˌspektəˈbɪləti/ n [U]

re·spect·ful /rɪˈspektfəl/ adj feeling or showing RESPECT (1) ~**ly** adv

re·spec·tive /rɪˈspektɪv/ adj particular and separate ~**ly** adv each separately in the order mentioned

res·pi·ra·tion /ˌrespəˈreɪʃən/ n [U] fml breathing –**piratory** /ˈresprəˌtɔːri, -ˌtʊəri, rɪˈspaɪrə-/ adj: the respiratory system (= lungs, etc.)

res·pi·ra·tor /ˈrespəˌreɪtə/ n apparatus to help people breathe

res·pite /ˈrespɪt/ n [C;U] **1** short rest from effort, pain, etc. **2** delay before something unwelcome happens

re·spond /rɪˈspɒnd/ vi **1** answer **2** act in answer

respond to phr vt (esp. of a disease) get better as a result of

re·sponse /rɪˈspɒns/ n **1** [C] answer **2** [C;U] action done in answer

re·spon·si·bil·i·ty /rɪˌspɒnsəˈbɪləti/ n **1** [U] condition or quality of being responsible: I take full responsibility for losing it. **2** [C] something for which one is RESPONSIBLE (2) **3** [U] trustworthiness

re·spon·si·ble /rɪˈspɒnsəbəl/ adj **1** having done or caused something (bad); guilty **2** having a duty to do or look after something **3** trustworthy **4** (of a job) needing a trustworthy person to do it **5** be responsible for be the cause of –**bly** adv

re·spon·sive /rɪˈspɒnsɪv/ adj answer readily with words or feelings: (fig.) a disease responsive to treatment

rest¹ /rest/ n **1** [C;U] (period of) freedom from action or something tiring **2** [U] not moving: It came to rest (= stopped) just here. **3** [C] support, esp. for the stated thing: a headrest **4** set someone's mind/fears at/to rest free someone from anxiety ~**ful** adj peaceful; quiet

rest² v vi/t (allow to) take a rest **2** vt lean; support **3** vi lie buried: Let him rest in peace. **4** rest assured be certain

rest on phr vt **1** (of a proof, argument, etc.) depend on **2** lean on **3** (of eyes) be directed towards

rest with phr vt be the responsibility of

rest³ n **1** the rest ones that still remain; what is left **2** for the rest apart from what has already been mentioned

res·tau·rant /ˈrestrənt, -ˌrɒnt, ˈrestə-/ n place where meals are sold and eaten

res·tau·ra·teur /ˌrestərəˈtɜː/ n restaurant owner

rest home /ˈ· ·/ n NURSING HOME

res·ti·tu·tion /ˌrestəˈtjuːʃən/ n [U] fml giving something back to its owner, or paying for damage

res·tive /ˈrestɪv/ adj unwilling to keep still or be controlled ~**ly** adv

rest·less /ˈrestlɪs/ adj **1** giving no rest or sleep **2** unable to stay still, esp. from anxiety or lack of interest ~**ly** adv

res·to·ra·tion /ˌrestəˈreɪʃən/ n [C;U] restoring

re·stor·a·tive /rɪˈstɒrətɪv, -ˈstʊər-/ n, adj (food, medicine, etc.) that brings back health and strength

re·store /rɪˈstɔː, rɪˈstʊə/ vt **1** give back **2** bring back into existence **3** bring back to a proper state, esp. of health **4** put back into a former position **5** repair (an old painting, building, etc.) restorer n

re·strain /rɪ'streɪn/ vt prevent from doing something; control ~ed adj calm and controlled **restraint** n 1 [U] quality of being restrained or act of restraining oneself 2 [C] something that restrains: *the re-straints of life in a small town*

re·strict /rɪ'strɪkt/ vt keep within a certain limit ~ive adj that restricts one ~ion /-'strɪkʃən/ n [C;U]

rest·room /'rest-rum, -rʊm/ n room in a public building with a toilet

re·struc·ture[1] /ˌriː'strʌktʃə/ vt arrange (a system or organization) in a new way

re·struc·ture[2] /ˌriː'strʌktʃə/ vt change the way a business, system, etc., is organized **restructuring** n [U]

rest stop /'· ·/ n 1 place along the road where people in cars can stop to rest, etc. 2 act of doing this

re·sult /rɪ'zʌlt/ n 1 [C;U] what happens because of an action or event 2 [C;U] (a) noticeable good effect 3 [C] situation of defeat or victory at the end of a game 4 [C] answer to a calculation ♦ vi happen as an effect or RESULT (1) ~ant adj resulting

    result in phr vt cause

re·sume /rɪ'zuːm/ v 1 vi/t begin again after a pause 2 vt fml return to

ré·su·mé, resume /'rezəˌmeɪ, 'reɪ-, ˌrezə'meɪ, ˌreɪ-/ n 1 shortened form of a speech, book, etc. 2 short written account of a person's education and past employment

re·sump·tion /rɪ'zʌmpʃən/ n [U] act of resuming

re·sur·gence /rɪ'sɜːdʒəns/ n [U] becoming active again

res·ur·rect /ˌrezə'rekt/ vt bring back into use or fashion ~ion /-'rekʃən/ n 1 [U] fig. rebirth 2 [the+S] return of dead people to life at the end of the world 3 [the] (cap.) return of Christ to life after his death

re·sus·ci·tate /rɪ'sʌsəˌteɪt/ vt bring a person back to life –tation /rɪˌsʌsə'teɪʃən/ n [U]

re·tail /'riːteɪl/ n [U] sale of goods in stores to customers, for not reselling to anyone else ♦ adv ~er n ♦ vi/t sell by retail

re·tain /rɪ'teɪn/ vt 1 keep; avoid losing 2 hold in place 3 employ (esp. a lawyer)

re·tain·er /rɪ'teɪnə/ n 1 servant 2 wires used to keep teeth in position 3 money paid in advance for services to a lawyer, etc.

re·tal·i·ate /rɪ'tæliˌeɪt/ vi pay back evil with evil –atory /-liəˌtɔːri, -ˌtʊəri/ adj –ation /rɪˌtæli'eɪʃən/ n [U]

re·tard /rɪ'tɑːd/ vt make slow or late ~ed adj slow in development of the mind

re·ten·tion /rɪ'tenʃən/ n [U] state or action of retaining (RETAIN)

re·ten·tive /rɪ'tentɪv/ adj able to remember things well

re·think /riː'θɪŋk/ vt **rethought** /-'θɔːt/ think again and perhaps change one's mind about **rethink** /'riːθɪŋk/ n [S]

ret·i·cent /'retəsənt/ adj unwilling to say much –cence n [U]

ret·i·na /'retɪn-ə/ n area at the back of the eye which receives light

ret·i·nue /'retɪˌnjuː/ n group traveling with and helping an important person

re·tire /rɪ'taɪə/ vi 1 leave one's job, usu. because of age 2 leave a place of action 3 fml go away, esp. to a quiet place 4 fml go to bed ♦ vt dismiss from work and pay a PENSION to ~ment n [U] **retired** adj having stopped working **retiring** adj liking to avoid company

re·tort /rɪ'tɔːt/ n quick or angry reply ♦ vt make a retort

re·touch /ˌriː'tʌtʃ/ vt improve (a picture) with small additions

re·trace /rɪ'treɪs, riː-/ vt go back over: *She retraced her steps.* (= went back the way she had come)

re·tract /rɪ'trækt/ vi/t 1 draw back or in: *The cat retracted its claws.* 2 take back (a statement or offer one has made) ~able adj ~ion /-'trækʃən/ n [U]

re·tread /'riːtred/ n tire with a new covering of rubber ♦ /ˌriː'tred/ vt make (a retread)

re·treat /rɪ'triːt/ vi 1 move backwards, esp. when forced 2 escape (from something unpleasant) ♦ n 1 [C;U] (act of) retreating 2 [the+S] military signal for this 3 [C] place one goes to for safety and peace

re·trench /rɪ'trentʃ/ vi fml arrange to lessen (one's spending) ~ment n [C;U]

re·tri·al /ˌriː'traɪəl, 'riːtraɪəl/ n new trial of a law case

ret·ri·bu·tion /ˌretrɪ'bjuːʃən/ n fml deserved punishment

re·trieve /rɪ'triːv/ vt 1 find and bring back 2 fml put right **retrieval** n [U] retrieving

retriever n dog that retrieves shot birds

ret·ro·ac·tive /ˌretrouˈæktɪv/ adj (of law, decision, etc.) effective from a particular date in the past

ret·ro·spect /ˈretrəˌspekt/ n **in retrospect** looking back to the past ~**ive** /ˌretrəˈspektɪv/ adj **1** thinking about the past **2** (of a law) having an effect on the past ◆ n a show of the work of a painter, SCULPTOR, etc., from his or her earliest years up to the present time

re·turn[1] /rɪˈtɜrn/ v **1** vi come or go back **2** vt give or send back **3** vt give (a VERDICT) **4 return a favor** do a kind action in return for another

return[2] n **1** [C;U] (act of) coming or giving back **2** [C] profit **3** [C] official statement or set of figures: a tax return **4 in return for** in exchange (for) **5 Many happy returns!** (used as a birthday greeting)

re·u·nion /riˈyunyən/ n **1** [C] meeting of former fellow workers, students, or friends after a separation **2** [U] state of being brought together again

Rev. abbrev. for: REVEREND

rev /rev/ vt -vv- increase the speed of (an engine) ◆ sl for REVOLUTION (3)

re·vamp /riˈvæmp/ vt give a new and improved form to

re·veal /rɪˈvil/ vt allow to be seen or known

rev·el /ˈrevəl/ v -l- lit pass the time in dancing, etc. ~**er** n person taking part in revelry ~**ry** n [U] wild, noisy dancing and feasting

revel in phr vt enjoy greatly

rev·e·la·tion /ˌrevəˈleɪʃən/ n **1** [U] making known of something secret: forced to resign by the revelation of his unpleasant activities **2** [C] (surprising) fact made known

re·venge /rɪˈvendʒ/ n [U] punishment given in return for harm done to oneself ◆ vt do something in revenge

rev·e·nue /ˈrevəˌnu/ n [U] income, esp. received by the government

re·ver·be·rate /rɪˈvɜrbəˌreɪt/ vt (of sound) be continuously repeated in waves ~**ration** /rɪˌvɜrbəˈreɪʃən/ n [C;U]

re·vere /rɪˈvɪr/ vt fml respect and admire greatly

rev·e·rence /ˈrevrəns/ n [U] fml great respect and admiration

Rev·e·rend /ˈrevrənd/ n (title of respect for) a Christian priest

rev·e·rent /ˈrevrənt/ adj showing (religious) reverence ~**ly** adv

rev·e·ren·tial /ˌrevəˈrenʃəl/ adj showing reverence ~**ly** adv

rev·er·ie /ˈrevəri/ n [C;U] pleasant dreamlike state while awake

re·vers·al /rɪˈvɜrsəl/ n **1** [C;U] (case of) being reversed **2** [C] defeat or piece of bad luck

re·verse /rɪˈvɜrs/ adj opposite in position: the reverse side | in reverse order ◆ n **1** [U] opposite **2** [U] position of a vehicle's controls that causes backward movement **3** [C] REVERSAL (2) **4** [C] back side of a coin, etc. ◆ **1** vi/t go or cause (a vehicle) to go backwards **2** vt change around or over to the opposite: reverse the order | reverse a decision

reverse dis·crim·i·na·tion /ˌ... ...ˈ.../ n [U] practice or principle of favoring people who are often treated unfairly, esp. because of their sex or race

re·vert /rɪˈvɜrt/ v **revert to** phr vt go back to (a former condition, habit, or owner)

re·view /rəˈvyu/ vt **1** consider and judge (an event or situation) **2** hold a REVIEW (2) **3** give a REVIEW (2a) of ◆ n **1** [C;U] (act of) REVIEWing **(1) 2 a** [C] (written) expression of judgment on a new book, play, etc. **b** magazine containing such judgments **3** grand show of armed forces, in the presence of a leader, general, etc. ~**er** n

re·vise /rɪˈvaɪz/ v **1** vt improve and make correct (written material) **2** vt change (an opinion, intention, etc.)

re·vi·sion /rɪˈvɪʒən/ n **1** [C;U] (act of) revising **2** [C] revised piece of writing

re·vi·tal·ize /riˈvaɪtlˌaɪz/ vt put new strength or power into

re·vive /rɪˈvaɪv/ v **1** vi/t become or make conscious or healthy again: (fig.) The photo revived (= brought to mind) old memories. **2** vi/t come or bring back into use or existence **3** vt perform (an old play) again after many years **revival** n **1** [C;U] rebirth **2** [C] new performance of an old play

rev·o·ca·tion /ˌrevəˈkeɪʃən/ n [U] revoking

re·voke /rɪˈvouk/ vt put an end to (a law, decision, permission, etc.)

re·volt /rɪˈvoult/ v **1** vi (try to) take power violently from those in power **2** vt (cause) to feel sick and shocked ◆ n [C;U]

(example of) the act of REVOLTing (1) ~**ing**
adj extremely nasty ~**ingly** *adv: revolt-
ingly adv*

rev·o·lu·tion /ˌrɛvəˈluʃən/ *n* **1** [C;U] (time
of) great social change, esp. of a political
system by force **2** [C] complete change
in ways of thinking or acting **3** [C] one
complete circular movement ~**ary** *adj* **1**
of a REVOLUTION (1) **2** completely new
and different ~**ary** *n* person who favors
or joins in a REVOLUTION (1) ~**ize** *vt* cause
a REVOLUTION (2) in

re·volve /rɪˈvɑlv/ *vi/t* spin around on a
central point
   revolve around *phr vt* have as a
center or main subject

re·volv·er /rɪˈvɑlvər/ *n* small gun with a
revolving container for bullets

re·vue /rɪˈvyu/ *n* theatrical show with
short acts, songs, jokes, etc.

re·vul·sion /rɪˈvʌlʃən/ *n* [U] feeling of
being REVOLTed (2)

re·ward /rɪˈwɔrd/ *n* **1** [C;U] (something
gained in) return for work or service **2**
[C] money given for helping the police ♦
vt give a reward to or for ~**ing** *adj* giving
personal satisfaction

re·wind /ˌriˈwaɪnd/ *vt* go back to the
beginning of (a TAPE, film, etc.)

re·work /ˌriˈwək/ *vt* put (music, writing,
etc.) into a new or different form (in
order to use again)

re·write /ˌriˈraɪt/ *vt* write again, using different words so as to be clearer or more
effective ♦ /ˈriˌraɪt/ *n*

rhap·so·dy /ˈræpsədi/ *n* **1** expression of
too great praise and excitement **2** piece
of music of irregular form –**dic** /ræp-
ˈsɑdɪk/ *adj*

rhet·o·ric /ˈrɛtərɪk/ *n* [U] **1** art of speaking
to persuade **2** words which sound fine
but are insincere or meaningless ~**al**
/rɪˈtɔrɪkəl, -ˈtɑr-/ *adj* **1** asked or asking only
for effect, and not expecting an answer: *a
rhetorical question* **2** of or showing
rhetoric ~**ally** *adv*

rheu·ma·tism /ˈrumətɪzəm/ *n* [U] disease
causing joint or muscle pain –**matic**
/ruˈmætɪk/ *adj* of, suffering from, or being
rheumatism

rheu·ma·toid ar·thri·tis /ˌrumətɔɪd ɑr-
ˈθraɪtɪs/ *n* [U] disease that lasts a long
time, causing pain and stiffness in the
joints

rhine·stone /ˈraɪnstoʊn/ *n* diamond-like
jewel made from glass or a transparent
rock

rhi·no /ˈraɪnoʊ/ *n* -**nos** rhinoceros

rhi·no·ce·ros /raɪˈnɑsərəs/ *n* large
African or Asian animal with thick skin
and either 1 or 2 horns on its nose

rhom·bus /ˈrɑmbəs/ *n* figure with 4 equal
straight sides

rhu·barb /ˈrubɑrb/ *n* [U] plant with
large leaves and thick red stems that are
eaten

rhyme /raɪm/ *v* **1** *vi* (of words or lines in
poetry) end with the same sound: *"Cat"
rhymes with "mat."* **2** *vt* put together
(words) ending with the same sound ♦ *n*
1 [U] (use of) rhyming words at ends of
lines in poetry **2** [C] word that rhymes
with another **3** [C] short simple rhyming
poem **4 rhyme or reason** (any) sense or
meaning

rhyth·m /ˈrɪðəm/ *n* [C;U] regular,
repeated pattern of sounds or movements: (fig.) *the rhythm of the seasons*
–**mic** /ˈrɪðmɪk/, –**mical** *adj* –**mically** *adv*

rhythm and blues /ˌ··· ˈ·/ *n* popular
form of Black music

rhythm meth·od /ˈ·· ˌ·-/ *n* [*the*+S] method
of CONTRACEPTION which depends on
having sex only at a time when the
woman is not likely to CONCEIVE

rib /rɪb/ *n* **1** any of the curved bones
enclosing the chest **2** curved rod for
strengthening a frame **3** thin raised
line in a pattern ♦ *vt* -**bb**- laugh at
(someone) ~**bed** *adj* having a pattern of
RIBS (3)

rib·ald /ˈrɪbəld/ *adj fml* (of jokes or laughter) rude and disrespectful

rib·bon /ˈrɪbən/ *n* long, narrow band of
cloth

rib cage /ˈ· ·/ *n* all one's RIBS (1)

rice /raɪs/ *n* [U] (plant with) a seed that is
widely eaten

rich /rɪtʃ/ *adj* **1** having a lot of money or
property **2** having a lot: *a city rich in
ancient buildings* **3** expensive, valuable,
and beautiful **4** (of food) containing a lot
of cream, eggs, sugar, etc. **5** (of a sound
or color) deep, strong, and beautiful **6**
infml amusing but often rather annoy-
ing ♦ *n* [(*the*) P] rich people ~**ly** *adv* **1**
splendidly **2** fully: *richly deserved* ~**ness**
n [U]

rich·es /ˈrɪtʃɪz/ *n* [U] *esp. lit* wealth

rick·ets /'rɪkɪts/ n [U] children's disease in which bones become soft and bent

rick·et·y /'rɪkəti/ adj weak and likely to break

rick·shaw /'rɪkʃɔ/ n small East Asian carriage pulled by a man

ric·o·chet /'rɪkəˌʃeɪ/ n sudden change of direction by a bullet, stone, etc., when it hits a hard surface ◆ v -t- change direction in a ricochet

rid /rɪd/ v (**rid** or **ridded**, pres. p. **-dd-**) **rid of** phr vt **1** make free of **2 get rid of:** **a** free oneself from **b** drive or throw away or destroy

rid·dance /'rɪdns/ n **good riddance** (said when one is glad that someone or something has gone)

rid·dle¹ /'rɪdl/ n **1** difficult and amusing question **2** mystery

riddle² v **riddle with** phr vt make full of holes

ride¹ /raɪd/ v **rode** /roʊd/, **ridden** /'rɪdn/ **1** vi/t travel along on (a horse, etc., a bicycle, or a motorcycle) **2** vi travel on a bus **3** vt remain safe (and floating) through: a ship riding a storm **4 let something ride** let something continue, taking no action **5 ride high** have great success **6 ride roughshod over** act in a hurtful way towards **rider** n **1** person riding esp. a horse **2** statement added to esp. an official declaration or judgment

   ride out phr vt come safely through (bad weather, trouble)

   ride up phr vi (of clothing) move upwards or out of place

ride² n **1** journey on an animal, in a vehicle, etc. **2 take someone for a ride** deceive someone

ridge /rɪdʒ/ n long narrow raised part, where 2 slopes meet

rid·i·cule /'rɪdɪˌkyul/ n [U] unkind laughter ◆ vt laugh unkindly at

ri·dic·u·lous /rɪ'dɪkyələs/ adj silly **~ly** adv

rife /raɪf/ adj widespread; common

rif·fle /'rɪfl/ v **riffle through** phr vt turn over (papers, etc.) quickly, searching

riff-raff /'rɪfræf/ n [U] derog worthless, badly behaved people

ri·fle¹ /'raɪfəl/ n gun with a long barrel, fired from the shoulder

rifle² vt search through and steal from

rift /rɪft/ n crack: (fig.) a rift in their friendship

rig¹ /rɪg/ vt **-gg-** fit (a ship) with sails, ropes, etc.

   rig up phr vt make quickly and roughly

rig² n **1** way a ship's sails and MASTs are arranged **2** apparatus: a drilling rig **~ging** n [U] all the ropes, etc., holding up a ship's sails

rig³ vt **-gg-** arrange dishonestly for one's own advantage

right¹ /raɪt/ adj **1 a** on the side of the body away from the heart **b** in the direction of one's right side: the right bank of the river **2** just; proper; morally good **3** correct **4** in a proper or healthy state; to put the trouble right | Are you all right?

right² n **1** [U] RIGHT¹ (1) side of direction **2** [U] what is RIGHT¹ (2) **3** [C;U] morally just or legal claim: You've no right to (= should not) say that. **4** [U] political parties that favor less change and less state control **5 in one's own right** because of a personal claim that does not depend on anyone else **6 in the right** not wrong or deserving blame **~ness** n [U]: the rightness of their claim — see also RIGHTS

right³ adv **1** towards the RIGHT² (1,2) correctly **2** exactly: right in the middle **3** completely: Go right back to the beginning! **4** yes; I will: "See you tomorrow." "Right!" — see also ALL RIGHT **6 right away** at once

right⁴ vt put back to a correct position or condition

right an·gle /'· ˌ·/ n angle of 90 degrees

right·eous /'raɪtʃəs/ adj **1** morally good **2** having just cause: righteous indignation **~ly** adv **~ness** n [U]

right·ful /'raɪtfəl/ adj according to a just or legal claim **~ly** adv

right-hand /'· ·/ adj on the right side **~ed** adj using the right hand for most actions **~er** n righthanded person

right-hand man /ˌ· · '·/ n most useful and valuable helper

right·ly /'raɪtli/ adv **1** correctly **2** justly

right-mind·ed /ˌ· '·-·/ adj having the right opinions, principles, etc.

right of way /ˌ· · '·/ n [U] right of a vehicle or person to go first

rights /raɪts/ n [P] **1** political, social, etc., advantages to which someone has a just claim, morally or in law **2 by rights** in justice; if things were done properly **3 set/put someone/something to rights** make someone/something just, healthy, etc. **4 the rights and wrongs of** the true facts of **5 within one's rights** not going beyond one's just claims

right-to-life /ˌ· ·ˈ·/ *adj* opposing ABORT*ion* **–lifer** *n*

right wing /ˌ· ˈ·◂/ *adj, n* [U] (of) a political party of the RIGHT² (4)

ri·gid /ˈrɪdʒɪd/ *adj* **1** stiff **2** not easy to change **~ly** *adv* **~ity** /rɪˈdʒɪdəti/ *n* [U]

rig·ma·role /ˈrɪɡməˌroʊl/ *n* [S;U] long confused story or set of actions

rig·or /ˈrɪɡə/ *n* [U] **1** severity **2** *fml* exactness and clear thinking

rig·or mor·tis /ˌrɪɡə ˈmɔrtɪs/ *n* [U] stiffening of the muscles after death

rig·or·ous /ˈrɪɡərəs/ *adj* **1** careful and exact **2** severe **~ly** *adv*

rile /raɪl/ *vt* annoy

rim /rɪm/ *n* edge, esp. of a round object ♦ *vt* **-mm-** be around the edge of

rind /raɪnd/ *n* [C;U] thick outer covering of certain fruits, cheese, etc.

ring¹ /rɪŋ/ *n* **1** (metal) circle worn on the finger **2** circular place: *smoke rings* **3** circular mark or arrangement: *a ring of troops around the building* **4** enclosed space where things are shown, performances take place, or esp. people BOX or WRESTLE **5** group of people who work together, esp. dishonestly: *a drug ring* **6 run rings around** do things much better and faster than ♦ *vt* form or put a ring around

ring² *v* rang /ræŋ/, rung /rʌŋ/ **1** *vt/i* cause (a bell) to sound **2** *vi* (of a bell, telephone, etc.) sound **3** *vi* be filled with sound **4 ring a bell** remind one of something **5 ring the changes** introduce variety in **6 ring true/false** sound true/untrue ♦ *n* [C] (making) a bell-like sound **2** certain quality: *It had a ring of truth.* (= sounded true)

  ring out *phr vi* (of a voice, bell, etc.) sound loudly and clearly

  ring up *phr vt* record (money paid) on a CASH REGISTER

ring·er /ˈrɪŋə/ *n* — see DEAD RINGER

ring fin·ger /ˈ· ˌ··/ *n* the finger next to the smallest finger, esp. on the left hand

ring·lead·er /ˈrɪŋˌlidə/ *n* person who leads others to do wrong

ring·let /ˈrɪŋlɪt/ *n* long, hanging curl of hair

ring·mas·ter /ˈrɪŋˌmæstə/ *n* person who directs CIRCUS performances

ring·side /ˈrɪŋsaɪd/ *adj, adv, n* (at) the edge of a RING¹ (4)

ring·worm /ˈrɪŋwəm/ *n* [U] disease causing red rings on the skin

rink /rɪŋk/ *n* specially prepared surface for skating (SKATE)

rink·y-dink /ˈrɪŋki ˌdɪŋk/ *adj* small and unimpressive

rinse /rɪns/ *vt* wash in clean water, so as to get rid of soap, dirt, etc. ♦ *n* **1** [C] act of rinsing **2** [C;U] liquid hair coloring

ri·ot /ˈraɪət/ *n* **1** [C] noisy, violent crowd behavior **2** [S] large, impressive show: *The garden is a riot of color.* **3** [S] *infml* very funny and successful occasion or person **4 run riot: a** become violent and uncontrollable **b** (of a plant) grow too thick and tall ♦ *vi* take part in a riot **~er** *n* **~ous** *adj* wild and disorderly

rip /rɪp/ *vt/i* **-pp- 1** tear quickly and violently **2 let something rip** *infml* remove control and let things develop in their own way ♦ *n* long tear

  rip off *phr vt* *infml* **1** charge too much **2** steal **rip-off** /ˈ· ·/ *n* something for which too much is charged or paid

RIP *abbrev. for:* rest in peace (= words written on the stone over a grave)

ripe /raɪp/ *adj* **1** (fully grown and) ready to be eaten: *a ripe apple* **2** ready; suitable: *land ripe for industrial development* **3** grown-up and experienced: *He's reached the ripe old age of 90.* **~ness** *n* [U]

rip·en /ˈraɪpən/ *vt/i* make or become ripe

rip·ple /ˈrɪpəl/ *vi/t* **1** move in small waves **2** make a sound like gently running water ♦ *n* [C] **1** very small wave or gently waving movement **2** sound of or like gently running water

rip-roar·ing /ˌ· ˈ··◂/ *adj* noisy and exciting

rise¹ /raɪz/ *vi* rose /roʊz/, risen /ˈrɪzən/ **1** go up; get higher: (fig.) *My spirits rose.* (= I became happier.) **2** (of the sun etc.) come above the horizon **3** (of land) slope upward **4** stand up **5** *fml* get out of bed **6** (of wind) get stronger **7** increase in size or number: *Let the bread rise.* | *rising crime rate* **8** REBEL¹: *They rose up against their leaders.* **9** come back to life after being dead **10** (esp. of a river) begin **11** move up in rank **12 rise to the occasion** show that one can deal with a difficult matter **rising** n UPRISING

rise² n **1** [C] increase **2** [U] act of growing greater or more powerful **3** reaction **4** [C] upward slope **5 give rise to** cause

risk /rɪsk/ n [C;U] **1** chance that something bad may happen **2** (in insurance) (a person or thing that is) a danger **3 at risk** in danger **4 at one's own risk** agreeing to bear any loss or danger **5 run/take a risk** do dangerous things ♦ vt **1** place in danger **2** take the chance of: *Are you willing to risk failure?* **~y** adj dangerous

ri·sot·to /rɪˈsɒtəʊ, -ˈzɒt-/ n [C;U] rice dish with chicken, vegetables, etc.

ris·qué /rɪˈskeɪ/ adj (of a joke, etc.) slightly rude

rite /raɪt/ n ceremonial (religious) act with a fixed pattern

rit·u·al /ˈrɪtʃuəl/ n [C;U] (ceremonial) act or acts always repeated in the same form ♦ adj done as a rite: *ritual murder*

ritz·y /ˈrɪtsi/ adj showy and expensive

ri·val /ˈraɪvəl/ n person with whom one competes ♦ vt -l- be as good as **~ry** n [C;U] competition

riv·en /ˈrɪvən/ adj fml split violently apart

riv·er /ˈrɪvə/ n wide natural stream of water

riv·et /ˈrɪvɪt/ n metal pin used for fastening heavy metal plates together ♦ vt **1** fasten with rivets **2** attract and hold (someone's attention) strongly **~ing** adj very interesting

ri·vi·e·ra /ˌrɪviˈeərə/ n stretch of coast where people vacation

roach /rəʊtʃ/ n COCKROACH

road /rəʊd/ n **1** smooth prepared track for vehicles with wheels: (fig.) *We're on the road to* (= on the way to) *success.* **2 on the road** traveling

road·block /ˈrəʊdblɒk/ n something placed across a road to stop traffic

road hog /ˈ· ·/ n fast, selfish careless driver

road·kill /ˈrəʊdkɪl/ n [U] infml animals killed by cars on a road

road·run·ner /ˈrəʊdˌrʌnə/ n bird that can run very quickly

road·side /ˈrəʊdsaɪd/ adj near the side of the road: *roadside cafe*

road trip /ˈ· ·/ n long trip in a car for pleasure

road·way /ˈrəʊdweɪ/ n middle part of a road, where vehicles drive

roam /rəʊm/ vi/t wander around with no clear purpose

roar /rɔr/ n deep, loud, continuing sound: *roars of laughter* ♦ v **1** vi give a roar **2** vt say forcefully **3** vi laugh loudly **~ing** adj, adv **1** very great: *We're doing a roaring trade.* (= doing very good business) **2** very: *roaring drunk*

roast /rəʊst/ vt cook (esp. meat) in an OVEN or over a fire ♦ adj roasted ♦ n large piece of roasted meat

rob /rɒb/ vt -bb- steal something from **~ber** n **~bery** n [C;U] (example of) the crime of robbing

robe /rəʊb/ n long flowing garment

rob·in /ˈrɒbɪn/ n small brown bird with a red front

ro·bot /ˈrəʊbɒt, -bət/ n machine that can do some of the work of a human being **~ics** /rəʊˈbɒtɪks/ n [U] study of the making and use of robots

ro·bust /rəʊˈbʌst, ˈrəʊbʌst/ adj strong (and healthy) **~ly** adv **~ness** n [U]

rock¹ /rɒk/ n **1** [C;U] stone forming part of the Earth's surface **2** [C] (large piece of) stone **3** emotionally strong person **4** [C] a diamond **5** ROCK 'N' ROLL **6 on the rocks: a** (of a marriage) likely to fail soon **b** (of a drink) with ice but no water

rock² /rɒk/ v **1** vi/t move regularly backwards and forwards or from side to side **2** vt shock greatly **3 rock the boat** spoil the existing good situation

rock and roll /ˌ· ·ˈ·/ n [U] ROCK 'N' ROLL

rock bot·tom /ˌ· ˈ··◂/ n [U] the lowest point

rock·er /ˈrɒkə/ n **1** curved piece of wood on which something rocks **2** ROCKING CHAIR **3 off one's rocker** infml crazy

rock·et /ˈrɒkɪt/ n object shaped like a tube driven through the air by burning gases, used for traveling into space, or as a MISSILE or FIREWORK ♦ vi rise quickly and suddenly

rock·ing chair /ˈ·· ˌ·/ n chair with ROCKERS

rocking horse /ˈ·· ˌ·/ n wooden horse with ROCKERS, for a child to ride on

rock 'n' roll /ˌrɒk ən ˈrəʊl/ n [U] popular modern music with a strong loud beat

rock·y /ˈrɒki/ adj **1** full of rocks **2** infml unsteady; not firm

rod /rɒd/ n long thin stiff pole or bar

rode /roʊd/ past t. of RIDE

ro·dent /ˈroʊdnt/ n small animal with long front teeth, such as a mouse, rat, or rabbit, that eats plants

ro·de·o /ˈroʊdiˌoʊ, roʊˈdeɪoʊ/ n -os public performance of COWBOY skills with horse riding, cattle catching, etc.

roe /roʊ/ n [C;U] mass of fish eggs, often eaten

ro·ger /ˈrɒdʒə/ interj (used in radio and signaling to say one has understood)

rogue /roʊg/ n old-fash dishonest person ♦ adj 1 (of a wild animal) bad-tempered and dangerous 2 not following the usual or accepted standards **roguish** adj playful and fond of playing tricks

role /roʊl/ n 1 character played by an actor 2 part someone takes in an activity

role mod·el /ˈ· ˌ·/ n admired person who others try to copy

roll¹ /roʊl/ v 1 vi/t turn over and over or from side to side: *The ball rolled into the hole.* 2 vt form into esp. a tube by curling round and round 3 vi move steadily and smoothly (as if) on wheels 4 vi swing from side to side on the sea 5 vt make flat with a ROLLER (1) or ROLLING PIN 6 vi make a long deep sound 7 vt cause (esp. film cameras) to begin working 8 vt cause (the eyes) to move around and around 9 **roll in the aisles** (esp. of people at the theater) laugh uncontrollably 10 **roll one's r's** pronounce the sound /r/ with the tongue beating rapidly against the roof of the mouth 11 **roll one's own** infml make one's own cigarettes instead of buying them ~**ing** adj 1 (of land) with low gentle slopes 2 **rolling in dough** infml extremely rich

roll in phr vi arrive in large quantities

roll out phr 1 vi get out of bed 2 vt UNROLL

roll up phr vi arrive

roll² n 1 act of rolling 2 rolled tube 3 small load of bread for one person 4 long deep sound (as if) of a lot of quick strokes: *a roll of drums* 5 official list of names 6 **on a roll** having several successes in a row: *He's on a roll.*

roll call /ˈ· ˌ·/ n calling a list of names to see who is there

roll·er /ˈroʊlə/ n 1 apparatus shaped like a tube for pressing, making smooth,

shaping, etc. 2 long heavy wave on the coast

Rol·ler·blade /ˈroʊləˌbleɪd/ n tdmk boot with a row of 4 small wheels fastened in a line under it

roller coast·er /ˈ·· ˌ·/ n small railroad with sharp slopes and curves, found in amusement parks

roller skate /ˈ·· ˌ/ n boot with 4 small wheels fastened under it, for moving along on **roller-skate** vi

rolling pin /ˈ·· ˌ/ n piece of wood, etc., shaped like a tube, for making pastry flat

ro·ly-po·ly /ˌroʊli ˈpoʊli◀/ adj infml (of a person) fat and round

ROM /rɒm/ n read-only memory; computer memory holding information that is continuously needed by the computer

Ro·man /ˈroʊmən/ n, adj (citizen) of Rome, esp. ancient Rome

Roman Cath·o·lic /ˌ· ˈ···/ n, adj (member) of the branch of the Christian religion led by the POPE ~**ism** /ˌ· ·ˈ····/ n [U]

ro·mance /roʊˈmæns, ˈroʊmæns/ n 1 [C] love affair 2 [U] ROMANTIC (2) quality 3 [C] story of love, adventure, etc. ♦ /roʊˈmæns/ adj (cap.) of a group of Western European languages descended from Latin

Roman nu·me·ral /ˌ· ˈ···/ n any of the signs (such as I, II, V, X, L) used for numbers in ancient Rome and sometimes now

ro·man·tic /roʊˈmæntɪk/ adj 1 showing warm feelings of love 2 of or suggesting love, adventure, strange happenings, etc. 3 having much imagination; not practical: *romantic notions* 4 showing romanticism ♦ n romantic person ~**ally** adv ~**ism** /-təˌsɪzəm/ n [U] admiration of feeling rather than thought, in art and literature ~**ize** vt make (something) seem more interesting or ROMANTIC (2) than it really is

Ro·ma·ny /ˈroʊməni/ n 1 [C] GYPSY 2 [U] gypsies' language

Ro·me·o /ˈroʊmiˌoʊ/ n -os romantic male lover

roof /ruf, rʊf/ n 1 top covering of a building, vehicle, etc. 2 upper part of the inside (of the mouth) ♦ vt put or be a roof on ~**ing** /ˈrufɪŋ, ˈrʊvɪŋ/ n [U] roof material

roof·top /ˈruftɑp, ˈrʊf-/ vt 1 roof 2 **from the rooftops** loudly, so that everyone can hear

rook /rʊk/ n 1 large black bird, like a CROW 2 one of the powerful pieces in the game of CHESS

rook·ie /'rʊki/ n 1 new soldier or police-man 2 first-year professional ATHLETE

room /rum, rʊm/ n 1 [C] division of a building, with its own floor, walls, and CEILING 2 [U] (enough) space 3 [U] need or possibility for something to happen: *room for improvement* ♦ vi have a place to live; have a room or rooms ~**y** adj with plenty of space inside

room·mate /'rum-meɪt, 'rʊm-/ n person sharing a room, apartment, or house

room ser·vice /'· ‚··/ n [U] hotel service providing food, etc., in people's rooms

roost /rust/ n 1 place where a bird sleeps 2 **rule the roost** be the leader ♦ vi 1 (of a bird) sit and sleep 2 **come home to roost** (of a bad action) have a bad effect on the doer, esp. after a period of time

roost·er /'rustər/ n fully grown male chicken

root[1] /rut/ n 1 part of a plant that goes down into the soil for food 2 part of a tooth, hair, etc., that holds it to the body 3 cause; beginning; origin 4 (in grammar) base part of a word to which other parts can be added 5 a number that when multiplied by itself a stated number of times gives another stated number 6 **take root** (of plants or ideas) become established and begin to grow ~**less** adj without a home **roots** n [P] 1 (one's connection with) one's place of origin 2 **pull up one's roots** move to a new place from one's settled home 3 **put down (new) roots** establish a (new) place, by making friends, etc. — see also GRASS ROOTS

root[2] v 1 vi/t (cause to) form roots: (fig.) *rooted to the spot* (= unable to move) | *deeply rooted* (= firmly fixed) 2 vi search by turning things over

root for phr vt support strongly

root out phr vt get rid of completely

root beer /'· ‚·/ n brown nonalcoholic drink with BUBBLES

rope[1] /roʊp/ n 1 [C;U] (piece of) strong thick cord 2 [C] fat twisted string (of the stated kind) 3 **give someone (plenty of) rope** allow someone (plenty of) freedom to act 4 **ropes** n [P] rules, customs, and ways of operating

rope[2] vt tie with a rope

rope in phr vt infml persuade or force to join an activity

rope off phr vt separate or enclose with ropes

ro·sa·ry /'roʊzəri/ n string of BEADS used by Roman Catholics for counting prayers

rose[1] /roʊz/ past t. of RISE

rose[2] n 1 brightly colored flower with a sweet smell growing on a bush with prickly stems 2 pale to dark pink color 3 — see also BED OF ROSES

ro·sé /roʊ'zeɪ/ n [U] light pink wine

rose-col·ored /'· ‚··/ — adj look at/see/ view the world through rose-colored glasses see the world, life, etc., as better and nicer than they really are

ros·in /'rɑzɪn/ n [U] substance rubbed on the BOWS[2] (2) of musical instruments with strings

ros·ter /'rɑstər/ n list of people's names and duties

ros·y /'roʊzi/ adj 1 (esp. of skin) pink 2 (esp. of future) giving hope

rot /rɑt/ vi/t -tt- decay ♦ n [U] 1 decay 2 process of getting worse or going wrong 3 infml foolish nonsense

ro·tate /'roʊteɪt/ vi/t 1 turn around a fixed point 2 (cause to) take turns or come around regularly **rotation** /roʊ'teɪʃən/ n 1 [U] action of rotating 2 [C] one complete turn 3 **in rotation** taking regular turns

ROTC /'rɑtsi/ n RESERVE OFFICERS TRAINING CORPS

rote /roʊt/ n [U] fml repeated study using memory rather than understanding

ro·tis·se·rie /roʊ'tɪsəri/ n apparatus for cooking meat by turning it around and around on a metal ROD

ro·tor /'roʊtər/ n 1 rotating (ROTATE) part of a machine 2 set of HELICOPTER blades

rot·ten /'rɑt'n/ adj 1 decayed; gone bad 2 infml nasty or unpleasant 3 **feel rotten** feel sick, tired, or unhappy

ro·tund /roʊ'tʌnd/ adj fml (of a person) fat and round

rouge /ruʒ/ n [U] red substance for col-oring the cheeks

rough[1] /rʌf/ adj 1 having an uneven surface 2 stormy and violent: *rough weather* 3 lacking gentleness, good manners, or consideration: *rough han-dling at the airport* 4 (of food and living conditions) not delicate; simple 5 not detailed or exact 6 unfortunate and/or

unfair **7** *infml* unwell **8 rough and**
ready simple and without comfort ~**ly**
adv **1** in a rough manner **2** about; not
exactly ~**en** *vi/t* make or become rough
~**ness** *n* [U]

rough² *n* [U] **1** areas of long grass on a
GOLF course **2 take the rough with the**
smooth accept bad things as well as
good things uncomplainingly

rough³ *v* **rough it** *infml* live simply and
rather uncomfortably

   rough up *phr vt infml* attack roughly,
usu. as a threat

rough·age /ˈrʌfɪdʒ/ *n* [U] coarse matter
in food, which helps the bowels to work

rough·house /ˈrʌfhaʊs/ *vi* disorderly,
noisy play esp. indoors –**housing**
/-ˌhaʊzɪŋ/ *n* [U]

rough·shod /ˈrʌfʃɑd/ *adv* — see ride
roughshod over (RIDE¹)

rou·lette /ruˈlet/ *n* [U] game of chance
played with a small ball and a spinning
wheel — see also RUSSIAN ROULETTE

round¹ /raʊnd/ *adj* **1** circular **2** shaped
like a ball **3** (of parts of the body) fat and
curved **4** (of a number) expressed to the
nearest 10, 100, 1000, etc. ~**ness** *n* [U]

round² *adv* **1** around **2** with a circular
movement: *The wheels went round.* **3**
surrounding a central point: *Gather*
round. **4 year round** during the whole
year

round³ *prep.* around

round⁴ *n* **1** number or set (of events): *a*
continual round of parties **2** regular
delivery trip: *do one's rounds* (= make
one's usual visits) **3 a** (in GOLF) complete
game **b** (in boxing (BOX²)) period of fighting in a match **c** (in tennis, football, etc.)
stage in a competition **d** one single shot
from a gun **4** long burst: *a round of*
applause **5** type of song for 3 or 4 voices,
in which each sings the same tune, one
starting a line after another has just
finished it

round⁵ *vt* **1** go around: *rounding the*
corner **2** make: *rounding his lips*

   round off *phr vt* **1** reduce or increase
to a whole number **2** end suitably and
satisfactorily

   round on *phr vt* turn and attack

   round up *phr vt* **1** gather together (scattered things) **2** increase (an exact figure)
to the next highest whole number

round·a·bout /ˈraʊndəˌbaʊt/ *adj* indirect

round·ly /ˈraʊndli/ *adv fml* **1** completely
2 forcefully

round trip /ˌ· ˈ·◂/ *n* trip to a place and
back again **round-trip** *adj*: *round-trip*
ticket

round-up /ˈraʊndʌp/ *n* gathering
together of scattered things, animals, or
people

rouse /raʊz/ *vt* **1** *fml* waken **2** make more
active, interested, or excited **rousing**
adj that makes people excited

rout /raʊt/ *n* complete defeat ♦ *vt* defeat
completely

route /rut, raʊt/ *n* way from one place to
another — see also EN ROUTE ♦ *vt* send by
a particular route

rou·tine /ruˈtin/ *n* **1** [C;U] regular fixed
way of doing things **2** [C] set of dance
steps, songs, etc. ♦ *adj* **1** regular; not
special **2** dull ~**ly** *adv* –**ize** *vt*

rov·ing /ˈroʊvɪŋ/ *adj* traveling or moving
from one place to another: *a roving*
reporter

row¹ /roʊ/ *n* **1** neat line of people or
things **2 in a row** one after the other
without a break

row² *vi/t* move (a boat) through the
water with OARS

row·boat /ˈroʊˌboʊt/ *n* small boat moved
with OARS

row·dy /ˈraʊdi/ *adj* noisy and rough ♦ *n*
–**dily** *adv* –**diness** *n* [U] ~**ism** *n* [U]
rowdy behavior

row house /ˈroʊ ˌhaʊs/ *n* house in a row
of houses connected to each other

roy·al /ˈrɔɪəl/ *adj* of a king or queen ~**ly**
adv splendidly

royal blue /ˌ·· ˈ·◂/ *adj* of a dark blue color

roy·al·ty /ˈrɔɪəlti/ *n* **1** [U] people of the
royal family **2** [C] payment made to the
writer of a book, piece of music, etc., out
of the money from its sales

rpm *abbrev. for*: revolutions per minute

RSVP please reply (written on invitations)

rub /rʌb/ *vi/t* **-bb-** **1** press against (something or each other) with a repeated up
and down or round and round movement
2 rub it in *infml* keep talking about
something that another person wants to
forget **3 rub salt in the wound** make
someone's suffering even worse **4 rub**
shoulders with *infml* meet socially and
treat as equals **5 rub someone the**
wrong way *infml* annoy ♦ *n* **1** [C] act of
rubbing **2** [*the*+S] cause of difficulty:

There's the rub. ~**bing** *n* copy made by rubbing paper laid over the top

rub down *phr vt* **1** dry by rubbing **2** make smooth by rubbing

rub in *phr vt* make (liquid) go into a surface by rubbing

rub off *phr vi* come off a surface (onto another) by rubbing: (fig.) *I hope some of her good qualities rub off on you.*

rub·ber¹ /'rʌbə/ *n* **1** [U] elastic substance used for keeping out water, making tires, etc. **2** [C] CONDOM ~**y** *adj*

rubber² *n* competition, esp. in cards, which usu. consists of an odd number of games

rubber band /ˌ· '·, '·· ·/ *n* thin circle of rubber for fastening things together

rub·ber·neck /'rʌbənek/ *vi/t* look at continuously with great interest ♦ *n* person who does this

rubber stamp /ˌ· '·/ *n* piece of rubber with raised letters or figures, for printing ♦ *vt* approve or support (a decision) officially, without really thinking about it

rub·bish /'rʌbɪʃ/ *n* [U] **1** waste material to be thrown away **2** nonsense

rub·ble /'rʌbəl/ *n* [U] broken stone and bricks, esp. from a destroyed building

ru·ble /'rubal/ *n* unit of money in Russia

ru·by /'rubi/ *n* deep red precious stone

ruck·us /'rʌkəs/ *n* [S] noisy angry argument or disagreement

rud·der /'rʌdə/ *n* blade at the back of a boat or aircraft to control its direction

rud·dy /'rʌdi/ *adj* **1** (of the face) pink and healthy looking **2** *lit* red

rude /rud/ *adj* **1** not polite; having bad manners **2** concerned with sex: *a rude joke* **3** sudden and violent: *a rude shock* **4** *old use* roughly made ~**ly** *adv* ~**ness** *n* [U]

ru·di·men·ta·ry /ˌrudə'mentəri◁/ *adj* **1** (of facts, knowledge, etc.) at the simplest level **2** small and not fully usable: *rudimentary wings*

ru·di·ments /'rudəmənts/ *n* [*the*+P] simplest parts of a subject, learned first

ruf·fle¹ /'rʌfəl/ *vt* **1** make uneven **2** trouble; upset

ruf·fle² *n* band of cloth sewn in folds as a decoration around the edges of a shirt, skirt, etc. ~**d** *adj*

rug /rʌg/ *n* thick decorative floor mat

rug·by /'rʌgbi/ *n* [U] type of European football

rug·ged /'rʌgɪd/ *adj* large, rough, and looking strong –**ly** *adv* ~**ness** *n* [U]

ru·in /'ruɪn/ *n* **1** [U] destruction **2** [C] also **ruins** *pl.* — remains of a building that has fallen down or been (partly) destroyed ♦ *vt* **1** spoil **2** cause total loss of money to ~**ed** *adj* (of a building) partly or wholly destroyed ~**ous** *adj* causing destruction or total loss of money

rule¹ /rul/ *n* **1** [C] something that tells one what must be done: *the rules of the game* **2** [U] period or way of ruling: *under foreign rule* **3** [C] RULER (2) **4 as a rule** usually **ruling** *n* official decision

rule² *v* **1** *vi/t* be in charge of (a country, people, etc.) **2** give an official decision **3** *vt* draw (a line) with a ruler

rule out *phr vt* **1** remove from consideration **2** make impossible

rule of thumb /ˌ· · '·/ *n* [C;U] quick inexact way of calculating or judging

rul·er /'rulə/ *n* **1** person who rules **2** narrow flat rod for measuring or drawing straight lines

rul·ing /'rulɪŋ/ *n* official decision esp. by a court of law

rum /rʌm/ *n* [U] strong alcoholic drink made from sugar

rum·ble¹ /'rʌmbəl/ *vi* make a deep, continuous rolling sound

rumble² *n* **1** [S] deep rolling sound **2** [C] street fight

ru·mi·nate /'rumənent/ *vi* think deeply

rum·mage /'rʌmɪdʒ/ *vi* turn things over untidily in searching

rummage sale /'·· ˌ·/ *n* sale of used articles, esp. to raise money for a church, CHARITY, etc.

ru·mor /'rumə/ *n* [C;U] (piece of) information, perhaps untrue, spread from person to person ~**ed** *adj* reported unofficially

rump /rʌmp/ *n* part of an animal above the back legs: *rump steak*

rum·ple /'rʌmpəl/ *vt* make untidy; disarrange

run¹ /rʌn/ *v* **ran** /ræn/, **run**, *pres. p.* -**nn**- **1** *vi* (of people and animals) move faster than a walk **2** *vt* take part in (a race) by running **3** *vi/t* (cause to) work: *The car ran into a tree.* **4** *vi/t* (cause to) work: *This machine runs on/by electric-*

ity. **5** *vi* (of a public vehicle) travel as arranged **6** *vt* control (an organization or system) **7** *vi* go; pass: *The road runs south.* **8** *vi* continue in operation, performance, etc.: *The play ran for 2 years in L.A.* **9** *vi/t* (cause liquid) to flow: *run a bath* | *running water* **10** *vi* pour out liquid: *The baby's nose is running.* **11** *vi* (melt and) spread by the action of heat or water **12** *vi* become: *Supplies are running low.* **13** *vi* try to get elected **14** *vt* print in a newspaper **15** *vt* bring into a country illegally and secretly **16** *vi* to appear often: *Intelligence runs in that family.* **17** *vt* take (someone or something) to somewhere in a vehicle: *I'll run you home.* **18 run for it** escape by running **19 run short: a** use almost all one has and not have enough left **b** become less than enough

run across *phr vt* meet or find by chance

run after *phr vt* **1** chase **2** try to gain the attention and company of

run along *phr vi* go away

run away *phr vi* go away (as if) to escape

run away/off with *phr vt* **1** gain control of: *Don't let your temper run away with you.* **2** go away with (a lover) **3** steal

run down *phr v* **1** *vt* knock down and hurt with a vehicle **2** *vt* chase and catch **3** *vi* (esp. of a clock or BATTERY) lose power and stop working **4** *vt* say unfair things about

run into *phr vt* **1** meet by chance **2** cause (a vehicle) to meet (something) with force

run off *phr vt* print (copies)

run on *phr vi* continue (for too long)

run out *phr vi* **1** come to an end, so there is none left **2** have none left: *We've run out of gas.*

run over *phr v* **1** *vt* knock down and drive over **2** *vi* overflow

run through *phr vt* **1** repeat for practice **2** read or examine quickly **3** push one's weapon right through

run to *phr vt* reach (the stated amount): *the total runs to $55.60.*

run up *phr vt* **1** raise (a flag) **2** cause oneself to have (bills or debts)

run up against *phr vt* be faced with (a difficulty)

run² *n* **1** [C] act of running **2** [C] ship or train journey **3** [S] continuous set of similar events, performances, etc.: *a run of bad luck* | *The play had a run of 3 months.* **4** [S] **a** eager demand to buy: *a big run on ice cream* **b** general desire to sell money or take one's money out: *a run on a bank* **5** [S] freedom to use: *He gave me the run of his library.* **6** [C] animal enclosure: *a chicken run* **7** point won in baseball **8** [C] sloping course: *a ski run* **9** [C] fault in a stocking, etc. **10 a (good) run for one's money: a** plenty of opposition in a competition **b** good results for money spent or effort made **11 in the long run** after a long period; in the end **12 on the run** trying to escape **13 the common/ordinary run (of)** the usual sort (of)

run·a·round /'· ·ₚ·/ *n* [*the*+S] *sl* delaying or deceiving treatment

run·a·way /'rʌnəˌweɪ/ *adj* **1** out of control: *runaway prices* **2** having escaped by running: *a runaway child* ♦ *n* child who has left home because of problems

run-down /'rʌndaʊn/ *n* detailed report

run-down /ₚ· ˈ·ˌ·/ *adj* **1** tired, weak, and sick **2** in bad condition

rung¹ /rʌŋ/ *past p. of* RING²

rung² *n* sideways bar in a ladder or on a chair

run·ner /'rʌnə/ *n* **1** person or animal that runs **2** smuggler (SMUGGLE): *a gunrunner* **3** thin blade on which something slides on ice or snow **4** stem with which a plant spreads itself along the ground

runner-up /ₚ·· ˈ·/ *n* **runners-up** one that comes second in a race, etc.

run·ning¹ /'rʌnɪŋ/ *n* **1** act or sport of running **2 in/out of the running** with some/no hope of winning

running² *adj* **1** (of water) flowing **2** continuous: *a running battle* | *a running commentary* **3** (of money) spent or needed to keep something working: *running costs* **4 in running order** (of a machine) working properly **5 take a running jump** run to a point where one starts a jump ♦ *adv* in a row: *I won 3 times running.*

running mate /'·· ·/ *n* (in politics) person with whom one is trying to get elected for a pair of political positions of greater and lesser importance

run·ny /'rʌni/ adj **1** in a more liquid form than usual **2** (of the nose or eyes) producing liquid

run-of-the-mill /ˌ·· '·◂/ adj ordinary; dull

run-on sen·tence /'·· ˌ·/ n sentence with too many CLAUSEs

runt /rʌnt/ n **1** small animal that is poorly developed physically **2** derog small unpleasant person

run through /'· ·/ n act of repeating (something) for practice

run·way /'rʌnweɪ/ n surface on which aircraft land and take off

ru·pee /ruˈpi, 'rupi/ n unit of money in India, Pakistan, etc.

rup·ture /'rʌptʃə/ n **1** [C;U] fml sudden breaking **2** [C] HERNIA ♦ v **1** vi/t fml break suddenly **2** vt give (oneself) a HERNIA

ru·ral /'rʊrəl/ adj of the country (not the town)

rush¹ /rʌʃ/ v **1** vi/t go or take suddenly and very quickly **2** vi hurry **3** vt deal with (too) hastily **4** vt force (someone) to eat hastily **5** vt attack suddenly and all together **6 rush someone off his/her feet** make someone hurry too much or work too hard ♦ n **1** [C] sudden rapid movement **2** [U] (need for) (too much) hurrying **3** [S] sudden demand **4** [U] period of great and hurried activity: *the Christmas rush*

rush² n grasslike water plant

rush·es /'rʌʃɪz/ n [P] (in film making) the first print of a film

rush hour /'· ˌ·/ n busy period when most people are traveling to or from work

rus·set /'rʌsɪt/ adj esp. lit brownish red ♦ n kind of potato

Rus·sian rou·lette /ˌrʌʃən ruˈlɛt/ n [U] dangerous game in which one fires a gun at one's head without knowing whether it is loaded

rust /rʌst/ n [U] **1** reddish brown surface formed on iron, steel, etc., that has been wet **2** the color of this ♦ vi/t (cause to) become covered with rust ~**y** adj **1** covered with rust **2** infml lacking recent practice

rus·tic /'rʌstɪk/ adj typical of the country, esp. in being simple

rus·tle /'rʌsəl/ v **1** vi/t (cause to) make slight sounds like dry leaves moving **2** vt steal (cattle or horses) –**tler** n

rustle up phr vt provide quickly

rut¹ /rʌt/ n **1** [C] deep narrow track left by a wheel **2** [S] dull fixed way of life ~**ted** adj having ruts

rut² n (season of) sexual excitement in some animals ♦ vi -**tt**- (of an animal) be in a rut

ruth·less /'ruθlɪs/ adj doing cruel things without pity ~**ly** adv ~**ness** n [U]

RV also **recreational vehicle** — n large vehicle for traveling and sleeping in while on vacation

rye /raɪ/ n [U] grass plant with grain used esp. for flour

S

S, s /ɛs/ the 19th letter of the English alphabet

S. *written abbrev. for*: south(ern)

Sab·bath /ˈsæbəθ/ n [S] religious day of rest, esp. Saturday (for Jews) or (for Christians) Sunday

sab·bat·i·cal /səˈbætɪkəl/ n, adj period with pay when one is free to leave one's ordinary job to travel and study

sa·ble /ˈseɪbəl/ n [C;U] (dark fur from) a small animal

sab·o·tage /ˈsæbəˌtɑːʒ/ n [U] intentional damage carried out secretly ♦ vt perform sabotage against

sab·o·teur /ˌsæbəˈtɜː/ n person who practices sabotage

sa·ber /ˈseɪbər/ n heavy military sword, usu. curved

saber-rat·tling /ˈ·· ˌ··/ n [U] talking about (military) power in a threatening way

sac /sæk/ n small bag-shaped part inside a plant or animal

sac·cha·rin /ˈsækərɪn/ n [U] chemical that tastes very sweet and is used instead of sugar

saccharine /ˌsækəˈriːn◄/ adj too romantic, in a silly insincere way

sach·et /sæˈʃeɪ/ n small cloth bag holding a nice-smelling substance

sack¹ /sæk/ n 1 [C] large simple bag of strong material 2 [the+S] *infml* bed 3 **hit the sack** *infml* go to bed ~**ing** n [U] sackcloth (1)

sack² vt destroy and rob (a defeated city)

sac·ra·ment /ˈsækrəmənt/ n important Christian ceremony, such as BAPTISM or marriage **~al** /ˌsækrəˈmɛntl◄/ adj

sa·cred /ˈseɪkrɪd/ adj 1 connected with religion 2 holy because connected with God or gods 3 that is solemn and must be respected **~ness** n [U]

sacred cow /ˌ·· ˈ·/ n derog thing so much accepted that not even honest doubts about it are allowed

sac·ri·fice /ˈsækrəˌfaɪs/ n 1 (an offering) to gods, esp. of an animal killed as part of a ceremony 2 loss or giving up of something of value ♦ v 1 vi/t offer

(something or someone) as a SACRIFICE (1) 2 vt give up or lose, esp. for some good purpose **–ficial** /ˌsækrəˈfɪʃəl◄/ adj

sac·ri·lege /ˈsækrəlɪdʒ/ n [C;U] treating a holy place or thing without respect **–legious** /ˌsækrəˈlɪdʒəs◄/ adj

sac·ro·sanct /ˈsækroʊˌsæŋkt, ˈsækrə-/ adj *often derog or humor* too holy or important to be treated disrespectfully or harmed

sad /sæd/ adj **-dd-** 1 unhappy 2 unsatisfactory **~ly** adv **~den** vt make or become SAD (1) **~ness** n [U]

sad·dle¹ /ˈsædl/ n 1 rider's seat on a horse, bicycle, etc. 2 **in the saddle**: a sitting on a SADDLE (1) b in control (of a job)

saddle² vt put a saddle on (a horse)

saddle with phr vt give (someone) (an unpleasant or difficult duty, responsibility, etc.)

sa·dis·m /ˈseɪdɪzəm/ n [U] unnatural fondness for cruelty to others, (sometimes to gain sexual pleasure) **–dist** n **–distic** /səˈdɪstɪk/ adj

sa·fa·ri /səˈfɑːri, səˈfæri/ n [C;U] trip to hunt or photograph animals, esp. in Africa

safe¹ /seɪf/ adj 1 out of danger 2 not likely to cause danger or harm 3 (in baseball) having reached base without being put out 4 **safe and sound** unharmed 5 **on the safe side** being more careful than may be necessary 6 **play it safe** take no risks **~ly** adv **~ness** n [U]

safe² n thick metal box with a lock; for keeping valuable things in

safe-de·pos·it box /ˈ· ·ˌ·· ˌ·/ n small box for storing valuable objects, esp. in a bank

safe·guard /ˈseɪfɡɑːrd/ n means of protection against something unwanted ♦ vt protect

safe·keep·ing /ˌseɪfˈkiːpɪŋ/ n [U] protection from harm or loss

safe sex /ˌ· ˈ·/ n [U] ways of having sex that reduce the risk of getting a sexual disease, esp. by using a CONDOM

safe·ty /ˈseɪfti/ n [U] condition of being safe

safety net /ˈ·· ˌ·/ n 1 system or arrangement that helps people who have serious problems: *the safety net of insurance* 2 large net for catching someone performing high above the ground if he/she falls

safety pin /ˈ·· ˌ·/ n bent pin with a cover at one end, used for fastening things

safety valve /ˈ·· ˌ·/ n 1 means of getting rid of possibly dangerous forces (in a machine) 2 something that allows strong feelings to be expressed in a non-violent way

saf·fron /ˈsæfrən/ n [U] 1 deep orange substance obtained from a flower, used for giving color and taste to food 2 orange-yellow color

sag /sæg/ vi -gg- 1 sink or bend downwards out of the usual position 2 become less active, happy, etc.: *My spirits sagged when I saw all the work I had to do.* **sag** n [S;U]

sa·ga /ˈsɑːɡə/ n 1 old story, esp. about adventure 2 long story

sage /seɪdʒ/ adj lit wise, esp. from long experience ♦ n wise person, esp. an old man

sage·brush /ˈseɪdʒbrʌʃ/ n [U] small bush growing on dry land in western N. America

Sag·it·tar·i·us /ˌsædʒəˈteəriəs/ n 1 [S] 9th sign of the ZODIAC, represented by a man with a BOW and ARROWS 2 someone born between November 22 and December 21

said /sed/ v past t. and p. of SAY ♦ adj law just mentioned

sail /seɪl/ n 1 piece of strong cloth that allows the wind to move a ship through the water 2 trip in a boat 3 blade of a WINDMILL, for catching the wind 4 **set sail** begin a trip at sea 5 **under sail** driven by sails and wind ♦ v 1 vi/t travel (across) by boat 2 vt direct or command (a boat) on water 3 vt be able to control a sailing boat: *Can you sail?* 4 vi begin a voyage 5 vi move smoothly or easily – see also **sail close to the wind** (CLOSE²) ~**ing** n [U] sport of riding in or directing a small boat with sails

sail·board /ˈseɪlbɔrd, -boʊrd/ n flat board with a sail used in the sport of WINDSURFING

sail·boat /ˈseɪlboʊt/ n small boat with one or more sails

sail·or /ˈseɪlər/ n person who works on a ship

saint /seɪnt/ n written abbrev. **St.** 1 person officially recognized after death as especially holy by the Christian church 2 infml a very good and completely unselfish person ~**ly** adj very holy

sake /seɪk/ n 1 **for the sake of: a** in order to help, improve, or bring advantage to **b** for the purpose of 2 **for Christ's/God's/goodness/pity's sake** infml (used to give force to an urgent request or sometimes an expression of annoyance): *For goodness sake, stop arguing!* | *For God's sake, what do you want from me!*

sal·ad /ˈsæləd/ n [C;U] a mixture of usu. raw vegetables served cold

salad bar /ˈ·· ˌ·/ n place in a restaurant where one can make one's own SALAD

salad days /ˈ·· ˌ·/ n [P] one's time of youth and inexperience

salad dress·ing /ˈ·· ˌ·/ n [C;U] sauce put on SALADS to add taste

sal·a·man·der /ˈsæləˌmændə/ n small animal like a LIZARD

sa·la·mi /səˈlɑmi/ n [U] large SAUSAGE usu. eaten cold

sal·a·ry /ˈsæləri/ n [C;U] fixed regular pay each month for a job, esp. for workers of higher rank –**ried** adj receiving a regular salary

sale /seɪl/ n 1 [C;U] (act of) selling 2 [C] special offering of goods at low prices 3 **for sale** offered to be sold, esp. privately 4 **on sale: a** offered to be sold, esp. in a store **b** offered at a lower price **salable** adj

sales /seɪlz/ adj of or for selling: *a sales forecast*

sales·clerk /ˈseɪlzklɜrk/ n person who helps customers in a store

sales·man /ˈseɪlzmən/ n -**men** /-mən/ a male salesperson

sales·man·ship /ˈseɪlzmənʃɪp/ n [U] skill in selling

sales·per·son /ˈseɪlzˌpɜrsən/ n -**people** /-ˌpipəl/ 1 a sales rep 2 SALESCLERK, esp. a skilled one

sales rep /ˈ·· ·/ n person who goes from place to place, usu. within a particular area, selling and taking orders for their company's goods

sales slip /ˈ·· ·/ n small piece of paper given in a store after buying something; RECEIPT

sales tax /ˈ·· ·/ n tax added onto the price of goods at the time of buying them

sales·wo·man /ˈseɪlzˌwʊmən/ n -**women** /-ˌwɪmɪn/ a female salesperson

sa·li·ent /ˈseɪliənt/ adj fml most noticeable or important

sa·line /ˈseɪlin, -lain/ adj containing salt

sa·li·va /səˈlaɪvə/ n [U] natural liquid produced in the mouth ~**ry** adj –**vate** /ˈsæləˌveɪt/ vi

sal·low /ˈsæloʊ/ adj (of the skin) yellow and looking unhealthy ~**ness** n [U]

salm·on /ˈsæmən/ n **salmon** [C;U] large fish with pink flesh of great value as food

sal·mo·nel·la /ˌsælməˈnelə/ n [U] bacteria that causes food poisoning

sal·on /səˈlɑn/ n stylish or fashionable small shop: a hairdressing salon

sa·loon /səˈlun/ n **1** large grandly furnished room for use of ship's passengers **2** public drinking place, esp. in the old West

sal·sa /ˈsælsə, ˈsɔl-/ n [U] **1** thick SAUCE made with onions, TOMATOes, and SPICY PEPPERS, eaten with Mexican food **2** Latin American dance, or the music played with this

salt¹ /sɔlt/ n **1** [U] common white substance used for preserving food and improving its taste: salt water **2** [C] chemical compound of an acid and a metal **3** [C] infml an old, experienced sailor: an old salt **4 the salt of the earth** person or people regarded as worthy of admiration and dependable **5 take something with a grain of salt** not necessarily believe all of something — see also **worth one's salt** (WORTH)

salt² vt put salt on

salt away phr vt save money (esp. for the future)

salt shaker /ˈ· ˌ··/ n small bottle with holes for shaking salt onto food

salt·y /ˈsɔlti/ adj containing or tasting of salt

sal·u·ta·ry /ˈsælyəˌteri/ adj causing an improvement in character, future behavior, health, etc.

sal·u·ta·tion /ˌsælyəˈteɪʃən/ n **1** [C;U] fml expression of greeting by words or actions **2** [C] word or phrase such as "Ladies and Gentlemen," "Dear Sir," "Dear Miss Jones," at the beginning of a speech or letter

sa·lute /səˈlut/ n **1** military sign of recognition: esp. raising the hand to the forehead **2** ceremonial firing of guns to honor someone **3 take the salute** (of a person of high rank) to stand while being SALUTEd by soldiers marching past ♦ v **1** vi/t make a SALUTE (1) (to) **2** vt fml honor and praise ~ vt fml greet

sal·vage /ˈsælvɪdʒ/ vt save (goods or property) from wreck or destruction ♦ n [U] act or process of salvaging

sal·va·tion /sælˈveɪʃən/ n [U] **1** (esp. in the Christian religion) the saving or state of being saved from SIN **2** something or someone that saves one from loss or failure

Salvation Ar·my /ˌ·· ˈ··/ n Christian organization with military uniforms and ranks, that helps poor people

salve /sæv/ n [C;U] medicinal cream for putting on a wound, sore place, etc. ♦ vt fml make (esp. feelings) less painful

sal·vo /ˈsælvoʊ/ n -**vos** or -**voes** firing of several guns together

Sa·mar·i·tan /səˈmærətˈn/ n see GOOD SAMARITAN

same¹ /seɪm/ adj **1** not changed or different; not another or other **2** alike in (almost) every way **3 one and the same** exactly the same **4 same here** infml me too **5 by the same token** in the same way **6 in the same boat** in the same unpleasant situation

same² pron **1** the same thing, person, condition, etc. **2 just/all the same** in spite of this **3 same to you** I wish you the same (a greeting or sometimes an angry wish) ~**ness** n [U] **1** very close likeness **2** lack of variety

same³ adv **the same (as)** in the same way (as)

sam·ple /ˈsæmpəl/ n small part representing the whole ♦ vt take and examine a sample of

san·a·to·ri·um /ˌsænəˈtoriəm, -ˈtouriəm/ n -**ums** or -**a** /-riə/ sort of hospital for sick people who are getting better but still need treatment, rest, etc.

sanc·ti·fy /ˈsæŋktəˌfaɪ/ vt make holy

sanc·ti·mo·ni·ous /ˌsæŋktəˈmouniəs/ adj fml disapproving of others because one thinks one is good, right, etc., and they are not ~**ly** adv ~**ness** n [U]

sanc·tion /ˈsæŋkʃən/ n **1** [U] fml formal or official permission, approval, or acceptance **2** [C] action taken against a person or country that has broken a law or rule **3** [C] something that forces people to keep a rule: a moral sanction ♦ vt fml **1** accept, approve, or permit, esp. officially **2** make acceptable: a custom sanctioned by long usage

sanc·ti·ty /ˈsæŋktəti/ n [U] holiness

sanc·tu·a·ry /'sæŋktʃuₑri/ n 1 [C] part of a (Christian) church considered most holy 2 [C;U] (place of) protection for someone being hunted by officers of the law 3 [C] area where animals are protected

sanc·tum /'sæŋktəm/ n 1 holy place inside a temple 2 *infml* private place or room where one can be quiet and alone

sand /sænd/ n [U] 1 loose material of very small grains, found on sea coasts and in deserts 2 **build on sand** plan or do something with no good reason to believe in its success ♦ vt 1 make smooth by rubbing with esp. SANDPAPER 2 put sand on, esp. to stop slipping **sands** n [P] 1 area of sand 2 moments in time (as if measured by sand in an HOURGLASS): *The sands of time are running out.* ~y adj 1 consisting of sand or having sand on the surface 2 (of hair) yellowish brown

san·dal /'sændl/ n light shoe with a flat bottom and bands to hold it to the foot

sand·bag /'sændbæg/ n bag filled with sand, esp. for forming a protective wall

sand·blast /'sændblæst/ vt clean or cut with a very fast stream of sand

sand·box /'sændˌbɒks/ n special area of sand for children to play in

sand·cas·tle /'sændˌkæsəl/ n 1 small model, esp. of a castle, built of sand 2 **sandcastles in the air** [P] impossible or impractical ideas or plans

S and L, S & L /ˌes ən 'el/ n SAVINGS AND LOAN

sand·pa·per /'sændˌpeɪpə/ n [U] paper covered with fine grainy material, for rubbing surfaces to make them smoother ♦ vt rub with sandpaper

sand·stone /'sændstoʊn/ n [U] soft rock formed from sand

sand·storm /'sændstɔːrm/ n desert storm in which sand is blown about

sand·wich /'sændwɪtʃ/ n 2 pieces of bread with other food between them ♦ vt fit (with difficulty) between 2 other things

sane /seɪn/ adj 1 healthy in mind; not crazy 2 sensible ~ly adv ~ness n [U]

sang /sæŋ/ v past t. of SING

san·guine /'sæŋgwɪn/ adj *fml* quietly hopeful

san·i·ta·ry /'sænəˌteri/ adj 1 concerned with preserving health, esp. by removing dirt 2 not dangerous to health; clean

sanitary pad /'···· ·/ n small mass of soft paper worn to take up MENSTRUAL blood

san·i·ta·tion /ˌsænə'teɪʃən/ n [U] methods of protecting public health, esp. by removing and treating waste

san·i·tize /'sænəˌtaɪz/ vt 1 make sanitary 2 *derog* make less unpleasant, dangerous, strongly expressed, etc., in order not to offend people

san·i·ty /'sænəti/ n [U] quality of being SANE

sank /sæŋk/ v past t. of SINK¹

San·ta Claus /'sæntə ˌklɔz/ n imaginary old man believed by children to bring presents at Christmas

sap¹ /sæp/ n [U] watery liquid that carries food in plants

sap² vt -pp- weaken or destroy, esp. over a long time

sap·ling /'sæplɪŋ/ n young tree

sap·py /'sæpi/ adj 1 foolish 2 too full of expressions of tender feelings

sap·phire /'sæfaɪə/ n [C;U] bright blue precious stone

sar·casm /'sɑrˌkæzəm/ n [U] saying the clear opposite of what is meant, in order to be (amusingly) offensive –castic /sɑr'kæstɪk/ adj –tically adv

sar·dine /sɑr'din/ n 1 small young fish often preserved in oil for eating 2 **like sardines** packed very tightly together

sar·don·ic /sɑr'dɒnɪk/ adj seeming to regard oneself as too important to consider a matter, person, etc., seriously ~ally adv

sa·ri /'sɑri/ n dress consisting of a length of cloth, worn by Hindu women

SASE n self-addressed stamped envelope

sash¹ /sæʃ/ n length of cloth worn around the waist or over one shoulder

sash² n window frame, esp. in a sort of window with 2 frames that slide up and down

sass /sæs/ n rude, disrespectful talk ♦ vt

SAT /sæt/ n Scholastic Aptitude Test, taken by those wishing to attend US universities

sat /sæt/ past t. and p. of SIT

Sa·tan /'seɪt'n/ n the Devil

sa·tan·ic /sə'tænɪk/ adj 1 very evil or cruel 2 of satanism ~ally adv

sat·an·ism /'seɪt'nˌɪzəm/ n [U] worship of the devil –ist n

sat·el·lite /ˈsætlˌaɪt/ n 1 heavenly body that moves around a larger one 2 artificial object moving around the Earth, moon, etc. 3 country or person that depends on another

satellite dish /ˈ··· ˌ·/ n large circular piece of metal for receiving television signals from SATELLITES (2)

sat·in /ˈsætˈn/ n [U] smooth shiny cloth made mainly from silk

sat·ire /ˈsætaɪə/ n [C;U] piece of writing, etc., showing the foolishness or evil of something in an amusing way –**irical** /səˈtɪrɪkəl/ adj –**irize** /ˈsætəˌraɪz/ vt

sat·is·fac·tion /ˌsætɪsˈfækʃən/ n 1 [C;U] (something that gives) a feeling of pleasure 2 [U] fml fulfillment of a need, desire, etc. 3 [U] fml certainty: It has been proved to my satisfaction. 4 [U] fml chance to defend one's honor

sat·is·fac·to·ry /ˌsætɪsˈfæktəri/ adj 1 pleasing 2 good enough –**rily** adv

sat·is·fy /ˈsætɪsˌfaɪ/ vt 1 please 2 fulfill (a need, desire, etc.) 3 fml fit (a condition, rule, standard, etc.) 4 persuade fully

sat·u·rate /ˈsætʃəˌreɪt/ vt 1 make completely wet 2 fill completely: The house market is saturated. –**rated** adj (of fat or oil) having chemicals combined in an unhealthy way –**ration** /ˌsætʃəˈreɪʃən/ n [U]

Sat·ur·day /ˈsætədi, -ˌdeɪ/ n the 7th day of the week, after Friday

Sat·urn /ˈsætən/ n the PLANET 6th in order from the sun, with large rings around it

sauce /sɔs/ n [C;U] 1 thick liquid put on food [C] 2 cooked fruit eaten with meat: cranberry sauce

sauce·pan /ˈsɔs·pæn/ n metal cooking pot with a handle

sau·cer /ˈsɔsə/ n small plate for putting a cup on — see also FLYING SAUCER

sau·na /ˈsɔnə, ˈsaʊnə/ n (a room or building for) a type of bath in steam

saun·ter /ˈsɔntə, ˈsɑn-/ vi walk in a slow, calm manner

saus·age /ˈsɔsɪdʒ/ n [C;U] finely cut meat in a tube of thin skin

sau·té /sɔˈteɪ/ vt cook quickly in a little hot oil

sav·age /ˈsævɪdʒ/ adj 1 forcefully cruel or violent 2 uncivilized ♦ n member of an uncivilized tribe ♦ vt attack and bite fiercely ~**ly** adv

sav·age·ry /ˈsævɪdʒri/ n [C;U] (act of) savage behavior

sa·van·na /səˈvænə/ n [U] flat grassy land in a warm part of the world

save¹ /seɪv/ v 1 vt make safe from danger or destruction 2 vi/t keep and add to an amount of (money) for later use 3 vt avoid the waste of (money, time, etc.) 4 vt keep for future use or enjoyment later 5 vt make unnecessary 6 vt (of a GOAL-KEEPER) stop one's opponents from getting the ball into the net 7 **save one's skin/neck** infml escape from a serious danger 8 **to save one's life** infml even with the greatest effort: I can't play the piano to save my life. ♦ n act of saving (SAVE (6)) **saver** n **savings** n [P] money saved, esp. in a bank

save² prep fml except

saving grace /ˌ·· ˈ·/ n the one good thing that makes something acceptable

savings account /ˈ·· ˌ·/ n bank account for saving

savings and loan /ˌ·· · ˈ·/ also S & L — n business organization into which people pay money in order to save it and gain interest, and which lends money to people who want to buy houses

savings bond /ˈ·· ˌ/ n BOND (2) sold by the government in amounts up to $1000, on which it pays interest

sa·vior /ˈseɪvjə/ n 1 one who saves from danger or loss 2 (usu. cap.) Jesus Christ

sa·vor /ˈseɪvə/ n [S;U] 1 taste or smell 2 (power to excite) interest ♦ vt enjoy slowly and purposefully

sa·vor·y /ˈseɪvəri/ adj tasting good

sav·vy /ˈsævi/ n [U] practical understanding or skill

saw¹ /sɔ/ past t. of SEE

saw² n tool with a thin blade and teeth for cutting hard materials ♦ vi/t **sawed**, **sawed**, or **sawn** /sɔn/ cut (as if) with a saw

saw³ n short common saying

saw·dust /ˈsɔdʌst/ n [U] wood dust made by a saw in cutting

saw·mill /ˈsɔˌmɪl/ n factory where trees are cut into boards

sax·o·phone /ˈsæksəˌfoʊn/ also **sax** /sæks/ infml — n metal musical instrument of the WOODWIND family, used esp. in JAZZ

say¹ /seɪ/ **said** /sɛd/ 1 vt pronounce (a sound, word, etc.) 2 vi/t express (a thought, opinion, etc.) in words 3 vt give as a general opinion; claim **4** *vt* suppose; suggest: *Let's say they accept your idea—what then? | Would you accept, say,* (= for example) *$500?* **5 go without saying** be clear; not need stating **6 hard to say** difficult to judge **7 say for oneself/something** offer as an excuse or defense: *You're late again. What have you got to say for yourself? | The idea has little to be said for it.* **8 say to more!** *infml* your/the meaning is clear **9 say to oneself** think **10 that is to say** expressed another (more exact) way **11 they say** it is usually thought **12 to say nothing of** including **13 when all is said and done** it must be remembered that **14 you don't say!** (an expression of slight surprise)

say² *n* [S;U] **1** power or right of (sharing in) acting or deciding **2 have one's say** (have the chance to) express one's opinion

say·ing /ˈseɪ-ɪŋ/ *n* common wise statement

scab /skæb/ *n* **1** hard mass of dried blood formed over a wound **2** *derog* one who works while others are on STRIKE

scads /skædz/ *n* [P] *infml* large numbers or quantities: *scads of money*

scaf·fold /ˈskæfəld, -foʊld/ *n* raised stage for the official killing of criminals **-ing** *n* [U] structure of poles and boards around a building for workmen to stand on

scald /skɔld/ *vt* burn with hot liquid **scald** *n*

scale¹ /skeɪl/ *n* **1** [C] set of marks on an instrument, used for measuring **2** [C] set of figures for measuring or comparing: *a temperature scale* **3** [C;U] relationship between a map or model and the thing it represents: *a scale of 1 inch to the mile* **4** [C;U] size or level in relation to other or usual things: *a large-scale business operation* **5** [C] set of musical notes at fixed separations **6 to scale** according to a fixed rule for reducing the size of something in a drawing, etc.

scale² also **scales** *pl.* — *n* weighing apparatus

scale³ *n* **1** any of the small flat stiff pieces covering fish, snakes, etc. **2** grayish material formed inside hot water pipes, pots in which water is boiled, etc. ♦ *vt* remove the scales from

scale⁴ *vt* **1** climb up **2** increase/reduce, esp. by a fixed rate

scal·lop /ˈskɑləp, ˈskæləp/ *n* small sea animal (MOLLUSK) with a shell, used for food

scalp /skælp/ *n* skin on top of the head: (fig.) *He wants the Mayor's scalp.* (= wants to see him punished for doing wrong) ♦ *vt* cut off the scalp of

scal·pel /ˈskælpəl/ *n* small sharp knife used by doctors in operations

scalp·er /ˈskælpər/ *n derog* person who offers tickets for the theater, etc., at very high prices

scam /skæm/ *n sl* clever and dishonest plan or course of action

scam·per /ˈskæmpər/ *vi* run quickly and usu. playfully

scan /skæn/ *v* **-nn- 1** *vt* examine closely, esp. making a search **2** *vt* look at quickly without careful reading **3** *vt* produce a picture of, using a computer or electronic apparatus ♦ *n* act of scanning **~ner** *n* instrument for scanning (1): *a brain scanner*

scan·dal /ˈskændl/ *n* **1** [C] (something causing) a public shock **2** [U] talk which brings harm or disrespect to someone **~ize** *vt* offend (someone's) feelings of what is right or proper **~ous** *adj* morally shocking

Scan·di·na·vi·an /ˌskændəˈneɪviən/ *adj* of Denmark, Norway, Sweden, Finland, and/or Iceland

scant /skænt/ *adj* hardly enough

scant·y /ˈskænti/ *adj* hardly (big) enough **-ily** *adv*

scape·goat /ˈskeɪpgoʊt/ *n* one who takes the blame for others' faults

scar /skɑr/ *n* mark left when a wound gets better ♦ *vt* **-rr-** mark with a scar

scarce /skers/ *adj* **1** less than wanted; hard to find **2 make oneself scarce** *infml* go away or keep away, esp. in order to avoid trouble **~ly** *adv* **1** hardly; almost not **2** (almost) certainly not **scarcity** *n* [C;U] being scarce; lack

scare /sker/ *vt* frighten ♦ *n* **1** [S] sudden fear **2** [C] (mistaken or unreasonable) public fear: *scare stories about war in the newspapers* **scary** *adj* frightening

scare·crow /ˈskerkroʊ/ *n* figure dressed in old clothes set up in a field to scare birds away from crops

scared /skɛrd/ *adj* frightened or nervous: *scared of flying*

scarf /skɑrf/ *n* **scarves** /skɑrvz/ *or* **scarfs** piece of cloth worn around the neck or head

scar·let /ˈskɑrlɪt/ *adj* bright red

scarlet fe·ver /ˌ··ˈ··/ *n* [U] serious disease marked by a painful throat and red spots on the skin

scat /skæt/ *vi* **-tt-** (*usu. imperative*) *infml* go away fast

scath·ing /ˈskeɪðɪŋ/ *adj* bitterly cruel in judgment **~ly** *adv*

scat·ter /ˈskæt̬ə/ *v* **1** *vi/t* separate widely **2** *vt* spread widely (as if) by throwing **~ed** *adj* far apart; irregularly separated

scat·ter·brain /ˈskæt̬əˌbreɪn/ *n* careless or forgetful person **~ed** *adj*

scav·enge /ˈskævɪndʒ/ *vi/t* **1** (of an animal) feed on (waste or decaying flesh) **2** search for or find (usable objects) among unwanted things **–enger** *n*

sce·na·ri·o /sɪˈnɛriˌoʊ, -ˈnær-/ *n* **-os 1** written description of the action in a film or play **2** description of a possible course of events

scene /sin/ *n* **1** (in a play) division (within an act) **2** single piece of action in one place in a play or film **3** background for action of a play: *There are few scene changes.* **4** place where something happens: *the scene of the crime* **5** event regarded as like something in a play or film: *scenes of merrymaking* **6** show of angry feelings esp. between 2 people in public **7** an area of activity: *He's new to the film/political scene.* **8 behind the scenes** secretly **9 on the scene** present: *a report from our man on the scene in Africa* **10 set the scene** prepare **11 steal the scene** get all the attention and praise expected by someone else at a show, party, etc.

sce·ne·ry /ˈsinəri/ *n* [U] **1** natural surroundings, esp. in the country **2** painted background and other articles used on stage

sce·nic /ˈsinɪk/ *adj* showing attractive natural scenery

scent /sɛnt/ *n* **1** [C] pleasant smell **2** [C] smell followed by hunting animals ♦ *vt* **1** tell the presence of by smelling **2** get a feeling of the presence of **3** fill with pleasant smells

scep·ter /ˈsɛptə/ *n* ceremonial rod carried by a ruler

sched·ule /ˈskɛdʒul, -dʒəl/ *n* **1** planned list or order of things to be done **2** list of times for trains, buses, etc. **3 ahead of/on/behind schedule** before/at/after the planned or expected time ♦ *vt* plan for a certain future time **–uled** *adj* **1** being a regular service **2** planned for a particular time

sche·mat·ic /skiˈmæt̬ɪk, skɪ-/ *adj* showing the main parts but leaving out details **~ally** *adv*

scheme /skim/ *n* clever dishonest plan ♦ *vi* make SCHEMES

schis·m /ˈsɪzəm, ˈskɪzəm/ *n* [C;U] separation between parts originally together, esp. in the church **~atic** /sɪzˈmæt̬ɪk, skɪz-/ *adj*

schiz·o·phre·ni·a /ˌskɪtsəˈfriniə/ *n* [U] disorder in which the mind becomes separated from the feelings **–phrenic** /-ˈfrɛnɪk/ *adj, n* (of) someone with schizophrenia

schlep /ʃlɛp/ *v* **-pp-** *infml* **1** *vt* carry or drag (something heavy) **2** *vi* spend a lot of time and effort in getting from one place to another

schlock /ʃlɑk/ *adj* cheap and of poor quality

schmaltz /ʃmɑlts, ʃmɔlts/ *n* [U] *infml* art or esp. music which brings out feelings in a too easy, not serious or delicate, way **~y** *adj*

schmooze /ʃmuz/ *vi* talk socially about unimportant things

schmuck /ʃmʌk/ *n* *infml* fool

schol·ar /ˈskɑlə/ *n* **1** person with great knowledge of a (non-science) subject **2** holder of a SCHOLARSHIP (1) **~ly** *adj* **1** concerned with serious detailed study **2** of or like a SCHOLAR (1)

schol·ar·ship /ˈskɑləʃɪp/ *n* **1** [C] payment so that someone can attend a college **2** [U] exact and serious study

scho·las·tic /skəˈlæstɪk/ *adj* of schools and teaching

school[1] /skul/ *n* **1** [C;U] (attendance or work at) a place of education for people under 18 years **2** [C] body of students (and teachers) at such a place: *She was liked by the whole school.* **3** [C;U] teaching establishment: *a barber school* **4** [C;U] (in some universities) department concerned with one subject: *the School of Law* **5** [C;U] *infml* UNIVERSITY *Where did you go to school?* **6** [C] group of people with the same methods, style, etc: *Rem-*

brandt and his school ♦ *vt fml* teach, train, or bring under control

school² *n* large group of fish swimming together

school board /ˌ· ˈ·/ *n* local committee in charge of education

school of thought /ˌ· · ˈ·/ *n* group with the same way of thinking, opinion, etc.

school·teach·er /ˈskuːlˌtiːtʃə/ *n* teacher at a school below college level

schoo·ner /ˈskuːnə/ *n* large fast sailing ship

schwa /ʃwɑː/ *n* vowel sound shown in this dictionary as /ə/ or /ə/

sci·ence /ˈsaɪəns/ *n* 1 [U] (study of) knowledge which depends on testing facts and stating general natural laws 2 [C] a branch of such knowledge, such as PHYSICS, chemistry, or BIOLOGY b anything which may be studied exactly

science fic·tion /ˌ·· ˈ·/ *n* [U] stories about imaginary future (scientific) developments

sci·en·tif·ic /ˌsaɪənˈtɪfɪk◄/ *adj* 1 of science 2 needing or showing exact knowledge or use of a system ~**ally** *adv*

sci·en·tist /ˈsaɪəntɪst/ *n* person who works in a science

sci-fi /ˈsaɪ faɪ/ *n infml* science fiction

scis·sors /ˈsɪzəz/ *n* [P] cutting tool with 2 joined blades

scoff /skɒf, skɑːf/ *vi* speak laughingly and disrespectfully

scoff·law /ˈskɒflɔː, ˈskɑːf-/ *n* someone who disobeys laws about parking, etc.

scold /skəʊld/ *vt* speak angrily and complainingly to (a person doing wrong)

scoop /skuːp/ *n* 1 sort of deep spoon for lifting and moving liquids or loose material 2 news report printed, broadcast, etc., before one's competitors can do so ♦ *vt* 1 take up or out (as if) with a SCOOP (1) 2 make a news report before (another newspaper)

scoot /skuːt/ *vi* go quickly and suddenly

scoot·er /ˈskuːtə/ *n* 1 child's vehicle with 2 wheels, pushed along by one foot 2 low vehicle with two small wheels, an enclosed engine, and usu. a wide curved part at the front to protect the legs

scope /skəʊp/ *n* [U] 1 area within the limits of a question, subject, etc. 2 space or chance for action or thought

scorch /skɔːtʃ/ *n* 1 *vt* burn the surface (of something) without destroying com-

pletely 2 *vt infml* travel very fast ♦ *n* burned mark ~**er** *n* something very exciting, angry, fast, etc.

score¹ /skɔː/ *n* 1 number of points won in a game, examination, etc. 2 a written copy of a piece of music b music for a film or play 3 reason: *Don't worry on that score.* 4 old disagreement or hurt kept in the mind: *to have a score to settle with someone* 5 **know the score** understand the true and usu. unfavorable facts of a situation

score² *v* 1 *vi/t* make (a point) in a game 2 *vi* record the points made in a game 3 *vt* gain (a success, victory, etc.) 4 *vi/t* make (a clever point) esp. in an argument: *She always tries to score (points) off other people in a conversation.* 5 *vt* arrange (music) for a particular combination of instruments 6 *vt* cut one or more lines on 7 *sl* (usu. of a man) have sex with someone 8 *sl* obtain and use unlawful drugs **scorer** *n* person who SCORES² (1, 2)

score³ *determiner, n* **score** *esp. lit* 20 **scores** /skɔːz/ *n* [P] a lot

score·board /ˈskɔːbɔːd, ˈskɔːbʊəd/ *n* board on which a SCORE¹ (1) is recorded

scorn /skɔːn/ *n* [U] strong (angry) disrespect ♦ *vt* refuse to accept or consider because of scorn or pride ~**ful** *adj* ~**fully** *adv*

Scor·pi·o /ˈskɔːpiəʊ/ *n* 1 [S] 8th sign of the ZODIAC, represented by a SCORPION 2 someone born between October 24 and November 21

scor·pi·on /ˈskɔːpiən/ *n* small animal with a long poisonous stinging tail

Scotch /skɒtʃ/ *adj* Scottish ♦ *n* [U] WHISKEY made in Scotland

Scotch tape /ˌ· ˈ·/ *n tdmk* band of thin clear sticky material ♦ *vt* put together with Scotch tape

scot-free /ˌskɒt ˈfriː/ *adj* without harm or esp. punishment

Scot·tish /ˈskɒtɪʃ/ *adj* of Scotland

scoun·drel /ˈskaʊndrəl/ *n* wicked, selfish, or dishonest man

scour¹ /skaʊə/ *vt* search (an area) thoroughly

scour² *vt* clean by hard rubbing with a rough material ~**er** *n* piece of rough nylon for cleaning pots and pans

scourge /skɜːdʒ/ *n* cause of great harm or suffering ♦ *vt* cause great harm or suffering to

scout /skaʊt/ n 1 member of an association (**the Boy Scouts** or **Girl Scouts**) for training boys or girls in character and helping themselves 2 soldier sent ahead of an army to find out about the enemy 3 person who looks for good young sports people, actors, etc., for new teams, shows, etc.: *a talent scout* ♦ vi go looking for something

scowl /skaʊl/ n angry FROWN ♦ vi make a scowl

scram /skræm/ vi -mm- [*often imperative*] *infml* get away fast

scram·ble /ˈskræmbəl/ v 1 vi move or climb quickly and untidily 2 vi struggle or compete eagerly or against difficulty 3 vt cook (an egg) with the white and yellow parts mixed together 4 vt mix up (a radio or telephone message) so that it cannot be understood ♦ n [S] act of scrambling (SCRAMBLE (1))

scrap[1] /skræp/ n 1 [C] small piece 2 [U] unwanted material (to be) thrown away: *She sold the car for scrap.* (= as metal to be used again) ♦ vt -pp- get rid of

scrap[2] n sudden short fight or argument ♦ vt -pp- fight or argue

scrap·book /ˈskræpbʊk/ n book of empty pages on which pictures cut from magazines, etc., are stuck

scrape /skreɪp/ v 1 vi/t (cause) to rub roughly against a surface 2 vt remove or clean by pulling or pushing an edge repeatedly across a surface 3 vi live, keep a business, etc., with no more than the necessary money 4 vi succeed by doing work of the lowest acceptable quality: *She scraped through the exam.* 5 **scrape a living** get just enough food or money to stay alive 6 **scrape the bottom of the barrel** take, use, suggest, etc., something of the lowest quality ♦ n 1 act or sound of scraping 2 mark or wound made by scraping 3 difficult situation

scrape up/together phr vt gather (enough money) with difficulty

scrap·py /ˈskræpi/ adj always wanting to argue or fight

scratch /skrætʃ/ vi/t 1 rub and tear or mark with something pointed or rough 2 rub (a part of the body) lightly and repeatedly 3 remove (oneself, a horse, etc.) from a race or competition 4 **scratch a living** get just enough food or money to stay alive 5 **scratch**

someone's back do someone a favor, expecting they will return it 6 **scratch the surface** deal with only the beginning of a matter or only a few of many cases ♦ n 1 [C] mark or sound made by scratching 2 [S] act of SCRATCHing (2) 3 **from scratch** (starting) from the beginning 4 **without a scratch** without even the smallest amount of hurt or damage ~y adj 1 (of a record, etc.) spoiled by scratches 2 (of clothes) hot, rough, and uncomfortable

scratch pa·per /ˈ· ͵·/ n [U] used paper for making notes, shopping lists, etc.

scrawl /skrɔl/ vt write carelessly or awkwardly ♦ n (piece of) careless or irregular writing

scraw·ny /ˈskrɔni/ adj unpleasantly thin

scream /skrim/ vi/t 1 cry out in a loud high voice: *The wind screamed around the house.* 2 draw attention, as if by such a cry ♦ n 1 [C] sudden loud cry 2 [S] *infml* very funny person, thing, joke, etc.

screech /skritʃ/ vi 1 make an unpleasant high sharp sound, esp. in terror or pain 2 (of machines, BRAKES, etc.) make such a noise 3 **screech to a halt/standstill** stop very suddenly (as if) making this noise ♦ n very high unpleasant noise

screen /skrin/ n 1 [C] something, esp. a movable upright frame, that protects, shelters, or hides 2 [C] surface on which a movie is shown 3 [U] the movie industry: *star of stage, screen and radio* | *screen test* (= test of one's ability to act in a film) | *She first appeared on the screen* (= acted in her first film) *last year.* 4 [C] front glass surface of an electrical instrument, esp. a television or computer, on which pictures or information appear 5 [C] wire net covering a window or door to keep insects out ♦ vt 1 shelter, protect, or hide (as if) with a screen 2 test so as to remove those that do not reach the proper standard 3 show or broadcast (a movie or television show) — see also SMALL SCREEN ~ing n 1 [C;U] (a) showing of a film 2 [U] process of SCREEN (2) ing

screen·play /ˈskrinpleɪ/ n story written for a movie or television

screen·writ·er /ˈskrinˌraɪtə/ n someone who writes SCREENPLAYS

screw /skru/ n 1 metal pin having a head with a cut across it, a point at the other end, and a raised edge winding round it so that when twisted into wood, etc., it holds firmly 2 act of turning one of these 3 PROPELLER, esp. in a ship 4 taboo sl a act of having sex b someone considered as a person to have sex with **5 have a screw loose** humor be slightly crazy **6 put the screws on someone** infml to force someone to do as one wishes, esp. by threatening ♦ v 1 vt fasten with one or more screws 2 vi/t tighten or fasten by turning 3 vi/t taboo sl have sex (with) 4 sl cheat: We really got screwed by that salesman.

screw up phr vt 1 twist (a part of the face) to express disapproval or uncertainty: She screwed up her eyes to read the sign. 2 vt confuse or annoy 3 vi/t sl a ruin b deal with badly: He really screwed up on that job. **4 screw up one's courage** stop oneself from being afraid **5 screwed up** infml very worried and confused

screw·ball /ˈskruːbɔl/ n 1 SCREWY person 2 type of throw with a BASEBALL

screw·driv·er /ˈskruːdraɪvə/ n tool with a blade that fits into the top of a screw, for turning it

screw·y /ˈskruːi/ adj infml strange or slightly crazy

scrib·ble /ˈskrɪbəl/ v 1 vi write (meaningless marks) 2 vt write carelessly or hastily ♦ n [S;U] meaningless or careless writing

scribe /skraɪb/ n person employed to copy things in writing

scrimp /skrɪmp/ vi **scrimp and save** save money slowly and with great difficulty

script /skrɪpt/ n 1 [C] written form of a play, film, or broadcast 2 [C;U] particular alphabet: Arabic script 3 [S;U] fml writing by hand **~ed** adj having a SCRIPT (1)

scriptwriter /ˈskrɪptˌraɪtə/ n writer of SCRIPTS (1)

scrip·ture /ˈskrɪptʃə/ also **scriptures** pl. — n [U] 1 the Bible 2 holy book(s) of the stated religion **–tural** adj

scroll /skrəʊl/ n 1 rolled piece of paper, esp. containing official writing 2 decoration or shape like this in stone or wood

scro·tum /ˈskrəʊtəm/ n -ta /-tə/ or -tums bag of flesh holding the TESTICLES

scrounge /skraʊndʒ/ vi/t get (something) without work or payment or by persuading others **scrounger** n

scrub /skrʌb/ v -bb- 1 vi/t clean or remove by hard rubbing 2 vt no longer do or have; CANCEL ♦ n [S] act of scrubbing

scrub[2] n [U] low plants covering the ground thickly

scruff /skrʌf/ n flesh at the back (of the neck)

scruf·fy /ˈskrʌfi/ adj dirty and untidy

scrump·tious /ˈskrʌmpʃəs/ adj infml (of food) extremely good

scrunch /skrʌntʃ/ vt crush

scrunch up phr vt press together closely

scru·ple /ˈskruːpəl/ n 1 [C] moral principle which keeps one from doing something 2 [U] conscience

scru·pu·lous /ˈskruːpjʊləs/ adj 1 fml very exact 2 exactly honest **–ly** adv

scru·ti·ny /ˈskruːtɪni/ n [U] careful and thorough examination **–nize** vt examine closely

scu·ba div·ing /ˈskuːbə ˌdaɪvɪŋ/ n [U] sport of swimming under water with special breathing apparatus

scuff /skʌf/ vt make rough marks on the smooth surface of (shoes, a floor, etc.) ♦ n mark made by scuffing

scuf·fle /ˈskʌfəl/ n disorderly fight among a few people **scuffle** vi

sculp·tor /ˈskʌlptə/ n artist who makes sculptures

sculp·ture /ˈskʌlptʃə/ n 1 [U] art of shaping solid representations 2 [C;U] (piece of) work produced by this ♦ vt make by shaping

scum /skʌm/ n 1 [S;U] (unpleasant) material formed on the surface of liquid 2 [P] sl worthless immoral people: the scum of the earth

scum·bag /ˈskʌmbæg/ n sl unpleasant person who cannot be trusted or respected

scur·ri·lous /ˈskʌrələs, ˈskʌr-/ adj fml containing very rude, improper, and usu. untrue statements **~ly** adv **~ness** n [U]

scur·ry /ˈskʌri, ˈskʌri/ vi hurry, esp. with short quick steps ♦ n [U] movement or sound of scurrying

scur·vy /ˈskɜːvi/ n [U] disease caused by lack of VITAMIN C

scut·tle /ˈskʌtl/ vi rush with short quick steps

scuz·zy /ˈskʌzi/ adj sl dirty or of low quality

scythe /saɪð, saɪθ/ n tool with a long curving blade fixed to a handle, for cutting grass ♦ /saɪð/ vt cut (as if) with a scythe

sea /si/ n [C] a particular (named) part of salty water: *the Caribbean Sea* **b** body of water (mostly) enclosed by land: *the Mediterranean Sea* **3** [C] any of a number of broad plains on the Moon: *the Sea of Tranquility* **4** [C] large quantity spread out in front of one: *a sea of faces* **5 at sea: a** on a trip on the ocean **b** *infml* not understanding **6 by sea** on a ship **7 go to sea** become a sailor

sea·a·nem·o·ne /'. .,.../ n simple flower-like sea animal

sea·board /'sibord, -boord/ n the part of a country along a sea coast

sea·food /'sifud/ n [U] fish and fishlike animals from the ocean which can be eaten, esp. SHELLFISH

sea·gull /'sigʌl/ n GULL

sea·horse /'sihors/ n small fish with a head and neck like those of a horse

seal[1] /sil/ n **1** official mark put on an official paper, often by pressing a pattern into it **2** something fastened across an opening to protect it **3** tight connection to keep gas or liquid in or out **4 set the seal on** bring to an end in a suitable way ♦ vt **1** fix a SEAL (1) onto **2** fasten or close (as if) with a SEAL (2, 3): (fig.) *My lips are sealed.* **3** make (more) certain, formal, or solemn **4 seal someone's fate** *fml* make someone's death or punishment certain

seal off *phr vt* close tightly so as not to allow entrance or escape

seal[2] n large ocean animal with a smooth body and broad flat limbs for swimming

sea lev·el /'. ,../ n the average height of the ocean, used as a standard for measuring heights on land

sea li·on /'. ,../ n large SEAL[2] of the Pacific Ocean

seam /sim/ n **1** line of stitches joining 2 pieces of cloth, etc. **2** narrow band of minerals between other rocks **3 burst at the seams** *infml* be very full

sea·man /'simən/ n -men /-mən/ n **1** sailor, esp. of low rank **2** man skilled in handling ships at sea ~**ship** n [U] skill in handling a ship and directing its course

seam·less /'simlıs/ adj done or made so well that one cannot notice where 1 part ends and another begins **2** without any SEAMS (1): *seamless stockings* ~**ly**, *adv*

seam·stress /'simstrəs/ n woman who sews and makes clothes

seam·y /'simi/ adj unpleasant and immoral –**iness** n [U]

sé·ance /'seɪɑns/ n meeting where people try to talk to the spirits of the dead

sear /sɪr/ vt burn with sudden powerful heat ~**ing** adj **1** burning **2** causing or describing very strong feelings, esp. of a sexual kind

search /sətʃ/ vi/t **1** look through or examine (a place or person) carefully and thoroughly to try to find something **2 search me!** *infml* I don't know! ♦ n **1** act of searching **2 in search of** searching for ~**ing** adj sharp and thorough: *a searching look* ~**er** n

search·light /'sətʃlaɪt/ n large powerful light that can be turned in any direction

search par·ty /'. ,../ n group of searchers, esp. for a lost person

search war·rant /'. ,../ n official written order allowing the police to search a place

sea·shell /'siʃɛl/ n shell covering some types of sea animals

sea·shore /'siʃɔr, -ʃoor/ n [U] land along the edge of the sea

sea·sick /'si,sɪk/ adj sick because of a ship's movement ~**ness** n [U]

sea·son /'sizən/ n **1** spring, summer, autumn, or winter **2** period of the year marked by a particular thing: *the rainy/holiday/football season* **3 in/out of season** (of food) at/not at the best time of year for eating **4 Season's Greetings!** (a greeting on a Christmas card) ♦ vt **1** give a special taste to (a food) by adding salt, pepper, a SPICE, etc. **2** dry (wood) gradually for use ~**able** adj *fml* suitable or useful for the time of year ~**al** adj happening or active only at a particular season ~**ed** adj having much experience ~**ing** n [C;U] something that seasons food

season tick·et /'. `../ n ticket usable for a number of sports events, performances, etc., during a fixed period of time

seat /sit/ n **1** place for sitting **2** the part on which one sits **3** place as a member of an official body: *to lose one's seat in the House* **4** place where a particular activity happens **5 in the driver's seat** *infml* in control **6 take a back seat (to someone)** *infml* allow someone else to take control or have the more important job **7 take/have a seat** please sit down

♦ *vt* **1** cause or help to sit: *be seated* (= please sit down) **2** have room for seats for ~**ing** *n* [U] seats

seat belt /ˈ· ·/ *n* protective belt around a seated person in a car, plane, etc.

sea ur·chin /ˈ· ·ˌ·/ *n* small sea animal with a prickly shell, shaped like a ball

sea·weed /ˈsiwid/ *n* [U] plant that grows in the sea

se·cede /sɪˈsid/ *vi* formally leave an official group or organization **secession** /-ˈsɛʃən/ *n* [U]

secluded /sɪˈkludɪd/ *adj* very quiet and private **seclusion** /sɪˈkluʒən/ *n* [U]

sec·ond¹ /ˈsɛkənd/ *determiner, adv, pron* 2nd

second² *n* **1** length of time equal to 1/60 of a minute **2** *infml* moment

second³ *n* **1** [C] imperfect article sold cheaper **2** [C] helper of a fighter in a boxing match (BOX²) or DUEL **3 second to none** *infml* the best **seconds** [P] *infml* 2nd servings of food at a meal

second⁴ /sɪˈkɑnd/ *vt* support formally (a formal suggestion at a meeting) ~**er** *n*

sec·ond·a·ry /ˈsɛkənˌdɛri/ *adj* **1** (of education or a school) for children past sixth grade **2** not main: *of secondary importance* **3** developing from something earlier: *a secondary infection* –**rily** *adv*

second best /ˌ·· ˈ·/ *adj* not as good as the best

second class /ˌ·· ˈ·/ *n* [U] traveling conditions cheaper than FIRST CLASS on a plane, etc. **second-class** *adj* below the highest quality

second cous·in /ˌ·· ˈ··/ *n* the child of one's parent's COUSIN

second fid·dle /ˌ·· ˈ··/ *n* position of having to report to the person in control

second-guess /ˌ·· ˈ·/ *vt infml* **1** make a judgment about (someone or something) only after an event has taken place **2** try to say in advance what (someone) will do, how (something) will happen, etc.

second-hand /ˌ·· ˈ·/ *adj, adv* **1** owned or used by someone else before; not new **2** (of information) not directly from its origin

second na·ture /ˌ·· ˈ··/ *n* [U] very firmly fixed habit

second-rate /ˌ·· ˈ·/ *adj* of low quality

second thought /ˌ·· ˈ·/ *n* **1 on second thought** said when you change an earlier decision or opinion: *On second thought, I think I will have a drink.* **2 have second thoughts** think that a past decision or opinion may not be right

second wind /ˌsɛkənd ˈwɪnd/ *n* [S] return of one's strength during hard physical activity, when it seemed one had become too tired to continue

se·cre·cy /ˈsikrəsi/ *n* [U] **1** keeping secrets **2** being secret

se·cret /ˈsikrɪt/ *adj* **1** that no one else knows or must know about **2** undeclared ♦ *n* **1** matter kept hidden or known only to a few **2** special way of doing something well: *the secret of baking perfect bread* **3** mystery **4 in secret** in a private way or place –**ly** *adv*

secret a·gent /ˌ·· ˈ··/ *n* person gathering information secretly, esp. for a foreign government

sec·re·ta·ry /ˈsɛkrəˌtɛri/ *n* **1** person who prepares letters, keeps records, arranges meetings, etc., for another **2** government official or high nonelected official: *the Secretary of State* **3** officer of an organization who keeps records, writes official letters, etc. –**rial** /ˌsɛkrəˈtɛriəl/ *adj*

se·crete /sɪˈkrit/ *vt* (esp. of an animal or plant organ) produce (a usu. liquid substance) **secretion** /sɪˈkriʃən/ *n* [C;U] (production of) a usu. liquid substance

se·cre·tive /ˈsikrətɪv, sɪˈkritɪv/ *adj* hiding one's thoughts or plans ~**ly** *adv* ~**ness** *n* [U]

secret ser·vice /ˌ·· ˈ··/ *n* government department dealing with special police work, esp. protecting high government officers

sect /sɛkt/ *n* small group within or separated from a larger (esp. religious) group

sec·tar·i·an /sɛkˈtɛriən/ *adj* of or between sects, esp. as shown in great strength and narrowness of beliefs ~**ism** *n* [U]

sec·tion /ˈsɛkʃən/ *n* **1** [C] separate part of a larger object, place, group, etc. **2** [C;U] representation of something cut through from top to bottom ~**al** *adj* **1** in sections (to be) put together **2** limited to one particular group or area

sec·tor /ˈsɛktə/ *n* **1** part of a field of activity, esp. in business or trade — see also PRIVATE SECTOR, PUBLIC SECTOR **2** area of military control

sec·u·lar /ˈsɛkyələr/ adj not connected with or controlled by a church

se·cure /sɪˈkyʊr/ adj **1** protected against danger or risk **2** fastened firmly **3** certain: a secure job **4** having no anxiety ♦ vt **1** close tightly **2** make safe **3** fml ~**ly** adv

se·cu·ri·ty /sɪˈkyʊrəti/ n **1** [U] state of being secure **2** [U] (department concerned with) protection, esp. against law breaking, violence, enemy acts, escape from prison, etc.: strict security measures | a maximum security prison **3** [U] property of value promised to a lender in case repayment is not made **4** [C] document giving the owner the right to some property: government securities

security deposit /ˈ··· ·ˌ·/ n amount of money given to the owner of a house or apartment before renting it, to be returned later if nothing is damaged

se·dan /sɪˈdæn/ n large car with a fixed roof and 2 or 4 doors

se·date /sɪˈdeɪt/ adj calm or quiet ♦ vt make sleepy or calm, esp. with a drug **sedation** /-ˈdeɪʃən/ n [U]

sed·a·tive /ˈsɛdətɪv/ n drug that makes one calm, esp. by causing sleep

sed·en·ta·ry /ˈsɛdn̩ˌtɛri/ adj fml used to or needing long periods of sitting and only slight activity

sed·i·ment /ˈsɛdəmənt/ n [S;U] solid material that settles to the bottom of a liquid ~**ary** /ˌsɛdəˈmɛntri, -ˈmɛntəri/ adj

se·di·tion /sɪˈdɪʃən/ n [U] speaking, actions, etc., encouraging people to disobey the government –**tious** adj

se·duce /sɪˈdus/ vt persuade to have sex with one **2** persuade to do esp. something bad by making it seem attractive **seducer** n **seduction** /sɪˈdʌkʃən/ n [C;U]

seductive /sɪˈdʌktɪv/ adj very desirable or attractive

see /si/ v saw /sɔ/, seen /sin/ **1** vi have or use the power of sight **2** vt notice, recognize, or examine by looking **3** vi/t come to know or understand: I can't see why you don't like it. **4** vt form an opinion or picture of in the mind: I see little hope of any improvement. **5** vt visit, meet, or receive as a visitor **6** vi/t (try to) find out: I'll see if he's there. **7** vt make sure; take care: See that you're ready at 8 o'clock. **8** vt go with: I'll see you home. **9** vt be the occasion of (an event or course in

history) **10** vt have experience of: We've seen some good times together. | That sofa has seen better days. **11** (I'll) see you/ be seeing you (soon/later/next week, etc.) (used when leaving a friend) **12** let me see (used for expressing a pause for thought) **13** see fit decide to **14** seeing is believing: a I'll believe it when I see it, but not before **b** Now I've seen it, so I believe it **15** see one's way (clear) to feel able or willing to **16** see red become very angry **17** see the back/last of someone have no more to do with **18** see the light: a understand or accept an idea **b** have a religious experience which changes one's belief **c** come into existence **19** see things think one sees something that is not there **20** so I see what you say is already clear **21** (you) see (used in explanations)

see about phr vt **1** deal with **2** consider further **3** We'll see about that! infml I will prevent that happening (or continuing!)

see in phr vt find attractive in: I don't know what she sees in him.

see off phr vt go to the airport, station, etc., with (someone who is starting a trip)

see out phr vt **1** last until the end of **2** go to the door with (someone who is leaving)

see through phr vt **1** not be deceived by **2** provide for, support, or help until the end of (esp. a difficult time)

see to phr vt attend to; take care of

seed /sid/ n [C;U] **1** usu. small hard plant part that can grow into a new plant **2** [C] something from which growth begins: seeds of future trouble **3** [U] lit SEMEN **4** [C] SEEDed (3) player **5** go to seed: a (of a plant) produce seed after flowers have been produced **b** (of a person) lose one's freshness, esp. by becoming lazy, careless, old, etc. ♦ vt **1** (of a plant) grow and produce seed **2** plant seeds in (a piece of ground) **3** place (esp. tennis players at the start of a competition) in order of likelihood to win ~**less** adj

See·ing Eye dog /ˌ·· ·ˈ· ·/ n tdmk dog trained to guide blind people

seed·ling /ˈsidlɪŋ/ n young plant grown from a seed

seed mon·ey /ˈ· ˌ··/ n [U] money needed to start up a business, program, etc.

seed·y /ˈsiːdi/ adj **1** looking poor, dirty, and uncared for **2** infml slightly unwell and/or in low spirits –**iness** n [U]

see·ing /ˈsiː-ɪŋ/ also **seeing that** /ˈ··· ·/ — conj as it is true that; since

seek /siːk/ v **sought** /sɔːt/ fml or lit **1** vi/t search (for) **2** vt ask for **3** vt try

seem /siːm/ v give the idea or effect of being; appear: She seems happy. ~**ing** adj that seems to be, but perhaps is not real: his seeming calmness ~**ingly** adv according to what seems to be so (but perhaps is not)

seen /siːn/ v past p. of SEE

seep /siːp/ vi (of liquid) flow slowly through small openings in a material ~**age** n [S;U] slow seeping flow

see·saw /ˈsiːsɔː/ n **1** board balanced in the middle for people to sit on at opposite ends so that when one end goes up the other goes down **2** up and down movement ♦ vi move up and down esp. between opponents or opposite sides: seesawing prices

seethe /siːð/ vi **1** be in a state of anger or unrest **2** (of a liquid) move about as if boiling

see-through /ˈ· ·/ adj (esp. of a garment) that can be (partly) seen through

seg·ment /ˈsɛgmənt/ n any of the parts into which something may be cut up or divided ♦ /sɛgˈmɛnt/ vt divide into segments ~**ation** /ˌsɛgmənˈteɪʃən/ n [U]

seg·re·gate /ˈsɛgrəˌgeɪt/ vt separate or set apart, esp. from a different social or racial group –**gation** /ˌsɛgrəˈgeɪʃən/ n [U]

seis·mic /ˈsaɪzmɪk/ adj of or caused by EARTHQUAKES

seis·mo·graph /ˈsaɪzməˌgræf/ n instrument for measuring the force of EARTHQUAKES

seize /siːz/ vt **1** take possession of by force or official order; (fig.) She was seized by a sudden idea. **2** take hold of eagerly, quickly, or forcefully **seizure** /ˈsiːʒər/ n **1** [U] act of seizing **2** [C] sudden attack of illness

seize up phr vt (of part of a machine) become stuck and stop working

sel·dom /ˈsɛldəm/ adv not often; rarely

se·lect /sɪˈlɛkt/ v choose as best, most suitable, etc., from a group ♦ adj **1** limited to members of the best quality or class **2** of high quality ~**or** n ~**ion** /-ˈlɛkʃən/ n **1** [U] act of selecting or fact of

being selected **2** [C] something or someone selected **3** [C] collection of things to choose from — see also NATURAL SELECTION

se·lec·tive /sɪˈlɛktɪv/ adj **1** careful in choosing **2** having an effect only on certain things ~**ly** adv –**tivity** /sɪˌlɛk-ˈtɪvəti, ˌsɛlɛk-/ n ~**ness** /sɪˈlɛktɪvnɪs/ n [U]

selective ser·vice /·ˌ··· ˈ·· ·/ n [S] system of choosing men for military service

self /sɛlf/ n selves /sɛlvz/ [C;U] whole being of a person, including their nature, character, abilities, etc.

self-ab·sorbed /ˌ· ··ˈ·/ adj paying all one's attention to oneself and one's own affairs

self-ap·point·ed /ˌ· ·ˈ··/ adj chosen by oneself to do something, unasked and usu. unwanted

self-as·sured /ˌ· ·ˈ·/ adj confident –**surance** n [U]

self-cen·tered /ˌ· ··ˈ·/ adj interested only in oneself ~**ness** n [U]

self-con·fi·dent /ˌ· ··ˈ·/ adj sure of one's own power to succeed ~**ly** adv –**dence** n [U]

self-con·scious /ˌ· ·ˈ·/ adj nervous and uncomfortable about oneself as seen by others ~**ly** adv ~**ness** adj [U]

self-con·tained /ˌ· ·ˈ·/ adj **1** complete in itself; independent **2** not showing feelings or depending on others' friendship

self-con·trol /ˌ· ·ˈ·/ n [U] control over one's feelings –**trolled** adj

self-de·feat·ing /ˌ· ··ˈ··/ adj making a situation have a bad result for oneself

self-de·fense /ˌ· ·ˈ·/ n [U] act or skill of defending oneself: He shot the man in self-defense. (= only to protect himself)

self-de·ter·mi·na·tion /ˌ· ···ˈ··/ n [U] country's right to govern itself

self-dis·ci·pline /ˌ· ···ˈ/ n [U] ability to make oneself do the things one ought to do

self-em·ployed /ˌ· ·ˈ·/ adj earning money from one's own business, rather than being paid by an employer

self-es·teem /ˌ· ·ˈ/ n [U] one's good opinion of one's own worth

self-ev·i·dent /ˌ· ···ˈ/ adj plainly true without need of proof ~**ly** adv

self-ex·plan·a·to·ry /ˌ· ·····ˈ/ adj easily understood

self-help /ˌ· ˈ/ n [U] use of one's own efforts to deal with one's problems ♦ adj: self-help books

self·im·age /ˌ ˈ··/ n idea about oneself, esp. in comparison to others: *a positive self-image*

self·im·prove·ment /ˌ ·ˈ··/ n [U] trying to learn more skills or deal with problems better

self·in·dul·gent /ˌ ·ˈ··◂/ adj too easily allowing oneself pleasure or comfort –**gence** n [U]

self·in·terest /ˌ ˈ·ˌ, ˌ ·ˈ··/ n [U] concern for what is best for oneself ~**ed** adj

self·ish /ˈsɛlfiʃ/ adj concerned with one's own advantage without care for others ~**ly** adv ~**ness** n [U]

self·less /ˈsɛlfləs/ adj concerned with others' advantage without care for oneself ~**ly** adv ~**ness** n [U]

self-made /ˌ ˈ·◂/ adj having gained success and wealth by one's own efforts alone

self-por·trait /ˌ ˈ··/ n picture made, drawn, etc., of oneself

self-pos·sessed /ˌ ·ˈ·◂/ adj calm and confident –**session** n [U]

self-re·spect /ˌ ·ˈ·/ n [U] proper pride in oneself ~**ing** adj

self-re·straint /ˌ ·ˈ·/ n [U] ability to control what one does or says in upsetting situations

self-right·eous /ˌ ˈ·◂/ adj (too) proudly sure of one's own rightness or goodness ~**ly** adv ~**ness** n [U]

self-sac·ri·fice /ˌ ˈ·ˌ·/ n [U] the giving up of things that one cares deeply about, esp. in order to help others

self-serv·ice /ˌ ˈ··◂/ adj, n [U] (working by) the system in which buyers take what they want and pay at a special desk

self-styled /ˌ ˈ·◂/ adj given the stated title by oneself, usu. without any right to it

self-suf·fi·cient /ˌ ·ˈ·◂/ adj able to provide everything one needs without outside help –**ciency** n [U]

sell¹ /sɛl/ v **sold** /soʊld/ **1** vi/t give (property or goods) to someone in exchange to be bought: *Bad news sells newspapers.* **3** vt offer (goods) for sale **4** vi be bought: *The magazine sells for $5.* **5** vt make acceptable or desirable by persuading **6** **sell oneself: a** make oneself or one's ideas seem attractive to others **b** give up one's principles for money or gain **7** **sell one's soul (to the devil)** act dishon-

orably in exchange for money, power, etc. **8** **sell someone down the river** put someone in great trouble by being disloyal to them **9** **sell something/ someone short** value something or someone too low ~**er** n

sell off phr vt get rid of by selling, usu. cheaply

sell out phr v **1** vi/t (cause to) sell all of (what was for sale): *The tickets are sold out; there are none left.* **2** vi be disloyal or unfaithful, esp. for payment

sell-out /ˈ· ˌ/ n **1** performance, match, etc., for which all tickets have been sold **2** act of disloyalty or unfaithfulness

sell up phr vi sell something (esp. a business) completely

sell² n [S] deception — see also HARD SELL, SOFT SELL

selves /sɛlvz/ pl. of SELF

se·man·tic /sɪˈmænɪk/ adj of meaning in language ~**ally** adv –**tics** n [U] study of meaning

sem·blance /ˈsɛmbləns/ n [S] appearance; outward form or seeming likeness: *a semblance of order*

se·men /ˈsiːmən/ n [U] liquid carrying SPERM, passed through the male sex organs

se·mes·ter /səˈmɛstə/ n either of the 2 teaching periods in the year in some schools

sem·i·cir·cle /ˈsɛmiˌsɜːkəl/ n half a circle

sem·i·co·lon /ˈsɛmiˌkoʊlən/ n mark (;) used to separate independent parts of a sentence

sem·i·con·duc·tor /ˌsɛmikənˈdʌktə/ n substance which allows the passing of an electric current more easily at high temperatures

sem·i·fi·nal /ˈsɛmiˌfaɪnl, ˌsɛmaɪ-, ˌsɛmaɪˈfaɪnl◂, ˌsɛmaɪ-/ n either of 2 matches, those who win play in a FINAL

sem·i·nal /ˈsɛmənəl/ adj **1** fml influencing future development in a new way **2** containing or producing SEMEN

sem·i·nar /ˈsɛməˌnɑːr/ n small study group

sem·i·na·ry /ˈsɛməˌnɛri/ n college for training esp. Roman Catholic priests

Se·mit·ic /səˈmɪtɪk/ adj of a race of people including Jews and Arabs

sen·ate /ˈsɛnɪt/ n (usu. cap.) **1** higher of the 2 parts of the body that makes laws in the US, France, etc. **2** highest council of state in ancient Rome **3** governing council in some universities –**ator** *n* member of a senate –**atorial** /ˌsɛnəˈtɔːriəl, -ˈtoʊr-/ *adj*

send /sɛnd/ *sent* /sɛnt/ **1** *vt* cause to go or be taken, without going oneself: *He sent her a birthday card.* **2 send packing** send away quickly **3 send word** send a message ~**er** *n*

   send away *phr vi* **1** send to another place **2** order goods to be sent by mail

   send down *phr vt* **1** cause to go down

   send for *phr vt* ask or order to come: *Send for a doctor!*

   send off *phr vt* **1** mail (a letter, parcel, etc.) **2** SEND **away**/**send-off** /ˈ·ˌ·/ *n* show of good wishes at the start of a journey, new business, etc.

   send on *phr vt* **1** send (a letter) to the receiver's next address **2** send (belongings) in advance to a point on a journey

   send out *phr vt* **1** send from a central point **2** (of a natural object) produce: *The sun sends out light.* **3** obtain something from somewhere else: *We can send out for coffee later.*

   send up *phr vt* **1** cause to go up **2** send someone to prison

se·nile /ˈsiːnaɪl, ˈsɛnaɪl/ *adj* of or showing old age, esp. in weakness of mind **senil·ity** /sɪˈnɪləti/ *n* [U]

sen·ior /ˈsiːnyər/ *n, adj* **1** (someone) older **2** person in the last year of high school or college **3** (someone) of high or higher rank –**ity** /sinˈyɔrəti, -ˈyɑr-/ *n* [U] **1** being senior **2** official advantage gained by length of service in an organization

Senior *adj* the older, esp. of two men in the same family who have the same name

senior cit·i·zen /ˌ·· ˈ···/ *n* older person, esp. one over 65 and RETIREDd

sen·sa·tion /sɛnˈseɪʃən/ *n* **1** [C;U] feeling, such as of heat or pain, coming from the senses **2** [C] general feeling in the mind or body **3** [C] (cause of) excited interest ~**al** *adj* **1** wonderful **2** causing excited interest or shock ~**ally** *adv*

sen·sa·tion·al·ism /sɛnˈseɪʃənlˌɪzəm/ *n* [U] the intentional producing of excitement or shock, esp. by books, magazines, etc., of low quality

sense /sɛns/ *n* **1** [C] intended meaning **2** [U] understand and esp. practical understand-ing and judgment **3** [C] any of the 5 natural powers of sight, hearing, feeling, tasting, and smelling — see also SIXTH SENSE **4** [C;U] power to understand and judge a particular thing: *a poor sense of direction* **5** [S] feeling, esp. one that is hard to describe **6 in a sense** partly; in one way of speaking **7 make sense: a** have a clear meaning **b** be a wise course of action **8 make sense (out) of** understand **9 (there's) no sense (in)** no good reason for ♦ *vt* feel in the mind: *I could sense danger.* **senses** *n* [P] powers of (reasonable) thinking: *He must have taken leave of his senses.* (= gone crazy) ~**less** *adj* **1** showing a lack of meaning, thought, or purpose **2** unconscious

sen·si·bil·i·ty /ˌsɛnsəˈbɪləti/ also **sensi-bilities** *pl.* — *n* [U] delicate feeling about style or what is correct, esp. in art or behavior

sen·si·ble /ˈsɛnsəbəl/ *adj* **1** having or showing good sense; reasonable **2 sen-sible of** *fml* recognizing; conscious of –**bly** *adv*

sen·si·tive /ˈsɛnsətɪv/ *adj* **1** quick to feel or show the effect of: *sensitive to light* **2** easily offended **3** showing delicate feelings or judgment: *a sensitive perfor-mance* **4** knowing or being conscious of the feelings and opinions of others **5** (of an apparatus) measuring exactly **6** needing to be dealt with carefully so as not to cause trouble or offense: *a sensi-tive issue* ~**ly** *adv* –**tivity** /ˌsɛnsəˈtɪvəti/ *n* [U]

sen·si·tize /ˈsɛnsəˌtaɪz/ *vt* make sensitive

sen·sor /ˈsɛnsə/ *n* apparatus for discov-ering the presence of something, such as heat or sound

sen·so·ry /ˈsɛnsəri/ *adj fml* of or by the physical senses

sen·su·al /ˈsɛnʃuəl/ *adj* **1** of physical feelings **2** interested in or suggesting physical, esp. sexual, pleasure ~**ity** /ˌsɛnʃuˈæləti/ *n* [U]

sen·su·ous /ˈsɛnʃuəs/ *adj* **1** giving plea-sure to the senses **2** SENSUAL (2) ~**ly** *adv* ~**ness** *n* [U]

sent /sɛnt/ *v past t. and p. of* SEND

sen·tence /ˈsɛntˠns, -təns/ *n* **1** group of words forming a complete statement, command, question, etc. **2** (order given by a judge which fixes) a punishment for a criminal found guilty in court **3** give/

pass/pronounce sentence (of a judge) say the order for a punishment **4 under sentence of death** having received a death sentence ♦ *vt* (of a judge) give a punishment to

sen·ti·ment /ˈsɛntəmənt/ *n* **1** [U] tender feelings of pity, love, sadness, etc., or remembrance of the past **2** [C] *fml* thought or judgment caused by a feeling ~**al** /ˌsɛntəˈmɛntl/ *adj* **1** caused by sentiment **2** showing too much sentiment, esp. of a weak or unreal kind ~**ally** *adv* ~**ality** /ˌsɛntəmənˈtæləti/ *n* [U]

sentiments /ˈsɛntəmənts/ *n fml* [P] opinion

sen·try /ˈsɛntri/ *n* soldier guarding a building, entrance, etc.

sep·a·ra·ble /ˈsɛpərəbəl/ *adj fml* that can be separated **–bly** *adv*

sep·a·rate¹ /ˈsɛpəˌreɪt/ *v* **1** *vi/t* move, set, keep, or break apart **2** *vi* stop living together as husband and wife **–ration** /ˌsɛpəˈreɪʃən/ *n* **1** [C;U] the act of separating or the fact of being separated **2** [C;U] (a time of) being or living apart **3** [U] *law* a formal agreement by a husband and wife to live apart

sep·a·rate² /ˈsɛprɪt/ *adj* **1** different: *a word with 3 separate meanings* **2** not shared: *We have separate rooms.* **3** apart ~**ly** *adv*

se·pi·a /ˈsipiə/ *n* [U] red-brown color

Sep·tem·ber /sɛpˈtɛmbə/ *n* the 9th month of the year

septic tank /ˈsɛptɪk tæŋk/ *n* large container in which body waste matter is broken up and changed by bacteria

sep·ul·cher /ˈsɛpəlkə/ *n* *lit* burial place **–chral** /sɪˈpʌlkrəl/ *adj fml* or *lit* like or suitable for a grave

se·quel /ˈsikwəl/ *n* **1** something that follows, esp. as a result **2** film etc., which continues where an earlier one ended

se·quence /ˈsikwəns/ *n* **1** [C] group following each other in order **2** [U] order in which things follow each other **3** [C] scene in a film

se·ques·tered /sɪˈkwɛstəd/ *adj* **1** *lit* quiet and hidden **2** *law* (of a JURY) kept away from the public

se·quin /ˈsikwɪn/ *n* small round shiny piece sewn on a garment for decoration

se·quoi·a /sɪˈkwɔɪə/ *n* REDWOOD

ser·e·nade /ˌsɛrəˈneɪd/ *n* piece of music played or sung to a woman by a lover ♦ *vt* sing or play a serenade to

se·rene /səˈrin/ *adj* completely calm and peaceful ~**ly** *adv* **serenity** /səˈrɛnəti/ *n* [U]

serf /sɜf/ *n* slave-like farm worker in former times ~**dom** *n* [U] state or fact of being a serf

ser·geant /ˈsɑrdʒənt/ *n* **1** army officer above a CORPORAL **2** policeman of middle rank

sergeant ma·jor /ˌ·· ˈ··/ *n* officer of high rank

se·ri·al¹ /ˈsɪriəl/ *adj* of, happening, or arranged in a SERIES

serial² *n* written or broadcast story appearing in parts at fixed times ~**ize** *vt* print or broadcast as a serial

serial kill·er /ˈ··· ˌ··/ *n* someone who has killed several people in the same way, one after the other

serial num·ber /ˈ··· ˌ··/ *n* number marked on something to show which one it is in a series

se·ries /ˈsɪriz/ *n* **series** group of things of the same or similar things coming one after another or in order

se·ri·ous /ˈsɪriəs/ *adj* **1** causing worry and needing attention **2** not cheerful or funny **3** needing or having great skill or thought ~**ly** *adv* ~**ness** *n* [U]

ser·mon /ˈsɜmən/ *n* talk given by a priest as part of a church service

ser·pent /ˈsɜpənt/ *n* *lit* snake

ser·rat·ed /səˈreɪtɪd, ˈsɛreɪtɪd/ *adj* having (an edge with) a row of V shapes like teeth

se·rum /ˈsɪrəm/ *n* **serums** or **sera** /-rə/ [C;U] liquid containing substances that fight sickness, put into a sick person's blood

ser·vant /ˈsɜvənt/ *n* person paid to do personal services for someone, esp. in their home — see also PUBLIC SERVANT

serve /sɜv/ *v* **1** *vi/t* do work (for); give service (to): *to serve in the army* **2** *vt* provide with something necessary or useful: *The pipeline serves the whole town.* **3** *vt* offer (food, a meal, etc.) for eating **4** *vt* attend to (a customer in a store) **5** *vt* spend (a period of time): *She served (2 years) in prison.* **6** *vi/t fml* be good enough to satisfy for (a purpose) **7** *vi/t* (esp. in tennis) begin play by hitting (the ball) to one's opponent **8** *vt law* deliver (an official order to appear in court) **9 if my memory serves me**

(right) if I remember correctly **10 serve someone right** be suitable punishment ♦ *n* act or manner of serving (SERVE (7))

server /'sɜːvə/ *n* **1** something used in serving food **2** player who serves in tennis **3** main computer in a NETWORK that controls other computers

ser·vice /'sɜːvɪs/ *n* **1** [C;U] act or work done for someone **2** [U] attention to guests in a hotel, restaurant, etc., or to customers in a store **3** [C;U] (operation of) an organization doing useful work: *a bus service | telephone service* **4** [C;U] (duty in) the army, navy, etc. **5** [C] religious ceremony **6** [C;U] examination of a machine to keep it in good condition **7** [C] SERVE **8** [C] set of dishes, etc.: *a dinner service* **9 at your service** *fml* willing to help **10 of service** *fml* useful; helpful ♦ *vt* repair or put in good condition ♦ *adj* something for the use of people working in a place, rather than the public: *service stairs*

ser·vice·a·ble /'sɜːvɪsəbəl/ *adj* fit for (long or hard) use; useful

service charge /'·· ./ *n* amount added to a bill to pay for a particular service

ser·vice·man /'sɜːvɪsˌmæn, -mən/ **—woman** /-ˌwʊmən/ *fem.* — *n* **-men** /-ˌmɛn, -mən/ member of the army, navy, etc.

service sta·tion /'·· ˌ··/ *n* GARAGE

ser·vile /'sɜːvaɪl, -vaɪl/ *adj* behaving like a slave **—vility** /sɜː'vɪləti/ *n* [U]

serv·ing /'sɜːvɪŋ/ *n* amount of food for 1 person

ser·vi·tude /'sɜːvətjuːd/ *n* [U] *lit* state of being a slave or one who is forced to obey another

ses·a·me /'sɛsəmi/ *n* [U] plant whose seeds and oil are used in cooking

ses·sion /'sɛʃən/ *n* **1** formal meeting or group of meetings of a LEGISLATURE or court **2** period of time used for a particular purpose: *a recording/drinking session*

set¹ /sɛt/ *v* **set**, *pres. p.* **-tt- 1** *vt* put (to stay) in the stated place: *to set a ladder against a wall* **2** *vt* fix; establish: *set a date for the wedding* **3** *vt* put into the correct condition for use: *set the clock/the table* **4** *vt* cause to be: *set a prisoner free | Her words set me thinking.* **5** *vt* put: *set a load down* **6** *vi* APPLY oneself: *set to work* **7** *vt* put the action of (a film, story, etc.) in the stated place and time **8** *vi/t* (cause to) become solid: *The jelly has*

set. **9** *vi* (of the sun, moon, etc.) go below the horizon **10** *vt* write or provide music for (a poem or other words to be sung) **11** *vt* fix (a precious stone) into (a piece of jewelry) **12** *vt* put (a broken bone) into a fixed position to mend **13** *vt* arrange (hair) when wet to be in a particular style when dry **14** *vt* arrange for printing **15 set an example** offer a standard for other people to follow **16 set eyes on** see **17 set light/fire to** cause (something) to burn **18 set one's heart/hopes on** want very much **19 set one's mind against** oppose **20 set one's mind to** decide firmly on

set about *phr vt* begin

set back *phr vt* **1** place at esp. the stated distance behind something: *The house is set back 15 feet from the road.* **2** delay **3** cost (a large amount)

set in *phr vi* (of bad weather, disease, etc.) begin (and continue)

set off *phr v* **1** *vi* begin a journey **2** *vt* cause to explode **3** *vt* cause (sudden activity) **4** *vt* make (one thing) look better by putting it near something different: *A white belt set off her blue dress.*

set out *phr v* **1** *vt* arrange or spread out in order **2** *vi* begin a journey **3** *vt* begin with a purpose

set to *phr vi* begin eagerly or determinedly

set up *phr vt* **1** put into position **2** prepare (a machine, instrument, etc.) for use **3** establish or arrange (an organization, plan, etc.) **4** provide with what is necessary or useful

set² *adj* **1** given or fixed for study: *a set program* **2** determined: *He's very set on going.* **3** fixed; PRESCRIBED: *set hours* **4** unmoving: *a set smile* **5** at a fixed price: *a set dinner* **6** *infml* ready: *I'm all set, so we can go.*

set³ *n* **1** group forming a whole: *a set of gardening tools* **2** television or radio receiving apparatus **3 a** scenery, etc., representing the place of action in a stage play **b** place where a film is acted **4** group of games in a tennis match **5** group of people of a particular social type: *the smart set* **6** act of setting (SET¹(13)) one's hair

set·back /'sɛtˌbæk/ *n* something that delays or prevents successful PROGRESS

set·ter /'sɛtə/ *n* dog with long hair, used by hunters

set·ting /ˈsɛtɪŋ/ n **1** the going down (of the moon, sun, etc.) **2** way or position in which an instrument is prepared for use **3 a** set of surroundings **b** time and place where the action of a book, film, etc., happens **4** set of articles (dishes, knives, forks, etc.) arranged at one place on a table for eating: *a place setting*

set·tle /ˈsɛtl/ v **1** vi start to live in a place **2** vi/t (place so as to) stay or be comfortable **3** vi/t come or bring to rest, esp. from above: *Dust had settled on the furniture.* **4** vi/t make or become quiet, calm, etc.: *Settle down, children!* **5** vt decide on firmly; fix: *That settles it!* (= *That has decided the matter.)* **6** vt provide people to live in (a place) **7** vi/t bring (a matter) to an agreement **8** vt pay (a bill) **settled** *adj* **settler** n member of a new population

settle down *phr vi* **1** (cause to) sit comfortably **2** give one's serious attention (to a job, etc.): *I must settle down to some work today.* **3** establish a home and have a quiet life **4** become used to a way of life, job, etc.

settle for *phr vt* accept (something less than hoped for)

settle in *phr vi/t* (help to) get used to a new home, job, etc.

settle on *phr vt* decide or agree on; choose

settle up *phr vi* pay what is owed

set·tle·ment /ˈsɛtlmənt/ n **1** [U] movement of a new population into a new place to live there **2** [C] area of houses built recently, with few people **3** [C;U] agreement or decision ending an argument **4** [C;U] payment of money claimed **5** [C] a formal gift or giving of money: *He made a settlement on his daughter when she married.*

set·up /ˈsɛtʌp/ n **1** arrangement; organization **2** competition deliberately made easy

sev·en /ˈsɛvən/ determiner, n, pron **7** ~**th** determiner, adv, n, pron 7th

sev·en·teen /ˌsɛvənˈtiːn◂/ determiner, n, pron **17** ~**th** determiner, adv, n, pron 17th

Seventh Day Ad·vent·ist /ˌsɛvənθ deɪ ædˈvɛntɪst/ n, adj (member) of a Christian group believing that Christ will soon come again to Earth

seventh heav·en /ˌ·· ˈ·◂/ n complete happiness

sev·en·ty /ˈsɛvənti/ determiner, n, pron **70** –**tieth** determiner, adv, n, pron 70th

seven-year itch /ˌ··· ·ˈ·/ n dissatisfaction after 7 years of marriage

sev·er /ˈsɛvə/ vt fml divide in 2, esp. by cutting: (fig.) *sever diplomatic relations* ~**ance** n [U]

sev·er·al /ˈsɛvrəl/ determiner, pron more than a few but not very many; some ♦ adj fml separate: *They went their several ways.*

severance pay /ˈsɛvrəns ˌpeɪ/ n [U] money paid by a company to a worker losing his job through no fault of his own

se·vere /səˈvɪr/ adj **1** causing serious harm, pain, or worry **2** not kind or gentle **3** completely plain and without decoration ~**ly** adv **severity** /səˈvɛrəti/ n [U]

sew /soʊ/ vi/t **sewed**, **sewn** /soʊn/ join (esp. cloth) with thread

sew up *phr vt* **1** close or repair by sewing **2** settle satisfactorily

sew·age /ˈsuːɪdʒ/ n [U] waste material and water carried in sewers

sew·er /ˈsuːə/ n large underground pipe for carrying away human waste and water, esp. in a city

sex /sɛks/ n **1** [U] condition of being male or female **2** [C] set of all male or female people **3** [U] (activity connected with) SEXUAL INTERCOURSE: *to have sex (with someone)* ♦ vt find out whether (an animal) is male or female

sex ap·peal /ˈ· ·ˌ·/ n [U] power of being sexually exciting to other people

sex ed·u·ca·tion /ˈ· ··ˌ··/ n [U] school subject including education about sexual activity and relationships

sex·is·m /ˈsɛkˌsɪzəm/ n [U] (unfair treatment coming from) the belief that one sex is better, cleverer, etc., than the other –**ist** adj, n

sex or·gan /ˈ· ˌ·/ n part of the body used in producing children

sex·tu·plet /sɛksˈtʌplɪt, -ˈtuːp-, ˈsɛkstʊplɪt/ n any of 6 children born together

sex·u·al /ˈsɛkʃuəl/ adj of or connected with sex ~**ly** adv: *sexually active* ~**ity** /ˌsɛkʃuˈæləti/ n [U] interest in the, the expression of, or the ability to take part in sexual activity

sexual ha·rass·ment /ˌ··· ˈ···, ˌ··· ·ˈ·/ n [U] unwanted sexual remarks, looks, or touching, esp. at work

sexual in·ter·course /ˌ··· ˈ··/ n [U]
physical act between 2 people in which
the sex organs are brought together

sex·y /ˈseksi/ adj sexually exciting –**ily**
adv –**iness** n [U]

SF written abbrev. for: SCIENCE FICTION

sh, shh /ʃ/ interj (used for demanding
silence)

shab·by /ˈʃæbi/ adj 1 untidy, not cared
for, and worn out 2 unfair and ungenerous –**bily** adv –**biness** n [U]

shack¹ /ʃæk/ n small roughly built shack
or hut

shack² v **shack up** phr vi infml (of a
person, or persons) live together
without being married

shack·le /ˈʃækəl/ n metal band for fastening the arms or legs: (fig.) the shackles of slavery ◆ vt fasten (as if) with
shackles

shade /ʃeɪd/ n 1 [U] slight darkness,
made esp. by blocking of direct sunlight
2 [C] something which provides shade or
reduces light: a lampshade 3 [C] degree
or variety of color: shades of blue 4 [C]
slight difference: shades of meaning 5
[S] slightly: a shade too loud 6 **put
someone/something in the shade**
make someone/something seem much
less important by comparison ◆ v 1 vt
shelter from direct light 2 vt represent
shadow on (an object in a picture) 3 vi
change gradually **shady** adj 1 in or producing shade 2 probably dishonest

shades /ʃeɪdz/ n [P] 1 infml SUNGLASSES 2
shades of this reminds me of

shad·ow /ˈʃædoʊ/ n 1 [U] SHADE (1): Most
of the room was in shadow. 2 [C] dark
shape made on a surface by something
between it and direct light: The tree cast
a long shadow across the lawn. 3 [C] dark
area: shadows under her eyes 4 [S] slightest bit: not a shadow of a doubt 5 [C] a
form from which the real substance has
gone: After his illness he was only a
shadow of his former self. 6 **be afraid of
one's own shadow** be habitually afraid
or nervous ◆ vt 1 make a shadow on 2
follow and watch closely, esp. secretly ~**y**
adj 1 hard to see or know about clearly
2 full of shade

shaft¹ /ʃæft/ n 1 thin rod forming the
body of a weapon or tool, such as a spear
or ax 2 bar which turns to pass power
through a machine: a propeller shaft 3
long passage going down: a mine shaft

4 either of 2 poles that an animal is fastened between to pull a vehicle **5** beam
(of light) **6** lit something shot like an
arrow: shafts of wit

shaft² vt sl treat unfairly and very
severely

shag·gy /ˈʃægi/ adj being or covered
with long uneven untidy hair –**giness** n
[U]

shake /ʃeɪk/ v **shook** /ʃʊk/, **shaken**
/ˈʃeɪkən/ 1 vi/t move up and down and
from side to side with quick short movements 2 vi/t hold (someone's right hand)
and move it up and down, to show esp.
greeting or agreement 3 vt trouble; upset
4 vi (of a voice) tremble 5 vt get rid of:
shake a feeling/habit 6 **shake one's head**
move one's head from side to side to
answer "no" ◆ n 1 [C] act of shaking 2
[C] infml moment 3 [C] infml MILK SHAKE
4 [S] infml treatment of the stated type: a
fair shake — see also SHAKES **shaky** adj
shaking; unsteady **shakily** adv

    shake off phr vt get rid of; escape from

    shake up phr vt 1 make big changes in
(an organization), esp. to improve it 2
mix by shaking 3 upset **shake-up** /ˈ· ·/ n
rearrangement of an organization

shake·down /ˈʃeɪkdaʊn/ n infml 1 act of
getting money dishonestly 2 place prepared as a bed 3 last test operation of a
new ship or aircraft

shakes /ʃeɪks/ n infml 1 [the+P] nervous
shaking of the body from disease, fear,
etc. 2 **no great shakes** not very good

shall /ʃəl; strong ʃæl/ v aux fml (used with
I and we) 1 (expresses the future tense)
2 (used in questions or offers): Shall I (=
would you like me to) go?

shal·lot /ʃəˈlɒt, ˈʃælət/ n vegetable like a
small onion

shal·low /ˈʃæloʊ/ adj 1 not deep 2 lacking
deep or serious thinking **shallows** n [P]
shallow area in a river, lake, etc.

sham /ʃæm/ n 1 [C] something that is not
what it appears or is said to be 2 [U]
falseness: PRETENSE 3 adj not real ◆ vi/t
-**mm**- put on a false appearance

sha·man /ˈʃɑmən, ˈʃeɪ-/ n tribal medicine
man

sham·bles /ˈʃæmbəlz/ n [P] (place or
scene of) great disorder

shame /ʃeɪm/ n 1 [U] painful feeling
caused by knowledge of guilt, inability,
or failure 2 [U] ability to feel this 3 [U]

loss of honor **4** [S] something one is sorry about: *It's a shame you can't come.* **5 put someone/something to shame** show someone/something to be less good by comparison ♦ *vt* **1** bring dishonor to **2** cause to feel shame ~**ful** *adj* which one ought to feel ashamed of ~**fully** *adv* ~**fulness** *n* [U] ~**ful** *adj* **1** not feeling suitably ashamed: *a shameless liar* **2** done without shame ~**lessly** *adv* ~**lessness** *n* [U]

sham·poo /ʃæmˈpuː/ *n* -**poos** [C;U] liquid soap for washing the hair ♦ *vt* -**pooed**, *present p.* -**pooing** wash with shampoo

sham·rock /ˈʃæmrɒk/ *n* [U] plant with 3 leaves on each stem that is the national sign of Ireland

shan·ty /ˈʃænti/ *n* small roughly built house

shan·ty·town /ˈʃæntitaʊn/ *n* (part of) a town where poor people live in shanties

shape /ʃeɪp/ *n* **1** [C;U] outer form of something: *a cake in the shape of a heart* **2** [U] general character or nature of something **3** [U] (proper) condition, health, etc. **4 get/put something into shape** arrange or plan something properly **5 in any shape or form** of any kind; at all **6 take shape** begin to be or look like the finished form ♦ *v* **1** *vt* give a particular shape to: *the influences that shape one's character* **2** *vi* develop in the stated way ~**less** *adj* ~**ly** *adj* (of a person) having an attractive shape

shape up *phr vi* **1** develop well or in the stated way **2** (usu. used threateningly or angrily) begin to work more effectively, behave better, etc.

shard /ʃɑːrd/ *n* broken piece of a bowl, cup, etc.

share /ʃeər/ *n* **1** part belonging to, owed to, or done by a particular person **2** part of the ownership of a business company, offered for sale to the public ♦ *v* **1** *vi/t* have, use, pay, etc., with others or among a group **2** *vt* divide and give out in shares **3 share and share alike** have an equal share in everything

share·crop·per /ˈʃeərɪkrɒpər/ *n* poor farmer who rents the land he works on

shark /ʃɑːrk/ *n* **1** shark or sharks large dangerous fish with sharp teeth **2** *infml* a person clever at getting money from others in dishonest ways

sharp /ʃɑːrp/ *adj* **1** having or being a thin cutting edge or fine point: *a sharp knife* **2** not rounded: *a sharp nose* **3** causing a sensation like that of cutting, pricking, biting, or stinging: *a sharp wind* | the *sharp taste of lemon juice* **4** quick and strong: *a sharp pain* | *a sharp blow to the head* **5** sudden: *a sharp turn* **6** clear in shape or detail: *a sharp photo* **7** quick and sensitive in thinking, seeing, etc. **8** angry **9** (in music) above the right note **10** *infml* attractive ♦ *adv* exactly at the stated time ♦ *n* (in music) sharp note ~**ly** *adv* ~**en** *vi/t* become or make sharp or sharper ~**ener** *n*: *a pencil sharpener* ~**ness** *n* [U]

sharp·shoot·er /ˈʃɑːrpˌʃuːtər/ *n* person skilled in shooting

shat·ter /ˈʃætər/ *v* **1** *vi/t* break suddenly into very small pieces **2** *vt* shock very much **3** *vt infml* tire very much

shave /ʃeɪv/ *v* **1** *vi/t* cut off (a beard or face hair) with a RAZOR or shaver **2** *vt* cut hair from (a part of the body) **3** *vt* cut off (very thin pieces) from (a surface) **4** *vt* come close to or touch in passing ♦ *n* act of shaving — see also CLOSE SHAVE **shaver** *n* **1** electric shaving tool **2** *infml* small boy **shaving** *n* very thin piece cut off from a surface

shaving cream /ˈ··· ·/ *n* [U] soapy paste put on the face to make shaving easier

shawl /ʃɔːl/ *n* large piece of cloth worn over the head or shoulders or wrapped around the body

s/he /ˌʃiː ə ˈhiː/ *pron* (used in writing when the subject of a sentence could be either male or female

she /ʃiː/ *pron* (used for the female subject of a sentence) ♦ *n* a female: *a she-goat*

sheaf /ʃiːf/ *n* **sheaves** /ʃiːvz/ **1** bunch of grain plants tied together **2** many things held or tied together: *a sheaf of notes*

shear /ʃɪər/ *v* **sheared**, **sheared** or **shorn** /ʃɔːrn, ʃoʊrn/ **1** *vt* cut off wool from (a sheep) **2** *vi/t* break under a sideways or twisting force **3 be shorn of** have (something) completely removed from one **shears** *n* [P] large cutting tool like scissors

she·bang /ʃɪˈbæŋ/ *n* **the whole shebang** *infml* everything

shed[1] /ʃed/ *n* lightly built (wooden) building on one floor

shed[2] *vt* **shed** *pres. p.* -**dd**- **1** cause to flow out: *shedding tears* (= crying) **2** get rid of (outer skin, leaves, hair, etc.) naturally **3** get rid of (something not wanted or needed) **4 shed blood** cause wounding or esp. killing **5 shed light on** help to explain

she'd /ʃid/ *short for:* **1** she would **2** she had

sheen /ʃin/ *n* [S;U] shiny surface

sheep /ʃip/ *n* **sheep 1** animal that eats grass, farmed for its wool and meat **2** person who is easily led — see also BLACK SHEEP ~**ish** *adj* **1** like a SHEEP (2) **2** uncomfortable because one knows one has done something wrong or foolish ~**ishly** *adv* ~**ishness** *n* [U]

sheep·dog /ˈʃipdɒg/ *n* dog trained to control sheep

sheer[1] /ʃɪr/ *adj* **1** pure; nothing but: *He won by sheer luck.* **2** very steep **3** (of cloth) very thin ♦ *adv* straight up or down

sheer[2] *vi* change direction quickly

sheet /ʃit/ *n* **1** large piece of cloth used on a bed **2** broad, regularly shaped piece of a thin or flat material: *a sheet of glass/paper* **3** a broad stretch of something: *a sheet of ice* **4** moving or powerful wide mass: *The rain came down in sheets.*

sheikh /ʃik, ʃeɪk/ *n* Arab chief or prince ~**dom** *n*

shelf /ʃelf/ *n* **shelves** /ʃelvz/ **1** flat (narrow) board fixed against a wall or in a frame, for putting things on **2** narrow surface of rock under water **3 on the shelf** delayed for an uncertain time

shelf life /ˈ· ·/ *n* length of time a product stays fresh in a store

shell[1] /ʃel/ *n* **1** [C;U] hard outer covering of a nut, egg, fruit, or certain types of animal: *a snail shell* **2** [C] outer surface or frame of something: (fig.) *He's only a shell of a man.* **3** [C] explosive for firing from a large gun **4 come out of one's shell** begin to be friendly or interested in others

shell[2] *vt* **1** remove from a SHELL[1](1) or POD **2** fire SHELLS[1] (3) at

    shell out *phr vt infml* pay

she'll /ʃil; *strong* ʃil/ *short for:* **1** she will **2** she shall

shel·lac /ʃəˈlæk/ *n* [U] shiny paintlike coat for wood, etc.

shell·fish /ˈʃelˌfɪʃ/ *n* **-fish 1** [C] water animal with a soft body inside a shell:

Oysters and lobsters are shellfish. **2** [U] such animals as food

shel·ter /ˈʃeltər/ *n* **1** [C] building or enclosure giving protection **2** [U] protection, esp. from bad weather ♦ *v* **1** *vt* give shelter to **2** *vi* take shelter

shelve /ʃelv/ *v* **1** *vt* put aside until a later time **2** *vi* slope gradually

shelves /ʃelvz/ *pl. of* SHELF

shep·herd /ˈʃepərd/ **shepherdess** /ˈʃepərdɪs/ *fem.* — *n* person who takes care of sheep ♦ *vt* lead or guide like sheep

sher·bet /ˈʃərbɪt/ *n* [C;U] dish of ice with a usu. fruit taste

sher·iff /ˈʃerɪf/ *n* elected law officer in a local area

sher·ry /ˈʃeri/ *n* [U] pale or dark brown strong wine (originally) from Spain

she's /ʃiz/ *short for:* **1** she is **2** she has

shh /ʃ/ *interj* SH

shield /ʃild/ *n* **1** something carried as a protection from being hit **2** representation of this, used for a COAT OF ARMS, BADGE, etc. **3** protective cover ♦ *vt* protect

shift /ʃift/ *v* **1** *vi/t* move from one place to another **2** *vt* get rid of; remove **3 shift for oneself** take care of oneself ♦ *n* **1** change in position or direction **2** (period worked by) a group of workers which takes turns with others: *the night shift* **3** loose fitting simple dress ~**less** *adj* lazy and lacking in purpose ~**y** *adj* looking dishonest; not to be trusted ~**ily** *adv* ~**iness** *n* [U]

shift key /ˈ· ·/ *n* KEY in a TYPEWRITER, etc., pressed to print a capital letter

shim·mer /ˈʃɪmər/ *vi* shine with a soft trembling light

shin /ʃin/ *n* the part of the leg below the knee

shine /ʃaɪn/ *v* **shone** /ʃoʊn/ **1** *vi/t* (cause to) give off light **2** *vt* (*past t.and p.* **shined**) polish **3** *vi* be clearly excellent ♦ *n* [S] **1** brightness **2** act of polishing **3 (come) rain or shine** whatever happens **4 take a shine to** start to like **shiny** *adj* bright

shin·gle /ˈʃɪŋgəl/ *n* unit of roof covering ~**gly** *adj*

shin·gles /ˈʃɪŋgəlz/ *n* [U] disease producing painful red spots, esp. around the waist

shin·ny /ˈʃɪni/ *vi* climb using hands and legs, esp. quickly and easily

ship /ʃɪp/ n 1 large boat 2 large aircraft or space vehicle 3 **when one's ship comes in** when one becomes rich ♦ vt -pp- 1 send by ship 2 send over a large distance by road, air, etc. ~**per** n dealer who ships goods ~**ping** n [U] ships as a group

ship·ment /ˈʃɪpmənt/ n 1 [C] load of goods sent by sea, road, or air 2 [C;U] sending, carrying, and delivering goods

ship·shape /ˈʃɪpʃeɪp/ adj clean and neat

ship·wreck /ˈʃɪp-rek/ n [C;U] destruction of a ship, by hitting rocks or by sinking ♦ vt 1 cause to suffer shipwreck 2 ruin

ship·yard /ˈʃɪp-yard/ n place where ships are built or repaired

shirk /ʃɜːk/ vi/t avoid (unpleasant work) because of laziness, lack of determination, etc. ~**er** n

shirt /ʃɜːt/ n 1 cloth garment for the upper body with SLEEVES and usu. a collar 2 **keep one's shirt on** not lose one's temper 3 **lose one's shirt** to lose all one has

shirt·sleeves /ˈʃɜːtˌsliːvz/ n **in (one's) shirtsleeves** wearing nothing over one's shirt

shit /ʃɪt/ n [U] taboo 1 solid waste from the bowels 2 something of no value: *I don't give a shit.* (= I don't care) 3 worthless or unpleasant person ♦ vi -tt- taboo pass solid waste from the bowels ♦ interj taboo (expressing anger or annoyance) ~**ty** adj taboo sl unpleasant

shiv·er /ˈʃɪvə/ vi shake, esp. from cold or fear ♦ n feeling of shivering ~**y** adj

shoal[1] /ʃəʊl/ n dangerous bank of sand near the surface of water

shoal[2] n large group of fish swimming together

shock[1] /ʃɒk/ n [C;U] 1 (state or feeling caused by) an unexpected and usu. very unpleasant event 2 violent force from a hard blow, crash, explosion, etc., or from electricity ♦ vt cause unpleasant or angry surprise to ♦ adj very surprising: *shock tactics* ~**ing** adj 1 very offensive, wrong, or upsetting 2 very bad: *I've got a shocking cold.*

shock[2] n thick mass (of hair)

shock ab·sorb·er /ˈ· ·ˌ··/ n apparatus fitted to a vehicle to lessen the effect of violent movement

shod /ʃɒd/ past t. and p. of SHOE

shod·dy /ˈʃɒdi/ adj 1 cheaply and badly done 2 ungenerous; dishonorable –**dily** adv –**diness** n [U]

shoe /ʃuː/ n 1 covering worn on the foot 2 **fill someone's shoes** take the place and do the job of someone 3 **in someone's shoes** in someone's position: *I'd hate to be in your shoes.* ♦ vt **shod** put a HORSESHOE on

shoe·horn /ˈʃuːhɔːn/ n curved piece of plastic or metal for helping put a shoe on easily ♦ vt force (something) to fit somewhere

shoe·lace /ˈʃuːleɪs/ n thin cord for fastening a shoe

shoe·string /ˈʃuːstrɪŋ/ n **on a shoestring** with a very small amount of money

shone /ʃɒn/ v past t. and p. of SHINE

shoo /ʃuː/ interj (used for driving away esp. birds and animals) ♦ vt drive away (as if) by saying "shoo"

shoo-in /ˈʃuː ɪn/ n someone expected to win easily in an election or race

shook /ʃʊk/ v past t. of SHAKE

shoot /ʃuːt/ v **shot** /ʃɒt/ 1 vi fire a weapon 2 vt (of a person or weapon) send out (bullets, etc.) with force: (fig.) *She shot him an angry glance.* 3 vt hit, wound, or kill with a bullet, etc. 4 vi move very quickly or suddenly: *The car shot past us.* | *Pain shot up my arm.* | (fig.) *Prices have shot up.* 5 vi/t make a photograph (or film) (of) 6 vi kick, throw, etc., a ball to make a point in a game 7 vt play (a game of BILLIARDS, POOL, etc.) 8 **shoot one's mouth off** talk foolishly about what one does not know about or should not talk about 9 **shoot the bull/the breeze** infml have an informal, not very serious conversation ♦ n 1 new growth from a plant 2 occasion for shooting, esp. of animals

shoot down phr vt 1 bring down (a flying aircraft) by shooting 2 REJECT (an idea)

shoot up phr v 1 vi go upwards, increase, or grow quickly 2 vt infml damage or wound by shooting 3 vi/t sl take (a drug) directly into the blood using a needle

shooting star /ˈ·· ˈ·/ n METEOR

shoot-out /ˈ· ·/ n battle between fighters with hand guns, usu. to decide a quarrel

shop[1] /ʃɒp/ n 1 [C] small building or room where goods are sold 2 a small department in a large store **3** [U] subjects connected with one's work: *Let's not talk shop.*

shop² *v* **-pp-** *vi* visit stores to buy things ~**per** *n* ~**ping** *n* [U] activity of visiting stores to buy things

shop around *phr vt* compare prices or values in different stores before buying: (fig.) *Shop around before deciding which club to join.*

shop·keep·er /ˈʃɑpˌkipə/ *n* person in charge of a small store

shop·lift /ˈʃɑpˌlɪft/ *vi* steal from a shop ~**er** *n*

shopping cen·ter /ˈ··ˌ··/ *n* **shopping mall** /ˈ··ˌ·/ *n* — see MALL

shore¹ /ʃɔr, ʃoʊr/ *n* [C;U] **1** land along the edge of a sea, lake, etc. **2 on shore** on land; away from one's ship

shore² *v* **shore up** *phr vt* support (something in danger of falling), esp. with wood

shorn /ʃɔrn, ʃoʊrn/ *past p.* of SHEAR

short¹ /ʃɔrt/ *adj* **1** measuring a small or smaller than average amount in distance, length, or height **2** lasting only a little time, or less time than usual or expected **3** a shorter (and often more usual) way of saying: *The word "disco" is short for "discotheque."* **4** not having or providing what is needed: *I'm short of money.* **5** rudely impatient **6 in short order** quickly **7 make short work of** deal with or defeat quickly **8 short and sweet** short and direct in expression **9 short of: a** not quite reaching **b** except for **10 short on** without very much or enough (of): *He's a nice fellow but short on brains.*

short² *adv* **1** suddenly: *He stopped short.* **2 fall short (of)** be less than (good) enough (for) **3 go short (of)** be without enough (of) **4 run short (of): a** not have enough left **b** become less than enough

short³ *n* **1** result; UPSHOT **2** short film shown before the main film at a theater **3** SHORT CIRCUIT **4 for short** as a shorter way of saying it **5 in short** all I mean is; to put it into as few words as possible — see also SHORTS

short·age /ˈʃɔrtɪdʒ/ *n* [C;U] amount lacking; not enough

short·cake /ˈʃɔrtˌkeɪk/ *n* [C;U] sweet cake eaten with fruit and cream

short-change /ˌ·ˈ·/ *vt* **1** give back less than enough money to a buyer **2** fail to reward fairly

short cir·cuit /ˌ·ˈ·/ *n* faulty electrical connection where the current flows the wrong way and usu. puts the power supply out of operation

short-circuit *vi/t* (cause to) have a short circuit

short·com·ing /ˈʃɔrtˌkʌmɪŋ/ *n* fault; failing

short cut /ˈ· ·/ *n* quicker more direct way

short·en /ˈʃɔrtn/ *vi/t* make or become shorter

short·en·ing /ˈʃɔrtn-ɪŋ/ *n* [U] fat for cooking

short·fall /ˈʃɔrtfɔl/ *n* amount by which something fails to reach the expected total

short·hand /ˈʃɔrt-hænd/ *n* [U] system of special signs for fast writing

short-lived /ˌʃɔrtˈlɪvd◂/ *adj* lasting only a short time

short·ly /ˈʃɔrtli/ *adv* **1** soon **2** impatiently **3** in a few words

shorts /ʃɔrts/ *n* [P] **1** short pants **2** men's short UNDERPANTS

short shrift /ˌ·ˈ·/ *n* [U] unfairly quick or unsympathetic treatment

short-sight·ed /ˌʃɔrtˈsaɪtɪd/ *adj* not considering what may happen in the future ~**ly** *adv* ~**ness** *n* [U]

short·stop /ˈʃɔrtstɑp/ *n* baseball player between 2nd and 3rd base

short-term, short term /ˌ· ˈ·◂/ *adj, n* (concerning) a short period of time; (in or for) the near future: *short-term planning*

shot¹ /ʃɑt/ *v past t. and p.* of SHOOT

shot² *n* **1** [C] (sound of) shooting a weapon **2** [C] hit, kick, etc., of a ball in sport **3** [C] person who shoots with the stated skill **4** [C] attempt: *I'll have a shot at it.* **5** [U] metal balls for shooting from shotguns or CANNONS **6** [C] **a** photograph **b** single part of a film made by one camera without interruption **7** [C] INJECTION: *a shot of penicillin* **8** [C] sending up of a spacecraft or ROCKET: *a moon shot* **9** [C] a small drink (esp. of WHISKEY) all swallowed at once **10 a shot in the arm** something which acts to bring back a better, more active condition **11 a shot in the dark** a wild guess unsupported by arguments **12 like a shot** quickly and eagerly — see also BIG SHOT

shot·gun /'ʃɑt'gʌn/ n gun fired from the shoulder, usu. having two barrels, used esp. to kill birds ♦ adv infml in the front seat on the passenger side of a car: riding shotgun

shotgun wed·ding /ˌ·· ˈ·-/ n wedding that has to take place, esp. because the woman is going to have a baby

should /ʃəd; strong ʃʊd/ v aux 1 a ought to b will probably 2 (used after that in certain expressions of feeling): It's odd that you should mention him. (= The fact that you have mentioned him is odd.) 3 fml (used instead of shall in conditional sentences with I and we as the subject and a past tense verb): I should be surprised if he came. 4 (to express humor or surprise): As I left the house, who should I meet but my old friend Sam. 5 I should think I believe 6 I should think so!/not! of course!/of course not!

shoul·der /'ʃoʊldə/ n 1 a the part of the body at each side of the neck where the arms are connected b part of a garment which covers this part of the body 2 part where something widens slopingly: the shoulder of a bottle 3 side of the road 4 head and shoulders above very much better than 5 rub shoulders with meet socially 6 shoulder to shoulder: a side by side b together; with the same intentions ♦ vt accept (a heavy responsibility, duty, etc.)

shoulder blade /'·· ˌ·/ n either of 2 flat bones in the upper back

should·n't /'ʃʊdnt/ v short for: should not

shout /ʃaʊt/ vi/t speak or say very loudly ♦ vt loud cry or call

shout down phr vt prevent a speaker being heard by shouting

shove /ʃʌv/ vi/t 1 push, esp. roughly or carelessly 2 infml move oneself: Shove over and let me sit down. ♦ n strong push

shov·el /'ʃʌvəl/ n tool with a long handle and a broad blade for lifting loose material ♦ vi/t -l- move or work (as if) with a shovel

show¹ /ʃoʊ/ v showed, shown /ʃoʊn/ 1 vt allow or cause to be seen: Show me your ticket. 2 vi be able to be seen: The stain won't show. 3 vt go with and guide or direct: May I show you to your seat? 4 vt explain, esp. by actions: Show me how to do it. 5 vt make clear; prove: This piece of work shows what you can do when you try. 6 vt cause to be felt in one's actions:

They showed their enemies no mercy. 7 vi sl for SHOW up (2) 8 it goes to show it proves the point 9 to show for as a profit or reward from

show off phr v 1 vi derog behave so as to try to get attention and admiration 2 vt show proudly or to the best effect

show up phr v 1 vt make clear the (esp. unpleasant) truth about 2 vi arrive; be present

show² n 1 [C] performance, esp. in a theater or on television or radio 2 [C] collection of things for the public to look at: a flower show 3 [S] showing of some quality; DISPLAY: a show of temper 4 [S] outward appearance: a show of interest 5 [U] (seemingly) splendid appearance or ceremony 6 [S] effort; act of trying: They've put up a very good/poor show this year. 7 get this show on the road infml start to work 8 on show being shown to the public — see also steal the show (STEAL) ~y adj (too) colorful, bright, etc.

show busi·ness /'· ˌ··/ n [U] job of people who work in television, films, the theater, etc.

show·case /'ʃoʊkeɪs/ n a set of shelves enclosed in glass on which objects are placed for looking at in a store, etc.: (fig.) The factory is a showcase for American industry.

show·down /'ʃoʊdaʊn/ n settlement of a quarrel in an open direct way

show·er /'ʃaʊə/ n 1 short fall of rain (or snow) 2 fall or sudden rush of many small things: a shower of sparks 3 (apparatus for) washing the body by standing under running water 4 party for a stated purpose: bridal shower ♦ v 1 vi fall in showers 2 vt scatter or cover in showers 3 vi take a SHOWER (3) ~y adj with showers of rain

show·ing /'ʃoʊɪŋ/ n 1 [S] performance: a poor showing 2 [C] act of putting on view

show·man /'ʃoʊmən/ n -men /-mən/ 1 person whose business is producing public entertainment, etc. 2 person who is good at gaining public attention ~ship n [U]

shown /ʃoʊn/ past p. of SHOW

show-off /'· ˌ·/ n person who SHOWS off (1)

show·room /'ʃoʊrum, -rʊm/ n room where things to be sold are shown to the public: a Chevrolet showroom

shrank /ʃræŋk/ past t. of SHRINK

shrap·nel /'ʃræpnəl/ n [U] metal scattered from an exploding bomb

shred /ʃred/ n 1 small narrow piece torn or roughly cut off 2 slightest bit: *not a shred of evidence* ♦ vt **-dd-** cut or tear into shreds **~der** n apparatus for shredding papers

shrew /ʃru/ n 1 very small mouselike animal 2 bad-tempered angry woman **~ish** adj

shrewd /ʃrud/ adj 1 showing good practical judgment 2 likely to be right: *a shrewd estimate* **~ly** adv

shriek /ʃrik/ vi/t, n (cry out with) a wild high cry

shrift /ʃrɪft/ n see SHORT SHRIFT

shrill /ʃrɪl/ adj (of a sound) high and (painfully) sharp **shrilly** /'ʃrɪl-li, 'ʃrɪli/ adv **~ness** n [U]

shrimp /ʃrɪmp/ n small sea creature with 10 legs, that is often eaten

shrine /ʃraɪn/ n 1 holy place, where one worships 2 box containing the remains of a holy person's body

shrink[1] /ʃrɪŋk/ v **shrank** /ʃræŋk/, **shrunk** /ʃrʌŋk/ 1 vi/t (cause to) become smaller 2 vi move back and away **~age** n [U] loss in size

shrink from phr vt avoid, esp. from fear

shrink[2] n infml PSYCHOANALYST or PSYCHIATRIST

shrinking vi·o·let /ˌ·· '···/ n SHY person

shrink-wrapped /'· ·/ adj (of goods) wrapped tightly in plastic **~wrap** n [U]

shriv·el /'ʃrɪvəl/ vi/t **-l-** (cause to) become smaller by drying and twisting into small folds

shroud /ʃraʊd/ n 1 cloth for covering a dead body 2 something that covers and hides ♦ vt cover and hide

shrub /ʃrʌb/ n low bush

shrub·be·ry /'ʃrʌbəri/ n [C;U] mass or group of shrubs

shrug /ʃrʌg/ vi/t **-gg-** raise (one's shoulders), esp. showing doubt or lack of interest ♦ n act of shrugging

shrug off phr vt treat as unimportant or easily dealt with

shrunk /ʃrʌŋk/ past p. of SHRINK

shrunk·en /'ʃrʌŋkən/ adj having been shrunk

shuck /ʃʌk/ vt remove the outer covering of (CORN, OYSTERS, etc.)

shud·der /'ʃʌdə/ vi shake uncontrollably for a moment ♦ n act of shuddering

shuf·fle /'ʃʌfəl/ v 1 vi/t mix up (playing cards) so as to produce a chance order 2 vi walk by dragging one's feet slowly along ♦ n 1 [C] act of shuffling cards 2 [S] slow dragging walk

shun /ʃʌn/ vt **-nn-** avoid with determination

shush /ʃʌʃ, ʃʊʃ/ interj (used for demanding silence)

shut /ʃʌt/ v **shut**, pres. p. **-tt-** 1 vi/t close: *Shut the door.* 2 vt keep or hold by closing a door, window, etc.: *He shut himself in his room.*

shut down phr vi/t (cause to) stop operation, esp. for a long time or forever **shutdown** /'ʃʌt'daʊn/ n

shut off phr vi/t 1 stop in flow or operation, esp. by turning a handle or pressing a button 2 keep separate or away

shut out phr vt defeat completely

shut up phr v 1 vi/t (cause to) stop talking 2 vt keep enclosed

shut-in /'· ·/ n person too ill or old to go outside

shut-out /'ʃʌtaʊt/ n game in which one side makes no points

shut·ter /'ʃʌtə/ n 1 part of a camera which opens to let light fall on the film 2 movable cover for a window 3 **put up the shutters** infml close a business at the end of the day or forever ♦ vt close (as if) with SHUTTERS (2)

shut·tle /'ʃʌtl/ n 1 (vehicle used on) a regular short journey: *a shuttle service between downtown and the university | the Boston to New York air shuttle* 2 reusable spacecraft 3 part that carries thread in weaving ♦ vt move by a SHUTTLE (1)

shut·tle·cock /'ʃʌtlˌkak/ n light feathered object struck in BADMINTON

shy[1] /ʃaɪ/ adj 1 nervous in the company of others 2 (of animals) unwilling to come near people 3 **once bitten, twice shy** a person who has been tricked will be more careful in the future **~ly** adv **~ness** n [U]

shy[2] vi (esp. of a horse) make a sudden (frightened) movement

shy away from phr vt avoid something unpleasant

shys·ter /'ʃaɪstə/ n infml dishonest person, esp. a lawyer

Si·a·mese twin /ˌsaɪəmiz ˈtwɪn/ *n* either of 2 people whose bodies are joined from birth

sib·ling /ˈsɪblɪŋ/ *n fml* brother or sister

sick /sɪk/ *adj* **1** ill **2** throwing or about to throw food up out of the stomach: *We felt sick as soon as the ship began to move.* **3** feeling annoyance, dislike, and loss of patience: *I'm sick of your complaints.* | *His hypocrisy makes me sick!* **4** cruel in an unnatural or unhealthy way: *a sick joke* **5 worried sick** very worried ~**ness** *n* **1** [C;U] illness **2** [U] feeling SICK (2)

sick·en /ˈsɪkən/ *v* **1** *vt* cause to feel SICK (3) **2** *vi* become ill ~**ing** *adj* extremely displeasing or unpleasant

sick·le /ˈsɪkəl/ *n* small tool with a curved blade for cutting long grass

sick·ly /ˈsɪkli/ *adj* **1** weak and unhealthy **2** pale to an unhealthy degree **3** causing a sick feeling

sick pay /ˈ· ˌ/ *n infml* money received from an employer when one is too ill to work

sick·le cell a·ne·mi·a /ˌsɪkəl sɛl əˈnimiə/ *n med* illness caused by problems with the blood, esp. in black people

side¹ /saɪd/ *n* **1** surface that is not the top, bottom, front, or back **2** edge; border: *A square has 4 sides.* **3** either of the 2 surfaces of a thin flat object **4** part in relation to a central line: *I live on the other side of town.* **5** place or area next to something: *On one side of the window was a mirror, and on the other a painting.* | *He never leaves his mother's side.* **6** part or quality to be considered: *Try to look at both sides of the question.* **7** (group holding) a position in a quarrel, war, etc.: *I'm on your side.* | *I never take sides.* (= support one side against the other) **8** sports team **9** part of a line of a family that is related to a particular person: *an uncle on my father's side* (= my father's brother) **10 get on the right/wrong side of someone** *infml* win/lose someone's favor **11 on the right/wrong side of** younger/older than (a stated age) **12 on the side** as a (sometimes dishonest) additional activity: *She does some teaching on the side.* **13 on the big/small/etc. side** rather; too big/small/etc. **14 on/to one side: a** out of consideration or use for the present **b** away from other people for a private talk **15 side by side** next to (one) another **16**

–sided having the stated number or kind of sides

side² *vi* support the stated SIDE¹ (7): *She sided with me.*

side·burns /ˈsaɪdbɜnz/ *n* [P] hair on the sides of a man's face

side·car /ˈsaɪdkɑr/ *n* small seat with wheels fastened to the side of a motorcycle

side ef·fect /ˈ· ˌˌ/ *n* effect in addition to the intended one

side is·sue /ˈ· ˌˌ/ *n* question or subject apart from the main one

side·kick /ˈsaɪdˌkɪk/ *n infml* a (less important) helper or companion

side·line /ˈsaɪdlaɪn/ *n* **1** activity in addition to one's regular job **2** line marking the limit of play on a sports field **3 on the sidelines** not taking part in an activity ◆ *vt* cause not to be included in an activity because of injury, lack of skill, etc.

side or·der /ˈ· ˌˌ/ *n* dish eaten in a restaurant in addition to the main dish

side·sad·dle /ˈsaɪdˌsædl/ *adv* riding a horse with both legs on the same side

side·show /ˈsaɪdʃoʊ/ *n* separate small show at a fair or CIRCUS

side·split·ting /ˈsaɪdˌsplɪtɪŋ/ *adj* very funny

side·step /ˈsaɪdstɛp/ *vi/t* -**pp**- **1** step aside to avoid (esp. a blow) **2** avoid (an unwelcome question, problem, etc.)

side·swipe /ˈsaɪdswaɪp/ *vt* hit while passing the side of ◆ *n*

side·track /ˈsaɪdtræk/ *vt* cause to leave one subject or activity and follow another (less important) one

side·walk /ˈsaɪdwɔk/ *n* hard path at the side of a road to walk on

side·ways /ˈsaɪdweɪz/ *adv* **1** with one side (not the back or front) forward or up **2** towards one side

sid·ing /ˈsaɪdɪŋ/ *n* [U] protective covering of boards on the outside of houses

si·dle /ˈsaɪdl/ *v* **sidle up** *phr vi* walk secretively or nervously up (to someone)

siege /sidʒ/ *n* operation by an army surrounding a city, etc., to force the people inside to accept defeat

si·es·ta /siˈɛstə/ *n* short sleep in the afternoon

sieve /sɪv/ *n* **1** tool with a net or holes for letting liquid or small objects through **2 head/memory like a sieve** a mind that forgets quickly ♦ *vt* put through or separate with a sieve

sift /sɪft/ *v* **1** *vt* put (something non-liquid) through a sieve **2** *vi/t* examine (things in a mass or group) closely: *sifting the evidence*

sigh /saɪ/ *vi* let out a deep breath slowly and with a sound, usu. expressing sadness, satisfaction, or tiredness: (fig.) *The wind sighed in the trees.* (= made a sound like sighing) ♦ *n* act or sound of sighing

sight /saɪt/ *n* **1** [U] power of seeing **2** [S;U] the seeing of something: *I caught sight of her* (= noticed her) *in the crowd.* **3** [C] something seen **4** [U] range of what can be seen: *The train came into sight.* **5** [C] something worth seeing: *the sights of San Francisco* **6** [C] part of an instrument or weapon which guides the eye in aiming **7** [S] something which looks very bad or laughable **8** [S] *infml* a lot: *She earns a sight more than I do.* **9 a sight for sore eyes** a person or thing that one is glad to see **10 at first sight** at the first time of seeing or considering **11 at/on sight** as soon as seen or shown **12 in sight: a** in view **b** near **13 know someone by sight** recognize someone without knowing them personally or without knowing their name **14 set one's sights on** direct one's efforts (towards) — see also SECOND SIGHT ♦ *vt* see for the first time ~**ed** *adj* able to see ~**ing** *n*: case of someone or something being sighted: *several sightings of rare birds* ~**less** *adj* blind

sight·see·ing /ˈsaɪtˌsiː-ɪŋ/ *n* [U] visiting places of interest –**seer** /-siə/ *n*

sign /saɪn/ *n* **1** mark which represents a known meaning: *+ is the plus sign.* **2** movement of the body intended to express a meaning **3** notice giving information, a warning, etc. **4** something that shows the presence or coming of something else: *There are signs that the economy may be improving.* **5** also **star sign** — any of the 12 divisions of the year represented by groups of stars (Leo, Taurus, etc.) **6 a sign of the times** something that is typical of the way things are just now ♦ *vi/t* **1** write (one's name) on (a written paper), esp. officially or to show that one is the writer **2** SIGNAL (1) **3** SIGN **up** ~**er** *n*

sign away *phr vt* give up (ownership, etc.) formally by signing a paper

sign on *phr vi/t* (cause to) join a working force by signing a paper

sign up *phr vi/t* (cause to) sign an agreement to take part in something or take a job

sig·nal /ˈsɪɡnəl/ *n* **1** sound or action which warns, commands, or gives a message: *a danger signal* **2** action which causes another to happen **3** apparatus by a railroad track to direct train drivers **4** message sent by radio or television waves ♦ *vi* -**l**- give a signal

sig·na·to·ry /ˈsɪɡnəˌtɔri, -ˌtoʊri/ *n fml* signer of an agreement, esp. among nations

sig·na·ture /ˈsɪɡnətʃə/ *n* person's name written by himself or herself — see also TIME SIGNATURE

sig·nif·i·cant /sɪɡˈnɪfəkənt/ *adj* **1** of noticeable importance or effect **2** having a special meaning, indirectly expressed ~**ly** *adv* –**cance** *n* [S;U]

significant oth·er /ˌ··· ˈ··/ *n infml* someone one is having a serious sexual relationship with

sig·ni·fy /ˈsɪɡnəˌfaɪ/ *v fml* **1** *vt* mean **2** *vi/t* make known (esp. an opinion) by an action **3** *vi* matter

sign lan·guage /ˈ· ˌ··/ *n* language of hand movements, used by DEAF people

sign·post /ˈsaɪnpoʊst/ *n* sign showing directions and distances

si·lence /ˈsaɪləns/ *n* **1** [C;U] (period of) absence of sound **2** [U] not speaking or making a noise **3** [U] failure to mention a particular thing ♦ *vt* cause or force to be silent ~**r** *n* apparatus put on the end of a gun so as to make less noise when fired

si·lent /ˈsaɪlənt/ *adj* **1** free from noise **2** not speaking **3** failing or refusing to express an opinion, etc. **4** (of a letter) not pronounced ~**ly** *adv*

silent part·ner /ˌ·· ˈ··/ *n* business partner who does no active work in the business

sil·hou·ette /ˌsɪluˈɛt, ˈsɪluˌɛt/ *n* dark shape seen against a light background ♦ *vt* cause to appear as a silhouette

sil·i·con /ˈsɪlɪkən, -kən/ *n* [U] simple non-metal substance found commonly in natural compounds

silicon chip /ˌ··· ˈ·/ *n* a CHIP[1] (4) in a computer or other ELECTRONIC machinery

silk /sɪlk/ n [U] (smooth cloth from) fine thread produced by silkworms **~en** adj **1** silky **2** made of silk **~y** adj soft, smooth, and/or shiny

silk·worm /ˈsɪlk-wɜːm/ n CATERPILLAR which produces silk

sill /sɪl/ n shelflike part at the bottom of a window

sil·ly /ˈsɪli/ adj not serious or sensible; foolish **–liness** n [U]

si·lo /ˈsaɪləʊ/ n **1** round tower-like enclosure for storing silage **2** underground base for firing MISSILES

silt /sɪlt/ n [U] loose mud brought by a river or current ♦ vt **silt up** phr vi/t fill or become filled with silt

sil·ver /ˈsɪlvə/ n **1** [U] soft, whitish precious metal **2** [U] spoons, forks, dishes, etc., made of silver **3** [U] coins made of, or colored, silver **4** [C] silver MEDAL ♦ adj **1** made of silver **2** of the color of silver **~y** adj **1** like silver in shine and color **2** having a pleasant metallic sound

silver an·ni·ver·sa·ry /ˌ··· ·····/ n the date that is exactly 25 years after the date of an event

sil·ver·smith /ˈsɪlvəsmɪθ/ n maker of jewelry, etc., in silver

sil·ver·ware /ˈsɪlvəweə/ n forks, knives, and spoons even if they are not silver

sim·i·lar /ˈsɪmələ/ adj almost but not exactly the same; alike **~ly** adv **~ity** /ˌsɪməˈlærəti/ n **1** [U] quality of being similar **2** [C] way in which things are similar

sim·i·le /ˈsɪməli/ n expression which describes one thing by comparing it with another (as in *as white as snow*)

sim·mer /ˈsɪmə/ vi/t cook gently in (nearly) boiling liquid: (fig.) *simmering with anger/excitement*

simmer down phr vi become calmer

sim·ple /ˈsɪmpəl/ adj **1** without decoration; plain **2** easy **3** consisting of only one thing or part **4** (of something nonphysical) pure: *the simple truth* **5** easily tricked; foolish **–ply** adv **1** in a simple way **2** just; only: *I simply don't know.* **3** really; completely: *a simply gorgeous day*

simple-mind·ed /ˌ·· ·····/ adj **1** foolish **2** simple and unthinking in mind

sim·ple·ton /ˈsɪmpəltən/ n mentally weak trusting person

sim·pli·ci·ty /sɪmˈplɪsəti/ n [U] **1** quality of being simple **2** simplicity itself very easy

sim·pli·fy /ˈsɪmpləfaɪ/ vt make simpler **–fication** /ˌsɪmpləfəˈkeɪʃən/ n [C;U]

sim·plis·tic /sɪmˈplɪstɪk/ adj derog treating difficult matters as if they were simple **~ally** adv

sim·u·late /ˈsɪmjəleɪt/ vt give the appearance or effect of **–lation** /ˌsɪmjəˈleɪʃən/ n [U]

sim·ul·ta·ne·ous /ˌsaɪməlˈteɪniəs/ adj happening or done at the same moment **~ly** adv

sin /sɪn/ n [C;U] **1** offense against God or a religious law **2** infml something that should not be done: *He thinks it's a sin to stay in bed after 8 o'clock.* **3** live in sin old-fashioned or humor (of 2 unmarried people) live together as if married ♦ vi **-nn-** do wrong **~ful** adj wicked **~ner** n

since /sɪns/ adv **1** at a time between then and now: *She left in 1979, and I haven't seen her since.* **2** from then until now: *He came here 2 years ago and has lived here ever since.* **3** ago: *I've long since forgotten his name.* ♦ prep from (a point in past time) until now: *I haven't seen her since 1979.* ♦ conj **1 a** after the past time when: *I haven't seen her since she left.* **b** continuously from the time when: *We've been friends since we met at school.* **2** because: *Since you can't answer, I'll ask someone else.*

sin·cere /sɪnˈsɪr/ adj free from deceit or falseness; honest and true **~ly** adv **–cerity** /sɪnˈsɛrəti/ n [U]

sin·ew /ˈsɪnjuː/ n [C;U] strong cord connecting a muscle to a bone **~y** adj

sing /sɪŋ/ v **sang** /sæŋ/, **sung** /sʌŋ/ **1** vi/t produce (music, songs, etc.) with the voice **2** vi make or be filled with a ringing sound: *It made my ears sing.* **~er** n gathering of many people to sing

sing. abbrev. of: SINGULAR

singe /sɪndʒ/ vt burn slightly

sin·gle¹ /ˈsɪŋgəl/ adj **1** being (the) only one: *a single sheet of paper* **2** considered by itself; separate: *He understands every single word I say.* **3** unmarried **4** for the use of only one person: *a single bed* ♦ n **1** record with only one short song on each side **2** unmarried person **3** $1 BILL — see also SINGLES **–gly** adv one by one; not in a group

single² v **single out** phr vt choose from a group for special attention

single file /ˌ·· ˈ·/ adv, n (in) a line of people, vehicles, etc., one behind another

sin·gle-hand·ed /ˌ·ˈ·· ◂/ adj without help from others ~**ly** adv

sin·gle-mind·ed /ˌ·ˈ·· ◂/ adj having one clear aim or purpose ~**ly** adv

sin·gles /ˈsɪŋɡəlz/ n singles (tennis) match between 2 players

sing·song /ˈsɪŋsɒŋ/ n [S] repeated rising and falling of the voice in speaking

sin·gu·lar /ˈsɪŋɡjələ/ adj **1** (of a word) representing only one thing **2** fml unusually great ♦ n SINGULAR (1) word or form ~**ly** adv fml particularly

sin·is·ter /ˈsɪnɪstə/ adj threatening or leading to evil

sink¹ /sɪŋk/ v sank /sæŋk/, sunk /sʌŋk/ **1** vi/t (cause to) go down below a surface, out of sight, or to the bottom (of water) **2** vi get smaller **3** vi fall from lack of strength: He sank into a chair. **4** vi lose confidence or hope: My heart sank. **5** vt make by digging: sink a well **6** vt put (money, labor, etc.) into

sink in phr vi become fully and properly understood

sink² n kitchen or bathroom BASIN for washing

sink·ing feel·ing /ˈ·· ˌ·/ n [S] infml uncomfortable feeling in stomach raised by fear or helplessness, esp. because something bad is about to happen

si·nus /ˈsaɪnəs/ n any of the spaces filled with air in the bones behind the nose

sip /sɪp/ vi/t -pp- drink with very small mouthfuls ♦ n very small amount drunk

si·phon /ˈsaɪfən/ n **1** tube for removing liquid by natural pressure **2** bottle for holding and forcing out a drink filled with gas ♦ vt remove with a siphon: (fig.) The new road will siphon off traffic from the business district.

sir /sə/ n **1** (used respectfully when speaking to an older man or one of higher rank) **2** (used at the beginning of a formal letter): Dear Sir, ...

sire /saɪə/ n **1** horse's male parent **2** lit (used when speaking to a king) ♦ vt (esp. of a horse) be the father of

si·ren /ˈsaɪrən/ n **1** apparatus for mak·ing a loud, long warning sound: a police/air-raid siren **2** dangerous beautiful woman

sir·loin /ˈsəlɔɪn/ n [U] BEEF cut from the best part of the lower back

sis·sy /ˈsɪsi/ n girlish or cowardly boy ♦ adj like a sissy

sis·ter /ˈsɪstə/ n **1** female relative with the same parents **2** female member of a religious group **3** female member of the same group (used esp. by supporters of the WOMEN'S MOVEMENT) ♦ adj belonging to the same group: our sister organization ~**hood** n **1** [U] being (like) sisters **2** [C] society of women leading a religious life ~**ly** adj like a sister

sister-in-law /ˈ·· ·ˌ·/ n sisters-in-law sister of one's husband or wife; one's brother's wife

sit /sɪt/ v sat /sæt/, present p. -tt- **1** vi rest on a seat or on the ground with the upper body upright **2** vi/t (cause to) take a seat **3** vi (of an official body) have one or more meetings **4** vi (take up a position to) be painted or photographed **5** be sitting pretty be in a very good position **6** sit tight keep in the same position; not move

sit around phr vt do nothing, esp. while waiting or while others act

sit back phr vi rest and take no active part

sit down phr vi SIT (2)

sit in phr vi take another's regular place, e.g. in a meeting

sit in on phr vi attend without taking an active part

sit on phr vt **1** be a member of (a committee, etc.) **2** delay taking action on

sit out phr vt not take part

sit up phr v **1** vi/t (cause or help to) rise to a sitting postition from a lying one **2** vi sit properly upright in a chair **3** vi stay up late; not go to bed **4** vi show sudden interest, surprise, or fear: Her speech really made them sit up (and take notice).

sit·com /ˈsɪtˌkɑm/ n [C;U] humorous television show typically having a number of standard characters who appear in different stories each week

site /saɪt/ n place where a particular thing happened or is done ♦ vt put or esp. build in a particular position

sit-in /ˈ· ·/ n method of expressing dissatisfaction and anger in which a group of people enter a public place, stop its usual services, and refuse to leave

sit·ter /ˈsɪtə/ n BABYSITTER

sit·ting /ˈsɪtɪŋ/ n **1** serving of a meal for a number of people at one time **2** act of having one's picture made **3** meeting of an official body

sitting duck /ˌ·· ˈ·/ n one easy to attack or cheat

sitting room /ˈ·· ˌ·/ n fml LIVING ROOM

sit·u·at·ed /ˈsɪtʃuˌeɪtɪd/ adj **1** in the stated place or position **2** in the stated situation: *How are you situated for money?* (= have you got enough?)

sit·u·a·tion /ˌsɪtʃuˈeɪʃən/ n **1** set of conditions, facts, and/or events **2** fml position with regard to surroundings **3** fml job

six /sɪks/ determiner, n, pron **6** ~**th** determiner, adv, n, pron **6**th

six-pack /ˈ·· ·/ n six drinks sold together; *six-pack of beer*

six·teen /ˌsɪksˈtiːn◂/ determiner, n, pron **16** ~**th** determiner, adv, n, pron **16**th

sixth sense /ˌ· ˈ·/ n ability to know things without using any of the 5 ordinary senses

six·ty /ˈsɪksti/ determiner, n, pron **60** –**tieth** determiner, adv, n, pron **60**th

siz·a·ble /ˈsaɪzəbəl/ adj fairly large

size¹ /saɪz/ n **1** [C;U] (degree of) bigness or smallness **2** bigness: *A town of some size.* **3** [C] standard measurement: *These shoes are size 9.* **4** -**sized** of the stated size **5 cut someone down to size** show someone to be really less good, important, etc. **6 that's about the size of it** that's a fair statement of the matter

size² v **size up** phr vt form an opinion or judgment about

siz·zle /ˈsɪzəl/ vi make a sound like food cooking in hot fat

skate¹ /skeɪt/ n **1** blade fixed to a shoe for moving along on ice **2** ROLLER SKATE

skate² vi **1** move on skates **(skate) on thin ice** infml (to be) doing something risky **skater** n

skate over/around phr vt avoid treating seriously

skate·board /ˈskeɪtˌbɔːrd, -ˌboʊrd/ n short board with 2 small wheels at each end for standing on and riding

skel·e·ton /ˈskelətn/ n **1** structure consisting of all the bones in the body **2** structure on which more is built or added **3 skeleton in the closet** a secret of which a person or family is ashamed ◆ adj enough simply to keep an operation going: *a skeleton staff* –**tal** adj

skeleton key /ˈ··· ·/ n key that fits an old-fashioned lock

skep·tic /ˈskeptɪk/ n skeptical person ~**al** adj unwilling to believe ~**ally** adv –**ticism** /-tɪˌsɪzəm/ n [U] doubt

sketch /sketʃ/ n **1** simple, quickly made drawing **2** short description **3** short humorous scene ◆ vi/t draw a sketch (of) ~**y** adj not thorough or complete

skew /skyu/ vt cause to be not straight or exact: DISTORT ~**ed** adj

skew·er /ˈskyuər/ n long pin put through meat for cooking

ski /ski/ n **skis** long thin piece of wood, plastic, etc., fastened to boots for traveling on snow ◆ vi **skied**, present p. **skiing** travel on skis ~**er** n

skid /skɪd/ vi -**dd**- (of a vehicle or wheel) slip sideways out of control ◆ n act of skidding

skill /skɪl/ n [C;U] special ability to do something well ~**ed** adj having or needing skill: *a skilled job*

skil·let /ˈskɪlɪt/ n large pan for frying food

skill·ful /ˈskɪlfəl/ adj having or showing skill ~**ly** adv

skim /skɪm/ v -**mm**- **1** vt remove from the surface of a liquid **2** vi/t read quickly to get the main ideas **3** vi/t (cause to) move quickly (nearly) touching (a surface)

skim milk /ˌ· ˈ·/ n [U] milk from which all the fat has been removed

skimp /skɪmp/ vi/t spend, provide, or use less (of) than is needed ~**y** adj not enough

skin /skɪn/ n **1** [U] natural outer covering of the body **2** [C] skin of an animal for use as leather, etc. **3** [C] natural outer covering of some fruits and vegetables: *banana skins* **4** [C;U] the solid surface that forms over some liquids **5 by the skin of one's teeth** only just **6 get under someone's skin** annoy or excite someone deeply **7 no skin off someone's nose** infml not something that upsets or causes disadvantage to someone **8 save one's skin** save oneself, esp. in a cowardly way, from death, etc. **9 skin and bone(s)** very thin ◆ vt -**nn**- remove the skin from ~**ny** adj very thin

skin-deep /ˌ· ˈ· ◂/ adj on the surface only

skin·flint /ˈskɪnˌflɪnt/ n someone who dislikes giving or spending money

skin·head /ˈskɪnhed/ n young white person with very short hair who often behaves violently toward nonwhite people

skin-tight /ˌ ˈ ◂/ adj (of clothes) fitting tightly against the body

skinny-dip /ˈskɪni ˌdɪp/ vi swim without clothes

skip /skɪp/ v -pp- 1 vi move in a light dancing way 2 vi/t leave out (something in order); not deal with (the next thing) 3 vi move in no fixed order 4 vi jump over a rope passed repeatedly beneath one's feet 5 vi/t leave hastily and secretly: *The thieves have skipped the country.* 6 vi fail to attend or take part in (an activity) ♦ n light, quick stepping and jumping movement

skip·per /ˈskɪpə/ n captain of a ship or sports team ♦ vt act as captain; lead

skir·mish /ˈskɜːmɪʃ/ n short military fight, not as big as a battle

skirt[1] /skɜːt/ n woman's outer garment that hangs from the waist

skirt[2] vi/t 1 be or go around the outside (of) 2 avoid (a difficult subject)

skit /skɪt/ n short acted scene making fun of something

skit·tish /ˈskɪtɪʃ/ adj (esp. of a cat or horse) easily excited and frightened

skulk /skʌlk/ vi hide or move about slowly and secretly, through fear or shame or for some evil purpose

skull /skʌl/ n head bone, enclosing the brain

skunk /skʌŋk/ n 1 small black and white animal which gives out an unpleasantly smelly liquid when attacked 2 *infml* person who is bad, unfair, etc.

sky /skaɪ/ n 1 space above the Earth, where clouds and the sun, moon, and stars appear 2 **the sky's the limit** there is no upper limit, esp. to the amount of money that can be spent

sky·div·ing /ˈskaɪˌdaɪvɪŋ/ n [U] sport of falling by PARACHUTE

sky-high /ˌ ˈ ◂/ adj, adv at or to a very high level

sky·light /ˈskaɪlaɪt/ n window in a roof

sky·line /ˈskaɪlaɪn/ n shape or view of esp. city buildings against the sky

sky·rock·et /ˈskaɪˌrɒkɪt/ vi increase suddenly and steeply

sky·scrap·er /ˈskaɪˌskreɪpə/ n very tall city building

slab /slæb/ n thick flat piece with usu. 4 sides: *a stone slab*

slack /slæk/ adj 1 (of a rope, etc.) not pulled tight 2 not careful or quick 3 not firm; weak: *slack discipline* 4 not busy ♦ n **take up the slack** tighten a rope, etc. ♦ vi 1 be lazy 2 reduce in speed, effort, etc. **slacks** n [P] informal pants **~en** vi/t make or become slack **~ness** n [U]

slain /sleɪn/ *past p. of* SLAY

sla·lom /ˈslɑːləm/ n SKI race down a very winding course

slam /slæm/ v -mm- 1 vi/t shut loudly and forcefully 2 vt push or put in a hurried and forceful way: *She slammed on the brakes.* 3 vt attack with words ♦ n noise of a door being slammed — see also GRAND SLAM

slan·der /ˈslɑːndə/ n [C;U] (act of) saying something false and damaging about someone ♦ vt harm by making a false statement **~ous** adj

slang /slæŋ/ n [U] very informal language that includes new and sometimes not polite words and meanings and is often used among particular groups of people, and not usu. in serious speech or writing

slant /slɑːnt/ v 1 vi/t (cause to) be at an angle 2 vt usu. *derog* express in a way favorable to a particular opinion ♦ n 1 [S] slanting direction or position 2 [C] particular way of looking at or expressing facts or a situation

slap /slæp/ n 1 hit with the flat hand 2 **slap in the face** an action (seeming to be) aimed directly against someone else ♦ vt -pp- 1 give a slap to 2 place quickly, roughly, or carelessly ♦ adv also **slap-bang** /ˌ ˈ ◂/ — directly; right: *slap in the middle of lunch*

slap·dash /ˈslæpdæʃ/ adj careless

slap·stick /ˈslæpˌstɪk/ n [U] humorous acting with fast violent action and simple jokes

slash /slæʃ/ v 1 vi/t cut with long sweeping violent strokes: (fig.) *a slashing attack on the government* 2 vt reduce very greatly ♦ n 1 long sweeping cut or blow 2 straight cut making an opening in a garment

slat /slæt/ n thin, narrow, flat piece of wood, plastic, etc. **~ted** adj

slate[1] /sleɪt/ n 1 [U] dark gray easily split rock 2 [C] piece of this used in rows for covering roofs 3 [C] small board of this, used for writing on with chalk 4 [C] imaginary record of (mistakes of) the past: *a clean slate* ♦ vt place on a SCHEDULE

slaugh·ter /'slɔːtə/ vt **1** kill (many people) cruelly or wrongly **2** kill (an animal) for food **3** infml defeat severely in a game ♦ n [U] slaughtering

slaugh·ter·house /'slɔːtəˌhaʊs/ n building where animals are killed for food

slave /sleɪv/ n **1** person who is owned by (and works for) another **2** person completely in the control of: a slave to drink ♦ vi work hard with little rest

slave driv·er /'· ˌ··/ n person who makes one work very hard

slav·ery /'sleɪvəri/ n [U] **1** system of having slaves **2** condition of being a slave

slav·ish /'sleɪvɪʃ/ adj **1** showing complete obedience to and willingness to work for others **2** copied too exactly, without being at all original ~ly adv

slay /sleɪ/ vt esp. lit **slew** /sluː/, **slain** /sleɪn/ kill

slea·zy /'sliːzi/ adj dirty, looking poor, and suggesting immorality

sled /slɛd/ vi, n -dd- (travel on) a vehicle for sliding along snow on 2 metal blades

sledge·ham·mer /'slɛdʒˌhæmə/ n heavy hammer with a long handle

sleek /sliːk/ adj **1** (of hair or fur) smooth and shining **2** stylish and without unnecessary decoration ~ly adv

sleep /sliːp/ n **1** [U] natural unconscious resting state **2** [S] act or period of sleeping **3** get to sleep succeed in sleeping **4** go to sleep: **a** begin to sleep **b** (of an arm, leg, etc.) become unable to feel, or feel PINS AND NEEDLES **5** put to sleep kill (a suffering animal) mercifully ♦ vi **slept** /slɛpt/ **1** rest in sleep **2** provide beds or places for sleep (for a number of people): The house sleeps 6. ~**er** n **1** sleeping person **2** train with beds **3** book, play, record, etc., that has a delayed or unexpected success ~**y** adj **1** tired **2** inactive or moving slowly ~**ily** adv

sleep around phr vi derog have sex with a lot of different people

sleep in phr vi sleep late in the morning

sleep off phr vt get rid of (a feeling or effect) by sleeping: Sleep it off. (= sleep until one is no longer drunk)

sleep on phr vt delay deciding on (a matter) until the next day

sleep through phr vt fail to be woken by

sleep together phr vi (of 2 people) have sex

sleep with phr vt have sex with

sleeping bag /'·· ˌ·/ n large cloth bag for sleeping in

sleeping pill /'·· ˌ·/ n PILL which helps a person to sleep

sleeping sick·ness /'·· ˌ··/ n [U] serious African disease which causes great tiredness

sleep·less /'sliːpləs/ adj **1** not providing sleep: a sleepless night **2** unable to sleep ~ly adv ~ness n [U]

sleep·walk·er /'sliːpˌwɔːkə/ n person who walks around while asleep –**ing** n [U]

sleet /sliːt/ n [U] partly frozen rain ♦ vi (of sleet) fall

sleeve /sliːv/ n **1** part of a garment for covering (part of) an arm **2** envelope for keeping a record in **3** have/keep something up one's sleeve keep something secret for use at the right time in the future

sleigh /sleɪ/ n large SLED pulled by a horse or horses

sleight of hand /ˌslaɪt əv 'hænd/ n [U] **1** skill and quickness of the hands in doing tricks **2** clever deception

slen·der /'slɛndə/ adj **1** gracefully or pleasingly thin **2** small and hardly enough: slender resources

slept /slɛpt/ v past t. and p. of SLEEP

sleuth /sluːθ/ n DETECTIVE

slew¹ /sluː/ v past t. of SLAY

slew² n large number of things

slice /slaɪs/ n **1** thin flat piece cut off: a slice of bread | (fig.) a slice of the profits **2** kitchen tool with a broad blade for serving food **3** a slice of life a representation of life as it really is ♦ v **1** vt cut into slices **2** vi/t hit (a ball) so that it moves away from a straight course

slick¹ /slɪk/ adj **1** smooth and slippery **2** skillful and effective, so as to seem easy **3** clever and able to persuade, but perhaps not honest ~ly adv

slick² n area of oil floating on esp. the sea

slick·er /'slɪkə/ n **1** infml an expensively dressed, confident, but probably untrustworthy person: a city slicker **2** coat made to keep out the rain

slide /slaɪd/ v **slid** /slɪd/ **1** vi/t go or send smoothly across a surface **2** vi move quietly and unnoticed **3** let something

slide let a situation or condition continue, esp. getting worse, without taking action, usu. because of laziness ♦ *n* 1 slipping movement 2 fall: *a slide in living standards* 3 apparatus for sliding down 4 piece of film through which light is passed to show a picture on a surface 5 small piece of thin glass to put an object on for seeing under a microscope

slide pro·ject·or /ˈ· ·ˌ·ˈ/ *n* apparatus for making SLIDES (4) appear on a screen

sliding scale /ˌ· ˈ·/ *n* system of pay, taxes, etc., calculated by rates which may very according to changing conditions

slight¹ /slaɪt/ *adj* 1 small in degree: *a slight improvement* 2 thin and delicate 3 **in the slightest** at all ~**ly** *adv* 1 a little: *slightly better* 2 in a SLIGHT (2) way: *He's very slightly built.*

slight² *vt* treat disrespectfully or rudely ♦ *n* INSULT

slim /slɪm/ *adj* -**mm**- 1 attractively thin 2 (of probability, hope, etc.) very small ~**ly** *adv*

slim down /ˌ· ˈ·/ *phr v* 1 *vi* become thinner by eating less, exercising, etc. 2 *vi/t* reduce in size or number

slime /slaɪm/ *n* unpleasant, thick, sticky liquid **slimy** *adj* 1 unpleasantly slippery 2 *derog* trying to please in order to gain advantage for oneself

sling /slɪŋ/ *vt* **slung** /slʌŋ/ 1 throw roughly or with effort 2 hang 3 **sling mud** at say unfair and damaging things about (esp. a political opponent) ♦ *n* piece of cloth hanging from the neck to support a damaged arm

sling·shot /ˈslɪŋʃɑt/ *n* stick shaped like a Y, with a rubber band, for shooting small stones

slink /slɪŋk/ *vi* **slunk** /slʌŋk/ move quietly and secretly, as if in fear or shame

slip¹ /slɪp/ *v* -**pp**- 1 *vi* slide out of place unexpectedly or by accident 2 *vi/t* move or put smoothly or unnoticed 3 *vi/t* put on or take off (a garment) quickly 4 *vi* get worse or lower: *slipping standards* 5 *vi* make a mistake 6 *vt* fail to be remembered by: *It slipped my mind.* (= I forgot) 7 give secretly: *I slipped the waiter some money.* 8 **let slip: a** fail to take (a chance) **b** make known accidentally ♦ *n* 1 small mistake 2 woman's undergarment like a skirt or loose dress 3 young, attractively SLIM person: *a slip*

of a girl 4 **give someone the slip** escape from someone

slip² *n* small or narrow piece of paper

slip·page /ˈslɪpɪdʒ/ *n* [C;U] (amount of) slipping

slipped disc /ˌ· ˈ·/ *n* painful displacement of one of the connecting parts between the bones of the SPINE

slip·per /ˈslɪpə/ *n* light soft shoe worn indoors

slip·per·y /ˈslɪpəri/ *adj* 1 very smooth or wet, so one cannot easily hold or move on it 2 not to be trusted

slip·shod /ˈslɪpʃɑd/ *adj* carelessly done

slip-up /ˈ· ·/ *n* usu. slight mistake

slit /slɪt/ *n* long, narrow cut or opening ♦ *vt* **slit**; *present p.* -**tt**- make a slit in

slith·er /ˈslɪðə/ *vi* 1 move smoothly and twistingly 2 slide in an unsteady manner

sliv·er /ˈslɪvə/ *n* small thin piece cut or broken off

slob /slɑb/ *n* rude, dirty, lazy, or carelessly dressed person

slob·ber /ˈslɑbə/ *vi* let SALIVA come out of the mouth; DROOL

slo·gan /ˈsloʊgən/ *n* short phrase expressing a political or advertising message

slop¹ /slɑp/ *vi/t* -**pp**- go or cause (a liquid) to go over the side of a container: *You're slopping paint everywhere!*

slop around *phr vi infml* play in or move about in anything wet or dirty

slop² *n* [U] 1 [usu. P] food waste, esp. for feeding animals 2 *derog* tasteless liquid food

slope /sloʊp/ *vi* lie neither completely upright nor completely flat ♦ *n* 1 piece of sloping ground 2 degree of sloping

slop·py /ˈslɑpi/ *adj* 1 (of clothes) loose, informal, and careless 2 not careful or thorough enough 3 silly in showing feelings ~**pily** *adv* ~**piness** *n* [U]

slosh /slɑʃ/ *v, vi/t* move or cause (liquid) to move about roughly and noisily, making waves ~**ed** *adj infml* drunk

slot /slɑt/ *n* 1 long, straight, narrow hole 2 place or position in a list, system, organization, etc. ♦ *vi/t* -**tt**- 1 (be) put into a SLOT (1) 2 fit into a SLOT (2)

slot ma·chine /ˈ· ·ˌ·/ *n* machine with a long handle, into which people put money to try to win more money

slouch /slaʊtʃ/ vi walk, stand, or sit with round shoulders, looking tired ♦ n lazy, useless person: *She's no slouch when it comes to tennis.* (= she's very good)

slough /slʌf/ vi **slough off** phr vt **1** (esp. of a snake) throw off (dead outer skin) **2** esp. lit get rid of as something worn out or unwanted

slov·en·ly /'slʌvənli/ adj **1** untidy **2** very carelessly done **–liness** n [U]

slow /sloʊ/ adj **1** having less than a usual speed; not fast **2** taking a long time: *a slow job* **3** (of a clock) showing a time that is earlier than the right time **4** not quick in understanding **5** not active: *Business is slow.* ♦ vi/t make or become slower ♦ adv slowly: *slow-moving traffic* **~ly** adv **~ness** n [U]

slow·down /'sloʊdaʊn/ n **1** lessening of speed or activity **2** decision to work slowly as a kind of STRIKE² (1)

slow·poke /'sloʊpoʊk/ n infml person who acts slowly

sludge /slʌdʒ/ n [U] thick soft mud

slug¹ /slʌg/ n small, soft limbless creature, like a SNAIL with no shell

slug² vt -gg- hit hard

slug³ n **1** bullet **2** infml amount of strong alcoholic drink taken at one swallow

slug·gish /'slʌgɪʃ/ adj not very active or quick **~ly** adv **~ness** n [U]

slum /slʌm/ n city area of bad living conditions and old unrepaired buildings ♦ vi amuse oneself by visiting a place on a much lower social level: *go slumming* **~my** adj

slum·ber /'slʌmbə/ vi, n lit sleep

slumber par·ty /'·· ,··/ n party at which a group of children sleep at one child's house

slump /slʌmp/ vi **1** drop down suddenly and heavily **2** decrease suddenly ♦ n **1** sudden decrease, esp. in business **2** time of seriously bad business conditions and high unemployment

slung /slʌŋ/ v past t. and p. of SLING

slunk /slʌŋk/ v past t. and p. of SLINK

slur¹ /slɜː/ vt -rr- pronounce unclearly

slur² vt -rr- make unfair damaging remarks about ♦ n: *a slur on my reputation*

slurp /slɜːp/ vt drink noisily **slurp** n

slush /slʌʃ/ n [U] **1** partly melted snow **2** books, films, etc., full of silly love stories **~y** adj

slush fund /'· ·/ n money secretly kept for dishonest payments

slut /slʌt/ n derog sexually immoral woman **~ty** adj

sly /slaɪ/ adj **1** secretly deceitful or tricky **2** playfully unkind: *a sly joke* **3 on the sly** secretly **~ly** adv **~ness** n [U]

smack¹ /smæk/ vt **1** hit with the flat hand **2** open and close (one's lips) noisily in eagerness to eat ♦ n **1** blow with the open hand **2** sl [U] HEROIN ♦ adv exactly; right: *smack in the middle*

smack² v **smack of** phr vt have a taste or suggestion of

small /smɔːl/ adj **1** of less than usual size, amount, importance, etc. **2** young: *small children* **3** doing only a limited amount of business **4** slight: *small hope of success* **5 feel small** feel ashamed or humble ♦ n [the+S] narrow middle part (of the back) **~ness** n [U]

small claims court /· ˌ· '·/ n court of law dealing with cases involving small amounts of money

small for·tune /· '··/ n [S] very large amount of money

small fry /'· ·/ n young or unimportant person

small-mind·ed /ˌ· '··◄/ adj having narrow or ungenerous views

small po·ta·toes /ˌ· ·'··/ n [U] infml person or thing of little importance

small·pox /'smɔːlpɒks/ n [U] serious infectious disease which leaves marks on the skin

small screen /'· ·/ n [the+S] television

small talk /'· ·/ n [U] light conversation on non-serious subjects

small-time /ˌ· '·◄/ adj limited in activity, ability, profits, etc.

smarm·y /'smɑːmi/ adj unpleasantly and falsely polite

smart¹ /smɑːt/ adj **1** intelligent **2** quick or forceful: *a smart blow on the head* **~ly** adv **~ness** n [U]

smart² vi, n (cause or feel) a stinging pain: (fig.) *She was still smarting over his unkind words.*

smart al·eck /'smɑːt ˌælɪk/ n annoying person who pretends to know everything

smart card /'· ·/ n small plastic card able to be used in many ways, e.g. as a key, bank card, ID CARD, etc.

smash /smæʃ/ v **1** vi/t break into pieces violently **2** vi/t go, drive, hit forcefully:

The car smashed into a lamppost. **3** *vt* put an end to: *The police have smashed the drugs ring.* **4** *vt* hit (the ball) with a SMASH (2) ♦ *n* **1** (sound of) a violent breaking **2** hard downward, attacking shot, as in tennis **3** very successful new play, film, etc.: *a smash hit* **4** SMASH-UP

smash-up /ˈ- ˌ/ *n* serious road or railroad accident

smat·ter·ing /ˈsmætərɪŋ/ *n* limited knowledge: *a smattering of German*

smear /smɪr/ *vt* **1** spread (a sticky or oily substance) untidily across (a surface) **2** make unproved charges against (someone) in order to produce unfavorable public opinion ♦ *n* **1** mark made by smearing **2** unfair, unproved charge against someone: *a smear campaign*

smell /smɛl/ *v* **1** *vi* have or use the sense of the nose **2** *vt* notice, examine, etc., (as if) by this sense: *I think I smell gas!* | *I could smell trouble coming.* **3** *vi* have a particular smell: *The bread smells stale.* **4** *vi* have a bad smell **5 smell a rat** guess that something wrong or dishonest is happening ♦ *n* **1** [U] power of using the nose to discover the presence of gases in the air **2** [C] quality that has an effect on the nose: *a flower with a sweet smell* **3** [C] bad smell **~y** *adj* smelling bad

smelt /smɛlt/ *vt* melt (ORE) for removing the metal

smid·gen /ˈsmɪdʒɪn/ *n* [S] *infml* small amount

smile /smaɪl/ *n* pleased or amused expression in which the mouth is turned up at the ends ♦ *vi* make a smile **smil·ingly** *adv*

smirk /smɜrk/ *vi, n* (make) a silly SELF-SATISFIED smile

smith /smɪθ/ *n* maker of metal things: *a silversmith*

smith·e·reens /ˌsmɪðəˈrinz/ *n* (in)to **smithereens** into extremely small pieces

smit·ten /ˈsmɪtˈn/ *adj* suddenly in love

smock /smɑk/ *n* long, loose shirtlike garment, esp. for protecting one's clothes from paint, dirt, etc.

smog /smɑg, smɔg/ *n* [U] thick dark unpleasant mist in cities

smoke /smoʊk/ *n* **1** [U] usu. white, gray, or black gas produced by burning **2** [S] act of smoking tobacco **3 go up in smoke** end or fail without results, esp. suddenly ♦ *v* **1** *vi/t* suck in smoke from

(a cigarette, pipe, etc.) **2** *vi* give off smoke: *smoking chimneys* **3** *vt* preserve (fish, meat, etc.) with smoke **smoker** *n* **1** person who smokes **2** apparatus for smoking meat, fish, etc. **smoky** *adj* **1** filled with smoke **2** tasting of or looking like smoke **smoking** *n* [U] practice or habit of smoking cigarettes, etc.

smoke out *phr vt* fill a place with smoke to force (a person, animal, etc.) to come out from hiding

smoke·screen /ˈsmoʊkskrin/ *n* **1** cloud of smoke produced to hide something **2** something that hides one's real intentions

smoke·stack /ˈsmoʊkstæk/ *n* **1** tall chimney of a factory or ship **2** chimney on a steam engine or ship

smok·ing gun /ˌ- ˈ-/ *n* definite proof of who is responsible for something or how something really happened

smol·der /ˈsmoʊldər/ *vi* **1** burn slowly with (almost) no flame **2** have violent but unexpressed feelings

smooch /smutʃ/ *vi* kiss and hold lovingly

smooth¹ /smuð/ *adj* **1** having an even surface; not rough **2** (of a liquid mixture) without lumps **3** even in movement, without sudden changes: *a smooth flight* **4** (too) pleasant or polite **~ly** *adv* **~ness** *n* [U]

smooth² *vt* make smooth(er)

smooth over *phr vt* make (difficulties) seem small or unimportant

smor·gas·bord /ˈsmɔrgəsˌbɔrd, -ˌboʊrd/ *n* meal in which people serve themselves from a table with many types of foods on it

smoth·er /ˈsmʌðər/ *vt* **1** cover thickly or in large numbers: *a face smothered in/with spots* **2** die or kill from lack of air **3** keep from developing or happening: *smother a yawn*

smudge /smʌdʒ/ *n* dirty mark with unclear edges ♦ *vi/t* make or become dirty with a smudge

smug /smʌg/ *adj* **-gg-** too pleased with oneself **~ly** *adv* **~ness** *n* [U]

smug·gle /ˈsmʌgəl/ *vt* take in or out secretly or illegally **-gler** *n* **-gling** *n* [U] taking goods from one country to another without paying the necessary tax

smut /smʌt/ *n* **1** [U] morally offensive talk, stories, etc. **2** [C] small piece of dirt **~ty** *adj* rude

snack /snæk/ n amount of food smaller than a meal ♦ vi eat a snack **~bar** small restaurant for quick meals

snag /snæg/ n 1 hidden or unexpected difficulty 2 rough or sharp part of something that may catch and hold things passing it ♦ vt **-gg-** catch on a SNAG(2)

sna·fu /ˈsnæfu, snæˈfu/ n confused situation

snail /sneɪl/ n small limbless creature with a soft body and a shell on its back, that moves slowly

snake /sneɪk/ n 1 long, thin, limbless creature, often with a poisonous bite 2 deceitful person 3 **a snake in the grass** a false friend ♦ vi move twistingly

snap /snæp/ v **-pp-** 1 vi/t close the jaws quickly (on): *The dog snapped at my ankles.* 2 vi/t break suddenly and sharply 3 vi/t move with a sharp sound: *The lid snapped shut.* 4 vi speak quickly and angrily 5 vt infml to photograph 6 **snap one's fingers** make a noise by moving the second finger quickly along the thumb 7 **snap out of it** free oneself quickly from a bad state of mind 8 **snap someone's head off** answer someone in a short rude way ♦ n 1 act or sound of snapping 2 informal photograph ♦ adj done without warning or long consideration: *snap judgments* **~py** adj 1 stylish; fashionable 2 hasty; quick: *Make it snappy!* (= Hurry up!)

snap up phr vt take or buy quickly and eagerly

snap·shot /ˈsnæpʃɑt/ n informal photograph taken quickly

snare /snɛr/ n 1 trap for small animals 2 deceiving situation ♦ vt catch in a snare

snarl[1] /snɑrl/ vi 1 (of an animal) make a low angry sound 2 speak angrily ♦ n act or sound of snarling

snarl[2] v **snarl up** phr vt mix together so as to make movement difficult: *The traffic had gotten snarled up.* **snarl-up** /ˈ-ˌ-/ n confused state, esp. of traffic

snatch /snætʃ/ vi/t take (something) quickly and often violently or wrongfully ♦ n 1 act of snatching 2 short incomplete part: *overhearing snatches of conversation*

snaz·zy /ˈsnæzi/ adj infml stylishly attractive **-zily** adv

sneak /snik/ vi **sneaked** or **snuck** /snʌk/ go or take quietly and secretly ♦ n derog sl school child who gives informa-

tion about the wrongdoings of others **~er** n light shoe worn for sports **~ing** adj 1 secret: *a sneaking admiration* 2 not proved but probably right: *a sneaking suspicion* **~y** adj acting or done secretly or deceitfully

sneak pre·view /ˌ· ˈ·· / n a chance to see something new, esp. a film, before anyone else has done so

sneer /snɪr/ vi express proud dislike and disrespect, esp. with an unpleasant curling smile ♦ n sneering look or remark

sneeze /sniz/ vi, n (have) a sudden uncontrolled burst of air from the nose

snick·er /ˈsnɪkə/ vi laugh quietly or secretly in a disrespectful way **snicker** n

snide /snaɪd/ adj indirectly but unpleasantly expressing a low opinion **~ly** adv

sniff /snɪf/ v 1 vi breathe in loudly, esp. in short repeated actions 2 vi/t do this to discover a smell (in or on) 3 vt take (a harmful drug) through the nose ♦ n act or sound of sniffing **~er** n

sniff at phr vt dislike or refuse proudly

sniff out phr vt discover or find out (as if) by smelling

snip /snɪp/ vt **-pp-** cut with quick short strokes, esp. with scissors ♦ n 1 act of snipping 2 small amount

snipe /snaɪp/ vi 1 shoot from a hidden position 2 make an unpleasant indirect attack in words **sniper** n

snip·pet /ˈsnɪpɪt/ n small bit: *a snippet of information*

snit /snɪt/ n **in a snit** infml unreasonably annoyed

sniv·el /ˈsnɪvəl/ vi **-l-** act or speak in a weak, complaining, crying way

snob /snɑb/ n person who pays too much attention to social class, and dislikes people of a lower class **~bery** n [U] behavior of snobs **~bish** adj

snoop /snup/ vi search around or concern oneself with other people's affairs without permission **~er** n

snoot·y /ˈsnuti/ adj infml proudly rude **-ily** adv **-iness** n [U]

snooze /snuz/ vi, n (have) a short sleep

snore /snɔr/ vi breathe noisily while asleep ♦ n act or sound of snoring

snor·kel /ˈsnɔrkəl/ n breathing tube for swimmers under water ♦ vi go snorkeling

snort /snɔrt/ **1** *vi* make a rough noise by forcing air down the nose, often in impatience or anger **2** *vt* SNIFF (3) ♦ *n* act or sound of snorting

snot /snɑt/ *n* **1** [U] *infml* thick liquid produced in the nose **2** [C] *sl derog* person who thinks he/she is better than others ~**ty** *adj*

snout /snaʊt/ *n* animal's long nose: *a pig's snout*

snow¹ /snoʊ/ *n* **1** [U] frozen rain that falls in white pieces (FLAKES) and often forms a soft covering on the ground ~**y** *adj*

snow² *vi* (of snow) fall

snow in *phr vt* prevent from traveling by a heavy fall of snow

snow under *phr vt* cause to have more of something than one can deal with: *snowed under with work*

snow·ball /'snoʊbɔl/ *n* ball of pressed snow, as thrown by children ♦ *vi* increase faster and faster

snow·bird /'snoʊbɜrd/ *n* someone, esp. an old person, who moves to a warmer place every winter when the place where they live becomes too cold

snow·board /'snoʊbɔrd, -boʊrd/ *n* long wide board used for moving down snow-covered hills as a sport ~**ing** *n* [U]

snowbound /'snoʊbaʊnd/ *adj* snowed in

snow·drift /'snoʊˌdrɪft/ *n* deep mass of snow piled up by the wind

snow·flake /'snoʊfleɪk/ *n* single piece of snow

snow·job /'snoʊdʒɑb/ *n* act of deceiving, esp. by use of too much information

snow·man /'snoʊmæn/ *n* **-men** /-mɛn/ figure of a person made out of snow

snow·mo·bile /'snoʊməˌbil/ *n* motor vehicle for traveling over snow

snow·plow /'snoʊplaʊ/ *n* apparatus or vehicle for clearing away snow

snow·storm /'snoʊstɔrm/ *n* very heavy fall of snow

snow·suit /'snoʊsut/ *n* article of clothing made in one piece, covering legs and arms, worn in winter

snub¹ /snʌb/ *vt* **-bb-** treat (someone) rudely, esp. by paying no attention to them ♦ *n* act of snubbing

snub² *adj* (of a nose) short and flat

snuck /snʌk/ *v past t. and p. of* SNEAK

snuff¹ /snʌf/ *n* [U] powdery tobacco for breathing into the nose

snuff² *vt* put out (a candle) by pressing the burning part

snuff out *phr vt* put a sudden end to

snug /snʌg/ *adj* **1** giving warmth, comfort, protection, etc. **2** (of clothes) fitting closely and comfortably

snug·gle /'snʌgəl/ *vi* settle into a warm comfortable position

so¹ /soʊ/ *adv* **1** to such a (great) degree: *It was so dark I couldn't see.* **2** (used instead of repeating something): *He hopes he'll win and I hope so too.* **3** also: *He hopes he'll win and so do I.* **4** very: *We're so glad you could come!* **5** in this way **6** yes; it is true: *"There's a fly in your soup." "So there is!"* **7** *fml* therefore **8 and so on/forth** and other things of that kind **9** or so more or less: *It'll only cost 15¢ or so.* **10 so as to**: **a** in order to **b** in such a way as to **11 so long!** *infml* goodbye **12 so many/much**: **a** a certain number/amount: *a charge of so much a day* **b** an amount equal to: *These books are just so much waste paper!*

so² *conj* **1** with the result that: *It was dark, so I couldn't see.* **2** therefore: *He had a headache, so he went to bed.* **3** with the purpose (that): *I gave him an apple so (that) he wouldn't go hungry.* **4** (used at the beginning of a sentence) **a** (with weak meaning): *So here we are again.* **b** (expressing discovery): *So that's how they did it!* **5 so what?** Why is that important?; Why should I care?

so³ *adj* **1** true: *Is that really so?* **2 just so** arranged exactly and tidily

soak /soʊk/ *vi/t* **1** (cause to) remain in liquid, becoming completely wet **2** (of liquid) enter (a solid) through the surface **3** *vt sl* make (a customer) pay too much ♦ *n* [C;U] (act of) soaking ~**ed** *adj* thoroughly wet, esp. from rain ~**ing** *adv, adj* very (wet)

soak up *phr vt* draw in (a liquid) through a surface: (fig.) *to soak up the sun* | *to soak up information*

so-and-so /'. .ˌ./ *n* **1** one not named **2** unpleasant or annoying person

soap /soʊp/ *n* **1** [U] usu. solid substance used with water for cleaning esp. the body **2** [C] *infml* SOAP OPERA ~**y** *adj*

soap·box /'soʊpbɑks/ *n* **on one's soapbox** stating one's opinions loudly and forcefully

soap op·e·ra /'. .ˌ./ *n* continuing television story about the daily life and troubles of the same set of characters

soar /sɔr, soʊr/ vi **1** (of a bird) fly high without moving the wings **2** rise steeply: *Prices soared.*

sob /sɑb/ vi **-bb-** cry while making short bursts of sound breathing in ♦ n act or sound of sobbing

so·ber /ˈsoʊbə/ adj **1** not drunk **2** fml thoughtful, serious, or solemn; not silly ♦ vi/t make or become SOBER (2): *a sobering thought* ~**ly** adv

sober up phr vi/t make or become SOBER (1)

sob sto·ry /ˈ· ˌ··/ n story intended to make the hearer or reader cry, feel pity, or feel sorry

so-called /ˌ· ˈ·◄/ adj (undeservedly but) commonly described in the stated way

soc·cer /ˈsɑkə/ n [U] game played with a round ball between 2 teams of 11 players

so·cia·ble /ˈsoʊʃəbəl/ adj fond of being with others; friendly –**bly** adv –**bility** /ˌsoʊʃəˈbɪləti/ n [U]

so·cial /ˈsoʊʃəl/ adj **1** of human society or its organization **2** living together by nature **3** based on rank in society: *social class* **4** for or spent in time or activities with friends (rather than work): *an active social life* ♦ a *social* **♦** n informal gathering: *ice-cream social* ~**ly** adv

social climb·er /ˌ·· ˈ·◄/ n derog person who tries to get accepted into a higher social class

so·cial·ism /ˈsoʊʃəlɪzəm/ n [U] political system aiming at establishing a society in which everyone is equal –**ist** adj, n

so·cial·ite /ˈsoʊʃəlaɪt/ n person who goes to many fashionable parties

so·cial·ize /ˈsoʊʃəlaɪz/ vi spend time with others in a friendly way

social sci·ence /ˌ·· ˈ··/ n [C;U] study of people in society, including SOCIOLOGY, ECONOMICS, etc.

Social Se·cu·ri·ty /ˌ·· ·ˈ···/ n [U] money for old people paid to the government by workers and employers

social work /ˈ·· ˌ·/ n [U] work done to help the old, sick, unemployed, etc. ~**er** n

so·ci·e·ty /səˈsaɪəti/ n **1** [U] everyone considered as a whole: *Society has a right to expect obedience to the law.* **2** [C;U] group of people who share laws, organization, etc.: *modern Western society* **3** [C] organization of people with similar aims or interests: *She joined the university film society.* **4** [U] fashionable

people **5** [U] fml being with other people –**tal** adj of society

so·ci·o·ec·o·nom·ic /ˌsoʊsioʊˌɛkəˈnɑmɪk, ˌsoʊʃioʊ-, -ˌikə-/ adj based on a combination of social and money conditions

so·ci·ol·o·gy /ˌsoʊsiˈɑlədʒi, ˌsoʊʃi-/ n [U] study of society and group behavior –**ogist** n –**ogical** /ˌsoʊsiəˈlɑdʒɪkəl, ˌsoʊʃiə-/ adj

sock¹ /sɑk/ n cloth covering for the foot

sock² vt sl strike hard ♦ n forceful blow

sock·et /ˈsɑkɪt/ n hole into which something fits, esp. an electrical PLUG

sod /sɑd/ n [C;U] (piece of) earth with grass and roots growing in it

so·da /ˈsoʊdə/ n [U] **1** SODA WATER: *a whiskey and soda* **2** drink with BUBBLES **3** fruit drink with ice cream **4** SODIUM

soda pop /ˈ·· ˌ·/ n sweet nonalcoholic FIZZY drink

soda wa·ter /ˈ·· ˌ··/ n [U] water filled with gas, esp. for mixing with other drinks

sod·den /ˈsɑdn/ adj very wet

so·di·um /ˈsoʊdiəm/ n [U] silver-white metal found naturally only in compounds

sod·o·my /ˈsɑdəmi/ n [U] fml or law any of various sexual acts, esp. ANAL sex between males

so·fa /ˈsoʊfə/ n comfortable seat for 2 or 3 people

soft /sɔft/ adj **1** not hard or stiff **2** smooth to the touch: *soft skin* **3** quiet **4** restful and pleasant: *soft colors* **5** with little force; gentle: *a soft breeze* **6** easy: *a soft job* **7** too kind **8** not in good physical condition **9** dealing with ideas not facts: *one of the soft sciences like PSYCHOLOGY* **10** not of the worst or most harmful kind: *Marijuana is a soft drug.* **11** (of a drink) containing no alcohol and usu. sweet and served cold **12** (in English pronunciation) **a** (of the letter c) having the sound /s/ and not /k/ **b** (of the letter g) having the sound /dʒ/ and not /g/ **13** (of water) free from minerals that stop soap from forming LATHER easily **14** infml foolish: *He's soft in the head.* ~**ly** adv ~**ness** n [U]

soft·ball /ˈsɔftbɔl/ n (ball used in) a game like baseball

soft-boiled /ˌ· ˈ·◄/ adj (of an egg) boiled not long enough for the yellow part to become solid

soft drink /ˈ· ˌ·/ n any nonalcoholic drink

soft·en /ˈsɒfən/ vi/t (cause to) become soft(er) or more gentle ~**er** n: *a water softener*

soften up phr vt break down opposition of (someone)

soft-heart·ed /ˌsɒftˈhɑːtɪd◂/ adj easily made to act kindly or feel sorry for someone

soft op·tion /ˌ ˈ ◂/ n course of action which will give one less trouble

soft-ped·al /ˌ ˈ ◂/ vt make (a subject, fact, etc.) seem unimportant

soft sell /ˌ ˈ ◂/ n [U] selling by gentle persuading

soft spot /ˈ ˌ◂/ n fondness

soft touch /ˌ ˈ◂/ n infml someone from whom it is easy to get what one wants because they are kind, easily deceived, etc.

soft·ware /ˈsɒft-weər/ n [U] set of PROGRAMS that control a computer

soft·wood /ˈsɒft-wʊd/ n [U] cheap, easily cut wood from trees such as PINE and FIR

sog·gy /ˈsɒɡi/ adj completely (and unpleasantly) wet –**giness** n [U]

soil[1] /sɔɪl/ n [U] top covering of the earth in which plants grow; ground

soil[2] vt fml make dirty

so·journ /ˈsɒdʒən/ vi fml live for a time in a place

sol·ace /ˈsɒlɪs/ n [C;U] (something that gives) comfort for someone full of grief or anxiety

so·lar /ˈsəʊlə/ adj of or from the sun

solar cell /ˌ ˈ ◂/ n apparatus for producing electric power from sunlight

solar pan·el /ˌ ˈ ◂/ n number of SOLAR CELLS working together

solar sys·tem /ˈ ˌ ◂/ n sun and the PLANETS going around it

sold /səʊld/ v past t. and p. of SELL

sol·der /ˈsɒdə, ˈsɔː-/ n [U] easily meltable metal used for joining metal surfaces ♦ vt join with solder

sol·dier[1] /ˈsəʊldʒə/ n member of an army

soldier on phr vi continue working steadily in spite of difficulties

sole[1] /səʊl/ n bottom surface of the foot or of a shoe

sole[2] n flat fish often used for food

sole[3] adj 1 only 2 unshared: *sole responsibility* ~**ly** adv only

sol·emn /ˈsɒləm/ adj 1 without humor or lightness; serious 2 (of a promise) made

sincerely and meant to be kept 3 of the grandest, most formal kind ~**ly** adv ~**ness** n [U] ~**ity** /səˈlɛmnəti/ n 1 [U] solemnness 2 [C] formal act proper for a grand event

sol·fa /ˌsɒlˈfɑː/ n system of names given to different musical notes

so·lic·it /səˈlɪsɪt/ v 1 vt fml ask for 2 ask people on the street to buy goods 3 vi esp. law advertise oneself as a PROSTITUTE

so·lic·i·tous /səˈlɪsɪtəs/ adj fml helpful and kind ~**ly** adv ~**ness** n [U]

sol·id /ˈsɒlɪd/ adj 1 not liquid or gas 2 not hollow 3 firm and well made 4 that may be depended on 5 in or showing complete agreement: *The strike was 100 percent solid.* 6 not mixed with any other (metal): *a watch of solid gold* 7 infml continuous: *waiting for 4 solid hours* 8 having length, width and height ♦ n solid object or substance ~**ly** adv –**ity** /səˈlɪdəti/ n [U] quality or state of being solid

sol·i·dar·i·ty /ˌsɒlɪˈdærəti/ n [U] loyalty within a group

so·lid·i·fy /səˈlɪdɪfaɪ/ vi/t (cause to) become solid or hard

solid-state /ˌ ˈ ◂/ adj having electrical parts, esp. TRANSISTORS, that run without heating or moving parts

so·lil·o·quy /səˈlɪləkwi/ n speech made by an actor alone on stage

sol·i·taire /ˌsɒləˈteə/ n [U] 1 card game for one player 2 (piece of jewelry having) a single jewel, esp. a diamond

sol·i·ta·ry /ˈsɒlətəri/ adj 1 (fond of being) alone 2 in a lonely place 3 single

sol·i·tude /ˈsɒlətjuːd/ n [U] fml state of being alone

so·lo /ˈsəʊləʊ/ n solos something done by one person alone, esp. a piece of music for one performer ♦ adj, adv 1 without a companion or esp. instructor 2 as or being a musical solo ~**ist** n performer of a musical solo

sol·stice /ˈsɒlstɪs, ˈsəʊl-/ n time of the longest and shortest days of the year

sol·u·ble /ˈsɒljəbəl/ adj 1 that can be dissolved (DISSOLVE) 2 fml solvable –**bility** /ˌsɒljəˈbɪləti/ n [U]

so·lu·tion /səˈluːʃən/ n 1 [C] answer to a problem or question 2 [C;U] liquid with a solid mixed into it

solve /sɒlv/ vt find an answer to or explanation of **solvable** adj

sol·vent¹ /ˈsɒlvənt/ adj not in debt –vency n [U]

solvent² n [C;U] liquid that can turn solids into liquids

som·ber /ˈsɒmbə/ adj sadly serious or dark ~ly adv ~ness n [U]

some¹ /sʌm/ determiner **1** an unknown or unstated person: She went to work for some computer firm (or other). **2** quite a large number or amount of: The fire lasted for some time. **3** infml no kind of: Some friend you are! **4** fine or important: That was some speech you made! **5** some ... or (an)other one or several which the speaker cannot or does not care to state exactly: He's staying with some friend or other. ♦ pron **1** an amount or number of the stated thing(s) **2** certain ones but not all ♦ adv **1** about (the stated number): Some 50 people came. **2** rather; a little: "Are you feeling better?" "Some, I guess."

some more an additional amount (of)

some² /səm; strong sʌm/ determiner a certain number or amount of: I bought some bread. | Some people like tea, others prefer coffee

some·bod·y /ˈsʌmbədi, -ˌbɒdi/ pron someone ♦ n [U] a person of some importance: He thinks he's really somebody.

some·day /ˈsʌmdeɪ/ adv at an unknown time in the future: Someday I'll be famous.

some·how /ˈsʌmhaʊ/ adv **1** in some way not yet known or stated **2** for some reason: Somehow I don't believe her.

some·one /ˈsʌmwʌn/ pron **1** a person (but not a particular or known one) **2** or someone or a person like that: We need a builder or someone.

some·place /ˈsʌmpleɪs/ adv SOMEWHERE

som·er·sault /ˈsʌməˌsɒlt/ n rolling movement in which the feet go over the head and then back to the ground **somersault** vi

some·thing /ˈsʌmθɪŋ/ pron **1** some unstated or unknown thing **2** better than nothing: At least we have the car, that's something. **3** make something of oneself/one's life be successful **4** or something (to show that the speaker is not sure): He's a director or something. **5** something of a(n) rather a(n); a fairly good **6** something like: **a** rather like **b** infml about: There were something like 1000 people there. **7** something over/under rather more/less than **8**

something to do with (having) a connection with

some·time /ˈsʌmtaɪm/ adv at some uncertain or unstated time ♦ adj fml former

some·times /ˈsʌmtaɪmz/ adv on some occasions but not all

some·what /ˈsʌmwɒt, -hwɒt/ adv a little; rather

some·where /ˈsʌmwɛr, -hwɛr/ adv **1** (at or to) some place **2** get somewhere begin to succeed

son /sʌn/ n **1** someone's male child **2** (used by an older man to a much younger man or boy): What's your name, son?

so·na·ta /səˈnɑːtə/ n piece of music in usu. 3 or 4 parts, for 1 or 2 instruments

song /sɒŋ/ n **1** [C] short piece of music with words for singing **2** [U] act or art of singing **3** [C;U] musiclike sound of birds **4 for a song** very cheaply

song and dance /ˌ·ˈ·/ n [S;U] infml an unnecessary or unwelcome expression of excitement, anger, etc.

son·ic /ˈsɒnɪk/ adj of or concerning the speed of sound or sound

son-in-law /ˈ· · ˌ/ n **sons-in-law** daughter's husband

son·net /ˈsɒnɪt/ n poem of 14 lines

so·nor·ous /səˈnɔːrəs, -ˈnʊər-, ˈsɒnərəs/ adj having a pleasantly full loud sound ~ly adv **-ity** /səˈnɒrəti, -ˈnɑːr-/ n

soon /suːn/ adv **1** within a short time **2** quickly; early: How soon can you finish it? **3** willingly: I'd sooner stay here. **4 as soon as** at once after; when **5 no sooner ... than** when ... at once: No sooner had she arrived than it was time to go. **6 sooner or later** certainly, although one cannot be sure when

soot /sʊt/ n [U] black powder produced by burning ~y adj ~iness n [U]

soothe /suːð/ vt **1** make less angry or excited **2** make less painful **soothingly** adv

sop¹ /sɒp/ n something offered to gain someone's favor or stop them complaining

sop² v -pp- **sop up** phr vt take up (liquid) into something solid

so·phis·ti·cat·ed /səˈfɪstɪˌkeɪtɪd/ adj **1** experienced in and understanding the ways of society **2** highly developed and including the best or most modern systems **-ion** /səˌfɪstɪˈkeɪʃən/ n [U]

soph·is·try /ˈsɒfəstri/ n [U] fml use of false deceptive arguments

soph·o·more /ˈsɒfəˌmɔr, -ˌmoʊr, ˈsɒfmɔr, ˈsɒfmoʊr/ n student in 10th grade of high school or the second year of high school or college

sop·o·rif·ic /ˌsɒpəˈrɪfɪk◂/ adj causing sleep

sop·ping /ˈsɒpɪŋ/ adv, adj very (wet)

so·pra·no /səˈprænoʊ, -ˈprɑ-/ n -nos 1 (someone, esp. a woman, with) the highest human singing voice 2 instrument which plays notes in the highest range

sor·bet /ˈsɔrbeɪ, ˈsɔrbət/ n [U] sweet frozen food made from fruit juice, sugar, and water

sor·cer·y /ˈsɔrsəri/ n [U] doing of magic with the help of evil spirits **sorcerer, sorceress** /ˈsɔrsərəs/ fem. — n

sor·did /ˈsɔrdɪd/ adj 1 completely lacking fine or noble qualities; low 2 dirty and badly cared for ~ly adv ~ness n [U]

sore /sɔr, soʊr/ adj 1 painful, esp. from a wound or hard use 2 likely to cause offense: Don't joke about his weight: it's a sore point with him. 3 angry ♦ n painful, usu. infected place on the body ♦ adv lit sorely ~ly adv fml very much: sorely needed ~ness n [U]

so·ror·i·ty /səˈrɔrəti, -ˈrɑr-/ n society of women in a college with their own RESIDENCE

sor·row /ˈsɑroʊ, ˈsɔr-/ n [C;U] sadness; grief ♦ vi grieve ~ful adj ~fully adv ~fulness n [U]

sor·ry /ˈsɑri, ˈsɔri/ adj 1 feeling sadness, pity, or sympathy 2 ashamed of or unhappy about an action and wishing one had not done it 3 causing pity mixed with disapproval: You look a sorry sight. ♦ interj 1 (used for excusing oneself or expressing polite refusal, disagreement, etc.) 2 (used for asking someone to repeat something one has not heard)

sort¹ /sɔrt/ n 1 group of people, things, etc., all sharing certain qualities; kind 2 person: She's not such a bad sort. 3 **of sorts** of a poor or doubtful kind 4 **out of sorts** feeling unwell or annoyed 5 **sort of** infml rather

sort² /vi/t put (things) in order

sort out phr vt separate from a mass or group

SOS n urgent message for help

so-so /ˈ. ./ adj, adv neither very bad(ly) nor very good/well

souf·flé /suˈfleɪ/ n [C;U] light airy baked dish of eggs and flour

sought /sɔt/ v past t. and p. of SEEK

sought-af·ter /ˈ. ˌ../ adj wanted because of rarity or high quality

soul /soʊl/ n 1 part of a person that is not the body and is thought not to die 2 person: Not a soul (= no one) was there. 3 perfect example: Your secret is safe with him; he's the soul of discretion. 4 most active part or influence: She's the life and soul of any party. 5 attractive quality of sincerity: The performance lacks soul. 6 SOUL MUSIC 7 **heart and soul** (with) all one's power and feeling 8 **keep body and soul together** have enough money, etc., to live ~ful adj expressing deep feeling ~fully adv ~less adj having no attractive or tender human qualities ~ly adv

soul food /ˈ. ./ n [U] old-fashioned cooking of the southern US

soul mu·sic /ˈ. ˌ../ n [U] type of popular music usu. performed by black singers

soul-search·ing /ˈ. ˌ../ n deep examination of one's mind and conscience

sound¹ /saʊnd/ n 1 [C;U] what is or may be heard 2 [S] idea produced by something read or heard: From the sound of it, I'd say the matter was serious. ♦ v 1 vi seem when heard: His explanation sounded suspicious. 2 vi/t (cause to) make a sound: Sound the trumpets. 3 vt signal by making sounds: Sound the alarm. 4 vt pronounce 5 vt measure the depth of (water, etc.) using a line with a weight on the end

sound off phr vi express an opinion freely and forcefully

sound out phr vt try to find out the opinion or intention of

sound² adj 1 not damaged or diseased 2 showing good sense or judgment: sound advice 3 thorough 4 (of sleep) deep and untroubled 5 **as sound as a bell** in perfect condition ~ly adv ~ness n [U]

sound³ adv **sound asleep** deeply asleep

sound bar·ri·er /ˈ. ˌ../ n point at which an aircraft, etc., reaches the speed of sound

sound·bite /ˈsaʊndbaɪt/ n short phrase used by politicians or advertisers to represent the most important part of what they are saying

sound ef·fects /'· ·ˌ·/ *n* [P] sounds produced to give the effect of natural sounds in a radio or television broadcast or film

sound·proof /'saʊndpruːf/ *adj* that sound cannot get through or into ♦ *vt* make soundproof

sound·track /'saʊndtræk/ *n* recorded music from a film

soup /suːp/ *n* [U] liquid cooked food often containing pieces of meat or vegetables ♦ *v* **soup up** *phr vt* increase the power of (an engine, etc): *soup up an old car*

sour /saʊə/ *adj* **1** tasting acid: *sour green apples* **2** tasting bad because of chemical action by bacteria: *sour milk* **3** bad-tempered; unfriendly **4** **go/turn sour** go wrong ♦ *vi/t* (cause to) become sour ~**ly** *adv* ~**ness** *n* [U]

source /sɔːs, soʊrs/ *n* where something comes from; cause

sour cream /ˌ· '·/ *n* [U] thick white cream with a sour taste, used on food and in cooking

sour·dough /'saʊədoʊ/ *n* [U] type of bread with a slightly sour taste

sour grapes /ˌ· '·/ *n* [U] pretending to dislike what one really desires, because it is unobtainable

south /saʊθ/ *n* (*often cap.*) **1** the direction which is on the right of a person facing the rising sun **2** [*the*+S] **a** the part of a country which is further south than the rest **b** the southeastern states of the US ♦ *adj* **1** in the south **2** (of wind) from the south ♦ *adv* towards the south ~**ward** /'saʊθwəd/ *adj, adv*

south·east /ˌsaʊθ'iːst◂/ *n, adj, adv* (direction) exactly between south and east ~**ern** /-'iːstən/ *adj*

south·er·ly /'sʌðəli/ *adj* south

south·ern /'sʌðən/ *adj* of the south part of the world or of a country ~**er** *n* (*often cap.*) person who lives in or comes from the southern part of a country

south·west /ˌsaʊθ'wɛst◂/ *n, adj, adv* (direction) exactly between south and west ~**ern** /-'wɛstən/ *adj*

sou·ve·nir /ˌsuːvə'nɪr, 'suːvəˌnɪr/ *n* object kept as a reminder of an event, journey, place, etc.

sov·e·reign /'sɒvrɪn/ *n fml* king, queen, etc. ♦ *adj* (of a country) independent and governing itself ~**ty** *n* [U] **1** complete freedom and power to act or govern **2** quality of being a sovereign state

So·vi·et /'soʊvi-ɪt, -viˌet/ *adj* of the former USSR or its people

sow[1] /soʊ/ *vi/t* **sowed**, **sown** /soʊn/ or **sowed** plant (seeds) on (a piece of ground) ~**er** *n*

sow[2] /saʊ/ *n* female pig

soy·bean /'sɔɪbiːn/ *n* bean of an Asian plant which produces oil and is made into a special dark liquid used in Chinese cooking (**soy sauce**)

spa /spɑː/ *n* place with a spring of mineral water where people come to improve their health

space /speɪs/ *n* **1** [U] something measurable in length, width, or depth; room: *There's not enough space in the cupboard for all my clothes.* **2** [C;U] quantity or bit of this: *looking for a parking space* **3** [U] what is outside the Earth's air; where the stars and PLANETS are **4** [U] what surrounds all objects and continues outwards in all directions: *staring into space* **5** [C;U] period of time: *within the space of a few years* ♦ *vt* place apart; arrange with spaces between

  space out *phr vt* forget

space-age /'· ·/ *adj* very modern

space·craft /'speɪs-krɑːft/ *n* vehicle able to travel in SPACE (3)

space·ship /'speɪsˌʃɪp/ *n* (esp. in stories) spacecraft for carrying people

space shut·tle /'· ˌ·/ *n* spacecraft that can be used more than once

space sta·tion /'· ˌ·/ large spacecraft intended to stay above the Earth and act as a base for scientific tests, etc.

space·suit /'speɪs-suːt/ *n* special garment worn in SPACE (3), covering the whole body

spa·cious /'speɪʃəs/ *adj* having a lot of room: *a spacious office* ~**ness** *n* [U]

spade[1] /speɪd/ *n* **1** tool with a broad blade for digging **2** **call a spade a spade** speak the plain truth without being delicate or sensitive

spade[2] *n* playing card with one or more figures shaped like black leaves on it

spa·ghet·ti /spə'ɡeti/ *n* [U] long, round, thin form of PASTA: *spaghetti and meatballs*

span /spæn/ *n* **1** length between two limits, esp. of time: *over a span of 3 years* **2** length of time over which something continues: *concentration span* **3** (part of) a bridge, arch, etc., between supports **4** distance from the end of the thumb to the little finger in a spread hand ♦ *vt* -**nn**- **1** form an arch or bridge over **2** include in space or time

span·gle /'spæŋgəl/ *n* small shiny piece sewn on for decoration ♦ *vt* decorate with spangles

span·iel /'spænyəl/ *n* dog with long ears and long wavy hair

spank /spæŋk/ *vt* hit (esp. a child) with the open hand for punishment, esp. on the BUTTOCKS **spank** *n*

spar[1] /spar/ *vi* -**rr**- **1** practice boxing (BOX[2]) **2** fight with words

spar[2] *n* pole supporting a ship's ropes or sails

spare /spɛr/ *vt* **1** give up (something that is not needed): *We have no money to spare.* (= we have only just enough) **2** keep from using, spending, etc.: *No expense was spared.* (= a lot of money was spent) **3** not give (something unpleasant): *Spare me the gory details.* **4** *esp. lit* not punish or harm **5 spare a thought** stop and consider ♦ *adj* **1** kept for use if needed: *a spare tire* **2** free: *spare time* **3** rather thin ♦ *n* SPARE PART

spare part /ˌ· '·/ *n* machine part to take the place of one that is damaged

spare·ribs /'spɛrˌrɪbz/ *n* [P] (dish of) pig's RIBS with their meat

spark /spark/ *n* **1** small bit of burning material flying through the air: (fig.) *His murder was the spark that set off the war.* **2** electric flash passing across a space **3** very small but important bit: *not a spark of humor* ♦ *vi* **1** produce a spark **2** lead to (esp. something unpleasant) **3** encourage

spark off *phr vt* cause (esp. something violent or unpleasant)

spar·kle /'sparkəl/ *vi* shine in small flashes: (fig.) *Her conversation sparkled with wit.* (= was bright and interesting) ♦ *n* [C;U] act or quality of sparkling –**kling** *adj* **1** full of life and brightness **2** (of wine) giving off gas in small BUBBLES

spark plug /'· ·/ *n* part inside an engine that makes a SPARK (2) to light the gas and start the engine

spar·row /'spærou/ *n* very common small brownish bird

sparse /spars/ *adj* scattered; not filled with crowds ~**ly** *adv* ~**ness** *n* [U]

spar·tan /'spart°n/ *adj* simple, severe, and without attention to comfort

spas·m /'spæzəm/ *n* **1** sudden uncontrolled tightening of muscles **2** sudden short period of uncontrolled activity: *spasms of coughing*

spas·mod·ic /spæz'madɪk/ *adj* happening irregularly or non-continuously: *spasmodic interest* ~**ally** *adv*

spat /spæt/ *v past t. and p. of* SPIT

spate /speɪt/ *n* [S] large number or amount coming together at the same time

spa·tial /'speɪʃəl/ *adj fml* of or in SPACE (1) ~**ly** *adv*

spat·ter /'spætə/ *vi/t* scatter (drops of liquid) or be scattered on (a surface)

spat·u·la /'spætʃələ/ *n* (kitchen) tool with a wide flat blade for spreading, mixing, etc.

spawn /spɔn/ *n* [U] eggs of water animals like fishes and FROGS ♦ *vi* **1** produce spawn **2** produce esp. in large numbers

spay /speɪ/ *vt* remove part of a female animal's sex organs so she cannot produce young

speak /spik/ *v* **spoke** /spouk/, **spoken** /'spoukən/ **1** *vt* say things; talk **2** *vi* express thoughts, ideas, etc., in some other way than this: *Actions speak louder than words.* **3** *vt* say; express: *Is he speaking the truth?* **4** *vt* be able to talk in (a language) **5** *vi* make a speech **6** *vi* mean in the stated way what is said: *generally/personally speaking, I agree* **7 on speaking terms** willing to talk and be polite to another **8 so to speak** as one might say **9 speak one's mind** express one's thoughts (too) directly **10 to speak of** worth mentioning ~**er** *n* **1** person making a speech **2** person who speaks a language **3** LOUDSPEAKER

speak for *phr vt* express the thoughts, opinions, etc. of

speak out *phr vi* speak boldly, freely, and plainly

speak up *phr vi* **1** speak more loudly **2** SPEAK **out**

speak·eas·y /'spikˌizi/ *n* (esp. in the 1920s and 1930s) place for going to buy and drink alcohol illegally

spear /spɪr/ *n* weapon consisting of a pole with a sharp point ♦ *vt* push or throw a spear into

spear·head /ˈspɪrhɛd/ n forceful beginner and/or leader of an attack or course of action ♦ vt lead forcefully

spear·mint /ˈspɪrˌmɪnt/ n [U] common MINT plant with a fresh taste

spe·cial /ˈspɛʃəl/ adj 1 of a particular kind; not ordinary 2 particularly great or fine: a special occasion ♦ n 1 something not of the regular kind 2 infml an advertised reduced price in a store ~ly adv 1 for one particular purpose 2 unusually

special ed·u·ca·tion /ˌ·· ··ˈ··/ n [U] education for children who have physical or mental problems

special ef·fects /ˌ·· ·ˈ·/ n [P] images or sounds of something that does not really exist or did not really happen, esp. in a movie

spe·cial·ist /ˈspɛʃəlɪst/ n 1 person with skill or interest in a particular subject 2 doctor who specializes in a particular sort of disease, etc.

spe·cial·ize /ˈspɛʃəˌlaɪz/ vi limit one's study, business, etc., to one particular area –**ization** /ˌspɛʃələˈzeɪʃən/ n [C;U]

spe·cial·ty /ˈspɛʃəlti/ n 1 person's particular field of work or study 2 finest product

spe·cies /ˈspiʃiz, -siz/ n -**cies** group of similar types of animal or plant

spe·cif·ic /spɪˈsɪfɪk/ adj 1 detailed and exact: specific instructions 2 particular; fixed or named: a specific tool for each job ~**ally** adv

spe·ci·fi·ca·tion /ˌspɛsəfəˈkeɪʃən/ n 1 [C] detailed plan or set of descriptions or directions 2 [U] act of specifying

spe·ci·fy /ˈspɛsəˌfaɪ/ vt state exactly

spe·ci·men /ˈspɛsəmən/ n 1 single typical thing or example 2 piece or amount of something to be shown, tested, etc.: The doctor needs a specimen of your blood.

speck /spɛk/ n very small piece or spot: a speck of dust

speck·le /ˈspɛkəl/ n any of a number of small irregular marks –**led** adj

spec·ta·cle /ˈspɛktəkəl/ n 1 something unusual that one sees, esp. something grand and fine 2 object of laughing, disrespect, or pity **spectacles** n old-fash [P] GLASSES

spec·tac·u·lar /spɛkˈtækyələr/ adj unusually interesting and grand ♦ n spectacular entertainment ~**ly** adv

spec·ta·tor /ˈspɛkˌteɪtər/ n person watching an event or sport

spec·ter /ˈspɛktər/ n fml or lit for: GHOST –**tral** adj

spec·trum /ˈspɛktrəm/ n -**tra** /-trə/ 1 set of bands of different colors into which light may be separated by a PRISM 2 broad and continuous range: both ends of the political spectrum

spec·u·late /ˈspɛkyəˌleɪt/ vi 1 make guesses 2 buy things to sell later in the hope of profit –**lator** n –**lative** /-lətɪv, -ˌleɪtɪv/ adj –**lation** /ˌspɛkyəˈleɪʃən/ n [C;U]

sped /spɛd/ v past t. and p. of SPEED

speech /spitʃ/ n 1 [U] act, power, or way of speaking 2 [C] set of words spoken formally to a group of listeners — see also FREE SPEECH ~**less** adj unable to speak because of strong feeling, shock, etc.

speed /spid/ n 1 [C] rate of movement: a speed of 2000 miles an hour 2 [U] quickness of movement or action: traveling at speed (= fast) 3 [U] sl for AMPHETAMINE ♦ v **speeded** or **sped** /spɛd/ 1 vi/t go or take quickly 2 vi drive illegally fast ~**y** adj fast

speed up phr vi/t (cause to) go faster

speed lim·it /ˈ· ˌ·ˈ·/ n fastest speed one is allowed to drive on a road

speed·om·e·ter /spɪˈdɑmətər/ n instrument showing how fast a vehicle is going

speed·way /ˈspidweɪ/ n place where cars are raced around a closed track

spell[1] /spɛl/ v 1 vi form words (correctly) from letters 2 vt name in order the letters of (a word) 3 vt (of letters) form (a word): B-O-O-K spells "book." 4 vt have as an effect: His disapproval spells defeat for our plan. ~**er** n ~**ing** n way a word is spelled

spell out phr vt explain in the clearest possible way

spell[2] n 1 unbroken period of time: spells of sunshine 2 quickly passing attack of illness: a dizzy spell

spell[3] n (words producing) a condition produced by magical power: (fig.) The first time we saw Venice, we fell under its spell.

spell·bind /ˈspɛlbaɪnd/ vt hold the complete attention of –**bound** /-baʊnd/ adj

spelling bee /ˈ·· ˌ·/ n competition in or between schools to find the best spellers

spend /spɛnd/ vt **spent** /spɛnt/ 1 pay (money) for goods or services 2 pass or use (time): He spent 3 years in prison. ~**er**

n **spent** *adj* **1** already used; no longer for use **2** worn out

spend·thrift /'spɛndˌθrɪft/ *n* person who wastes money

sperm /spɜːm/ *n* male sex cell which unites with the female egg to produce new life

spew /spyu/ *vi/t* (cause to) come out in a rush or flood

sphere /sfɪr/ *n* **1** mass in the shape of a ball **2** area or range of existence, meaning, action, etc.: *this country's sphere of influence* **spherical** /'sfɛrɪkəl, 'sfɪr-/ *adj* ball-shaped

sphinx /sfɪŋks/ *n* ancient Egyptian image of a lion with a human head

spice /spaɪs/ *n* **1** [C;U] vegetable product used for giving taste to food **2** [S;U] (additional) interest or excitement ♦ *vt* add spice to **spicy** *adj* **1** containing (much) spice **2** slightly improper or rude

spi·der /'spaɪdə/ *n* small creature with 8 legs, of which many types make WEBS to catch insects ~**y** *adj* long and thin like a spider's legs

spiel /ʃpil, spil/ *n* *infml* long explanation, often used to try to persuade people

spike /spaɪk/ *n* **1** pointed piece, esp. of metal **2** metal point fixed to the bottom of a (sports) shoe **3** group of grains or flowers on top of a stem **4** high, thin heel of a woman's shoe ♦ *vt* **1** drive a spike into **2** add a strong alcoholic drink to (a weak or nonalcoholic one) **3** stop (esp. an article in a newspaper) from being printed or spread **spiky** *adj*

spill /spɪl/ *vi/t* **spilled** (cause to) pour out accidentally and be lost: *I've spilled some coffee on the carpet.* | (fig.) *The crowd spilled into the streets.* **2 spill the beans** *infml* tell a secret too soon or to the wrong person ♦ *n* fall from a horse, bicycle, etc.

spin /spɪn/ *v* **spun** /spʌn/, *pres. p.* **-nn- 1** *vi/t* turn around and around fast **2** *vi/t* make (thread) by twisting (cotton, wool, etc.): (fig.) *spin a yarn* (= tell a story) **3** *vt* produce in threadlike form: *a spider spinning a web* ♦ *n* **1** [C] act of spinning **2** [S;U] fast turning movement **3** [C] short trip (in a car) for pleasure **4** [S] a steep drop: *The news sent prices into a spin.* **5** [U] way of saying or reporting something that makes it seem to have particular qualities, used esp. in politics

and advertising **6 in a spin** in a confused state of mind ~**ner** *n*

spin out *phr vt* cause to last long enough or too long

spin·ach /'spɪnɪtʃ/ *n* [U] vegetable with large soft leaves

spin·al cord /ˌspaɪnl 'kɔrd/ *n* thick cord of important nerves enclosed in the SPINE (1)

spin·dle /'spɪndl/ *n* **1** machine part around which something turns **2** pointed rod onto which thread is twisted ~**dly** *adj* long, thin, and looking weak

spin doc·tor /'· ˌ··/ *n* someone who describes events in politics, in a way that influences people's opinions about them

spine /spaɪn/ *n* **1** row of bones down the center of the back **2** prickly animal or plant part **3** side of a book along which the pages are fastened ~**less** *adj* weak and cowardly **spiny** *adj* prickly

spine-chil·ling /'· ˌ··/ *adj* very frightening

spin-off /'· ·/ *n* (useful) indirect product of a process

spi·ral /'spaɪrəl/ *n, adj* **1** (curve) winding around and around a central line or away from a central point **2** process of continuous upward or downward change ♦ *vi* **-l-** move in a spiral

spir·it /'spɪrɪt/ *n* **1** [C] person's mind or soul **2** [C] a being without a body, such as a GHOST **3** [U] quality of enthusiastic determination or brave effort: *a woman with spirit* | *team spirit* **4** [C] person of the stated kind of temper: *a free spirit* **5** [C] central quality or force: *the spirit of the law* (= its real intention) **6** [S;U] feeling in the mind towards something; ATTITUDE: *Please take my remarks in the spirit in which they were intended, and don't be offended.* **7 in spirit** in one's thoughts **8** ~**spirited** having the stated feelings or spirits: *high-spirited* ♦ *vt* take secretly or unseen **spirits** *n* **1** [P] state of one's mind: *in high spirits* (= cheerful) **2** strong alcoholic drink ~**ed** *adj* full of SPIRIT (3) ~**edly** *adv* ~**less** *adj* without SPIRIT (3) ~**lessness** *n* [U]

spir·i·tu·al /'spɪrɪtʃuəl/ *adj* **1** of the spirit rather than the body **2** religious ♦ *n* religious song originally sung by blacks ~**ly** *adv*

spit /spɪt/ *v* **spat** /spæt/; *pres. p.* **-tt- 1** *vi/t* throw out (liquid or other contents) from the mouth with force **2** *vt* say with effort

or anger **3** *vi* rain very lightly ♦ *n* [U]
SALIVA

spit² *n* **1** thin rod on which meat is
cooked over a fire **2** small usu. sandy
point of land running out into a stretch
of water

spit and pol·ish /ˌ· · ˈ·./ *n* [U] great military attention to a clean and shiny
appearance

spite /spaɪt/ *n* [U] **1** desire to annoy or
harm **2 in spite of** taking no notice of:
They continued, in spite of my warning.
♦ *vt* annoy or harm intentionally ~**ful**
adj

spitting im·age /ˌ·· ˈ·./ *n* exact likeness

splash /splæʃ/ *v* **1** *vi/t* **a** (cause to) fall or
move about in drops or waves, esp.
wildly or noisily: *Rain splashed against
the window.* **b** throw a liquid against
(something): *He splashed his face with
cold water.* **2** *vt* report as if very important, esp. in a newspaper ♦ *n* **1** (sound or
mark made by) splashing **2** forceful
effect: *make a splash in society*

splash·y /ˈsplæʃi/ *adj* big, bright, and
very noticeable

spleen /spliːn/ *n* **1** organ that controls the
quality of the body's blood supply
2 vent one's spleen express one's
annoyance

splen·did /ˈsplɛndɪd/ *adj* **1** grand in
appearance or style **2** very fine; excellent
~**ly** *adv*

splen·dor /ˈsplɛndə/ *n* [U] excellent or
grand beauty

splice /splaɪs/ *vt* fasten end to end to
make one continuous length

splint /splɪnt/ *n* flat piece for keeping a
broken bone in place

splin·ter /ˈsplɪntə/ *n* small sharp piece,
esp. of wood, broken off ♦ *vi/t* break
into splinters

split /splɪt/ *v* **split**; *pres. p.* **-tt- 1** *vi/t*
divide along a length, esp. by a blow or
tear **2** *vi/t* divide into separate parts **3**
vt share **4** *vi/t* separate into opposing
groups or parties: *Did you know John
and Mary had split up?* (= their marriage
or relationship had ended) **5 split hairs**
concern oneself with small, unimpor-
tant differences ♦ *n* **1** cut, break, or division made by splitting — see also SPLITS
~**ting** *adj* (of a headache) very bad

split-lev·el /ˌ· ˈ·./ *adj* (of a house)
having a ground floor on two levels

split per·son·al·i·ty /ˌ· ··ˈ··/ *n* set of 2
very different ways of behaving present
in one person

splits /splɪts/ *n* [*the*+P] movement in
which a person's legs are spread wide
and touch the floor along their whole
length

split sec·ond /ˌ· ˈ··◂/ *n* very short
moment

splurge /splɜːdʒ/ *vi* spend more than one
can usu. afford

splut·ter /ˈsplʌtə/ *vi* **1** talk quickly, as if
confused **2** make a wet spitting (SPIT)
noise **splutter** *n*

spoil /spɔɪl/ *v* **spoiled** or **spoilt** /spɔɪlt/ **1**
vt destroy the value, worth, or pleasure
of; ruin **2** *vt* treat very or too well: *Go on,
spoil yourself, have another piece of cake.*
3 *vi* decay **spoils** *n* [P] *fml* or *lit* things
taken without payment

spoil·sport /ˈspɔɪlspɔːt, -spoʊrt/ *n* person
who ruins others' fun

spoke¹ /spoʊk/ *v past t. of* SPEAK

spoke² *n* any of the bars connecting the
outer ring of a wheel to the center

spok·en /ˈspoʊkən/ *v past p. of* SPEAK

spoken for /ˈ·· ·/ *adj infml* closely
connected with a person of the opposite
sex

spokes·per·son /ˈspoʊksˌpɜːsən/
spokes·man /-mən/ *masc.,* **spokes-
wom·an** /-ˌwʊmən/ *fem. — n* person
chosen to speak officially for a group

sponge /spʌndʒ/ *n* **1** [C] simple sea creature with a rubber-like body **2** [C;U]
piece of this or plastic like it, which can
suck up water and is used for washing ♦
v **1** *vt* clean with a sponge **2** *vi derog*
get things from people free by taking
advantage of their generosity **sponger** *n*
person who SPONGES (2) **spongy** *adj* not
firm

sponge cake /ˈ· ·/ *n* [U;C] light cake
made from eggs, sugar, and flour

spon·sor /ˈspɒnsə/ *n* **1** company or
person giving money to help others to do
something **2** person who takes responsibility for a person or thing ♦ *vt* act
as a sponsor for: *a concert sponsored by
American Express* ~**ship** *n* [U]

spon·ta·ne·ous /spɒnˈteɪniəs/ *adj* happening naturally, without pressure or
another's suggestion ~**ly** *adv* **–taneity**
/ˌspɒntəˈniːəti, -ˈneɪ-/ *n* [U]

spoof /spuːf/ n funny untrue copy or description

spook /spuːk/ vt cause (esp. an animal) to be suddenly afraid ♦ n infml for GHOST

spook·y /'spuːki/ adj causing fear in a strange way –**ily** adv

spool /spuːl/ n wheel-like object onto which things are wound

spoon /spuːn/ n kitchen tool consisting of a small bowl with a handle, used esp. for eating ♦ vt take up with a spoon

spoon-feed /'·ˌ·/ vt 1 feed with a spoon 2 teach (people) in very easy lessons

spoon·ful /'spuːnfʊl/ n amount that a spoon can hold

spo·rad·ic /spə'rædɪk/ adj happening irregularly –**ally** adv

spore /spɔː, spɔːr/ n very small cell that acts like a seed: a mushroom's spores

sport /spɔːt, spɔːrt/ n 1 activity needing physical effort and skill and usu. done as a competition according to rules 2 friendly or kind person ♦ vt wear or show publicly: sporting a brand new coat ~**ing** adj fair and generous ~**y** infml right for sports

sports·cas·ter /'spɔːtsˌkæstə, 'spɔːrts-/ n person who talks about sports on television or radio **sportscast** n

sports car /'·ˌ·/ n low fast car

sports·man /'spɔːtsmən, 'spɔːr-/ **sports·wom·an** /-ˌwʊmən/ fem. — n -**men** /-mən/ person who plays sports ~**ship** n [U] fairness to one's opponent, esp. in sports

sports·wear /'spɔːtsˌweə/ n [U] clothes for informal occasions

spot /spɒt/ n 1 usu. round part different from the main surface: a black spot on his white shirt 2 small diseased mark on the skin 3 place: a beautiful spot for a picnic 4 small or limited part of something: one of the brighter spots in the news 5 a specific position in a SEQUENCE 6 infml difficult situation 7 SPOTLIGHT 8 place in a broadcast: a guest spot on TV 9 **hit the spot** sl satisfy a want or need 10 **on the spot: a** at once **b** at the place of the action **c** in a position of having to make the right action or answer: The question really put me on the spot. — see also SOFT SPOT ♦ vt -**tt- 1** see; recognize **2** mark with spots **3** allow as an advantage in a game ~**less** adj completely clean ~**ty** adj with some parts less good than others

spot check /'·ˌ·/ n examination of a few chosen by chance to represent all **spot-check** vt

spot·light /'spɒtlaɪt/ n 1 (light from) a large lamp with a directable beam 2 public attention ♦ vt direct attention to

spouse /spaʊs, spaʊz/ n fml or law husband or wife

spout /spaʊt/ n 1 opening from which liquid comes out: the spout of a teapot 2 forceful (rising) stream of liquid 3 infml **up the spout** ruined ♦ vi/t come or throw out in a forceful stream **spout off** phr vi derog pour out in a stream of words

sprain /spreɪn/ vt damage (a joint in the body) by sudden twisting **sprain** n

sprang /spræŋ/ v past t. of SPRING

sprawl /sprɔːl/ vi/t spread out awkwardly or ungracefully ♦ n sprawling position or area

spray /spreɪ/ vi/t send or come out in a stream of small drops (onto) ♦ n 1 [U] water blown in very small drops 2 [C;U] liquid to be sprayed out from a container under pressure: hair spray (= to keep hair in place) 3 [C] small branch with its leaves and flowers

spread /spred/ v **spread** 1 vi/t (cause to) become longer, broader, wider, etc. 2 vi/t (cause to) have an effect or influence or become known over a wider area: The fire/news soon spread. 3 vi cover a large area or period 4 vt put over (a surface): Spread butter on the bread. ♦ n 1 [U] act or action of spreading 2 [U] soft food for spreading on bread: cheese spread 3 [C] large or grand meal

spread·sheet /'spredʃiːt/ n type of computer PROGRAM that allows figures (e.g. about sales, taxes, and profits) to be shown in groups on a SCREEN (4) so that quick calculations (CALCULATE) can be made

spree /spriː/ n period of much wild fun, spending, drinking, etc.

sprig /sprɪg/ n small end of a stem with leaves

spright·ly /'spraɪtli/ adj cheerful and active –**liness** n [U]

spring[1] /sprɪŋ/ v **sprang** /spræŋ/, **sprung** /sprʌŋ/ **1** vi move quickly and suddenly as if by jumping: The soldiers sprang to attention. | (fig.) The engine sprang into life. **2** vi/t open or close with a SPRING (2): The box sprang open. (= opened suddenly) | *to spring a trap* **3** *vt* produce (as) (a surprise): *She sprang the news on us.* **4 spring a leak** (of a ship, container, etc.) begin to let liquid through a hole, etc.

spring from *phr vt* have as its origin

spring up *phr vi* come into existence suddenly

spring² *n* **1** [C;U] season between winter and summer **2** [C] length of wound metal that comes up again after being pressed down **3** [C] place where water comes naturally from the ground **4** [U] elastic quality **5** [C] act of springing ~y *adj* elastic

spring·board /ˈsprɪŋbɔrd, -boʊrd/ *n* **1** bendable board for people who DIVE **2** strong starting point

spring break /ˌ· ˈ·/ *n* school or college vacation in the spring, usu. about 2 weeks long

spring chick·en /ˌ· ˈ··/ *n humor* someone who is young: *He's no spring chicken.*

spring-clean /ˌ· ˈ·/ *vi/t* clean (a house, etc.) thoroughly **spring cleaning** /ˈ· ··/ *n* [U]

sprin·kle /ˈsprɪŋkəl/ *vt* scatter (small drops or bits) on or over (a surface) **–kler** *n* apparatus for sprinkling drops of water

sprint /sprɪnt/ *vi* run very fast **sprint** *n* ~**er** *n*

sprout /spraʊt/ *vi/t* send or come out as new growth ♦ *n* new growth on a plant

spruce¹ /sprus/ *adj* neat and clean ♦

spruce up *phr vt* make (esp. oneself) spruce

spruce² *n* tree of northern countries with short leaves shaped like needles

sprung /sprʌŋ/ *v past p. of* SPRING

spry /spraɪ/ *adj* (esp. of older people) active

spud /spʌd/ *n infml* potato

spun /spʌn/ *v past t. and p. of* SPIN

spunk·y /ˈspʌŋki/ *adj* very enthusiastic

spur /spɜr/ *n* **1** sharp object fitted to a rider's boot, used to make a horse go faster **2** event or influence leading to action **3** length of high ground coming out from a mountain range **4 on the spur of the moment** without preparation or planning ♦ *vt* **-rr-** urge or encourage forcefully

spu·ri·ous /ˈspyʊriəs/ *adj* **1** based on incorrect reasoning **2** pretended; false ~**ly** *adv* ~**ness** *n* [U]

spurn /spɜrn/ *vt* refuse or send away with angry pride

spurt /spɜrt/ *vi/t* **1** make a SPURT (1) **2** (cause to) flow out suddenly or violently ♦ *n* **1** sudden short increase of effort or speed **2** spurting of liquid or gas

sput·ter /ˈspʌtə/ *vi* make repeated soft explosive sounds

spy /spaɪ/ *n* **1** person employed to find out secret information **2** person who watches secretly ♦ *v* **1** *vi* watch or search secretly **2** *vt* catch sight of

sq. *written abbrev. for*: square

squab·ble /ˈskwɑbəl/ *vi, n* (have) a quarrel about unimportant things

squad /skwɑd/ *n* group of people working as a team

squad car /ˈ· ·/ *n* police car

squad·ron /ˈskwɑdrən/ *n* large group of soldiers with TANKS (2), of fighting ships, or of aircraft in the airforce

squal·id /ˈskwɑlɪd/ *adj* **1** very dirty and unpleasant **2** of low moral standards ~**ly** *adv*

squall /skwɔl/ *n* sudden strong wind usu. with rain or snow ♦ *vi* cry violently ~**y** *adj*

squal·or /ˈskwɑlə/ *n* [U] SQUALID (1) conditions

squan·der /ˈskwɑndə/ *vt* spend foolishly and wastefully

square¹ /skwɛr/ *n* **1** shape with 4 straight equal sides forming 4 right angles **2** broad open area with buildings around it in a town **3** result of multiplying a number by itself ♦ *adj* **1** being a SQUARE (1) **2** of an area equal to a square with sides of the stated length: *1 square foot* **3** forming (nearly) a right angle: *a square jaw* **4** fair; honest: *a square deal* **5** having paid and settled what is owed

square² *v* **1** *vt* put into a square shape **2** *vt* divide into squares **3** *vt* multiply by itself: *2 squared is 4.* **4** *vi/t* (cause to) fit a particular explanation or standard **5** *vt* cause (totals of points or games won) to be equal **6** *vt* pay or pay for **7** *vt* pay or settle dishonestly: *There are government officers who will have to be squared.* ♦ *adv* squarely ~**ly** *adv* directly: *He looked her squarely in the eye.*

square up *phr vi* settle a bill

square dance /ˈ· ·/ *n* type of country dance in which 4 pairs of dancers face each other in a square **–dancing** *n* [U]

square knot /ˌ· ˈ·/ n double knot that will not undo easily

square meal /ˌ· ˈ·/ n infml good satisfying meal

square one /ˌ· ˈ·/ n [U] the starting point

square root /ˌ· ˈ·/ n number which when squared (SQUARE² (3)) equals a particular number: 2 is the square root of 4.

squash /skwɑʃ, skwɒʃ/ v 1 vt make flat; crush 2 vi/t push or fit into a small space 3 vt force into silence or inactivity ♦ n 1 [S] act or sound of squashing 2 [C;U] any of a group of vegetables with hard skins, including ZUCCHINI and PUMPKINS 3 [U] game played in a court with 4 walls with RACKETS and a small ball ~y adj soft and easy to squash

squat /skwɑt/ vi -tt- 1 sit with the legs drawn up under the body 2 live in an empty building without permission ♦ adj ungracefully short or low and thick ~ter n person who SQUATS (2)

squawk /skwɔk/ vi 1 (of a bird) make a loud rough cry 2 complain loudly ♦ squawk n

squeak /skwik/ vi, n (make) a short, very high quiet sound ~y adj: a squeaky door

squeal /skwil/ n a long, very high cry ♦ vi 1 make a squeal 2 sl give secret information about one's criminal friends to the police ~er n

squeam·ish /ˈskwimɪʃ/ adj easily shocked or upset by unpleasant things ~ly adv ~ness n [U]

squeeze /skwiz/ v 1 vt press firmly (together), esp. from opposite sides 2 vt get or force out (as if) by pressure: squeeze the juice from an orange 3 vi/t fit or go by forcing or pushing: She squeezed through the narrow opening. 4 vt cause many difficulties to: Higher lending rates are squeezing small businesses. ♦ n 1 act of squeezing 2 difficult situation caused by high costs or not enough supplies

squelch /skwɛltʃ/ v 1 vt prevent completely from acting; SUPPRESS 2 vi, n (make) the sound of soft mud being pressed ~y adj

squid /skwɪd/ n squid or squids sea creature with 10 arms at the end of its long body used for food

squig·gle /ˈskwɪgəl/ n short wavy or twisting line

squint /skwɪnt/ vi 1 look with almost closed eyes 2 have a SQUINT (1) ♦ n 1 condition in which the eyes look in different directions 2 act of SQUINTing (1)

squirm /skwɜrm/ vi twist the body about, esp. from discomfort, shame, or nervousness

squir·rel /ˈskwɜrəl/ n small furry animal that climbs trees

squirt /skwɜrt/ vi/t, n (force or be forced out in) a thin stream

squish·y /ˈskwɪʃi/ adj infml pastelike; soft and wet

Sr. written abbrev. for: SENIOR

SS abbrev. for: STEAMSHIP

St. written abbrev. for: 1 Street 2 SAINT

stab /stæb/ vt -bb- strike forcefully (into) with a pointed weapon ♦ n 1 act of stabbing 2 try: I'll have a stab at it. 3 a stab in the back an attack from someone supposed to be a friend ~bing adj (of pain) sharp and sudden ~bing n [C;U]: a big increase in the number of stabbings reported to police

sta·ble¹ /ˈsteɪbəl/ adj not easily moved, upset, or changed –bilize vi/t –bilizer n –bility /stəˈbɪləti/ n [U]

stable² n 1 building where horses are kept 2 group of things with one owner ♦ vt keep in a stable

stac·cat·o /stəˈkɑtoʊ/ adj, adv played with very short notes

stack /stæk/ n 1 neat pile: a stack of dishes 2 large pile of dried grass stored outdoors 3 also stacks pl. — large amount ♦ vt 1 make into a neat pile (on) 2 blow one's stack sl become very angry and shout

stack up phr vi measure, esp. in comparison to some others: How does your new car stack up?

sta·di·um /ˈsteɪdiəm/ n -diums or -dia /-diə/ large building containing a sports field and seats for SPECTATORS

staff /stæf/ n 1 the workers in a place 2 long, thick stick or pole ♦ vt provide workers for

staff·er /ˈstæfər/ n someone who works for an organization: Mercury News staffers

stage /steɪdʒ/ n 1 raised floor on which plays are performed: He wants to go on the stage. (= become an actor) 2 a center of action or attention: on the center of the political stage 3 state reached at a particular time in a course of events: The project was canceled at an early stage. 4 part of a journey or long race 5 any of the separate driving parts of a ROCKET ♦ vt **1** perform or arrange for public show **2** cause to happen, esp. for public effect

stage·coach /ˈsteɪdʒkoʊtʃ/ n (in former times) carriage pulled by horses, providing a regular passenger service

stage fright /ˈ· ·/ n [U] nervousness felt by some people before performing in front of a lot of people

stage man·ag·er /ˈ· ,··/ n person in charge of a theater stage

stag·ger /ˈstæɡə/ v **1** vi/t walk in an unsteady manner, almost falling **2** vt shock greatly **3** vt arrange so as to happen at different times ♦ n unsteady movement, as if about to fall

stag·nant /ˈstæɡnənt/ adj **1** (esp. of water) not flowing or moving, and often smelling bad **2** not developing or growing –nate /ˈstæɡneɪt/ vi become STAGNANT (2) –nation /stæɡˈneɪʃən/ n [U]

staid /steɪd/ adj serious and dull by habit ~ness n [U]

stain /steɪn/ vi/t discolor in a way that is hard to repair ♦ n **1** stained place or spot **2** mark of guilt or shame

stained glass /ˌ· ˈ·/ n [U] colored glass for making patterns in windows

stain·less steel /ˌ·· ˈ·/ n [U] steel that does not RUST

stair /steər/ n step in a set of stairs

stairs /steərz/ n [P] number of steps for going up or down, esp. indoors: a flight of stairs

stair·case /ˈsteərkeɪs/ n set of stairs with its supports and side parts

stake /steɪk/ n **1** pointed post for driving into the ground **2** share in something so that one is interested in whether it succeeds or fails **3** money risked on the result of something **4** post to which a person was tied for being killed, esp. by burning **5 at stake** at risk ♦ vt **1** risk the loss of (something) on a result **2 stake a claim** state that something should belong to one

stake out phr vt carefully watch (a building, etc.), expecting that some criminal activity will be seen **stakeout** /ˈsteɪk-aʊt/ n act of doing this

stale /steɪl/ adj **1** no longer fresh: stale bread/ (fig.) news **2** no longer interesting or new ~ness n [U]

stale·mate /ˈsteɪlmeɪt/ n **1** (in CHESS) position in which neither player can win **2** situation in which neither side in a quarrel can get an advantage

stalk¹ /stɔk/ n thin plant part with 1 or more leaves, fruits, or flowers on it

stalk² v **1** vt hunt by following closely and secretly **2** vi walk stiffly or proudly ~er n

stall¹ /stɔl/ n **1** small shop with an open front or other selling place in a market **2** indoor enclosure for an animal

stall² vi/t **1** (cause to) stop because there is not enough speed or engine power **2** delay ♦ n act of stalling

stal·lion /ˈstælyən/ n male horse kept for breeding

stal·wart /ˈstɔlwət/ adj, n strong and dependable (person)

stam·i·na /ˈstæmənə/ n [U] strength to keep going

stam·mer /ˈstæmə/ vi/t speak or say with pauses and repeated sounds ♦ n habit of stammering

stamp /stæmp/ v **1** vi/t put (the feet) down hard **2** vt mark by pressing: The title was stamped in gold on the book.| (fig.) His manners stamped him as a military man. **3** vt stick a stamp onto ♦ n **1** small piece of paper for sticking onto esp. a letter, package, etc., to be posted **2** tool for pressing or printing onto a surface: a date-stamp **3** mark made by this: (fig.) a remark which bears the stamp of truth **4** act of stamping the foot

stamp out phr vt put an end to

stam·pede /stæmˈpid/ n **1** sudden rush of frightened animals **2** sudden mass movement **3** RODEO ♦ vi/t (cause to) go in a stampede or unreasonable rush

stance /stæns/ n **1** way of standing **2** way of thinking; ATTITUDE

stand¹ /stænd/ v stood /stʊd/ **1** vi support oneself on one's feet in an upright position **2** vi rise to a position of doing this: They stood (up) when he came in. **3** vi be in height: He stands 5 feet 10 inches. **4** vi/t (cause to) rest in a position, esp. upright or on a base: The clock stood on the shelf. **5** vi be in a particular state of affairs: How do things stand at the moment? **6** vi be in a position (to gain or lose): He stands to win a fortune if his number's called. **7** vt like; bear: I can't stand whiskey. **8** vi remain true or in force: My offer still stands. **9** vt pay the cost of (something) for (someone else): He stood them a wonderful meal. **10**

know how/where one stands (with someone) know how someone feels about one 11 stand a chance have a chance 12 standing on one's head with no difficulty at all: *I could do the job standing on my head.* 13 stand on one's hands/head support oneself on the hands/head and hands, with the feet in the air 14 stand on one's own two feet be able to do without help from others 15 stand something on its head change or upset violently 16 stand to reason be clear to all sensible people

stand by *phr v* 1 *vt* remain loyal to 2 *vt* keep (a promise, agreement, etc.) 3 *vi* be present or near 4 *vi* remain inactive when action is needed 5 *vi* wait in readiness

stand down *phr vi* leave the witness box in court

stand for *phr vt* 1 represent; mean: *US stands for United States.* 2 have as a principle 3 accept without complaining

stand in *phr vi* take the place of the usual person for a time

stand out *phr vi* 1 have an easily seen shape, color, etc. 2 be clearly the best

stand up *phr vt* 1 remain in good condition in spite of: *Will it stand up to continuous use?* 2 be accepted as true: *The charges will never stand up in court.* 3 fail to meet (someone, esp. of the opposite sex) as arranged: *He stood me up again.*

stand up for *phr vt* defend; support

stand² *n* 1 place for selling or showing things 2 piece of furniture for putting things on: *a hatstand* 3 building with an open front for watchers at a sports ground 4 raised stage: *the judge's stand* 5 strong effort of defense 6 place from which people called to a court speak; WITNESS STAND — see also ONE-NIGHT STAND

stan·dard /ˈstændəd/ *n* 1 level of quality that is considered proper or acceptable 2 something fixed as a rule for measuring weight, value, etc. 3 ceremonial flag ♦ *adj* of the usual kind; ordinary **~ize** *vt* make all the same in accordance with a single STANDARD (2) **–ization** /ˌstændə-dəˈzeɪʃən/ *n* [U]

standard of liv·ing /ˌ·· ˈ···/ *n* degree of wealth and comfort in daily life that a person, country, etc., has

standard time /ˈ·· ˌ·/ *n* [U] time used in the US from fall to spring, one hour earlier than DAYLIGHT (SAVING) TIME

stand-by /ˈstændbaɪ/ *n* 1 one kept ready for use 2 **on standby: a** ready for action **b** able to travel, as in a plane, only if there is a seat no one else wants

stand-in /ˈ·· ˌ/ *n* person who takes the place or job of someone else for a time

stand·ing /ˈstændɪŋ/ *n* [U] 1 rank, esp. based on experience or respect 2 continuance: *a friend of long standing* (= who has been a friend for a long time) ♦ *adj* continuing in use or force: *a standing invitation*

stand-off /ˈstændɒf/ *n* situation in which neither side in a fight or battle can gain an advantage

stand-off-ish /ˌstændˈɒfɪʃ/ *adj* rather unfriendly **~ly** *adv* **~ness** *n* [U]

stand·point /ˈstændpɔɪnt/ *n* POINT OF VIEW

stand·still /ˈstændˌstɪl/ *n* [S] condition of no movement; stop

stand-up /ˈstænd ˌʌp/ *adj* (of comedy) involving 1 person telling jokes as a performance ♦ *n* [C;U]

stank /stæŋk/ *v past t. of* STINK

stan·za /ˈstænzə/ *n* division of a poem

sta·ple¹ /ˈsteɪpəl/ *n* piece of wire put through sheets of paper and bent to fasten them together ♦ *vt* fasten with staples **stapler** *n*

staple² *adj* used all the time; usual; ordinary ♦ *n* main product: *a staple among American products*

star /stɑr/ *n* 1 very large mass of burning gas in space, seen as a small bright spot in the night sky 2 figure with 5 or more points, used as a sign of something: *a five star hotel* (= a very good hotel) 3 heavenly body regarded as determining one's fate: *born under an unlucky star* 4 famous performer: *a movie star* 5 **stars in one's eyes** an unthinking feeling that some wonderful thing is really possible 6 **see stars** see flashes of light, esp. as a result of being hit on the head ♦ *v* **-rr-** 1 *vi/t* appear or have as a main performer: *a film starring Charlie Chaplin* 2 *vt* mark with STARS (2) **~ry** *adj* filled with stars

star·board /ˈstɑrbəd/ *n* [U] right side of a ship or aircraft for a person inside it facing the front

starch /stɑrtʃ/ *n* [U] 1 white, tasteless substance that is an important part of foods such as grain and potatoes 2 substance for making cloth stiff ♦ *vt* stiffen with STARCH (2) ~**y** *adj* **1** full of, or like, STARCH **2** stiffly correct and formal –**ily** *adv*

star·dom /'stɑːdəm/ *n* [U] state of being a famous performer

stare /steɪ/ *vi* look for a long time with great attention ♦ *n* long steady look

stare down *vt* look at someone till they turn away

star·fish /'stɑːfɪʃ/ *n* flat sea animal with 5 arms forming a star shape

stark /stɑːk/ *adj* **1** hard, bare, or severe in appearance **2** complete: *stark terror* ♦ *adv* completely: *stark naked* | *stark raving mad* (= completely crazy)

star·let /'stɑːlɪt/ *n* young actress hoping to become famous

star·ling /'stɑːlɪŋ/ *n* common green-black European bird

starry-eyed /ˌ·ˈ·◂/ *adj* full of unreasonable hopes

Stars and Stripes /ˌ· ·ˈ·/ *n* [the+S] the flag of the US

star-stud·ded /ˈ· ˌ··/ *adj* filled with famous performers

start¹ /stɑːt/ *v* **1** *vi/t* begin **2** *vi/t* (cause to) come into existence: *How did the trouble start?* **3** *vi/t* (cause to) begin operation: *The car won't start.* **4** *vi* begin a trip **5** *vi* make a sudden sharp movement, esp. from surprise **6 start something** cause trouble ~**er** *n* **1** person, etc., in a race or match at the start **2** person who gives the signal for a race to begin **3** instrument for starting a machine **4** first part of a meal **5 for starters** first of all

start² *n* **1** [C] beginning of activity **2** [the+S] first part or moments **3** [C] place of starting **4** [C;U] amount by which one is ahead of another **5** [C] sudden sharp movement — see also FLYING START, HEAD START

start·le /'stɑːtl/ *vt* give a sudden slight shock to

start-up /ˈ· ·/ *adj* related to beginning and developing a new business: *start-up costs*

starve /stɑːv/ *vi/t* **1** (cause to) suffer from great hunger **2** (cause to) not have enough: *starved of affection/funds* **starva·tion** /stɑːˈveɪʃən/ *n* [U]

stash /stæʃ/ *vt infml* store secretly; hide ♦ *stash n*

state¹ /steɪt/ *n* **1** [C] particular way of being; condition: *the current state of our economy* **2** [C] *infml* a very nervous, anxious condition: *Don't get in(to) such a state.* **3** [C;U] government or political organization of a country: *industry controlled by the state* | *state secrets* **4** [C] nation; country **5** [C] area within a nation that governs itself: *the states of the US* **6** [U] official grandness and ceremony ~**less** *adj* belonging to no country ~**lessness** *n* [U] ~**ly** *adj* **1** formal; ceremonious **2** grand in style or size ~**liness** *n* [U]

state² *vt* say or mention, esp. formally or in advance

State De·part·ment /ˈ· ˌ··/ *n* [the] the US government department which deals with foreign affairs

state house /ˈ· ˌ·/ *n* building for the state government

state·ment /'steɪtmənt/ *n* **1** (formal) written or spoken declaration **2** list showing money paid, received, etc.

state-of-the-art /ˌ· · · ˈ·◂/ *adj* using the most modern methods or materials

state·wide /'steɪtˈwaɪd/ *adj* in all parts of a state: *a statewide ban on the sale of alcohol*

states·man /'steɪtsmən/ *n* **-men** /-mən/ respected political or government leader — see also ELDER STATESMAN ~**ship** *n* [U]

stat·ic /'stætɪk/ *adj* **1** not moving or changing **2** of or being electricity that collects on the surface of objects ♦ *n* [U] electrical noise spoiling radio or television signals

sta·tion /'steɪʃən/ *n* **1** (building at) a place where the stated public vehicles regularly stop: *a bus station* **2** building for the stated service or activity: *a polling station* (= where people vote) **3** broadcasting company or apparatus **4** *fml* one's position in life; social rank: *She married beneath her station.* — see also SPACE STATION ♦ *vt* put (esp. a person) into a certain place for esp. military duty

sta·tion·a·ry /'steɪʃənəri/ *adj* not moving

sta·tion·er·y /'steɪʃənəri/ *n* [U] paper, pens, pencils, envelopes, etc.

station wag·on /ˈ·· ˌ··/ *n* car with a door at the back and folding back seats

sta·tis·tics /stəˈtɪstɪks/ *n* **1** [P] numbers which represent facts or measurements **2** [U] science that deals with and explains these –**tical** *adj* –**tically** *adv*

statistician /ˌstætəˈstɪʃən/ n person who works with statistics

stat·ue /ˈstætʃuː/ n (large) stone or metal likeness of a person, animal, etc.

stat·u·ette /ˌstætʃuˈet/ n small statue that goes on a table or shelf

stat·ure /ˈstætʃə/ n [C;U] fml 1 degree to which someone is regarded as important or worthy of admiration 2 person's height

sta·tus /ˈsteɪtəs, ˈstæ-/ n 1 [C;U] rank or condition in relation to others 2 [U] high social position 3 [C] state of affairs at a particular time

status quo /ˌsteɪtəs ˈkwoʊ, ˌstæ-/ n existing state of affairs

stat·ute /ˈstætʃuːt/ n fml law

stat·u·to·ry /ˈstætʃətɔːri, -ˌtoʊri/ adj fixed or controlled by law

staunch /stɔːntʃ, stɑːntʃ/ adj dependably loyal; firm **~ly** adv **~ness** n [U]

stave /steɪv/ v **stave off** phr vt keep away: just enough food to stave off hunger

stay /steɪ/ vi 1 remain in a place rather than leave 2 continue to be; remain: trying to stay healthy 3 live in a place for a while: staying at a hotel 4 **stay put** not move 5 **stay the course** last or continue for the whole length of ♦ n 1 period of living in a place 2 law stopping or delay: a stay of execution (= not carrying out a punishment)

  stay on phr vt remain after the usual leaving time

STD n sexually transmitted disease; a disease passed on by sexual activity: an STD clinic

stead·fast /ˈstedfæst/ adj fml or lit 1 firmly loyal 2 not moving or movable **~ly** adv **~ness** n [U]

stead·y /ˈstedi/ adj 1 firm; not shaking: a steady hand 2 not varying wildly; regular: a steady speed 3 not likely to change: a steady job 4 dependable ♦ vi/t make or become steady **–ily** adv **–iness** n [U]

steak /steɪk/ n [C;U] flat piece of meat, esp. BEEF or fish

steal /stiːl/ v stole /stoʊl/, stolen /ˈstoʊlən/ 1 vi/t take (what belongs to someone else) without permission 2 vi move secretly or quietly 3 vt take secretly or improperly: stealing a look at someone 4 **steal the show** get all the attention and praise depected by someone else, at a

show or other event ♦ n [S] infml something for sale very cheaply

stealth /stelθ/ n [U] acting quietly and secretly or unseen **~y** adj

steam /stiːm/ n [U] 1 water gas produced by boiling 2 power produced by steam under pressure: The ship sailed full steam ahead. (= at its fastest speed) 3 **let off steam** get rid of anger or unwanted ENERGY 4 **under one's/its own steam** by one's/its own power or effort ♦ v 1 vi give off steam 2 vi travel by steam power 3 vt cook with steam 4 vt use steam on: He steamed the letter open. **~er** n 1 ship driven by steam power 2 container for cooking food with steam **~y** adj 1 of or containing steam 2 infml EROTIC

  steam up phr vi/t 1 cover or become covered with a mist of cooling water 2 infml make angry or excited **steamed-up** adj infml excited and angry

steam·roll /ˈstiːmroʊl/ vt force into spite of all opposition: He was steamrolled into signing the agreement.

steam·roll·er /ˈstiːmˌroʊlə/ n vehicle with heavy metal wheels for making new road surfaces flat

steam·ship /ˈstiːmˌʃɪp/ n a large non-naval ship driven by steam power

steel /stiːl/ n [U] hard, strong metal made from iron ♦ vt make (esp. oneself) unfeeling or determined **~y** adj like steel in color or hardness

steel band /ˈ· ˌ·/ n Caribbean band playing drums cut from metal oil BARRELS

steep[1] /stiːp/ adj 1 rising or falling at a large angle 2 (esp. of a price) too high **~ly** adv **~ness** n [U]

steep[2] vt 1 keep in liquid 2 **steeped in** thoroughly filled or familiar with

stee·ple /ˈstiːpəl/ n high, pointed church tower

steer[1] /stɪr/ vt 1 direct the course of (esp. a boat or road vehicle) 2 **steer clear (of)** keep away (from); avoid

steer[2] n young male animal of the cattle family with its sex organs removed

steering wheel /ˈ·· ˌ·/ n wheel turned to make a vehicle go left or right

stel·lar /ˈstelə/ adj of the stars

stem[1] /stem/ n 1 part of a plant on which leaves or smaller branches grow 2 narrow, upright support: the stem of a wineglass

stem² /vt -mm- stop (the flow of)
stem from phr vt result from

stench /stentʃ/ n very strong bad smell

sten·cil /'stensəl/ n 1 card, etc., with patterns or letters cut in it 2 mark made by putting paint, etc., through the holes in this onto paper, etc. ♦ vt -l- make (a copy of) with a stencil

sten·to·ri·an /sten'tɔːriən, -'toʊr-/ adj fml (of the voice) very loud

step¹ /step/ n 1 act of moving by raising one foot and bringing it down somewhere else 2 the sound this makes 3 short distance: It's just a step away from here. 4 flat edge, esp. in a set one above the other, on which the foot is placed for going up or down 5 act, esp. in a set of actions, which should produce a certain result: We must take steps (= take action) to improve matters. 6 movement of the feet in dancing 7 in/out of step: a moving/not moving the feet at the same time as others in marching b in/not in accordance or agreement with others 8 step by step gradually 9 watch one's step behave or act carefully

step² vi -pp- 1 go by putting one foot usu. in front of the other 2 bring the foot down 3 step on it! go faster 4 step on someone's toes a annoy someone to by rudeness b cause someone to act by being pushy 5 step out of line act differently from others or from what is expected

step down/aside phr vi leave one's job, position, etc.

step in phr vi INTERVENE

step up phr vt increase

step·broth·er /'step,brʌðə/ n boy or man whose father or mother has married your father or mother

step-by-step /ˌ· · ˈ·◄/ adj (of a plan, method, etc.) dealing with things carefully and in a particular order

step·daugh·ter /'step,dɔːtə/ n daughter your husband or wife has from a previous relationship

step·fa·ther /'step,fɑːðə/ n man married to your mother who is not your father

step·lad·der /'step,lædə/ n folding ladder with 2 parts joined at the top

step·moth·er /'step,mʌðə/ n woman married to your father, who is not your mother

steppe /step/ n large treeless area in Russia and parts of Asia

stepping stone /ˈ·· ˌ·/ n 1 any of a row of large stones for walking across a stream on 2 way of improvement or getting ahead

step·sis·ter /'step,sistə/ n girl or woman whose father or mother has married your father or mother

step·son /'step,sʌn/ n son your husband or wife has from a previous relationship

ster·e·o /'sterioʊ, 'stɪr-/ adj using a system of sound recording in which the sound comes from 2 different places ♦ n -os 1 [C] apparatus for playing records, CASSETTES, CDs, etc. 2 [U] stereo sound —see also PERSONAL STEREO

ster·e·o·type /'steriəˌtaɪp, 'stɪr-/ n usu. derog fixed set of ideas about what a particular type of person or thing is like ♦ vt derog treat as an example of a fixed general type —**typical** /ˌsteriə'tɪpɪkəl, ˌstɪr-/ adj

ster·ile /'sterəl/ adj 1 which cannot produce young 2 free from all (harmful) bacteria, etc. 3 lacking new thought, imagination, etc. 4 (of land) not producing crops —**ility** /stə'rɪləti/ n [U] —**ilize** /'sterəlaɪz/ vt make STERILE (1,2) —**ilization** /ˌsterələ'zeɪʃən/ n

ster·ling /'stɜːlɪŋ/ adj 1 (of silver) over 92% pure silver 2 of the highest standard, esp. in being loyal and brave

stern¹ /stɜːn/ n severe and serious: a stern look/reprimand ~**ly** adv ~**ness** n [U]

stern² n back part of a ship

ste·roid /'sterɔɪd, 'stɪə-/ n chemical that has a strong effect on the workings of the body

steth·o·scope /'steθəˌskoʊp/ n tube with which doctors can listen to people's hearts beating

stew /stuː/ vi/t cook slowly and gently in liquid ♦ n 1 [C;U] dish of stewed meat and vegetables 2 [S] confused anxious state of mind

stew·ard /'stuːəd/ n 1 stewardess -dɪs/ fem. — person who serves passengers on a ship, plane, etc. 2 person in charge of HOUSEHOLD duties

stick¹ /stɪk/ n 1 small thin piece of wood 2 thin wooden or metal rod used for support while walking, for hitting things, etc. 3 thin rod of any material: a stick of chalk/celery 4 get the short end of the stick infml be the one who must do the unpleasant job that no one else wants to do — see also STICKS

stick² v **stuck** /stʌk/ **1** vt push: *She stuck her fork into the meat.* **2** vi/t fasten or be fastened with glue or a similar substance **3** vi/t (cause to) become fixed in position: *He got his finger stuck in the hole.* **4** vt infml put: *Stick your coat down over there.* ~**er** n **1** LABEL with a message or picture, which can be stuck to things **2** infml determined person

 stick around phr vi not go away

 stick by phr vt continue to support

 stick out phr v **1** vi/t come out beyond a surface: *Her ears stick out.* **2** vt continue to the end of (something difficult) **3 stick one's neck out** infml take a risk

 stick to phr vt **1** refuse to leave or change: *stick to one's decision* **2 stick to one's guns** infml continue to express one's beliefs or carry on a course of action in spite of attacks

 stick together phr vi (of 2 or more people) stay loyal to each other

 stick up for phr vt defend (someone) by words or actions

 stick with phr vt **1** stay close to **2 stick with it** infml continue in spite of difficulties

stick-in-the-mud /ˈ···ˌ/ n person who will not change or accept new things

stick·ler /ˈstɪklə/ n person who demands the stated quality: *a stickler for punctuality*

sticks /stɪks/ n [the+P] infml a country area far from modern life

stick shift /ˈ·ˌ/ n GEAR shift

stick·up /ˈstɪk-ʌp/ n infml robbery carried out by threatening with a gun

stick·y /ˈstɪki/ adj **1** like or covered with glue or a similar substance **2** difficult; awkward: *a sticky situation* **3 come to/meet a sticky end** (suffer) ruin, death, etc. ~**iness** n [U]

stiff /stɪf/ adj **1** not easily bent or changed in shape **2** formal; not friendly **3** strong, esp. in alcohol **4** difficult; severe: *stiff competition* ♦ adv extremely: *I was scared stiff.* ♦ n sl ordinary working person **2** dead body ~**ly** adv ~**en** vi/t make or become stiff ~**ness** n [U]

sti·fle /ˈstaɪfəl/ v **1** vi/t (cause to) be unable to breathe properly **2** vt keep from happening: *stifling a yawn*

stig·ma /ˈstɪgmə/ n feeling of shame ~**tize** vt describe very disapprovingly

still¹ /stɪl/ adv **1** (even) up to this/that moment: *He's still here.* **2** in spite of that: *It's raining. Still, we must go out.* **3** even: *a still greater problem* **4** yet: *He gave still another reason.*

still² adj **1** not moving **2** without wind **3** silent; calm **4** (of a drink) not containing gas ~**ness** n [U]

still³ n photograph of a scene from a (movie) film

still⁴ n apparatus for making alcohol

still-birth /ˈstɪlbɜːθ, ˌstɪlˈbɜːθ/ n child born dead

still-born /ˈstɪlbɔːn, ˌstɪlˈbɔːn◁/ adj born dead

still life /ˌ·ˈ·◁/ n **still lifes** [C;U] painting of objects, esp. flowers and fruit

stilt /stɪlt/ n either of a pair of poles for walking around on high above the ground

stilt·ed /ˈstɪltɪd/ adj very formal and unnatural

stim·u·late /ˈstɪmjəˌleɪt/ vt **1** cause to become more active, grow faster, etc. **2** fml excite (the body or mind) –**lant** n **1** drug which gives one more power to be active **2** stimulus –**lation** /ˌstɪmjəˈleɪʃən/ n [U]

stim·u·lus /ˈstɪmjələs/ n –**li** /-laɪ/ something that causes activity

sting /stɪŋ/ vi/t **stung** /stʌŋ/ **1** have, use, or prick with a STINGER **2** (cause to) feel sharp pain: (fig.) *stinging criticism* ♦ n **1** wound caused by this **2** sharp pain organ used by certain insects and plants for attack or protection, producing pain ~**er** n

stin·gy /ˈstɪndʒi/ adj infml ungenerous; –**gily** adv

stink /stɪŋk/ vi **stank** /stæŋk/, **stunk** /stʌŋk/ **1** give off a strong bad smell **2** infml be very unpleasant or bad: *Your plan stinks.* ♦ n strong bad smell

 stink out phr vt fill with a stink

stint /stɪnt/ n limited or fixed amount of time, shared work, etc. ♦ vi give too small an amount (of): *not stint on luxuries*

sti·pend /ˈstaɪpɛnd/ n fixed or regular pay, esp. for a SCHOLARSHIP

stip·u·late /ˈstɪpjəˌleɪt/ vt state as a necessary condition –**lation** /ˌstɪpjəˈleɪʃən/ n [C;U] statement of conditions

stir /stɚ/ v **-rr-** **1** vt move around and mix (esp. liquid) with a spoon, etc. **2** vi/t make or cause a slight movement (in): *She stirred in her sleep.* **3** vt excite: *a stirring tale of adventure* **4** vi infml cause trouble between others ♦ n **1** [C] act of stirring **2** [S] (public) excitement

stir up phr vt **1** cause (trouble) **2** upset

stir-fry /ˈ. ./ v quickly cook (meat, vegetables, etc.) in a little oil over high heat **stirfry** n [C;U]

stir-rup /ˈstɚəp, ˈstrəp/ n metal piece shaped like a D, for a rider's foot to go in

stitch /stɪtʃ/ n **1** [C] amount of thread put with a needle through cloth or through skin to close a wound **2** [C] single turn of the yarn around the needle in knitting (KNIT) **3** [S] sharp pain in the side caused by running **4** [S] infml clothes: *He didn't have a stitch on.* (= was completely NAKED) **5 in stitches** laughing helplessly ♦ vi/t sew

stock /stak/ n **1** [C] supply: *a large stock of food* **2** [C;U] (supply of) goods for sale: *Do you have any blue shirts in stock?* **3** [C;U] ownership of a company, divided into shares: *stocks and bonds* **4** [U] liquid made from meat, bones, etc., used in cooking **5** [U] farm animals, esp. cattle **6** [C;U] a family line, of the stated sort: *She comes from farming/good stock.* **7 take stock (of)** consider a situation carefully so as to make a decision ♦ vt keep supplies of ♦ adj commonly used, esp. without much meaning: *stock excuses*

stock up phr vi provide oneself with a full store of goods

stock-ade /staˈkeɪd/ n strong fence for defense

stock-brok-er /ˈstakˌbroʊkɚ/ n someone who buys and sells STOCKS (3) for others

stock ex-change /ˈ. .ˌ./ n place where STOCKS are bought and sold

stock-hold-er /ˈstakˌhoʊldɚ/ n person who owns STOCK (3) in a company

stock-ing /ˈstakɪŋ/ n closely fitting garment for a woman's foot and leg

stock-man /ˈstakmən/ n **-men** /-mən/ man who looks after farm animals

stock mar-ket /ˈ. ˌ.ˌ/ n STOCK EXCHANGE

stock-pile /ˈstakpaɪl/ n large store for future use ♦ vt make a stockpile of

stock-y /ˈstaki/ adj thick, short, and strong **-ily** adv **-iness** n [U]

stock-yard /ˈstakyard/ n place where cattle are kept before being sold or killed for their meat

sto-ic /ˈstoʊɪk/ n person who remains calm and uncomplaining ~al adj patient when suffering, like a stoic ~ally adv ~ism /-ˌsɪzəm/ n [U] stoical behavior

stoke /stoʊk/ vt fill (an enclosed fire) with FUEL **stoker** n

stole¹ /stoʊl/ v past t. of STEAL

stole² n long piece of material worn over the shoulders

sto-len /ˈstoʊlən/ v past p. of STEAL

stol-id /ˈstalɪd/ adj showing no excitement when strong feelings might be expected

stom-ach /ˈstʌmək/ n **1** [C] baglike organ in the body where food is digested (DIGEST¹) **2** [C] front part of the body below the chest **3** [S;U] desire; liking: *He's got no stomach for a fight.* ♦ vt accept without displeasure; bear

stom-ach-ache /ˈstʌməkˌeɪk/ n pain in the stomach

stomp /stamp, stɔmp/ vi walk heavily

stone /stoʊn/ n **1** [C] fairly large piece of rock **2** [U] rock **3** [C] piece of hard material formed in an organ of the body ♦ vt throw stones at **stoned** adj infml under the influence of drugs **stony** adj **1** containing or covered with stones **2** cruel

Stone Age /ˈ. ./ n earliest known time in human history, when stone tools were used

stone's throw /ˈ. ./ n [S] short distance

stone-wall /ˈstoʊnwɔl/ vi/t refuse to obey

stood /stʊd/ v past t. and p. of STAND

stooge /studʒ/ n person who habitually does what another wants

stool /stul/ n seat without back or arm supports

stoop /stup/ vt **1** bend the upper body forwards and down **2** stand like this habitually ♦ n **1** [S] habitual stooping position **2** [C] PORCH

stoop to phr vt fall to a low standard of behavior by allowing oneself to do (something)

stop¹ /stap/ v **-pp-** **1** vi/t (cause to) no longer be moving or operating **2** vi/t (cause to) end: *The rain has stopped.* **3** vt prevent **4** vi pause **5** vt block: *The pipe's stopped up.* **6** vt stop from being given or paid: *stop a check* ~**per** n object for closing a bottle

stop in phr vi visit

stop off phr vi make a short visit to a place while making a journey elsewhere

stop over phr vi make a short stay before continuing a journey

stop² n 1 act of stopping or the state of being stopped 2 BUS STOP 3 **pull all the stops out** do everything possible to complete an action 4 **put a stop to** stop (esp. an undesirable activity)

stop·gap /'stɒpgæp/ n something that fills a need for a time

stop·light /'stɒplaɪt/ n traffic light

stop·o·ver /'stɒpˌoʊvə/ n short stay between parts of a journey

stop·page /'stɒpɪdʒ/ n 1 [C] stopping, esp. of work 2 [C;U] blocked state

stop·watch /'stɒpwɒtʃ/ n watch that can be started and stopped to measure periods exactly

stor·age /'stɔːrɪdʒ, 'stoʊrɪdʒ/ n [U] (price paid or place for) storing

store /stɔːr, stoʊr/ vt 1 make and keep a supply of for future use 2 keep in a special place while not in use ♦ n 1 building or room where goods are sold 2 supply for future use 3 place for keeping things 4 **in store: a** being stored **b** about to happen: *There's trouble in store.* 6 **set ... store by** feel to be of (the stated amount of) importance **stores** n [S;P] (building or room containing) military or naval goods and food

store·keep·er /'stɔːrˌkiːpə, 'stoʊr-/ n someone who owns or is in charge of a store

stork /stɔːrk/ n large bird with a long beak, neck, and legs

storm /stɔːrm/ n 1 rough weather condition with rain, strong wind, etc. 2 sudden violent show of feeling: *a storm of protest* 3 **take by storm: a** conquer by a sudden violent attack **b** win great approval from (those who watch a performance) ♦ v 1 vt attack (a place) with sudden violence 2 vi go angrily ~**y** adj

sto·ry¹ /'stɔːri, 'stoʊri/ n 1 account of events, real or imagined 2 news article 3 lie: *Have you been telling stories again?* 4 **the same old story** the usual excuse or difficulty

story² n floor or level in a building

sto·ry·book /'stɔːrɪbʊk, 'stoʊr-/ adj as perfectly happy as in a fairy story for children

story line /'·· ·/ n events in a film, book, or play

stout /staʊt/ adj 1 rather fat 2 brave and determined 3 strong and thick ♦ n [U] strong dark beer ~**ly** adv ~**ness** n [U]

stove /stoʊv/ n enclosed apparatus that can be heated for cooking or to provide warmth

stow /stoʊ/ vt put away or store, esp. on a ship

stow away phr vi hide on a ship or plane in order to make a free journey

stow·a·way /'stoʊəˌweɪ/ n person who stows away

strad·dle /'strædl/ vt 1 have one's legs on either side of 2 be, land, etc., on either side of (something), rather than in the middle

strag·gle /'strægəl/ vi move, grow, or spread untidily –**gler** n one who is behind a main group –**gly** adj growing or lying untidily

straight¹ /streɪt/ adj 1 not bent or curved 2 level or upright 3 neat; tidy 4 honest, open, and truthful 5 (of the face) with a serious expression 6 (of alcohol) without added water 7 correct: *set the record straight* 8 sl HETEROSEXUAL ~**ness** n [U]

straight² adv 1 in a straight line 2 directly (and without delay): *Get straight to the point.* 3 clearly: *I can't think straight.* 4 **go straight** leave a life of crime

straight and nar·row /ˌ· ·ˈ·· ·/ n [U] honest life

straight·en /'streɪtⁿn/ vt (cause to) become straight, level, or tidy

straighten out phr vt remove the confusions or difficulties) in: *straighten out one's business affairs*

straighten up phr vi 1 get up from a bent position 2 improve one's behavior

straight·for·ward /ˌstreɪtˈfɔːrwəd/ adj 1 honest and open, without hidden meanings 2 simple ~**ly** adv ~**ness** n [U]

strain¹ /streɪn/ v 1 vt damage (a body part) through too much effort or pressure 2 vi make (too) great efforts 3 vt separate (a liquid and solid) by pouring through esp. a strainer 4 vt force beyond acceptable or believable limits: *straining the truth* ♦ n [C;U] 1 (force causing) the condition of being tightly stretched 2 troubling influence 3 damage caused by straining a body part ~**ed** adj 1 not natural in behavior; unfriendly 2 tired or nervous ~**er** *n* instrument with a net for STRAIN*ing* (3) things

strain[2] *n* **1** breed or type of plant or animal **2** *lit* tune

strait /streɪt/ also **straits** *pl.* — *n* narrow water passage between 2 areas of land

straits *n* [P] difficult situation: *in dire straits*

strait·jack·et /'streɪtˌdʒækɪt/ *n* **1** garment for a violently crazy person that prevents arm movement **2** something preventing free development

strait·laced /ˌstreɪt'leɪst◂/ *adj* having severe, old-fashioned ideas about morals

strand /strænd/ *n* single thin thread, wire, etc.

strand·ed /'strændɪd/ *adj* in a helpless position, unable to get away

strange /streɪndʒ/ *adj* **1** unusual; surprising **2** unfamiliar ~**ly** *adv* ~**ness** *n* [U]

strang·er /'streɪndʒə/ *n* **1** unfamiliar person **2** person in an unfamiliar place

stran·gle /'stræŋgəl/ *vt* **1** kill by pressing the throat to stop breathing **2** stop the proper development of **–gler** *n* **–gula·tion** /ˌstræŋgjə'leɪʃən/ *n* [U]

stran·gle·hold /'stræŋgəlˌhoʊld/ *n* strong control which prevents action

strap /stræp/ *n* strong narrow band used as a fastening or support: *a luggage strap* ♦ *vt* **-pp-** fasten with straps

strap·ping /'stræpɪŋ/ *adj* big and strong

stra·ta /'streɪtə, 'strætə/ *n pl.* of STRATUM

strat·a·gem /'strætədʒəm/ *n* trick or plan for deceiving or gaining an advantage

stra·te·gic /strə'tiːdʒɪk/ *adj* **1** part of a plan, esp. in war **2** right for a purpose ~**ally** *adv*

strat·e·gist /'strætədʒɪst/ *n* person skilled in (military) planning

strat·e·gy /'strætədʒi/ *n* **1** [U] skillful (military) planning **2** [C] particular plan for winning success

strat·os·phere /'strætəsˌfɪr/ *n* outer air surrounding the Earth, starting at about 15 miles above the Earth

stra·tum /'streɪtəm, 'stræ-/ *n* **-ta** /-tə/ **1** band of a particular rock **2** part of something thought of as divided into different levels

straw /strɔ/ *n* **1** [U] dried stems of grain plants, such as wheat **2** [C] single such stem **3** [C] thin tube for sucking up liquid — see also LAST STRAW

straw·ber·ry /'strɔˌbɛri/ *n* (plant with) a small red juicy fruit

straw poll /ˌ·'·/ *n* unofficial examination of opinions before an election, to see what the result is likely to be

stray /streɪ/ *vi* wander away ♦ *n* animal lost from its home ♦ *adj* **1** wandering; lost **2** single; not in a group

streak /strik/ *n* **1** thin line or band, different from what surrounds it **2** bad quality of character: *a stubborn streak* **3** period marked by a particular quality: *a lucky streak* **4 like a streak (of lightning)** very quickly ♦ *v* **1** *vi* move very fast **2** *vt* cover with streaks ~**y** *adj* marked with streaks

stream /strim/ *n* **1** small river **2** something flowing: *a stream of traffic* | (fig.) *a stream of abuse* **3 go with/against the stream** agree/not agree with a general way of thinking, etc., in society **4 on stream** in(to) production ♦ *v* **1** *vi* flow strongly **2** *vi* move in a continuous flowing mass **3** *vi* float in the air ~**er** *n* long narrow piece of paper for throwing

stream·line /'strimlaɪn/ *vt* **1** give a smooth shape which moves easily through water or air **2** make more simple and effective **–lined** *adj*

street /strit/ *n* **1** road in a town **2 up/down one's street** in one's area of interest

street·car /'stritˌkɑr/ *n* usu. electric bus that runs on metal tracks set in the road

street gang /'· ·/ *n* group of young men who steal, fight, and kill in big cities

street peo·ple /'· ˌ··/ *n* homeless people who live in the streets

street·wise /'strit⌐waɪz/ *adj* *infml* smart enough to succeed and live well in the hard world of the city streets

strength /streŋkθ, streŋθ, strenθ/ *n* **1** [U] (degree of) being strong **2** [U] way in which something is good or effective: *the strengths and weaknesses of the plan* **3** [U] force measured in numbers: *The police are at full strength.* **4 on the strength of** persuaded or influenced by ~**en** *vi/t* become or make strong or stronger

stren·u·ous /'strɛnyuəs/ *adj* **1** needing great effort **2** showing great activity: *a strenuous denial* ~**ly** *adv* ~**ness** *n* [U]

stress /strɛs/ *n* [C;U] **1** (worry resulting from) pressure caused by difficulties **2** force of weight caused by pressure **3** sense of special importance **4** degree of force put on a part of a word when spoken, or on a note in music: *In "under" the main stress is on "un."* ♦ *vt* **1** mention strongly **2** put STRESS (4) on **~ed (out)** *adj* worried, tired, and unable to relax **~ful** *adj* causing worry

stretch /stretʃ/ *v* **1** *vi/t* (cause to) become wider or longer **2** *vi* spread out: *The forest stretched for miles.* **3** *vi* be elastic **4** *vi* straighten one's limbs to full length: *stretch out your arms* **5** *vt* allow to go beyond exact limits: *stretch a rule* **6** **stretch one's legs** have a walk esp. after sitting for a long time ♦ *n* **1** [C] act of stretching **2** [U] elasticity **3** [C] long area of land or water **4** [C] continuous period: *14 hours at a stretch* (= without stopping) **5** **at full stretch** using all one's powers **~y** *adj* elastic

stretch·er /ˈstretʃər/ *n* covered frame for carrying a sick person

strew /struː/ *vt* **strewed, strewn** /struːn/ *or* **strewed** *esp. lit* **1** scatter **2** lie scattered over

strick·en /ˈstrɪkən/ *adj* showing the effect of trouble, illness, etc.: *stricken with grief*

strict /strɪkt/ *adj* **1** severe in making people behave properly **2 a** exact: *strict instructions* **b** complete: *in strict secrecy* **~ly** *adv* **~ness** *n* [U]

stride /straɪd/ *vi* **strode** /strod/, **stridden** /ˈstrɪdn/ walk with long steps ♦ *n* **1** long step **2** **make strides** improve or do well **3** **take something in one's stride** deal with a difficult situation easily and without complaint

stri·dent /ˈstraɪdnt/ *adj* with a hard sharp sound or voice **~ly** *adv* **–dency** *n* [U]

strife /straɪf/ *n* [U] trouble and quarreling between people

strike¹ /straɪk/ *v* **struck** /strʌk/ **1** *vt* hit sharply **2** *vt* make a (sudden) attack **3** *vt* harm suddenly: *They were struck down with illness.* **4** *vt* light (a match) **5** *vi/t* **a** make known (the time), esp. by the hitting of a bell: *The clock struck 3.* (= rang 3 times, for 3 o'clock) **b** (of time) be made known in this way **6** *vi* stop working because of disagreement **7** *vt* find; meet: *strike oil/difficulties* **8** *vt* have a particular effect on: *Her behavior struck me as odd.* | **struck down with fear 9** *vt* come suddenly to mind **10** *vt* produce (a coin or similar object) **11** *vt* make (an agreement): *strike a bargain/*

balance **12** **strike a chord** remind someone of something **13** **strike a note of** express (a need for): *The book strikes a warning note.* **14** **strike it rich** find sudden wealth

strike off *phr vt* remove (someone or their name) from (an official list)

strike out *phr vi* **1** go purposefully in the stated direction **2** **strike out on one's own** take up an independent life **3** CROSS **out**

strike up *phr vt* **1** begin playing or singing **2** start or make (a friendship)

strike² *n* **1** act or time of striking (STRIKE¹ (6)): *The workers are on strike.* **2** attack, esp. by aircraft **3** success in finding esp. a mineral in the earth: *an oil strike* **4** point against the BATTER³ in baseball

strik·er /ˈstraɪkər/ *n* person on STRIKE² (1)

strik·ing /ˈstraɪkɪŋ/ *adj* very noticeable, esp. because beautiful or unusual **~ly** *adv*

striking dis·tance /ˈ·· ˌ·/ *n* **within striking distance** very close (to)

string¹ /strɪŋ/ *n* **1** [C;U] thin cord **2** [C] thin cord or wire stretched across a musical instrument to give sound **3** [C] set of objects on a thread: *a string of pearls* **4** [C] set of things, events, etc., following each other closely: *a whole string of complaints* **5** **no strings attached** (esp. of an agreement) with no limiting conditions **6** **pull strings** use secret influence **strings** *n* [P] all the (players of) VIOLINS, CELLOS, etc., in an ORCHESTRA **~y** *adj* **1** (of food) full of unwanted threadlike parts **2** unpleasantly thin, so that the muscles show

string² *vt* **strung** /strʌŋ/ **1** put STRINGS (2) on (a musical instrument or RACKET¹) **2** put with others onto a thread **3** **highly strung** (of a person) very sensitive and easily excited **4** **strung up** very excited, nervous, or worried

string along *phr v* **1** *vt* encourage the hopes of deceitfully **2** *vi* go (with someone else) for a time, esp. for convenience

string out *phr vt* spread out in a line

string up *phr vt* **1** hang high **2** kill by hanging

string bean /ˈ· ·/ *n* bean with a long eatable seed container

strin·gent /ˈstrɪndʒənt/ *adj* (esp. of rules, limits, etc.) severe **~ly** *adv*

string·er /'strɪŋə/ n reporter who works part of the time in a distant place

strip /strɪp/ v -pp- **1** vt remove (the covering or parts of) **2** vi/t undress, usu. completely ♦ n **1** narrow piece: a strip of paper/land **2** street with stores, gas stations, restaurants, etc., on both sides ~**per** n **1** [C] STRIPTEASE performer **2** [C;U] tool or liquid for removing things: paint stripper

strip down phr vt remove the parts of (esp. an engine)

strip off phr vt take away (something of value) from

stripe /straɪp/ n **1** band of a different color **2** sign usu. shaped like a V worn on a uniform to show rank ~**striped** adj

strip·tease /'strɪptiz, ˌstrɪp'tiz/ n [U] removal of clothes by a person, performed as a show

strive /straɪv/ vi **strove** /strouv/ or **strived, striven** /'strɪvən/ or **strived** fml or lit make a great effort

strode /stroud/ v past t. of STRIDE

stroke[1] /strouk/ vt **1** pass the hand over gently **2** treat in a kind way, esp. to gain favor

stroke[2] n **1** hit, esp. with a weapon **2** act of stroking **3** line made by a single movement of a pen or brush **4** act of hitting a ball **5** (single movement or set of movements that is repeated in) a method of swimming **6** sudden bursting of a blood tube in the brain **7** unexpected piece of luck) **8** sound of a clock striking: on the stroke of (= exactly at) 6 o'clock **9** at a stroke with one direct action

stroll /stroul/ vi, n (take) a slow walk for pleasure ~**er** n **1** person who strolls or is strolling **2** small chair on wheels for a child

strong /strɔŋ/ adj **1** having great power **2** not easily becoming broken, changed, destroyed, or ill **3** having a powerful effect on the mind or senses: a strong smell **4** (of a drink, drug, etc.) having a lot of the substance which gives taste, produces effect, etc.: This coffee's too strong. **5** having the stated number of members: a club 50 strong **6** (still) going strong continuing with ENERGY, good health, etc. **7** strong on: a good at doing **b** eager and active in dealing with ~**ly** adv

strong·hold /'strɔŋhould/ n **1** fort **2** place where a particular activity is common

strong lan·guage /ˌ· '··/ n [U] swearing; curses

strong point /'· ·/ also **strong suit** — n something one is good at

strong-willed /ˌ· '·◄/ adj having a lot of determination; STUBBORN

strove /strouv/ v past t. of STRIVE

struck /strʌk/ v past t. and p. of STRIKE

struc·ture /'strʌktʃə/ n **1** [C;U] way in which parts are formed into a whole **2** [C] large thing built ♦ vt arrange so that each part is properly related to others –**tural** adj –**turally** adv

strug·gle /'strʌgəl/ vi **1** make violent movements, as in fighting **2** make a great effort ♦ n hard fight or effort

strum /strʌm/ vi/t play carelessly or informally on (esp. a GUITAR, BANJO, or other instrument with strings)

strung /strʌŋ/ v past t. and p. of STRING

strut[1] /strʌt/ n supporting rod in a structure

strut[2] vi -tt- walk proudly

strych·nine /'strɪknaɪn, -nin/ n [U] poisonous drug

stub /stʌb/ n **1** short remaining part of esp. a pencil **2** part of a ticket returned to the user to show he has paid ♦ vt -bb- hit (one's toe) against something ~**by** adj short and thick: stubby fingers

stub out phr vt put out (a cigarette) by pressing

stub·ble /'stʌbəl/ n [U] **1** short growth of beard **2** remains of cut wheat –**bly** adj

stub·born /'stʌbən/ adj **1** having a strong will; (unreasonably) determined **2** difficult to use, move, change, etc. ~**ly** adv ~**ness** n [U]

stuc·co /'stʌkou/ n [U] PLASTER stuck (as decoration) onto walls

stuck[1] /stʌk/ v past t. and p. of STICK

stuck[2] adj **1** unable to go further because of difficulties **2** stuck with having to do or have, esp. unwillingly

stuck-up /ˌ· '·◄/ adj infml too proud in manner

stud[1] /stʌd/ n **1** button-like fastener that can be removed, esp. for collars **2** nail with a large head ♦ vt -dd- cover (as if) with STUDS[1] (2)

stud[2] n **1** number of horses kept for breeding **2** [U] kind of POKER GAME **3** sl man who has sex a lot and thinks he is very good at it

stu·dent /ˈstudnt/ n 1 person studying esp. at a high school, college, or university 2 person with a stated interest: *a student of life*

student bod·y /ˌ·· ˈ·-/ n all the students in a school, college, etc.

stu·di·o /ˈstudiˌoʊ/ n 1 place where films, recordings, or broadcasts are made 2 room for a painter, photographer, etc. to work in

studio a·part·ment /ˌ··· ·ˈ··/ n very small one-room apartment with kitchen and bathroom

stu·di·ous /ˈstudiəs/ adj 1 fond of studying 2 careful ~ly adv ~ness n [U]

stud·y /ˈstʌdi/ n 1 [U] also **studies** pl. — act of studying 2 [C] thorough enquiry into a particular subject, esp. including a piece of writing on it 3 [C] room for working in; office 4 [C] drawing or painting of a detail: *a study of a flower* 5 [C] piece of music for practice ♦ v 1 vi/t spend time in learning 2 vt examine carefully **studied** adj carefully thought about or considered, esp. before being expressed: *a studied remark*

stuff[1] /stʌf/ n [U] 1 matter; material 2 one's possessions or the things needed to do something 3 **do one's stuff** show one's ability as expected 4 **know one's stuff** be good at what one is concerned with 5 **That's the stuff!** *infml* That's the right thing to do/say!

stuff[2] vt 1 fill 2 push so as to be inside 3 put STUFFING (2) inside 4 fill the skin of (a dead animal) to make it look real 5 cause (oneself) to eat as much as possible ~**ing** n [U] 1 filling material 2 food cut up and put inside a chicken, etc., before cooking

stuff up phr vt block

stuffed shirt /ˌ· ˈ·, ˈ· ·/ n dull person who thinks himself important

stuff·y /ˈstʌfi/ adj 1 (having air) that is not fresh 2 derog formal and old-fashioned —**ily** adv —**iness** n [U]

stum·ble /ˈstʌmbəl/ vi 1 catch one's foot on something and start to fall 2 stop and/or make mistakes in speaking

stumble across/on/upon phr vt meet or find by chance

stumbling block /ˈ·· ˌ·/ n something preventing action or development

stump[1] /stʌmp/ n 1 base of a tree that has been cut down 2 useless end of

something long that has been worn down, cut off, etc. ~**y** adj short and thick in body

stump[2] v 1 vt leave (someone) unable to reply 2 vi walk heavily or awkwardly 3 vi/t make political speeches (in a place) in order to gain votes

stun /stʌn/ vt -**nn**- 1 make unconscious 2 shock greatly 3 delight ~**ning** adj very attractive

stung /stʌŋ/ v past t. and p. of STING

stunk /stʌŋk/ v past p. of STINK

stunt[1] /stʌnt/ n 1 dangerous act of skill 2 action intended to attract attention: *publicity stunts* 3 **pull a stunt** do a trick, sometimes silly

stunt[2] vt prevent full growth (of)

stunt man /ˈ· ·/ **stunt woman** /ˈ· ˌ·/ fem. — n person who does STUNTS (1) in films, etc.

stu·pe·fy /ˈstupəˌfaɪ/ vt fml 1 surprise (and annoy) extremely 2 make unable to think —**faction** /ˌstupəˈfækʃən/ n [U]

stu·pen·dous /stuˈpɛndəs/ adj surprisingly great or good

stu·pid /ˈstupɪd/ adj foolish ~**ly** adj ~**ity** /stuˈpɪdəti/ n [U]

stu·por /ˈstupə/ n [C;U] nearly unconscious unthinking state

stur·dy /ˈstɜrdi/ adj 1 strong and firm 2 determined —**dily** adv —**diness** n [U]

stut·ter /ˈstʌtə/ vi/t speak or say with difficulty in pronouncing esp. the first consonant of words ♦ n habit of stuttering

sty[1], **stye** /staɪ/ n infected place on the eyelid

sty[2] n PIGSTY

style /staɪl/ n 1 [C;U] (typical) manner of doing something: *the modern style of architecture | written in a formal style* 2 [C] fashion, esp. in clothes 3 [U] high quality of social behavior or appearance 4 [C] type or sort 5 **in style** in a grand way ♦ vt 1 —DESIGN 2 give (a title) to: *He styles himself "Sir."* **stylish** adj fashionable and attractive **stylist** n 1 person who invents styles or fashions 2 person with a (good) style of writing **stylize** vt present in a simple style rather than naturally **stylistic** /staɪˈlɪstɪk/ adj of STYLE (1)

sty·lus /ˈstaɪləs/ n -**luses** or -**li** /-laɪ/ needle-like instrument that in a RECORD PLAYER that picks up sound signals from a record

suave /swɑv/ *adj* with smooth (but perhaps insincere) good manners –**ly** *adv* ~**ness** *n* [U]

sub /sʌb/ *n infml* 1 SUBMARINE 2 SUBSTITUTE 3 long bread roll filled with meat, cheese, etc.

sub·com·mit·tee /ˈsʌbkəˌmɪti/ *n* small group formed from a committee

sub·con·scious /ˌsʌbˈkɑnʃəs/ *adj, n* (present at) a hidden level of the mind, not consciously known about –**ly** *adv*

sub·con·ti·nent /ˈsʌbˈkɑntˈn-ənt, ˌsʌb-ˌkɑn-, -tənənt/ *n* large mass of land smaller than a CONTINENT, esp. India

sub·con·tract /ˌsʌbˈkɑntrækt, ˌsʌbkən-ˈtrækt/ *vt* hire someone else to do (work which one has agreed to do) ~**or** /ˈsʌbkənˌtræktə/ *n* person or firm that has had work subcontracted to it

sub·cul·ture /ˈsʌbˌkʌltʃə/ *n* behavior, beliefs, activities, etc., of a group in society different from the rest of society: *the drug subculture*

sub·di·vide /ˌsʌbdəˈvaɪd, ˈsʌbdəˌvaɪd/ *vt* divide into even smaller parts –**division** /ˈsʌbdəˌvɪʒən/ *n* [C;U] 1 act of doing this 2 land area divided into lots for building houses

sub·due /səbˈdu/ *vt* 1 gain control of 2 make gentler –**dued** *adj* 1 of low brightness or sound 2 unusually quiet in behavior

sub·ject[1] /ˈsʌbdʒɪkt/ *n* 1 thing being dealt with, represented, or considered: *the subject of the painting/of the conversation* 2 branch of knowledge being studied 3 word that comes before a main verb and represents the person or thing that performs the action of the verb or about which something is stated 4 member of a state: *British subjects* ◆ *adj* 1 tending; likely: *He's subject to ill health.* 2 not independent: *a subject race* 3 subject to depending on: *subject to your approval* (= if you approve)

subject[2] /səbˈdʒɛkt/ *vt fml* defeat and control ~**ion** /-ˈdʒɛkʃən/ *n* [U] 1 act of subjecting 2 state of being severely controlled by others

   subject to *phr vt* cause to experience or suffer

sub·jec·tive /səbˈdʒɛktɪv/ *adj* 1 influenced by personal feelings (and perhaps unfair) 2 existing only inside the mind; not real ~**ly** *adv* –**tivity** /ˌsʌbdʒɛkˈtɪvəti/ *n* [U]

sub·ju·gate /ˈsʌbdʒəˌgeɪt/ *vt* defeat and make obedient –**gation** /ˌsʌbdʒəˈgeɪʃən/ *n* [U]

sub·junc·tive /səbˈdʒʌŋktɪv/ *adj, n* (of) a verb form expressing doubt, wishes, unreality, etc.: *In "if I were you" the verb "were" is in the subjunctive.*

sub·let /sʌbˈlɛt, ˈsʌblɛt/ *vt* -**let**, *pres. p.* -**tt**- rent (property rented from someone) to someone else

sub·lime /səˈblaɪm/ *adj* 1 very noble or wonderful 2 *infml* complete and usu. careless or unknowing –**ly** *adv*

sub·lim·i·nal /sʌbˈlɪmənl/ *adj* at a level which the ordinary senses are not conscious of

sub·ma·chine gun /ˌsʌbməˈʃin gʌn/ *n* light MACHINE GUN

sub·ma·rine /ˈsʌbməˌrin, ˌsʌbməˈrin/ *n* (war)ship which can stay under water ◆ /ˌsʌbməˈrin◄/ *adj* under or in the sea

sub·merge /səbˈmɜrdʒ/ *vi/t* 1 (cause to) go under the surface of water 2 cover or competely hide –**mersion** /-ˈmɜrʒən/ *n* [U] act of submerging or state of being submerged

sub·mit /səbˈmɪt/ *v* -**tt**- 1 *vi* admit defeat 2 *vt* offer for consideration 3 *vt esp. law* suggest –**mission** /-ˈmɪʃən/ *n* 1 [C;U] submitting 2 [U] *fml* opinion 3 [U] *fml* obedience 4 [C] *law* request; suggestion 5 [C] something SUBMITted (2) –**missive** /-ˈmɪsɪv/ *adj* too obedient

sub·or·di·nate[1] /səˈbɔrdn-ɪt/ *adj* less important ◆ *n* someone of lower rank

sub·or·din·ate[2] /səˈbɔrdnˌeɪt/ *vt* put in a subordinate position –**ation** /səˌbɔrdn-ˈeɪʃən/ *n* [U]

sub·poe·na /səˈpinə/ *n* written order to attend a court of law **subpoena** *vt*

sub·scribe /səbˈskraɪb/ *vi* pay regularly, esp. to receive a magazine –**scriber** *n*

   subscribe to *phr vt* agree with; approve of

sub·scrip·tion /səbˈskrɪpʃən/ *n* 1 act of subscribing (to) 2 amount paid regularly, esp. to belong to a society, receive a magazine, etc.

sub·se·quent /ˈsʌbsəkwənt/ *adj* coming afterwards or next ~**ly** *adv*

sub·ser·vi·ent /səbˈsɜrviənt/ *adj* too willing to obey ~**ly** *adv* –**ence** *n* [U]

sub·side /səbˈsaɪd/ *vi* 1 return to its usual level; become less: *The flood waters/The wind/His anger subsided.*

2 (of land or a building) sink down **subsidence** /səbˈsaɪdns, ˈsʌbsədəns/ n [U]

sub·sid·i·a·ry /səbˈsɪdiˌɛri/ adj connected with but less important than the main one ♦ n subsidiary company

sub·si·dy /ˈsʌbsədi/ n money paid, esp. by government, to make prices lower, etc. –**dize** vt give a subsidy to (someone) for (something): subsidized crops

sub·sist /səbˈsɪst/ vi fml remain alive ~**ence** n [U] **1** ability to live, esp. on little money or food **2** state of living with little money or food

sub·stance /ˈsʌbstəns/ n **1** [C] material; type of matter: a sticky substance **2** [U] fml truth: There is no substance to these rumors. **3** [U] fml real meaning, without the unimportant details **4** [U] fml wealth **5** [U] importance, esp. in relation to real life: There was no real substance in the speech.

substance a·buse /ˈ·· ·ˌ·/ n [U] habit of taking too many illegal drugs

sub·stand·ard /ˌsʌbˈstændəd◂/ adj not as good as average or usual

sub·stan·tial /səbˈstænʃəl/ adj **1** solid; strongly made **2** satisfactorily large: a substantial meal **3** noticeably large (and important): substantial changes **4** concerning the main part **5** wealthy ~**ly** adv **1** in all important ways: They are substantially the same. **2** quite a lot

sub·stan·ti·ate /səbˈstænʃiˌeɪt/ vt fml prove the truth of –**ation** /səbˌstænʃiˈeɪʃən/ n [U]

sub·stan·tive /ˈsʌbstəntɪv/ adj fml having reality, actuality, or importance

sub·sti·tute /ˈsʌbstəˌtut/ n one taking the place of another ♦ v **1** vt put in place of another **2** vi act or be used instead –**tution** /ˌsʌbstəˈtuʃən/ n [C;U]

sub·ter·fuge /ˈsʌbtəˌfyudʒ/ n [C;U] deceiving or slightly dishonest trick(s)

sub·ter·ra·ne·an /ˌsʌbtəˈreɪniən◂/ adj underground

sub·ti·tles /ˈsʌbˌtaɪtlz/ n [P] translation printed over a foreign film

sub·tle /ˈsʌtl/ adj **1** hardly noticeable: subtle differences **2** clever in arrangement: a subtle plan **3** very clever in noticing and understanding –**tly** adv –**tlety** n [C;U]

sub·tract /səbˈtrækt/ vt take (a number or amount) from a larger one ~**ion** /-ˈtrækʃən/ n [C;U]

sub·urb /ˈsʌbəb/ n outer area of a town, where people live ~**an** /səˈbəbən/ adj

sub·ur·bi·a /səˈbəbiə/ n [U] (life and ways of people who live in) suburbs

sub·vert /səbˈvət/ vt try to destroy the power and influence of –**versive** /-ˈvəsɪv, -ˈzɪv/ adj trying to destroy established ideas or defeat those in power –**version** /-ˈvəʒən/ n [U]

sub·way /ˈsʌbweɪ/ n underground electric railroad in a big city

suc·ceed /səkˈsid/ v **1** vi do what one has been trying to do **2** vi do well, esp. in gaining position or popularity **3** vt follow after **4** vi/t be the next to take a rank or position (after): Hammond succeeded Jones as chairman.

suc·cess /səkˈsɛs/ n **1** [U] degree of succeeding; good result **2** [C] person or thing that succeeds ~**fully** adv

suc·ces·sion /səkˈsɛʃən/ n **1** [U] following one after the other: in quick succession **2** [S] many following each other closely: a succession of visitors **3** [U] SUCCEEDing (4)

suc·ces·sive /səkˈsɛsɪv/ adj following each other closely in time ~**ly** adv

suc·ces·sor /səkˈsɛsə/ n person who takes an office or position formerly held by another

suc·cinct /səkˈsɪŋkt/ adj clearly expressed in few words ~**ly** adv

suc·cor /ˈsʌkə/ vt, n [U] lit help

suc·cumb /səˈkʌm/ vi fml stop opposing

such /sʌtʃ/ predeterminer, determiner **1** of that kind: I dislike such people. | some flowers, such as (= for example) roses **2** to so great a degree: He's such a kind man. **3** so great; so good, bad, or unusual: He wrote to her every day, such was his love for her. ♦ pron **1** (things) of that kind **2** any/no/some such any/no/some (person or thing) like that: No such person exists. **3** as such properly so named

such-and-such /ˈ· · ·ˌ·/ predeterminer infml a certain (time, amount, etc.) not named

suck /sʌk/ v **1** vi/t draw (liquid) in with the muscles of the mouth **2** vt hold (something) in one's mouth and move one's tongue against it: sucking one's *thumb* **3** *vt* draw powerfully: *The current sucked them under.* **4** *vi sl* be of poor quality: *this film sucks* such *n*

suck·er /ˈsʌkə/ *n* **1** person or thing that sucks **2** flat piece which sticks to a surface by suction **3 a** easily cheated person **b** someone who likes the stated thing very much: *a sucker for ice cream* **4** *infml* LOLLIPOP

suc·tion /ˈsʌkʃən/ *n* [U] drawing away air or liquid, esp. to lower the air pressure between 2 objects and make them stick to each other

sud·den /ˈsʌdn/ *adj* happening unexpectedly and quickly ~**ly** *adv* ~**ness** *n* [U]

suds /sʌdz/ *n* [P] mass of soapy BUBBLES

sue /suː/ *vi/t* bring a legal claim (against)

suede /sweɪd/ *n* [U] soft leather with a rough surface

suf·fer /ˈsʌfə/ *v* **1** *vi* experience pain or difficulty **2** *vt* experience (something unpleasant) **3** *vt* accept without dislike: *He doesn't suffer fools gladly.* **4** *vi* grow worse: *His work has suffered since his illness.* ~**ing** *n* [C;U]

suf·fice /səˈfaɪs/ *vi/t* *fml* **1** be enough (for) **2 suffice it to say that** ... I will say only that ...

suf·fi·cient /səˈfɪʃənt/ *adj* enough ~**ly** *adv* –**ciency** *n* [S;U] *fml*

suf·fix /ˈsʌfɪks/ *n* group of letters or sounds added at the end of a word (as in kind*ness*, quick*ly*)

suf·fo·cate /ˈsʌfəkeɪt/ *vi/t* (cause to) die because of lack of air –**cation** /ˌsʌfəˈkeɪʃən/ *n* [U]

suf·frage /ˈsʌfrɪdʒ/ *n* [U] right to vote in national elections

sug·ar /ˈʃʊɡə/ *n* [U] sweet white or brown plant substance used in food and drinks ♦ *vt* put sugar in ~**y** *adj* **1** containing or tasting of sugar **2** too sweet, nice, kind, etc., in an insincere way

sug·ar beet /ˈʃʊɡə ˌbiːt/ *n* root vegetable from which sugar is made

sug·ar cane /ˈʃʊɡə ˌkeɪn/ *n* [U] tall tropical plant from whose stems sugar is obtained

sug·gest /səˈdʒest, səˈdʒest/ *vt* **1** state as an idea for consideration: *I suggest we do it this way.* **2** give signs (of): *The latest figures suggest that business is improving.* ~**ive** *adj* **1** (perhaps) showing

thoughts of sex **2** *fml* which leads the mind into a particular way of thinking ~**ion** /səɡˈdʒestʃən, səˈdʒes–/ *n* [C;U] act of suggesting or something suggested

su·i·cide /ˈsuːəˌsaɪd/ *n* **1** [C;U] killing oneself **2** [C] person who does this **3** [U] action that destroys one's position –**cidal** /ˌsuːəˈsaɪdl◂/ *adj* **1** likely or wishing to kill oneself **2** likely to lead to death or destruction

suit¹ /suːt/ *n* **1** short coat with pants or skirt of the same material **2** garment for a special purpose: *a bathing suit | a suit of armor* **3** any of the 4 sets of playing cards **4 follow suit** do the same as everyone else

suit² *vt* **1** be convenient for; satisfy **2** match or look good on (someone): *That hairstyle doesn't suit you.* **3 be suited (to/for)** be suitable **4 suit oneself** do what one likes

sui·ta·ble /ˈsuːtəbəl/ *adj* right or good enough for a purpose –**bly** *adv* –**bility** /ˌsuːtəˈbɪləti/ *n* [U]

suit·case /ˈsuːtˌkeɪs/ *n* case for carrying clothes and possessions when traveling

suite /swiːt/ *n* **1** set of hotel rooms **2** piece of music made up of several parts

sui·tor /ˈsuːtə/ *n* *lit* man wishing to marry a particular woman

sul·fur /ˈsʌlfə/ *n* [U] substance found esp. as a light yellow powder

sul·fu·ric ac·id /sʌlˌfjʊrɪk ˈæsɪd/ *n* [U] powerful acid

sulk /sʌlk/ *vi* be silently bad-tempered ~**y** *adj* ~**ily** *adv* ~**iness** *n* [U]

sul·len /ˈsʌlən/ *adj* showing silent dislike, bad temper, lack of interest, etc. ~**ly** *adv* ~**ness** *n* [U]

sul·ly /ˈsʌli/ *vt* *lit* spoil

sul·tan /ˈsʌltn/ *n* (*often cap.*) Muslim ruler

sul·try /ˈsʌltri/ *adj* **1** (of weather) hot, airless, and uncomfortable **2** causing or showing strong sexual desire

sum¹ /sʌm/ *n* **1** total produced when numbers are added together **2** amount (of money) **3** simple calculation

sum² *v* –**mm**– **sum up** *phr v* **1** *vi/t* summarize **2** *vt* consider and form a judgment of

sum·ma·ry /ˈsʌməri/ *n* short account giving the main points ♦ *adj* **1** short **2** done at once without attention to formalities: *summary dismissal* –**rize** *vt* make a summary of

sum·mer /ˈsʌmə/ n [C;U] hot season between spring and autumn ~**y** adj like or suitable for summer

summer school /ˈ·· ˌ·/ n program of study offered in the summer to high school and college students

sum·mit /ˈsʌmɪt/ n 1 highest point 2 top of a mountain 3 meeting between heads of government

sum·mon /ˈsʌmən/ vt order officially to come

summon up phr vt get (a quality in oneself) ready for use

sum·mons /ˈsʌmənz/ n, vt order to appear in a court of law

sump·tu·ous /ˈsʌmptʃuəs/ adj expensive and grand ~**ly** adv

sum to·tal /ˌ· ˈ··/ n [the+S] the whole, esp. when less than expected or needed

sun /sʌn/ n 1 [the+S] star around which the Earth moves 2 [the+S;U] sun's light and heat: *sitting in the sun* 3 [C] star around which PLANETS may turn 4 **under the sun** at all ♦ vt -**nn**- place (oneself) in sunlight ~**ny** adj 1 having bright sunlight 2 cheerful

sun·bathe /ˈsʌnbeɪð/ vi sit or lie in strong sunlight –**bather** n

sun·beam /ˈsʌnbiːm/ n a beam of sunlight

Sun Belt /ˈ· ˌ·/ n [the+S] southern and southwestern parts of the US

sun·block /ˈsʌnblɒk/ n [C;U] SUNSCREEN

sun·burn /ˈsʌnbɜːn/ n [U] sore skin caused by too much strong sunlight –**burnt** /-bɜːnt/, ~**ed** adj

sun·dae /ˈsʌndi, -deɪ/ n ice cream dish with fruit, nuts, etc.

Sun·day /ˈsʌndi, -deɪ/ n the 1st day of the week, before Monday

sun·dial /ˈsʌnˌdaɪəl/ n apparatus producing a shadow which shows the time

sun·down /ˈsʌndaʊn/ n [U] sunset

sun·dry /ˈsʌndri/ adj 1 various 2 **all and sundry** all types of people; everybody **sundries** n [P] various small articles, esp. for personal use

sung /sʌŋ/ v past p. of SING

sun·glass·es /ˈsʌnˌglɑːsɪz/ n [P] glasses with dark glass for protection from sunlight

sunk /sʌŋk/ v past p. of SINK

sunk·en /ˈsʌŋkən/ adj 1 that has (been) sunk 2 below the surrounding level: *sunken eyes* | *a sunken garden*

sun·light /ˈsʌnlaɪt/ n [U] light from the sun

sun·lit /ˈsʌnˌlɪt/ adj brightly lit by the sun

sunny-side up /ˌ·· · ˈ·/ adj (of an egg) cooked in fat without being turned over

sun porch /ˈ· ·/ n glass room that lets the sunlight into the house

sun·rise /ˈsʌnraɪz/ n [U] time when the sun appears after the night

sun roof /ˈ· ·/ n window in the roof of a car

sun·screen /ˈsʌnskriːn/ n [C;U] skin cream used to avoid burning the skin from strong sunlight

sun·set /ˈsʌnset/ n [C;U] time when the sun disappears as night begins

sun·shine /ˈsʌnʃaɪn/ n [U] strong sunlight

sun·spot /ˈsʌnspɒt/ n dark, cooler area on the sun's surface

sun·stroke /ˈsʌnstrəʊk/ n [U] illness caused by too much strong sunlight

sun·tan /ˈsʌntæn/ n brownness of the skin caused by being in strong sunlight

su·per /ˈsuːpə/ adj wonderful; extremely good ♦ n infml abbrev. for: SUPERINTENDENT (2)

su·perb /suˈpɜːb/ adj excellent; wonderful ~**ly** adv

Su·per Bowl /ˈ·· ˌ·/ n [the+S] important football game to decide the best team

su·per·con·duc·tor /ˌsuːpəkənˈdʌktə/ n metal which at very low temperatures allows electricity to pass freely

su·per·fi·cial /ˌsuːpəˈfɪʃəl◂/ adj 1 on the surface; not deep 2 not thorough or complete ~**ly** adv ~**ity** /ˌsuːpəˌfɪʃiˈæləti/ n [U]

su·per·flu·ous /suˈpɜːfluəs/ adj more than is necessary; not needed ~**ly** adv

su·per·high·way /ˌsuːpəˈhaɪˌweɪ/ n large road for fast travel over long distances

su·per·hu·man /ˌsuːpəˈhjuːmən, -ˈjuː-◂/ adj (as if) beyond or better than human powers

su·per·im·pose /ˌsuːpərɪmˈpəʊz/ vt put (something) over something else, esp. so that both can be (partly) seen

su·per·in·tend·ent /ˌsuːpərɪnˈtendənt/ n 1 person in charge 2 person in charge of keeping a building in good order

su·pe·ri·or /səˈpɪriə, suː-/ adj 1 of higher rank 2 better 3 of high quality 4 derog (as if) thinking oneself better than others ♦ *n* person of higher rank ~**ity** /səˌpɪriˈɒrəti, -ˈɑr-, sʊ-/ *n* [U]

su·per·la·tive /səˈpɜrlətɪv, sʊ-/ *adj* **1** *gram* expressing "most" **2** extremely good ♦ *n gram* superlative form of an adjective or adverb

su·per·mar·ket /ˈsupərˌmɑrkɪt/ *n* large food store where one serves oneself

su·per·mod·el /ˈsupərˌmɑdl/ *n* very famous fashion MODEL

su·per·nat·u·ral /ˌsupərˈnætʃərəl◄/ *adj* of or caused by the power of spirits, gods, and magic ~**ly** *adv*

su·per·pow·er /ˈsupərˌpaʊər/ *n* very powerful nation

su·per·sede /ˌsupərˈsid/ *vt* take the place of

su·per·son·ic /ˌsupərˈsɑnɪk◄/ *adj* (flying) faster than the speed of sound

su·per·star /ˈsupərˌstɑr/ *n* very famous performer

su·per·sti·tion /ˌsupərˈstɪʃən/ *n* [C;U] (unreasonable) belief or guessing based on old ideas about luck, magic, etc. –**tious** *adj*

su·per·struc·ture /ˈsupərˌstrʌktʃər/ *n* upper structure built on a base

su·per·vise /ˈsupərˌvaɪz/ *vt* watch (people or work) to make sure things are done properly –**visor** *n* –**visory** /ˌsupərˈvaɪzəri◄/ *adj* –**vision** /ˌsupərˈvɪʒən/ *n* [U]

sup·per /ˈsʌpər/ *n* [C;U] evening meal

sup·plant /səˈplænt/ *vt* take the place of

sup·ple /ˈsʌpl/ *adj* bending easily and gracefully ~**ness** *n* [U]

sup·ple·ment /ˈsʌpləmənt/ *n* **1** additional amount to supply what is needed **2** additional separate part of a newspaper, magazine, etc. ♦ /ˈsʌpləˌment/ *vt* make additions to ~**ary** /ˌsʌpləˈmentəri, -ˈmentri◄/ *adj* additional

sup·ply /səˈplaɪ/ *vt* **1** provide (something) **2** provide things to (someone) for use ♦ *n* **1** amount for use: *a supply of food* **2** (system for) supplying: *the supply of electricity* **3** **in short supply** scarce — see also MONEY SUPPLY –**plier** *n* **supplies** *n* [P] things necessary for daily life, esp. food

supply and de·mand /ˌ‧‧ ‧ ‧ˈ‧/ *n* [U] balance between the amount of goods for sale and the amount that people actually want to buy

sup·port /səˈpɔrt, -ˈpoʊrt/ *vt* **1** bear the weight of, esp. so as to prevent from

falling **2** approve of and encourage **3** be loyal to: *supporting the local merchants* **4** provide money for (someone) to live on **5** strengthen (an idea, opinion, etc.) ♦ *n* **1** [U] state of being supported **2** [C] something that supports **3** [U] active approval and encouragement **4** [U] money to live on ~**er** *n* person who supports a particular activity or team, defends a particular principle, etc. ~**ive** *adj* providing encouragement, help, etc.

sup·pose /səˈpoʊz/ *vt* **1** consider to be probable: *As she's not here, I suppose she must have gone home.* **2** **be supposed to: a** ought to; should **b** be generally considered to be ♦ *conj* **1** (used for making a suggestion): *Suppose we wait a while.* **2** what would/will happen if? ~**dly** /-zɪdli/ *adv* as believed; as it appears –**posing** *conj* suppose

sup·po·si·tion /ˌsʌpəˈzɪʃən/ *n* **1** [U] act of supposing or guessing **2** [C] guess

sup·press /səˈpres/ *vt* **1** bring to an end by force **2** prevent from being shown or made public: *suppressing her anger/the truth* –**ion** /-ˈpreʃən/ *n* [U]

su·preme /səˈprim, sʊ-/ *adj* **1** highest in degree: *supreme happiness* | *the supreme sacrifice* (= giving one's life) **2** most powerful ~**ly** *adv* extremely **supremacy** /səˈpreməsi/ *n* [U]

Supreme Court /‧‧ ‧/ *n* [*the+*S] highest court in the US or in a particular state

sur·charge /ˈsɜrtʃɑrdʒ/ *n* (demand for) an additional payment ♦ *vt* make (someone) pay a surcharge

sure /ʃʊr/ *adj* **1** having no doubt **2** certain (to happen): *You're sure to* (= certainly will) *like it.* **3** confident (of having): *I've never felt surer of success.* **4** **be sure to** don't forget to **5** **make sure: a** find out (if something is really true) **b** take action (so that something will certainly happen) **6** **sure of oneself** certain that one's actions are right ♦ *adv* **1** certainly **2** **for sure** certainly so **3** **sure enough** as was expected ~**ly** *adv* **1** I believe, hope, or expect: *Surely you haven't forgotten?* **2** safely ~**ness** *n* [U]

sure·fire /ˈʃʊrfaɪr/ *adj* certain to succeed

sure·foot·ed /ˌʃʊrˈfʊtɪd◄/ *adj* able to walk, climb, etc., in difficult places without falling

sure thing /ˌ· ˈ·/ *n infml* something that is expected to be a success: *The nightclub was a sure thing.*

surf /sɜːf/ *n* [U] white waves filled with air breaking on a shore ♦ *v* **1** *vi* ride as a sport over breaking waves near the shore, on a SURFBOARD **2 surf the Net** look for interesting information on the INTERNET **~ing** *n* [U] sport of surfing **~er** *n* person who goes surfing

sur·face /ˈsɜːfɪs/ *n* **1** outer part of an object **2** top of liquid **3** what is easily seen, not the main (hidden) part ♦ *adj* **1** not deep; SUPERFICIAL: *surface friendliness* ♦ *vi* come up to the surface of water: (fig.) *He doesn't usually surface* (= get out of bed) *until noon.*

surface mail /ˈ·· ·/ *n* [U] mail carried by land or sea

surf·board /ˈsɜːfbɔːd, -ˌboʊrd/ *n* board for riding on surf

surge /sɜːdʒ/ *n* **1** sudden powerful forward movement **2** sudden increase of strong feeling ♦ *vi* **1** move forwards like powerful waves **2** (of a feeling) arise powerfully

sur·geon /ˈsɜːdʒən/ *n* doctor who does SURGERY (1)

sur·ge·ry /ˈsɜːdʒəri/ *n* **1** [C;U] (performing of) a medical operation: *He was in surgery for 5 hours.* **2** [U] branch of medicine concerned with such treatment

sur·gi·cal /ˈsɜːdʒɪkəl/ *adj* **1** of or used for surgery **2** (of a garment) worn as treatment for a particular physical condition **~ly** *adv*

sur·ly /ˈsɜːli/ *adj* having a bad temper and manners **surliness** *n* [U]

sur·mount /səˈmaʊnt/ *vt* **1** succeed in dealing with (a difficulty) **2** be on top of

sur·name /ˈsɜːneɪm/ *n* person's family name; LAST NAME

sur·pass /səˈpæs/ *vt fml* go beyond, esp. be better than

sur·plus /ˈsɜːplʌs, -plɒs/ *n, adj* (amount) additional to what is needed or used

sur·prise /səˈpraɪz, səˈpraɪz/ *n* [C;U] **1** (feeling caused by) an unexpected event **2 take by surprise** come on (someone) unprepared ♦ *vt* **1** cause surprise to **2** find, catch, or attack when unprepared

sur·pris·ing /səˈpraɪzɪŋ, səˈpraɪ-/ *adj* unusual; causing surprise **~ly** *adv*

sur·real /səˈriːl/ *adj* having a strange, dreamlike unreal quality **~ism** *n* [U]

modern art or literature that treats subjects in a surreal way **~ist** *n, adj* (artist or writer) concerned with surrealism

sur·ren·der /səˈrendə/ *v* **1** *vi/t* give up or give in to the power (esp. of an enemy); admit defeat **2** *vt fml* give up possession of ♦ *n* [C;U] act of surrendering

sur·rep·ti·tious /ˌsʌrəpˈtɪʃəs◂, ˌsʌr-/ *adj* done secretly, esp. for dishonest reasons **~ly** *adv*

sur·ro·gate /ˈsʌrəgeɪt, -gɪt, ˈsʌr-/ *n, adj* (person or thing) acting or used in place of another: *a surrogate mother* (who has a baby for another woman unable to have children) **-gacy** *n*

sur·round /səˈraʊnd/ *vt* be or go all around on every side ♦ *n* (decorative) edge or border **~ing** *adj* around and near **~ings** *n* [P] place and conditions of life

sur·veil·lance /səˈveɪləns/ *n* [U] close watch kept on someone or something

sur·vey[1] /səˈveɪ, ˈsɜːveɪ/ *vt* **1** look at or examine as a whole **2** examine the condition of (a building) **3** measure (land) **~or** /səˈveɪə/ *n* person whose job is to SURVEY[1] (2,3)

survey[2] /ˈsɜːveɪ/ *n* **1** act of surveying: *a survey of public opinion/of a house* **2** general description

sur·vive /səˈvaɪv/ *vi/t* continue to live or exist (after), esp. after coming close to death: *She survived the accident.* **-vival** *n* **1** [U] act of surviving **2** [C] something which has survived from an earlier time **-vivor** *n*

sus·cep·ti·ble /səˈseptəbəl/ *adj* **1** easily influenced (by) **2** likely to suffer (from) **-bility** /səˌseptəˈbɪləti/ *n*

sus·pect /səˈspekt/ *vt* **1** believe to be so; think likely: *I suspected he was ill but didn't want to warn him.* **2** believe to be guilty ♦ /ˈsʌspekt/ *n* person suspected of guilt ♦ *adj* of uncertain truth, quality, legality, etc.

sus·pend /səˈspend/ *vt* **1** *fml* hang from above **2** hold still in liquid or air **3** make inactive for a time: *The meeting was suspended while the lights were repaired.* **4** prevent from taking part for a time, esp. for breaking rules **~ers** *n* [P] bands over the shoulders to keep pants up

sus·pense /səˈspens/ *n* [U] state of unsureness causing anxiety or pleasant excitement

sus·pen·sion /səˈspɛnʃən/ *n* **1** [U] act of suspending or fact of being suspended **2** [C] apparatus fixed to a vehicle's wheels to lessen the effect of rough roads

suspension bridge /·ˈ·· ·/ *n* bridge hung from strong steel ropes fixed to towers

sus·pi·cion /səˈspɪʃən/ *n* **1** [U] **a** a case of suspecting or being suspected (SUSPECT (2)): *under suspicion of murder* **b** lack of trust: *treat someone with suspicion* **2 a** a feeling of SUSPECTING: *I have a suspicion you're right.* **b** belief about someone's guilt: *They have their suspicions.* **3** [S] slight amount **–cious** *adj* **1** suspecting guilt, bad or criminal behavior, etc. **2** making one suspicious: *suspicious behavior* **–ciously** *adv*

sus·tain /səˈsteɪn/ *vt* **1** keep strong **2** keep in existence over a long period **3** *fml* suffer: *The car sustained severe damage.* **4** *fml* hold up (the weight of) **~able** *adj* able to continue or last for a long time

swab /swɑb/ *n* small stick with a piece of material on the end of it ♦ *vt* **-bb-** clean (a wound) with a swab

swag·ger /ˈswægə/ *vi* walk or behave (too) confidently or proudly **swagger** *n* [S;U]

swal·low[1] /ˈswɑloʊ/ *v* **1** *vi/t* move (the contents of the mouth) down the throat **2** *vt* accept patiently or with too easy belief: *It was an obvious lie, but he swallowed it.* **3** *vt* hold back (uncomfortable feelings); not show or express: *swallow one's pride* ♦ *n* act of swallowing or amount swallowed

swallow up *phr vt* take in and cause to disappear

swallow[2] *n* small bird with a tail with 2 points

swam /swæm/ *v past t. of* SWIM

swamp /swɑmp, swɔmp/ *n* [C;U] (area of) soft wet land ♦ *vt* cause to have (too) much to deal with **~ed** *adj* having too much to deal with **~y** *adj* wet like a swamp

swan /swɑn/ *n* large white water bird with a long neck

swank·y /ˈswæŋk/ *adj infml* very fashionable or expensive

swan song /ˈswɑn sɔŋ/ *n* one's last performance or piece of artistic work

swap /swɑp/ *vi/t* **-pp-** exchange (goods or positions) so that each person gets

what they want ♦ *n* **1** exchange **2** something (to be) exchanged

swarm /swɔrm/ *n* large moving mass of insects: (fig.) *swarms of tourists* ♦ *vi* move in a crowd or mass

swarm with *phr vt* be full of (a moving crowd)

swash·buck·ling /ˈswɑʃˌbʌklɪŋ, ˈswɔʃ-/ *adj* full of showy adventures, sword fighting, etc.

swat /swɑt/ *vt* **-tt-** hit (an insect), esp. so as to kill it

SWAT /swɑt/ *n* special police kept ready for special action

sway /sweɪ/ *v* **1** *vi/t* swing from side to side **2** *vt* influence, esp. so as to change opinion ♦ *n* [U] **1** swaying movement **2** *lit* influence

swear /swɛr/ *v* **swore** /swɔr, swoʊr/, **sworn** /swɔrn, swoʊrn/ **1** *vi* curse **2** *vi/t* make a solemn promise or statement, esp. by taking an OATH (1): *She swore to tell the truth/swore that she had been there.* **3** cause to take an OATH

swear by *phr vt* have confidence in (something)

swear in *phr vt* **1** cause (a witness) to take the OATH (1) in court **2** cause to make a promise of responsible action, etc.: *The new President was sworn in.*

sweat /swɛt/ *n* **1** [U] body liquid that comes out through the skin **2** [S] anxious state **3** [S] *infml* hard work **4 no sweat** *infml* (used for saying that something will not cause any difficulty) ♦ *vi* **1** produce sweat **2** be very anxious or nervously impatient **3 sweat blood** *infml* work unusually hard **~y** *adj* **1** covered in or smelly with sweat **2** unpleasantly hot

sweat·er /ˈswɛtə/ *n* (woolen) garment for the upper body

sweat·pants /ˈswɛtˌpænts/ *n* pants worn esp. for running and other sports

sweats /swɛts/ *n* [P] set of cotton shirt and pants, worn esp. for running and other sports

sweat·shirt /ˈswɛtˌʃət/ *n* loose cotton garment for the upper body

sweat·shop /ˈswɛtˌʃɑp/ *n* business that pays its workers very little money

sweep[1] /swip/ *v* **swept** /swɛpt/ **1** *vt* clean or remove by brushing **2** *vi/t* move (over) or carry quickly and powerfully: *A wave of panic swept over her.* | *We were swept along by the crowd.* **3** *vi* lie in a curve across land **4** *vi* win completely and easily, as in an election **5** *vi* (of a person) move in a proud, firm manner **6 sweep someone off their feet** fill someone with sudden love or excitement **7 sweep something under the rug** keep (something bad or shocking) secret ~**er** *n* ~**ing** *adj* **1** including many or most things: *sweeping changes* **2** too general: *a sweeping statement*

sweep aside *phr vt* refuse to pay any attention to

sweep² *n* **1** act of sweeping **2** long curved line or area of country: (fig.) *the broad sweep of her narrative* (= covering all parts of the subject) **3** person who cleans chimneys **4** sweepstake

sweep·stakes /ˈswiːpsteɪks/ *n* contest in which people win money or prizes

sweet /swiːt/ *adj* **1** tasting like sugar **2** pleasing to the senses: *sweet music* **3** charming; lovable: *What a sweet little boy!* — see also **short and sweet** (SHORT¹) —**en** *vt* **1** make sweeter **2** *infml* give money or presents in order to persuade —**ly** *adv* ~**ness** *n* [U]

sweet·en·er /ˈswiːtn-ə, -nə/ *n* **1** substance used instead of sugar to make food or drink taste sweet **2** *infml* money, a present, etc., given in order to persuade someone

sweet·heart /ˈswiːthɑːt/ *n* **1** person whom one loves **2** (used when speaking to someone you love): *Yes, sweetheart.*

sweet·ie /ˈswiːti/ *n* (used when speaking to someone you love)

sweet po·ta·to /ˌ· ·ˈ·-/ *n* root looking like an orange potato, cooked and eaten as a vegetable

sweet talk /ˈ· ·/ *n* [U] *infml* insincere talk intended to please or persuade **sweet-talk** /ˈ· ·/ *vt*

sweet tooth /ˌ· ˈ·, ˈ· ·/ *n* [S] liking for sweet and sugary things

swell /swel/ *vi/t* **swelled**, **swollen** /ˈswəʊlən/ **or swelled 1** increase gradually to beyond the usual or original size: *a swollen finger.* **2** fill or be filled, giving a full round shape ♦ *n* **1** [S] rolling up and down movement of the surface of the sea **2** [C] *often derog* classy person ♦ *adj* excellent ~**ing** *n* **1** act of swelling **2** swollen place on the body

swel·ter·ing /ˈswɛltərɪŋ/ *adj* unpleasantly hot

swept /swept/ *v past t. and p. of* SWEEP

swerve /swɜːv/ *vi*, *n* (make) a sudden change of direction

swift¹ /swɪft/ *adj* quick ~**ly** *adv* ~**ness** *n* [U]

swift² *n* small brown bird like a SWALLOW², that flies quickly

swig /swɪg/ *vt* -**gg**- *infml* drink, esp. in large mouthfuls **swig** *n*

swill /swɪl/ *vt* **1** wash with great streams of water **2** *infml* drink, esp. in large amounts ♦ *n* [U] **1** partly liquid pig food **2** unpleasant food

swim /swɪm/ *v* **swam** /swæm/, **swum** /swʌm/; *present p.* -**mm**- **1** *vi* move through water using the limbs, FINS, etc. **2** *vt* cross by doing this: *swim the English Channel* **3** *vi* be full of or surrounded with liquid **4** *vi* seem to spin around and around: *My head was swimming.* **5 swim with the tide** follow the behavior of other people around one ♦ *n* **1** [S] act of swimming **2 in the swim (of things)** knowing about and concerned in what is going on in modern life ~**mer** *n*

swimming pool /ˈ·· ·ˌ/ *n* large container filled with water and used for swimming

swim·suit /ˈswɪmsuːt/ *n* piece of clothing worn by women or girls when swimming

swin·dle /ˈswɪndl/ *vt* cheat, esp. so as to get money ♦ *n* act of swindling **swindler** *n*

swine /swaɪn/ *n* **swine 1** *fml or lit* pig **2** *sl* unpleasant person

swing /swɪŋ/ **swung** /swʌŋ/ **1** *vi/t* move backwards and forwards or around and around from a fixed point: *Soldiers swing their arms as they march.* **2** *vi/t* move in a smooth curve: *The door swung shut.* **3** *vi* turn quickly **4** *vi* start smoothly and rapidly: *We're ready to swing into action.* ♦ *n* **1** [C] act of swinging, esp. a BAT at a baseball **2** [C] children's swinging seat fixed from above by ropes or chains **3** [C] noticeable change: *a big swing in public opinion* **4** [S] JAZZ music of the 1930s and 1940s with a strong regular active beat **5 in full swing** having reached a very active stage

swipe /swaɪp/ *vt* **1** hit hard **2** *infml* steal **3** pass (an electronic card) through an apparatus ♦ *n* sweeping blow — see also SIDESWIPE

swirl /swəl/ vi/t move with twisting turns ♦ n twisting mass

swish /swɪʃ/ vi/t **1** move through the air with a sharp whistling noise **2** (of a man) walk like a woman ♦ n act of swishing

Swiss /swɪs/ adj of Switzerland

switch /swɪtʃ/ n **1** apparatus for stopping or starting an electric current **2** sudden complete change ♦ vi/t change or exchange: *They switched jobs.* | *The lights have switched to green.*

   switch off/on phr vt turn (an electric light or apparatus) off/on with a switch

   switch over phr vi change completely

switch·blade /'swɪtʃbleɪd/ n knife with a blade operated by a spring, used as a weapon

switch·board /'swɪtʃbɔrd, -boʊrd/ n place where telephone lines in a large building are connected

swiv·el /'swɪvəl/ vi/t -l- turn around (as if) on a central point

swol·len[1] /'swoʊlən/ v past p. of SWELL

swol·len[2] adj **1** (of a body part) bigger than usual because of injury or sickness **2** (of a river) containing more water than usual

swoon /swun/ vi lit **1** experience deep joy, desire, etc. **2** FAINT

swoop /swup/ vi come down sharply, esp. to attack **swoop** n **1** swooping action **2** in one fell swoop all at once

sword /sɔrd, soʊrd/ n **1** weapon with a long sharp metal blade and a handle **2** cross swords (with) be opposed (to), esp. in argument

swore /swɔr, swoʊr/ v past t. of SWEAR

sworn /swɔrn, swoʊrn/ v past p. of SWEAR

swum /swʌm/ v past p. of SWIM

swung /swʌŋ/ v past t. and p. of SWING

syc·a·more /'sɪkəˌmɔr, -ˌmoʊr/ n common tree with broad leaves

syc·o·phant /'sɪkəfənt/ n person who praises people insincerely to gain personal advantage **~ic** /ˌsɪkəˈfænrɪk◂/ adj **~ically** adv **–phancy** /-fənsi, -ˌfænsi/ n [U]

syl·la·ble /'sɪləbəl/ n part of a word containing a single vowel sound: *There are two syllables in "window": "win-" and "-dow."* **–labic** /səˈlæbɪk/ adj

syl·la·bus /'sɪləbəs/ n arrangement of subjects for study over a period of time

sym·bol /'sɪmbəl/ n something that represents something else: *The dove is the*

symbol of peace. **~ism** n [U] use of symbols **~ize** vt represent by or as a symbol **~ic** /sɪmˈbɑlɪk/ adj representing: *The snake is symbolic of evil.* **~ically** adv

sym·me·try /'sɪmətri/ n [U] **1** exact likeness in size, shape, etc., between opposite sides **2** effect of pleasing balance **symmetrical** /sɪˈmetrɪkəl/ adj

sym·pa·thy /'sɪmpəθi/ n [U] **1** sensitivity to and pity for others' suffering **2** agreement and/or understanding: *I am in sympathy with their aims.* **–thize** vt feel or show sympathy **sympathies** n [P] feelings of support or loyalty **–thetic** /ˌsɪmpəˈθetɪk◂/ adj feeling or showing sympathy **–thetically** adv

sym·pho·ny /'sɪmfəni/ n piece of music for an ORCHESTRA, usu. in 4 parts

sym·po·si·um /sɪmˈpoʊziəm/ n -ums or -a /-ziə/ meeting to talk about a subject of study

symp·tom /'sɪmptəm/ n **1** outward sign of a disease **2** outward sign of inner change, new feelings, etc. **~atic** /ˌsɪmptəˈmætɪk◂/ adj being a symptom of

syn·a·gogue /'sɪnəˌgɑg, -ˌgɔg/ n building where Jews worship

sync /sɪŋk/ n in sync/out of sync a happening or moving at the same time or rate, or not doing this: *The drummer was out of sync with the band* **b** doing or saying things that are suitable or unsuitable for a situation: *Our message must be in sync with voter's concerns*

syn·chro·nize /'sɪŋkrəˌnaɪz/ vt **1** cause to happen at the same time or speed **2** cause (watches, etc.) to show the same time **–nization** /ˌsɪŋkrənəˈzeɪʃən/ n [U]

syn·di·cate[1] /'sɪndəkɪt/ n group of people or companies combined for usu. business purposes

syn·di·cate[2] /'sɪndəˌkeɪt/ vt sell (written work, pictures, PROGRAMS (3), etc.) to many different newspapers, stations or magazines

syn·drome /'sɪndroʊm/ n **1** set of medical SYMPTOMs which represent an illness **2** any pattern of qualities, happenings, etc., typical of a general condition

syn·o·nym /'sɪnəˌnɪm/ n word with the same meaning as another **~ous** /sɪˈnɑnəməs/ adj

sy·nop·sis /sɪˈnɑpsɪs/ n short account of something longer

syn·tax /ˈsɪntæks/ *n* [U] way in which words are ordered and connected in sentences –**tactic** /sɪnˈtæktɪk/ *adj*

syn·the·sis /ˈsɪnθəsɪs/ *n* -**ses** /-sɪz/ **1** [U] combining of separate things, ideas, etc., into a complete whole **2** [C] something made by synthesis –**size** *vt* make by synthesis, esp. make (something similar to a natural product) by combining chemicals –**sizer** *n* electrical instrument, like a piano, that can produce many sorts of different sounds, used esp. in popular music

syn·thet·ic /sɪnˈθɛtɪk/ *adj* artificial ~**ally** *adv*

syph·i·lis /ˈsɪfəlɪs/ *n* [U] very serious illness passed on through sex

sy·phon /ˈsaɪfən/ *n*, *v* SIPHON

sy·ringe /səˈrɪndʒ/ *n* (medical) instrument with a hollow tube for sucking in and pushing out liquid, esp. through a needle ♦ *vt* clean with a syringe

syr·up /ˈsɪrəp, ˈsɜəp/ *n* [U] **1** sweet liquid, esp. sugar and water **2** mixture of sugar, water, and medicine: *cough syrup*

sys·tem /ˈsɪstəm/ *n* **1** [C] group of related parts which work together forming a whole: *a computer system* | *the digestive system* **2** [C] ordered set of ideas, methods, or ways of working: *the American system of government* **3** [C] the body, thought of as a set of working parts: *Traveling always upsets my system.* **4** [U] orderly methods **5** [*the* + S] society seen as something which uses and limits INDIVIDUALS: *to fight the system* — see also EXPERT SYSTEM, OPERATING SYSTEM ~**atic** /ˌsɪstəˈmætɪk◄/ *adj* based on orderly methods and careful organization; thorough ~**atically** *adv*

systems an·a·lyst /ˈ.. ˌ.../ *n* someone who studies (esp. business) activities and uses computers to plan ways of carrying them out, etc.

T

T, t /tiː/ *the 20th letter of the English alphabet*

tab /tæb/ *n* **1** small piece of paper, cloth, metal, etc., fixed to something to hold it by, open it with, etc. **2 keep tabs on** watch closely

tab·by /ˈtæbi/ *n* cat with dark and light bands of fur

ta·ble /ˈteɪbəl/ *n* **1** piece of furniture with a flat top on upright legs **2** set of figures arranged in rows across and down a page **3 turn the tables on** gain an advantage over (someone who had an advantage over you) — see also WATER TABLE ♦ *vt* leave until a later date for consideration

ta·ble·spoon /ˈteɪbəlˌspuːn/ *n* spoon for serving and measuring food

tab·let /ˈtæblɪt/ *n* **1** small solid piece of medicine **2** many sheets of paper fastened together **3** flat piece of stone or metal with words on it

table ten·nis /ˈ·· ˌ··/ *n* [U] indoor game in which a small ball is hit across a net on a table

tab·loid /ˈtæblɔɪd/ *n* newspaper with small pages and many pictures

ta·boo /təˈbuː, tæ-/ *n* -**boos** [C;U] strong social or religious custom forbidding something ♦ *adj* strongly forbidden by social custom: *taboo words*

tab·u·late /ˈtæbjəˌleɪt/ *vt* arrange as a TABLE (2) -**lar** *adj* -**lation** /ˌtæbjəˈleɪʃən/ *n* [U]

ta·cit /ˈtæsɪt/ *adj* accepted or understood without being openly expressed: *tacit approval* ~**ly** *adv*

tack /tæk/ *n* **1** small nail **2** sailing ship's direction: (fig.) *a new tack on the crime problem* **3** long loose stitch ♦ *v* **1** *vt* fasten with tacks **2** *vi* change the course of a sailing ship

tack·le /ˈtækəl/ *n* **1** [C] act of stopping or taking the ball away from an opponent in sports **2** [U] apparatus used in certain sports: *fishing tackle* **3** [C;U] (system of) ropes and wheels for heavy pulling and lifting ♦ *v* **1** *vt* take action in order to deal with **2** *vt* speak to fearlessly so as to deal with a problem **3** *vi/t* stop or rob with a tackle (1), esp. in football

tack·y /ˈtæki/ *adj* **1** sticky **2** of low quality: *a tacky hotel/remark* (= in bad TASTE (3)) -**iness** *n* [U]

ta·co /ˈtɑːkoʊ/ *n* Mexican food made with a TORTILLA (= thin flat bread) rolled around meat, beans, cheese, etc.

tact /tækt/ *n* [U] skill of speaking or acting without offending people ~**ful** *adj* ~**fully** *adv* ~**less** *adj* ~**lessly** *adv*

tac·tic /ˈtæktɪk/ *n* plan or method for gaining a desired result **tactics** *n* [U] art of arranging and moving military forces in battle **tactical** *adj* **1** of tactics **2** done to get a desired result in the end: *a tactical retreat* **tactician** /tækˈtɪʃən/ *n* person skilled in tactics

tac·tile /ˈtæktəl, -taɪl/ *adj* of or able to be felt by the sense of touch

tad·pole /ˈtædpoʊl/ *n* small creature that grows into a FROG or TOAD

taf·fy /ˈtæfi/ *n* [U] (piece of) sticky candy

tag /tæɡ/ *n* **1** [C] small piece of paper or material fastened to something to show who owns it, its cost, etc. **2** [U] game in which one child chases the others until he/she touches one of them ♦ *vt* -**gg- 1** fasten a tag to **2** provide with a name or NICKNAME **3** put (a player) out in baseball by touching him with the ball

tag along *phr vi* go with someone by following closely behind or when not welcome

tag on *phr vt* add

tail¹ /teɪl/ *n* **1** long movable growth at the back of a creature's body **2** last or back part (of something long): *the tail of an aircraft* **3** person employed to follow someone **4 turn tail** turn around ready to run away **tails** *n* [P] **1** side of a coin without a head on it **2** man's formal coat with a long back divided into 2 parts below the waist

tail² *vt* follow (someone) closely, esp. without their knowledge

tail away/off *phr vi* lessen gradually

tail·gate /ˈteɪlɡeɪt/ *vi/t* drive too close (to the car ahead) ~**gater** *n*

tail·light /ˈteɪl-laɪt/ *n* one of 2 red lights at the back of a vehicle

tai·lor /ˈteɪlə/ *n* person who makes garments ♦ *vt* fit to a particular need ~**made** /ˌ·· ˈ·◄/ *adj* exactly right for a particular need, person, etc.

tail·pipe /'teɪlpaɪp/ n pipe through which waste gases leave a vehicle

taint /teɪnt/ vt, n [S] (spoil with) a small amount of decay, infection, or bad influence

take¹ /teɪk/ v took /tʊk/, **taken** /'teɪkən/ vt move from one place to another: *Take the chair into the garden.* | *Take the children with you.* | *I had a tooth taken out.* **2** vt remove without permission: *Someone's taken my pen.* **3** vt subtract: *What do you get if you take 5 from 12?* **4** vt get possession of; seize: *Rebels have taken the airport.* **5** vt get by performing an action: *Take his temperature.* | *He took notes.* | *Take a seat.* **6** vt start to hold: *She took my arm.* **7** vt use for travel: *I take the train to work.* **8** vt be willing to accept: *Will you take a check?* **9** vt accept as true or worthy of attention: *Take my advice.* | *I took his suggestion seriously.* **10** vt be able to contain: *The bus takes 55 passengers.* **11** vt be able to accept; bear: *I can't take his rudeness.* **12** vt need: *The journey takes* (= lasts) *2 hours.* | *It took 10 men to pull down the wall.* **13** vt do; perform: *He took a walk/a bath.* **14** vt put into the body: *take some medicine/a deep breath* **15** vt make by photography **16** vt have (a feeling): *take offense/pity* **17** vi have the intended effect; work: *Did the vaccination take?* **18** vt become: *take ill* **19** vt understand: *I take it you know each other.* **20** **take care of** look after **21** **take it easy** *infml* RELAX **22** **take one's time: a** use as much time as is necessary **b** use too much time **23** **take part** join in with others **24** **take place** happen **25** **take the cake** win **26** **take the floor** begin to speak in a group

take aback phr vt surprise and confuse

take after phr vt look or behave like (an older relative)

take apart phr vt **1** separate into pieces **2** sl harm a place or person

take back phr vt **1** admit that (what one said) was wrong **2** cause to remember a former period in one's life: *That takes me back!*

take in phr vt **1** reduce the size of (a garment) **2** provide a home for **3** include **4** understand fully **5** deceive

take off phr v **1** vt remove (a garment) **2** vi (of a plane, etc.) rise into the air to begin a flight **3** vi fml leave without warning: *One day he just took off.* **4** vt

copy the speech or manners of, esp. for humor; MIMIC **5** vt have as a vacation from work: *I took Tuesday off.*

take on phr vt **1** begin to have (a quality or appearance) **2** start to quarrel or fight with **3** accept (work, responsibility, etc.) **4** start to employ

take out phr vt **1** go somewhere with (someone) as a social activity **2** obtain officially: *take out insurance* **3** **take it out of someone** use all the strength of someone

take out on phr vt express (one's feelings) by making (someone) suffer: *He tends to take things out on his wife.*

take over phr vi/t gain control of and responsibility for (something)

take to phr vt **1** like, esp. at once **2** begin as a practice or habit: *He took to drink.* **3** go to (one's bed, etc.) for rest, escape, etc.

take up phr vt **1** begin to interest oneself in: *I've taken up the guitar.* **2** complain, ask, or take further action about: *I'll take the matter up with my lawyer.* **3** fill or use (space or time), esp. undesirably **4** accept (someone's) offer: *I'll take you up on that.* **5** continue (a story, etc.) **6** shorten (a garment) by folding up the bottom

take up with phr vt **1** become friendly with **2** be very interested in: *She's very taken up with her work.*

take² n **1** filming of a scene **2** takings

take·off /'teɪk-ɔf/ n **1** [C;U] rising of a plane, etc., from the ground **2** amusing copy of someone's typical behavior

take·out /'teɪk-aʊt/ n (meal from) a restaurant that sells food to eat elsewhere

take·o·ver /'teɪkˌoʊvə/ n act of gaining control of esp. a business company

tak·er /'teɪkə/ n [usu. pl.] infml person willing to accept an offer

tak·ings /'teɪkɪŋz/ n [P] money received, esp. by a store

tal·cum pow·der /'tælkəm ˌpaʊdə/ also **talc** infml — n [U] crushed mineral put on the body to dry it or make it smell nice

tale /teɪl/ n **1** story **2** false story; lie

tal·ent /'tælənt/ n [S;U] special natural ability or skill ~ed adj

talk /tɔk/ v **1** vi speak: *Can the baby talk yet?* | *Is there somewhere quiet where we* *can talk?* **2** *vi* give information by speaking, usu. unwillingly: *We have ways of making you talk.* **3** *vi* speak about others' affairs; GOSSIP **4** *vt* speak about: *It's time to talk business.* ♦ *n* **1** [S] conversation **2** [C] informal LECTURE **3** [U] way of talking: *baby talk* **4** [*the*+S] subject much talked about: *Her sudden marriage is the talk of the town.* **5** [U] empty or meaningless speech **6 talk turkey** speak openly (about difficult matters) — see also SMALL TALK, SWEET TALK **talks** *n* [P] formal exchange of opinions ~**er** *n*

talk back *phr vi* reply rudely

talk down to *phr vt* speak to (someone) as if one were more important, clever, etc.

talk into/out of *phr vt* persuade (someone) to do/not to do (something)

talk over *phr vt* speak about thoroughly and seriously

talk up *phr vt* speak favorably about, esp. to win support

talk·a·tive /ˈtɔkətɪv/ *adj* liking to talk a lot

talking point /ˈ·· ·/ *n* subject of conversation or argument

talking-to /ˈ·· ·/ *n* angry talk in order to blame or CRITICIZE

talk show /ˈ· ·/ *n* television or radio show in which people answer questions about themselves or discuss important subjects

tall /tɔl/ *adj* **1** of greater than average height **2** of the stated height from top to bottom: *He is 6 feet tall.*

tall or·der /ˌ· ˈ·/ *n* [S] something unreasonably difficult to do

tal·low /ˈtæloʊ/ *n* [U] hard animal fat used for candles

tall tale /ˌ· ˈ·/ *n* story that is difficult to believe

tal·ly /ˈtæli/ *n* recorded total of money spent, points made in a game, etc. ♦ *vi* be exactly equal; match

tal·on /ˈtælən/ *n* sharp powerful curved nail on a hunting bird's foot

tam·bou·rine /ˌtæmbəˈrin/ *n* drumlike musical instrument with small metal plates around the edge

tame /teɪm/ *adj* **1** not fierce or wild **2** dull; unexciting ♦ *vt* make (an animal) tame ~**ly** *adv* ~**ness** *n* [U] **tamer** *n*

tam·per /ˈtæmpə/ *v* **tamper with** *phr vt* touch or change without permission, esp. causing damage

tam·pon /ˈtæmpɑn/ *n* mass of cotton put into a woman's sex organ to take up the monthly bleeding

tan /tæn/ *v* **-nn- 1** *vt* change (animal skin) into leather by treating with TANNIN **2** *vi/t* turn brown, esp. by sunlight ♦ *n* **1** [C] brown skin color from sunlight **2** [U] yellowish brown color

tan·dem /ˈtændəm/ *n* **1** bicycle for 2 riders **2 in tandem** with both working closely together

tan·gent /ˈtændʒənt/ *n* **1** straight line touching the edge of a curve **2 go/fly off at a tangent** change suddenly to a different course of action or thought ~**ial** /tænˈdʒɛnʃəl/ *adj* not concerned with the main subject

tan·ge·rine /ˌtændʒəˈrin, ˈtændʒəˌrin/ *n* sort of small orange

tan·gi·ble /ˈtændʒəbəl/ *adj* **1** clear and certain; real: *tangible proof* **2** touchable –**bly** *adv*

tan·gle /ˈtæŋɡəl/ *vi/t* (cause to) become a confused mass of twisted threads ♦ *n* confused mass or state

tan·go /ˈtæŋɡoʊ/ *n* **-gos** Latin-American dance

tang·y /ˈtæŋi/ *adj* having a strong sharp taste or smell

tank /tæŋk/ *n* **1** large liquid or gas container **2** enclosed armored military vehicle

tank·er /ˈtæŋkə/ *n* ship, road vehicle, etc., carrying large quantities of liquid or gas

tan·nin /ˈtænɪn/ *n* [U] reddish acid found in parts of certain plants

tan·ta·lize /ˈtæntəˌlaɪz/ *vt* cause to desire something even more strongly by keeping it just out of reach –**lizing** *adj*

tan·ta·mount /ˈtæntəˌmaʊnt/ *adj* having the same effect as (as): *Her answer is tantamount to a refusal.*

tan·trum /ˈtæntrəm/ *n* sudden uncontrolled attack of angry bad temper

tap[1] /tæp/ *vt* **-pp- 1** use or draw from: *tapping our reserves of oil* **2** listen secretly by making an illegal connection to (a telephone)

tap[2] *vi/t, n* **-pp-** (strike with) a light short blow: *She tapped her fingers on the table/tapped me on the shoulder.*

tap dance /ˈ· ·/ *n* dance in which one makes loud sounds on the floor with special shoes **tap-dance** *vi*

tape /teɪp/ n [C;U] 1 (long piece of) narrow material: *Stick it on with some tape.* 2 (long piece of) narrow plastic MAGNETic material on which sounds or pictures are recorded ♦ vt 1 record on tape (2) 2 fasten or tie with tape (1)

tape deck /ˈ· ·/ n tape recorder

tape mea·sure /ˈ· ·ˌ·/ n narrow band of cloth or bendable metal used for measuring

ta·per /ˈteɪpə/ vi/t make or become gradually narrower towards one end ♦ n thin candle

tape re·cord·er /ˈ· ·ˌ··/ n electrical apparatus for recording and playing sound with TAPE (2)

tap·es·try /ˈtæpɪstri/ n [C;U] (piece of) cloth with pictures or patterns woven into it

tap wa·ter /ˈ· ·ˌ·/ n [U] water taken from a FAUCET

tar /tɑr/ n [U] black meltable substance used for making roads, preserving wood, etc. ♦ vt **-rr-** 1 cover with tar 2 **tarred with the same brush** having the same faults 3 **beat the tar out of** beat badly

ta·ran·tu·la /təˈræntʃələ/ n large hairy poisonous SPIDER

tar·dy /ˈtɑrdi/ adj fml or lit 1 late, esp. at school **-dily** adv **-diness** n [U] 2 slow in acting or happening

tar·get /ˈtɑrgɪt/ n 1 something aimed at in shooting practice 2 place, thing, or person at which an attack is directed 3 total or object which one tries to reach: *a production target of 500 cars a week* ♦ vt cause to be a target

tar·iff /ˈtærɪf/ n tax on goods coming into a country

tar·mac /ˈtɑrmæk/ n [U] area where aircraft take off and land

tar·nish /ˈtɑrnɪʃ/ vi/t make or become discolored or less bright: *tarnished silver*/(fig.) *reputations*

tar·ot /ˈtæroʊ/ n set of 22 special cards used for telling the future

tarp /ˈtɑrˌpɔlɪn, ˈtɑrpəlɪn/ n (sheet or cover of) heavy WATERPROOF cloth

tart¹ /tɑrt/ adj bitter **~ness** n [U]

tart² n sexually immoral woman

tart³ n pastry container holding fruit or JAM

tar·tan /ˈtɑrtⁿn/ n [C;U] (woolen cloth with) a pattern of bands crossing each other, esp. representing a particular Scottish CLAN

tar·tar /ˈtɑrtə/ n [U] chalklike substance that forms on teeth

tartar sauce /ˈ·· ˌ·/ n food made from MAY-ONNAISE and PICKLES, eaten with fish

task /tæsk/ n 1 piece of (hard) work (to be) done 2 **take someone to task** speak severely to someone for a fault or failure

task force /ˈ· ·/ n military or police group set up for a special purpose

tas·sel /ˈtæsəl/ n tied bunch of threads hung in a decorative way

taste /teɪst/ n 1 [C;U] quality by which a food or drink is recognized in the mouth: *Sugar has a sweet taste.* 2 [U] sense which recognizes food or drink as sweet, salty, etc. 3 [U] ability to make (good) judgments about beauty, style, fashion, etc. 4 [C;U] personal liking: *These expensive tastes in clothes.* ♦ v 1 vt experience or test the taste of 2 vi have a particular taste: *These oranges taste nice.* 3 vt lit experience: *having tasted freedom* **~ful** adj showing good TASTE (3) **~less** adj 1 not tasting of anything 2 showing bad TASTE (3) **tasty** adj tasting pleasant

taste bud /ˈ· ·/ n group of cells on the tongue used in tasting

tat·ters /ˈtætəz/ n **in tatters: a** (of clothes) old and torn **b** ruined **-tered** adj (dressed in clothes that are) in tatters

tat·tle /ˈtætl/ vt/i tell (a secret)

tat·tle·tale /ˈtætlˌteɪl/ n person who tattles

tat·too /tæˈtuː/ n **-toos** pattern made by tattooing ♦ vt make (a pattern) on the skin (of) by pricking with a needle and then putting colored DYEs in **~ist** n

taught /tɔt/ past t. and p. of TEACH

taunt /tɔnt, tɑnt/ vt try to upset with unkind remarks or by laughing at faults or failures ♦ n taunting remark

Tau·rus /ˈtɔrəs/ n 1 [S] 2nd sign of the ZODIAC, represented by a BULL 2 someone born between April 20 and May 20

taut /tɔt/ adj stretched tight **~ly** adv **~ness** n [U]

taw·dry /ˈtɔdri/ adj cheaply showy; showing bad TASTE (3) **-driness** n [U]

taw·ny /ˈtɔni/ adj brownish yellow

tax /tæks/ n [C;U] money which must be paid to the government ♦ vt 1 make (someone) pay a tax 2 charge a tax on: *Cigarettes are heavily taxed.* 3 push to the limits of what one can bear: *Such stupid questions tax my patience.* **~able** *adj* that can be TAXed (2) **~ation** /tæk-'seɪʃən/ *n* [U] (money raised by) taxing **~ing** /'tæksɪŋ/ *adj* needing great effort

tax-de·duct·i·ble /ˌ· ·'···· ◂/ *adj* that may legally be subtracted from one's total income before it is taxed

tax-ex·empt /ˌ· ·'· ◂/ *adj* not taxed, or not having to pay tax: *tax-exempt income*

tax·i[1] /'tæksi/ also **tax·i·cab** /'tæksikæb/ — *n* car with a driver which carries passengers for money

taxi[2] *vi* (of an aircraft) move along the ground before taking off or after landing

tax·i·der·my /'tæksɪˌdəmi/ *n* [U] filling the skins of dead animals so that they look real **–mist** *n*

taxi stand /'·· ˌ·/ *n* place where taxis wait for riders

tax·pay·er /'tæksˌpeɪə/ *n* someone who pays taxes

tax shel·ter /'· ˌ··/ *n* plan or method for legally avoiding paying tax

TB *abbrev. for:* TUBERCULOSIS

tbs. *abbrev. for:* TABLESPOON

tea /ti/ *n* [C;U] **1** (drink made by pouring boiling water onto) the dried leaves of an Asian bush cut into pieces **2** drink made like tea from the stated leaves: *mint tea* **3 not one's cup of tea** not the sort of thing one likes: *Running isn't really my cup of tea.*

tea·bag /'tibæg/ *n* small paper bag full of tea leaves

teach /titʃ/ *v* **taught** /tɔt/ **1** *vi/t* give knowledge or skill of (something) to (someone): *He taught me French.* **2** *vt* show (someone) the bad results of doing something: *I'll teach you to be rude to me!* (= a threat) **~er** *n* person who teaches, esp. as a job **~ing** *n* [U] **1** job of a teacher **2** also **teachings** *pl.* — moral beliefs taught by someone of historical importance: *the teachings of Christ*

teach·er's pet /ˌ·· '·/ *n* *infml* teacher's favorite student, esp. one who is disliked by other students

teak /tik/ *n* [U] hard yellowish brown wood from Asia, used for furniture

team[1] /tim/ *n* **1** group of people who work or esp. play together: *a football team* **2 2** or more animals pulling the same vehicle

team[2] *v* **team up** *phr vi* work together for a shared purpose

team·mate /'timˌmeɪt/ *n* member of the same team

team·ster /'timstə/ *n* TRUCK driver, esp. one belonging to a labor union

team·work /'timwək/ *n* [U] (effective) combined effort

tea·pot /'tipɑt/ *n* container in which tea is made and served

tear[1] /tɛr/ *v* **tore** /tɔr, toʊr/, **torn** /tɔrn, toʊrn/ **1** *vt* pull apart by force, esp. so as to leave irregular edges **2** *vi* become torn **3** *vt* remove with sudden force: *He tore off his clothes.* **4** *vi* rush excitedly **5 be torn between** be unable to decide between **6 tear one's hair (out)** be very upset ♦ *n* hole made by tearing

   tear down *phr vt* pull down; destroy
   tear into *phr vt* attack violently
   tear up *phr vt* destroy completely by tearing

tear[2] /tɪr/ *n* **1** drop of salty liquid that flows from the eye, esp. because of sadness **2 in tears** crying **~ful** *adj* **~fully** *adv*

tear·drop /'tɪrdrɑp/ *n* single TEAR[2] (1)

tear gas /'tɪr gæs/ *n* [U] gas that stings the eyes

tear·jerk·er /'tɪrˌdʒəkə/ *n* very sad book, film, etc.

tease /tiz/ *v* **1** *vi/t* make jokes (about) or laugh (at) unkindly or playfully **2** *vt* annoy on purpose **3** *vt* separate the threads in (wool, etc.) ♦ *n* someone fond of teasing

tea·spoon /'tispun/ *n* small spoon used for eating and measuring

tech·ni·cal /'tɛknɪkəl/ *adj* **1** concerned with scientific or industrial subjects or skills **2** needing special knowledge in order to be understood: *His arguments are too technical for me.* **3** according to an (unreasonably) exact acceptance of the rules **~ly** *adv* — see also HIGH TECHNOLOGY

tech·ni·cal·i·ty /ˌtɛknɪ'kæləti/ *n* small (esp. unimportant) detail or rule

tech·ni·cian /tɛk'nɪʃən/ *n* highly skilled scientific or industrial worker

tech·nique /tɛk'nik/ *n* method of doing an activity that needs skill

tech·no·crat /'tɛknəˌkræt/ *n often derog* scientist or technician in charge of an organization

tech·nol·o·gy /tɛk'nɑlədʒi/ *n* practical science, esp. as used in industrial production **–gist** *n* **–gical** /ˌtɛknə'lɑdʒɪkəl ◂/ *adj*

ted·dy bear /ˈtɛdi ˌbɛr/ also **teddy** *infml* — *n* toy bear

te·di·ous /ˈtidiəs/ *adj* long and uninteresting ~**ly** *adv* ~**ness** *n* [U]

te·di·um /ˈtidiəm/ *n* [U] state of being tedious

tee /ti/ *n* small object on which a GOLF ball is placed to be hit ◆ *v*

tee off *phr vi* drive the ball from a tee

tee up *phr vi/t* place (the ball) on a tee

teem /tim/ *vi* to be full of or to be present in large numbers

teem with *phr vt* have (a type of creature) present in great numbers

teen·ag·er /ˈtinˌeɪdʒə/ *n* person of between 13 and 19 years old **teenage** *adj*

teens /tinz/ *n* [P] period of being a teenager

tee·ny wee·ny /ˌtini ˈwini◄/ *adj infml* extremely tiny

tee·ter /ˈtitə/ *vi* stand or move in an unsteady manner

teeter-tot·ter /ˈ·· ˌ·◄/ *n* SEESAW (1)

teeth /tiθ/ *pl. of* TOOTH

teethe /tið/ *vi* (of a baby) grow teeth

teething troub·les /ˈtiðɪŋ ˌtrʌbəlz/ *n* [P] problems in the early stages of using something

tee·to·tal·er /ˌtiˈtoʊtl-ə◄/ *n* someone who drinks no alcohol

Tef·lon /ˈtɛflɑn/ *n tdmk* [U] artificial substance to which things will not stick, used on kitchen pans, etc.

tel·e·com·mu·ni·ca·tions /ˌtɛlɔkəˌmyunəˈkeɪʃənz/ *n infml* [P] sending and receiving of messages by means of radio, telephone, SATELLITE, etc.

tel·e·com·mut·er /ˈtɛlɔkəˌmyutə/ *n* someone who works at home with a computer instead of in an office –**muting** *n* [U]

tel·e·gram /ˈtɛlɔˌgræm/ *n* message sent by telegraph

tel·e·graph /ˈtɛlɔˌgræf/ *n* [U] method of sending messages along wire by electric signals ◆ *vt* send a telegraph ~**ic** /ˌtɛlɔˈgræfɪk◄/ *adj*

te·lep·a·thy /təˈlɛpəθi/ *n* [U] sending of messages directly from one mind to another –**thic** /ˌtɛləˈpæθɪk◄/ *adj*

tel·e·phone /ˈtɛlɔˌfoʊn/ *n* [C;U] (apparatus for) the sending and receiving of sounds over long distances by electric means ◆ *vi/t* (try to) speak (to) by telephone

telephone pole /ˈ··· ˌ·/ *n* pole for supporting telephone wires

te·le·pho·to lens /ˌtɛlɔˌfoʊtoʊ ˈlɛnz/ *n* special LENS used for photographing very distant objects

tel·e·scope /ˈtɛlɔˌskoʊp/ *n* tube with a special piece of glass in it for looking at very distant objects ◆ *vi/t* **a** by one part sliding over another **b** by crushing –**scopic** /ˌtɛlɔˈskɑpɪk◄/ *adj* **1** of or related to a telescope **2** that telescopes

tel·e·thon /ˈtɛlɔˌθɑn/ *n* long television program intended to persuade people to give money to a CHARITY

tel·e·vise /ˈtɛlɔˌvaɪz/ *vt* broadcast on television

tel·e·vi·sion /ˈtɛlɔˌvɪʒən/ *n* [C;U] (apparatus for receiving) the broadcasting of pictures and sounds by electric waves

tell /tɛl/ *v* told /toʊld/ **1** *vt* make (something) known to (someone) in words: *Are you telling me the truth?* | *Tell me how to do it.* **2** *vt* warn; advise: *I told you it wouldn't work.* **3** *vt* order: *I told him to do it.* **4** *vi/t* find out; know: *How can you tell which button to press?* | *It was so dark that I couldn't tell if it was you.* **5** all told when all have been counted **6** tell time read the time from a watch or clock **7** there's no telling it is impossible to know **8** you're telling me (used as a strong way of saying) I know this already

tell off *phr vt* speak severely to (someone who has done something wrong)

tell on *phr vt* **1** have a bad effect on **2** *infml* (used esp. by children) inform against (someone)

tell·er /ˈtɛlə/ *n* bank clerk

tell·ing /ˈtɛlɪŋ/ *adj* sharply effective: *a telling argument*

tell·tale /ˈtɛlteɪl/ *adj* being a small sign that shows something: *a few telltale hairs on the murderer's sleeve*

temp /tɛmp/ *n infml* secretary employed for a short time ◆ *vi infml* work as a temp

tem·per /ˈtɛmpə/ *n* **1** [C] state of mind; MOOD: *He's in a good/bad temper.* **2** [C;U] angry or impatient state of mind **3** keep one's temper stay calm **4** lose one's temper become angry ◆ *vt* **1** harden (esp. metal) by special treatment **2** make less severe: *justice tempered with mercy*

tem·pe·ra·ment /ˈtɛmprəmənt/ *n* person's character with regard to being calm, easily excited, etc. ~**al** /ˌtɛmprə-

¹**men·tl◂/** *adj* **1** having or showing frequent changes of temper **2** caused by temperament ~**ally** *adv*

tem·pe·rate /ˈtempərɪt/ *adj* **1** (of an area's weather) neither very hot nor very cold **2** *fml* avoiding too much of anything

tem·pe·ra·ture /ˈtemprətʃə/ *n* **1** [C;U] degree of heat or coldness: *the average temperature* **2** [S] body temperature higher than the correct one; fever

tem·pest /ˈtempɪst/ *n lit* violent storm

tem·plate /ˈtempleɪt/ *n* **1** shape used as a guide for cutting metal, wood, etc. **2** computer FILE used to make others

tem·ple¹ /ˈtempəl/ *n* building where people worship a god or gods, esp. in the Jewish and Mormon religions

temple² *n* flattish area on each side of the forehead

tem·po /ˈtempoʊ/ *n* **-pos 1** rate of movement or activity **2** speed of music

tem·po·ra·ry /ˈtempəˌreri/ *adj* lasting for only a limited time –**rily** /ˌtempəˈrerəli/ *adv*

tempt /tempt/ *vt* (try to) persuade (someone) to do something wrong –**ation** /tempˈteɪʃən/ *n* **1** [U] act of tempting **2** [C] something that tempts, esp. by being very attractive –**ing** *adj* very attractive

ten /ten/ *determiner, n, pron* 10

te·na·cious /təˈneɪʃəs/ *adj* bravely firm ~**ly** *adv* –**city** /təˈnæsəti/ *n* [U]

ten·ant /ˈtenənt/ *n* person who pays rent for the use of a building, land, etc. –**ancy** *n* **1** [C] length of time a person is a tenant **2** [U] use of land, etc., as a tenant

tend¹ /tend/ *vt* be likely: *She tends to lose* (= often loses) *her temper if you disagree with her.*

tend² *vt* take care of

ten·den·cy /ˈtendənsi/ *n* **1** likelihood of often happening or behaving in a particular way **2** special liking and natural skill: *She has artistic tendencies.*

ten·der¹ /ˈtendə/ *adj* **1** not difficult to bite through **2** needing careful handling; delicate **3** sore **4** gentle, kind, and loving ~**ly** *adv* ~**ness** *n* [U]

tender² *v fml* **1** *vt* present for acceptance: *She tendered her resignation.* **2** *vt* offer in payment of debt — see also LEGAL TENDER

ten·der·heart·ed /ˌtendəˈhɑrtɪd◂/ *adj* easily made to feel love, pity, or sorrow

ten·der·ize /ˈtendəˌraɪz/ *vt* make (meat) softer by preparing it in a special way ~**r** *n*

ten·don /ˈtendən/ *n* strong cord connecting a muscle to a bone

ten·dril /ˈtendrəl/ *n* thin curling stem by which a plant holds on to things

ten·e·ment /ˈtenəmənt/ *n* large building divided into APARTMENTS, esp. in a poor city area

ten·et /ˈtenɪt/ *n fml* principle; belief

ten·nis /ˈtenɪs/ *n* [U] game played by hitting a ball over a net with a RACKET

tennis shoe /ˈ·· ˌ/ *n* comfortable shoe worn for sports

ten·or /ˈtenə/ *n* **1** (man with) the highest man's singing voice **2** instrument with the same range of notes as this: *a tenor saxophone* **3** *fml* general meaning (of something written or spoken)

tense¹ /tens/ *adj* **1** stretched tight **2** nervously anxious ♦ *vi/t* (cause to) become tense ~**ly** *adv* ~**ness** *n* [U]

tense² *n* form of a verb showing time and continuity of action: *the future tense*

ten·sion /ˈtenʃən/ *n* **1** [C;U] degree to which something is (able to be) stretched **2** [U] nervous anxiety caused by problems, uncertain waiting, etc. **3** [C;U] anxious, untrusting, and possibly dangerous relationship: *racial tensions in the inner city* **4** [U] *tech* electric power: *high-tension cables*

tent /tent/ *n* cloth shelter supported usu. by poles and ropes, used esp. by campers

ten·ta·cle /ˈtentəkəl/ *n* long, snakelike boneless limb of certain creatures: *the tentacles of an octopus*

ten·ta·tive /ˈtentətɪv/ *adj* **1** not firmly arranged or fixed: *a tentative agreement* **2** not firm in making statements or decisions ~**ly** *adv*

ten·ter·hooks /ˈtentəˌhʊks/ *n* **on tenterhooks** anxiously waiting

tenth /tenθ/ *determiner, adv, n, pron* 10th

ten·u·ous /ˈtenyuəs/ *adj* slight: *a tenuous connection* ~**ly** *adv* ~**ness** *n* [U]

ten·ure /ˈtenyə/ *n* [U] **1** act, right, or period of holding a job or land **2** right to keep one's job, esp. as a university teacher

te·pee /ˈtipi/ *n* round tent with a pointed top used by Native Americans

tep·id /ˈtepɪd/ *adj* only slightly warm: *tepid water* | (fig.) *tepid enthusiasm*

te·quil·a /təˈkilə/ *n* strong alcoholic drink made in Mexico

term /təm/ *n* **1** word or expression, esp. as used in a particular activity: *"Tort" is a legal term.* **2** fixed period: *a 4-year term as president* **3** division of the school or university year: *the summer term* **4** **in the long/short term** over a long/short period — see also TERMS ♦ *vt* name; call; describe as

ter·mi·nal /'təmənl/ *adj* of or being an illness that will cause death ♦ *n* **1** main building for passengers or goods at an airport, port, etc. **2** apparatus for giving instructions to and getting information from a computer **3** place for electrical connections: *the terminals of a battery* ~**ly** *adv*

ter·mi·nate /'təməneɪt/ *vi/t fml* (cause to) come to an end –**nation** /ˌtəmə'neɪʃən/ *n* [U]: *the termination of a pregnancy*

ter·mi·nol·o·gy /ˌtəmə'nɑlədʒi/ *n* [U] (use of) particular TERMS (3) *legal terminology* –**logical** /ˌtəmən'lɑdʒɪkəl/ *adj*

ter·mi·nus /'təmənəs/ *n* -**ni** /-naɪ/ or -**nuses** end of a transportation line

ter·mite /'təmaɪt/ *n* antlike insect that eats wood

terms /təmz/ *n* [P] **1** conditions of an agreement or contract **2** conditions of sale **3** **come to terms** reach an agreement **4** **come to terms with** accept (something unwelcome) **5** **on good/bad/friendly terms** having a good, bad, etc., relationship

ter·race /'tɛrɪs/ *n* **1** level area cut from a slope **2** flat area next to a building ♦ *vt* form into TERRACES (1)

ter·ra cot·ta /ˌtɛrə 'kɑtə◂/ *n* [U] (articles of) reddish brown baked clay

ter·rain /tə'reɪn/ *n* [C;U] (area of) land of the stated sort: *rocky terrain*

ter·res·tri·al /tə'rɛstriəl/ *adj fml* of the Earth or land, as opposed to space or the sea

ter·ri·ble /'tɛrəbəl/ *adj* **1** extremely severe: *a terrible accident* **2** extremely bad or unpleasant: *a terrible dinner* –**bly** *adv* **1** extremely, severely, or badly **2** extremely: *terribly sorry*

ter·ri·er /'tɛriə/ *n* type of small active dog

ter·rif·ic /tə'rɪfɪk/ *adj* **1** excellent **2** very great ~**ally** *adv* extremely

ter·ri·fy /'tɛrəfaɪ/ *vt* frighten extremely: *a terrified horse*

ter·ri·to·ry /'tɛrətɔri, -ˌtouri/ *n* [C;U] **1** (area of) land, esp. as ruled by one gov-ernment: *This island is French territory.* **2** area belonging to (and defended by) a particular person, animal, or group **3** area for which one person or group is responsible –**rial** /ˌtɛrə'tɔriəl◂, -'tour-/ *adj* **1** of or being land or territory **2** (of animals, birds, etc.) showing a tendency to guard one's own TERRITORY (2)

ter·ror /'tɛrə/ *n* [U] extreme fear

ter·ror·is·m /'tɛrəˌrɪzəm/ *n* [U] use of violence for political purposes –**ist** *n*

ter·ror·ize /'tɛrəˌraɪz/ *vt* fill with terror by threats or acts of violence

ter·ry /'tɛri/ also **ter·ry·cloth** /'tɛriˌklɔθ/ — *n* thick cotton cloth used esp. for making TOWELS

terse /təs/ *adj* using few words, often to show anger ~**ly** *adv* ~**ness** *n* [U]

TESOL /'tɛsɑl/ *n* [U] teaching English to speakers of other languages

test /tɛst/ *n* **1** set of questions or jobs to measure someone's knowledge or skill: *a history/driving test* **2** short medical examination: *an eye test* **3** use of something to see how well it works: *nuclear weapon tests* **4** **put to the test** find out the qualities of (something) by use ♦ *vt* **1** study or examine with a test **2** provide difficult conditions for: *a testing time* (= a difficult period) *for the country* **3** search by means of tests: *The company is testing for oil.*

tes·ta·ment /'tɛstəmənt/ *n* **1** *fml for:* WILL² (5) **2** (*cap.*) either of the 2 main parts of the Bible: *the Old Testament*

test-drive /'· ·/ *vt* try driving (a car) to decide whether one wants to buy it ♦ **test drive** *n*

tes·ti·cle /'tɛstɪkəl/ *n* either of the 2 round organs that produce SPERM in male animals

tes·ti·fy /'tɛstəfaɪ/ *vi/t* **1** make a solemn statement of truth **2** show (something) clearly; prove

tes·ti·mo·ni·al /ˌtɛstə'mouniəl/ *n* **1** formal written statement of someone's character and ability **2** something given or done to show respect, thanks, etc.

tes·ti·mo·ny /'tɛstəˌmouni/ *n* formal statement of facts, esp. in a court of law

test tube /'· ·/ *n* small glass tube, closed at one end, used in scientific tests ♦ *adj* made by man in a test tube: *a test tube baby*

tet·a·nus /'tɛtˀn-əs, -nəs/ *n* [U] serious disease, caused by infection of a cut, which causes the muscles to stiffen

teth·er /ˈtɛðə/ n **1** rope, etc., to which an animal is tied **2 the end of one's tether** the condition of being unable to bear any more difficulties, annoyances, etc. ♦ vt fasten with a tether

text /tɛkst/ n **1** [C;U] main body of printed words in a book **2** [C;U] exact original words of a speech, etc. **3** [C] textbook **4** [C] sentence from the Bible used by a priest in a SERMON ~**ual** /ˈtɛk-stʃuəl/ adj

text·book /ˈtɛksfbʊk/ n standard book used for studying a particular subject, esp. in schools ♦ adj **1** as it ought to be; IDEAL: textbook journalism **2** typical

tex·tile /ˈtɛkstaɪl, ˈtɛkstl̩/ n woven material

tex·ture /ˈtɛkstʃə/ n [C;U] quality of roughness, smoothness, or fineness of a surface or substance

TGIF humor Thank God It's Friday

than /ðən; strong ðæn/ conj, prep **1** (used in comparing things): This is bigger than that. **2** when; as soon as: No sooner had we started to eat than the doorbell rang.

thank /θæŋk/ vt express one's gratefulness to **thanks** n [P] **1** (words expressing) gratefulness **2 thanks to** because of ~**ful** adj **1** glad **2** grateful ~**fully** adv ~**less** adj not likely to be rewarded with thanks or success

thanks /θæŋks/ interj thank you

thanks·giv·ing /ˌθæŋksˈgɪvɪŋ/ n [C;U] (an) expression of gratefulness, esp. to God

Thanksgiving Day /ˌ··ˈ·ˌ/ n national holiday on the fourth Thursday in November

thank you /ˈ·ˈ·/ interj **1** (used for politely expressing thanks or acceptance) **2 no, thank you** (used for politely refusing an offer)

that¹ /ðæt/ determiner, pron those /ðoʊz/ **1** (being) the person, thing, or idea which is understood or has just been mentioned or shown: Look at that man over there. | Who told you that? | I'd like these apples, not those. **2 that's that** that is the end of the matter

that² /ðət; strong ðæt/ conj **1** (used) for introducing CLAUSES): She said that she couldn't come. **2** (used as a RELATIVE PRONOUN) which/who(m): This is the book that I bought.

that³ /ðæt/ adv to such a degree; so: It wasn't that difficult.

thaw /θɔ/ v **1** vi/t change from a solid frozen state to being liquid or soft **2** vi become friendlier, less formal, etc. ♦ n **1** period when ice and snow melt **2** increase in friendliness

the /ðə; before vowels ði; strong ði/ definite article, determiner **1** (used for speaking or writing of a particular thing): the sky | Close the door. **2** (used with some names of places etc.): the Rhine | the Pacific **3** (used before a singular noun to make it general): The lion is a wild animal. **4** (used for making an adjective into a noun): I like the French. (= French people) | To do the impossible. **5** (used with measures) each: paid by the hour | sold by the yard **6** (used before names of musical instruments): She plays the piano. **7** (used before the plural of 20, 30, etc., to show a period of 10 years): music of the 60s ♦ adv **1** (used in comparisons, to show that 2 things happen together): The more he eats, the fatter he gets. **2** (in comparisons to show that someone or something is better, worse, than before): She looks (all) the better for having quit her job. **3** (to show that someone or something is more than any other): She's the cleverest/the most sensible of them all.

the·a·ter /ˈθiətə/ n **1** building where plays are performed or movies are shown **2** the work of people involved with plays: He's in the theater. **3** large room where public talks are given **4** area of activity in a war –**atrical** /θiˈætrɪkəl/ adj **1** of the theater **2** too showy; not natural

the·at·er·go·er /ˈθiətəˌgoʊə/ n person who goes regularly to THEATERS (1)

thee /ði/ pron lit (object form of **thou**) you

theft /θɛft/ n [C;U] stealing

their /ðə; strong ðɛr/ determiner of them; their house

theirs /ðɛrz/ pron of them; their one(s): It's theirs.

them /ðəm, əm; strong ðɛm/ pron (object form of **they**): I want those books; give them to me.

theme /θim/ n **1** subject of a talk, piece of writing, etc. **2** repeated idea, image, or tune in writing, music, etc.

theme park /'· ·/ n enclosed outdoor area containing amusements which are all based on a single subject (e.g. space travel)

theme song /'· ·/ n short piece of music used regularly to introduce a famous person or television program

them·selves /ðəm'sɛlvz, ðɛm-/ pron 1 (reflexive form of they): They saw themselves on television. 2 (strong form of they): They built it themselves. 3 (all) by themselves: a alone b without help 4 to themselves not shared

then /ðɛn/ adv 1 at that time: I was happier then. 2 next; afterwards:... and then we went home. 3 in that case; as a result: Have you done your homework? Then you can watch television. 4 besides; also

the·ol·o·gy /θi'ɑlədʒi/ n [U] study of religious ideas and beliefs –ologian /ˌθiə'loudʒən/ n –ological /ˌθiə'lɑdʒɪkəl/ adj

theo·rem /'θiərəm, 'θɪrəm/ n MATHEMATICAL statement that can be proved by reasoning

the·o·ry /'θiəri, 'θɪri/ n 1 [C] statement intended to explain a fact or event 2 [U] general principles and methods as opposed to practice –retical /ˌθiə'rɛtɪkəl/ adj existing in or based on theory, not practice or fact –rize /'θiəˌraɪz/ vi form a theory

ther·a·peu·tic /ˌθɛrə'pyutɪk/ adj 1 for the treating or curing of disease 2 having a good effect on one's health or state of mind: I find swimming/knitting very therapeutic.

ther·a·py /'θɛrəpi/ n [C;U] treatment of illnesses of the body or mind –pist n

there[1] /ðɛr/ adv 1 at or to that place: He lives over there. 2 (used for drawing attention to someone or something): There goes John. 3 all there healthy in mind 4 there and then at that exact place and time 5 there you are: a here is what you wanted b I told you so ♦ interj (used for comforting someone or expressing victory, satisfaction, etc.): There, there. Stop crying. | There, I knew I was right.

there[2] pron (used for showing that something or someone exists or happens, usu. as the subject of **be**, **seem**, or **appear**): There's someone at the door to see you.

there·a·bouts /ˌðɛrə'baʊts, 'ðɛrəˌbaʊts/ adv near that place, time, number, etc.

there·af·ter /ðɛr'æftə/ adv fml after that

there·by /ðɛr'baɪ, 'ðɛrbaɪ/ adv fml by doing or saying that

there·fore /'ðɛrfɔr, -fou r/ adv for that reason; as a result

there·up·on /'ðɛrəˌpɑn, -ˌpɔn, ˌðɛrə'pɑn, -'pɔn/ adv fml 1 about that matter 2 without delay

ther·mal /'θəməl/ adj of, using, producing, caused by or keeping in heat: thermal underwear (= for use in cold weather) ♦ n rising current of warm air

ther·mo·dy·nam·ics /ˌθəmoudaɪ'næmɪks/ n [U] scientific study of heat and its power in driving machines

ther·mom·e·ter /θə'mɑmətə/ n instrument for measuring temperature

Ther·mos /'θəməs/ n tdmk bottle with a VACUUM between its 2 walls, for keeping liquids hot or cold

ther·mo·stat /'θəməˌstæt/ n apparatus for keeping a machine, room, etc., at an even temperature

the·sau·rus /θɪ'sɔrəs/ n dictionary with words arranged in groups according to similarities in meaning

these /ðiz/ pl. of THIS

the·sis /'θisɪs/ n -ses /-siz/ 1 long piece of writing on a particular subject, done to gain a higher university degree 2 opinion or statement supported by reasoned arguments

they /ðeɪ/ pron (used as the subject of a sentence) 1 those people, animals, or things 2 people in general: They say prices are going to rise. 3 (used to avoid saying he or she): If anyone knows, they should tell me.

they'd /ðeɪd/ short for: 1 they had 2 they would

they'll /ðeɪl, ðɛl/ short for: they will

they're /ðə/ strong ðɛr, ðeɪə/ short for: they are

they've /ðeɪv/ short for: they have

thick /θɪk/ adj 1 having a large or the stated distance between opposite surfaces: thick walls | walls 2 feet thick 2 (of liquid) not flowing easily 3 difficult to see through: thick mist 4 full of; covered with: furniture thick with dust 5 with many objects set close together: a thick forest 6 sl stupid ♦ adv 1 thickly 2 thick

and fast quickly and in large numbers ♦ *n* [*the+*S] part, place, etc., of greatest activity: *in the thick of the action* **2 through thick and thin** through both good and bad times ~**ly** *adv* ~**en** *vi/t* make or become thicker ~**ness** *n* **1** [C;U] being thick **2** [C] LAYER

thick-skinned /ˌ ˈ· ◄/ *adj* not easily offended

thief /θiːf/ *n* **thieves** /θiːvz/ person who steals

thigh /θaɪ/ *n* top part of the leg in humans and some animals

thim·ble /ˈθɪmbəl/ *n* small cap put over the end of the finger when sewing

thin /θɪn/ *adj* **-nn-** **1** having a small distance between opposite surfaces **2** not fat **3** (of a liquid) flowing (too) easily; weak **4** with few objects widely separated: *a thin audience* **5** easy to see through: *thin mist* **6** lacking force or strength: *a thin excuse* **7 thin end of the wedge** something which seems unimportant but will open the way for more serious things of a similar kind ♦ *adv* thinly ♦ *vi/t* make or become thinner ~**ly** *adv* ~**ness** *n* [U]

thin air /ˌ ˈ·/ *n* [U] *infml* state of not being seen or not existing

thing /θɪŋ/ *n* **1** [C] unnamed or unnameable object: *What do you use this thing for?* **2** [C] remark, idea, or subject: *What a nasty thing to say!* **3** [C] act; activity: *the first thing we have to do* **4** [C] event: *A funny thing happened today.* **5** [S] that which is necessary or desirable: *Cold beer's just the thing on a hot day.* **6** [S] the fashion or custom: *the latest thing in shoes* **7** [S] *sl* activity satisfying to one personally: *Tennis isn't really my thing.* **8 first thing** early in the morning **9 for one thing** (used for introducing a reason) **10 have a thing about** have a strong like or dislike for **11 a good/bad thing** it's sensible/not sensible: *It's a good thing we found you.* (= it's lucky) **12 make a thing of** give too much importance to **13 the thing** is what we must consider is **things** *n* [P] **1** general state of affairs; situation **2** one's personal possessions: *Pack your things.*

thing·a·ma·jig /ˈθɪŋəməˌdʒɪg/ *n infml* thing (1)

think /θɪŋk/ *v* **thought** /θɔːt/ **1** *vi* use the mind to make judgments **2** *vt* have an opinion; believe: *Do you think it will*

rain? **3** *vt* understand; imagine: *I can't think why you did it.* **4** *vt* have as a plan: *I think I'll go swimming tomorrow.* **5 think aloud** to speak one's thoughts as they come ~**er** *n*

think about *phr vt* consider seriously before making a decision

think of *phr vt* **1** form a possible plan for **2** have as an opinion about: *What do you think of that?* **3** take into account: *But think of the cost!* **4** remember **5 not think much of** have a low opinion of **6 think better of** decide against **7 think highly/well/little of** have a good/bad, etc., opinion of someone or something **8 think nothing of** regard as usual or easy

think out/through *phr vt* consider carefully and in detail

think over *phr vt* consider seriously

think up *phr vt* invent (esp. an idea)

think·ing /ˈθɪŋkɪŋ/ *n* [U] opinion: *What's the director's thinking on this?* ♦ *adj* thoughtful; able to think clearly

think tank /ˈ· ˌ/ *n* committee of experts established to produce ideas and give advice

thin-skinned /ˌ ˈ· ◄/ *adj* easily offended

third /θɜːd/ *determiner, adv, n, pron* 3rd

third de·gree /ˌ· ·ˈ·/ *n* [*the+*S] hard questioning and rough treatment

third par·ty /ˌ· ˈ·◄/ *n* **1** person other than the 2 main people concerned **2** person other than the holder protected by an insurance agreement

Third World /ˌ· ˈ·◄/ *n* [*the*] the countries of the world which are industrially less developed

thirst /θɜːst/ *n* **1** [S;U] desire for drink **2** [U] lack of drink: *I'm dying of thirst* **3** [S] strong desire: *the thirst for knowledge* ~**y** *adj* feeling or causing thirst

thir·teen /ˌθɜːˈtiːn/ *determiner, n, pron* 13 ~**th** *determiner, adv, n, pron* 13th

thir·ty /ˈθɜːti/ *determiner, n, pron* 30 ~**tieth** *determiner, adv, n, pron* 30th

this /ðɪs/ *determiner, pron* **these** /ðiːz/ **1** (one) going to be mentioned, or shown: *I'll come this morning.* | *Do it like this.* (= in the way about to be shown) **2** (one) near or nearer in place, time, thought, etc.: *Give me these, not those.* **3** *infml* a certain: *There were these two men standing there . . .* ♦ *adv* to this degree: *It was this big.*

this·tle /ˈθɪsəl/ n plant with prickly leaves and usu. purple flowers

thong /θɒŋ, θɑŋ/ n narrow length of leather used esp. for fastening

thongs /θɒŋz, θɑŋz/ n [P] leather or rubber shoes held on the foot with a thong

thorn /θɔrn/ n 1 sharp growth on a plant 2 **thorn in one's flesh/side** continual cause of annoyance ~**y** adj 1 prickly 2 difficult to deal with

thor·ough /ˈθɜroʊ, ˈθʌroʊ/ adj 1 complete in every way: *a thorough search* 2 careful about details ~**ly** adv ~**ness** n [U]

thor·ough·bred /ˈθɜrəbred, ˈθʌrə-/ n, adj (animal, esp. a horse) from parents of one very good breed

thor·ough·fare /ˈθɜrəˌfɛr, ˈθʌrə-/ n fml large public road

those /ðoʊz/ pl. of THAT

though /ðoʊ/ conj, adv 1 in spite of the fact (that): *Though it's hard work, I enjoy it.* 2 but: *I'll try, though I don't think I can.* 3 **as though** as if

thought[1] /θɔt/ v past t. & p. of THINK

thought[2] n 1 [C] something thought; idea, etc. 2 [U] thinking 3 [U] serious consideration 4 [U] intention: *I had no thought of causing any trouble.* 5 [C;U] attention; regard: *acting with no thought to her own safety* — see also SECOND THOUGHT ~**ful** adj 1 thinking deeply 2 paying attention to the wishes, needs, etc., of others ~**fully** adv ~**less** adj showing a selfish or careless lack of thought ~**lessly** adv

thou·sand /ˈθaʊzənd/ determiner, n, pron **thousand** or **thousands** 1000 ~**th** determiner, adv, n, pron 1000th

thrall /θrɔl/ n [U] lit state of being completely interested: *He held me in thrall.*

thrash /θræʃ/ n 1 vt beat (as if) with a whip or stick 2 vt defeat thoroughly 3 vi move wildly or violently

thread /θrɛd/ n 1 [C;U] very fine cord made by spinning cotton, silk, etc. 2 [C] line of reasoning connecting the parts of an argument or story 3 [C] raised line that winds around the outside of a screw 4 **hang by a thread** be in a very dangerous position ♦ vt 1 put thread through the hole in (a needle) 2 put (a film or TAPE) in place on an apparatus 3 put (things) together on a thread 4 **thread one's way through** go carefully through (crowds, etc.)

thread·bare /ˈθrɛdbɛr/ adj (of cloth) very worn: (fig.) *a threadbare* (= too often used) *excuse*

threat /θrɛt/ n 1 [C;U] expression of an intention to harm or punish someone 2 [C] something or someone regarded as a possible danger

threat·en /ˈθrɛtn/ v 1 vt make a threat (against): *They threatened to blow up the plane.* 2 vt give warning of (something bad): *The sky threatened rain.* 3 vi (of something bad) seem likely: *Danger threatens.*

three /θri/ determiner, n, pron 3

three-D /ˌθri ˈdiˑ◂/ n [U] three-dimensional form or a appearance

three-di·men·sion·al /ˌ·ˈ·····◂/ adj having length, depth, and height

three R's /ˌθri ˈɑrz/ n [the+P] reading, writing, and ARITHMETIC, considered as forming the base of children's education

thresh·old /ˈθrɛʃhoʊld, -ʃoʊld/ n 1 point of beginning: *scientists on the threshold of* (= about to make) *a research breakthrough* 2 piece of stone or wood across the bottom of a doorway

threw /θru/ v past t. of THROW

thrice /θraɪs/ adv lit 3 times

thrift /θrɪft/ n [U] not spending too much money ~**y** adj ♦ n SAVINGS AND LOAN

thrift shop /ˈ·◂/ also **thrift store** — n store that sells used goods cheaply

thrill /θrɪl/ n (something producing) a sudden strong feeling of excitement, fear, etc. ♦ vi/t (cause to) feel a thrill ~**er** n book, film, etc., telling a very exciting (crime) story

thrive /θraɪv/ vi develop well and be healthy, strong, or successful

throat /θroʊt/ n 1 passage from the mouth down inside the body 2 front of the neck

throb /θrɒb/ vi -**bb**- (of a machine, the action of the heart, etc.) beat heavily and regularly ♦ n throbbing

throes /θroʊz/ n [P] 1 lit sudden violent pains, esp. caused by dying 2 **in the throes of** struggling with (some difficulty)

throne /θroʊn/ n ceremonial seat of a king, queen, etc.: (fig.) *He ascended the throne.* (= became king)

throng /θrɒŋ, θrɑŋ/ n large crowd ♦ vi/t go as or fill with a throng

throt·tle /ˈθrɑtl/ vt seize (someone) by the throat to stop them breathing ♦ n VALVE controlling the flow of gas, etc., into an engine

through /θru/ *prep, adv* **1** in at one side (of) and out at the other: *Water flows through this pipe.* | *I opened the door and went through.* **2** from beginning to end (of): *I read through the letter.* **3** so as to finish successfully: *Did you get through your exam?* **4** past: *He drove through a red light.* ♦ *prep* **1** by means of; because of: *The war was lost through bad organization.* **2** up to and including: *Wednesday through Saturday* ♦ *adv* **1** so as to be connected by telephone **2** **through and through** completely ♦ *adj* **1** finished; done: *Are you through yet?* **2** having no further relationship: *I'm through with him!* **3** allowing a continuous journey: *a through train*

through·out /θru'aʊt/ *prep, adv* in, to, through, or during every part (of)

throw /θroʊ/ *v* **threw** /θru/, **thrown** /θroʊn/ **1** *vi/t* send (something) through the air with a sudden movement of the arm **2** *vt* move or put forcefully or quickly: *The two fighters threw themselves at each other.* | *I'll just throw on some clothes.* **3** *vt* cause to fall to the ground: *Her horse threw her.* **4** *vt* direct: *I think I can throw some light on the mystery.* **5** *vt* operate (a SWITCH) **6** *vt* shape from wet clay when making POTTERY **7** *vt* make one's voice appear to come from somewhere other than one's self **8** *vt infml* arrange (a party) **9** *vt* confuse; shock: *Her reply really threw me.* **10** **throw a fit** have a sudden uncontrolled attack of anger **11** **throw oneself into** to start to work very busily at **12** **throw oneself on/upon** put complete trust in **13** **throw one's weight around** give orders to others, because one thinks one is important **14** **throw oneself at** *phr vt* **a** rush violently towards someone **b** attempt forcefully to win someone's love ♦ *n* **1** act of throwing **2** distance thrown **~er** *n*

throw away *phr vt* **1** get rid of **2** waste (an opportunity, chance, etc.)

throw in *phr vt* **1** supply additionally without increasing the price **2** **throw in the towel** admit defeat

throw off *phr vt* **1** recover from **2** escape from **3** confuse

throw open *phr vt* allow people to enter

throw out *phr vt* **1** get rid of **2** refuse to accept

throw over *phr vt* end a relationship with

throw together *phr vt* build or make hastily

throw up *phr v* **1** *vi* VOMIT **2** *vt* bring to notice: *The investigation has thrown up some interesting facts.* **3** *vt* build hastily

throw·a·way /'θroʊəweɪ/ *adj* made to be used and then gotten rid of: *a throwaway camera*

thrush /θrʌʃ/ *n* common singing bird with a spotted breast

thrust /θrʌst/ *vi/t* **thrust** push forcefully and suddenly ♦ *n* **1** [C] act of thrusting **2** [U] engine's power of moving forwards **3** [U] (main) meaning

thud /θʌd/ *vi, n* **-dd-** (make) the dull sound of something heavy falling

thug /θʌg/ *n* violent criminal

thumb[1] /θʌm/ *n* **1** short thick finger set apart from the others **4** **all thumbs** *infml* very awkward with the hands **3** **stick out like a sore thumb** *infml* seem out of place **4** **thumb one's nose at** *infml* make fun of **5** **thumbs up/down** *infml* an expression of approval/disapproval **6** **under someone's thumb** *infml* under the control of someone — see also GREEN THUMB, RULE OF THUMB

thumb[2] *v* **thumb a ride** ask passing motorists for a ride by signaling with one's thumb — see HITCHHIKE

thumb through *phr vi/t* look through (a book) quickly

thumb·nail /'θʌmneɪl/ *n* nail of the thumb ♦ *adj* small or short: *a thumbnail description/sketch*

thumb·tack /'θʌmtæk/ *n* small nail pushed in with the thumb

thump /θʌmp/ *v* **1** *vt* hit hard **2** *vi* make a repeated dull sound: *My heart thumped.* ♦ *n* (sound of) a heavy blow

thun·der /'θʌndər/ *n* [U] **1** loud explosive noise that follows lightning: (fig.) *the thunder of distant guns* **2** **steal someone's thunder** spoil the effect of someone's action by doing it first ♦ *v* **1** *vi* produce thunder **2** *vi* produce or go with a loud noise **3** *vt* shout loudly **~ous** *adj* very loud: *thunderous applause*

thun·der·bolt /'θʌndərboʊlt/ *n* **1** thunder and lightning together **2** event causing great shock

thun·der·clap /ˈθʌndəˌklæp/ n a single loud crash of thunder

thun·der·head /ˈθʌndəˌhed/ n large dark cloud likely to bring rain

thun·der·storm /ˈθʌndəˌstɔrm/ n storm with THUNDER and LIGHTNING

thun·der·struck /ˈθʌndəˌstrʌk/ adj shocked

Thurs·day /ˈθɜrzdi, -deɪ/ n the 5th day of the week, between Wednesday and Friday

thus /ðʌs/ adv fml 1 in this way 2 with this result 3 **thus far** up until now

thwart /θwɔrt/ vt prevent from happening or succeeding

thy·roid /ˈθaɪrɔɪd/ n organ in the neck that controls growth and activity

tic /tɪk/ n sudden unconscious movement of the muscles

tick¹ /tɪk/ n short repeated sound of a watch or clock

tick² v 1 vi make a TICK¹ (1) 2 **make someone/something tick** infml provide a person/thing with reasons for behaving, working, etc., in a particular way

tick off phr vt infml cause anger

tick over phr vi continue working at slow steady rate

tick³ n very small insect that sucks blood from whatever it bites

ticker-tape pa·rade /ˈtɪkə teɪp pəˌreɪd/ n a PARADE celebrating someone when CONFETTI is thrown from tall buildings onto the street below

tick·et /ˈtɪkɪt/ n 1 piece of paper or card showing that payment for a service has been made: a bus/movie ticket 2 piece of card showing the price, size, etc., of goods 3 printed notice of an offense against traffic laws 4 infml exactly the thing needed: This hammer is just the ticket.

tick·le /ˈtɪkəl/ v 1 vt touch (someone's body) lightly to produce laughter, a feeling of nervous excitement, etc.: Stop tickling my toes! 2 vi give or feel a prickly sensation 3 vt delight or amuse ♦ n [C;U] (act or feel of) tickling —**lish** adj 1 sensitive to being tickled 2 (of a problem or situation) rather difficult

tic-tac-toe /ˌtɪk tæk ˈtoʊ/ n children's game in which 2 players draw X's and O's in a pattern of 9 squares

tid·al wave /ˈtaɪdl weɪv/ n very large dangerous ocean wave: (fig.) a tidal wave of public disapproval

tid·bit /ˈtɪdˌbɪt/ n small piece of particularly nice food: (fig.) a few tidbits of information

tide¹ /taɪd/ n 1 regular rise and fall of the sea: The tide's out. (= has fallen to its lowest point) 2 current caused by this: strong tides 3 feeling or tendency that moves or changes like the tide: the tide of public opinion **tidal** adj

tide² v **tide over** phr vt help (someone) through (a difficult period)

tid·ings /ˈtaɪdɪŋz/ n [P] lit news

ti·dy /ˈtaɪdi/ adj 1 neat 2 infml fairly large: a tidy income ♦ vi/t make (things) tidy **tidily** adv **tidiness** n [U]

tie¹ /taɪ/ n 1 band of cloth worn around the neck 2 a card, string, etc., used for fastening something 3 something that unites: the ties of friendship 4 something that limits one's freedom 5 result in which each competitor gains an equal number of points, votes, etc.

tie² v **tied**; pres. p. **tying** 1 vt fasten by knotting: tie a parcel/one's shoe laces 2 vt make (a knot or BOW²) (3) 3 vi/t finish (a game or competition) with a TIE¹ (5)

tie down phr vt 1 limit the freedom of 2 force to be exact

tie in phr vi have a close connection

tie up phr vt 1 limit free use of (money, property, etc.) 2 connect 3 **tied up** very busy

tie-breaker /ˈtaɪˌbreɪkə/ n play to decide who wins a tennis SET³ (4) or other competition

tie-in /ˈ·ˌ·/ n product that is connected in some way with a new film, television show, etc.

tier /tɪr/ n 1 any of a number of rising rows of esp. seats 2 level of organization

tie tack /ˈ·ˌ·/ n decorative CLIP for holding a TIE¹ (1) in place

ti·ger /ˈtaɪgə/ **tigress** /ˈtaɪgrɪs/ fem. — n 1 large Asian wild cat that has yellowish fur with black bands 2 fierce or brave person — see also PAPER TIGER

tight /taɪt/ adj 1 firmly fixed in place; closely fastened: The cases were packed tight in the back. | Is the roof watertight? 2 fully stretched 3 fitting (too) closely; leaving no free room or time: tight shoes | a tight schedule 4 difficult to obtain:

Money is tight just now. **5** marked by close competition: *a tight game/finish* **6** *sl* ungenerous with money **7** *sl* drunk **8** in a close relationship **9 in a tight corner/spot** in a difficult position ♦ *adv* tightly ~**ly** *adv* ~**en** *vi/t* make or become tighter ~**ness** *n* [U] **tights** *n* [P] very close-fitting garment covering the legs and lower body

tight-fist·ed /ˌtaɪtˈfɪstɪd◄/ *adj* very ungenerous with money ~**ness** *n* [U]

tight-lipped /ˌ ˈ ◄/ *adj* **1** having the lips pressed together **2** not saying anything

tight-rope /ˈtaɪtˈroʊp/ *n* rope tightly stretched high above the ground, on which someone walks

tight-wad /ˈtaɪtˈwɑd/ *n infml* someone who hates spending or giving money

tile /taɪl/ *n* thin shaped piece of baked clay, etc., used for covering roofs, walls, floors, etc. ♦ *vt* cover with tiles

till¹ /tɪl/ *prep, conj* until

till² /tɪl/ *n* drawer where money is kept in a store

till³ /tɪl/ *vt lit* cultivate (the ground)

til·ler /ˈtɪlə/ *n* long handle for turning a boat's RUDDER

tilt /tɪlt/ *vi/t* (cause to) slope (as if) by raising one end ♦ *n* [C;U] **1** slope **2 (at) full tilt** at full speed

tim·ber /ˈtɪmbə/ *n* **1** [U] wood for building **2** [U] growing trees **3** [C] wooden beam, esp. in a ship

time /taɪm/ *n* **1** [U] continuous measurable quantity from the past, through the present, and into the future **2** [S;U] period: *It happened a long time ago.* | *I don't have (the) time to do it.* (= I am too busy doing other things) **3** period in which an action is completed, esp. in a race: *Her time was just under 4 minutes.* **4** [U] particular point stated in hours, minutes, seconds, etc.: *The time is 4 o'clock.* **5** [C;U] particular point in the year, day, etc.: *We both arrived at the same time.* | *in summertime* | *It's time we were leaving.* **6** [C] occasion: *I've been here several times.* **7** [C] experience connected with a period or occasion: *We had a great time at the party.* **8** [C] period in history: *in ancient times* **9** [U] point when something should happen: *The plane arrived on time.* (= not early or late) **10** [U] rate of speed of a piece of music **11 ahead of one's time** with ideas not accepted in the

period in which one lives **12 all the time** continuously **13 at a time** singly/in groups of 2/3, etc.: *We went into her office 2 at a time.* **14 at all times** always **15 at one time** formerly **16 at the same time:** a together **b** however; NEVERTHELESS **17 at times** sometimes **18 behind the times** old-fashioned **19 buy time** *infml* delay an action or decision in order to give oneself more time **20** *sl* **do time** go to prison **21 for a time** for a short period **22 for the time being** for a limited period at present **23 from time to time** sometimes **24 have no time for someone** dislike someone **25 in no time** very quickly **26 in time:** a after a certain amount of time has passed **b** early or soon enough **27 take one's time** not hurry **28 the time of one's life** have a very enjoyable experience **29 time and (time) again/time after time** repeatedly — see also TIMES ♦ *vt* **1** arrange the time at which (something) happens **2** measure the time taken by or for **3** (in sports) make (a shot) at exactly the right moment ~**less** *adj* **1** unending **2** not changed by time ~**ly** *adj fml* happening at just the right time: *a timely warning* **timer** *n* person or machine that measures or records time — see also OLD TIMER

time and a half /ˌ ·· ˈ ·/ *n* rate of payment equal to 1½ times the usual rate: *we get paid time and a half on weekends.*

time bomb /ˈ· ·/ *n* **1** bomb set to explode at a particular time **2** situation likely to become very dangerous

time card /ˈ· ·/ *n* card on which one's hours worked are marked by a machine

time-con·sum·ing /ˈ· ·ˌ··/ *adj* requiring a long time to do: *time-consuming work*

time frame /ˈ· ·/ *n* period of time in which something is expected to happen

time-hon·ored /ˈ· ˌ··/ *adj* having existed or worked well for a long time: *a time-honored tradition*

time lim·it /ˈ· ˌ··/ *n* period of time in which something must be done

times /taɪmz/ *n* (used to show an amount that is calculated by multiplying something the stated number of times): *Their house is at least 3 times the size of ours.* ♦ *prep* multiplied by: *3 times 3 is 9.*

time sig·na·ture /ˈ· ˌ··/ *n* mark, esp. 2 numbers, to show what speed music should be played at

time·ta·ble /ˈtaɪmˌteɪbəl/ n (list of) the order of events in a program, etc.

time warp /ˈ. ./ n infml feeling that one is in a different time in history or in the future

time zone /ˈ. ./ n area within which all clocks are set to the same time: *the mountain time zone*

tim·id /ˈtɪmɪd/ adj fearful; lacking courage ~**ly** adv ~**ity** /tɪˈmɪdəti/ n [U]

tim·ing /ˈtaɪmɪŋ/ n [U] ability to decide the right time to do something: *good/bad timing*

tin /tɪn/ n 1 [U] soft whitish metal ~**y** adj 1 of or like tin 2 having a thin metallic sound

tin can /ˌ. ˈ., ˈ. ./ n small closed metal container in which food is sold

tin·foil /ˈtɪnfɔɪl/ n [U] very thin, bendable sheet of shiny metal

tinge /tɪndʒ/ vt give a small amount of color to: *black hair tinged with gray* | (fig.) *admiration tinged with jealousy* ♦ [S] small amount

tin·gle /ˈtɪŋgəl/ vi, n [S] (feel) a slight, not unpleasant, stinging sensation

tin·ker /ˈtɪŋkə/ vi work without a definite plan or useful results, making small changes, esp. when trying to repair or improve something

tin·kle /ˈtɪŋkəl/ vi 1 make light metallic sounds 2 infml urinate (URINE) ♦ n 1 tinkling sound 2 act of tinkling (2)

tin·sel /ˈtɪnsəl/ n [U] 1 threads of shiny material used for (Christmas) decorations 2 something showy that is really cheap and worthless

tint /tɪnt/ n place or delicate shade of a color ♦ vt give a tint to

ti·ny /ˈtaɪni/ adj extremely small

tip¹ /tɪp/ n 1 (pointed) end of something: *the tips of one's fingers* 2 part stuck on the end: *cigarettes with filter tips* 3 **on the tip of one's tongue** not quite able to be remembered ♦ vt -**pp**- put a tip on

tip² /tɪp/ v -**pp**- 1 vi/t (cause to) fall over 2 vi/t (cause to) lean at an angle

tip³ n small amount of money given to someone who does a service ♦ vi/t -**pp**- give a tip (to)

tip⁴ n helpful piece of advice ♦ vt -**pp**- suggest as likely to succeed

tip off phr vt give a warning or piece of secret information

tip-off /ˈ. ./ n 1 piece of secret information 2 beginning of play in BASKETBALL

tip·sy /ˈtɪpsi/ adj infml slightly drunk

tip·toe /ˈtɪptoʊ/ n **on tiptoe** on one's toes with the rest of the foot raised ♦ vi walk on tiptoe

ti·rade /ˈtaɪreɪd, taɪˈreɪd/ n long, angry speech

tire¹ /ˈtaɪə/ vi/t (cause to) become tired ~**less** adj never getting tired ~**some** adj 1 annoying 2 uninteresting

tire² n thick band of rubber around the outside edge of a wheel

tired /ˈtaɪəd/ adj 1 needing rest or sleep 2 no longer interested: *I'm tired of doing this; let's go for a walk.* 3 showing lack of imagination or new thought: *tired ideas* ~**ness** n [U]

tis·sue /ˈtɪʃu/ n 1 [C;U] the material animals and plants are made of; cells: *lung tissue* 2 [U] thin light paper, esp. for wrapping 3 [C] paper handkerchief 4 [C] fml something formed as if by weaving threads together: *a tissue of lies*

ti·tan·ic /taɪˈtænɪk/ adj very great in degree: *a titanic struggle*

ti·ta·ni·um /taɪˈteɪniəm/ n [U] light strong metal used in compounds

tit for tat /ˌtɪt fə ˈtæt/ n [U] something unpleasant given in return for something unpleasant one has suffered

tit·il·late /ˈtɪtlˌeɪt/ vt excite, esp. sexually –**lation** /ˌtɪtlˈeɪʃən/ n [U]

ti·tle /ˈtaɪtl/ n 1 [C] name of a book, play, painting, etc. 2 [C] word such as "Mrs.," "President," or "Doctor" used before someone's name to show rank, office, or profession 3 [S;U] legal right to ownership 4 [C] position of a person who has won: *the world heavyweight boxing title*

title deed /ˈ.. ./ n document showing ownership of property

TLC n tender loving care; very kind and special treatment

TNT n [U] powerful explosive

to /tə; before vowels tu; strong tu/ prep 1 in a direction towards: *the road to Fredonia* 2 a (used before a verb to show it is the INFINITIVE): *I want to go.* b (used in place of infinitive): *We didn't want to come but we had to.* 3 in order to: *I came by car to save time.* 4 so as to be in: *I was sent to prison.* 5 as far as: *from beginning to end* 6 for the attention or possession of: *I told/gave it to her.* 8 in connection with: *the answer to a question* 9 in relation or comparison with: *That's nothing to what it could have been.* | *We won by 6 points to 3.* **10** (of time) before: *It's 10 to 4.* **11** per: *This car gets 30 miles to the gallon.* ♦ /tu/ *adv* **1** so as to be shut: *Pull the door to.* **2** into consciousness: *She came to.*

toad /toʊd/ *n* animal like a large FROG

toad·stool /ˈtoʊdstul/ *n* (uneatable) FUNGUS

toad·y /ˈtoʊdi/ *vi* be too nice to someone of higher rank, esp. for personal advantage ♦ *n* person who toadies

to and fro /ˌtu ənd ˈfroʊ/ *adv* forwards and backwards or from side to side: *The door swung to and fro in the breeze.*

toast /toʊst/ *n* **1** [U] bread made brown by heating **2** [C] act of ceremonial drinking to show respect or express good wishes: *They drank a toast to their guest.* ♦ *vt* **1** make brown by heating **2** warm thoroughly **3** drink to TOAST (2) to ~**er** *n* electrical apparatus for making TOAST (1) ~**y** *adj* comfortably warm

to·bac·co /təˈbækoʊ/ *n* [U] dried leaves of a certain plant prepared esp. for smoking in cigarettes, pipes, etc.

to·bog·gan /təˈbagən/ *n* long board for carrying people over snow **toboggan** *vi*

to·day /təˈdeɪ/ *adv, n* [U] **1** (on) this day **2** (at) this present time

tod·dle /ˈtadl/ *vi* **1** walk, esp. with short unsteady steps **2** *infml* walk; go ~**dler** *n* child who has just learned to walk

toe[1] /toʊ/ *n* **1** any of the 5 small movable parts at the end of the foot **2** part of a shoe or sock covering these **3 on one's toes** fully ready for action

toe[2] *v* **toe the line** act obediently

tof·fee /ˈtɔfi, ˈtafi/ *n* [C;U] (piece of) a hard brown candy made from sugar and butter

to·fu /ˈtoʊfu/ *n* white soft food made from SOYBEANS

to·ga /ˈtoʊgə/ *n* loose outer garment worn in ancient Rome

to·geth·er[1] /təˈgɛðər/ *adv* **1** in or into a single group, body, or place **2** with each other **3** at the same time **4** in agreement; combined **5 together with** in addition to ~**ness** *n* [U] friendliness

together[2] *adj infml* **1** (of a person) very much in control of life, actions, etc. **2 get it together** have things under control

tog·gle /ˈtagəl/ *n* **1** wooden button in a bar or WEDGE shape **2** electrical apparatus with two positions

toil /tɔɪl/ *n* [U] *lit* hard work ♦ *vi lit* work or move with great effort

toi·let /ˈtɔɪlɪt/ *n* **1** [C] a seatlike apparatus for receiving and taking away the body's waste matter **2** [U] *fml* act of washing, dressing oneself, etc.

toilet pa·per /ˈ·· ˌ··/ *n* [U] paper for cleaning oneself after passing waste matter from the body

toi·let·ries /ˈtɔɪlətriz/ *n* [P] things used in washing, making oneself clean, etc.

to·ken /ˈtoʊkən/ *n* **1** outward sign: *They wore black as a token of mourning.* **2** small part that represents something larger — see also **by the same token** (SAME[1]) ♦ *adj* **1** being a small part representing something greater **2** *derog* done so as to seem acceptable: *a token effort*

told /toʊld/ *v past t. and p. of* TELL

tol·e·rate /ˈtalə₁reɪt/ *vt* **1** permit (something one disagrees with) **2** suffer (someone or something) without complaining ~**rable** /ˈtalərəbəl/ *adj* fairly good; not too bad ~**rably** *adv fml* fairly ~**rance** *n* **1** [C;U] ability to suffer pain, hardship, etc., without being harmed or damaged: *a low tolerance to cold* **2** [U] allowing people to behave in a way one disagrees with, without getting annoyed **3** [U] toleration (1) ~**rant** *adj* showing or practicing tolerance (2) ~**ration** /ˌtalə₁ˈreɪʃən/ *n* [U] **1** allowing opinions, customs, etc., different from one's own to be freely held or practiced **2** tolerance (2)

toll[1] /toʊl/ *n* **1** tax paid for using a road, bridge, etc. **2** bad effect of illness, misfortune, etc.: *The death toll in the accident was 9.*

toll[2] *vi/t* ring (a bell) or be rung slowly and repeatedly

toll booth /ˈ· ˌ·/ *n* place where one pays to use a particular road, bridge, etc.

toll-free /ˌ· ˈ·◂/ *adj, adv* (of a telephone call or number) not costing any money

tom·a·hawk /ˈtaməˌhɔk/ *n* Native American ax

to·ma·to /təˈmeɪtoʊ/ *n* -**toes** soft red fruit eaten raw or cooked as a vegetable

tomb /tum/ *n* (large decorative cover for) a grave

tom·boy /ˈtambɔɪ/ *n* spirited young girl who enjoys rough and noisy activities

tom·cat /ˈtɑmkæt/ n male cat

tome /toʊm/ n lit or humor large heavy book

to·mor·row /təˈmɔroʊ, -ˈmɑr-/ adv on the day following today ♦ n 1 [U] day after today 2 [S;U] future

tom-tom /ˈtɑmtɑm/ n long narrow drum played with the hands

ton /tʌn/ n 1 a measure of weight equal to 2000 pounds 2 also **tons** pl. — a very large amount 3 **come down on someone like a ton of bricks** infml turn the full force of one's anger against someone, usu. as a punishment **tons** adv sl very much

tone¹ /toʊn/ n 1 [C] quality of sound, esp. of a musical instrument or the voice 2 [C] variety or shade of a color 3 [U] general quality or nature 4 [U] proper firmness of the body's organs and muscles **tonal** adj

tone² v

tone down phr vt reduce in force

tone up phr vt make stronger, brighter, more effective, or healthy, etc.

tone-deaf /ˈ· ·/ adj unable to tell the difference between musical notes

ton·er /ˈtoʊnə/ n [U] black powder used in computer PRINTERs, PHOTOCOPIERs, etc.

tongs /tɑŋz, tɔŋz/ n [P] 2 movable arms joined at one end, for holding and lifting things

tongue /tʌŋ/ n 1 movable organ in the mouth used for talking, tasting, licking (LICK), etc.: (fig.) She has a sharp tongue. (= a severe or unkind way of speaking) 2 object like this in shape or purpose: tongues of flame 3 lit language 4 **hold one's tongue** remain silent 5 (with) **tongue in cheek** saying or doing something one does not seriously mean

tongue-tied /ˈ· ·/ adj unable to speak freely, esp. because of nervousness

tongue twist·er /ˈ· ˌ··/ n word or phrase difficult to say

ton·ic /ˈtɑnɪk/ n 1 [C] something, esp. a medicine, that increases health or strength 2 [U] tonic water: a gin and tonic

tonic wa·ter /ˈ·· ˌ··/ n [U] gassy water usu. mixed with alcoholic drink

to·night /təˈnaɪt/ adv, n (during) the night of today

ton·sil /ˈtɑnsəl/ n either of 2 small organs at the back of the throat

ton·sil·li·tis /ˌtɑnsəˈlaɪtɪs/ n [U] painful soreness of the tonsils

too /tu/ adv 1 to a greater degree than is necessary or good: You're driving too fast. 2 also: I've been to Montreal, and to Quebec too. 3 in fact 4 **only too** very

took /tʊk/ v past t. of TAKE

tool /tul/ n instrument held in the hand, such as an ax, hammer, etc.

toot /tut/ vt make a short warning sound with (a horn) **toot** n

tooth /tuθ/ n **teeth** /tiθ/ 1 small bony object growing in the mouth, used for biting 2 any of the pointed parts standing out from a comb, SAW, COG, etc. 3 ability to produce an effect: The present law has no teeth. 4 **armed to the teeth** very heavily armed 5 **fight tooth and nail** fight very violently 6 **get one's teeth into** do a job very actively and purposefully 7 **in the teeth of** against and in spite of: in the teeth of fierce opposition 8 **lie through one's teeth** lie shamelessly 9 **set someone's teeth on edge** give someone an unpleasant sensation caused by certain acid tastes or high sounds — see also SWEET TOOTH **~less** adj **~y** adj

tooth·ache /ˈtuθeɪk/ n pain in a tooth

tooth·brush /ˈtuθbrʌʃ/ n small brush for cleaning one's teeth

tooth·paste /ˈtuθpeɪst/ n [U] paste for cleaning one's teeth

tooth·pick /ˈtuθˌpɪk/ n short, thin pointed stick for removing food from the teeth

top¹ /tɑp/ n 1 the highest or upper part: the top of a tree 2 the best or most important part or place: at the top of the class 3 cover: bottle tops 4 **at the top of (one's) voice** as loudly as possible 5 **from top to bottom** all through; completely 6 **from top to toe** (of a person) completely 7 **get on top of** infml too much for: This work is getting on top of me. 8 **on top of: a** able to deal with **b** in addition to 9 **on top of the world** infml very happy — see also **blow one's top** (blow¹) **~less** adj leaving the breasts bare ♦ adj highest, best, etc.: at top speed (= very fast)

top² vt **-pp- 1** be higher, better, or more than: Our profits have topped $1 million. **2** form a top for: a cake topped with whipped cream **3 top the bill** be chief actor or actress in a play

top off *phr vt* complete successfully by a last action

top³ *n* child's toy that spins around

to·paz /'toʊpæz/ *n* [C;U] (precious stone cut from) a yellowish mineral

top brass /ˌ ˈ·/ *n* [U;P] *sl* officers of high rank, esp. in the armed forces

top dog /ˌ ˈ·/ *n* person in the most advantageous or powerful position

top drawer /ˌ ˈ·◂/ *n* highest level of society, etc.

Top 40 /ˌtɒp ˈfɔrti/ *n* 40 most popular songs (at a given time or now)

top hat /ˌ· ˈ·/ *n* man's formal tall usu. black hat

top-heav·y /ˌ· ˈ·◂/ *adj* too heavy at the top

top·ic /'tɒpɪk/ *n* subject for conversation, writing, etc.

top·ic·al /'tɒpɪkəl/ *adj* of or being a subject of present interest ~ly *adv*

top-notch /ˌ· ˈ·◂/ *adj* being one of the best

to·pog·ra·phy /tə'pɒgrəfi/ *n* [U] (science of describing) the shape and height of land **–phical** /ˌtɒpə'græfɪkəl/ *adj*

top·ple /'tɒpəl/ *vi/t* (cause to) become unsteady and fall down: (fig.) *The scandal toppled the government.*

top-se·cret /ˌ· ˈ·◂/ *adj* that must be kept extremely secret

top·sy-tur·vy /ˌtɒpsi ˈtɜrvi◂/ *adj, adv* in complete disorder and confusion

torch /tɔrtʃ/ *n* **1** mass of burning material carried by hand to give light **2** lamp that blows a flame (e.g. for burning off paint) ♦ *vt sl* set fire to

tore /tɔr, toʊr/ *v past t. of* TEAR¹

tor·ment¹ /'tɔrment/ *n* [C;U] very great suffering

torment² /tɔr'mɛnt/ *vt* cause torment to ~**or** *n*

torn /tɔrn, toʊrn/ *v past p. of* TEAR

tor·na·do /tɔr'neɪdoʊ/ *n* **-does** *or* **-dos** very violent wind that spins at great speed

tor·pe·do /tɔr'pidoʊ/ *n* **-does** long narrow explosive apparatus driven by a motor, which is fired through the sea to destroy ships ♦ *vt* attack or destroy (as if) with a torpedo

tor·rent /'tɔrənt, 'tar-/ *n* violently rushing stream of water: (fig.) *torrents of abuse* **–rential** /tə'rɛnʃəl, tɔ-/ *adj: torrential rain*

tor·rid /'tɒrɪd, 'tar-/ *adj* **1** (esp. of weather) very hot **2** full of strong feelings and uncontrolled activity, esp. sexual: *a torrid love affair*

tor·so /'tɔrsoʊ/ *n* **-sos** human body without the head and limbs

tort /tɔrt/ *n law* wrongful but not criminal act

tor·til·la /tɔr'tiyə/ *n* flat bread eaten with Mexican food

tor·toise /'tɔrtəs/ *n* land animal with a hard shell, that moves slowly

tor·toise·shell /'tɔrtəsˌʃɛl, 'tɔrtəsˌʃɛl/ *n* [U] material from a tortoise's or TURTLE's shell, brown with yellowish marks

tor·tu·ous /'tɔrtʃuəs/ *adj* **1** twisted; winding **2** not direct in speech, thought or action ~**ly** *adv*

tor·ture /'tɔrtʃə/ *vt* cause great pain or suffering to out of cruelty, as a punishment, etc. ♦ *n* **1** act of torturing **2** [C;U] severe pain or suffering **–turer** *n*

toss /tɒs/ *v* **1** *vt* throw **2** *vi/t* (cause to) move about rapidly and pointlessly: *He tossed and turned all night, unable to sleep.* **3** *vt* move or lift (part of the body) rapidly: *She tossed her head.* **4** *vt* mix lightly: *toss a salad* **5** *vi/t* throw (a coin) to decide something according to which side lands upwards: *There's only one cookie left — let's toss for it.* ♦ *n* [C] act of tossing

toss-up /ˈ· ·/ *n* [S] even chance; unsureness

tot¹ /tɒt/ *n* very small child

tot² *v* **-tt- tot up** *phr vt* add up

to·tal /'toʊtl/ *adj* complete; whole ♦ *n* **1** complete — see also GRAND TOTAL, SUM-TOTAL amount **2 in total** when all have been added up ♦ *vt* **-l- 1** be when added up: *His debts totaled $9000.* **2** destroy completely: *His car was totaled in the accident.* ~**ly** *adv: totally different* ~**ity** /toʊ'tæləti/ *n* [U] *fml* completeness

to·tal·i·tar·i·an /toʊˌtælə'tɛriən/ *adj* of or based on a centrally controlled system of government that does not allow any political opposition ~**ism** *n* [U]

tote /toʊt/ *vt infml* carry, esp. with difficulty

totem pole /'toʊtəm ˌpoʊl/ *n* **1** tall wooden pole with faces cut into it and painted **2 low man on the totem pole** person in a low position who does the dull work

tot·ter /ˈtɑtə/ vi move or walk in an unsteady manner, as if about to fall: (fig.) their tottering economy

touch¹ /tʌtʃ/ v 1 vi/t be separated (from) by no space at all: Their hands touched. 2 vi/t feel or make connection (with), esp. with the hands: The model is fragile, don't touch (it). | I never touch alcohol. 4 vt compare with: Nothing can touch a cold drink on a hot day! 5 vt cause to feel pity, sympathy, etc.: a touching story 6 touch base (with someone) in order to keep in CONTACT ~ed adj 1 grateful 2 slightly crazy ~y adj easily offended or annoyed ~ily adv ~iness n [U]

  touch down phr vi (of a plane or spacecraft) land

  touch off phr vt cause (a violent event) to start

  touch on/upon phr vt talk about shortly

  touch up phr vt improve with small additions

touch² n 1 [U] sense of feeling 2 [C] way something feels: the silky touch of her skin 3 [C] act of touching 4 [U] connection, esp. so as to receive information: He's gone to Paris, but we keep in touch by letter. 5 [S] particular way of doing things: a woman's touch 6 [C] small details: putting the finishing touches to the plan 7 [S] special ability: I'm losing my touch. 8 [S] slight attack of an illness: a touch of the flu 9 [S] slight amount: It needs a touch more salt. 10 keep in touch continue CONTACT 11 lose touch lose contact — see also SOFT TOUCH

touch-and-go /ˌ· ·ˈ·◂/ adj of uncertain result; risky

touch·down /ˈtʌtʃdaʊn/ n 1 act of gaining 6 points in football 2 landing of a plane or spacecraft

touch foot·ball /ˈ· ˌ··/ n football game where players touch rather than TACKLE

touch·y /ˈtʌtʃi/ adj 1 easily offended or annoyed 2 (of a question, subject, etc.) requiring careful speech, because of the possibility of causing offense

tough /tʌf/ adj 1 not easily weakened or broken 2 difficult to cut or eat: tough meat 3 difficult: a tough job/problem 4 not kind, severe: a tough new law against drunken driving 5 unfortunate: tough luck ♦ n [C] rude or troublesome

young man ~ly adv ~en vi/t make or become tougher ~ness n [U]

tou·pee /tuˈpeɪ/ n small WIG worn by a man

tour /tʊr/ n 1 act of traveling around a country, walking around a building, etc., looking at interesting things 2 period of duty in a job, esp. in a foreign country 3 journey to take part in performances, sports matches, etc. ♦ vi/t visit as a tourist ~ism n [U] 1 traveling for pleasure, esp. during one's vacation 2 the business of providing vacations for tourists ~ist n person traveling for pleasure

tour de force /ˌtʊr də ˈfɔrs, -ˈfoʊrs/ n [S] show of great skill

tour·na·ment /ˈtʊrnəmənt, ˈtɜ-/ n 1 competition: a chess/tennis tournament 2 (in former times) competition of fighting skill

tour·ni·quet /ˈtʊrnɪkɪt, ˈtɜ-/ n something twisted tightly around a limb to stop bleeding

tout /taʊt/ vt derog 1 publicize as being valuable: touting his new ideas 2 try to persuade people to buy (one's goods or services)

tow /toʊ/ vt pull (esp. a vehicle) with a rope or chain ♦ n 1 act of towing 2 in tow following closely behind

to·ward /tɔrd, toʊrd, təˈwɔrd/ prep 1 in the direction of: He walked toward me. | She had her back toward me. 2 just before the time: We arrived toward noon. 3 in relation to: What are their feelings toward us? 4 for the purpose of: Each week we save $5 toward our vacation.

tow·a·way zone /ˈtoʊəweɪ ˌzoʊn/ n area where cars cannot be left or they will be removed

tow·el /ˈtaʊəl/ n piece of cloth or paper for drying things ♦ vt -l- rub or dry with a towel

tow·er /ˈtaʊə/ n 1 tall (part of a) building: a church tower 2 tall metal framework for signaling or broadcasting ♦ vi be very tall: (fig.) Intellectually he towers above (= is much better than) them all. ~ing adj very great: a towering rage

town /taʊn/ n 1 [C] large group of houses and other buildings where people live and work 2 [C] all the people who live in such a place 3 [U] the business or shopping center of a town 4 [S] (life in) towns and cities in general 5 go to town act or behave freely or wildly **6 (out) on the town** enjoying oneself, esp. at night **7 paint the town red** have a very enjoyable time, esp. in a wild or noisy manner

town hall /ˌ. ˈ./ n public building for a town's local government

town·house /ˈtaʊnhaʊs/ n house sharing 1 or more walls with another house or houses

town·ship /ˈtaʊnʃɪp/ n part of a COUNTY

tow truck /ˈ. ./ n strong truck for pulling vehicles that cannot move

tox·ic /ˈtɒksɪk/ adj poisonous: toxic waste (= harmful waste products from industry) ~**ity** /tɒkˈsɪsəti/ n [U]

tox·in /ˈtɒksɪn/ n poison produced in plants and animals

toy[1] /tɔɪ/ n **1** object for children to play with **2** small breed of dog

toy[2] v **toy with** phr v t **1** consider (an idea) not very seriously **2** play with or handle purposelessly

trace[1] /treɪs/ vt **1** find, esp. by following a course **2** copy lines or the shape of something using transparent paper ♦ n **1** [C;U] mark or sign showing the present presence of someone or something: She had vanished without trace. (= completely) **2** [C] small amount of something: traces of poison in his blood

trace[2] n rope, chain, etc. fastening a cart or carriage to the animal pulling it

track[1] /træk/ n **1** marks left by a person, animal, or vehicle that has passed before **2** narrow (rough) path or road **3** railroad line **4** course for racing **5** piece of music on a record or TAPE (2) **6** group of students of similar ability **7 cover one's tracks** keep one's movements, activities, etc., secret **8 in one's tracks** infml where one is; suddenly **9** keep/lose track of keep/ fail to keep oneself informed about a person, situation, etc. **10 make tracks** leave, esp. in a hurry **11 off the beaten track** not well known or often visited **12 on the right/wrong track** thinking or working correctly/incorrectly **13 a one-track mind** infml a tendency to think only of one thing or subject

track[2] vt **1** follow the TRACK[1] (1) of **2** sort (students) according to ability ~**er** n

track down phr vt find by hunting or searching

track and field /ˌ. ˈ ./ n [U] sports involving running races, jumping, and throwing objects

track meet /ˈ. ./ n sports competition including different running, jumping, and throwing events

track rec·ord /ˈ. ˌ../ n degree to which someone or something has performed well or badly up to now

tract[1] /trækt/ n **1** wide stretch of land **2** system of related organs in an animal: the digestive tract

tract[2] n fml short article on a religious or moral subject

trac·tion /ˈtrækʃən/ n [U] **1** type of pulling power: steam traction **2** force that prevents a wheel from slipping **3** medical treatment with a pulling apparatus used to cure a broken bone or similar injury (INJURE)

trac·tor /ˈtræktə/ n motor vehicle for pulling farm machinery

trade[1] /treɪd/ n **1** [U] business of buying, selling, or exchanging goods, esp. between countries **2** [C] particular business: the wine trade **3** [C] job, esp. needing skill with the hands: the printer's trade **4** [S] stated amount of business: doing a good trade — see also FREE TRADE

trade[2] v **1** vi buy and sell goods **2** vt exchange: I traded my radio for a typewriter. | (fig.) trading insults

trade in phr vt give in part payment for something new: I traded my old car in.

trade off phr vt balance (one situation or quality) against another, with the aim of producing an acceptable or desirable result

trade·mark /ˈtreɪdmɑrk/ n **1** sign or word put on a product to show who made it **2** thing by which a person or thing may habitually be recognized

trade name /ˈ. ./ n name given by a producer to a particular product

trade-off /ˈ. ./ n balance between two (opposing) situations or qualities

trade se·cret /ˌ. ˈ../ n information about a product known only to its makers

trade wind /ˈ. ./ n wind blowing almost continually towards the EQUATOR

tra·di·tion /trəˈdɪʃən/ n **1** [C] opinion, custom, principle, etc., passed down from the past to the present **2** [U] (passing down of) such customs, etc.: By tradition, brides in the West wear white. ~**al** adj ~**ally** adv

traf·fic /ˈtræfɪk/ n [U] **1** (movement of) vehicles on the road, planes in the sky, etc. **2** trade, esp. in illegal things **3** business done in carrying passengers or goods ♦ v **-ck- traffic in** phr vt trade in (esp. illegal things) **~ker** n: drug traffickers

traffic cop /ˈ·· ˌ·/ n infml official who controls the parking of vehicles on streets

traffic jam /ˈ·· ˌ·/ n long line of vehicles on the road that cannot move, or that only move very slowly

traffic lights /ˈ·· ˌ·/ n [P] set of colored lights for controlling road traffic

tra·ge·dy /ˈtrædʒədi/ n [C;U] **1** serious play that ends sadly **2** [U] these plays considered as a group **3** terrible, unhappy, or unfortunate event

tra·gic /ˈtrædʒɪk/ adj **1** of or related to TRAGEDY (2) **2** very sad, unfortunate, etc. **~ally** adv

trail /treɪl/ n **1** track or smell followed by a hunter: we're on their trail. (= following them closely) **2** path across rough country **3** stream of dust, smoke, people, etc., behind something moving ♦ v **1** vi/t drag or be dragged along behind **2** vt track **3** vi (of a plant) grow along a surface **~er** n **1** vehicle pulled by another **2** vehicle fastened to a car and used as a vacation home **3** MOBILE HOME **4** small pieces of a new film shown to advertise it

trailer park /ˈ·· ˌ·/ n area where TRAILERS (3) are parked and used as homes

train¹ /treɪn/ n **1** line of railroad cars pulled by an engine **2** set of related things one after another: It interrupted my train of thought. **3** part of a long garment that spreads over the ground behind the wearer **4** long line of moving people, animals or vehicles

train v **1** vi/t give or be given instruction, practice, or exercise: training a dog to jump over a fence **2** vt aim (a gun, etc.) **3** vt direct the growth of (a plant) **~ee** n person being trained **~er** n **~ing** n [S;U] **1** practical instruction **2** in/out of training in/not in a healthy condition for a sport, test of skill, etc.

traipse /treɪps/ vi walk without purpose or aim

trait /treɪt/ n fml particular quality of someone or something

trai·tor /ˈtreɪtə/ n someone disloyal, esp. to their country

tra·jec·to·ry /trəˈdʒektəri/ n fml curved path of an object fired or thrown through the air

tramp /træmp/ vi **1** walk heavily **2** sound of heavy walking **3** walk steadily, esp. over a long distance ♦ n wandering person with no home or job who begs for food or money

tram·ple /ˈtræmpəl/ vi/t step (on) heavily; crush under the feet

tram·po·line /ˌtræmpəˈlin, ˈtræmpəˌlin/ n frame with springy material on which people jump up and down

trance /træns/ n sleeplike condition of the mind

tran·quil /ˈtræŋkwəl/ adj pleasantly calm, quiet, or free from worry **~ize** vt make calm (esp. with tranquilizers) **~izer** n drug for reducing anxiety and making people calm **~ity** /træŋˈkwɪləti/ n [U] calmness

trans·act /trænˈsækt, -ˈzækt/ vt fml do and complete (a piece of business) **~ion** /-ˈsækʃən, -ˈzæk-/ n **1** [U] act of transacting **2** [C] piece of business **transactions** /trænˈzækʃənz/ n [P] records of meetings of a society

trans·at·lan·tic /ˌtrænzətˈlæntɪk◂/ adj connecting or concerning countries on both sides of the Atlantic Ocean

tran·scend /trænˈsend/ vt fml or lit go beyond (a limit or something within limits) **~ent** adj going far beyond ordinary limits

trans·con·ti·nen·tal /ˌtrænzkɑntəˈnentl, ˌtræns-/ adj crossing a CONTINENT: the first transcontinental railroad

tran·scribe /trænˈskraɪb/ vt **1** write an exact copy of **2** write down (something said) **3** arrange (a piece of music) for instrument or voice other than the original

tran·script /ˈtrænˌskrɪpt/ n **1** exact written or printed copy **2** official document listing all classes taken and grades received **~ion** /trænˈskrɪpʃən/ n **1** [U] act or process of transcribing **2** [C] transcript(1)

trans·fer¹ /trænsˈfɜ, trænsˈfɜ/ v **-rr- 1** vi/t move from one place, job, etc., to another **2** vt give ownership of property to another person **3** vi move from one vehicle to another **~able** adj

trans·fer² /ˈtrænsfɜ/ n **1** [C;U] act or process of transferring **2** [C] something transferred **~ence** /trænsˈfɜns, ˈtræns-fərəns/ n [U]

trans·form /træns'fɔrm/ vt change completely ~**ation** /ˌtrænsfə'meɪʃən/ n [C;U]: *the transformation of heat into power* ~**er** /træns'fɔrmə/ n apparatus for changing electrical force, esp. to a different VOLTAGE

trans·fu·sion /træns'fyuːʒən/ n [C;U] act of putting one person's blood into another's body

trans·gress /trænz'grɛs/ v fml 1 vt go beyond (a proper or legal limit) 2 vi do wrong ~**ion** /-'grɛʃən/ n [C;U] ~**or** /-'grɛsə/ n

tran·sient /'trænzʒənt/ adj fml lasting or staying for only a short time ♦ n person staying in a place only a short time ~**ence** n [U]

tran·sis·tor /træn'zɪstə/ n 1 small apparatus for controlling the flow of electric current 2 small radio with TRANSISTORS ~**ize** vt provide with transistors (1)

tran·sit /'trænzɪt/ n [U] going or moving of people or goods from one place to another: *The parcel was lost in transit.*

tran·si·tion /træn'zɪʃən/ n [C;U] (act of) changing from one state to another ~**al** adj

tran·si·tive /'trænzətɪv/ adj (of a verb) that must have an object or a phrase acting like an object

tran·si·to·ry /'trænzətɔri, -ˌtouri/ adj TRANSIENT

trans·late /'trænzleɪt, ˌtrænz'leɪt/ vi/t change (speech or writing) into a different language ~**lation** /-'leɪʃən/ n [C;U] ~**lator** n

trans·lit·e·rate /trænz'lɪtəreɪt/ vt fml write in a different alphabet

trans·lu·cent /trænz'lusənt/ adj allowing light to pass through (although not transparent)

trans·mit /trænz'mɪt/ v -tt- 1 vi/t broadcast: *transmit a radio distress signal* 2 vt pass to another person: *transmit a disease* 3 vt allow to pass through itself: *Water transmits sound.* ~**mission** /-'mɪʃən/ n [U] 1 act of transmitting 2 [C] television or radio broadcast 3 [C] parts of a vehicle that carry power to the wheels ~**ter** n broadcasting apparatus

trans·par·ent /træns'pærənt, -'pɛr-/ adj 1 that can be seen through 2 fml easily understood 3 fml clear and certain: *a*

transparent lie ~**ency** n 1 [U] quality of being transparent 2 [C] SLIDE (4)

tran·spire /træn'spaɪə/ vt fml 1 become known 2 happen

trans·plant /træns'plænt/ vt 1 move (a plant) from one place and plant it in another 2 move (an organ, piece of skin, hair, etc.) from one part of body to another, or one person to another ♦ /'trænsplænt/ n 1 something transplanted 2 act or operation of transplanting an organ: *a heart transplant*

trans·port /træns'pɔrt, -'pourt/ v carry (goods, people, etc.) from one place to another ♦ n [U] ~**ation** /ˌtrænspɔ'teɪʃən/ (means or system of) transporting: *travel by public transportation* ~**er** n long vehicle on which several cars can be carried

trans·pose /træns'pouz/ vt fml 1 change the order or position of (2 or more things) 2 change the KEY of a piece of music ~**position** /ˌtrænspə'zɪʃən/ n [C;U]

trans·ves·tite /trænz'vɛstaɪt/ n person who likes to wear the clothes of the opposite sex ~**tism** n [U]

trap /træp/ n 1 apparatus for catching and holding an animal: *a mousetrap* 2 plan for deceiving (and catching) a person: *The police set a trap to catch the thief.* 3 vehicle with 2 wheels, pulled by a horse 4 sl mouth: *Keep your trap shut!* 5 (in GOLF) sandy place from which it is difficult to hit the ball ♦ vt -pp- 1 place or hold firmly with no hope of escape: *The miners were trapped underground.* 2 trick; deceive 3 catch (an animal) in a trap ~**per** n

trap·door /ˌtræp'dɔr, -'dour/ n small door in a roof or floor

tra·peze /trə'piz/ n short bar hung high above the ground used by ACROBATS to swing on

trap·pings /'træpɪŋz/ n [P] articles of dress or decoration, esp. as an outward sign of rank

trash /træʃ/ n [U] 1 something of extremely low quality or value 2 waste material to be thrown away ~**y** adj

trash·can /'træʃkæn/ n container for waste materials

trau·ma /'trɔmə, 'traumə/ n damage to the mind caused by a shock or terrible experience ~**tic** /trə'mætɪk, trɔ-, trau-/ adj deeply and unforgettably shocking

trav·el[1] /ˈtrævəl/ v -l- 1 vi/t make a journey (through) 2 vt cover (the stated distance) on a journey 3 vi go, pass, move, etc.: At what speed does light travel? 4 **travel light** travel without many bags, etc. ♦ n [U] traveling: foreign travel ~ed adj experienced in travel: a much traveled writer ~er person on a journey **travels** n [P] journeys, esp. to foreign countries

travel a·gen·cy /ˈ·· ˌ··/ n business that arranges travel and vacations

travel a·gent /ˈ·· ˌ·/ n someone who makes people's travel arrangements

traveler's check /ˈ··· ˌ/ n check that can be exchanged abroad for foreign money

traveling sales·man /ˌ··· ˈ·/ n person who travels from place to place trying to get orders for goods

trav·el·og, -ogue /ˈtrævəˌlɔg, -ˌlɑg/ n film or talk describing foreign travel

tra·verse /trəˈvɜrs/ vt fml pass across, over, or through

trav·es·ty /ˈtrævəsti/ n something that completely misrepresents the nature of the real thing: The trial was a travesty of justice. (= was very unjust)

trawl /trɔl/ vi/t, n (fish with) a large net drawn along the sea bottom ~er n boat that uses a trawl

tray /treɪ/ n flat piece of plastic, metal, etc., for carrying things, esp. food

treach·er·y /ˈtrɛtʃəri/ n 1 [U] disloyalty or deceit [C] disloyal or deceitful act –rous adj 1 very disloyal or deceitful 2 full of hidden dangers: treacherous currents –rously adv

tread /trɛd/ v trod /trad/, trodden /ˈtradn/ 1 vi fml put one's foot when walking; step 2 vt fml walk along: tread a path 3 vt press firmly with the feet 4 **tread water** keep upright in water by moving the legs ♦ n 1 [S] act, way, or sound of walking 2 [C;U] pattern of raised lines on a tire 3 [C] part of a stair on which the foot is placed

tread·mill /ˈtrɛdˌmɪl/ n something providing repeated uninteresting work

trea·son /ˈtrizən/ n [U] disloyalty to one's country, esp. by helping its enemies ~**able** adj law of or being treason

trea·sure /ˈtrɛʒər/ n 1 [U] wealth in gold, jewels, etc. 2 [C] very valuable object or person ♦ vt keep or regard as precious: treasured memories

trea·sur·er /ˈtrɛʒərə/ n person in charge of an organization's money

trea·su·ry /ˈtrɛʒəri/ n government department that controls and spends public money

treat /trit/ vt 1 act or behave towards: He treated his horses very cruelly. 2 deal with or handle: Treat the glass carefully. | He treated my request as a joke. 3 try to cure medically 4 put through a chemical or industrial action: metal treated against rust 5 pay for (someone's) food, drink, amusement, etc. ♦ n 1 something that gives great pleasure, esp. when unexpected: What a treat to have real champagne! 2 act of treating (TREAT (5)) someone: The meal's my treat, so put away your money. ~**ment** n 1 [U] act or way of treating someone or something 2 [C] substance or method for treating someone or something

trea·tise /ˈtritɪs/ n serious book on a particular subject

treat·y /ˈtriti/ n formally signed agreement between countries

treble /ˈtrɛbəl/ n [U] upper half of the whole range of musical notes

tree /tri/ n 1 tall plant with a wooden trunk or stem, that lives for many years 2 treelike bush: a rose tree ~**less** adj

trek /trɛk/ vi, n -kk- (make) a long hard journey, esp. on foot

trel·lis /ˈtrɛlɪs/ n light upright wooden framework on which plants are grown

trem·ble /ˈtrɛmbəl/ vi 1 shake uncontrollably 2 be very worried: I tremble to think what may happen. **tremble** n [S]

tre·men·dous /trɪˈmɛndəs/ adj 1 very great in amount or degree 2 wonderful: What a tremendous party! ~**ly** adv

trem·or /ˈtrɛmə/ n shaking movement: an earth tremor (= a small EARTHQUAKE) | a tremor in his voice

trench /trɛntʃ/ n long narrow hole cut in the ground, esp. as a protection for soldiers

trench coat /ˈ· ·/ n long coat that ties at the waist

trend /trɛnd/ n 1 general direction or course of development: a rising trend of violent crime 2 **set a/the trend** start or popularize a fashion ~**y** adj infml very fashionable

trend·set·ter /ˈtrɛndˌsɛtə/ n person who starts or popularizes the latest fashion –**ting** adj

trep·i·da·tion /ˌtrepəˈdeɪʃən/ n [U] fml anxiety

tres·pass /ˈtrespæs/ vi go onto privately owned land without permission ♦ n 1 [C] lit for SIN 2 [C;U] (act of) trespassing ~**er** n

tress·es /ˈtresɪz/ n [P] lit woman's long hair

tri·al /ˈtraɪəl/ n 1 [C;U] (act of) hearing and judging a person or case in a court of law: He's on trial for murder. 2 [C;U] (act of) testing to find out if something is good: We gave her the job for a trial period. 3 [C] cause of worry or trouble 4 **stand trial** be tried in court 5 **trial and error** trying several methods and learning from one's mistakes

trial run /ˌ· ·ˈ·/ n testing of something new to see if it works properly

tri·an·gle /ˈtraɪˌæŋgəl/ n figure or shape with 3 straight sides and 3 angles –**gular** /traɪˈæŋgyələr/ adj

tribe /traɪb/ n people of the same race, beliefs, language, etc., living together under the leadership of a chief: a tribe of Amazonian Indians **tribal** adj

tri·bu·nal /traɪˈbyunl, trɪ-/ n sort of court that deals with particular matters

trib·u·ta·ry /ˈtrɪbyəˌteri/ n river that flows into a larger river

trib·ute /ˈtrɪbyut/ n [C;U] something said or given to show respect or admiration: The chairman paid tribute to (= praised) their hard work.

trick /trɪk/ n 1 clever act or plan to deceive or cheat someone 2 something done to make someone look stupid: children playing tricks on their teacher 3 amusing or confusing skillful act: magic/card tricks 4 quick or clever way to do something 5 cards played or won in a single part of a card game 6 **do the trick** fulfill one's purpose ♦ vt deceive ♦ adj full of hidden difficulties: a trick question ~**ery** n [U] use of deceiving tricks ~**y** adj 1 difficult to deal with: a tricky problem 2 (of a person or actions) clever and deceitful

trick·le /ˈtrɪkəl/ vi flow in drops or a thin stream ♦ n [S] thin slow flow: (fig.) a trickle of inquiries

trick-or-treat /ˌ· · ·ˈ·/ vi (of children) go to people's houses on HALLOWEEN and ask for TREATS (1) under threat of playing tricks on people who refuse

trick·ster /ˈtrɪkstər/ n deceiver; cheater

tri·cy·cle /ˈtraɪsɪkəl/ n bicycle with 3 wheels

tried /traɪd/ v past t. and p. of TRY

tried-and-true /ˌ· · ·ˈ·/ adj known to be worthy

tri·fle¹ /ˈtraɪfəl/ n 1 [C] fml something of little value or importance 3 **a trifle** fml fairly: You were a trifle rude. –**fling** adj fml of little value or importance

trifle² v **trifle with** phr vt treat without seriousness or respect

trig·ger /ˈtrɪgər/ n piece pulled with the finger to fire a gun ♦ vt start (esp. a number of things that happen one after the other)

trigger-hap·py /ˈ·· ˌ·/ adj too eager to use violent methods

trig·o·nom·e·try /ˌtrɪgəˈnɑmətri/ n [U] MATHEMATICS dealing with the relationship between the sides and angles of TRIANGLES

trill /trɪl/ vi/t, n (sing, play, or pronounce with) a rapidly repeated sound

tril·lion /ˈtrɪlyən/ determiner, n, pron 1,000,000,000,000

tril·o·gy /ˈtrɪlədʒi/ n group of 3 related books, plays, etc.

trim /trɪm/ vt -**mm**- 1 make neat by cutting 2 decorate, esp. around the edges 3 move (sails) into the correct position for sailing well ♦ n 1 [S] act of cutting (esp. hair) 2 **in (good) trim** [U] proper condition ♦ adj -**mm**- pleasingly neat ~**ming** n decoration or useful addition: roast turkey with all the trimmings (= vegetables, potatoes, SAUCE, etc.)

Trin·i·ty /ˈtrɪnəti/ n [the] (in the Christian religion) the union of the 3 forms of God (the Father, Son, and Holy Spirit) as one God

trin·ket /ˈtrɪŋkɪt/ n small decorative object of low value

tri·o /ˈtrioʊ/ n -os 1 group of 3 2 piece of music for 3 performers

trip /trɪp/ v -**pp**- 1 vi/t (cause to) catch the foot and lose balance: I tripped over a stone and fell down. 2 vi/t (cause to) make a mistake: He tried to trip me up with awkward questions. 3 vi lit move or dance with quick light steps ♦ n 1 short journey, esp. for pleasure 2 act of tripping (TRIP (1)) 3 period under the influence of a drug that changes one's mind

tripe /traɪp/ n [U] wall of a cow's stomach used as food

trip·le /'trɪpəl/ adj having 3 parts or members ♦ vi/t increase to 3 times the amount or number

trip·let /'trɪplɪt/ n any of 3 children born to the same mother at the same time

trip·li·cate /'trɪpləkɪt/ n in triplicate in 3 copies, one of which is the original

tri·pod /'traɪpɑd/ n support with 3 legs, esp. for a camera

trite /traɪt/ adj (of a remark) common and uninteresting

tri·umph /'traɪəmf/ n [C;U] (joy or satisfaction caused by) a complete victory or success ♦ vi be victorious ~**al** /traɪ'ʌmfəl/ adj of or marking a triumph ~**ant** /traɪ'ʌmfənt/ adj (joyful because one is) victorious ~**antly** adv

triv·i·a /'trɪviə/ n [P] 1 trivial things 2 facts of general knowledge: a trivia quiz

triv·i·al /'trɪviəl/ adj 1 of little worth or importance 2 ordinary ~**ality** /ˌtrɪvi-'æləti/ n [C;U] ~**ize** /'trɪviəˌlaɪz/ vt

trod /trɑd/ v past t. of TREAD

trod·den /'trɑdn/ v past p. of TREAD

Tro·jan horse /ˌtroʊdʒən 'hɔrs/ n something or someone that attacks or weakens something secretly from within

trol·ley /'trɑli/ n small train driven by electricity along tracks in a street

trom·bone /trɑm'boʊn/ n brass musical instrument with a long sliding tube

troop /trup/ n 1 (moving) group of people or animals 2 group of soldiers esp. on horses 3 **-er** member of state police ♦ vi move in a group **troops** n [P] soldiers

tro·phy /'troʊfi/ n 1 prize for winning a competition or test of skill 2 something kept as a reminder of success

trop·ic /'trɑpɪk/ n line around the world at 23½° north (**the tropic of Cancer**) and south (**the tropic of Capricorn**) of the EQUATOR **tropics** n [P] hot area between these lines ~**al** 1 adj of the tropics 2 very hot: tropical weather

trot¹ /trɑt/ n [S] 1 horse's movement, slower than a CANTER 2 slow run

trot² vi **-tt-** move at the speed of a trot

trot out phr vt repeat in an uninteresting, unchanged way: trotting out the same old excuses

trots /trɑts/ n [the+P] infml DIARRHEA

trou·ba·dour /'trubəˌdɔr, -ˌdoʊr/ n traveling singer and poet of former times

trou·ble /'trʌbəl/ n 1 [C;U] (cause of) difficulty, worry, annoyance, etc.: I didn't have any trouble doing it; it was easy. 2 [U] state of being blamed: He's always getting into trouble with the police. 3 [S;U] inconvenience or more than usual work or effort: I took a lot of trouble to get it right. 4 [C;U] political or social disorder 5 [U] failure to work properly: engine/heart trouble 6 **ask/look for trouble** behave so as to cause difficulty or danger for oneself ♦ v 1 vi/t worry 2 vt cause inconvenience to 3 vi make an effort; BOTHER ~**some** adj annoying

trou·ble·shoot·er /'trʌbəlˌʃutər/ n person who finds and removes causes of trouble in machines, organizations, etc.

trough /trɒf/ n 1 long container for animals' food 2 long hollow area between waves 3 area of low air pressure

trounce /traʊns/ vt defeat completely

troupe /trup/ n company of entertainers

trou·sers /'traʊzərz/ n fml PANTS

trout /traʊt/ n trout river (or sea) fish used for food

trow·el /'traʊəl/ n 1 tool with a flat blade for spreading cement, etc. 2 garden tool like a small spade

tru·ant /'truənt/ n student who stays away from school without permission ♦ adj ~**ancy** n [U]

truce /trus/ n [C;U] agreement for the stopping of fighting

truck /trʌk/ n large motor vehicle for carrying goods ♦ vt carry by truck ~**er** n truck driver

truck farm /'· ·/ n area for growing vegetables and fruit for sale

truck·ing /'trʌkɪŋ/ n [U] business of taking goods from place to place by truck

truck·load /'trʌkloʊd/ n amount of something that a truck can carry

truck stop /'· ·/ n cheap place to eat and buy gasoline near a HIGHWAY, used esp. by truck drivers

trudge /trʌdʒ/ vi walk slowly and with effort ♦ n long tiring walk

true /tru/ adj 1 in accordance with fact or reality 2 real: true love 3 faithful; loyal 4 exact: a true likeness 5 **come true** happen as was wished, expected, or dreamt **truly** adv 1 in accordance with the truth 2 really: a truly wonderful experience 3 sincerely: truly sorry ♦ n out

of **true** not having correct shape or balance

true-blue /ˌ. ˈ.◂/ adj completely loyal

truf·fle /ˈtrʌfəl/ n 1 underground FUNGUS highly regarded as food 2 expensive chocolate candy

trump¹ /trʌmp/ n 1 card of a sort (SUIT¹ (3)) chosen to be of higher rank than other suits in a game 2 **turn/come up trumps** do the right or needed thing, esp. unexpectedly at the last moment

trump² vt beat by playing a trump

trump up phr vt invent (a false charge or reason)

trump card /ˈ. ˌ./ n something that gives a clear and unquestionable advantage

trum·pet /ˈtrʌmpɪt/ n brass musical instrument producing high notes, consisting of a long usu. winding tube ♦ v 1 vi (of an elephant) make a loud sound 2 vt declare or shout loudly **~er** n trumpet player

trun·cate /ˈtrʌŋkeɪt/ vt shorten (as if) by cutting off the top or end

trunk /trʌŋk/ n 1 main stem of a tree 2 large box in which things are packed for traveling 3 ELEPHANT's long nose 4 body without the head or limbs 5 space at the back of a car for boxes, etc. **trunks** n [P] men's SHORTS for swimming

truss /trʌs/ vt 1 tie up firmly and roughly 2 tie (a bird's) wings and legs in place for cooking ♦ n 1 medical supporting belt worn by someone with a HERNIA 2 framework of beams built to support a roof, bridge, etc

trust¹ /trʌst/ n 1 [U] firm belief in the honesty, goodness, worth, etc., of someone or something 2 [C;U] arrangement for) the holding and controlling of money for someone else: a charitable trust 3 [C] group of companies working together to limit competition 4 [U] fml responsibility: employed in a position of trust 5 **take on trust** accept without proof

trust² vt 1 believe in the honesty and worth of, esp. without proof 2 allow someone to do or have something: Can he be trusted with a gun? 3 depend on 4 fml hope, esp. confidently: I trust you enjoyed yourself. **~ful**; also **~ing** adj (too) ready to trust others **~fully**, **~ingly** adv **~y** adj lit dependable

trust in phr vt fml have faith in

trust ac·count /ˈ. ·ˌ·/ n bank account for saving money

trust·ee /trʌˈstiː/ n 1 person in charge of a TRUST¹ (2) 2 member of a group controlling the affairs of a company, college, etc.

trust·wor·thy /ˈtrʌstˌwɜːði/ adj dependable

truth /truːθ/ n **truths** /truːðz/ 1 [U] that which is true: Are you telling the truth? 2 [U] quality of being true: I doubted the truth of what he said. 3 [C] true fact — see also MOMENT OF TRUTH **~ful** adj 1 (of a statement) true 2 habitually telling the truth **~fully** adv **~fulness** n [U]

try /traɪ/ v 1 vi/t make an attempt: I tried to persuade him, but failed. 2 vt test by use and experience: Have you tried this new soap? | We need to try the idea out in practice. 3 vt examine in a court of law: He was tried for murder. 4 vt cause to suffer, esp. with small annoyances: Her constant questions try my patience. 5 vt attempt to open (a door, window, etc.) ♦ n attempt adj known to be good from experience

try on phr vt put on (a garment, etc.) to see if it fits or looks well

try out phr vt 1 test by use or experience 2 **try out for** compete for a position on a team, etc: try out for football

try·ing /ˈtraɪ-ɪŋ/ adj difficult and unpleasant: It's been a very trying day

try·out /ˈtraɪ-aʊt/ n occasion when someone is tested to decide whether he/she is good enough to join a sports team, etc.

tset·se fly /ˈtɛtsi flaɪ, ˈtsɛtsi-, ˈsɛtsi-/ n African fly that causes SLEEPING SICKNESS

T-shirt /ˈtiː ʃɜːt/ n light informal collarless garment for the upper body

tsp. abbrev. for: teaspoon

tub /tʌb/ n 1 round container for washing, packing, storing, etc. 2 BATHTUB

tu·ba /ˈtuːbə/ n large brass musical instrument that produces low notes

tub·by /ˈtʌbi/ adj infml rather fat

tube /tuːb/ n 1 hollow round pipe 2 small soft metal or plastic container for paint, paste, etc., which you get out by pressing: a tube of toothpaste 3 pipe in the body: the bronchial tubes **tubing** n [U] tubes **tubular** /ˈtuːbjələ/ adj 1 in the form of tubes 2 sl especially good

tu·ber·cu·lo·sis /tʊˌbɜːkjəˈloʊsɪs/ *n* [U] serious infectious disease that attacks esp. the lungs **tubercular** /tʊˈbɜːkjələ/ *adj*

tuck /tʌk/ *vt* 1 put (the edge of) into a tight place for neatness, protection, etc.: *Tuck your shirt in.* | *She tucked the newspaper under her arm.* 2 put into a private or almost hidden place: *a house tucked away among the trees* ♦ *n* narrow flat fold of material sewn into a garment

tuck in *phr vi* 1 eat eagerly 2 make (esp. a child) comfortable in bed by pulling the sheets tight

Tues·day /ˈtjuːzdi, -deɪ/ *n* the 3rd day of the week, between Monday and Wednesday

tuft /tʌft/ *n* small bunch (of hair, grass, etc.)

tug /tʌg/ *vi/t* **-gg-** pull hard ♦ *n* 1 sudden strong pull 2 also **tugboat** /ˈtʌgboʊt/ — small boat used for pulling and guiding ships in narrow places

tug-of-war /ˌ · · ˈ·/ *n* [C;U] sport in which 2 teams pull against each other on a rope

tu·i·tion /tuˈɪʃən/ *n* [U] money paid for education esp. to a university

tu·lip /ˈtuːlɪp/ *n* garden plant with large colorful flowers shaped like cups

tum·ble /ˈtʌmbəl/ *vi* 1 roll suddenly and helplessly, esp. rolling over 2 *infml* understand 3 perform GYMNASTICS without special equipment ♦ *n* fall

tumble down *phr vi* fall to pieces; COLLAPSE

tum·ble-down /ˈtʌmbəldaʊn/ *adj* nearly in ruins

tum·bler /ˈtʌmblə/ *n* drinking glass with a flat bottom and no handle

tumble·weed /ˈtʌmbəlˌwiːd/ *n* plant that breaks off and is blown in the wind

tum·my /ˈtʌmi/ *n infml* stomach

tu·mor /ˈtuːmə/ *n* mass of quickly growing diseased cells in the body

tu·mult /ˈtuːmʌlt/ *n* [S;U] confused noise and excitement **~uous** /tuˈmʌltʃuəs/ *adj* noisy

tu·na /ˈtuːnə/ *n* tuna *or* tunas [C;U] large sea fish used for food

tun·dra /ˈtʌndrə/ *n* [U] large flat area of land in cold northern areas, with no trees

tune /tuːn/ *n* 1 (pleasing) pattern of musical notes 2 **call the tune** be in a position to give orders 3 **change one's tune** change one's opinion, behavior,

etc. 4 **in/out of tune: a** at/not at the correct musical level **b** in/not in agreement or sympathy 5 **to the tune of** to the amount of ♦ *vt* 1 set (a musical instrument) to the correct musical level 2 put (an engine) in good working order **~ful** *adj* having a pleasant tune **tuner** *n* person who tunes musical instruments

tune in *phr vi* turn on a radio, esp. so as to listen to a particular radio station

tune out *phr vt* stop listening to

tung·sten /ˈtʌŋstən/ *n* hard metal used esp. in making steel

tune-up /ˈ· ·/ *n* occasion when a car's engine is cleaned and fixed

tu·nic /ˈtuːnɪk/ *n* 1 loose usu. belted garment which reaches to the knees 2 short coat forming part of a uniform

tun·nel /ˈtʌnl/ *n* usu. artificial underground passage for road, railway, etc. ♦ *vi/t* **-l-** make a tunnel (under or through)

tunnel vi·sion /ˈ·· ˌ·/ *n* [U] tendency to consider only one part of a question, without even trying to examine others

Tup·per·ware /ˈtʌpəˌweɪ/ *n* [U] *tdmk* type of plastic containers with tight-fitting lids, used for storing food

tur·ban /ˈtɜːbən/ *n* 1 Asian head covering made by winding cloth around the head 2 woman's small hat which fits high on the head

tur·bid /ˈtɜːbɪd/ *adj* 1 (of a liquid) not clear; muddy 2 confused

tur·bine /ˈtɜːbɪn, -baɪn/ *n* motor in which liquid or gas drives a wheel to produce circular movement

tur·bo·jet /ˈtɜːboʊˌdʒɛt/ *n* (aircraft) engine that forces out a stream of gases behind itself

tur·bu·lent /ˈtɜːbjələnt/ *adj* violent and disorderly or irregular **-lence** *n* [U] 1 being turbulent 2 turbulent air movements

turd /tɜːd/ *n taboo* 1 piece of solid waste passed from the body 2 *sl* offensive person

turf¹ /tɜːf/ *n* 1 [U] grass surface 2 [C] area of a town where a street GANG holds authority

turf² *vt* cover with turf

tur·gid /ˈtɜːdʒɪd/ *adj fml* (of language or style) too solemn and SELF-IMPORTANT

tur·key /ˈtɜːki/ *n* 1 [C;U] bird like a large chicken, used for food 2 *sl* play in theater or a film which does not succeed **3** *sl* stupid person **4 talk turkey** *infml* speak seriously and plainly esp. about business — see also COLD TURKEY

tur·moil /ˈtɜːmɔɪl/ *n* [S;U] state of confusion and trouble

turn¹ /tɜːn/ *v* **1** *vi/t* move around a central point: *The wheels turned.* **2** *vi/t* move so that a different side faces upwards or outwards: *She turned the pages.* **3** *vi* change direction: *Turn right at the end of the road.* | *He turned to crime.* (= became a criminal) **4** *vt* go around: *The car turned the corner.* **5** *vi* look around: *She turned to wave.* **6** *vt* aim; point: *They turned their hoses on the burning building.* | *I turned my thoughts to home.* **7** *vi/t* (cause to) become: *His hair has turned gray.* | *The witch turned the prince into a frog.* **8** *vi* go sour: *The milk's turned.* **9** *vt* pass: *It's just turned 3 o'clock.* | *She's turned 40.* **10 turn a phrase** *fml* say a clever thing neatly **11 turn one's hand** to begin to practice (a skill) **12 turn one's head** make one too proud **13 turn one's stomach** make one feel sick **14 turn tail** start to run away **15 turn the other cheek** react patiently to cruelty **16 turn the tables** bring about the opposite of a situation

turn against *phr vt* (cause to) become opposed to

turn away *phr vt* **1** refuse to let in **2** refuse to help

turn down *phr vt* **1** refuse **2** reduce the force, speed, loudness, etc., of (something) by using controls: *Can you turn that radio down?*

turn in *phr v* **1** *vt* no longer continue **2** *vi* go to bed **3** *vt* deliver to the police **4** *vt* give back; return **5** hand in; deliver: *He's turned in some very poor work lately.*

turn off *phr vt* **1** stop the flow or operation of: *turn off the tap/television* **2** *sl* cause to lose interest, often sexually

turn on *phr vt* **1** cause to flow or operate: *turn on the tap/television* **2** depend on **3** attack suddenly and without warning **4** *sl* excite or interest strongly, often sexually **5** *sl* (cause to) take an illegal drug, esp. for the first time **6** *vt* cause to know or appreciate: *He turned me on to Melville.*

turn out *phr v* **1** *vt* stop the operation of (a light) **2** *vt* drive out; send away **3** *vi* come out or gather (as if) for a meeting

or public event **4** *vt* produce: *The factory turns out 100 cars a day.* **5** *vt* empty (a cupboard, pocket, etc.) **6** happen to be in the end: *The party turned out a success.* **7** *vt* dress: *an elegantly turned-out woman*

turn over *phr vt* **1** think about; consider **2** deliver to the place **3** (of an engine) to run at the lowest speed **4** do business

turn over to *phr vt* give control of (something) to

turn to *phr vt* go to for sympathy, help, advice, etc.

turn up *phr v* **1** *vi* be found **2** *vi* arrive **3** *vi* find **4** *vt* turn over (a playing card) so that the number is showing: *turn up a King* **5** *vi* happen **6 turn up one's nose (at something or someone)** suggest by one's behavior that (something or someone) is not good enough for one

turn² *n* **1** act of turning (something) **2** change of direction **3** rightful chance or duty to do something: *It's my turn to speak.* | *We took turns doing it.* (= did it one after the other) **4** development: *She's taken a turn for the worse.* (= has become more ill) **5** point of change in time: *at the turn of the century* **6** attack of illness: *He had one of his funny turns.* **7** shock: *You did give me a turn, appearing like that suddenly!* **8 a good turn** a useful or helpful action **9 at every turn** in every place; at every moment **10 in turn** in proper order **11 out of turn** unsuitably: *I hope I haven't spoken out of turn.* **12 take turns** succeed in order

turn·ing point /ˈ·· ˌ·/ *n* point at which a very important change happens

tur·nip /ˈtɜːnɪp/ *n* [C;U] plant with a large, round whitish root used as a vegetable

turn-off /ˈ· ˌ·/ *n* **1** smaller road branching off from a main road **2** *infml* something that causes one to feel dislike or lose interest, esp. sexually

turn-on /ˈ· ˌ·/ *n* *infml* something that excites or interests one strongly, esp. sexually

turn·out /ˈtɜːnaʊt/ *n* **1** number of people who attend **2** occasion on which one empties all unwanted things from drawers, rooms, etc. **3** wide place in a narrow road

turn·o·ver /ˈtɜːnˌoʊvə/ *n* [S] **1** rate at which a particular kind of goods is sold **2** amount of business done **3** number of workers hired to fill the places of those who leave **4** small pie: *apple turnover*

turn·pike /'tənpaɪk/ *n* main road which drivers have to pay to use

turn·stile /'tənstaɪl/ *n* small gate that turns around, set in an entrance to admit people one at a time

turn·ta·ble /'tən,teɪbəl/ *n* **1** round spinning surface on which a record is placed to be played **2** machine including such a round surface

tur·pen·tine /'təpən,taɪn/ *n* [U] thin oil used esp. for cleaning off unwanted paint

tur·quoise /'təkwɔɪz/ *n* [C;U] (piece of) a precious green-blue mineral ♦ *adj* turquoise in color

tur·tle /'tətl/ *n* animal with 4 legs and a hard horny shell

tur·tle·neck /'tətl,nɛk/ *n* (garment with) a high collar that fits closely

tusk /tʌsk/ *n* very long pointed tooth, usu. one of a pair: *an elephant's tusks*

tus·sle /'tʌsəl/ *vi* infml fight roughly without weapons ♦ *n* rough struggle or fight

tut /tʌt/ *interj* (shows annoyance or disapproval)

tu·tor /'tutə/ *n* private teacher ♦ *vt* teach in private lessons ~**ial** /tu'tɔriəl, -'tour-/ *n* short period of instruction given by a TUTOR

tu·tu /'tutu/ *n* short stiff skirt worn by women BALLET dancers

tux·e·do /tʌk'sidoʊ/ also **tux** /tʌks/ *infml* — *n* -**dos** man's formal suit

TV /n [C;U] television

TV din·ner /ˌ· '·-/ *n* prepared frozen meal

twang /twæŋ/ *n* **1** quick ringing sound **2** sound of human speech (as if) produced partly through the nose ♦ *vi/t* (cause to) make a TWANG (1)

tweak /twik/ *vt* **1** pull to, seize, and twist: *He tweaked her ear.* **2** make a small improvement to (a computer program, engine, etc.) **tweak** *n*

tweed /twid/ *n* [U] coarse wool cloth

tweeds /twidz/ *n* [P] (suit of) tweed clothes

tweet /twit/ *vi, n* (make) the short, weak high noise of a small bird

tweet·er /'twitə/ *n* a LOUDSPEAKER that gives out high sounds

twee·zers /'twizəz/ *n* [P] small jointed tool with 2 parts for picking up and pulling out very small objects

twelfth /twɛlfθ, twɛlθ/ *determiner, adv, n, pron* 12th

twelve /twɛlv/ *determiner, n, pron* 12

twen·ty /'twɛnti/ *determiner, n, pron* 20 **-tieth** *determiner, adv, n, pron* 20th

twerp /twəp/ *n sl* small foolish person

twice /twaɪs/ *predeterminer, adv* **1** 2 times **2 think twice (about something)** consider (something) carefully

twig /twɪg/ *n* small thin stem on a tree or bush

twi·light /'twaɪlaɪt/ *n* [U] (faint darkish light at) the time when day is about to become night **-lit** *adj*

twill /twɪl/ *n* [U] strong woven cotton cloth

twin /twɪn/ *n* either of 2 people born to the same mother at the same time — also SIAMESE TWIN

twin bed /ˌ· '·/ *n* narrow bed for 1 person

twine /twaɪn/ *n* [U] strong string ♦ *vi/t* twist; wind

twinge /twɪndʒ/ *n* sudden sharp pain: (fig.) *a twinge of conscience*

twin·kle /'twɪŋkəl/ *vi* **1** shine with an unsteady light: *The stars twinkled.* **2** (of the eyes) be bright with cheerfulness, amusement, etc. ♦ *n* [S] **1** twinkling light **2** brightness in the eye

twirl /twəl/ *vi/t* **1** spin **2** curl ♦ *n* sudden quick spin or circular movement

twist /twɪst/ *v* **1** *vi/t* bend, turn, etc., so as to change shape: *She twisted the wire into the shape of a star.* **2** *vt* bind: *Twist the wires together.* **3** *vi* move windingly **4** *vt* turn: *She twisted her head around.* **5** *vt* hurt (a joint or limb) by turning it sharply **6** *vt derog* change the true meaning of **7 twist someone's arm** persuade someone forcefully or threateningly **8 twist someone around one's little finger** be able to get someone to do what one wants ♦ *n* **1** act of twisting **2** bend **3** unexpected development: *a strange twist of fate* **4** popular dance of the 1960s ~**er** *n* **1** dishonest cheating person **2** *infml* (small) TORNADO

twitch /twɪtʃ/ *vi/t* move with a twitch: *His eyelid twitched.* ♦ *n* repeated short, sudden unconscious muscle movement ~**y** *adj* nervous; anxious

twit·ter /'twɪtə/ *vi, n* [U] **1** (of a bird) (make) short high rapid sounds **2** state of nervousness or excitement

two /tu/ *determiner, n, pron* **1** (the number) **2** **2 in two** in two parts **3 one or two** a few **4 put two and two together** calculate the meaning of what one sees or hears **5 two can play at that game** (used as a threat to someone who has been unfair, unkind, etc., to oneself) **6 one's two cents worth** one's opinion on a subject

two-by-four, 2 × 4 /ˌ· ·ˈ·/ *n* piece of cut wood used in building

two·faced /ˌtuˈfeɪst◂/ *adj* deceitful; insincere

two·some /ˈtusəm/ *n* 2 people or things

two-time /ˈ· ·/ *vt* be unfaithful to (a girl or boy friend)

two-way /ˌ· ˈ·◂/ *adj* moving or allowing movement in both directions

ty·coon /taɪˈkun/ *n* rich, powerful business person

ty·ing /ˈtaɪ-ɪŋ/ *v pres. p. of* TIE

type /taɪp/ *n* **1** [C] sort; kind; example of a group or class: *She's just that type of person.* **2** [U] small blocks with raised letters on them, used in printing **3** [U] printed letters: *italic type* **4 true to type** behaving or acting (esp. badly) just as one would expect ♦ *vi/t* write with a TYPEWRITER or WORD PROCESSOR

type·cast /ˈtaɪpkæst/ *vt* **-cast** repeatedly give (an actor) the same kind of part

type·face /ˈtaɪpfeɪs/ *n* size and style of printed letters

type·script /ˈtaɪpˌskrɪpt/ *n* typed copy of something

type·writ·er /ˈtaɪpˌraɪtə/ *n* machine that prints letters by means of keys operated by one's fingers

ty·phoid /ˈtaɪfɔɪd/ *n* [U] infectious disease causing fever and often death, produced by bacteria in food or drink

ty·phoon /ˌtaɪˈfun◂/ *n* very violent tropical storm

ty·phus /ˈtaɪfəs/ *n* [U] infectious disease that causes fever, severe headaches, and red spots on the body

typ·i·cal /ˈtɪpɪkəl/ *adj* showing the usual or main qualities of a particular sort of thing: *a typical American movie, with lots of sex and violence* **~ly** *adv*

typ·ist /ˈtaɪpɪst/ *n* secretary employed mainly for typing (TYPE) letters

ty·po /ˈtaɪpoʊ/ *n* mistake in printing or typing (TYPE)

ty·pog·ra·phy /taɪˈpɑgrəfi/ *n* [U] **1** preparing matter for printing **2** arrangement and appearance of printed matter **-phic** /ˌtaɪpəˈgræfɪk◂/ *adj*

tyr·an·ny /ˈtɪrəni/ *n* [U] use of cruel or unjust ruling power **-ical** /tɪˈrænɪkəl, taɪ-/ *adj*

ty·rant /ˈtaɪrənt/ *n* cruel unjust ruler

U

U, u /yu/ the 21st letter of the English alphabet

u·biq·ui·tous /yu'bɪkwətəs/ adj fml happening or existing everywhere

ud·der /'ʌdə/ n organ of a cow, female goat, etc., that produces milk

UFO /ˌyu ɛf 'oʊ, 'yufoʊ/ n UFO's or UFOs strange object in the sky, thought of as a spacecraft from other worlds

ugh /ʊg, ʌg/ interj (expresses extreme dislike)

ug·ly /'ʌgli/ adj 1 unpleasant to see 2 very unpleasant or threatening: in an ugly mood **ugliness** n [U]

ugly duck·ling /ˌ·· '·-/ n person less attractive than others in early life but becoming attractive later

uh-huh /'ʌ hʌ, m'hm/ interj infml yes

uh oh /'ʌ ˌʔoʊ/ interj infml (said after making a mistake or realizing something bad)

UK n [the] the United Kingdom (of Great Britain and Northern Ireland)

u·ku·le·le /ˌyukə'leɪli/ n sort of small GUITAR

ul·cer /'ʌlsə/ n sore place where the skin is broken ~**ate** vi turn into or become covered with ulcers ~**ous** adj

ul·te·ri·or /ˌʌl'tɪriə/ adj kept secret, esp. because bad: an ulterior motive

ul·ti·mate /'ʌltəmɪt/ adj being or happening after all others: our ultimate destination ~**ly** adv in the end

ul·ti·ma·tum /ˌʌltə'meɪtəm/ n -**tums** or -**ta** /-tə/ statement of conditions to be met, not open to argument

ul·tra·ma·rine /ˌʌltrəmə'rin◄/ adj very bright blue

ul·tra·son·ic /ˌʌltrə'sɑnɪk◄/ adj (of a sound wave) beyond the range of human hearing

ul·tra·sound /'ʌltrəˌsaʊnd/ n [C;U] medical process using sound waves to produce images of the inside of the body

ul·tra·vi·o·let /ˌʌltrə'vaɪəlɪt◄/ adj (of light) beyond the purple end of the range of colors that can be seen by humans

um·bil·i·cal cord /ʌm'bɪlɪkəl ˌkɔrd/ n tube of flesh which joins an unborn creature to its mother

um·brel·la /ʌm'brɛlə/ n 1 folding frame covered with cloth, for keeping rain off the head 2 protecting power or influence 3 anything which covers or includes a wide range of different parts

um·pire /'ʌmpaɪə/ also **ump** /ʌmp/ infml — n judge in charge of certain games, such as baseball and tennis ♦ vi/t act as an umpire (for)

ump·teen /ˌʌmp'tin◄/ determiner, pron infml a large number (of) ~**th** n, determiner

UN abbrev. for: UNITED NATIONS

un·a·ble /ʌn'eɪbəl/ adj not able

un·a·bridged /ˌʌnə'brɪdʒd◄/ adj (of books) complete

un·ac·coun·ta·ble /ˌʌnə'kaʊntəbəl/ adj fml hard to explain; surprising ~**bly** adv

un·ac·cus·tomed /ˌʌnə'kʌstəmd◄/ adj 1 not used (to) 2 unusual

un·am·big·u·ous /ˌʌnæm'bɪgyuəs/ adj very clear; impossible to misunderstand

un·A·mer·i·can /ˌʌn ə'mɛrɪkən◄/ adj not supporting or loyal to American customs, ideas, etc.

u·nan·i·mous /yu'nænəməs/ adj with everyone agreeing: a unanimous decision ~**ly** adv ~**nimity** /ˌyunə'nɪməti/ n [U]

un·an·swer·a·ble /ʌn'ænsərəbəl/ adj that cannot be answered or argued against

un·armed /ˌʌn'ɑrmd◄/ adj not carrying any weapons

un·as·sum·ing /ˌʌnə'sumɪŋ/ adj quiet and unwilling to make claims about one's good qualities

un·at·tached /ˌʌnə'tætʃt◄/ adj 1 not connected 2 not married or ENGAGEd (1)

un·at·tend·ed /ˌʌnə'tɛndɪd◄/ adj alone, with no one present or in charge

un·au·thor·ized /ˌʌn'ɔθəraɪzd/ adj without official approval or permission

un·a·vail·ing /ˌʌnə'veɪlɪŋ◄/ adj having no effect ~**ly** adv

un·a·wares /ˌʌnə'wɛrz/ adv unexpectedly or without warning: I took/caught her unawares. (= surprised her by my presence)

un·bal·ance /ˌʌn'bæləns/ vt make slightly crazy: an unbalanced mind

un·beat·a·ble /ˌʌn'bitəbəl/ adj better than any other person or thing: unbeatable prices

un·be·knownst /ˌʌnbɪˈnoʊnst/, also **un·be·known** /-ˈnoʊn/ — adv without the stated person knowing: Unbeknownst to me, he had left.

un·blink·ing /ʌnˈblɪŋkɪŋ/ adj showing no emotion or doubt

un·born /ʌnˈbɔrn◂/ adj not yet born: an unborn child

un·bowed /ˌʌnˈbaʊd◂/ adj esp. lit not defeated

un·bri·dled /ʌnˈbraɪdld/ adj not controlled, and esp. too active or violent

un·bur·den /ʌnˈbɜrdn/ vt fml free (oneself, one's mind, etc.) by talking about a secret trouble

un·called-for /ʌnˈkɔld ˌfɔr/ adj not deserved, necessary, or right: uncalled-for rudeness

un·can·ny /ʌnˈkæni/ adj not natural or usual; mysterious ~nily adv

un·ce·re·mo·ni·ous /ˌʌnsɛrəˈmoʊniəs/ adj 1 informal 2 rudely quick ~ly adv: He was thrown out unceremoniously into the street.

un·cer·tain /ʌnˈsɜrtn/ adj 1 doubtful 2 undecided or unable to decide 3 likely to change: uncertain weather ~ly adv ~ty n [C;U]

un·chart·ed /ʌnˈtʃɑrtɪd◂/ adj esp. lit (of a place) not well known enough for maps to be made

un·cle /ˈʌŋkəl/ n brother of one's father or mother, or husband of one's aunt

un·clean /ˌʌnˈklin◂/ adj not (religiously) pure

Uncle Sam /ˌʌŋkəl ˈsæm/ n infml lit the US or its government

un·com·for·ta·ble /ʌnˈkʌmftəbəl, ʌn-ˈkʌmfətəbəl/ adj 1 not comfortable 2 embarrassed -bly adv

un·com·mon·ly /ʌnˈkɑmənli/ adv fml very: uncommonly good

un·com·pro·mis·ing /ʌnˈkɑmprəˌmaɪzɪŋ/ adj (bravely) unchangeable in one's opinions, actions, etc.

un·con·di·tion·al /ˌʌnkənˈdɪʃənl◂/ adj not limited by or depending on any agreements or conditions: an unconditional guarantee

un·con·scious /ʌnˈkɑnʃəs/ adj 1 having lost consciousness 2 not intentional

un·con·sti·tu·tion·al /ˌʌnkɑnstəˈtuʃənl◂/ adj against the principles of a constitution, and so not legal

un·con·ven·tion·al /ˌʌnkənˈvɛnʃənl◂/ adj very different from the way people usually behave, think, dress, etc.

un·count·a·ble /ʌnˈkaʊntəbəl/ adj that cannot be counted: "Furniture" is an uncountable noun — you can't say "two furnitures."

un·couth /ʌnˈkuθ/ adj fml rough, with bad manners

un·cov·er /ʌnˈkʌvər/ vt 1 remove a covering from 2 find out (something unknown or kept secret)

un·cut /ˌʌnˈkʌt◂/ adj 1 (of a film, book, etc.) with nothing taken out 2 pure; with nothing added

un·daunt·ed /ʌnˈdɔntɪd◂, -ˈdɑn-/ adj not at all discouraged or frightened

un·de·cid·ed /ˌʌndɪˈsaɪdɪd◂/ adj not yet having (been) decided; in doubt

un·de·ni·a·ble /ˌʌndɪˈnaɪəbəl◂/ adj clear and certain -bly adv

un·der /ˈʌndər/ prep 1 below; covered by: The ball rolled under the table. | (fig.) She wrote under the name of George Eliot. 2 less than: under $5 3 working for; controlled by: She has 3 secretaries under her. | Spain under Franco. 4 (expresses various states or relationships): He was under threat of (= was threatened with) dismissal. | I was under the impression (= thought) that you'd gone. 5 in the state or act of: under discussion/contract 6 under age too young in law, esp. for drinking alcohol, driving a car, etc. 7 under cover of hidden (by): They escaped under cover of darkness. ♦ adv 1 in or to a lower place 2 less: children of 9 or under

un·der·a·chieve /ˌʌndərəˈtʃiv/ v perform below the level of ability or expectation -chiever n

un·der·age /ˌʌndərˈeɪdʒ◂/ adj too young to legally buy alcohol, drive a car, etc.: underage drinkers

un·der·bel·ly /ˈʌndərˌbɛli/ n esp. lit weak or undefended part of a place, plan, etc.

un·der·brush /ˈʌndərˌbrʌʃ/ n [U] bushes and low plants growing around trees

und·er·charge /ˌʌndərˈtʃɑrdʒ/ vi/t take too small an amount of money from (someone)

un·der·class·man /ˈʌndərˌklæsmən/ n -men /-mən, -ˌmɛn/ college student in the beginning years

un·der·clothes /ˈʌndərˌkloʊz, -ˌkloʊðz/ n [P] UNDERWEAR

un·der·coat /ˈʌndəˌkoʊt/ n covering of paint that goes under the main covering

un·der·cov·er /ˌʌndəˈkʌvə◂/ adj acting or done secretly, esp. as a SPY

un·der·cur·rent /ˈʌndəˌkʌrənt, -ˌkʌr-/ n 1 hidden current of water beneath the surface 2 hidden tendency: an undercurrent of discontent

un·der·cut /ˌʌndəˈkʌt, ˈʌndəˌkʌt/ vt -cut; pres. p. -tt- sell things more cheaply than (a competitor)

un·der·dog /ˈʌndəˌdɔg/ n one always treated badly by others or expected to lose in a competition

un·der·done /ˌʌndəˈdʌn◂/ adj not completely cooked

un·der·es·ti·mate /ˌʌndəˈestəˌmeɪt/ v 1 vi/t guess, too low a value (for) 2 vt have too low an opinion of ♦ /-stəmət/ n ESTIMATE which is too small

un·der·fed /ˌʌndəˈfed◂/ adj having not enough food

un·der·foot /ˌʌndəˈfʊt/ adv beneath the feet: The path was stony underfoot.

un·der·go /ˌʌndəˈgoʊ/ vt -went /-ˈwent/, -gone /-ˈgɔn/ experience (esp. something unpleasant or difficult)

un·der·grad·u·ate /ˌʌndəˈgrædʒuɪt/ n person attending college for a first degree

un·der·ground /ˈʌndəˌgraʊnd/ adj 1 below the Earth's surface 2 secret; representing a political view not acceptable to the government ♦ n secret group fighting or opposing the rulers of a country ♦ /ˌʌndəˈgraʊnd/ adv go underground hide from political view for a time

un·der·hand /ˌʌndəˈhænd◂/ also **un·der·hand·ed** /-ˈhændɪd◂/ — adj (secretly) dishonest

underhand² /ˈʌndəˌhænd/ adj, adv (in sports) with the hand below the shoulder

un·der·line /ˌʌndəˈlaɪn, ˌʌndəˈlaɪn/ vt 1 draw a line under 2 give additional force to, so as to show importance

un·der·ling /ˈʌndəlɪŋ/ n person of low rank

un·der·ly·ing /ˌʌndəˈlaɪ-ɪŋ◂/ adj (of a reason, cause, etc.) most important but not easy to discover

un·der·mine /ˌʌndəˈmaɪn, ˈʌndəˌmaɪn/ vt 1 weaken or destroy gradually: Criticism undermines his confidence. 2 wear away the earth beneath

un·der·neath /ˌʌndəˈniθ/ prep, adv under; below

un·der·paid /ˌʌndəˈpeɪd◂/ adj earning less money than one deserves

un·der·pants /ˈʌndəˌpænts/ n [P] underclothes for the lower part of the body

un·der·pass /ˈʌndəˌpæs/ n path or road under another road, railroad, etc.

un·der·priv·i·leged /ˌʌndəˈprɪvəlɪdʒd◂/ adj poor and living in bad social conditions

un·der·score /ˌʌndəˈskɔr, -ˈskoʊr/ vt UNDERLINE

un·der·shirt /ˈʌndəˌʃɜt/ n undergarment for the upper body

un·der·side /ˈʌndəˌsaɪd/ n lower side or surface

un·der·signed /ˈʌndəˌsaɪnd/ n fml whose signature is/are beneath the writing: We, the undersigned . . .

un·der·staffed /ˌʌndəˈstæft◂/ adj not having enough workers, or having fewer workers than usual

un·der·stand /ˌʌndəˈstænd/ v -stood /-ˈstʊd/ 1 vi/t know or find the meaning (of): She spoke in Russian, and I didn't understand. 2 vt know or feel closely the nature of (a person, feelings, etc.) 3 vt take or judge (as the meaning) 4 vt fml have been informed: I understand you wish to join. 5 vt add (something unexpressed) in the mind to make a meaning complete 6 make oneself understood make one's meaning clear to others, esp. in speech ~able adj 1 that can be understood 2 reasonable ~ably adv ~ing n 1 [U] mental power; ability to understand 2 [C] private informal agreement 3 [U] sympathy ♦ adj sympathetic

un·der·state /ˌʌndəˈsteɪt, ˌʌndəˈsteɪt/ vt express less strongly than one could or should ~ment n [C;U]

un·der·stud·y /ˈʌndəˌstʌdi/ n actor able to take over from another in a particular part if necessary ♦ vt be an understudy for

un·der·take /ˌʌndəˈteɪk/ vt -took /-ˈtʊk/, -taken /-ˈteɪkən/ fml 1 take up or accept (a position, work, etc.) 2 promise -taking /ˈʌndəˌteɪkɪŋ, ˌʌndəˈteɪ-/ n 1 piece of work; job 2 fml promise

un·der·tak·er /ˈʌndəˌteɪkə/ n funeral arranger -ing n [U]

un·der·tone /ˈʌndəˌtoʊn/ n 1 low voice 2 hidden meaning or feeling

un·der·wa·ter /ˌʌndəˈwɔtə◂, -ˈwɑ-/ adj, adv below the surface of water: underwater photography

un·der·wear /'ʌndəˌwɛr/ n [U] clothes worn next to the body under other clothes

un·der·went /ˌʌndəˈwɛnt/ v past t. of UNDERGO

un·der·world /'ʌndəˌwɜːld/ n 1 criminals considered as a social group 2 home of the dead in ancient Greek stories

un·der·write /ˌʌndəˈraɪt/ vt -wrote /-ˈroʊt/, -written /-ˈrɪtˈn/ fml support, esp. with money –writer /'ʌndəˌraɪtə/ n person who makes insurance contracts

un·de·si·ra·ble /ˌʌndɪˈzaɪrəbəl/ adj fml not wanted; unpleasant ♦ n someone regarded as immoral, criminal, or socially unacceptable –bility n /ˌʌndɪˌzaɪrəˈbɪləti/ [U]

un·de·vel·oped /ˌʌndɪˈvɛləpt◁/ adj (usu. of a place) not having industry, building, etc.

un·dies /'ʌndiz/ n [P] infml (women's) UNDERWEAR

un·dis·put·ed /ˌʌndɪˈspjuːtɪd◁/ adj agreed by everyone: the undisputed leader

un·di·vid·ed /ˌʌndɪˈvaɪdɪd◁/ adj complete

un·do /ʌnˈduː/ vt -did /-ˈdɪd/, -done /-ˈdʌn/ 1 unfasten (something tied or wrapped) 2 remove the effects of: The fire undid months of hard work. ~ing n [S] cause of someone's ruin, failure, etc.

un·doubt·ed /ʌnˈdaʊtɪd◁/ adj known for certain to be (so) ~ly adv

un·dress /ʌnˈdrɛs/ v 1 vi take one's clothes off 2 vt take (someone's) clothes off ♦ n fml lack of clothes ~ed adj wearing no clothes

un·due /ʌnˈduː/ adj too much; unsuitable –unduly adv: not unduly worried

un·du·late /'ʌndʒəˌleɪt/ vi rise and fall like waves –lation /ˌʌndʒəˈleɪʃən/ n [C;U]

un·dy·ing /ʌnˈdaɪ-ɪŋ/ adj lit which will never end

un·earth /ʌnˈɜːθ/ vt 1 dig up 2 discover

un·eas·y /ʌnˈiːzi◁/ adj worried; anxious –ily adv –iness n [U]

un·em·ployed /ˌʌnɪmˈplɔɪd◁/ adj not having a job ♦ n [the+S] people without jobs

un·em·ploy·ment /ˌʌnɪmˈplɔɪmənt/ n [U] 1 condition of lacking a job 2 lack of jobs for numbers of people in society 3 infml government money paid to those without work: collecting unemployment

un·en·vi·a·ble /ʌnˈɛnviəbəl/ adj not to be wished for, esp. because of difficulty

un·e·qualed /ʌnˈiːkwəld/ adj the greatest possible

un·e·quiv·o·cal /ˌʌnɪˈkwɪvəkəl/ adj totally clear in meaning

un·er·ring /ʌnˈɜːrɪŋ, -ˈɛr-/ adj without making a mistake

un·eth·i·cal /ʌnˈɛθɪkəl/ adj morally wrong

un·e·ven /ʌnˈiːvən/ adj 1 not smooth, straight, or regular 2 ODD (2) 3 varying in quality: uneven work (= often fairly bad) ~ly adv ~ness n [U]

un·ex·pect·ed /ˌʌnɪkˈspɛktɪd◁/ adj surprising because of not being expected: his unexpected death ~ly adv

un·ex·pur·gat·ed /ʌnˈɛkspəˌɡeɪtɪd/ adj (of a book, play, etc.) with nothing that is considered improper taken out; complete

un·fail·ing /ʌnˈfeɪlɪŋ/ adj continuous ~ly adv

un·fair /ʌnˈfɛr◁/ adj not right or fair: an unfair decision ~ly adv ~ness n [U]

un·faith·ful /ʌnˈfeɪθfəl/ adj having sex with someone other than one's regular partner

un·fa·mil·iar /ˌʌnfəˈmɪljə/ adj not known to one: unfamiliar face

un·fit /ʌnˈfɪt/ adj not suitable or good enough for a particular purpose: land unfit for farming

un·flap·pa·ble /ʌnˈflæpəbəl/ adj always calm, esp. in difficult situations

un·fold /ʌnˈfoʊld/ v 1 vt open from a folded position 2 vi/t (cause to) become clear, more fully known, etc.: as the story unfolded

un·fore·seen /ˌʌnfəˈsiːn◁, -fɔː-/ adj unexpected and not planned for: unforeseen delays

un·for·get·ta·ble /ˌʌnfəˈɡɛtəbəl/ adj too strong in effect to be forgotten –bly adv

un·for·tu·nate /ʌnˈfɔːtʃənɪt/ adj 1 that makes one sorry 2 unlucky ~ly adv

un·found·ed /ʌnˈfaʊndɪd◁/ adj not supported by facts

un·furl /ʌnˈfɜːl/ vt unroll and open (a flag, sail, etc.)

un·god·ly /ʌnˈɡɒdli/ adj 1 not religious 2 infml (of time) very inconvenient

un·glued /ʌnˈɡluːd/ adj infml emotionally upset

un·grate·ful /ʌnˈɡreɪtfəl/ adj 1 not grateful 2 lit (of work) giving no reward or result

un·guard·ed /ˌʌnˈgɑrdɪd◂/ adj unwisely careless, esp. in speech

un·hap·py /ʌnˈhæpi/ adj not happy; feeling sad, worried, or annoyed –**piness** n [U]

un·heard-of /ʌnˈhɜrd əv/ adj very unusual

u·ni·corn /ˈyunəˌkɔrn/ n imaginary horselike animal with a single horn

un·i·den·ti·fied /ˌʌnaɪˈdɛntəˌfaɪd◂, -ˌʌnə-/ adj not recognized, or not known by name

u·ni·form /ˈyunəˌfɔrm/ n sort of clothes worn by all members of a group: *nurse's/army uniform* ♦ adj the same all over; regular ~**ly** adv ~**ed** adj: *uniformed soldiers* ~**ity** /ˌyunəˈfɔrməti/ n [U]

u·ni·fy /ˈyunəˌfaɪ/ vt bring together so as to be a single whole or all the same –**fication** /ˌyunəfəˈkeɪʃən/ n [U]

u·ni·lat·e·ral /ˌyunəˈlætərəl◂/ adj done by only one group: *unilateral disarmament*

un·im·por·tant /ˌʌnɪmˈpɔrt'nt◂, -ˈpɔrtnt/ adj not important

un·i·ni·ti·at·ed /ˌʌnɪˈnɪʃiˌeɪtɪd/ n [the+P] fml people who are not among those who have special knowledge or experience

un·in·sured /ˌʌnɪnˈʃʊrd◂/ adj having no insurance

un·in·ter·est·ed /ʌnˈɪntrɪstɪd, -təˌrɛs-/ adj not interested

u·nion /ˈyunyən/ n 1 [C] club or society, esp. a LABOR UNION 2 [C] group of states: *the Soviet Union* 3 [U] fml joining 4 [C;U] lit (unity in) marriage

u·nique /yuˈnik/ adj 1 being the only one of its type 2 unusual 3 better than any other ~**ly** adv

u·ni·sex /ˈyunəˌsɛks/ adj of one type for both male and female

u·ni·son /ˈyunəsən/ n [U] 1 being together in taking action 2 everyone singing or playing the same note

u·nit /ˈyunɪt/ n 1 group within a larger organization: *the hospital's intensive care unit* 2 amount forming a standard of measurement: *The dollar is a unit of currency.* 3 whole number less than 10 4 piece of furniture, etc., which can be fitted with others of the same type

u·nite /yuˈnaɪt/ v 1 vt join 2 vi become one 3 vi act together for a purpose

United King·dom /ˌ···ˈ···/ n [the] England, Scotland, Wales, and Northern Ireland

United Na·tions /ˌ··· ˈ··/ [the] international organization that tries to find peaceful solutions to world problems

United States /ˌ·· ˈ·/ [the] also **United States of America** /ˌ··· · · ˈ···/, **US**, **USA** — n republic in North America, made up of 50 states with their own governments

u·ni·ty /ˈyunəti/ n [U] being united or in agreement

u·ni·verse /ˈyunəˌvɜrs/ n [the+S] everything which exists in all space –**versal** /ˌyunəˈvɜrsəl◂/ adj among or for everyone or in every place: *universal agreement* –**versally** adv

u·ni·ver·si·ty /ˌyunəˈvɜrsəti/ n 1 place of education at the highest level, where degrees are given 2 members of this place

un·just /ˌʌnˈdʒʌst◂/ adj not fair or reasonable

un·kempt /ˌʌnˈkɛmpt◂/ adj (esp. of hair) untidy

un·kind /ˌʌnˈkaɪnd◂/ adj not kind; cruel or thoughtless

un·known quan·ti·ty /ˌ·· ˈ···/ n 1 person or thing whose qualities and abilities are not yet known 2 (in MATHEMATICS) a number represented by the letter x

un·law·ful /ʌnˈlɔfəl/ adj not legal ~**ly** adv

un·lead·ed /ʌnˈlɛdɪd/ adj (of gasoline) not containing any LEAD

un·leash /ʌnˈliʃ/ vt allow (feelings, forces, etc.) to act with full force

un·less /ənˈlɛs, ʌn-/ conj except if: *Don't come unless I ask you to.*

un·like·ly /ʌnˈlaɪkli◂/ adj 1 not expected; improbable 2 not likely to happen or be true

un·lim·it·ed /ʌnˈlɪmɪtɪd◂/ adj without a fixed limit: *a rental car with unlimited mileage*

un·list·ed /ʌnˈlɪstɪd◂/ adj (of telephone numbers) not included in the list of numbers in the telephone book

un·load /ʌnˈloʊd/ v 1 vt remove (a load) from (something) 2 vi/t remove bullets from (a gun) or film from (a camera) 3 vt get rid of

un·loose /ʌnˈlus/ vt lit set free

un·loos·en /ʌnˈlusən/ vt loosen

un·luck·y /ʌnˈlʌki◂/ adj 1 having bad luck 2 causing or resulting from bad luck

un·mask /ʌnˈmæsk/ vt show the hidden truth about

un·men·tio·na·ble /ʌnˈmɛnʃənəbəl/ adj too shocking to be spoken about

un·mit·i·gat·ed /ʌnˈmɪtəˌgeɪtɪd◂/ adj in every way (bad): *an unmitigated disaster*

un·nat·u·ral /ʌnˈnætʃərəl/ adj **1** unusual **2** against ordinary good ways of behaving: *unnatural sexual practices*

un·nec·es·sar·y /ʌnˈnesəˌseri/ adj **1** not needed, or more than is needed: *unnecessary delays* –rily /ʌnˈnesəˈserəli/ adv

un·nerve /ʌnˈnɜːv/ vt take away (someone's) confidence or courage

un·ob·tru·sive /ʌnəbˈtruːsɪv, -zɪv/ adj not (too) noticeable ~ly adv

un·of·fi·cial /ʌnəˈfɪʃəl◁/ adj **1** without approval or permission: *unofficial reports* **2** not made publicly known, or not done as part of official duties: *the President's unofficial visit*

un·or·tho·dox /ʌnˈɔːθəˌdɒks/ adj different from what is usual or expected

un·pack /ʌnˈpæk/ vi/t remove (possessions) from (a container)

un·pleas·ant /ʌnˈplezənt/ adj **1** not enjoyable **2** unkind

un·plug /ʌnˈplʌg/ vt -gg- disconnect (electrical apparatus) by removing its PLUG from a SOCKET

un·pop·u·lar /ʌnˈpɒpjələ/ adj not liked by most people

un·pre·ce·dent·ed /ʌnˈpresəˌdentɪd/ adj never having happened before

un·pro·fes·sion·al /ʌnprəˈfeʃənl/ adj not behaving as one should in a profession or activity: *unprofessional conduct*

un·pro·voked /ʌnprəˈvəʊkt◁/ adj (of anger, attacks, etc.) directed at someone who has done nothing to deserve it

un·qual·i·fied /ʌnˈkwɒləˌfaɪd/ adj **1** not limited **2** not having suitable knowledge or experience

un·ques·tio·na·ble /ʌnˈkwestʃənəbəl/ adj which cannot be doubted; certain –bly adv

un·rav·el /ʌnˈrævəl/ v -l- **1** vi/t become or cause (threads, cloth, etc.) to become separated or unwoven **2** vt make clear (a mystery)

un·real /ʌnˈrɪəl◁/ adj seeming imaginary or unlike reality ~ity /ʌnriˈæləti/ n [U]

un·rea·son·a·ble /ʌnˈriːzənəbəl/ adj **1** wrong or unfair **2** behaving in a way that is silly or not sensible ~bly adv

un·re·lent·ing /ʌnrɪˈlentɪŋ◁/ adj continuing for a long time: *unrelenting rain*

un·re·mit·ting /ʌnrɪˈmɪtɪŋ◁/ adj fml (of something difficult) never stopping

un·re·quit·ed /ʌnrɪˈkwaɪtɪd◁/ adj fml not given in return: *unrequited love*

un·rest /ʌnˈrest/ n [U] troubled or dissatisfied confusion, often with fighting

un·ri·valed /ʌnˈraɪvəld/ adj better than any other

un·roll /ʌnˈrəʊl/ vi/t open from a rolled condition

un·ru·ly /ʌnˈruːli/ adj **1** behaving wildly: *unruly children* **2** hard to keep in place: *unruly hair*

un·safe /ʌnˈseɪf/ adj **1** dangerous: *unsafe equipment* **2** (of a person) in danger of being hurt

un·sat·is·fac·to·ry /ʌnsætɪsˈfæktəri/ adj not good enough -torily adv

un·sa·vor·y /ʌnˈseɪvəri/ adj unpleasant or unacceptable in moral values

un·scathed /ʌnˈskeɪðd/ adj not harmed

unscrew /ʌnˈskruː/ vt **1** remove the screws from **2** take (a lid) off

un·scru·pu·lous /ʌnˈskruːpjələs/ adj not caring about honesty and fairness

un·sea·so·na·ble /ʌnˈsiːzənəbəl/ adj unusual for the time of year, esp. bad –bly adv

un·seat /ʌnˈsiːt/ vt **1** remove from a position of power **2** (of a horse) throw off (a rider)

un·seem·ly /ʌnˈsiːmli/ adj not proper or suitable (in behavior)

un·seen /ʌnˈsiːn◁/ adj, adv not noticed or seen

un·set·tle /ʌnˈsetl/ vt make more anxious, dissatisfied, etc. -tled adj (of weather, a political situation, etc.) likely to get worse

un·sight·ly /ʌnˈsaɪtli/ adj ugly

un·skilled /ʌnˈskɪld/ adj (of workers or jobs) not having or requiring special skills or training

un·so·cial /ʌnˈsəʊʃəl◁/ adj unsuitable for combining with family and social life: *working unsocial hours*

un·spea·ka·ble /ʌnˈspiːkəbəl/ adj terrible –bly adv

un·spec·i·fied /ʌnˈspesəˌfaɪd/ adj not clearly or definitely stated

un·spo·ken /ʌnˈspəʊkən/ adj understood, but not discussed: *an unspoken agreement*

un·sta·ble /ʌnˈsteɪbəl/ adj **1** likely to change suddenly, with difficult or dangerous results: *an unstable economy* **2** dangerous and likely to fall over

un·stuck /ʌnˈstʌk/ *adj* not fastened

un·sung /ˌʌnˈsʌŋ◀/ *adj lit* not famous (though deserving to be)

un·sure /ˌʌnˈʃʊr◀/ *adj* 1 not certain 2 **unsure of oneself** lacking confidence

un·swerv·ing /ʌnˈswɜːvɪŋ/ *adj* firm: *unswerving loyalty*

un·think·a·ble /ʌnˈθɪŋkəbəl/ *adj* that cannot be considered or accepted; impossible

un·til /ənˈtɪl, ʌn-/ *prep, conj* 1 up to (the time that): *Don't start until he arrives.* 2 as far as: *We stayed on the train until Pittsburgh.*

un·to /ˈʌntu/ *prep lit* to

un·told /ˌʌnˈtoʊld◀/ *adj* very great: *untold damage*

un·touch·a·ble /ʌnˈtʌtʃəbəl/ *adj* in such a strong position as to be unaffected by anything or unable to be punished

un·true /ʌnˈtru/ *adj* not giving the right facts; false

un·truth /ʌnˈtruθ/ *n fml* **-truths** /-ˈtruðz, -ˈtruθs/ lie **~ful** *adj* dishonest or not true **~fully** *adv*

un·used[1] /ʌnˈyuzd◀/ *adj* not being used, or never used

un·used[2] /ʌnˈyust/ *adj* **unused to** not experienced in dealing with: *unused to driving at night*

un·u·su·al /ʌnˈyuʒuəl, -ʒəl/ *adj fml* 1 not common 2 interesting because different from others **~ly** *adv* 1 very 2 in an unusual way

un·var·nished /ʌnˈvɑrnɪʃt/ *adj* without additional description

un·veil /ʌnˈveɪl/ *vt* 1 remove a covering from 2 show publicly for the first time

un·want·ed /ˌʌnˈwɑntɪd◀, -ˈwɒn-, -ˈwɔn-/ *adj* not wanted or needed: *unwanted visitors*

un·war·rant·ed /ʌnˈwɔrəntɪd, -ˈwɑr-/ *adj* (done) without good reason

un·well /ʌnˈwel/ *adj* (slightly) sick

un·wiel·dy /ʌnˈwildi/ *adj* awkward to move, handle, or use

un·will·ing /ʌnˈwɪlɪŋ/ *adj* not wanting to do something: *unwilling to help*

un·wind /ʌnˈwaɪnd/ *v* **-wound** /-ˈwaʊnd/ 1 *vi/t* undo (something wound) or become undone: *unwinding a ball of yarn* 2 *vi* become calmer and free of care

un·wit·ting /ˌʌnˈwɪtɪŋ◀/ *adj* not knowing or intended: *their unwitting accomplice*

un·writ·ten rule /ˌʌnrɪtˈn ˈrul/ *n* usual custom (not officially stated)

un·zip /ʌnˈzɪp/ *vt* **-pp-** unfasten the ZIPPER on (a bag, garment, etc.)

up /ʌp/ *adv* 1 to or at a higher level: *She climbed up onto the roof.* | *He turned up his collar.* 2 (shows increase): *Turn the radio up.* (= louder) 3 to the north: *driving up to Canada* 4 out of bed: *We stayed up late.* 5 so as to be completely finished: *Eat up your vegetables.* 6 into small pieces: *She tore it up.* 7 firmly; tightly: *He tied up the package.* 8 together: *Add up the figures.* 9 more loudly: *Speak up!* 10 on top: *right side up* 11 **up against** having to face (something difficult) 12 **up and down: a** higher and lower: *jumping up and down* **b** backwards and forwards: *walking up and down* 13 **up to: a** towards and as far as: *He walked up to me and asked my name.* **b** until: *up to now* **c** good, well, or smart enough for: *He's not up to the job.* **d** the duty or responsibility of: *I'll leave it up to you.* (= you must decide) **e** doing (something bad): *What are you up to?* 14 **Up with** We want or approve of: *Up with the workers!* ♦ *prep* 1 to or at a higher level on: *walking up the stairs* 2 at or at the top or far end of: *They live just up the road.* ♦ *adj* 1 directed up: *the up escalator* 2 at a higher level: *Profits are up.* 3 **be up** be happening: *What's up?* 4 **be well up in/on** know a lot about 5 **up and about** out of bed (again) and able to walk 6 **up for: a** intended or being considered for **b** on trial for **c** **up for** wanting to do or experience: *Are you up for a movie?* ♦ *vt* *sl* increase

up-and-com·ing /ˌ· · ˈ··◀/ *adj* new and likely to succeed

up-and-up /ˌ· · ˈ·/ *n* **on the up-and-up** honest

up·bring·ing /ˈʌpˌbrɪŋɪŋ/ *n* [S] (way of) training and caring for a child

up·chuck /ˈʌpˌtʃʌk/ *vt* VOMIT

up·com·ing /ˈʌpˌkʌmɪŋ/ *adj* about to happen

up·date /ˌʌpˈdeɪt, ˈʌpdeɪt/ *vt* 1 make more modern 2 supply with the latest information ♦ /ˈʌpdeɪt/ *n* report of the latest information

up·front /ˌʌpˈfrʌnt/ *adj* very direct and making no attempt to hide one's meaning

up·grade /ˌʌpˈgreɪd, ˈʌpgreɪd/ *vt* 1 give a more important position to 2 improve by modernizing: *upgrade a computer system* ♦ /ˈʌpgreɪd/ *n*: *software upgrade*

up·heav·al /ʌpˈhivəl/ n [C;U] great change and confusion, with much activity

up·held /ʌpˈhɛld/ past t. and p. of UPHOLD

up·hill /ʌpˈhɪl◂/ adj, adv 1 up a slope 2 difficult: an uphill task

up·hold /ʌpˈhoʊld/ vt -held /-ˈhɛld/ 1 prevent from being weakened or taken away 2 declare (a decision) to be right ~er n

up·hol·ster /ʌpˈhoʊlstə, əˈpoʊl-/ vt cover and fill (furniture) ~er n ~y n [U] material covering and filling furniture

up·keep /ˈʌpkip/ n [U] (cost of) keeping something repaired and in order

up·lift /ʌpˈlɪft/ vt fml encourage cheerful or holy feelings in

up·on /əˈpɑn, əˈpɔn/ prep fml for: ON¹ (1,3,4,6,7)

up·per /ˈʌpə/ adj at or nearer the top: the upper arm ♦ n 1 top part of a shoe 2 sl drug that speeds you up

upper class /ˌ·· ˈ·◂/ n highest social class, **upper-class** adj

upper hand /ˌ·· ˈ·/ n [the+S] control

up·per·most /ˈʌpəˌmoʊst/ adv in the highest or strongest position

up·right /ˈʌp-raɪt/ adj 1 exactly straight up; not bent or leaning 2 completely honest ♦ n upright supporting beam

up·ris·ing /ˈʌpˌraɪzɪŋ/ n act of the ordinary people suddenly and violently opposing those in power

up·roar /ˈʌp-rɔr, -roʊr/ n [S;U] confused noisy activity, esp. shouting ~ious /ʌpˈrɔriəs, -ˈroʊr-/ adj very noisy, esp. with laughter

up·root /ʌpˈrut, -ˈroʊt/ vt 1 tear (a plant) from the earth 2 remove from a home, settled habits, etc.

ups and downs /ˌ· · ˈ·/ n [P] good and bad periods

up·scale /ˈʌpskeɪl/ adj being or using goods produced to meet the demand of the wealthier social groups

up·set /ʌpˈsɛt/ vt -set; pres. p. -tt- 1 turn over, esp. accidentally, causing confusion or scattering 2 cause to be worried, sad, angry, etc. 3 make slightly ill ♦ n /ˈʌpsɛt/ 1 slight illness: a stomach upset 2 unexpected result

up·shot /ˈʌpʃɑt/ n result in the end

up·side down /ˌʌpsaɪd ˈdaʊn/ adj 1 with the top turned to the bottom 2 in disorder

up·stage /ʌpˈsteɪdʒ/ vt take attention away from (someone) for oneself

up·stairs /ˌʌpˈstɛrz◂/ adv, adj on or to a higher floor

up·stand·ing /ˌʌpˈstændɪŋ◂/ adj 1 tall and strong 2 honest

up·start /ˈʌpstɑrt/ n someone who has risen too suddenly or unexpectedly to a high position

up·state /ˈʌpsteɪt/ n, adj (esp. northern) part of a state away from cities

up·stream /ˌʌpˈstrim/ adv, adj moving against the current of a river

up·take /ˈʌpteɪk/ n [U] ability to understand: He's pretty slow on the uptake.

up·tight /ˌʌpˈtaɪt◂/ adj infml anxious and nervous

up-to-date /ˌ· · ˈ·◂/ adj 1 modern 2 including or having all the latest information

up·town /ˌʌpˈtaʊn◂/ adj, n (of the) northern part of a city: the uptown bus

up·turn /ˈʌptərn/ n a favorable change

up·ward /ˈʌpwərd/ adj going up **upwards** adv more than

upwardly-mo·bile /ˌ··· ˈ·◂/ adj able or wishing to move into a higher social class and become more wealthy **upward mobility** /ˌ·· ·ˈ···/ n

u·ra·ni·um /yuˈreɪniəm/ n [U] radioactive (RADIOACTIVITY) metal used in producing atomic power

U·ra·nus /yuˈreɪnəs, ˈyʊrənəs/ n the PLANET 7th in order from the sun

ur·ban /ˈərbən/ adj of towns

ur·bane /əˈbeɪn/ adj smoothly polite ~ly adv –banity /-ˈbænəti/ n [U]

ur·chin /ˈərtʃɪn/ n small dirty, untidy child — see also SEA URCHIN

urge /ərdʒ/ vt 1 try strongly to persuade: He urged me to reconsider. 2 drive forwards: He urged the horses onward with a whip. ♦ n strong desire or need

ur·gent /ˈərdʒənt/ adj that must be dealt with at once ~ly adv **urgency** n [U]

u·ri·nal /ˈyʊrənl/ n container or building for (men) urinating

u·rine /ˈyʊrɪn/ n [U] liquid waste passed from the body **urinary** adj **urinate** vi pass urine from the body **urination** /ˌyʊrəˈneɪʃən/ n [U]

urn /ərn/ n 1 large metal container for serving tea or coffee 2 container for the ashes of a burned dead body

us /əs; strong ʌs/ pron (object form of we)

US also **USA** — *abbrev. for:* **1** the United States (of America) **2** of the United States: *the US Navy*

us·age /ˈyusɪdʒ/ *n* **1** [C;U] way of using a language: *a book on English usage* **2** *fml* (type or degree of) use

use¹ /yus/ *n* **1** [U] using or being used **2** [U] ability or right to use something: *He lost the use of his legs.* **3** [C;U] purpose: *A machine with many uses.* **4** [U] advantage; usefulness: *It's no use complaining.* (= complaining will have no effect) **5 in use** being used **6 make use of** use **7** of use useful ~**fully** *adv* ~**fulness** *n* [U] ~**less** *adj* **1** not useful **2** unable to do anything properly ~**lessly** *adv*

use² /yuz/ *vt* **1** employ for a purpose; put to use: *Oil can be used as a fuel.* **2** finish; CONSUME (2) **3** take unfair advantage of; EXPLOIT **usable** *adj* **used** *adj* that has already had an owner: *used cars* **user** *n*

  use up *phr vt* finish completely

use³ /yus/ *vi* (used in the past tense for showing what always or regularly happened): *I used to go there every week, but I no longer do.*

used to /ˈyust tə; *final or before a vowel* yust tu/ *adj* no longer finding (something) strange or annoying because it has become familiar: *I'm used to the noise.*

user-friend·ly /ˌ··ˈ···◂/ *adj* easy to use or understand

ush·er /ˈʌʃə/ *n* someone who shows people to their seats in a public place ♦ *vt fml* bring by showing the way: (fig.) *The bombing of Hiroshima ushered in the nuclear age.*

USS *n* United States Ship; title for a ship in the US navy

USSR *abbrev. for:* Union of Soviet Socialist Republics; the former Soviet Union

u·su·al /ˈyuʒuəl, -ʒəl/ *adj* in accordance with what happens most of the time: *He lacked his usual cheerfulness.* ~**ly** *adv* in most cases; generally

u·surp /yuˈsɝp, yuˈzɝp/ *vt fml* steal (someone else's power or position) ~**er** *n*

u·su·ry /ˈyuʒəri/ *n* [U] *fml* lending money to be paid back at an unfairly high rate of interest ~**rer** *n*

u·ten·sil /yuˈtɛnsəl/ *n fml* object with a particular use, esp. a tool or container

u·te·rus /ˈyutərəs/ *n* round organ inside women and female MAMMALs in which babies or young develop

u·til·i·tar·i·an /yuˌtɪləˈtɛriən/ *adj fml, sometimes derog* made to be useful rather than decorative

u·til·i·ty /yuˈtɪləti/ *n* **1** [U] *fml* degree of usefulness **2** [C] public service, such as water supplies, electricity, etc.

u·til·ize /ˈyutlˌaɪz/ *vt fml for:* USE² (1) **-ization** /ˌyutlə-ˈzeɪʃən/ *n* [U]

ut·most /ˈʌtˈmoʊst/ *adj fml* very great: *done with (the) utmost care* ♦ *n* [U] the most that can be done: *I did my utmost to prevent it.*

u·to·pi·a /yuˈtoʊpiə/ *n* [C;U] perfect society **-pian** *adj* impractically trying to bring social perfection

ut·ter¹ /ˈʌtə/ *adj* (esp. of something bad) complete: *utter nonsense* ~**ly** *adv*

utter² *vt fml* make (a sound) or produce (words) ~**ance** *n fml* **1** [U] speaking **2** [C] something said

U-turn /ˈyu tɝn/ *n* **1** turning movement in a vehicle which takes one back in the direction one came from **2** complete change, resulting in the opposite of what has gone before

V

V, v /viː/ the 22nd letter of the English alphabet

v abbrev. for: verb

va·can·cy /ˈveɪkənsi/ n unfilled place, such as a job or hotel room

va·cant /ˈveɪkənt/ adj 1 empty 2 (of a job) having no worker to do it 3 showing lack of interest or serious thought ~**ly** adv

va·cate /ˈveɪkeɪt/ vt fml cease to use or live in: *Please vacate your seats.*

va·ca·tion /veɪˈkeɪʃən, və-/ n 1 [C] time of rest from work, school, etc. 2 [U] fml vacating ♦ vi take a vacation

vac·cine /ˈvæksiːn/ n [C;U] substance put into the body to protect it against disease –**cinate** /ˈvæksəneɪt/ vt put a vaccine into –**cination** /ˌvæksəˈneɪʃən/ n [C;U]

vac·u·ous /ˈvækjuəs/ adj fml 1 showing foolishness: *a vacuous grin* 2 with no purpose or meaning ~**ly** adv –**uity** /væˈkjuːəti, və-/ n [U]

vac·uum /ˈvækjum/ n 1 vacuum cleaner 2 space completely without air or other gas: (fig.) *Her death left a vacuum (= emptiness) in our lives.* ♦ vt clean with a vacuum cleaner

vacuum clean·er /ˈ·· ˌ·-/ n electric apparatus for sucking up dirt from floors, etc.

vacuum-packed /ˌ·· ˈ·◄/ adj wrapped in plastic with all air removed

vag·a·bond /ˈvægəbɒnd/ n lit person who lives a wandering life

va·gi·na /vəˈdʒaɪnə/ n passage from the outer female sex organs to the UTERUS

va·grant /ˈveɪgrənt/ n fml or law person with no home who wanders around and usu. begs **vagrancy** /ˈveɪgrənsi/ n [U] being a vagrant

vague /veɪg/ adj 1 not clearly seen, described, understood, etc. 2 unable to express oneself clearly ~**ly** adv ~**ness** n [U]

vain /veɪn/ adj 1 admiring oneself too much 2 unsuccessful; unimportant: *a vain attempt* 3 **in vain** unsuccessfully 4 **take someone's name in vain** talk disrespectfully about someone ~**ly** adv

val·ance /ˈvæləns/ n piece above a window to hide curtain tops

val·e·dic·tion /ˌvæləˈdɪkʃən/ n [C;U] fml or lit (act of) saying goodbye –**tory** /-ˈdɪktəri/ adj used in valediction

val·e·dic·to·ri·an /ˌvælədɪkˈtɔːriən, -ˈtoʊr-/ n student who received the best grades all through high school or college, and gives a speech at GRADUATION

va·len·cy /ˈveɪlənsi/ n measure of the power of atoms to form compounds

val·en·tine /ˈvæləntaɪn/ n (card sent to) a lover chosen on **Valentine's Day** (February 14th)

val·et /ˈvæleɪ, ˈvælɛɪ, ˈvælɪt/ n 1 person who parks cars at restaurants, etc. 2 hotel servant who cleans and presses clothes

val·iant /ˈvæljənt/ adj esp. fml or lit very brave ~**ly** adv 1 very bravely 2 very hard: *He tried valiantly (but without success) to pass the exam.*

val·id /ˈvælɪd/ adj 1 (of a reason, argument, etc.) firmly based and acceptable 2 that can legally be used: *a ticket valid for 3 months* –**ly** adv –**ate** vt fml make valid **validity** /vəˈlɪdəti/ n [U]

Val·i·um /ˈvæliəm/ n tdmk widely used calming drug

val·ley /ˈvæli/ n land between 2 lines of hills or mountains

val·or /ˈvælə/ n [U] esp. fml or lit great bravery –**orous** adj

val·u·a·ble /ˈvæljəbəl, ˈvæljuəbəl/ adj 1 worth a lot of money 2 very useful ♦ n something VALUABLE (1)

val·u·a·tion /ˌvæljuˈeɪʃən/ n 1 [C;U] calculating how much something is worth 2 [C] value decided on

val·ue /ˈvælju/ n 1 [S;U] usefulness or importance, esp. compared with other things: *The map was of great value in finding the way.* 2 [C;U] worth in esp. money: *goods to the value of $500* 3 [U] worth compared with the amount paid: *a restaurant offering the best value in town* ♦ vt 1 calculate the value of 2 consider to be of great worth

values /ˈvæljuːz/ n [P] standards or principles; people's ideas about the worth of certain qualities: *moral values* **valueless** adj –**uer** /ˈvæljuə/ n

valve /vælv/ n 1 part inside a pipe which opens and shuts to control the flow of liquid or gas through it 2 closed airless glass tube for controlling a flow of electricity

vam·pire /'væmpaɪə/ n imaginary evil creature that sucks people's blood

van /væn/ n covered road vehicle or railroad car for carrying esp. goods

van·dal /'vændl/ n person who destroys beautiful or useful things ~**ism** [U] needless damage to esp. public buildings ~**ize** vt destroy or damage intentionally

vane /veɪn/ n bladelike turning part of a machine — see also WEATHER VANE

van·guard /'vængɑrd, 'vængɑrd/ n 1 leading part of some kind of advancement in human affairs: scientists in the vanguard of medical research 2 front of a marching army

va·nil·la /və'nɪlə/ n [U] plant substance with a strong smell, used in food ♦ adj usual; ordinary

van·ish /'vænɪʃ/ vi 1 disappear 2 cease to exist

van·i·ty /'vænəti/ n [U] 1 being too proud of oneself 2 quality of being without lasting value

van·quish /'væŋkwɪʃ, 'væn-/ vt esp. lit defeat completely

vap·id /'væpɪd/ adj fml dull

va·por /'veɪpə/ n [U] gaslike form of a liquid, such as mist or steam
vaporize /'veɪpəraɪz/ vi/t change into vapor

var·i·a·ble /'vɛriəbəl, 'vær-/ adj that changes or can be changed; not fixed or steady ♦ n variable amount –**bly** adv

var·i·ance /'vɛriəns, 'vær-/ n fml **at variance (with)** not in agreement (with)

var·i·ant /'vɛriənt, 'vær-/ n, adj (form, etc.) that is different and can be used instead: variant spellings

var·i·a·tion /ˌvɛri'eɪʃən, ˌvær-/ n 1 [C;U] (example or degree of) varying: price variations 2 [C] any of a set of pieces of music based on a single tune

var·i·cose veins /ˌværəkoʊs 'veɪnz/ n [P] swollen blood tubes, esp. in the legs

var·ied /'vɛrid, 'vær-/ adj 1 VARIOUS (1) 2 (always) changing: a varied life

var·i·e·gat·ed /'vɛriəgeɪtɪd, 'vɛrɪgeɪtɪd, 'vær-/ adj marked irregularly with different colors –**gation** /ˌvɛriə'geɪʃən, ˌvɛri'geɪʃən, ˌvær-/ n [U]

va·ri·e·ty /və'raɪəti/ n 1 [U] not being always the same: a job lacking variety 2 [S] group containing different sorts of the same thing: a wide variety of colors 3 [C] sort: a new variety of wheat 4 [U] entertainment with many short performances of singing, dancing, telling jokes, etc.

var·i·ous /'vɛriəs, 'vær-/ adj 1 different from each other: There are various ways of doing it. 2 several ~**ly** adv

var·nish /'vɑrnɪʃ/ n [C;U] liquid that gives a hard shiny surface to esp. wooden articles ♦ vt cover with varnish
varnish over phr vt cover up (something unpleasant)

var·si·ty /'vɑrsəti/ n [C;U] main team that represents a school or college in sports

var·y /'vɛri, 'væri/ v 1 vi be different (from each other): Houses vary in size. 2 vi/t change, esp. continually: varying one's work methods

vase /veɪs, veɪz, vɑz/ n deep decorative pot for esp. flowers

va·sec·to·my /və'sɛktəmi/ n operation for cutting the tubes that carry SPERM in a man, to prevent him from becoming a father

vast /væst/ adj extremely large: a vast desert/improvement ~**ly** adv

vat /væt/ n large liquid container for industrial use: a whiskey vat

Vat·i·can /'vætɪkən/ n (palace in Rome which is) the center of government of the Roman Catholic Church

vault¹ /vɔlt/ n 1 room with thick walls, for storing valuable things 2 underground room, esp. for storing things or for dead bodies 3 place where money is kept safe in a bank 4 arched roof

vault² vi jump using the hands or a pole to gain more height ♦ n act of vaulting ~**er** n

V chip /'vi tʃɪp/ n computer CHIP in a television that allows parents to prevent their children from watching programs containing sex or violence

VCR n videocassette recorder; machine for recording television shows or watching VIDEOTAPES

VD n [U] VENEREAL DISEASE

veal /vil/ n [U] meat from a young cow

veer /vɪr/ vi change direction

veg /vɛdʒ/ v -**gg- veg out** phr vi sl relax and not do anything important

ve·gan /'vidʒən, 'vigən, 'veɪ-/ n person who eats no food that comes from animals ♦ adj

vege·ta·ble /'vɛdʒtəbəl/ n 1 plant grown for food to be eaten with the main part of a meal, rather than with sweet things:

Potatoes and carrots are vegetables. **2** human being who exists but has little or no power of thought

veg·e·tar·i·an /ˌvedʒəˈteriən/ n person who eats no meat ♦ adj **1** of or related to vegetarians **2** made up only of vegetables

veg·e·tate /ˈvedʒəˌteɪt/ vi lead a dull, inactive life

veg·e·ta·tion /ˌvedʒəˈteɪʃən/ n [U] plants

veg·gies /ˈvedʒiz/ n infml [P] vegetables

ve·he·ment /ˈviəmənt/ adj fml forceful ~**ly** adv –**mence** n [U]

ve·hi·cle /ˈviːɪkəl/ n **1** something in or on which people or goods are carried, such as a car, bicycle, etc. **2** means of expressing or showing something: *He bought the newspaper company as a vehicle for his own political views.*

veil /veɪl/ n **1** covering for a woman's face or head **2** something that covers and hides: *a veil of mist* ♦ vt cover (as if) with a veil: *veiled in secrecy* ~**ed** adj expressed indirectly: *veiled threats*

vein /veɪn/ n **1** tube carrying blood back to the heart **2** thin line running through a leaf or insect's wing **3** crack in rock, containing metal **4** small but noticeable amount: *a vein of cruelty* **5** state of mind: *in a sad vein*

Vel·cro /ˈvelkrou/ n tdmk [U] cloth with special surfaces that fasten to each other

ve·loc·i·ty /vəˈlɑsəti/ n fml speed

vel·vet /ˈvelvɪt/ n [U] cloth with a soft furry surface on one side only ~**y** adj soft like velvet

ven·det·ta /venˈdetə/ n situation that lasts for a long time, in which one person repeatedly tries to harm another

vend·ing ma·chine /ˈvendɪŋ məˌʃiːn/ n machine into which one puts money to obtain small articles

vend·or /ˈvendə/ n fml seller

ve·neer /vəˈnɪr/ n **1** thin covering of wood on an article **2** false outer appearance: *a veneer of respectability* ♦ vt cover with a veneer

ven·e·ra·ble /ˈvenərəbəl/ adj fml deserving respect or honor because of great age or wisdom

ven·e·rate /ˈvenəˌreɪt/ vt fml treat (someone or something old) with great respect or honor –**ration** /ˌvenəˈreɪʃən/ n [U]

ve·ne·re·al dis·ease /vəˌnɪriəl dɪˈziːz/ n [C;U] disease passed on by sexual activity

ve·ne·tian blind /vəˌniːʃən ˈblaɪnd/ n window covering with long flat bars that can be turned to let in or shut out light

ven·geance /ˈvendʒəns/ n **1** [U] harm done in return for harm done to oneself: *He took vengeance on his tormentors.* **with a vengeance** infml very greatly

venge·ful /ˈvendʒfəl/ adj esp. lit fiercely wishing to take vengeance –**ly** adv

ven·i·son /ˈvenəsən/ n [U] deer meat

ven·om /ˈvenəm/ n **1** liquid poison produced by certain animals **2** great anger or hatred ~**ous** adj: *a venomous snake/ book*

vent[1] /vent/ n **1** opening or pipe by which gas, smoke, etc., escape **2** **give vent to** express freely: *giving vent to his anger*

vent[2] v **vent on** phr vt express by making (someone or something) suffer: *venting her fury on the cat*

ven·ti·late /ˈventɪˌleɪt/ vt let or bring fresh air into (a room, building, etc.) –**lator** n **1** apparatus for ventilating **2** apparatus for pumping air into and out of the lungs of someone who cannot breathe properly –**lation** /ˌventəˈleɪʃən/ n [U]

ven·tri·cle /ˈventrɪkəl/ n space in the bottom of the heart that pushes blood out into the body

ven·tril·o·quist /venˈtrɪləkwɪst/ n someone who can make their voice seem to come from someone or somewhere else –**quism** /-ləˌkwɪzəm/ n [U]

ven·ture /ˈventʃə/ v **1** vi risk going: *She ventured too near the cliff edge, and fell over.* **2** vt fml dare to say ♦ n (new and risky) course of action: *her latest commercial venture*

venture cap·i·tal /ˈ·· ˌ···/ n [U] money lent to start up a new business company, esp. a risky one

ven·ture·some /ˈventʃəsəm/ adj ready to take risks

ven·ue /ˈvenyu/ n law place where something happened or where a case is tried

Ve·nus /ˈviːnəs/ n the PLANET 2nd in order from the sun

ve·rac·i·ty /vəˈræsəti/ n [U] fml truthfulness

ve·ran·da /vəˈrændə/ n open area with a floor and roof beside a house

verb /vɜːb/ n word or group of words that is used in describing an action, experience, or state, such as *wrote* in *She wrote a letter,* or *put on* in *He put on his coat*

verb·al /'vɜbəl/ *adj* **1** spoken, not written **2** of words and their use **3** of a verb ~**ly** *adv* in spoken words

verb·al·ize /'vɜbəˌlaɪz/ express (something) in words

verbal noun /ˌ·· '·/ *noun* describing an action, formed by adding -*ing* to the verb: *In the sentence "The building of the bridge was slow work," "building" is a verbal noun.*

ver·ba·tim /ˌvɜ'beɪtɪm/ *adv, adj* repeating the actual words exactly

ver·bose /vɜ'boʊs/ *adj fml* using too many words –**bosity** /-'basəti/ *n* [U]

ver·dant /'vɜdənt/ *adj lit* green with growing plants

ver·dict /'vɜdɪkt/ *n* **1** decision made by a JURY at the end of a trial about whether the prisoner is guilty **2** judgment; opinion

verge¹ /vɜdʒ/ *n* **on the verge of** nearly; about to

verge² *v* **verge on** *phr vt* be near to: *dark gray, verging on black*

ver·i·fy /'vɛrəˌfaɪ/ *vt* make certain that (something) is true –**fiable** *adj* –**fication** /ˌvɛrəfə'keɪʃən/ *n* [U]

ver·i·ta·ble /'vɛrətəbəl/ *adj fml* (used to give force to an expression) real: *a veritable feast* –**bly** *adv*

ver·min /'vɜmɪn/ *n* [P] **1** insects and small animals that do damage **2** people who are a trouble to society

ver·mouth /vɜ'muθ/ *n* [U] drink made from wine with substances added that have a strong taste

ver·nac·u·lar /vɜ'nækyələ/ *adj, n* (in or being) the language spoken in a particular place

ver·sa·tile /'vɜsətl, -ˌtaɪl/ *adj* that can do many different things or has many uses –**tility** /ˌvɜsə'tɪləti/ *n* [U]

verse /vɜs/ *n* **1** [U] writing in the form of poetry, esp. with RHYMES — see also BLANK VERSE, FREE VERSE **2** [C] single division of a poem **3** [C] short numbered group of sentences in the Bible or other holy book

versed /vɜst/ *adj fml* experienced; skilled: *thoroughly versed in the arts of diplomacy*

ver·sion /'vɜʒən/ *n* **1** form of something that is slightly different from others of the same sort: *This dress is a cheaper version of the one we saw in the other store.* **2** one person's account of an event: *The 2 eyewitnesses gave different versions of the accident.*

ver·sus /'vɜsəs/ *prep* in competition with; against

ver·te·bra /'vɜtəbrə/ *n* -**brae** /-bri, -breɪ/ small bone in the BACKBONE

ver·te·brate /'vɜtəbrɪt, -ˌbreɪt/ *n* animal with a BACKBONE

ver·ti·cal /'vɜtɪkəl/ *adj* forming a 90° angle with the ground or bottom; upright ~**ly** *adv*

ver·ti·go /'vɜtɪˌgoʊ/ *n* [U] unpleasant feeling of being unsteady at great heights

verve /vɜv/ *n* [U] forcefulness and eager enjoyment

ve·ry /'vɛri/ *adv* **1** to a great degree: *a very exciting book* **2** in the greatest possible degree: *I did my very best to help.* **3 very good** (used as a respectful form of agreement) **of course 4 very well** *fml* (used as a form of agreement, often with some degree of unwillingness) ♦ *adj* **1** (used for giving force to an expression) actual: *He died in that very bed.* **2 the very idea!** (used for expressing surprise at something said by someone else)

ves·sel /'vɛsəl/ *n* **1** ship or large boat **2** (round) container, esp. for liquids **3** tube that carries liquid through a body or plant

vest¹ /vɛst/ *n* garment without arms worn under a coat

vest² *v* **vest in/with** *phr vt fml* give the legal right to possess or use (power, property, etc.) to (someone)

vested in·terest /ˌ·· '··, ˌ·· '···/ *n* a personal reason for doing something, because one gains advantage from it

ves·ti·bule /'vɛstəˌbyul/ *n fml* **1** room or passage through which larger rooms are reached **2** enclosed passage at each end of a railroad car which connects it with the next car

ves·tige /'vɛstɪdʒ/ *n* **1** (small) remaining part; *the last vestiges of imperial power* **2** slightest bit: *not a vestige of truth*

ves·try /'vɛstri/ *n* room in a church for esp. changing into vestments

vet /vɛt/ *n infml* animal doctor

vet·e·ran /'vɛtərən/ *n, adj* **1** (person) with long service or (former) experience, esp. as a soldier **2** (thing) that has grown old with long use

vet·e·ri·na·ry /ˈvetərəˌneri, ˈvetrə-/ adj of the medical care of animals ~**rian** /ˌvetərəˈnerɪən, ˌvetrə-/ n animal doctor

ve·to /ˈviːtoʊ/ vt -**toed**; pres. p. -**toing** officially refuse to allow ♦ n vetoes [C;U] (act of) vetoing

VHS n [U] common type of VIDEOTAPE

vi·a /ˈvaɪə, ˈviːə/ prep traveling through

vi·a·ble /ˈvaɪəbəl/ adj able to succeed in actual use: an economically viable plan –**bility** /ˌvaɪəˈbɪləti/ n [U]

vial /ˈvaɪəl/ n small glass container

vibe /vaɪb/ n [C] sl feeling that one gets from a person, place, situation etc.: I was getting bad vibes from this guy.

vi·brant /ˈvaɪbrənt/ adj 1 powerful and exciting 2 (of color or light) bright and strong ~**ly** adv **vibrancy** n [U]

vi·brate /ˈvaɪbreɪt/ vi/t (cause to) move with a slight continuous shake **vibration** /vaɪˈbreɪʃən/ n [C;U]

vi·car·i·ous /vaɪˈkeriəs/ adj experienced indirectly, by watching, reading, etc.: vicarious pleasure ~**ly** adv

vice /vaɪs/ n [C;U] 1 criminal activity involving sex or drugs 2 a fault of character: Laziness is his one vice. b bad habit: Smoking is my only vice.

vice pres·i·dent /ˌ·ˈ···◂/ n 1 person 2nd in rank to the president of a country 2 someone responsible for a part of a large company: vice president for marketing

vice squad /ˈ· ·/ n part of the police force dealing with vice (1)

vice ver·sa /ˌvaɪsə ˈvɚsə, ˌvaɪs-/ adv the opposite way around

vi·cin·i·ty /vəˈsɪnəti/ n [U] area which is near: (fig.) a price in the vicinity of $50,000.

vi·cious /ˈvɪʃəs/ adj 1 showing an unpleasant desire to hurt: a vicious kick 2 dangerous: a vicious-looking knife ~**ly** adv

vicious cir·cle /ˌ·· ˈ··/ n situation in which unpleasant causes and effects lead back to the original starting point

vic·tim /ˈvɪktəm/ n one who suffers as the result of something: the murderer's victim (= the person he killed) | the victims of the plane crash ~**ize** vt cause to suffer unfairly ~**ization** /ˌvɪktəməˈzeɪʃən/ n [U]

vic·tor /ˈvɪktɚ/ n fml or lit person who wins

vic·to·ry /ˈvɪktəri/ n [C;U] winning: her victory in the election/golf tournament –**torious** /vɪkˈtɔriəs, -ˈtoʊr-/ adj 1 that has won: the victorious team 2 showing victory: a victorious shout

vict·uals /ˈvɪtlz/ n humor food

vid·e·o /ˈvɪdioʊ/ adj for (recording and) showing pictures on television ♦ n -**os** [C;U] videotape recording ♦ vt -**oed**; pres. p. -**oing** videotape

vid·e·o·cas·sette /ˌvɪdioʊkəˈset/ n flat plastic case containing a VIDEOTAPE

vid·e·o·tape /ˈvɪdioʊˌteɪp/ n [C;U] band of MAGNETIC material on which moving pictures are recorded ♦ vt record on videotape

vie /vaɪ/ vi **vied**, pres. p. **vying** compete

view /vyu/ n 1 [C;U] what one can see: The train came into view around the corner. | You get a beautiful view of the sea from this window. 2 [C] opinion: In my view, he's a fool. 3 **in view of** taking into consideration: In view of the unusual circumstances, we'll cancel it. 4 **on view** being shown to the public 5 **with a view to** with the intention of ♦ vt 1 consider; regard: I view the matter very seriously. 2 examine by looking 3 watch television ~**er** n person watching television

view·point /ˈvyupoɪnt/ n POINT OF VIEW

vig·il /ˈvɪdʒəl/ n act of staying (awake and) watchful for some purpose

vig·i·lance /ˈvɪdʒələns/ n [U] watchful care –**lant** adj fml always prepared for possible danger –**lantly** adv

vig·i·lan·te /ˌvɪdʒəˈlænti/ n sometimes derog person who tries by unofficial means to punish crime

vi·gnette /vɪˈnyet/ n short effective written description

vig·or /ˈvɪgɚ/ n [U] active strength or force –**orous** adj –**orously** adv

Vi·king /ˈvaɪkɪŋ/ n Scandinavian attacker (and settler) in northern and western Europe from the 8th to the 10th centuries

vile /vaɪl/ adj 1 fml low, shameful, and worthless: a vile slander 2 extremely unpleasant: vile food ~**ly** /ˈvaɪl-li/ adv

vil·i·fy /ˈvɪləˌfaɪ/ vt fml say unfairly bad things about –**fication** /ˌvɪləfəˈkeɪʃən/ n [C;U]

vil·lage /ˈvɪlɪdʒ/ n collection of houses in a country area, smaller than a town –**lager** n person who lives in a village

vil·lain /ˈvɪlən/ n **1** (esp. in stories) bad person **2** infml criminal ~**ous** adj threatening great harm; evil

vin·ai·grette /ˌvɪnɪˈɡret/ n [U] mixture of oil, VINEGAR, etc., put on SALADS

vin·di·cate /ˈvɪndəˌkeɪt/ vt **1** free from blame **2** prove (something that was in doubt) to be right **–cation** /ˌvɪndəˈkeɪʃən/ n [S;U]

vin·dic·tive /vɪnˈdɪktɪv/ adj wishing to harm someone who has harmed you ~**ly** adv ~**ness** n [U]

vine /vaɪn/ n climbing plant, esp. one that produces GRAPES

vin·e·gar /ˈvɪnɪɡə/ n [U] liquid with an acid taste, used in preparing food ~**y** adj

vine·yard /ˈvɪnyəd/ n piece of land with vines for making wine

vin·tage /ˈvɪntɪdʒ/ n particular year in which a wine is made ♦ adj **1** of the best quality (of cars, clothing, etc.) old but well preserved **3 vintage year** a very good year for the stated thing

vi·nyl /ˈvaɪnl/ n [U] firm bendable plastic

vi·o·la /viˈoʊlə/ n musical instrument like a large VIOLIN

vi·o·late /ˈvaɪəˌleɪt/ vt **1** act against (something solemnly promised or officially agreed): violate a treaty **2** fml come violently into (and spoil) **3** have sex (with a woman) by force **–lation** /ˌvaɪəˈleɪʃən/ n [C;U]

vi·o·lent /ˈvaɪələnt/ adj using, showing or produced by great damaging force: He became violent and began to hit her. | a violent storm | a violent death ~**ly** adv **–lence** n [U] **1** extreme (and damaging) force **2** use of force to hurt people

vi·o·let /ˈvaɪəlɪt/ n small plant with purple flowers that smell sweetly — see also SHRINKING VIOLET

vi·o·lin /ˌvaɪəˈlɪn/ n small wooden musical instrument with 4 strings played by drawing a BOW² (2) across the strings ~**ist** n

VIP n person of great influence or fame

vi·per /ˈvaɪpə/ n small poisonous snake

vir·gin /ˈvɜdʒɪn/ n person who has not had sex ♦ adj unused; unspoiled ~**ity** /vəˈdʒɪnəti/ n [U] state of being a VIRGIN

Vir·go /ˈvɜɡoʊ/ n **1** [S] 6th sign of the ZODIAC, represented by a VIRGIN **2** someone born between August 23 and September 22

vir·ile /ˈvɪrəl/ adj having the strong and forceful qualities expected of a man, esp. in matters of sex **–ility** /vəˈrɪləti/ n [U]

vir·tu·al /ˈvɜtʃuəl/ adj **1** almost or unofficially the stated thing: Though her husband was king, she was the virtual ruler of the country. **2** produced by a computer and intended to seem real: a virtual shopping mall ~**ly** adv almost; very nearly

virtual re·al·i·ty /ˌ... ...ˈ.../ n [U] environment produced by a computer, intended to surround the viewer and seem almost real

vir·tue /ˈvɜtʃu/ n **1** [U] fml condition of being morally good **2** [C] morally good quality, such as truthfulness or loyalty **3** [C;U] advantage: The plan's great virtue is its simplicity. **4 by virtue of** as a result of; by means of **–tuous** adj morally good

vir·tu·o·so /ˌvɜtʃuˈoʊsoʊ/ n **-si** /-si, -zi/ extremely skilled (musical) performer **–osity** /-ˈɒsəti/ n [U] virtuoso's skill

vir·u·lent /ˈvɪryələnt, ˈvɪrə-/ adj **1** (of a poison, disease, etc.) very powerful and dangerous **2** fml full of bitter hatred: virulent abuse ~**ly** adv **–lence** n [U]

vi·rus /ˈvaɪrəs/ n **1** extremely small living thing that causes infectious disease: the flu virus **2** set of instructions secretly put into a computer, that can destroy stored information **viral** adj

vi·sa /ˈvizə/ n official mark put on a PASSPORT to allow someone to enter or leave a particular country

vis·cous /ˈvɪskəs/ adj (of a liquid) thick and sticky **–cosity** /vɪsˈkɒsəti/ n [U]

vise /vaɪs/ n tool with metal jaws for holding things firmly

vis·i·ble /ˈvɪzəbəl/ adj **1** that can be seen **2** noticeable **–bly** adv noticeably: He was visibly shaken by the unpleasant experience. **–bility** /ˌvɪzəˈbɪləti/ n [U] **1** clearness with which things can be seen over a particular distance **2** ability to give a clear view

vi·sion /ˈvɪʒən/ n **1** [U] ability to see **2** [U] wise understanding of the future **3** [C] picture in the mind: I had visions of missing (= thought I might miss) my plane. **4** [C] something supposedly seen when in a sleeplike state or as a religious experience

vi·sion·a·ry /ˈvɪʒəˌneri/ adj **1** having VISION (2) **2** grand but impractical ♦ n visionary person

vis·it /ˈvɪzɪt/ v 1 *vi/t* go to and spend time in (a place) or with (a person): *We visited my uncle in Detroit.* 2 *vt* go to (a place) to make an official examination 3 *vt* stay with ♦ *n* act or time of visiting: *We paid him a visit.* (= visited him) ~**or** *n*

visit on *phr vt* direct (anger, etc.) against

visit with *phr vt* talk socially with

vi·sor /ˈvaɪzɚ/ *n* face or eye protector on a hat or HELMET

vis·ta /ˈvɪstə/ *n* view stretching away into the distance

vi·su·al /ˈvɪʒuəl/ *adj* 1 of or done by seeing 2 having an effect on the sense of sight: *the visual arts* ~**ly** *adv* ~**ize** *vt* imagine, esp. as if by seeing

vi·tal /ˈvaɪtl/ *adj* 1 extremely necessary or important 2 necessary to stay alive 3 full of life and force ~**ly** *adv* in the highest possible degree

vi·tal·i·ty /vaɪˈtæləti/ *n* [U] 1 cheerful forceful quality 2 ability to remain alive or effective

vital sta·tis·tics /ˌ·· ·ˈ··/ *n* [P] information kept by the state about births, deaths, marriages, etc.

vit·a·min /ˈvaɪtəmɪn/ *n* chemical substance found in certain foods and important for growth and good health: *Oranges contain vitamin C.*

vi·tro /ˈvitroʊ/ see IN VITRO

vi·va·cious /vɪˈveɪʃəs, vaɪ-/ *adj* (esp. of a woman) full of life and fun ~**ly** *adv* ~**city** /vɪˈvæsəti, vaɪ-/ *n* [U]

viv·id /ˈvɪvɪd/ *adj* 1 (of light or color) bright and strong 2 producing sharp clear pictures in the mind: *a vivid description* ~**ly** *adv*

viv·i·sec·tion /ˌvɪvɪˈsɛkʃən/ *n* [U] performing of operations on animals to test medical treatments, new products, etc.

V-neck /ˈvi nɛk/ *n* neck opening of a dress, shirt, etc., shaped like a V

vo·cab·u·la·ry /vəˈkæbyəˌlɛri, voʊ-/ *n* 1 [C;U] words known, learned, used, etc.: *a child's limited vocabulary* 2 [C] short list of words with their meanings

vo·cal /ˈvoʊkəl/ *adj* 1 of or produced by the voice: *vocal music* 2 expressing one's opinion loudly ~**ly** *adv* ~**ist** *n* singer

vocal cords /ˈ·· ·/ *n* [P] muscles in the throat that produce sounds when air passes through them

vo·ca·tion /voʊˈkeɪʃən/ *n* job, esp. one which you do because you have a particular ability ~**al** *adj* of or for a job: *vocational training*

vo·cif·er·ous /voʊˈsɪfərəs/ *adj fml* expressing oneself forcefully or noisily ~**ly** *adv*

vod·ka /ˈvɑdkə/ *n* [U] strong colorless alcoholic drink

vogue /voʊg/ *n* [C;U] popular fashion: *Short skirts were in vogue then.* ♦ *adj* popular at present: *vogue words*

voice /vɔɪs/ *n* 1 [C;U] sound(s) produced in speaking or singing: *a loud/kind voice* | *She shouted at the top of her voice.* (= very loudly) 2 [C] ability to produce such sounds: *She's lost her voice.* 3 [S;U] right to express oneself: *I have no voice in* (= influence over) *the decision.* ♦ *vt* express in words, esp. forcefully: *voicing their opinions*

voice mail /ˈ· ·/ *n* [U] system in which telephone messages are recorded so that one can listen to them later

voice-o·ver /ˈ·· ··/ *n* voice of an unseen person on a film or television show

void /vɔɪd/ *n* empty space ♦ *adj law* having no value or effect ♦ *vt* make void

vol·a·tile /ˈvɑlətl, -ˌtaɪl/ *adj* 1 quickly changing, esp. easily becoming angry or dangerous 2 (of a liquid) easily changing into gas ~**tility** /ˌvɑləˈtɪləti/ *n* [U]

vol·ca·no /vɑlˈkeɪnoʊ/ *n* -**noes** or -**nos** mountain which sometimes throws out hot gases and melted rock ~**canic** /-ˈkænɪk/ *adj* 1 of a volcano 2 violently forceful

vo·li·tion /voʊˈlɪʃən, və-/ *n* 1 WILL² (1) and (2) 2 of one's own volition *fml* because one wishes, not because told to by someone else

vol·ley /ˈvɑli/ *n* 1 many shots fired together: (fig.) *a volley of blows/curses* 2 kicking or hitting of a ball before it has hit the ground ♦ *v* 1 *vi* (of guns) be fired together 2 *vi/t* hit or kick (as) a VOLLEY (2)

vol·ley·ball /ˈvɑliˌbɔl/ *n* [U] team game played by hitting a large ball across a net with the hands

volt /voʊlt/ *n* unit of electrical force ~**age** /ˈvoʊltɪdʒ/ *n* [C;U] electrical force measured in volts

vol·ume /ˈvɑlyəm, -yum/ *n* 1 [U] (degree of) loudness of sound: *Turn down the volume on the TV.* 2 [U] size of something measured by multiplying its length by its height by its width **3** [C] any of a set of books: *volume 9 of the encyclopedia* **4** [C;U] amount: *the increasing volume of passenger traffic* **5 speak volumes (for something)** show or express (something) very clearly or fully

vo·lu·mi·nous /vəˈluːmənəs/ *adj fml* **1** filling or containing a lot of space: *a voluminous skirt/suitcase* **2** producing or containing (too) much writing

vol·un·ta·ry /ˈvɑlənˌteri/ *adj* acting or done willingly, without being forced **–arily** /ˌvɑlənˈterəli, ˈvɑlənˌter-/ *adv*

vol·un·teer /ˌvɑlənˈtɪr/ *n* person who has volunteered ♦ *v* **1** *vi/t* offer to do something without payment or reward, or without being forced: *Jenny volunteered to clear up afterwards.* **2** *vt* tell without being asked: *He volunteered a statement to the police.*

vo·lup·tu·ous /vəˈlʌptʃuəs/ *adj* **1** suggesting or expressing sexual pleasure **2** giving a fine delight to the senses

vom·it /ˈvɑmɪt/ *vi* throw up (the contents of the stomach) through the mouth ♦ *n* [U] swallowed food thrown back up through the mouth

voo·doo /ˈvuːduː/ *n* [U] set of magical religious practices in esp. Haiti

vo·ra·cious /vəˈreɪʃəs, vɔ-, voʊ-/ *adj* eating or wanting a lot of food: (fig.) *a voracious reader* (= who reads a lot) **~ly** *adv* **–city** /-ˈræsəti/ *n* [U]

vor·tex /ˈvɔrteks/ *n* **-texes** or **-tices** /-təˌsiz/ **1** powerful circular moving mass of water or wind **2** *lit* situation that makes one powerless: *sucked into the vortex of war*

vote /voʊt/ *v* **1** *vi* express one's choice officially, esp. by marking a piece of paper or raising one's hand: *Which candidate will you vote for in the election?* |

As we can't reach an agreement, let's vote on it. **2** *vt* agree, by a vote, to provide (something) **3** *vt infml* agree as the general opinion: *I vote we leave now.* ♦ *n* **1** [C;U] (choice or decision made by) voting: *I'll cast my vote for Tom Smith.* | *Let's put the matter to a vote.* **2** [U] number of such choices made by or for a particular person or group: *an increase in the Republican vote* **3** [U] right to vote in political elections **voter** *n*

vouch /vaʊtʃ/ *v* **vouch for** *phr vt* state one's firm belief in the good qualities of, based on experience

vouch·er /ˈvaʊtʃər/ *n* **1** ticket usable instead of money **2** official paper given to prove that money has been paid

vow /vaʊ/ *vt, n* (make) a solemn promise or declaration of intention: *He vowed he would never steal again.*

vow·el /ˈvaʊəl/ *n* speech sound made without closing the air passage in the mouth or throat: *In English, vowels are represented by the letters* a, e, i, o, u.

voy·age /ˈvɔɪ-ɪdʒ/ *n* long journey by ship ♦ *vi lit* make a voyage **–ager** *n*

voy·eur /vwaˈyɜr, vɔɪˈə/ *n* person who gets sexual excitement by (secretly) watching others have sex **~ism** *n* [U]

vs. *abbrev. for:* VERSUS

vul·gar /ˈvʌlgər/ *adj* **1** very rude or having bad manners **2** showing bad judgment in matters of beauty, style, etc. **~ly** *adv* **–ity** /vʌlˈgærəti/ *n* [U]

vul·ne·ra·ble /ˈvʌlnərəbəl/ *adj* **1** easy to attack **2** (of a person) easily harmed; sensitive **–bility** /ˌvʌlnərəˈbɪləti/ *n* [U]

vul·ture /ˈvʌltʃər/ *n* **1** large tropical bird which feeds on dead animals **2** person who has no mercy and who uses people

vy·ing /ˈvaɪ-ɪŋ/ *v pres. p. of* VIE

W

W, w /ˈdʌbəlyu/ the 23rd letter of the English alphabet

W. *written abbrev. for:* **1** west(ern) **2** WATT

wack·y /ˈwæki/ *adj esp.* silly **–iness** *n* [U]

wad /wɑd/ *n* **1** many thin things pressed or folded thickly together: *a wad of $10 bills* **2** small thick soft mass: *a wad of cotton* **3 shoot one's wad** spend all of one's money at one time

wad·dle /ˈwɑdl/ *vi* walk like a duck

wade /weɪd/ *vi/t* walk through (water) **wader** *n* **1** bird that wades to find its food **2** either of a pair of high rubber boots to protect the legs while wading

  wade into *phr vt* begin (to attack) forcefully and with determination

  wade through *phr vt* do or complete (something long or dull) with an effort

wa·fer /ˈweɪfə/ *n* **1** thin COOKIE or CRACKER **2** thin round piece of special bread used in the Christian ceremony of COMMUNION

wafer-thin /ˌ··ˈ·◂/ *adj* extremely thin

waf·fle /ˈwɑfəl/ *n* light sweet cake marked with raised squares

waft /wɑft, wæft/ *vi/t* move lightly (as if) on wind or waves

wag[1] /wæg/ *vi/t* **-gg-** shake (esp. a body part) or be shaken from side to side: *The dog wagged its tail.* **wag** *n*

wag[2] *n infml* amusing man

wage /weɪdʒ/ *vt* carry on (a war)

wa·ger /ˈweɪdʒə/ *n, vi fml for:* BET

wag·es /ˈweɪdʒɪz/ also **wage** [S] — *n* [P] payment for work done: *He gets his wages every Friday.*

wag·on /ˈwægən/ *n* **1** strong vehicle usu. pulled by a horse or horses **2** small vehicle with a handle used by children **3 on the wagon** no longer willing to drink alcohol

waif /weɪf/ *n esp. lit* child or animal that is homeless or not cared for

wail /weɪl/ *vi, n* (make) a long cry (as if) in grief or pain

waist /weɪst/ *n* **1** narrow part of the human body below the chest **2** narrow part of a garment or apparatus

waist·band /ˈweɪstbænd/ *n* strengthened part of pants, a skirt, etc., that fastens around the waist

waist·line /ˈweɪstlaɪn/ *n* (length or height of) an imaginary line around the waist: *(fig.) No sugar for me — I'm watching my waistline.* (= trying not to become fatter)

wait /weɪt/ *v* **1** *vi* do nothing in the expectation of something happening: *I had to wait 2 hours for the bus!* | *Are you waiting to use the phone?* **2** *vt* not act until: *You'll have to wait your turn.* **3** *vi* remain unspoken, unheard, etc.: *My news can wait till later.* **4 wait and see** delay an action or decision until the future becomes clearer **5 wait tables** serve meals, esp. as a regular job ♦ *n* [S] act or period of waiting **~er, ~ress** /-trɪs/ *fem.* — *n* someone who serves food to people

  wait on *phr vt* **1** serve food to, esp. in a restaurant **2 wait on someone hand and foot** serve someone very humbly

waiting list /ˈ·· ˌ·/ *n* list of people who will be dealt with later

waiting room /ˈ·· ˌ·/ *n* room at a station, doctor's office, etc., where people wait

waive /weɪv/ *vt fml* state that (a rule, claim, etc.) is no longer in effect **waiver** *n* written statement waiving a right, etc.

wake[1] /weɪk/ *vi/t* woke /wook/ *or* waked, woken /ˈwookən/ *or* waked (cause to) stop sleeping: *I woke up late.* **~ful** *adj* sleepless **waking** *adj* of the time when one is awake: *all my waking hours*

wake[2] *n* **1** track left by a ship: *(fig.) The car left clouds of dust in its wake.* **2 in the wake of** as a result of: *war, with hunger and disease in its wake*

wake[3] *n* gathering to grieve over a dead person

walk /wɔk/ *v* **1** *vi* move slowly on foot so that at least one foot is always touching the ground **2** *vt* walk along: *He'd walked the streets looking for work.* **3** *vt* go with on foot: *I'll walk you to the bus stop.* **4** *vt* take (an animal) for a walk ♦ *n* **1** [C] (short) journey on foot: *Let's go for a walk.* | *The station's just a 5-minute walk from here.* **2** [S] way of walking **3** [C] place, path, or course for walking

  walk all over *phr vt* treat badly

  walk into *phr vt* **1** get caught by (something) through carelessness **2** get (a job) very easily

walk off/away with phr vt **1** steal and take away **2** win easily

walk out phr vi **1** leave suddenly and disapprovingly **2** go on STRIKE² (1)

walk out on phr vt leave suddenly

walk·er /'wɔkə/ n **1** someone who walks **2** metal frame used by old or sick people for support while walking

walk·ie-talk·ie /ˌwɔki 'tɔki/ n radio for talking as well as listening, that can be carried

walk-in /ˈ· ·/ adj **1** big enough for a person to walk into : a walk-in closet **2** that can be used without arranging a time before coming: a walk-in medical center

walking stick /'·· ·/ n stick for support while walking

Walk·man /'wɔkmən/ n tdmk for PERSONAL STEREO

walk of life /ˌ· · '·/ n position in society, esp. one's job

walk-on /ˈ· ·/ n small usu. non-speaking part in a play

walk·out /'wɔk-aʊt/ n **1** action of disapprovingly leaving a meeting, organization, etc. **2** STRIKE² (1)

walk·o·ver /'wɔkˌəʊvə/ n easy victory

walk·way /'wɔk-weɪ/ n path usu. above the ground connecting 2 buildings or parts of a building

wall /wɔl/ n **1** side of a room or building: pictures hanging on the wall **2** upright surface of brick or stone, for enclosing something: the boundary wall | (fig.) a wall of flames **3** enclosing or inside surface: the walls of a blood vessel **4** bang one's head against a (brick) wall infml try to do the impossible **5** go up the wall infml get very angry **6** push to the wall force into a bad situation ~ed adj surrounded with a wall

wall off phr vt separate with a wall

wall up phr vt close or enclose with a wall

wal·let /'wɔlɪt/ n small flat case for paper money, CREDIT CARDs, etc.

wall·flow·er /'wɔlˌflaʊə/ n **1** garden plant with flowers that smell sweet **2** person who gets left out of social activity

wal·low /'wɔləʊ/ vi move, roll, or lie around happily in deep mud, water, etc.: wallowing in a hot bath / (fig.) in self-pity

wall·pa·per /'wɔlˌpeɪpə/ n [U] decorative paper (for) covering the walls of a room

♦ vt cover the walls of (a room) with wallpaper

Wall Street /'· ·/ n center of the American business and money world, in New York

wall-to-wall /ˌ· · '·◂/ adj covering the whole floor: wall-to-wall carpet

wal·nut /'wɔlnʌt/ n **1** eatable nut shaped like a brain **2** [U] wood from its tree, used for furniture

wal·rus /'wɔlrəs, 'wɔl-/ n -ruses or -rus large sea animal with 2 very long teeth that point downwards

waltz /wɔlts/ vi, n (do) a slow dance for a man and a woman

wand /wɒnd/ n stick used by someone doing magic tricks

wan·der /'wɒndə/ v **1** vi/t move about without a fixed course or purpose: the wandering tribes of the Sahara. | (fig.) The discussion seems to have wandered from its main point. **2** vi be or become confused and unable to make or follow ordinary conversation ~er n ~ings n [P] long travels

wane /weɪn/ vi get gradually smaller ♦ n **on the wane** becoming smaller or weaker

wan·na·be /'wɒnəbi/ n sl someone who tries to look or behave like a famous or popular person or become involved in a group

want /wɒnt, wɑnt, wɔnt/ vi **1** have a strong desire for: I don't want to go. **2** wish the presence of: Your mother wants you. **3** wish to find; hunt: He's wanted by the police for murder. **4** need: The house wants painting. **5** fml lack: to be found wanting (= not considered good, strong, etc., enough) ♦ n **1** [C;U] lack: The plants died for/from want of water. **2** [U] severe lack of things necessary for life ~ing adj fml **1** lacking **2** not good enough

want for phr vt fml lack: The children want for nothing.

want ad /'· ·/ n small newspaper advertisement for a thing or person wanted

wan·ton /'wɒntˀn, 'wɒn-/ adj fml **1** (of something bad) having no just cause: wanton disregard of the rules **2** (esp. of a woman) sexually improper

war /wɔr/ n [C;U] (example or period of) armed fighting between nations: The 2 countries are at war. | World War II | (fig.) waging a war against poverty and ignorance ~ring adj fighting (each other)

war·ble /'wɔrbəl/ vi (esp. of a bird) sing with a continuous varied note –**bler** n any of various songbirds

war crime /'· ·/ n illegal act done while fighting a war

ward[1] /wɔrd/ n **1** part of a hospital for a particular group of sick people **2** political division of a city **3** person legally protected by another: *The children were made wards of court.*

ward[2] v **ward off** phr vt keep away (something bad)

war·den /'wɔrdn/ n person in charge of a place or people

war·drobe /'wɔrdroʊb/ n person's collection of clothes

ware·house /'wɛrhaʊs/ n -**houses** /-haʊzɪz/ large building for storing things or selling things in quantity

wares /wɛrz/ n [P] esp. lit things for sale

war·fare /'wɔrfɛr/ n [U] war

war game /'· ·/ n pretended battle to test military plans

war·head /'wɔrhɛd/ n explosive front end of a MISSILE

war·like /'wɔrlaɪk/ adj fierce; liking to fight

warm[1] /wɔrm/ adj **1** having enough heat or pleasant heat: *a warm bath* **2** able to keep one warm: *warm clothes* **3** showing strong good feelings: *a warm welcome* **4** seeming cheerful or friendly: *warm colors*

warm[2] vi/t make or become warm ~**ly** adv

warm to phr vt **1** begin to like **2** become interested in

warm up phr vi/t prepare for action or performance by exercise or operation in advance

war·mon·ger /'wɔrmʌŋgər, -ˌmɑŋ-/ n derog person who wants war

warmth /wɔrmθ/ n [U] being warm

warn /wɔrn/ v **1** vi/t tell of something bad that may happen, or of how to prevent it **2** vt give knowledge of some future need or action: *We warned them we'd be away.* ~**ing** n [C;U] **1** telling in advance: *They attacked without warning.* **2** something that warns: *That's the second warning we've had.*

warp /wɔrp/ vi/t turn or twist out of shape: *a warped plank/(fig.) mind* ♦ n **1** warped place **2** threads running along the length of cloth

war·path /'wɔrpæθ/ n **on the warpath** angry and looking for someone to fight or punish

warped /wɔrpt/ adj **1** having ideas thought to be unusual or not normal: *a warped sense of humor* **2** bent or twisted into the wrong shape

war·rant /'wɔrənt, 'wɑr-/ n **1** [C] official paper allowing something: *The police have a warrant for her arrest.* **2** [U] fml proper reason for action ♦ v **1** cause to seem right or reasonable **2** promise (that something is so)

warrant of·fi·cer /'·· ˌ···/ n one just below an officer in rank

war·ran·ty /'wɔrənti, 'wɑr-/ n written GUARANTEE

war·ri·or /'wɔriə, 'wɑr-/ n lit soldier

war·ship /'wɔrˌʃɪp/ n naval ship used for war

wart /wɔrt/ n small hard swelling on the skin

war·time /'wɔrtaɪm/ n [U] period during which a war is going on

war·y /'wɛri/ adj careful; looking out for danger –**ily** adv

was /wəz; strong wʌz, wɑz/ v 1st and 3rd person sing. past t. of BE

wash /wɑʃ, wɔʃ/ v **1** vt clean with liquid **2** vi be able to be cleaned with liquid without damage: *This shirt doesn't wash well.* **3** vi wash oneself **4** vt carry by the force of moving water: *crops washed away by the floods* **5** vi/t esp. lit flow (against or over) continually **6** vi be (easily) believed: *His story won't wash.* **7** **wash one's dirty linen (in public)** make public unpleasant subjects which ought to be kept private **8** **wash one's hands of** refuse to have anything more to do with or to accept responsibility for ♦ n **1** [S] act of washing **2** [U] things to be washed **3** [S;U] movement of water caused by a passing boat **4** **come out in the wash** infml **a** (of something shameful) become known **b** turn out all right in the end **5** **in the wash** being washed ~**able** adj ~**ing** [U] clothes that are to be washed or have just been washed

wash down phr vt **1** clean with a lot of water **2** swallow with the help of liquid

wash out phr vt **1** cause to wash free of an unwanted substance **2** destroy or prevent by the action of water, esp. rain

wash up phr v **1** vi wash one's face and hands **2** vt (of the sea) bring in to the shore

wash·cloth /ˈwɑʃkləθ, ˈwɔʃ-/ n -**cloths** /-kləðz, -kləθs/ small cloth for washing the face

washed-out /ˌ·ˈ·◂/ adj **1** faded **2** very tired **3** prevented because of rain: *The game was washed-out.*

washed-up /ˌ·ˈ·◂/ adj infml with no further possibilities of success

wash·er /ˈwɑʃə, ˈwɔ-/ n **1** ring of metal, plastic, etc., for making a joint tight under a screw, between 2 pipes, etc. **2** person or machine that washes

washing ma·chine /ˈ·· ·ˌ·/ n machine for washing clothes

wash·out /ˈwɑʃaʊt, ˈwɔʃ-/ n failure

wash·room /ˈwɑʃrum, ˈwɔʃ-, -rʊm/ n public RESTROOM

was·n't /ˈwʌzənt, ˈwɑ-/ short for: was not

wasp /wɑsp, wɔsp/ n black and yellow bee-like insect ~**ish** adj sharply bad-tempered and cruel ~**ishness** n [U]

WASP, Wasp /wɑsp/ n often derog White Anglo-Saxon Protestant; an American whose family was originally from N. Europe, esp. considered as a member of the class which has power or influence in society ~**ish** adj

waste /weɪst/ n **1** [S;U] loss through wrong use or less than full use: *a waste of time* | *Don't let it go to waste.* (= be wasted) **2** [U] used or unwanted matter: *industrial/ bodily waste* **3** [U] wide, empty lonely stretch of water or land ◆ vt **1** use wrongly or not at all: *wasting his money on silly things* **2** fml make (the body) extremely thin ◆ adj **1** (of ground) empty and unused **2** gotten rid of as used or useless: *waste paper/products* ~**ful** adj tending to waste things ~**fully** adv

waste·bas·ket /ˈweɪstˌbæskɪt/ n small container for throwing away unwanted paper, etc.

wast·ed /ˈweɪstɪd/ adj sl having drunk too much alcohol or taken too many drugs

watch /wɑtʃ, wɔtʃ/ v **1** vi/t look (at) attentively: *Watch me and you'll see how it's done.* **2** vt be careful about: *Watch what you're doing with that knife!* **3** **watch it!** be careful **4** **watch one's step** act with great care **5** **watch the clock** be waiting for one's working day to end rather than thinking about one's work ◆ n **1** [C] small clock worn esp. on the wrist **2** [S;U] act of watching: *The police are keeping (a) watch on their activities.* **3** [C;U] period of duty on a ship ~**er** n ~**ful** adj careful to notice things

watch for phr vt look for; expect and wait for

watch out phr vi take care

watch out for phr vt **1** keep looking for **2** be careful of

watch over phr vt guard and protect; take care of

watch·dog /ˈwɑtʃdɒg, ˈwɔtʃ-/ n **1** dog kept to guard property **2** person or group that tries to prevent loss, waste, or undesirable practices

watch·man /ˈwɑtʃmən, ˈwɔtʃ-/ n -**men** /-mən/ guard, esp. of a building

watch·word /ˈwɑtʃˌwɜd, ˈwɔtʃ-/ n **1** PASSWORD **2** word or phrase expressing a guiding principle

wa·ter /ˈwɑtə, ˈwɔ-/ n [U] **1** liquid found as rain, in the sea, etc., and commonly drunk **2** a mass of this: *She dived into the water.* | *After the flood the fields were under water.* | *The goods came by water.* (= by boat) **3** **above water** out of difficulty: *keep one's head above water* (= keep oneself out of difficulty) **4** **hold water** be true or reasonable: *Your story doesn't hold water.* **5** **like water** in great quantity: *The wine flowed like water* **6** **pass water** urinate (URINE) **7** **throw cold water on** point out difficulties (in a plan, idea, etc.) — see also HOT WATER ◆ v **1** vt pour water on (a plant or area) **2** vt supply (esp. animals) with water **3** vi (of the mouth or eyes) form or let out watery liquid **waters** n [P] **1** sea near or around a country: *in Icelandic waters* **2** water of the stated river, lake, etc. ~**y** adj **1** containing too much water **2** very pale

water down phr vt **1** weaken by adding water **2** reduce the force of: *a watered-down report*

wa·ter·bed /ˈwɔtəˌbɛd, ˈwɑ-/ n bag filled with heated water for sleeping on

water can·non /ˈ·· ˌ·/ n apparatus for shooting out a powerful stream of water, esp. for controlling crowds

wa·ter·col·or /ˈwɔtəˌkʌlə, ˈwɑ-/ n **1** [C;U] paint mixed with water rather than oil **2** [C] picture painted with this

wa·ter·cress /ˈwɔtəˌkrɛs, ˈwɑ-/ n [U] water plant with leaves used as food

wa·ter·fall /ˈwɔtəˌfɔl, ˈwɑ-/ n very steep fall of water in a river, etc.

wa·ter·front /ˈwɔtəˌfrʌnt, ˈwɑ-/ n land along a stretch of water, esp. in a port

wa·ter·hole /ˈwɔtəˌhoʊl, ˈwɑ-/ n pool where animals come to drink

watering can /ˈ·· ˌ·/ n container for pouring water onto garden plants

watering hole /ˈ·· ˌ·/ n place where people gather to drink

wa·ter·logged /ˈwɔtəˌlɒgd, -ˌlɑgd, ˈwɑ-/ adj 1 (of ground) very wet 2 (of a boat) full of water

wa·ter·mark /ˈwɔtəˌmɑrk, ˈwɑ-/ n 1 partly transparent mark in paper 2 mark that shows a level reached: *the high watermark of her success*

wa·ter·mel·on /ˈwɔtəˌmɛlən, ˈwɑ-/ n large round green fruit with juicy red flesh

water po·lo /ˈ·· ˌ·/ n [U] game played by 2 teams of swimmers with a ball

wa·ter·proof /ˈwɔtəˌpruf, ˈwɑ-/ adj, n (an outer garment) which does not allow water, esp. rain, through ♦ vt make waterproof

wa·ter·shed /ˈwɔtəˌʃɛd, ˈwɑ-/ n 1 direction towards which water flows 2 point of very important change

wa·ter·side /ˈwɔtəˌsaɪd, ˈwɑ-/ n [U] edge of a river, lake, etc.

water ski·ing /ˈ·· ˌ·/ n [U] sport of being pulled across water on SKIS –er n

water sup·ply /ˈ·· ˌ·/ n flow of water provided for a building or area, and system of lakes, pipes, etc., that provides it

water ta·ble /ˈ·· ˌ·/ n level below which water can be found in the ground

wa·ter·tight /ˈwɔtəˌtaɪt, ˈwɑ-/ adj 1 which water cannot pass through 2 allowing or having no mistakes or possibility of doubt: *a watertight plan*

wa·ter·way /ˈwɔtəˌweɪ, ˈwɑ-/ n stretch of water which ships travel along

wa·ter·works /ˈwɔtəˌwɜks, ˈwɑ-/ 1 place from which a public water supply is provided 2 *infml* body's system for removing water from the body 3 **turn on the waterworks** start to cry, esp. to get attention, or what one wants

watt /wɑt/ n measure of electrical power

wave /weɪv/ v 1 vi/t move (one's hand or something in it) as a signal: *We waved as the train pulled out.* 2 vt direct with a movement of the hand: *The policeman*

waved the traffic on. 3 vi move gently from side to side in the air: *The flags waved.* 4 vi/t (cause to) curve regularly: *waved hair* ♦ n 1 raised moving area of water, esp. on the sea 2 movement of the hand in waving 3 feeling, way of behaving, etc., that suddenly starts and increases: *a wave of nausea* | *a crime wave* 4 form in which light, sound, etc., move: *radio waves* 5 evenly curved part of the hair **wavy** adj having regular curves

wave aside phr vt push aside without giving attention to (esp. ideas, etc.)

wave·length /ˈweɪvlɛŋθ, -lɛŋθ, -lɛnθ/ n 1 distance between 2 WAVES (4) 2 radio signal sent out on radio WAVES that are a particular distance apart: (fig.) *We're on completely different wavelengths.* (= are completely different, cannot understand each other, etc.)

wa·ver /ˈweɪvə/ vi be uncertain or unsteady in direction or decision: *Her loyalty never wavered.*

wax[1] /wæks/ n [U] solid meltable fatty or oily substance –y adj

wax[2] 1 vi (esp. of the moon) get gradually larger 2 vi lit (of a person) become: *He waxed eloquent as he described his plans.* 3 vt put wax on, esp. as a polish

wax·works /ˈwæksˌwɜks/ n –works (place) with models of people made in wax

way /weɪ/ n 1 [C] road, path, etc., to follow in order to reach a place: *She asked me the way to the station.* | *We lost our way.* 2 [C] direction: *He went that way.* 3 [S] distance: *We're a long way from home.* 4 [C] method: *Do it this way.* 5 [C] manner: *the cruel way in which he treats his animals* 6 [C] single part of a whole; detail; point: *In many ways I agree with you, but I don't think you're completely right.* 7 **by the way** (used to introduce a new subject in speech) 8 **by way of: a** by going through **b** as a sort of: *a few sandwiches by way of lunch* 9 **get one's own way** do or get what one wants in spite of others 10 **go one's own way** do what one wants 11 **go out of the/one's way (to do)** take the trouble (to do); make a special effort: *I went out of my way to pick her up and she didn't even thank me.* 12 **have a way with one** have an attractive quality which persuades others 13 **have it both**

ways gain advantage from 2 opposing opinions or actions **14 out of/in the way** (of) (not) blocking space for forward movement: *You're in the way; move!* **15 make one's way** go **16 make way for** leave so as to allow to develop freely **17 no way** *infml* no: *"Will you help me?" "No way!"* **18 out of the way** unusual or not commonly known **19 see one's way (clear) to (doing)** feel able to do **20 under way** moving forwards — see also RIGHT OF WAY ♦ *adv* far: *That's way outside my area.* **ways** *n* [P] customs; habits: *mend one's ways* (= improve one's manners, etc.)

way·far·er /ˈweɪˌfɛərə/ *n lit* traveler

way·lay /ˌweɪˈleɪ, ˈweɪleɪ/ *vt* **-laid** /ˈweɪˌleɪd, ˌweɪˈleɪd/, **-laying**, **-laid 1** attack (a traveler) **2** find or stop (someone) to speak to them

way·side /ˈweɪsaɪd/ *n lit* side of the road or path

ways and means /ˌ· ·ˈ·/ *n* [P] **1** method of doing something **2** plans to raise money, esp. for the government

way·ward /ˈweɪwəd/ *adj* **1** difficult to guide or control **2** not well aimed

we /wiː/ *pron* (*used as the subject of a sentence*) the people speaking; oneself and one or more others

weak /wiːk/ *adj* **1** having little power: *weak muscles/eyes* **2** easily becoming broken, changed, destroyed, or ill: *a weak heart* **3** having little taste: *weak coffee* **4** unable to control people: *a weak teacher* **5** not reaching a good standard: *His math is pretty weak.* **~ly** *adv* **~en** *vi/t* (cause to) become weaker **~ness** *n* **1** [U] fact or state of being weak **2** [C] part that spoils the rest: *The plan's only weakness is its cost.* **3** [C] fault in character **4** [C] strong liking: *a weakness for chocolate*

weak-kneed /ˌ· ˈ·◂/ *adj* cowardly

weak·ling /ˈwiːk.lɪŋ/ *n derog* weak person

wealth /wɛlθ/ *n* **1** [U] (large amount of) money and possessions **2** [S] *fml* large number: *a wealth of examples* **~y** *adj* rich

wean /wiːn/ *vt* gradually give (a baby) solid food instead of milk

  wean from *phr vt* gradually persuade to give up (something one disapproves of)

weap·on /ˈwɛpən/ *n* something to fight with, such as a gun or sword **~ry** *n* [U] weapons

wear /wɛr/ *v* **wore** /wɔr, woʊr/, **worn** /wɔrn, woʊrn/ **1** *vt* have (esp. clothes) on the body **2** *vt* have (a particular expression) on the face **3** *vi/t* (cause to) show the effects of continued use, rubbing, etc.: *You've worn a hole in your sock.* | (fig.) *That excuse is wearing thin.* (= becoming unbelievable) **4** *vi* last in the stated condition: *an old person who has worn well* **5** *vt infml* find acceptable **6** **wear the pants** have control or authority: *She wears the pants in that family.* ♦ *n* [U] **1** clothes: *evening wear* | *men's wear* **2** act of wearing esp. clothes **3** damage from use: *signs of wear* **4** quality of lasting in use: *There's a lot of wear in these shoes.*

  wear down *phr vt* weaken

  wear off *phr vi* (of a feeling, effect, etc.) become gradually less

  wear on *phr vi* pass slowly in time

  wear out *phr v* **1** *vi/t* (cause to) be reduced to nothing or a useless state by use **2** *vt* tire greatly

wear and tear /ˌ· ·ˈ·/ *n* [U] damage from use; WEAR (3)

wear·y /ˈwɪri/ *adj* very tired ♦ *vi/t* (cause to) become weary **-ily** *adv* **-iness** *n* [U]

wea·sel[1] /ˈwiːzəl/ *n* small fierce furry animal

weasel[2] *v* **weasel out** *phr vi infml* escape a duty by clever dishonest means

weath·er /ˈwɛðə/ *n* [U] **1** particular condition of wind, sunshine, rain, snow, etc.: *a day of fine weather* **under the weather** slightly sick ♦ *v* **1** *vt* pass safely through (a storm or difficulty) **2** *vi/t* change from the effects of air, rain, etc.: *weathered stone*

weather-beat·en /ˈ·· ˌ·/ *adj* marked or damaged by the wind, sun, etc.

weather fore·cast /ˈ·· ˌ·/ *n* description of weather conditions as they are expected to be

weath·er fore·cast·er /ˈ·· ˌ··/ *n* person who describes future weather conditions, esp. on television or radio

weather vane /ˈ·· ·/ *n* small apparatus that is blown around to show the direction of the wind

weave /wiːv/ *v* **wove** /woʊv/, **woven** /ˈwoʊvən/ **1** *vi/t* form threads into (material) by drawing them singly under and over a set of longer threads **2** *vt* twist;

wind: *a bird's nest woven from straws* **3** vt produce (a story) esp. from a suggestion **4** (*past t. and p.* **weaved**) vi move twistingly: *The cyclist weaved through the traffic.* ♦ *n* style or pattern of woven material: *a loose weave* **weaver** *n*

Web /wɛb/ *n* [*the*] INTERNET

web *n* **1** net of thin threads made by a SPIDER: (fig.) *a web of lies* **2** skin between the toes of certain swimming birds and animals ~**bed** /wɛbd/ *adj* having a WEB (2) between the toes

web·bing /ˈwɛbɪŋ/ *n* [U] strong woven bands used for belts, supports, etc.

web·site /ˈwɛbˌsaɪt/ *n* document on the INTERNET giving information about a subject or product

wed /wɛd/ *vi/t* **wedded** *or* **wed** *esp. lit* marry

we'd /wid/ *short for:* **1** we had **2** we would

wed·ding /ˈwɛdɪŋ/ *n* marriage ceremony

wedding ring /ˈ·· ˌ·/ *n* ring worn to show that one is married

wedge /wɛdʒ/ *n* **1** piece of wood, etc. shaped like a V, for keeping something in place or splitting something **2** piece shaped like a V: *a wedge of glass* **3** something shaped like this: *shoes with wedge heels* — see also **thin end of the wedge** (THIN) ♦ *vt* fix firmly (as if) with a wedge: *Wedge the door open.* | *I got wedged between 2 people on the bus.*

wed·lock /ˈwɛdlɒk/ *n* [U] *lit* **out of wedlock** of unmarried parents

Wednes·day /ˈwɛnzdi, -deɪ/ *n* 4th day of the week, between Tuesday and Thursday

wee /wi/ *adj* **1** very small **2** very early; *in the wee hours of the morning*

weed¹ /wid/ *n* **1** unwanted wild plant **2** physically·weak person ~**y** *adj* **1** thin and weak **2** full of weeds

weed² *vi/t* remove weeds from (a garden)

   weed out *phr vt* get rid of (less good ones)

week /wik/ *n* **1** period of 7 days, usu. thought of as starting on Sunday and ending on Saturday **2** period worked during a week: *a 35-hour week* **3** **week after week** also **week in, week out** — continuously

week·day /ˈwikdeɪ/ *n* day other than Saturday or Sunday

week·end /ˈwikɛnd/ *n* period between Friday evening and Monday morning: *We usually go away (on) weekends.*

week·ly /ˈwikli/ *adj, adv* (happening) every week or once a week ♦ *n* magazine or newspaper which appears once a week

weep /wip/ *vi* **wept** /wɛpt/, **weeping** *fml or lit* cry ~**ing** *adj* (of a tree) with branches hanging down

wee·vil /ˈwivəl/ *n* small insect which eats (and spoils) grain, seeds, etc.

weigh /weɪ/ *v* **1** *vt* find the weight of: *weigh oneself* **2** *vi* have the stated weight: *It weighs 6 lbs.* **3** *vt* consider or compare carefully **4** *vt* raise (an ANCHOR)

   weigh down *phr vt* make heavy with a load: (fig.) *weighed down with grief*

   weigh in *phr vi* have weight measured officially, esp. in sports

   weigh on *phr vt* worry: *His responsibilities weighed on him.*

   weigh up *phr vt* form an opinion about, esp. by balancing opposing arguments

weight /weɪt/ *n* **1** [C;U] (measured) heaviness of something: *The weight of the sack is 2 lbs.* **2** [C] something heavy: *lifting weights* **3** [C] piece of metal of known heaviness, used for weighing things **4** [U] system of standard measures of heaviness: *metric weight* **5** [U] value; importance: *I don't attach much weight to these rumors.* **6** [C] (something that causes) a feeling of anxiety: *a great weight off my mind* **7** **pull one's weight** do one's full share of work **8** **put on/lose weight** (of a person) become heavier/lighter **9** **throw one's weight around** give orders to others ♦ *vt* **1** make heavy, esp. by fastening weights **2** include conditions in (something) that give a (dis)advantage: *a competition weighted against younger children* ~**less** *adj*: *a weightless flight in space* ~**y** *adj* **1** heavy **2** *fml* important and serious

weight·lift·ing /ˈweɪtˌlɪftɪŋ/ also **weight training** — *n* [U] sport of lifting heavy weights –*er n*

weird /wɪrd/ *adj* **1** strange; unusual: *a weird shriek* **2** unusual and not sensible or acceptable: *weird ideas* ~**ly** *adv* ~**ness** *n* [U]

weird·o /ˈwɪrdoʊ/ *n, -os sl* strange person

wel·come /ˈwɛlkəm/ *interj* (a greeting to someone who has arrived) ♦ *vt* **1** greet (someone newly arrived), esp. with friendliness **2** wish to have; like: *I'd welcome some help.* ◆ *adj* **1** acceptable and wanted: *A cool drink is always welcome on a hot day.* **2** allowed freely (to have): *I have plenty of paper; you're welcome to some.* **3 You're welcome** (a polite expression when thanked for something) ◆ *n* greeting

weld /wɛld/ *vt* join (metal) by melting ~**er** *n*

wel·fare /'wɛlfɛr/ *n* [U] **1** comfort, health, and happiness: *I was concerned for her welfare.* (= thought she might be in trouble) **2** help with living conditions, social problems, etc. **3 on welfare** receiving money from the government to live on

well[1] /wɛl/ *adv* **better** /'bɛtər/, **best** /bɛst/ **1** in a good way: *He sings well.* | *a well-dressed man* **2** thoroughly: *They were well beaten.* **3** much; quite: *She finished well within the time allowed.* **4** suitably; properly: *I couldn't very well refuse.* **5 as well:** **a** also: *She came as well.* **b** with as good a result: *We might just as well have stayed at home.* **6 as well as** in addition to **7 come off** well be lucky in the end **8 do well** succeed or improve **9 do well out of** gain profit from **10 do well to** act wisely to **11 just as well** it is fortunate (that); there's no harm done **12 may well** could suitably **13 pretty well** almost **14 well and truly** completely **15 well underway** off to a good start **16 Well done!** (said when someone has been successful) ◆ *adj* **better, best 1** in good health **2** in an acceptable state ◆ *interj* **1** (expresses surprise) **2** (introduces an expression of surprise, doubt, etc.)

well[2] *n* **1** place where water can be taken from underground **2** OIL WELL **3** deep narrow space inside a building, for stairs or an ELEVATOR (2) ◆ *vi* flow

we'll /wɪl; *strong* wil/ *short for:* **1** we will **2** we shall

well-ad·jus·ted /ˌ· ·'··◂/ *adj* (of a person) fitting in well with society

well-ad·vised /ˌ· ·'·◂/ *adj* sensible

well-be·ing /ˌwɛl'biː·ɪŋ/ *n* [U] personal and physical comfort, esp. good health and happiness

well-bred /ˌ· '·◂/ *adj* having or showing high social rank, with good manners

well-con·nec·ted /ˌ· ·'··◂/ *adj* knowing or esp. related to people of high social rank or influence

well-done /ˌ· '·◂/ *adj* thoroughly cooked

well-groomed /ˌ· '·◂/ *adj* neat and clean

well-heeled /ˌ· '·◂/ *adj infml* rich

well-in·formed /ˌ· ·'··◂/ *adj* knowing a lot about several subjects or parts of a particular subject

well-in·ten·tioned /ˌ· ·'··◂/ *adj* acting in the hope of good results, though often failing

well-known /ˌ· '·◂/ *adj* known by many people; famous

well-mean·ing /ˌ· '··◂/ *adj* well-intentioned

well-off /ˌ· '·◂/ *adj* **1** rich **2** lucky

well-pre·served /ˌ· ·'··◂/ *adj* (of someone or something old) still in good condition

well-read /ˌwɛl 'rɛd◂/ *adj* having read many books and got a lot of information

well-round·ed /ˌ· '··◂/ *adj* **1** (of a person) having had a wide variety of experience in life **2** (of education, background, etc.) complete, giving knowledge of many subjects

well-spok·en /ˌ· '··◂/ *adj* having a socially acceptable way of speaking

well-to-do /ˌ· ·'·◂/ *adj* rich

well-wish·er /'· ˌ·◂/ *n* person who wishes another to succeed, have good luck, etc.

well-worn /ˌ· '·◂/ *adj* (of a phrase) too much used

Welsh /wɛlʃ/ *adj* of Wales

welt /wɛlt/ *n* mark on the skin where one has been hit

wel·ter /'wɛltər/ *n* [S] confused mixture: *a welter of statistics*

wel·ter·weight /'wɛltərˌweɪt/ *n* boxer (BOX[2]) of middle weight

went /wɛnt/ *v past t. of* GO

wept /wɛpt/ *v past t. and p. of* WEEP

were /wɜr/ *v past t. of* BE

we're /wɪr; *strong* wɪr/ *short for:* we are

were·wolf /'wɛrwʊlf, 'wɪr-/ *n* (in stories) person who sometimes turns into a WOLF (1)

west /wɛst/ *n* **1** (*often cap.*) direction towards which the sun sets **2** [*the*+S] (*cap.*) western Europe and the US ◆ *adj* **1** in the west **2** (of wind) from the west ◆ *adv* towards the west ~**ward** *adj, adv*

west·er·ly /'wɛstərli/ *adj* west

west·ern /'wɛstən/ adj of the west part of the world or of a country ♦ n story or film about life in the middle of the US in the past, with COWBOYS and gun fights ~**er** n someone who lives in or comes from the WEST (2)

west·ern·ize /'wɛstənaɪz/ vt cause to have or copy the customs typical of America and Europe

wet /wɛt/ adj -tt- 1 covered with or being liquid: wet grass/paint 2 rainy: a wet day 3 weak in character and unable to get things done ♦ n [the + S] rainy weather ♦ vt wet or wetted; pres. p. -tt- make wet ~**ness** n [U]

wet·back /'wɛtˌbæk/ n derog someone from Mexico who has come to the US illegally

wet blan·ket /ˌ· ˈ··/ n person who discourages others or prevents them from enjoying themselves

wet dream /ˌ· ˈ·/ n sexually exciting dream resulting in a male ORGASM

wet suit /ˈ· ˌ·/ n rubber garment for keeping the body warm in sea sports

we've /wiv/ short for: we have

whack /wæk/ vt hit with a noisy blow ♦ n 1 (noise) of a hard blow 2 trial or attempt 3 **out of whack** out of order; in poor condition

whale /weɪl/ n 1 extremely large fishlike animal 2 **a whale of a time** a very enjoyable time **whaler** n a person who hunts whales **b** ship from which whales are hunted **whaling** n [U] hunting whales

whale watch·ing /ˈ· ˌ··/ n [u] sport of watching whales from boats

wham /wæm/ n (sound of) a hard blow

wharf /wɔrf, hwɔrf/ n **wharfs** or **wharves** /wɔrvz, hwɔrvz/ place where ships are tied up to unload and load goods

what /wʌt, wɑt, hwʌt, hwɑt; weak wət, hwət/ predeterminer, determiner, pron 1 (used in questions about an unknown thing or person): What are you doing? | What color is it? 2 the thing(s) that: He told me what to do. 3 (shows surprise): What a strange hat! 4 **what for?** why? 5 **what if?** what will happen if? 6 **what's more** and this is more important 7 **what's what** the true state of things: to know what's what 8 **what's up?** Any news? what's happening? ♦ adv 1 (used esp. in questions when no answer is expected) in what way: What do you

care? (= I don't think you care at all) 2 **what with** (used for introducing the cause of something, esp. something bad)

what·ev·er /wɑtˈɛvə, hwɑt-/ determiner, pron 1 no matter what: Whatever I said, he'd disagree. 2 anything: They eat whatever they can find. 3 fml (shows surprise) what: Whatever is that peculiar thing? ♦ adj at all: I have no money whatever.

what·not /ˈwʌtˌnɑt, ˈwɑt-, ˈhwʌt-, ˈhwɑt-/ n [U] infml anything (else): carrying his bags and whatnot

wheat /wit, hwit/ n [U] (plant producing) grain from which flour is made

wheel /wil, hwil/ n 1 circular frame which turns to allow vehicles to move, to work machinery, etc. 2 movement by which a group of marching soldiers curve to the left or right 3 [the+S] the STEERING WHEEL of a car or ship 4 **at the wheel: a** driving or guiding a car or ship **b** in control 5 **wheels within wheels** hidden influences having effects on surface behavior ♦ v 1 vt move (a wheeled object) with the hands 2 vi turn around suddenly 3 vi (of birds) fly around and around in circles 4 **wheel and deal** vi infml make deals, esp. in business or politics, in a skillful and perhaps dishonest way ~**ed** adj having wheels

wheel·bar·row /ˈwilˌbærou, ˈhwil-/ n small 1-wheeled cart pushed by hand

wheel·chair /ˈwil-tʃɛr, ˈhwil-/ n wheeled chair for someone who cannot walk

wheeler-deal·er /ˌ··· ˈ··/ n someone skilled at doing clever (but perhaps not always honest) deals, esp. in business or politics

wheel·ie /ˈwili, ˈhwili/ n act of riding a bicycle on its back wheel

wheeze /wiz, hwiz/ vi make a noisy whistling sound in breathing ♦ n wheezing sound **wheezy** adj

when /wɛn, hwɛn; weak wən, hwən/ adv, conj 1 at what time; at the time that: When will they come? | He looked up when she came in. 2 considering that; although: Why did you do it when I told you not to?

when·ev·er /wɛnˈɛvə, hwɛ-, wə-, hwə-/ adv, conj 1 at whatever time 2 every time

where /wɛr, hwɛr/ adv, conj at or to what place; at or to the place that: Where do you live? | Sit where you are.

where·a·bouts /ˈwɛrəˌbauts, ˈhwɛr-, ˌwɛrəˈbauts, ˌhwɛr-/ adv where in general (not exactly): *Whereabouts did I leave my glasses?* ♦ /ˈhwɛərəˌbaʊts, ˈwɛr-/ *n* [U] place where a person or thing is

where·as /wɛrˈæz, hwɛr-/ *conj fml* (shows an opposite) but: *They live in a house, whereas we have an apartment.*

where·by /wɛrˈbaɪ, hwɛr-/ *adj fml* by means of which

where·u·pon /ˌwɛrəˈpɑn, -ˈpɔn, ˌhwɛr-, ˈwɛrəˌpɑn, -ˌpɔn, ˈhwɛr-/ *conj* without delay after and because of which: *He stood up to speak, whereupon everyone cheered.*

wher·ev·er /wɛrˈɛvə, hwɛr-, wə-, hwə-/ *adv* **1** to or at whatever place **2** (shows surprise) where

where·with·al /ˈwɛrwɪˌðɔl, -ˌθɔl, ˈhwɛr-/ *n* [U] enough supplies or money

whet /wɛt, hwɛt/ *vt* **-tt- 1** sharpen (a knife, etc.) **2 whet someone's appetite** make someone wish for more

wheth·er /ˈwɛðə, ˈhwɛ-/ *conj* if . . . or not: *I'm trying to decide whether to go.*

whey /weɪ, hweɪ/ *n* [U] watery part of milk

which /wɪtʃ, hwɪtʃ/ *determiner, pron* **1** (used in questions, when a choice is to be made): *Which shoes shall I wear, the red ones or the brown?* **2** (shows what thing is meant): *This is the book which I told you about.* **3** (used to add more information about something): *The train, which only takes an hour, is quicker than the bus.* — see also EVERY WHICH WAY

which·ev·er /wɪˈtʃɛvə, hwɪ-/ *determiner, pron* **1** any (one) of the set that: *Take whichever seat you like.* **2** no matter which: *It has the same result, whichever way you do it.*

whiff /wɪf, hwɪf/ *n* [S] **1** temporary smell of something **2** a breath in: *A few whiffs of gas and she'll fall asleep.*

while¹ /waɪl, hwaɪl/ *n* [S] **1** length of time: *He's been gone quite a while.* (= a fairly long time) **2 once in a while** sometimes, but not often **3 worth one's/someone's while** WORTHWHILE to one/someone: *We'll make it worth your while.* (= pay you) ♦ *conj* **1** during the time that: *They arrived while we were having dinner.* **2** although: *While I agree with your reasons, I can't allow it.* **3** WHEREAS **4** and what is more

while² *v* **while away** *phr vt* pass (time) in a pleasantly lazy way

whim /wɪm, hwɪm/ *n* sudden (often unreasonable) idea or wish

whim·per /ˈwɪmpə, ˈhwɪm-/ *vi* make small, weak trembling cries **whimper** *n*

whim·sy /ˈwɪmzi, ˈhwɪm-/ *n* whim –**sical** *adj* fanciful; with strange ideas

whine /waɪn, hwaɪn/ *vi* **1** make a high sad sound **2** complain (too much) in an unnecessarily sad voice ♦ *n: the whine of the jet engines*

whip¹ /wɪp, hwɪp/ *n* **1** long piece of esp. rope or leather on a handle, used for striking sharp blows **2** (person who gives) an order to a member of Congress to attend and vote

whip² *v* **-pp- 1** *vt* hit with a whip **2** *vi/t* move quickly: *He whipped out his gun.* **3** *vt* beat (esp. cream or eggs) until stiff **4** *vt infml* defeat ~**ping** *n* beating as a punishment

whip up *phr vt* **1** cause (feelings) to become stronger, etc. **2** make quickly

whip·lash /ˈwɪp-læʃ, ˈhwɪp-/ *n* **1** blow from a whip **2** harm done by sudden violent movement of the head and neck, as in a car accident: *a whiplash injury*

whir /wə, hwə/ *vi, n* **-rr-** (make) the regular sound of something turning and beating against the air

whirl /wəl, hwəl/ *vi/t* move around and around very fast ♦ *n* **1** [S] act or sensation of whirling: (fig.) *My head's in a whirl.* (= confused) **2** [C] very fast (confused) movement or activity **3 give something a whirl** *infml* try something

whirl·pool /ˈwəlpul, ˈhwəl-/ *n* fast circular current of water

whirl·wind /ˈwəlˌwɪnd, ˈhwəl-/ *n* tall tube of air moving dangerously at high speed: (fig.) *a whirlwind romance* (= happening very quickly)

whisk /wɪsk, hwɪsk/ *vt* **1** remove, either by quick light brushing or by taking suddenly: *She whisked my cup away before I'd finished.* **2** beat (esp. eggs), esp. with a whisk ♦ *n* small apparatus held in the hand, for beating eggs, cream, etc.

whis·ker /ˈwɪskə, ˈhwɪ-/ *n* long stiff hair near an animal's mouth **whiskers** *n* [P] hair on the sides of a man's face

whis·key /ˈwɪski, ˈhwɪ-/ *n* [U] strong alcoholic drink made from grain

whis·per /ˈwɪspə, ˈhwɪ-/ *v* **1** *vi/t* speak or say very quietly **2** *vt* suggest or pass (information) secretly: *It's whispered he* *may resign.* ♦ *n* **1** very quiet voice **2** RUMOR

whis·tle /ˈwɪsəl, ˈhwɪ-/ *n* **1** simple (musical) instrument played by blowing **2** high sound made by air blowing through a narrow opening ♦ *v* **1** *vi* make a WHISTLE (2), esp. by blowing through the lips: (fig.) *The wind whistled around us.* **2** *vt* produce (a tune) by doing this

whis·tle-blow·er /ˈwɪsəlˌbloʊə, ˈhwɪ-/ *n* person who calls attention to illegal or wrong activity

white /waɪt, hwaɪt/ *adj* **1** of the color of snow and milk **2** pale **3** of a race with pale skin **4** (of coffee) without milk or cream ♦ *n* **1** [U] white color **2** [C] WHITE (3) person **3** [C] part of an egg surrounding the central yellow part

whiten /ˈwaɪtn/ *vi/t* (cause) to become white(r)

white-col·lar /ˌ· ˈ·◂/ *adj* of or being office workers, indoor workers, etc.

white el·e·phant /ˌ· ˈ···◂/ *n* useless article

white flag /ˌ· ˈ·/ *n* sign that one accepts defeat

white heat /ˌ· ˈ·/ *n* [U] temperature at which metal turns white

White House /ˈ· ·/ *n* [*the*] **1** official Washington home of the US president **2** EXECUTIVE branch of the US government

white lie /ˌ· ˈ·/ *n* harmless lie

white meat /ˌ· ˈ·/ *n* [U] lighter-colored meat from chicken, esp. from the breast

white pages /ˈ· ˌ·/ *n* [P] book with an alphabetical list of people's names, addresses, and telephone numbers

white-tie /ˌ· ˈ·◂/ *adj* (of parties and other social occasions) at which the men wear white BOW TIES and tails (TAIL²)

white trash /ˌ· ˈ·/ *n* [U] *derog* poor, uneducated white people

white·wash /ˈwaɪtˌwɑʃ, -ˌwɔʃ, ˈhwaɪt⌝-/ *n* **1** [U] white liquid for covering walls **2** [C;U] *derog* attempt to hide something wrong **3** [C] complete defeat ♦ *vt* **1** cover with WHITEWASH (1) **2** make (what is bad) seem good

whit·tle /ˈwɪtl, ˈhwɪtl/ *vt* cut thin pieces off (wood): (fig.) *We've whittled the list of candidates down* (= reduced it) *to 5.*

whiz /wɪz, hwɪz/ *vi* -**zz**- move very fast (and noisily) ♦ *n* **1** [S] whizzing sound **2** [C] *infml* someone who is very fast, clever, or skilled in the stated activity

whiz kid /ˈ· ·/ *n* person who makes quick successes in life

who /hu/ *pron* (used esp. as the subject of a sentence) **1** what person?: *Who said that?* **2** (shows what person is meant): *the people who live in that house* **3** (adds more information about a person): *This is my father, who lives in Lockport.*

whoa /woʊ, hwoʊ, hoʊ/ *interj* (call to a horse to stop)

who-dun·it /ˌhuˈdʌnɪt/ *n* story, film, etc., about a crime mystery

who·ev·er /huˈevə/ *pron* **1** anyone at all: *I'll take whoever wants to go.* **2** no matter who: *Whoever it is, I don't want to see them.* **3** (shows surprise) who: *Whoever can that be at the door?*

whole /hoʊl/ *adj* **1** all; complete: *I spent the whole day in bed.* | *She swallowed it whole.* (= not divided up) **2** swallow something whole accept something without questioning it ♦ *n* **1** complete amount, thing etc. **2** on the whole generally; mostly wholly /ˈhoʊl-li/ *adv*: *not wholly to blame*

whole·food /ˈhoʊlfud/ *n* [C;U] food in a simple natural form

whole-heart·ed /ˌ· ˈ··◂/ *adj* with all one's ability, interest, etc.; full: *whole-hearted support*

whole num·ber /ˌ· ˈ··/ *n* INTEGER

whole·sale /ˈhoʊlseɪl/ *adj, adv* **1** sold in large quantities to stores (rather than directly to customers) **2** *usu. derog* very great or complete: *wholesale slaughter* **–saler** *n* seller of goods wholesale

whole·some /ˈhoʊlsəm/ *adj* **1** good for the body: *wholesome food* **2** having a good moral effect **~ness** *n* [U]

whole wheat /ˌ· ˈ·◂/ *adj* (made from flour) without the covering of the grain being removed

whom /hum/ *pron fml* (object form of who): *To whom did you speak?*

whoop /hup, hwup, wup/ *vi* **1** make a loud cry, as of joy **2** whoop it up *infml* enjoy oneself a lot ♦ *n* a loud shout of joy

whoo·pee /ˈwʊpi, ˈhwʊ-, wʊˈpi, hwʊ-/ *interj* (cry of joy)

whoop·ing cough /ˈhupɪŋ ˌkɔf, ˈhʊp-/ *n* [U] (children's) disease with attacks of serious coughing and difficult breathing

whoops /wʊps, hwʊps, wups/ *interj* (said when one has made a mistake)

whoosh /wʊʃ, hwuʃ, wɔʃ, hwɔʃ/ *vi, n* (move quickly with) a rushing sound

whop·per /ˈwɒpə, ˈhwɑ-/ n infml 1 big thing 2 big lie –**ping** adj, adv very (big): a whopping (great) bonus

whore /hɔr, hoʊr/ n lit or derog for: PROSTITUTE

whose /huz/ determiner, pron of whom: Whose car is that? (= who does it belong to?) | That's the man whose house burned down.

why /waɪ, hwaɪ/ adv, conj 1 for what reason: Why did you do it? 2 the reason why: Is that why you did it? 3 **why not** (used in suggestions): Why not sell it? (= I suggest you sell it) ♦ n the whys and wherefores (of) reasons and explanations (for)

wick /wɪk/ n burning thread in a candle or lamp

wick·ed /ˈwɪkɪd/ adj 1 morally bad; evil 2 playfully bad: a wicked twinkle in his eye 3 sl excellent –**ly** adv –**ness** n [U]

wick·er /ˈwɪkə/ n [U] (objects made from) woven CANES, sticks, etc. ♦ adj made of wicker: wicker baskets

wide /waɪd/ adj 1 large from side to side: The car's too wide to go through the gate. 2 covering a large range: wide experience ♦ adv 1 completely (open or awake) 2 (in sports) away from the correct or central point 3 **wide of the mark** not suitable, correct, etc., at all –**ly** adv over a wide range: It's widely believed (= believed by many people) that carrots are good for the eyes. **widen** vi/t make or become wider

wide-eyed /ˌ ˈ ◄/ adj 1 with eyes very fully open 2 accepting or admiring things too easily

wide·spread /ˌwaɪdˈsprɛd◄/ adj common

wid·ow /ˈwɪdoʊ/ n woman whose husband has died

wid·ow·er /ˈwɪdoʊə/ n man whose wife has died

width /wɪdθ, wɪtθ/ n [C;U] size from side to side

wield /wild/ vt have and/or use (power, influence, etc.)

wie·ner /ˈwinə/ n FRANKFURTER

wife /waɪf/ n **wives** /waɪvz/ woman to whom a man is married

wig /wɪg/ n covering of false hair for the head

wig·gle /ˈwɪgəl/ vi/t move with quick small movements: He wiggled his toes.

wig·wam /ˈwɪgwɑm/ n round Native American hut

wild /waɪld/ adj 1 **a** living in natural conditions, not changed by human beings: wild animals **b** (of people) not civilized 2 uncontrollably violent 3 showing very strong feelings, esp. of anger 4 showing lack of thought or control: a wild guess/throw 5 infml having a very eager liking: He's wild about football. 6 infml good ♦ n [U] natural areas full of animals and plants, with few people ♦ adv 1 **go wild** be filled with feeling, esp. anger or joy 2 **run wild** behave as one likes, without control –**ly** adv: wildly (= too greatly) optimistic

wil·der·ness /ˈwɪldənɪs/ n unchanging stretch of land, etc., with no sign of human presence

wild·fire /ˈwaɪldfaɪə/ n **like wildfire** very quickly

wild-goose chase /ˌ ˈ ◄ ./ n useless search for something that cannot be found

wild·life /ˈwaɪldlaɪf/ n [U] animals living in natural conditions

wild oats /ˌ ˈ ◄/ n **sow one's wild oats** behave wildly, esp. having many sexual partners while young

will¹ /wəl, əl, l; strong wɪl/ v aux 3rd person sing. **will**, pres. t. negative short form **won't** 1 (expresses the future tense): Will it rain tomorrow? 2 be willing to: I won't go! 3 (used in requests): Shut the door, will you? 4 (shows what always happens): Oil will float on water. 5 (used like **can** to show what is possible): This car will hold 5 people. 6 (used like **must** to show what is likely): That will be the mailman at the door now.

will² /wɪl/ n 1 [C;U] power of the mind to make decisions and act in accordance with them: You need a strong will to give up smoking. — see also FREE WILL 2 [U] what someone wishes or intends: She was forced to sign a confession against her will. 3 [U] stated feelings toward someone: I bear you no ill will. 4 [S] force and interest: They set to work with a will. 5 [C] official statement of the way someone wants their property to be shared out after they die 6 **at will** as one wishes 7 **of one's own free will** according to one's own will 8 –**willed** having a certain kind of WILL² (1) ♦ vt 1 make or intend to happen, esp. by the power of the mind 2 leave to someone in a WILL² (5)

will·ful /ˈwɪlfəl/ adj **1** doing what one wants in spite of other people **2** (of something bad) done on purpose ~**ly** adv ~**ness** n [U]

will·ing /ˈwɪlɪŋ/ adj ready; not refusing: Are you willing to help? **2** done or given gladly: willing help **3** eager: a willing helper ~**ly** adv ~**ness** n [U]

wil·low /ˈwɪloʊ/ n tree which grows near water, with long thin branches ~**y** adj pleasantly thin and graceful

will·pow·er /ˈwɪlˌpaʊə/ n [U] strength of WILL² (1)

wil·ly-nil·ly /ˌwɪli ˈnɪli/ adv regardless of whether it is wanted, or not

wilt /wɪlt/ v **1** vi/t become or cause (a plant) to become less fresh and start to die **2** vi (of a person) become tired and weaker

wil·y /ˈwaɪli/ adj clever, esp. at getting what one wants **wiliness** n [U]

wimp /wɪmp/ n weak or useless person, esp. a man ~**ish** adj

win /wɪn/ v **won** /wʌn/, pres. p. -**nn**- **1** vi/t be first or best (in) beating one's opponent(s): Who won the race? **2** vt be given as the result of success: I won $100 in the competition. **3** vt gain: trying to win his friendship **4** vi be right in a guess or argument **5 win hands down** win easily ♦ n (esp. in sports) victory; success ~**ner** n ~**ning** adj very pleasing or attractive: a winning smile ~**nings** n [P] money won

win over phr vt gain the support of by persuading

wince /wɪns/ vi move back suddenly (as if) from something unpleasant, often twisting the face

winch /wɪntʃ/ n apparatus that turns to pull up heavy objects ♦ vt pull up with a winch

wind¹ /wɪnd/ n **1** [C;U] strongly moving air **2** [U] breath or breathing: — see also SECOND WIND **3 get wind of** hear about, esp. accidentally or unofficially **4 see/find out which way the wind blows** find out what the situation is before taking action **5** (**something**) **in the wind** (something, esp. that is secret or not generally known) that is about to happen/being done **6 take the wind out of someone's sails** infml take away someone's confidence or advantage, esp. by saying or doing something unexpected ♦ vt make breathless ~**y** adj with a lot of wind: a windy day

wind² /waɪnd/ v **wound** /waʊnd/ **1** vt turn around and around: wind a handle **2** vt make into a twisted round shape: winding yarn **3** vi go twistingly: The path winds through the woods. **4** vt tighten the working parts of by turning: I wound the clock (up). **5** vt move by turning a handle: Wind down the car window. **6** vt place around several times: She wound a bandage around his arm.

wind down phr vi **1** (of a clock or watch) work more slowly before at last stopping **2** (of a person) to rest until calmer, after work or excitement **3** cause to be no longer in operation, esp. gradually: They're winding down their business in Hong Kong.

wind up phr v **1** vt bring to an end **2** vi get into the stated unwanted situation in the end: I wound up having to pay for it myself.

wind·bag /ˈwɪndbæg/ n person who talks too much

wind·break·er /ˈwɪndˌbreɪkə/ n light JACKET

wind·chill /ˈwɪndˌtʃɪl/ n [S] combination of cold weather and strong winds, which makes temperature feel colder

wind·fall /ˈwɪndfɔl/ n **1** unexpected lucky gift **2** fruit blown from a tree

wind in·stru·ment /ˈwɪnd ˌɪnstrəmənt/ n musical instrument played by blowing air through it

wind·mill /ˈwɪndˌmɪl/ n apparatus used to pump water, make electricity, etc., driven by large sails turned by the wind

win·dow /ˈwɪndoʊ/ n opening (filled with glass) in the wall of a building, in a car, etc., to let in light and air — see also FRENCH DOORS

win·dow·pane /ˈwɪndoʊˌpeɪn/ n one whole piece of glass in a window

window-shop /ˈ··· / vi -**pp**- look at goods in store windows without necessarily intending to buy

wind·pipe /ˈwɪndpaɪp/ n air passage from the throat to the lungs

wind·shield /ˈwɪndʃild/ n piece of transparent material across the front of a vehicle, for the driver to look through

windshield wip·er /ˈ·· ˌ·/ also **wiper** — n one of 2 movable arms which clears rain from the windshield of a car

wind·surf·ing /ˈwɪndˌsɜfɪŋ/ n [U] sport of riding on SAILBOARDS -**er** n

wind·swept /ˈwɪndswɛpt/ *adj* **1** open to continual strong wind: *a windswept beach* **2** as if blown into an untidy state: *a windswept appearance*

wind tun·nel /ˈwɪnd ˌtʌnl/ *n* enclosed place through which air is forced at fixed speeds to test aircraft

wine[1] /waɪn/ *n* [C;U] alcoholic drink made from GRAPES

wine[2] *vt* **wine and dine** (cause to) have a meal and wine

wing /wɪŋ/ *n* **1** limb used by a bird, insect, etc., for flying **2** part standing out from a plane which supports it in flight **3** part standing out from the side: *the west wing of the palace* **4** (in sports) far left or right of the field **5** group with different opinions or purposes from the main organization: *the left wing of the Democratic Party* **6 on the wing** (of a bird) flying **7 take wing** fly (away) **8 under someone's wing** being protected, helped, etc., by someone ♦ *v* **1** *vi* fly (as if) on wings **2** *vt* wound slightly **wings** *n* [P] **1** sides of a stage, where an actor is hidden from view **2 in the wings** hidden and waiting for action ~**ed** *adj* having wings ~**er** *n* **1** player on the WINGS (4) **2** person on the stated WING (5)

wink /wɪŋk/ *vi/t* **1** close and open (an eye) quickly **2** flash or cause (a light) to flash on and off ♦ *n* **1** [C] winking of the eye **2** [S] even a short period of sleep: *I didn't get a wink all night.* (= didn't sleep at all) — see also FORTY WINKS

win·o /ˈwaɪnoʊ/ *n* -os *sl* someone who drinks a lot of cheap wine and lives on the streets

win·ter /ˈwɪntə/ *n* cold season between fall and spring ♦ *vi* spend the winter –**try** /ˈwɪntri/ *adj*

win-win sit·u·a·tion /ˌ•ˈ•• ••••/ *n* [S] situation that will end well for everyone involved

wipe /waɪp/ *vt* **1** rub (a surface or object) to remove (dirt, liquid, etc.): *Wipe your shoes on the mat.* | *She wiped the tears away.* **2 wipe the floor with someone** make someone feel deeply ashamed by severe scolding or by defeat in an argument ♦ *n* act of wiping

wipe off *phr vt* get rid of on purpose: *to wipe off a debt*

wipe out *phr vt* **1** destroy or remove all of **2** *sl* make very tired

wipe up *phr vt* remove with a cloth: *Wipe up that mess!*

wip·er /ˈwaɪpə/ *n* WINDSHIELD WIPER

wire /waɪə/ *n* [C;U] (piece of) thin threadlike metal: *a wire fence* | *electric wires* ♦ *vt* **1** connect up wires (esp. an electrical system) **2** fasten with wire(s) **3** send a TELEGRAM to **wiring** *n* [U] system of (electric) wires **wiry** *adj* thin, but with strong muscles

wired /waɪəd/ *adj* **1** with hidden recording equipment attached **2** *sl* feeling very active, excited, and awake

wire-tap·ping /ˈ•• ˌ••/ *n* [U] listening secretly to other people's telephone conversations with an electrical connection

wis·dom /ˈwɪzdəm/ *n* [U] quality of being wise

wisdom tooth /ˈ•• ˌ•/ *n* large back tooth that grows later than the others

wise[1] /waɪz/ *adj* **1** sensible **2** having long experience and much knowledge **3 none the wiser** knowing no more, after being told **4** -**wise**: **a** in the manner of **b** in the direction of: *clockwise* **c** in connection with: *taxwise* ~**ly** *adv*

wise[2] *v* **wise up** *phr vi/t* (cause to) learn or become conscious of the true situation or true nature of someone or something

wise·crack /ˈwaɪzkræk/ *vi, n* (make) a clever joke

wise guy /ˈ• ˌ•/ *n* annoying person who pretends to know everything

wish /wɪʃ/ *vt* **1** want (something impossible): *I wish I hadn't agreed.* | *I wish I were a bird.* **2** *vi* want and try to cause something (as if) by magic: *If you wish hard enough you may get what you want.* **3** *vt* hope that (someone) will have (something), esp. expressed as a greeting: *We wished him a safe journey.* **4** *vt fml* want ♦ *n* **1** feeling of wanting something: *the wish for these peace talks to succeed* **2** thing wished for **3** attempt to make a wanted thing happen (as if) by magic

wish·bone /ˈwɪʃboʊn/ *n* chicken bone shaped like a V pulled apart before making a wish

wishful think·ing /ˌwɪʃfəl ˈθɪŋkɪŋ/ *n* false belief that something is true or will happen simply because one wishes it

wish·y-wash·y /ˈwɪʃi ˌwaʃi, -ˌwɒʃi/ *adj* without determination or clear aims and principles

wist·ful /ˈwɪstfəl/ *adj* sad because of unfulfilled hopes or thoughts of the past ~**ly** *adv* ~**ness** *n* [U]

wit[1] /wɪt/ n 1 [U] ability to say clever, amusing things 2 [C] witty person 3 [U] also **wits** pl. — power of thought; cleverness: He hadn't the wit to say no. | (fig.) It scared me out of my wits. (= very much) 4 **at one's wits end** too worried by difficulties to know what to do next 5 **have/keep one's wits about one** be ready to act quickly and sensibly ~**ty** adj having or showing WIT[1] (1) ~**tily** adv

wit[2] v to wit lit or law that is (to say)

witch /wɪtʃ/ n woman with magic powers

witch·craft /'wɪtʃkræft/ n [U] performing of magic

witch·doc·tor /'wɪtʃdɒktə/ n man who cures people by magic

with /wɪð, wɪθ/ prep 1 in the presence or company of: I went to the movies with Jim. 2 having: a book with a green cover 3 by means of; using: Cut it with scissors. | Fill it with jam. 4 in support of: Are you with us or against us? 5 against: competing with foreign companies 6 with regard to; in the case of: Be careful with that glass. | He's in love with you. 7 at the same time and rate as: This wine improves with age. 8 (used in comparisons): The window is level with the street. 9 in spite of: With all his faults, I still like him. 10 because of: trembling with fear 11 **in with** a friend of (a person or group) 12 **with it** giving proper attention to what is going on 13 **with me/you** following my/your argument: I'm not with you, what do you mean? 14 **with that** at once after that; then

with·draw /wɪð'drɔ, wɪθ-/ v **-drew** /-'dru/, **-drawn** /-'drɔn/ 1 vt take away or back: She withdrew $50 from her bank account. | I withdraw that remark. 2 vi/t move away or back: I withdrew from (= left) the room. 3 vi/t (cause to) not take part: She withdrew from the election. ~**al** n [C;U] (act of) withdrawing **-drawn** adj quiet and not interested in other people

with·draw·al symp·toms /·'·· ,·'·/ n [P] painful or unpleasant effects which are the result of breaking or stopping a habit, esp. the taking of a drug

with·er /'wɪðə/ vi/t (cause to) become dry, pale, and lifeless: The heat had withered the plants. ~**ing** adj sharply severe: withering scorn

with·hold /wɪθ'hoʊld, wɪð-/ vt **-held** /-'hɛld/ refuse to give: withhold payment

with·in /wɪ'ðɪn, wɪ'θɪn/ adv, prep 1 not more than: He'll arrive within an hour. 2 inside: within the city limits

with·out /wɪ'ðaʊt, wɪ'θaʊt/ prep, adv 1 not having; lacking: a jar without a lid | He went out without telling me. 2 **do/go without** continue as usual in spite of the lack (of)

with·stand /wɪθ'stænd, wɪð-/ vt **-stood** /-'stʊd/ bear or support

wit·ness /'wɪtnɪs/ n 1 person who saw something happen 2 person who gives information to a court of law 3 person who watches another sign an official paper, and then signs it as proof of having seen the first signer 4 **bear witness** to show or prove (a quality) ♦ vt 1 be present at and see 2 watch or sign as a WITNESS (3) 3 be a sign or proof of

witness stand /'·· ,·/ n enclosed area where witnesses stand in a court

wives /waɪvz/ pl. of WIFE — see also OLD WIVES' TALE

wiz·ard /'wɪzəd/ n 1 (in stories) old man with magical powers 2 extremely skillful person: a computer wizard ~**ry** n [U]

wob·ble /'wɒbəl/ vi/t move in an unsteady manner from side to side: Don't wobble the table. **wobble** n **-bly** adj wobbling: wobbly legs

woe /woʊ/ n fml or lit 1 [U] great sorrow 2 [C] trouble ~**ful** adj 1 esp. lit very sad 2 (of something bad) very great: woeful ignorance ~**fully** adv

wok /wɒk/ n deep round Chinese cooking pan

woke /woʊk/ v past t. of WAKE

wok·en /'woʊkən/ v past p. of WAKE

wolf /wʊlf/ n **wolves** /wʊlvz/ 1 fierce wild animal of the dog family 2 man who wants women for sex only 3 **cry wolf** call for help unnecessarily 4 **keep the wolf from the door** earn enough to eat and live 5 **a wolf in sheep's clothing** person who seems harmless but is hiding evil intentions ♦ vt eat quickly in large amounts

wom·an /'wʊmən/ n **women** /'wɪmɪn/ 1 adult female person 2 women in general 3 female nature or qualities 4 **woman of the world** an experienced woman who knows how people behave ~**hood** n [U] quality or time of being a woman ~**ly** adj having good qualities suitable to a woman

wom·an·ize /ˈwʊməˌnaɪz/ *vi* (of a man) habitually pay attention to many women for sexual purposes **-izer** *n*

womb /wuːm/ *n* round organ inside female MAMMALs in which young develop

won /wʌn/ *v past t. and p. of* WIN

won·der /ˈwʌndə/ *n* **1** [U] feeling of strangeness, surprise, and usu. admiration **2** [C] wonderful or surprising thing **3** do/work wonders bring unexpectedly good results **4** (it's) no/little/small wonder it is not surprising; naturally ♦ *vi/t* **1** express a wish to know, in words or silently: *I wonder how you work this machine.* **2** be surprised: *We wondered at the life she chose.* ♦ *adj* unusually good or effective: *a wonder drug* **-ful** *adj* unusually good; causing pleasure or admiration **-fully** *adv* **-ment** *n* [U]

won·drous /ˈwʌndrəs/ *adj lit* wonderful

won't /wəʊnt/ *short for:* will not

woo /wuː/ *vt* **1** *lit* try to make (a woman) love and marry one **2** try to gain the support of

wood /wʊd/ *n* **1** [U] substance of which trees are made **2** [C] also woods *pl.* — place where trees grow, smaller than a forest **3** [the+S] barrels **4** out of the woods free from danger, difficulty, etc. **-ed** *adj* covered with trees **-en** *adj* **1** made of wood **2** stiff; unbending **-y** *adj* of or like wood

wood·chuck /ˈwʊdtʃʌk/ also groundhog — *n* small furry animal that lives underground and sleeps all winter

wood·peck·er /ˈwʊdˌpɛkə/ *n* bird with a long beak that makes holes in trees

wood·wind /ˈwʊdˌwɪnd/ *n* [U;P] (players of) WIND INSTRUMENTS made of wood

wood·work /ˈwʊdwɜːk/ *n* [U] **1** skill of making wooden objects **2** parts of a house that are made of wood

wood·worm /ˈwʊdwɜːm/ *n* [U] damaged condition of wood caused by the young of certain BEETLEs, which make holes

woof /wʊf/ *n, interj* sound made by a dog

woof·er /ˈwʊfə/ *n* LOUDSPEAKER that gives out deep sounds

wool /wʊl/ *n* [U] **1** soft thick hair of sheep **2** material made from this **3** pull the wool over someone's eyes trick someone by hiding the facts **-en** *adj* made of wool **-y** *adj* of or like wool

woo·zy /ˈwuːzi, ˈwɒzi/ *adj infml* having an unsteady feeling in the head **-iness** *n* [U]

word /wɜːd/ *n* **1** [C] (written representation of) 1 or more sounds which can be spoken to represent an idea, object, etc. **2** [S] shortest (type of) statement: *Don't say a word* (= anything) *about it to anyone.* **3** [S] short conversation: *I'd like a word with you.* **4** [U] message or piece of news: *He sent word that he wanted to see me.* **5** [S] promise: *I give you my word that I'll do it.* **6** [C] suggestion or recommendation (RECOMMEND): *Put in a good word for her.* **7** by word of mouth by speaking and not by writing **8** eat one's words admit to having said something wrong **9** get a word in edgeways *infml* get a chance to speak **10** have a word with someone (speak to someone) secretly, esp. giving advice or asking a question **11** (have) the last word (on) (make) the remark that finishes an argument, etc. **12** have words (with) argue angrily (with) **13** in other words expressing the same thing in different words **14** (not) in so many words (not) directly expressed in those words but only suggested **15** put words in(to) someone's mouth: a tell someone what to say **b** claim falsely that someone has said a particular thing **16** take someone's word for it accept what someone says as correct **17** the last word in the most recent development in **18** word for word in exactly the same words ♦ *vt* express in words **-ing** *n* [U] words in which something is expressed **-y** *adj* using or containing more words than necessary

word-per·fect /ˌ· ˈ··/ *adj* repeating or remembering every word correctly

word pro·cess·or /ˈ· ˌ···/ *n* small computer for esp. ordinary office work **-cessing** *n* [U]

wore /wɔː, wʊə/ *v past t. of* WEAR

work¹ /wɜːk/ *n* **1** [U] activity done to produce something or gain a result rather than for amusement **2** [U] job; business: *I go to work by train.* **3** [U] something produced by work, esp. of the hands: *This mat is my own work.* (= I made it) | (fig.) *The murder was the work of a madman.* **4** [C] object produced by painting, writing, etc.: *a work of art* | *the works of Shakespeare* **5** all in a day's work not unusual **6** at work (on) doing something, esp. work **7 go/set to work (on)** start doing **8 have one's work cut out for one** have something difficult to do, esp. in the time allowed **9 in/out of** work having a job/unemployed **10 make short work of** finish quickly and easily — see also WORKS

work² v **1** vi do an activity which uses effort, esp. as one's job: *She works at the factory.* **2** vi (of a machine, plan, etc.) operate (properly): *It works by electricity.* | *Your plan will never work.* **3** vt make (a person) do work: *They work us too hard.* **4** vt make (a machine) do work: *How do you work this thing?* **5** vt make (one's way) by work or effort **6** vi/t make or become by small movements: *This little screw has worked itself loose.* **7** vt produce (an effect): *This medicine works wonders.* **8** vt arrange, esp. unofficially: *We'll work it so that we can all go together.* **9** vi move or act for a certain result: *This will work against you in the future.*~**able** adj which can be put into effect; usable: *a workable plan* ~**er** n **1** person who works: *an office worker* **2** member of the WORKING CLASS

work off phr vt get rid of by work or effort: *He worked off his anger by chopping wood.*

work out phr v **1** vt calculate (the answer to) **2** vi have a result; develop: *The plan worked out very well in practice.* **3** vt plan; decide: *We're trying to work out how to get there.* **4** vi reach the stated amount by being calculated: *The cost works out at $10 each.* **5** vi exercise

work up phr vt **1** excite the feelings of: *He gets very worked up about exams.* **2** cause oneself to have: *I couldn't work up much enthusiasm for it.*

work·a·hol·ic /ˌwəːkəˈhɒlɪk, -ˈhɑ-/ n person who likes to work too hard

work·bench /ˈwəːkbentʃ/ n (a table with) a hard surface for working on with tools

work·book /ˈwəːkbʊk/ n school book with questions and exercises

work·fare /ˈwəːkfeəʳ/ n [U] system in which poor people must do some work, in exchange for money from the government

work·force /ˈwəːkfɔːʳs/ n all the workers in a factory or in industry generally

work·horse /ˈwəːkhɔːʳs/ n person who does most of the (dull) work

work·ing /ˈwəːkɪŋ/ adj **1** used for work: *working clothes* **2** (of time) spent in work **3** useful as a base for further development: *a working hypothesis*

working class /ˌ·· ˈ·ʳ/ n social class of people who work with their hands **working-class** adj

working or·der /ˌ·· ˈ·ʳ/ n [U] state of working well, with no trouble

work·ings /ˈwəːkɪŋz/ n [P] **1** way something works or acts: *the workings of an engine/of his mind* **2** parts of a mine which have been dug out

work·load /ˈwəːkləʊd/ n amount of work that a person or machine is expected to do in a particular period of time

work·man /ˈwəːkmən/ n **-men** /-mən/ man who works with his hands, esp. in a particular skill or trade ~**like** adj showing the qualities of a good workman ~**ship** n [U] (signs of) skill in making things

work·out /ˈwəːk-aʊt/ n period of physical exercise

works /wəːks/ n **works 1** [P] moving parts of a machine **2** [C] factory: *a dye works* **3 give someone the works** sl **a** give someone everything: *They gave us supper, wine, chocolates, the works.* **b** attack violently

work·sheet /ˈwəːkʃiːt/ n piece of paper with questions, exercises, etc., for students

work·shop /ˈwəːkʃɒp/ n **1** room where heavy repairs and jobs on machines are done **2** period of group activity and study: *a drama workshop*

work·sta·tion /ˈwəːkˌsteɪʃən/ n part of an office where 1 person works, with a desk, computer, etc.

world /wəːld/ n **1** [the+S] **a** the Earth: *the richest man in the world* **b** particular part of it: *the Old World* **2** [the+S] the universe **3** [the+S] group of living things: *the animal world* **4** [the+S] a particular area of human activity: *the world of football* **5** [the+S] people generally: *We don't want the whole world* (= everyone) *to know about it.* **6** [the+S] human life and its affairs: *the ways of the world* **7** [C] PLANET: *life on other worlds* **8** large number or amount: *This medicine did me a world of good.* **9** [the+S] fml material standards: *to give up the world to serve God* **10 all the world to** very important to **11 for all the world like/as if** exactly like/as if **12 (have) the best of both worlds** (to have) the advantage which each choice offers, without having to choose between them **13 in the world** (in a question expressing surprise): *Where in the world have you been?* **14 not for the world** certainly not: *I wouldn't hurt her for the world.* **15 on top of the world** very happy **16 out of this world** unusually good; wonderful **17 worlds apart** completely different ~**ly** *adj* **1** material: *all my worldly goods* (= everything I own) **2** too much concerned with human society, rather than religious things ~**liness** *n* [U]

world-class /ˌ·'·◄/ *adj* among the best in the world

world-fam·ous /ˌ·'··◄/ *adj* known all over the world

world pow·er /ˌ·'··/ *n* nation with very great power and influence

World Ser·ies /ˌ·'··/ *n* [the] last series of baseball games played each year to decide the best professional team in the US and Canada

world·wide /ˌwəʳld'waɪd◄/ *adj, adv* in or over all the world

World Wide Web /ˌ·'·'·/ *n* [the] INTERNET

worm /wɜːm/ *n* **1** small thin creature with no bones or limbs, like a tube of flesh **2** worthless, cowardly, etc., person ♦ *vt* move by twisting or effort: *We wormed our way through the crack in the wall.* | (fig.) *He wormed his way into her affections.*

worn /wɔːn, woʊrn/ *v past p. of* WEAR

worn-out /ˌ·'·◄/ *adj* **1** no longer usable **2** very tired

wor·ry /'wɜːi, 'wʌri/ *v* **1** *vi/t* (cause to) be anxious or uncomfortable: *worrying about the exams* | *Heights don't worry me.* **2** *vt* (esp. of a dog) chase and bite (an animal) ♦ *n* [C;U] **1** feeling of anxiety **2** (person or thing that causes) anxiety –**ried** *adj* anxious ~**ing** *adj*

wor·ry·wart /'wɜːiˌwɔːt, 'wʌ-/ *n infml* person who worries a lot about unimportant things

worse /wɜːs/ *adj* **1** (*comparative of* BAD) of lower quality; more bad **2** more ill (than before) **3 none the worse (for)** not harmed (by) **4 the worse for wear** harmed by use over a period ♦ *adv* in a worse way or to a worse degree ~**n** [U] something worse **worsen** *vi/t* (cause to) become worse

wor·ship /'wɜːʃɪp/ *n* [U] (showing of) strong (religious) feelings of love, respect, and admiration ♦ *vi/t* show worship (to): *to worship God* | *She worships her brother.* (= admires him too) greatly) ~**er** *n*

worst /wɜːst/ *adj* (*superlative of* BAD) of lowest quality; most bad ♦ *n* **1 worst** worst thing or part: *These ones are the worst.* **2 at (the) worst** if the worst happens **3 get the worst of** suffer most from **4 if worst comes to worst** if there is no better way **5 (in) the worst way** very much ♦ *adv* (*superlative of* BADly) most badly: *the worst-dressed man in the office*

worth /wɜːθ/ *prep* **1** of the stated value: *a painting worth $5000* **2** deserving: *That film isn't worth seeing.* **3 for all one is worth** with all possible effort **4 for what it's worth** though I'm not sure it's of any value **5 worth it** useful; worthwhile **6 worth one's salt** worthy of respect or of being so called **7 worth one's/someone's while** worthwhile to one/someone ♦ *n* [U] value ~**less** *adj* **1** of no value **2** (of a person) of bad character

worth·while /ˌwɜːθ'waɪl◄, ·'hwaɪl◄/ *adj* with a good enough result to deserve the trouble taken

wor·thy /'wɜːði/ *adj* **1** deserving respect or serious attention **2** deserving: *worthy of admiration* **3** good but not very exciting or interesting –**thily** *adv* –**thiness** *n* [U]

would /wəd, əd, d; *strong* wʊd/ *v* *aux* **1** (*past of* will): *They said they would meet us at 10:30.* **2** (shows what is likely or possible): *What would you do if you won a million dollars?* **3** (shows what always happened): *We would meet for a drink after work.* **4** (shows choice): *I'd rather have eggs.* **5** (expressing a polite request): *Would you lend me your pencil?*

would-be /'·◄ ·/ *adj* which one wants or intends to be, but isn't: *a would-be musician*

wouldn't /'wʊdnt/ *short for*: would not

wound¹ /wuːnd/ *n* damaged place on the body, esp. caused by a weapon: *a bullet wound* ♦ *vt* cause a wound to: *a wounded leg* | (fig.) *wounded pride*

wound² /waʊnd/ *v past t. and p. of* WIND²

wound-up /ˌwaʊnd 'ʌp◄/ *adj* anxiously excited

wove /woʊv/ *v past t. of* WEAVE

wov·en /'woʊvən/ *v past p. of* WEAVE

wow /waʊ/ *interj infml* (expresses surprise and admiration) ♦ *n* [S] *sl* a great success ♦ *vt sl* cause surprise and admiration in someone

wrap /ræp/ *vt* **-pp- 1** cover in material folded over: *I wrapped the box in brown paper | She had a bandage wrapped around her finger.* **2 wrap someone around one's little finger** make someone do what one wants ♦ *n* **1** garment for covering a woman's shoulders **2 under wraps** secret ~**per** *n* loose paper cover ~**ping** *n* [C;U] ma·terial for folding around and covering something

wrap up *phr vt* **1** wear warm clothes **2** complete (a business arrangement, meeting, etc.) **3** summarize (SUMMARY) **4 wrapped up in** giving complete attention to

wrap-up /'· ·/ *n* SUMMARY

wrath /ræθ/ *n* [U] *fml or lit* strong fierce anger ~**ful** *adj*

wreak /rik/ *vt esp. lit* perform or bring about (something violent or unpleasant)

wreath /riθ/ *wreaths* /riðz/ *n* usu. circular arrangement of flowers or leaves **a** given at a funeral **b** placed on the head as a sign of honor **c** used as Christmas decoration

wreck /rɛk/ *n* **1** [C] sunken or destroyed ship **2** [C] something in a very bad condition: *Have you seen the old wreck he drives around in!* **3** [U] *fml* ruin; destruction: *the wreck of our hopes* **4** [C] person whose health is destroyed ♦ *vt* destroy: *a ship wrecked on the rocks | The bad weather wrecked our plans.* ~**age** *n* [U] broken parts of a destroyed thing

wren /rɛn/ *n* very small brown bird

wrench /rɛntʃ/ *vt* **1** pull hard with a twist **2** twist and damage (a joint of the body) ♦ *n* **1** act of or damage caused by wrenching **2** separation that causes suffering of the mind **3** metal tool with jaws or a hollow end, for twisting NUTs (2)

wrest /rɛst/ *vt* **1** pull (away) violently **2** *esp. lit* obtain with difficulty

wres·tle /'rɛsəl/ *vi/t* fight by trying to hold or throw one's opponent: (fig.) *wrestling with a difficult problem* ~**tler** *n* person who wrestles as a sport

wretch /rɛtʃ/ *n* **1** unfortunate person **2** annoying person

wretch·ed /'rɛtʃɪd/ *adj* **1** very unhappy **2** of a bad type which makes one unhappy: *a wretched headache* **3** annoying: *Why*

can't that wretched child behave himself! ~**ly** *adv* ~**ness** *n* [U]

wrig·gle /'rɪgəl/ *vi/t* move from side to side: *He wriggled uncomfortably on the hard seat.* ♦ *n* wriggling movement

wriggle out of *phr vt* escape (a difficulty) by clever tricks

wring /rɪŋ/ *vt* **wrung** /rʌŋ/, **wringing 1** twist or press (wet clothes) to remove (water) **2** twist (the neck) hard, causing death **3** press hard on, esp. hands: *wringing her hands in sorrow* **4** obtain by severe or cruel methods: *Her torturers wrung a confession out of her.* **5 wringing wet** very wet ~**er** *n* machine for wringing clothes

wrin·kle /'rɪŋkəl/ *n* **1** small line or fold, esp. on the skin owing to age **2** *infml* useful suggestion or trick ♦ *vi/t* (cause to) form wrinkles –**kly** *adj*

wrist /rɪst/ *n* joint between the hand and the arm

wrist·watch /'rɪst-wɑtʃ/ *n* watch with a band for fastening around the wrist

writ /rɪt/ *n* official legal paper telling someone (not) to do a particular thing

write /raɪt/ *v* **wrote** /roʊt/, **written** /'rɪt⁻n/ **1** *vi/t* make (marks representing letters or words) with a tool, esp. a pen or pencil **2** *vt* think of and record, esp. on paper: *He wrote a report on the match.* **3** *vt* complete by writing words: *write a check* **4** *vi/t* produce and send (a letter): *He writes to me every week.* **5** *vi* be a writer (of books, plays, etc.): *She writes for television.* **6 be written on/all over** clearly showing because of the expression on: *Guilt was written all over his face.* **7 writ large** *lit* on a larger or grander scale **writer** *n* writing *n* [U] **1 a** anything written by hand **b** style of writing by hand **2** written work or form: *Put it down in writing.* **3** activity of writing books, etc. **writings** *n* [P] written works

write down *phr vt* record (esp. what has been said) in writing

write out *phr vt* write in full

write up *phr vt* write (again) in a complete and useful form **write-up** /'· ·/ *n* written report giving a judgment

writhe /raɪð/ *vi* twist the body (as if) in great pain

writ·ten /'rɪt⁻n/ *v past p. of* WRITE

wrong /rɒŋ/ *adj* **1** not correct: *the wrong answer* **2** morally bad **3** not in a proper or healthy state: *There's something* *wrong with the engine.* **4** not suitable: *the wrong time to visit* ♦ *adv* **1** wrongly **2 go wrong: a** stop working properly **b** make a mistake **c** end badly ♦ *n* **1** [U] morally bad behavior **2** [C] *fml* unjust or bad action **3 in the wrong** mistaken or deserving blame ♦ *vt* be unfair to or cause to suffer ~**ful** *adj* unjust or illegal: *wrongful arrest* ~**fully** *adv*

wrong·do·ing /ˌrɔŋˈduɪŋ, ˈrɔŋˌduɪŋ/ *n* [C;U] (example of) bad or illegal behavior **wrongdoer** /ˈrɔŋˌduɚ/ *n* [C]

wrote /roʊt/ *v past t. of* WRITE

wrought /rɔt/ *adj lit* made: *wrought of steel*

wrought i·ron /ˌ· ˈ·· ◂/ *n* [U] iron shaped into a useful, pleasing form

wrung /rʌŋ/ *v past t. and p. of* WRING

wry /raɪ/ *adj* showing a mixture of amusement and dislike, disappointment, etc.: *a wry smile* ~**ly** *adv*

WWW *abbrev. for:* WORLD WIDE WEB

X, x[1] /ɛks/ the 24th letter of the English alphabet

X[2] *adj* (of a film) which is not suitable for persons under 18

xen·o·pho·bi·a /ˌzɛnəˈfoʊbiə/ *n* [U] unreasonable fear and dislike of foreigners –**bic** *adj*

Xe·rox /ˈzɪrɑks, ˈzirɑks/ *vt, n tdmk* (make) a photographic copy on an electric copying machine

X·mas /ˈkrɪsməs, ˈɛksməs/ *n infml* CHRISTMAS

X-ray /ˈɛks reɪ/ *n* **1** powerful unseen beam which can pass through solid things, used esp. for photographing conditions inside the body **2** photograph taken with this **3** medical examination with this **x-ray** *vt* photograph, examine, or treat with X-rays

xy·lo·phone /ˈzaɪləˌfoʊn/ *n* musical instrument with many small wooden bars hit with a hammer

Y

Y, y /waɪ/ the 25th letter of the English alphabet

yacht /jɑt/ n **1** light sailing boat used esp. for racing **2** large pleasure boat with a motor ~**ing** n [U] sailing in a yacht

yachts·man /ˈjɑtsmən/ **yachts·woman** /-ˌwʊmən/ fem. — n -**men** /-mən/ sailor in a yacht

yak[1] /jæk/ n cow of central Asia with long hair

yak[2] vi -**kk**- derog talk continuously about unimportant things

yam /jæm/ n tropical plant with a root eaten as a vegetable

yank /jæŋk/ vi/t pull suddenly and sharply **yank** n

Yan·kee /ˈjæŋki/ n derog American person esp. from the north

yap /jæp/ vi -**pp**- derog **1** (of a dog) BARK continuously **2** talk noisily about unimportant things

yard[1] /jɑrd/ n a measure of length equal to 3 feet or .9144 meters

yard[2] n **1** area around a house with grass, flowers, and trees **2** area enclosed for the stated activity or business: a lumberyard

yard sale /ˈ· ·/ n sale of used articles

yard·stick /ˈjɑrdˌstɪk/ n **1** measuring stick one yard long **2** standard of measurement or comparison

yar·mul·ke /ˈjɑrməlkə, ˈjɑməkə/ n special small hat worn by Jewish men

yarn[1] /jɑrn/ n **1** [U] long continuous thread esp. in making cloth **2** [C] story

yawn /jɔn/ vi **1** open the mouth wide and breathe deeply, esp. from tiredness **2** be(come) wide open: a yawning chasm ♦ n **1** act of yawning **2** infml something dull

yd. written abbrev. for: YARD(s)[1]

yeah /jɛə/ adv infml yes

year /jɪr/ n **1** period of 365 (or 366) days, or 12 months, esp. as measured from January 1 to December 31 **2** period of about a year in the life of an organiza-

tion: the school year **3** all year round during the whole year **4** year after year continuously for many years **5** year in, year out regularly each year ~**ly** adj, adv (happening) every year or once a year

year·book /ˈjɪrbʊk/ n book printed each year about students, events, etc., at a high school or college

year·ling /ˈjɪrlɪŋ/ n animal between 1 and 2 years old

year·long /ˈjɪrlɔŋ/ adj lasting a whole year

yearn /jɜrn/ vi esp. lit have a strong (sad) desire: I yearn for your return. ~**ing** n [C;U] esp. lit strong desire

yeast /jist/ n [U] form of very small plant with a chemical action used for producing alcohol in making wine and beer and for making bread light and soft ~**y** adj

yell /jɛl/ vi/t, n shout

yel·low /ˈjɛloʊ/ adj **1** of the color of gold **2** infml cowardly ♦ vi/t (cause to) become yellow ~**ish** adj

yellow fe·ver /ˌ· ˈ·· / n [U] serious tropical disease

yellow pag·es /ˌ· ˈ·· / n [the+P] book with telephone numbers of businesses

yelp /jɛlp/ vi, n (make) a sharp high cry, esp. of pain

yen[1] /jɛn/ n yen unit of Japanese money

yen[2] n strong desire

yes /jɛs/ adv **1** (used for accepting or agreeing) **2** (used for replying to a call)

yes-man /ˈ· · / n derog someone who always agrees with their leader or employer

yes·ter·day /ˈjɛstədi, -ˌdeɪ/ adv, n (on) the day before today

yes·ter·year /ˈjɛstəˌjɪr/ n [U] esp. lit the recent past

yet /jɛt/ adv **1** up until this time: He hasn't arrived yet. **2** in the future, and in spite of how things seem now: We may yet win. **3** even: a yet bigger problem **4** still: I have yet to be told. (= I have still not been told) **5** as yet YET(1) ♦ conj but even so: strange yet true

Yid·dish /ˈjɪdɪʃ/ adj, n (language) of European Jews

yield /jild/ v **1** vt produce: a tree which yields a large crop **2** vt fml give up control of: yield a position of advantage **3** vi fml or lit admit defeat **4** vi allow other traffic to go first ♦ *n* amount produced: *a high yield of fruit* ~**ing** *adj* **1** not stiff or fixed **2** (too) easily persuaded

yip·pee /ˈyɪpi, yɪˈpi/ *interj* (shout of delight or success)

yo /yoʊ/ *interj sl* (used to greet someone, get their attention, or as a reply to a greeting)

yo·del /ˈyoʊdl/ *vi/t* **-l-** sing with many changes between the natural voice and a very high voice

yo·ga /ˈyoʊgə/ *n* [U] Hindu system of control of the mind and body, often including special exercises

yo·gurt /ˈyoʊgət/ *n* [U] milk that has thickened and turned slightly acidic through the action of certain bacteria

yoke /yoʊk/ *n* **1** bar joining 2 animals for pulling a vehicle or heavy load **2** frame across someone's shoulders for carrying 2 equal loads **3** *lit* controlling power: *the hated yoke of their conquerors* **4** part of a garment from which the rest hangs ♦ *vt* join (as if) with a yoke

yolk /yoʊk/ *n* [C;U] yellow part of an egg

yon·der /ˈyɑndə/ *adj, adv* that; over there

you /yə, yʊ; *strong* yu/ *pron* (used as subject or object) **1** person or people being spoken to: *I love you.* **2** anyone; one: *You can't trust such people.* **3** (used for addressing someone, esp. angrily): *You fool!*

you'd /yəd, yʊd; *strong* yud/ *short for*: **1** you had **2** you would

you'll /yəl, yʊl; *strong* yul/ *short for*: **1** you will **2** you shall

young /yʌŋ/ *adj* **younger** /ˈyʌŋgə/, **youngest** /ˈyʌŋgɪst/ in an early stage of

life or development ♦ *n* [P] **1** young people generally **2** young animals

young·ster /ˈyʌŋstə/ *n* person

your /yə; *strong* yʊr, yɔr, yoʊr/ *determiner* of you: *your house*

you're /yə; *strong* yʊr, yɔr, yoʊr/ *short for*: you are

yours /yʊrz, yɔrz, yoʊrz/ *pron* **1** of you; your one(s) **2** (used at the end of a letter): *Sincerely, yours, Janet Smith.* **3 yours truly: a** (polite phrase written at the end of a letter) **b** *infml* I; me; myself

your·self /yəˈsɛlf/ *pron* **-selves** /-ˈsɛlvz/ **1** (reflexive form of **you**): *Don't hurt yourself.* **2** (strong form of **you**): *Did you make it yourself?* **3 (all) by yourself: a** alone **b** without help **4 to yourself** not shared

youth /yuθ/ *n* **youths** /yuðz, yuθs/ **1** [U] period of being young **2** [C] *often derog* young person, esp. male **3** [U;P] young people as a group: *the youth of today* ~**ful** *adj* (seeming) young

you've /yəv, yʊv; *strong* yuv/ *short for*: you have

yo-yo /ˈyoʊ yoʊ/ *n* **1** toy held in the hand, made of joined circular parts that move up and down a string **2** *sl* stupid person

yuck /yʌk/ *interj* (expression of disgust)

yuck·y /ˈyʌki/ *adj infml* extremely unpleasant

Yule /yul/ *n* [U] *lit for*: CHRISTMAS

yum /yʌm/ *interj* (said when one thinks something tastes very good)

yum·my /ˈyʌmi/ *adj infml* tasting very good

yup·pie /ˈyʌpi/ *n* young person in a professional job with a high income, esp. one who enjoys spending money and having a fashionable way of life

Z

Z, z /ziː/ the 26th and last letter of the English alphabet

za·ny /ˈzeɪni/ *adj* amusingly foolish

zap /zæp/ *v* **-pp-** *infml* **1** *vt* attack and/or destroy **2** *vi/t* move quickly and forcefully

zeal /ziːl/ *n* [U] *fml* eagerness ~**ous** /ˈzɛləs/ *adj* eager; keen ~**ously** *adv*

zeal·ot /ˈzɛlət/ *n* someone who is (too) eager in their beliefs

ze·bra /ˈzibrə/ *n* **-bra** *or* **-bras** horselike African animal with broad black and white lines

zen·ith /ˈzinɪθ/ *n* highest or greatest point of development, success, etc.

ze·ro¹ /ˈzɪroʊ, ˈzɪroʊ/ *n* **-ros** *or* **-roes 1** (sign representing) the number 0 **2** point between + and – on a scale: *The temperature was below zero.* (= below the freezing point of water) **2** nothing: *zero growth*

zero² *v* **zero in on** *phr vt* **1** aim a weapon directly at **2** aim one's attention directly towards

zero hour /ˈ·· ˌ·/ *n* [U] time at which something important is to begin

zest /zɛst/ *n* **1** [S;U] pleasantly exciting quality: *The danger adds zest to the affair.* **2** [S;U] eagerness: *a zest for life* ~**ful** *adj*

zig·zag /ˈzɪgzæg/ *vi, n* **-gg-** (go in) a line shaped like a row of z's: *The path zigzags up the hill.*

zil·lion /ˈzɪlyən/ *also* **zillions** *pl.* — *determiner, n, pron infml* extremely large number

zinc /zɪŋk/ *n* [U] blue-white metal

zing /zɪŋ/ *n* [U] exciting or spirited taste or quality

zip¹ /zɪp/ *vi* **1** fasten with a ZIPPER **2** *vi/t* move very quickly and forcefully

zip² *n* [U] exciting or spirited quality

Zip code /ˈ·· ˌ·/ *n* numbers added to an address to make it more exact for delivering letters

zip·per /ˈzɪpə/ *n* fastener with 2 sets of teeth and a sliding piece that joins the edges of an opening by drawing the teeth together

zit /zɪt/ *n* [P] *sl* spot on the skin

zo·di·ac /ˈzoʊdiˌæk/ *n* [*the*+S] imaginary belt in space along which the sun, moon, and nearest PLANETS seem to travel, divided into 12 equal parts used in ASTROLOGY

zom·bie /ˈzɑmbi/ *n* **1** *derog* someone who moves or acts very slowly or lifelessly **2** dead person made to move by magic

zone /zoʊn/ *n* area marked off from others by particular qualities or activities: *a war/danger zone* ♦ *vt* give a particular purpose to (an area): *a part of town zoned for industrial development* **zonal** *adj* **zoning** *n* [U]

zoo /zu/ *n* **zoos** park where many types of wild animals are kept for show

zo·ol·o·gy /zoʊˈɑlədʒi/ *n* [U] scientific study of animals –**gist** *n* **zoological** /ˌzoʊəˈlɑdʒɪkəl/ *adj*

zoom /zum/ *vi* **1** go quickly with a loud noise **2** (of a movie camera) move quickly between a distant and a close view **3** increase suddenly and greatly

zoom lens /ˈ· ˌ·/ *n* curved piece of glass by which a camera can zoom in and out while keeping the picture clear

zuc·chi·ni /zuˈkini/ *n* **-ni** *or* **-nis** green SQUASH

Word beginnings

Afro- /ˈæfrou/ **1** of Africa: *an Afro-American* **2** African and: *Afro-Asian peoples*

Anglo- /ˈæŋglou/ **1** of England or Britain: *an Anglophile* (someone who loves Britain) **2** English or British and: *an Anglo-American treaty*

ante- /ˈænti/ before: *antediluvian* –compare POST-

anti- /ˈæntai/ against; not in favor of; trying to prevent or destroy: *an anti-cancer drug* | *an antitank gun* | *He's very anti-war.* -compare PRO-

arch- /ɑrtʃ/ chief; main: *our archenemy*

astro- /ˈæstrou/ of or about the stars and space: *astrophysics*

audio- /ˈɔdiou/ of, for, or using sound, esp. recorded sound: *audiovisual teaching aids* –compare VIDEO-

Austro- /ˈɔstrou/ **1** Australian and: *Austro-Malayan* **2** Austrian and: *the Austro-Italian border*

be- /bi/ (makes verbs and adjectives) cause to be or have: *a bespectacled judge* (= wearing glasses) | *She befriended me.*

bi- /bai/ two; twice: *a biannual publication* (= coming out twice a year)

bio- /baiou/ connected with (the study of) living things: *biochemistry*

centi- /ˈsɛntə/ hundredth part: *a centimeter* (= a hundredth of a meter)

co- /kou/ with; together: *my co-author, who wrote the book with me*

counter- /ˈkauntə/ done in return or so as to have an opposite effect or make ineffective: *a counterattack* | *counter-espionage operations*

cross- /krɔs/ going between the stated things: *cross-cultural influences*

de- /di/ **1** (showing an opposite): *a de-populated area* (= which all or most of the population has left) **2** to remove: *to dethrone a king* | *to debug a computer program* **3** to make less: *devalue the currency*

deca- /ˈdɛkə/ ten: *a decaliter* (= ten liters)

deci- /ˈdɛsə/ tenth part: *a deciliter* (= a tenth of a liter)

dis- /dis/ **1** not; the opposite of: *I disagree.* | *He is dishonest.* **2** removal: *nuclear disarmament*

em- /im, ɛm/ (*before* **b**, **m**, *or* **p**) EN-: *emboldened*

en- /in/ (makes verbs) cause to be (more): *Enlarge the hole.*

equi- /ˈɛkwə/ equally: *two points equidistant from a third*

Euro- /yurou/ of Europe, esp. the EU: *the Europarliament*

ex- /ɛks/ former: *my ex-fiance*

extra- /ˈɛkstrə/ not (usu.) included; beyond; outside: *extracurricular lessons* | *extravehicular activity by astronauts*

fore- /fɔr/ **1** before; in advance: *I was forewarned of their visit.* **2** in or at the front: *a boat's foresail*

foster- /ˈfɔstə/ giving or receiving parental care although not of the same family: *my fosterparents*

Franco- /ˈfræŋkou/ **1** of France: *a Francophile* (= someone who loves France) **2** French and: *the Franco-Prussian war*

geo- /dʒiou/ connected with the study of the Earth or its surface: *geophysics*

hecto- /ˈhɛktou/ hundred: *a hectoliter* (= a hundred liters) -compare CENTI-

hydro- /ˈhaidrou/ concerning or using water: *hydroelectricity*

hyper- /haipə/ very or too much: *hyperactive* | *hypercritical*

il- /il/ (*before* **l**) not: *illiberal*

im- /im/ (*before* **b**, **m**, *or* **p**) IN-: *impossible*

in- /in/ **1** not: *indecisive* | *insane* **2** inwards: *a sudden inrush of water*

inter- /intə/ between or including both or all: *the intercity train service* | *an interdominational marriage ceremony*

ir- /ir/ (*before* **r**) not: *irrational*

kilo- /kilə/ thousand: *a kilogram* (= a thousand grams) -compare MILLI-

mal- /mæl/ bad(ly); wrong(ly): *a malformed body* | *maladministration*

maxi- /ˈmæksi/ unusually large or long -compare MINI-

mega- /ˈmɛgə/ **1** million: *a ten-megaton nuclear bomb* **2** *sl* very great: *a movie megastar*

micro- /ˈmaikrou/ **1** (esp. with scientific words) extremely small: *a microcomputer* **2** using a microscope: *microsurgery* **3** millionth part: *a microsecond* (= a millionth of a second)

mid- /mid/ middle; in the middle of: *midwinter* | *mid-Atlantic* | *She's in her mid-20s.* (= is about 25 years old)

milli- /mɪlə/ thousandth part: *a milliliter* (= a thousandth of a liter) -compare KILO-

mini- /mɪni/ unusually small or short: *a miniskirt* | *a TV miniseries*

mis- /mɪs/ **1** bad(ly); wrong(ly): *He mistreats his dog.* | *I misheard what you said.* **2** lack of; opposite of: *mistrust* | *misfortune*

mono- /mɑnoʊ/ one; single; UNI-: *monosyllabic* | *a monoplane* (with one wing on each side) -compare POLY-

multi- /mʌlti/ many: *a multipurpose tool* | *a multistory building*

non- /nɑn/ not: *nonaddictive* | *nonprofitmaking*

over- /oʊvə/ **1** too much: *an overindulgent parent* | *an overcooked dish* –compare UNDER- **2** above; across: *We took the overland route.*

poly- /pɑli/ many: *polysyllabic* -compare MONO-

post- /poʊst/ after; later than: *the postwar years* -compare PRE-

pre- /pri/ before; earlier than: *the prewar years* | *a prelunch drink* -compare POST-

pro- /proʊ/ in favor of; supporting: *a prodemocracy movement* -compare ANTI-

pseudo- /sudoʊ/ only pretending to be, false: *pseudo-intellectuals*

psycho- /saɪkoʊ/ connected with (illness of) the mind: *psychotherapy* | *psychosexual disorders*

quasi- /kwɑzi/ seeming to be; almost like: *a quasijudicial function*

re- /ri/ again: *The body was dug up and then reburied.*

self- /sɛlf/ of or by oneself or itself: *a self-charging battery* | *self-deception* | *She's completely self-taught.*

semi- /sɛmi; sɛmaɪ/ **1** half: *a semicircle* **2** partly; incomplete(ly): *semipermanent* | *in the semidarkness*

step- /stɛp/ related through a parent who has remarried

sub- /sʌb/ **1** under, below: *subsoil* | *subzero temperatures* **2** smaller part of: *a subcategory* **3** less than; worse than: *subhuman intelligence* **4** next in rank below: *a sublieutenant* -compare SUPER-

super- /supə/ greater or more than: *superhuman strength* | *supertankers* (= very large ships) *carrying oil* -compare SUB-

trans- /trænz, træns/ across; on or to the other side of: *a transatlantic flight*

tri- /traɪ/ three: *trilingual* (= speaking three languages)

ultra- /ʌltrə/ very, esp. too: *ultramodern* | *ultracautious*

un- /ʌn/ **1** (makes adjectives and adverbs) not: *uncomfortable* | *unfairly* | *unwashed* **2** (makes verbs) make or do the opposite of: *She tied a knot, and then untied it.*

under- /ʌndə/ **1** too little: *undercooked potatoes* | *underproduction* **2** below: *an undersea cable* -compare OVER-

vice- /vaɪs/ next in rank below: *the vice-chairman of the committee*

video- /vɪdioʊ/ of, for, or using recorded pictures, esp. as produced by a video (2): *a videocassette*

Word endings

-able /əbəl/ also **-ible** (in adjectives) that can have the stated thing done to it: a washable fabric

-age /ɪdʒ/ (in nouns) **1** the action or result of doing the stated thing: to allow for shrinkage (= getting smaller) | several breakages (= things broken) **2** the cost of doing the stated thing: Postage is extra. **3** the state or rank of: in his dotage

-al /əl/ **1** (in adjectives) of; connected with: autumnal mists | a musical performance **2** (in nouns) (an example of the) act of doing something: the arrival of the bus | several rehearsals

-an /ən/ -IAN: the Republican candidate

-ance /əns/ (in nouns) (an example of) the action, state or quality of doing or being the stated thing: his sudden appearance (= he appeared suddenly) | her brilliance (= she is brilliant)

-ant /ənt/ (in adjectives and nouns) (person or thing) that does the stated thing: in the resultant confusion | a bottle of disinfectant

-ar /ə/ **1** (in adjectives) of; connected with; being: the Polar regions **2** (in nouns) -ER²: a liar

-arian /ɛəriən/ (in nouns) person who supports and believes in: a libertarian (= person who supports freedom)

-ary /ɛri/ (in adjectives) being: with his customary (= usual) caution | her legendary (= very famous) courage

-ate /ət, eɪt/ **1** (in verbs) (cause to) become or have: a hyphenated word **2** (in adjectives) having: a fortunate (= lucky) woman

-ation /əʃən/ (in nouns) (an) act or result of doing the stated thing: the continuation of the story

-ative /ətɪv, eɪtɪv/ (in adjectives) **1** liking or tending to have or do: argumentative | talkative **2** for the purpose of the stated thing: a consultative meeting

-bound /baʊnd/ (in adjectives) limited, kept in, or controlled in the stated way: a fog-bound aircraft

-cy /si/ (makes nouns from adjectives ending in /t/ or /tɪk/) -ITY: several inaccuracies in the report

-d /d, t/ (after e) -ED: a wide-eyed stare

-dom /dəm/ (in nouns) **1** condition of being the stated thing: freedom | boredom **2** country or area ruled by: a kingdom **3** people of the stated sort: despite the opposition of officialdom

-ean /iən/ -IAN

-ed /d, əd, t/ **1** (makes regular past t. and p. of verbs): We landed safely. **2** (in adjectives) having or wearing the stated thing; with: a long-tailed dog | a costumed actor

-ee /i/ (in nouns) **1** person to whom the stated thing is done: an employee | a trainee **2** person who is or does the stated thing: an absentee

-eer /ɪr/ (in nouns) person who does or is connected with the stated thing: a mountaineer | The auctioneer asked for bids.

-en /ən/ **1** (in adjectives) made of: a wooden box **2** (in verbs) make or become (more): unsweetened tea | The sky darkened.

-ence /əns/ (in nouns) -ANCE: its existence | reference | occurrence

-ent /ənt/ -ANT: nonexistent

-er¹ /ə/ (in comparative of short adjectives and adverbs) more: faster | colder

-er² /ə/ (in nouns) **1** person or thing that does the stated thing: a singer | a football player (= person who plays football) | an electric water heater **2** person who comes from or lives in the stated place: a New Yorker

-ery /əri, ɛri/ (in nouns) **1** the stated condition; -NESS: bravery **2** the stated art or practice; -ING (2): millinery **3** place where the stated thing is done: a brewery

-es /əz/ (after /s,z,ʃ,tʃ,dʒ/) -s: bosses | matches

-ese /iz/ (in nouns and adjectives) (language) of the stated country: Do you speak Japanese? | Portuguese food

-esque /ɛsk/ (in adjectives) in the manner or style of; like: statuesque beauty | Kafkaesque

-ess /əs/ (in nouns) female: an actress (= a female actor) | a lioness

-est /ɪst/ (in superlative of short adjectives and adverbs) most: slowest | loveliest

-eth /əθ/ -TH: the twentieth time

-ette /ɛt/ (in nouns) small: a kitchenette

-ey /i/ (esp. after y) -Y: clayey soil

-fold /fəʊld/ (in adjectives and adverbs) multiplied by the stated number: a four-fold increase

-free /fri/ (*in adjectives*) -LESS (1): *a care-free attitude*

-friendly /frɛndli/ (*in adjectives*) not difficult for the stated people to use: *a user-friendly computer*

-ful /fəl/ **1** (*in adjectives*) having or giving: *a sinful man* | *a restful day* **2** /fʊl/ (*in nouns*) amount contained by: *a handful of coins* | *two spoonfuls of sugar*

-hood /hʊd/ (*in nouns*) condition or period of being the stated thing: *falsehood* | *during her childhood*

-ial /əl/ -AL (1): *a commercial transaction* | *the presidential car*

-ian /iən, ən/ **1** (*in adjectives and nouns*) of or connected with the stated place or person: *Parisian restaurants* | *I speak Russian.* **2** (*in nouns*) person who studies the stated subject; EXPERT: *a historian* | *a theologian*

-ible /ɪbəl/ -ABLE: *deductible*

-ic /ɪk/ *also* **-ical** /ɪkəl/ (*in adjectives*) connected with; having or showing: *The design is completely symmetric/symmetrical* | *an historic occasion* | *a historical novel*

-icide /əsaɪd/ (*in nouns*) killing of: *infanticide*

-ics /ɪks/ (*in nouns*) science or skill: *linguistics* | *aeronautics*

-ie /i/ -Y (2)

-ify /əfaɪ/ (*in verbs*) make or become: *purify* | *simplify*

-ine /aɪn, ɪn/ **1** of or concerning: *equine* (= of horses) **2** made of; like: *crystalline*

-ing /ɪŋ/ **1** (makes pres. p. of verbs): *I'm coming.* | *a sleeping child* **2** (makes nouns from verbs): *Eating chocolate makes you fat.* | *a fine painting*

-ish /ɪʃ/ **1** (*in nouns and adjectives*) (language) of the stated country: *I speak Swedish.* | *British customs* **2** (*in adjectives*) **a** typical of: *a foolish man* | *girlish giggles* **b** rather: *a reddish glow* **c** about the stated number: *He's fortyish.* | *Come at sixish.*

-ism /ɪzəm/ (*in nouns*) **1** set of beliefs: *Buddhism* | *socialism* **2** quality or way of behaving: *heroism* | *male chauvinism* **3** way of speaking: *Americanisms*

-ist /ɪst/ (*in nouns*) **1** person who works with or does the stated thing: *A violinist plays the violin.* | *A machinist works machines.* **2** (*in adjectives and nouns*)

(follower) of a set of beliefs: *a Buddhist* **3** making unfair differences between people based on the stated thing: *racist* | *agist*

-ite /aɪt/ -IST (2): *a Trotskyite*

-itude /ətud/ (*in nouns*) the state or degree of being: *exactitude* | *certitude* (= being certain)

-ity /əti/ (*in nouns*) the stated condition or quality; -NESS: *stupidity* | *sublimity*

-ive /ɪv/ (*in adjectives*) tending to do the stated thing: *a creative child* | *a supportive partner*

-ize /aɪz/ (*in verbs*) make or become: *popularizing a new brand of soap* | *to modernize our procedures*

-less /lɪs/ (*in adjectives*) **1** without: *a windless day* | *We are powerless to act.* **2** that never does the stated thing: *a tireless worker*

-let /lɪt/ (*in nouns*) small: *a piglet*

-like /laɪk/ (*in adjectives*) typical of: *childlike innocence*

-ly /li/ **1** (*in adverbs*) in the stated way: *Drive carefully!* **2** (*in adjectives and adverbs*) every: *an hourly report* | *I see him daily.* **3** (*in adjectives*) typical of: *brotherly love* **4** (*in adverbs*) from the stated point of view: *Musically she's very gifted.*

-man /mən, mæn/ **1** man who comes from the stated place: *a Frenchman* **2** person with the stated job or skill: *a mailman*

-manship /mənʃɪp/ (*in* [U] *nouns*) the art or skill of a person of the stated type: *seamanship* | *horsemanship*

-ment /mənt/ (*in nouns*) act or result of doing the stated thing; -ING (2): *enjoyment* | *encouragement*

-most /moʊst/ -EST: *the northernmost parts of the country*

-ness /nɪs/ (*in nouns*) the stated condition or quality: *loudness* | *gentleness*

-nik /nɪk/ (*in nouns*) person who is connected with or enthusiastic about: *a peacenik*

-ology /ɑlədʒi/ (*in nouns*) science or study of: *toxicology* (= the study of poisons) | *musicology*

-or /ə/ -ER²: *a sailor*

-ory¹ /ɔri, əri/ (*in nouns*) place or thing used for doing the stated thing: *an observatory*

-ory² (*in adjectives*) that does the stated thing: *a congratulatory telegram*

-ous /əs/ (*in adjectives*) having; full of: *a dangerous place* | *a spacious room*

-phile /faɪl/ (*in nouns*) person who likes the stated thing or place very much: *an Anglophile* (= who likes England)

-phobe /foʊb/ (*in nouns*) person who dislikes the stated thing or person very much: *an Anglophobe* (= who dislikes England)

-phobia /foʊbiə/ (*in nouns*) great dislike: *Anglophobia*

-proof /pruf/ **1** (*in adjectives*) treated or made so as not to be harmed by the stated thing: *a bulletproof car* | *an oven-proof dish* **2** (*in verbs*) to treat or make in this way: *to soundproof a room*

-r /ə/ (*after e*) -ER

-ridden /rɪdən/ (*in adjectives*) **1** suffering from the effects of: *guiltridden* **2** too full of: *mosquito ridden*

-ry /ri/ (in nouns) -ERY: *sheer wizardry*

-s /z, s/ **1** (*makes the pl. of nouns*): *one cat and two dogs* **2** (*makes the 3rd person pres. sing. of verbs*): *She laughs too much.*

-'s 1 (*forms the possessive case of sing. nouns and of plural nouns that do not end in -s*): *my sister's husband* | *yesterday's class* | *the sheep's heads* **2** the home of: *I met him at Mary's.*

-s' (*forms the possessive case of plural nouns*): *the girls' dresses*

-scape /skeɪp/ (*in nouns*) a wide view of the stated area: *some old Dutch seascapes*

-ship /ʃɪp/ (*in nouns*) **1** condition of having or being the stated thing: *a business in partnership with his brother* | *kingship* **2** the stated skill: *her masterly musicianship*

-some /səm/ **1** (*in adjectives*) causing; producing: *a troublesome problem* **2** (*in nouns*) group of the stated number of people or things: *a twosome*

-speak /spik/ *often derog* (*in nouns*) the special language, esp. slang words, used in the stated business or activity: *computerspeak*

-st /st/ (*after e*) -EST

-th /θ/ (*makes adjectives from numbers, except those ending in 1, 2 or 3*): *the seventh day*

-tion /ʃən/ (*in nouns*) -ION

-tude /tud/ (*in nouns*) -ITUDE: *disquietude*

-ty /ti/ -ITY: *cruelty*

-ure /yə/ (*in nouns*) act or result of doing the stated thing; -ING (2): *the closure of the factory*

-ward /wəd/ also **-wards** /wədz wədz/ (*in adjectives and adverbs*) in the stated direction: *the homeward journey* | *traveling northwards*

-ware /wɛr/ (*in nouns*) containers, tools, etc., made of the stated material or for the stated purpose: *pewterware* | *kitchenware* (= for cooking)

-ways /weɪz/ -WISE: *sideways*

-wise /waɪz/ (*in adverbs*) **1** in the stated way or direction: *walked crabwise* **2** with regard to: *very inexperienced business-wise*

-y /i/ **1** (*in adjectives*) of; like; having: *a lemony smell* | *a noisy room* **2** (*makes nouns more informal; used esp. when speaking to children*): *my mommy* | *a nice little doggy* **3** (*in nouns*) -ITY: *jealousy*

Irregular verbs

verb	past tense	past participle
abide	abided, abode	abided
arise	arose	arisen
awake	awoke, awakened	awoken
baby-sit	baby-sat	baby-sat
be	*see dictionary entry*	
bear	bore	borne
beat	beat	beaten
become	became	become
befall	befell	befallen
begin	began	begun
behold	beheld	beheld
bend	bent	bent
beseech	besought, beseeched	besought, beseeched
beset	beset	beset
bet	bet	bet
bid	bade, bid	bade, bid
bind	bound	bound
bite	bit	bitten
bleed	bled	bled
bless	blessed	blessed
blow	blew	blown
break	broke	broken
breed	bred	bred
bring	brought	brought
broadcast	broadcast	broadcast
build	built	built
burn	burned, burnt	burned, burnt
burst	burst	burst
buy	bought	bought
cast	cast	cast
catch	caught	caught
chide	chided, chid	chid, chidden
choose	chose	chose
cleave	cleaved, cleft, clove	cleaved, cleft, clove
cling	clung	clung
come	came	come
cost	cost	cost
creep	crept	crept
cut	cut	cut
deal	dealt /delt/	dealt
dig	dug	dug
dive	dived, dove	dived

verb	past tense	past participle
do	did	done
draw	drew	drawn
dream	dreamed, dreamt	dreamed, dreamt
drink	drank	drunk
drive	drove	driven
dwell	dwelled, dwelt	dwelled, dwelt
eat	ate	eaten
fall	fell	fallen
feed	fed	fed
feel	felt	felt
fight	fought	fought
find	found	found
flee	fled	fled
fling	flung	flung
fly	flew	flown
forbear	forbore	forborne
forbid	forbade, forbad	forbidden
forecast	forecast	forecast
foresee	foresaw	foreseen
foretell	foretold	foretold
forget	forgot	forgotten
forgive	forgave	forgiven
forgo	forwent	forgone
forsake	forsook	forsaken
freeze	froze	frozen
get	got	gotten
give	gave	given
go	went	gone
grind	ground	ground
grow	grew	grown
hamstring	hamstrung	hamstrung
hang	hung	hung
hang (sense 4)	hanged	hanged
have	had	had
hear	heard	heard
heave	heaved, hove	heaved, hove
hew	hewed	hewn, hewed
hide	hid	hidden
hit	hit	hit
hold	held	held
hurt	hurt	hurt
keep	kept	kept
kneel	knelt, kneeled	knelt, kneeled
knit	knitted, knit	knitted, knit
know	knew	known

verb	past tense	past participle
lay	laid	laid
lead	led	led
leap	leapt, leaped	leapt, leaped
leave	left	left
lend	lent	lent
let	let	let
lie	lay	lain
light	lit, lighted	lit, lighted
lose	lost	lost
make	made	made
mean	meant	meant
meet	met	met
mislay	mislaid	mislaid
mislead	misled	misled
mistake	mistook	mistaken
misunderstand	misunderstood	misunderstood
mow	mowed	mown
outdo	outdid	outdone
outgrow	outgrew	outgrown
outshine	outshone	outshone
overcome	overcame	overcome
overdo	overdid	overdone
overhang	overhung	overhung
overload	overloaded	overladen
overrun	overran	overrun
oversee	oversaw	overseen
oversleep	overslept	overslept
overtake	overtook	overtaken
overthrow	overthrew	overthrown
partake	partook	partaken
pay	paid	paid
prove	proved	proven, proved
put	put	put
read	read /red/	read /red/
repay	repaid	repaid
rethink	rethought	rethought
rid	rid	rid
ride	rode	ridden
ring	rang	rung
rise	rose	risen
run	ran	run
saw	sawed	sawn, sawed
say	said	said
see	saw	seen
seek	sought	sought

verb	past tense	past participle
sell	sold	sold
send	sent	sent
set	set	set
sew	sewed	sewn, sewed
shake	shook	shaken
shear	sheared	shorn, sheared
shed	shed	shed
shine	shone	shone
shoe	shod	shod
shoot	shot	shot
show	showed	shown, showed
shrink	shrank, shrunk	shrunk
shut	shut	shut
sing	sang	sung
sink	sank, sunk	sunk
sit	sat	sat
slay	slew	slain
sleep	slept	slept
slide	slid	slid
sling	slung	slung
slink	slunk	slunk
slit	slit	slit
sow	sowed	sown, sowed
speak	spoke	spoken
speed	sped, speeded	sped, speeded
spend	spent	spent
spin	spun	spun
spit	spat, spit	spat, spit
split	split	split
spread	spread	spread
spring	sprang, sprung	sprung
stand	stood	stood
steal	stole	stolen
stick	stuck	stuck
sting	stung	stung
stink	stank, stunk	stunk
strew	strewed	strewn
stride	strode	stridden
strike	struck	struck
string	strung	strung
strive	strove	striven, strived
swear	swore	sworn
sweep	swept	swept
swell	swelled	swollen, swelled
swim	swam	swum

verb	past tense	past participle
swing	swung	swung
take	took	taken
teach	taught	taught
tear	tore	torn
tell	told	told
think	thought	thought
thrive	thrived, throve	thrived
throw	threw	thrown
thrust	thrust	thrust
tread	trod	trodden
undergo	underwent	undergone
understand	understood	understood
undertake	undertook	undertaken
undo	undid	undone
unwind	unwound	unwound
uphold	upheld	upheld
upset	upset	upset
wake	woke	woken
wear	wore	worn
weave	wove	woven
wed	wedded, wed	wedded, wed
weep	wept	wept
wet	wet	wet
win	won	won
wind /wamd/	wound	wound
withdraw	withdrew	withdrawn
withhold	withheld	withheld
withstand	withstood	withstood
wring	wrung	wrung
write	wrote	written

Ashru